Asian Americans

Experiences and Perspectives

Edited by

Timothy P. Fong
California State University, Sacramento

Larry H. Shinagawa
Sonoma State University

Prentice Hall, Upper Saddle River, New Jersey 07458

Library of Congress Cataloging-in-Publication Data

Asian Americans : experiences and perspectives / edited by Timothy P. Fong, Larry H. Shinagawa.
    p.   cm.
    ISBN 0-13-742966-5
    1. Asian Americans.   I. Fong, Timothy P.   II. Shinagawa, Larry Hajime.
E184.06A8433   2000
305.895073—dc21   99-22781
                                                          CIP

Editorial Director: Charlyce Jones Owen
Editor in Chief: Nancy Roberts
Managing Editor: Sharon Chambliss
Project Manager: Merrill Peterson
Prepress and Manufacturing Buyer: Mary Ann Gloriande
Cover Director: Jayne Conte
Cover Designer: Bruce Kenselaar
Marketing Manager: Christopher DeJohn

This book is dedicated to our students and our colleagues
in Asian American studies

Printed in the United States of America

ISBN   0-13-742966-5

PRENTICE-HALL INTERNATIONAL (UK) LIMITED, London
PRENTICE-HALL OF AUSTRALIA PTY. LIMITED, Sydney
PRENTICE-HALL CANADA INC., Toronto
PRENTICE-HALL HISPANOAMERICANA, S.A., Mexico
PRENTICE-HALL OF INDIA PRIVATE LIMITED, New Delhi
PRENTICE-HALL OF JAPAN, INC., Tokyo
PEARSON EDUCATION ASIA PTE. LTD., Singapore
EDITORA PRENTICE-HALL DO BRASIL, LTDA., Rio de Janeiro

Contents

Chapter 4

Education Issues   **123**

Chapter 5

Employment and Occupation   **191**

Chapter 6

Popular Culture, Imagery, and Stereotypes   **243**

Chapter 10

Future Directions in Asian American Studies   **410**

Contributors   **446**

Preface

This anthology was created with two purposes in mind. First, it serves as a companion text to the book *The Contemporary Asian American Experience: Beyond the Model Minority.*[1] The anthology offers readers the opportunity to review many of the original sources cited in *The Contemporary Asian American Experience* and to assess them independently. Second, it became clear as this project evolved that this anthology could also be used as a stand-alone text suitable as a core resource for anyone interested in the Asian American experience. As a compendium or a stand-alone text, this anthology is extremely serviceable because it provides a sufficient number of selections for instructors to tailor readings for a variety of Asian American and ethnic studies courses, or any course in other disciplines dealing with race and ethnic relations. The interdisciplinary approach of this anthology will enable readers to appreciate the writing and research findings of scholars of various academic backgrounds, as well as those of community activists and journalists. Most of the selections in this anthology are reprinted in their entirety with references included. Some selections, however, were edited. Great efforts were made to maintain the key concepts, content, and arguments of each edited selection.

Narrowing the number of selections was a difficult task, because the field of Asian America studies is burgeoning. Of course, many selections were considered but not included. Today resources abound; the 1997 Annual Bibliography of the *Amerasia Journal*, a prominent periodical for Asian American studies, cited 2,628 articles and books about Asian and Pacific Islander Americans.[2] In addition, several major publishers now devote an entire series to the publication of works on and about Asian Americans. Currently, Temple University Press, University of Washington Press, UCLA Asian American Studies Center, Stanford University, University of Illinois Press, and Altamira Press/Sage Publications each have a series focusing on Asian American literary, social, and historical themes. Exciting new books and articles about Asian Americans were published even as we were completing this anthology.

A number of considerations went into our selection decisions. One was to achieve balanced representation. Representation meant balancing the number and length of selections within range of cutting-edge issues we chose for this anthology. Representation also meant balancing the perspectives of the various Asian American ethnic groups and Asian American

[1] Timothy P. Fong, *The Contemporary Asian American Experience: Beyond the Model Minority* (Upper Saddle River, New Jersey: Prentice Hall, 1998).

[2] See *Amerasia Journal* 23:3 (Winter 1997–1998): 233–298.

women and men. A second consideration was our desire to incorporate selections from community activists and journalists, as well as scholars, all of whom are vital to the comprehensive development of Asian American studies. A third consideration was our desire to achieve a balance between *content* and *pedagogy*. This anthology was highly influenced by the publication of *Teaching Asian America: Diversity & the Problem of Community*, edited by Lane Ryo Hirabayashi. Essays in Hirabayashi's volume focus on what is taught, and what should be taught, in Asian American studies courses as we begin the new millennium.[3]

Our anthology strives to present the best ideals of the Asian American movement in terms that students can understand and adapt to their own needs. We are highly cognizant of the diversity within Asian America, and we are keenly conscious of the diverse readership this anthology will have. As a result, we consider this anthology to be an important introductory primer for the Asian American experience, rather than an exhaustive treatise; it is also an invitation and an encouragement for the reading audience to advance its knowledge of Asian Americans. We believe the knowledge gained from the selections in this anthology will serve the reader very well as she or he continues on a personal and intellectual exploration into Asian American studies.

No published work can be completed without the help of many people. We want to first thank administrative assistant Janice Ornellas. She was especially helpful in keeping all of the selections organized and in obtaining the necessary reprint permission forms. Her proofreading and copyediting skills were invaluable in getting the text ready for publication. This anthology would not have been completed without her. Librarians Francis Hui, Lena Chang, and Louise Cheng deserve special mention for their superb research assistance. Their professionalism and caring attitudes were greatly appreciated. Thanks also go to Maria Elena Marquez, Consuelo Lopez, Bethany Garland, and Sokhoeuth Moeurn. All four were high school students who were responsible for helping to photocopy selections used in this anthology and for getting them "production ready." Highest praises go to Prentice Hall managing editor Sharon Chambliss, editor Angela Stone, production editor Merrill Peterson, and copyeditor Barbara Milligan. Sharon oversaw the entire project and was especially supportive throughout. Angela guided this project along and gave us both the good swift kick we needed to keep moving. Merrill was remarkably efficient in moving the raw materials of this anthology into publication. Barbara's keen eye and expert advice helped to keep the text clear and readable.

Very special thanks go to our families, Elena Almanzo and Gabriel Almanzo Fong, and Sun, Nathan, Chibo, Mitch, and Grant Shinagawa. They are the light of our lives. We especially want to thank them for their understanding, assistance, personal support, and encouragement during the long and arduous task of bringing this anthology to life.

Timothy P. Fong
California State University, Sacramento

Larry H. Shinagawa
Sonoma State University

---

[3]Lane Ryo Hirabayashi, ed., *Teaching Asian America: Diversity & the Problem of Community* (Savage, Maryland: Rowman & Littlefield Publishers, 1998).

Introduction

Asian Americans are one of the fastest growing populations in the United States and one of the most diverse in terms of class, culture, political orientation, and social experience. Among their populations are some of the highest achieving ethnic groups in the U.S., as well as those deeply affected by discrimination, linguistic barriers, and cultural differences. Since the founding of the first Asian American studies program at San Francisco State College (now University) in 1968, the field of Asian American studies has expanded rapidly. Today, the Association of Asian American Studies (AAAS) officially counts several dozen departments and programs across the nation that teach Asian American studies in one form or another.[1] Interest in Asian Americans has escalated rapidly due in large part to the growth of the Asian Pacific American population. The 1990 census counted over 7.2 million Asian and Pacific Islander Americans (2.9 percent of the total U.S. population), a threefold increase from 1970. Indeed, at its current rate, some demographers project this population will increase to 20 million by the year 2020.[2] Interest in Asian Americans has also come as a result of their high concentration in higher education, influence in various occupations, our growing awareness of interdependence with Asia and the Pacific Rim, and increased consciousness of the significance of multicultural diversity in contemporary American life.

In this context, we present this anthology to encourage readers to think comprehensively and critically about the social issues facing Asian Americans. The works included examine the social, economic, cultural, and political roles that Asian Americans have played, and continue to play, in contemporary American life. Several features make this anthology an essential part of an Asian American introductory or contemporary issues course. The objectives of this anthology are to:

- Educate students about the experiences and perspectives of Asian Americans
- Implicitly advance a multicultural, comparative, and interdisciplinary approach to regarding the Asian American experience
- Present works that are theoretically engaging, current, diverse, and well researched

---

[1] Directory of Asian American Studies Programs (Ithaca, New York: Asian American Studies Program, Cornell University, 1998).

[2] Paul Ong, "The Growth of the Asian Pacific American Population: Twenty Million in 2020," in *The State of Asian Pacific America: Policy Issues to the Year 2020* (Los Angeles: LEAP Asian Pacific American Public Policy Institute and UCLA Asian American Studies Center, 1993), pp. 11–24.

- Provide an academic context for students to break away from stereotyped thinking about Asian Americans
- Furnish a sufficient number of selections for instructors to tailor readings for specific courses

PERSPECTIVE

This anthology focuses on the four founding principles of ethnic studies (Wong, Chapter 10). The first is self-determination, which embodies control of one's own destiny. For Asian Americans, this involves challenging stereotypical images and negative attitudes, confronting discriminatory education policies and workplace discrimination, and working to make change. These issues will continue to be an ongoing part of the Asian American experience in the future. The second founding principle is developing solidarity among American racial minorities. The image of Asian Americans as the "model minority" has for decades been used to separate Asian Americans from other racial minority groups. Certain politicians and academics have highlighted Asian American "success," particularly in education and employment, in order to fuel competition and animosity between groups. The issues raised in this anthology clearly demonstrate that Asian Americans have never been immune to the scourge of racism, discrimination, and xenophobia. Understanding the historical and contemporary context of issues important to Asian Americans is vital to understanding similar issues confronted by others and for working positively with others (Osajima, Chapter 10).

The third founding principle of ethnic studies is educational relevance. Most, if not all, of the issues raised in this anthology will touch the Asian American students at some point in their lives. Non–Asian American students will have greater insights into the Asian American experience. The relevance of the materials presented expand shared experiences, create discussion, and stimulate collective action. At the same time, readers will also recognize that Asian American diversity is highly relevant. Differences in gender, ethnicity, class, nativity, and sexual orientation, as well as biraciality and multiraciality among Asian Americans are acknowledged throughout this anthology. Cognizance of the "differential power and agency" between and among various Asian American groups is also delineated (Hune, Chapter 2).

The fourth principle of ethnic studies is to utilize an interdisciplinary approach to examine the experiences of racialized minorities in the United States. This anthology includes the works of sociologists, historians, educators, literary critics, anthropologists, and psychologists, as well as journalists and community activists, to analyze the Asian American experience in the U.S. This interdisciplinary and multidimensional approach is necessary in order to cover the broad range of issues that face Asian Americans. Despite our best efforts, we acknowledge that the issues and discipline areas included here are by no means exhaustive. For example, literary works and autobiographical essays were seriously considered for inclusion in this volume, but page limitations and cost considerations restricted our ability to use all the materials we had hoped to include. Nonetheless, we believe that this anthology provides an important introduction to Asian American studies.

In addition to the four founding principles of ethnic studies, this anthology centers the Asian American experience within the broader context of the American experience. We have challenged the dominant bipolar white-black paradigm of race relations that has effectively made Asian Americans (as well as Latinos and Native Americans) virtually invisible by placing them somewhere between white and black, but in nowhere particular. Centering the Asian American experience involves much more than merely acknowledging its existence in today's society. Rather, it is the full recognition that the historical and contemporary Asian American experience is essential to understanding the complex racial dynamics that have unfolded, and continue to unfold, in the United States (Okihiro, Chapter 2). Centering the Asian American experience is also a major part of the movement in almost all colleges and universities. Campuses across the nation now view education of and for a diverse citizenry as integral to their missions of public leadership and service. At the same time, there is an ongoing debate over curriculum and content, and over how to address fundamental issues of equality, difference, and society. Asian Americans and the Asian American experience are an integral part of this debate (Takaki, Chapter 4, and Williams et al., Chapter 4).

RACE AND ETHNIC RELATIONS: AN ASIAN AMERICAN PERSPECTIVE

One way of centering the Asian American experience within the broader American experience is to review the dominant literature on race and ethnic relations from an Asian American perspective. Over the course of the twentieth century, a wide variety of theories have developed to explain race and ethnic relations in the United States. While there is no race and ethnic relations theory specific to just Asian Americans, it is useful to understand and contextualize the historical and contemporary Asian American experience within various theoretical frameworks. These theoretical frameworks have tended to focus on migration, contact, accommodation and adaptation, conflict, and the persistence of stratification. The dominant theoretical frameworks in this area are classified as **symbolic interactionalist, structural functionalist**, and **social conflict**. These frameworks are useful in explaining why race and ethnic relations appear in different forms, from peaceful acceptance to violent exclusion. Symbolic interactionism is fundamentally concerned with the micro (interpersonal) level of society—how people act toward one another and how they make sense of their daily lives. One interactionalist approach focuses on how **racial socialization** contributes to feelings of solidarity with one's own racial-ethnic group. Racial socializing is a process of social interaction relative to one's personal and group identity, intergroup and individual relationships, and position in the social stratification system.[3] In other words, a person of the dominant majority group may see race relations as smooth, while a person of a minority group may see nothing but problems. This has been called the **Rashomon model**, based on the classic Japanese film portraying different interpretations of the same incident.[4] Another interactionalist approach can be seen in **bias theories**, which emphasizes the prejudiced attitudes of majority members.[5] According to this perspective, prejudiced attitudes are the source of discriminatory actions that maintain racial

[3]Diana Kendall, *Social Problems in a Diverse Society* (Needham Heights, MA: Allyn & Bacon, 1998), p. 50.

[4]Harry H. L. Kitano, *Race Relations* (Upper Saddle River, NJ: Prentice Hall, 1997), p. 8.

[5]Gunnar Myrdal, *An American Dilemma* (New York: Pantheon, 1962).

and ethnic minority oppression and marginalization. These attitudes are a reflection of an individual's dependence on *stereotypes*. Stereotypes tend to mislead us through false generalizations, are often based on negative information, are emotionally anchored, are difficult to change, and are easily ingrained into one's personality and psychological makeup. Within this framework is **scapegoating theory**, which postulates that interactions between people are affected if individuals from the dominant group view racial or ethnic minorities as unwanted, inferior, and/or threatening.[6] Symbolic interactionalism is useful as a microsociological perspective but does fully consider the larger picture. Social interaction is often affected by social structures, institutions, groups, and cultures far beyond the awareness and control of individuals. As a result, structural functionalist and social conflict theories developed. Both have a macrosociological perspective, but they are ideologically quite divergent.

To functionalists, social order and stability are of primary concern, and patterns of inclusion are emphasized. One functionalist perspective focuses on **assimilation**, the process by which racial and ethnic minorities adopt the dominant group's culture as their own. In the United States, **Anglo-conformity** is the most complete pattern of assimilation. This complete form of assimilation can be expressed as $A + B + C = A$, where A is the dominant group, while B and C are different minority groups. Racial and ethnic minorities B and C lose their cultural traits to become part of the dominant group, A.

Amalgamation, or the **melting-pot theory**, is the process by which diverse racial and ethnic groups are blended together to form a new society that incorporates the special contributions of each group. The formula for this pattern is $A + B + C = D$. Here A, B, and C are distinct groups who come together to form D—a unique society unlike any of its original components. Another functionalist viewpoint emphasizes **cultural pluralism**. Here, different racial and ethnic groups coexist, each displaying its own separate identities and culture. In its most negative extreme, cultural pluralism occurs in a segregated society. *Segregation* is the social and geographic separation within a society of people based on race and/or ethnicity, class, religion, or other social characteristic. The most positive expression of cultural pluralism seen today is the movement toward acceptance of *multiculturalism* on college campuses and communities across the nation. Cultural pluralism can be seen as $A + B + C = A + B + C$, which shows that various groups retain their culture cultural identities and have the opportunity to exist on their own terms while interacting with each other.[7]

These functionalist perspectives offer the most popular explanations for majority-minority relations because of their focus on the trajectory of progressive inclusion of various groups into the American mainstream. Asian American scholars have pointed out, however, historic anti-Asian sentiment exemplified in the Chinese exclusion law of 1882 through to the internment of Japanese Americans in 1942, as well as continuing attacks against Asian immigrants and hate crimes against Asian Americans occurring today. In response to these and other criticisms, the social conflict theories emerged.

---

[6]Juan L. Gonzales, Jr., *Racial and Ethnic Groups in America*, second edition (Dubuque, Iowa: Kendall/Hunt Publishing Company, 1993), p. 32.

[7]Milton Gordon, *Assimilation in American Life: The Role of Race, Religion, and National Origins* (New York: Oxford University Press, 1964).

Social conflict theories examine competition and the constant power struggle for control of scarce resources as the causes of social stratification and inequality. According to conflict theorists, certain groups of people are privileged while others are disadvantaged and oppressed. In the United States the rich are privileged relative to the poor *(class)*, whites are privileged relative to people of color *(race)*, and men are privileged relative to women *(gender)*. The **class perspective** on race and ethnic relations highlights the role of the capitalist class in racial exploitation. As an example, Oliver Cox (1945) argued that capitalist support of the institution of slavery was due primarily because it was the cheapest form of labor, and the racist ideology rationalizing the enslavement of African Americans was a secondary factor.[8] Conversely, the **internal colonialism theory** places racial oppression at the center of its analysis. Robert Blauner (1972) cites three conditions that differentiate the experiences of racial minorities (African Americans, Native Americans, Chicanos, and Asian Americans) from ethnic European immigrants: forced entry (slavery and annexation), unfree labor (strict job segregation), and cultural destruction (the destruction of slave families, forced conversion of Native Americans to Christianity, laws prohibiting the immigration of Asian women, and English-only laws). These conditions work to perpetuate racial stratification and ideological racism, serving to benefit white groups at the expense of people of color.[9]

Critics have questioned the "either/or" quality of the class and internal colonial perspectives. Edna Bonacich (1972) offers an expansion of these perspectives in her description of the **split labor market theory**. This theory divides the U.S. labor force into two employment sectors: the primary labor market and the secondary labor market. The primary labor market is recognized for offering better wages, working conditions, and benefits. Those in the secondary labor market usually earn poor wages, suffer harsh working conditions, and have few, if any, benefits. The two labor markets are racially stratified, with whites dominating the primary labor market and people of color and women dominating the secondary labor market. The capitalist class pits the two labor markets against one another, thus creating a *race-class* conflict.[10] In this theory, the capitalist class is not omnipotent; there are times when white workers in the primary market are politically strong enough to exercise their influence. Chapter 1 describes many examples of white working-class antagonism fomenting anti-Asian sentiment. The results of this antagonism were the passage of discriminatory laws and immigration restrictions aimed at preventing Asians from competing against the interests of higher-paid workers.

A major weakness of the split labor market theory is in its inability to address the experiences of racial minorities who are not relegated to the confines of the working class. Indeed, certain Asian American immigrant groups have occupied a certain economic niche as *petite bourgeoisie*—that is, merchants who own their own businesses. It was from this observation that Bonacich and John Modell (1975) forwarded the **middleman minority theory**. Key to this theory is its recognition of the status of some racial and ethnic groups as merchants that is different, yet similar, to that of cheap labor. These merchants typically work long hours, earn very little net income, and make extensive use of unpaid family, or

---

[8]Oliver C. Cox, *Caste, Class & Race* (New York: Doubleday & Company, Inc., 1948).
[9]Robert Blauner, *Racial Oppression in America* (New York: Harper & Row, 1972).
[10]Edna Bonacich, "A Theory of Ethnic Antagonism: The Split Labor Market," *American Sociological Review* 37 (1972): 547–559.

underpaid coethnic, workers.[11] Many of these small business owners have either been excluded from mainstream employment or are unable to find stable employment because of their lack of English language fluency. Lastly, the types of businesses they tend to operate (for example, "mom 'n' pop" grocery stores, liquor stores, restaurants, and so on) often sell products, manufactured by large corporations, to low-income communities who would not usually have easy access to that merchandise. Good examples of middleman minorities are the Chinese Americans in Mississippi who owned and operated stores that catered to rural African American customers, and Korean Americans whose businesses are located in inner-city New York, Los Angeles, Chicago, and Atlanta. While the split labor market theory helps to explain popular white antagonism toward racial minorities, the middleman minority theory also explains the antagonism between and within racial minorities themselves.

An important alternative to the split labor market and middleman minority theories is the **ethnic enclave** perspective, which presupposes that enclave economies function quite well separate from, and in competition with, the U.S. mainstream economy. This perspective was central to sociologist Min Zhou's study of New York's Chinatown (1992). The success of an enclave economy is dependent on three key factors. First, there is an ethnic population and consumer market large enough to support a number of ethnic businesses. Second, enclave businesses often pay workers less and work them long hours, which gives the stores a competitive edge. Third, the owner-worker relationship in the enclave economy is viewed more as an apprenticeship rather than as an exploitative relationship. Ethnic enclave businesses provide jobs and opportunities for less privileged immigrant workers who are excluded from the primary labor market, and in all likelihood would face even greater discrimination in the secondary labor market of the mainstream economy.[12] Critics of the enclave economy perspective contend that success in ethnic enclaves is really based on the exploitation of coethnics. They question whether or not these low-paying jobs truly offer immigrant workers long-term opportunities. Also important is evidence that immigrant men benefit from the enclave economy far more than immigrant women. This focus on ethnic enclave economies is distinct from earlier assimilationist theories that assume the dilution of ethnicity and ethnic solidarity. Instead, enclave economies serve to strengthen and maintain ethnic bonds. The study of enclave economies also serves to highlight the complex positive as well as negative inner workings within the ethnic enclave, rather than focus only on exploitation by outsiders.

Attention to gender stratification within ethnic communities can be extended to the broad social conflict area, referred to as **gendered racism**. This perspective emerged in response to the fact that most theories of racial and ethnic relations neglected gender stratification against women of color. From this perspective, male dominance, or patriarchy, is not analyzed separately from race and class oppression. Many studies of women of color have added another sector of labor beyond the primary and secondary markets described earlier. The primary market historically has been

[11]Edna Bonacich and John Modell, *The Economic Basis of Ethnic Solidarity: Small Business in the Japanese American Community* (Berkeley: University of California Press, 1980).

[12]Min Zhou, *Chinatown: The Socioeconomic Potential of an Urban Enclave* (Philadelphia: Temple University Press, 1992).

dominated by white men, and the secondary market has been dominated by men of color and white women, while a third market is dominated primarily by women of color. Several scholars have focused on the Asian American women's experience through a gendered racism perspective. Lucie Cheng Hirata (1979) has examined the lives of Chinese American prostitutes, Evelyn Nakano Glenn (1956) has done research on Japanese American domestic servants, and Bonacich et al. (1994) have analyzed the clothing apparel industry and focused on women who work in garment factory sweatshops.[13]

Theories within the symbolic interactionalism, structural functionalism, and social-conflict frameworks all have useful attributes. However, none of these specific theories encompasses the totality of the contemporary Asian American experience. They tend to situate themselves within a particular historical period or ideological framework, which makes them rather rigid in several ways. First, these theoretical perspectives understandably concentrate on explaining a particular phenomenon or event and are less concerned with changes in time and context. Second, they tend to view race and ethnic relations dualistically—white and nonwhite—with relatively little attention given to distinctions between and within minority groups. Third, these theoretical perspectives tend to treat the micro view of immediate situations and human interaction, and the macro view, which focuses on the large social phenomena of society as mutually exclusive rather than as interconnected.

The emergence of **racial formation theory** is especially significant in light of the preceding concerns. Sociologists Michael Omi and Howard Winant examine "race" as a macro- and micro-level social construct rather than as a biological concept. For them, race is a matter of social structure and sociocultural representation, which have individual meaning and significance for collective action. Omi and Winant describe racial formation as the sociohistorical process by which racial categories are created, reified, challenged, and transformed.[14] A key concept of racial formation is the significance of the *racial state*—for example, U.S. government policies that have resulted in identifying and marginalizing racial minority groups. The U.S. Constitution counting African American slaves as three-fifths a person, the passage of the Naturalization Law of 1790 permitting citizenship to only white immigrants, government-supported genocide and forced relocation of Native Americans, deportation of Mexican Americans, and Japanese internment during World War II are just a few examples of the state's complicity in the exploitation of people of color. At the same time, as these governmental abuses continued, people of color, with the help of supportive whites, mobilized to challenge oppression and discrimination. The Civil Rights movement of the 1960s is a good example of popular protest leading to tremendous change in government policy. Racial formation theory explains the trajectory of race relations in the United States as quite fluid, rather than as one-dimensional.

---

[13]Lucie Cheng Hirata, "Free, Indentured and Enslaved: Chinese Prostitutes in Nineteenth Century America," Signs 5 (1979): 3–29; Evelyn Nakano Glenn, *Issei, Nisei, War Bride: Three Generations of Japanese American Women in Domestic Service* (Philadelphia: Temple University Press, 1986); and Edna Bonacich, Lucie Cheng, Norma Chinchilla, Nora Hamilton, and Paul Ong (eds.), *Global Production: The Apparel Industry in the Pacific Rim* (Philadelphia: Temple University Press, 1994).

[14]Michael Omi and Howard Winant, *Racial Formation in the United States: From the 1960s to the 1990s* (New York: Routledge, 1994).

Omi and Winant's recognition of the complex nature of race relations is manifested in their understanding that all racisms are not alike in either their origins or their consequences. They contend that racism, like the concept of "race," has changed over time. It is obvious that the same kind of racism found in attitudes, institutions, and policies of nineteenth-century America does not exist today. The lack of distinction regarding racism leads only to pessimism and denial of all the efforts and progress made to end racial injustice. From an Asian American perspective, racial formation accounts for differential experiences of exclusion, incorporation, and autonomy experienced by various Asian American groups during specific, and sometimes overlapping, periods of time.

Omni and Winant also emphasize distinctions between *racial awareness, racial essentialism, and strategic essentialism*. Racial awareness is a conscious and open recognition of the distinct experiences of individuals and racial groups. This is the antithesis of the current popular call for the U.S. to be "color-blind" concerning racial issues and concerns. At the same time, racial awareness should not be confused with racial essentialism. Racial essentialism is the stereotype of "sameness" and the denial or flattening of differences within a particular racially defined group. Racial essentialism may seem a rather benign concept, but it can have deadly consequences. In 1982, Vincent Chin, a twenty-seven-year old Chinese American was beaten to death by two autoworkers who allegedly blamed Japan for problems in the U.S. auto industry and thought Chin was Japanese. A more recent incident occurred in April 1997, when Kuanchung Kao was shot and killed by police officers in Rohnert Park, California, a community one hour north of San Francisco. The police officers involved allegedly assumed Kao, who was legally drunk on the night of the incident, to be a potentially dangerous martial arts expert. Kao had no martial arts training, but the officers perceived Kao as more of a threat than the average intoxicated man and may have acted with excessive force. Despite inherent dangers of racial essentialism, racial formation theory acknowledges that there are times when Asian Americans must band together in order to defend their rights and interests. This strategic essentialism is a necessary reaction to the racial essentialism imposed by others that negatively and uniformly affect all Asian American groups as a whole.[15] Examples of strategic essentialism are seen in the pan-Asian American protests and activities following the Chin and Kao killings (Eljera, Chapter 9).

With the emergence of racial formation theory there evolved many other new perspectives on the Asian American experience. These perspectives incorporate postmodern, transnational, and gay and lesbian points of view and are highlighted in Chapter 10.

ORGANIZATION OF THE ANTHOLOGY

This anthology is organized by themes and issues, rather than by specific ethnic group. Our choice reflects a wholistic view of the Asian American experience and better serves to compare and contrast the diverse Asian American perspectives. The first two chapters provide the necessary contextual background that will be useful throughout the text.

[15]*Ibid.*, pp. 69–76.

Chapter 1 presents a historical overview of Asians in the United States, starting with the earliest sojourners and continuing through to the most recent wave of Asian immigrants and refugees. Included in this chapter is a section with the most up-to-date demographic and socioeconomic statistics on Asian Americans. Chapter 2 provides important critical perspectives by leading Asian American scholars. Chapters 3 through 10 are issue-focused, addressing the key social issues and their effects on Asian Americans.

Chapter 3 examines the formation of new communities. The large number of Asian immigrants and refugees to the United States since the 1965 Immigration Reform Act has helped to create conspicuous ethnic enclaves in various regions across the U.S. The urban Chinatown or Japantown are no longer representative of the contemporary Asian American community. The influence of Asian Americans is seen on the community level and also throughout all levels of education. Chapter 4 draws attention to issues facing Asian Americans in both primary school and higher education. Although the popular media has focused on Asian American "whiz kids" who excel far ahead of their classmates, this chapter reveals some of the challenges faced by Asian Americans in education. Asian Americans are a significant component of the ever-growing diversity within all levels of education. This chapter highlights the need for an enlightened education policy and curriculum change. Because they have attained higher levels of education, it is assumed that better employment opportunities will follow. However, the relative "success" of Asian Americans in the professional and managerial ranks is questionable. Chapter 5 explores some of the challenges faced by Asian Americans in the workplace and draws particular attention to issues important for both highly educated Asian American workers and less-educated unskilled laborers.

Chapter 6 shifts to issues of popular culture, imagery, and stereotypes. This chapter reviews the long history of negative images of Asian Americans in popular culture and also calls attention to contemporary concerns. From popular culture, Chapter 7 progresses to individualized family issues. The authors explore the family dynamics of various Asian American ethnic groups, to illuminate important similarities as well as differences. It is important to note that the differences in family experiences are not only a matter of ethnicity, but also are contextual and situational. Family dynamics continue to be examined in Chapter 8, but they move beyond traditional family groupings. This chapter includes articles on intermarriage, multiraciality, and the experiences of gay and lesbian Asian Americans.

Chapter 9 focuses on Asian American involvement in politics. This includes electoral politics as well as nonelectoral, grass-roots organizing. Both have their place in providing Asian Americans with more visibility and voice in the political arena. Involvement in the political process is important to Asian Americans if they want to have an impact on public policy issues affecting their civil and human rights. Despite steady progress in both electoral and nonelectoral political efforts, recent media attention on political fundraising scandals involving Asian government officials and Asian American power-brokers has placed Asian American political involvement in a negative light. Activists have been quick to confront racist stereotyping by some partisan politicians, by observing that a small number of allegedly illegal fundraising practices were being confused with legitimate Asian American political activities. Finally, Chapter 10 draws from authors who examine future directions and possibilities. These thought-provoking essays offer impor-

102,620 Chinese men and only 3,868 Chinese women in the United States, a male-female ratio of 26:1.[4] Despite these conditions, Chinese workers continued to come to the United States.

Following the completion of the transcontinental railroad in 1869, large numbers of unemployed Chinese workers had to find new sources of employment. Many found work in agriculture where they cleared land, dug canals, planted orchards, harvested crops, and were the foundation for successful commercial production of many California crops. Others settled in San Francisco and other cities to manufacture shoes, cigars, and clothing. Still others started small businesses such as restaurants, laundries, and general stores. Domestic service such as houseboys, cooks, and gardeners were also other areas of employment for the Chinese. In short, the Chinese were involved in many occupations that were crucial to the economic development and domestication of the western region of the United States.[5] Unfortunately, intense hostility against the Chinese reached its peak in 1882 when Congress passed the Chinese Exclusion Act intended to "suspend" the entry of Chinese laborers for ten years. Other laws were eventually passed that barred Chinese laborers and their wives permanently.[6]

The historical experience of Japanese in the United States is both different yet similar to that of the Chinese. One major difference is that the Japanese emigrated in large numbers to Hawaii and were not significant in United States until the 1890s. In 1880 there were only 148 Japanese living in the U.S. mainland. In 1890 this number increased to 2,000, mostly merchants and students. However, the population increased dramatically when an influx of 38,000 Japanese workers from Hawaii arrived in the U.S. mainland between 1902 and 1907.[7] The second difference was the fact the Japanese were able to fully exploit an economic niche in agriculture that the Chinese had only started. The completion of several national railroad lines and the invention of the refrigerator car were two advancements that brought forth tremendous expansion in the

California produce industry. The early Japanese were fortunate to arrive at an opportune time, and about two thirds of the Japanese found work as agricultural laborers. Within a short time the Japanese were starting their own farms in direct competition with non-Japanese farms. By 1919 the Japanese controlled over 450,000 acres of agricultural land. Although this figure represents only 1 percent of active California agricultural land at the time, the Japanese were so efficient in their farming practices that they captured 10 percent of the dollar volume of the state's crops.[8]

The third major difference was the emergence of Japan as an international military power at the turn of the century. Japan's victory in the Russo-Japanese War (1904–1905) impressed President Theodore Roosevelt and he believed a strategy of cooperation with the Japanese government was in the best interest of the United States. Roosevelt blocked calls for complete Japanese exclusion and instead worked a compromise with the Japanese government in 1907 known as the "Gentleman's Agreement." This agreement halted the immigration of Japanese laborers but allowed Japanese women into the United States. With this in mind, the fourth difference was the fact that the Japanese in the United States were able to actually increase in population, start families, and establish a rather stable community life.[9]

Filipino immigration began after the United States gained possession of the Philippines following the Spanish-American War in 1898. The first Filipinos to arrive were a few hundred pensionados, or students supported by government scholarships. Similar to the Japanese experience, a large number of Filipinos went directly to Hawaii before coming to the U.S. mainland. Between 1907 and 1919 over 28,000 Filipinos were actively recruited to work on sugar plantations in Hawaii. Filipinos began to emigrate to the United States following the passage of the 1924 Immigration Act, which prohibited all Asian immigration to this country and there was a need for agricultural and service labor.[10]

Because Filipinos lived on American territory, they were "nationals" who were free to travel in the United States without restriction. In the 1920s over 45,000 Filipinos arrived in Pacific Coast ports, and a 1930 study found 30,000 Filipinos working in California. These Filipinos were overwhelmingly young, single males. Their ages ranged between 16 and 29, and there were 14 Filipino men for every Filipina. Sixty percent of these Filipinos worked as migratory agricultural laborers, and 25 percent worked in domestic service in Los Angeles and San Francisco. The rest found work in manufacturing and as railroad porters. Unlike the Japanese, Filipinos did not make their mark in agriculture as farmers, but as labor union organizers.[11] Both Filipino farm worker activism and Japanese farm competition created a great deal of resentment among white farmers and laborers.

Koreans and Asian Indians slightly predated the Filipinos, but arrived in much smaller numbers. Between 1903 and 1905 over 7,000 Koreans were recruited for plantation labor work in Hawaii, but after Japan established a protectorate over Korea in 1905, all emigration was halted.[12] In the next five years, Japan increased its economic and political power and formally annexed Korea in 1910. Relatively few Koreans lived in the United States between 1905 and 1940. Among those included about 1,000 workers who migrated from Hawaii, about 100 Korean "picture brides," and a small number of American-born Koreans. The Korean population in the United States during that time was also bolstered by roughly 900 students, many of whom fled to their home country because of their opposition to Japanese rule. Like other Asian immigrant groups, Koreans found themselves concentrated in California agriculture working primarily as laborers, although a small number did become quite successful farmers.[13]

The first significant flow of Asian Indians occurred between 1904 and 1911, when just over 6,000 arrived in the United States. Unlike the other Asian groups, Asian Indians did not work in Hawaii prior to entering the American main-land, but they worked primarily in California agriculture. Similar to the Chinese, Filipinos, and Koreans, they had an extremely high male to female ratio. Of the Asian Indians who immigrated to the United States between 1904 and 1911, there were only three or four women, all of whom were married.[14] Eighty to ninety percent of the first Asian Indian settlers in the United States were Sikhs, a distinct ethno-religious minority group in India. Despite this fact, these Sikhs were often called Hindus, which they are not. Sikhs were easily recognizable from all other Asian immigrant groups because of their huskier build, they wore turbans, and they kept their beards. But like other Asians in the United States at the time, they also worked primarily in California's agricultural industry. Asian Indians worked first as farm workers, and like the Japanese, also formed cooperatives, pooled their resources, and began independent farming.[15] Immigration restrictions, their relatively small numbers, and an exaggerated male-female ratio prevented Asian Indians from developing a lasting farm presence. One major exception can be found in the Marysville–Yuba City area of Northern California, where Asian Indian Sikhs are still quite active in producing cling peaches.[16]

Anti-Asian Laws and Sentiment

The United States is a nation that proclaims to welcome and assimilate all newcomers. But the history of immigration, naturalization, and equal treatment under the law for Asian Americans has been an extremely difficult one. In 1790 Congress passed the first naturalization law limiting citizenship rights to only a "free white person."[17] In 1870, during the period of reconstruction following the end of the Civil War, Congress amended the law and allowed citizenship for "aliens of African nativity and persons of African descent."[18] For a while there was some discussion on expanding naturalization rights to Chinese immigrants, but that idea was rejected by politicians from western states.[19] This rejection is exemplary of the intense anti-Chinese sentiment at the time.

As early as 1850 California imposed a Foreign Miners Tax, which required the payment of $20 a month from all foreign miners.[20] The California Supreme Court ruled in *People v. Hall* (1854), that Chinese could not testify in court against a white person. This case threw out the testimony of three Chinese witnesses and reversed the murder conviction of George W. Hall, who was sentenced to hang for the murder of a Chinese man one year earlier.[21] In 1855 a local San Francisco ordinance levied a $50 tax on all aliens ineligible for citizenship. Since Chinese were ineligible for citizenship under the Naturalization Act of 1790, they were the primary targets for this law.[22]

The racially distinct Chinese were the primary scapegoats for the depressed economy in the 1870s, and mob violence erupted on several occasions through to the 1880s. The massacre of 21 Chinese in Los Angeles in 1871 and 28 Chinese in Rock Springs, Wyoming, in 1885 are examples of the worst incidents. It is within this environment that Congress passed the 1882 Chinese Exclusion Act. The act suspended immigration of Chinese laborers for only ten years, but it was extended in 1892 and 1902. The act was eventually extended indefinitely in 1904.[23] The intense institutional discrimination achieved the desired result: The Chinese population declined from 105,465 in 1880 to 61,639 in 1920.[24]

Anti-Chinese sentiment easily grew into large-scale anti-Asian sentiment as immigrants from Asia continued to enter the United States. During the same period that the Chinese population declined, the Japanese population grew and became highly visible. As early as 1910 there were 72,157 Japanese Americans compared to 71,531 Chinese Americans in the United States.[25] The Japanese farmers in California were particularly vulnerable targets for animosity. One of the most sweeping anti-Asian laws was aimed at the Japanese Americans, but affected all other Asian

American groups as well. The 1913 Alien Land Law prohibited "aliens ineligible to citizenship" from owning or leasing land for more than three years. Initially the Japanese Americans were able to bypass the law primarily because they could buy or lease land under the names of their American-born offspring (the Nisei), who were U.S. citizens by birth. The law was strengthened in 1920, however, and the purchase of land under the names of American-born offspring was prohibited.[26]

Several sweeping anti-immigration laws were passed in the first quarter of the twentieth century that served to eliminate Asian immigration to the United States. A provision in the 1917 Immigration Act banned immigration from the so-called "Asian barred zone," except for the Philippines and Japan. A more severe anti-Asian restriction was further imposed by the 1924 National Origins Act, which placed a ceiling of 150,000 new immigrants per year. The 1924 act was intended to limit Eastern and Southern European immigration, but a provision was added that ended any immigration by aliens ineligible for citizenship.[27]

Asian Americans did not sit back passively in the fact of discriminatory laws; they hired lawyers and went to court to fight for their livelihoods, naturalization rights, and personal liberties. Sometimes they were successful, oftentimes they were not. In the case of *Yick Wo v. Hopkins* (1886), Chinese successfully challenged an 1880 San Francisco Laundry Ordinance, which regulated commercial laundry service in a way that clearly discriminated against the Chinese. Plaintiff Yick Wo had operated a laundry service for 22 years, but when he tried to renew his business license in 1885 he was turned down because his storefront was made out of wood. Two hundred other Chinese laundries were also denied business licenses on similar grounds, while 80 non-Chinese laundries were approved—even those in wooden buildings. The Supreme Court ruled in favor of Yick Wo, concluding there was "no reason" for the denial of the business license "except to the face and nationality" of the petitioner.[28]

The inability to gain citizenship was a defining factor throughout the early history of Asian Americans. The constitutionality of naturalization based on race was first challenged in the Supreme Court case of *Ozawa v. United States* (1922). Takao Ozawa was born in Japan but immigrated to the United States at an early age. He graduated from Berkeley High School in California and attended the University of California for three years. Ozawa was a model immigrant who did not smoke or drink, he attended a predominantly white church, his children attended public school, and English was the language spoken at home. When Ozawa was rejected in his initial attempt for naturalization, he appealed and argued that the provisions for citizenship in the 1790 and 1870 acts did not specifically exclude Japanese. In addition, Ozawa also tried to argue that Japanese should be considered "white."

The Court unanimously ruled against Ozawa on both grounds. First, the Court decided that initial framers of the law and its amendment did not intend to *exclude* people from naturalization but, instead, only determine who would be *included*. Ozawa was denied citizenship because the existing law simply didn't include Japanese. Second, the Court also ruled against Ozawa's argument that Japanese were actually more "white" than other darker-skinned "white" people such as some Italians, Spanish, and Portuguese. The Court clarified the matter by defining a "white person" to be synonymous with a "person of the Caucasian race." In short, Ozawa was not Caucasian (though he thought himself to be "white") and, thus, was ineligible for citizenship.[29]

Prior to the *Ozawa* case, Asian Indians already enjoyed the right of naturalization. In *United States v. Balsara* (1910), the Supreme Court determined that Asian Indians were Caucasian and approximately 70 became naturalized citizens. But the Immigration and Naturalization Service (INS) challenged this decision, and it was taken up again in the case of *United States v. Thind* (1923). This time the Supreme Court reversed its earlier decision and ruled that Bhagat Singh Thind could not be a citizen because he was not "white." Even though Asian Indians were classified as Caucasian, this was a scientific term that was inconsistent with the popular understanding. The Court's decision stated: "It may be true that the blond Scandinavian and the brown Hindu have a common ancestor in the dim reaches of antiquity, but the average man knows perfectly well that there are unmistakable differences between them today."[30] In other words, only "white" Caucasians were considered eligible for U.S. citizenship. In the wake of the *Thind* decision, the INS was able to cancel retroactively the citizenship of Asian Indians between 1923 and 1926.

Asian Americans also received disparate treatment compared to other immigrants in their most private affairs, such as marriage. In the nineteenth century, anti-miscegenation laws prohibiting marriage between blacks and whites were common throughout the United States. In 1880 the California legislature extended restrictive anti-miscegenation categories to prohibit any marriage between a white person and a "negro, mulatto, or Mongolian." This law, targeted at the Chinese, was not challenged until Salvador Roldan won a California Court of Appeals decision in 1933. Roldan, a Filipino American, argued that he was Malay, not Mongolian, and he should be allowed to marry his white fiancée. The Court conceded that the state's anti-miscegenation law was created in an atmosphere of intense anti-Chinese sentiment, and agreed Filipinos were not in mind when the initial legislation was approved. Unfortunately, this victory was short-lived. The California State legislature amended the anti-miscegenation law to include the "Malay race" shortly after the Roldan decision was announced.[31]

World War II and the Cold War Era

For Asian Americans, World War II was an epoch; but the profound impact was distinct for different Asian American groups. For over 110,000 Japanese Americans, World War II was an agonizing ordeal soon after Japan's attack of Pearl Harbor on December 7, 1941. The FBI arrested thousands of Japanese Americans who were considered potential security threats immediately after the Pearl Harbor bombing raid. Arrested without evidence of disloyalty were the most visible Japanese American community leaders, including businessmen, Shinto and Buddhist priests, teachers in Japanese language schools, and editors of Japanese language newspapers. Wartime hysteria rose to a fever pitch, and on February 19, 1942, President Franklin Roosevelt issued Executive Order 9066. This order established various military zones and authorized the removal of anyone who was a potential threat. While there were a small number of German and Italian aliens detained and relocated, this did not compare to the mass relocation of Japanese Americans on the West Coast of the United States.[32]

The order to relocate Japanese Americans because of military necessity, and the threat they posed to security, was a fabrication. There was considerable debate even among military leaders over the genuine need for mass relocation, and the government's own intelligence reports found no evidence of Japanese American disloyalty. "For the most part the local Japanese are loyal to the United States or, at worst, hope that by remaining quiet they can avoid concentration camps or irresponsible mobs," one report stated. "We do not believe that they would be at least any more disloyal than any other racial group in the United States with whom we went to war."[33] This helps to explain why 160,000 Japanese Americans living in Hawaii were not interned. More telling was the fact that Japanese Americans in the continental United States were a small but much resented minority. Despite government reports to the contrary, business leaders, local politicians, and the media fueled antagonism against the Japanese Americans and agitated for their abrupt removal.[34]

With only seven days' notice to prepare once the internment order was issued, and no way of knowing how long the war would last, many Japanese Americans were forced to sell their homes and property at a mere fraction of their genuine value. It is estimated that the Japanese Americans suffered economic losses alone of at least $400 million. By August 1942 all the Japanese on the West Coast were interned in ten camps located in rural regions of California, Arizona, Utah, Idaho, Wyoming, and Arkansas. Two thirds of the interned Japanese American men, women, and children were U.S. citizens, whose only crime was their ancestry; even those with as little as one-eighth Japanese blood were interned. The camps themselves were crude, mass facilities surrounded by barbed wire and guarded by armed sentries. People were housed in large barracks with each family living in small cramped "apartments." Food was served in large mess halls, and toilet and shower facilities were communal. Many of the camps were extremely cold in the winter, hot in the summer, and dusty all year round. The camps remained open for the duration of the war.[35]

After the first year of the camps, the government began recruiting young Japanese American men to help in the war effort. The military desperately needed Japanese Americans to serve as interpreters for Japanese prisoners of war and translators of captured documents. But to the military's incredulity, most American-born Japanese had only modest Japanese language skills and had to take intense training in the Military Intelligence Service Language School before they could perform their duties.[36] It was, however, the heroic actions of the 100th Infantry Battalion, which later merged with the 442nd Regimental Combat Team, that stand out the most among historians. The two segregated units engaged in numerous campaigns and served with distinction throughout Europe. By the end of the war in Europe, for example, the Nisei soldiers of the 442nd suffered over 9,000 casualties, while earning over 18,000 individual decorations of honor. The 442nd was the most decorated unit of its size during all of World War II.[37]

Compared to the Japanese American experience, other Asian American groups fared far better during and after World War II. Changes for Chinese Americans were particularly dramatic. Prior to the war, the image of the Chinese was clearly negative compared to the Japanese. A survey of Princeton undergraduates in 1931 thought the top three traits of the Chinese were the fact they were "superstitious, sly, and conservative," while Japanese were considered "intelligent, industrious, and progressive."[38] Immediately after the bombing of Pearl Harbor, Chinese store owners put up signs indicating they were not Japanese, and in some cases Chinese Americans wore buttons stating, "I am Chinese." To alleviate any further identification problems, *Time* magazine published an article on December 22, 1941, explaining how to tell the difference between Chinese and "Japs." The article compared photographs of a Chinese man and a Japanese man, highlighting the distinguishing facial features of each.[39] Just months later, a 1942 Gallup Poll characterized the Chinese as "hardworking, honest, and brave," while Japanese were seen as "treacherous, sly, and cruel."[40]

Employment opportunities outside of the segregated Chinatown community became available to Chinese Americans for the first time during the war, and continued even after the war ended. Chinese Americans trained in various professions and skilled crafts were able to find work in war-related industries that had never been open to them before. In addition, the employment of Chinese American women increased threefold during the 1940s. Leading the way were clerical positions, which increased from just 750 in 1940 to 3,200 in 1950. In 1940 women represented just one in five Chinese American professionals, but by 1950 this increased to one in three. On another level, Chinese actors suddenly found they were in demand for film roles—usually playing evil Japanese characters. Shortly after the war, writers such as Jade Snow Wong and Pardee Lowe discovered the newfound interest and appreciation of Chinese Americans could be turned into commercial success through the publication of their memoirs.[41]

On the military front, Asian Americans also distinguished themselves. Over 15,000 Chinese Americans served in all branches of the military, unlike the Japanese Americans who were placed only in segregated infantry units and in the Military Intelligence Service. Similarly, over 7,000 Filipino Americans volunteered for the army and formed the First and Second Filipino Infantry Regiments. About 1,000 other Filipino Americans were sent to the Philippines to perform reconnaissance and intelligence activities for General Douglas MacArthur.[42] Equally significant was the War Bride's Act of 1945, which allowed war veterans to bring wives from China and the Philippines as non-quota immigrants. This resulted in a rapid and dramatic shift in the historic gender imbalance of both groups. For example, between 1945 and 1952, nine out of ten (89.9 percent) Chinese immigrants were female, and 20,000 Chinese American babies were born by the mid-1950s. Similarly, between 1951 and 1960 seven out of ten (71 percent) Filipino immigrants were female.[43]

On the broad international front, alliances with China, the Philippines, and India eventually began the process of changing the overtly discriminatory immigration laws against Asians: The Chinese Exclusion Law was repealed in 1943 and an annual quota of 105 immigrants from China was allotted; in 1946 Congress approved legislation that extended citizenship to Filipino immigrants and permitted the entry of 100 Filipino immigrants annually; also in 1946, the Luce-Cellar Act ended the 1917 "Asian barred zone," allowed an immigration quota of 100 from India, and for the first time permitted Asian Indians to apply for citizenship since the *United States v. Thind* case of 1923. Though these changes were extremely modest, they carried important symbolic weight by helping to create a favorable international opinion of the United States during and immediately after the war.[44]

Geopolitical events during the Cold War era of the 1950s and 1960s immediately following World War II continued to have important ramifications for Asian Americans. After the 1949

United States immigration policy also allowed virtually unrestricted immigration to certain categories of people including spouses, children under 21, and parents of U.S. citizens. These provisions served to accelerate immigration from Asia to the United States. While the primary goal of the 1965 Immigration Reform Act was to encourage family reunification, a much higher percentage of Asian immigrants initially began entering the United States under the established occupational and non-preference investment categories. In 1969, for example, 62 percent of Asian Indians, 43 percent of Filipinos, and 34.8 percent of Koreans entered the United States under the occupational and investor categories. By the mid-1970s, however, 80 to 90 percent of all Asian immigrants entered the United States through one of the family categories.[48] Still, studies clearly show that most post-1965 Asian immigrants tend to be more middle-class, educated, urbanized, and they arrive in the United States in family units rather than as individuals, compared to their pre-1965 counterparts.[49]

The framers of the 1965 law did not anticipate any dramatic changes in the historical pattern of immigration, but it is clear that Asian immigrants

have taken advantage of almost every aspect of the 1965 Immigration Reform Act. Asians were just 7.7 percent of all immigrants to the United States between 1955 and 1964; this rose to 22.4 percent between 1965 and 1974, and increased to 43.3 percent between 1975 and 1984. The percentage of Asian immigrants remained steady for several years but declined sharply in the late 1980s and early 1990s (see Table 2). This decline was due to the sudden increase of mostly Mexicans who were able to apply for legal status following the passage of the Immigration Reform and Control Act of 1986 (IRCA). By the early 1990s, 2.67 million aliens received permanent residence status under IRCA.[50]

This "amnesty" provision was only a part of IRCA, which was fully intended to control illegal immigration into the United States. IRCA also required that all employers verify the legal status of all new employees, and it imposed civil and criminal penalties against employers who knowingly hire undocumented workers.[51] While IRCA closed the "back door" of illegal immigration, another reform, the Immigration Act of 1990, was enacted to keep open the "front door" of legal immigration. Indeed, this law actually authorizes

TABLE 2
Percent of Immigrants Admitted by Region, Fiscal Years 1955–1994

Region	1955–1964	1965–1974	1975–1984	1985–1990	1991–1994
All	100.0	100.0	100.0	100.0	100.0*
Europe	50.2	29.8	13.4	8.9	14.9
North/West	28.6	11.0	5.2	4.0	4.6
South/East	21.6	18.7	8.1	4.9	10.3
Asia	7.7	22.4	43.3	33.5	33.0
North America	26.4	19.0	14.8	28.8	27.0
Caribbean	7.0	18.0	15.1	12.0	10.4
Central America	2.4	2.5	3.7	7.2	5.9
South America	5.1	6.0	6.6	6.2	5.5
Africa	.7	1.5	2.4	2.6	2.0
Oceania	.4	.7	.8	.5	.5

*May not add to 100 due to rounding.

Source: U.S. Immigration and Naturalization Service, *Statistical Yearbook of the Immigration and Naturalization Service* (Washington, DC: Government Printing Office, 1996), Table C, p. 21.

an *increase* in legal immigration to the United States. In response to uncertain economic stability at home, growing global economic competition abroad, and the dramatically changed face of immigration, the 1990 law sent a mixed message to Asian immigrants.

First of all, the law actually authorized an increase in legal immigration, but at the same time placed a yearly cap on total immigration for the first time since the 1920s. For 1992 to 1995, the limit is 700,000 persons, and 675,000 thereafter. While this appears to be an arbitrary limit, it still allows for an unlimited number of visas for immediate relatives of U.S. citizens. This may not have a negative effect on Asian immigration since, as a group, Asians have the highest rate of naturalization compared to other immigrants.[52] Second, the law encourages immigration of more skilled workers to help meet the needs of the U.S. economy. The number of visas for skilled workers and their families increased from 58,000 to 140,000, while the number for unskilled workers was cut in half to just 10,000. This may prove to be a benefit to Asians who, since 1965, have been among the best-educated and best-trained immigrants this nation has ever seen. Third, the 1990 immigration law also seeks to "diversify" the new immigrants by giving more visas to countries who have sent relatively few migrants to the United States in recent years. This program has been popular with lawmakers who want to assist emigrants from Western European countries, at the expense of Asians. For example, up to 40 percent of the initial visas allocated for the diversity category were for Ireland. Noted immigration attorney Bill Ong Hing found sections of the Immigration Act of 1990 "provide extra independent and transition visas that are unavailable to Asians."[53]

The lasting legacy of the civil rights movement on immigration policy was the emphasis on fairness, equality, and family reunification. But the increased emphasis on highly skilled immigrants found in the 1990 immigration law indicates some loosening of those ideals and priorities. It is clear from the above descriptions

of Asian American history that the conditions for the post-1965 Asian migrants are quite distinct from pre-1965 migrants. This seemingly obvious observation reflects the fact that international migration is not a simple, stable, nor homogeneous process. Even with this in mind, the most popular frame of reference for all movement to the United States continues to be the European immigrant experience throughout the nineteenth and early twentieth centuries. The popular European immigrant analogy is highlighted in the words of welcome written on the Statute of Liberty:

> Give me your tired, your poor
> Your huddled masses yearning to breathe free
> The wretched refuse of your teeming shore.
> Send these, the homeless, tempest-tost to me,
> I lift my lamp beside the golden door!

The European immigrant experience, however, is by no means universal, and is only part of what scholars today see as a much broader picture of the international movement of people and capital. Understanding the broader dynamics of global economic restructuring is useful in comparing and contrasting post-1965 Asian immigrants with other immigrants and minority groups in the United States.

Global Economic Restructuring

What makes people want to leave their home country and migrate to another country? The most commonly accepted answer is found within what is known as the push-pull theory. This theory generally asserts that difficult economic, social, and political conditions in the home country force, or push, people away. On the other hand, these people are attracted, or pulled, to another country where conditions are seen as more favorable. Upon closer examination, however, this theoretical viewpoint does run into some problems. Most significantly, the push-pull theory tends to see immigration flows as a natural, open, and spontaneous process, but does not adequately take into account the structural factors and policy changes that directly affect immigration flows. This is because earlier migration studies based on European immigration limited their focus on poor countries that sent low-skilled labor to affluent countries with growing economies that put newcomers to work. The push-pull theory is not incorrect, but is considered to be incomplete and historically static. Recent studies have taken a much broader approach to international migration and insist that in order to understand post-1965 immigration from Asia, it is necessary to understand the recent restructuring of the global economy.[54]

Since the end of World War II, global restructuring has involved the gradual movement of industrial manufacturing away from developed nations such as the United States to less developed nations in Asia and Latin America where labor costs are cheaper. This process was best seen in Japan in the 1950s through 1970s, and accelerated rapidly in the 1980s to newly industrialized Asian countries, namely Taiwan, Hong Kong, Singapore, and South Korea. Other Asian countries such as India, Thailand, Indonesia, Malaysia, and the Philippines also followed the same economic course with varying degrees of success. In the 1990s mainland China has increased its manufacturing and export capacity dramatically, and is steering on the same economic path of other Asian nations.

Among the effects of global restructuring on the United States is the declining need to import low-skilled labor because manufacturing jobs are moving abroad. At the same time, there is an inclining need to import individuals with advanced specialized skills that are in great demand. According to research by Paul Ong and Evelyn Blumenberg (1994), this phenomena is evidenced in part by the increasing number of foreign-born students studying at U.S. colleges.[55] In the 1954–1955 academic year the United States was host to just 34,232 foreign exchange students; this number increased to over 440,000 in 1994.[56] Over

half of all foreign students in the United States are from Asian countries, and most major in either engineering, science, or business. A 1993 report by the National Science Foundation found that over half of the doctorate degrees in engineering, mathematics, and computer science were earned by foreign graduate students.[57] Many of these foreign graduate students planned to work in the United States and eventually gained permanent immigrant status. Companies in the United States have, of course, been eager to hire foreign-born scientists and engineers. Not only are highly skilled immigrants valuable to employers as workers, many also start their own high-tech businesses. For example, Subramonian Shankar, is the co-founder and president of American Megatrends, Inc., a company that manufactures personal-computer motherboards and software in Norcross, Georgia. AMI started business in 1985 and now has a work force of 130 people, made up of native-born Americans and immigrants. "I couldn't have done this in India," Shankar says proudly.[58]

The medical profession is another broad area where Asian immigrants have made a noticeable impact. Researchers Paul Ong and Tania Azores (1994) found that Asian Americans represented 4.4 percent of the registered nurses and 10.8 percent of the physicians in the United States in 1990. Ong and Azores estimate that only a third of Asian American physicians and a quarter of Asian American nurses were educated in the United States. Graduates of overseas medical and nursing schools have been coming to the United States since the passage of the 1946 Smith-Mundt Act, which created an exchange program for specialized training. While this exchange was intended to be temporary, many medical professionals were able to become permanent immigrants. A physician shortage in the United States during the late 1960s and early 1970s, coupled with the elimination of racial immigration quotas in 1965, brought forth a steady flow of foreign-trained M.D.s from Asian countries. A 1975 United States Commission on Civil Rights report found 5,000 Asian medical school graduates entered the United States annually during the early 1970s. But, under pressure from the medical industry, Congress passed the 1976 Health Professions Educational Act, which restricted the number of foreign-trained physicians who could enter the United States. Despite the passage of this law, almost 30,000 physicians from Asia immigrated to the United States between 1972 and 1985, and data up to 1990 show roughly half of all foreign-trained physicians entering the United States have come from Asia.[59]

Asia is also the largest source for foreign nurses. In particular, over half of all foreign-trained nurses come from the Philippines. One 1988 study conservatively estimated 50,000 Filipino nurses were working in the United States at the time. Filipino nurses find work in the United States attractive because they can earn up to 20 times the salary they can make in the Philippines, and their English-speaking abilities make them highly desired by employers. Filipino nurses are also attracted to the United States because of liberal policies that eventually allow them to stay permanently. While most foreign-trained nurses are brought to work initially on a temporary basis, the passage of the Immigration Nursing Relief Act of 1989 allows nurses to adjust to permanent status after three years of service.[60]

The general explanations for the origins of migration found that the push-pull theory continues still to have some value today. Opportunities for large numbers of professionals in Asian countries are still difficult and limited, while opportunities and relatively high salaries are available in the United States. Political instability throughout Asia also continues to be an important push factor for Asian immigrants and refugees. At the same time, this immigration process is not totally natural or spontaneous, as witnessed by foreign student and immigration policies encouraging well-trained individuals to come to the United States. Overall, the changing character of the push and pull in terms of the types of migrants entering the United States and the new skills they bring are very much a result of dynamic global economic restructuring. Global economic restructuring is an important context for understanding not only why Asian immigrants have come to the United States but also how well they have adjusted and been accepted socially, economically, and politically. It is important to note that not all Asian immigrants are middle-class and successful professionals; there is also a sizable number of other Asian immigrants, especially refugees, who have found their lives in America extremely difficult. The extreme diversity among Asian Americans is due in large part to the third major event affecting migration from Asia—the Vietnam War.

The Vietnam War and Southeast Asian Refugees

Since 1975 large numbers of Southeast Asian refugees have entered the United States, and today California is the home for most of them (see Table 3). Roughly three quarters of all Southeast Asian refugees are from Vietnam, with the rest from Laos and Cambodia. Unlike most other post-1965 Asian immigrants who came to the United States in a rather orderly fashion seeking family reunification and economic opportunities, Southeast Asian refugees arrived as part of an international resettlement effort of people who faced genuine political persecution and bodily harm in their home countries. Southeast Asian refugees to the United States can be easily divided into three distinct waves: the first wave arrived in the United States in 1975 shortly after the fall of Saigon; the second wave arrived between 1978 and 1980; and the third entered the United States after 1980 and continues to this day. The United States has accepted these refugees not only for humanitarian reasons but also because of a recognition that U.S. foreign policy and military actions in Southeast Asia had a hand in creating much of the calamity that has befallen the entire region.

U.S. political interests in Southeast Asia actually began during World War II, although for years efforts were limited to foreign aid and military advisers. Direct military intervention rapidly

quota of 50,000 refugees per year, funded resettlement programs, and allowed refugees to
become eligible for the same welfare benefits as
U.S. citizens after 36 months of refugee assistance (this was changed to 18 months in 1982).
The third wave of Southeast Asians are technically not considered refugees, but are in actuality
immigrants. This has been facilitated by the 1980
Orderly Departure Program (ODP), an agreement
with Vietnam that allows individuals and families
to enter the United States. ODP was a benefit for
three groups: relatives of permanently settled
refugees in the United States, Amerasians, and
former reeducation camp internees. By the end of
1992, over 300,000 Vietnamese immigrated to the
United States, including 80,000 Amerasians and
their relatives, as well as 60,000 former camp
internees and their families.[67] . . .

It is obvious that Southeast Asian refugees/
immigrants have been a rapidly growing and
extremely diverse group. According to the 1990
census, there were 1,001,054 Southeast Asians in
the United States, or 13 percent of the total population of Asian Americans. Individually, the
census counted 614,547 Vietnamese, 149,014
Laotians, 147,411 Cambodians, and 90,082
Hmong. Some have argued that these census
figures are an undercount of the actual numbers
of people from Southeast Asian countries. Researchers point to the fact that the total number of
arrivals to the United States from Southeast Asia is
roughly the same as census figures. This is an
anomaly because the census figure should be
about 20 percent larger to reflect the number of
American-born Southeast Asians. There are,
however, several reasons for this disparity. First of
all, new arrivals from Southeast Asia who have
little knowledge of the English language may
simply not have responded to census questionnaires. This certainly is a general concern for all
Asian American groups. Second, and probably
most important, it is estimated that between 15
and 25 percent of those from Vietnam, Cambodia,
and Laos are actually ethnic-Chinese. It is quite
possible that many ethnic-Chinese from Southeast

Asia answered the appropriate census question of
ethnicity without regard to their nationality. Third,
no one is exactly sure how Amerasians identified
themselves on the 1990 census, or if they even
participated at all. While a factor, it is important to
note that most of the Amerasians from Vietnam
did not actually enter the United States until after
the 1990 census was taken. All references to the
Southeast Asian population should keep these
considerations in mind.[68]

CONCLUSION

This reading briefly describes the history and
recent growth of the Asian population in the United
States. It also highlights the significance of the
1965 Immigration Reform Act, global economic
restructuring, and the Vietnam War as three broad
events that profoundly impacted both the number
and type of migrants who have come to the United
States from Asian countries. In order to examine
post-1965 Asian Americans comprehensively, it is
particularly important to look not only at the rapid
growth of the population but also at a multitude of
other factors, such as personal history, nativity,
length of time in the United States, pre-migration
experiences and traumas, education, socioeconomic class background, and gender. . . .

NOTES

1. Shih-shan Henry Tsai, *The Chinese Experience in
   America* (Bloomington: Indiana University Press, 1986),
   p. 1; also see Stan Steiner, *Fusahang: The Chinese Who
   Built America* (New York: Harper & Row, 1979), pp.
   24–35; Elena S. H. Yu, "Filipino Migration and Community Organization in the United States," *California Sociologist* 3:2 (1980); 76–102; and Joan M. Jensen, *Passage
   from India: Asian Indian Immigrants in North America*
   (New Haven: Yale University Press, 1988), pp. 12–13.

2. Sucheng Chan, *Asian Californians* (San Francisco:
   MTL/Boyd & Fraser, 1991), pp. 5–6.

3. Ronald Takaki, *Strangers from a Different Shore* (Boston:
   Little, Brown and Company, 1989), pp. 79, 114.

4. Stanford Lyman, *Chinese Americans* (New York: Random
   House, 1974), pp. 86–88.

5. Chan, *Asian Californians*, pp. 27–33.

6. Lyman, *Chinese Americans*, pp. 63–69.

7. Yuji Ichioka, *The Issei: The World of the First Generation Japanese Immigrant's, 1885–1924* (New York: The Free Press, 1988), pp. 64–65.

8. Roger Daniels, *Concentration Camps: North America Japanese in the United States and Canada During World War II* (Malabar, FL: Robert A. Kreiger, 1981), p. 7.

9. Bill Ong Hing, *Making and Remaking Asian America Through Immigration Policy, 1850–1990* (Stanford, CA: Stanford University Press, 1993), pp. 28–30.

10. Chan, *Asian Californians*, p. 7.

11. Edwin B. Almirol, *Ethnic Identify and Social Negotiation: A Study of a Filipino Community in California* (New York: AMS Press, 1985), pp. 52–59; and H. Brett Melendy, "Filipinos in the United States," in Norris Hundlkey, Jr. (ed.), *The Asian American: The Historical Experience* (Santa Barbara: Cleo Books, 1977), pp. 101–128.

12. Takaki, *Strangers from a Different Shore*, pp. 53–57.

13. Chan, *Asian Californians*, pp. 7, 17–19, 37; and Warren Y. Kim, *Koreans in America* (Seoul: Po Chin Chai Printing Co., 1971), pp. 22–27.

14. Joan M. Jensen, *Passage from India: Asian Indian Immigrants in North America* (New Haven: Yale University Press, 1988), pp. 24–41; and Rajanki K. Das, *Hindustani Workers on the Pacific Coast* (Berlin and Leipzig: Walter De Bruyter & Co., 1923), p. 77.

15. Das, *Hindustani Workers*, pp. 66–67.

16. Bruce La Brack, "Occupational Specialization Among Rural California Sikhs: The Interplay of Culture and Economics," *Amerasia Journal* 9:2 (1982): 29–56.

17. Naturalization Act of 1790, I Stat. 103 (1790).

18. Act of 14 July 1870, 16 Stat. 256.

19. Roger Daniels, *Asian Americans: Chinese and Japanese in the United States* (Seattle: University of Washington Press, 1988) p. 43.

20. Chan, *Asian Californians*, p. 42.

21. Robert F. Heizer and Alan F. Almquist, *The Other Californians: Prejudice and Discrimination under Spain, Mexico, and the United States to 1920* (Berkeley: University of California Press, 1971), p. 129.

22. Takaki, *Strangers from a Different Shore*, p. 82.

23. Lyman, *Chinese Americans*, pp. 55–85.

24. Takaki, *Strangers from a Different Shore*, pp. 111–112.

25. Juan L. Gonzales, *Racial and Ethnic Groups in America*, second edition (Dubuque, Iowa: Kendall/Hunt Publishing Co., 1993), p. 136; and Juan L. Gonzales, *Racial and Ethnic Families in America*, second edition (Dubuque, Iowa: Kendall/Hunt Publishing Co., 1993), p. 3.

26. Chan, *Asian Californians*, pp. 44–45.

27. Hing, *Making and Remaking Asian America*, pp. 32–39.

28. *Yick Wo v. Hopkins*, 118 U.S. 356 (1886); and Lyman, *Chinese Americans*, p. 79.

29. *Takao Ozawa v. United States*, 260 U.S. 178 (1922); Heizer and Alquist, *The Other Californians*, pp. 192–193; and Ichioka, *The Issei*, pp. 210–226.

30. *United States v. Bhagat Singh Thind*, 261 U.S. 204 (1923); Jensen, *Passage from India*, pp. 255–260; and Gurdial Singh, "East Indians in the United States," *Sociology and Social Research* 30:3 (1946): 208–216.

31. Megumi Dick Osumi, "Asians and California's Anti-Miscegenation Laws," in Nobuya Tsuchida (ed.), *Asian and Pacific American Experiences: Women's Perspectives* (Minneapolis: Asian/Pacific American Learning Resource Center, University of Minnesota, 1982), pp. 1–37; and Takaki, *Strangers from a Different Shore*, pp. 330–331.

32. William Petersen, *Japanese Americans* (New York: Random House, 1971), pp. 66–100; Roger Daniels, *Concentration Camps: U.S.A.* (New York: Holt, Rinehart & Winston, 1971), pp. 75, 81–82; and Jacobus tenBroek, Edward N. Barnhart, and Floyd W. Matson, *Prejudice, War, and the Constitution* (Berkeley: University of California Press), pp. 118–120.

33. Cited in Commission on Wartime Relocation and Internment of Civilians, *Personal Justice Denied* (Washington, DC: Government Printing Office, 1982), pp. 52–53.

34. Takaki, *Strangers from a Different Shore*, pp. 379–392.

35. Commission on Wartime Relocation and Internment of Civilians, *Personal Justice Denied*, p. 217; tenBroek, Barnhart, and Matson, *Prejudice, War, and the Constitution*, pp. 155–177, 180–181; and Daniels, *Concentration Camps: North America*.

36. Chan, *Asian Californians*, p. 101.

37. Petersen, *Japanese Americans*, p. 87.

38. Cited in Marvin Karlins, Thomas L. Coffman, and Gary Walters, "On the Fading of Social Stereotypes: Studies of Three Generations of College Students," *Journal of Personality and Psychology* 13 (1990): 4–5.

39. *Time*, December 22, 1941, p. 33.

40. Cited in Harold Isaacs, *Images of Asia: American Views of China and India* (New York: Harper & Row, 1972), pp. xviii–xix.

41. Chan, *Asian Californians*, pp. 103–104; and Lyman, *Chinese Americans*, pp. 127, 134.

42. Takaki, *Strangers from a Different Shore*, pp. 357–363, 370–378; Manuel Buaken, "Life in the Armed Forces," *New Republic* 109 (1943); 279–280; and Bienvenido Santos, "Filipinos in War," *Far Eastern Survey* 11 (1942): 249–250.

43. Harry H. L. Kitano and Roger Daniels, *Asian Americans: Emerging Minorities*, second edition (Englewood Cliffs, New Jersey: Prentice Hall, 1995), p. 42, Table 4–2; and Monica Boyd, "Oriental Immigration: The Experience of Chinese, Japanese, and Filipino Populations in the United States," *International Migration Review* 10 (1976): 48–60, Table 1.

44. Chan, *Asian Californians*, pp. 105–106.

45. Diane Mark and Ginger Chih, *A Place Called Chinese America* (San Francisco: The Organization of Chinese Americans, 1982), pp. 105–107.

46. Chan, *Asian Californians*, pp. 108–109.

47. Ibid., pp. 109–110.

48. Hing, *Making and Remaking Asian America*, Appendix B, pp. 189–200; Table 9, p. 82.

49. Hing, *Making and Remaking Asian America*, pp. 79–120; Luciano Mangiafico, *Contemporary American Immigrants: Patterns of Filipino, Korean, and Chinese Settlement in the United States* (New York: Praeger Publishers, 1988), pp. 1–26; James T. Fawcett and Benjamin V. Carino (eds.), *Pacific Bridges: The New Immigration from Asia and the Pacific Islands* (Staten Island, NY: Center for Migration Studies, 1987); and Herbert R. Barringer, Robert W. Gardner, and Michael J. Levine (eds.), *Asian and Pacific Islanders in the United States* (New York: Russell Sage Foundation, 1993).

50. U.S. Immigration and Naturalization Service, *Statistical Yearbook of the Immigration and Naturalization Service, 1993* (Washington, DC: Government Printing Office, 1994), p. 20.

51. Roger Daniels, *Coming to America* (New York: Harper-Collins Publishers, 1990), pp. 391–397.

52. U.S. Immigration and Naturalization Service, *Statistical Yearbook of the Immigration and Naturalization Service, 1994* (Washington, DC: Government Printing Office, 1996), p. 126, Chart O.

53. Hing, *Making and Remaking Asian America*, pp. 7–8.

54. Paul Ong, Edna Bonacich, and Lucie Cheng (eds.), *The New Asian Immigration in Los Angeles and Global Restructuring* (Philadelphia: Temple University Press, 1994), pp. 3–100; and Edna Bonacich, Lucie Cheng, Norma Chinchilla, Nora Hamilton, and Paul Ong (eds.), *Global Production: The Apparel Industry in the Pacific Rim* (Philadelphia: Temple University Press, 1994), pp. 3–20.

55. Paul Ong and Evelyn Blumenberg, "Scientists and Engineers," in Paul Ong (ed.) *The State of Asian Pacific America: Economic Diversity, Issues & Policies* (Los Angeles: LEAP Asian Pacific American Public Policy Institute and UCLA Asian American Studies Center, 1994), pp. 113–138. It is important to note that I am distinguishing between foreign exchange students who are overseas nationals from Asian American students who happen to be foreign born.

56. Ibid., p. 173; and U.S. Department of Commerce, *Statistical Abstract of the United States, 1995* (Washington, DC: Government Printing Office, 1995), p. 188. Table 295.

57. Cited in *Statistical Abstract, 1995*, p. 619, Table 997.

58. Michael J. Mandel and Christopher Farrell, "The Immigrants: How They're Helping to Revitalize the U.S. Economy," *Business Week*, July 13, 1992, pp. 114–120, 122.

59. Paul Ong and Tania Azores, "Health Professionals on the Front-Line," in Paul Ong (ed.), *The Sate of Asian Pacific America: Economic Diversity, Issues & Policies*, pp. 139–164.

60. Paul Ong and Tania Azores, "The Migration and Incorporation of Filipino Nurses," in Ong et al. (eds.), *The New Asian Immigration in Los Angeles and Global Restructuring*, pp. 166–195; and Mangiafico, *Contemporary American Immigrants*, pp. 42–43.

61. Literature on the Vietnam conflict is voluminous. For an excellent and readable overview see Stanley Karnow, *Vietnam: A History* (New York: Penguin Books, 1991).

62. The quota for refugees under the 1965 Immigration Reform Act was only 17,400, so President Gerald Ford instructed the attorney general to use his "parole" power to admit the 130,000 refugees. The use of parole was also used to bring European refugees to the United States during the 1950s. For more details, see Hing, *Making and Remaking Asian America*, pp. 123–128, and Paul J. Strand and Woodrow Jones, Jr., *Indochinese Refugees in America: Problems of Adaptation and Assimilation* (Durham, NC: Duke University Press, 1985).

63. Chan, *Asian Californians*, p. 128; and Chor-Swan Ngin, "The Acculturation Pattern of Orange County's Southeast Asian Refugees," *Journal of Orange County Studies* 3:4 (Fall 1989–Spring 1990): 46–53.

64. Ngin, "The Acculturation Pattern of Orange County's Southeast Asian Refugees," p. 49; and Ngoan Le, "The Case of the Southeast Asian Refugees: Policy for a Community 'At-Risk'," in *The State of Asian Pacific America: Policy Issues to the Year 2020* (Los Angeles: LEAP Asian Pacific American Public Policy Institute and UCLA Asian American Studies Center, 1993), pp. 167–188.

65. For more details see Strand and Jones, *Indochinese Refugees in America*; Barry I. Wain, *The Refused: The Agony of Indochina Refugees* (New York: Simon & Schuster, 1981); and U.S. Committee for Refugees, *Uncertain Harbors: The Plight of Vietnamese Boat People* (Washington, DC: Government Printing Office, 1987).

66. Chan, *Asian Californians*, pp. 121–139; Kitano and Daniels, *Asian Americans: Emerging Minorities*, pp. 170–191; U.S. Committee for Refugees, *Cambodians in Thailand: People on the Edge* (Washington, DC: Government Printing Office, 1985); and U.S. Committee for Refugees, *Refugees from Laos: In Harm's Way* (Washington, DC: Government Printing Office, 1986).

67. U.S. Committee for Refugees, *Uncertain Harbors*, pp. 19–20; and Ruben Rumbaut, "Vietnamese, Laotian, and Cambodian Americans," in Pyong Gap Min (ed.), *Asian Americans: Contemporary Trends and Issues* (Thousand Oaks, CA: Sage Publications, 1995), p. 240.

68. Ruben Rumbaut and J. R. Weeks, "Fertility and Adaptation: Indochinese Refugees in the United States," *International Migration Review* 20:2 (1986): 428–466; and Rumbaut, "Vietnamese, Laotian, and Cambodian Americans," pp. 239–242.

Reading 2

Contemporary Asian American Sociodemographic Status

Larry H. Shinagawa

More than any current "racial" group in the United States, Asian Pacific Americans are affected by immigration. Historically, the ebbs and flows of Asian and Pacific Islander immigration have been chiefly responsible for the size and diversity of the Asian Pacific American populations. While immigration came in spurts, and with virtual stops, between 1850 and 1965, the majority of Asian and Pacific Islander immigration occurred after the passage of the Immigration and Nationality Act Amendments of 1965.[1] This law and its successors caused an amazing growth of the Asian Pacific American population. Between 1960 and 1990 the Asian Pacific American population increased from 1 million to over 7 million, illustrating a 700 percent growth factor. Between 1970 and 1990 the Asian Pacific American population more than tripled (3.62 times). More recently, the Asian Pacific American population doubled in size between 1980 and 1990 (1.96 times). In 1990, there were 7,273,662 Asian Pacific American individuals, represented by 31 diverse groups. By 1990, they constituted 2.9 percent of all Americans.

According to the 1994 Current Population Survey, the Asian Pacific American population was estimated at 8.8 million. In 1994, as in 1990, they constituted roughly 3 percent of America's population. Since 1990, the Asian Pacific American population has grown by an average of 4.5 percent per year. Eighty-six percent of the growth is attributable to immigration. The remainder was due to natural increase.[2]

Source: Bill Ong Hing and Ronald Lee, eds., *Reframing the Immigration Debate* (Los Angeles: LEAP Asian Pacific American Policy Institute and UCLA Asian American Studies Center, 1996), pp. 59–126. Reprinted with the permission of Larry Shinagawa.

By the year 2000, Asian Pacific Americans are projected to reach 12.1 million and represent 4.3 percent of America's population.[3] Until the year 2000, 75 percent of the Asian Pacific American population growth will be attributable to immigration. By the year 2050, the Asian Pacific American population will have increased 5 times its size from 1995.[4] By then, it will comprise 10 percent of the total U.S. population.

Regionally, the Western states, and California in particular, will continue to be the favorite locations of Asian Pacific Americans. Between 1993 and 2020, there will be an increase in the Western Asian Pacific American population by 8 million persons. By the year 2000, 40.5 percent of all Asian Pacific Americans will live in California, as compared to 40.0 percent in 1995 and 39.1 percent in 1990. By the year 2000, California is projected to have almost 10 million Asian Pacific Americans. By 2020, Texas and New York will each have more than 1 million Asian Pacific Americans.[5]

MAJOR ASIAN PACIFIC AMERICAN GROUPS

In 1990, Chinese Americans constituted the largest Asian Pacific American population, with 1,645,472 individuals. Over one-fifth (22.6 percent) of all Asian Pacific Americans were Chinese Americans and they represented about .7 percent of all Americans. Closely following them were Filipino Americans with a population of 1,406,770. Nearly one-fifth (19.3 percent) of Asian Pacific Americans were Filipino Americans and they constituted .6 percent of all Americans. Smaller in size, in

31

in Washington, Korean Americans in Virginia, and Asian Indian Americans in Florida. In Massachusetts, Chinese Americans were the largest population with 53,792, followed by Asian Indian Americans with 19,719.

The distribution of Asian Pacific Americans in the top ten cities with the largest Asian Pacific American populations showed the typical bi-coastal pattern and the regional concentration in Chicago and in Houston. According to the 1990 STFlC, Asian Pacific Americans represented 28 percent of San Francisco's population, 19 percent of San Jose, 11 percent of San Diego, 9 percent of Los Angeles, 7 percent of New York City, and 5 percent of Boston. These cities were among the 20 largest in the United States. The top ten cities with the largest Asian Pacific American population were, by descending order: New York City, New York; Los Angeles, California; Honolulu, Hawaii; San Francisco, California; San Jose, California; San Diego, California; Chicago, Illinois; Houston, Texas; Seattle, Washington; and Long Beach, California.

Among counties in the United States Los Angeles County had the largest Asian Pacific American population (954,485), followed by Honolulu County, Hawaii; Queens County, New York; Santa Clara County, California; Orange County, California; San Francisco County, California; San Diego County, California; Alameda County, California; Cook County, Illinois; and Kings County, New York. . . . Among these counties, the three counties with the largest Asian Pacific American percentage concentration were Honolulu, Hawaii (63 percent); San Francisco, California (29.1 percent); and Santa Clara, California (17.5 percent). Among the top ten counties, six of these counties were in California and seven out of ten were in the West.

According to the Summary Tape File 3C, the counties and cities with the largest population of a specific Asian Pacific American ethnic group were as follows: Chinese Americans (Los Angeles, CA; New York, NY); Filipino Americans (Los Angeles, CA; Los Angeles, CA); Japanese Americans (Honolulu, HI; Honolulu, HI); Asian Indian American (Queens, NY; New York, NY); Korean American (Los Angeles, CA; Los Angeles, CA); Vietnamese Americans (Orange, CA; San Jose, CA); Hawaiian Americans (Honolulu, HI; Honolulu, HI); Laotian American (Fresno, CA; Fresno, CA); Cambodian American (Los Angeles, CA; Long Beach, CA); Thai American (Los Angeles, CA; Los Angeles, CA); Hmong American (Fresno, CA; Fresno, CA); Guamanian American (Los Angeles, CA; San Diego, CA); Samoan American (Honolulu, HI; Honolulu, HI); Tongan American (Salt Lake, UT; Salt Lake City, UT).[10]

ASIAN PACIFIC AMERICAN EDUCATION

In 1994, among Asian Pacific American men 25 years and older 9 out of 10 had at least a high school diploma. Among Asian Pacific American women of the same age range, 8 out of 10 had at least a high school diploma. Two-fifths of Asian Pacific Americans 25 years of age or older had at least a bachelor's degree (46 percent of men, 37 percent of women, as opposed to White/European Americans of the same age, 28 percent of men, 21 percent of women).

According to William O'Hare, based on his analysis of the March 1991 Current Population Survey, 49 percent of Asian Pacific Americans between the ages of 16 and 24 were attending school only, 19 percent were attending school and working, 21 percent were working only, and 11 percent were neither working nor going to school. In comparison, 26 percent of non-Hispanic Whites were attending school only, 26 percent were going to school and working, 40 percent were working only, and 8 percent were neither working nor going to school.[11]

Among the specific Asian groups in the 1990 census, Asian Indians had the highest proportion, earning at least a bachelor's degree (58 percent) and Tongans, Cambodians, Laotians, and Hmongs the lowest (6 percent or less each).[12] Educational attainment continues to be high for the Asian Pacific American population as a whole. According the U.S. National Science Foundation, in 1993 7 percent of all doctorates were awarded to Asian Pacific Americans.[13]

In 1994, nearly 9 out of 10 Asian Pacific American males 25 years and older, and 8 out of 10 comparable females had at least a high school diploma. High school graduation rates vary widely among Asian Pacific American groups.[14] The 1990 census, the latest where subgroup information was available, showed that among Asians the rates varied from 31 percent for Hmongs, who are the most recent Asians to immigrate, to 88 percent for Japanese, who have been in the country for several generations. Within the Pacific American group, the proportion with at least a high school diploma ranged from 64 percent for Tongans to 80 percent for Hawaiians.[15]

ASIAN PACIFIC AMERICAN AGE AND SEX

The median age of Asian Pacific Americans, according to the 1994 March Current Population Survey, was 32.4 years, as compared to 36.6 for non-Hispanic Whites. Less than half (48.7 percent) of Asian Pacific Americans were male and 51.3 percent were female.[16]

According to the 1992 March Current Population Survey, Asian Pacific Americans had the highest proportion of persons of working age. Sixty-five percent of Asian Pacific Americans were between the ages of 18 and 64, as compared to 61 percent among non-Hispanic Whites, 59 percent among African Americans, 60 percent among Hispanic Americans, and 58 percent among Native Americans.[17]

Asian Pacific American females had a median age of 31.1 years while males had a median age of 29.0 years; 51.2 percent were female while 48.8 percent were male.

Disparities in the median age appear when we examine the native-born general population and the native-born Asian Pacific American population. While the general population has a median age of 32.5 among native-born, Asian Pacific Americans

have a median age of only 15.8 among the native-born. With the exception of Japanese Americans, the median age of the selected Asian Pacific American groups among the native-born are markedly lower than among the general population. These lower figures reflect the youthful population structure of immigrant Asian Pacific American populations. For example, among the native-born Asian Indian Americans, the median age was 8.8 years. Among Korean Americans, the median age was 9.0. The lowest median age among native-born Asian Pacific Americans was among Cambodian Americans, with a median age of 4.7 years.

Most Asian Pacific Americans, even among the foreign-born, are youthful, with the general age being lower than that of the general population. Many of the Asian and Pacific Islander immigrants have arrived since 1980, and among that population, they tend to be more youthful than among their cohorts who arrived prior to 1980. Also, most of the foreign-born remain not citizens (59 percent). Among those who are not naturalized, they tend to be of older age than those who are, though only slightly (35.7 as compared to 35.0). The Hmong American population has the highest proportion of persons not naturalized (90 percent).

The elderly constituted 6 percent of the Asian and Pacific Islander population in 1990 and could reach 16 percent of this group in 2050. . . .

ASIAN PACIFIC AMERICAN HOUSEHOLDS AND FAMILY STRUCTURE

According to the 1991 Current Population Survey, marital status for persons 15 years and older was as follows: 31.1 percent never married, 56.4 percent married with spouse present, 3.4 percent married with spouse absent, 5.1 percent widowed, and 4 percent divorced. Comparable statistics for non-Hispanic Whites are 22 percent never married, 58.1 percent married with spouse present, 2.6 percent married with spouse absent, 7 percent widowed, and 8 percent divorced.[18] Asian Pacific

Americans also had the smallest percentage of families headed by women (11.4 percent).

In 1990, among Asian Pacific Americans, 31.2 percent of all Asian Pacific American husbands and 40.4 percent of all Asian Pacific American wives were intermarried. 18.9 percent of Asian Pacific American husbands were interethnically married and 12.3 percent were interracially married. Among the interracially married, 9.9 percent of these husbands married non-Hispanic Whites. Among Asian Pacific American wives, 16.2 percent were interethnically married, and 24.2 percent were interracially married. Among the interracially married, 20.8 percent of Asian Pacific American wives had married non-Hispanic Whites. Japanese American wives and Filipino American wives had the highest proportion of intermarriages (51.9 percent and 40.2 percent, respectively).[19] The high proportions of intermarriages among Japanese Americans was accountable by the large presence of wives of U.S. servicemen.

In 1994, the average number of persons per family for Asian Pacific Americans and Non-Hispanic Whites were 3.8 and 3.1, respectively. 73 percent of Asian Pacific American families had three or more persons in 1994, compared with 55 percent of non-Hispanic White families. 22 percent of all Asian Pacific American families had five or more persons, compared with 12 percent of non-Hispanic White families.

Six in ten Asian and Pacific Islander families had related children under 18 years old, compared with almost half (49 percent) of non-Hispanic White families. In each group, about 80 percent of related children under 18 years old lived with two parents.

ASIAN PACIFIC AMERICAN HOUSEHOLD AND FAMILY INCOME

In 1993, the median income of Asian and Pacific Islander families ($44,460) was similar to that of non-Hispanic White families ($41,110). The median income for Asian and Pacific Islander families maintained by women with no spouses present ($28,920) was higher than that for comparable non-Hispanic White families ($21,650). Male householder families with no spouse present had median family incomes that were not statistically different ($23,130 for Asian Pacific American and $30,170 for non-Hispanic Whites).

Asian Pacific American married-couple families had a higher median income than comparable non-Hispanic White families ($49,510 compared with $45,240). Both the husband and wife worked in about 60 percent of all Asian Pacific American and non-Hispanic White married-couple families. However, the husband was the only earner in 18 percent of Asian Pacific Americans and in 15 percent of non-Hispanic White married couple families. The 1990 census showed that 20 percent of Asian Pacific American families, compared with 13 percent of non-Hispanic White families, had three or more earners.

The 1990 STF3A data showed that of Asia Pacific America householders under the age of 25, 23.1 percent had a household income of less than $5,000. Compared to other age groups, this age category of householders had the largest percentage with an income of $5,000 or less. At the other end of the household income spectrum, Asian Pacific American householders in California between the ages 45 and 54 had the largest percentage (11.8 percent) of household income $100,000 or more.

ASIAN PACIFIC AMERICAN INDIVIDUAL INCOMES

In 1993, Asian and Pacific Islander males 25 years and older who worked year-round, full-time had median earnings ($31,560) higher than comparable females ($25,430). Asian and Pacific Islander and non-Hispanic White females with at least a bachelor's degree had similar earnings ($31,780 versus $32,920), while comparably educated Asian and Pacific Islander males ($41,220) earned about $87 for every $100 of non-Hispanic White males' earnings ($47,180).

In 1990, Asian Pacific American males who worked year-round, full-time had median incomes of $26,764 as compared to $28,881 for non-Hispanic White males. Among comparable Asian Pacific American females, they received median incomes of $21,323, and the median income for non-Hispanic White females was $20,048.

Per-capita income among Asian Pacific Americans in 1990 was $13,420, as compared to $15,265 for non-Hispanic Whites. In the West, per capita income among Asian Pacific Americans was $13,774, as compared to $15,444 for non-Hispanic Whites. In California, per-capita income among Asian Pacific Americans in 1990 was $13,733, as compared to $19,028 for non-Hispanic Whites. Thus, Asian Pacific American per-capita income was 27.8 percent below the non-Hispanic White population.

OCCUPATIONS

In 1993, one out of six Asian Pacific American men 25 or older worked in executive occupations. Twenty-one percent of them worked in professional occupations. Of women the same age, 18 percent worked in executive occupations, 20 percent worked in professional occupations, and 23 percent worked in administrative support (such as clerical) occupations. Less than half a percent of rural landowners were Asian Pacific American.

When we compare the occupational characteristics of Asian Pacific Americans with non-Hispanic White Americans, noticeable patterns are apparent [see Table 1]. Asian Pacific American men are less likely to be in executive positions than non-Hispanic White men (16.3 percent compared to 18.5 percent), but Asian Pacific American women are more likely [than Asian Pacific American men] to be in such positions in comparison to non-Hispanic White women (17.5 percent compared to 18.9 percent).

The largest differences between the two groups occurred in service occupations, where the percentage of Asian Pacific American men was three times that of non-Hispanic White men (10 and 3 percent, respectively), and in precision production, craft, and repair jobs (12 and 19 percent, respectively).

The proportions of Asian Pacific American men and women in most occupations were similar, except in administrative support, farming, precision production, and transportation.

MARKET POWER

According to the Asian and Pacific Islander Center for Census Information and Services (ACCIS), in 1993 Asian Pacific Americans represented a 94 billion dollar consumer market.[20] In 1987, businesses owned by Asian Pacific Americans had gross receipts of over 33 billion dollars.[21] Asian Pacific Americans earned a total of 79 billion dollars of wage and salary income in 1990.[22]

ASIAN PACIFIC AMERICAN POVERTY

Despite higher educational attainments and a similar median family income, the poverty rate for Asian Pacific American families (14 percent) was higher than that for non-Hispanic White families (8 percent) in 1993. Only 16 percent of both poor Asian Pacific American and non-Hispanic White families had a householder who worked year-round, full-time.

Twelve percent of Asian and Pacific Islander and 5 percent of non-Hispanic White married-couple families lived in poverty. There was no statistical difference in the poverty rates for Asian and Pacific Islander and non-Hispanic White female householder families with no spouse present, 19 and 25 percent, respectively.

In 1993, 15 percent of Asian Pacific Americans were poor, compared with 10 percent of non-

TABLE 1
Occupation of Asian Pacific Americans and Non-Hispanic Whites
Percent of Workers in Occupation, by Sex, 1993

Occupation	Asian Pacific American		Non-Hispanic White	
	Men	Women	Men	Women
Executive, administrative, and managerial	16.3	17.5	18.5	18.9
Professional	21.5	20.3	15.6	18.4
Technical	5.5	4.5	3.1	4.6
Sales	10.9	9.6	13.0	10.8
Administrative, including clerical	8.5	22.5	5.5	28.0
Private household/domestic	—	1.0	—	0.3
Protective service	1.6	0.6	3.0	0.6
Service	10.1	11.0	3.4	8.7
Farming, fishing, and forestry	2.0	0.1	3.3	0.9
Precision production, craft, and repair	11.7	3.8	19.2	2.6
Machine operators, assemblers, and inspectors	7.0	7.8	6.1	4.7
Transportation and material movers	3.5	0.2	6.4	0.6
Handler, equip. cleaners, helpers, laborers	1.4	1.1	3.1	0.9
Total	100%	100%	100%	100%

— Under 0.1 percent

Hispanic Whites. Twenty-eight percent of all poor Asians and Pacific Islanders 15 years old and over worked, compared with 42 percent of poor non-Hispanic Whites.

Asian Pacific American families and Asian Pacific American individuals on average are more likely to be in poverty. Between 1990 and 1994, poverty among Asian Pacific American families rose from 11.9 in 1990 to 13.5 percent in 1994. Among individuals, it rose from 14.1 percent in 1990 to 15.3 percent in 1994.

ASIAN PACIFIC AMERICAN LANGUAGE

In California in 1990, according to STF3A, of those who speak an Asian Pacific American language, 18.2 percent of those 5 to 17 years, 24 percent of those 18 to 64 years, and 51.3 percent of those 65 years and over responded they speak English "not well" or "not at all." Of the persons age 5 to 17 who speak an Asian Pacific American language, 43.3 percent are in a household where there is no one who speaks English "well" or

"very well." 41 percent of persons age 65 and over are in a household where there is no one who speaks English "well" or "very well."

In California in 1990, there were 665,605 households that spoke an Asian Pacific American language; among these, 32.8 percent were classified as linguistically isolated; i.e., there were no persons in the household over the age of 13 who responded that he/she spoke English "well" or "very well."

In California in 1990, languages spoken at home for persons 5 years and over included Chinese (575,447), Tagalog (464,644), Korean (215,845), Vietnamese (233,074), Japanese (147,451), Indic (119,318), and Mon-Khmer (59,622).

NOTES

1. Bill Ong Hing, *Making and Remaking Asian America Through Immigration Policy, 1850–1990* (Stanford, Calif.: Stanford Press, 1993), pp. 38–44.

2. U.S. Bureau of the Census, *Population Profile of the United States, 1995* (Washington, DC: U.S. Government Printing Office, 1995), p. 48.

3. U.S. Bureau of the Census, *Population Projections for States, by Age, Sex, Race, and Hispanic Origin: 1993 to 2020*, P25–1111 (Washington, DC: U.S. Government Printing Office, 1994), Table 3.

4. U.S. Bureau of the Census, *Population Profile* . . . , p. 7.

5. Ibid., p. 13.

6. U.S. Bureau of the Census, Summary Tape File 1A.

7. Computations from the 5 percent 1990 Public Use Microdata Sample (PUMS).

8. U.S. Bureau of the Census, *The Asian and Pacific Islander Population in the United States: March 1991 and 1990*, Current Population Reports, Population Characteristics, P20–459 (Washington, DC: U.S. Government Printing Office, 1992), Table 1.

9. Examination of the PUMS for 1980 and 1990 indicate that the majority of the growth can be attributed to the presence of foreign-born immigrants.

10. Figures from special tabulations of the 1990 STF1C.

11. William P. O'Hare, *America's Minorities: The Demographics of Diversity* (Washington, DC: Population Reference Bureau, 1992), p. 31.

12. Special tabulations of the 5 percent 1990 PUMS.

13. National Science Foundation, *Science and Engineering Doctorate Awards: 1993* (Washington, DC: National Science Foundation, 1993), Table 3, p. 19.

14. U.S. Bureau of the Census, *Population Profile* . . . , p. 49.

15. Special tabulations of the 5 percent 1990 PUMS.

16. U.S. Bureau of the Census, *The Asian and Pacific Islander Population* . . . , p. 4.

17. O'Hare, p. 18.

18. U.S. Bureau of the Census, *The Asian and Pacific Islander Population* . . . , p. 13.

19. Larry Hajime Shinagawa and Gin Yong Pang, "Asian American Pan-Ethnicity and Intermarriage," *Amerasia Journal*, Spring 1996.

20. Glass Ceiling Commission, *Good for Business: Making Full Use of the Nation's Human Capital. The Environmental Scan* (Washington, DC: U.S. Government Printing Office, 1995), p. 10.

21. U.S. Bureau of the Census, *Survey of Minority-Owned Business Enterprises: Asian Americans, American Indians, and Other Minorities* (Washington, DC: U.S. Government Printing Office, 1991), Table A, p. 3.

22. Special tabulations of the 5 percent 1990 PUMS.

CHAPTER 2

Critical Perspectives

This chapter focuses upon the important critical perspectives of Asian American studies. These articles are intended to conceptually connect the significance of history, identity, and community in order to better understand the Asian American experience. All three selections apply the lessons of history and connect them to contemporary issues. Taken together, these selections provide a useful context for readings in the chapters that follow.

Sucheng Chan offers an important overview of written works about the Asian American experience and shows the evolution of Asian American studies as an academic discipline. Her article outlines four general periods of Asian American historiography, or the historical study of Asian Americans. The periods presented here are slightly different from the periods of Asian American history described in Chapter 1, because Chan focuses on the published writings of Asian Americans rather than on the historical events themselves. The first period (1870s to the early 1920s) centered on debating the social, political, and economic costs and benefits of the early immigration from China and Japan. The second period (1920s to the 1960s) saw a great deal of writing by social scientists attempting to explain the assimilation and social organization of Asians in the United States, as well as studies of the experience of Japanese Americans sent to internment camps during World War II. The third period (1960s to the early 1980s) was shaped by scholars taking a critical, or revisionist, perspective to challenge negative portrayals of Asian Americans. The fourth period (1980s to the present) shows the tremendous growth of Asian American studies scholarship and its attention to both historical and contemporary issues.

Gary Y. Okihiro asks the poignant question "Is Yellow Black or White?" to raise important issues around preconceived notions of Asian American racial identity. He takes the reader on a fascinating journey to explore the similarities between the African American and the Asian American experience. Okihiro shows that during certain periods in U.S. history, Asian Americans have been seen alternatively as either "nearly white" or "just like blacks." Additionally, he recognizes that Asian Americans have also been viewed as invisible, due to the limitations of the black-white dyad so dominant in U.S. race relations.

Shirley Hune, in her article, compares and contrasts "traditional" and "emergent" paradigms and their implications for the future of Asian American studies. First, Hune reiterates the need to examine race relations beyond black-white, to a more diverse perspective that includes interracial and intraracial dynamics. Second, she highlights the importance of seeing race and racism as more than static and isolated concepts, but as constantly changing phenomena that are at the center of American life. Third, Hune recognizes that Asian American communities must evolve beyond a paradigm of victimization and oppression to the reality of differential power and agency. Fourth, Hune criticizes the traditional approach of studying racial and ethnic groups in a separate and linear fashion and advocates for greater comparative and panethnic studies. Lastly, Hune identifies the limitations of examining Asian American communities in isolation from larger global and diasporic events and trends.

Reading 3

Asian American Historiography

Sucheng Chan

Writings about Asians in America have appeared since the Chinese—the first group of Asians to enter the United States in sizable numbers—arrived in the middle of the nineteenth century. The Asian American historiographical tradition is thus one and a half centuries old. It may be divided into four periods. The first, characterized by partisanship, lasted from the 1870s to the early 1920s. The second, from the 1920s to the 1960s, was dominated by social scientists. The third, during which revisionist works appeared, extended from the 1960s to the early 1980s. Only in the fourth period, which began in the early 1980s, have professional historians played a leading role in creating historical knowledge about Asian Americans.

Though virtually none of the studies published during the first three periods were written by historians, they nevertheless are of historical interest because they reflect the temper of the times in which they were produced. Authored by missionaries, diplomats, politicians, labor leaders, journalists, propagandists, and scholars trained in sociology, economics, social psychology, and political science, this literature is quite voluminous. I shall identify its salient features before turning my attention to books published in the last fifteen years.[1]

The first books about Asians in the United States were highly partisan because the immigration of Chinese and Japanese was enormously controversial. Missionaries William Speer and Otis Gibson and diplomat George F. Seward, who had all worked in China, were the most vocal defenders of Chinese immigration.[2] They tried to calm American fears about the growing Chinese

presence in the United States by discussing various facets of Chinese civilization and by depicting the Chinese as a hard-working, harmless people. A number of Chinese diplomats and community leaders in the United States also published writings (in English) to promote a positive image of the Chinese.[3] Arrayed against them were such anti-Chinese writers as M. B. Starr, Pierton W. Dooner, and Robert Woltor, whose sensationalist accounts kindled anxieties about a potential Yellow Peril invasion.[4] Anti-Chinese feelings were so strong that it was impossible to discuss Chinese immigration without betraying where one stood. Even the first scholarly work in Asian American history, *Chinese Immigration* by sociologist Mary Roberts Coolidge, published in 1909, was openly partisan (Coolidge was pro-Chinese).[5]

No sooner had exclusionary laws begun to reduce the number of Chinese in the United States than Japanese immigration became an issue and a second set of partisan authors appeared. Sidney L. Gulick, a former missionary in Japan and an activist in the peace movement during the World War I era, defended the Japanese influx in numerous books, articles, and pamphlets.[6] He was joined in his efforts by Japanese writers fluent in English.[7] The most scholarly among them was Yamato Ichihashi of Stanford University, who marshaled an impressive amount of information to persuade the American public that the Japanese were assimilating (contrary to popular assumptions) and were not causing any problems.[8] In countering the charges against their countrymen, these well-educated Japanese writers revealed a strong class bias. They tried to placate Euro-Americans by insisting that while Japanese immigrant laborers might indeed behave objectionably, higher-class Japanese like themselves were just as

Source: Pacific Historical Review LXV:3 (August 1996): 363–399. Copyright © 1996 by the American Historical Association, Pacific Coast Branch. Reprinted with the permission of Sucheng Chan and the University of California Press.

refined as Euro-Americans and should therefore be welcomed.

Works pitted against continued Japanese immigration came in the form of sociological studies, novels, and propaganda tracts by writers as diverse as Homer Lea, Montaville Flowers, Jesse F. Steiner, Lothrop Stoddard, Wallace Irwin, Peter B. Kyne, and V.S. McClatchy. Each articulated a great fear—images of an America overrun by Japanese, whom the authors recognized were not an inferior race.[9] Precisely because these anti-Japanese spokespersons could not be certain whether Euro-Americans or Japanese would win in a "race war," they wanted to make sure that the racial frontier along the Pacific Coast would remain impregnable. In their view, Japanese immigrants, however small their numbers, could not be allowed to establish even the tiniest foothold along the American and Canadian shores of the Pacific.

Books published during the second historiographical period were less impassioned. Written mainly by social scientists, they concentrated on three topics: the assimilation of Asian Americans, the social organization of Asian communities in America, and the incarceration of Japanese Americans during World War II.

The most notable studies on assimilation were done by sociologists affiliated with the University of Chicago. Robert E. Park, the leading light in the sociology department at Chicago, hypothesized that all immigrants passed through a race relations cycle consisting of four stages of interaction with the host society: contact, competition, accommodation, and assimilation. Only two groups did not fit this paradigm—African Americans and Asian Americans. Park and his colleagues thus were intrigued by the "Negro problem" and the "Oriental problem." Their chance to investigate the latter came in late 1923, when Park was appointed the director of research for the Survey of Race Relations on the Pacific Coast—a project initiated by the Institute of Social and Religious Research to improve race relations by gathering "objective" data. The project never achieved its goal due to a shortage of funds and opposition from anti-Asian groups. However, several books based on the information collected were published by sociologists William C. Smith, Roderic D. McKenzie, Emory Bogardus, and Eliot Grinnell Mears, who understood quite well the dilemma faced by the "Orientals" they studied.[10] As Romanzo Adams put it in a preface he wrote for one of Smith's books, "The real question is not one of the capacity of the Orientals, but of our ability to give them a fair opportunity. . . . America should understand the young men and women of Oriental ancestry . . . have been born in our own country. . . . These young people are American citizens.. . . . [They] are a part of us. . . . Whether they shall make their due contribution to American life or whether they shall be an irritant depends largely on the way Americans of the older stock meet them."[11]

The Chicago School's immense intellectual influence can also be seen in more than a dozen M.A. theses and Ph.D. dissertations on Filipino immigrant life written by graduate students under the mentorship of Emory Bogardus at the University of Southern California, in two books on Filipinos by Bruno Lasker and Paul G. Cressey, in several studies done in Hawaii by Romanzo Adams, Andrew W. Lind, and Clarence E. Glick; and in a sociology dissertation on Chicago's Chinese laundrymen by Paul C.P. Siu.[12] These sociological studies are pertinent to Asian American historiography because they have themselves become valuable historical documents.

Educational psychologists at Stanford University also produced several important studies about the adaptation of Asian Americans in the 1930s. Edward K. Strong, Jr., and Reginald Bell reported that the general abilities of Asian students were not inferior to those of Euro-American students.[13] However, given the prevalence of racial prejudice, Strong and Bell advised their "Oriental" students to be realistic in their career choices and to refrain from applying for jobs for which they would not be considered.

A second topic that fascinated social scientists, as well as journalists, from the 1930s through the 1960s was the social organization (more derisively called the "social pathology") of Asian ghetto communities in America.[14] These studies include the earliest book-length publications by Asian American sociologists such as Rose Hum Lee and S. Frank Miyamoto who were trained at the University of Chicago.

During World War II, several teams of social scientists seized the opportunity provided by the incarceration of 112,000 persons of Japanese ancestry in so-called relocation camps to investigate how people function in confined situations. Sociologists, demographers, political scientists, and anthropologists dutifully recorded the minutiae of life behind barbed wire. The publications on this topic are voluminous but easily available. Since Roger Daniels has reviewed many of them in his 1974 essay (see note 1), they will not be discussed here.[15]

Several books published during the second period do not fit into any of the above three categories. The *Anti-Chinese Movement in California*, by Elmer C. Sandmeyer, has the distinction of being the first major study in Asian American history written by a professional historian. It was published in 1939—nine decades after Chinese began to settle along the Pacific Coast. Seven years later, Milton R. Konvitz produced the first study in Asian American legal history. Next, Fred W. Riggs examined the political maneuvers leading to the repeal, in 1943, of the Chinese exclusion laws. Hilary Conroy followed with a book about how the Japanese government, the Hawaiian government, and American sugar planters negotiated the terms under which tens of thousands of Japanese came to work in Hawaii's sugar plantations.[16]

During both the first and second historiographical periods, regardless of what topic was under investigation, the Asian presence in the United States was almost invariably framed as a "problem." Because Asian Americans allegedly failed to assimilate, they were considered deficient or deviant. It was not until the early 1970s

that young Asian American activists on college and university campuses rebelled against such negative portrayals of their forebears and themselves. They rejected the assimilationist paradigm and proposed several alternatives. One was classical Marxism, which enabled them to see Asian Americans as workers exploited by a capitalist system. A second was the internal colonialism model, which allowed them to think of Asian ethnic communities as internal colonies. A third perspective depicted Asian Americans as brothers and sisters of people in Asian nations who had suffered under Western imperialism. The second and third models addressed the same phenomenon at different geographic sites—the European and American colonization of Africa, Latin America, and Asia and their peoples, including those who had been transported to North America as immigrants, indentured migrant laborers, or slaves. According to their view, racial minorities in the United States were a "Third World within," whose members shared a common history of oppression with people living in the "Third World without." In their own eyes, the Asian American activists who sought to "decolonize" research and to establish ethnic studies programs during the late 1960s and 1970s were engaged in a struggle that was simultaneously anticapitalist, antiracist, and anti-imperialist.

The campus activists produced few book-length studies. The best repositories for their radical perspectives are three anthologies published by the Asian American Studies Center at UCLA and an edited volume produced by UCLA scholars.[17] By emphasizing structural oppression and systemic victimization, these often polemical writings unwittingly depicted Asian Americans as mere cogs in a capitalist, racist system.

During this same period, several general histories with more moderate perspectives and emphasizing the contributions made by Asians to American history and society also appeared. Betty Lee Sung, Thomas W. Chinn, Him Mark Lai, Philip Choy, Bill Hosokawa, Harry H.L. Kitano, Francis L.K. Hsu, the editorial board of the United Japanese Society of Hawaii, and Robert A. Wilson all pleaded for inclusiveness.[18] Their books sold well as the ethnic consciousness movement spread among Asian Americans and newly established college courses in Asian American studies created a need for textbooks. However, their contributionist stance helped to keep old assimilationist assumptions alive.

The assimilation model continued to hold sway even during a time of profound and pervasive social upheaval because it resonates so deeply with the American sense of nationhood. As Philip Gleason has pointed out, America's national identity has been based not so much on such primordial sentiment as a shared ancestry, language, or religion as on a set of political values and practices. It is a peoplehood constructed primarily upon an ideological foundation.[19] Since ideology can be learned and is mutable, native-born Americans assume that immigrants should be able—indeed, are morally obligated—to shed the political beliefs and cultural baggage they bring with them and to adopt the values and behavior befitting Americans.

The facile assumption that all immigrants can and should transform themselves overlooks the fact that people of color have encountered enormous hurdles–legal, political, social, and economic—whenever they have tried to enter mainstream society. Thus, before the assimilation model can be dismantled, scholars must demonstrate convincingly that American society has never been the egalitarian paradise it is said to be. A number of Euro-American historians took up that revisionist task in the 1960s and 1970s. Roger Daniels emphasized the racist nature of the anti-Japanese movement and showed how even the California Progressives, who were supposed to be such liberal and enlightened reformers, did not hesitate to "draw the color line." Stuart Creighton Miller argued persuasively that anti-Chinese attitudes had not been confined to California and had, in fact, predated the arrival of Chinese on American soil. Alexander Saxton chronicled how the labor movement relied on anti-Chinese rhetoric and actions to consolidate itself. Robert McClellan

argued that negative images of the Chinese were based on the "private needs" of Euro-Americans and not on the realities of Chinese life. Delbert L. McKee analyzed the draconian means used to implement the Chinese exclusion laws.[20] The only book published during this period that did not focus on the anti-Chinese movement was written by sociologist James Loewen, who studied the Chinese in the Mississippi Delta, where they functioned as middlemen between white and black Americans.[21] Each of these fine studies demonstrated convincingly that the racism and class prejudice shown towards Asian immigrants and their American heirs were not temporary aberrations but were, rather, tendencies deeply embedded in the very social fabric of the United States. One indication of how much scholarly assumptions were changing during this period is the fact that only one scholar, Gunther Barth, still faulted the Chinese for their own suffering.[22]

By the late 1970s, the *Sansei* (third-generation Japanese Americans) had become numerous enough to allow scholars to assess intergenerational changes, so social scientists wrote several books on this topic.[23] A number of historical studies also appeared. Douglas W. Nelson chronicled life in one of the so-called relocation camps, Frank F. Chuman authored the first legal history of Japanese Americans, while John Modell showed how Japanese in Los Angeles, a city with a weak labor movement, managed to find a niche for themselves.[24] Modell then teamed up with sociologist Edna Bonacich to analyze the relationship between class and ethnic solidarity in Japanese American communities.[25]

Regardless of which conceptual frameworks various authors used, during the first three historiographical periods Asian immigrants and their American-born children were seldom portrayed as individuals with personalities, motives, or agency. To catch glimpses of the humanity of Asian Americans, one must turn to books containing their direct testimonies in the form of autobiographies and oral histories, of which there are quite a number.[26]

Unlike the noisy and combative shift from the assimilationist paradigm to one emphasizing oppression and victimization, the next change in analytical framework that occurred in the early 1980s has elicited little notice. The new element that has crept into historical studies of Asian Americans done in the last decade and a half is the concept of agency—a central idea in the new social history. Asian immigrants (old and new) and their American-born progeny, as individuals and as members of groups, have been increasingly depicted as people capable of weighing alternatives, making choices, asserting control over the circumstances they face, and helping to change the world in which they live. The fundamental question that many of today's Asian American historians ask is, "Is human action determined by economic forces and social conditioning or it is the result of human agency and subjectivity?" Most of them have not adopted either of the polar positions implied by this question. Instead, they tend to interpret evidence dialectically: on the one hand, they recognize that structures do limit the ability of individuals to act as subjects or agents in the making of their own history; on the other hand, they acknowledge that it is human action that creates those structures. Agency and structure thus must both be described and analyzed. Just as the radical writings of the early 1970s that highlighted structure and ignored agency told only partial and simplistic stories, so attempts to privilege agency to the neglect of structural constraints are equally unsatisfactory, given the long and complex history of oppression that has haunted the Asian American past.

The best of the historical studies about Asian Americans produced in the last decade and a half have helped—to borrow the words of the British social historian, E.P. Thompson—to "rescue" various groups of Asian Americans from "the enormous condescension of posterity" by according them their rightful places in U.S. history.[27] Cumulatively and persistently, the point is being made that the particular historical experiences of Asian Americans, however parochial or trivial they may seem to the academic gatekeepers in the historical profession, did and do *matter* in the larger story of the nation.

The turn toward social history in Asian American historical scholarship came with the publication of *China and the Overseas Chinese in the United States* by Shih-shan Henry Tsai.[28] Relying largely on Chinese-language sources, Tsai presented cogently the Chinese point of view (or, at least, the point of view of certain Chinese diplomats and government officials) and displayed effectively the aggressive efforts made by the Chinese to defend their right to immigrate and to earn a living in America.

Two other studies enlarge our understanding of Asian emigration and immigration: *Imingaisha*, by Alan T. Moriyama, and *The Korean Frontier in America*, by Wayne Patterson.[29] These carefully researched books document the significant roles played by individuals who manipulated the relations among nations to enable certain classes of people from chosen localities in Japan and Korea to emigrate to Hawaii. By demonstrating that international migrations cannot be explained simply by postulating general "push" and "pull" factors, Moriyama and Patterson have helped us understand why particular migration patterns developed and how they were perpetuated. (An M.A. thesis by Mary Dorita discusses a similar process for Filipinos.[30])

To date, no comparable studies of Chinese or Asian Indian emigration have yet been done, so our knowledge of why and how those two groups left their homelands continues to be based largely on inference and on conjecture about generic structural conditions. However, there is a fine book about how international politics affected the lives of immigrants from India. In *Passage from India*, Joan Jensen chronicled how, as British colonial subjects, certain Indian immigrants in the United States and Canada who were active in efforts to free India from colonial rule were subjected to extensive surveillance by British intelligence agents who relied on their American counterparts for help.[31] The U.S. government, in support of its ally, Great Britain, stripped several dozen Asian Indians of the naturalized U.S. citizenship they had earlier acquired.

Among the more significant facts unearthed in recent studies of Asian immigration is that Asians came to the United States by multiple (some hitherto unsuspected) routes and points of entry. In *Chinese in the Post-Civil War South*, Lucy M. Cohen, an anthropologist with a keen eye for historical details, discovered that a small number of Chinese had entered the American South via the Caribbean.[32] These pioneers, along with several hundred Chinese brought to the South to build railroads, ended up working in cotton plantations and eventually dispersed into the local communities. Before they disappeared from the historical record, they left traces of their militance: they went on strike against employers who failed to pay them or to treat them equally with other workers.

Sandy Lydon uncovered yet another point of entry while doing research for *Chinese Gold*.[33] He found evidence to suggest that some Chinese may have sailed in junks (Chinese ships) across the Pacific to Monterey Bay, settling in the region as fishermen specializing in the harvesting of shrimp and abalone. Combining information preserved in local newspapers and myriad other written sources with oral history interviews, Lydon has produced the best local history of a Chinese immigrant community to date.

After their arrival, Asian immigrants had to find ways to earn a living. In *This Bittersweet Soil*, Sucheng Chan, a political scientist-turned-historian, used information painstakingly collected from the unpublished schedules of U.S. censuses of population and of agriculture and from the archives of over forty counties in California to recover the long lost story of how Chinese helped develop California agriculture, the state's most important economic enterprise.[34] By combining research methods used in agricultural economics, economic history, cultural geography, historical anthropology, historical sociology, and history, Chan pieced together a vast number of small details to demonstrate how Chinese farmers and farm laborers did not just provide "cheap labor,"

as formerly depicted, but adapted skills brought from China to grow crops under California's peculiar climatic conditions and to bargain shrewdly with landowners to maximize their income.

Asian immigrants encountered many difficulties in their struggle for survival. How complex these hurdles were can best be seen in *The Issei* by Yuji Ichioka, who plumbed an impressive array of Japanese-language sources to reveal the inner organization of Asian immigrant communities—communities segmented by class, gender, and political and ideological differences.[35] *Issei* (Japanese-immigrant) workers not only experienced multiple forms of discrimination at the hands of Euro-American employers and Japanese labor contractors due to their race and class status, but also suffered from the cynical actions of the Japanese government, which repeatedly sacrificed the immigrants' interests whenever the exigencies of international relations dictated.

One aspect of Japanese American history that Ichioka did not cover extensively is the Issei's achievement in agriculture, not only in California, but throughout the American West. That story is told in minute detail in *Planted in Good Soil* by Masakazu Iwata.[36] This two-volume work illuminates the extraordinary diversity of western agriculture as well as the broad range of skills the Japanese brought to the task of cultivating the soil. Conditions in different locations differed greatly, so knowledge and skills developed in one setting could not be applied automatically to another. The technical requirements of agriculture shaped the nature of the communities that sprang up in farming areas. The social life within one California farming community settled by Japanese has been richly depicted by Valerie J. Matsumoto in *Farming the Home Place*.[37]

Since an overwhelming majority of the Asian immigrants who came in the late nineteenth and early twentieth centuries were male workers, labor history is an important component of Asian American history.[38] It is almost fully developed in studies of Hawaii. Four books offer glimpses of the living and working conditions of the islands' plantation workers, as well as the many strikes—some multiethnic—that they engaged in.[39] Ronald Takaki looked at workers of various ethnic origins while Robert N. Anderson and his coauthors focused on Filipinos. These two books emphasizing work culture are examples of the "new" labor history. Edward D. Beechert, on the other hand, has paid far more attention to how labor laws were passed and enforced to control the plantation work force. He has also analyzed in greater depth the strikes and the organizations that the workers formed—an approach that places his study more squarely in the "old" labor history tradition. Gary Okihiro added a new dimension to the story by arguing persuasively that the anti-Japanese movement in Hawaii and the antilabor stance of the islands' sugar plantation owners arouse from the same source: the desire by Hawaii's ruling oligarchy to preserve its own racial and economic privileges. One method the elite effectively used was to turn the class antagonism between plantation owners and their workers into a racial conflict. The planters called the workers' fight for better wages and working conditions "blood unionism" and depicted it as part of a larger scheme by Japan to colonize Hawaii.

Renqiu Yu has likewise demonstrated insightfully how race and class were intertwined in the struggles undertaken by another group of Asian immigrant workers—Chinese and laundrymen—who challenged the traditional leaders of New York's Chinatown for influence and power in the community.[40] Members of the elite did not hesitate to use coercive tactics to maintain their own position. One weapon they relied on was the Chinese exclusion laws: the leaders reported or threatened to report individuals they wished to discredit or even to eliminate to immigration officials who would then investigate them for possible arrest or deportation. The manner in which certain individuals manipulated laws formulated on the basis of racial discrimination against *all* Chinese to enhance their personal status is not a pretty story, but it is one that needs to be told and Yu has told it well.

The most fully developed study in Asian American labor history is *Organizing Asian American Labor* by Chris Friday.[41] Using a wide range of sources, he explicitly links Asian American history to U.S. labor history. The book shows more clearly than does any other study the multiple and intersecting socioeconomic, interracial, and intraethnic hierarchies that circumscribed the lives of Asian American workers in the Pacific Northwest, while still allowing them some room to maneuver. Both the agency of individuals and the structural constraints under which they lived and worked are compellingly portrayed in this exhaustively researched study.

Though earning a living occupied a very large part of the waking hours of Asian immigrants, they did manage to find time for a social life within their own communities and to interact in selected yet complicated ways with the larger society, as shown in more than a dozen books published since the mid-1980s.[42] The most conceptually sophisticated of these books examine ethnic identities and the processes called acculturation, accommodation, and assimilation in a far more multidimensional way than did social scientists of an earlier era, who thought of assimilation as a monolithic, linear, unidirectional process. Even though in everyday speech, *acculturation, accommodation, adaptation,* and *assimilation* tend to be used interchangeably, scholars have become aware—since sociologist Milton Gordon first pointed it out to them in his important 1964 book, *Assimilation in American Life*—that these phenomena are not synonymous.[43]

In *Korean Immigrants in America*, a study of Koreans who arrived in Chicago and Los Angeles after 1965, sociologists Won Moo Hurh and Kwang Chung Kim observed that their respondents were simultaneously experiencing ethnic confinement and adhesive adaptation. Many Koreans are confined to their own ethnic communities because of their limited English, foreign schooling, and not-always-appropriate job experiences. Due to the prejudice and discrimination that nonwhite groups in the United States face, they have been able to earn a living only in the secondary labor market or in their own ethnic enclaves.[44] Adhesive adaption refers to the tendency of Korean immigrants to adopt only selected aspects of Euro-American behavior—those useful for achieving economic success—*while* retaining their "traditional" values and patterns of social interaction. This dualistic mode of adaption takes place partly because of residential, occupational, and social segregation and partly because of the Korean immigrants' strong attachment to their homeland.

Anthropologist Margaret Gibson, in studying Asian Indian students in a city in the Sacramento Valley of California, reported a similar pattern in *Accommodation without Assimilation*. The students not only did quite well in school but often outperformed their Euro-American peers—apparently by following the advice of their immigrant parents who encouraged them to abide by the school's regulations while adopting only "desirable" aspects of Euro-American behavior rather than assimilating completely.

Not only do conditions in the host society affect the assimilation of immigrants, so do changing international relations. Karen Leonard, an historian-turned-anthropologist, examined families formed by men from the Punjab region of India and the Mexican or Mexican American women they married in *Making Ethnic Choices*, a work of meticulous scholarship.[45] In these biethnic families, the strength of conjugal as well as intergenerational bonds fluctuated with changing conditions in the outside world. Though Punjabi men in India were patriarchal, in California they could not exercise their full power vis-à-vis their wives or children because California's anti-alien land laws forbade Asian immigrants to own agricultural land. Whatever land the men acquired had to be vested in the names of their Mexican wives or American-born children. But when Congress passed a law in 1946 giving Indian immigrants the right of naturalization, some of the Punjabi farmers became U.S. citizens and finally gained title to their land under their own names. After immigration laws were liberalized in 1965, some aging men brought long-separated family members from India to the United States and turned control of the land over to these newly arrived relatives when they themselves became too infirm to operate their farms. In some instances they even deprived their Mexican wives and Punjabi-Mexican children of an inheritance. Such behavior shows that even though many Punjabi immigrants had adapted well to life in America, once legal and political conditions made it possible for them to do so, they reasserted their attachment to the land of their origins.

While scholars have postulated that assimilation increases over time—and it does, in general—the process is much more complicated than meets the eye. In *Japanese American Ethnicity*, social psychologist Stephen Fugita and sociologist David O'Brien investigated Japanese Americans—the Asian ethnic group with the largest percentage of American-born members and therefore, presumably, the greatest assimilation—and discovered a seeming paradox: many Japanese Americans have retained an unexpectedly strong sense of ethnic identity and a high level of involvement in ethnic community activities even though, as a whole, they have achieved almost complete structural assimilation, and exhibit a very high rate of out-marriage. The explanation lies in their preferred style of interpersonal interaction—one based on what Fugita and O'Brien call the "core cultural orientations" that predated the immigration of Japanese into the United States: an emphasis on interpersonal harmony and the forging of consensus to ensure the smooth functioning of the group and its long-term collective survival. Despite the ease with which most Japanese Americans fit into the larger society, many of them apparently still prefer to socialize with people with a more pronounced group orientation—that is, people who are less individualistic than most Euro-Americans tend to be.

The next two noteworthy books to be published both explore the relationship between class status and ethnic identity. One study was done in Hawaii, the other in southern California. Though Hawaii is often depicted as a multiracial paradise, historically its social structure has been built upon a clearly demarcated racial hierarchy. This means that those in power expect the groups below them to "stay in their place." Thus, as historian Eileen Tamura has shown so well in *Americanization, Acculturation, and Ethnic Identity*, leaders of the Americanization movement in Hawaii, who wanted the *Nisei* (second-generation Japanese Americans) to learn English, convert to Christianity, and discard all vestiges of Japanese culture had a very different idea of what assimilation entailed than the Nisei themselves did. Whereas the Americanizers wanted the Nisei to remain on the sugar plantations as diligent, loyal, and docile lower-class workers, the Nisei desired a middle-class existence—a life *away from* the plantations. The Nisei knew they could attain this goal only if they became sufficiently well-educated, not just in terms of academic knowledge and vocational skills, but also in terms of the manners exhibited by members of the middle class. Thus, when they assimilated, they did so for a reason quite different from the one impelling members of the islands' oligarchy.

Next to an education in American public schools, conversion to Christianity has been considered the most effective facilitator of assimilation. However, in a study of Japanese Protestants, *"For the Sake of Our Japanese Brethren,"* historian Brian Hayashi discovered that members of an immigrant group do not always ascribe the same meaning to their actions as outside observers may do. While Japanese American Protestants strongly favored learning English, observing American holidays, and adopting American customs, they did so in order to demonstrate that they were cosmopolitan and that Japanese were as good as Euro-Americans, and not because they thought assimilation *per se* was desirable. Just as importantly, many of the church members not only had come from a relatively high social standing in Japan but they also had achieved considerable economic success in America. To them, establishing and maintaining good relations with white people—which required them to be cognizant of American ways—was one way to perpetuate their privileged socioeconomic status. At the same time, because they had close ties with Japanese diplomats stationed in the United States, many of them retained a strong identification with Japan.

One aspect of the interaction between Asian immigrant groups and the host society that has received a great deal of scholarly attention is the propensity of certain groups that arrived after 1965 to engage in small business. Five books on this topic are especially deserving of attention.[46]

In *Immigrant Entrepreneurs*, sociologists Ivan Light and Edna Bonacich argued that there are so many Korean immigrant entrepreneurs in the United States today because Korea has been exporting middle-class workers—a result of that country's role in providing cheap labor in the world economic system. Since the end of World War II, Korean society, in their view, has been shaped so decisively by U.S. military, political, and economic interventions that American foreign policy has helped create the conditions making possible Korean emigration to the United States and the emergence of Koreans as entrepreneurs there. While recognizing that more short-term factors, such as the ethnic and class resources of the immigrants, as well as labor market disadvantages, have also played a role in pushing Korean immigrants into small business, Light and Bonacich characterized the Korean entrepreneurs' hard work and frugality as a form of self-exploitation.

In contrast to Light and Boncich's world-system framework, sociologist Pyong Gap Min emphasized a situation phenomenon he called "status inconsistency" in *Ethnic Business Enterprise*, a study of Korean small businesses in Atlanta, Georgia. Status inconsistency exists when there is a high incidence of underemployment in an immigrant population—that is, when well-educated people are forced by circumstances to take low-paid, low-status jobs. Though many post-1965 Korean immigrants came with college degrees and white-collar work experience, they have not been able to find jobs commensurate with their education. Threatened with downward mobility, they conclude that the best channel for upward mobility open to people like themselves is small business. Even though many have had no business experience, two-thirds of the individuals Min surveyed think it is easier to operate a small business in the United States than in Korea because the U.S. government interferes less than the Korean government in the economic activities of its citizens, there is a more efficient supply and demand system in America, and bank loans are easier to get. Thus, according to Min, "host discrimination" is a less important factor channeling Korean immigrants into small business than the latter's perception that they would face greater disadvantages in nonbusiness occupations. While it is understandable that Min's respondents would want to offer as dignified an interpretation of their situation as possible, their tendency to minimize the impact of "host discrimination" leaves unanswered the question of why there are more disadvantages in nonbusiness occupations. Min's study illustrates the difficulty of balancing an author's desire to depict the people he or she studies as individuals in control of their lives and the danger of accepting everything they say at face value.

Standing midway between the analysis of Light and Bonacich and the conclusions of Min is sociologist In-Jin Yoon's comparative study of Koreans in Chicago and Los Angeles. In *On My Own*, Yoon called shopkeeping a "bittersweet livelihood" and made several points not found in earlier studies. First, he argued that it is too restrictive to use the middleman minority concept to characterize. Korean immigrant entrepreneurship, given the fact that Korean merchants engage in many kinds of business, some catering primarily to other Koreans, some mainly to other minorities, and some to the larger multiethnic market. Second, Yoon found that while small businesses may enhance internal ethnic solidarity, the fierce competition among them also simultaneously increases conflicts among Koreans, widening class divisions within the immigrant population. Finally, Yoon asserted that political mobilization by African Americans who boycotted Korean stores has been an important factor in escalating the antagonism between the two groups.

Though books about Asian immigrant entrepreneurship have focused mainly on Koreans, scholars have also looked at other groups. In *Chinatown*, a study of the Chinese in New York City, sociologist Min Zhou claimed that Chinatown does not "necessarily block immigrants from moving up socioeconomically in the larger society" (p. 226). In contrast to the activist scholars of the 1960s and 1970s who strongly condemned the exploitative working conditions in Chinatown—which sociologist Paul Takagi has called a "gilded ghetto"—Zhou saw low-paid menial jobs as "part of a time-honored path toward upward social mobility" among Chinese immigrants. Since Chinatown has a "structural duality"—with a "protected sector" serving mostly Asian customers and an "export sector" selling goods and services to people outside the enclave—it can, in Zhou's view, actually facilitate the entry of immigrants into the larger society (pp. 220–222).

While the academic debate about the economic adaptation of Asian immigrants was going on, the rosy picture of their economic achievements was shattered by the civil unrest in Los Angeles following the 1992 acquittal of the four Los Angeles police officers who had beaten African American motorist Rodney King. Because so much of the destruction was inflicted on Korean-owned or operated businesses, journalists and other commentators have singled out the conflicts between African American customers and Korean storeowners as a major cause of the disorders (wrongly, in my view). Many articles have been published about the "first multiethnic riot" in American history, but *Blue Dreams*, by Nancy Abelmann and John Lie, is the first book-length study of this episode. In it, the authors, an anthropologist and a sociologist, respectively, present a multiplicity of Korean American voices, expressing views seldom heard, if at all, in earlier writings about the upheaval. In 1966, more Korean Americans became audible in *East to America*, an anthology of more than three dozen oral histories compiled by literary scholar Elaine H. Kim and sociologist

Eui-Young Yu (cited in note 26). Both books demonstrated the complex ways Korean immigrants and Korean Americans have responded to their economic losses and their psychological trauma. What happened to them was a painful rite of passage that forced them to admit to themselves that they *are*, after all, a racial minority in America, subject to all the disabilities that status entails, even though they have often been praised as a model minority. Korean Americans were left to fend for themselves when law enforcement officers concentrated on protecting neighborhoods inhabited largely by Euro-Americans. So much hostility was vented against Korean Americans because they served as a surrogate target (in place of the Euro-American-controlled power structure) for the pent-up frustrations felt by those who participated in the arson and looting.

Other manifestations of contemporary interracial tensions are described in *The First Suburban Chinatown*, by ethnic studies scholar Tim Fong, and *The Politics of Diversity*, by sociologist John Horton. Both books record the economic, social, political, and cultural transformation of Monterey Park, a once-sleepy suburban "bedroom community" in southern California.[47] Many of the Chinese from Taiwan and Hong Kong who have moved into Monterey Park have been affluent and well educated. The business they have established are not just Mom-and-Pop stores but include well-capitalized banks, real estate companies, and supermarkets. As Chinese investors bought buildings and lots, erected high-rise structures, and hung Chinese-language signs over their businesses, old-time residents—not just Euro-Americans but also Latino-Americans, Chinese Americans, and Japanese Americans—felt besieged: the new, rich immigrants were taking over their city. The antagonism toward the new immigrants crossed ethnic lines and racial tensions infused the contest over fast-paced development versus slow or controlled growth—tensions soothed eventually only by the emergence of moderate leaders sensitive to the conflicting perspectives and interests of their multiethnic constituency.

Yet another dimension of the interaction between Asian Americans and the larger society, their resistance to oppression, is highlighted in books on Asian American legal and political history. The research in legal history has concentrated heavily on the Chinese, given the staggering number of court cases involving them. Though Milton Konvitz's pioneering study appeared five decades ago, it is only in recent years that legal historians have begun to mine the voluminous available records. Two well-crafted books and several books chapters (as well as dozens of journal articles that cannot be cited due to space limitations) attest to the robust promise of this area of scholarly research.[48]

In *Search of Equality*, by Charles J. McClain, an attorney and historian, and *Laws Harsh as Tigers*, by historian Lucy E. Salyer, skillfully analyze the case files and published federal and state court decisions to reveal the great persistence and extraordinary sophistication with which the Chinese contested the exclusion laws and other discriminatory statutes decade after decade. Not only are these studies interesting in themselves, they also illustrate how well assimilated some Chinese in fact were in terms of their understanding of legal procedures and democratic rights. McClain demonstrates convincingly that landmark cases involving Chinese litigants made important contributions to the development of American legal doctrine in general, while Salyer shows persuasively how Chinese challenges to the exclusion laws helped shape U.S. immigration law in particular.

In more recent years, Asian American resistance has occurred in the political arena more than in the courts. Three books illuminate how Asian American have mobilized to protest discrimination and to demand their civil and human rights.[49] In *Asian American Panethnicity*, sociologist Yen Le Espiritu examined the Asian American movement, Asian American participation in electoral politics, struggles for social service funding, the controversy over ethnic enumeration in the U.S. census, and reactions to anti-Asian violence to pinpoint the circumstances that enabled a panethnic identity to develop—that is, a recognition by Asians of various national/ethnic origins that they shared common interests as *Asian* Americans. She concluded that Asian Americans panethnicity is a form of reactive solidarity. Historian William Wei, in *The Asian American Movement*, looked at the various aspects of that movement—including the growth of ethnic consciousness, Asian American women's groups, the alternative press, Asian American studies programs, reformist community organizations, radical Maoist organizations, and electoral politics—and discovered that the Asian American movement began as a middle-class reform effort to achieve racial equality, social justice, and political empowerment. In *The Retreat from Race*, sociologist Dana Y. Takagi analyzed the latest development that riled Asian Americans and brought them together politically: the decline in the number of Asian American students admitted to the nation's top universities, both public and private. Takagi argued that the controversy has reverberated beyond university campuses and has affected race relations in society at large as academic and political leaders have shied away from discussing various problems in racial terms.

The most sustained struggle undertaken by Asian Americans in recent years has been the effort of Japanese Americans to secure redress for their World War II incarceration. The corpus of works on the internment has grown steadily. *Justice at War*, by Peter Irons, a political scientist and legal scholar, exposed the hypocrisy of government officials who deliberately concealed pertinent evidence from the U.S. Supreme Court. A second book edited by Irons, *Justice Delayed*, contains the text of most of the cases considered by the U.S. Supreme Court. *Keeper of Concentration Camps*, by historian Richard Drinnon, examines the career of the former director of the War Relocation Authority in a most critical (some would say hostile) manner. *Exile Within*, by Thomas James, an historian of education, tells the ironic story of how Japanese American children were taught ideas about democracy while their families were denied the fundamental civil liberties that all Americans are supposed to enjoy. *Jewel in the Desert*, by historian Sandra Taylor, follows a group of Japanese Americans as they journey from the San Francisco Bay area to the camp established at Topaz, Utah, and eventually back to the "real world." *Righing a Wrong*, by Leslie T. Hatamiya, a congressional legislative aide, chronicles the legislative process that led to the passage of the 1988 Civil Liberties Act, which provided a redress of $20,000, as well as an official apology, to each surviving internee. *Legacy of Injustice*, by psychologist Donna K. Nagata, explores the impact of the internment on second-and third-generation Japanese Americans, while *Breaking the Silence*, by anthropologist Yazuko I. Takezawa, offers an ethnographic account of the redress movement in Seattle and analyzes how that effort affected the ethnic identity of its participants. The essays in *Japanese Americans*, edited by Roger Daniels, Sandra C. Taylor, and Harry H.L. Kitano, examine the multifaceted impact of the wartime incarceration as well as the redress and reparations movement not only on Japanese Americans but also on some non-Japanese who worked in the camps or lived in the surrounding communities.[50]

The insights from these books, unfortunately, do not seem to have been disseminated to the wider scholarly community. Thus, it was still possible in 1995 for the late Page Smith, an award-winning U.S. historian, to publish *Democracy on Trial*, without taking this body of writings into account.[51] Smith pays no attention to the government's suppression of evidence in the U.S. Supreme Court cases involving Gordon Hirabayashi, Minoru Yasui, Fred Korematsu, and Mitsuye Edno; calls WRA director Dillon Myer "the most vocal and eloquent defender of the evacuees" (p. 419); claims that mass removal and incarceration was a "decision nobody made" (pp. 102–103) as it resulted from a contest between "two strong-willed" individuals, U.S. Attorney General Francis Biddle and Western Defense Commander Lt. General John DeWitt (p. 102); and quotes approvingly a sociologist who thought that most of the evacuees "have come through the experience with surprisingly undamaged personalities" (p. 424). Smith concludes that "the decision was based exclusively on military considerations (however mistaken those considerations may have been) and that racial prejudice, while it indisputedly existed, had no direct effect on the long slow slide into evacuation" (p. 433). He states that "[t]hose who condemn the relocation as a 'racist decision' have to climb over a mountain of evidence that many Japanese living in California were ardent Japanese nationalists" (p. 428) and "that a number of Japanese patriotic organizations existed, a complex and intricate network of associations dedicated to advancing the interests of the Emperor" (p. 124), but he does not evaluate whatever evidence may exist for these allegations (the book contains no footnotes).

Compared to the above topics, some areas of Asian American history are still relatively undeveloped: women's and family history and cultural history. The first book on Asian American familial relations appeared in 1985. *Transforming the Past*, by anthropologist Sylvia J. Yanagisako, examined first-and second-generation Japanese Americans in Seattle. Yanagisako used anthropological theory to explain how and why the same kinship relations—those between husbands and wives, parents and children, and siblings—can mean quite different things to members of the two generations, who think in terms of a "symbolic opposition" between Japanese and American norms.[52] In the following year, the first book-length study of Asian-American women, *Issei, Nisei, War Bride*, by sociologist Evelyn Nakano Glenn, was published.[53] It combines oral histories conducted in the San Francisco Bay area with sociological theory to place the individual experiences of the women who were interviewed within the conceptual framework of international labor migration in a capitalist world-system. The three books that followed—*Chinese Women of America,* by Judy Yung; *Japanese American Women,* by Mei T. Nakano; and *Making Waves*, an anthology collectively edited by Asian Women

United of California—have been widely used in the classroom.[54]

Asian American women's and family history made important strides in the 1990s with the publication of four books, all of them feminist in orientation.[55] While sociologist Nazli Kibria, anthropologist Nancy Donnelly, and historian Judy Yung have been careful to show that feminist assumptions developed in the middle-class Euro-American women's movement cannot be applied uncritically to groups of Asian American women, historian Benson Tong, in his eagerness to demonstrate that even the most oppressed individuals—in this instance, Chinese prostitutes in nineteenth-century San Francisco—possessed agency, overstated the extent to which these women were able to overcome the restrictive conditions under which they lived and imputed more feminist consciousness to them than can be justified by the available evidence.

Based upon ethnographic fieldwork in Philadelphia, Kibria painted a highly nuanced portrait of gender and intergenerational relations within Vietnamese refugee families in the 1980s in *Family Tightrope*. Two of her findings are especially significant. First, she discovered that few Vietnamese refugee families in the United States exist in the form traditionally associated with Vietnam's kinship structure. Decades of war and revolution, as well as the fearful escape from Vietnam itself and the difficulties encountered while resettling in America, had all disrupted family life and changed the roles of various family members. In the United States, those families with the greatest flexibility seem best able to take advantage of the limited economic opportunities available to them. Second, though there is greater gender equality in these refugee families, many of the Vietnamese women voluntarily curb their own "liberation" because something else is more important to them: parental control over children. They realize that if they wish, as mothers, to guide and discipline their children, then they cannot afford to undermine too much the authority of those children's fathers, their own husbands. In short, their desire to maintain generational hierarchy is greater than their inclination to reduce gender inequality.

In studying the Hmong, tribespeople from Laos, Donnelly observed in *Changing Lives of Refugee Hmong Women* how living in a new society with very different values—a society in which government agencies can and do intervene in family life—many men feel their power and prestige are constantly being undermined. As a community, the Hmong have had to rethink very seriously what it means to be Hmong: what values and behaviors lie at the center of Hmong identity? Though adult Hmong strongly desire to continue practicing various aspects of their culture, Donnelly noted that when they gather every year to celebrate Hmong New Year in Seattle, the songs they sing, the dances they perform, and the rites they carry out are no longer "lived rituals" but "cultural displays"—"icons of a remembered past rather than natural expressions of an understood reality" (p. 64). Far more important to them than these external cultural emblems that can be hauled out for periodical performance is their ability to preserve the gender and age hierarchies of a patriarchal culture in their everyday lives. Some Hmong say that being able to do that is even more crucial than retaining the ability to speak the Hmong language.

In the case of both the Vietnamese and Hmong refugees, then, changes in the statues and role of women apparently pose the gravest threat to the preservation of a group's cultural identity. That women and the social controls imposed upon their behavior are the fulcrum upon which the acculturation process turns is a conclusion that nonfeminist scholars may not have reached.

Unlike Kibria and Donnelly who could conduct ethnographic fieldwork, Tong and Yung, who studied earlier periods, had to undertake far more painstaking research because the documentary record in Asian American women's history is extremely thin. For *Unsubmissive Women*, Tong searched valiantly through numerous newspapers, government documents, missionary records, private family papers, memoirs, business directories, fire maps prepared by insurance companies,

and the manuscript schedules of three U.S. censuses of population to find information to reconstruct the sad story of Chinese prostitutes in San Francisco during the latter half of the nineteenth century. He also relied on a few extant autobiographical accounts to breathe life into the stories of these women. However, he probably underestimated the degradation and violence they faced. Yung had an easier task as she wrote about the twentieth century. Because many of the women could still be interviewed, *Unbound Feet* reverberates with their voices. Yung wove together vignettes from her own family history and more than fifty oral histories, along with all the written sources she could find, to paint an engrossing collective portrait of Chinese American women in San Francisco from the turn of the century to World War II. These books represent the first steps in a long journey to recover the buried past and to make visible the hidden present of a "minority within a minority."

Asian American cultural history has received even less attention than women's history. This is surprising in light of the common practice of relying on "cultural differences" to explain the behavior and status of Asian Americans. Since the early 1980s, only a handful of books on the cultural aspects of Asian American history has been published. One examines Chinese theater in America and three investigate representations of Asians in American popular culture. Two other look at how Asian religious traditions are being modified as they are transplanted to the United States.

Flying Dragons, Flowing Streams, by cultural historian Ronald Riddle, is a history of Cantonese opera in San Francisco. Not only Chinese but also some Euro-Americans attended these lively performances with their resplendent costumes and amazing acrobatics. *The Yellow Peril*, by literary scholar William Wu; *Romance and the "Yellow Peril,"* by film scholar Gina Marchetti; and *Marginal Sights*, by the theater arts specialist James Moy, on the other hand, all examine how Asians have been depicted in mainstream America culture—mainly as a "Yellow Peril." Wu looked at fiction, Marchetti analyzed films, Moy examined museum displays, circuses, performance arts, cartoons, photographs, films, plays, and pornography. Fantasies of rape, the threat of captivity, interracial seduction, white men always coming to the rescue, and tragic and transdecendent love permeated each of these media. Employing a postmodernist vocabulary, Moy showed how both Euro-American playwrights and audiences have been fascinated by the "Other." With their understanding of racial differences based upon a process of fetishization, this fascination created, perpetuated, and justified the Sinophobic attitudes of a white America. Since stereotypes tend to take on a life of their own, the caricatures and stereotypes developed over the course of more than a century have continued to influence Euro-American perceptions of Asian Americans to this day.[56]

The fact that immigrants from Asia brought non-Christian religions with them also encouraged Euro-Americans to see them as irredeemably alien. While earlier studies of Asian American religious activities investigated the transformation of Buddhism on American soil, *Transplanting Religious Traditions*, by John Fenton, and *Religion and Immigrants from India and Pakistan*, by Raymond B. Williams, examine the contemporary introduction of Hinduism, Islan, Sikhism, and Janism into the United States through the efforts of immigrants from South Asia.[57]

Although creative writings by Asian Americans and Asian American literary studies are important aspects of Asian American cultural history, a consideration of this growing corpus is outside the scope of this essay. More than half a dozen books of literary criticism and an extensive bibliography are now available as guides to the novels, short stories, plays, and poetry written by Asian Americans.[58]

Despite the steady progress in Asian American historical scholarship, significant gaps remain. The most glaring is the absence of book-length studies on Filipino Americans. The number of journal articles published in the last two decades on this group, compared to other Asian ethnic groups, is also very small, and both the quality of the scholarship and the topical coverage are uneven. The first analytical study of one aspect of Filipino American history has been written not by an historian or social scientist, but by a literary critic.[59]

Even though the refugees from Vietnam, Laos, and Cambodia arrived much later than did the Filipinos, they have received far more scholarly attention. The number of journal articles on these groups is now enormous.[60] Among the more substantial books, all by social scientists, *Refugees as Immigrants*, edited by David W. Haines, summarizes a great deal of the survey research done during the first decade of the refugees' resettlement in the United States. *The Boat People and Achievement in America*, by Nathan Caplan and his associates, reports the findings of the largest of these survey research projects, which was carried out in five cities; and *Refugee Communities*, by Steven J. Gold, compares the experiences of Vietnamese and Soviet Jewish refugees.[61] Recent U.S. refugee policy has been explored in *Indochinese Refugees in America*, by Paul J. Strand and Woodrow Jones, Jr.; *Calculated Kindness*, by Gil Loescher and John A. Scanlan; *Alien Winds*, by James W. Tollefson; *The Indochinese Refugee Dilemma* by Valerie O'Connor Sutter; and *States and International Migrants,* by Jeremy Hein.[62]

For those who do not have the time or desire to read the books discussed in this essay, several works of synthesis are available. *Asian America*, by Roger Daniels; *Strangers from a Different Shore*, by Ronald Takaki; *Asian Americans*, by Sucheng Chan; and *Margins and Mainstreams*, by Gary Y. Okihiro, were written by historians; *Asian Americans*, by Harry H. L. Kitano and Roger Daniels, and *Asian Americans*, edited by Pyong Gap Min, contain contributions by social scientists; while *Making and Remaking Asian America*, by Bill Ong Hing, is the work of a law professor.[63] Anthropologist Paul J. Rutledge and sociologist Jeremey Hein produced the first two works of synthesis on refugees from Southeast Asia—*The Vietnamese Experience in America* and *From Vietnam, Laos, and Cambodia*, respectively.[64] Each of these works offers a convenient overview, but readers who rely solely on them will miss tasting the veritable intellectual feast that Asian American history can now claim to offer.

NOTES

1. Earlier historiographical assessments include Roger Daniels, "Westerners from the East: Oriental Immigrants Appraised," *Pacific Historical Review*, XXXV (1966), 373–383; Daniels, "American Historians and East Asian Immigrants," ibid., XLIII (1974), 449–472; and Shirley Hune, *Pacific Migration to the United States: Trends and Themes in Historical and Sociological Literature* (Washington, D.C., 1977).

2. William Speer, *The Oldest and Newest Empire* (Cincinnati, 1870); Otis Gibson, *The Chinese in America* (Cincinnati, 1877); and George F. Seward, *Chinese Immigration in Its Social and Economic Aspects* (New York, 1881).

3. K. Scott Wong, "Cultural Defenders and Brokers: Chinese Responses to the Anti-Chinese Movement," in K. Scott Wong and Sucheng Chan, eds., *Claiming America: Constructing Chinese American Identities during the Exclusion Era*.

4. M.B. Starr, *The Coming Struggle* (San Francisco, 1873); Pierton W. Dooner, *Last Days of the Republic* (San Francisco, 1880); and Robert Woltor, *A Short and Truthful History of the Taking of Oregon and California by the Chinese in the Year A.D. 1899* (San Francisco, 1882).

5. Mary Roberts Coolidge, *Chinese Immigration* (New York, 1909).

6. The most important of these works were Sidney L. Gulick, *The American Japanese Problem* (New York, 1914); and Gulick, *American Democracy and Asiatic Citizenship* (New York, 1918).

7. These include Kiyoshi Karl Kawakami, *Asia at the Door: A Study of the Japanese Question in Continental United States, Hawaii and Canada* (New York, 1914); Kawakami, *The Real Japanese Question* (New York, 1921); Kiichi Kanzaki, *California and the Japanese* (San Francisco, 1921); T. Iyenaga and Kenoske Sato, *Japan and the California Problem* (New York, 1921); Iichiro Tokutomi, *Japanese-American Relations* (New York, 1922); and Kiyo Sue Inui, *The Unsolved Problem of the Pacific: A Survey of International Contacts, Especially in Frontier Communities, with Special Emphasis upon California* (Tokyo, 1925). Kawakami was a prolific writer and propagandist; Kanzaki was general secretary of the Japanese Association of America; Iyenaga and Sato were political scientists who had taught and studied, respectively, at the University of Chicago; Tokutomi was a member of Japan's House of Peers and editor-in-chief of the newspaper, *Kokumin Shimbun*; while Inui had taught international relations at Occidental College, the University of Southern California, and Tokyo University and had

served as one of Japan's delegates to the League of Nations.

8. Yamato Ichihashi, *Japanese Immigration: Its Status in California* (San Francisco, 1915); and Ichihashi, *Japanese in the United States* (Stanford, Calif., 1932).

9. Homer Lea, *The Valor of Ignorance* (New York, 1909); Montaville Flowers, *The Japanese Conquest of American Opinion* (New York, 1917); Jesse F. Steiner, *The Japanese Invasion: A Study in the Psychology of Inter-Racial Contacts* (Chicago, 1917); Lothrop Stoddard, *The Rising Tide of Color against White World-Supremacy* (New York, 1920); Wallace Irwin, *Seed of the Sun* (New York, 1920); Peter B. Kyne, *The Pride of Palomar* (New York, 1921); and V.S. McClatchy, "Japanese Immigration and Colonization: Skeleton Brief," 67 Cong., 1 sess. *Sen.Doc. 55* (1921).

10. William C. Smith, *The Second Generation Oriental in America* (Honolulu, 1927); Roderic D. McKenzie, *Oriental Exclusion: The Effect of American Immigration Laws, Regulations, and Judicial Decisions upon the Chinese and Japanese on the American Pacific Coast* (Chicago, 1928); Emory S. Bogardus, *Immigration and Race Attitudes* (Boston, 1928); William C. Smith, *Americans in Process: A Study of Our Citizens of Oriental Ancestry* (Ann Arbor, 1937); and Eliot Grinnel Mears, *Resident Orientals on the American Pacific Coast: Their Legal and Economic Status* (New York, 1928). The Survey of Race Relations collected several hundred life histories and reams of miscellaneous information. These materials are housed at the Hoover Institution on War, Revolution, and Peace located at Stanford University.

11. Romanzo Adams, "Introduction," in Smith, *Americans in Process*, xii–xiv.

12. Bruno Lasker, *Filipino Immigration to Continental United States and to Hawaii* (Chicago, 1931); Paul G. Cressey, *The Taxi Dance Hall: A Sociological Study in Commercialized Recreation and City Life* (Chicago, 1932); Romanzo C. Adams, *Interracial Marriage in Hawaii* (New York, 1937); Andrew W. Lind, *An Island Community: Ecological Succession in Hawaii* (Chicago, 1938); Clarence E. Glick, *Sojourners and Settlers: Chinese Migrants in Hawaii* (Honolulu, 1980); and Paul C.P. Siu, *The Chinese Laundryman: A Study of Social Isolation* (New York, 1987). Though not published until the 1980s Glick's dissertation was completed in 1938, while Siu, who had begun his research in 1938, submitted his dissertation in 1953.

13. Edward K. Strong, Jr., and Reginald Bell, *Vocational Aptitudes of Second-Generation Japanese in the United States* (Stanford, Calif. 1933); Edward K. Strong, Jr., *Japanese in California* (Stanford, Calif., 1933); Reginald Bell, *Public School Education*.

14. Books on this topic that are still of considerable interest include Leong Gor Yun, *Chinatown Inside Out* (New York, 1936); Charles C. Dobie, *San Francisco's Chinatown* (New York, 1936); S. Frank Miyamoto, *Social Solidarity among the Japanese in Seattle* (Seattle, 1939); Rose Hum Lee, *The Growth and Decline of Chinese Communities in the Rocky Mountain Region*, (New York, 1978); and Lee, *The Chinese in the U.S.A.* (Hong Kong, 1960). One book

on Chinese American communities that does not fit into the Chicago school's intellectual mold is S.W. Kung, *Chinese in American Life: Some Aspects of Their History, Status, Problems, and Contributions* (Seattle, 1962).

15. Three groups of social scientists did research on the incarcerated Japanese Americans: one group employed by the War Relocation Authority; another associated with the Japanese American Evacuation and Resettlement Study (JERS) directed by Dorothy Swaine Thomas of the University of California, Berkeley; and a third group called the Bureau of Sociological Research led by Alexander H. Leighton. Of the early works, Carey McWilliams, *Prejudice: Japanese Americans, Symbol of Racial Intolerance* (Boston, 1944) and Morton Grodzins, *Americans Betrayed: Politics and the Japanese Evacuation* (Chicago, 1949) were the most critical of the government's actions, while Dorothy S. Thomas and Richard S. Nishimoto, *The Spoilage: Japanese-American Evacuation and Resettlement during World War II* (Berkeley and Los Angeles, 1946); Dorothy S. Thomas, *The Salvage* (Berkeley and Los Angeles, 1952); and Jacobus ten Broek, Edward N. Barnhart, and Floyd W. Matson, *Prejudice, War and the Constitution: Causes and Consequences of the Evacuation of Japanese Americans in World War II* (Berkeley and Los Angeles, 1954) were apologists. Retrospective assessments of JERS may be found in Yuji Ichioka, ed., *Views from Within: The Japanese American Evacuation and Resettlement Study* (Los Angeles, 1989). Other books published in the years immediately after World War II include Alexander H. Leighton, *The Governing of Men: General Principles and Recommendations Based on Experience at a Japanese Relocation Camp* (Princeton, N.J., 1945); Leonard Broom and Ruth Riemer, *Removal and Return: The Socio-Economic Effects of the War on Japanese Americans* (Berkeley and Los Angeles, 1949); and Leonard Broom and John I. Kitsuse, *The Managed Casualty: The Japanese-American Family in World War II* (Berkeley and Los Angeles, 1956). Dillon Myer, the director of the WRA, has told his version of the story in *Uprooted Americans: The Japanese Americans and the War Relocation Authority during World War II* (Tucson, 1971). Roger Daniels's writings are especially authoritative: *Concentration Camps USA: Japanese Americans and World War II* (New York, 1971); *The Decision to Relocate the Japanese Americans* (New York, 1975); and *Prisoners Without Trial: Japanese Americans in World War II* (New York, 1993). Recent revisionist analyses will be discussed below.

16. Elmer C. Sandmeyer, *The Anti-Chinese Movement in California* (Urbana, Ill., 1939); Milton R. Konvitz, *The Alien and the Asiatic in American Law* (Ithaca, N.Y., 1946); Fred W. Riggs, *Pressure on Congress: A Study of the Repeal of Chinese Exclusion* (New York, 1950); and Hilary Conroy, *The Japanese Frontier in Hawaii, 1868–1898* (Berkeley and Los Angeles, 1953).

17. Amy Tachiki *et al.*, eds., *Roots: An Asian American Reader* (Los Angeles, 1971); Jesse Quinsaat *et al.*, *Letters in Exile: An Introductory Reader on the History of Pilipinos in America* (Los Angeles, 1976); Emma Gee,

ed., *Counterpoint: Perspectives on Asian America* (Los Angeles, 1976); and Lucie Cheng and Edna Bonacich, eds., *Labor Immigration under Capitalism: Asian Workers in the United States before World War II* (Berkeley and Los Angeles, 1984).

18. Betty Lee Sung, *Mountain of Gold: The Story of the Chinese in America* (New York, 1967); Thomas W. Chinn, Him Mark Lai, and Philip P. Choy, *A History of the Chinese in California: A Syllabus* (San Francisco, 1969); Bill Hosokawa, *Nisei: The Quiet Americans* (New York, 1969); Harry H.L. Kitano, *Japanese Americans: The Evolution of a Subculture* (Englewood Cliffs, N.J., 1969); Francis L.K. Hsu, *The Challenge of the American Dream: The Chinese in the United States* (Belmont, Calif., 1971); United Japanese Society of Hawaii, *A History of Japanese in Hawaii* (Honolulu, 1971); and Robert A. Wilson and Bill Hosokawa, *East to America: A History of the Japanese in the United States* (New York, 1980). A number of books published a few years later also proved useful as textbooks, especially since they extended coverage to other Asian groups. These include H. Brett Melendy, *Asians in America: Filipinos, Koreans, and East Indians* (Boston, 1977); Hyung-chan Kim, *The Korean Diaspora: Historical and Sociological Studies of Korean Immigration and Assimilation in North America* (Santa Barbara, 1977); Bong-Youn Choy, *Koreans in America* (Chicago, 1979); Tricia Knoll, *Becoming Americans: Asian Sojourners, Immigrants, and Refugees in the Western United States* (Portland, Ore., 1982); and Fred Cordova, *Filipinos: Forgotten Asian Americans, a Pictorial Essay, 1763, circa 1963* (Seattle, 1983).

19. Philip Gleason, "American Identity and Americanization," in Stephan Thernstrom, ed., *Harvard Encyclopedia of American Ethnic Groups* (Cambridge, Mass., 1980), 31–58.

20. Roger Daniels, *The Politics of Prejudice: The Anti-Japanese Movement in California and the Struggle for Japanese Exclusion* (Berkeley and Los Angeles, 1962); Stuart Creighton Miller, *The Unwelcome Immigrant: The American Image of the Chinese, 1785–1882* (Berkeley and Los Angeles, 1969); Alexander Saxton, *The Indispensable Enemy: Labor and the Anti-Chinese Movement in California* (Berkeley and Los Angeles, 1971); Robert McClellan, *The Heathen Chinee: A Study of American Attitudes toward China, 1890–1905* (Columbus, Oh., 1971); and Delber L. McKee, *Chinese Exclusion versus the Open Door Policy, 1900–1906; Clashes over China Policy during the Roosevelt Era* (Detroit, 1977).

21. James W. Loewen, *The Mississippi Chinese: Between Black and White* (Cambridge, Mass., 1971).

22. Gunther Barth, *Bitter Strength: A History of the Chinese in the United States, 1850–1870* (Cambridge, Mass., 1964).

23. John W. Connor, *Tradition and Change in Three Generations of Japanese Americans* (Chicago, 1977); Darrel Montero, *Japanese Americans; Changing Patterns of Ethnic Affiliation over Three Generations* (Boulder, Colo., 1980); Gene N. Levine and Colbert Rhodes, *The*

Japanese American Community: A Three-Generation Study (New York, 1981).

24. Douglas W. Nelson, *Heart Mountain: The History of an American Concentration Camp* (Madison, Wis., 1976); Frank F. Chuman, *The Bamboo People: The Law and Japanese-Americans* (Del Mar, Calif., 1976); and John Modell, *The Economics and Politics of Racial Accommodation: The Japanese of Los Angeles, 1900–1942* (Urbana, Ill., 1977).

25. Edna Bonacich and John Modell, *The Economic Basis of Ethnic Solidarity: Small Business in the Japanese American Community* (Berkeley and Los Angeles, 1980).

26. Listed in chronological order, these include Yan Phou Lee, *When I Was a Boy in China* (Boston, 1887); Yung Wing, *My Life in China and America* (New York, 1909); Younghill Kang, *East Goes West: The Making of an Oriental Yankee* (New York, 1937); No-Yong Park, *Chinaman's Chance: An Autobiography* (Boston, 1940); Pardee Lowe, *Father and Glorious Desendant* (Boston, 1943); Jade Snow Wong, *Fifth Chinese Daughter* (New York, 1945); Carlos Bulosan, *American Is in the Heart: A Personal History* (New York, 1946); Manuel Buaken, *I Have Lived with the American People* (Caldwell, Ida., 1948); Monica Sone, *Nisei Daughter* (Boston, 1953); Chung Kim Ai, *My Seventy-Nine Years in Hawaii* (Hong Kong, 1960); Dalip Singh Saund, *Congressman from India* (New York, 1960); Daniel K. Inouye with Lawrence Elliot, *Journey to Washington* (Englewood Cliffs, N.J., 1967); Daniel I. Okimoto, *American in Disguise* (New York, 1971); Victor G. Nee and Brett de Bary Nee, *Longtime Californ': A Documentary Study of an American Chinatown* (New York, 1972); Jim Yoshida with Bill Hosokawa, *The Two Worlds of Jim Yoshida* (New York, 1972); Jeanne Wakatsuki Houston and James Houston, *Farewell to Manzanar* (Boston, 1973); Kazuo Ito, *Issei: A History of Japanese Immigrants in North America* (Seattle, 1973); John Modell, ed., *The Kikuchi Diary: Chronicle from an American Concentration Camp—The Tanforan Journals of Charles Kikuchi* (Urbana, Ill., 1973); Jade Snow Wong, *No Chinese Stranger* (New York, 1975); Michiyo Laing, *et al.* eds., *Issei Christians: Selected Interviews from the Issei Oral History Project* (Sacramento, 1977); Roberto V. Vallangca, *Pinoy: The First Wave* (San Francisco, 1977); Akemi Kikumura, *Through Harsh Winters: The Life of a Japanese Immigrant Woman* (Novato, Calif., 1981); Nobuya Tsuchida, ed., *Asian and Pacific American Experiences: Women's Perspectives* (Minneapolis, 1982); Elaine H. Kim, *With Silk Wings: Asian American Women at Work* (Oakland, Calif., 1983); Eileen Sunada Sarasohn, ed., *The Issei: Portrait of a Pioneer, an Oral History* (Palo Alto, Calif., 1983); Karl G. Yoneda, *Ganbatte: Sixty-Year Struggle of a Kibei Worker* (Los Angeles, 1983); Asian American Studies Center, University of California, Los Angeles, and Chinese Historical Society of Southern California, *Linking Our Lives: Chinese American Women of Los Angeles* (Los Angeles, 1984); Filipino Oral History Project, *Voices: A Filipino American Oral History* (Stockton, Calif., 1984); Michi Kodama-Nishimoto *et al.*, eds., *Hanahana: An Oral History Anthology of Hawaii's Working People* (Honolulu, 1984); John Tateishi, *And Justice for All: An Oral History of the Japanese American Detention Camps* (New York, 1984); Mike Masaoka with Bill Hosokawa, *They Call Me Moses Masaoka: An American Saga* (New York, 1987); Caridad Concepcion Vallangca, *The Second Wave: Pinay and Pinay (1945–1960)* (San Francisco, 1987); Gene Oishi, *In Search of Hiroshi: A Japanese-American Odyssey* (Rutland, Vt., 1988); James Freeman, *Hearts of Sorrow: Vietnamese-American Lives* (Stanford, Calif., 1989); Le Ly Hayslip with Jay Wurts, *When Heaven and Earth Changed Places: A Vietnamese Woman's Journey from War to Peace* (New York, 1989); Wanwadee Larsen, *Confessions of a Mail Order Bride: American Life Through Thai Eyes* (Far Hills, N.J., 1989); Lucy Nguyen-Hong-Nhiem and Joel Martin Halpern, eds., *The Far East Comes Near: Autobiographical Accounts of Southeast Asian Students in America* (Amherst, Mass., 1989); Joanna C. Scott, *Indochina's Refugees: Oral Histories from Laos, Cambodia and Vietnam* (Jefferson, N.C., 1989); Katsuyo K. Howard, comp., *Passages: An Anthology of Southeast Asian Refugee Experience* (Fresno, Calif., 1990); Mary Paik Lee, *Quiet Odyssey: A Pioneer Korean Woman in America* (Seattle, 1990); Akemi Kikumura, *Promises Kept: The Life of an Issei Man* (Novato, Calif., 1991); Joyce C. Lebra, *Women's Voices in Hawaii* (Niwot, Colo., 1991); Russell C. Leong, ed., *Moving the Image: Independent Asian Pacific Media Arts* (Los Angeles, 1991); David Mura, *Turning Japanese: Memoirs of a Sansei* (New York, 1991); John Tenhula, *Voices from Southeast Asia: The Refugee Experience in the United States* (New York, 1991); Craig Scharlin and Lilia V. Villanueva, *Philip Vera Cruz: A Personal History of Filipino Immigrants and the Farmworkers Movement* (Los Angeles, 1992); Le Ly Hayslip with James Hayslip, *Child of War, Woman of Peace* (New York, 1993); Maria Hong, ed., *Growing Up Asian American: An Anthology* (New York, 1993); Usha Welaratna, *Beyond the Killing Fields: Voices of Nine Cambodian Survivors in America* (Stanford, 1993); Women of South Asian Descent Collective, ed., *Our Feet Walk the Sky: Women of the South Asian Diaspora* (San Francisco, 1993); Sucheng Chan, ed., *Hmong Means Free: Life in Laos and America* (Philadelphia, 1994); Jade Ngoc Quang Huynh, *South Wind Changing* (Minneapolis, 1994); Nguyen Qui Duc, *Where the Ashes Are: The Odyssey of a Vietnamese Family* (Reading, Mass., 1994); Yen Le Espiritu, *Filipino American Lives* (Philadelphia, 1995); Garrett Hongo, *Volcano: A Memoir of Hawai'i* (New York, 1995); Peter Hyun, *In the New World: The Making of a Korean American* (Honolulu, 1995); K. Connie Kang, *Home Was the Land of Morning Calm: A Saga of a Korean-American Family* (Reading, Mass., 1995); Easurk Emsen Charr, *The Golden Mountain: The Autobiography of a Korean Immigrant, 1895–1960* (Urbana, Ill., 1996); and Elaine H. Kim and Eui-young Yu, *East to America: Korean American Life Stories* (New York, 1996).

27. E. P. Thompson, *The Making of the English Working Class* (London, 1965), 12–13.

28. Shih-shan Henry Tsai, *China and the Overseas Chinese in the United States, 1868–1911* (Fayetteville, Ark., 1983).

29. Alan T. Moriyama, *Imingaisha: Japanese Emigration Companies and Hawaii, 1894–1908* (Honolulu, 1985); and Wayne Patterson, *The Korean Frontier in America: Immigration to Hawaii, 1896–1910* (Honolulu, 1988).

30. Mary Dorita, *Filipino Immigration to Hawaii* (San Francisco, 1975).

31. Joan M. Jensen, *Passage from India: Asian Indian Immigrants in North America* (New Haven, 1988).

32. Lucy M. Cohen, *The Chinese in the Post-Civil War South: A People without a History* (Baton Rouge, La., 1984). Marina E. Espina, a librarian, has discovered that Filipinos arrived in the American South more than a century before the first Chinese came to the United States. Marina E. Espina, *Filipinos in Louisiana* (New Orleans, 1988).

33. Sandy Lydon, *Chinese Gold: The Chinese in the Monterey Bay Region* (Capitola, Calif., 1985).

34. Sucheng Chan, *This Bittersweet Soil: The Chinese in California Agriculture, 1860–1910* (Berkeley and Los Angeles, 1986).

35. Yuji Ichioka, *The Issei: The World of the First Generation Japanese Immigrants, 1885–1924* (New York, 1988).

36. Masakazu Iwata, *Planted in Good Soil: A History of the Issei in the United States Agriculture* (2 vols., New York, 1992).

37. Valerie J. Matsumoto, *Farming the Home Place: A Japanese American Community in California, 1919–1982* (Ithaca, N.Y., 1993). There are half a dozen other books on Japanese American farming communities, the most analytical of which is Timothy J. Lukes and Gary Y. Okihiro, *Japanese Legacy: Farming and Community Life in California's Santa Clara Valley* (Cupertino, Calif., 1985).

38. For a thorough review of writings in Asian American labor history, see Chris Friday, "Asian American Labor and Historical Interpretation," *Labor History,* XXXV (1994), 524–564.

39. Ronald Takaki, *Pau Hana: Plantation Life and Labor in Hawaii* (Honolulu, 1983); Robert N. Anderson with Richard Coller and Rebecca F. Pestano, *Filipinos in Rural Hawaii* (Honolulu, 1984); Edward D. Beechert, *Working in Hawaii: A Labor History* (Honolulu, 1985); and Gary Y. Okihiro, *Cane Fires: The Anti-Japanese Movement in Hawaii, 1865–1945* (Philadelphia, 1991).

40. Renqiu Yu, *To Save China, to Save Ourselves: The Chinese Hand Laundry Alliance of New York* (Philadelphia, 1992).

41. Chris Friday, *Organizing Asian American Labor: The Pacific Coast Canned-Salmon Industry, 1870–1942* (Philadelphia, 1994).

42. In chronological order, these include Maxine P. Fisher, *The Indians of New York City: A Study of Immigrants from India* (Columbia, Mo., 1980); Illsoo Kim, *New Urban Immigrants: The Korean Community in New York* (Princeton, N.J., 1981); Edwin B. Almirol, *Ethnic Identity and Social Negotiation: A Study of a Filipino Community in California* (New York, 1985); Margaret A. Gibson, *Accommodation without Assimilation: Sikh Immigrants in an American High School* (Ithaca, N.Y., 1988); Bruce La Brack, *The Sikhs of Northern California, 1904–1975* (New York, 1988); Sathi S. Dasgupta, *On the Trail of an Uncertain Dream: Indian Immigrant Experience in America* (New York, 1989); Arthur W. Helweg and Usha M. Helweg, *An Immigrant Success Story: East Indians In America* (Philadelphia, 1990); Stephen S. Fugita and David J. O'Brien, *Japanese American Ethnicity: The Persistence of Community* (Seattle, 1991); Karen Isaksen Leonard, *Making Ethnic Choices: California's Punjabi-Mexican Americans* (Philadelphia, 1992); Eileen H. Tamura, *Americanization, Acculturation, and Ethnic Identity: The Nisei Generation in Hawaii* (Urbana, Ill., 1994); and Brian Masary Hayashi, *"For the Sake of Our Japanese Brethren": Assimilation, Nationalism, and Protestantism among the Japanese of Los Angeles, 1895–1942* (Stanford, Calif., 1995).

43. In *Assimilation in American Life: The Role of Race, Religion, and National Origins* (New York, 1964), Milton M. Gordon differentiated among seven different kinds of stages of assimilation: *acculturation* (adopting the cultural values and behavioral standards of the host society); *structural assimilation* (large-scale entrance into the cliques, clubs, and institutions of the host society); *marital assimilation* or *amalgamation* (a high incidence of interracial or interethnic marriage); *identificational assimilation* (a sense of peoplehood based exclusively on the host society); *attitude receptional assimilation* (an absence of prejudice on the part of the host society); *behavior receptional assimilation* (an absence of discrimination by the host society); and *civic assimilation* (an absence of conflict in public life among the different groups). While some of the above processes depend largely on the extent to which members of an immigrant, ethnic, or racial minority group change their values and behavior, other processes can occur only when members of the majority or host society are receptive to such changes.

44. Jobs in the *primary* labor market are well-paid, long-term, and stable, come with good fringe benefits, and offer the possibility of advancement, while those in the *secondary* labor market are poorly paid, seasonal, devoid of fringe benefits, and provide no or very limited channels for upward mobility. In *ethnic enclaves*, immigrants in small businesses supposedly can earn incomes equal to or even exceeding those in the primary labor market, while wage workers, though poorly paid, supposedly can learn the ropes in preparation for self-employment. Other advantages provided by ethnic enclaves are the availability of credit to borrowers who might not qualify for regular bank loans and existence of ethnic ties that facilitate job placements.

45. Antimiscegenation laws, which existed in more than three dozen states to prohibit marriages between Americans of European and African ancestry, were expanded in certain states to bar marriages between Asian Americans and Euro-Americans. Male immigrants from India who settled in states with antimiscegenation laws could usually only marry women of color from non-Asian origins because almost no females from India came. For a history of antimiscegenation laws as they affected Asians

in California, see Megumi Dick Osumi, "Asians and California's Anti-Miscegenation Laws," in Nobuya Tsuchida, ed., *Asian and Pacific American Experiences: Women's Perspectives* (Minneapolis, 1982), 1–37.

46. Ivan Light and Edna Bonacich, *Immigrant Entrepreneurs: Koreans in Los Angeles, 1965–1982* (Berkeley and Los Angeles, 1988); Pyong Gap Min, *Ethnic Business Enterprise: Korean Small Business in Atlanta* (New York, 1988); In-Jin Yoon, *On My Own: Korean Immigration, Entrepreneurship, and Korean-Black Relations in Chicago and Los Angeles* (Chicago, 1996); Min Zhou, *Chinatown: The Socioeconomic Potential of an Urban Enclave* (Philadelphia, 1992); and Nancy Abelmann and John Lie, *Blue Dreams: Korean Americans and the Los Angeles Riots* (Cambridge, Mass., 1995).

47. Timothy P. Fong, *The First Suburban Chinatown: The Remaking of Monterey Park, California* (Philadelphia, 1994); and John Horton, *The Politics of Diversity: Immigration, Resistance, and Change in Monterey Park, California* (Philadelphia, 1995).

48. Charles J. McClain, *In Search of Equality: The Chinese Struggle against Discrimination in Nineteenth-Century America* (Berkeley and Los Angeles, 1994); Lucy E. Salyer, *Laws Harsh as Tigers: Chinese Immigrants and the Shaping of Modern Immigration Law* (Chapel Hill, N.C., 1995); the first four chapters in Sucheng Chan, ed., *Entry Denied: Exclusion and the Chinese Community in America, 1882–1943* (Philadelphia, 1991); and the essays in Hyung-chan Kim, ed., *Asian Americans and the Supreme Court: A Documentary History* (Westport, Conn., 1992).

49. Yen Le Espiritu, *Asian American Panethnicity: Bridging Institutions and Identities* (Philadelphia, 1992); William Wei, *The Asian American Movement* (Philadelphia, 1993); and Dana Y. Takagi, *The Retreat from Race: Asian-American Admissions and Racial Politics* (New Brunswick, N.J., 1992).

50. Peter Irons, *Justice at War: The Story of the Japanese American Internment Cases* (New York, 1983); Peter Irons, ed., *Justice Delayed: The Record of the Japanese American Internment Cases* (Middletown, Conn., 1989); Richard Drinnon, *Keeper of Concentration Camps: Dillon S. Myer and American Racism* (Berekely and Los Angeles, 1987); Thomas James, *Exile Within: The Schooling of Japanese Americans, 1942–1945* (Cambridge, Mass., 1987); Sandra C. Taylor, *Jewel of the Desert: Japanese American Internment at Topaz* (Berkeley and Los Angeles, 1993); Leslie T. Hatamiya, *Righting a Wrong: Japanese Americans and the Passage of the Civil Liberties Act of 1988* (Stanford, Calif., 1993); Donna K. Nagata, *Legacy of Injustice: Exploring the Cross-Generational Impact of the Japanese American Internment* (New York, 1933); Yazuko I. Takezawa, *Breaking the Silence: Redress and Japanese American Ethnicity* (Ithaca, N.Y., 1995); and Roger Daniels, Sandra C. Taylor, and Harry H. L. Kitano, eds., *Japanese Americans: From Relocation to Redress* (1986; rev. ed., Seattle, 1991). An earlier revisionist work should also be noted: Michi Weglyn, *Years of Infamy: The Untold Story of America's Concentration Camp*, (New York, 1976). So

should the official report of the Commission on Wartime Relocation and Internment of Civilians, *Personal Justice Denied* (Washington, D.C., 1982).

51. Page Smith, *Democracy on Trial: The Japanese American Evacuation and Relocation in World War II* (New York, 1995).

52. Sylvia Junko Yanagisako, *Transforming the Past: Traditions and Kinship among Japanese Americans* (Stanford, Calif., 1985).

53. Evelyn Nakano Glenn, *Issei, Nisei, War Bride: Three Generations of Japanese American Women in Domestic Service* (Philadelphia, 1986).

54. Judy Yung, *Chinese Women of America: A Pictorial History* (Seattle, 1986); Mei T. Nakano, *Japanese American Women: Three Generations, 1890–1990* (San Francisco, 1990); and Asian Women United of California, ed., *Making Waves: An Anthology of Writings by and about Asian Women* (Boston, 1989).

55. Nazli Kibria, *Family Tightrope: The Changing Lives of Vietnamese Americans* (Princeton, N.J., 1973); Nancy D. Donnelly, *Changing Lives of Refugee Hmong Women* (Seattle, 1994); Benson Tong, *Unsubmissive Women: Chinese Prostitutes in Nineteenth-Century San Francisco* (Norman, Okla. 1994); and Judy Yung, *Unbound Feet: A Social History of Chinese Women in San Francisco* (Berkeley and Los Angeles, 1995).

56. Ronald Riddle, *Flying Dragons, Flowing Streams: Music in the Life of San Francisco's Chinese* (Westport, Conn., 1983); William F. Wu, *The Yellow Peril: Chinese Americans in American Fiction, 1850–1940* (Hamden, Conn., 1982); Gina Marchetti, *Romance and the "Yellow Peril": Race, Sex, and Discursive Strategies in Hollywood Fiction* (Berkeley and Los Angeles, 1993); and James S. Moy, *Marginal Sights: Staging the Chinese in America* (Iowa City, 1993).

57. John Y. Fenton, *Transplanting Religious Traditions: Asian Indians in America* (New York, 1988); and Raymond Brady Williams, *Religions of Immigrants from India and Pakistan: New Threads in the American Mosaic* (Cambridge, England, 1988).

58. Elaine H. Kim, *Asian American Literature: An Introduction to the Writings and Their Social Context* (Philadelphia, 1981); Marlon Hom, *Songs of Gold Mountain: Cantonese Rhymes from San Francisco Chinatown* (Berkeley and Los Angeles, 1987); King-Kok Cheung and Stan Yogi, eds., *Asian American Literature: An Annotated Bibliography* (New York, 1988); Amy Ling, *Between Worlds: Women Writers of Chinese Ancestry* (New York, 1990); Stephen H. Sumida, *And the View from the Shore: Literary Traditions of Hawaii* (Seattle, 1991); Esther Mikyung Ghymn, *The Shapes and Styles of Asian American Prose Fictions* (New York, 1992); Shirley Geok-lin Lim and Amy Ling, eds., *Reading the Literatures of Asian America* (Philadelphia, 1992); King-Kok Cheung, *Articulate Silences: Hisaye Yamamoto, Maxine Hong Kingston, Joy Kogawa* (Ithaca, N.Y., 1993); and Sau-Ling Cynthia Wong, *Reading Asian American Literature: From Necessity to Extravagance* (Princeton, N.J., 1993). The bibliog-

raphy compiled by King-Kok Cheung and Stan Yogi, published by the Modern Languages Association, is available on CD-Rom and is updated periodically.

59. Epifanio San Juan, Jr., *The Philippine Temptation: Dialectics of Philippine-U.S. Literary Relations* (Philadelphia, 1996).

60. For a fairly comprehensive listing of works published between 1977 and 1992, see Sucheng Chan, "A Selected Bibliography and List of Films on the Vietnamese, Cambodian, and Laotian Experience in Southeast Asia and the United States," in Franklin Ng et al., *New Visions in Asian American Studies: Diversity, Community, Power* (Pullman, Wash., 1994), 63–110.

61. David W. Haines, ed., *Refugees as Immigrants: Cambodians, Laotians, and Vietnamese in America* (Totowa, N.J., 1989); Nathan Caplan, John K. Whitmore, and Marcella H. Choy, *The Boat People and Achievement in America: A Study of Family Life, Hard Work, and Cultural Values* (Ann Arbor, 1989); and Steven J. Gold, *Refugee Communities: A Comparative Field Study* (Newbury Park, Calif., 1992). Nathan Caplan et al. have published a segment of their larger study as *Children of the Boat People: A Study of Educational Success* (Ann Arbor, 1991).

62. Paul J. Strand and Woodrow Jones, Jr., *Indochinese Refugees in America: Problems of Adaptation and Assimilation* (Durham, N.C., 1985); Gil Loescher and John A. Scanlan, *Calculated Kindness: Refugees and America's Half-Open Door, 1945–Present* (New York, 1986); James W. Tollefson, *Alien Winds: The Reeducation of America's Indochinese Refugees* (New York, 1989); Valerie O'Connor Sutter, *The Indochinese Refugee Dilemma* (Baton Rouge, La., 1990); and Jeremy Hein, *States and International Migrants: The Incorporation of Indochinese Refugees in the United States and France* (Boulder, Colo., 1993).

63. Roger Daniels, *Asian America: Chinese and Japanese in the United States since 1850* (Seattle, 1988); Ronald Takaki, *Strangers from a Different Shore: A History of Asian Americans* (Boston, 1989); Sucheng Chan, *Asian Americans: An Interpretive History* (Boston, 1991); Gary Y. Okihiro, *Margins and Mainstreams: Asians in American History and Culture* (Seattle, 1994); Harry H.L. Kitano and Roger Daniels, *Asian Americans: Emerging Minorities* (1988; rev. ed., Englewood Cliffs, N.J., 1994); Pyong Gap Min, ed., *Asian Americans: Contemporary Trends and Issues* (Thousand Oaks, Calif., 1995); and Bill Ong Hing, *Making and Remaking Asian America Through Immigration Policy, 1850–1990* (Stanford, Calif., 1993). Shih-shan Henry Tsai, *The Chinese Experience in America* (Bloomington, Ind., 1986) and Harry H.L. Kitano, *Generations and Identity: The Japanese Americans* (Needham Heights, Mass., 1993) provide overviews of single groups.

64. Paul James Rutledge, *The Vietnamese Experience in America* (Bloomington, Ind., 1992); and Jeremy Hein, *From Vietnam, Laos, and Cambodia: A Refugee Experience in the United States* (New York, 1995).

Reading 4

Is Yellow Black or White?

Gary Y. Okihiro

. . . Between 1985 and 1990 in New York City, there were three major protests against Korean storeowners in African communities, while in Los Angeles, as one boycott ended in the summer of 1991, another began, and within a six-month period, five Korean grocery stores were firebombed. In a Los Angeles courtroom, the television monitors showed fifteen-year-old Latasha Harlins punch Soon Ja Du and turn to leave the store, when Du lifts a gun and fires pointblank at Harlin's head, killing her. On December 15, 1991, Yong Tae Park died of bullet wounds received during a robbery on his liquor store the previous day; Park was the seventh Korean storeowner killed in Los Angeles by African male suspects that year. "Black Power. No Justice, No Peace! Boycott Korean Stores! The Battle for Brooklyn," the poster read. "Crack, the 'housing crisis,' and Korean merchants is a conspiracy to destabilizing our community. . . . The Korean merchants are agents of the U.S. government in their conspiracy to destabilize the economy of our community. They are rewarded by the government and financed by big business."[1] In south central Los Angeles in April and May 1992, following the acquittal of police officers in the beating of African American Rodney G. King, Koreatown was besieged, eighteen-year-old Edward Song Lee died in a hail of bullets, nearly fifty Korean merchants were injured, and damage to about 2,000 Korean stores topped $400 million. Parts of Japantown were also hit, and losses to Japanese businesses exceeded $3 million. Is Yellow black or white?

Source: Gary Y. Okihiro, *Margins and Mainstreams: Asian American History and Culture* (Seattle: University of Washington Press, 1994). Reprinted by permission.

In laying the intellectual foundation for what we now call the model minority stereotype, social scientists William Caudill and George De Vos stated their hypothesis: "there seems to be a significant compatibility (but by no means identity) between the value systems found in the culture of Japan and the value systems found in American middle class culture." That compatibility, they cautioned, did not mean similarity but rather a sharing of certain values and adaptive mechanisms, such that "when they [Japanese and white middle-class Americans] meet under conditions favorable for acculturation . . . Japanese Americans, acting in terms of their Japanese values and personality, will behave in ways that are favorably evaluated by middle class Americans."[2] Although Caudill and De Vos tried to distinguish between identity and compatibility, similarity and sharing, subsequent variations on the theme depicted Asians as "just like whites." And so, is yellow black or white?

The question is multilayered. Is yellow black or white? is a question of Asian American identity. Is yellow black or white? is a question of Third World identity, or the relationships among people of color. Is yellow black or white? is a question of American identity, or the nature of America's racial formation.[3] Implicit within the question is a construct of American society that defines race relations as bipolar—between black and white—and that locates Asians (and American Indians and Latinos) somewhere along the divide between black and white. Asians, thus, are "near-whites" or "just like blacks."[4] The construct is historicized, within the progressive tradition of American history, to show the evolution of Asians from minority to majority status, or "from hardship and discrimination to become a model of self-respect and achievement in today's America."[5] "Scratch a Japanese-American," social scientist Harry Kitano was quoted as saying, "and you find a Wasp," and Asians have been bestowed the highest accolade of having "outwhited the Whites."[6] The construct, importantly, is not mere ideology but is a social practice that assigns to Asian Americans, and indeed to all minorities, places within the social formation. Further, the designations, the roles, and the relationships function to institute and perpetuate a repression that begets and maintains privilege. Asian Americans have served the master class, whether as "near blacks" in the past or as "near-whites" in the present or as "marginal men" in both the past and the present. Yellow is emphatically neither white nor black; but insofar as Asians and Africans share subordinate position to the master class, yellow is a shade of black, and black, a shade of yellow.

We are a kindred people, African and Asian Americans. We share a history of migration, interaction and cultural sharing and commerce and trade. We share a history of European colonization, decolonization, and independence under neo-colonization and dependency. We share a history of oppression in the United States, successively serving as slave and cheap labor, as peoples excluded and absorbed, as victims of mob rule and Jim Crow. We share a history of struggle for freedom and the democratization of America, of demands for equality and human dignity, of insistence on making real the promise that all men and women are created equal. We are a kindred people, forged in the fire of white supremacy and struggle, but how can we recall that kinship when our memories have been massaged by white hands, and how can we remember the past when our storytellers have been whispering, amid the din of Western civilization and Anglo-conformity?

We know each other well, Africans and Asians. Some of the first inhabitants of South and Southeast Asia were a people called "Negrito," who were gatherers and hunters and slash-and-burn cultivators. They may have been absorbed or expelled by the Veddoids, a later group of immigrants to the Indian subcontinent, but remnants survive today as the Semang of the Malay Peninsula, the Mincopies of the Andaman Islands, and the Negritos of the Philippines. One branch of the Dravidians, who arrived in South Asia probably after 1000 B.C.E., were black people, who at first apparently intermarried with the lighter-skinned Indo-Aryan branch of Dravidians, but who were later denigrated in the caste system that evolved on the Gangetic plains.[7]

Trade, if not migration, between Africa and Asia predated the arrival of Portuguese ships in the Indian Ocean by at least a thousand years. African ambergris, tortoiseshell, rhinoceros horns, and especially ivory left African ports for Arabia, India, Indonesia, and China. The *Periplus of the Erythraean Sea*, a handbook compiled by a Greek-Egyptian sailor sometime during the first three centuries C.E., described Indonesian food crops, such as coconuts, and cultural items, such as sewn boats, along the East African coast perhaps as far south as Mozambique, and historians believe that Indonesians may have settled on Madagascar in the early centuries C.E., but after the time of the *Periplus*.[8] The Chinese Ch'eng-shih Tuan, in his *Yu-yang-tsa-tsu* written in the ninth century C.E., described East Africa, or the "land of Po-pa-li," where the women were "clean and well-behaved" and where the trade products were ivory and ambergris.[9]

From the eighth through twelfth centuries, the Hindu kingdom of Sri Vijaya, centered on Sumatra, was the dominant mercantile power in the Indian Ocean; it controlled the sea routes between India and China and likely traded directly with people along the East African coast. About the same time, the Chola kingdom in southeast India sent traders to East Africa, where their cowrie currency, system of weights, and trade beads became standard and widespread. By the thirteenth century, both Sri Vijaya and the Chola kingdom fell into decline, and the west Indian Ocean became an Islamic sphere. Still, the Ming dynasty, which gained control of China in 1368, sent a fleet to East Africa in 1417 and again in

1421, and Ming porcelain has been found in abundance among the ruins of mosques, tombs, houses, and palaces on the islands and on the mainland along the East African coast. Fei-Hsin, a junior officer on the 1417 expedition, described the townspeople of Mogadishu: "the men wear their hair in rolls which hang down all round and wrap cotton cloths round their waists" and the women "apply a yellow varnish to their shaven crowns and hang several strings of disks from their ears and wear silver rings round their necks."[10]

Besides the trade in goods, Africans and Asians engaged in a slave trade that was "probably a constant factor" in the Indian Ocean from the tenth to the thirteenth centuries.[11] Much of that trade was conducted by Africanized Muslims, who sent African slaves to the shores of the Persian Gulf, to India, and to China. In the year 1119, "most of the wealthy in Canton possessed negro slaves," and East African slave soldiers were used extensively by the Sassanian kings of Persia during the seventh century and by the Bahmanid kings of the Deccan in India during the fourteenth and fifteenth centuries.[12] Africans in Asia sometimes rose from the ranks of slaves to become military and political leaders, such as Malik Sarvar of Delhi, who became the sultan's deputy in 1389, was appointed governor of the eastern province, and eventually ruled as an independent king. Perhaps most influential was Malik Ambar, who was born in Ethiopia around 1550, sold into slavery in India, and rose to become a commander and ruler in the Decan. Ferista, a contemporary Arab historian, called Ambar "the most enlightened financier of whom we read in Indian history," and he reported that "the justice and wisdom of the government of Mullik Ambar have become proverbial in the Deccan."[13] The East African slave trade remained small in volume until the nineteenth century, when European colonies in the Americas and the Indian Ocean opened a larger market for slaves.[14]

The creation of that global system of labor and the conjunction of Africans, Asians, and Europeans began long before the nineteenth century. African and Asian civilizations contributed much to the dawning of European civilization in the Greek city-states. The armies of the Islamic Almoravids ranged across the Sudan and North Africa to Carthage and the Iberian Peninsula, and the Mongol armies of Chingiz Khan penetrated the European heartland. The invaders brought not only devastation but also religion, culture, and science. That intimacy would later be denied by the Europeans, who, after crusades to expel the "infidels" from Christendom and after the rise of nationalism and mercantile capitalism, conceived an ideology that justified their expansion and appropriation of land, labor, and resources in Africa, Asia, and the Americas. That ideology, in the name of religion and science, posited the purity and superiority of European peoples and cultures, unsullied by the anti-Christian, uncivilized non-Europeans—the Other—and found expression in European colonization of the Third World.

Seeking first the kingdom of gold, Europeans set sail for Asia down the African coast and around the Cape of Good Hope to India and China, and later west across the Atlantic Ocean to India, where instead they stumbled into the landmass they named the Americas. Colonization followed trade just as surely as capital required labor. European plantations in the Americas devoured the native inhabitants and, unstated, demanded African laborers from across the Atlantic in the miserable system of human bondage that supplied an outlet for European manufacturers and produced the agricultural products that enriched the metropole. The reciprocal of European development was Third World underdevelopment, and the web spun by European capitalism crisscrossed and captured the globe, creating a world-system in which capital and labor flowed as naturally as the ocean currents that circled the Atlantic and Pacific.

Some of the earliest Asians in the Americas came by way of the Spanish galleon trade between Manila and Acapulco in the early seventeenth century. Chinese and Filipino crew members and servants on those Spanish ships settled in Mexico, and Filipino "Manilamen" found their way to Louisiana, where, in 1763, they created the oldest continuous Asian American communities in North America.[15] The Filipinos named their fishing and shrimping settlements Manila Village, St. Malo, Leon Rojas, Bayou Cholas, and Bassa Bassa. But the main body of Asian migration to the Americas came after the termination of the African slave trade in the nineteenth century and the consequent need for a new source of labor for the plantations, mines, and public works in Central and South America, Africa, and the islands of the Pacific and Caribbean.

A forerunner of the nineteenth-century coolie trade and the successor of the earlier East African slave trade was the use of Asian and African slaves on board European ships in the Indian Ocean and a European carrying trade that took Asian slaves from Bengal, southern India and Sri Lanka, the Indonesian archipelago, the Philippines, and Japan to Dutch and Portuguese possessions in Asia and Africa. Beginning in the early sixteenth century, largely because of the debilitating effects of disease upon European sailors, Arab, South Asian, Malay, and African slaves frequently màde up the majority of the crews on Portuguese vessels plying Indian Ocean waters.[16] Asian slaves were joined by Africans taken from Madagascar and East Africa and were brought to the Dutch settlement at the Cape of Good Hope after 1658. By 1795, there were 16,839 slaves in the colony, and in 1834, the year slavery was abolished at the Cape, there were approximately 34,000 slaves.[17] The slaves produced mixed offspring with the indigenous San and Khoikhoi and with whites, forming the group the Europeans called the Cape Coloured. South Asians arrived on the East Coast of eighteenth-century America as indentured workers and slaves. Brought to Massachusetts and Pennsylvania on board English and American trade vessels possibly during the 1780s and 1790s, South Asians with Anglicized names such as James Dunn, John Ballay, Joseph Green, George Jimor, and Thomas Robinson served indentures, were sold and bought as slaves, likely married

African American women, and became members of the local African American communities.[18]

In 1833, slavery was formally abolished in the British Empire, but during the period of transition, slaves over six years of age served apprenticeships from four to six years as unpaid and later as paid labor. Apprenticeships ended in the British colonies in 1838, leading to the claim by sugar planters of a chronic labor shortage and a determination "to make us, as far as possible, independent of our negro population," according to John Gladstone, father of Robert and William Gladstone and one of the largest slaveholders and proprietors of estates in British Guiana.[19] Slavery, as pointed out by historian Hugh Tinker, produced both "a system and attitude of mind" that enabled a new system of slavery—coolieism—that incorporated many of the same oppressive features of the old.[20]

White planters saw the "new slaves" as subhuman and mere units of production. In 1836, anticipating the end of African slave apprenticeships, John Gladstone inquired about purchasing a hundred coolies from Gillanders, Arbuthnot & Company, who had supplied thousands of South Asians to Mauritius. The firm assured Gladstone that the Dhangars, or "hill coolies" of India, were "always spoken of as more akin to the monkey than the man. They have no religion, no education, and in their present state no wants beyond eating, drinking and sleeping: and to procure which they are willing to labour."[21] In May 1838, the first contingent of what would become a veritable stream of indentured labor arrived in British Guiana. The 396 Asian Indians were contracted to work nine to ten hours a day (as compared with seven and a half hours daily under apprenticeships) for sixteen cents (compared with thirty-two cents for free workers). In addition to economic exploitation, the indentured laborers were subject to disease and harsh treatment, particularly during the "seasoning," or breaking-in, period, resulting in numerous runaways and high mortality rates. From May 1845 to December 1849, 11,437 Asian Indians were indentured on sugar estates in British Guiana. Of that total as of December

1849, only 6,417 still remained on the estates, whereas 643 were listed as sick, vagrants, paupers, or children, 2,218 had died on the estates in jails and hospitals or were found dead elsewhere, and 2,159 were unaccounted for, of whom more than half were probably dead. Even those who had served their period of contract were left to wander "about the roads and streets, or lie down, sicken and die" or were castigated as "vagrants" who were stereotyped as "eating every species of garbage . . . filthy in [their] habits, lazy and addicted to pilfering."[22] Little wonder that Asian Indian indentures composed and sang this song as they sailed for Trinidad:

What kind plate,
What kind cup,
With a ticket to cut
in Trinidad,
O people of India
We are going to die there.[23]

Chinese and Asian Indian "coolies" were sold and indentured to European and American ship captains in a barter called by the Chinese "the buying and selling of pigs." The Chinese coolies, or "pigs," were restrained in "pigpens"; one such barracoon on Amoy in 1852 was described in a British report: "the coolies were penned up in numbers from 10 to 12 in a wooden shed, like a slave barracoon, nearly naked, very filthy, and room only sufficient to lie; the space 120 by 24 feet with a bamboo floor near the roof; the number in all about 500."[24] On shore, the coolies were stripped naked and on their chest were painted the letters *C* (California), *P* (Peru), or *S* (Sandwich Islands), denoting their destinations. Once on board the ship, they were placed below deck in the hold, where they were usually confined for the duration of the transpacific passage. Overcrowding and a short supply of food and water led to revolts, suicides, and murders. Fearing a revolt, the crew of an American ship, the *Waverly*, drove the Chinese coolies below deck and closed the hatch on October 27, 1855: "on opening them some twelve or fourteen hours

afterwards it was found that nearly three hundred of the unfortunate beings had perished by suffocation."[25] Chao-ch'un Li and 165 other coolies petitioned the Cuba Commission about ill-treatment and abuse: "When quitting Macao," they testified, "we proceeded to sea, we were confined in the hold below; some were even shut up in bamboo cages, or chained to iron posts, and a few were indiscriminately selected and flogged as a means of intimidating all others; whilst we cannot estimate the deaths that, in all, took place, from sickness, blows, hunger, thirst, or from suicide by leaping into the sea."[26] As many as a third of the coolies died during the journey across the Pacific on board ships bound for the Americas. During the years 1860 to 1863, for example, of the 7,884 Chinese coolies shipped to Peru, 2,400, or 30.4 percent, died en route.[27] The African slave and Asian coolie were kinsmen and kinswomen in that world created by European masters.

Between 1848 and 1874, 124,813 Chinese coolies reached Cuba from Macao, Amoy, Canton, Hong Kong, Swatow, Saigon, and Manila. Within Cuba's plantation system, wrote historian Franklin W. Knight, the Chinese became "coinheritors with the Negroes of the lowliness of caste, the abuse, the ruthless exploitation. . . . Chinese labor in Cuba in the nineteenth century was slavery in every social aspect except the name."[28] Coolies were sold in the open market, following advertisements that appeared in the local newspapers. Prospective buyers inspected the human merchandise, lined up on a platform, before the bargaining began, and the Asians were "virtually sold to the planters."[29] Conditions on Cuba's plantations were desperate. Chien T'ang, Chao Chang, A-chao Wen, and about three hundred of their compatriots in labor testified that they worked daily from between 2 and 4 a.m. until midnight, including Sundays, and others described the harsh treatment they received at the hands of overseers and masters. Confinement, shackling with chains, flogging, and cutting off fingers, ears, and limbs were methods employed to ensure docility and productivity in the workplace. A-pa Ho reported that for making a cigarette, "I was flogged with a rattan rod so severely that my flesh was lacerated and the bones became visible." A-chen Lu stated: "I have seen men beaten to death, the bodies being afterwards buried, and no report being made to the authorities"; A-sheng Hsieh told of Chen and Liang, who committed suicide after having been severely beaten. "The administrator accused them of cutting grass slowly," testified Hsieh, "and directing four men to hold them in a prostrate position, inflicted with a whip, a flogging which almost killed them. The first afterwards hanged himself, and the second drowned himself."[30]

In the United States, white planters similarly saw Chinese laborers as the "coinheritors with the Negroes of the lowliness of caste, the abuse, the ruthless exploitation." Before the Civil War, southern planters saw African slaves as a counter to immigration to their region by, in the words of Edmund Ruffin, "the hordes of immigrants now flowing from Europe." After the war, the planters saw free blacks as a troublesome presence and sought to deport and colonize them outside the United States and to replace them with Europeans and Asians.[31] In 1869, Godfrey Barnsley, a Georgia planter and New Orleans factory predicted that Mississippi Valley planters would recruit "large numbers of Chinese to take the place of negroes as they are said to be better laborers[,] more intelligent and can be had for $12 to $13 per month and rations." William M. Lawton, chair of the Committee on Chinese Immigrants for the South Carolina Agricultural and Mechanical Society, put it more bluntly: "I look upon the introduction of Chinese on our Rice lands, & especially on the unhealthy cotton lands as new and essential machines in the room of others that have been destroyed [or are] wearing out, year by year."[32] Africans and Asians, according to that point of view, were mere fodder for the fields and factories of the master class.

Africans and Asians, however, were not the same. After the Civil War, southern employers viewed African Americans not only as essential laborers but also as political liabilities insofar as

they voted and voted Republican.[33] The problem, thus, was how to maintain white political supremacy while employing cheap and efficient "colored" workers, thereby ensuring white economic supremacy. William M. Burwell, in an essay published in the July 1869 issue of *De Bow's Review*, described the challenge: "We will state the problem for consideration. It is: To retain in the hands of the whites the control and direction of social and political action, without impairing the content of the labor capacity of the colored race." Asian migrant workers, it seemed to some southerners, provided the ideal solution to the problem in that they were productive laborers and noncitizens who could not vote. Further, Asian workers would be used to discipline African workers and depress wages. On June 30, 1869, the *Vicksburg Times*, a proponent of Asian migration, editorialized: "Emancipation has spoiled the negro, and carried him away from fields of agriculture." The *Times* went on to exult at the impending arrival of several hundred Chinese coolies: "Our colored friends who have left the farm for politics and plunder, should go down to the *Great Republic* today and look at the new laborer who is destined to crowd the negro from the American farm." Arkansas Reconstruction governor Powell Clayton observed: "Undoubtedly the underlying motive for this effort to bring in Chinese laborers was to punish the negro for having abandoned the control of his old master, and to regulate the conditions of his employment and the scale of wages to be paid him."[34]

African and Asian workers, nonetheless, were related insofar as they were both essential for the maintenance of white supremacy, they were both members of an oppressed class of "colored" laborers, and they were both tied historically to the global network of labor migration as slaves and coolies. As anthropologist Lucy M. Cohen has shown, the planters in the American South were members of a Caribbean plantation complex, and the plans they formulated for Chinese migration drew from their cultural bonds with West Indian societies.[35] For example, during the 1850s, Daniel Lee of the *Southern Cultivator* and

J.D.B. De Bow of *De Bow's Review*, despite their preference for African slaves, informed their readers about the growing use of Asian coolie labor in the plantations of the West Indies, and after the Civil War in October 1865, John Little Smith, an eminent jurist, reported in several southern newspapers that, according to an American ship captain who had taken Chinese coolies to Cuba, the Chinese were the "best and cheapest labor in the world" and would make good plantation workers and unparalleled servants.[36]

Despite their interest in Asian coolies, southern planters were stymied by the 1862 act of Congress that had prohibited American involvement in the coolie trade. To skirt federal restrictions on the importation of Asian workers, the planters and labor contractors crafted a distinction between coolies, who were involuntary and bonded labor, and Asian migrants, who were voluntary and free labor. That distinction, they noted, enabled the comparatively easy entry of Chinese into California, and when a shipload of Chinese from Cuba was impounded in 1867 at the port of New Orleans, planter Bradish Johnson argued: "What if the government should forbid the employment of the thousands of Chinese who have worked on the railroads, on the mines, and agriculture of California? No reason had been found for their exclusion and they were valuable for that country. The cultivators of cane and cotton would not be made an exception."[37] Johnson won his point, and the case was discontinued. Meanwhile, planters held Chinese labor conventions, such as the 1869 Memphis convention that drew delegates from Alabama, Arkansas, Georgia, Kentucky, Louisiana, Mississippi, Missouri, South Carolina, Tennessee, and California, representing agricultural, railroad, and other business interests, and formed immigration committees and companies, and labor agents continued to bring Chinese workers, under contract, to the South, procuring them from Cuba, California, and China. After 1877, when white supremacist Democrats had broken the grip of Reconstruction through fraud and violence, southern planters reverted to a pref-

erence for African American workers, and interest in Asians declined and vanished.[38]

Although advocates of Chinese labor in the South learned to distinguish slave from coolie, and coolie from migrant, the migration of Asians to America cannot be divorced from the African slave trade, or from the coolie trade that followed in its wake. Both trades were systems of bonded labor, and both trades formed the contexts and reasons for the entry of Asians into America. Contract labor was the means by which Chinese and Japanese migrated to the Hawaiian kingdom and the American South, whereas the credit-ticket system was the means by which many Chinese gained admittance into California. But a system that advanced credit to laborers and constrained those workers to a term of service until the debt was paid was a scant advance over the earlier forms of coolie and contract labor,[39] and, perhaps more importantly, all of the successive systems of labor—from slave to coolie to contract to credit-ticket—were varieties of migrant labor and functioned to sustain a global order of supremacy and subordination.[40] The lines that directed Africans and Asians to America's shore converge at that point, and the impetus for that intersection came from the economic requirement and advantage of bonded labor buttressed by the relief in the centrality of whiteness and the marginality of its negation—nonwhiteness.

African Americans recognized early on the wide embrace of racism and equated racism directed at Asians with racism directed at Africans. Frederick Douglass pointedly declared that the southern planters' scheme to displace African with Asian labor was stimulated by the same economic and racist motives that supported the edifice of African slavery. The white oligarchy of the South, he stated, "believed in slavery and they believe in it still." During the late 1870s and early 1880s, when a Chinese exclusion bill was being debated in the Congress, Blanche K. Bruce of Mississippi, the lone African American senator, spoke out and voted against the discriminatory legislation, and the *Christian Recorder*, an African American newspaper in Boston, editorialized:

"Only a few years ago the cry was, not 'The Chinese must go,' but 'The niggers must go' and it came from the same strata of society. There is not a man to-day who rails out against the yellow man from China but would equally rail out against the black man if opportunity only afforded."[41]

In his *Observations Concerning the Increase of Mankind*, published in 1751, Benjamin Franklin divided humankind along the color line of white and nonwhite. The number of "purely white people," he noted with regret, was greatly exceeded by the number of blacks and "Tawneys," who inhabited Africa, Asia, and the Americas. Whites had cleared America of its forests and thereby made it "reflect a brighter light"; therefore, argued Franklin, "why should we . . . darken its people? Why increase the sons of Africa, by planting them in America, where we have so fair an opportunity, by excluding all Blacks and Tawneys, of increasing the lovely White . . . . ?"[42] According to historian Alexander Saxton, the same racism that sought to increase the "lovely White" and that justified the expulsion and extermination of American Indians and the enslavement of Africans was carried, like so much baggage, west across the American continent, where it was applied to Asians, the majority of whom resided along the Pacific coast.[43]

Franklin's binary racial hierarchy found expression in a book written by Hinton R. Helper of North Carolina, who would become a chief Republican antislavery polemicist. Describing his visit to California in his *The Land of Gold*, published in 1855, Helper wrote of the inhabitants of a small coastal town north of San Francisco: "Bodega contains not more than four hundred inhabitants, including 'Digger' Indians, 'niggers,' and dogs, the last by far the most useful and decent of the concern." Of the Chinese, Helper charged that the "semibarbarians" had no more right to be in California than "flocks of blackbirds have in a wheat field," and he offered his view of American race relations: "No inferior race of men can exist in these United States without becoming subordinate to the will of the Anglo-Americans. . . . It is so with the Negroes in the South; it is so with the Irish in

the North; it is so with the Indians in New England; and it will be so with the Chinese in California."[44] Within months after the end of the Civil War, the *New York Times* warned of allied dangers: "We have four millions of degraded negroes in the South . . . and if there were to be a flood-tide of Chinese population—a population befouled with all the social vices, with no knowledge or appreciation of free institutions or constitutional liberty, with heathenish souls and heathenish propensities . . . we should be prepared to bid farewell to republicanism."[45] In popular culture, the stereotype character of the "heathen chinee" made its debut in American theater by way of the blackface minstrel shows, and Chinese were paired with black sambos in Wild West melodramas.[46]

The institutionalization of Africans and Asians as the Other, as nonwhites, was embraced in American law and proposed legislation. California's state assembly passed two companion bills excluding from the state both Chinese and African Americans, modeled on the black codes of midwestern states.[47] In 1854, Justice Charles J. Murray delivered the California Supreme Court's ruling on *The People v. George W. Hall*, in which Hall, a white man, was convicted of murder based upon the testimony of Chinese witnesses. Murray outlined the precedents that established that "no black or mulatto person, or Indian, shall be allowed to give evidence in favor of, or against a white man," and he considered the generic meaning of the terms "black" and "white." The words, Murray contended, were oppositional, and "black" meant "nonwhite," and "white" excluded all persons of color. In addition, the intent of the law was to shield white men "from the testimony of the degraded and demoralized caste" and to protect the very foundations of the state from the "actual and present danger" of "a race of people whom nature has marked as inferior, and who are incapable of progress or intellectual development beyond a certain point . . . differing in language, opinions, color, and physical conformation; between whom and ourselves nature has placed an impassable difference."[48] The Chinese testimony thus was inadmissible, and Hall's conviction was reversed.

Like exclusion, antimiscegenation laws helped to maintain the boundary between white and nonwhite. Virginia banned interracial marriages in 1691.[49] Besides withholding state sanction of interracial cohabitation, antimiscegenation laws sought to prevent race mixing and the creation of "hybrid races" and the "contamination" and lowering of the superior by the inferior race. The issue of Chinese and white parents, predicted John F. Miller at California's 1878 constitutional convention, would be "a hybrid of the most despicable, a mongrel of the most detestable that has ever afflicted the earth." California enacted its antimiscegenation law two years later, prohibiting marriages between whites and nonwhites, "negro, mulatto, or Mongolian."[50] Based on the same reasons for antimiscegenation laws, African, Asian, and American Indian children were excluded in 1860 from California's public schools designated for whites, and the state's superintendent of pubic instruction had the power to deny state funds to schools that violated the law. Nonwhite children attended separate schools established at public expense.[51]

Asian laborers might have been ideal replacements for African slaves because they were productive and incapable of becoming citizens, but they were also useful in that they were neither white nor black. Although some believed that the addition of yet another group of people to society would only add to the complexity and hence difficulty of race relations, others saw the entrance of Asians as a way to insulate whites from blacks. Asians were simultaneously members of the nonwhite Other, despite their sometime official classification as white, and an intermediate group between white and black. The foundations of that social hierarchy can be found in the economic relations of the plantation system. Franklin Knight informs us that in nineteenth-century Cuba, Asians were classified as whites, yet "their conditions of labor tended to be identical to those of slaves," and on plantations with a mixed labor force, Asians "bridged the gap between black and white," assisting slaves in the fields and factories but, unlike slaves, performing simple semiskilled tasks and handling machines.[52]

In Louisiana before the 1870 census, Chinese were counted as whites in the absence of a separate category for people who were neither white nor black.[53] Despite that classification, whites perceived Asians as belonging to the economic, if not social, caste assigned to Africans. In 1927, taking up a Chinese American challenge by Gong Lum to Mississippi's Jim Crow schools, the U.S. Supreme Court, citing its 1896 landmark decision *Plessy v. Ferguson*, which set forth the "separate but equal" doctrine, affirmed the state supreme court's ruling that Chinese were nonwhite and hence "colored" and thus could be barred from schools reserved for whites. A Chinese man who married an African American woman during the 1930s recalled: "Before 1942, the Chinese had no status in Mississippi whatever. They were considered on the same status as the Negro. If a Chinese man *did* have a woman, it *had* to be a Negro." Mississippi planter William Alexander Percy described Delta society in his autobiography, *Lanterns on the Levee*, published in 1941: "Small Chinese storekeepers are almost as ubiquitous as in the South Seas. Barred from social intercourse with the whites, they smuggle through wives from China or, more frequently, breed lawfully or otherwise with the Negro."[54]

The Chinese, however, occupied an ambiguous position racially, as reflected in Louisiana's census. In 1860, Chinese were classified as whites; in 1870, they were listed as Chinese; in 1880, children of Chinese men and non-Chinese women were classed as Chinese; but in 1900, all of those children were reclassified as blacks or whites and only those born in China or with two Chinese parents were listed as Chinese.[55] In Mississippi, according to sociologist James W. Loewen, the Chinese were initially assigned "a near-Negro position" with no more legal rights or political power, but neither whites nor blacks "quite thought of them *as* Negroes," and they later served in some respects "as middlemen between white and black."[56] In fact, that function both mediated and advanced the prevailing social relations.

In 1925, two months after the founding of A. Philip Randolph's Brotherhood of Sleeping Car Porters, the Pullman Company hired Filipinos to serve on its private cars as attendants, cooks, and busboys. African Americans, who had for more than fifty years worked in those capacities, were henceforth relegated to the position of porter and denied mobility to easier, more-lucrative positions. At first, the Brotherhood called Filipinos "scab labor" and sought their elimination from Pullman lines; however, during its most desperate years, the 1930s, the Brotherhood, unlike the racist American Federation of Labor that had excluded both Africans and Asians, recognized the hand of capital in dividing workers and saw the common plight of black and yellow: "We wish it understood," explained a policy statement, "that the Brotherhood has nothing against Filipinos. They have been used against the unionization of Pullman porters just as Negroes have been used against the unionization of white workers . . . We will take in Filipinos as members . . . We want our Filipino brothers to understand that it is necessary for them to join the Brotherhood in order to help secure conditions and wages which they too will benefit from."[57]

Amid such examples of solidarity, African Americans were severely tested by the capitalist system, which deliberately pitted African against Asian workers, whereby Asians were used to discipline African workers and to depress their wages. The root cause of African and Asian American oppression was further clouded by mutual ethnocentrism and prejudice that frequently devolved from the ideas and practices of the master class. It is not surprising, therefore, that some African Americans, like Howard University professor Kelly Miller, saw a danger in linking the claims of African and Asian Americans. "The Negro is an American citizen whose American residence and citizenry reach further back than the great majority of the white race," wrote Miller.

"He has from the beginning contributed a full share of the glory and grandeur of America and his claims to patrimony are his just and rightful due. The Japanese, on the other hand, is the eleventh hour comer, and is claiming the privilege of those who have borne the heat and burden of the day."[58]

What is surprising, instead, was the extent and degree of solidarity felt by African Americans toward Asian Americans. The *Chicago Defender* explained that Chinese and Japanese learned from racist America, having been "taught to scorn the Race or lose the little footing they may now boast," and Mary Church Terrell believed that Japanese shunned African Americans in an attempt to avoid the stigma of inferiority that whites had placed upon blacks.[59] And despite dismay over Asian American ethnocentrism, African Americans steadfastly realized that the enemy was white supremacy and that anti-Asianism was anti-Africanism in another guise. Thus, in 1906 and 1907, when the San Francisco school board ruled that Japanese children had to attend "Oriental schools" and when President Theodore Roosevelt intervened to avoid an international incident, the *Colored American Magazine* declared: "We are with the President in the California muddle, for as California would treat the Japanese she would also treat the Negroes. It is not that we desire to attend schools with the whites at all, per se, but the principle involved in the attempt to classify us as inferiors—not because we are necessarily inferior, but on the grounds of color—forms the crux of our protest."[60]

The Philippine-American war, like many of America's imperialist wars, provided an extraordinary test for American minorities. The late nineteenth century, America's period of manifest destiny and expansionism overseas, was a time of severe repression at home for African Americans. Shouldering the white man's burden was an opportunity for making domestic claims and gains, but at the expense of peoples of color with whom African Americans identified: the Cubans, Puerto Ricans, and Filipinos. Bishop Henry M. Turner of the African Methodist Episcopal church characterized the U.S. presence in the Philippines as "an unholy war of conquest" against "a feeble band of sable patriots," and Frederick L. McGhee, a founder of the Niagara Movement, observed that America was out "to rule earth's inferior races, and if they object make war upon them," and thus concluded that African Americans could not support the war against the Filipinos.[61] From the Philippines, an African American soldier wrote home to Milwaukee, where his letter was published in the *Wisconsin Weekly Advocate* on May 17, 1900:

> I have mingled freely with the natives and have had talks with American colored men here in business and who have lived here for years, in order to learn of them the cause of their [Filipino] dissatisfaction and the reason for this insurrection, and I must confess they have a just grievance. . . . [Americans] began to apply home treatment for colored peoples: cursed them as damned niggers, steal [from] and ravish them, rob them on the street of their small change, take from the fruit vendors whatever suited their fancy, and kick the poor unfortunate if he complained, desecrate their church property, and after fighting began, looted everything in sight, burning, robbing the graves.
>
> I have seen with my own eyes carcasses lying bare in the boiling sun, the results of raids on receptacles for the dead in search of diamonds. The [white] troops, thinking we would be proud to emulate their conduct. . . . One fellow . . . told me how some fellows he knew had cut off a native woman's arm in order to get a fine inlaid bracelet . . . They talked with impunity of "niggers" to our soldiers, never once thinking that they were talking to home "niggers" and should they be brought to remember that at home this is the same vile epithet they hurl at us, they beg pardon and make some effiminate [*sic*] excuse about what the Filipino is called.
>
> I want to say right here that if it were not for the sake of the 10,000,000 black people in the United States, God alone knows on which side of the subject I would be.

General Robert P. Hughes, a commander in the Philippines, entertained some doubt over "which side of the subject" African American troops fell

when he reported: "The darkey troops . . . . mixed with the natives at once. Whenever they came together they became great friends." And according to a contemporary report, white troops deserted because they found the Army irksome, whereas black troops deserted "for the purpose of joining the insurgents," whose cause they saw as the struggle of all colored people against white domination. Perhaps the most famous African American deserter was David Fagan of the Twenty-fourth Infantry, who joined the Filipino freedom fighters and fought the Yankee imperialists for two years.[62] After the war—the war in which General "Howlin' Jake" Smith ordered his men to "kill and burn, kill and burn, the more you kill and the more you burn the more you please me" and the war that cost over 600,000 Filipino lives for the sake of "civilizing" those who remained—about 500 African Americans, many of whom had married Filipino women, chose to stay in the Philippines.[63]

Asians, like African Americans, resisted their exploitation and subjugation, and in the shared struggle for equality secured the blessings of democracy for all peoples. On this point, we must be clear. Inclusion, human dignity, and civil rights are not "black issues," nor are they gains for one group made at the expense of another. Likewise, the democratization of America fought for by African and Asian Americans was advantageous for both groups. The "separate but equal" doctrine of *Plessy v. Ferguson*, for instance, was a basis for the 1927 case *Gong Lum v. Rice*, and both were cited as precedents in the 1954 *Brown v. Board of Education* decision.[64] In addition to those parallel and conjoining struggles for freedom, African and Asian American lives converge like rivers through time. In full knowledge of intergroup conflicts and hatreds among America's minorities and their sources and functions, I will recall here only acts of antiracialism and solidarity between Asian and African Americans.[65]

During the late 1840s and early 1850s, African Americans gathered with Chinese and whites at San Francisco's Washerwoman's Bay to wash clothes, and relations between Chinese and

Africans were apparently friendly. William Newby, a prominent African American leader in the city, reported to Frederick Douglass "that the Chinese were the most mistreated group in the state and that blacks were the only people who did not abuse them." Both shared with Indians, Newby pointed out, the "same civil rights disabilities," insofar as they were denied the franchise and debarred from the courts.[66] In 1869, the first Japanese settlers arrived in California and established the Wakamatsu Tea and Silk Farm Colony near Sacramento. The colony failed, but among that group of adventurers was Masumizu Kuninosuke, who married an African American woman, had three daughters and a son, and operated a fish store in Sacramento for many years.[67] Sacramento Chinese shared their church with African Americans for some time during the nineteenth century, and in San Francisco, Jean Ng, an African American married to a Chinese American, was buried in a Chinese cemetery. In 1913, Charley Sing, a Mobile, Alabama, Chinese laundryman, tried to get permission to marry Lilie Lambert, an African American.[68] A Filipino band made sweet music under the baton of its African American conductor, Walter Loving, at the San Francisco Panama-Pacific International Exposition in 1915, and touring African American musicians sometimes stayed at Chinese-owned lodging houses in San Francisco.[69] In 1927, Lemon Lee Sing, a sixty-eight-year-old Chinese laundryman in New York City, sought permission to adopt Firman Smith, an abandoned African American child he had found sleeping in a hallway. Sing fed and clothed Firman, enrolled him in school, and ultimately won from the courts custody of the child.[70] Sam Lee, a Chinese restaurant owner in Washington, D.C., refused to fire one of his African American employees, despite threats on his life, while in Chicago, in 1929, a Chinese restaurant was dynamited for serving African Americans.[71]

Many of us, Asian and Pacific Americans, several generations native-born, came of age during America's imperialist war in Vietnam and the African American freedom struggle of the 1960s. Many of us found our identity by reading Franz Fanon and Malcom X, Cheikh Anta Diop and W.E.B. Du Bois, Leopold Senghor and Langston Hughes. Many more of us, however, have migrated to the United States since 1965; we came of age in Reagan's America, the era of yuppies and yappies, and wasn't that the time when history came to an end?—announced, significantly, by an Asian American.[72] During fall semester 1990, I asked my Asian American students with whom they felt a closer kinship: African or European Americans? They almost universally expressed affinity with whites, and I recall how in 1944, amid strident, anti-Japanese wartime propaganda and concentration camps for Japanese Americans, the *Negro Digest* conducted a poll among its readers. To the question, "Should negroes discriminate against Japanese?" 66 percent in the North and West and 53 percent in the South answered "No."[73] During spring semester 1991, I asked my Asian American students the same question, and all of them claimed kinship with African Americans, and I recalled how in 1960, Yuri Kochiyama, born in San Pedro, California, and interned during the war at the Jerome concentration camp in Arkansas, and her husband, a veteran of World War II, enrolled in the Harlem Freedom School established by Malcom X to learn African American history and to engage in the struggle for civil rights.[74]

We are a kindred people, African and Asian Americans. We share a history of migration, cultural interaction, and trade. We share a history of colonization, oppression and exploitation, and parallel and mutual struggles for freedom. We are a kindred people, forged in the fire of white supremacy and tempered in the water of resistance. Yet that kinship has been obscured from our range of vision, and that common cause, turned into a competition for access and resources. We have not yet realized the full meaning of Du Bois's poetic insight: "The stars of dark Andromeda belong up there in the great heaven that hangs above his tortured world. Despite the crude and cruel motives behind her shame and exposure, her degradation and enchaining, the fire and freedom of black Africa, with the uncurbed might of her consort Asia, are indispensable to the fertilizing of the universal soil of mankind, which Europe alone never would nor could give this aching world."[75]

Is yellow black or white? In 1914, Takao Ozawa, a Japanese national, filed for naturalization on the basis of his over twenty-eight-year residence in the United States and the degree of his "Americanization." Further, Ozawa contended, Asians were not specifically excluded under the naturalization laws, and thus he should be considered a "free white person." The U.S. Supreme Court rendered its decision on November 13, 1922, rejecting Ozawa's application and claim. Only whites and Africans were accorded the privilege of naturalization, wrote Associate Justice George Sutherland, and although the founding fathers might not have contemplated Asians within the meaning of either black or white, it was evident that they were not included within the category of "free white persons." Ruled Sutherland: "the appellant is clearly of a race which is not Caucasian, and therefore belongs entirely outside the zone on the negative side."[76] The marginalization of Asians— "entirely outside the zone"—was accompanied by their negation as "nonwhites"—"on the negative side"—in this institutionalization of the racial state. Yellow is not white.

But yellow is not black either, and the question posed is, in a real sense, a false and mystifying proposition. The question is only valid within the meanings given to and played out in the American racial formation, relations that have been posited as a black and white dyad. There are other options. Whites considered Asians "as blacks" or, at the very last, as replacements for blacks in the post-Civil War South, but whites imported Chinese precisely because they were not blacks and were thus perpetual aliens, who could never vote. Similarly, whites upheld Asians as "near-whites" or "whiter than whites" in the model minority stereotype, and yet Asians experienced and continue to face white racism "like blacks" in educational and occupational barriers and ceilings and in anti-Asian abuse and physical violence. Further, in both instances, Asians were

used to "discipline" African Americans (and other minorities according to the model minority stereotype). That marginalization of Asians, in fact, within a black and white racial formation, "disciplines" both Africans and Asians and constitutes the essential site of Asian American oppression. By seeing only black and white, the presence and absence of all color, whites render Asians, American Indians, and Latinos invisible, ignoring the gradations and complexities of the full spectrum between the racial poles. At the same time, Asians share with Africans the status and repression of nonwhites—as the Other—and therein lies the debilitating aspect of Asian-African antipathy and the liberating nature of African-Asian unity.

On November 27, 1991, about 1,200 people gathered outside Los Angeles City Hall to participate in a prayer vigil sponsored by the African-Korean American Christian Alliance, a group formed the previous month. A newspaper reporter described the "almost surreal" scene:

> Elderly Korean American women twirling and dancing with homeless men in front of the podium. Koreans and street people in a human chain, holding hands but not looking at each other. Shoes and clothing ruined by cow manure, which had been freshly spread over the rally grounds in an unfortunate oversight. Alliance co-chair Rev. Hee Min Park startled rally-goers when he began quoting from Marther Luther King's famous "I have a dream" speech. Black homeless people listened in stunned silence at first, as the pastor's voice with a heavy immigrant accent filled the slain black minister's familiar words. Then a few began chanting "Amen" in response to Park's litany.[77]

Park's articulation of King's dream reminds me of Maxine Hong Kingston's version of the story of Ts'ai Yen, a Han poetess kidnapped by "barbarians," in her book *The Woman Warrior*. Although she had lived among them for twelve years, Ts'ai Yen still considered the people primitive, until one evening, while inside her tent, she heard "music tremble and rise like desert wind." Night after night the barbarians blew on their flutes, and try as she might, Ts'ai Yen could not block out the sound. "Then, out of Ts'ai Yen's tent, which was apart from the others, the barbarians heard a woman's voice singing, as if to her babies, a song so high and clear, it matched the flutes." After she was ransomed, Ts'ai Yen brought her songs back to her people, who sang them to their own instruments. Concluded Kingston, "They translated well."[78]

NOTES

1. Poster of the December 12th Movement, Brooklyn Chapter, 1990.

2. William Caudill and George De Vos, "Achievement, Culture and Personality: The Case of the Japanese Americans," *American Anthropologist* 58 (1956): 1107.

3. For a definition of racial formation, see Michael Omi and Howard Winant, *Racial Formation in the United States: From the 1960s to the 1980s* (New York: Routledge & Kegan Paul, 1986), pp. 57–86.

4. See, e.g., James W. Loewen, *The Mississippi Chinese: Between Black and White* (Cambridge: Harvard University Press, 1971).

5. *U.S. News & World Report*, December 26, 1966. See also Dan Caldwell, "The Negroization of the Chinese Stereotype in California," *Southern California Quarterly* 53 (June 1971): 123–31, on the convergence of the Chinese and African American physiognomy; and Dennis M. Ogawa, *From Japs to Japanese: The Evolution of Japanese-American Stereotypes* (Berkeley: McCutchan Publishing, 1971), on the progression of Japanese American stereotypes.

6. "Success Story: Outwhiting the Whites," *Newsweek*, June 21, 1971.

7. Hugh Tinker, *South Asia: A Short History* (Honolulu: University of Hawaii Press, 1990), pp. 1–5.

8. J.E.G. Sutton, *The East African Coast: An Historical and Archaeological Review* (Dar es Salaam: East African Publishing House, 1966), p. 8.

9. G.S.P. Freeman-Grenville, ed., *The East African Coast: Select Documents from the First to the Earlier Nineteenth Century* (London: Oxford University Press, 1962), p. 8.

10. Gervase Mathew, "The East African Coast until the Coming of the Portuguese," in *History of East Africa*, ed. Roland Oliver and Gervase Mathew (London: Oxford University Press, 1963), 1:116, 120–21.

11. Ibid., p. 106.

12. Ibid, pp. 101, 108, 121.

13. Joseph E. Harris, *The African Presence in Asia: Consequences of the East African Slave Trade* (Evanston: Northwestern University Press, 1971), pp. 78–79, 91–98.

14. Ibid., pp. 7–10; and Edward A. Alpers, *The East African Slave Trade* (Dar es Salaam: East African Publishing House, 1967), pp. 4–5.

15. Marina E. Espina, *Filipinos in Louisiana* (New Orleans: A.F. Laborde & Sons, 1988), p.1.

16. Arnold Rubin, *Black Nanban: Africans in Japan during the Sixteenth Century* (Bloomington: African Studies Program, Indiana University, 1974), pp. 1–2, 9.

17. R.L. Watson, *The Slave Question: Liberty and Property in South Africa* (Hanover: Weslyan University Press, 1990), pp. 9–10; and Robert Ross, *Cape of Torments: Slavery and Resistance in South Africa* (London: Routledge & Kegan Paul, 1983), pp. 11, 13.

18. Joan M. Jensen, *Passage from India: Asian Indian Immigrants in North America* (New Haven: Yale University Press, 1988), pp. 12–13.

19. Alan H. Adamson, *Sugar without Slaves: The Political Economy of British Guiana, 1838–1904* (New Haven: Yale University Press, 1972), pp. 31, 41.

20. Hugh Tinker, *A New System of Slavery: The Export of Indian Labour Overseas, 1830–1920* (London: Oxford University Press, 1974), p. 19. For overviews of Asian Indian and Chinese migration and indentureship in the Caribbean, see K.O. Laurence, *Immigration into the West Indies in the 19th Century* (Mona, West Indies: Caribbean Universities Press, 1971); and William A. Green, *British Slave Emancipation: The Sugar Colonies and the Great Experiment, 1830–1865* (London: Oxford University Press, 1976), pp. 276–86, 289–93.

21. Tinker, *New System of Slavery*, p. 63.

22. Adamson, *Sugar without Slaves*, p. 48. Asian Indian and Chinese indentured laborers inherited, in the minds of the white planters, the alleged vices of African slaves in Trinidad. See David Vincent Trotman, *Crime in Trinidad: Conflict and Control in a Plantation Society, 1838–1900* (Knoxville: University of Tennessee Press, 1986), pp. 69, 87–88.

23. Noor Kumar Mahabir, *The Still Cry: Personal Accounts of East Indians in Trinidad and Tobago during Indentureship (1845–1917)* (Tacarigua, Trinidad: Calaloux Publications, 1985), p. 41. For life on the sugar estates, see Adamson, *Sugar without Slaves*, pp. 104–59; and Judith Ann Weller, *The East Indian Indenture in Trinidad* (Rio Piedras, P.R.: Institute of Caribbean Studies, University of Puerto Rico, 1968).

24. Cited in Ching-Hwang Yen, *Coolies and Mandarins: China's Protection of Overseas Chinese during the Late Ch'ing Period (1851–1911)* (Singapore: Singapore University Press, 1985), p. 59.

25. Shih-shan H. Tsai, "American Involvement in the Coolie Trade," *American Studies* 6, nos. 3 and 4 (December 1976): 54. For a more detailed account of U.S. involvement in the coolie trade and coolie resistance, see Robert J. Schwendinger, *Ocean of Bitter Dreams: Maritime Relations between China and the United States, 1850–1915* (Tucson: Westernlore Press, 1988), pp. 18–62.

26. Yen, *Coolies and Mandarins*, pp. 61–62.

27. Persia C. Campbell, *Chinese Coolie Emigration to Countries within the British Empire* (London: P.S. King & Son, 1923), p. 95; and Watt Stewart, *Chinese Bondage in Peru* (Durham: Duke University Press, 1951), pp. 62, 66, 97. See also Yen, *Coolies and Mandarins*, p. 62.

28. Franklin W. Knight, *Slave Society in Cuba during the Nineteenth Century* (Madison: University of Wisconsin Press, 1970), p. 119. African slavery in Cuba, of course, was gover by slave codes that differed significantly from the institutions that regulated the coolie system. On the complementarity and distinctions between African slavery and Chinese indentured labor, see Rebecca J. Scott, *Slave Emancipation in Cuba: The Transition to Free Labor, 1860–1899* (Princeton: Princeton University Press, 1985), pp. 29–35, 109–10.

29. Yen, *Coolies and Mandarins*, p. 63; and Knight, *Slave Society*, p. 116.

30. Yen, *Coolies and Mandarins* pp. 64, 66–68. For a comparison, see Jan Breman, *Taming the Coolie Beast: Plantation Society and the Colonial Order in Southeast Asia* (Delhi: Oxford University Press, 1989); and Wing Yung, *My Life in China and America* (New York: Henry Holt, 1909), p. 195, on Chinese coolies in Peru.

31. James L. Roark, *Masters without Slaves: Southern Planters in the Civil War and Reconstruction* (New York: W.W. Norton, 1977), p. 165. See also Rowland T. Berthoff, "Southern Attitudes toward Immigration, 1865–1914," *Journal of Southern History* 17, no. 3 (August 1951): 328–60; and George E. Pozzetta, "Foreigners in Florida: A Study of Immigration Promotion, 1865–1910," *Florida Historical Quarterly* 53, no.2 (October 1974): 164–80.

32. Roark, *Masters without Slaves* p. 167.

33. Loewen, *Mississippi Chinese*, pp. 21–24.

34. Ibid., p. 23.

35. Lucy M. Cohen, *Chinese in the Post–Civil War South: A People without a History* (Baton Rouge: Louisiana State University Press, 1984); idem, "Entry of Chinese to the Lower South from 1865 to 1879: Policy Dilemmas," *Southern Studies* 17, no. 1 (Spring, 1978): 5–37; and idem, "Early Arrivals," *Southern Exposure*, July/August 1984, pp. 24–30.

36. Cohen, "Entry of Chinese," pp. 8–12.

37. Ibid., p. 20.

38. Loewen, *Mississippi Chinese*, p. 26.

39. Cohen, *Chinese in the Post–Civil War South*, p. 44; and Gunther Barth, *Bitter Strength: A History of the Chinese in the United States, 1850–1870* (Cambridge: Harvard University Press, 1964), p. 67. See also Shih-shan Henry Tsai, *The Chinese Experience in America* (Bloomington: Indiana University Press, 1986), pp. 3–7; idem, "American Involvement"; Roger Daniels, *Asian America: Chinese and Japanese in the United States since 1850* (Seattle: University of Washington Press, 1988), pp. 13–15; and Sucheng Chan, *This Bitter-Sweet Soil: The Chinese in California Agriculture, 1860–1910* (Berkeley and Los Angeles: University of California Press, 1986), pp. 21, 26.

40. June Mei, "Socioeconomic Origins of Emigration: Guangdong to California, 1850 to 1882," in *Labor Immigration under Capitalism: Asian Workers in the United States before World War II*, ed. Lucie Cheng and Edna Bonacich (Berkeley and Los Angeles: University of California Press, 1984), p. 220; and Sucheng Chan, *Asian Americans: An Interpretive History* (Boston: Twayne Publishers, 1991), p. 4.

41. David J. Hellwig, "Black Reactions to Chinese Immigration and the Anti-Chinese Movement: 1850–1910," *Amerasia Journal* 6, no. 2 (1979): 27, 30, 31. See also Philip S. Foner, "Reverend George Washington Woodbey: Early Twentieth Century California Black Socialist," *Journal of Negro History* 6, no. 2 (April 1976): 149–50. In their 1943 struggle for repeal of the exclusion laws, Chinese Americans recognized a common cause with African Americans in their quest for equality. Renqiu Yu, "Little Heard Voices: The Chinese Hand Laundry Alliance and the *China Daily News'* Appeal for Repeal of the Chinese Exclusion Act in 1943," in *Chinese America: History and Perspectives, 1990*, ed. Marlon K. Hom et al. (San Francisco: Chinese Historical Society of America, 1990), pp. 28–29, 31–32.

42. Quoted in Takaki, *Iron Cages*, p. 14.

43. Alexander Saxton, *The Indispensable Enemy: Labor and the Anti-Chinese Movement in California* (Berkeley and Los Angeles: University of California Press, 1971), pp. 19–45; and idem, *The Rise and Fall of the White Republic: Class Politics and Mass Culture in Nineteenth Century America* (London: Verso, 1990). See also Luther W. Spoehr, "Sambo and the Heathen Chinese: Californians' Racial Stereotypes in the Late 1870s," *Pacific Historical Review* 42, no. 2 (May 1973): 185–204; and Miller, *Unwelcome Immigrant*.

45. Saxton, *Indispensable Enemy*, p. 18; and Caldwell, "Negroization of the Chinese Stereotype," p. 127.

46. Cited in Ronad Takaki, *Strangers from a Different Shore: A History of Asian Americans* (Boston: Little, Brown & Co., 1989), pp.100–101.

47. Saxton, *Indispensable Enemy*, p. 20.

48. Ibid., p. 19–20. For comparison of Chinese and African American intelligence, see U.S. Congress, Senate, *Report of the Joint Special Committee to Investigate Chinese Immigration*, 44th Cong., 2d sess., 1877, pp. 942, 1133–34.

48. Quoted in Wu, *"Chink!"* pp. 36–43.

49. George M. Fredrickson, *The Arrogance of Race: Historical Perspectives on Slavery, Racism, and Social Inequality* (Middletown: Wesleyan University Press, 1988), p. 196. Cf. Takaki, *Strangers from a Different Shore*, p. 101, who, like Winthrop Jordan, claims that a 1664 Maryland law that discouraged the marriage of "Negro slaves" with "freeborne English women" by imposing a penalty requiring such women and their children to be consigned into slavery should be viewed as ban on interracial marriage. Fredrickson, however, argues that before the 1690s, bans of interracial unions were largely class as opposed to race-based.

50. Takaki, *Strangers from a Different Shore*, pp. 101–2.

51. Elmer Clarence Sandmeyer, *The Anti-Chinese Movement in California* (Urbana: University of Illinois Press, 1973), p. 50; Victor Low, *The Unimpressible Race: A Century of Educational Struggle by the Chinese in San Francisco* (San Francisco: East/West Publishing Co., 1982), pp., 6–37: and Charles M. Wollenberg, *All Deliberate Speed:*

Segregation and Exclusion in California Schools, 1855–1975 (Berkeley and Los Angeles: University of California Press, 1976), pp. 30, 31, 39–43.

52. Knight, *Slave Society*, p. 71.

53. Cohen, *Chinese in the Post-Civil War South*, p. 167.

54. Loewen, *Mississippi Chinese*, pp. 59, 61, 66–68.

55. Cohen, *Chinese in the Post-Civil War South*, pp. 167–68. Sociologists Omi and Winant point out that racial classification is "an intensely political process" and is not a mere academic exercise but denies or provides access to resources and opportunities (Omi and Winant, *Racial Formation*, pp. 3–4).

56. Loewen, *Mississippi Chinese*, p. 60. Similarly, the biracial offspring of Africans, Europeans, and American Indians occupied an ambiguous social and legal position in the South. See Adele Logan Alexander, *Ambiguous Lives: Free Women of Color in Rural Georgia, 1789–1879* (Fayetteville: University of Arkansas Press, 1991).

57. Barbara M. Posadas, "The Hierarchy of Color and Psychological Adjustment in an Industrial Environment: Filipinos, the Pullman Company, and the Brotherhood of Sleeping Car Porters," *Labor History* 23, no. 3 (1982): 363.

58. Kelly Miller, *The Everlasting Stain* (Washington, D.C.; Associated Publishers, 1924), p. 163.

59. David J. Hellwig, "Afro-American Reactions to the Japanese and the Anti-Japanese Movement, 1906–1924," *Phylon* 38, no. 1 (March 1977: 103.

60. *The Colored American Magazine* 12, no. 3 (March 1907): 169.

61. Willard B. Gatewood, Jr,. *"Smoked Yankees" and the Struggle for Empire: Letters from Negro Soldiers, 1898–1902* (Urbana: University of Illinois Press, 1971), p. 13; and William Loren Katz, *The Black West* (Seattle: Open Hand Publishing, 1987), pp. 323–24. On African American soldiers and the Vietnam War, see Byron G. Fiman, Jonathan F. Borus, and M. Duncan Stanton, "Black-White and American-Vietnamese Relations among Soldiers in Vietnam," *Journal of Social Issues* 31, no.4 (1975): 39–48.

62. Gatewood, *"Smoked Yankees,"* pp. 14, 15.

63. Luzviminda Francisco, "The First Vietnam: The Philippine-American War, 1899–1902," *in Letters in Exile: An Introductory Reader on the History of Philipinos in America*, ed. Jesse Quinsaat (Los Angeles: UCLA Asian American Studies Center, 1976), pp. 15, 19; and Gatewood, *"Smoked Yankees,"* p. 15.

64. Richard Kluger, *Simple Justice: The History of* Brown v. Broad of Education *and Black America's Struggle for Equality* (New York: Vintage Books, 1975), pp. 120–22, 191, 423, 448, 554, 565–66, 670, 703–4.

65. On African and Asian American conflicts, see Arnold Shankman's three publications: "'Asiatic Ogre' or 'Desirable Citizen'? The Image of Japanese Americans in the Afro-American Press, 1867–1933," *Pacific Historical Review* 46, no. 4 (November 1977): 567–87; "Black on Yellow: Afro-Americans View Chinese-Americans," *Phylon* 39, no. 1 (Spring 1978): 1–17; and *Ambivalent Friends: Afro-Americans View the Immigrant* (Westport: Greenwood Press, 1982).

66. Rudolph M. Lapp, *Blacks in Gold Rush California* (New Haven: Yale University Press, 1977), pp. 104–5.

67. Bill Hosokawa, *Nisei: The Quiet Americans* (New York: William Morrow, 1969), pp. 31–33.

68. Lapp, *Blacks in Gold Rush California*, pp. 104–5, 109–10; Douglas Daniels, *Pioneer Urbanites: A Social and Cultural History of Black San Francisco* (Philadelphia: Temple University Press, 1980), p. 97; and Shankman, *Ambivalent Friends*, pp. 31–32. On marriages between Africans and Asians in the South, see Loewen, *Mississippi Chinese*, pp. 135–53; Cohen, *Chinese in the Post-Civil War South*, pp. 149–72; and Doris Black, "The Black Chinese," *Sepia*, December 1975, pp. 19–24.

69. Kenneth G. Goode, *California's Black Pioneers: A Brief Historical Survey* (Santa Barbara: McNally & Loftin, 1974), p. 110; and Shankman, *Ambivalent Friends*, p. 30.

70. Shankman, "Black on Yellow," pp. 15–16.

71. Ibid., p. 16.

72. Francis Fukuyama, "The End of History?" *National Interest* 16 (Summer 1989): 3–18. The symbol of a man of color, particularly a man of Japanese ancestry, schooled in the West proclaiming "the triumph of the West" added substance to the finality of that "triumph," especially to those dubbed by Allan Bloom "we faithful defenders of the Western Alliance" (Allan Bloom, "Responses to Fukuyama," *National Interest* 16 [Summer 1989]: 19).

73. *Negro Digest*, September 1944, p. 66.

74. Yuri Kochiyama, "Because Movement Work is Contagious," *Gidra*, 1990, pp. 6, 10.

75. W.E.B. Du Bois, *The World and Africa, An Inquiry into the Part Which Africa Has Played in World History* (New York: International Publishers, 1965), p. 260.

76. Frank F. Chuman, *The Bamboo People: The Law and Japanese-Americans* (Del Mar, Calif.: Publisher's Inc., 1976), pp. 70–71. See also Yuji Ichioka, *The Issei: The World of the First Generation Japanese Immigrants, 1885–1924* (New York: Free Press, 1988), pp. 210–26.

77. *Korea Times*, December 9, 1991. In Los Angeles, after meeting between the Korean American Grocers Association and several African American gang leaders on May 25, 1992, the merchants announced plans to hire gang members, and a participant in the negotiations reported a "total bond between the two groups," which included the widely feared gangs the Bloods and the Crips (*Asian Week*, May 29, 1992; and *Korea Times*, June 8, 1992).

78. Maxine Hong Kingston, *The Woman Warrier: Memories of a Girlhood among Ghosts* (New York: Alfred A. Knopf, 1976), pp. 241–43.

Rethinking Race: Paradigms and Policy Formation

Shirley Hune

Thomas Kuhn has defined paradigms as world-views, values, and techniques held in common by members of a given community. Paradigms in the scientific community often become simplified as models or examples that govern its practitioners more than the subject matter itself. As "exemplary past achievements," paradigms are difficult to change.[1] More important, paradigms endure outside of the scientific community and reflect the dominant belief system of the general society.

Race relations models or theories are outgrowths of paradigms. They become habits of mind and patterns of behavior taught to subsequent generations of scholars. Racial paradigms are also embedded in ideologies, policies, and practices and are integrated into the formal structures and institutions of U.S. society as well as our everyday lives.[2] People who benefit from existing racial paradigms have a vested interest in maintaining them and tend to resist innovation. But sometimes paradigms shift as new models emerge to challenge traditional ways of defining problems and, in some cases, begin to replace existing models. As Kuhn has observed, paradigm shifts are begun typically by newcomers to the field who are less encumbered by existing approaches.[3] I would add that paradigm shifts are also initiated by outsiders to a particular community whose experiences offer alternative views to established ways of explaining the same phenomena. It is not surprising then that Ethnic Studies as a new field would begin to transform existing modes of thought and contribute to recent shifts in theoretical orientation.

Source: *Amerasia Journal* 21:1 & 2 (1995): 29-40. Reprinted with the permission of Shirley Hune and the Asian American Studies Center, UCLA.

I employ the term *rethinking* here to refer to new directions in race relations that are both being conceived and in need of development given the current social realities. I frame this rethinking within the concept of *shifting paradigms*, which I have utilized elsewhere,[4] and highlight below in five racial paradigms. While in my view these racial paradigms have not shifted in the sense that they have replaced traditional frameworks, they are beginning to change how problems and policies are perceived and developed. The results are what I call here *emergent paradigms*. I will focus my comments on the implications of dominant and emergent racial paradigms on policy formation and their significance for Asian American Studies.

1. From black/white paradigm or vertical dynamics and integration to the multiplicity of racial dynamics. For decades, research agendas have analyzed racial interactions in the U.S. almost exclusively as black/white relations. As the predominant racial model, the individual and community development of African Americans is viewed within a vertical dynamic with whites at the apex. All power and race relations have come to be seen within this framework of subordinate/majority dynamics.

Black/white relations is *the* model for Asian American/white, Latino/white, and Native American/white relations. Studies of separate and distinct vertical dynamics and integration of each group with the dominant white group prevail. Hence Asian American Studies is replete with examinations of each Asian American ethnic group's relations with whites. Furthermore, Asian American struggles for justice and their strategies of resistance, conflict resolution, cooperation, and empowerment are measured primarily against African Americans. Gary Okihiro has asked, "Is Yellow Black or White?" He suggests that the black/white paradigm marginalizes Asian Americans along a continuum where they are seen by the dominant culture "as Blacks" or as "near-Whites" depending upon the historical situation.[5] In rethinking racial paradigms, we need to go beyond binary and vertical relations and to consider standpoints other than that of whites and of being subordinate. The well-being and daily interactions of Asian Americans are not determined solely within Asian American/white vertical dynamics. Our past, present, and certainly future power relations have been and will continue to be inter-linked both horizontally and vertically with other subordinate racial groups as well as vertically with the dominant majority. The relations between Asian American small business owners and their non-Asian American employees and cliental, new multiracial and multiethnic residential patterns, biracial families, the growing class disparities within racial/ethnic groups, the shift in party affiliation and voting preferences of racial groups from Democrats to Republicans and other indicators give rise to rethinking race relations.

The emergent paradigm gives greater attention to the multiplicity of racial dynamics. It considers race relations in their complexities with the intersection of multiple racial groups and class differentiations along with gender, immigrant generation and age as a more accurate portrayal of the nation's race realities.[6] Changing majority/minority and minority/minority perspectives are evident in two recent hotly contested issues in California.

First, Proposition 187, which denies most social services, medical benefits and public education to illegal immigrants, was approved by 53 percent of the voters in November 1994, with racial groups holding different views. Exit polls differed somewhat. About 70 percent of Latinos opposed 187, while white voters favored it by over 60 percent and blacks and Asians were split. Similarly, the debates over a proposed California Civil Rights Initiative that would eliminate the use of race, sex, color, ethnicity or national origin as a criterion for either discriminating against or granting preferential treatment to any individual or group in public employment, public education or public contracting, indicate changes in majority and minority views towards affirmative action. With the proposed Initiative likely to appear on the California state ballot in November 1996, a March 1995 *Los Angeles Times* poll found that 48 percent of African Americans oppose the Initiative and 71 percent of whites, 54 percent of Asians, and 52 percent of Latinos support it.[7] Both proposals have become politicized and expose splits within racial groups, possible divisions between minority groups, and suggest the potential for new alliances.

A binary paradigm is inadequate in a multiracial context. What is needed is a framework that incorporates multiple racial groups and explores the complexity of current and future inter-group dynamics. Furthermore, the dominant black/white paradigm reinforces the exclusion of Asian Americans and others from public and private agendas because they are viewed as being neither black nor white. In contrast, a multiplicity paradigm will contribute to the inclusion of Asian Americans in American public policy.

2. From race and racism as static concepts and one aspect of American life and politics to racial formation and racism as dynamic, expansive and at the center of American life and politics. Intertwined with the black/white paradigm is another longstanding racial model that presumes race in America to be a relatively unchanging set of categories, experiences and outcomes governed largely by biology.[8] In turn, the paradigm of racism has focused on laws that discriminate and privileges civil and political rights in achieving equality. The assumption is that social and economic justice will follow once legal discrimination is abolished.

Current rethinking, notably the writings of Omi and Winant, views race as a historical process and a social construction whose meaning is contested collectively and individually and whose practice is embedded in all aspects of American life.[9] The emergent paradigm extends the struggle against racism beyond civil and political rights to broad issues of economic, social and cultural rights. It also views race relations as a dynamic that is continuously being redefined. For example, the study of race relations is expanding to incorporate the environmental justice movement. Policies and programs in support of Asian Pacific Americans, therefore, need to be active, view race as central, and connect race with the overall quality of life of the community.[10]

3. From Asian Pacific American communities as victim paradigm to differential power and agency. Much of race relations literature and analysis has placed communities of color in the victim mode. Communities and researchers of color sometimes assume this position. While this may have held some truth in the past, current and future race realities suggest that this depiction is limited. For example, the concept of internal colonialism as a descriptor of residential and commercial social and spatial relations ignores class differences within Asian American communities and between Asian American employers and their co-ethnic and non co-ethnic employees and clientele. Similarly, while noting the bifurcated educational achievement of Asian Americans, the differential attainments of various Asian Americans ethnic groups and the high educational accomplishments of many low-income Asian Americans cannot be ignored.

The emergent paradigm considers that Asian American communities like other communities of color have differential power. The old model of passive objects is being replaced with analyses of subject and agency. Those involved in policy studies are redefining community development and challenging the top-down approach. Where communities once waited for those with political and economic resources to define solutions and develop appropriate public and private policies, the shift in thinking is to view communities as

agents of change who can plan and develop for themselves, from their own perspectives, and not always to the wide acceptance of other residents.[11] Community empowerment, particularly of low-income members, gives greater attention to a bottom-up, community-based approach appropriate to the needs of a specific community, its size, strengths and resources.[12] Hence Asian American community development, how growth, preservation and conservation are defined and the use and allocation of resources by whom and for whom become central issues of empowerment. This paradigm also acknowledges that Asian Americans have a social responsibility to address the needs and concerns of disadvantaged peoples within and outside their own communities.

4. From ethnic-specific and homogenous studies to heterogenous, comparative and panethnic studies. A traditional paradigm in immigration studies and race relations is to treat each ethnic group linearly and as a separate and relatively homogenous entity. Hence, we find studies on individual Asian American communities—the Chinese, Japanese, Filipinos, and now Koreans, Vietnamese, Asian Indians, Cambodians, Thais and so forth—from their first years in the U.S. to the present. The lives of first generation immigrant males are privileged and the experiences of the first wave of Asian immigrant groups dominate the scholarship. This approach was a necessary beginning for Asian American Studies as it sought to reclaim its historic place in American history and culture. However, this paradigm results in descriptions of ethnic-specific experiences that are circumscribed, while assumed to be representative of the entire community. Consequently, policy recommendations that address the needs of a particular Asian American ethnic group or Asian Americans in general presume a one-size-fits-all solution that does not meet the range and complexity of contemporary communities.

The emergent paradigm recognizes the heterogeneity of Asian America and of each Asian American group. For example, recent studies that focus on gender and generation as variables in the work world and family politics of Japanese and Vietnamese Americans disclose the rich and intricate interplay of sharing and tensions that abound within these communities.[13] Other studies remind us that Asian Americans are not defined by urban and working class experiences alone, but are also rural or suburban and middle-class.[14]

The new thinking needs to discern the role of social class, gender, ethnicity, sexual orientation, the perspectives and experiences of different generations, political and economic dynamics, specific historical situations, political affiliations, regionality, nationality and other dimensions that challenge the limitations of the existing homogenous ethnic-specific paradigm. The emergent heterogeneity paradigm may finally given attention to neglected areas of research within our communities, to comparative studies between ethnic groups and panethnic studies of Asian Pacific American communities. It also suggests that public policies need to be refined if they are to adequately meet the needs of our communities and their many segments.

The emphasis on creating a homogeneous Asian American experience in Asian American Studies has caused us to overlook variations and distinctions. The shift to incorporating diversity carries with it a rebalancing of ethnic group realities, including the fact of dissimilar political and economic eras. Asian Americans who have dissimilar political and economic experiences, for example, often possess different world-views. At the same time, it highlights the need to appraise the strengths and weakness of Asian American panethnicity as a political strategy and an ethnic identity.[15]

5. From Asian Pacific American communities as an American experience to global and diasporic studies. Asian Pacific immigration as a racial paradigm in the U.S. is predominantly viewed as a phenomenon of American exceptionalism. Once more the dynamic is primarily linear—one leaves the Pacific Rim, settles in the U.S., works, establishes a family, and a community emerges. The emphasis is on inter-group

dynamics in the receiving society, the adaptation of newcomers, and the uniqueness of the United States as an immigrant nation.[16]

The emerging paradigm views the immigrant experience as circular and global. It recognizes that Asian emigration is diasporic and that Asians in the United States is only one part of the story.[17] The Asian experience abroad has historically been global, but the new realities of contemporary international migration have contributed to its recent (re)"discovery." There is new recognition that the transnational flow of capital, labor, technology, information, cultural motifs, and consumer habits are not simply one-way, but circular.[18] Consequently, there is a need to address families, economic enterprises, community formation, political and social movements and other aspects of the Asian American experience as transnational and global.

Asian American Studies had its historic origins in the demand for ethnic studies in the late 1960s. As a mass-based curricula and research agenda, it challenged American higher education as an elite and Eurocentric institution. It has also been in direct tension with the more established and largely state-sponsored Asian Studies programs. If racial paradigms have dominated ethnic studies, area studies programs have been driven by Cold War paradigm and U.S. hegemonic interests. Given their different beginnings, missions, and frameworks of analysis, Asian American Studies sought to forge its own identity distinct from Asian Studies. In so doing, it attracted many scholars originally trained in area studies who favored the democratizing tendencies of Asian American Studies. At the same time given their divergent intellectual and political interests, Asian Studies kept its distance from Asian American Studies, while university administrators tried to figure out the difference between the two fields.[19] This form of academic labor market segmentation, however, has contributed to the narrowing of the intellectual boundaries of Asian American Studies. For example, we know little about the impact of Asian emigration on the sending states or of the relations between communities of origin and communities of settlement.

The end of the Cold War era and the rise of globalization is leading to new academic pursuits, such as global and diasporic studies. Diasporic studies can expand the parameters of the Asian experience abroad from a largely American experience to a global one and serve as a bridge between ethnic studies and area studies. It can link Asian American scholars with those studying Asian Pacific experiences in Asia itself, Europe, the Americas, Africa, and the Middle East. The internationalization of Asian American Studies can contribute to the decentering of Asian Studies from a paradigm of regionality and one of importance when it is of national interest to the West. The linkage is a potential for intellectual exchange. However, it will continue to be problematic as long as area studies are privileged in the academy and Asian Studies retains its Cold War paradigm. New linkages do not replace or take away from Asian American Studies developing as a field in its own right. Nonetheless, global forces are transforming all aspects of our lives. Hence policy studies directed at Asian Pacific Americans cannot be limited by concepts of national borders and American exceptionalism.

Conclusions. I have confined my discussion to five shifting racial paradigms to suggest what researchers are thinking about today. Emerging paradigms, however, do not negate the persistence of dominant race relations models. The most important distinction of these emerging paradigms is that they are being formulated largely by scholars and practitioners pushing at the margins of traditional disciplines, many of whom are people of color and women. They are the newcomers to academic disciplines and outsiders to the academy that Kuhn identifies as less fearful of novelty and open to changing paradigms.

The theoretical repositioning on race and its impact on Asian American Studies raise some concerns. First, the rethinking is part of a resurgence of interest in race-specific theories to

explain inequality in America and reflects the debates over race-specific policies to redress injustice.[20] Race matters to and for Asian Pacific Americans. But so do class and gender. Race matters differently depending on one's social class and gender.[21] Race itself can become a dominant paradigm contributing to a serious lack of attention to other factors. Asian Americanists cannot afford to neglect such factors as class, gender, generation and others in rethinking race theory.

The new multiracial realities have been part of our landscape for some time. The changing demographics, the Los Angeles uprising of 1992, and the resurgence of anti-immigration activities have led researchers to give them new attention. Secondly, the rethinking of racial paradigms is just that—*rethinking*. The *doing* of new kinds of research in race relations is still in the making. Replication is easier than innovation. Institutional barriers, including surmounting the zealously guarded boundaries of academic units and disciplines, also complicate the conduct and implementation of interdisciplinary studies. However, when new forms of research are not carried out, old paradigms predominate.

Finally, what is the relationship between theory and practice. When Asian American Studies was founded, it represented a new paradigm that challenged the existing academic elite and traditional scholarship. Participants saw themselves as part of a different way of thinking, being, and doing in the academy that included new forms of scholarship, pedagogy, and research. Asian American faculty and students also saw themselves as a bridge between campus and community. Underlying this original mission was the notion that the privilege of education would contribute to the liberation of the less privileged and the increased democratization of U.S. society.[22] It has been said that each generation rewrites history in its own image. Similarly, social movements and organizations often revise their mission to reflect the context of their times. In striving for legitimacy in the academy, much of current theory and scholarship, especially in the area of cultural studies, is remotely connected to and often incomprehensible to those for whom Asian American Studies is said to represent. We need to consider whether the paradigm of Asian American Studies is shifting from its original mission and links with community and the less privileged to one in which our practice is centered exclusively in the university. If the primary engagement of Asian American Studies is with and for other academicians and if the new theoretical positioning maintains the status quo rather than changes it, we are moving in the direction of becoming another elite.

In summary, old racial paradigms are limited in explaining existing conditions, but persist. In rethinking race, new paradigms are emerging that speak to the multiplicity of racial dynamics, the ever-changing, but centrality of race and racism in America, the differential power and agency of communities, the increased attention to heterogeneous, comparative and panethnic studies as well as viewing Asian Pacific American communities in the context of global and diasporic studies. Each of these emergent paradigms, in turn, impacts on policy formation.

Rethinking race also has implications for Asian American Studies. One consideration is that race-specific paradigms will contribute to the neglect of other factors, such as class, gender, and generation. Another is that when the conduct of research is not commensurate with theoretical developments and new empirical studies are not forthcoming, old racial paradigms will continue to determine Asian Pacific American research. Finally and most important, the relationship between current theoretical repositioning and the practice of Asian American Studies is not clear. New paradigms are not necessarily transformative. Furthermore, current practices that disconnect Asian American Studies from community and place the academy at its center shift the paradigm of Asian American Studies from social transformation to the production of a new academic elite. In rethinking race, we also need to reexamine our practices. It is my hope that the new theoretical repositioning will not neglect the links to community, but reinforce and further the historic mission of Asian American Studies.

NOTES

1. Thomas Kuhn, *The Structure of Scientific Revolutions*, second edition, enlarged (Chicago: The University of Chicago Press, 1970), 171–94.
2. The October-November 1994 alleged hoax concocted by Susan Smith of a black man stealing her car with her two sons in it when she had drowned her children in the car in a lake near Union, South Carolina is only the most recent dramatic incident of a well-established racial paradigm to blame black males for individual or societal wrongs. "Woman's False Charge Revives Hurt for Blacks," *New York Times*, November 6, 1994.
3. Kuhn, 144–59.
4. Shirley Hune, "An Overview of Asian Pacific American Futures: Shifting Paradigms." In *The State of Asian Pacific America: Policy Issues to the Year 2020* (Los Angeles: LEAP Asian Pacific American Public Policy Institute and UCLA Asian American Studies Center, 1993), 1–9.
5. Gary Y. Okihiro, *Margins and Mainstreams* (Seattle: University of Washington Press, 1994), 31–63.
6. For examples of multiracial economic relations, see James W. Loewen, *The Mississippi Chinese: Between Black and White*, second edition (Prospect Heights, Illinois: Waveland Press, 1988), and Edward T. Chang, "Jewish and Korean Merchants in African American Neighborhoods: A Comparative Perspective" in *Los Angeles—Struggles toward Multiethnic Community*, edited by Edward T. Chang and Russell C. Leong (Seattle: University of Washington Press, 1995), 5–22. For a study of political dynamics, see Leland T. Saito, "Asian Americans and Latinos in San Gabriel Valley, California: Interethnic Political Cooperation and Redistricting 1990–92" in Chang and Leong, 55–68. For studies of multiracial identity, see Karen I. Leonard, *Making Ethnic Choices: California's Punjabi Mexican Americans* (Philadelphia: Temple University Press, 1992) and Maria P. P. Root, editor, *Racially Mixed People in America* (Newbury Park, California: SAGE Publications, 1992).
7. The statewide exit poll of the *Los Angeles Times*, November 10, 1994, indicated that 63 percent of whites, 47 percent blacks, 23 percent Latinos, and 47 percent Asians voted for Proposition 187, while the *USA Today*, November 11, 1994, found that 64 percent of whites, 56 percent blacks, 31 percent Latinos, and 57 percent Asians supported it. At this writing, Proposition 187 is being reviewed by the courts and is yet to be implemented. "The Times Poll. Most Call Prop. 187 Good, Want It Implemented Now," *Los Angeles Times*, March 13, 1995. The *Los Angeles Times* affirmative action poll has been criti-

cized for poorly worded questions that may have confused respondents. "The Times Poll. Most Back Anti-Bias Policy but Spurn Racial Preferences," *Los Angeles Times*, March 30, 1995.

8. The view that the differential outcomes of racial groups is based upon biology persists. Recent examples include, *The Bell Curve* by Richard J. Herrnstein and Charles Murray (New York: The Free Press, 1994). The authors argue that I.Q. scores are race-based and that African Americans are intellectually inferior. Similarly in the November 1994 remarks of President Francis Lawrence of Rutgers University, he stated that black students did not have the "genetic, hereditary background" to have a higher average on their SAT scores. See "Lawrence Must Go," *New York Times*, February 11, 1995. Both the book and Lawrence's remarks have been soundly challenged.

9. Michael Omi and Howard Winant, *Racial Formation in the United States* (New York: Routledge and Kegan Paul, 1986).

10. See, for example, *The State of Asian Pacific America: Policy Issues to the Year 2020* (Los Angeles: LEAP Asian Pacific American Public Policy Institute and UCLA Asian American Studies Center, 1993); Paul Ong, editor, *The State of Asian Pacific America: Economic Diversity, Issues and Policies* (Los Angeles: LEAP Asian Pacific American Public Policy Institute and UCLA Asian American Studies Center, 1994); and Robert D. Bullard, editor, *Confronting Environmental Racism* (Boston: South End Press, 1993).

11. Timothy P. Fong, *The First Suburban Chinatown* (Philadelphia: Temple University Press, 1994).

12. Paul Ong, editor, *Beyond Asian American Poverty* (Los Angeles: LEAP Asian Pacific American Public Policy Institute, 1993).

13. Evelyn Nakano Glenn, *Issei, Nisei, Warbride* (Philadelphia: Temple University Press, 1986) and Nazli Kibria, *Family Tightrope: The Changing Lives of Vietnamese Americans* (Princeton, New Jersey: Princeton University Press, 1993).

14. Recent rural studies include, Valerie J. Matsumoto, *Farming the Home Place* (Ithaca, New York: Cornell University Press, 1993) and Gary Y. Okihiro, "Fallow Field: The Rural Dimension of Asian American Studies" in *Frontiers of Asian American Studies* edited by Gail M. Nomura, Russell Endo, Stephen H. Sumida and Russell C. Leong (Pullman: Washington State University Press, 1989). The emergence of "middle-class" Asian American communities in the suburbs is discussed, for example, in Fong, *The First Suburban Chinatown* and in Hsiang-shui Chen's *Chinatown No More: Taiwan Immigrants in Contemporary New York* (Ithaca, New York: Cornell University Press, 1992).

15. Yen Le Espiritu, *Asian American Panethnicity* (Philadelphia: Temple University Press, 1992).

16. Shirley Hune, *Pacific Migration to the United States: Trends and Themes in Historical and Sociological Litera-* ture (Washington, DC: Research Institute on Immigration and Ethnic Studies, Smithsonian Institution, 1977), 1-21. Also reprinted in *Asian American Studies: An Annotated Bibliography and Research Guide*, edited by Hyung-chan Kim (New York: Greenwood Press, 1989), 17–30.

17. See, for example, the articles in the special issue of *Amerasia Journal*—Asians in the Americas 5:2 (1989) including a discussion of diaspora in Russell C. Leong's "Asians in the Americas: Interpreting the Diaspora Experience," vii–xviii.

18. See, for example, Haiming Liu, "The Trans-Pacific Family: A Case Study of Sam Chang's Family History," *Amerasia Journal* 18:2 (1992), and Paul Ong, Edna Bonacich, and Lucie Cheng, editors, *The New Asian Immigration in Los Angeles and Global Restructuring* (Philadelphia: Temple University Press, 1994).

19. For a discussion of the different origins, missions, and frameworks of ethnic studies and area studies, see *Asian Americans: Comparative and Global Perspectives*, edited by Shirley Hune, Hyung-chan Kim, Stephen S. Fugita and Amy Ling, "Part One, Comparing Old and New Area Studies" with articles by Shirley Hune, Evelyn Hu-DeHart, Gary Y. Okihiro and Sucheta Mazumdar (Pullman: Washington State University, 1991), 1–44. See also, Shirley Hune, "Opening the American Mind and Body: The Role of Asian American Studies," *Change* (November/December 1989): 56–63.

20. See, for example, Omi and Winant, 1986 and Mari J. Matsuda, Charles R. Lawrence III, Richard Delgado and Kimberle Williams Crenshaw, *Words That Wound: Critical Race Theory, Assaultive Speech and the First Amendment* (Boulder, Colorado: Westview Press, 1993).

21. In a controversial book in 1978, William J. Wilson noted the improving position of the black middle class in contrast to the deteriorating circumstances of the black underclass. *The Declining Significance of Race* (Chicago: The University of Chicago Press) launched a debate as to the relative importance of race and class in the African American community. By 1993, Cornell West (*Race Matters*, Boston: Beacon Press) was reminding the nation that race still matters for African Americans. See also, Dana Y. Takagi, *The Retreat from Race* (New Brunswick, New Jersey: Rutgers University Press, 1992), and Kenyon S. Chan and Shirley Hune, "Racialization and Panethnicity: From Asians in America to Asian Americans" in *Toward a Common Destiny: Improving Race and Ethnic Relations in America*, edited by W. Halley and A. W. Jackson (San Francisco: Jossey-Bass, 1995): 205–33, for a discussion of the significance of race for Asian Americans in education admissions.

22. Russell Endo and William Wei, "On the Development of Asian American Studies Programs" in *Reflections on Shattered Windows*, edited by G. Okihiro, S. Hune, A. Hansen and J. Liu (Pullman: Washington State University Press, 1988) and Hune, *Change*, 1989.

CHAPTER 3

Asian American Communities

Asian Americans have historically settled in the western United States, particularly in California and Hawaii. Today, however, Asian American communities can be found in urban, suburban, and rural areas across the nation. Almost half of all Asian Americans (44.3 percent) live in the midwestern, northeastern, and southern portions of the U.S. The selections in this chapter provide a glimpse of these new and emerging Asian American communities. These communities emerge for purposes of social and economic support, as well as a sense of identity. While Asian Americans generally congregate in large urban centers such as San Francisco, New York, and Los Angeles, lesser-known areas have also become popular places for settlement. Unfortunately, the growth of Asian American communities is not always welcomed by established residents. Negative reactions to Asian American newcomers can be indirect and subtle, but it also can be quite direct and violent.

Chor-Swang Ngin's article provides an excellent description of the early influx of Southeast Asian refugees to Orange County, California. According to the 1990 Census, almost a quarter of a million Asian Americans (249,192) live in Orange County, representing just over ten percent of the population. The focus of Ngin's work is the varying acculturation patterns among Southeast Asian refugees. She highlights five factors that must be taken into account: (1) the diversity of class and ethnic background of the Southeast Asian refugees, (2) their status and experience as refugees, (3) the size of the Southeast Asian refugee population, (4) the socioeconomic position of Southeast Asians in Orange County, and (5) opposition from the established community.

Tom L. Chung's article is based on the study of three decades of demographic and social changes in eastern Massachusetts. He focuses his analysis on an ethnic enclave framework but recognizes the diversity among Asian Americans. He then describes three economically distinguishable enclaves. "One-step-up enclaves" represent middle-class Asian Americans who are not necessarily new immigrants but who are arrivals from other areas. "New immigrant enclaves" are found in low-income areas, where they face a multitude of problems associated with poverty, such as poor living conditions, high crime rates, and underfunded school systems. "Suburban enclaves" are located in the most affluent areas, with all the advantages that come with upper-middle-class status. The Asian American residents of suburban enclaves are predominantly well-educated professionals and entrepreneurs. Ironically, even Asian American residents of suburban enclaves report incidences of discrimination and unfair treatment by local authorities.

Bert Eljera reports on Daly City, California, a city with a population that is 44 percent Asian American, but best known as home to the largest concentration of Filipinos in the United States. He describes the demographic shift from the 1970s, when whites were the majority, to 1990, when Filipinos became the largest ethnic group in the city. Despite some initial resistance, Filipino Americans appear to have integrated smoothly into all areas of life in Daly City, including the public schools, churches, and local politics. Located just ten minutes from San Francisco, Daly City is a natural location for a new Asian American community.

The emergence of an Asian American community in a seemingly unusual location is described in Jeff Yang's article on Dekalb County, Georgia. Asian Americans represent only about 3 percent of the population in Dekalb County, but are quite conspicuous because of the growth of ethnic businesses along the major commercial corridors. The local reception of Asian immigration has been, at best, mixed. While some business leaders see the change as an opportunity, others fear the area will be "overrun by foreigners." This antagonism against the sudden influx of Asians and the businesses they start in their new community is not unique. It is a scenario that has been repeated many times in numerous cities across the nation.

The most obvious example is the urban unrest demonstrated in south-central Los Angeles in 1992. Korean American and other Asian American merchants became the targets of rage following the acquittal of four white L.A. police officers who were accused of beating an African American, Rodney King. Over two thousand Korean-owned businesses were either damaged or destroyed during the riot. Together, Korean and other Asian American businesses suffered over $400 million in property losses, nearly half the total of all property losses in the city. Angela Oh's essay illustrates the anger and sadness that Korean Americans continue to suffer as a result of those devastating days of violence and arson in 1992.

The Acculturation Pattern of Orange County's Southeast Asian Refugees

Chor-Swang Ngin

In the past decade, Orange County has become home to about 130,000 Southeast Asian refugees.[1] The urban landscape along Bolsa Avenue in Westminster has changed from a mixture of strawberry fields, dusty used car lots, and machine shops along dirt sidewalks to mini-malls housing about 1,200 Vietnamese and Chinese businesses. How are these new immigrants welcome in Orange County? What is the acculturation pattern experienced by the refugees? Is it similar to the acculturation patterns of other Asian groups (e.g., Japanese or Chinese), or is there a pattern specific to the refugees themselves? This article will examine some of the experiences of Southeast Asians' acculturation in Orange County.

Before 1975, there were few Vietnamese, Cambodians or Laotians in Orange County. In a span of about fifteen years, of the more than 909,000 Southeast Asian refugees resettled in the United States, about 359,800 have settled in California and of those 130,000 in Orange County. In Orange County, most Southeast Asians live in Garden Grove, Westminster, Stanton, Huntington Beach, Santa Ana, and Costa Mesa.[2] They have also settled in the outlying areas of Mission Viejo, Irvine, Placentia, and Yorba Linda. Some of the families have bought homes and started small businesses. In the area of employment, many former Vietnamese professionals, after retraining and recertification, have become part of the American middle-class work force.[3] Others, with the help of refugee resettlement agencies and mutual-aid associations, have found work in electronic assembly, manufacturing, sales, and service.

Source: Journal of Orange County Studies 3/4, Fall 1989/Spring 1990, 46–53. Reprinted by permission.

Southeast Asian newcomers appear to be settling into Orange County with remarkable ease and speed, [whereas] the early Chinese settlers who came during the second half of the nineteenth century, and the Japanese who came later, were subjected to various discriminatory practices. For example, the Chinese in California were the only group subjected to the Foreign Miners' License Tax, and the Japanese were prohibited from owning land. Various legal barriers and discriminations against the Chinese and the Japanese eventually affected all other Asian groups. In addition, the Japanese Americans on the West Coast were thrust into a climate of anti-Asian hysteria that eventually led to the interment of 120,000 Japanese Americans during the Second World War. Repeated attempts made by the Asian American community at repealing these laws were turned down. The result was one of self-segregation of the various Asian immigrant groups into Chinatowns and other ethnic ghettoes.

Compared to this history of discrimination against early Asian Americans, the Southeast Asians have been received with less overt discrimination. No overt legislation that directly discriminates against Southeast Asians has been implemented to date. In an incident involving Vietnamese fishermen and members of the Ku Klux Klan who were disputing fishing rights along the Texas coast, the Vietnamese had full protection of the legal system, something earlier immigrants did not have.[4] A recent investigation by the Governor's Community Relations Commission also found no reported racial crimes directed against Southeast Asian refugees in Orange County. Local police departments that were interviewed in that investigation reported only extortion and burglary committed by the refugees on the refugees.[5]

What then has made the Southeast Asian newcomers' resettlement in the United States so unlike the earlier Asian immigrants whose experience was marked by legal barriers and anti-Asian hysteria? One possible explanation is the vastly different circumstances under which these two groups came to the United States. Attracted by the economic opportunities and "pulled" by labor needs in America, early Asian immigrants came to "seek fortune" in a new land. Southeast Asians, by contrast, were escaping the ravages of war and governments under communism. When Saigon fell to the Communists in 1975, the U.S. government felt that it was its moral obligation to help war allies—members of the former Vietnamese army and the Hmong who served in the CIA's secret army—and protect these allies from possible persecution from the new Communist governments.[6] Therefore when the first group of Vietnamese evacuees came to Camp Pendleton, there was an organized effort to help the refugees. Similarly, when the Hmong came, Americans recognized them for their contribution in the Vietnam War. American families in Orange County and throughout the country adopted and sponsored refugees, rented houses for them, brought furniture, clothes and food, and helped with the initial period of adjustment. As war refugees escaping from Communist-controlled countries, they are also entitled to a variety of refugee assistance programs— programs unheard of when Chinese, Japanese, Korean, and Filipino immigrants came earlier in the century. In Orange County, resettlement agencies provide programs in English as a Second Language (ESL) classes, job-placement, housing, citizenship application, and other social adjustment needs.

This broad view that Southeast Asians have been received very differently from Chinese and Japanese in earlier generations is not meant to imply that their entry into the United States and Orange County has been entirely without hostility. Their tendency to concentrate in a few communities and to turn these into conspicuously different areas has triggered various acts of resentment ranging

from sign defacement to public criticism. Sporadic beatings of school children and opinion polls suggesting strong feelings against the continued influx of Southeast Asians are reminders that some residents of the county still view them as "foreigners." The newcomers' method of adaptation and the public's reaction to it are some of the factors that affect the newcomers' acculturation (to be discussed later).

Noting that the transition of Southeast Asian refugees into Orange County has been relatively free from reported incidents of racial violence, and that the refugees have received assistance provided by refugee resettlement programs, what does this mean in terms of the Southeast Asian refugees' acculturation pattern? Would this relatively "happy" reception mean that acculturation will be more rapid?

To answer this question, we need to consider two concepts of acculturation or assimilation: the cultural, and social-structural models.[7] Cultural assimilation means taking on the ways of the host society, such as dress, diet, and life style. Social-structural assimilation refers to large-scale entrance of new peoples into cliques, clubs, and institutions of the host society. Other types of assimilation include marital, identificational, and civic.

While the experience of Southeast Asians in Orange County is still very recent, their acculturation process and the extent to which they have assimilated in any of these ways may be viewed in the context of: (1) the diversity of class and ethnic background of the Southeast Asian refugees; (2) their status and experience as refugees; (3) the size of the Southeast Asian refugee population; (4) the socioeconomic position of Southeast Asians in Orange County; and (5) opposition from the established community.

THE DIVERSITY OF SOUTHEAST ASIAN REFUGEE GROUPS

Southeast Asian immigration in the United States is characterized by ethnic and cultural diversity which in turn affects each group's adaptation to the new country. About 61.9 percent of the Southeast Asian refugees resettled permanently in the United States are from Vietnam; the rest are from Cambodia and Laos.[8] Besides the three major ethnic groups of Vietnamese, Khmer, and Lao, and the ethnic Chinese from urban Vietnam, Cambodia, and Laos, there are twenty distinct ethnic and linguistic groups with widely varying social and economic backgrounds. Most of the Vietnamese newcomers (100,000) have settled in Orange County, Cambodians (about 40,000) in Long Beach, and Lao and Hmong in Fresno and Stockton in central California. Each group has also built "ethnic towns" to serve the many needs of its newcomers. The largest among them is the Vietnamese community of Little Saigon in Westminster. The Cambodian community in Orange County consists mostly of about two-thousand people concentrated in a few apartments in the South Minnie Street area of Santa Ana. The rest of them are scattered throughout the county. The large number of Cambodians in Long Beach, however, have established a sort of a "Cambodian town" along Anaheim Boulevard near downtown Long Beach. Ethnic Chinese from both Vietnam and Cambodia have resettled in the existing Chinatowns in Los Angeles and Monterey Park as well as in Little Saigon and Cambodiatown.[9]

Over the years, the composition of the refugees has changed considerably, coming in several distinctive waves of arrivals. The first waves of refugees were largely Vietnamese and arrived following the fall of Saigon in 1975. This initial group was comprised primarily of the better educated, urban professional class. Smaller numbers of refugees also came from Laos and Cambodia into Thailand in those early days, and the United States maintained a small resettlement program throughout that period. About 30 percent from the first wave spoke English well or fluently upon arrival.[10] Adjustment to American society was comparatively easy for this first group. Many from these urban and privileged classes have gained economic self-sufficiency, even though many worked in jobs not commensurate with their qualifications. For example, a former lawyer from Vietnam may now work as a legal aide. Former government officers and schoolteachers, because of their education, are now working as counselors or refugee coordinators. While the professionals from this group may work in Little Saigon, many lived outside of it in other suburban Orange County communities. A middle-class Khmer who lives in Yorba Linda told me that, "If you look at my house, you can't even tell it belongs to a Cambodian family. We have lawns just like everybody else. Inside our house, we have American furniture. Maybe we are like an Asian American family."

The children from this group are rapidly acquiring the English language and local life style. Members of this more acculturated group perceived a difference between themselves and those who arrived later on, whom they dubbed the "FOB"—"Fresh Off the Boat." The young adult children of the first wave, a few of whom were American-born and most of them American educated, are relatively more acculturated as a group. They speak and write English with ease and are either attending college or have generally taken jobs in a cross section of American economic sectors. Even though many still understand or speak their native languages, many are no longer able to read or write them except for the most rudimentary words. Many have also tried hard to become more acceptable by modifying their appearance, particularly hair style and dress, to conform to the local fashion. Others have tried to "blend in" by taking on American first names, especially after they have become American citizens. The young also prefer eating hamburgers and riding skateboards to eating Southeast Asian foods and attending family functions.

The young adults find their Asian parents putting too much pressure on academic performance and severely restrictive in their freedom to socialize with their peers and the opposite sex. Parents, on the other hand, having grown up in Southeast Asia, find adjustment to American life extremely difficult. In the new country, they gain comfort in familiar foods and kinsmen and friends who speak the same language. They find their parental authority constantly challenged by American cultural values emphasizing individual freedom and choice, making children growing up here difficult to control. Furthermore, the loss of the traditional support system—traditional religious leaders, educators and elders from their home country who would have helped reinforce the shared value of respect for the parents and the elders—makes maintaining their cultural heritage difficult.

Different pressures on parents and children have resulted in conflicts between the generations. Creative solutions to these conflicts included the example of Dr. Thanh Van Le, who, instead of objecting to his children eating hamburgers, deliberately introduced them to expensive Vietnamese, Chinese, and French cuisines. He presented all these as different parts of the Vietnamese experience and history. By doing so, he felt that his children were able to retain a part of their Vietnamese heritage without perceiving their parents as cultural chauvinists. Young adult children caught in this conflict with their parents over dating the opposite sex have, for example, solved the problem by meeting their friends in public places, such as the library on weekdays or Little Saigon's Asian Garden Mall on weekends.

In the group's relationship with the larger non-Asian society, a few individuals speak of being comfortable enough to move outside of their own ethnic group into non-Asian areas. However, that step is often tentative because of the perception that non-Asians do not like Southeast Asian refugees. The result is that, except for a few individuals who have crossed that ethnic boundary into another ethnic community, there is much self-segregation.

The tendency to be affiliated with one's own group is also evident in the hundreds of ethnically based associations and clubs. Some of the organizations' goals are multiple; others are based on single-issue, ad-hoc needs. Examples of the former are the mutual-aid associations such as the Vietnamese Community of Orange County, Vietnamese Chambers of Commerce, Lao Family

Community, Cambodian Family, and United Cambodian Community. These groups help newcomers adapt to America through ESL classes, job training, and childcare. Examples of the latter organizations include the lesser known Vietnam/Cambodia/Laos Chinese Newspaper Reporters' Association, the Vietnamese Chinese American Friendship Association, the Vietnamese Physicians' Association, Cambodian Womens' Association, the Families of Vietnamese Political Prisoners Association, and the Association of Former Political Prisoners of Communist Vietnam in Southern California.

In other words, there is not much integration into the larger American society through large-scale entrance of membership into mainstream organizations among either the older and younger adults from this first wave. Thus, despite the superficial assimilation into American culture in the forms of dress and hair styles, speaking the English language, taking on jobs in all economic sectors, owning homes throughout the county, and an occasional preference for hamburgers, group affiliation, interpersonal relationships, dating practices, and food preference remain distinctively Asian.

The next large resettlement of newcomers, the second wave, began in 1978–1979 with the large-scale movement of boat people from Vietnam, land arrivals from Cambodia, and the continued presence of Laotians, including Hmong, Mien and other highland tribes. These new arrivals were more heterogeneous, including a large number of ethnic Chinese, and represented a more diverse socioeconomic strata of society. The proportion of those fluent in English upon arrival was far lower—about 7 percent. The acculturation pattern of this group has been far slower and more complex than the first.

The acculturation process of the more educated and urban professional Vietnamese, Chinese, and Khmer from the second group is similar to that of the first group. However, the experience of the majority of more rural newcomers is significantly different from the first group. The later group of rural newcomers tend to concentrate in their already established ethnic communities.

The recent arrivals of young Vietnamese adults find transition into American high school particularly difficult because many have had their education interrupted while languishing for years in refugee camps. They find playing "catch up" in the American high schools virtually impossible, with the result that many eventually have dropped out of school. Without an American high school education and unable to speak English, many find society and culture outside of the Southeast Asian community foreign to them. Mr. My Ta, a Vietnamese aide in an Orange County high school, reported that many of the high school dropouts spend their time sipping French coffee and listening to Vietnamese rock music at the malls in Little Saigon by day and congregating at the local pool halls by night. Without English, the only work available to them is in Little Saigon. The men tend to work in restaurants and supermarkets while the women work as manicurists, seamstresses, and hair dressers. Many hope that through years of hard work they can own a business of their own. To some others, that path to the American dream seems impossible, and they have therefore joined gangs as a way to combat boredom and hopelessness. A bright spot in the bleak future of the young adults is detected by My Ta who observed that some of them are discovering that auto mechanic courses provide profitable work opportunities without requiring extensive English skills. Many are therefore seeking to enroll in the adult classes of the Regional Opportunity Program (ROP) in Orange County.

Among the Khmer refugees in Orange County, the process of adapting into American society will be even more difficult. Under Pol Pot's regime, education was nonexistent. For adult Khmer newcomers, most of them women with young children, daily survival in America is still a struggle. Instead of languishing in refugee camps, many seek shelter in the protective shield of the Cambodian community in South Minnie Street in Santa Ana.

The adjustment process of those who came in the later waves, compared to those from the first group, has been and will be even more difficult. Some of the factors affecting their adaptation are discussed below.

SOUTHEAST ASIANS AS REFUGEES

The acculturation of the Southeast Asian refugees is also affected by their status as refugees. Unlike a contemporary immigrant whose decision to migrate to a new country is usually well thought out, a refugee does not make plans to migrate. When the Vietnamese evacuees were airlifted out of Saigon right after the fall of that city, many thought the evacuation was only temporary.[11] Similarly, the Cambodians who escaped to the Thai border were most concerned with leaving Pol Pot's reign of terror and had only vague notions of going to France or the United States. They did not have a clear idea of what they would do in the country of resettlement. This lack of psychological preparation to start a new life has contributed to the complaints of homesickness and an inability to adjust to a new country among large number of refugees. In a Boston study, it was found that 48 percent of the Cambodians studied suffered from homesickness.[12] In Orange County, similar concerns have been heard about refugees wishing to return to Southeast Asia. A common practice used by resettlement counselors in the county involves advising refugees to forget about returning to Southeast Asia, as it only impedes the process of their adjustment in the United States.

As war refugees, the newest immigrants to America have also suffered greatly from the trauma of war and escape. The plight of the Vietnamese who escaped by boats to neighboring countries has stirred the world through such personal accounts as those of Nhat Tien, Duong Phuc and Vu Thanh Thuy in *Pirates on the Gulf of Siam* (1981). The horror suffered by Cambodian refugees under Pol Pot's reign of terror equals that of the Nazi holocaust. Some survivors see their escape as a sign of new hope and purpose in life, but many others bear the scars of violence for years. In addition, refugees also suffered from an extraordinary degree of family disorganization as family members were either killed or separated from those who managed to escape and resettle in the United States. Among Cambodian refugees on Minnie Street most households consist of widowed, mother-child households. The men have either died from Pol Pot's regime or are still fighting for their country's independence in the Thai border camps. Among many of the newcomers who find adjustment most difficult are those who are without their families. Therefore, the psychological orientation of Southeast Asian refugees who are still coping with the trauma of war is on rebuilding a familiar cultural surrounding. Their most visible products in attempting to create the ambiance of the homeland are the ethnic towns mentioned earlier.

In rebuilding their lives, Southeast Asians have also tried to establish cultural links to Asia by the founding of Khmer, Vietnamese, and Laotian temples, Vietnamese Christian churches, and Cham Muslim Societies. In addition, there are also Vietnamese language schools, Khmer dance and music groups, Vietnamese and Cambodian chambers of commerce and numerous professional and trade organizations. Traditional festivals are also celebrated to maintain a sense of cultural identity and continuity.

Ethnic community organizations and ethnic support networks serve the important social, emotional, spiritual, and psychological needs of the recent arrivals. They also serve as important intermediaries between the new arrivals and American society. Mr. Tu Tran, a nineteen-year-old college student, compared his own experience with that of those who came recently: "Adjustment in some way is easier for the later groups because they have the support of Little Saigon and other ethnic communities. They know immediately what to wear and how to act appropriately in American society by observing their countrymen who have come before. When I came nine years ago, I did not know what to do because there were so few of us." Paradoxically, however, as ethnic communi-

ties and social networks help the new arrivals adjust to a new country, they may actually prevent them from integrating into the larger society.[13]

As refugees who have recently escaped the war and turmoil in their home countries, their lives are still intertwined with political events in Southeast Asia. The 1989 forced repatriation of Vietnamese Boat People from Hong Kong brought about protests and debates in the Vietnamese community in Orange County. The recent successful negotiation between the United States government and the Vietnamese government on the emigration of released Vietnamese political prisoners and family members also brought about the formation of organizations to represent the interests of this newer group of immigrants. Similarly, conferences and meetings have been held in the last two years highlighting events in Cambodia.

For many newcomers, some of their loved ones are still in the refugee camps in Thailand, Malaysia, and Hong Kong. Their futures are uncertain. The wait sometimes ends tragically. A brother of a Khmer resettlement counselor in Santa Ana recently committed suicide, for example, after attempts to immigrate into the United States failed.

The newcomers' relationship to those in Asia is most visible in the remittance of money and sending of medicine and other goods to Vietnam that can be resold in the black market. Many newcomers work two or three jobs in order to fulfill the obligation of helping those in the homeland. Personal enjoyment and leisure are often placed on hold among those exploring every possibility of family reunification. Life for them is the narrow focus of their immediate concerns. Issues in the larger American communities remain foreign even though they may be living in the midst of them.

THE SIZE OF THE SOUTHEAST ASIAN REFUGEE POPULATION

The acculturation of the Southeast Asian newcomers is also affected by the size of its population. The Vietnamese in Orange County are a large enough group to form the self-sustaining ethnic town of Little Saigon. This means that for many recent arrivals, after their initial contact with the resettlement and social-service personnel, interaction with the larger society is either minimal or nonexistent. This social isolation is evident even among educated, English-speaking Vietnamese professionals practicing in Little Saigon. The clients of the lawyers, doctors, and accountants tend to be other Vietnamese and other Southeast Asians.

Restaurants and other businesses in Little Saigon are able to survive through their dependence on mainly Asian and Southeast Asian customers, though these businesses' viability also depends on razor-thin profit margins, owners and family members working long hours, and employees receiving low wages.

Those living near Little Saigon can obtain most of their basic needs—from groceries, restaurants, doctors, pool parlors to funeral homes—without going outside of the community. Even among those who speak English and work with non-Asians, socialization after work is still within the community. Furthermore, Southeast Asians who live outside Little Saigon will shop and use the businesses in that community on weekends.

The Cambodian population in Orange County is much smaller and does not have the equivalent of a Little Saigon, as mentioned earlier. The Cambodian community in Orange County on South Minnie Street consists mostly of apartments, a Buddhist temple, and a Cham temple in a predominantly Latino area. It does not have Cambodian shops except for a Khmer law office nearby. Like the Vietnamese in Little Saigon, Cambodian women do not shop in the Caucasian-owned supermarkets in their neighborhood but wait until the weekends when their adult children or husbands are free to drive them into Little Saigon or Long Beach.[14] In other words, the newcomers' needs—from food to entertainment, from marriage partners to ethnic identification—are being provided by the ethnic community.

It is not likely that this pattern of settlement will change in the near future, as the population in the Southeast Asian community will continue to increase. The population has experienced a positive natural growth rate, i.e., more births than deaths. Population increase will also come from secondary migration from other parts of the United States and California as people move to Orange County to be reunited with their families and, equally important, to be near these ethnic communities. Migration will continue to come from Southeast Asia under the quota allotted to refugees. In the last few years, Southeast Asians have an annual quota of between 40,000 to 50,000. Finally, Southeast Asians who have become citizens are eligible to sponsor their immediate relatives to enter the United States as immigrants. The size of this increase, however, will depend upon the exit visas granted by the governments of Vietnam, Cambodia and Laos. If these three countries decide to relax the ban on the emigration of their people, family unification could create a chain migration that portends an even larger Southeast Asian population in the future.

THE SOCIOECONOMIC POSITION OF SOUTHEAST ASIANS IN ORANGE COUNTY

The acculturation process of Southeast Asian refugees into Orange County also depends on their economic self-sufficiency. The profile of a successfully integrated refugee in Orange County is one who has a college education, speaks English, and has full-time employment. Knowledge of the English language is an important factor in economic adaptation and for full participation in American institutions. Yet most refugees, especially those who came after the first wave, do not fit that profile.

A recent study conducted by the Immigrant and Refugee Planning Center revealed the following refugee characteristics: 70 percent of the refugees are unemployed, 68 percent of all Orange County Southeast Asian refugees live in households supplemented by some form of government aid, and

88 percent of the refugees rent their homes. The number one concern of the refugees in Orange County is unemployment, followed by language barrier, racial prejudice, housing costs, and the well-being of their families in Southeast Asia.

While this picture appears bleak, there are reports that suggest a distinct pattern in Southeast Asian refugees' resettlement. Their degree of economic independence is related to their length of stay in the country, with significant decrease in assistance even within the first three years after arrival.[15] In Orange County, it is also evident that the groups that arrived earlier have already contributed to the booming Orange County economy by providing a labor force that is hard working, thrifty, competitive, and with strong family values. Employers surveyed about their experience of having Southeast Asians as employees are overwhelmingly positive.

OPPOSITION FROM THE ESTABLISHED COMMUNITY

Despite evidence of Southeast Asians' economic contribution, there is an undercurrent of resentment toward the newcomers in Orange County. The noticeable occurrences have ranged from the repeated defacement of the sign "Little Saigon" along Garden Grove Freeway to the remarks of Westminster Councilman Frank Fry who denied a Vietnamese military veterans' request for a parade while telling the Vietnamese that

> It's my opinion that you're all Americans and you'd better be Americans. If you want to be South Vietnamese, go back to South Vietnam. That may be unfair, but that's my opinion, and I'm sure that is the opinion of a lot of people around here.[16]

There are also occurrences that went unreported by media. Anti-Asian incidents in Little Saigon included vandalism and physical attacks on individuals, shouting of racial epithets on residents and shoppers, shooting of BB guns into businesses, and

more resentfully, harassment of elderly people by pushing their shopping carts into roadside gutters. A community leader charged that these incidents went unnoticed because the police practiced a policy of benign neglect. A criminal justice student studying Southeast Asian gangs theorized that many newcomers are reluctant to report attacks on them because they fear retribution from the criminals. Furthermore, they perceived the American police departments as "corrupt" because criminals, instead of being punished, are able to use bail for their release. Given such a view, ordinary Southeast Asian residents see no possibility of protection for themselves should they report their attackers. My own observation found the newcomers unaware of their rights. Many are afraid of authority figures, are fearful that their jobs or welfare checks would be taken away should they make any waves. Moreover, many do not see America as home yet, and they suffer the silence of people without a country to go home to.

The resentment and intolerance towards the Southeast Asian newcomer can perhaps be attributed to the establishment and the phenomenal growth of the Vietnamese community in a pre-existing white, middle- and working-class community. The problem is also exacerbated by unique experiences of the newcomers as refugees: large numbers of them seeking to reunite with friends and families as a way to rebuild their lives, to be closer to an existing ethnic and cultural community as a way to psychologically recover from the loss of their homeland. The lack of English language skills among the newcomers also caused them to turn to Little Saigon as a viable place to establish economic independence by starting businesses. All of the foregoing, however, is not well understood by the larger society. Most still remember the shame and the loss of American lives suffered from the Vietnam War. Southeast Asian newcomers are remembered as part of the unpleasant American past. Resentment of the "enemy" gaining economic ascendence in the host community is understandable, especially when the locals erroneously believed that Southeast Asian refugees receive government grants to buy houses, cars, and to start businesses, when in fact many depended on pooling of income, thrift, and hard work to get by. The perception that the newcomers refuse to give up their cultural heritage, as in the parade requested by the Vietnamese veterans, and the conspicuously Asian facade of Little Saigon, has therefore created rumbles among those who have accepted the presence of other Asians.

How then does this negative attitude and constant minor harassment affect the acculturation of the Southeast Asian newcomers into American society? The answer to this question requires an assessment of the difference in perception of the various Southeast Asian groups by the larger society as well as the socioeconomic and cultural factors that affect acculturation. A detailed analysis is beyond the scope of this paper. However, it is possible to suggest that those with the advantage of education, especially English language ability, wealth, and some marketable skills will adapt quickly through economic independence. On the other hand, individuals lacking those skills and unable to adapt may draw closer to the protective shield provided by the ethnic communities. Given the size of those who belong to the second category, and the psychological importance of the ethnic communities to the Southeast Asian refugees, it is conceivable that important ethnic towns will remain for a long time. The ethnic towns, in turn, will help retain an American version of the Vietnamese and Khmer cultures.

As to the future of the ethnic communities, Southeast Asian community leaders feel that individual insensitivities fuel intolerance, and therefore there is a need to take appropriate action against them to prevent racial tensions of a greater magnitude. They emphasize not only education to promote cultural understanding but also programs that actually bring non-Southeast Asians into contacts with Southeast Asians. An example is the "Ethnic Host Family Dinner" started by the Intercultural Development Center at California State University, Fullerton, where non-Southeast Asian students are invited to Vietnamese homes for

dinner. Acceptance of Southeast Asians may also be facilitated by appreciation of their contributions to local culture and history. Hmong reverse applique and embroidery has already been appraised by the established art world as an important cultural contribution. Cambodian textiles by the Khmer Women Weavers have had major exhibitions in museums in the Southland. A recent exhibit of Cambodian silver artifacts in Long Beach also received rave reviews. Plays by Khmer playwright Kan Noun, for example, reached both the Khmer and larger American audience. A . . . play, *The Dead Accused*, ran for three weeks at the Long Beach Found Theatre in early 1989. Traditional Southeast Asian music and dances, taught and performed at weddings and ceremonies, have also been included in local and regional international fairs and festivals. The most interesting experiment was a "jam session" of American jazz musicians and Southeast Asian musicians conducted by Prany Sananikone, a Lao musician and assistant executive director of the United Cambodian Community, Inc. In the session, the jazz musicians were attempting to integrate the "sounds" of traditional Southeast Asian music into the contemporary jazz modes. For the Southeast Asian musicians, it was a rare event where they were able to perform with and be appreciated by musician of a totally different cultural tradition.

At the university level, archives have been established at the University of California, Irvine, and California State University, Long Beach, not only as repositories for Southeast Asian cultural heritage but also to make research material available for others interested in this part of recent American history.

At the popular level, Southeast Asian ethnic restaurants have sprung up throughout the Southland. The 1989 edition of the *Vietnamese Business Directory of Southern California* listed 160 restaurants. Of these, there were thirty-one Vietnamese pho or noodle houses, a number of Vietnamese French restaurants, and a large number of Teochew-style Chinese restaurants, a regional cooking-style from northern Guandong Province in China. Unlike the Toisan and Sanyap speakers of the Guandong Province who came to America during the later part of the nineteenth century, the Teochew speakers migrated to Southeast Asia. While the Chinese immigrants from Guandong Province introduced Cantonese-style food to the Americans, it is the ethnic Teochew Chinese from Cambodia and Vietnam who are introducing Teochew-style cooking into America.

The immediate problems faced by Southeast Asian refugees include the ability to find a job and to assume individual financial responsibility. Language and cultural barriers will prevent them from gaining the basic tools needed to survive in Orange County. If Southeast Asian refugees cannot gain an economic foothold in Orange County and if the refugees cannot see themselves with a positive image in the new land, it is difficult for them to integrate into the larger society. As mentioned earlier, the prospect of the Southeast Asian refugees successfully adapting into American society will depend on the educational and class background of the different groups of arrivals. Given the large number of those who lack these advantages, the path ahead remains a long struggle.

NOTES

1. The designation "Southeast Asian" is used throughout the paper to refer to the people from Vietnam, Cambodia, and Laos, instead of the more precise term "Indochinese." Besides Vietnam, Cambodia, and Laos, "Southeast Asia" as a geographical designation also includes the countries of Burma, Thailand, Malaysia, Singapore, Indonesia, and the Philippines. This less precise term is chosen because, from the standpoint of ethnic studies, "Indochina" has colonial implications whereas "Southeast Asia" is a more neutral geographical designation. Several leaders in the community I have spoken with also prefer the terms "Southeast Asia" to "Indochina" and "Southeast Asian" to "Indochinese." Ordinary people from Vietnam, Cambodia, and Laos never refer to themselves by either term. They simply say they are Vietnamese, Cambodian or Khmer, Hmong, Lao, Vietnamese Chinese, Cambodian Chinese, etc.

    Substantial numbers of Southeast Asians are also coming in with immigrant status as they are sponsored by relatives who are now permanent residents and American citizens. Therefore, technically speaking, some of the recent arrivals are also immigrants, and not refugees.

Exact figures on the Southeast Asian population in Orange County are difficult to obtain. Until the 1990 census is processed, some of the data appearing in the newspapers and other sources are mere estimates. The figure 135,000 was quoted by Mai Cong of the Vietnamese Community of Orange County, Inc., at the Symposium on Vietnamese Former Political Prisoners, 28 October 1989, Marriott Hotel, Anaheim, California. Orange County demographer, Allen Lutz of the Social Service Agency uses a figure lower than 100,000.

2. Beth Baldwin, *Capturing the Change: the Impact of Indochinese Refugees in Orange County* (Santa Ana: Immigration and Refugee Planning Center, 1982).

3. The process of integration into American professional work force is not without problems, The American medical establishment, for example, refused to recognize the training Vietnamese physicians had because either their documents were lost in the war or they were left behind as the doctors fled from Vietnam (*Los Angeles Times*, Orange County Edition, 11 November 1988).

4. Tricia Knoll, *Becoming Americans: Sojourners, Immigrants and Refugees in the Western United States*. (Portland: Coast-to-Coast Books, 1982), 198.

5. Even though this report states that there have been no racial crimes committed against Southeast Asian refugees, community leaders such as Hoa Duong, Executive Director of the Orange County Community Resources Opportunity Project, Inc. in Santa Ana, sensed an uneasiness and tension, which is evidenced by an increase in incidences of harassment and discrimination directed against Southeast Asian refugees. She and others feel that there should be more documentation of this type of racial harassment and discrimination even though they are not "crimes" per se.

    The view of the police departments is also contradicted by another community leader, Frank Jao. In a guest lecture given at a class at California State University, Long Beach on November 4, 1989, Jao described several racial incidences directed against Southeast Asians along Bolsa Boulevard. See discussion later in the paper.

    Individual Southeast Asians in the community have also told me about racial slurs being hurled at them as they drive through Little Saigon, but many suffered the hurt in silence, unaware that others have no right to insult them because of their race. Whenever I ask individuals to describe their experience of racial incidents, this response is quite typical: "You mean you won't get mad at me if I tell you about those insults that white people have used to shout at me? Are you sure it is ok to tell you those things?"

6. *Nguoi Viet*, 8 October 1989.

7. Milton Gordon, *Assimilation in American Life* (New York: Oxford University Press,) 1964.

8. Percentages on the Vietnamese were based on the following figures in the *Refugee Reports*, 12 September 1988.

Vietnamese	547,205
Cambodian	143,597
Laotian	192,098

One should note that those coming from Vietnam are not all ethnic Vietnamese, but included a large number of ethnic Chinese and Khmer. Both groups have lived in Vietnam for centuries.

9. It is reported that half of Los Angeles' Chinatown's estimated 1,400 businesses are either owned or operated by ethnic Chinese from Vietnam, despite initial resentment by the older residents. See Penelope McMillan, "Vietnamese Chinese Give Chinatown a New Look," *Los Angeles Times,* 24 November 1984.

10. Jeff Crisp, "A Lengthy and Difficult Road," *Refugees* (June 1989): 32–33.

11. Thi Luu Dinh, "Adaptation of a Group of Vietnamese Women in Los Angeles" (Master's thesis, UCLA, 1982).

12. Candace Waldron, *Health Issues for Cambodian Women: Needs Assessment Summary* (Boston: Massachusetts Department of Public Health, 1987).

13. This dilemma is not unique to Southeast Asians. Other Asian immigrant groups as well as many European immigrants set up ethnic neighborhoods, cultural organizations, and economic associations for a generation or two. But Southeast Asians today offer the most striking example of this paradoxical aspect of acculturation. Maryanne Blank, executive director of St. Anselm's Indochinese Refugee Resettlement Agency, called Little Saigon "a curse" in that it is like a crutch that individuals could lean on and never have to leave the ethnic community.

14. An interesting meeting between the Cambodian women and the manager of a local American supermarket (arranged by Marianne Salamida, the Director of the Neighborhood Center in Minnie Street) revealed that the women found the supermarket lacking the major sundries of an average Cambodian family: twenty-five and fifty pound bags of rice, fresh fish, spices, fresh herbs and the vegetables used in Southeast Asian cooking. The women also found the "food baskets" given out by the center not usable because of the many unfamiliar American canned foods. Sensitive to the needs of the Cambodian women, the center was actively looking for donations of rice.

15. Crisp, "A Lengthy and Difficult Road," 32–33.

16. Quoted in *Los Angeles Times,* Orange County Edition, 14 April 1989. Even this well-publicized event supports the point that hostility toward refugees has been relatively mild, for this remark received widespread criticism, and Fry soon apologized for it.

Asian Americans in Enclaves—They Are Not One Community: New Modes of Asian American Settlement

Tom L. Chung

The focus of most studies about Asian Americans has been primarily on either "community needs" or cultural differences (e.g., attitude toward Western style health care), which mainly reflect the passive aspects of Asian Americans' lives. The active aspects of Asia Americans, lives such as the interdependence of the various groups are overlooked. Consequently, Asia Americans are often referred to as "the Asian American community." Too often Asian Americans are lumped together as a single group in quantitative studies; while in qualitative studies, individual groups are conveniently taken or implied to be the representative of all Asian Americans. There are at least two obvious reasons why Asian Americans should not be considered as one community. First, in a geographic sense, Asian Americans do not always live close enough to develop a "community" relationship. Second, they come from very diverse backgrounds. When Asian Americans are assumed to be homogeneous, their differences are de-emphasized and their interrelationships are ignored. This pre-conception can be soundly dispelled through a study of three decades of demographic and social changes in eastern Massachusetts.

At the national level, the Asian American population in the U.S. has been increasing rapidly since the 1965 Hart-Celler Act, which placed an emphasis on family reunification. New Asian immigration increased so dramatically that the total U.S. Asian population doubled between each census since 1970. The census estimates of the

Source: *Asian American Policy Review* V (1995): 78-94. Reprinted by permission.

total U.S. Asian population grew from 1.5 million in 1970 to 3.7 million in 1980 to 7.5 million in 1990. This rapid increase in immigration helps explain the demographic shifts forward in eastern Massachusetts. For instance, on average in every year during the 1980s, the number of Asian Americans settling down in Greater Boston exceeded the total number of Chinatown residents, on average.[1] In addition to the population growth, the Massachusetts' Asian American population became more diverse. Along with a wave of professional and entrepreneurial immigrants between the mid-1960s and 1970s, there has also been a large influx of refugees and poorer, working class immigrants.[2] A century old geographic pattern of distribution in eastern Massachusetts was inevitably altered.

Prior to the mid-1950s, Massachusetts' Asian Americans settled primarily in Boston. Within Boston, the proportion living in Chinatown was consistently around 80% from 1890 to 1950.[3] Chinatown was the "Asian community" until 1953, when it began to lose land to urban renewal, highway construction (e.g., Massachusetts Turnpike, Northeast Expressway) and institutional expansion (e.g., New England Medical Center). In 1960, the proportion of Boston's Asian Americans residing in Chinatown had dropped to 31%.[4] By 1970, the proportion of Boston Asian Americans living in Chinatown shrank to 25%[5], and below 20% thereafter.[6] Land loss, however, was not the only cause of geographic dispersion. Indeed, the size of Chinatown's residential population had actually grown despite continuous land loss. It was the continuous influx of immigrants who settled in other areas, and the continuous emigration from Chinatown that has reduced Chinatown's role as a residential center.

A 1988 survey found that the median length of stay for Chinatown residents was seven years. If only those who moved out were counted, the average length of stay was four years.[7] Chinatown's share of the state's Asian population had decreased from 5.5% in 1980[8] to 2.3% by 1990.[9] Where have these people gone? Peter Kiang and Carlton Sagara observed the growth of the Asian American population in every Boston neighborhood.[10] Indeed, Boston's Asian population had doubled between 1980 and 1990, increasing by 195.6%, but Boston's proportion of Asian Americans in Massachusetts dropped because it had been outpaced by a 289.7% increase in the state's total Asian population.[11] One explanation for the settlement of the Asian American population is the emergence of ethnic enclaves beyond Chinatown and Boston.

DEFINITION OF ENCLAVES

For the purpose of this study, the concept of ethnic enclaves must be defined. The term ethnic is used because it cuts across race and culture. In addition, it takes into account of an "externally imposed ethnic identity" and does not assume cultural and emotional homogeneity. The "externally imposed ethnic identity," according to Yen Le Espiritu, results from a categorization process of lumping minorities together by a dominant group, regardless of their subgroup differences.[12] These subgroups, however, may eventually develop a common ethnic identity when they recognize that the larger society does not acknowledge their differences.

The term enclave is used instead of community because it does not presume any internal cohesiveness. It also avoids notion of being functionally or institutionally complete, a image too often associated with the term community. The term enclave also underscores the fact that an ethnically distinct settlement may be enclosed within or across political or administrative boundaries.

For many years, advocates and fund raisers have emphasized ethnicity in order to reach beyond geographic or administrative boundaries. Many Asian Americans still live close to Chinatown, creating clusters that are closely linked and highly visible. The geographical expansion of the Asian American population beyond Chinatown carries political and economic implications. Greater interaction with non-Asian neighbors inevitably increases the heterogeneity of Asian Americans. Meanwhile, Chinatown has more economic competition as Asian restaurants, churches and other services thrive outside of Chinatown. The impact of geography clearly affects the decision to purchase goods and services locally or in Chinatown. Ignoring geographic factors will only relegate studies of Asian Americans to incomplete inquiry. The term enclave heeds the geographic implication.

Based on their varied backgrounds, but under the same, externally-imposed ethnic identity, three categories of ethnic enclaves have emerged. For a better understanding of the proposed ethnic enclaves, a concrete example for each type (one-step-up,[13] new immigrant, and suburban) will be presented. As will be seen later, these enclaves have distinct and separate characteristics. More importantly, they and the Boston Chinatown create a dynamic set of inter-relationships, replacing the old relationship between the society and the "Asian American community."

THREE TYPES OF ETHNIC ENCLAVES

Earlier studies of Asian Americans, particularly historical studies on immigration law and Asian laborers, have reinforced the image of Asian Americans as a homogeneous group. Recent socio-economic data counter that image and support the view that Asian Americans are quite heterogeneous. While much media focus has portrayed Asian Americans as either poor or affluent, there is little information about those in the middle. The data describing the U-shaped distribution of socioeconomic status only serve to reinforce the stereo-type that Asian Americans, unlike other ethnic groups, are bimodal. This bimodal impression only reflects the socio-economic conditions at both ends of an expanding spectrum. An inconspicuous but emerging middle ground of Asian Americans has appeared. Their presence is strongest in the one-step-up enclaves, which are significantly different from the new immigrant and suburban enclaves.

The settlement of Asian Americans in eastern Massachusetts is, by no means, random. Although no longer confined to Boston, the overwhelming majority still concentrates around Greater Boston, where they settle in areas that match their socio-economic status. Table 1 shows that ethnic enclaves are located in three economically distin-guishable tiers of municipalities. Because standard data pertaining to Asian Americans within indi-vidual ethnic enclaves is not available, the overall municipality data provide the closest estimates for a systematic comparison. The ten municipalities presented here, albeit only a small portion of the 351 Massachusetts cities and towns, host about half of the state's Asian American population.

A discussion of enclaves, however, is not com-plete without Chinatown and its emerging role in eastern Massachusetts. The 1990 Census shows that the median Asian household income in Chinatown was only 41% of the city media,[14] which was in turn less than 80% of the state median (see Table 1). Because it has separate and distinct characteristics, it is neither a prototype of ethnic enclaves nor a center for Asian American social and political activ-ities. Chinatown, the original immigrant enclave, serves as the "hub" for the various ethnic enclaves. Amid rapid changes, Chinatown has managed to take on a new role as an ethnic crossing, a role that facilitates inter-enclave dynamics.

THE ONE-STEP-UP ENCLAVES

In Massachusetts, one-step-up enclaves are located in areas with easy access to Chinatown. In these enclaves, there is an increase of Asian Americans whose income and education attain-ment are much closer to that of the American mainstream (i.e., middle class). Most of them are not new immigrants but arrivals from other areas. While maintaining close ties with Chinatown, their attitudes and behaviors are no longer domi-nated by their homeland culture; they have fre-quent exchanges with other ethnic groups. In a decade or two, these one-step-up enclaves may replace Chinatown and other enclaves as the major mode of settlement.

An example of the one-step-up enclave is Quincy, Massachusetts, the first and largest of its kind. In the 1980s, Asian Americans began to settle down in Quincy at a rapid rate, so rapid that the city has been unable to accommodate most of their social service needs until recently. According to the 1980 Census, there were only 750 Asian Americans in Quincy. In the late 1980s, two independent studies estimated that the Asian population had grown to approximately 10,000.[15] Public agencies' inability to agree on how many Asian Americans lived in Quincy may help explain why the city was slow in responding to Asian American residents' needs. The 1990 Census acknowledged only 5,577 Asian resi-dents. In 1992, Quincy City Hall conducted its own census with a special effort to identify its Asian residents. It found 67% more Asian Ameri-cans than the 1990 U.S. Census did. Yet, this figure was still below earlier estimates. In 1993, the Quincy City Hall estimated the population figure to be 12,000. This latest figure is several times larger than the figure for Chinatown. Despite its size and the Chinese majority in Quincy's Asian American population, Quincy has not become another Chinatown. Instead, it has emerged as a new type of enclave.

Unlike Chinatown in its earlier days and the new immigrant enclaves today, Quincy mainly attracts immigrants who already have resided in the U.S. for several years. A 1989 survey esti-mated that only 16% of the city's Asian population came directly from foreign countries. Approxi-mately 56% of them came from Boston, 15% from

TABLE 1
Sample Municipal Settings of Ethnic Enclaves

	Total Population[1]	Asian Population[1]	Percentage Asian[1]	Median Household Income[1]	Median Per Capita Income[1]	Median Price Of Single Family Home[2]	Median Monthly Rent[2]	Rent/Own Unit Ratio[2]
State of Massachusetts	6,016,425			$36,952	$17,224	$162,800	$506	0.69
Asian		144,492	2.40%	$34,706	$12,665	NA	NA	1.5
City of Boston	574,283			$29,180	$15,581	$161,400	$546	2.24
Asian		30,388	5.30%	$22,504	$9,406	NA	NA	NA
Asian Ethnic Crossing								
Chinatown[3]		3,301	88.90%	$12,143	$7,573	NA	$456	22.26
New Immigrant Enclaves								
Dorchester[4]		3,725	4.40%	$30,000	$12,500	$153,000	$530	1.88
Lowell		11,493	11.10%	$29,351	$12,701	$131,100	$494	1.39
Chelsea		1,435	5.00%	$25,144	$11,559	$142,000	$501	2.56
Lynn		3,003	3.70%	$28,533	$13,026	$139,200	$507	1.16
One-step-up Enclaves								
Quincy		5,577	6.60%	$35,858	$17,436	$161,100	$599	1.05
Malden		2,815	5.20%	$34,344	$15,820	$162,900	$575	1.31
Somerville		2,824	3.70%	$32,455	$15,179	$165,800	$591	2.23
Suburban Enclaves								
Lexington		1,876	6.50%	$67,389	$30,718	$282,800	$902	0.22
Newton		3,760	4.50%	$59,719	$28,840	$293,400	$809	0.45
Brookline		4,585	8.40%	$45,598	$29,044	$377,800	$629	1.32

[1] 1990 Census data.

[2] From Edith Hornor, *Massachusetts Municipal Profile, 1991–1992.* Palo Alto, CA: Information Publications, 1991; and Irene Sege, "Increase the Diversity Shown in the Census." *The Boston Globe* (July 1, 1991): Metro Section, p. 1.

[3] There have been several delineations of Chinatown. Figures adopted here come from the Boston Redevelopment Authority (BRA).

[4] Dorchester figures are estimated from several BRA Dorchester sub-district 1990 Census summary reports.

other parts of Massachusetts, and 13% from other states.[16] More importantly, most Asian American households in Quincy are complete family units, rather than single persons or non-traditional families. In 1988, 66% of the Asian Americans in Quincy had school age children, and the percentage was expected to increase.[17] The fact that there are more home owners than renters,[18] which was not true for the city as a whole, suggests the permanence of their settlements.

While the median price of a house in Quincy is slightly higher than in most Boston neighborhoods, it is substantially lower than that of an upper-middle class suburb. Given the median income of residents of one-step-up enclaves, most cannot afford a home in an upper-middle class suburb. Nevertheless, Quincy Asian Americans generally have paid a higher price for a similar house than non-Asian Americans.[19] Possible explanations range from the reluctance of former residents to sell their property to Asian Americans to unfair practices by the real estate brokers.

There is no comprehensive assessment available on the financial status of Quincy's Asian population. The closest indicator is the median household income reported in the 1990 Census. The median Asian household income was slightly higher than the local median ($36,455 versus $35,858) but the median per capita income was below the local median ($11,140 versus $17,436).[20] The data suggests that many Asian American families have been able to purchase a home in the one-step-up enclave only when family members pool their resources together. A 1989 survey found that the average Asian household is larger. Approximately 52% of the respondents had 3–4 persons in their household (versus 31% among non-Asian Americans), and 33% had 5 or more persons in the household (versus 12% among non-Asian Americans).[21]

One reason Quincy may be desirable to Asian Americans is its accessibility to Chinatown via public transportation. In the late 1980s, 76% of the city's Asian Americans visited Chinatown at least once a week,[22] but only 54% of them owned a car.[23] At least during the initial stages, it appears

the goods and services sector in Quincy was not equipped to meet their basic needs. One study reported that one-third of the respondents did not even do their primary shopping in Quincy.[24] Were it not for the goods and services available in Chinatown, Asian Americans might not have considered Quincy a desirable area to settle.

As the number and size of Asian American family units increase in Quincy, the need for services such as pediatric, dental and child care has also increased. Yet by 1989, Quincy Hospital still had no full-time bilingual clinician. Asian Americans accounted for five out of every eighty residents rushed to the emergency room in 1989, but none of the ambulance paramedics spoke any Asian language, and there were no interpreters at the hospital. Not surprisingly, 70% of Quincy's Asian residents went outside of Quincy for health care services.[25] Furthermore, 84% of the respondents to a 1988 needs assessment survey doubted they knew about the range of services and support available in Quincy.[26]

As can be inferred from the available data, Asian Americans moving into a one-step-up enclave intend to settle down despite the aforementioned inadequacies. Even if their financial situation improves, many one-step-up enclave residents may decide to stay rather than leave for a suburban enclave. Suburban living is expensive and the suburban lifestyle requires a greater cultural adjustment. With a continuous influx, will Quincy become the new ethnic crossing? It is still too early to tell. Perhaps a "local ethnic crossing" will form in Quincy, but the available evidence suggests it will more likely become an additional layer of ethnic crossing, complementing rather than replacing Chinatown, the current ethnic crossing.

CHINATOWN IN TRANSITION

In its early days, Chinatown was a community comprised of predominantly single, young males that expected very little outside help. Traditional community organizations existed as informal networks among friends or colleagues. Over the last three decades, the services offered by traditional community organizations have not been sufficient to accommodate the influx of immigrants. Evidence of the inadequacy of the traditional network can be found in a 1987 employment study which asked clients where they would try to obtain their next job. Two-thirds, including many who used to rely upon an informal network for employment, would contact secondary organizations.[27]

Today people do not come to Chinatown just for their basic needs. They also look for specialized professional services. The broader range of services and goods is reflected by the occupational changes in the last three decades. Until the late-1960s, Chinatown predominantly offered personal service positions (82%).[28] The 1990 Census revealed that employment in the service sector (excluding personal service) in Chinatown increased to 17%. In addition, there was also an expansion of the finance, insurance, and real estate sector from almost negligible in the 1980 Census to 12%.[29] Inevitably, the increased presence of professionals who operate under professional codes and administrative procedures established outside of Chinatown diminished the old, informal system.

As more Asian Americans from other enclaves rely on Chinatown, Chinatown residents themselves are no longer the only target of the local agencies. In a 1987 employment study, a survey of employment program and English class enrollees found 12% came from one-step-up enclaves, 25% from new immigrant enclaves, 8% from suburban enclaves, and only 55% from Chinatown and adjacent areas.[30] A 1989 comprehensive needs assessment survey found only 52% of the clients using services in Chinatown lived in the area.[31] If these trends continue, the proportion of local resident clients using Chinatown's services will decline.

There is both direct and indirect evidence confirming the fact that Chinatown's businesses target Asian American patrons. In 1988, a Boston Redevelopment Authority study found that two-thirds of the "Chinatown users" were Asian

Americans (55% Chinese, 4% Chinese-Vietnamese, 3% Vietnamese, 1% Cambodian, 24% White, 8% Black, 2% Hispanic, and 3% others).[32] More importantly, 96% of these Chinatown users came at least once every month (54% daily, 2% more frequently than weekly, 18% weekly, 15% bi-weekly, and 7% monthly).[33] Tourists obviously do not visit with such frequency. The kind of businesses in Chinatown inform us of their primary targets. In 1988, half of the businesses in Chinatown were related to regular consumption (29.1% related to personal/professional services, 11.3% wholesale/factory, 8.7% grocery/drug store.) The remaining businesses were restaurants/bakeries (25.4%) and entertainment (12.0%). In contrast, only one-tenth of the Chinatown business targeted tourists: 10.3% were gift shops or specialty stores.[34] Chinatown still keeps a keen interest in tourism, but perhaps not as much as Ivan Light observed in his 1972 book, *Ethnic Enterprise in America.*[35]

By accommodating the needs of Chinese Americans and other Asian American groups, Chinatown has become more inclusive and effective in meeting the needs of all groups. There are a growing number of Vietnamese signs on grocery stores, drug stores, restaurants, video rental, jewelry and variety shops in Chinatown. The presence of Thai, Japanese, Cambodian and Laotian activities are also detectable. To some observers, Chinatown could be aptly renamed Asiatown.[36]

In sum, Chinatown is in transition. Its activities and resources have extended far beyond its geographic boundary. The expansion of its customer base and service sector reflect its role among the ethnic enclaves. Although Chinatown does not always assume a leadership role, it does provide resources, connections and a convenient location for facilitating exchanges among Asian Americans. In this sense, Chinatown serves as a crossing, and sometimes a center, for Asian Americans in eastern Massachusetts. When an ethnic crossing expands and extends itself to appeal to non-residents, local residential issues are no longer its only priority. Its attention is often extended beyond Chinatown. One example of this extension is regular coverage of suburban current events by one Chinese daily newspaper.

An ethnic crossing is the most convenient link among ethnic populations, because it has established relationships with other ethnic enclaves. Indeed, ethnic enclaves interact much more with the ethnic crossing than with each other. Services, commodities, information and other resources are usually channeled through the ethnic crossing before reaching individual enclaves. Hence, an ethnic crossing has a convenient location and easy access to public transportation. The distribution channels are particularly crucial to the initial stages of the new immigrant and the one-step-up enclaves. A close connection is still maintained when individual enclaves can secure basic supplies locally for the following reasons. First, while local providers take away some market share, the volume of exchange does not necessarily decrease if the whole ethnic population grows. Second, due to a broader set of economic connections and larger volume, the original ethnic crossing is able to offer more comprehensive packages of goods and services, usually at competitive prices. Third, the original ethnic crossing historically carries a symbolic appeal to the non-Asians. For example, when the mass media, politicians, and advertisers are looking for a representative of "the Asian American community," they conveniently turn to Chinatown.

THE NEW IMMIGRANT ENCLAVES

The new immigrant enclaves are situated in municipalities with the lowest median household income. Dorchester, a poor inner city neighborhood with a large Vietnamese population, is an example of a new immigrant enclave. Until recently the Vietnamese settlement in Dorchester was rather transient, and a commitment to the community simply did not exist. The Executive Director of the Vietnamese American Civic Association, the largest

Vietnamese service agency, believed thousands of Vietnamese may already have left for other towns such as Quincy or Malden.[37] One observation vividly illustrates the transience:

> There are few obligations to meet and few contracts to notify. The telephone number and utility bills still bear the name of the tenants who lived there two years ago, no one bothered to change it.[38]

Despite its size and growth, the Vietnamese population is not yet well organized politically. Many Vietnamese move several times within a few years after immigrating to the United States.[39] The high mobility rate makes it difficult to organize. Moreover, a 1989 Massachusetts state agency study cited a general distrust of organizations among the Vietnamese. This study reported that only 5 out of the 453 persons sampled belonged to any organization other than religious ones.[40] And when they did organize, their attention was more likely directed to issues in Vietnam than in their present environment.[41]

There are, however, indications of change in Dorchester; the Vietnamese population appears to be more stable.[42] The Dorchester Avenue area has about three dozen stores (e.g., video tapes, personal care, food and book) and agencies (e. g., insurance, travel, and human services.) Fliers in Vietnamese are posted along the streets. A local ethnic enclave capable of fulfilling basic needs appears to be taking shape. Recently *Sampan,* an Asian newspaper published in the Boston Chinatown, reported a number of Vietnamese Americans had moved back from outlying areas.[43] Many others return regularly to visit a Vietnamese doctor or to shop at Vietnamese stores, not unlike the Chinese Americans who return regularly to Chinatown.

While the Vietnamese population is not well organized, they were able to muster some organizational capacity after a highly publicized event. In June 1992, a racial slur made by a city council member and his subsequent refusal to apologize, aroused public outcry. The Vietnamese held meetings and organized protests, and for the first time, they rallied around local politics rather than their homeland politics.[44]

In general, new immigrant enclave members are poor, and contain more single persons or incomplete families. As seen in Table 1, they live in areas where the median household income is far below the state median. Cost is a determinant factor in their choice of residence. Cheap rent and utilities, as well as easy access to inexpensive transportation for work are major considerations. Housing that meets such constraints is more likely to be located in a rundown section of the inner city. Thus, new immigrants face problems other inner city poor are facing: poor housing facilities, high crime rate, noise pollution, and poor school systems. In addition, new immigrants are hindered by informational, cultural and language barriers, and may face service providers that are not sensitive to their needs. It is not surprising that this group underutilizes local human services.[45] When they finally decide to seek help, new immigrants often have no choice but to travel outside of their immediate neighborhood.

The need to seek help outside their immediate neighborhood may be a reason why Dorchester and other new immigrant enclaves have maintained a close link with Chinatown. As previously noted, approximately 25% of the 1987 Chinatown User survey respondents came from the new immigrant enclaves. These visits suggest that human service needs are not being met in the new immigrant enclaves. Among the new immigrants are refugees who suffered great emotional and physical distress in Southeast Asia. A 1989 Massachusetts state report suggested that Southeast Asian refugees tend to have more problems in their daily living adjustment than other groups.[46] Their resettlement is stressful due to language difficulty, downward mobility, a shift in the sex ratio, a change of family roles, and employment barriers.[47] A 1990 U.S. House Committee Report on Hunger report revealed that thirty-five percent of these refugee families were under the federal poverty guideline, two and a half times greater than the national level.[48]

In the health and human services field there has been an increase in exchange among enclaves. During the last decade, funding agencies such as the government and private foundations, have urged individual ethnic groups to form "coalitions" when they apply for grants.[49] Service providers in the new immigrant enclaves often have to work closely with Chinatown agencies, and their cooperation reinforces the connection between these enclaves. Meanwhile, Chinatown has been making substantial adjustments to the needs of other Asian Americans. For example, Chinatown agencies are hiring more non-Chinese workers. The largest social service agency, previously named Chinese American Civic Association (CACA), has adopted a new name by replacing the word "Chinese" with "Asian" (AACA). New programs in Chinatown have expanded to cover all Asian Americans, not just Chinese Americans, such as the SafeNet Hate Violence Prevention Program, which monitors incidents of hate crimes against the Asian Americans. Recently established agencies also prefer to call themselves "Asian" instead of "Chinese." Examples include the Asian Economic Development Council and the Asian Shelter Advocacy Project.

SUBURBAN ENCLAVES

As Asian Americans moved into the suburbs in greater numbers, they began to form suburban enclaves.[50] Despite their vast differences in socio-economic status, they nevertheless still share similar experiences and concerns with other Asian Americans in other enclaves, and they still maintain an exchange with Chinatown.

Lexington, a town that has been particularly appealing to Asian Americans, is an example of a suburban enclave. Asian Americans comprised 6.5% of the town population in 1990 (see Table 1), which is among the highest in the state. Lexington is known for its quality of life, an excellent school system, and a progressive atmosphere. According to the 1990 Census, Lexington ranked tenth in household income among the 351 cities and towns in Massachusetts. The median income among Asian residents was 17% higher than the town median.[51]

Even in a town like Lexington, Asian American residents still share concerns with other enclaves. In a police survey, Asian American respondents were more likely to think that the local police did not treat them with respect.[52] Lexington's Asian residents, like other residents, are mostly professionals and entrepreneurs. (A recent study on the membership of a suburban Asian association showed that almost all of the household heads and spouses finished college, 80% of the household heads hold a Master's degree, and 40% hold an M.D. or a Ph.D. degree.[53]) The local newspaper could only attribute their response to the race factor.[54]

In early 1994, an Asian parent group issued a statement presenting the fact that Asian American students comprised 11.5% of the school population, with further increases expected. The group questioned the inadequate representation of the Asian perspective in the educational curriculum after finding the public school system did not have a single Asian American full-time teacher or administrator.[55]

Lexington is one of the few politically mobilized ethnic enclaves,[56] but less so on the local issues. Even though the town elected an Asian American selectman in the mid-1980s, political participation on the local level is sporadic and inconsistent as Asian Americans in Lexington have shown greater interest in political affairs beyond Lexington. Mobilizing Lexington's three largest Asian groups, the Chinese, Indians and Koreans, can be difficult when they rarely interact beyond an individual level.

As previously detailed, a small percentage of the Chinatown service agency clients come from the suburbs. If the suburban enclaves like Lexington have local Asian restaurants, groceries, churches, and other services, why then do suburban Asian Americans still maintain a relationship with Chinatown?

Several hypotheses may be put forth. First, the increasing professionalism in services in China-town have created hundreds of positions that cannot be adequately filled by Chinatown residents alone. Businesses and non-profit organizations that try to recruit a qualified Asian American find that many live in the suburbs. Second, many Chinatown business owners live in the suburbs. Third, food supplies, at retail and wholesale, are abundant and competitively priced. Fourth, suburban Asian Americans looking for volunteer work can find plenty of opportunities in Chinatown. The pace of clientele growth has been so rapid that many programs are understaffed or even underfunded. Finally, Asian Americans everywhere share many common concerns: their children's academic performance, college admission quotas, the glass-ceiling, preservation of cultural heritage, hate crimes, stereotypes, changes in immigration laws, and current events in their native countries.[57]

A CONCEPTUAL FRAMEWORK— THE ETHNIC ENCLAVE COMPLEX

The majority of Asian Americans in eastern Massachusetts live in ethnic enclaves. An ethnic enclave is an aggregate of ethnic members who live nearby and communicate in a linguistically or culturally different way from their non-ethnic neighbors. Enclave members mingle with non-ethnic neighbors and share local concerns that are not necessarily ethnic. Yet, their interests could extend along ethnic links beyond local boundaries. Their interactions at times seem to be loosely organized when compared to the outdated notion of the "community."

An ethnic enclave is different from a community. The term ethnic enclave is inclusive, fluid and dynamic in its conceptualization of the diverse and rapidly changing experiences of the Asian American population. The ethnic enclave is a more open system than a community. The term "community" is static and structured, and assumes homogeneity and coherence. An enclave can be formed in a few years while a community takes much longer to develop. Even with the passage of time, there is no guarantee that an enclave can become a community. First, its geographic boundary is not always clearly delineated. Second, unlike members of a homogeneous community who predominantly interact with members of the same group, ethnic enclave members engage in contacts with both non-ethnic neighbors and ethnic non-neighbors.

The ethnic enclave complex acknowledges that Asian Americans come from different places of origin, via different paths and at different periods of time; they are not easily mobilized behind any single ethnic issue. Even with these differences, members of the ethnic enclave complex share certain physical and cultural characteristics, which are conspicuously different from those of the majority. Based on their similarities, a common identity is easily imposed externally. The externally imposed identity, as Espiritu argued, can be transformed and internalized to become a common identity. In other words, when the "ethnic-group-in-itself" begins to work toward common interests, it has the potential to become an "ethnic-group-for-itself."

In sum, the framework of the ethnic enclave complex directs our attention to the interactions among individual enclaves, and between the enclaves and society. The "community" concept does not facilitate such interactions. Whereas community problems are more likely to become important issues to society because of assumed homogeneity, the individual ethnic enclaves' problems, due to their uniqueness and small population size, are less urgent to society unless they are common across different locales. Hence, individual enclaves may find it difficult to attract social or political attention. Given its precarious societal support, an enclave has to rely upon other enclaves. That is, the incompleteness of individual enclaves presents a predisposition for the formation of an ethnic enclave complex. They become robust when they join forces with other enclaves, regardless of geographic boundary and socio-economic background. Within a larger entity, the ethnic enclave complex, they can become a stronger vehicle for social and political empowerment.

NOTES

1. Rolf Goetze, Mark Johnson, *City of Boston Neighborhood Area Series*, (Chinatown, Boston Redevelopment Authority, August 1991), p. 1

   There are many ways to define Chinatown and Greater Boston which leads to different population estimates. On average, the Chinatown population in the 1980s was around 4,000, including non-Asians. Estimates of the Chinatown population ranges from below 3,000 to over 5,000, according to various census and survey reports released by the Boston Redevelopment Authority. The estimate of Chinatown adopted for this article identified 3,301 Asians out of a total of 3,714 residents.

   The average annual influx of Asian immigrants to Massachusetts was about 7,000 (See Massachusetts Office of Refugees and Immigrants reports: *Refugees and Immigrants Demographic Update*, 1990, Volume I, No. 1 and *Refugees and Immigrants in Massachusetts: A Demographic Report*, 1989). About 4,200 settled in Greater Boston.

2. Bill Ong Hing, *State of Asian Pacific American Issues to the Year 2020*, (Leadership Education for Asian Pacifics, 1993), pp. 127–139.

3. Charles Sullivan, Kathlyn Hatch, *The Chinese in Boston* (Boston: Action for Community Development, 1973, 6th Edition), p. 20.

4. Ibid., p. 20.

5. Ibid., p. 20.

6. Jeffrey Brown, et al., *Profile of Boston's Chinatown Neighborhood*, (Boston: Boston Redevelopment Authority, 1987), Table 2.

7. Deborah Oriola, Gregory Perkins, *Chinatown User Survey* (Boston: Boston Redevelopment Authority, 1988), p. 4, 24.

8. Jeffrey Brown, et al, 1987, Table 2.

   This report listed 2,712 Asians in Chinatown and 49,501 in Massachusetts for 1980. The boundary of Chinatown in this report outlines a smaller area than that in the Goetze and Johnson report for 1990. Hence, if the data for the area designated in the Goetze and Johnson report were available in 1980, the percentage may be slightly larger.

9. Goetze, Johnson, 1991, p. 1.

   This report listed 3,301 Asians in Boston Chinatown and 143,392 in the state in 1990.

10. Peter Kiang, Carlton Sagara, eds., *Recognizing Poverty in Boston's Asian American Community* (Boston: The Boston Foundation, 1992), p. 26.

11 Ibid., p. 26.

12. Yen Le Espiritu, *Asian American Panethnicity: Bridging Institutions and Identities*, (Philadelphia: Temple University Press, 1992), pp. 5–7.

13. Bill Archer, Tom Conroy, *The Asians, Quincy's Newest Immigrants,* (The Patriot Ledger, 1989), p. 15.

14. Goetze, Johnson, op cit., p. 26.

15. Valerie Parker, et al., *Quincy Gateway City Newcomer Needs Assessment*, (Edmonds and Parker Housing and Community Services, Inc., 1988), 10–11. Also Archer, Conroy, op cit., p. 6.

16. Archer, Conroy, 1989, p. 8.

17. Ibid., p. 77.

18. Ibid., p. 16.

19. Ibid., p. 13.

    The Patriot Ledger reported that between 1984 and 1989, Asian Americans paid more than non-Asians for homes, even though the homes were assessed at about the same value. An unpublished 1992 study, *Quincy Real Estate Study*, by Thomas Flynn, replicated the findings.

20. Estimated by author using 1990 Census data.

21. Ibid., 5. Archer and Conroy, 1989, p. 12.

22. Ibid., p. 12.

23. Valerie Parker, et al., *Quincy Gateway City Newcomer Needs Assessment*, (Edmonds and Parker Housing and Community Services, Inc., 1988), p. 20.

24. Ibid., p. 20.

25. Archer, Conroy, 1989, pp. 61–63.

26. Parker, et al., 1988, p. 18.

27. Tom Lun-nap Chung, *Job Expectations and Opportunities of Asian American Clients*, (Boston: Boston Redevelopment Authority and the South Cove–Chinatown Neighborhood Council, 1988), p. 49.

28. Sullivan, Hatch, 1973, p. 61.

29. Goetze, Johnson, 1991, p. 12.

30. Chung, 1988, p. 9.

31. Tom Lun-nap Chung, and Henderson's Planning Group, *Needs Assessment for the Chinatown Community Center (Parcel C) Project*, (Boston Redevelopment Authority and South Cove–Chinatown Neighborhood Council, 1989), p. 4.

32. Oriola, Perkins, 1988, p. 6.

33. Ibid., p. 19.

34. Mary Bourguignon, *Chinatown Survey Area Land Use Report*, (Boston Redevelopment Authority, 1988), p. 8.

35. Ivan Light, *Ethnic Enterprise in America: Business and Welfare Among Chinese, Japanese, and Blacks*, (Berkeley: University of California Press, 1972), pp. 15–16.

36. Betsy Tong, Linda Matchan, "Vietnamese Edge into Chinatown," *The Boston Globe* (February 1, 1993): Metro Section, p. 1.

37. Michael Rezendes, "Vietnamese Leaders Hit O'Neil Remarks," *The Boston Globe* (June 11, 1992): Metro Section, p. 31.

38. Mai Lan Pham, "Strangers in Fields Corner: The Formation of a Vietnamese Community in Dorchester," *The Boston Review*, XVII, No. 5, 17.

39. Le Van Bia, *Descriptive Profile and Needs Assessment of Vietnamese People in Massachusetts*, (Department of Mental Health, 1989), pp. 21–23.

    This study found that over 80% of its sample had lived in the U.S. less than five years. Approximately 17.9% of its respondents had moved twice, 28.3% three to five times, and 2.9% more than five times.

40. Ibid., p. 27.

41. Pham, 1992, p. 19.

42. Robert O'Malley, "Fields Corner, Dorchester," *Sampan* (August 5, 1994): p. 8.

43. Ibid., p. 8.

44. 1992, Metro Section, Rezendes, 31. See also Irene Sege, "Vietnamese Find Their Voice After Boston Councilor's Remark," *The Boston Globe* (June 26, 1992): Metro Section, 1. Betsy Tong, "Asians Flexing Political Muscle," *The Boston Globe* (June 20, 1993): City Weekly, p. 1.

45. Massachusetts Department of Mental Health, 1989, 38–42. See also Johnathon Lyon, *Domestic Violence, Southeast Asian Refugees, and the Public Health: A Qualitative Study*, 1991, Tufts University, pp. 35–36.

46. Massachusetts Department of Mental Health, *Refugee Mental Health Needs Assessment, A Key Informant Study*, (Massachusetts Executive Office of Human Services, 1989), p. 14.

47. Lyon, 1991, p. 89.

48. Pham, 1992, p. 17.

49. Espiritu, 1992, pp. 92–94.

50. Until the early twentieth century, Euro-Americans successfully confined Asian Americans to restricted areas without laws enforcing segregation. See Sucheng Chan, *Asian Americans, An Interpretative History*, (Boston: Twayne Publishers, 1991), p. 57.

51. 1990 Census of Population and Housing Summary Tape Fine 3A, PO82.

    The median Lexington Asian household income is estimated to be $79,850. The town median is estimated to be $67,389.

52. Eva Heney, "Police Rate Well in Survey," *Lexington Minuteman* (June 9, 1994): p. 13.

53. Tom Lun-nap Chung, Cynthia Ker, Carrie Tang, Loraine Choi, *GBCCA Membership Survey* (Greater Boston Chinese Cultural Association, 1992), pp. 4–5.

54. Heney, 1994, p. 13.

55. The Lexington Asian Americans for Education, press release (March 15, 1994): p. 1.

56. Irene Sege, "Moving out and Moving up, Asian Americans Establish Growing Presence in Suburbs," *The Boston Globe* (May 19, 1991): Metro Section, p. 1.

57. Many of these concerns were expressed during and after the Massachusetts Asian American Commission Town Meeting in Bedford/Lexington, Chinatown and Quincy held in October and November 1994.

Reading 8

Filipinos Find Home in Daly City

Bert Eljera

It's 10 a.m., and a line is starting to form at the Manila Bay Cuisine, a fast-food restaurant at the Serramonte Center. *Adobo, minudo, kare-kare, dinuguan* and other Filipino delicacies are arrayed invitingly at the counter. At one table, Christilyn Cordoves and Elsa Lai are digging into their early lunch of steaming rice, barbecue, and *sinigang.* Over coffee at a nearby table, Tony Tolman and his buddies in the Thursday Club are swapping stories about the Philippines. At the Camelot Music store, Cherry Amores is checking out new CDs from Manila. Huddled on a bench outside the Burger King restaurant, World War II veterans, Felix Antonis, 74, and Ignacio Soriano, 79, are lamenting how hard it is for the elderly to live in America.

In most Philippine towns, people go to the plaza to chat and get caught up with the news. Whether it is to eat, shop, meet friends, or simply gripe, Serramonte Center is where Filipinos in Daly City, Calif., congregate. For Filipino Americans, the Serramonte Center is that plaza in a city that is now home to the largest concentration of Filipinos outside of Manila.

"When people talk of Daly City, they talk of Filipinos," said Lloyd Bumanlag, a Filipino American who sits on the city's planning commission. "I've seen Filipino movies in which a character would say: 'If I go to America, I'd go to Daly City'."

Over the past two decades, Filipino immigrants have flocked to Daly City, transforming the bedroom community into a mini-metropolis with a distinctly Pacific flavor.

About eight miles from San Francisco's downtown, Filipino restaurants dot the city's shopping

strips. *Bagoong, tinapa, daing, kamote, and kamoteng kahoy*—staple foods in rural Philippines—are readily available in dozens of Oriental stores. Philipino songs blare from music stores.

In churches and schools, Filipinos are a big presence. According to the 1990 census, the Filipino American population in Daly City is estimated at 25,000, about 27 percent of the city's 93,000 residents. Recent statistics also reflect those numbers. The Daly City Chamber of Commerce estimates that in 1994, the city's population was 99,000—now placed at more than 100,000—with Filipinos constituting 27 percent.

Other California cities—Delano, Watsonville, Stockton, and Lathrop—may have had large Filipino populations in the past. Regional centers, such as Los Angeles-Long Beach, San Francisco-Oakland, Cerritos-Artesia-Norwalk, and New York-New Jersey, continue to have a large number of Filipino residents, but no city has grown as fast as Daly City due to Filipino immigration. Between 1970 and 1980, for instance, Daly City's population increased 17.3 percent, rising from 66,922 to 78,519. The growth rate was three times that of the entire San Mateo County.

The city's growth rate remained at about 17.5 percent through the next decade, while the number of Filipino immigrants nearly doubled, from 14,421 in 1980 to 24,950 in 1990. This growth has been translated into political and economic muscle. Mike Guingona, Daly City's current mayor, is Filipino American. He got married last week and is now on his honeymoon in the Philippines.

"This city has been good to us," said Rolly Recio, a realtor who moved to Daly City from San Francisco in 1975. "We can raise our children

Source: AsianWeek, May 3, 1996, pp. 13–15. Reprinted by permission.

WHERE WE ARE

According to the 1990 census, Filipinos are the second largest Asian Pacific American ethnic group in the United States with a population of 1.4 million. Filipino Americans are largely concentrated in California, but they can also be found in large numbers in Illinois, New York, Washington, Houston, and New Jersey.

A former U.S. colony, the Philippines is one of the most westernized countries in Asia, and English is the official language. Since many Filipinos do not feel any strong language or cultural barriers, they do not tend to live in ethnic enclaves in the U.S., as with other Asian immigrants.

Filipinos can be found in some of the largest American cities and the smallest communities. Based on the 1990 census, the top 10 metropolitan areas where Filipino immigrants have settled are:

Metropolitan Area	Filipino Pop.	% of total pop.
Los Angeles-Long Beach	219,653	2.5
Honolulu	120,029	14.4
San Diego	95,945	3.8
San Francisco	88,560	5.5
Oakland	77,198	3.7
San Jose	61,518	4.1
Chicago	54,441	0.9
New York	49,156	0.6
Anaheim-Santa Ana	30,356	1.3
Vallejo-Fairfield-Napa	29,760	6.6

well, acquire property, and not be exposed to hostility and discrimination. We're free to pursue our American Dream."

Why Daly City? Most significant is the city's proximity to San Francisco, where most jobs are, Recio and other Filipino immigrants say. "You don't have to cross any bridge," Recio said. "You stay in your car 10 to 15 minutes, and public transportation is readily available." Cordoves and Lai said Daly City is close to their jobs in San Francisco. "It's hard to find a job anywhere else," said Cordoves, 39, a nursing assistant at Laguna Honda Hospital. "I prefer to stay here."

"Daly City is close to everything—the airport, San Francisco, San Jose," said Lai, who works at a Bank of America branch on Market Street. "There are lots of Filipinos here, too."

Convenient transportation is also a factor. Freeways and mass transit systems connect Daly City to the East Bay and North Bay areas. San Francisco International Airport is just nine miles away. San Jose and Silicon Valley are 45 miles to the south. The city is served by the Bay Area Rapid Transit system (BART), which has stations in Daly City and Colma; the San Mateo County Transit District (Sam-Trans); and the Municipal Railway of the City and County of San Francisco (Muni).

Another advantage of residing in Daly City is housing, which is relatively affordable compared with San Francisco and other Bay Area cities, according to recent studies by the Daly City Chamber of Commerce. As of last year, the average price for a single-family home is $242,000, and $149,000 for condominiums and townhouses. New housing units range from $100,000 to $500,000. But in the 1960s and early 1970s homes were selling at about $40,000— quite affordable for Filipino immigrants who endured crowded living conditions in tiny apartments in San Francisco.

Recio, who arrived in 1971, said San Francisco was—and remains—the port of entry for Filipino immigrants to the West Coast. Many would stay in San Francisco for about two to three years, save enough money for a house down payment, and then move to Daly City.

San Francisco is a natural gateway, a sort of way station for Filipino immigrants, said Tolman, a member of the Thursday Club, a group of Filipino retirees who meet once a week at the Serramonte Center. "San Francisco is the starting point," Tolman said. "You're close to your job, there's easy transportation, and you can stay with relatives or friends and save [money]." Pete Aguilar, a Thursday Club member, said he has lived in San Francisco, then Daly City, for 10 years, and now lives in San Bruno. Many of his friends have gone the San Francisco-to-Daly City route, too, he said. This migration from San

Francisco has pretty much been the story of Daly City.

The first big jump in the city's population occurred after the 1906 earthquake that devastated San Francisco, according to Bunny Gillespie who, along with her husband, Ken, are Daly City's official historians. A dairy farmer at the time, John Daly, after whom the city was named, provided food for the refugees, Bunny Gillespie said. W. Powell, owner of the Colma Lumber Co., also provided temporary shelter to the fire and quake victims. "The truly great effect of the earthquake lay in the movement of people rather than in physical damage," Samuel C. Chandler wrote in his 1973 book *Gateway to the Peninsula: A History of Daly City*. "For days and weeks, the people came from their demolished homes or from the unburned parks and streets where they had gone to escape the quake and the fire."

Land developers sold land to refugees who could afford it and, in time, the refugees became residents of the area which later became Daly City and Colma. The refugees liked the area and decided to stay. With assistance from the government and some developers, they built homes and criss-crossed the areas with roads. They brought street cars and businesses from San Francisco and turned the village, then known as Vista Grande, into a thriving town. On March 11, 1911, the residents voted to form a city and gave it a new name: Daly City, in honor of John Daly, who was credited for the growth of the town.

In the 1860s, when he was 13, Daly came to California from Boston by way of Panama, along with his mother, said Chandler, a former Daly City librarian, in his book. Daly's mother died on the trip. Daly survived by doing odd jobs for the dairymen of San Mateo County. At 15, he got a job carrying mail from Millbrae to Belmont in San Mateo County's version of the Pony Express. He later worked on a dairy ranch until he got enough money to start his own dairy business. Daly got married twice. He acquired the Holenworth Ranch, one of the largest at the time, in what is now known as the Top of the Hill. Within a few

years, his ranch house and barns were among the largest buildings in San Mateo County.

In 1907, shortly after the 1906 earthquake and fire that devastated San Francisco, Daly broke up his dairy and sold all the land, except for about four acres between San Jose Avenue and Mission Street, where he built a small house surrounded with flower gardens. Daly moved his family to San Francisco, where he died Jan. 1, 1923, at the age of 81. Until his death, Daly remained active in building the city that sprang from his lands.

"He was a good friend of the growing city," said Bunny Gillespie, the Daly City historian. "There was some controversy about the city being named after him, but it was put to a public vote and his name won."

When Daly City marked its 50th anniversary in 1961, the dairy and pig farms of Daly's days were long gone and the city's main thoroughfare, John Daly Boulevard, ran through the farmer's former ranch. The years after World War II saw a building boom in the city. In 1945, a San Francisco company, Harry Doelger Inc., bought land south of San Francisco's Lake Merced and built homes for more than 22,000 people. The Gellert brothers, Fred and Carl, also purchased land from the early settlers, and converted 950 acres into a thriving community, built around the Serramonte Center. Before 1939, there were 2,054 homes throughout the city. By 1990, there were 30,201 housing units, according to census data.

As the city's population grew, the ethnic composition also changed dramatically. In 1970, whites were the majority in every Daly City neighborhood. By 1990, Filipinos became the majority in the Hillside and Serramonte neighborhoods. The Gillespies' St. Francis Heights neighborhood—where Recio also moved into—was one of those which saw some of the most dramatic changes. When the Gillespies bought their home 40 years ago, St. Francis Heights was an all-white neighborhood of Irish and Italians, Ken Gillespie said.

"Three of four were World War II veterans," Ken Gillespie said. "They were moving from rental properties in San Francisco, able to buy homes through government loans." Homes were selling for about $28,000 then, according to Bunny Gillespie, 69, a former journalist. Now, the standard three-bedroom, two-bath homes cost about $250,000, she said.

Ken Gillespie said that when Asians—mostly Chinese and Filipinos—began buying homes in their neighborhood, many of the white folks were eager to sell. "It was not white flight, but the opportunity to make money, " he said. "It was a case of, "Wow, I can make 10 times of what I paid for this house." Bunny Gillespie said Filipinos were welcomed to the neighborhood, and they themselves made some friends right away. "Filipinos are a community of smiles," said Bunny Gillespie. "They are very family-oriented, religious people, and keep their homes beautiful." Ken Gillespie said he has learned some Filipino words, and had planned several times to visit the Philippines with some Filipino friends.

Recio, on the other hand, said he had detected some subtle discrimination from some whites, who were selling their homes at the time he moved into the St. Francis Heights neighborhood. "They will not tell you directly, but I believe—and this was supported by some studies—that there was some resistance in accepting the new immigrants," Recio said. However, he said, "There was no major backlash. We were free. We could live anywhere."

Recio, who ran unsuccessfully for the city council twice, is typical of the Filipinos who moved to Daly City in the 1970s. A business graduate from the University of the East in Manila, he was one of the Filipino professionals who came in large numbers after 1965. He worked as bookkeeper in a garment manufacturing company in San Francisco and, in 1975, bought a house on Highgate Drive in St. Francis Heights.

At one time, the three-bedroom, one-bath house had 11 people living in it, as Recio's parents, sisters, and relatives of his wife followed them to Daly City. "I should have installed a Statue of Liberty in my house," Recio said with a smile. "They all passed through there."

Most other Filipinos did the same thing. Often by necessity, they followed relatives and friends to Daly City. In time, they became the largest ethnic group.

In the Jefferson Elementary School District, 2,719 of 8,129 kindergarten to sixth grade students are of Filipono descent. Of 8,129 middle-school students, 2,719 are Filipinos as of October 1995. In the Jefferson Union High School District, 28.3 percent, or 1,508 of the 5,328 students are of Filipino ancestry. At Westmoor High

School, Filipinos make up 38.1 percent of the student population of 1,776.

Since about 80 percent of Filipinos are Catholics, most Catholic churches in Daly City and the nearby communities of Colma, South San Francisco, and San Bruno have seen an explosion in new members. At Holy Angels Church, which serves Colma and Daly City residents, Father John Clogerty, the parish priest, said about 70 percent of the 3,500-member congregation are Filipinos.

"They have energized the parish," Father Clogerty said. "They brought a great faith and that has influenced the community."

The parish's staff is mostly Filipino, including its assistant pastor, Father Arturo Albano, and the principal of the Holy Angels Catholic School, Sister Therese Improgo. Nearly 70 percent of the school's 320 students are Filipinos, Sister Improgo said. "Because of our strong faith, we believe in and support quality Catholic education," she said. "It's part of our culture, and parents are willing to make sacrifices."

Their Catholic faith has made it easier for Filipinos to be accepted by the community, said Father Clogerty, whose parish includes Irish and Italian members. "They don't have to construct new churches or schools," Father Clogerty said. "The transition is very easy." Yet other Asian immigrants have encountered some problems because of their religion. In Southern California, for instance, Vietnamese immigrants ran into some community opposition when they tried to build Buddhist temples in some neighborhoods.

At Holy Angels Church, next month Filipinos are planning to hold a *Santacruzan*, a traditional May festival in the Philippines honoring the Virgin Mary. The festival includes a beauty pageant featuring young Filipina women. Money raised from the festival will be donated to the church, according to Tito Rangasajo, a member of the Filipino American Club, which is organizing the event.

Councilwoman Madolyn Agrimonti, who was Daly City's mayor last year, said immigrants have contributed to the vibrant culture and economy of the city. "It's wonderful," said Agrimonti, the first Latino to sit on the council. "It's a touch of what the world is about." She said Daly City will continue to draw immigrants because of its affordable housing, excellent mass transit system, and its small-town feel—despite its recent growth. "We have the best of both worlds," Agrimonti said. "A small-town feeling with the convenience and amenities of the big city."

But as it continues to grow, it would become increasingly more difficult to provide basic services to the people, Agrimonti said. Some big city problems have started to appear. Street gangs have sprung up, including within the Filipino community, said Officer Bob Payne of the Daly City Police Department. About a dozen Filipino gangs have been identified—with Royal Pinoy Brotherhood, Flipside Crew, and Vigilantes among the largest. They have been involved in assaults, robberies, and drive-by shootings, Payne said. "It's a problem," Payne said. "On the school level, we do preventative programs, particularly among fifth graders." The police department has a juvenile task force of four officers, including a Chinese American and two women. There are five Filipino Americans on the city's 114-member force, Payne said.

Ultimately, however, Daly City can only truly become a home for Filipino Americans through the efforts of the Pinoys themselves, said Bumanlag, the planning commissioner. Pinoy is a term of endearment among Filipinos. He said one project that has been in the works for the past couple of years is a proposed cultural center, which will showcase Filipino American heritage. "It will be like a plaza area where people can meet," said Bumanlag, a marketing and communications consultant. "It will have a performing arts center, similar to Japantown." Japantown in San Francisco consists of about two blocks of shops, restaurants, galleries, and theaters showcasing Japanese art and cuisine. It is the site of the annual Cherry Blossom Festival. "We should get people excited about it," Bumanlag said. "We need City Hall to move. This will be great not just for Filipinos but for Daly City."

It's not by accident that Daly City has become home for many Filipinos in the United States. It has the qualities of a Philippine island: misty mornings, bright sunshine, the blue waters and roaring waves of the Pacific Ocean nearby. "It's like I'm back in the Philippines," said Christilyn Cordoves, treating herself to *halo-halo*, a Filipino milk shake of fresh fruits and nuts, after her lunch at the Serramonte Center's food court.

Reading 9

Dixie's Global Village

Jeff Yang

Dekalb County, GA—If you're looking for the new face of the South, head down to Atlanta and take a drive down the Buford Highway, just outside city limits. The signs tell all: Asian Square, Lupe's Boutique, Chinatown Mall, Carniceria Hispanica, a thousand signs printed in a dozen languages, plus, almost incidentally, English.

This is the Buford Corridor, a region that in a mere decade has evolved from a bastion of white, small-town Southernness into a polyglot patchwork of immigrant communities sharing the lingua franca of commerce—primarily Asian and Latino. It's not the only area in the South that's seen a rise in its immigrant population, but it's the one that's seen the greatest immediate change: Over the last 10 years, the Asian American population has doubled, the Latino population has quadrupled, and the number of businesses run by minority entrepreneurs has risen into the hundreds. Some white residents of the area have responded with resentment at being "overrun by foreigners," while others—in particular, business leaders in the region—have seen the arrival of the immigrants as a tremendous opportunity. Enter a new phase in Dekalb's development: Buford Corridor will be the site of the "International Village"—the New South's first and only model panethnic community.

"The International Village will provide an opportunity for immigrants and refugees, of various cultures, to successfully live, work, and socialize together," says the Dekalb Chamber of Commerce. "Native costumes will be encouraged." It will be "a unique experience for tourists and convention groups. A national model for social change, education, and environmental innovations. . . . A visitor will be able to enjoy a Greek lunch, stroll through Hispanic shops in the afternoon, and have dinner at a Korean restaurant."

THE COLOR OF MONEY

Dekalb's Chamber of Commerce is the vanguard of the Village team, and the Chamber's international development head, Ray Kemper, has made this project his mission. A sandy-haired, square-jawed, 30-ish Tennesseean, Kemper's vision of the Village is low budget, high concept. Despite lip service paid to social engineering in the original hype, the plans that have been drawn up seem to indicate that the International Village will be less a multicultural utopia than a Mall of [Ethnic] America. In fact, strip away the Village's community center, and what you're left with is a roofless food court, replete with colorful tchotchkes: open-air markets. Cultural festivals, Architectural style standards that "reinforce the international flavor," a Dragon's Trail tour that showcases local Asian eateries, some alternative transportation." "We've discussed having rickshaws," he says, spreading his hands flat on his paper-cluttered desk. "Something like that. The sky's the limit in our imagination. We want to strengthen the entrepreneurial spirit and offer those as options, whatever the market wants to create."

Originally, the Chamber of Commerce was hoping to have the Village in some stage of completion before the 1996 Olympics. That goal is gone, as it were, with the wind. The problem has

Source: "Dixie's Global Village" by Jeff Yang, first appeared in the Winter 1994 issue of *A. Magazine: Inside Asian America*, copyright 1994, Metro East Publications, Inc.; an earlier version of this story ("Mallticulturalism") appeared in the Village Voice, September 20, 1994. Reprinted by permission.

been that the Village was originally set to straddle both townships in the Corridor, Chamblee and Doraville. As the plans proceeded, however, Doraville's city council became increasingly critical of the Village's aims and ultimate effects, and finally dropped out of the project.

Doraville's defection is not a deadly setback. The Village will happen, with or without the town, and Kemper is confident that its impact will reach far beyond Buford Corridor, or Dekalb, or even, for that matter, the South itself. "This is major," he says with a broad, Southern-sunny smile. "I think we can really capitalize on the tremendous amount of diversity we have here."

Kemper's business-oriented agenda is textbook New South: commerce, internationalism, opportunity. The New South means business, and throughout the '80s, in Atlanta—the self-styled "Capital of the New South"—business was booming. Over the past few years, however, grey-flannel Atlanta has shown a bit of tattiness at the elbows. The Olympics, a major coup when won in 1992, are looming as a potential fiasco, with $1 billion in badly needed repairs behind schedule; last summer, a sewer-line cave-in killed two people and left a gaping sink hole in the center of midtown. Since 1991, Atlanta has fallen from first to 11th in *Fortune*'s annual list of cities with the best environments for corporate development—if not an indication of a coming bust, certainly a sign that the bloom may be off the Peach.

Still, the downdrift of Atlanta's corporate hot zone is less an indication of Southern decline, than a sign that energy is spiraling into the suburban outlands, where Asian and Latino immigrants are making their mark. The revolution occurring along Buford Highway's blacksnake curves of asphalt is, for all intents and purposes, a map of the future. And thus, the split between the Corridor's two townships—Chamblee's embrace of the project versus Doraville's adamant rejection—can be seen as a paradigm for how communities will come to uneasy terms with their sudden diversity, and in the process, put immigrants in the middle of a complex tug-of-war.

Certainly it seems that the embrace of immigration represented by the International Village is better than the fear and resentment represented by its opponents; the question is whether these are, indeed, the only choices available. In both cases, newcomers, regardless of their actual diversity, end up as a monolithic symbol of difference: the "immigrants," the "aliens," the "foreigners."

"I don't like to see the word 'immigrant,' because society is always labeling newcomers as 'immigrants,'" says Thomas Choi, a Doraville lawyer and president of the Korean Association of Greater Atlanta. "They forget that besides American Indians, everybody came to this country at some point in time. Some people's ancestors came 200 years ago; in my case—I'm first generation—I came here 20 years ago. We are all part of the American pie."

A TALE OF TWO TOWNSHIPS

Driving through Chamblee, you'll see shuttered apartments, condemned warehouses; this is a town that, Chamblee city officials agree, needs some work; assimilating new cultures into a mix that is already 55 percent people of color is a small price to pay for, say, real sidewalks.

Indeed, many white old-timers in Chamblee have already fled to towns beyond the Route 285 Perimeter. Many more will leave in a federally mandated buyout of 100 homes around the nearby Peachtree-Dekalb Airport. As a result, Chamblee is 150 percent behind the International Village. "Our attitude is this," says Chamblee councilman Lee Floyd, "Chamblee woke up one day and said, 'Gosh, there's a lot of folks here don't know what a backyard barbecue is.' Well, we can show them that. We're still Americans, we still love hot dogs and hamburgers. But nowadays, we'll take 'em with a little kimchee and a burrito too."

Chamblee's sister city Doraville is a different story. Much of the town is Anytown, USA: ball fields, small houses with well-tended gardens. Here the white community has anchors that go back generations. The town's biggest event is Thanksgiving weekend, when 380 Pee Wee football teams roll into town to play in a charity tournament, the Shriner's Crippled Children Classic.

In Doraville, everyone knows everyone else, or used to, and any kind of change is looked at with your basic down-home suspicion. "The mentality of the city council people is that they are so-called 'good old boys' says Choi. "They really don't care about the 'foreigners.' "

Doraville's City Hall is perched on a small hill, facing a looming billboard that asks, "IF WE CONTINUE TO BUY FOREIGN CARS, HOW WILL OUR CHILDREN WORK?" Here Gene Lively, mayor of Doraville for 12 years, holds court at a monthly session of the town's council. There's a warm camaraderie among these men, who've been working and living together for decades. "Have we been here a long time? We sure have," says Lively, a white-haired character with tinted pilot lenses and a casual slouch. "I've had no opposition since I was mayor, except once in 1973. When you got a good thing, you don't mess it up."

This is a town where Clintonite rhetoric would be greeted with a blank stare, and Clinton himself run out on a rail. At the council meeting, supplicants step forward with requests that in other townships would be rubber-stamped away. One local merchant brings in a large set of charts to illustrate his need to raise his sign to make it visible from the highway. An ex-serviceman with the incongruous hobby of bonsai asks for permission to build a small greenhouse. Each of these appeals are discussed with grave seriousness.

But the real debate begins when local businessman John Park makes a nervous presentation on the annual Korean Festival. It's a sore point with the council; last year's festivities ended up triggering a wave of enmity over the organizers' decision to fly the Korean flag on the City Hall flagpole—right underneath Georgia's Stars-and-Bars–embellished state flag.

"Let's get the flag situation straightened out," says Ray Jenkins, his voice concerned. "They can't fly their flag up here."

"Y'all remember the flak we got last year?" asks Lively, turning to Park. "You cannot fly our flag with your flag."

"We had a lady come up here and raise heck about that," says Jenkins. "Y'all don't know the rules of this country."

"You cannot fly *our* flag with your flag," says Lively. "Unless we are at war, something of that nature."

Park affirms that the festival organizers will post a cleanup bond and pay for extra security, and agrees that the Korean flag will be nowhere near the city hall for the duration. Point settled.

Later on, in his office, Lively expands on the trials that the old-timers in the town have faced: "This is just a small, sleepy town. Back 10 years ago, there was so many service stations here, we had to wear badges so we wouldn't sell gas to each other. It was real companion-like."

Since then, of course, there've been big changes in the town, not that he minds the new people so much—they've brought in business, of course— but . . . change is *change*. "In the last five years, it's been an absolute 360 degree turnaround. It used to be ALL American businesses, and now it's 90 percent foreign," he says. "All the different ethnic groups moving in, that we're not used to, that can't speak our language. We need to be able to communicate, especially on the way our laws are. I mean, it must be really different from the way it is in your country."

Lively and the council's line is simple, and drawn in the sand: "We know they're here, we can see them," says councilman Ray Jenkins. "But we don't want to be encouraging more of them to come. As far as changing this into an International Village is concerned, we're trying to stick to Doraville. This is *Doraville*."

DIVIDING THE PIE

Lively and Jenkins do have a point, of course. Beyond the general benefits of increased commerce in the area, the marketing of the Village as a locale of exotic cuisines and goods must necessarily trim down the white—and black—slices of the pie. A tourist to the area won't be looking for burgers, after all, but burritos and bibimbap; Joe's Down Home Diner won't be on the Dragon's Trail tour.

But even among those closest to its core, the Asian and Latino communities, the latter will clearly benefit less. Overseas Asian capital is poised to pour into the Village; the Asian-managed Summit Bank is ready with Small Business Administration loans for would-be Asian entrepreneurs. The area's Latinos have little by way of fiscal support and access to capital. Even SBA loans may be out of the question for a community skittish about dealing with the feds.

"When the Census was here in 1990, there were posters along Buford Highway saying, DO NOT ANSWER THE CENSUS, in Spanish," says Sara Rosello of Doraville's Latin American Association. "There's that fear of the government."

As a result, for many Latinos, the fruits of the Village may be meager—low-level service jobs in Asian restaurants, for instance. Stanley So, manager of Chamblee's Oriental Pearl, points out a table of off-duty Latino employees seated and eating at his restaurant. "We employ many Mexicans here, but just in the lower jobs—dishwashing," he says, noting that the waiters must, for appearances sake, be Asian. "That is true for most of the restaurants around here. With them, the labor costs is a little less, and they do a lot of work." If Latino leaders support the project, it's because any steady employment for the less-educated migrant worker population is better than nothing. "In any area, you need to have laborers, carpenters, electricians," notes Ray Ortega of the region's Hispanic Chamber of Commerce. "Not everybody can be an executive, so we're going to have some busboys. It's a philosophy you have to adopt."

Meanwhile, many of the old-time, white-owned businesses in the area have long since given up and sold out to "the foreigners." Lively and Jenkins still mourn the loss of Old Sarge's Army-Navy store, now being replaced by a warehouse-sized Korean market. Jack Halpern, however, does not. Halpern runs Halpern Enterprises, the Corridor's largest developer of commercial real estate, and for him, the exploding immigrant demand has been a bonanza. "I didn't totally grasp what this transition would mean for me as a property owner until I traveled to Los Angeles," Halpern says. "The Asians there told me Atlanta is where Los Angeles was 10 or 15 years ago. It's been sad to say goodbye to old friends, but whenever a vacant space appears, it's filled with an immigrant-owned business. For us property owners, that's a positive trend."

The surge of immigrant demand has sent commercial land values skyrocketing. Today, a half-acre along the highway might be worth $600,000, more than a similar lot in Downtown Atlanta; ultimately, the really big winners out of the International Village may end up being the two dominant Anglo businesses of the area, Halpern Enterprises and multimillionaire socialite Gerald Blonders's Tempo Management, whose apartments line the Highway like dominoes.

MALLTICULTURALISM

The project design sketches of the Village are attractive, in a generic postcard fashion. The roofs of buildings have a ribbed, gently canted pagoda motif, and the streets as rendered are clean and pedestrian-friendly. But even if the worst nightmares of its opponents—giant friezes of dancing dragons, garishly attired costumed mascots in fanciful ethnic garb—aren't made real, this snapshot from Buford's future is still a marked contrast from its present. This is ethnic America cleaned up for mass consumption, as seen through a storefront window. The only figures in the sketch are blond and carrying shopping bags; migrant workers and refugees are presumably employed somewhere behind the scenes, or the subject of their own exhibits in a grand Immigration Museum.

Compare this to Chamblee and Doraville today. The El Palenque mariachi hall, with its gently swaying Christmas lights. The Atlanta

Music Studio, a gaudy storefront Korean karaoke club. Lupe's Boutique, with its ceiling-to-floor racks of outfits for the Mexican dance known as *la quebradita*. Tiny *taquerias* and Chinese herb stores, their smells brewing together into a murky, tantalizing funk. These are the establishments that have spread across the Corridor like kudzu, jumbled but natural. At the Oriental Pearl, a young Singaporean woman is enjoying brunch with her companion. "We live in Charleston, actually," she says. "I know people there who come here every weekend, even though it's six hours away. I guess when people have a craving for dim sum, they'll do anything."

The "international village" is with us already, in Buford, in Flushing, Queens, in Fort Lee, New Jersey, in Wausau and Minneapolis and Houston and Los Angeles. It needn't be marketed, and it can't be suppressed; lose the hype, and it'll do just fine. On the outskirts of Chamblee, before the strip malls and shopping plazas fade out into open road, one entrepreneur's shingle says it all.

"Welcome to Chamblee," says the sign. "*Chao mung. Bienvenidas.*"

Reading 10

Still Bitter After All These Years

Angela E. Oh

In revisiting the familiar question, "What has happened among Korean Americans since the riots of April, 1992 in Los Angeles?" non-Koreans have the chance to learn a little more about a community that emerged in one of the most painful moments of Southern California history. Unfortunately for Korean Americans, this annual inquiry hurts not only for the obvious reasons—no real relief was ever realized and we must admit this fact—but it also hurts because the only thing that non-Koreans learn about Koreans is the tragedy of our passage into this society. While it is true that there are plenty of stories about loss and devastation, it is also true that there are stories of recovery, survival, and hope.

We can count on an annual barrage of inquiries from newspapers, radio programmers, and television producers developing stories focused on the tragedy that captured the attention of our nation for a brief moment, only to fall into the abyss of "old news" before any progress toward relief could be made and reported. (In another five years or so, the inquiries will likely stop because other tragedies of the magnitude in Los Angeles, 1992 will almost surely unfold.)

The cynical view is that the media scrounges for the drama that sells and competes in the market place. The less cynical view is that the implosion of 1992 provides a proper reason to re-examine critical urban issues such as economic disenfranchisement, race relations, police-community relations, and political empowerment. In either case, most of the 2,500 Korean American families who suffered the losses in Los Angeles in the spring of 1992 are not interested in talking.

Source: *AsianWeek*, April 25, 1997, p 7. Reprinted by permission.

These were deeply personal tragedies, never redressed; and the internal crises continue. There is no honor in revealing these deeply private matters. This fact should not surprise or disappoint anyone.

A few will speak up. Listening to Korean Americans who lost their only source of family income to the looting, vandalism, and arson, it is clear that the bitterness remains. No official from the police department or the City of Los Angeles ever acknowledged even the slightest contrition over the failure to respond to thousands of calls for help. Instead, a local ordinance which purported to streamline the rebuilding process in Los Angeles was adopted with exclusions for five types of businesses: swap meets, auto repair shops, pawn shops, gun shops, and "establishments dispensing alcoholic beverages for consideration." Guess what kinds of businesses were owned and operated by Korean immigrant families?

Yes, there was a basis for feelings of bitterness. Moreover, that basis for bitterness still exists. Those few individuals who have the courage to speak out are doing so for many different reasons. Some continue to live with the hardship of this local ordinance and want the public to know. Others hope to expose how stores are being closed one by one, after being duly labeled "a public nuisance" under the local land-use ordinance—yet another tool for dismantling family-owned businesses in Los Angeles. Still others simply want to vent their frustrations over the lack of justice, the lack of resources, financial struggles, and a feeling of complete alienation from anyone who did not feel the direct effects of the chaos.

When we turn to those voices in the Korean American community who are actively engaged in trying to build those proverbial "bridges" between cultures, classes, generations, and centuries, another compelling reality surfaces. We can only alter the course of things to come, not things that have already passed. Thus, many young Korean Americans—and a few older ones—dedicate their creativity and talent to efforts aimed at ensuring that the injustice and bigotry visited upon their families and friends will never happen again. True, the efforts to build those bridges have produced only modest results. But our Korean American community is a nascent one, with much to learn and even more to try and understand.

The building and rebuilding struggle is occurring in an era of extreme anti-immigrant sentiment, bitter political turmoil at all levels of government, and a period of deeply disturbing racial intolerance in our large urban centers. Yet, Korean Americans are involved in alliances on economic development, multi-ethnic youth leadership programs, intergenerational boards with community-based organizations, and politics (as contributors, candidates, field deputies, and appointees). This is happening in Los Angeles and across the country where Korean American communities are growing. Is it enough? Of course not. But in the course of empowerment struggles, the efforts put forth never seem to be enough.

For those who expected that the last five years would have produced more results (i.e., compensation for those whose losses exceeded $1 billion), the reality of the circumstances of ethnic Koreans living in Los Angeles has obviously not sunk in. As Korean Americans, we are only a fraction of the entire Asian Pacific American population of our city (which in total is about 10.5 percent). More than 80 percent of the ethnic-Korean population is foreign-born. Thus, it would be fair to assume that English is not the first language of most Koreans and that effective advocacy, both written and verbal, is still being learned.

Moreover, we are a very young population, with the median age being 31.7 years old and about 30 percent of the population in L.A. county under the age of 19. There are no elected officials of Korean descent serving on our local school boards, city council, county board of supervisors, state assembly, or state senate. In light of these facts, why would any thoughtful person believe more could be accomplished?

Without a doubt, it is horrible to know that families continue to struggle and in some quarters history has been revised—with newcomer Korean families being viewed as having deserved the brunt of losses suffered in Los Angeles. Having felt the heat of those buildings on April 30, 1992, as I drove into the area known as Koreatown; having witnessed all that came before, during, and after the riots in our city; and continuing to work on issues related to survival for many newcomer Korean families, it is clear that crises and hope exist hand in hand. For some, it was a rebellion; for Korean Americans it was *sa-i-gu*—and its real meaning can never be translated into the English language for consumption once a year.

CHAPTER 4

Education Issues

According to the U.S. Census Bureau study, "Asian and Pacific Islander Population in the United States: March 1998," 42 percent of all Asian Americans 25 years of age and over had completed at least four years of college. This compares with a rate of 24 percent for all Americans over 25 and 27 percent for all whites over 25. In addition, studies have found that Asian American high school students spend more time studying and Asian American parents have higher expectations for their children's education than other groups. Although the overall educational achievements by Asian Americans are impressive, this does not imply that there are no serious issues to be confronted and addressed. This chapter highlights just some of the major educational concerns for Asian Americans.

Peter Nien-Chu Kiang discusses the problems of racial harassment of Asian American students in primary school. Using case study examples, and quoting students directly, Kiang describes the effects of anti-Asian sentiment from schoolmates, teachers, and school administrators. Without peer or institutional support, Asian American students often have only themselves to rely upon, and often organize themselves to make a change in the hostile school environment. In one case, over seven hundred students from fifty high schools banded together to attend a Conference for Asian Pacific American Youth (CAPAY). In another case, Asian American students at Westlake High School in a suburban community outside of Boston, Massachusetts organized a protest against the drama department's performance of "Anything Goes" that included racial stereotypes of Chinese.

Shirley Hune and Kenyon S. Chan offer a comprehensive examination of the Asian American educational experience. Utilizing a multitude of statistical data, Hune and Chan reveal the opportunities and barriers faced by Asian American students in higher education. This analysis examines the similarities and differences between Asian American women and men in higher education, including comparisons within different Asian American groups, and other non-Asian groups. Their report ends with a number of recommendations to improve access and equity for Asian Americans in colleges and universities.

In the next article, Ronald Takaki provides an insightful and challenging argument advocating inclusive multicultural education. Takaki cites numerous conservative pundits who rail against a multicultural curriculum for fear it will create disunity and conflict. The dominant ethos of higher education has been centered on connecting universal themes, rather than the issues or experiences of any particular social group. Takaki bridges this dichotomy by acknowledging the importance of both "particularism" and "pluralism," which together can be insightful, enlightening, and uniting.

Teresa Kay Williams, Cynthia L. Nakashima, George Kitahara Kich, and G. Reginald Daniel further expand the idea of diversity. Their article advocates for the inclusion of multiracial and multiethnic studies throughout the curricula of higher education. The authors envision comparative ethnic studies as the model for the emerging area of multiracial and multiethnic studies; many student organizations have formed as a result of students taking an ethnic studies course. The attention to multiracial and multiethnic studies is also a result of the increasing number of people of mixed-race heritage who are entering college, continuing their groundbreaking research as graduate students and professionals, and then joining the academic ranks as young college professors.

We Could Shape It: Organizing for Asian Pacific American Student Empowerment[1]

Peter Nien-Chu Kiang

With the doubling of the school-age population of Asian Pacific Americans during the 1990s, the unmet needs of Asian Pacific Americans are escalating dramatically in schools throughout the country. In most settings, teachers, counselors, and administrators do not share the ethnic, linguistic, and racial backgrounds of their Asian Pacific American students. Constrained by limited resources, an increasingly hostile, anti-immigrant climate, and their own stereotypical assumptions, educators have been unable to respond effectively to the full range of academic, social, and personal challenges that face growing numbers of Asian Pacific American students (Trueba, Cheng, and Ima, 1993; Kiang and Lee, 1992).

At the same time, due to linguistic barriers, cultural differences, and economic pressures, Asian Pacific American parents, most of whom are immigrants, typically do not participate or intervene consistently in their children's schooling, even if they express high expectations at home for their children's educational success (Tran, 1992; Morrow, 1989; Kitano and Chinn, 1986). Thus Asian Pacific American students are often left on their own to manage and mediate their experiences in school.

This paper examines how Asian Pacific American high school students struggle to gain social support, cultural affirmation, and political empowerment. Four distinct case studies are highlighted: City Academy High School, an urban examination (elite) public school; City

Source: We Could Shape It: Organizing for Asian Pacific American Student Empowerment (University of Boston, Institute for Asian American Studies), November 1996. Reprinted by permission.

South High School, an urban neighborhood (non-elite) public school; Westlake High School, a wealthy, suburban public school; and the Conference/Coalition for Asian Pacific American Youth (CAPAY), a project of students and youth supported by university and community resources outside of school. Based on participant observation and extensive interviews with Asian Pacific American students in each setting, these case studies offer opportunities to listen, as Nieto and others urge, to the voices and views of urban immigrant/refugee students, suburban immigrant, and American-born students in a variety of institutional contexts (Nieto, 1994; Phelan, Davidson, and Cao, 1992; Poplin and Weeres, 1992).

The first three cases illustrate ways through which students in specific school settings analyze and respond to critical issues that affect them, including racial harassment, the need for bilingual/bicultural support services, and stereotypes in the curriculum. In each of these three cases, however, students' commitments to organize and make positive changes are not shared by most adults in their schools and ultimately go unfulfilled. The fourth case focuses on students from a variety of schools who become the core of a collaborative, community-based effort to organize a regional conference for Asian Pacific American youth. In contrast to the three school-based cases, students in the final case who had strong adult support succeed in establishing an ongoing student/youth network following their landmark conference, and in the process, empower and transform themselves. By sharing lessons from both the failures and successes of students' organizing efforts, this paper suggests how educators, parents, and community members can support students' efforts more effectively.

CONFRONTING RACIAL HARASSMENT: WHO CARES

I'm not going to walk home with tears running down my brown cheeks like the old days . . . I would stand up for my self because, if I don't, who will? Nobody stood up for me when I was spat at, kicked at, or cussed out just for being Cambodian (Pho, 1993, p. 14).

Issues of racial harassment severely affect Asian Pacific American students, as documented by the U.S. Commission on Civil Rights (1992) and other studies of school climate (Pompa, 1994; Sing and Lee, 1994; First and Willshire Carrera, 1988). The Commission's landmark report states:

The pervasive anti-Asian climate and the frequent acts of bigotry and violence in our schools not only inflict hidden injuries and lasting damage, but also create barriers to the educational attainment of the Asian American student victims (pp. 97–98).

Confirming the Commission's national findings, Michele Ott (1994) found, based on a survey of 266 Asian Pacific American students from a variety of urban and suburban school districts in New England, that:

- 54 percent of the respondents had been called names or harassed and 24 percent had been physically attacked in school;
- 9 out of 10 had heard of or witnessed an Asian Pacific American student being harassed, and 6 out of 10 had heard of or witnessed one being physically attacked;
- 69 percent had never reported any incident to a teacher;
- 25 percent felt that teachers would not care, and 30 percent believed that teachers would not do anything, even if incidents were reported; and

- of those students who had experienced harassment, one out of three had considered dropping out of school.

Ott's regional findings are further validated by ethnographic profiles of individual schools (Kiang, Nguyen, and Sheehan, 1995; Kiang and Kaplan, 1994; Kagiwada, 1989). In one urban high school, for example, Semons (1991) observes:

By far, the majority of the negative comments directed toward an outside group were targeted toward Asian students. Negative comments about Asians were overheard in the presence of teachers, who did nothing to interrupt them. Students could therefore infer that prejudice against Asians was acceptable, unlike prejudice against Blacks (p. 147).

Though not the situation in every school, similar dynamics are explored in the following case.

CASE STUDY 1: CITY ACADEMY HIGH SCHOOL

The City Academy is an urban school serving about 1,500 students in grades seven to twelve. The student population is approximately 19 percent Asian, 41 percent white, 33 percent Black, and 7 percent Latino. The school is one of the city's three elite, examination public high schools for which admissions are based on results from standardized tests administered by the school district during sixth grade. Four out of the school's 71 teachers are Asian Pacific American. There are no Asian Pacific American administrators. The headmaster is a Hispanic female. The curriculum is traditional with an emphasis on "classics," although students have opportunities to participate in educational and cultural activities sponsored by various cultural clubs after school.

Racial climate became a focus of the school's attention following a fight in the cafeteria started by a white male student who called Jenny,[2] a Chinese American female, "a fucking gook." After Jenny reported the incident, the school's headmaster scheduled a disciplinary hearing for the white male student, as required by district policy.

An ad hoc group of Asian Pacific American students, including leaders of the school's Chinese and Asian student clubs, quickly formed after the incident to demand that those responsible for racial harassment be seriously disciplined. These students also called for a more diverse curriculum and school-wide training in prejudice awareness and conflict resolution. To press their concerns, many of the school's Asian Pacific American students agreed to walk out of school en masse the next day when the disciplinary hearing was scheduled to take place. A modest multiethnic coalition also formed in solidarity.

The school administration responded immediately by threatening to suspend any student who walked out of school. Not wanting to jeopardize their academic standing, students agreed to cancel the walkout and, in its place, to meet as a group with the administration. Following the meeting, the school's headmaster expressed surprise at how marginalized the Asian Pacific American students felt from the larger school community. She asserted, "The kids have always worked together. We pride ourselves on having a nurturing atmosphere" (Tong, 1992, p. 19).

Student views, however, contrasted sharply with this. Angela, a Chinese American senior, recalled:

An Asian girl, Lisa, was having a hard time with some white boys who kept telling her to give up her seat to them. Two teachers came over to see what the trouble was and ended up telling Lisa just to give her seat over to the boys!

While describing examples of specific incidents among peers, many students also criticized school officials for denying that racism was a problem. Sunthon, a Lao American senior, stated, "It's totally swept under the rug, it's never discussed. It's a taboo subject and it goes completely unmentioned." Angela agreed, "The teachers did not seem to want to talk about what happened."

Asian Pacific American students were not alone in these views. Bill, a white male sophomore observed, "The topic of racism is not really ever discussed in classrooms, but Asians get the most mistreatment as far as racism goes." Tonisha, an African American senior, added, "I've been in the school for six years and this is actually the first incident I ever remember being discussed."

The school's elite reputation figured prominently in staff and student discourse about racial conflict. Many were reluctant to report incidents because of not wanting to damage the school's public image. Jenny explained, "They try to create the impression that this kind of stuff doesn't happen at our school because we are an exam school." However, students also expressed disappointment, if not bitterness, with the lack of support they received from the school's faculty and administration. Sunthon explained:

The school clearly had a choice between supporting its students or looking good. . . . We approached them and they immediately tried to say, "Oh, there's no such thing here," covering it all up. . . . The whole point of going to [the headmaster] was to set a precedent, to let the student body know. But she did nothing; no letters, nothing over the intercom, nothing in the student newspaper. . . . She has so much power and she has done nothing.

Kim, a Black sophomore, agreed, "Teachers don't want to talk about it, but we still bring it up. It's dying down and [the headmaster] wants it that way. We like her and she likes us, but when we go to her, she's too busy or she's in a meeting. Sometimes we think she's trying to save her own butt."

Recognizing the importance of having faculty who care, and especially having Asian Pacific American teachers as mentors. Angela explained:

Having younger teachers on the faculty is very important. Younger teachers have an easier time relating to students, they can understand what students are going through a lot better. . . . I can think of only one teacher—Mr. Siu who is Chinese—who really gets involved with his students.

However, students' disappointment also extended to some adults who were themselves Asian Pacific Americans. Kim recalled:

> *Even the [deputy] superintendent came. He's Asian and they [the Asian students] thought that he would side with them but he did not. He just kept putting them down. Whenever they thought they brought up a good point, he'd just put them down. He was really angry about the flyer which said "Asian American Student Rally."*

Through these experiences, Asian Pacific American students learned some hard lessons in how dynamics of race, culture, class, and power affect relationships in a school community. Although they had articulated a thoughtful, comprehensive set of proposals for school improvement that addressed such areas as school climate, the curriculum, faculty/staff hiring, student activities, and disciplinary policies, only one recommendation for a schoolwide diversity awareness orientation was adopted by the administration. Even then, students had to do the legwork of identifying trainers and community resources to make it happen. Pointing to the school's failure as an educational environment, Sunthon declared:

> *[In school] there was hardly anything about race relations, anything about what it means to be a person of color in this country. The discussion is just not happening. We don't have a place where we can talk about it, a time when people can come together and talk it out instead of confronting it outside. People are just walking past each other in the hallways, sitting in the same classrooms, but they are not talking with one another. I think that needs to change, to not be so fearful that if we talk about racism, if we talk about prejudice, it's gonna lead into an uproar or a riot. I mean, give young people some credit! I mean, we have minds, let us exercise them.*

In the end, Jenny, the 16–year-old "victim," expressed her biggest disappointment with the school's disciplinary decision after the hearing. She recalled:

> *I resented the fact that she [the headmaster] seemed to be defending the boy by trying to make me understand that he was under a lot of pressure. That really has nothing to do with the kinds of things he said to me. . . . The boy ended up only being suspended for the rest of the day immediately after the hearing. He basically got to have a half-day, and I have been told that he cannot be retried in the hopes that he might receive some harsher punishment. That is it.*

Despite her frustration, though, Jenny voiced no regrets for her own actions, noting that "After the incident, a lot of students spoke to me about how similar incidents have happened to them. . . . Maybe the younger students will realize how important it is to come forward if this kind of stuff happens."

DEVELOPING ASIAN STUDENT ORGANIZATIONS: CREATING NEW SPACE IN SCHOOL

> *We were coming from a meeting of the Asian Club and white students threw oranges at us. Before that we had been standing in the hall and the supervisor kicked us out. So we went outside and they threw oranges. So there is nowhere to go (Gibson, 1988, p. 143).*

When students at City Academy initially responded to the racial slur against Jenny, their first line of support came from the school's two Asian student organizations. In schools across the country, Asian Pacific American students have tried to establish their own clubs as a way of affirming each other, while also contributing to the broader school community. Organizations have taken the form of both pan-Asian and specific nationality clubs (Filipino or Korean, for example) as well as broader multicultural clubs and international or English as a Second Language (ESL) student associations. The impact of these groups individually and institutionally, however, has been uneven, depending in large part on how adults in particular schools and communities have chosen to relate to them, as the following case illustrates.

CASE 2: CITY SOUTH HIGH SCHOOL

The [Vietnamese Student] Association is going to provide opportunities for the "torn leaves" to help the "more torn leaves."[3]

City South High School is a non-selective urban high school with a student body that is 12 percent Asian, 24 percent Latino, 27 percent White, and 37 percent Black. Of the adults in the school, there are no Asian administrators, counselors, or regular education teachers. Khmer and Vietnamese bilingual teachers and para-professionals are the only Asian Pacific American staff inside the building.

Asian Pacific American students at City South, even more so than their peers at City Academy, vividly described examples of racial harassment, including name-calling and physical assault. One Vietnamese student sighed, "I feel like I get stepped on every day in that school." Like City Academy, however, the school's principal asserted, "we have not had confrontations, we have not had tensions" (Ellemont and Gorov, 1993, p. 1).

Through interviews conducted for a larger study with 15 Vietnamese students ranging from 10th through 12th grade, every student recounted examples of witnessing or experiencing harassment as part of their daily lives. While one said, "The white kid is always messing with the Asian," another noted, "I experience problem with Blacks more than any other group," and still others described conflicts with Hispanic and Haitian students.

In three years' time, the number of Vietnamese students at City South tripled from 30 to more than 100. Most were newly arrived immigrants. School officials never discussed the implications of this dramatic demographic change within the school community. Many non-Asian students, therefore, disregarded the Vietnamese students'

ethnic, linguistic. and cultural identities as Vietnamese and, instead, assigned them a racial identity under the label of "Chinese" and "Chinks." Confusion surrounding the Vietnamese students' presence was evident in the experiences of almost every student interviewed. Thuy, a junior, recalled:

When we pass by them they give you some kind of like a dirty look. . . . They say, "Look at that Chinese girl," and then they call like, "Chinks, go back to where you belong."

Whether because of personal experience, observation, or advice from friends and siblings, Vietnamese students at City South crafted individual survival strategies to get through school—typically by choosing to be quiet in class, rushing through the hallways in groups, confining themselves to particular tables in the cafeteria, and avoiding certain areas like the bathrooms where they expected racial conflict. Ky, a 12th grader, explained:

I try to keep myself very, very careful, you know. I think about where I'm going before I'm going there . . . My eyes open . . . so I can get out some situation quickly as I can.

A few students, however—those who had lived in the U.S. longer than five years and who were more proficient in English—asserted themselves as equal members of the school community. This challenged the school's social dynamics according to Kieu, another senior:

I see other Asian student. . . . After the class change they just go straight to the class or they walk in a whole group. . . . [But] Ky and I or even Thuy, it seems like we speak more English, and we walk like [we're] a part of the school. . . . That's why the problems started. . . . They want to be power in the school. . . . When I walk in school I feel like I'm equal to anybody else. And I guess that what they not wanted.

In this context, with the escalating needs of Vietnamese students going unrecognized at City South, Thuy, Ky, and Kieu decided to launch a

Vietnamese club for the school. Thuy's idea for the club grew out of her middle school experience in another state:

> *They have all kind of ESL, bilingual programs for Asian kids [at the middle school] . . . and they have this club called the ESL club . . . and all Asian kids can join the club and the teachers, the ESL teacher, she do a lot of activity with us. . . . Then I went to City South. I saw a lot of Vietnamese kids, right, they don't speak English at all, but the school didn't do anything for them. It's like either they learn or they don't. . . . So I felt kind of bad, and I start talk to my teacher. . . . I complain to her. And I say that they should have an ESL program or something you know. Or at least a Vietnamese club that we could help those students.*

Ky voiced similar sentiments, "I just miss the old school back in Vietnam, so I want to try to recall some of those memories. We wanted to form a club so we can all get together."

Assisted by a Vietnamese tutor from a local university, a Cambodian bilingual teacher, and another teacher of English, the group attracted roughly 30 students to its first meeting. Ky and Kieu delivered the welcome speech:

> *None of us wants, 10 to 20 years later when we travel half our lives, to not have any nice memory about our first steps into life at our student age. The Vietnamese Student Association is going to be the first means to help us to build those memories. . . . Of course, the Vietnamese Student Association is not going to be a place only for fun. But it is also the place for studying. . . . We will have occasions to improve and exchange our experiences as students and the initial difficulties when trying to adapt into new schools and a new society. We can share the good poems, the good novels and songs in order to help keep the national (Vietnamese) culture in our hearts. This is also a good way that we can prove to the foreigners that even though we have to take their culture daily, we are not going to forget to improve our national culture.[4]*

Participants in the first meeting discussed their hopes for the club to provide academic and ESL tutoring, advice about cultural expectations in U.S. society, and ways to share Vietnamese language and culture. After three well-attended meetings, however, the club had still not gained any backing from the school itself, particularly in terms of having an approved time and place to meet. While some teachers were willing to help when asked, others criticized the new club for encouraging segregation. Thuy observed, "They [school personnel] are not so happy about [the club] . . . it's so hard up here to do those things."

The club also faced internal conflicts, reflecting gender dynamics and differences in acculturation. Thuy recalled:

> *At every meeting when I open my mouth, he [Ky] always jump in and say let him handle it. . . . The guy try to be the head, you know. They don't want any young lady or woman to take their place. So every thing I say, he always jump in and cut me off. So that's a problem.*

These gender conflicts reflected important issues for the students to work through. Ky asserted, "Most of the girls I know who've been here more than two years, they always act that way. They're bolder, aggressive." Thuy countered:

> *A lot of Vietnamese kids go to school, whatever the people say, they just sit there. They sit there and be quiet. . . . I say no! I'm not gonna sit there and be quiet. I won't. I won't be quiet.*

Without adequate bilingual/bicultural faculty or staff in the school, no one helped the students analyze their attitudes or guided their actions. As a result, students were unable individually or collectively, to sustain their organizing initiative and overcome the lack of formal, institutional support they received from the school's administration.

Interestingly students found no guidance at home either. None had told their parents about either their interests in the club or their problems with racial harassment at school. A junior noted, "They don't know what happened, and they feel okay because they don't know everything. My mother and father don't speak English." Ky described the relationships between Vietnamese students and their parents in these terms:

> *Our parents not involved enough in our schools. One of the things is English barrier. They try and protect themselves inside their house . . . and sometime they too busy with their work, trying to earn a living, trying to survive in this society. So they try so hard they just forget about us. . . . I don't blame at all. They try so, make a living so hard.*

Though very conscious of the sacrifices and hardships their parents endured in order to provide a better life for their families, most students did not describe close relationships with their parents. While challenging Vietnamese students' silence in school, Thuy sighed that her parents viewed her as "too Americanized" at home. Kieu also felt discouraged that her parents did not understand the difficulties she faced at school. She revealed to them some of the more dramatic incidents of racism that she experienced only after they criticized her for receiving mediocre grades. Kieu explained, "I go home and struggle. When I go outside, outside I struggle."

Without space or sanction, the Vietnamese Student Association dissolved after two months and was not re-activated during the following year. Ironically, instead of embracing Vietnamese students' leadership and resourcefulness in responding to a growing need within the school, some adults at City South labeled students' efforts to organize themselves and support their newcomer peers as separatist and divisive. This dominant response by adults was both powerful and chilling. Similar dynamics play out in the next case that focuses on choices and priorities for the curriculum.

CONFRONTING THE CURRICULUM: ANYTHING GOES

> *Rich man cannot buy Chinese honor.*
> *I'll make it five thousand.*
> *Chinese honor sold.*
>   —dialogue from the musical,
>   *Anything Goes*[5]

In the previous two cases, urban Asian Pacific American students organized to improve their school environment by challenging racial harassment and addressing their own needs for academic, social, and cultural support. Adults, in large part, failed to respond meaningfully to the issues raised by students in each situation. Though focusing their efforts primarily on peer relations, the students in those cases acknowledged and linked their concerns to issues of curriculum development and the need for faculty to foster diversity awareness.

Sunthon at City Academy, for example, stated explicitly, "We should have a diversified curriculum, a multicultural curriculum to teach that people without white skin are not outsiders." Ky from City South asserted, "Talk about this [racial conflict] to kids. . . . Start from kindergarten, first grade, second grade . . . teach them to live together, to tolerate with people, respect people." In the next case, Asian Pacific American students directly confronted the curricular choices and priorities of their teachers.

CASE STUDY 3: WESTLAKE SUBURBAN HIGH SCHOOL

Westlake High School serves roughly 800 students in a wealthy, predominantly white, suburban town. Asian Pacific Americans comprise only 2 percent of the high-school student body. There is one teacher of color (African American) and no Asian Pacific American teachers, counselors, or administrators in the building.

As a high point of each spring school period, faculty in Westlake's Drama Department select a play or musical for the student Drama Club to perform publicly. Choosing the play represents a major curricular decision for the school, with significant, and sometimes controversial implications for faculty time and student learning. This was the case, especially when the play includes controversial content—as when Cole Porter's musical, *Anything Goes*, was selected. Written in the 1930s, *Anything Goes* includes two characters named "Ching" and "Ling" who are portrayed as subservient gamblers in need of Christian conversion and described in the script as "two Chinamen" (Bolton et al., 1977, p. 67). They and other characters speak pidgin English, like "so soree no sow wild oats in China, sowee wild rice" (Bolton et al., 1977, p. 103) and imitate Chinese nonsense syllables such as "Confucius say, Wa ho ding so le tow" (Bolton et al., 1977, p. 106).

Concerned about the high public profile and legitimacy that the musical would lend to racial stereotypes, Asian Pacific American students challenged the play's demeaning references to Chinese men and women as well as to Chinese language and music. With no active Asian student club in the school, the Diversity Club, which included students of many backgrounds who were committed to promoting multicultural awareness, took the lead.

After analyzing the script and developing what they considered to be reasonable demands for changes, members of the club led by Cara, a Chinese American senior, prepared a leaflet outlining their concerns, and distributed it in faculty mailboxes, albeit without approval. School administrators, however, removed the leaflet before most faculty saw it and criticized the students for "not following procedures." Students' demands included: "No Pidgin English," "No Fake Asian Languages," "Change the Names of Ching and Ling," and "Cut Out the Word 'Chinamen.'" Referring to the school's student handbook, students stated, "If this racist behavior (slurs) is not tolerated in the school halls, it should not be tolerated on stage for a public school play."

As tension about the musical and the Diversity Club's unmet demands intensified, club members agreed to meet directly with the Drama Department's faculty and Drama Club students to voice their differences. The meeting, however, only escalated the conflict further. Anita, a Chinese immigrant senior, described the reaction of the Drama Club students as: "Why are the Asians making a big fuss? It's just a play." Wendy, a Chinese immigrant junior, similarly recalled:

We were going through the play point by point, and there were lines specifically that Cara was going over, and people were asking what's wrong with that? She was trying to explain it and they wouldn't understand.

Asian Pacific American students were especially critical of the Drama Department chair who, as director of the play, defended his selection of *Anything Goes* based on the entertainment value of its music/dance numbers. Cara challenged him in the meeting, explaining that the play was offensive rather than entertaining for many Asian Pacific Americans. Radha, an Indian immigrant junior, described the chair's reaction:

He didn't handle it right because then he went bitching to his students. . . . Obviously he didn't want to hear what Cara was saying, and than his students became hostile and they were after us, too.

Wendy added, "He didn't handle the situation discreetly . . . maybe he was angry or maybe he was worried," to which Anita replied, "He might have been insulted because she [Cara] criticized his choice as a teacher, and then he was embarrassed so he had to cover it up or something."

The Drama Department chair rebutted students' demands by accusing them of advocating censorship. From that point on, the students never recovered from being placed on the defensive. Discussion among both students and faculty shifted to protecting First Amendment rights and artistic license rather than recognizing diversity and making responsible educational choices.

At a faculty meeting called to discuss the controversy, many teachers voiced support for the Drama Department chairs' position. Anita recalled, "There were [only] a couple of teachers who spoke on our behalf at the Faculty Meeting, but they didn't follow through, so nothing came of that."

In a letter to an Asian Pacific American parent who had expressed concern about the play, the principal articulated the school's official view:

While canceling the play would have been an option, I felt that it would be more educationally sound for the students and teachers to engage in dialogue about the concerns and feelings that they had about both the negative stereotyping in the play and the dangers of censorship in an educational community.

The show did go on. As a concession to the students, however, a statement on the inside back cover of the program booklet for the musical acknowledged that some in the school community had found the play racist and offensive. The statement also explained that the English and Social Studies departments had facilitated class discussions about Asian American stereotypes in order to understand the socio-historical context of the play.

Yet, when asked how thorough or systematic these discussions had been, Anita replied, "it did not happen. They were going to talk about it in English and History, and then they didn't." Students saw that only a couple of teachers actually tried, but had such limited knowledge of the issues, that the discussions seemed counter-productive. Wendy recalled:

One of our English teachers brought up the play and basically the whole class was arguing like why are these Asians so upset. . . . This other girl, she was Black, she understood, but the other people were basically like, "I don't care, it's just a play, it's just for fun." . . . I felt like the whole class was against the Asians, and I just felt hurt by it. . . . After class I just started crying, and then my English teacher came over to me and said, "I'm sorry you had to go through this." . . . She tried to do something, you know. She said maybe we can discuss it after the play, but then she never went through with it.

Like the first two cases, Westlake students were clearly disappointed in the lack of support they received from adults in the school. But unlike the first two cases where students' working-class, immigrant parents typically knew little about and did not participate directly in their children's school experiences, Westlake High Asian Pacific American parents, though also immigrants, tended to intervene more directly in their children's school lives, perhaps due to their own bilingual, highly educated professional backgrounds.

Yet, parent intervention did not mean support for student activism. If anything, the Westlake High parents played a major role in consciously limiting how intensively the students were able to advocate for their demands. Cara, for example, revealed in writing:

Just about everyone is upset, frustrated and fed up. Anita had a big fight with her parents last night because they want her to concentrate on school. My parents are concerned with the scholarship issue. It's a bummer but my Dad is the one who's gonna pay my college tuition. . . . We really do not have support from other parents/kids.

Indeed, Cara's parents were counting on her winning a major scholarship to a local university, but this depended on receiving outstanding recommendations from her teachers and the principal. Not wanting to risk those relationships, Cara's father halted her activism. He stated in a phone conversation at the time, "I don't think Cara should be involved in this any longer. Living in this country, I've learned you have to look out for number one."

Also in sharp contrast to City Academy and City South, no student at Westlake described experiences of direct physical harassment. As a much smaller minority population [2 percent compared with 19 percent at City Academy and 12 percent at City South], Asian Pacific American students' sense of their struggle at Westlake seemed more diffuse and less urgent. Anita analyzed the dynamics this way:

I don't think a lot of people realized that they're Asian. They're kind of separated here. There's no like Asian unity. Like a lot of my friends from other cities, there's so many Asians there, and it's kinda cool 'cause they hang out and stuff . . . but there's no sense of Asian unity here at all.

Radha echoed, "Most Asians here are passive, and I'm passive, too, so people don't really know each other and they don't make an effort to get together and have an Asian club."

As a result, Wendy concluded:

It made me realize even more that Asians are like, no one listens to them. Like if the African Americans came out and said something, probably the people in the school would have done something, but when the Asians come out, no one really does anything.

Radha also pointed to the dominant black-and-white paradigm of race relations as a barrier preventing Asian Pacific American issues from being addressed in meaningful ways at the school. She explained:

I went to a racism workshop like a week ago, and I was like, cool, let's talk about racism. So I went in and they were just talking about black-and-white problems and I was like, wait a second, there are Asian problems, you know. And they were like, oh yeah, and then they discussed it like for a minute.

Based on their direct experiences, Asian Pacific American students found their issues, concerns, and perhaps even their very presence, to be marginal at Westlake. In questioning the judgment of a senior faculty member and forcing a school-wide examination of bias in one aspect of the curriculum, their efforts were quickly undermined both by adults who labeled their intent as censorship and by non-Asian peers who viewed them as "over-sensitive." Wendy recalled:

It's like the day we were having that discussion in my English class, and everyone was focusing on me, like looking at me saying, "Don't you think you shouldn't censor stuff?" They were looking straight at me like "what's the problem?"

Although the Drama Club made some minor changes to the production in order to appease the Asian Pacific American students, the basic flaws remained. By the time the performances took place, the Asian Pacific American students had long given up their demands. Some had followed

their parents' wishes to disengage from the controversy, while others simply could not envision ways to overcome their marginalized minority position. An Asian Pacific American community leader, invited by some students to attend the performance, offered powerful testimony that confirmed the depth of students' disempowerment within this wealthy, suburban school:

I never felt so silenced in my life. It was like a sea of white, the whole auditorium, with everyone cheering and clapping, being really proud of their kids. But what about our kids? It's like we weren't even there.

In looking back at the chain of events leading to the performance, Anita, Radha, and Wendy placed some of the responsibility on their own Asian Pacific American community for having allowed others to define their image. But they also criticized inaction by the school administration, using language almost identical to students at both City South and City Academy. Wendy stated:

She is the principal, so I think she should care about what her students are concerned with. I mean, if they have any concerns, she should do something about it.

Anita added, "I think she just wants to sweep it under the rug, which she did." Radha agreed, "Again, just like other incidents that Westlake has swept under the rug and never dealt with at all."

For Cara, whose initial outrage had compelled her to challenge Westlake's faculty and curriculum, she concluded, perhaps wisely:

Other racial stuff is BOUND to occur in Westlake, believe me. Next time it will go further. We'll achieve more. I guess we all have to learn to be patient.

Although her tempered assessment of Westlake seems realistic, Cara needs to know that active intervention and dramatic change are possible if resources and support are consciously mobilized. This is the lesson from the following final case.

ORGANIZING FOR EMPOWERMENT: WE COULD SHAPE IT

We believe that youth united by a common purpose can make a difference. We aim to establish a forum for free dialogue and for positive change in our communities. Our initiatives are diverse and include avenues to abolish stereotypes, to educate ourselves and others about Asian Pacific America, to celebrate our heritage, and to improve race relations.

—Mission Statement, Coalition for Asian
Pacific American Youth[6]

The previous three case stories illustrate some of the substantial struggles waged in different settings by Asian Pacific American high-school students to organize and empower themselves. Without support from adults either at school or at home, these cases clearly do not represent victories or success stories. One might conclude, in fact, that while the desires for youth empowerment may be ardent—which by itself should be cause for respect and celebration—nevertheless, the prospects appear discouragingly slim.

In contrast, the final case focuses on the experiences of a core group of students who organized a landmark, regional conference for Asian Pacific American youth from which emerged an ongoing Asian Pacific American regional youth network.

CASE 4: CONFERENCE/ COALITION FOR ASIAN PACIFIC AMERICAN YOUTH

When an ad hoc group of adults and youth first gathered to discuss how community resources could support Asian Pacific American students confronting the issue of racial harassment in school, no one imagined that a few months later nearly 700 young people from more than 50 high schools would attend a Conference for Asian Pacific American Youth (CAPAY). The ad hoc group convened at first because such little support seemed to be coming from home or school.

Following a series of open-ended initial meetings, a core group of 50 students—primarily seniors from various high schools in the region—agreed to work with each other in planning a conference that would gather Asian Pacific American youth together, and provide opportunities for gaining awareness, sharing experiences, and raising voices in unity. Adults affiliated with a range of community, groups, local universities, and state agencies agreed, in turn, to pool resources to support the youths' organizing efforts. Although most of the core group of young people had never met or worked with each other before, they quickly immersed themselves in a collective process to make CAPAY happen, working as interns every day during the summer and every Sunday throughout the fall.

Organizing the conference brought together many students who had been active in their own schools, often as the only Asians in multicultural clubs or school-wide leadership bodies. After the first meeting, Samantha, a senior from an urban, predominantly Black and Hispanic community, admitted, "I was like shocked because in my school as far as Asians, I'm the one who does everything." Lisa, a senior from an affluent, predominantly white suburban town, recalled, "It was the first time in my life that I had been in a room with people who feel the same way I do. I'm so used to being like the only Asian speaking about Asian issues." Lauren, a Chinese immigrant senior from an urban school, added, "I'm always like the only Asian, but when I started working on this, it's like I can have friends that share the same interest, who have these common goals to work on."

For some, this experience was both thrilling and threatening—directly challenging and, at the same time, affirming their racial, cultural, and social identities. Amy, a Korean American senior from a suburban school, revealed:

When I first walked in, I swear, I just wanted to turn around and walk right out, I was so intimidated. I've never really been in a room with so many Asian students in my age group. I was like, what am I doing here? And then I started coming to the meetings, and I got more involved in it, and I was like, oh my god, you know this is really cool! Asians are cool! [laughs].

In addition to their urban/suburban and public/private differences in school and socioeconomic status, core group members' ethnicities included Lao, Vietnamese, Pakistani, Korean, Japanese, Chinese, Filipino, Vietnamese Chinese, Indian, Taiwanese, and Khmer. Sharing each others' backgrounds while working together on a common goal generated unforgettable learning. Chia Chia, a Taiwanese immigrant, exclaimed:

I learned a lot from the others. They broke all my stereotypes. Like Pakistani women having no rights, but then I met Attia. I never heard of Cambodia, Laos, etc., and I never thought they were Asians. But then I met Sarouem and Chan and Vira and Chantala. I've always thought Japanese believe they are the best and they don't care about other Asians. But Isamu showed me that he cares in a lot of ways. Many people broke my stereotypes and I'm glad.

Amidst this diversity, Ivan, a working-class Chinese senior from a suburban school, noted the affection and mutual commitments that emerged among the group, "It feels like a family and we're very close and somehow we have a lot of differences, but we are very open to each other. I don't see that often in other activities." Lauren also emphasized the community-building aspect of the process, especially appreciating "the friendship that we have all built or gained through organizing."

Vira, a Lao senior from an urban school, added:

The first meeting was so exciting! You had a roomful of Asian American youths talking about some of the things that concerned them. Just so many different types of people, and it really impacted me. There was a real sense of "This is for us," you know. And we could make it into whatever we wanted. We could shape it, we could develop it, and I think that was really powerful.

Others like Chantala, a Lao freshwoman in college, gained a similar sense of power and purpose from the conference planning process. She recalled realizing, "Instead of everything that's happening to us, it's how we are affecting the outcome." In contrast to the discouragement and disempowerment of students in the previous three cases, the structure, resources, and praxis developed for CAPAY all served to respect, support, and enable those who participated. The difference is striking and fundamental.

Planning for the conference plenary sessions and workshops introduced the organizers to a wealth of community resources and to older generations of activists with whom they could relate. Topics ranged from gangs and media stereotypes to inter racial dating and parent-youth relations to civil rights strategies and curriculum reform. Michele, a Filipina college student, noted, "Before, if I got an idea in my head, I would be like, too bad I can't do it. But all of us know the outlets to go now, we have connections we can make."

Members of the core group spoke in moving terms about the significance of working with the adult advisors. Amy commented, "At school, there are no Asian teachers or faculty members, and it's awesome seeing like cool Asian adults. . . . It's a really good influence." Ivan agreed:

In my entire school, there are no Asian teachers that are full-time. And it's a really negative aspect that I never really thought of until I started coming to CAPAY and then finding adults who are great leaders and who are also very good role models. And that makes such a difference because when I was younger, I didn't really have any Asian American role models, and it was so bad. . . . That really limited my options when I was younger, and that's why I was such an inactive kid.

The process and impact of the conference transformed those who organized it. Chantala exclaimed, "It's given me a much clearer sense of what I want to accomplish in life." Michele added, "Now I can look at the future as being something I can help try to mold and not just think that everything is not going to change. I have a brighter outlook." Amy rejoiced:

I've become really proud of who I am and where I come from, and I know that I've become stronger. I'm no longer that silent anymore. . . . I have really found myself.

Lisa similarly reflected:

CAPAY taught me how powerful the Asian community would be and how powerful I, as an Asian American woman, would be. I became "empowered"—full of hope and optimism. It boosted me and made me see the need to be more active. It instilled confidence, and gave me a voice.

Originally expecting 250 participants, the organizers had to change the date and location of the conference when over 600 students preregistered. Although many conference participants complained in the workshops and plenary sessions about "apathy" among their Asian Pacific peers, the overwhelming response to CAPAY ironically indicated just the opposite. Noting this irony, members of the core group analyzed student disinterest or apathy in light of their own evolution in becoming active. Lisa explained, "It's not because they don't want to know, but because they haven't been taught to know what they should know, and they haven't been given the chance to do something about it, to be empowered." With the CAPAY conference providing that first chance for many, Michele observed, "The more people get used to forums like a conference, the more they will feel that they can speak up some place."

Although most core members had already been active in their own schools prior to CAPAY, their work on the conference greatly advanced their own leadership skills. Attia, a Pakistani American junior and elected student government head from a suburban school, reflected:

Organization and leadership: I discovered new ways to think about these qualities. All of us were trying to accomplish the same goal, but in such different ways. We had a lot of conflicting ideas, yet we were good friends. I learned how to be more open and democratic. . . . It really is a process—brainstorming, working with people, putting it on paper, trying it out, implementing it, seeing what happens—that's something really cool that I learned. . . . This was the first big event that I had a real impact on. It's so easy to say, "oh, things will never change," so easy to let all this energy inside me become negative energy. But it's a lot more fun trying to solve things. You can always make things better.

Five months after the historic first conference, 60 youths gathered to reinvent CAPAY as an ongoing *Coalition* for Asian Pacific American Youth. Governed by a steering committee and general membership consisting entirely of youth and supported by an adult advisory group and the Asian American Studies program of a local public university, CAPAY continues to serve as a unique vehicle for networking, skill-building, and leadership-training among immigrant and American-born Asian Pacific youth of many nationalities, from urban and suburban backgrounds and both public and private schools. While sponsoring a major annual conference as well as retreats, a quarterly newsletter, a summer learn-and-serve program, and many other activities, CAPAY is working toward long-term institutionalization within the Asian Pacific American community.[7]

As CAPAY continues to evolve, it not only provides a valuable voice for youth, it actively enables individual young people to take on larger leadership roles in various Asian Pacific American communities. Several community organizations, for example, have invited CAPAY members to serve as speakers, to evaluate programs and services from a youth perspective, and even to become board members. CAPAY has also advanced the visions and prospects of a multiracial youth movement. While CAPAY members have participated in many multiracial youth conferences and rallies, some Latino students have discussed how to develop their own youth network, using CAPAY as an organizational model.

CAPAY is also significant as an alternative model to gangs for organizing Asian Pacific American youth. Asian youth gangs have proliferated in recent years, reflecting a variety of factors, including limited job opportunities, fragmented family support systems, and academic as well as social alienation due to linguistic and cultural barriers in school. Not unlike CAPAY, however, many gangs at the local level have formed explicitly to defend against racial harassment in school or in neighborhoods. According to a 21-year-old former Cambodian gang member, "Racism has shaped my life, my experience ever since the first day I set foot in this country. . . . In the gang, I watch your back, you watch my back. We look out for each other" (Kiang, 1994, pp. 141–142). For many youth, neither their parents nor their teachers have offered the requisite support and multicultural understanding needed to deal with the realities of racism in school and on the streets.

CONCLUSIONS

The voices and experiences shared in this paper point out several significant lessons. In both urban and suburban schools, Asian Pacific American youth are actively seeking positive change. At the same time, they face indifference, misunderstanding, and active opposition from adults as well as peers. Although Asian Pacific American students in urban settings seem to confront more frequent and blatant examples of racial violence, suburban students' degree of disempowerment also seems severe.

Particular incidents or issues such as the harassment of Jenny at City Academy or selection of the *Anything Goes* musical at Westlake led some Asian Pacific American students to plan rallies and assemblies, to draft petitions and public statements, and to form new organizations or activate existing ones to affect their situations in school. Through their organizing efforts, they seek to transform their schools into places "where we can talk" and "build those nice memories."

If asked, students also articulate connections between specific instances and a more general critique of learning environments at their schools. They point to gaps in the curriculum, for example, in the areas of Asian American Studies, multicultural awareness, and conflict resolution that reflect and reinforce the problems they experience. From their perspectives, "the discussion is just not happening" and "the school didn't do anything" to enable students or other members of the school community to understand, respect, and support each other. Even well-meaning teachers lack training in these critical areas and fail to "follow through" on their commitments.

As a result, students' hopes and demands for positive change in their schools go largely ignored or rejected. Yet, despite their frustrations, they feel their efforts are still important, if only to "help the more torn leaves" and set an example that encourages younger students "to come forward" so that "next time it will go further."

While denouncing administrators and teachers who ignore racial issues in order to protect their schools' images, students long for youth-centered, Asian Pacific American adult mentors and role models with whom they can identify. When provided with opportunities to collaborate with community-based Asian Pacific American adult activists, young people identify much more directly with the possibilities of making positive change for themselves, their schools, and their communities. They also quickly recognize the absence of comparable individuals within their schools and, in most cases, within their families.

Harassment, exclusion, and marginalization contrast sharply with the oft-repeated dreams of immigrant and refugee families who come to this country for the sake of the children. Yet parents do not offer significant support for students' organizing efforts in school. In urban settings, the students' immigrant and working-class parents have little direct involvement with their children's lives in school because of economic, linguistic, and cultural barriers that prevent their participation. In suburban settings, immigrant parents with professional class backgrounds may be more knowledgeable and comfortable in dealing with school matters, but they discourage and restrict their children's organizing activities, particularly if such activism leads to confrontations with school personnel.

The voices of Asian Pacific American students in this chapter deserve and demand recognition. Far greater communication and coordination are needed between youth and their families, schools, and communities. Over the long term, Asian Pacific American parents themselves need multilingual and multicultural leadership training and organizing to better understand their children's experiences and to gain greater accountability from schools, service agencies, and local governments.

Given the profound absence of family and school-based interventions to ensure Asian Pacific American children's daily physical and emotional integrity in school, community interventions like CAPAY are urgently needed. Providing an alternative model to the group empowerment, such as gangs, the CAPAY model not only affirms the efforts of young people, but provides them with relevant resources, skills, and an environment within which to transform themselves individually and collectively. The continuing programmatic success and personal impact of CAPAY suggest a larger need for Asian Pacific American communities to develop methods and structures to enable youth leadership more systematically.

If schools are to become authentic sites of learning, support, and growth for Asian Pacific American and indeed for all students, then organizing projects like CAPAY will need much broader development and a direct connection to the schools themselves. This could take place along the lines of Vira's vision:

What I really want to see is the impact on schools. . . . If Asian Americans aren't respected in the student body and if they are constantly being excluded or overlooked in discussions concerning race, how are they going to see themselves? That's

part of forging their identity. They won't see themselves as being powerful, they won't see themselves being adaptive. They'll see themselves as being really insignificant and hopeless. . . . We can use CAPAY as a way of legitimizing some of the concerns we have, like having more Asian American faculty and administrators. . . . If the school is serious about its Asian American students, they're going to listen to what CAPAY has to say.

CAPAY and projects like it create rich resources not only for advocacy but also for continuing research on the process of organizing and outcomes of the Asian Pacific American youth empowerment. These potential long-term contributions, like those of the young people themselves, seem limitless.

NOTES

1. This study was completed with funding from the Research Fellows Program of the Institute for Asian American Studies at the University of Massachusetts Boston and with research assistance from UMass Boston students, Chin-Lan Chen, Marty Cosgrove, Paul Davis, Jenny Kaplan, Carol Ann Neff, and Arlene Reidinger. Case 2 is adapted from a larger study conducted with Jenny Kaplan. Michelle Janmey and Amy Emura provided valuable editorial assistance. Finally, I am especially grateful to CAPAY and the many high-school students who shared their voices and visions with me. A version of this study is published under the same title in *Cherished Dreams: Educating Asian Pacific American Children*, edited by Li-Rong Lilly Cheng and Valerie Ooka Pang, SUNY Press, 1996.

2. With the exception of the CAPAY case study, the names of schools and individuals cited within are pseudonyms.

3. Translation of unpublished speech delivered to the Vietnamese Student Association, 8 May 1992. "Torn leaves" refers to being Vietnamese refugees.

4. Translation of unpublished speech delivered to the Vietnamese Student Association, 8 May 1992.

5. See Bolton, G., Wodehouse, P.G., Lindsay, H., and R. Crouse, 1977. *Anything Goes*. NY: Tams-Witmark Music Library, p. 103.

6. Drafted by Ivan Chan and ratified by CAPAY on 14 May 1994.

7. CAPAY's second conference took place in March 1995 and once again attracted 700+ youth from 60+ schools and communities. The conference also added separate sessions and a resource room for adult teachers and

parents who accompanied the youth as chaperones. A third conference, held in March 1996, enabled youth leadership teams from 50+ schools to plan and implement activities in celebration of Asian Pacific American Heritage Month in May—a first for most schools involved.

REFERENCES

Bolton, G., Wodehouse, P.G., Lindsay, H., and Crouse, R. 1977. *Anything Goes*. NY: Tams-Witmark Music Library.

Cosgrove, M. and Neff, C.A. 1992. Paper prepared for the University of Massachusetts Boston.

Ellemont, J. and Gorov, L. 1993. "South Boston High to Reopen in Stages." *Boston Globe*, May 8, 1 and 14.

First, J. and Willshire Carrera, J. 1988. *New Voices: Immigrant Students in U.S. Public Schools*. Boston: National Coalition of Advocates for Students.

Gibson, M.A. 1988. *Accommodation without Assimilation: Sikh Immigrants in an American High School*. Ithaca, NY: Cornell University Press.

Kagiwada, G. 1989. "The Killing of Thong Hy Huynh: Implications of a Rashomon Perspective." In Nomura, G., et al. (eds). *Frontiers of Asian American Studies*. Pullman, WA: Washington State University Press, 253–265.

Kaplari, J. 1992. "Vietnamese American Students at an Urban High School." Paper prepared for the University of Massachusetts Boston.

Kiang, P.N. 1994. "When Know-Nothings Speak English Only: Analyzing Irish and Cambodian Struggles for Community Development and Educational Equity." In K. Aguilar-San Juan (ed.) *The State of Asian America: Activism and Resistance in the 1990s*. Boston: South End Press, 125–145.

Kiang, P.N. and Kaplan, J. 1994. "Where Do We Stand? Views of Racial Conflict by Vietnamese American High-School Students in a Black-and-White Context," *The Urban Review* 26(2): 95–119.

Kiang, P.N. and Lee, V.W. 1992. "Exclusion or Contribution: Education K–12 Policy," *State of Asian Pacific America*. Los Angeles: LEAP Asian Pacific American Public Policy Institute and UCLA Asian American Studies Center, 25–48.

Kiang, P.N., Nguyen, N.L., and Sheehan, R.L. 1995. "Don't Ignore It: Documenting Racial Harassment in a Fourth Grade Vietnamese Bilingual Classroom," *Equity and Excellence in Education* 28(1): 31–35.

Kitano, M. and Chinn, P.C. (eds.) 1986. *Exceptional Asian Children and Youth*. Council for Exceptional Children.

Morrow, R.D. 1989. "Southeast Asian Parent Involvement: Can it be a Reality?" *Elementary School Guidance & Counseling* 23(2): 289–297.

Nieto, S. 1994. "Lessons from Students on Creating a Chance to Dream," *Harvard Educational Review* 64(4): 393–426.

Ott, M. 1994. "The Incidence of Anti-Asian Violence in High Schools." Honors thesis prepared for Bates College.

Phelan, P., Davidson, A.L., and Cao, H.T. 1992. "Speaking Up: Students' Perspectives on School," *Phi Delta Kappa*. 73: 695–704.

Pho, S.T. 1993. "No More Tears Will Run Down Our Brown Cheeks," *Asian Week*. May 28, 14.

Pompa, D. 1994. *Looking for America: Promising School-Based Practices for Intergroup Relations*. Boston: National Coalition of Advocates for Students.

Poplin, M. and Weeres, J. 1993. *Voices from the Inside: A Report on Schooling from Inside the Classroom*. CA: Institute for Education in Transformation, Claremont Graduate School.

Semons, M. 1991. "Ethnicity in the Urban High School: A Naturalistic Study of Student Experiences," *The Urban Review* 23(3): 137–158.

Sing, R. and Lee, V.W. 1994. *Delivering on the Promise: Positive Practices for Immigrant Students*. Boston: National Coalition of Advocates for Students.

Tong, B. 1992. "Students Protest Racial Incident," *Boston Globe*. November 13, 19.

Tran, M.L.T. 1992. "Maximizing Vietnamese Parent Involvement in Schools," *NASSP Bulletin*. 76–79.

Trueba, H.T., Cheng, L.R.L., and Ima, K. 1993. *Myth or Reality: Adaptive Strategies of Asian Americans in California*. London: Falmer Press.

U.S. Commission on Civil Rights. 1992. *Civil Rights Issues Facing Asian Americans in the 1990s*. Washington, D.C.

Reading 12

Educating Asian Pacific Americans: Struggles and Progress

Shirley Hune and Kenyon S. Chan

INTRODUCTION

The purpose of this report on Asian Pacific Americans (APAs) is to provide an in-depth analysis of the presence, progress, and complex outcomes of Asian Americans and Pacific Islanders in American education. APAs are too often left out of the discourse on race and education. First, studies omit APAs because the racial experience in the U.S. is interpreted largely in a black/white framework and neglects other racial/ethnic groups.[1] Secondly, APAs are frequently viewed as foreigners or permanent immigrants rather than as an American racial minority with a long and deep educational history in the U.S. Thirdly, APAs are excluded from the racial discourse on education because, it is argued, they are a "model minority" and not in need of attention from educators. When APAs are included, it is to emphasize their "success story" and to reaffirm inferred cultural explanations for their educational attainment.[2]

This report seeks to give educators and policy-makers a more informed, comprehensive, and balanced view of Asian Pacific American education. It is concerned with the education of native-born and foreign-born Americans of Asian and Pacific Islander descent and not with international students from Asia and the Pacific Rim.

Source: Excerpted from Hune, S. & Chan, K. (1997). Special Focus: Asian Pacific American Demographic and Educational Trends. In D. Carter & R. Wilson (Eds.) *Minorities in Education: 1996–1997* (Vol 15), pp. 39–67 and 103–107. Washington, D.C.: American Council on Education. Copyright © 1997. Reprinted by permission.

THE STRUGGLE FOR EDUCATIONAL RIGHTS, DESEGREGATION, AND EQUITY

Like other racial/ethnic groups in the U.S., Asian Pacific Americans have a history of denied public schooling, segregated schooling, and inequality in education. APAs have challenged their unequal treatment in public fora and in the courts. A number of distinguished cases and events are highlighted here.

The APA struggle for educational rights began with their initial settlements in America. Chinese parents in San Francisco had to petition the school board for their children's education. A small, but separate, school was opened in 1859 and subsequently closed by the school superintendent with the claim that there were too few students. Chinese parents again petitioned the school board and the California state legislature in the 1870s pointing out the injustice of paying taxes to support public education while their children were denied access because of race. Their pleas were ignored.[3]

In a case that reached the California State Supreme Court, Mary and Joseph Tape disputed the San Francisco school board's decision in 1884 to deny their American-born daughter Mamie the right to a public education because of her Chinese heritage. When the Court agreed that Chinese American students had a right to an education, the school board resisted and set up separate facilities for "Mongolians" rather than to have "race mixing," and established the "Oriental School" in San Francisco in 1885.[4]

The schooling of 93 Japanese and Korean immigrants became an international issue in 1905, after Japan protested the San Francisco's school board decision to have them attend the separate "Oriental School." Only after President Theodore Roosevelt negotiated a Gentlemen's Agreement in 1908, whereby Japan restricted the emigration of its laboring class to the U.S., did the school board permit Japanese students to enroll in public schools set aside for whites. International and federal interventions and a new diplomatic agreement were necessary here to desegregate schools for Japanese students in San Francisco.[5]

The 1954 *Brown v. Board of Education* Supreme Court decision remains the landmark case for school desegregation. APAs also have contested the legality of segregated schools. Efforts by Chinese Americans to end school segregation in the early 1900s failed in San Francisco when a federal court based its ruling on the "separate but equal" doctrine drawn from *Plessy v. Ferguson*, an 1896 Supreme Court decision. In affirming that separate facilities for blacks and whites were permissible as long as they were equal, although in practice they never were, *Plessy v. Ferguson* helped legitimate a system of institutionalized racism and legalized segregation in America that was extended to other racial groups.[6]

Another test case arose in the Mississippi Delta where Chinese Americans, brought there to work as sharecroppers in the 1870s, found themselves in a rigid hierarchical racial order between blacks and whites.[7] Gong Lum sought to have his daughter, Martha, enrolled in a white school in 1924 and pursued the matter to the U.S. Supreme Court. The Court based its ruling on *Plessy v. Ferguson*, ignored the violation of the equal protection clause of the 14th Amendment, and upheld the Mississippi court decision that only Caucasians could attend white schools. The 1927 *Gong Lum v. Rice* ruling concluded that as no public schools for "Mongolians" existed in Mississippi and Chinese Americans could attend a "colored" school, Martha Lum was not being denied an education.[8]

Some APA students did enroll in schools with whites and other students as few communities were willing to fund separate schools. However, they could still be found attending segregated schools in parts of California until the 1930s and in Mississippi until 1950.[9]

Asian Pacific Americans have had an historic role in expanding equal and quality education for all Americans. Chinese Americans in San Francisco filed a class action suit in federal court in 1970 arguing that schools were ill equipped to academically prepare limited-English students. In the landmark 1974 *Lau v. Nichols* decision, the U.S. Supreme Court redefined educational access and equity and called for new remedies. These have included bilingual programs, teachers, and teacher assistants. This action has benefited all immigrant and non-English speaking groups.[10]

APAs have struggled for equal treatment in higher education. Students demonstrated on university campuses during the late 1960s and early 1970s to demand increased access, minority faculty, and curriculum reform, especially Asian American Studies and other ethnic studies programs.[11] Higher education's failure to respond to APA issues led to new student actions at Hunter College, Northwestern University, UC Irvine and other institutions across the nation during the 1980s and 1990s. On some campuses, students adopted hunger strikes and sit-ins to have their educational concerns met.

APAs have challenged unequal treatment in student admissions. In examining the policies and practices of higher education institutions in the 1980s, including those of Brown, Harvard, Princeton, Stanford, UC Berkeley, and UCLA, APAs noted that their admission rate (i.e. the ratio of students admitted relative to the total number of applicants) was not commensurate with the growth in student applications and concluded that institutions were setting "quotas" on APA enrollment.[12]

Investigations revealed that some universities required APAs to have higher academic qualifications for admissions than other students. Others added supplemental and often subjective criteria to their admissions standards or reweighted criteria in a manner that negatively impacted APA students. Underlying these actions was the argument that Asian Americans were "overrepresented." Brown University admitted bias in its admissions procedures and revised its practices. Harvard University defended its practice of giving preferences to children of alumni and to recruited athletes, few of whom were APAs, resulting in lower admission rates for APA applicants than for whites.[13] APAs continue to question the "shifting sands" of admissions policies, including efforts to eliminate affirmative action. They have also challenged notions of "overrepresentation" and "parity" and how they are applied for decisions that discriminate against APAs.[14]

Asian Pacific Americans have opposed inequities in higher education employment. One recent case reached the U.S. Supreme Court and has changed academic procedures. Dr. Rosalie Tung, a nationally recognized scholar and faculty member in The University of Pennsylvania Wharton School of Business, was turned down for tenure in 1984. She then filed a complaint with the University grievance commission, which found that discrimination had taken place in her case, and also with the Equal Employment Opportunity Commission (EEOC) alleging race, sex, and national origin discrimination in her tenure review. Her case also involved *quid pro quo* sexual harassment on the part of her department chair, who deliberately solicited negative letters for her dossier.[15]

In the 1990 *University of Pennsylvania v. Equal Employment Opportunity Commission* ruling, the U.S. Supreme Court established an important precedent in academic employment. It ruled that the University had to disclose confidential tenure materials (files of the complainant and other faculty for "comparability") to the EEOC as part of its investigation of employment discrimination charges. While secrecy and closed meetings still surround promotion and tenure decisions, the Court ruling has forced universities to adopt a more open, impartial, and consistent review process and has benefited all faculty. One outcome is that the number of faculty filing tenure and promotion grievances has risen since the ruling.[16]

The strivings of APA students today and their family sacrifices in support of education are a continuation of the population's historic efforts to achieve equity. These efforts have recently been complicated by a powerful public image of APAs as a "model minority" group, which contends that APAs are all "successful" and not in need of remedies.

DEMYTHOLOGIZING THE "MODEL MINORITY" STEREOTYPE

Asian Pacific American students are perceived as well-behaved, diligent, high achievers, who persevere and are educationally successful in spite of socio-economic and language obstacles. They are also seen as being *less* "well-rounded" than the ideal student, making "narrow" academic choices, focused mostly on mathematics, the sciences, and engineering. This oversimplified profile of APA students as "whiz kids" with limited interests reinforces a popular stereotype of the population as a "model minority" and masks a more complicated appraisal of their education in the U.S.[17] APA students who do not fit this image, such as teenage mothers, gang members, or school drop-outs, are seldom portrayed in the media. Yet, these youth are becoming a growing and significant concern in the APA community.[18]

The image of APAs as a "model minority" group underlies much of American education's policies and practices toward them over the past three decades. It is a broad brush stroke that purports to paint a representative portrait of APAs and is a radical departure from their derogatory image as "yellow and brown hordes" so prominent from the 1840s to the end of World War II. However, this dominant "success story " image conceals disparities *within* and *among* APA ethnic groups in their educational achievements and ignores obstacles in their pipeline. While presumed a positive image, the "model minority" stereotype has hindered attention to real educational concerns.[19]

The "model minority" image is also applied to Asian Pacific Americans in the workplace where they are considered to be hard working, dutiful, well represented in the professions, and economically successful, but lacking in the communication skills and leadership qualities that are necessary for higher management positions. Here too, the stereotype conceals their wide range of occupations from garment workers to attorneys, a "glass ceiling" for professionals, high rates of poverty, and incomes and employment levels that are not commensurate with their schooling and work experience. APA returns on education and employment are complex, diverse, and unequally rewarded compared to white male counterparts and demonstrate the persistence of racial discrimination and other barriers.[20]

Nonetheless, the academic achievements and persistence of APA students cannot be ignored. Neither can APAs with low educational attainment be viewed as anomalies rather than as a representative part of this population. Cultural explanations predominate in explaining the school success or failure of individuals and racial/ethnic groups. Many academicians and social commentators look to "Asian cultures" to explain APA education. Such interpretations are a result of "orientalized" or exotic misunderstandings of Asian Pacific Americans, which consider APAs to be embodiments of "Asian cultures." APA cultures, however, are not fixed "Asian cultures" and do not exist in isolation. They are dynamic. Through negotiation, accommodation, and resistance to dominant American beliefs, norms, structures, and rewards, APAs create and recreate their cultures in adapting to changing conditions.[21]

Furthermore, APAs represent more than two dozen communities with different histories, religions, and values. They arrived with different socio-economic characteristics and have settled in the U.S. at different historical periods and under different circumstances. Many APAs are indigenous to what is now the U.S. Others are several generations American-born with little knowledge of traditional "Asian cultures." Cultural variables are also difficult to define, isolate, and control for research purposes. Data directly linking specific values and educational performance is lacking and conclusions rest largely on supposition and anecdotes. Moreover, cultural values identified with Asians, such as respect for education, are not unique nor exclusive to APAs, and are shared by many non-Asian groups.[22]

Some scholars have argued that APA educational "success" is due to their "immigrant ethos." Voluntary minorities, i.e. immigrants, and involuntary minorities or groups incorporated into U.S. society by colonization, conquest, annexation, or slavery, are seen as having different approaches to education. The experiences of involuntary minorities in America lead them to conclude that education is no guarantee of economic mobility. Immigrant racial minorities, on the other hand, have limited experience with American racism. They believe in the "American Dream" that hard work is rewarded. They tend to compare American opportunities with those in their homeland and remain positive of the instrumental role of education for their mobility, if not for themselves, certainly for their children. The "immigrant ethos" explanation sheds some light on why APAs work hard for good grades, but has limitations. It treats culture as a static phenomenon, views APAs as a homogeneous group, and ignores the experiences of American-born APAs and APAs who are low achievers.[23]

Cultural explanations give little consideration to socio-historical, structural, and societal influences, including the education system itself, and American society. Most importantly, they obscure alternative interpretations.[24] For example, the high academic achievement of many APAs can be better explained by public and institutional policies, such as changes in U.S. immigration laws and the settlement of international students from Asia and the Pacific Rim in the U.S., which have selectively recruited and retained highly educated APAs in America.

APA scholars were the first to call attention to the role of racism and other barriers in explaining the high participation rate of APAs in education.[25] APAs have had a long history of racial discrimination in the U.S. and subtle forms of bias continue to affect their lives. This experience has contributed to their struggles, past and present, to contest race-biased educational inequality.

APAs view education as a necessary means to achieve social mobility in a racially stratified society and as a "hedge" or protection from bias. Research that includes interviews with students and parents disclose that APAs, regardless of their class background, state economic necessity and the likelihood that racial discrimination will continue to impede their social mobility as reasons for their emphasis on education. The pursuit of education is pragmatic, goal-oriented, and job related. The notion of education for its own sake or as an aspect of "Asian cultures" is not the primary emphasis. Occupations which are valued in American society, provide financial security, and are not likely to be eliminated in the future, such as those in the sciences, engineering, and health care, are given priority.[26] This helps to explain why APAs are invested in schooling and illuminates their educational choices, but also does not deal with low-achieving students and obstacles in the pipeline. It assumes that hard work and persistence will be rewarded and that *all* APAs are academically motivated by structural and systemic barriers. Some APAs find the racial climate defeating and become low achievers or dropouts.

Recent studies of APAs provide additional insights on the social costs of racism and other barriers to achieve an education. Parents make personal and financial sacrifices. Korean parents have moved to neighborhoods with high academic public schools, sent their children to after-school programs for additional studies, and provided them with tutors for difficult subjects.[27]

Studies on APA high school students document that they spend more time doing homework to achieve higher grades (from 5 to 10 hours more per week than white students), study in groups to make up for individual deficiencies, take more advanced academic courses to be college-eligible, and are less likely to be absent from school or to cut classes than whites.[28]

New research has documented wide disparities in APA educational achievement and uncovered differences in how APAs respond to the pressures of the "model minority" stereotype. Many APA high school and college students have internalized the stereotype and feel they must be more academically prepared than other students and to do well in mathematics and the sciences to conform to the image. Students also note that the stereotype invokes hostility from other students who feel that APAs are unfair academic competitors. Other APAs resist the "model minority" image because they cannot or will not meet its expectations and pressures. They may fail in majors in which they lack interest or aptitude or drop out of school prematurely in order to demonstrate their defiance . Still other APA students have real academic needs, such as English language or mathematics deficiencies, which are not addressed by educators determined to maintain the "model minority" mystique.[29]

Like their peers, many APA students are actively engaged in a wide range of extracurricular activities from sports, student government, religious groups, to political activism. They are unjustly perceived as "nerds" and indeed resent this perception. Some APA students become politically active on campuses and in their communities to change the inequality in their environment.[30]

Qualitative studies on APAs who persist through college also reveal subtle forms of exclusion. They find that APA students and their concerns are ignored by faculty, staff, and administrators, in part, because of their presumed "success." APAs who challenge the Eurocentric, male-dominated, heterosexual curriculum and its theoretical paradigms find they are often silenced in the classrooms. Hence while APAs are obtaining college degrees in large numbers, they face "hidden injuries of race" and "everyday inequities" in their education.[31]

Deconstructing the "model minority" concept has been a continuous activity of many commentators over the past three decades. While this concept is certainly more "positive" than previous stereotypes of APAs, it reduces APA groups and individuals to a neatly conceived image that bears little resemblance to their real lives. It also has consequences, particularly for those unable or unwilling to live up to the image. APAs who are at-risk, have unmet academic needs, and are constricted in the educational pipeline, are being neglected. More balanced research giving attention to structural, institutional, and societal influences is needed to explicate Asian Pacific American educational trends. While the high achievement of many APAs is a significant accomplishment, it is not representative of all APAs and is a complicated story that shall be discussed in the next section.

EDUCATIONAL TRENDS

A comprehensive analysis of the demographic development of the APA community is not possible in this paper but such an analysis is necessary to fully contextualize the educational trends presented here. For a complete analysis of APA demographics see the monograph by Hune and Chan.[32]

Educational Attainment. Table 1 presents comparative educational attainment data for persons 25 years and older in 1994.[33] At first glance, it would appear that the APA population has a much higher educational attainment when compared to the total U.S. population and is identical to whites. Looking within levels of attainment, there are disparities. More APAs have 8th grade or less education than all Americans and all whites, while APAs with bachelor's degrees or more appear to be almost twice that of the U.S. population and for whites. These are national figures and a more accurate APA picture can be obtained by examining available data comparing APAs to populations residing in the West only, where APAs are concentrated.

TABLE 1.

Comparison of Educational Attainment by Race— 1994 Percentage of Persons 25 years old and over

United States	Total Population	Asian and Pacific Americans	Whites
8th grade or less	8.8	9.8	6.2
9th grade to h.s. graduate	44.6	30.0	44.3
Some college or associate degree	24.3	19.1	25.2
Bachelor's degree or more	22.2	41.2	24.3
% h.s. grad or more	80.9	84.8	84.9

Source: U.S. Department of Commerce, Bureau of the Census, 1994 Current Population Survey, *The Asian and Pacific Islander Population in the United States*, March 1994.

First, those residing in the West appear to have obtained more education than the country in general (Table 2). Whites in the West had the highest rate of high school graduation or beyond (90.3 percent). However, over 10 percent of

TABLE 2.

Comparison of Educational Attainment by Race— West Region Only—1994 Percentage of Persons 25 years old and over

West Only	Total Population	Asian and Pacific Americans	Whites
8th grade or less	9.1	10.8	3.1
9th grade to h.s. graduate	37.3	32.6	36.5
Some college or associate degree	29.4	21.9	32.3
Bachelor's degree or more	24.2	34.7	28.1
% h.s. grad or more	82.6	83.9	90.3

Source: U.S. Department of Commerce, Bureau of the Census, 1994 Current Population Survey, *The Asian and Pacific Islander Population in the United States*, March 1994.

APAs had an education of 8th grade or less, which is over three times the rate for the white population in the West. While APAs still lead whites in those with bachelor's degrees or more, the gap between APAs and whites closes in the West. APA bimodality is moderated slightly in the West.

Secondly, there are gender differences within the APA population and in comparison to whites. In the West, APA females have educational attainment rates of 14.5 percent with 8th grade or less and 80.3 percent high school or more completion rates which is lower than for APA males (10.8 percent and 83.9 percent, respectively). Thirteen percent of APA females completed 8th grade or less or 4.5 times the rate for white females. At the same time, APA women had higher college completion rates (32.5 percent) than white females (23.8 percent), reflecting again the bimodality of APA education.[34]

Thirdly, examining educational attainment by ethnic group within the APA population reveals that some groups are educationally at-risk. Table 3 shows high levels of persons with less than 5th grade education among refugee groups—Vietnamese, Cambodian, Hmong, and Laotian Americans. Southeast Asians also have lower high school completion and college participation rates than other APAs.

The educational attainment of Pacific Islander groups (particularly Hawaiians, Samoans, and Guamanians), who are largely U.S. born, with their full educational experience in the American educational system, is also problematic. While they appear to negotiate high school in reasonable numbers, although slightly less than others, their college experience and college completion proportions are very low in comparison to APAs as a whole and to the total population. The low rates of some college and college completions among at-risk groups raise questions about the need for possible educational intervention and suggest, once again, that focusing on aggregated data for APAs masks groups at serious educational risk.

Educational Attainment, Earnings and Poverty Rates. Educational attainment has not resulted in income parity for APAs when compared to the U.S. population or to whites (Table 4). APAs earn less than the aggregate of the U.S. population and whites in every educational attainment category, including those with bachelor's degrees or higher, except for those with some college or associate degrees.[35] Comparable data for other ethnic minorities in the same time period were not available.

The discrepancy between education and income for APAs is also revealed in family poverty rates. Rates of poverty by educational levels (Table 4) show that the poverty rate for APAs far exceeds the rate for the population as a whole and for whites at every educational level.[36] Thus, while APAs have progressed in education, they are not rewarded to the same extent as whites.

In summary, the educational attainment of APAs is generally high, but less than whites in the West. It is also complex and varied. Their educational bimodality reflects the emergence of a bifurcated APA population that is in large part an outgrowth of the socio-economic characteristics of post-1965 immigrants and refugees and the circumstances under which they have come to the U.S. The high percentage of APAs with bachelor's degrees or more also include immigrants with college degrees selectively recruited under the "professional and highly educated preference" category of the 1965 Immigration Act. Likewise, those who arrived as refugees include most of those with 8th grade or less. The low educational levels among at-risk APA communities and the lack of income parity across all educational levels warrant special attention. The disaggregation of data by ethnic groups gives a more precise analysis of APA education and other characteristics.

College Preparation and Beyond. The relatively high rates of Asian Pacific American students bound for college over the past two decades is well documented. APAs have a higher expecta-

TABLE 3.
At-Risk APA Groups—Education: 25 years and older (percentage)

	Total Pop.	All APAs	At-Risk Groups							
			Vietnamese	Cambodian	Hmong	Laotian	Hawaiian	Samoan	Guamanian	Other P.I.
Less than 5th grade	2.7	6.9	11.4	40.7	54.9	33.9	1.3	4.3	4.7	6.0
High school or more	75	77.5	61.2	34.9	31.1	40	79	70.6	72.3	69.4
Some college	45.2	59.0	43.7	23.1	20.6	20.9	40.9	34.8	41.0	41.3
Bachelor's or more	20.3	36.6	17.4	5.7	4.9	5.4	11.9	8.0	10.0	9.5

Source: U.S. Department of Commerce, Bureau of the Census, *1990 Census of Population, Social and Economic Characteristics (CP-2-1)*, 1993.

TABLE 4.
Median Earnings of Full-Time Workers 25 Years Old and Over by Educational Attainment (in dollars) and Family Poverty Rate by Educational Attainment (by percentage)—1993

	U.S.	APA	White
Median Income			
Not high school grad	17,020	14,459	19,022
High school grad	22,719	21,076	24,124
Some college or assoc. deg.	27,003	29,481	27,932
Bachelor's degree or more	40,240	36,844	41,094
Family Poverty Rate			
Not a high school grad	27.5	41.0	17.8
High school grad	12.7	13.4	8.4
Bachelor's or more	2.4	7.0	1.9

Source: U.S. Department of Commerce, Bureau of the Census, 1994 Current Population Survey, *The Asian and Pacific Islander Population in the United States*, March 1994.

tion of going to college than other racial/ethnic groups. For high school seniors in 1992, 77 percent of APAs expected to attend and complete a two or four year college program as compared to all teens (67 percent), whites (67 percent), African Americans (63 percent), and Hispanics (46 percent). All groups showed a significant increase in expectations from 1972.[37] Similarly, the College Board found that APAs were 6 percent of college-bound students in 1987 and 9 percent by 1996.[38]

APA students were better prepared for college than other racial/ethnic groups. They earned more academic credits than other teens in 1994 with 57 percent of APA high school graduates completing the "New Basics" curriculum as compared to all teens (51 percent), whites (54 percent), African Americans (45 percent), and Hispanics and American Indians/Alaskan Natives (44 percent). Furthermore, 44 percent of APA seniors took 20 or more year-long academic courses before grad-

uation, similar in proportion to whites and more than Hispanics (37 percent), and African Americans (27 percent).[39]

APA achievements, however, were uneven. APA seniors were less proficient readers than white seniors and seniors as a whole and more proficient in mathematics and science than other groups.[40] The College Board reported that APA seniors scored lower on the SAT 1 Verbal (496) than did all students (505) or white students (526), but higher than all other racial/ethnic groups reported. On the SAT 1 Math, APAs scored an average of 558, higher than any other group reported. College-bound APA seniors in 1996 also showed a 17 points improvement in both verbal and math SAT scores when compared to their 1987 counterparts.[41]

Limited English proficiency has been found to restrict APA opportunities in the educational pipeline. For example, limited English skills are a barrier to college eligibility and transfer to four-year institutions in California for APA students. Whereas, in contrast, limited mathematics skills are a barrier for Latino students, who often also require improved English skills. College-bound APAs who do not meet the English requirements of four-year institutions attend community colleges where they accumulate a disproportionately higher rate of ESL units than other groups. These units are not transferable to B.A. granting institutions and extend the years required for APAs to finish college.[42]

In addition to college preparation, racial/ethnic groups differ in their persistence to finish college. For high school graduates in 1989–90 who sought a bachelor's degree, 69 percent of APA students either finished their bachelor's degree by 1994 or continued to be enrolled in a bachelor's degree program compared to 64 percent for all students, 65 percent for whites, 53 percent for African Americans, and 54 percent for Hispanics.[43]

In summary, many more high school APAs have higher expectations to attend and complete college, take more academic courses, are generally better prepared to begin college, and persist to completion. Limited English proficiency may reflect the foreign-born origins of many APA families and the failure of their U.S. school experiences to provide adequate training. This limits their educational choices. Higher APA math scores may be a product of students whose own parents are professionals and educated in math and science areas and/or the misperception by students, parents, teachers, and guidance counselors that limited English speakers by concentrating in math and science can find success without mastering English. Overall, APA expectations, preparation, and perseverance are factors that should translate into strong college attendance and degree completion.

Higher Education Participation. For the most part, except for limited census data that will be presented in this section, the available data on APAs in higher education is aggregated for all ethnic groups within the APA community. As explained earlier in this special focus, aggregated APA data homogenizes their experiences and provides a distorted picture of the educational participation of groups *within* the APA population. Lacking sufficient and adequate disaggregate data contributes to over generalized and sometimes spurious interpretations of the APA experience in higher education. Therefore, due caution must be taken when exploring APA higher education data.

Careful preparation for college by many Asian Pacific American students contributes to high eligibility and increased college enrollment. Their high education participation also mirrors the growth in the APA population since 1965. Between 1984-1995, APAs were the second fastest growing racial/ethnic group at the undergraduate level

(101.7 percent) and graduate level (105.4 percent) after Hispanics (104.4 percent and 112.5 percent, respectively) and the fastest growing group at the professional school level, increasing 233.3 percent. In 1995, APA students represented 5.6 percent of all students enrolled in higher education, including 5.7 percent of undergraduates, 4.4 percent of graduate students, and 10.1 percent of professional school students (see Tables 3, 4, and 5 for complete data on all racial/ ethnic groups).

Table 5 shows the percentage of persons 18 to 24 years old enrolled in college by race and sex. More than half of all APAs in this age group were enrolled in college during the reporting period. This rate exceeds the rate for the total population and for whites. It is more than double the rate for Blacks, Hispanics, and American Indians.

Disaggregating higher education data by gender reveals differences. Women in all racial/ethnic groups, with the exception of APAs, have made up more than half of all students enrolled in higher education since 1986. APA women lagged behind APA men until 1994 when they slightly exceeded the enrollment of APA men. From 1984 to 1995, the enrollment of APA women rose by 124 percent, the most of any group.[44] The increase in APA enrollment is due, in part, to this rise in APA female students.

The decennial U.S. census data provides some disaggregated data on APA education (Figure 1). There is great variability in college enrollment within the 18 to 24 years old APA population in the 1990 census. Participation rates ranged from a high of 66 percent for Chinese Americans to a low of 26 percent for Laotian Americans.

TABLE 5.

Percent of Persons 18 to 24 Years Old Enrolled in College by Race and Sex (By Percentage)

	APA	TOTAL U.S.	White	Black	Hispanic	American Indian
Total	55.1	34.4	36.8	27.1	22.9	21.6
Males	56.0	32.7	35.7	23.3	20.4	20.2
Females	54.1	36.0	37.9	30.8	25.7	23.2

Source: U.S. Department of Commerce, Bureau of the Census, *1990 Census of Population, Social and Economic Characteristics (CP-2-1)*, 1993.

Of the 797,000 of APAs who participated in higher education in 1995, 60 percent were enrolled in four-year institutions with the remainder enrolled in two-year institutions. In comparison, 61 percent of all students, 63 percent of whites, 58 percent of Blacks, 44 percent of His-panics, and 50 percent of American Indians were enrolled in four-year institutions.[45] Eighty percent of APAs were enrolled in public institutions as compared to 78 percent of all students, 77 percent of whites, 79 percent of Blacks, 86 percent of His-panics, and 87 percent of American Indians.[46]

Degrees Earned and Fields of Study

Associate degrees. In 1994, Asian Pacific Americans earned 3.4 percent of all associate degrees in contrast to 2.3 percent in 1985. While APA males earning associate degrees increased steadily, rising 53 percent between 1985 and 1993, APA females doubled their associate degrees earned in this period (132 percent). The significant rise in APA women earning associate degrees allowed them to surpass their male coun-terparts by 1990, something women in other racial/ethnic groups had accomplished at least five years earlier.

Bachelor's degrees. APAs earned 4.8 percent of all bachelor's degrees in 1994, an increase from 2.6 percent in 1985. The number of APA bachelor's degrees increased from 25,395 in 1985 to 55,660 in 1994, a rise of 119 percent. In comparison, whites earned 80 percent of all bach-elor's degrees in 1994, an increase of 13.3 percent since 1985, which included a decrease of 1.2

FIGURE 1

College Enrollment of Persons 18–24 by APA Ethnic Group (By Percentage)

Source: U.S. Department of Commerce, Bureau of the Census, *1990 Census of Population, Social and Economic Characteristics (CP-2-1)*, 1993.

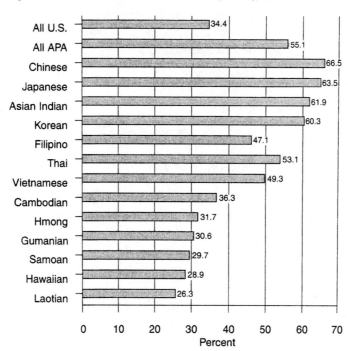

percent from 1993 to 1994. APA women made major gains in bachelor's degrees earned from 1985 to 1994 (increasing 142.6 percent) and reached parity with their male counterparts in 1992 when they obtained slightly more than half of all APA bachelor's degrees.

In 1994, APAs received nearly 10 percent of all science and engineering bachelor's degrees, but only 1 percent of education bachelor's degrees. They earned 5 percent of all bachelor's degrees in business and similar proportions in arts (4.7 percent), social sciences (4.6 percent), health (4.1 percent), and humanities (3.2 percent).

Business was the leading field of study selected by APAs at the bachelor's degree level in 1994, as it was for all students. Large numbers of APAs also majored in engineering-related fields, the social sciences, sciences, and the humanities. Health, arts, and education were selected by relatively small numbers of APA students (Figure 2).[47]

Fields selected by APA bachelor's degree earners varied by gender (Table 6). APA women dominated degrees in health-related subjects, education, humanities, and the arts. They slightly outnumbered APA men in the social sciences and business, but were surpassed by men in the sciences. APA men dominated engineering and engineering-related fields (77.6 percent), but less than the dominance of men in general in these fields of study (82 percent of all engineering bachelor's degrees).

Thus while engineering and the sciences are often selected fields of study by APAs, especially males, APA bachelor's degrees earned are distributed among all fields of study. APAs resembled

FIGURE 2

Bachelor's Degrees by Selected Fields—1994: APAs vs. Total Degree Earners (By Percentage)

Source: U.S. Department of Education, National Center for Education Statistics, Integrated Postsecondary Education Data System (IPEDS), "Completions" Survey.

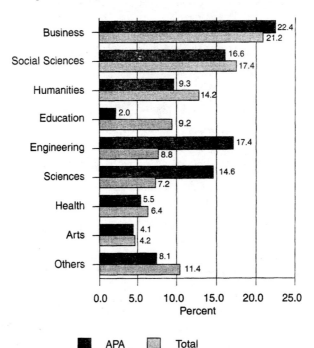

TABLE 6.

Number of APA Bachelor's Degrees Earned by Field and Percent of APA Women by Field—1994

	APA Men	APA Women	APA Total	% APA Women
Health	709	2361	3070	76.9
Education	270	852	1122	76.0
Humanities	1845	3339	5184	64.4
Arts	826	1455	2281	63.8
Social sciences	3962	5287	9249	57.2
Business	5619	6867	12,486	55.0
Sciences	4258	3895	8153	47.8
Engineering/ Computer sci.	7515	2164	9679	22.4
Other	1934	2502	4436	56.4
All Fields	26,938	28,722	55,660	51.6

Source: U.S. Department of Education, National Center for Education Statistics, Integrated Postsecondary Education Data System (IPEDS), "Completions" Survey, 1996.

all students in the selection of business as their first major and APA choices reflect gender differences. These data suggest that the stereotype of the APA math and science "nerd" is clearly a misperception. American-born and middle class APAs are also less likely to choose math and applied science careers than males from immigrant and working class families.[48] Hence, with each generation of American-born proceeding to college there is likely to be an even broader range of fields of study among APA students.

Master's degrees. APAs showed a strong and steady gain in master's degrees over the past decade, earning 4.0 percent (15,267) of all such degrees in 1994 compared to 2.8 percent (7,782) in 1985. In comparison, whites obtained 74.8 percent of all master's degrees in 1994, while African Americans accounted for 5.7 percent, Hispanics 3.1 percent, and American Indians 0.4 percent.

Of all master's degree earners, APAs were significantly represented in engineering/computer sciences (9.8 percent) and the sciences (6.0 percent). They earned 4.9 percent of all business degrees and were relatively small proportions of master's degree recipients in the arts (3.9 percent), health (3.6 percent), humanities (3.1 percent), social sciences (2.8 percent), and education (1.6 percent).[49]

Among APA master's degree recipients, 30 percent were in business in 1994, which parallels that of all master's degree recipients (Figure 3). Engineering and computer science accounted for 25.9 percent of APA master's degrees, which was significantly greater than the proportion for all degree earners (10.4 percent). APAs also earned 5.9 percent of all science master's degrees, slightly more than for all degree earners (3.9 percent). Education accounted for only 10 percent of APA master's degrees, in contrast to 25.7 percent for all degree earners. The proportion of master's degrees in all other fields was similar for APAs and the total population.

Women, in general, have earned more than half of all master's degrees each year since at least 1985. However, unlike all other racial/ethnic groups, APA women have yet to reach parity with APA male master's degree recipients. APA women more than doubled their master's degrees earned from 1985 to 1994 (up 139.5 percent), but accounted for only 46 percent of APA master's degrees in 1994. APA women outnumbered APA men in education, health, arts, humanities, and social sciences master's degrees, but were underrepresented in business, sciences, and engineering/computer sciences degrees (Table 7). Clearly, choice of master's fields continues to be

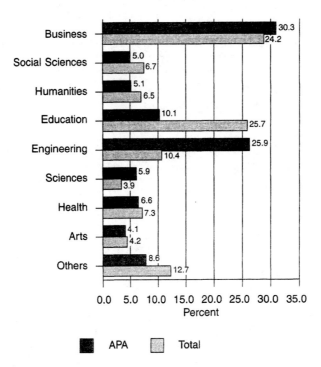

FIGURE 3
Master's Degrees by Selected Fields—1994: APAs vs.
Total Degree Earners (By Percentage)
Source: U.S. Department of Education, National Center for Education
Statistics, Integrated Postsecondary Education Data System (IPEDS),
"Completions" Survey.

gender-based. APA women are making gains at this level, although they continue to lag behind women in other racial/ethnic groups.

First Professional Degrees.[50] In 1994, APAs earned 7.8 percent (5,892) of all first professional degrees, an increase of 224.4 percent since 1985. While APA women continued to earn fewer first professional degrees than APA men (2,678 versus 3,214), they made the greatest gains of any racial/ethnic group, increasing 303 percent since 1985. Women in all racial/ethnic groups made major strides in first professional degrees over the past decade. However, they have yet to reach parity with their male counterparts.

Law and medicine accounted for 53 percent and 20.4 percent, respectively, of all first professional degrees conferred in 1994. APAs, on the other

hand, preferred medicine over law with 39 percent and 30.4 percent of their professional degrees in these fields, respectively. Dentistry was also a more popular degree for APAs (9 percent) than for all first professional degree earners (5 percent).[51]

APA men and women are earning first professional degrees in larger proportion than doctorates when compared to others. The ratio in 1994 for APAs was 5.3 professional degrees for every one doctorate earned compared to a ratio of 2.7 for all U.S. citizens and permanent residents, 2.5 for whites, 4.0 for Blacks, 3.5 for Hispanics, and 2.6 for American Indians. Perhaps APAs view first professional studies as having greater job security, prestige, and earning power than doctoral studies. This lends support to the hypothesis that APAs select education, training, and fields of study based on economic concerns rather than a

TABLE 7.
Number of APA Master's Degrees Earned by Field and Percent of APA Women by Field—1994

	APA Men	APA Women	APA Total	% APA Women
Health	311	696	1007	69.1
Education	405	1129	1534	73.6
Humanities	328	445	773	57.6
Arts	139	249	388	64.2
Social Sciences	323	438	761	57.6
Business	2752	1873	4625	40.1
Sciences	489	409	898	45.6
Engineering/				
Computer Sci.	2929	1011	3940	25.7
Other	549	792	1341	59.0
All Fields	8225	7042	15,267	46.1

Source: U.S. Department of Education, National Center for Education Statistics, Integrated Postsecondary Education Data System (IPEDS), "Completions" Survey, 1996.

presumed notion of fulfilling a cultural attribute of respect for education.

Doctorates. In 1995, American higher education produced 41,610 doctorates of which 27,603 were earned by U.S. citizens. APA U.S. citizens received 2.7 percent (1,138) of all doctorates earned or 4.1 percent of doctorates earned by U.S. citizens that year. In contrast, international students from Asia earned eight times the number of doctorates in 1995 as Asian Pacific Americans or 21 percent (8,558) of all doctorates earned.

APA doctorates have generally received all or most of their education in the U.S. and are not to be confused with Asian doctorates, most of whom were first educated in Asia, arrived in the U.S. as graduate students, and most often return to their countries of origin for employment. Many foreign students do remain in the U.S., become permanent residents and citizens, and find employment in industry and higher education. Observers of American colleges and universities often misconstrue Asian foreign students and APA students leading to the misperception that Asian Pacific Americans are overrepresented in higher education, which they are not. Separating APAs from Asian foreign students results in a modest representation of APAs at the doctoral level.

APA doctorates grew by 120 percent from 1985 to 1995 with an even more impressive gain (149 percent) recorded by APA women. Nonetheless, their absolute numbers, especially female doctorates, remain modest. APA females received 468 doctorates in 1995 or 41.1 percent of all APA doctorates, while women generally earned 46 percent of all U.S. doctorates that year. With the exception of African Americans, women continued to earn fewer doctorates than men in every racial/ethnic group, which has implications for women in the higher education employment pipeline, and partially explains their increasing, but still limited presence as faculty.

Within fields of study and for U.S. citizens only in 1995, APAs earned 255 or 10.7 percent of all doctorates in engineering. They also earned 266 doctorates in the life sciences (5.3 percent), 223 in the physical sciences (6.1 percent), 168 in the social sciences (3.3 percent), 81 in the humanities (2.0 percent), and 80 in education (1.4 percent). They appear well represented in engineering, life sciences, and physical sciences, but were underrepresented in the remaining fields of study.

Of the 1,138 APA doctoral degrees earned in 1995, most were in the life sciences (23.4 percent), engineering (22.5 percent), and the physical sciences (19.6 percent) (Figure 4). While APAs complete doctorates in the social sciences (14.8 percent), education (8.0 percent), and humanities (7.0 percent), their absolute numbers remain small compared to all doctorates awarded in these fields. APA doctoral degree recipients are more concentrated in science and engineering than at the bachelor's or master's levels, which reflect the interests of the larger APA male enrollment at the doctoral degree level as compared to APA women.

The Educational Pipeline: Opportunities and Barriers

The educational pipeline of Asian Pacific Americans in higher education since 1985 shows a strong and steady increase of students, especially at the bachelor's, master's, and first professional levels. This increase is partially demographic reflecting the growth in the overall APA population with the arrival of large numbers of immigrants and refugees since 1965. It is also part of a general increase in college and university enrollment as Americans of all racial/ethnic groups and socio-economic characteristics pursue higher education opportunities.

APA selection of fields of study at the bachelor's and master's levels, challenge their stereotype as primarily science and engineering majors. Their interests and career goals are complex, diverse, and gender-based, and not unlike other students. The diversification in APA fields of study at the doctoral level, while growing, is still somewhat restricted to science and engineering.

The APA pipeline, however, is not free flowing, and is constricted by gender and at the doctorate level. The little research that has been done on APA women in education suggests that there are structural and societal barriers that limit their progress. Mainstream American and APA cultures continue to view women's proper place as in the domestic sphere with roles as homemakers and caretakers. Education is important for women, but too much of it, it is believed, is likely to jeopardize a woman's marriage opportunities and her traditional role. In APA immigrant and working class households, in

FIGURE 4
Doctoral Degree by Selected Fields—1995: APAs vs. Total
Degree Earners (By Percentage)
Source: National Research Council, Doctorate Records File, 1995.

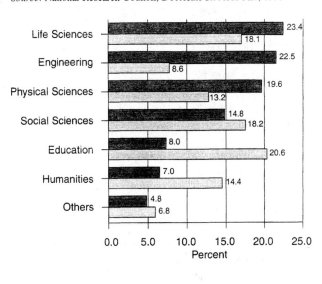

particular, children's help is especially critical to a family's economic well-being. Even as APA families support the education of both men and women, young women are expected to assume household responsibilities. They spend more time cooking, cleaning, and caring for younger siblings than their brothers. Hence some APA adolescent women select a less academic course of study in high school or limit their ambition to the B.A. level. This is compounded by the gender stereotyping of teachers and counselors leaving some APA women less academically prepared for college eligibility and college work than their male counterparts and with restricted educational and career goals.[52]

APA women who pursue higher education share a belief with their male counterparts in education as a necessity for economic survival. However, gender discrimination continues through the higher education pipeline. APA women, like women of all racial/ethnic groups, experience a "chilly climate" in universities and colleges where 66 percent of the faculty presently are men. Women continue to be valued less than men in the curriculum, the classroom, meetings with advisors, and in consideration for research and other opportunities. Hence qualified APA women are often not identified for and supported by faculty for graduate studies.[53] Moreover, they are frequently stereotyped as exotic sexual beings rather than as academics in their own right and experience sexual harassment, complicating their efforts to achieve educationally.[54] Thus the APA gender gap reflects women's inequality overall.

The APA pipeline is also constricted at the doctoral level where APA doctorates have not been commensurate with the numbers of bachelor's and master's degrees earned. The small number of APAs in doctoral programs is only partially explained by their choice of first professional studies in greater proportion than doctoral studies. The campus climate remains race- and gender-biased. The "chilly climate" that women experience in the pipeline is also experienced by racial minorities.

Numerous campus climate and other studies point to formal policies and informal practices

that limit minority doctorates even in a period of affirmative action, which is now under siege. APAs are generally overlooked having been deemed a "model minority" and not in need of advisement. They note the lack of staff who are sensitive to their academic and personal concerns. They are also marginalized in the curriculum. This unwelcoming academic climate plays a role in doctoral recruitment. The doctoral process itself is a barrier because of its exclusivity. Based on an apprenticeship model, it continues to rely on the willingness of faculty to serve as mentors. APAs and other students of color speak of the lack of faculty mentors generally, the small number of faculty of color and women on American campuses, the lack of courses that reflect their interests, such as Asian American Studies, and the difficulties they often encounter in having their perspectives and research interests respected and taken into consideration by faculty.[55]

Hence affirmative action remains an essential component of access and equity for APAs, but is only a first step. The progress of APAs in the educational pipeline cannot be measured solely in quantitative terms, but must also include the quality of their educational experience.

HIGHER EDUCATION EMPLOYMENT

Faculty profile. APA faculty increased steadily from 1983 to 1991, but declined by −4.8 percent between 1991 and 1993, the last reporting period. They were 4.7 percent of full-time faculty in 1993, which was down from 1991, but more than in 1983. APA faculty losses between 1991 and 1993 were due to a −7.7 percent decline in male full-time faculty at the junior ranks of assistant professor (−19.0 percent), instructor and lecturer (−11.1 percent), and other faculty (−28.3 percent), which was not offset by the 5.0 percent increase in APA female faculty in this period.

While the decrease of APA males at the junior level should be of concern, it may reflect a methodological change adopted in 1993 when the category "nonresident aliens" was added to the possible list of race/ethnicity selections, providing another classification for enumerating faculty. Up to 1991, racial/ethnic counts of faculty included non-resident aliens within other racial categories, including APAs. One estimate noted that foreign nationals comprised 42 percent of all full-time APA faculty in 1991, an increase from 40 percent in 1989.[56] Therefore, faculty data for APAs prior to 1991 included significant numbers of Asian foreign nationals, many of whom were first educated in their homelands then, for the most part, received their doctorates in the U.S., and were likely in the process of becoming permanent residents or citizens. Given the large numbers of Asian foreign nationals in doctoral programs and higher education employment, a negative effect on the enumeration of APA faculty is likely when Asian nonresident aliens are removed from the APA racial category and counted separately as was seen in 1993. The precise impact of this change on the tabulation of APA faculty, however, is not known. Trends in the hiring of APA male faculty over the next few years bear careful attention to determine if the negative growth of APA male faculty is mostly a statistical artifact or early signs of faculty hiring problems.[57]

The APA faculty profile is also changing. APA female faculty continue to grow, but still lag well behind their male counterparts. They nearly doubled their numbers from 1983 to 1993 (3,222 to 6,326), but APA men still comprise two-thirds of all APA faculty (Table 8). APA women have the largest gender gap of any racial/ethnic group.

Table 8 considers APA faculty by rank and sex in 1993. APA women comprised 25 percent of all full-time APA faculty and were concentrated at the junior ranks with the majority at the untenured level. They made up only 11.2 percent of all APA full professors. In contrast, APA males were concentrated at the full professor level with smaller numbers at the junior ranks. This trend in conjunction with the low tenure rate of APAs (discussed below) raises a serious issue for their faculty renewal and representation if there are fewer junior faculty moving through the ranks to replace a larger group of retiring senior faculty.

APA full-time faculty teach in most disciplines. However, their concentrations reflect interests that have become gender-biased. APA male faculty have a higher representation than their overall proportion in engineering, computer sciences, natural sciences, and first professional disciplines. APA female faculty are represented higher than their overall proportion in foreign languages and are well represented in the health sciences, especially nursing.[58]

Finally, no data on APA faculty could be found which disaggregates APA faculty by ethnic groups. Hence, disparities in ethnic group representation and progress have not been examined. Further study on APA faculty should give attention to their ethnic diversity or lack of it in recruitment and retention.

Tenure rate. Tenure rate varies by race and sex. Whites hold the highest rate of all racial/ethnic groups and men are tenured at a higher rate than women in each of the major

TABLE 8.
Number of APA Full-Time Faculty by Rank and Sex and Percent of APA Women by Rank—1993

	All Ranks	*Full*	*Associate*	*Assistant*	*Instructor/lecturer*	*Other*
All APA	25,269	7,033	5,471	7,586	2,700	2,479
APA males	18,943	6,245	4,367	5,277	1,390	1,664
APA females	6,326	788	1,104	2,309	1,310	815
% female	25%	11.2	20.2	30.4	48.5	32.9

Source: U.S. Department of Education, National Center for Education Statistics, "EEO-6 Higher Education Staff Information" Survey, 1994.

racial/ethnic groups. In 1983, APAs had the lowest tenure rate for all racial/ethnic groups at 61 percent, which rose modestly to 64 percent by 1993, compared to 71 percent for all faculty in both years. The tenure rate of APA males was 62 percent in 1983 and 67 percent by 1993 compared to 55 percent and 52 percent, respectively, for APA female faculty.[59] APA women have the lowest tenure rate for all racial/ethnic groups and have lost ground over the decade.

Administrative profile. APAs were less than one percent of all chief executive officers in higher education in 1996. Of the 20 APA presidents of colleges and universities, the majority of male APA presidents were found in 4-year institutions, while the only 2 female APA presidents headed 2-year institutions. Like other forms of management in government and the corporate world, APAs are poorly represented in higher levels of university administration, reflecting once again the "glass ceiling."[60]

Higher Education Employment: Opportunities and Barriers

APA faculty trends suggest a modest increase over the past decade, reflecting a general trend for faculty of color. The small numbers of APA female faculty generally and their concentration at the junior ranks along with the uncertainly of APA male recruitment at the entry levels is of concern.

The modest and uneven representation of APA faculty on American campuses is a reflection of their own choices and institutional barriers. In one study that looked at 1992 U.S. doctorate recipients, APAs were the least likely (26.6 percent) to plan employment with educational institutions compared to all U.S. doctorates (44.9 percent), whites (45.3 percent), African Americans (54.8 percent), Mexican Americans (54.1 percent), and American Indians (44.8 percent). APA doctorates in engineering, life sciences, and physical sciences have career opportunities in industry and self-employment as well as higher

education. Many find private industry a more secure and remunerative option than the academy. In addition, some APAs are wary of a faculty appointment, given the low tenure rate.[61]

For APAs seeking a career in higher education, opportunities are elusive. A recent study on faculty recruitment efforts over a five-year period finds that concerted efforts by colleges and universities to diversify their faculty in a tight job market is a myth and not reality. Recent highly qualified doctorates of all racial/ethnic groups, including white males, noted the many biases that still persist against minorities and women in the hiring process. Female and minority applicants interviewed for the study refuted the belief that they were being hotly pursued by institutions and were the recipients of competitive offers. Faculty recruitment and hiring has not changed significantly and faculty diversification, including the incorporation of APA faculty, remains largely rhetoric rather than action.[62] Low levels of APA faculty recruitment may also be an unintended consequence of the "model minority" stereotype, whereby it is believed that APAs are overrepresented in higher education and not in need of affirmative action policies.

Like other faculty of color and white women, APA faculty experience an unsupportive climate in higher education. Studies on the "revolving door," the "chilly climate," and campus climates disclose the overt and subtle ways in which they are treated differently. Institutions often view diverse faculty as replaceable parts rather than as long-term investments. APA faculty report little support and mentoring from their departments and a lack of respect for issues of importance to them. They are consulted when diversity issues arise, but rarely as colleagues with academic expertise. On those occasions when their specialization and skills are sought, they are expected to be "superstars." APAs generally carry a heavier workload than white male counterparts because of additional student advisement and committee service and the preparation of new courses in response to student demands. APA faculty with interests in "new" scholarship, such as ethnic studies and women's studies, find their research is given less value in tenure, promotion, and merit increase decisions. Most are "solo" in their department and are frequently seen as tokens. APA faculty experience racial and sexual incidents from students and staff as well as faculty.[63]

APA faculty also find bias in other areas. Their salaries are generally lower than their white counterparts even when rank and college affiliation are taken into consideration. English proficiency is an issue and is often perceived rather than real. Many APA faculty find that the perception of English language deficiency, such as speaking with an Asian accent, can be used to restrict their career advancement. APAs have filed language and accent discrimination grievances with the EEOC in other employment areas. In addition, higher education institutions provide little support for those with real language difficulties. Cultural bias in leadership styles and faculty participation can be a career impediment when they contribute to the marginalization of APA faculty from important department and university committees. Rate of promotion and tenure is also an issue. APA faculty at one institution were asked by their respective chairs to delay their request for promotion to enable non-APA colleagues to be put up before them.[64]

The low tenure rate of APA faculty raises serious questions about their equal treatment in higher education. That APAs from across the ethnic groups and disciplines and in a range of higher education institutions, large and small, public and private, have charged bias in their tenure review indicate that the problem is widespread. The increasing number of cases involving female APA faculty reflect an additional obstacle of sexual discrimination and suggest that women's growing presence on American campuses may be a challenge to traditional academe. A number of cases, such as that of Dr. Rosalind Tung, which was cited earlier in this special focus, were successfully challenged, but they reveal only the tip of the iceberg on bias cases against APAs. In many more cases, APAs like other minority and female faculty are unwilling to endure the long drawn out, often politicized, and highly secretive battle against higher education institutions which are better funded and can afford to hire legal teams.[65]

APAs seeking administrative positions find barriers. Many APAs assert that they are not being identified, mentored, or recruited for university management. Like faculty, they cite cultural biases, including disrespect for their leadership styles, perceived language limitations, such as speaking with an accent, and other forms of subtle discrimination as obstacles in the administrative career ladder.[66] Leadership training programs have not targeted APA faculty.

The discrepancy between APA faculty qualifications and scholarly achievements and their low tenure rate and underrepresentation in higher levels of university administration has drawn the attention of other researchers who have called for higher education to examine their policies and practices towards Asian Pacific Americans for obstacles in their progress in the pipeline.[67] While there are opportunities for APAs in higher education employment, structural barriers based on race, class, and gender, cultural biases, and questions of academic legitimacy in faculty research interests serve as impediments. Overall, an unwelcoming climate still exists on American campuses impacting the quality of the APA workplace environment as well. Hence, in higher education employment, there is little evidence of a "model minority" or "success story" here.

Consequently, APAs strongly support affirmative action. When the controversial Proposition 209, a California ballot initiative seeking to eliminate affirmative action in public employment, public education, and public contracting in the state, was passed by the voters of California in November, 1996, APAs voted 61 percent against the measure statewide and 76 percent against it in the four Southern California county areas where the largest number of APAs reside. The latter poll found bipartisan opposition to Proposition 209.[68] While there are differences of opinion among APAs on whether affirmative action helps or hurts their educational access and employment, the majority of APAs conclude that affirmative action or alternative policies and programs to ensure equal opportunities continue to be necessary until an equitable society is achieved.[69]

CONCLUSIONS AND RECOMMENDATIONS

Asian Pacific Americans are a complex and dynamic population, comprised of many different ethnic groups. Some APAs share similar cultures, socio-economic backgrounds, and experiences in the U.S., and some differ significantly. APAs include Hawaiians who are indigenous to the U.S., some communities with over a century of history in America, and new immigrants and refugees who arrived very recently. Their composition and definition remain quite fluid.

While the term APA implies commonalties within this community, it also obscures differences within and among ethnic groups that require attention. Disaggregating data on APAs helps identify issues that may be overlooked by educators, researchers, and policy-makers. Thus collecting both aggregated and disaggreggated data on APAs and the ethnic groups within the APA category is critical to understanding and serving this segment of the U.S. population.

Changes in U.S. immigration and refugee policies since 1965 have transformed the APA community into one of the fastest growing and most diverse racial/ethnic groups in the U.S. New APA communities have changed the ethnic composition and broadened the range of socio-economic characteristics within the APA population. They have also impacted American institutions, especially education and social services. While recent arrivals coincided with civil rights legislation, APAs continue to experience racial discrimination and other biases that limit their advancement and rewards, irrespective of high educational attainment, resulting in slower rates of career advancement and confrontations with the "glass ceiling" in many professions.

From their initial settlements in the mid 19th century to the present, APAs have sought access and equity in education and have challenged discriminatory treatment in the courts and other fora. Their actions have resulted in a number of landmark U.S. Supreme Court cases which have helped redefine equality of treatment in American education and benefited other Americans.

Historically, APAs have had a negative image as "yellow and brown hordes." Only recently have APAs been seen as a "model minority" whose educational achievements, it is argued, derive from their "Asian cultures" or from their "immigrant ethos." New research provides alternative interpretations as to why APAs concentrate significant effort in education and give greater attention to structural and societal factors in explaining APA educational trends. When asked, APAs express the view that education is a necessary means to achieve social mobility in this racially stratified society and a "hedge" against discrimination much more often than they cite some cultural tenet. New studies also give attention to the social costs APAs bear in trying to comply with the "model minority" image and to the multiple ways in which students respond to the stereotype. Some APA ethnic groups are at-risk educationally, challenging the notion of the "model minority." More research is needed to illuminate the complexities and disparities of APA educational progress.

Over the past three decades, APAs changed from a largely U.S.-born population to a predominantly foreign-born population of new immigrants and refugees who speak a language other than English. While they are found in every region of the U.S., they reside mostly in six states. APAs are concentrated "inside urbanized areas," which are high cost/high income locales. They generally live as married-couple families in larger households than the U.S. population and whites. They also live in more crowded conditions and pay more for their housing, both in home ownership and rent, than the U.S. population and whites.

Their economic profile is complex and diverse. Any analysis of their economic progress must take into account their concentration in high cost/high income areas, their larger family size, and the number of wage earners per family. APAs are significantly more economically secure than other peoples of color, but as individuals and families they have not reached parity with whites in median family income, per capita income, or level of poverty. High poverty rates among certain sectors, especially Southeast Asians and Pacific Islanders, deserve special attention. The image of APAs as a "success story" obstructs concern and support for those who are at-risk within the population.

APAs have a higher rate of labor participation than the general population and are in a wide range of occupational categories. The U.S. census categories are unsatisfactory in interpreting APA employment. Manager, for example, combines data on salaried administrators in private and non-profit sectors with the self-employed, which in the case of APAs can range from economically marginal small family businesses to large and profitable high tech firms.

Overall, APAs have high educational attainment compared to other racial/ethnic groups. A closer examination of APA data reveals wide differences within and among APA groups and includes a bimodal education pattern which reflects a socio-economically bifurcated population. In conjunction with high rates of college completion, APAs have high rates for those with 8th grade or less. Southeast Asian groups, many of whom arrived as refugees, and Pacific Islander groups, who are largely native to the U.S. and wholly educated here, are educationally at-risk. APA women, in general, obtain less education than their male counterparts.

APA men and women have higher expectations and are more academically prepared for college than other groups. Those with limited English skills, however, have restricted choices in the educational pipeline.

APA enrollment in higher education has increased considerably since 1970 and mirrors their growth in the population. APAs are more diverse in their fields of study than the "model minority" image purports and can be found in all disciplines and fields at the bachelor's and master's levels. Business, for example, was their first choice at the B.A. and M.A. levels. APA doctoral choices are becoming more diverse, but are still concentrated in the sciences and engineering. These foci reflect the predominance of males in Ph.D. studies and the perception of more secure employment opportunities in engineering and the sciences in comparison to fields in the liberal arts.

APA doctoral enrollment is not commensurate with the numbers of APAs who earn B.A.'s and M.A.'s. APAs are five times more likely to obtain a first professional degree than a doctorate. It may be that medicine, law, and dentistry have greater value for APAs than doctorates and lends support to the argument that education is viewed by APAs as an economic necessity rather than some "orientalized" interpretation of the data.

The APA educational pipeline is not free flowing. There are impediments for some APA groups at the B.A. level, for women generally, and for all APAs at the doctoral level. APA men and women are well represented at the associate's and bachelor's degrees level. APA women have lagged behind APA men at all degree levels. Beliefs in women's proper place as being in the domestic sphere and not the public sphere, the stereotyping of APA women as "exotics" and not academics, the privileging of men in the curriculum and classroom, and other aspects of the "chilly climate" that women face generally in higher education, impede APA women in the pipeline. Inhospitable classroom and campus climates, the lack of diverse faculty as mentors, the selectivity of the Ph.D. process, and the "model minority" image are other explanations for the modest representation of APAs at the doctorate level. Thus while APAs are taking advantage of educational opportunities, they also experience barriers, particularly at the doctorate level. Affirmative action policies remain imperative for APA access to higher education, especially graduate studies. The quality of their academic life is also a concern.

Until recently, APA faculty data included Asian educated and trained faculty, most of whom are in the sciences and engineering. Inclusion of non-resident aliens or foreign students within the APA category also obscures the actual state of APAs in higher education. A wide disparity exists between the proportion of APA faculty and the proportion of APA students on American campuses with little reason for optimism in closing this gap in the near future without the active and knowledgeable intervention of colleges and universities.

APA employment in higher education is not commensurate with doctoral degrees earned. APAs have demonstrated a modest increase in their numbers as faculty, but recent negative trends bear close attention. APA faculty have the widest gender gap for all racial/ethnic groups. Many APA doctorates choose private industry rather than higher education employment. APAs also have a low tenure rate. Hence APA faculty recruitment, retention, and renewal are issues to consider as senior faculty retire with smaller numbers of junior faculty being recruited to replace them. In addition, lack of mentorship, workload issues, and unequal treatment in tenure, promotion, and salaries hinder APAs in the higher education employment pipeline.

In the area of management, APAs are less than one percent of higher education administrators. Here again, the relatively high educational attainment of APAs does not transmit into comparable economic rewards and career advancement. Obstructions in the path to university management include cultural biases, perceived language limitations, accent discrimination, and lack of recruitment and mentorship. The small numbers of APAs who serve as university and college administrators and presidents are reflections again of the "glass ceiling."

Asian Pacific Americans are changing the educational landscape. Their educational accomplishments are significant, but are not shared by all APAs. Educational differences by gender, within an APA ethnic group, and among APA groups, require attention. Barriers and unequal rewards remain in the educational pipeline and in employment. In a time when the need for affirmative action is being seriously challenged, one need only consider the level of educational attainment and higher education employment of all peoples of color and to conclude that equity has yet to be achieved. The educational trends of African Americans, Latinas/os, and American Indians, both men and women, are of critical concern. This special focus has given attention to Asian Pacific Americans and their complexities and disparities. The following is a set of recommendations to address some of the issues raised in this study. They are not prioritized.

Recommendation 1: Demythologizing APAs as a "Model Minority"

Strong faculty, administrative, and staff development should be organized on campuses to demythologize Asian Pacific Americans as a "model minority" and to de-"orientalize" their educational aspirations and choices. Faculty, administrators, and staff must develop broader and "humanized" views of this group and understand the complexities and variabilities within the APA population, many of whom require attention and academic assistance. APA students and faculty are complex individuals and should not be treated on the basis of predetermined stereotypes.

Recommendation 2: Support for Affirmative Action

Racial and sex discrimination and other biases still exist. Affirmative action policies and programs in the educational system are still needed to remedy historic disadvantages and continuing unequal treatment in American society and its institutions, including the educational system. APAs should be included in affirmative action remedies. Institutions should revisit their policies and programs on a regular basis and revise them to address new population groups and expanding definitions of equity and quality education. A diverse student body, faculty, staff, and adminis-

tration benefits all members of the higher education community and the society at-large.

Recommendation 3: Changing Campus Climate

All colleges and universities should be positive,
thoughtful, and understanding environments for
APA students, faculty, and staff regardless of their
numbers on campus. All colleges and universities
should make every effort to include the APA
experience in their faculty and staff development.
Numerous campus climate reports have proposed
recommendations to address the "chilly climate"
for minorities and women. All higher education
institutions should ensure that APAs are included
in these remedies and that APA concerns are
addressed.

All colleges and universities need to distinguish
between real English language deficiency and perceived deficiency, for example, bias against Asian
accents, and prevent language bias in the recruitment and retention of students, faculty, staff, and
administrators. All colleges and universities should
establish open lines of communications between
faculty and administrators and APA students and
community to ensure and encourage dialogue and
a shared campus community.

Recommendation 4: Language Development Programs

Strong English language development programs
are needed for many APAs. Colleges and universities should collaborate with their K–12 partners and
local APA communities to develop English-as-a-
Second Language intervention programs for students who otherwise succeed in school. Narrowing
educational and career choices of APAs because of
lack of English preparation should not be tolerated.
Successful APA students focusing in the math and
science areas should be required to excel in English
language competency as well, and not be allowed to
progress under the illusion that English language
skills are not critical to these fields or to their

futures. Acquiring English language proficiency
involves the cooperation and support of K–12, students and their families, academic counselors,
faculty, and the education system, in general.

Greater support should be given to the
enhancement of existing Asian language programs on American campuses and to the development of language programs that reflect the new
Asian language groups in the U.S.

Recommendation 5: Curriculum Transformation and Infusion

In order to prepare all students for a multicultural
and global world, all colleges and universities
should ensure that their academic programs
reflect the diversity within the United States and
the world-at-large, and not simply the diversity in
their local communities. All colleges and universities should ensure that APAs are properly
included and treated within their mission and programmatic planning. The experiences and roles of
APAs in American society should be a part of the
curriculum in all colleges and universities.
Teacher education and related training, in particular, need to incorporate the APA experience in
their curriculum and practice. Departments, programs, and courses in Asian American Studies
should be encouraged and supported. In addition,
APA related materials should be infused
throughout the curriculum and all institutional
programs. Percentage of APAs on campus or in
the local community should not be the rationale
for including or excluding discussions on this
segment of the American mosaic.

Recommendation 6: Focus on High-risk APA Groups

Special attention should be focused on high-risk
ethnic groups within the APA population. The
large numbers of Southeast Asians who are at-risk
are likely a consequence of their being refugees
and adjustment issues may take several decades
to overcome. For Pacific Islanders, risk is more

complicated, since for the most part, their entire life and educational experience have been within the American context. More focused research and intervention programs should be designed to assist these high-risk APA groups.

Recommendation 7: Focus on APA Women and Gender Inequity

All colleges and universities should focus on the limited representation and quality of the educational experience of women generally, and APA women, specifically. APA women should be properly included and treated in the curriculum and all aspects of academic programming and campus life. Special attention should be given to the recruitment and retention of APA women, especially in graduate studies, and as faculty and administrators. Changing gender inequity for APA women in higher education involves the collaboration and support of K–12, students and their families, academic counselors, faculty, and the education system, in general.

Recommendation 8: Doctoral Recruitment and Retention

Strong recruitment and retention programs should be designed at doctoral degree granting universities to encourage APAs to pursue doctoral degrees. Articulation programs should be developed with four-year institutions having large numbers of APA students. All colleges and universities should identify and mentor qualified APA undergraduates for opportunities in graduate studies. Special attention should be given to ensure representation of APA women and the diversity of APA ethnic groups. Colleges and universities should distinguish between their Asian Pacific American graduate students and Asian foreign students. All doctoral programs should provide the necessary supports to their APA students, including faculty mentors, fellowships, research and publication opportunities, and other aid, to ensure their successful completion of the degree.

Recommendation 9: Opening the Higher Education Employment Pipeline

Strong faculty, staff, and administrator recruitment programs should be developed at all colleges and universities to ensure an open employment pipeline. Special attention should be focused on APA women at all levels, APA men at the junior faculty levels, and to ensure a diverse representation of APA ethnic groups. All colleges and universities should identify structural, attitudinal, and programmatic barriers that may account for the poor hiring and tenure rate of APA faculty and the lack of APA administrators.

Development of APA administrators, especially at levels of deans and higher, needs to be a top priority in higher education. National higher education organizations, government agencies, and foundations should concentrate effort in the development and mentorship of APA leaders and strong leadership training programs should be developed and supported.

Recommendation 10: Fostering Research on APAs

More data and better qualitative and quantitative research on Asian Pacific Americans should be supported. Very little is known about APAs in general, and especially of high-risk groups. Aggregated data, most commonly found in educational studies, are replete with problems. All institutional research offices in higher education should be encouraged to disaggregate campus data on APAs.

NOTES

1. In this paper, white refers to non-Hispanic whites; Hispanic origin refers to Hispanics of any race; American Indian includes American Indians, Eskimos, and Aleuts; and black is used interchangeably with African American. Asian Pacific Americans are defined in the Overview. The ACE report and tables may use slightly different definitions.

2. Lee, Stacey J. *Unraveling the "Model Minority" Stereotype.* New York: Teachers College Press, 1996, 3–5. See also Hune, Shirley. "Rethinking Race: Paradigms and Policy Formation." *Amerasia Journal* 21:1&2, 1995, 29–40.

3. McClain, Charles J. *In Search of Equality.* Berkeley: University of California Press, 1994, 134–144 and Wollenberg, Charles M. *All Deliberate Speed.* Berkeley: University of California Press, 1976, 28–47.

4. McClain, 1994.

5. Wollenberg, 1976, 48–72.

6. McClain, 1994 and Berry, Mary Frances and John W. Blassingame. *Long Memory: The Black Experience in America.* New York: Oxford University Press, 1982.

7. Loewen, James W. *The Mississippi Chinese.* Prospect Heights, Ill.: Waveland Press, 1988. Second ed.

8. Chang, Robert S. "Toward an Asian American Legal Scholarship: Critical Race Theory, Post-Structuralism, and Narrative Space." *California Law Review* 81:1241, 1993, 1294.

9. Chan, Sucheng. *Asian Americans: An Interpretive History.* Boston: Twayne, 1991, 59.

10. Wang, L. Ling-Chi. "Lau v. Nichols: History of a Struggle for Equal and Quality Education." In Gee, Emma et al. (Eds.), *Counterpoint*, 240–259. Los Angeles: UCLA Asian American Studies Center, 1976.

11. Wei, William. *The Asian American Movement.* Philadelphia: Temple University Press, 1993, and Umemoto, Karen. "'On Strike!' San Francisco State College Strike, 1968–69: The Role of Asian American Students." *Amerasia Journal* 15:1, 1989, 3–42.

12. Chan, Sucheng, and Ling-Chi Wang. "Racism and the Model Minority: Asian-Americans in Higher Education." In Altbach, Philip G. and Kofi Lomotey, (Eds.), *The Racial Crisis in American Higher Education*, 43–67. Albany: State University of New York Press, 1991; Takagi, Dana Y. *The Retreat from Race.* New Brunswick, NJ: Rutgers University Press, 1992; and Woo, Deborah. "The 'Overrepresentation' of Asian Americans: Red Herrings and Yellow Perils." *Sage Race Relations Abstracts* 15:2, May 1990, 1–36.

13. Takagi, 1992; Walker-Moffat, Wendy. *The Other Side of the Asian American Success Story*, 16. San Francisco: Jossey-Bass, 1995. and Woo, 1990. For contrasts in how Brown University, UC Berkeley, and Harvard University handled the admissions discrimination issue, see, *Civil Rights Issues Facing Asian Americans in the 1990s*, 1992, 109–129.

14. Woo, 1990 and Chin, Gabriel, Sumi Cho, Jerry Kang and Frank Wu. *Beyond Self-Interest: Asian Pacific Americans Toward a Community of Justice.* Los Angeles, 1996.

15. Cho, Sumi. "Converging Stereotypes in Racialized Sexual Harassment: Where the Model Minority Meets Suzie Wong." In Wing, Adrien, (Ed.), *Critical Race Feminism.* New York: New York University Press, 1997.

16. Cho, 1997 and Flanigan, Jackson L., Michael D. Richardson, Kenneth E. Lane and Dennis W. VanBerkum.

"Pennsylvania v. EEOC: Tenure Decisions and Confidentiality." *Thought and Action* 11:1, Spring 1995, 79–95.

17. For a detailed analysis of the evolution of the "model minority" stereotype in the media, see Osajima, Keith. "Asian Americans as the Model Minority: An Analysis of the Popular Press Image in the 1960's and 1980's." In Okihiro, Gary, Shirley Hune, Arthur Hansen and John Liu, (Eds.), *Reflections on Shattered Windows*, 165–174. Pullman: Washington State University Press, 1988.

18. For example, the *60 Minutes* television program manipulated a 1987 feature on "Why are Asian Americans doing so exceptionally well in school?" Boulder High School in Colorado was dropped from the *60 Minutes* feature when it was found that many Hmong and Cambodian students were teenage mothers or had less than exceptional test scores. Thus millions of Americans were presented only with the desired APA academic success story profile. See, Walker-Moffat, 1995, 8–9. Features on Asian Americans as a "success" group began in the late 1960s, but were especially focused on students during the 1980s. See, for example, Brand, David. "Cover Story: The New Whiz Kids." *Time*, August 31, 1987, 42–51; Butterfield, Fox, "Why Asians are Going to the Head of the Class," *New York Times Magazine*, August 3, 1986, 19–24; and Graubard, Stephen G. "Why Do Asian Pupils Win Those Prizes?" *New York Times*, January 29, 1988, A35. Some recent accounts are giving attention to at-risk APA students as well as National Merit scholars, see Seo, Diane. "In School, A Minority No Longer." *Los Angeles Times*, December 26, 1995, A1 and A30.

19. For more on the "model minority myth," see Chan and Hune, 1995.

20. Barringer, Herbert R., David T. Takeuchi and Peter Xenos. "Education, Occupational Prestige and Income of Asian Americans." *Sociology of Education* 63, 1990, 27–43; Kim and Lewis, 1994; Tang, Joyce. "The Career Attainment of Caucasian and Asian Engineers." *The Sociological Quarterly* 34:3, 1993, 467–496; and Woo, 1994.

21. Lee, 1996, 52–54.

22. Steinberg, Stephen. *The Ethnic Myth*, 270–271. Boston: Beacon Press, 1989. Updated and expanded ed.

23. For a discussion of the cultural ecology school and its proponents, J. Ogbu, M. E. Matute-Bianchi, M. A. Gibson and others, see Lee, 1996, 54–56.

24. Solorzano, Daniel and Ronald Solorzano. "The Chicano Educational Experience: A Proposed Framework for Effective Schools in Chicano Communities." *Educational Policy*, 9, 1995, 293–314.

25. For a more detailed discussion of the works of Asian American scholars, see Chan and Hune, 1995.

26. Lee, 1996, 54; Leung, S. Alvin. "Factors Affecting the Career Aspirations of Asian Americans." Paper presented at the annual meeting of American Psychological Association, August 1989; Seymour, Elaine and Nancy M. Hewitt. *Talking about Leaving: Factors Contributing to High Attrition Rates among Science, Mathematics and Engineering*

Undergraduate Majors. Final Report to the Alfred P. Sloan Foundation on an Ethnographic Inquiry at Seven Institutions. Boulder: Ethnography and Assessment Research Bureau of Sociological Research, University of Colorado, 1994; and Sue, S. and Okazaki, S. "Asian American Educational Achievements: A Phenomenon in Search of an Explanation." *American Psychologist* 45:8, 1990, 913–920.

27. Min, Pyong Gap. "Korean Americans." In Min, Pyong Gap, (Ed.), *Asian Americans: Contemporary Trends and Issues*, 224. Thousand Oaks: Sage, 1995.

28. Wong, Morrison. "The Education of White, Chinese, Filipino and Japanese Students: A Look at 'High School and Beyond.' " *Sociological Perspectives* 33, 1990, 355–374.

29. Lee, 1996 and *The Diversity Project: Final Report*, 21–27. UC Berkeley: Institute for Social Change, 1991.

30. Lee, 1996 and Wong, 1990.

31. Hune, Shirley. "Higher Education as Gendered Space: Asian American Women and Everyday Inequities." In Ronai, Carol, Barbara A. Zsembik and Joe R. Feagin, (Eds.), *Everyday Sexism in the Third Millennium*. New York: Routledge, 1997; Kosasa-Terry, Geraldine E. "Localizing Discourse." In Ng, Franklin, Judy Yung, Stephen S. Fugita and Elaine H. Kim, (Eds.), *New Visions in Asian American Studies*, 211–221. Pullman: Washington State University Press, 1994; and Osajima, Keith. "Hidden Injuries of Race." In Revilla, Linda A., Gail M. Nomura, Shawn Wong and Shirley Hune, (Eds.), *Bearing Dreams, Shaping Visions*, 81–91. Pullman: Washington State University Press, 1993.

32. Hune, S. and K. Chan (1997). Special Focus: Asian Pacific American Demographic and Educational Trends. In D. Carter and R. Wilson (Eds.) *Minorities in Education*. (Vol 15), pp. 39–67 and 103–107. Washington, D.C.: American Council on Education.

33. U.S. Department of Commerce, Bureau of the Census, 1994 Current Population Survey, *The Asian and Pacific Islander Population in the United States*, March 1994.

34. 1994 Current Population Survey.

35. 1994 Current Population Survey (Table 4).

36. 1994 Current Population Survey (Table 4).

37. Smith, Thomas. *Issues in Focus: Minorities in Higher Education*, National Center for Education Statistics, 1996.

38. College Board. *Profile of College-Bound Students in the High School Class of 1996*. College Board, 1996.

39. Smith, 1996. The National Commission on Excellence in Education defines "New Basics" as a core curriculum composed of 4 units of English and 3 units each of science, social studies, and mathematics. See, *A Nation at Risk*. Washington, D.C.: U.S. Government Printing Office, 1983.

40. Smith, 1996.

41. College Board. *College Board Reports Continuing Upward Trend in Average Scores on SAT I*. College Board, 1996.

42. Kowarsky, Judy. "Preparation for Transfer: An Orange County Community College Case Study." In Hurtado, Aida,

Richard Figueroa and Eugene E. Garcia, (Eds.). *Strategic Interventions in Education: Expanding the Latina/Latino Pipeline*, 214–267. Santa Cruz, CA: University of California, Santa Cruz, 1996 and *Asian Pacific Americans in the CSU: A Follow-up Report*. The California State University, Office of the Chancellor: Report of the Asian Pacific American Education Advisory Committee, 1994.

43. Smith, 1996.

44. Carter, Deborah J. and Reginald Wilson. *15th Annual Status Report Minorities in Higher Education 1996–1997*, Washington, D.C.: American Council on Education, 1997. Table 4.

45. Calculated from *15th Annual Status Report Minorities in Higher Education 1996–1997*, 1997, Table 3.

46. Calculated from *15th Annual Status Report Minorities in Higher Education 1996–1997*, 1997, Table 5.

47. U.S. Department of Education, National Center for Education Statistics, Integrated Postsecondary Education Data System (IPEDS), "Completions" survey. Some categories used in this supplement are aggregations of more definitive categories and are more inclusive than the data reported annually in Table 14 by ACE's Minorities in Higher Education Status Reports. Social science includes social sciences, history, and psychology. Sciences include life sciences, physical sciences, and math. Engineering includes engineering and computer/information sciences. Humanities include English language and literature/letters, foreign languages and literatures, liberal arts and sciences, general studies, and humanities, communications, philosophy and religion, and theological studies/religious vocations. Arts include performing and visual arts.

48. Hsia, Jayjia. *Asian Americans in Higher Education and at Work*. Hillsdale, NJ: Lawrence Erlbaum Associates, 1988, 129.

49. U.S. Department of Education, National Center for Education Statistics, Integrated Postsecondary Education Data System (IPEDS), "Completions" survey.

50. First Professional degrees consist of eleven subfields, including medicine, law, dentistry, and divinity.

51. U.S. Department of Education, National Center for Education Statistics, Integrated Postsecondary Education Data System (IPEDS), "Completions" survey, 1993–94 and "Consolidated" survey, 1994.

52. Gibson, Margaret A. *Accommodation without Assimilation*. Ithaca: Cornell University Press, 1988 and Mau, Rosalind Y. "Barriers to Higher Education for Asian/Pacific-American Females." *The Urban Review* 22, 1990, 183–197.

53. Hune, 1997.

54. Cho, 1997.

55. See, for example, Astin, Alexander W., Jesus G. Trevino and Tamara L. Wingard. *The UCLA Campus Climate for Diversity*. Los Angeles: Higher Education Research Institute, UCLA, 1991; *The Diversity Project: Final Report*. Berkeley: Institute for the Study of Social Change, University of California, 1991; Justus, Joyce Bennett, Sandra B.

Freitag and L. Leann Parker. *The University of California in the 21st Century: Successful Approaches to Faculty Diversity*. Berkeley: Office of the President, University of California System, 1987; Osajima, Keith. "Breaking the Silence: Race and the Educational Experiences of Asian American College Students." In Michele Foster, (Ed.). *Readings on Equal Education*, 115–134. New York: AMS Press, 1991.; Swoboda, Marian J., (Ed.). *Retaining and Promoting Women and Minority Faculty Members: Problems and Possibilities*. Madison: The University of Wisconsin System, 1990; and Chan and Wang, 1991.

56. Carter, Deborah J. and Eileen M. O'Brien. *Employment and Hiring Patterns for Faculty of Color*. American Council on Education, Research Briefs 4:6, 1. Washington, D.C., 1993.

57. U.S. Equal Employment Opportunity Commission. *EEO-6 Higher Education Staff Information Survey 1975–1991* counted non-resident alien full-time faculty within the major racial/ethnic categories. In 1994 the data shifted to the U.S. Department of Education, National Center for Education Statistics, Integrated Postsecondary Education Data System (IPEDS), "Completions" survey, 1993–94 and "Consolidated" survey, 1994 where non-resident aliens were separated into a distinct category and account for 2 percent of full-time faculty or approximately 11,000 persons who previously would have been distributed among other racial/ethnic categories. How many of these persons are of Asian descent are unknown. This may account for part of the decrease in APA males found in 1993.

58. Zimbler, Linda J. *Faculty and Instructional Staff: Who Are They and What Do They Do?* Washington, D.C.: Department of Education, National Center for Education Statistics, Survey Report, 1993 National Study of Postsecondary Faculty, 1994, 7, 14–15.

59. Carter, Deborah and Reginald Wilson. *Fourteenth Annual Status Report Minorities in Higher Education*. Washington, D.C.: American Council on Education, 1995–96, 1996, 84.

60. Woo, 1994.

61. Ottinger, Cecilia, Robin Sikula and Charles Washington. *Production of Minority Doctorates*. American Council on Education Research Briefs, 4:8, 8. Washington, D.C., 1993.

62. Smith, Daryl G. with Lisa E. Wolf and Bonnie E. Busenberg. *Achieving Faculty Diversity: Debunking the Myths*. Washington, D.C.: Association of American Colleges and Universities, 1996.

63. *Asian, Hispanic, and Native American Task Force Report*. University of Maryland, College Park, 1996; Carter and O'Brien, 1993; Hune, 1997; Sandler, Bernice R. and Roberta M. Hall. *The Campus Climate Revisited: Chilly for Women Faculty, Administrators, and Graduate Students*. Washington, D.C.: Project on the Status and Education of Women, Association of American Colleges, 1986; and Swoboda, 1990.

64. *Asian, Hispanic, and Native American Task Force Report*, 1996 and Woo, 1994, 47–52, 148–150.

65. Cho, Sumi K. "Confronting the Myths: Asian Pacific American Faculty in Higher Education." In Wang, Ling-Chi, (Ed.). *Affirmative Action and Discrimination: Ninth Annual Asian Pacific Americans in Higher Education Conference Proceedings*. Asian Pacific Americans in Higher Education, 1996; Cho, 1997; and Minami, Dale. "Guerilla War at UCLA: Political and Legal Dimensions of the Tenure Battle." *Amerasia Journal* 16, 1990, 81–107.

66. Miller, Susan Katz. "Asian-Americans Bump against Glass Ceilings." *Science* 258, 13 November 1992, 1224–1228 and Woo, 1994, 90–96.

67. Escueta, Eugenia and Eileen O' Brien. *Asian Americans in Higher Education: Trends and Issues*. American Council on Education Research Briefs 2:4, 9. Washington, D.C., 1991.

68. "Affirmative Action: Controversy in California." *Crosscurrents*, 19:2, Fall/Winter, 1996 (UCLA). . . .

69. For examples of APA responses to the affirmative action debate see Chin, Gabriel, Sumi Cho, Jerry Kang and Frank Wu, 1996 and *Perspectives on Affirmative Action*. Los Angeles: LEAP Asian Pacific American Public Policy Institute, 1996.

Reading 13

Multiculturalism: Battleground or Meeting Ground?

Ronald Takaki

It is very natural that the history written by the victim does not altogether chime with the story of the victor.

Jose Fernandez of California, 1874[1]

In 1979, I experienced the truth of this statement when I found myself attacked by C. Van Woodward in the *New York Review of Books*. I had recently published a broad and comparative study of blacks, Chinese, Indians, Irish, and Mexicans, from the American Revolution to the U.S. war against Spain. But, for Woodward, my *Iron Cages: Race and Culture in Nineteenth-Century America* was too narrow in focus. My analysis, he stridently complained, should have compared ethnic conflicts in the United States to those in Brazil, South Africa, Germany, and Russia. Such an encompassing view would have shown that America was not so "bad" after all.

The author of scholarship that focused exclusively on the American South, Woodward was arguing that mine should have been cross-national in order to be "balanced." But how, I wondered, was balance to be measured? Surely, any examination of the "worse instances" of racial oppression in other countries should not diminish the importance of what happened here. Balance should also insist that we steer away from denial or a tendency to be dismissive. Woodward's contrast of the "millions of corpses" and the "horrors of genocide" in Nazi Germany to racial violence in the United States seemed both heartless and

Source: The Annals of the American Academy of Political and Social Science 530, (Nov. 1993): 109–121. Copyright © 1993 by Sage Publications. Reprinted by permission of Sage Publications, Inc.

beside the point. Enslaved Africans in the American South would have felt little comfort to have been told that conditions for their counterparts in Latin America were "worse." They would have responded that it mattered little that the black population in Brazil was "17.5 million" rather than "127.6 million" by 1850, or whether slavery beyond what Woodward called the "three-mile limit" was more terrible and deadly.

What had provoked such a scolding from this dean of American history? One might have expected a more supportive reading from the author of *The Strange Career of Jim Crow*, a book that had helped stir our society's moral conscience during the civil rights era. My colleague Michael Rogin tried to explain Woodward's curious reaction by saying that the elderly historian perceived me as a bad son. History had traditionally been written by members of the majority population; now some younger scholars of color like me had received our Ph.D.'s and were trying to "re-vision" America's past. But our critical scholarship did not chime with the traditional version of history. Noting my nonwhiteness, Woodward charged that I was guilty of reverse discrimination: my characterization of whites in terms of rapacity, greed, and brutality constituted a "practice" that could be described as "racism." Like a father, Woodward chastised me for catering to the "current mood of self-denigration and self-flagellation." "If and when the mood passes," he lamented, "one would hope a more balanced perspective on American history will prevail."[2]

Looking back at Woodward's review today, we can see that it constituted one of the opening skirmishes of what has come to be called the culture war. Some of the battles of this conflict have erupted in the political arena. Speaking before the 1992 Republican National Convention, Patrick Buchanan urged his fellow conservatives to take back their cities, their culture, and their country, block by block. This last phrase was a reference to the National Guard's show of force during the 1992 Los Angeles riot. On the other hand, in his first speech as President-elect, Bill Clinton recognized our ethnic and cultural diversity as a source of America's strength.

But many of the fiercest battles over how we define America are being waged within the academy. There minority students and scholars are struggling to diversify the curriculum, while conservative pundits like Charles J. Sykes and Dinesh D'Souza are fighting to recapture the campus.[3]

The stakes in this conflict are high, for we are being asked to define education and determine what an educated person should know about the world in general and America in particular. This is the issue Allan Bloom raises in his polemic, *The Closing of the American Mind*. A leader of the intellectual backlash against cultural diversity, he articulates a conservative view of the university curriculum. According to Bloom, entering students are "uncivilized," and faculty have the responsibility to "civilize" them. As a teacher, he claims to know what their "hungers" are and "what they can digest." Eating is one of his favorite metaphors. Noting the "large black presence" at major universities, he regrets the "one failure" in race relations—black students have proven to be "indigestible." They do not "melt as have *all* other groups." The problem, he contends, is that "blacks have become blacks": they have become "ethnic." This separatism has been reinforced by an academic permissiveness that has befouled the curriculum with "Black Studies" along with "Learn Another Culture." The only solution, Bloom insists, is "the good old Great Books approach."[4]

Behind Bloom's approach is a political agenda. What does it mean to be an American? he asks. The "old view" was that "by recognizing and accepting man's natural rights," people in this society found a fundamental basis of unity. The immigrant came here and became assimilated. But the "recent education of openness," with its celebration of diversity, is threatening the social contract that had defined the members of American society as individuals. During the civil rights movement of the 1960s, Black Power militants had aggressively affirmed a group identity. Invading college campuses, they demanded "respect for blacks as blacks, not as human beings simply," and began to "propagandize acceptance of different ways." This emphasis on ethnicity separated Americans from each other, shrouding their "essential humankindness." The black conception of a group identity provided the theoretical basis for a new policy, affirmative action, which opened the doors to the admission of unqualified students. Once on campus, many black students agitated for the establishment of black studies programs, which in turn contributed to academic incoherence, lack of synopsis, and the "decomposition of the university."[5]

Bloom's is a closed mind, unwilling to allow the curriculum to become more inclusive. Fortunately, many other educators have been acknowledging the need to teach students about the cultural diversity of American society "Every student needs to know," former University of Wisconsin chancellor Donna Shalala has explained, "much more about the origins and history of the particular cultures which, as Americans, we will encounter during our lives."[6]

This need for cross-cultural understanding has been grimly highlighted by recent racial tensions and conflicts such as the black boycott of Korean stores, Jewish-black antagonism in Crown Heights, and especially the 1992 Los Angeles racial explosion. During the days of rage, Rodney King pleaded for calm: "Please, we can get along here. We all can get along. I mean, we're all stuck here for a while. Let's try to work it out." But how should "we" be defined?[7]

Earlier, the Watts riot had reflected a conflict between whites and blacks, but the fire this time in 1992 Los Angeles highlighted the multiracial reality of American society. Race includes Hispanics and Asian Americans. The old binary language of race relations between whites and blacks, *Newsweek* observed, is no longer descriptive of who we are as Americans. Our future will increasingly be multiethnic as the twenty-first century rushes toward us: the western edge of the continent called California constitutes the thin end of an entering new wedge, a brave new multicultural world of Calibans of many different races and ethnicities.[8]

If "we" must be more inclusive, how do we "work it out"? One crucial way would be for us to learn more about each other—not only whites about peoples of color, but also blacks about Koreans, and Hispanics about blacks. Our very diversity offers an intellectual invitation to teachers and scholars to reach for a more comprehensive understanding of American society. Here the debate over multiculturalism has gone beyond whether or not to be inclusive. The question has become, How do we develop and teach a more culturally diverse curriculum?

What has emerged are two perspectives, what Diane Ravitch has usefully described as "particularism" versus "pluralism." But, by regarding each as exclusive, even antagonistic, Ravitch fails to appreciate the validity of both viewpoints and the ways they complement each other.[9]

Actually, we need not be forced into an either-or situation. Currently, many universities offer courses that study a particular group, such as African Americans or Asian Americans. This focus enables students of a specific minority to learn about their history and community. These students are not necessarily seeking what has been slandered as self-esteem courses. Rather, they simply believe that they are entitled to learn how their communities fit into American history and society. My grandparents were Japanese immigrant laborers, and even after I finished college with a major in American history and completed a Ph.D. in this field, I had learned virtually nothing about why they had come to America and what had happened to them as well as

other Japanese immigrants in this country. This history should have been available to me.

The particularistic perspective led me to write *Strangers from a Different Shore: A History of Asian Americans.* This focus on a specific group can also be found in Irving Howe's *World of Our Fathers: The Journey of the East European Jews to America,* Mario Garcia's *Desert Immigrants: The Mexicans of El Paso, 1880–1920,* Lawrence Levine's *Black Culture and Black Consciousness,* and Kerby Miller's *Emigrants and Exiles: Ireland and the Irish Exodus to North America.*[10]

Increasingly, educators and scholars are recognizing the need for us to step back from particularistic portraits in order to discern the rich and complex mosaic of our national pluralism. While group-specific courses have been in the curriculum for many years, courses offering a comparative and integrative approach have been introduced recently. In fact, the University of California at Berkeley has instituted an American cultures requirement for graduation. The purpose of this course is to give students an understanding of American society in terms of African Americans, Asian Americans, Latinos, Native Americans, and European Americans, especially the immigrant groups from places like Ireland, Italy, Greece, and Russia.

What such curricular innovations promise is not only the introduction of intellectually dynamic courses that study the crisscrossed paths of America's different groups but also the fostering of comparative multicultural scholarship. This pluralistic approach is illustrated by works like my *Different Mirror: A History of Multicultural America* as well as Gary Nash's *Red, White, and Black: The Peoples of Early America,* Ivan Light's *Ethnic Enterprise in America: Business and Welfare among Chinese, Japanese, and Blacks,* Reginald Horsman's *Race and Manifest Destiny: The Origins of American Racial Anglo-Saxonism,* and Benjamin Ringer's *"We the People" and Others: Duality and America's Treatment of Its Racial Minorities.*[11]

Even here, however, a battle is being fought over how America's diversity should be conceptualized. For example, Diane Ravitch avidly supports the pluralistic perspective, but she fears national division. Stressing the importance of national unity, Ravitch promotes the development of multiculturalism based on a strategy of adding on: to keep mainstream Anglo-American history and expand it by simply including information on racism as well as minority contributions to America's music, art, literature, food, clothing, sports, and holidays. The purpose behind this pluralism, for Ravitch, is to encourage students of "all racial and ethnic groups to believe that they are part of this society and that they should develop their talents and minds to the fullest." By "fullest," she means for students to be inspired by learning about "men and women from diverse backgrounds who overcame poverty, discrimination, physical handicaps, and other obstacles to achieve success in a variety of fields." Ravitch is driven by a desire for universalism: she wants to affirm our common humanity by discouraging our specific group identities, especially those based on racial experiences. Ironically, Ravitch, a self-avowed proponent of pluralism, actually wants us to abandon our group ties and become individuals.[12]

This privileging of the "unum" over the "pluribus" has been advanced more aggressively by Arthur Schlesinger in *The Disuniting of America.*

In this jeremiad, Schlesinger denounces what he calls "the cult of ethnicity"—the shift from assimilation to group identity, from integration to separatism. The issue at stake, he argues, is the teaching of *"bad* history under whatever ethnic banner." After acknowledging that American history has long been written in the "interests of white Anglo-Saxon Protestant males," he describes the enslavement of Africans, the seizure of Indian lands, and the exploitation of Chinese railroad workers. But his discussion on racial oppression is perfunctory and parsimonious, and he devotes most of his attention to a defense of traditional history. "Anglocentric domination of schoolbooks was based in part on unassailable facts," Schlesinger declares. "For better or worse,

American history has been shaped more than anything else by British tradition and culture." Like Bloom, Schlesinger utilizes the metaphor of eating. "To deny the essentially European origins of American culture is to falsify history," he explains. "Belief in one's own culture does not require disdain for other cultures. But one step at a time: no culture can hope to ingest other cultures all at once, certainly not before it ingests its own." Defensively claiming to be an inclusionist historian, Schlesinger presents his own credentials: "As for me, I was for a time a member of the executive council of the *Journal of Negro History. . . .* I have been a lifelong advocate of civil rights."[13]

But what happens when minority peoples try to define their civil rights in terms of cultural pluralism and group identities? They become targets of Schlesinger's scorn. This "exaggeration" of ethnic differences, he warns, only "drives ever deeper the awful wedges between races," leading to an "endgame" of self-pity and self-ghettoization. The culprits responsible for this divisiveness are the "multicultural zealots," especially the Afrocentrists. Schlesinger castigates them as campus bullies, distorting history and creating myths about the contributions of Africans.[14]

What Schlesinger refuses to admit or is unable to see clearly is how he himself is culpable of historical distortion: his own omissions in *The Age of Jackson* have erased what James Madison had described then as "the black race within our bosom" and "'the red on our borders.'" Both groups have been entirely left out of Schlesinger's study: they do not even have entries in the index. Moreover, there is not even a mention of two marker events, the Nat Turner insurrection and Indian Removal, which Andrew Jackson himself would have been surprised to find omitted from a history of his era. Unfortunately, Schlesinger fails to meet even his own standards of scholarship: "The historian's goals are accuracy, analysis, and objectivity in the reconstruction of the past."[15]

Behind Schlesinger's cant against multiculturalism is fear. What will happen to our national ideal of *"e pluribus unum?"* he worries. Will the center hold, or will the melting pot yield to the Tower of Babel? For answers, he looks abroad. "Today," he observes, "the nationalist fever encircles the globe." Angry and violent "tribalism" is exploding in India, the former Soviet Union, Indonesia, Guyana, and other countries around the world. "The ethnic upsurge in America, far from being unique, partakes of the global fever." Like Bloom and Ravitch, Schlesinger prescribes individualism as the cure. "Most Americans," he argues, "continue to see themselves primarily as individuals and only secondarily and trivially as adherents of a group." The dividing of society into "fixed ethnicities nourishes a culture of victimization and a contagion of inflammable sensitivities." This danger threatens the "brittle bonds of national identity that hold this diverse and fractious society together." The Balkan present, Schlesinger warns, may be America's prologue.[16]

Are we limited to a choice between a "disuniting" multiculturalism and a common American culture, or can we transform the "culture war" into a meeting ground? The intellectual combats of this conflict, Gerald Graff suggests, have the potential to enrich American education. As universities become contested terrains of different points of view, gray and monotonous cloisters of Eurocentric knowledge can become brave new worlds, dynamic and multicultural. On these academic battlegrounds, scholars and students can engage each other in dialogue and debate, informed by the heat and light generated by the examination of opposing texts such as Joseph Conrad's *Heart of Darkness* and Chinua Achebe's *Things Fall Apart.* "Teaching the conflicts has nothing to do with relativism or denying the existence of truth," Graff contends. "The best way to make relativists of students is to expose them to an endless series of different positions which are *not* debated before their eyes." Graff turns the guns of the great books against Bloom. By viewing culture as a debate and by entering a process of intellectual clashes, students can search for truth, as did Socrates "when he taught the conflicts two millennia ago."[17]

Like Graff, I welcome such debates in my teaching. One of my courses, "Racial Inequality in America: A Comparative Historical Perspective," studies the character of American society in relationship to our racial and ethnic diversity. My approach is captured in the phrase "from different shores." By "shores," I intend a double meaning. One is the shores from which the migrants departed, places such as Europe, Africa, and Asia. The second is the various and often conflicting perspectives or shores from which scholars have viewed the experiences of racial and ethnic groups.

By critically examining these different shores, students address complex comparative questions. How have the experiences of racial minorities such as African Americans been similar to and different from those of ethnic groups such as Irish Americans? Is race the same as ethnicity? For example, is the African American experience qualitatively or quantitatively different from the Jewish American experience? How have race relations been shaped by economic developments as well as by culture— moral values about how people think and behave as well as beliefs about human nature and society? To wrestle with these questions, students read Nathan Glazer's analysis of assimilationist patterns as well as Robert Blauner's theory of internal colonialism, Charles Murray on black welfare dependency as well as William Julius Wilson on the economic structures creating the black underclass and Thomas Sowell's explanation of Asian American success as well as my critique of the "myth of the Asian-American model minority."[18]

The need to open American minds to greater cultural diversity will not go away. Faculty can resist this imperative by ignoring the changing racial composition of student bodies and the larger society, or they can embrace this timely and exciting intellectual opportunity to revitalize the social sciences and humanities. "The study of the humanities," Henry Louis Gates observes, "is the study of the possibilities of human life in culture. It thrives on diversity. . . . The new [ethnic studies] scholarship has invigorated the traditional disciplines." What distinguishes the university from other battlegrounds, such as the media and politics, is that the university has a special commitment to the search for knowledge, one based on a process of intellectual openness and inquiry. Multiculturalism can stoke this critical spirit by transforming the university into a crucial meeting ground for different viewpoints. In the process, perhaps we will be able to discover what makes us an American people.[19]

Whether the university can realize this intellectual pursuit for collective self-knowledge is uncertain, especially during difficult economic times. As institutions of higher learning face budget cuts, calls for an expansion of the curriculum often encounter hostility from faculty in traditional departments determined to protect dwindling resources. Furthermore, the economic crisis has been fanning the fires of racism in society: Asian Americans have been bashed for the seeming invasion of Japanese cars, Hispanics accused of taking jobs away from Americans, and blacks attacked for their dependency on welfare and the special privileges of affirmative action.

This context of rising racial tensions has conditioned the culture war. Both the advocates and the critics of multiculturalism know that the conflict is not wholly academic; the debate over how America should be defined is related to power and privilege. Both sides agree that history is power. Society's collective memory determines the future. The battle is over what should be remembered and who should do the remembering.

Traditionally excluded from the curriculum, minorities are insisting that America does not belong to one group and neither does America's history. They are making their claim to the knowledge offered by the university, reminding us that Americans originated from many lands and that everyone here is entitled to dignity. "I hope this survey do a lot of good for Chinese people," an immigrant told an interviewer from Stanford in the 1920s. "Make American people realize that Chinese people are humans. I think very few American people really know anything about Chinese." As different groups find their voices,

they tell and retell stories that liberate. By writing about the people on Mango Street, Sandra Cisneros explained, "the ghost does not ache so much." The place no longer holds her with "both arms. She sets [Cisneros] free." Indeed, stories may not be as innocent or simple as they might seem. They "aren't just entertainment," observed Native American novelist Leslie Marmon Silko.[20]

On the other side, the interests seeking to maintain the status quo also recognize that the contested terrain of ideas is related to social reality. No wonder conservative foundations like Coors and Olin have been financing projects to promote their own political agenda on campuses across the country, and the National Association of Scholars has been attacking multiculturalism by smearing it with a brush called "political correctness." Conservative critics like Bloom are the real campus bullies: they are the ones unwilling to open the debate and introduce students to different viewpoints. Under the banner of intellectual freedom and excellence, these naysayers have been imposing their own intellectual orthodoxy by denouncing those who disagree with them as "the new barbarians," saluting Lynne Cheney, the former head of the National Endowment for the Humanities, for defending traditional American culture, and employing McCarthyite tactics to brand ethnic studies as "un-American."[21]

How can the university become a meeting ground when the encounter of oppositional ideas is disparaged? What Susan Faludi has observed about the academic backlash against women's liberation can be applied to the reaction to multiculturalism. "The donnish robes of many of these backlash thinkers cloaked impulses that were less than scholarly," she wrote. "Some of them were academics who believed that feminists had cost them in advancement, tenure, and honors; they found the creation of women's studies not just professionally but personally disturbing and invasive, a trespasser trampling across *their* campus." Her observation applies to multiculturalism: all we need to do is to substitute "minority scholars" for "feminists," and "ethnic studies" for "women's studies." The intellectual backlashers are defending "their" campuses against the "other."[22]

The campaign against multiculturalism reflects a larger social nervousness, a perplexity over the changing racial composition of American society. Here Faludi's insights may again be transferrable. The war against women, she notes, manifests an identity crisis for men: what does it mean to be a man? One response has been to reclaim masculinity through violence, to "kick ass," the expression George Bush used to describe his combat with Geraldine Ferraro in the 1984 vice-presidential debate. Eight years later, during the Persian Gulf war against Saddam Hussein, Bush as President demonstrated masculine power in Desert Storm. In a parallel way, it can be argued, the expanding multicultural reality of America is creating a racial identity crisis: what does it mean to be white?[23]

Demographic studies project that whites will become a minority of the total U.S. population some time during the twenty-first century. Already in major cities across the country, whites no longer predominate numerically. This expanding multicultural reality is challenging the traditional notion of America as white. What will it mean for American society to have a non-white majority? The significance of this future, *Time* observed, is related to our identity—our sense of individual self and nationhood, or what it means to be American. This demographic transformation has prompted E. D. Hirsch to worry that America is becoming a "Tower of Babel," and that this multiplicity of cultures is threatening to tear the country's social fabric. Nostalgic for a more cohesive culture and a more homogeneous America, he contends, "If we *had* to make a choice between the one and the *many,* most Americans would choose the principle of unity, since we cannot function as a nation without it." The way to correct this fragmentization, Hirsch argues, is to promote the teaching of "shared symbols." In *Cultural Literacy: What Every American Needs to Know*, Hirsch offers an appendix of terms designed to create a sense of national identity and unity—a list that leaves out much of the histories and cultures of minorities.[24]

The escalating war against multiculturalism is being fueled by a fear of loss. " 'Backlash politics may be defined as the reaction by groups which are declining in a felt sense of importance, influence, and power,' " observed Seymour Martin Lipset and Earl Raab. Similarly, historian Richard Hofstadter described the impulses of progressive politics in the early twentieth century in terms of a "status revolution"—a widely shared frustration among middle-class professionals who had been displaced by a new class of elite businessmen. Hofstadter also detected a "paranoid style in American politics" practiced by certain groups such as nativists who suffered from lost prestige and felt besieged by complex new realities. Grieving for an America that had been taken away from them, they desperately fought to repossess their country and "prevent the final destructive act of subversion."[25]

A similar anxiety is growing in America today. One of the factors behind the backlash against multiculturalism is race, what Lawrence Auster calls "the forbidden topic." In an essay published in the *National Review,* he advocates the restriction of immigration for nonwhites. Auster condemns the white liberals for wanting to have it both ways—to have a common culture and also to promote racial diversity. They naively refuse to recognize the danger: when a "critical number" of people in this country are no longer from the West, then we will no longer be able to employ traditional reference points such as "our Western heritage" or speak of "our Founding Fathers." American culture as it has been known, Auster warns, is disappearing as "more and more minorities complain that they can't identify with American history because they 'don't see people who look like themselves' in that history." To preserve America as a Western society, Auster argues, America must continue to be composed mostly of people of European ancestry.[26]

What Auster presents is an extreme but logical extension of a view shared by both conservatives like Bloom and liberals like Schlesinger: they have bifurcated American society into "us" versus "them." This division locates whites at the center and minorities at the margins of our national identity. "American," observed Toni Morrison, has been defined as "white." Such a dichotomization denies our wholeness as one people. " 'Everybody remembers,' " she explained, " 'the first time they were taught that part of the human race was Other. That's a trauma. It's as though I told you that your left hand is not part of your body.' "[27]

In their war against the denied parts of American society, the backlashers are our modern Captain Ahabs. In their pursuit of their version of the white whale, they are in command; like Ahab directing his chase from the deck of the *Pequod,* they steer the course of the university curriculum. Their exclusive definition of knowledge has rendered invisible and silent the swirling and rich diversity below deck. The workers of the *Pequod* represent a multicultural society—whites like Ishmael, Pacific Islanders like Queequeg, Africans like Daggoo, Asians like Fedallah, and American Indians like Tashtego. In Melville's powerful story, Ishmael and Queequeg find themselves strangers to each other at first. As they labor together, they are united by their need of mutual survival and cooperation. This connectedness is graphically illustrated by the monkeyrope. Lowered into the shark-infested water to secure the blubber hook into the dead whale, Queequeg is held by a rope tied to Ishmael. The process is perilous for both men. "We two, for the time," Ishmael tells us, "were wedded; and should poor Queequeg sink to rise no more, then both usage and honor demanded that, instead of cutting the cord, it should drag me down in his wake." Though originally from different shores, the members of the crew share a noble class unity. Ahab, however, is able to charm them, his charisma drawing them into the delirium of his hunt. Driven by a monomaniac mission, Ahab charts a course that ends in the destruction of everyone except Ishmael.[28]

On college campuses today, the voices of many students and faculty from below deck are challenging such hierarchical power. In their search for cross-cultural understandings, they are trying to re-vision America. But will we as Americans continue to perceive our past and peer into our future as through a glass darkly? In the telling and retelling of our particular stories, will we create communities of separate memories, or will we be able to connect our diverse selves to a larger national narrative? As we approach a new century dominated by ethnic and racial conflicts at home and throughout the world, we realize that the answers to such questions will depend largely on whether the university will be able to become both a battleground and a meeting ground of varied viewpoints.

NOTES

1. David J. Weber, ed., *Foreigners in Their Native Land: Historical Roots of the Mexican Americans* (Albuquerque: University of New Mexico Press, 1973), p. vi.
2. C. Van Woodward, "America the Bad?" *New York Review of Books*, 22 Nov. 1979; Ronald Takaki, *Iron Cages: Race and Culture in Nineteenth-Century America* (New York: Knopf, 1979).
3. Charles J. Sykes, *The Hollow Men: Politics and Corruption in Higher Education* (Washington, DC: Regnery Gateway, 1990); Dinesh D'Souza, *Illiberal Education: The Politics of Race and Sex on Campus* (New York: Free Press, 1991).
4. Allan Bloom, *The Closing of the American Mind: How Higher Education Has Failed Democracy and Impoverished the Souls of Today's Students* (New York: Simon & Schuster, 1987), pp. 19, 91–93, 340–41, 344.
5. Ibid., pp. 27, 29, 33, 35, 89, 90, 347.
6. *University of Wisconsin—Madison: The Madison Plan* (Madison: University of Wisconsin, 1988).
7. Rodney King's statement to the press; see *New York Times*, 2 May 1992, p. 6.
8. "Beyond Black and White," *Newsweek*, 18 May 1992, p. 28.
9. Diane Ravitch, "Multiculturalism: E Pluribus Plures," *American Scholar*, 59(3): 337–54 (Summer 1990).
10. Ronald Takaki, *Strangers from a Different Shore: A History of Asian Americans* (Boston: Little, Brown, 1989); Irving Howe, *World of Our Fathers: The Journey of the East European Jews to America and the Life They Found and Made* (New York: Simon & Schuster, 1976); Lawrence W. Levine, *Black Culture and Black Consciousness: Afro-American Folk Thought from Slavery to Freedom* (New York: Oxford University Press, 1977);

Mario T. Garcia, *Desert Immigrants: The Mexicans of El Paso, 1880–1920* (New Haven, CT: Yale University Press, 1981); Kerby A. Miller, *Emigrants and Exiles: Ireland and the Irish Exodus to North America* (New York: Oxford University Press, 1985).

11. Ronald Takaki, *A Different Mirror: A History of Multicultural America* (New York: Little, Brown, 1993); Gary Nash, *Red, White, and Black: The Peoples of Early America* (Englewood Cliffs, NJ: Prentice-Hall, 1974); Ivan Light, *Ethnic Enterprise in America: Business and Welfare among Chinese, Japanese, and Blacks* (Berkeley: University of California Press, 1972); Reginald Horsman, *Race and Manifest Destiny: The Origins of American Racial Anglo-Saxonism* (Cambridge, MA: Harvard University Press, 1981); Benjamin Ringer, *"We the People" and Others: Duality and America's Treatment of Its Racial Minorities* (New York: Tavistock, 1983).

12. Ravitch, "Multiculturalism," pp. 341, 354.

13. Arthur M. Schlesinger, Jr., *The Disuniting of America: Reflections on a Multicultural Society* (Knoxville, TN: Whittle Communications, 1991), pp. 2, 24, 14, 81–82.

14. Ibid., pp. 58, 66.

15. James Madison, quoted in Takaki, *Iron Cages*, p. 80; Arthur M. Schlesinger, Jr., *The Age of Jackson* (Boston: Little, Brown, 1945); idem, *Disuniting of America*, p. 20.

16. Schlesinger, *Disuniting of America*, pp. 2, 21, 64.

17. Gerald Graff, *Beyond the Culture Wars: How Teaching the Conflicts Can Revitalize American Education* (New York: Norton, 1992), p. 15.

18. Nathan Glazer, *Affirmative Discrimination: Ethnic Inequality and Public Policy* (New York: Basic Books, 1975); Robert Blauner, *Racial Oppression in America* (New York: Harper & Row, 1972); Charles Murray, *Losing Ground: American Social Policy, 1950–1980* (New York: Basic Books, 1984); William Julius Wilson, *The Truly Disadvantaged: The Inner City, the Underclass, and Public Policy* (Chicago: University of Chicago Press, 1987); Thomas Sowell, *Ethnic America: A History* (New York: Basic Books, 1981); Takaki, *Strangers from a Different Shore*. For an example of the debate format, see Ronald Takaki, *From Different Shores: Perspectives on Race and Ethnicity in America* (New York: Oxford University Press, 1987).

19. Henry Louis Gates, Jr., *Loose Canons: Notes on the Culture Wars* (New York: Oxford University Press, 1992), p. 114.

20. Pany Lowe, interview, 1924, Survey of Race Relations, Hoover Institution Archives, Stanford, CA; Sandra Cisneros, *The House on Mango Street* (New York: Vintage, 1991), pp. 109–10; Leslie Marmon Silko, *Ceremony* (New York: New American Library, 1978), p. 2.

21. Dinesh D'Souza, "The Visigoths in Tweed," in *Beyond PC: Towards a Politics of Understanding*, ed. Patricia Aufderheide (St. Paul, MN: Graywolf Press, 1992), p. 11; George Will, "Literary Politics," *Newsweek*, 22 Apr. 1991, p. 72; Arthur Schlesinger, Jr., "When Ethnic Studies Are Un-American," *Wall Street Journal*, 23 Apr. 1990.

22. Susan Faludi, *Backlash: The Undeclared War against American Women* (New York: Doubleday, 1992), p. 282.

23. Ibid., p. 65.

24. William A. Henry III, "Beyond the Melting Pot," *Time*, 9 Apr. 1990, pp. 28–31; E. D. Hirsch, Jr., *Cultural Literacy: What Every American Needs to Know* (Boston: Houghton, Mifflin, 1987), pp. xiii, xvii, 2, 18, 96, 152–215.

25. Lipset and Raab quoted in Faludi, *Backlash*, p. 231; Richard Hofstadter, *The Age of Reform: From Bryan to F.D.R.* (New York: Random House, 1955), pp. 131–73.

26. Lawrence Auster, "The Forbidden Topic," *National Review*, 27 Apr. 1992, pp. 42–44.

27. Toni Morrison, *Playing in the Dark: Whiteness in the Literary Imagination* (Cambridge, MA: Harvard University Press, 1992), p. 47; Bonnie Angelo, "The Pain of Being Black," *Time*, 22 May 1989, p. 121. Copyright © 1989 Time Inc. Reprinted by permission.

28. Herman Melville, *Moby Dick* (Boston: Houghton Mifflin, 1956), pp. 182, 253, 322–23.

Being Different Together in the University Classroom: Multiracial Identity as Transgressive Education

Teresa Kay Williams, Cynthia L. Nakashima, George Kitahara Kich, and G. Reginald Daniel

In the spring of 1992, the University of California, Santa Barbara's Asian American Studies program (now a full-fledged department) offered the first course ever on Asian-descent multiracials. Half of the students in the class were multiracial and transracially adopted. Another 10% consisted of monoracially identified European Americans, and the remaining 40% were monoracially identified Asian Americans. All of the multiracial students were a mixture of Asian and European ancestries except for one student who was Filipino and Mexican. On the first day of class, students introduced themselves and explained why they were interested in taking the course. A Euro-American student prefaced her remarks by stating, "As you can tell, I'm obviously white." She was immediately challenged by her multiracial classmates. One multiracial student asked her to explain what "obviously white" meant. As this Euro-American student attempted to articulate the taken-for-granted assumptions of racial designations in American society, describing skin color, physical features, geographical origins, and so on, another multiracial student pointed out to her that many of the Eurasians in the class in fact looked "more obviously white" than she did, according to the phenotypical standards of "race" to which this Euro-American student subscribed. One multiracial student after another easily poked holes in this Euro-American student's loosely threaded explanation of race. The multiracial students indicated how many of them possessed lighter complexions, lighter hair and eye coloring, and more phenotypical characteristics associated with European ancestry than did this self-

professed "obviously white" woman. For the next 10 weeks, this Euro-American female student was put on the defensive by the multiracial and transracially adopted students in the class. For the first time in her life, she was forced to interrogate her taken-for-granted assumptions about race and to question her social location in American society, not only in relation to monoracially identified groups of color, but also in relation to multiracial peoples with European ancestry.

We have come to realize from our years of teaching race relations and multiracial identity that these kinds of conflicts and confrontations are critical, if not necessary. It is only through these classroom experiences that both students and professors are able to interrogate interactively and integratively our own theoretical, conceptual understandings of the world around us; grapple with painful, perplexing contradictions; connect them to our everyday lives; and engage in the transformative power of transgressive education. (hooks, 1994)

A "critical mass" (Root, 1992b, 1994b) of multiracial students, faculty, and staff personnel in higher education has allowed for a multiracial and multiethnic studies "field" to emerge. This chapter highlights the importance of the growing number of courses by, for, and about biracial and multiracial peoples offered on university campuses and the role that ethnic studies has played in fostering a multidisciplinary, education-as-empowerment framework within which biracial and multiracial student activism, scholarly research, and teaching are taking place. This chapter discusses the value and necessity of integrating the study of racially and culturally blended peoples into academic curricula at the college and university level. We raise questions of pedagogy and methodology of teaching courses about such a complex group of peoples who neither had a social script to follow nor a legitimate space of academic inquiry in which to write and construct one until now (Natasha Hansen, personal communication, October 1994).

THE PROBLEMS OF CURRENT CROSS-CULTURAL AND MULTICULTURAL STUDIES

General cross-cultural or multicultural education courses in the social sciences, literature, humanities, law, medicine, and fine arts typically have not included modules or lectures on multiracial peoples, or even on interracial marriages. A major unstated focus of these courses is often to educate and enlighten Euro-Americans about the impact of race, ethnicity, and culture. These courses, although well-intentioned, often have an underlying paternalistic view about peoples of color. They legitimize the separation and inequality across racial and ethnic groups; they foster learning about *other* peoples' cultures; and they assume, if not perpetuate, the notion of race with distinct borders. Curiously, the fact of interracial relationships is all too often missing. Subsequently, multiraciality is erased out of textual and experiential existence.

In multiculturally sensitive fields, there are often options and even requirements for taking a class on one or two of the major "ethnic" groups in the United States, which almost always means a topic on a racial minority group. For example, in the state of California, one of the academic requirements for state licensure as a psychotherapist is to take a graduate course in "cross-cultural mores and values, including a familiarity with the wide range of racial and ethnic backgrounds common among California's population" (Board of Behavioral Science Examiners, 1990, p. 6). Courses and textbooks used to fulfill this requirement (e.g., Atkinson et al., 1989; Chin, De La Cancela, & Jenkins, 1993; Dana, 1993; Ho, 1992; McGoldrick, Pearce, & Giordano, 1982; Sue & Sue, 1990; Vargas & Koss-Chioino, 1992) are generally surveys, attempting to do too much in too little space and time. They often carry the cross-cultural load for the rest of the curriculum.

The texts and course materials in multicultural or cross-cultural education have often been criticized for

1. being too reductionistic and anthropologically distanced (e.g., studying "the Natives" or "the exotic *other*");
2. presenting materials without a social and political framework;
3. failing to recognize diversity within groups and ascribing cultural practices and beliefs across members of a group; and/or
4. focusing on clinical case examples that simplistically limit or expand the possibilities for change for the racial or ethnic client.

Moreover, the implication for students of these cross-cultural or multicultural classes (and even ethnic studies classes, as we shall explain later) is that (a) the historical separation of the races is normal, (b) that the differences between cultures are insurmountable, and (c) that there exists such a thing as a "bona fide" monoracial group. Furthermore, students are not challenged to think about how race is constructed. Thus, taken-for-granted, faulty notions of race . . . are pedagogically duplicated and legitimized.

Except for brief references—usually to make the claim that race is a faulty concept, but nevertheless a significant one because of its sociological application—there is little or no mention of interracial relationships, marriages, and families or the biracial offspring and the complexity of their identities and social locations in traditional studies of race and ethnic relations. However, U.S. history of race and ethnic relations is embedded in a history of laws and regulations concerning interracial contact, sexuality, and economics, mostly in the forms of restriction and prohibition (Tenzer, 1990). Understanding personal, family, and community dynamics without an understanding of this history presents students with an ahistorical view of entrenched and deterministic racial and ethnic conflict. For instance, many students are surprised and dismayed to understand that the antimiscegenation laws in the United States were ruled unconstitutional by the U.S. Supreme Court as recently as 1967. Upon learning about the U.S. antimiscegenation laws, a biracial Eurasian student at UC Santa Barbara, who took a course on multiracials of Asian descent titled, "The World of Amerasians," wrote in her journal entry,

I am appalled! In some states, my parents' love for each other was illegal when they first got married—speaking of "forbidden fruit." There was a time when my siblings and I could have been treated as illegal products of an illegal union. I always thought I was different from "full-blooded" Asians because being part-white, [that] my history was not one of racial discrimination. After I read about these laws, I called my father and asked him what it was like. This is the first time my father and I ever really talked about my parents' marriage from a racial perspective.

By reading how blood quantum laws were instituted by the U.S. government, students learn concretely how race came to be employed as one of the single most significant markers of status, privilege, and power. For example, on learning how multiracial individuals and intermarried couples were incarcerated in concentration camps along with monoracially identified, intramarried Japanese Americans during World War II, the structural manipulation of racial definitions is illuminated. Furthermore, by studying the realities of interracial families, students can understand more easily the contradictory context in which racial and ethnic identities are constructed in a society that is embedded in the paradox of the "melting pot myth." That is to say, the "melting pot truth" has only been extended to Euro-American individuals, whose multiple European identities have been allowed to (or perhaps forced to) "melt" together, join forces, and then reap the personal,

economic, and legal rewards of such a privileged identity. The study of interracial relations, sexuality, and marriage, as well as the treatment and placement of the biracial offspring, therefore can provide critical insight into how and why race became such an effective tool to differentiate, rank, and offset groups of people. Race-difference paradigms, which dominate the literature on race relations, are directly challenged by introducing the study of multiracial peoples.

Most texts intended for use in general cross-cultural or multicultural education classes do not explicitly state this, yet they appear to be directed at training and increasing the awareness of Euro-American teachers, therapists, and professionals as they interact in an increasingly multicolored world. Current personal realities become engaged with the need for class time focused on helping students to process their feelings, their perceived realities, and their current judgments. For instance, reading the history of the slavery process in the United States often generates feelings of guilt on the part of Euro-American students, sparking debates about current responsibility for the consequences. Some Euro-American students sometimes express distanced and somewhat paternalistic views of the *other* as having been the unfortunate victims of prior racism, without understanding the systematic, personal, and institutional processes of cumulative disempowerment and continued dehumanization of peoples of color. The impact of modern racism requires a deeper level of self-awareness, sensitivity, and critical thinking.

If there are students of color in these classes, sensitivity to their presence and their reactions to materials presented in class or in the texts becomes important. They may become inadvertent spokespersons for their entire group. As representatives of their groups, students of color in these classes are treated as the norm for all members of their group, the exception to the norm of their group, or even the scapegoat for the covert and overt hostility by other class members. When the majority of the students in the class are Euro-

American, the "outsider" perspective of students of color often becomes the focus of class discussions. As a necessary introduction for Euro-Americans to the racialized realities, ethnic rituals, and worldviews of peoples of color, these sessions can sometimes provoke impatience on the part of students of color as they ask why do we have to take on the role of educating white people.

Furthermore, within this type of classroom context, the multiracial person disappears into a monoracial projection fostered by teachers, fellow students, or both. Unless interracial themes, histories, and concepts are presented as part of the course, either the credibility of the multiracial individual as a person of color is questioned and resisted or, if he or she possesses European ancestry, it is not acknowledged due to a hypodescent mentality that devalues ancestries of color and then locates biracial individuals into the lower status racial group. The dynamics of modern racism, which creates invisible minorities and then discounts the racism that produced their realities, are again repeated with multiracial students.

If peoples' heritages are treated as if they are monoracial without understanding the consistent and persistent, yet unsuccessful campaign by the American government to prevent interracial unions, then the idea of race and its racist origins are never fully interrogated. That is to say, race continues to be treated as biologically based (i.e., genetic, natural), rather than as a socially constructed, politically maintained category (Omi & Winant, 1986). Both students of color and Euro-American students, whose understanding of their social realities in American society may be different, are invested in the race-difference paradigms that legitimize their separate and unequal social locations. For many students, questioning the differences among the concepts of race, ethnicity, nationality, culture, and heritage become a confusing emotional process. By studying the history of interracial blending, by interacting with people from different backgrounds in the form of casual classroom contact, or by engaging in intimate interpersonal friendships and companionships across racial boundaries in the present, students and teachers personally realize the importance of interracial relationships in comprehending the highly racialized world in which we live and operate.

In cross-cultural and multicultural studies, students recognize that these courses are about so-called "monoracial" peoples and about how they are supposed to relate to these different peoples. However, when students are introduced to the extent of the legacy of racial and cultural blending in American history and its effects on present-day multiracial trends, they gradually begin to see how their own family genealogies connect with others. They not only wonder about the facts of their own histories, but they become curious as to why these facts seem to have remained hidden. If and only when the shared family histories of these students who have been forcibly socialized to experience separate racial statuses are recognized, appreciated, and nurtured can false, rigid, and unequal boundaries be transgressed and transformed. At a time when cross-cultural and multicultural education continues to duplicate the same racial and cultural hierarchies that it proposes to defeat, the implementation of topics on multiracials becomes necessary to provide effective conceptual tools for understanding the complex structure of race relations and their day-to-day impact within the realm of interpersonal experiences.

ETHNIC STUDIES AS MODEL FOR MULTIRACIAL AND MULTIETHNIC STUDIES

The university has privileged dispassionate, apolitical, and depersonalized inquiry and deemed it "quality" education. The struggle for the inclusion and integration of the voices and experiences of marginalized peoples into academia has always been and necessarily remains political, personal, and passionate. Peoples of color, multiracial individuals, gays, lesbians, and bisexuals, women, members of the working class, people with disabilities, and those who belong to all of these groups have been forced to create and sustain their own analytical and personal spaces within university contexts. In an academic world that has often been hostile to marginalized populations, ethnic studies programs and departments have become locations of analytical and personal refuge for students and faculty of color, at times even referred to as an "academic ghetto."

Ethnic studies on college campuses, unlike the "traditional" disciplines, arose out of a student and community empowerment movement in which students of color and their Euro-American allies organized, rallied, and protested under the threat of guns, police batons, and punitive administrative actions. As a result of the grassroots mobilization of students, community members, and supportive faculty and staff, many colleges and universities have come to include the histories and experiences of non–Anglo Protestant groups into their curriculum and language references. About 25 years have passed since colleges and universities first began implementing ethnic studies classes, programs, research centers, and departments. The action-oriented, bottom-up, multidisciplinary educational model of ethnic studies has allowed for a critical and transgressive self-interrogation of its fields in order to explain its scholarship and membership. As a result, ethnic studies, perhaps more so than any other field in higher education, has been at the forefront of including the histories and experiences of multiply marginalized groups such as multiracial peoples.

Scholars interested in doing research and teaching in the area of multiracial identity have often found institutional support in a variety of ethnic studies settings. Indeed, several courses on multiracial individuals, groups, and families have been offered sporadically by individual instructors interested in this subject matter within various departments, and others have included topics relating to biracial children, interracial dating and marriage, and multiracial populations in general social science, literature, humanities,

and ethnic studies courses. However, the only two regularly offered courses on multiracial peoples built into the core curriculum are (a) UC Berkeley's "People of Mixed Racial Descent" course, first designed and introduced into the ethnic studies curriculum by Dr. Terry Wilson in the late 1970s, and (b) UC Santa Barbara's "The World of Amerasians," introduced into the Asian American studies department curriculum and institutionalized by its chairperson, Dr. Sucheng Chan. Both of these courses on multiracial peoples are offered through ethnic studies departments. Moreover, both courses have served as a catalyst for the formation and revitalization of multiracial student organizations such as UC Berkeley's MISC and UC Santa Barbara's Variations. Out of these courses and groups have also come student-published journals, such as *Voices of Identity, Rage,* and *Deliverance* (No Collective, 1992) from UC Berkeley and *Inside/Out: Poetry and Prose by People of Mixed Heritage* (Littlejohn, 1994) from UC Santa Cruz and student-produced documentaries like Deidre Natsuno Howard's *And We Are Whole* and Erika Schmitt's *Variations on Race* from UC Santa Barbara.

Other ethnic studies courses have also inspired multiracial students to become agents of identity proclamation and change. Several of the multiracial individuals who took Jere Takahashi's Japanese American history class at UC Berkeley formed the Hapa Issues Forum, which now meets regularly, puts out a newsletter, and organizes a yearly conference on issues facing Asian descent multiracials. When Professor Ronald Takaki introduced his graduate teaching assistant, Cynthia Nakashima, to his comparative race and ethnic relations class at UC Berkeley as a scholar doing research on mixed-race identity, a biracial student of European and African ancestries and another of African and Pilipino ancestries approached Nakashima and together they started the Students of Interracial Descent (SID), which has since become Multiethnic/Interracial Students' Coalition (MISC). Students are now organizing multiracial associations on college campuses, putting on forums and conferences, and conducting groundbreaking research on multiracial populations and identity development, in turn further encouraging faculty to continue teaching courses on these topics. For example, when Dr. Terry Wilson proposed and taught the first course ever on multiracial people at UC Berkeley in the 1970s, it was designed as a seminar. Each year, the enrollment increased due to its extraordinary popularity. In 1990, when 480 students showed up, Dr. Wilson changed it to a lecture course, which now takes in about 250 students. In Fall 1994, when Cynthia Nakashima taught this course, she had five teaching assistants—all of whom were mixed-race women of various blends doing groundbreaking multiracial research from a variety of disciplines.

Ethnic studies has functioned as an ideal intellectual environment for the discourse on multiraciality due to its interdisciplinary approach. Ethnic studies' lack of disciplinary borders is compatible with the examination of multiracial individuals—by definition, a group that crosses many sociopolitical boundaries. The deconstructionist and postmodern leanings among ethnic studies scholars have also been methodologically and theoretically useful for questioning cultural constructions and presumptions of social boundaries as they relate to multiracial peoples. For example, with tremendous support from UCLA's Asian American Studies Reading Room coordinator, Marjie Lee, Steven Masami Ropp, an active member of Hapa Issues Forum and a UCLA graduate student, has spearheaded the compilation of an extensive, multidisciplinary, selected bibliography project on Asian descent multiracials, *Prism Lives, Emerging Voices*. Ropp has designed this bibliographical project so it could "facilitate multiracial scholars to consider works from a multitude of academic fields, seek out broader level connections and constructs in terms of theory and structure, and to develop this growing field on multiracial identity and experience" (Ropp, Williams, & Rooks, 1995, p. 1).

In examining multiracial peoples' experiences and identity development, ethnic studies has also had its limitations and shortcomings. The administrative and pedagogical thrust in ethnic studies programs mirrors the dominant assimilationist, race-difference paradigms—even when these programs harshly criticize the paradigms and take into account power relations between racial minority groups and the superordinate Euro-American group. It is no surprise that much of the emphasis on intergroup relations in ethnic studies' research and teaching therefore has been on minority-majority relations. Ethnic studies programs are often designed to examine their own group or intraracial and panethnic dynamics in relationship to the superordinate Euro-American group. The question of whose educational needs ethnic studies should meet is debated in terms of how it would be beneficial to the students of that program's specific racial, ethnic affiliation or to Euro-Americans. We might want to ask why it is never assumed or expected that African American students should take Asian American studies, that Asian/Pacific Islander American students should take Chicano/Latino studies, that Native American students should take black studies, or that all students should take a class on multiracial populations, and so on.

The divisions among the various ethnic studies programs across university campuses (in which budget and planning, faculty hiring, and curricula and course offerings are directly involved) pose a major problem for understanding the social realities of groups that defy single racial and ethnic identifications. For example, when examining the histories, literary character analyses, or identity development of Afro-Asians or black Native Americans, should one implement a class on these groups from within black studies, Asian American studies, Chicano/Latino studies, or Native American studies? Ideally, courses on multiracial populations would be cross-listed in and offered from within all ethnic studies. However, at a time of budget cuts and freezes, when ethnic studies programs are often among the financially hardest hit, each program would rather protect and preserve courses dealing with topics specifically about its own group, understandably. Thus the challenges that often face the multiracial individual in a zero-sum, either-or society also confront students and faculty trying to foster a multiracial consciousness in an either-or ethnic studies setup, coupled with the competition for seemingly ever-dwindling resources.

For now, the ethnic studies avenues open to scholars interested in teaching and doing research on multiracial identity are as follows:

1. To work with supportive ethnic studies faculty and implement courses on multiracial peoples within specific ethnic studies programs and departments, such as the courses on multiracial people taught at UC Berkeley and UC Santa Barbara;

2. To incorporate topics of interracial marriage and multiracial peoples into general ethnic studies courses already offered; and

3. To bridge and coalesce the all-too-often socially and politically disjointed ethnic studies programs by offering courses on interracial relationships and multiracial populations that are cross-listed, such as the courses on multiracial identity taught by Dr. G. Reginald Daniel at UCLA through the center for both Latin American and Afro-American studies and funded by the Counsel on Educational Development, or Dr. Vicki Mays's course on interracial relationships at UCLA, cross-listed in psychology and Afro-American studies.

When the critical mass of multiracial students, staff, and faculty grows in numbers and departmental influence and administrative clout, a "multiracial/multiethnic studies" department may not be unimaginable.

METHODS OF TEACHING BIRACIALITY AND MULTIRACIALITY

There are two ways in which the study of multiracial populations has been introduced and integrated into college and university courses. The first is to include this topic in the general courses on race and ethnicity, such as Asian American

history, comparative race relations, African American women's experience, introduction to Chicano studies, contemporary Native American and Euro-American relations, Chicana/Latina literature, cross-cultural psychology, cultural anthropology, methods classes, and so on. Dr. G. Reginald Daniel, who has taught, "Betwixt and Between: Multiracial Identity in Global Perspective and Close Encounters: Racial and Cultural Blending in the Americas" at UCLA has said,

> Ideally the topic on multiracial identity not only should be dealt with in courses dealing specifically with the topic in order to give students a more detailed and in-depth analysis, but also should be incorporated into general courses on race and ethnicity. My fundamental goal is to provide all students with an examination of the multiracial experience in the larger world arena in order to facilitate an understanding of the complex issues surrounding the newly emerging multiracial consciousness in the United States. By so doing, I feel it may be possible to define ways of nurturing this consciousness in manner [sic] that could help move race relations toward a broader basis of cooperation and collaboration. (Daniel & Collins, 1994, p. 2)

Kevin Yoshida, a biracial Euro-American and Japanese American student, was pleasantly surprised when he took the general sociological survey course on race and ethnic relations at Santa Monica College in Spring 1992. This course included readings from *Racially Mixed People in America* (Root, 1992b) throughout the semester, along with other general race relations texts and a specific discussion on intermarriage and multiracial identity the last two weeks of the course. After taking this course, Yoshida (personal communication, 1992) remarked,

> This was one of the only courses I've taken in college that has allowed me to connect my multiple identities and understand my humanity in its fullness. I am biracial Japanese American and white; I am fluently bilingual in English and Spanish. I am a gay man of color. I am a multira-

cial, international person. I am many things simultaneously. This course legitimized who I am and how I live.

Leslie Hunter, a binational, biracial woman of African American and Honduran ancestries, took the same general sociology course on race and ethnic relations at Santa Monica College 2 years later in Spring 1994. For a group project assignment, Hunter volunteered to work on the topic of black-Latino conflict in Los Angeles. During the week that multiracial identity was covered, Hunter generously and openly shared her personal experiences with the class. Although she often felt each of her parent groups treated her as the *other*, she articulated that being both African American and Latina—at times simultaneously and at other times situationally—best described who she is. Until Hunter mentioned her African ancestry, most students in the class simply assumed she was Latina.

The voices and faces of students like Yoshida and Hunter directly contest faulty notions people have about how biracial people should look, act, and be named. Personal testimonies like those articulated by Yoshida and Hunter in class and in their writings bring to life the theoretical models that seem abstract to most students and show how teaching about multiraciality can have personally transformative experiences for multiracial students and the students they encounter in the classrooms.

Scholars such as Dr. Sucheng Chan (UC Santa Barbara), Dr. Jere Takahashi (UC Berkeley), Dr. Ronald Takaki (UC Berkeley), Dr. Robert Blauner (UC Berkeley), Dr. Melinda Micco (Mills College), Dr. Darrell Darrisaw (Carleton College, Minnesota), Dr. Amy Mass (Whittier College, California), Dr. Maria Root (University of Washington), Dr. Christine Hall (University of Arizona), Dr. Paul Spickard (Brigham Young University—Hawai'i), and others have used guest lecturers and panels of speakers and included readings on multiracial individuals in one or two class sessions of the course as a method of integrating this subject matter into their courses. Other scholars, including Root, Hall, Mass, and

Spickard, as well as Dr. Jack Forbes (UC Davis), Dr. Gerald Vizenor (UC Berkeley, UC Santa Cruz) and Caroline Streeter (Stanford) have also taught specific courses on multiracial peoples and/or have woven the discussion of multiraciality throughout their general courses as well.

A far more challenging and ideal way to include multiraciality on a regular basis is the total incorporation of racially mixed people into the curriculum. Cynthia Nakashima includes mixed-race issues throughout her introduction to Asian American history course at UC Berkeley. For example, Nakashima begins by looking at early intermarriage rates and interracial families in the context of Asian male labor immigration (i.e., the Chinese, Filipinos, and South Asian Indians) and European American hostility. The gender imbalance caused by the restriction of Asian female immigration may explain why outmarriage frequently occurred among some Asian men in the United States and not others (e.g., Chinese men and Native Hawaiian women in Hawai'i; Chinese men and African American women in the American South; Filipino men and Euro-American and Mexican women in the West Coast; South Asian Indian men and Mexican women in California, Chinese and Japanese men with Euro-American women on the East Coast, etc.). Nakashima also examines the dominant racial ideology and the corresponding laws regarding miscegenation between Euro-Americans and Asians as an important and telling aspect of the viewing of Asians as racial *others* in the United States. Ethnicity, gender, geographical location, and class are accounted for when Nakashima interrogates the intermarriage patterns of early Asian immigrants and Asian Americans in the United States (Gulick, 1914; Leonard, 1992; Posadas, 1989; Spickard, 1989). She also discusses the impact of antimiscegenation laws on the numbers and racial combinations of intermarriages and points out that a sizable number of second-generation Asian Americans may have been mixed race because there were so few Asian women at the time.

World War II has had a significant impact on the lives of Asian Americans (Chan, 1991). Nakashima also lectures on how World War II was important for interracially married couples and for multiracial, Asian-descent Americans as well because:

1. Racial ideology had begun to turn away from biological determinism and away from hybrid degeneracy.
2. Internment of Japanese Americans tested the line between Asian and European American; interracially married families were interned, although gender and race of the parents qualitatively altered the life experiences of internees.
3. World War II and U.S. military dominance in Asia created the "war bride" and Amerasian phenomena.
4. U.S. military presence in Hawai'i also brought Asian Americans in Hawai'i together with servicemen of various racial and ethnic ancestries.

Following World War II, the structural and demographic changes in the United States also affected interracial families and Asian-descent multiracials. During the 1960s civil rights and racial/ethnic power movements, the last of the antimiscegenation laws were struck down, and the biracial baby boom began. Post-1965 issues are around mail-order brides, sex tours, the homecoming act for Vietnamese Amerasians, and the withdrawal of U.S. bases in the Philippines leave thousands of Pilipino Amerasians behind. Nakashima's approach to integrating mixed-race issues throughout general ethnic studies can also be adapted to including discussions on women of color and gays, lesbians, and bisexuals of color in these courses.

Finally, one could design and organize a complete course on multiracial identity in which an interdisciplinary ethnic studies approach is taken, such as the courses taught by Dr. Jack Forbes (UC Davis), Dr. Terry Wilson (UC Berkeley), Dr. G. Reginald Daniel (UCLA), Teresa Kay Williams (UC Santa Barbara), Cynthia Nakashima (UC Berkeley), Dr. Melinda Micco (Mills College) or a more single-discipline course on this subject matter, such as the courses taught by Dr. Gerald Vizenor in literature (UC Berkeley), Teresa Kay Williams in sociology (UCLA), and Dr. George

Kitahara Kich in graduate level cross-cultural psychology. These courses have a profound impact on both monoracially identified and biracial and multiracial students. Having entire courses on this subject matter give academic legitimacy to multiracial peoples by locating their identities into the structure of knowledge. They teach students that the realities of multiracial groups illuminate the salience of race and ethnic relations in an ever-transforming world community and give them analytical tools to question, challenge, and transgress take-for-granted, normalized assumptions upon which this salience rests.

Multiracial students have become accustomed to not having their identities and realities affirmed in academic disciplines. "Learning about one's culture" or "finding one's roots" is often done through monoracial exploration of one heritage over another. Natasha Hansen, a first-year graduate student, expressed her amazement when she stumbled across a course on multiracial identity offered by UCLA's sociology department in Fall 1994. Hansen explained,

> Frantically searching for a third course to take in the schedule of classes, I was pleasantly surprised to come upon a course titled, "Within, Between, and Beyond Race: Racially Mixed People in the U.S." Actually, I was not pleasantly surprised, I was shocked. Because I am a black and white biracial woman, I have become accustomed to being socially located on the margins. This being the case, being able to take a class that focuses on and centralizes my plural racial identity seemed unbelievable.

Treacy White, a biracial Japanese Euro-American woman, described her reactions upon taking a course on multiracial people of Asian descent at UC Santa Barbara in Spring 1992, when the first course on this topic was offered. She has written in her first journal assignment,

> I don't know where to begin! Should I begin with how excited I am about this class? Should I begin with asking myself who I am? Or should I begin

with my own experiences as being biracial and Amerasian? No. I think I will begin with my reactions to all the things I've learned from Maria P. Root's [1992b] book thus far.

I have to admit that as I opened this book I found myself getting excited. Never have I read any literature about people like myself. It feels good to know that my kind of racial background has been acknowledged and has actually spurred interest in people. As I read chapter one I was actually nodding my head in agreement with what Root was saying. Being half Japanese and half white, I have always had qualms about committing myself to one or the other culture. I don't think I am Asian enough to say I am Asian American and I am not completely white so I can't say that I am. So what am I? I do not want to divide myself. I don't want [to] separate what makes me a complete person, but society seems to allow me only to be one or the other. Now it seems that some people are finally saying I don't have to deny part of my heritage.

Lee Corbett, a Korean American man adopted into a Euro-American family, became an outspoken campus activist after taking a class on the multiracial identity of Asian-descent Americans at UC Santa Barbara. He is one of the several founding members of UC Santa Barbara's multiracial organization, Variations, which grew out of the political quest of the students who took this course. In a personal letter he wrote to the instructor years later, Corbett reflected,

That was the first class that presented models that captured the struggles I went through as a multiethnic, Asian American man adopted into a European American family. Your class has been invaluable for my own personal and intellectual growth.

Examining the racial and cultural multiplicity embodied by multiracial individuals permits many monoracially identified students to make connections with their multiple realities. Que Dang, a UC Santa Barbara graduate, had taken a course on multiracial people of Asian descent as an elective for her Asian American studies' major in Spring 1993. Dang explained what she had gained from taking this course:

That was the only Asian American Studies class I took in which I was not part of the numerical majority. Most of the students were biracial, but at the same time, I could relate to the racial and cultural duality of biracial people because I was born in Vietnam and came to the U.S. at the age of two and being a refugee in a country that thinks of itself as an immigrant nation. I have also dealt with the bicultural struggles of being Vietnamese and being American within my family. At the time I took the class, I was dating someone African American. Our visual, phenotypical differences were an issue for the people around me perhaps more so than when I've dated European American men. I saw the class as pertaining to my prospective children. I'll most likely marry someone who is not Vietnamese so the class gave me insight on what I may expect when I marry and have children.

Euro-American students who can move beyond the notion of "studying other people's fascinating cultures" can also participate in a liberating educational process that transgresses the invisible power dynamics between themselves and students of color in the classroom. Myra Mayesh has taken the general sociology course, "Race and Ethnic Relations," at Santa Monica College in which multiracial identity models were treated as central to understanding intergroup dynamics. After talking this course, Mayesh recognized how she too could understand her many selves in relationship to her racial status in American society. Mayesh has explained,

This course has been one of the most enriching experiences, yet one of the most academically challenging courses I've taken. . . . As a European American woman, I have only had to see my gender in relationship to my sexual orientation and perhaps socioeconomic status. Not only has this course challenged me to look at my racial status, gender, sexual orientation, and class in relationship to one another, but by looking at multiple racial realities as both black and white—rather than black or white—it provides a model for my other dualities.

As these students' statements illuminate, there are benefits to being an "insider majority group member"; one possesses the shared values, assumptions, and even similar physical appearances with the majority of the class, including the instructor. Being an insider majority group member gives students the sense that they are part of a larger collective.

Students of color who take ethnic studies courses often express how comfortable it is sitting in a classroom filled with co-ethnics and taking courses taught by professors of color, who speak their same consciousness. Although the disadvantages are numerous and perhaps obvious (e.g., alienation, exclusion, invisiblity, etc.), there are also advantages to being an "outsider minority group," a racially and culturally marginalized member in the classroom setting. Students of color, multiracial students, female students, gays, lesbians, and bisexual students are accustomed to sitting on the sidelines in terms of class participation, course materials, texts, and so on. Euro-American students, who often experience being an outsider minority group member when they take ethnic studies classes, learn for the first time what it is like when your group is not addressed by the course materials or, when covered, is not always portrayed in an accurate or flattering way. Euro-American students hear some students of color angrily refer to them as "whites" and "white people" as they experience their individuality dismissed and humanity objectified. Euro-American students learn what it feels like to be marginalized in text and in physical presence within this artificial setting of the classroom.

Being forced to occupy an outsider minority group position allows students to see themselves in relationship to the contextual majority group whose human existence, perspective, and worldview are validated at the expense of theirs. Multiracial students often experience being insiders and outsiders simultaneously in these settings, where fellow classmates and instructors alike have no clue as to what being biracial and multiracial entails.

In *Teaching to Transgress,* bell hooks (1994) explains how teaching and learning can be transformative acts, restoring for us the vision of edu-

cation as a form of liberation. The classroom must be seen as an important revolutionary site, where critical thinking can and must be nurtured. hooks stated this powerfully:

> The classroom with all its limitations remains the location of possibility. In that field of possibility we have the opportunity to labor for freedom, to demand of ourselves and our comrades an openness of mind and heart that allows us to face reality even as we collectively imagine ways to move beyond boundaries, to transgress. This is education as the practice of freedom. (p. 231)

As attacks are waged on affirmative action programs and multiculturally focused curricula with accusations that "politically correct cops" are "closing the American mind" (Bloom, 1987; D'Souza, 1991), universities are in desperate need of more courses that provide safe spaces for healing, understanding, and compassion among monoracially identified students of color, monoracially identified Euro-Americans, and multiracial students of various sexual orientations, socioeconomic statuses, and physical abilities. The new and exciting emergent field of multiracial studies has the potential to fulfill the promise of education that transgresses boundaries, that inspires critical thinking, that dismantles hierarchies, that moves and transforms the world.

CONCLUSION

The university has traditionally been an exclusive location, as the ivory tower metaphor implies, where knowledge has been produced and transmitted. All members of the society take part in creating knowledge, but only those with MAs and PhDs next to their names are credited with this task, thereby excluding the nonformally trained from the material rewards of producing and transmitting knowledge. It is through our conscious efforts as students, professors, and activists to continue the inclusion and incorporation of all members of our society into the production of knowledge and to connect what is studied in our classrooms to the everyday lives of our students that we can reclaim a university from which all can benefit, not just an exclusive group of well-trained professionals. The study of multiracial populations through multidisciplinary research methods and rigorous analytical thinking provides us with insight into the social realities of individuals who live along and across ever-expanding borders.

In addition to immigration, economic restructuring, and increased structural intergroup contact at primary and secondary levels of interaction, multiracial populations are contributing to the much-debated demographic changes in the United States. Multiracial people should not simply be seen as mere interracial and intercultural ambassadors put on this earth to bridge the gaps between and across groups because this view absolves the monoracially identified populations from their responsibilities of cooperation and coalition building. Rather, we should be asking how biracial and multiracial peoples process their personal and social selves in a variety of contexts; how they gain entry into and negotiate membership into various groups; how they are perceived and treated by subordinate and superordinate groups; and under what conditions newly recognized identities are mounted and sustained. What do these boundary-defying populations tell us about how boundaries are constructed, maintained, violated, and deconstructed? How do the studies of biracial and multiracial identities fit into the structure of knowledge?

Students who have been asking these questions have been at the forefront challenging the increasingly volatile racial climates on college campuses. In order to network with other biracial and multiracial students who are navigating the uncharted waters of this new multiracial consciousness, students at Kansas State, Harvard, Yale, Brown, Stanford, New York, Michigan, University of Southern California, UC Berkeley, UC Santa Cruz, UC Irvine, UC Santa Barbara, and other campuses have formed multiracial student associations. Some biracial students in these multiracial organizations have also jointly retained membership in traditional racial and ethnic student organizations (Black Student Union, Asian Pacific Coalition, MECHA, American Indian Students Association, etc.).

These organizations, along with courses on multiracial topics, are crucial to the social and political institutionalization of an identity that would otherwise remain individually based. Multiracial identity has been seen as temporary and transitional—a stage in development before people either become an appendage to the subordinate racial group through social customs and hypodescent laws or become part of the superordinate group through straight-line assimilation into the core society. The emergence of university courses and student organizations by, for, and about biracial and multiracial people strongly indicates that this identity deserves social and academic legitimacy and institutional sustenance. What multiracial studies in higher education can offer is the abolition of hierarchies and transgression of boundaries that separate us from the totality of our humanity and divide us from one another.

BIBLIOGRAPHY

Atkinson, D., Morten, G., & Sue, D. (Ed.). (1989). *Counseling American minorities: A cross-cultural perspective* (3rd ed.). Dubuque, IA: William C. Brown.

Bloom, A. (1987). *The Closing of the American mind.* New York: Simon & Schuster.

Chan, S. (1991). *Asian Americans: An interpretive history.* Boston: Twayne.

Chin, J. L., De La Cancela, V., & Jenkins, Y. (Ed.). (1993). *Diversity in psychotherapy.* New York: Praeger.

Dana, R. H. (1993). *Multicultural assessment perspectives for professional psychology.* Boston: Allyn & Bacon.

Daniel, G. R., & Collins, III, J. U. (1994). *Pluralism and integration: The dynamics of ethnic relations reconsidered.* Unpublished manuscript.

D'Souza, D. (1991) *Illiberal education.* New York: Free Press.

Gulick, S. L. (1914). *The American Japanese problem.* New York: Scribner.

Ho, M. K. (1992). *Minority children and adolescents in therapy.* Newbury Park, CA: Sage.

hooks, b. (1994). *Teaching to transgress: Education as the practice of freedom.* New York: Routledge.

Leonard, K. I. (1992). *Making ethnic choices: California's Punjabi Mexican Americans.* Philadelphia, PA: Temple University Press.

McGoldrick, M., Pearce, J., & Giordano, J. (Ed.). (1982). *Ethnicity and family therapy.* New York: Guilford.

Omi, M., & Winant, H. (1986). *Racial formation in the United States from the 1960s to the 1980s.* New York: Routledge & Keagan Paul.

Posadas, B. M. (1989). Mestiza girlhood: Interracial families in Chicago's Filipino American community since 1925. In Asian Women United of California (Ed.), *Making waves: An anthology of writings by and about Asian American women* (pp. 273–282). Boston: Beacon.

Root, M. P. P. (Ed.). (1992b). *Racially mixed people in America.* Newbury Park, CA: Sage.

Root, M. P. P. (1994b, Summer). Reasons racially mixed persons identify as people of color. In M. Garcia (Ed.), *FOCUS: Newsletter for the Psychological Study of Ethnic Minority Issues in the American Psychological Association,* pp. 1–5.

Ropp, S. M., Williams, T. K., & Rooks, C. (1995). *Prism lives/emerging voices of multiracial Asians: A selective, partially annotated bibliography.* Los Angeles: University of California Press.

Spickard, P. R. (1989). *Mixed blood: Intermarriage and ethnic identity in twentieth-century America.* Madison: University of Wisconsin Press.

Sue, D. W., & Sue, D. (1990). *Counseling the culturally different: Theory and practice* (2d ed.). New York: John Wiley.

Tenzer, L. R. (1990). *A completely new look at interracial sexuality: Public opinion and select commentaries.* Manahawkin, NJ: Scholars' Publishing House.

Vargas, L. A., & Koss-Chioino, J. D. (Ed.). (1992). *Working with culture.* San Francisco: Jossey-Bass.

CHAPTER 5

Employment and Occupation

The image of Asian Americans as the "model minority" is commonly reinforced in the popular media with summary statistics showing high levels of education, occupational status, and higher-than-average family incomes. According to the U.S. Commission on Civil Rights (1992), however, the model minority image is not only misleading, it is indeed harmful to Asian Americans. This impression diverts attention away from serious social and economic problems that affect many segments of the Asian American population, detracts from both the subtle and the overt racial discrimination encountered by Asian Americans, places undue pressure on young Asian Americans to succeed educationally and professionally, and fuels competition and resentment between Asian Americans and other groups. This chapter offers a critical look at the Asian American experience in various workplace settings that directly challenges the model minority image and offers a view seldom seen in the mainstream media.

Deborah Woo's selection, "The Inventing and Reinventing of 'Model Minorities': the Cultural Veil Obscuring Structural Sources of Inequality," presents a comprehensive overview of the model minority phenomenon. Beginning with a historical context of the emergence of the model minority image, she sets forth an extensive analysis of its persistence. According to Woo, the five reasons for maintenance of the model minority image are (1) media celebration of a few dramatic examples of "rags-to-riches" stories, (2) the existence of a sizable and visible group of highly educated professionals, (3) failure to disaggregate census data, (4) unexamined assertions about the relationship between culture and mobility, and (5) specific political or ideological purposes served by the image. In addition, Woo raises the issue of a "glass ceiling" used against Asian Americans that limits their mobility regardless of education, hard work, and experience. She contends that the existence of a glass ceiling challenges the model minority image of unobstructed Asian American economical mobility.

The detailed work of Pan Suk Kim and Gregory Lewis demonstrates the glass ceiling in action. Their article examines Asian Americans in federal government employment, offering a complex longitudinal analysis. The authors discovered interesting and troubling differences between Asian American men and Asian American women. Their research describes how highly educated and experienced Asian American men do not experience a glass ceiling in terms of high-grade positions and salaries, although they are much less likely to be in supervisory or management positions. Employment status discrepancies between Asian American women and white women actually *increased* between 1978 and 1992, despite adjustments made for similar education, seniority, age, veteran, and handicap status. The authors also found that Asian Americans without college degrees appeared to experience employment disadvantages relative to whites.

Language discrimination is a major issue confronting Asian Americans in the workplace. Accent discrimination and "English-only" rules are important because of the large proportion of immigrants and non-native English speakers among Asian Americans in all levels of employment. Everyone agrees that communication skills are important, but Asian Americans are increasingly frustrated by employers who arbitrarily discriminate on the subjective basis of language fluency rather than on the quality of work. Richard J. P. Cavosora reports on one case involving five Filipino security guards who were removed from their jobs after someone complained about having trouble communicating with an unidentified guard over the telephone. No effort was made to determine whether or not any of the guards were actually involved in the phone incident, and there were no prior complaints about the job performance of any of the guards. Since the early 1990s there has been an increase in reports of disciplinary actions and dismissals of employees based on an employer's subjective assessment of a worker's ability to communicate and its impact on the workplace. As a result, many Asian Americans are filing discrimination lawsuits and taking their cases to court.

The popular media image of the model minority has primarily concentrated on successful Asian American professionals and entrepreneurs. Yet it is important to realize that a significant number of Asian Americans do not fall into these categories, earning their living paycheck by paycheck. Miriam Ching Louie's article chronicles the experiences of Asian immigrant women working in the garment industry, and the organizing efforts of Asian Immigrant Women Advocates (AIWA). AIWA has been instrumental in drawing attention to "sweatshop" conditions in sewing factories in the U.S. and empowering immigrant women workers to fight for their rights. AIWA spearheaded a three-year nationwide campaign to boycott Jessica McClintock clothing products in order to call attention to exploitative labor practices throughout the garment industry. In 1996 Jessica McClintock, Inc. (JMI) and AIWA resolved the issues that separated them. The agreement called for cooperative efforts by both parties to ensure workers' rights as well as to promote awareness of fair labor practices. Although not legally responsible or required, JMI agreed to donate money to establish an education fund, sponsor scholarships, and provide garment workers with bilingual state and federal publications to better educate them on fair labor standards. The precedent-setting McClintock boycott pressured other garment industry companies to negotiate better worker protections and establish toll-free confidential hotlines for garment workers to report violations in their workplaces.

The selections in this chapter not only offer an overview of the workplace experiences faced by Asian Americans, but also illustrates how Asian Americans are fighting back against unfair and unequal treatment. Through individual and collective efforts, Asian Americans are making a mark in the workplace and challenging the quiet, unassuming model minority image.

Reading 15

The Inventing and Reinventing of "Model Minorities": The Cultural Veil Obscuring Structural Sources of Inequality

Deborah Woo

With but a few changes in detail, the same fable can be—and has been—told about the Japanese, Irish, Jews, Italians, Greeks, Swedes and many more. Its form is always the same: a people beset by hardships and oppression in their own country bravely cross the seas to America, a land which promises freedom and opportunity. Once arrived, however, they encounter prejudice, oppression, and difficult times. However, they never lose faith in the dream that originally compelled them. They work hard, refuse to be discouraged by the abuses that harm their lives and hinder their progress, and eventually—usually in the second, or sometime the third generation—succeed. History is, thus, nicely encapsulated within the American Protestant ethic . . . (Lyman, 1973: 71)

Sociologist Stanford Lyman thus indicated how success stories about Chinese in America were part of "America's perpetual morality tale about its minorities." This imagery has not only been extended to other Asian Americans but been firmly implanted through the recitation of statistical data.

During the 1970s when the Asian American population was largely Japanese Americans and Chinese Americans, gross statistical profiles of these groups pointed to their high educational and occupational achievement (Varon, 1967). Conversely, one found relatively low rates of divorce (Sanborn, 1977; Barringer et al., 1995: 136–144), unemployment (Jaco and Wilber, 1975), crime[1] and

Source: An expanded version of Chapter 1 in Deborah Woo, *Glass Ceilings and Asian Americans: The New Face of Workplace Barriers* (Walnut Creek, CA: Alta Mira Press, 1999). Reprinted by permission.

delinquency (Beach, 1932; Kitano, 1969; Takagi and Platt, 1978; Strong, 1934), and mental illness (Jew and Brody, 1967). As the fastest growing of minority groups in the United States (O'Hare and Felt, 1991; Gardner et al., 1985; Bureau of the Census, 1993),[2] Asian Americans are the most highly educated of all groups, including white males, and are projected in the next decade to make up a disproportionate share of the professional workforce (Ong and Hee, 1993; Fullerton, 1989).

While supporting facts for the morality tale are often based on census data, the myth is kept alive by media accounts. It is here, in fact, where demography is aligned with culturally appealing explanations. A strong work ethic, high value placed on educational achievement, and stable family relations are routinely cited as among the most influential factors promoting upward mobility. Underlying it all is a theme of hard work and determination that echoes the stories told by Horatio Alger (1832–1899). A Harvard educated man and ordained minister, Alger had penned hundreds of stories about penniless boys who pulled themselves out of poverty by their own "bootstraps." As works of fiction intended to inspire, they valorized honesty and diligence, the heroes representing not so much extraordinary individuals but ones who made modest though significant efforts. The "Asian" Horatio Alger myth can be seen as an extension of such tales woven around aspiring immigrants in this country. In the more recent period, the substance of the narrative has been slightly altered to incorporate high-tech success, but the form of these stories remains very much the same.

This presentation discusses how the *cultural* assumptions underlying the thesis ignore certain *structural* or *class* issues. In doing so, it calls into question a fundamental premise of model minority logic—namely, that cultural factors are the primary ingredients for success. Apart from Horatio Alger's legacy, a culturalist approach to understanding social issues has enjoyed great favor in the United States, whereas a long history of class analysis has dominated European thought on stratification.[3] The controversy between cultural and class analyses came to a head in the United States during the unrest and agitation of the 1960s, with the emergence of the "culture of poverty" idea. American leftists saw this idea as "victim-blaming," as the social problems of American blacks were attributed to a "culture of poverty," an "unstable family structure" and way of life that promoted failure or low achievement (Moynihan, 1965; Valentine, 1968). By the same logic, discriminatory actions on the part of employers and a host of institutions could be dismissed as causes of continuing racial segregation and its consequences for employment (Massey and Denton, 1993; Wilson, 1997).

As a result, cultural explanations in general become politically suspect among that generation of scholars and activists, particularly as the melting pot ideal, along with culturally-based mobility assumptions, were empirically contradicted by research evidence (Glazer and Moynihan, 1963; Steinberg, 1982).[4] Culture of poverty ideas, however, would resurface in a new form, namely, through an inverted discourse that premised achievement on an enabling cultural repertoire of values associated with Asian Americans as "model minorities."

By the 1980s and 1990s the model minority thesis was being used as a wedge in arguments against affirmative action (*Asian American Policy Review*, 1996). With the publication of *The Bell Curve* in 1994, genetic twist was added to these racial explanations, as social inequalities were reduced to "natural" differences in inherited intelligence between the races. The relatively inferior status of blacks vis-a-vis whites and Asians was reframed as one of basic intelligence, and by implication, a problem that could not be remedied through government intervention (Herrnstein and Murray, 1994).

For these reasons, where issues of social inequality in matters of race and ethnicity are concerned, Asian Americans occupy a critical place in our thinking about ethnic politics. They are not only a common empirical reference point for evaluating relative progress and achievement among different groups but an ideological one as well. Critics of the ideological agenda have disputed the statistical facts themselves, along with the cultural theory purporting to explain them. The concept of "model minority" has been criticized as simplistic, masking extreme inequalities within and between different Asian American groups, as well as deflecting attention from structural issues that might better account for success or failure. Although such critiques have produced a certain retreat from uncritical use of the term in public discourse,[5] in the larger public arena the image of a successfully assimilating minority continues to be seductive, forming an inescapable backdrop for a wide array of issues where Asian Americans have been drawn into broader social and political analyses of American society.

An analysis of the various factors responsible for the persistence of the model minority thesis therefore has significant theoretical implications. The basic argument in this chapter is that model minority theory has withstood counterevidence and counterarguments by ushering available facts under its own umbrella, and that this has been possible due to inattention to the problematic aspects of doing so. In a review and analysis of images in the popular press in the 1960s and 1980s, Keith Osajima pointed out how subsequent versions of the thesis have been based on "remarkably pliable constructs," enabling critical research findings to be embraced and subsumed under the core thesis of success, though the fundamental thesis remained largely unchanged (Osajima, 1988). In this way, simplistic portrayals became slightly more "complex" in the 1980s. The bulk of the following analysis is aimed at reviewing some of the major critiques of the thesis, introducing others which deserve attention, and thereby explaining how the thesis has survived into the 1990s.

ASIAN AMERICANS AS "MODEL MINORITIES": A LEGACY OF THE 1960S

Up until the late 1960s, the Asian population in the United States was a fraction of what it is today and still largely invisible. The introduction of national immigration quotas in the 1920s had sharply curtailed Asian immigration, reducing it to a trickle. Until the abolishment of these quotas in 1965, the maximum annual immigration permitted from Asia was 2,990, compared to a total allowance of 149,667 for Europe (Chan, 1991: 146). Subsequent immigration would fundamentally transform the social composition of Asian American communities by increasing the dominance of the foreign-born population and the presence of a large proportion of professionals (Hing, 1993). It was the experiences, however, of native-born Chinese and Japanese Americans, who formed the large majority of the Asian American population prior to 1965, that would be the original stimulus for media stories of success.

There is no question that this nation has absorbed immigrants with extraordinary differences in history, religion, race, class, and national origin (Levine, 1996). As evidenced by the acculturation of subsequent generations and increasing rates of outmarriage,[6] a certain degree of assimilation or acculturation occurs simply as a matter of time and increasing social contact, with relations of power setting the terms for that contact. Yet, it has been the persistence of racial inequalities that has served as an ongoing challenge to faith in the inevitability of assimilation, as well as a catalyst to demands for change.

During the 1960s, the need to reexamine and address issues of racial inequality was pronounced. Racial unrest was one of several sources of societal discontent, which together with the war in Vietnam, led to demands for government reforms that had not been equaled since the Great Depression of the 1930s. Over and against such moves towards fundamental institutional change were competing attempts to recast the causes of social inequality in terms of individual effort and hard work.

Thus, for example, on December 26, 1966, *U.S. News and World Report* printed an article entitled "Success Story of One Minority in the U.S.," in which it was suggested that blacks and other minorities were making unreasonable demands for government assistance. "At a time when it is being proposed that hundreds of billions be spent to uplift Negroes and other minorities, the nation's 300,000 Chinese-Americans are moving ahead on their own, with no help from anyone else" (p. 73). Earlier in the year, *The New York Times* had published a piece called "Success Story, Japanese American Style," in which the emphasis upon self-help was implicitly, if not explicitly, a point of admiration. "By any criterion we choose, the Japanese Americans are better off than any other group in our society, including native-born whites. They have established this remarkable record, moreover, by their own almost totally unaided effort" (p. 25).

Such news coverage quickly caught the attention of Asian Americans in the scholarly community, who have been sharply critical of such portrayals ever since (Kitano and Sue, 1973[7]; Kim, 1973; Suzuki, 1977; Kim and Hurh, 1983; Osajima, 1988; Suzuki, 1989). The concern was twofold: (1) that there were unwarranted assumptions made about the progress of Asian Americans, and (2) that the comparisons with other racial groups were invidious and insidious, generating ill feelings with the moral injunction that underachievers, particularly "certain" minorities, "re-form" themselves after this "model."

While the 1980s would generate research and objective evidence countering unqualified accounts of Asian American success, the print media continued to promote a picture of extraordinary accomplishment. Thus, for example, in 1982 the *Oakland Tribune* noted that Chinese Americans had among the highest per capita incomes, echoing the impressive accomplishments which have marked overseas Chinese communities.

They have been inordinately successful on both sides of the Pacific. U.S. census figures indicate that Asian Americans, including 705,000 of Chinese extraction, now have the nation's highest per capita income, echoing the achievements that have made Hong Kong, Singapore, and Taipei nodal points of booming Asia. (*Oakland Tribune*, May 26, 1982)

As the Immigration Act of 1965 introduced new ethnic dimensions into the Asian American population, making it more diverse than ever before,[8] success stories have been reproduced for other Asian ethnic groups as well, including Japanese, Koreans, and Southeast Asians (Caudill and DeVos, 1956; Kim and Hurh, 1983; Osajima, 1988; Caplan et al., 1985, 1992, 1994). Even diverging cultural values did not undermine the popular view that had brought this population center stage, namely, Horatio Alger dreams and belief in a "cultural formula for success."

THE PERSISTENCE AND ELASTICITY OF THE "MODEL MINORITY THESIS"

Insofar as they represent living embodiments of certain ideals and their related ethical injunctions, Asian Americans have enjoyed a certain status as prima facie testimonials to these myths. The model minority thesis has persisted, however, for other reasons. It is in the face of a cumulative body of contradicting evidence that a closer examination is called for. Five reasons are offered to explain this tenacity: (1) media celebration of a few dramatic examples of "rags-to-riches" stories, (2) the existence of a sizable and visible group of highly educated professionals, (3) failure to disaggregate census data, (4) unexamined assertions about the relationship between

culture and mobility, including a dearth of studies on the relative role of culture and social class background, and (5) the specific political or ideological purposes served by the thesis.

The thread throughout this discussion is that the thesis was never based on careful, systematic analysis but rather has been a loose grab-bag of assumptions. Expediently put together, there is a flexibility to the reasoning which is stretched to accommodate contradictions, both empirical and logical. The major crutch supporting the thesis is itself ideological—the myth of the American Dream.

Media Celebration of a Few Dramatic Examples of "Rags-to-Riches" Stories

Good journalism minimally implies careful coverage and documentation of the facts on some topic. At its very best, it goes beyond the mere reporting of facts and brings an analysis, critical perspective or comprehension of the issues. Where Asian Americans have walked onto the stage, it is the way in which they have been cast as players that has made their appearance "newsworthy." The stories of individuals here are rarely simply about individuals but about a racial set or cultural mold. This is true whether the subject is an imbroglio as serious as campaign finance contributions with an "Asian Connection" (Wu and Nicholson, 1997) or "human interest stories" which are told for their broad popular appeal as morality tales. This section speaks to the latter, with the particular goal of showing how the value of such cultural narratives derives less from representations that conform with some objective reality than from how they function to support the dominant ideology that fits the American Dream (Hsu, 1996).

In April of 1998, the *Washington Post* retold a familiar fable, now rendered in the form of high-tech success. The opening line thus read: "The classic dream of entrepreneurial American came true in Landover yesterday: Jeong Kim, a Korean-born immigrant who once worked the night shift at 7–Eleven to put himself through school, sold his company—for $1 billion." In selecting this news account for his "Osgood Files," radio commentator Charles Osgood similarly opined: "This is a story that Horatio Alger would love to tell." The impetus for the report was the merger of Jeong Kim's company Yurie with Lucent Technology, and Kim's appointment as president of Lucent's Carrier Networks division, making him one of the 100 richest high-tech executives in the country. Such mergers reflect the timbre of our time, though what is considered unmistakably noteworthy and thereby "newsworthy" was the more personal narrative of bootstrap success, matched only by the company's "rocket ascendancy."

At 14, Kim had come to the United States from Seoul with his Korean-born parents, and eventually attended Johns Hopkins University, where he studied electrical engineering and then went on to the University of Maryland, where he received his Ph.D. in engineering. After serving seven years in the navy, where he was the officer of a nuclear submarine, he went to work as a contract engineer at the Naval Research Laboratory. It is here where he began to develop the idea for a multimedia technology that would enable reporters to pipe almost instant voice, data and video feeds from action taking place at international "hot spots," battlefields or elections. Founded on this technology in 1992, his company Yurie made its impact almost immediately, soon marketing to federal agencies and later to [the] world-wide market.

Although initially framed as a "classic" story of entrepreneurial success, the *Washington Post* account later reveals that Kim had not pulled himself entirely up by his bootstraps. Yurie had, like other companies, been "born from government contracts," having received $305,000 Defense Department money through a separate program for small, minority-owned businesses (*Washington Post*, April 18, 1998). The coherence of the story as a cultural narrative is affected by this last observation, and it is to the credit of the writers that they sought to explore this issue. Nevertheless, in the end, it is the original framing of the report that will be remembered.

Over the years, the media has been saturated with stories about individual dreams which are realized through sheer perseverance. On July 16, 1998, CBS News' *48 Hours* dedicated an entire program, "Making It," to this theme, where the dream now encompasses individual aspirations that surpass even Horatio Alger's expectations in terms of the pot at the end of the rainbow: "Only in America: a place where you can reach for your dreams and make it big, against all odds, aiming for that million dollar payday." Stories about Asian Americans which have been tailored to mirror the ethos of the American Dream generally attribute this population's resourcefulness and resilience to cultural values (Osajima, 1988). This culturally-based perceptive is also given legitimacy by academics (Caudill and DeVos, 1956; Petersen, 1971; Sowell, 1981). Whether because of a general public thirst that remains unquenched, or because of particular circumstances surrounding their own condition, ethnic insiders, in turn, have relished success stories where desperate circumstances, back-breaking or mind-numbing work, are transcended through pluck, ingenuity, and above all, the ability to endure and persevere.

The story of David Tsang is illustrative of how such accounts derive their appeal as inspirational stories. A successful entrepreneur and founder of three high-technology companies in the Bay Area, his life is told in a style that conforms with the contours of the fabled climb from rags-to-riches. A "shy young man of 19," he arrives with only "$300 in his pocket and a shabby suitcase" in a country which "seemed like an intimidating, unfriendly land." Despite being alone (with his only contact a "distant friend of his father") and facing obstacles that include corporate politics and his having "just the barest knowledge of English," Tsang "persevered." In the end, this discipline pays off, and after some thirty years, Tsang is described as someone who continues to work 10- to 12-hour days and 6-day weeks, who "prides himself in never giving up," and now offers himself as a role model to "younger, potential Asian American entrepreneurs" (*AsianWeek*, March 8, 1996).

In yet another news account, Chong-Moon Lee, also a Silicon Valley entrepreneur, is described as one who persisted despite desperate circumstances which forced him to live on "21-cent packages of Ramen noodles," near bankruptcy, and frequenting pawn shops in order to pay a $168 phone bill (*AsianWeek*, November 3, 1995). Lee eventually not only recoups but becomes a major benefactor. Thus, the *San Francisco Chronicle*'s coverage of his story underscored his meteoric rise as follows: "From the depths of longing for a hamburger he couldn't afford and contemplating suicide, this entrepreneur rose to such success he was able to give $15 million to S.F.'s Asian Art Museum. Chong-Moon Lee makes Horatio Alger look like a Slacker" (*San Francisco Chronicle*, November 5, 1995).

Although such journalism pieces serve as inspirational stories, the problem occurs when they are elevated to the level of social analyses and models for others to emulate, without there also being a commensurate effort to integrate and analyze the role played by other pertinent factors. What these accounts often fail to do is draw the link between biography, history, and society, which C. Wright Mills saw as necessary for escaping the entrapment created by framing the problems in everyday life as individual "troubles," rather than as public "issues."

> *Troubles* occur within the character of the individual and within the range of his immediate relations with others; they have to do with his self and with those limited areas of social life of which he is directly and personally aware. Accordingly, the statement and the resolution of troubles properly lie within the individual as a biographical entity and within the scope of his immediate milieu—the social setting that is directly open to his personal experience and to some extent his willful activity. A trouble is a private matter. . . .
>
> *Issues* have to do with matters that transcend these local environments of the individual and the range of his inner life. They have to do with the organization of many such milieux into the institutions of an historical society as a whole, with the ways in which various milieux overlap and interpenetrate to form the larger structure of social and historical life. An issue is a public matter. . . . (Mills, 1959: 8)

Individuals who have worked their way up from poverty to wealth are the anomaly, not the rule (Domhoff, 1998: 100–101), though the afterglow left from media attention directed at these anomalies belies the more sociological truth of advantage due to social class privilege. The celebrated success story of Chong-Moon Lee might itself, on closer examination, be qualified in important ways. As a first-generation Korean-born immigrant, Lee certainly faced difficulties a native-born American would not have. He also had, however, certain social advantages and connections, including royal descent. One of his ancestors had been a king who invented the Korean language in the fourteenth century and whose family ruled the country until the Japanese take-over in 1905. Prior to his own immigration and founding of Diamond Multimedia Systems in 1982, Lee had been a university professor as well as successful pharmaceuticals executive in the family business of manufacturing antibiotics. In other words, while his personal success itself is not at issue, his particular biography deviates significantly from the typical Horatio Alger one of humble beginnings. If it is to be treated as a morality tale, then it would seem that the moral of the story is that "making it" in American society is unlikely, given the formidable odds for someone even from such an elite background as Lee. Conversely, the more poignant social commentary is the fact that many who adhere to an ethic of hard work have faced hurdles that are insurmountable. This is not to say that exceptions to this larger pattern cannot be found, but the point is that they *are* exceptions.

Whether or not details about social origins are omitted or included, narrative as ideology is crafted to suggest that the all-important factors were individual character, high moral standards, and motivation. The contradictions in Chong-Moon Lee's life were bracketed discursively, so that by the end of the narrative, an extraordinary history of privilege, with all of its tangible and intangible resources, recedes into the background. In other biographies, we know little about whether or not *other* factors were relevant in propelling such individuals out of desperate circumstances. David Tsang's background, for example, is not fully revealed. We are told that his father was a teacher, which one might infer provided at least a certain level of status, security, and economic means, but this background is otherwise sketchy. Even when there are facts contradicting the idea of humble beginnings or of individual "bootstrappers," the major theme of the American Dream is preserved. Those who identify with this dominant ethos generally buy into the model minority assumption that education will bring with it equality and achievement (Lee, 1996). The life trajectories of those on the bottom, however, are rarely examined for the purpose of empirically specifying the limits of cultural determinism. An implicit assumption or hope is that it will be simply a matter of time and cultural fortitude before those less fortunate close the gap between themselves and their more successful counterparts.

A. Magazine's cover story a few years ago was similarly opaque about the backgrounds of those individuals identified in the title of the article as "Power Brokers: The 25 Most Influential People in Asian America." Directed towards a young Asian American audience, the magazine did not intend any serious coverage of these personages. As the editors themselves state in the paragraph below, they wanted merely to spotlight those they believed to be having a significant influence not simply on "Asian America" but on the country as a whole.

> The powerful are artists of the social canvas: agenda-makers, trendsetters, and gate keepers. As a result, the process we followed in choosing these individuals as the nation's 25 most powerful Asian Americans relied less on science than instinct. What we sought was a list of those Asian Americans who had touched more people and done more to alter the cultural fabric than any others. Some of those included are symbolic figures—pioneers who have made historic breakthroughs; others are behind-the-scenes decision-makers, whose effects are quieter, but no less important. Some are young faces just beginning the upward arcs of their contributing careers; others are veterans whose notable achievements are a matter of record. There are familiar names included, and there are some which are surprising. But, like power itself, we know how mutable this list is and how arbitrary. By this time next year, this order will have changed, and some new names will have replaced old. Until then, we'll be watching these 25 closely. Because they aren't just influencing the direction of Asian America. They're setting the pace for America as a whole. (*A. Magazine*, 1993: 25)

Given that such profiles are offered up decontextualized, the omission of a frame leaves the door open to their being seen as Asian-spun versions of the American Dream. As pointed out in another article in this same issue, the value is in having such individuals as role models, especially where there appear to be barriers to achieving the American Dream. The reference here is to glass ceiling barriers, where the rare few who make it are seen as exemplars for other aspirants: "an Asian who demonstrates talent for leadership at an important American organization sends out the message that Asian Americans *can* do the job, and ultimately empowers the entire community" (Chen, 1993: 71). Despite the hopefulness behind this conclusion, the viability of role models may be contingent, however, upon other factors as well, ones not so easily emulated.

In their own review of "Asian Americans in the Power Elite," Zweigenhaft and Domhoff (1998) argue that social class plays a critical role in mobility. When looking into the family backgrounds of the Asian Americans in the corporate elite, they found that many did not make the climb from the very bottom of the social ladder but rather from already high rungs of that ladder. Thus, they reported that:

. . . Chang-Lin Tien, former Chancellor of the University of California, Berkeley, and a director of Wells Fargo Banks, reports that he arrived in the United States at the age of 21 as a penniless immigrant, unable to speak the language, but he also was born into a wealthy banking family in Wanchu, and his wife's father was a high-ranking officer in Chiang Kai Shek's army. . . .

Perhaps the best-known Chinese American—best known because she is a television "personality" —provides yet another example. Connie Chung is the daughter of a former intelligence officer in Chiang Kai Shek's army. . . .

Pei-Yuan Chia, former vice chair of Citibank, was the highest ranking Asian-American executive and corporate director at a world-class American corporation until his unexpected retirement in 1996 at age 56. He also was a prototypical Chinese-American member of the power elite. Born in Hong Kong in 1939, he grew up in a family with a "long line of bankers.". . .

Zweigenhaft and Domhoff's book is replete with such examples for other groups, women as well as other ethnic minorities, where the biographical details alone contradict Alger's moral message. Indeed, the true moral behind such life stories seems to be that the American Dream is primarily open to those who come with certain material advantages and social connections.

The Existence of a Sizable and Visible Group of Highly Educated Professionals

A rosy portrait of structural assimilation into American society has been made by pointing to major inroads which Asian Americans have made into both higher education and professional work. There is no denying the existence of a sizable and visible group of highly educated professionals. Rather, it is the conceptual or theoretical leaps from such observations that need to be reexamined, especially the view that they are the contemporary Horatio Alger's heroes.

To remain true to the myth of humble beginnings, one would have to ignore the fact that the 1965 Immigration Act contained special provisions that specifically recruited professionally trained personnel to these shores. As a select group of immigrants, they arrive either already educated and trained, or from sufficiently affluent social class backgrounds which enable them to pursue their education abroad. In fact, the vast majority of Asian students who receive postgraduate degrees from American institutions are foreign-born (Escueta and O'Brien, 1991), with many choosing to remain in the United States after they have graduated. In their study of diversity in America's "power elite," Zweigenhaft and Domhoff acknowledge that there were few "authentic bootstrappers" among Asian Americans, especially Chinese who formed the majority of Asian American directors in Fortune 1000 Boards (Zweigenhaft and Domhoff, 1998: 144): "Unlike most Chinese immigrants to the United States before the 1970s, who came from low-income backgrounds, the great majority of Chinese Americans at the top levels of American society are from well-to-do or well-educated families in China, Taiwan, and Hong Kong" (Zweigenhaft and Domhoff, 1998: 141).

In general, those in the upper echelons, especially corporate executives, board members, and directors, tended also to be overwhelmingly from the upper strata of society as well. This generalization was found to be true for Jews, women, blacks, Latinos, Asian Americans, and gays and lesbians. Women and minorities who found their way into the power elite were also likely to have to be "better educated than the white males already a part of it." For this reason, the authors state that class was not the only factor that would explain the composition of those in the power elite. One had to also have cultural capital in the form of degrees from high-status institutions. (Zweigenhaft and Domhoff, 1998: 179).

Other studies have similarly noted that those from elite universities and colleges were best groomed or primed for the high-status track (Kingston and Lewis, 1990), and that wealth, social connections, and elite educational credentials went far towards explaining disparities in social mobility (Useem and Karabel, 1990).

Whether it is education or social class which has the greater [influence] on mobility, the convergence of high educational and social status among the sizable and visible group of Asian professionals in the United States obscures this distinction. In other words, the lateral mobility of such immigrants to the United States is premised on their affluence, as is any subsequent vertical rise up the ladder.

Failure to Disaggregate Census Data

Of all the criticisms brought to bear on the model minority thesis, the most common one is directed towards the glib and facile generalizations that gloss over important internal differences within this population. At one time, German Americans were blanketly viewed as a rapidly assimilating minority because their internal diversity was overlooked. In a 1996 publication entitled "German Americans: Paradoxes of a 'Model Minority,'" Walter Kamphoefner said that by the 1970s, different sources had already commented on the rapid and complete assimilation of German Americans into American society. Yet, this perception of complete assimilation was erroneously based on the fact that the public made no distinction between "old immigrants" and "new immigrants." [9]

Like German Americans, Asian Americans include many "old" as well as "new immigrants."[10] The native-born descendants of these old immigrants are more likely to be more culturally assimilated than recent immigrants from Asia. Length of time in the U.S, in fact, was found to have an important bearing on *both* income and acculturation. Income levels tended to increase while poverty levels decreased, the longer Asian Americans had been in the United States. All *native* Asian Americans, in fact, with the exception of Vietnamese, did better than blacks or Hispanics in terms of both income and poverty levels (Barringer et al., 1995: 154–155).

There are *other* aspects of internal diversity within the Asian American population which also undermine the notion of uniform cultural or structural assimilation. Like earlier German Americans, there are segments of this population which are more accustomed to rural life[11] and more likely than their urban counterparts to resist the pulls of mainstream American society (Knoll, 1982; Walker-Moffat, 1995).

Analysts, furthermore, have noted that Asian American populations tend to concentrate at the extremes of various indicators of social status— i.e. at both the high and low ends, creating what is called a "bimodal" distribution.[12] Statistical "averages" obscure this fact, and the continuing failure to disaggregate these data perpetuates a picture of high achievement, whether we are talking about educational achievement or occupational mobility.

In the case of education achievement, there are large clusters of Asian Americans who are high achievers and the college-bound. In addition, however, there are students, whose high school records are not only less promising, but indicative of retention problems, including delinquency (Hune and Chan, 1997; Trueba et al., 1993).

Failure to disaggregate statistical data in other ways has also resulted in spurious comparisons with the white population that suggest Asian Americans are not only doing well but "outdoing whites." (Suzuki, 1989). The common belief that they earn more than other groups, including majority males, was significantly qualified once other factors were "controlled for." These included the number of wage earners per family, region of residence, the nature of managerial work, and whether income calculations are based on mean or median income.

National income averages are misleading since Asian Americans tend to reside in metropolitan areas of high-income states, whereas the general population or non-Hispanic whites are more geographically dispersed. In 1990, three-fifths of Asian Americans lived in just three states —California, Hawaii, and New York (Lott, 1998: 59). Thus, if we look at the median annual income for Asian Americans *nationwide* for that year, it was $36,000, whereas that for non-Hispanic whites was $31,100. Disaggregating *national income data* for this same year *reverses* this very picture. From comparisons based on four metropolitan areas: specifically, the median annual income for Asian Pacific Americans was $37,200, compared to $40,000 for non-Hispanic whites (Ong and Hee, 1994: 34). Not only are Asian American incomes *lower* but when one recalls where they live, their dollars also have lower buying power.

Like national income figures, the use of "mean income" can similarly obscure. Given the bimodal character of the Asian American population, median income rather than mean income is the preferred measure, the median being that point above and below which 50 percent of all cases fall. When such adjustments in calculation were made, the median incomes of Japanese, Chinese, Filipino, Koreans, Asian Indians, and Vietnamese, were invariably lower than the mean (Barringer et al., 1995: 152–153).

Even when median income is utilized, other crucial differences are still camouflaged. Thus, median family incomes were reported in 1979 to be "considerably higher for all Asian Americans than for whites" (with the exception of Vietnamese). Taking into account such factors [as] the number of wage-earners per household and geographical area of residence sharply alters the comparative picture. The U.S. General Accounting Office explicitly drew attention to this fact when it reported on 1985 incomes. Specifically, it reported that while Asian American households earned $2,973 a month, 28 percent more than the average U.S. household income of $2,325, this difference *disappeared,* once one looked at *per capita* income (U.S. General Accounting Office, 1990: 20–21). In other words, Asian Americans did not necessarily *earn more,* but household incomes tended to be higher because they were more likely to have *more income earners,* including unpaid family members.

Where census data are used to gauge the existence of glass ceiling barriers, managerial data are seldom disaggregated to distinguish between fundamentally different managerial levels in the corporate hierarchy or between different sectors of the economy.[13] The distinction between managers in mainstream corporate America and those in ethnic enclaves is especially critical for Asian Americans, since these managerial structures are not comparable. As the following chapter will discuss at greater length, managerial status for Asian Americans often takes the form of self-employment, which may be an indicator not so much of an entrepreneurial spirit but of downward mobility and disaffection with mainstream employment. Even if this propensity for small business involvement is considered a viable opportunity structure, participation in it does not occur across all Asian Americans groups.[14]

In sum, these general methodological issues have critical theoretical implications when assessing the relative progress of Asian Americans vis-a-vis other racial or immigrant groups. While there have been some moves to achieve a better picture of the existing demographic diversity among Asian Americans in census data, analyzing these patterns is another matter.

Unexamined Assertions about the Relationship between Culture and Mobility

Although Asian cultural values have been credited for much individual or group success, it would seem critical to examine the relationship between culture and mobility. There has, however, been a dearth of studies in this regard. One cannot, in other words, *assume* the operation of certain values, or assuming their existence, predict where they will lead.

For one, census data are not a good source of cultural data, except perhaps for language. Thus, sociologist Herbert Barringer and his associates (1995: 168) noted in their comprehensive review of the literature on the status of Asian Americans: "census data offer precious little in support of cultural theories." This state of affairs, of course, has not kept people from reading into such data— from assuming, inferring, or imputing the influence of culture as a causal factor. As noted at the outset of this chapter, statistical data provide a certain profile of successful adjustment among Asian Americans. For each statistic, a cultural value can be invoked to explain the rate in question: high educational attainment rates (e.g., value placed on learning, on the scholarly tradition), low employment rates (e.g., strong work ethic), low divorce or delinquency rates (e.g., a strong value placed on the family), low rates of psychiatric hospitalization (e.g., a philosophical attitude of acceptance), and so on.

Notwithstanding that cultural values may be operating at some level, cultural theorizing and empirical research has not kept pace with demographic changes in the population. Second, despite the implied determinism to cultural explanations of mobility, they are unable to explain notable exceptional patterns of deviations even where the values in question are not at issue. The cultural motivation that is often assumed to underlie educational achievement and entrepreneurial activity falls short in both regards.

With respect to the first point, most critiques of the model minority thesis have acknowledged diversity in the Asian American population and have repeatedly pointed to the fact that "not all" Asian Americans have made similar progress.[15] Only by ignoring this cultural diversity as well as the differential within these populations is it possible to exclusively posit success on an enabling body of cultural values. During the 1960s, Chinese and Japanese were the two largest Asian ethnic populations in the United States, and Confucianism was a major part of their cultural orientation, which also included Buddhism, as well as elements of American culture. Since then, the Asian American population has become much more diverse. While the 1970 census included four designated census categories for Asian groups (Chinese, Japanese, Filipino, and Koreans) and one Pacific group (Hawaiians), by the 1980 census, the number of Asian American groups had increased to twelve, with as many as six Pacific groups (Lott, 1991: 58).

A comparison of select Asian subgroups in terms of value orientation and objective status would seem to support the idea of Confucian as this enabling body of values. Where the Confucian tradition has been strongest (e.g., among the Chinese and Japanese), one finds greater clustering of these individuals at the upper end of the income, educational, and occupational ladders. Conversely, those groups where the historical and cultural trail to Confucianism is moot or absent (e.g., among Hmong, Khmer, and Cambodians) are ones where poverty is also higher (Trueba et al., 1993: 44).

When still other Asian ethnic groups are brought into the picture, however, it is questionable whether Confucian values themselves can be credited. Thus, for example, Korean Americans fall somewhere between Chinese and Japanese in terms of educational attainment. Despite a strong Confucian tradition in Korea, a significant portion of those who immigrated to the United States in the early 1900s as well as in recent years have been Christian (Abelman and Lie, 1995: 198, fn 7; Kim, 1981: 187–207; Knoll, 1982: 116–121). In the case of both Asian Indians and Filipinos, college completion rates exceed that of other Asian ethnic groups, including the Chinese and Japanese, and yet "neither Filipinos nor Asian Indians can be said to be influenced by Confucianism and they equal or surpass East Asians in educational attainment" (Barringer et al., 1995: 164). In other words, there is no single overarching cultural umbrella that satisfactorily explains these similarly high achievement levels.

The model minority thesis has managed to survive because it has managed to stretch or reinvent itself *discursively*, as opposed to through new empirical research (e.g., that which shows how different subcultural tendencies achieve the same ends). Thus, where Confucian values have not fit the picture, the picture of success has been repainted with broader brush strokes positing values related to "hard work" as the key differentiating factor between the poor and the successful.

Yet a second reason why such broad cultural generalizations are insufficient lies in exceptions to their implied determinism. Values alone—seen as "wants," "preferences," or subjective inclinations—are inadequate for understanding action or conduct. Yet given that such assertions continue to be made, it is hard to explain why those who adhere strongly to the same values are not similarly positioned in life.[16]

Some of the relatively greater educational progress of Asian Americans over blacks can be linked not simply to cultural values but to pre-existing experiences or structures of support. These include pre-immigration work experiences, either prior professional training or commercial involvement, as well as access to capital for investment (Carnoy, 1995). Money for educational pursuits or business adventures came through family borrowing, rotating credit associations, and more recently, for a select group of entrepreneurs, through large-scale venture capital firms (Park, 1996). For those with little education or English fluency, entrepreneurialism established an economic *floor* for pursuing educational ambitions. In other words, while first-generation immigrant parents might themselves be uneducated and illiterate, their ability to set up small shops makes it possible for their children to climb out of poverty.

While both education and entrepreneurialism offer ways out of poverty, the ability to take advantage of such opportunities is itself influenced by factors other than culture. In the case of Korean Americans, for example, it has been suggested that the relative contribution to mobility played by Confucian or Christian cultural traditions may be less important than situational or structural factors (Min, 1996). If culture were the determining factor, they would have gladly foregone commercial pursuits in favor of government or academic jobs.[17] As Abelmann and Lie explain, among immigrants to the U.S., entrepreneurialism represents a form of downward mobility:

> Commercial pursuits, especially shopkeeping were less prestigious, if not frowned upon. . . .
>
> . . . many 1970s immigrants had graduated from college, including extremely prestigious universities such as Seoul National University (SNU). . . For an SNU graduate to "make it" as a greengrocer or a dry cleaner in the United States is akin to an elite

U.S. university graduate's succeeding as a convenience store owner in opulent Japan. . . .

> . . . The incongruous image of a college-educated European American opening up a shop in a poor inner-city neighborhood should make us question the idea that Korean Americans are somehow naturally inclined toward opening and running small businesses.
>
> . . . Korea immigrant entrepreneurship should . . . be seen as a concatenation of conscious decisions, albeit made under strong structural constraints. (Abelmann and Lie, 1995: 123–125, 129)

Instead, self-employment was taken up because of negative factors, such as language barriers, the nontransferability of professional credentials or college degrees, and other structural constraints to white-collar and professional employment, including racial discrimination (Abelmann and Lie, 1995: 126–147).

As long as culture is viewed simply as a property of individuals [rather] than of structures, cultural explanations will give short shrift to structural explanations. Attributing the *absence* of small business activity among American descendants of slaves to the absence of entrepreneurial values is one such example. For the absence of such values can themselves be linked to the disappearance of such *structures* as the esusu, an African form of the rotating credit association.[18] As a result, blacks have been more dependent upon white employers and government policies for establishing the economic floor from which educational gains can be made. The educational progress of black children, in turn, has been most rapid when public policy measures were directed towards improving schools and alleviating poverty (Carnoy, 1995).

The presumption of entreprenurial values among Koreans could be seen as an error of imputation, and not a weakness with theories of cultural endowment. If so, it is a recurring error of no small consequence. Yet, the problems with cultural explanations have less to do with the substance of the logic than with how they are invoked. As Portes and Rumbaut (1990: 77) pointed out, they are "always *post-factum*," i.e., invoked after a group has already achieved success, but are otherwise unable to predict success. Moreover, the numerous empirical exceptions to the theory cannot be neatly encompassed by such explanations.[19]

Finally, although education is now almost a *prerequisite* for mobility, culture need not be. In their book *Inequality by Design*, sociology professors at the University of California, Berkeley (Fischer et al., 1996) drew upon a cumulative body of research to show how social inequalities are significantly affected by social class background as well as by social or national policy arrangements. Social status was shown to have direct implications for IQ. For example, even though Koreans have achieved high levels of education in the United States, their lower, minority status in Japan is manifested in lower IQ scores. In the United States, however, IQ differences between Koreans and Japanese fade (Fischer et al., 1996: 172, 191–193, 199). Rather than being a direct measure of innate intelligence, IQ was more a measure of how academic performance was contingent upon social background and circumstances. Again, as we saw earlier, social class background might better explain important differences among Asian Americans, as well as between Asian Americans and other racial-ethnic groups.

To return to the point about census data raised at the beginning of this section, census data are not designed to address cultural theories. Despite this limitation, we might make the best of this situation were we to approach such statistics as a basis for *generating* theories. Besides cultural explanations, one might posit a range of structural explanations for the rates in question. For example, even when student achievement can be traced to parental pressures to perform, the motivation need not be culturally-based. Parental exhortations to "work hard," for example, may be derived from the realization that discrimination makes it necessary for a minority to work "twice as hard" in order to succeed. This alternative, structural perspective has yet to get the attention it deserves, even in the educational context where the model minority

thesis prevails. In the occupational sphere, there is some research which has noted that the motivation behind ongoing education among Asian Americans is not cultural but "structural"—a response to blocked mobility (Sue and Okazaki, 1990).

Specific Political or Ideological Purposes Served by the Thesis

As pointed out in different ways throughout this chapter, cultural explanations obscure structural conditions, institutional policies, and particularly the relative social class privilege that has assisted the large majority of those who "make it." Insofar as the model minority view has lent itself towards obscuring these issues, it has served to maintain the status quo. As such, it has not been subject to careful study, but has persisted because of this ideological purpose.[20] Were there not blacks and other minorities who form a prominent part of the picture of sustained economic disadvantage, the thesis would not exist.

Given the value placed on social equality in the United States, gross inequities have been a source of national embarrassment, ill ease, and the source of social if not *ideological* crisis. In this context, "model minorities" serve as a sign of the ongoing viability of the American Dream. Where there are inequities, these are largely reduced to matters of individual will or choice: If Asian Americans can apparently make it, then why not blacks, other minorities, or other groups? Thus, for example, success on the part of individual Jews has occasioned some to wonder aloud why blacks do not imitate or emulate those strategies.

> Jews have moved up in American life by utilizing middle-class skills—reason, orderliness, conservation of capital, and a high valuation and use of education. . . . Finding that playing by the "rules of the game"—reward based on merit, training and seniority—has worked for them, many Jews wonder why Negroes do not utilize the same methods for getting ahead. (Friedman, cited in Steinberg, 1982: 88)

The Jewish Horatio Alger story itself has been critiqued in ways which parallel some of the analysis in the previous pages. Sociologist Stephen Steinberg made several pointed criticisms in this regard: (1) that success was not uniformly distributed throughout the Jewish population, (2) that even those who had managed to climb the occupational hierarchy still found their mobility limited, (3) that Jewish cultural values have limited explanatory power, and (4) that structural considerations had a vital bearing on the degree to which pre-immigration skills interfaced well with the needs of the American economy. For these reasons, he said "the popular image of Jews as a middle-class monolith tends to be overdrawn," and that even by the mid-1960s, one still found that "almost a quarter of all employed Jewish males in New York City were manual workers, and another unspecified number worked in low-paying white-collar occupations" (Steinberg, 1982: 90). Those who manage to escape from the "working class" into the professions were far from being an "economic elite."

> The most important qualification of the Jewish success story is that American Jews by no means constitute an economic elite. The Jewish middle class has been concentrated mostly in small business and the professions; Jews are conspicuously absent from the managerial hierarchies of major corporations. This was first established in 1936. . . . Only two industries had significant Jewish representation—the apparel industry and the movie and broadcasting industries. (Steinberg, 1982: 90–91)

Zweigenhaft and Domhoff's more recent study partially supports Steinberg's earlier findings. As late as the 1970s there were few Jews in the executive ranks of large Fortune-level companies. Unlike Gentiles, they were more likely to be in smaller Fortune-level companies, to have joined as "outsiders with expertise" rather than coming up through the ranks, or to be in companies "owned or founded by Jews."

> . . . Jews were well represented in the corporate elite but were more likely to be in small *Fortune*-level

companies rather than large ones. We also found that they had traveled different pathways in getting to the corporate elite than had their Gentile counterparts. Whereas Gentile executives were most likely to have advanced through the managerial ranks of the corporation, the Jewish directors were more likely to have joined the boards as outsiders with expertise in such areas as investment banking, corporate law, or public relations—unless they had risen through the ranks of companies owned or founded by Jews. (Zweigenhaft and Domhoff, 1998: 20).

Since the 1970s, however, Jews have made such significant inroads into the largest Fortune-level boards that the authors conclude they are now "most certainly overrepresented in the corporate elite" (Zweigenhaft and Domhoff, 1998: 23).

Despite the ideology of a classless society, Zweigenhaft and Domhoff (1998: 176–181) specified four factors they believe to be critical to the assimilation of Jews (as well as to the assimilation of other minorities and women): identity management, class, education, and light skin. Steinberg, for his part, directly questioned the viability of the Jewish Horatio Alger myth as *cultural* ideology. While acknowledging that cultural values certainly played an important role in promoting literacy, study, and intellectual achievement, he emphasized the fact that pre-immigration skills were also critical. Jews from Eastern Europe arrived with industrial skills which intersected well with the needs of the burgeoning American industrial economy. In this respect, they were different from other immigrants, including Asians who arrived at the turn of the century,[21] though they share certain similarities with those Asian immigrants in the post-1965 who would also be included as part of the model minority picture.

Ironically, although the small business endeavors of both Jewish and Asian American merchants have been similarly attributed to cultural traits, in both instances what is frequently omitted in such accounts is the fact that these ventures do not necessarily conform with the respective occupational ideals of these groups. Many Korean

American businessmen are from the ranks of the college-educated, who have been unable to make it in mainstream America. East European Jews, for their part, were motivated to become merchants and shopkeepers, primarily because of discriminatory laws which restricted their ability to own land. For these reasons, rather than any cultural predilection, they ended up in livelihoods such as moneylending and liquor trades, occupations in which they might not otherwise have engaged. The enmity which they thereafter attracted to themselves led to programs which eventually forced their emigration (Cowan and Cowan, 1989: 14, 21–27; Steinberg, 1982: 94; Schwarz, 1956: 296).

Although the casting of Asian Americans as "model minorities" has temporarily supplanted the standard reference point for assimilation, which has been the European immigrant experience on this continent (Steinberg, 1982), the persuasiveness and appeal of such logic—as ideology—is contingent on several factors. However empirical studies may challenge the *validity* of the model minority thesis, it has persisted because it serves both an ideological and political purpose. On the one hand, it is couched in values consistent with middle-class American values and taps into familiar cultural beliefs and myths associated with Horatio Alger and the American Dream. On the other hand, the dominant attitude towards Asian Americans has depended on whether they represent a greater or lesser threat than other groups to the existing hierarchy. While dubbed a "model minority," Asian Americans have rarely, if ever, been seriously elevated as a model for majority whites, especially where competition between the two has been direct. It is precisely in these situations where the thesis is no longer considered tenable that ideology and politics become most salient and apparent to those who run up against a new logic, if not new, unexpected barriers.

Thus, where Asian American admissions to colleges and universities have been associated with declining white enrollments, praise is at best faint and more often likely to be accompanied by concerns about Asian American "overrepresentation"

and by unflattering characterizations of them as "nerds," who are "academically narrow" or lacking in socially desirable qualities (*San Jose Mercury*, February 23, 1998; Woo, 1996, 1990; Takagi, 1992: 58, 60–61). In work spheres where Asian American professionals have appeared in significant numbers, their mobility has been impeded by "glass ceilings" and negative assessments of their managerial potential. Whatever the justifications for their exclusion, the idea of them as "model" no longer surfaces.

Cultural Ideologies and Their Social-Historical Contexts: The Limits of Ideology

The analysis in this chapter has suggested that cultural explanations are at best only partially accurate in accounting for what we know about Asian Americans as an aggregate. In fact, the social soil from which the idea of a model minority germinated may say more about the politics of power than it does about the factors underlying achievement. The questions concerning us here are of a different order than those which motivated the original formulation of the thesis. Instead of asking, "What are the cultural factors behind success?" the appearance of a glass ceiling prompts one instead to ask: "What are the rationales or justifications offered to explain differential progress? If cultural factors are inadequate, to what extent are structural factors at issue? What place, if any, do cultural explanations occupy within this structure or scheme of things?" For the moment, let it suffice to say that these questions themselves can be seen as a product of a social, historical context that breathes life into these questions.

Historically specific, the model minority thesis is premised on the fundamental assumption that educational achievement is the *sine qua non* of success. For this reason, it is unlike its Horatio Alger counterpart, which was created earlier in the nation's history when higher education served as finishing schools for the elite. For the masses of ordinary people then, both agrarian and new emerging industrial sectors of America were still able to provide opportunities to make a living without so much as a high school diploma. It is only in postwar decades that the nation has firmly embraced an ideology that links education achievement with occupational mobility. The postwar economy was an expanding one and the GI bill made it possible for education to be widely pursued. In this way, structural opportunities were created for educational achievement to become a form of social or cultural capital that could be converted into job security, greater socioeconomic benefits, professional autonomy or authority. In this new ideological formulation, education would substantially counter and overcome the effects of racial discrimination and racial privilege. However, . . . the prerequisites for mobility go beyond education. Glass ceilings, specifically, point to the limits of ideology by suggesting ongoing "artificial" barriers.

NOTES

1. Between the years 1870–1890, when the anti-Chinese movement gained momentum, until it ultimately led to the 1882 Exclusion Act, Chinese were incarcerated in California State Prisons at a rate higher than their proportion of the population, particularly for crimes involving economic gain (e.g. burglary and larceny). For example, while only 8 percent of the California population in 1870, they were 14 percent of those imprisoned. By 1890, the Exclusion Act had clearly had its effect: not only did the Chinese population drop to 5 percent but the prison rate fell to 2 percent (Shimabukuro, 1980).

2. While the Census Bureau has published different population estimates for Asian and Pacific Islanders, there is little question that their rate of growth has surpassed other groups, including blacks, Hispanics, and non-Hispanic whites. Now the third largest minority, after blacks and Hispanics, they are expected to approximate 9.9 million by the year 2000, or 4 percent of the U.S. population. By 1990, they were already 7.3 million, having doubled their size since 1980. The 1980 figures themselves represent a doubling of the population since 1970. In 1970, the Asian American population numbered 1.4 million. By 1980, that population had more than doubled to 3.5 million, or 1.5 percent of the total U.S. population of 226.5 million.

3. Part of this difference can be attributed to the relative diversity—or lack thereof—in these respective countries or continents. Given the racial homogeneity of Great Britain during Marx's time, inequality was largely reflected in social class differences.

4. Chapters from Steinberg's book were based on materials published in the 1970s.

5. Reference to the term "model minority thesis" is most commonly made in Asian American academic circles where the construct survives as a short-hand way of referring to the hidden cultural assumptions which continue to underlie social or political debates where Asian Americans figure as a successful minority.

6. Insofar [as] interracial marriage with the white, mainstream majority of Americans is the result not only of greater contact in both business and social affairs but also of greater social acceptance, such rates have been treated as an important indicator of assimilation (Kitano and Sue, 1973). More recent interpretations, however, suggest that trends towards intra-marriages among Asian Americans point to an alternative view of acculturation, namely, the assimilation of ideas in the context of social and economic experiences associated with the experience of "race" in America (Shinigawa and Pang, 1996).

7. This volume was a special issue devoted to "Asian Americans: A Success Story?"

8. The 1990 census contains information not only on nine major subcategories of "Asian or Pacific Islanders," but on at least twenty "other" Asian ethnic groups.

9. Germans had arrived as early as the eighteenth century and their mass migration to the United States during the 1840s and 1850s was such that by World War I German Americans already included many second-generation descendants. Descendants of older immigrants could be expected to be completely assimilated and invisible by the 1970s simply because they had arrived so much earlier. Another reason offered, however, for the overall perception of complete assimilation was "Anglo Saxon race ideology at the turn of the century," which, according to Kamphoefner, "caused people to see what they wanted to see." The allusion here was to the "anti-German hysteria of World War I" and some psychological need to counter negative attitudes towards Germany as an enemy nation with positive attitudes towards German Americans as "easily Americanized."

10. The German American population, however, suffered few curbs on its numbers through restricted immigration. Unlike Asian immigration, national immigration quotas in the 1920s had had little effect on German immigration because aliens from the western hemisphere were exempted from such quotas and specifically classified as "nonquota" immigrants.

11. According to Kamphoefner, those German Americans who were less assimilated were geographically isolated in rural areas. Patterns of cultural survival were most evident here. These included use of the German language, social resistance to prohibition and anti-alcohol legislation, and other signs of cultural preservation, including a "locational persistence" associated with peasant attitudes towards landownership as a major form of security. Attitudes in this regard were so tenacious that sacrifices on behalf of landholding might well be pursued at the expense of children's education.

12. The "modal" tendency simply refers to the "frequency" of an occurrence on any given measure or indicator.

13. Dual labor or split labor market theorists have referred to these respective sectors as "primary" and "secondary," or as "core" and "periphery."

14. Filipinos, for example, have been underrepresented in small business, whereas Koreans are heavily concentrated here, more so than other Asian Americans and or other immigrant groups. According to Min, "The Korean group shows the highest rate of self-employment among seventeen recent immigrant groups classified in the 1980 Census, while the Filipino group ranks fifteenth, ahead only of the Portuguese and Haitian groups. . . ." Min theorized about a number of differences between Filipino and Korean immigrants that might explain their differential distribution. For one, there is a higher representation of Filipino immigrants as professional or white-collar workers in non-Filipino firms, which itself might be traced to the fact that the Philippines is an English-speaking country. By contrast, Koreans would have had greater language barriers than Koreans to entering the U.S. general labor market. In addition, as immigrants they have had more of a previous history of working in an industrial business economy, which can be seen as giving them an "advantage" when it came to starting up small businesses (Min, 1986–87: 56).

15. Even among Japanese and Chinese Americans, who were the original inspiration for the model minority thesis, one can find high poverty levels among recent immigrants (Barringer et al., 1995: 155).

16. Culture of poverty theories notwithstanding, blacks themselves have highly valued education as a path to mobility, leading some researchers to explore the gap between these abstract and concrete attitudes, and their different implications for predicting achievement or mobility outcomes (Zweigenhaft and Domhoff, 1998: 186, 190). For this same reason, sociologist Ann Swidler argued against this conventional view of culture in favor of defining culture as a repertoire of skills, habits, or styles that organize action (Swidler, 1986).

17. Kwoh (1947: 86–87, 114) has similarly explained the paucity of businessmen among American-born Chinese graduates to the low prestige and lack of real opportunity for mobility afforded by such work, along with the expectations associated with their college training.

18. The particular form which slavery itself took in the United States led to the disappearance of the esusu. Specifically, its disappearance has been attributed to the patriarchal relationship between the American plantation owners and their slaves. In contrast to West Indian slaves, whose absentee owners permitted them to develop their own subsistence economy (if only out of necessity, because the slave population here was much larger relative to slaveowners), American slaves were discouraged from independently cultivating their own plots of land or else devoting themselves to trades and crafts. Moreover, they were legally denied the right to maintain their own traditions, customs, and language, and otherwise positioned to "absorb the culture of the slaveowner" (Light, 1987). In his study of the Mississipi Chinese, James Loewen discusses and explains in detail how a variety of situational and structural factors positioned the Chinese so that they were able to become prosperous in the grocery business because they were able to enter a "ready-made niche" that was unavailable to blacks. The importance of situational factors is also underscored by the fact that Mississippi Chinese were more concentrated in the grocery business to an extent not found in other Chinese immigrants ("with identical geographic and class origins") elsewhere in the United States (Loewen, 1988: 32–57).

19. Portes and Rumbaut (1990: 77–78) also noted several other weaknesses associated with cultural theories of small business success: Given flourishing businesses among a diverse range of ethnic groups, there is a "theoretical untidiness" in isolating "unique entrepreneurial 'values'" for groups from a wide range of religiocultural backgrounds. The problem of explanation, moreover, is compounded by the fact that others from the same backgrounds are not entrepreneurially inclined (e.g., why Chinese Buddhists and not Buddhist Cambodians?). Similarly, sojourner theories of entrepreneurship might explain why some temporary residents might be motivated to accumulate profits in order to return home but the exceptions to this theory are also numerous (e.g., entrepreneurial activity among Eastern European Jews intending to stay in the U.S. or among Cuban refugees with little prospects of return). Finally, situational theories of disadvantage do not fully explain why some Asian minorities (Chinese and Japanese) have high rates of employment while other groups (Filipinos and Mexicans) are underrepresented in self-employment.

20. According to Karl Mannheim, dominant groups, given that the existing order supports their own group interests, will be particularly invested in an ideology that supports the status quo.

    The concept "ideology" reflects the one discovery which emerged from political conflict, namely, that ruling groups in their thinking become so intensively interest-bound to a situation that they are simply no longer able to see certain facts which would undermine their sense of domination. There is implicit in the word "ideology" the insight that in certain situations the collective unconscious of certain groups obscures the real condition of society both to itself and to others and thereby stabilizes it (Mannheim, 1936: 40).

21. These included Koreans, Asian Indians, Japanese, and Filipinos, although the last two groups contributed to the bulk of this immigration.

REFERENCES

Abelman, Nancy, and John Lie. *Blue Dreams: Korean Americans and the Los Angeles Riots.* Cambridge, MA and London, England: Harvard University Press, 1995.

"Arts Philanthropist." *AsianWeek* November 3, 1995.

Asian American Policy Review. Vol. VI. "Affirmative Action," 1996.

Barringer, Herbert, Robert W. Gardner, and Michael J. Levin (eds.). *Asians and Pacific Islanders in the United States*. New York: Russell Sage Foundation, for the National Committee for Research on the 1980 Census, 1995.

Beach, W.G. *Oriental Crime in California*. Palo Alto, CA: Stanford University Press, 1932.

Bureau of the Census. *We the American Asians*. Washington, D.C.: U.S. Government Printing Office, Population Reference Bureau, September 1993.

Caplan, Nathan. "Study Shows Boat Refugees' Children Achieve Academic Success." *Refugee Reports* VI (10): 1–6, October 11, 1985.

Caplan, Nathan, Marcella H. Choy, and John K. Whitmore. *Children of the Boat People: A Study of Educational Success*. Ann Arbor: The University of Michigan Press, 1994.

Caplan, Nathan, Marcella H. Choy, and John K. Whitmore. "Indochinese Refugee Families and Academic Achievement." *Scientific American* 266 (2): 36–42, February 1992.

Carnoy, Martin. *Faded Dreams: The Politics and Economics of Race in America*. New York: Cambridge University Press, 1995.

Caudill, William, and George DeVos. "Achievement, Culture and Personality: The Case of Japanese Americans." *American Anthropologist* 58: 1102–1126, 1956.

Chan, Sucheng. *Asian Americans: An Interpretive History*. Boston: Twayne, 1991.

Chen, Joanne. "The Asian American Dream?" *A. Magazine* 2(3): 16–17, 70–71, Fall 1993.

"Chinese in a Global Economy." *Oakland Tribune* May 26, 1982.

"Chong-Moon Lee." *San Francisco Chronicle* November 5, 1995.

Cowan, Neil M., and Ruth Schwartz Cowan. *Our Parents' Lives: The Americanization of Eastern European Jews*. New York: Basic Books, 1989.

Domhoff, William. *Who Rules America? Power and Politics in the Year 2000*. Mountain View, CA: Mayfield Publishing Company, 1998.

"East, West Teaching Traditions Collide." *San Jose Mercury* February 23, 1998.

Escueta, Eugenia, and Eileen O'Brien. "Asian Americans in Higher Education: Trends and Issues." *Research Briefs, American Council on Education* 2 (4): 1–11, 1991.

Fischer, Claude S., Michael Hout, Martin Sanchez Jankowski, Samuel R. Lucas, Ann Swidler, and Kim Voss. *Inequality By Design: Cracking the Bell Curve Myth*. Princeton, New Jersey: Princeton University Press, 1996.

Fullerton, Howard N., Jr. "New Labor Force Projections, Spanning 1988 to 2000." *Monthly Labor Review* 3–12, November 1989.

Gardner, Robert W., Bryant Robey, and Peter C. Smith. "Asian Americans: Growth, Change, and Diversity." *Population Bulletin* Vol. 40, No. 4: 1–44, October 1985.

Glazer, Nathan, and Daniel Patrick Moynihan. *Beyond the Melting Pot: The Negroes, Puerto Ricans, Jews, Italians, and Irish of New York City*. Cambridge, MA: The M.I.T. Press and Harvard University Press, 1963.

Herrnstein, Richard J., and Charles Murray. *The Bell Curve: Intelligence and Class Structure in American Life*. New York: Free Press, 1994.

Hing, Bill Ong. "Social Forces Unleashed after 1969." Chapter Three in *Making and Remaking Asian America Through Immigration Policy: 1850–1990*. Stanford, CA: Stanford University Press, 1993.

Hsu, Ruth. "Will the Model Minority Please Identify Itself? American Ethnic Identity and Its Discontents." *Diaspora* 5 (1): 37–64, Spring 1966.

Hune, Shirley, and Kenyon S. Chan. "Special Focus: Asian Pacific American Demographic and Educational Trends," pp. 39–67 in Deborah J. Carter and Reginald Wilson, *Minorities in Higher Education, Fifteen Annual Status Report, 1996–1997*. Washington, D.C.: American Council on Education, April 1997.

"For Immigrant, A Billion-Dollar High-Tech Deal: Maryland Entrepreneur to Sell Firm He Founded." *Washington Post* April 28, 1998.

Jaco, Daniel E., and George L. Wilber. "Asian Americans in the Labor Market." *Monthly Labor Review* 33–38, July 1975.

Jew, Charles C., and Stuart A. Brody. "Mental Illness among the Chinese: I. Hospitalization Rates over the Past Century." *Comprehensive Psychiatry* 9 (2): 129–134, 1967.

Kamphoefner, Walter D. "German Americans: Paradoxes of a Model Minority," pp. 152–160 in Silvia Pedraza and Ruben Rumbaut (eds.), *Origins and Destinies: Immigration, Race, and Ethnicity in America*. Belmont, CA: Wadsworth, 1996.

Kim, Bok Lim. "Asian Americans: No Model Minority." *Social Work* 18: 44–53, 1973.

Kim, Chung, and Won Moo Hurh. "Korean Americans and the Success Image: A Critique." *Amerasia Journal* 10 (2): 3–21, 1983.

Kingston, Paul William, and Lionel S. Lewis (eds.). *The High-Status Track: Studies of Elite Schools and Stratification*. Albany, New York: SUNY, 1990.

Kitano, Harry. *Japanese Americans: The Evolution of a Subculture*. Englewood Cliffs, New Jersey: Prentice-Hall, 1969.

Kitano, Harry H.L., and Stanley Sue. "The Model Minorities." *The Journal of Social Issues* 29: 1–9, 1973.

Knoll, Tricia. *Becoming Americans: Asian Sojourners, Immigrants, and Refugees in the Western United States*. Portland, Oregon: Coast to Coast Books, 1982.

Lee, Stacy. *Unraveling the "Model Minority" Stereotype: Listening to Asian American Youth*. New York: Teachers' College Press, 1996.

Levine, Larry. *The Opening of the American Mind*. Boston: Beacon Press, 1996.

Light, Ivan. "Ethnic Enterprise in America: Japanese, Chinese, and Blacks," pp. 83–93 in Ron Takaki (ed.), *From Different Shores: Perspectives on Race and Ethnicity in America*. New York: Oxford University Press, 1987.

Loewen, James W. *The Mississippi Chinese: Between Black and White*. Prospect Heights, Illinois: Waveland Press, 1988.

Lott, Juanita T. "Policy Implications of Population Changes in the Asian American Community." *Asian American Policy Review* II: 57–64, Spring 1991.

Lyman, Stanford Morris. Review of Betty Lee Sung, *The Story of the Chinese in America*, in *Journal of Ethnic Studies* 1 (1): 71–72, Spring 1973.

Mannheim, Karl. *Ideology and Utopia*. New York: Harcourt, Brace & World, 1936.

Massey, Douglas S., and Nancy A. Denton. *American Apartheid: Segregation and the Making of the Underclass*. Cambridge, MA: Harvard University Press, 1993.

Mills, C. Wright. *The Sociological Imagination*. New York: Oxford University Press, 1959.

Min, Pyong Gap. "The Entrepreneurial Adaptation of Korean Immigrants," pp. 302–314 in Silvia Pedraza and Ruben Rumbaut (eds.), *Origins and Destinies: Immigration, Race, and Ethnicity in America*. Belmont, California: Wadsworth, 1996.

Min, Pyong Gap. "Filipino and Korean Immigrants in Small Business: A Comparative Analysis." *Amerasia Journal* 13 (1): 53–71, 1986–87.

Moynihan, Daniel Patrick. *The Negro Family: The Case for National Action*. Washington, D.C.: U.S. Department of Labor, 1965.

O'Hare, William P., and Judy C. Felt. *Asian Americans: America's Fastest Growing Minority Group*. Washington, D.C.: Population Reference Bureau, No. 19 in a series of occasional papers, Population Trends and Public Policy, pp. 1–16, February 1991.

Ong, Paul, and Suzanne J. Hee. "Economic Diversity," in Paul Ong (ed.), *The State of Asian Pacific America: Economic Diversity, Issues and Policies*. Los Angeles: LEAP Asian Pacific American Policy Institute and UCLA Asian American Studies Center, 1994.

———. "Work Issues Facing Asian Pacific Americans: Labor Policy," pp. 141–152 in *The State of Asian Pacific America: Policy Issues to the Year 2020*. Los Angeles: LEAP Asian Pacific American Policy Institute and UCLA Asian American Studies Center, 1993.

Osajima, Keith. "Asian Americans as the Model Minority: An Analysis of the Popular Press Image in the 1960s and 1980s," pp. 165–175 in Gary Y. Okihiro, Shirley Hune, Arthur A. Hansen, and John M. Liu (eds.), *Reflections on Shattered Windows*. Pullman, Washington: Washington State University Press, 1988.

Park, Edward Jang-Woo. "Asian American Entrepreneurs in the High Technology Industry in Silicon Valley," pp. 155–177 in Bill Ong Hing and Ronald Lee (eds.), *Reframing the Immigration Debate: a Public Policy Report*. Los Angeles: LEAP Asian Pacific American Public Policy Institute, 1996.

Petersen, William. *Japanese Americans.* New York: Random House, 1971.

Portes, Alejandro, and Ruben G. Rumbaut. *Immigrant America: A Portrait.* Berkeley and Los Angeles: University of California Press, 1990.

"Power Brokers: The 25 Most Influential People in Asian America." *A. Magazine,* Vol. 2 (3): 25–34, Fall 1993.

Sanborn, Kenneth O. "Intercultural Marriage in Hawaii," pp. 41–50 in Wen-shing Tseng, John F. McDermott, and Thomas W. Maretzki (eds.), *Adjustment in Intercultural Marriage.* Honolulu: University of Hawaii Press, 1977.

Shimabukuro, Milton. "Chinese in California State Prisons, 1870–1890," pp. 221–224 in Genny Lim (ed.), *The Chinese American Experience: Papers from the Second National Conference on Chinese American Studies.* San Francisco: The Chinese Historical Society of America and The Chinese Culture Foundation of San Francisco, 1980.

Shinigawa, Larry Hajime, and Gin Yong Pang. "Asian American Panethnicity and Intermarriage." *Amerasia Journal* 22 (2): 127–152, 1996.

"Silicon Valley Pioneer." *AsianWeek* March 8, 1996.

Sowell, Thomas. "The Chinese" and "The Japanese," Chapters 6 and 7 in Thomas Sowell, *Ethnic America: A History.* New York: Basic Books, 1981.

Steinberg, Stephen. *The Ethnic Myth: Race, Ethnicity, and Class in America.* Boston: Beacon Press, 1982.

Strong, Edward K. *The Second-Generation Japanese Problem.* Palo Alto, CA: Stanford University Press, 1934.

"Success Story, Japanese American Style." *New York Times* January 9, 1966.

"Success Story of One Minority in the U.S." *U.S. News and World Report* December 26, 1966.

Sue, Stanley, and Sumie Okazaki. "Asian American Educational Achievements: A Phenomenon in Search of an Explanation." *American Psychologist* 45 (8): 913–920, August 1990.

Suzuki, Bob. "Education and Socialization of Asian Americans: A Revisionist Analysis of the Model Minority Thesis." *Amerasia* 4: 23–51, 1977.

Suzuki, Bob H. "Asian Americans as the 'Model Minority': Outdoing Whites? or Media Hype?" *Change*: 13–19, November/December 1989.

Takagi, Dana Y. *The Retreat from Race: Asian-American Admissions and Racial Politics.* New Brunswick, New Jersey: Rutgers University Press, 1992.

Takagi, Paul, and Tony Platt. "Behind the Gilded Ghetto: An Analysis of Race, Class, and Crime in Chinatown." *Crime and Social Justice*: 2–25, Spring–Summer 1978.

Trueba, Henry T., Lilly Cheng, and Kenji, Ima. *Myth or Reality: Adaptive Strategies of Asian Americans in California.* Washington, D.C.: Falmer Press, 1993.

U.S. General Accounting Office. *Asian Americans: A Status Report* GAO/HRD-90–36FS, March 1990.

Useem, Michael, and Jerome Karabel. "Pathways to Top Corporate Management," pp. 175–207 in Paul William Kingston and Lionel S. Lewis (eds.), *The High-Status Track: Studies of Elite Schools and Stratification.* Albany, NY: SUNY, 1990.

Valentine, Charles A., *Culture and Poverty: Critique and Counter-Proposals.* Chicago and London: University of Chicago Press, 1968.

Varon, Barbara F. "The Japanese Americans: Comparative Occupational Status, 1960 and 1950." *Demography* 4: 809–819, 1967.

Walker-Moffat, Wendy. *The Other Side of the Asian American Success Story.* San Francisco: Jossey-Bass, 1995.

Wilson, William Julius. *When Work Disappears: The World of the New Urban Poor.* NY: Vintage, 1997.

Woo, Deborah. "Asian Americans in Higher Education: Issues of Diversity and Access." *Race, Gender & Class* 3 (3): 11–37, Spring 1996.

Woo, Deborah. "The 'Overrepresentation' of Asian Americans: Red Herrings and Yellow Perils." *Sage Race Relations Abstracts* 15 (2), May 1990.

Wu, Frank, and May Nicholson. "Facial Aspects of Media Coverage on the John Huang Matter." *Asian American Policy Review* VII: 1–37, Spring 1997.

Zweigenhaft, Richard L., and William Domhoff. *Diversity in the Power Elite: Have Women and Minorities Reached the Top?* New Haven: Yale University Press, 1998.

Reading 16

Asian Americans in the Public Service: Success, Diversity, and Discrimination

Pan Suk Kim and Gregory B. Lewis

Although high levels of schooling and occupational achievement suggest that Asian Americans have succeeded in American society (Taylor and Kim 1980, p. 2), their image as a "model minority" conceals both their diversity and the discrimination they continue to face. In this article we investigate that diversity and discrimination and analyze the status of Asian Americans in the public sector, particularly the federal civil service. We begin with a general profile of Asian Americans in the United Sates, then narrow the focus to federal employees. We examine trends in employment and compensation of Asian Americans relative to nonminorities and questions whether Asians face a "glass ceiling" that keeps them out of the top levels of the federal bureaucracy, perhaps by channeling them into professional occupations and away from supervisory authority.

GENERAL PROFILE OF ASIAN AMERICANS

The first Asians to arrive in the United States in large numbers were the Chinese who arrived as laborers in the mid-nineteenth century. The Chinese Exclusion Act of 1882 banned the immigration of Chinese laborers, but not merchants and students (Daniels, 1988). Shortly thereafter, large numbers of Japanese laborers immigrated and were followed by Filipinos and considerable numbers of Koreans, Indians, and other Asians.

Source: *Public Administration Review*, 54:3 (May/June 1994): 285–290. Reprinted by permission.

Restrictive immigration laws such as the Immigration Acts of 1917 and 1924 produced a 40-year break in Asian immigration starting in the 1920s (*Ozawa* v. *United States*, 260 U.S. 178, 1922; *Thind* v. *United States*, 261 U.S. 204, 1923). In 1965, when the United States lifted its anti-Asian immigration restrictions (by abandoning the national origins system of immigration), a new wave of immigration from Southeast Asia and other Asian countries began (U.S. Commission on Civil Rights, 1992); Takaki, 1989; U.S. Commission on Civil Rights, 1980).

By 1990, the U.S. Asian and Pacific Islander population was about 7.3 million, of whom 95 percent were Asian (U.S. Bureau of the Census, 1991). Asian Americans (hereinafter, the terms "Asians" and "Asian Americans" include Pacific Islanders) are the fastest growing minority group in the United States, primarily because of immigration, especially in the aftermath of the Vietnam War. Their numbers grew by 55 percent in the 1960s, by 141 percent in the 1970s, and by 76 percent in the 1980s (O'Hare and Felt, 1991). Asians nearly doubled their share of the U.S. population during the 1980s, increasing from 1.6 percent in 1980 to 2.9 percent of the population in 1990. The U.S. Census Bureau (1992a) projects that by 2020, Asians may comprise 7 percent of the U.S. population.

Although Asians have been classified as a single minority group in official U.S. statistics since 1976 (before that they were included in "other races"), they vary widely in culture, language, and recency of immigration. In 1980, nearly two-thirds of all Asian Americans (compared to only 6 percent of the U.S. population) were foreign-born, and one-quarter of Asian adults had immigrated in the previous five years, with considerable variation by national/ethnic origin (Table 1). Only about one-fourth of Japanese Americans were foreign born, compared to two-thirds of Chinese, Filipinos, and Indians, and 90 percent or more of Vietnamese, Cambodians, and Laotians.

Asian Americans are falsely perceived to be largely exempt from economic problems such as high unemployment or poverty (O'Hare and Felt, 1991). Their average family income exceeded the U.S. average by about 28 percent in 1985 primarily because Asian American households are generally larger; their per capita income was lower than the U.S. average and that of non-His-

panic whites (U.S. General Accounting Office, 1990). High family incomes also reflect the concentration of Asian Americans in high cost-of-living areas—94 percent lived in metropolitan areas in 1991, compared to only 77 percent of whites (U.S. Bureau of the Census, 1992b).

The high median family income of Asians as a group hides their diversity. According to 1980 census data (the most recent available by national origin), the median family income for Asian Americans was $2,700 higher than that for the U.S. population as a whole (Table 1). The Japanese median family income exceeded that of white non-Hispanics by 30 percent and the other populous Asian groups (Chinese, Filipinos, and Asian Indians) also

TABLE 1
Characteristics of Asians by Nationality of Origin

National or Ethnic Origin	Percentage of Asians	Percentage Foreign Born	Family Income[a]	High School Diploma (%)	College Educated[b](%)
Chinese	22	63	22,600	71	37
Filipino	21	65	23,700	74	37
Japanese	19	28	27,400	82	26
Indian	10	70	25,000	80	52
Korean	10	82	20,500	78	34
Vietnamese	7	90	12,800	62	13
Hawaiian	5	2	19,200	68	10
Laotian	1	94	5,200	31	6
Thai	1	82	19,400	72	32
Samoan	1	36	14,200	61	7
Guamanian	1	10	18,200	68	8
Cambodian	c	94	8,700	43	8
Pakistani	c	85	20,900	87	58
Indonesian	c	83	20,500	90	33
Tongan	c	75	16,700	66	13
Hmong	c	91	5,000	22	3
OtherAsians[d]	1	n/a	n/a	n/a	n/a
All Asian Americans	100[e]	62	22,700	75	33
Total U.S. population	f	6	20,000	67	16

[a] Figures are based on 1979 income and rounded to the nearest 100.

[b] Percentage of all persons age 25 and over who have completed at least four years of college.

[c] Less than 1 percent.

[d] Includes other Pacific Islanders.

[e] Percents may not add to total due to rounding.

[f] Asian Americans, including Pacific Islander Americans, numbered 3.7 million of 1.6 percent of the U.S population.

Source: U.S. General Accounting Office, *Asian Americans: A Status Report*. Washington, DC: U.S. Government Printing Office, March 1990, pp. 13 and 26 (The 1990 GAO report is based on 1980 census data published in 1988 by the U.S. Bureau of the Census): and U.S. Bureau of the Census, *We, the Asian and Pacific Islander Americans*. Washington, DC: U.S. Government Printing Office, September 1988, pp. 13 and 16.

fared better than white non-Hispanic families. Southeast Asian Americans (Cambodian, Laotian, and Hmong) had median family incomes far less than the national average in 1979 (U.S. Bureau of the Census, 1983, 1988). These groups were also the most likely to be foreign born, however, and were probably the most recent immigrants, so more recent data might reveal different patterns.

Educational achievements of Asian Americans are high: in 1991, similar percentages of Asians and whites age 25 or older had finished high school (82 percent and 80 percent, respectively), but Asians were almost twice as likely to have finished four years of college (39 percent compared to 22 percent) (Usdansky, 1992; U.S. Bureau of the Census, 1992b, p. 5). According to 1980 census data (the most recent available by national origin), educational attainment was lower in 1980 (only 75 percent instead of 82 percent of Asians had completed high school) and varied substantially by national origin. Over 80 percent of Japanese, Indonesians, Pakistanis, and Asian-Indians had completed high school, but the majority of Cambodian, Laotian, and Hmong had not (Table 1).

High educational attainment, however, does not prevent discrimination. Among male high school graduates in 1990, median earnings were only 79 percent as high for Asians as for whites. Asian male college graduates earned only 90 percent as much as white male college graduates. Asian females earned about 95 percent as much as comparable white females, both at high school and college levels of educators (U.S. Bureau of the Census, 1992b).

ASIAN AMERICANS IN THE PUBLIC SERVICE

Asian American employment has increased rapidly in all sectors of the U.S. economy: by 108 percent in the private sector between 1978 and 1990, by 82 percent in the state and local sector between 1980 and 1990, and by 46 percent in the federal sector between 1982 and 1990 (U.S.

Equal Employment Opportunity Commission, 1991). No other group remotely approaches these rates of employment growth. Overall, Asian Americans comprise 2.6 percent of the civilian labor force. Oddly, they are overrepresented in the federal service (3.5 percent) and the U.S. Postal Service (4.3 percent) but underrepresented in the state and local sector (2.0 percent).

This pattern of underrepresentation holds for state, county, city, and town governments (though not for special districts). It also holds for positions in elementary and secondary education, where Asians made up only 0.7 percent of school teachers, principals, and assistant principals in the fiscal year 1990–91 (U.S. Equal Employment Opportunity Commission, 1991). Asian Americans are overrepresented among college and university faculty, however, while non-Asian minorities are underrepresented. In 1990, Asians comprised only 15 of 7,065 elected mayors/chairmen in municipal governments; only 8 of 5,056 chief appointed administrative officers (CAOs)/managers; and only 6 of 1,524 assistant managers or assistant CAOs. Overall, fewer than 1 percent of municipal officials are Asians (International City Management Association, 1991).

In federal white-collar employment, the mean annual salary of white non-Hispanics was $33,500 in 1990. On average, Asian Americans earned 97 percent as much. Hispanics 82 percent, African Americans 76 percent, and American Indians 74 percent as much. In the federal General Schedule and equivalent pay systems, the mean grade of Asian Americans (8.9) approached that of whites (9.3), while those of Hispanics (7.9), African Americans (7.2), and American Indians (7.1) lagged far behind (U.S. Office of Personnel Management, 1990, p. 44). Overall, Asians had a grade distribution much more like that of whites than of other minorities, but at the top levels, Asians were underepresented. They held only 73 of 8,136 positions (0.9 percent) in the federal Senior Executive Service (SES), whereas white non-Hispanics held 92.0 percent of SES positions (U.S. Equal Employment Opportunity Commission, 1990).

ASIAN AMERICANS
IN THE FEDERAL SERVICE

The extensive literature on representation and employment discrimination in the federal bureaucracy has focused mostly on African Americans and women (e.g., Krislov, 1967, 1974; Meier, 1975, 1984; Kranz, 1976; Rosenbloom, 1977; Lewis, 1988; Kellough, 1990). It shows that women and minorities are concentrated at the lower job levels, hold less prestigious occupations in the federal bureaucracy, and earn substantially less than white males with similar qualifications. Only two studies (Taylor and Kim, 1980; Kim, 1993) focus on Asian Americans in the U.S. public service, although a few more general studies mention them in passing. They suggest that the situation for Asian Americans differs somewhat from that for other minority groups. Asian males tend to be concentrated in higher level occupations than other minorities (i.e., a higher proportion of Asians hold managerial and professional occupations) (U.S. Bureau of the Census, 1992b), and their salaries approach those of white males, but they still earn less than comparable white males. Asian females face double discrimination, but they seem to be held back more by their gender than their race.

We investigated several questions in this study. First, previous research (Taylor and Kim, 1980; Lewis, 1988) demonstrated that Asians were in lower grades and earned lower salaries than comparable white non-Hispanics, but the last detailed look at this issue (Taylor and Kim, 1980) used data that are now 15 years old. We examined whether grade gaps between comparable Asians and white non-Hispanics have widened or narrowed over time, and whether they are wider for men or women. We used a standard methodology in the economics of discrimination literature. Using multiple regression analysis, we controlled for a number of factors known to influence career success. We asked whether Asians earned less than white non-Hispanics with the same levels of education, experience, and age who were also comparable in veterans' preference and disability status. Because

other factors also affect career success, the persistence of grade gaps after controlling for age, education, federal experience, veterans' preference, and disability status does not prove discrimination, but it does indicate problems that the government needs to investigate. Second, Asians are the group most similar to whites in grade, salary, and education, yet they remain underrepresented at grades 13 and above. Does this suggest that Asians face a glass ceiling, a general pattern of fair treatment until they reach the portals of power, at which point they find themselves restricted from top positions largely reserved for white males? Conversely, the rapid expansion of Asian American employment in the federal service may come largely from the newer immigrants, who may be less assimilated into American society. Is discrimination concentrated on this group? Third, Asians seem to choose or be directed to professional rather than administrative occupations in the federal government. Does this lead them to less supervisory and managerial power than comparably qualified white non-Hispanics?

We analyzed a 1 percent sample of federal personnel records for 1978, 1985, and 1992, taken from the Central Personnel Data File (CPDF). The CPDF, which is maintained by the U.S. Office of Personnel Management (OPM), is the best data set available for studying federal careers, but it classifies all Asians and Pacific Islanders as a single group. This makes it impossible to determine to what extent the expansion of Asian employment represents older, assimilated nationalities or newer immigrant groups. To simplify the analysis and isolate the impact of being Asian rather than nonminority, we eliminated all blacks, Hispanics, and Native Americans from the data set and analyzed men and women separately. Because the patterns for men and women differ so much, we discuss them separately below.

Asian and White Non-Hispanic Men

Consistent with previous studies, white men held a higher mean grade in federal jobs than Asian men in our sample (10.9 vs. 10.4) in 1992

TABLE 2

Characteristics of Asians and White Non-Hispanics in the Federal Service, 1978, 1985, and 1992

Characteristic	Asian Females	White Females	Asian Males	White Males
Mean Grade				
1992	7.7	8.1	10.4	10.9*
1985	6.9	6.7	9.8	10.5**
1978	6.7	5.9*	9.8	10.2
Percentage with				
Supervisory Authority				
1992	7	12*	15	27**
1985	9	8	15	26***
1978	8	6	23	19
Mean Years				
of Education				
1992	14.4	13.7***	15.3	15.2
1985	14.1	13.3***	15.2	15.0
1978	13.6	12.9*	15.0	14.6
Mean Years				
of Federal Service				
1992	10.2	12.4***	11.6	14.1***
1985	9.5	11.0*	11.7	13.8**
1978	12.5	10.4*	12.9	13.2
Sample Size				
1992	203	4,436	209	5,569
1985	123	4,283	163	5,691
1978	76	3,883	110	5,965

* Asian-white difference significant at .05 level.

**Asian-white difference significant at .01 level

***Asian-white difference significant at .0001 level.

Source: U.S. Office of Personnel Management, *Central Personnel Data File*, 1 percent sample, machine-readable data set.

(Table 2), and they were almost twice as likely as Asian men to be supervisors (27 percent vs. 15 percent). Both differences were significant at the .05 level or better, allowing us to conclude that the basic patterns held true for the entire federal work force. The supervisory situation was much worse for Asians in 1992 than in 1978, when Asian men had the edge in the sample (although the difference was not statistically significant). The gap between the mean grades of Asians and whites was slightly wider in 1992 (10.4 vs. 10.9) than in 1978 (9.8 vs. 10.2) but narrower than in 1985 (9.8 vs. 10.5), suggesting no special trend.

Patterns for both education and federal experience suggest possible explanations for the worsening of the situation for Asians. Asians had more education than whites in each year in our sample (though none of the differences were statistically significant), but whites gained steadily in years of service between 1978 and 1992. White men's mean length of federal service rose by 0.9 of a year between 1978 and 1992, but that of Asian men declined by 1.3 years. Because experience influences grade levels, Asians' relative decline in seniority could have caused their grade levels to slip relative to that of whites.

Multiple regression supports that explanation (Table 3). In 1992, Asian men tended to be 0.3 of a grade lower than white men with the same amount of education, federal experience, and age who had

---

TABLE 3
Differences between Expected Grades of Comparable Asians and Whites, 1978, 1985, and 1992

Characteristic	Women	Men
All Employees		
1992	0.6***	0.3*
1985	0.2	0.5**
1978	−0.0	0.6**
With High School or Less		
1992	1.6***	1.0*
1985	0.6	1.4*
1978	0.5	1.1
With Some College		
1992	0.1	1.0**
1985	0.0	1.1**
1978	−0.1	1.3**
With Bachelor's Degrees		
1992	0.1	−0.2
1985	0.4	−0.3
1978	−0.2	−0.2
With Graduate Degrees		
1992	1.9**	−0.2
1985	−0.8	0.5
1978	−0.4	0.9

* Coefficient significant at 0.5 level.

** Coefficient significant at .01 level.

***Coefficient significant at .0001 level.

Note: Numbers are unstandardized regression coefficients on the variable WHITE, which was coded 1 for whites and 0 for Asians. All regression models include years of education, years of service, years of service squared, age, age squared, and two dummy variables indicating whether the employee received veterans' preferences or was classified as disabled.

Source: U.S. Office of Personnel Management, *Central Personnel Data File,*1 percent sample, machine-readable data set.

the same handicap and veteran status. Earlier gaps between the grades of comparable Asians and white non-Hispanics had been wider (0.6 grade in 1978 and 0.5 grade in 1985). Thus, the gap tentatively attributed to discrimination rather than to the other factors in the model actually narrowed in the 1980s, despite the fact that the gap between the mean grades widened. In short, Asian men are in lower grades than comparable white men (consistent with an argument of discrimination), but the trend is toward greater equality.

Do the well-educated Asians nearing the glass ceiling feel the pinch of discrimination more than their less-educated brethren? For the men, the answer is a clear "no." In the 1992 sample, Asian men with bachelor's or graduate degrees had slightly higher grades than comparable white men (that is, white men of the same level of education, age, length of service, veteran status, and handicap status), but Asian men who had not gone beyond high school or who had started college but had not finished were one grade behind comparable white men. (The latter differences were statistically significant, while the former were not.) Trends over time suggest improvements in treatment for Asians with some college and, especially, for those with graduate degrees (where whites had a statistically significant 0.9 grade advantage in 1978 but had a statistically insignificant 0.2 grade disadvantage in 1992). Gaps held reasonably constant for those with college diplomas or with high school only.

In 1992, identical percentages of Asian and white men in the sample held professional or administrative positions. Much higher percentages of Asians than whites (50 and 34, respectively) held professional jobs, however, whereas much higher percentage of whites than Asians (39 and 23, respectively) filled administrative positions. Logic analysis confirms that Asians were more likely to be professionals than whites with the same years of education, federal experience, age, and with the same veteran and handicap status, while the opposite held true for administrative occupations.

Does this division of labor between professional and administrative occupations help explain why Asians attain less supervisory authority? No.

Logit analysis confirms that Asian men are less likely to be supervisors than comparable white men. That difference remains virtually unchanged when controlling for occupational category in the logit analysis. Asian men are less likely than comparable white men to be administrators; they are also less likely to be supervisors; but there appears to be little connection between the two facts.

In sum, as a group, well-educated Asian men face little or no discrimination in achieving high grade positions and salaries, but they are less successful in attaining supervisory or managerial authority. Their choice of, or channeling into, professional rather than administrative occupations does not seem to explain this discrepancy. Less-educated Asian men face much greater obstacles to attaining the same grades as comparably educated and experienced white men. Asians without college diplomas were at least one grade behind comparable whites in all three years examined, although the gaps seemed to be narrowing somewhat. Asians' communication skills, especially less fluency in English, might account for some of the grade differences, if this group is made up largely of newer immigrants.

Asian and White Non-Hispanic Women

The story for Asian women is more complex and troubling. As shown in Table 2, the mean grades of Asian and white non-Hispanic women in our sample did not differ significantly in 1992 (7.7 vs. 8.1), although the mean grade of Asians had been significantly higher in 1978 (6.7 vs. 5.9). In 1992, 12 percent of the whites and only 7 percent of the Asians wielded supervisory authority (a difference significant at the .05 level), but in 1978 and 1985, Asian women in the sample had a (statistically insignificant) advantage over white women in supervisory authority.

The relative standing of Asian women in mean grades and supervisory status fell between 1978 and 1992, despite the fact that Asians had had significantly more education than whites in all three years and that the education gap did not shrink at all over the period. On the other hand, Asians had two more years of federal service than whites in 1978, but whites had two more years of federal service than Asians in 1992. The declining relative seniority of Asian women could be partially responsible for their declining status.

Multiple regression, however, shows that is not a complete explanation (Table 3). In 1978, white and Asian women with the same education, seniority, age, veteran status, and handicap status had nearly identical grades. By 1985, Asian women were a statistically insignificant 0.2 of a grade behind, and by 1992, that gap had widened to a statistically significant 0.6 of a grade. Thus, while the unexplained grade gap between Asians and whites was narrowing for the men, it was widening for the women.

Analysis by level of education suggests that the problem is primarily at the high school and graduate school level. White and Asian women with some college or a bachelor's degree held very similar grades in all three years, but Asians with high school only or with graduate degrees were 1.6 or 1.9 grades, respectively, below comparable whites in 1992. Both differences were clearly significant, and much larger than the gaps in 1978 and 1985. These findings provide marginal support for arguments of both the glass ceiling and discrimination against recent immigrants, but the evidence does not fall neatly into a coherent whole.

Similar percentages of Asian and white non-Hispanic women held professional or administrative positions in 1992 (47 percent vs. 45 percent). As with the men, however, the Asians were more likely than the whites to be in professional occupations (24 percent vs. 16 percent) and less likely to be in administrative occupations (23 percent vs. 29 percent). Logit analysis did not reveal significant differences between the two groups in choice of, or channeling into, professional or administrative occupations.

Logit analysis confirmed that in 1992 white women were significantly more likely to wield supervisory authority than comparably educated and experienced Asian women. Again, occupational differences between Asians and whites explained none of that difference in supervisory authority, although finer distinctions among occupations might reveal some effect.

Overall, Asian women fell in status relative to white women between 1978 and 1992. Asians and whites did not differ significantly in grades or supervisory authority in 1978, but by 1992 white women had a clear, statistically significant advantage on both measures. That advantage was apparent among both the most and least educated women (although not those in between), offering little insight into why the situation is worsening for Asian American women. This is especially surprising when the trend has been toward greater equality, not only for Asian men but for all minority and female groups. The most likely explanation is that white women are the group that has gained most from affirmative action in recent years (Lewis, 1988). Asian women have gained on white men, but not as rapidly as white women have, leading Asian women to fall behind relative to white women.

CONCLUSION

Asian Americans have often been stereotyped as the model minority (Taylor and Kim, 1980; Petersen, 1970), based partly on high family incomes, educational attainment, and occupational status (Hurh and Kim, 1989; Chun, 1980). As favorable as it might seem, this stereotype has damaging consequences. First, it masks the very real social and economic problems faced by many segments of the Asian American population and may result in the needs of poorer, less successful Asian Americans being overlooked. Second, emphasis on the model minority stereotype may also divert public attention from the existence of discrimination, even against more successful Asian Americans, in general employment practices and in discriminatory admissions policies in institutions of higher learning. Finally, the origin of this stereotype may be an effort to discredit other minorities by arguing that if Asian Americans can succeed, so can

other minorities. Many Asian Americans resent being used in this fashion (Daniels, 1988; U.S. Commission on Civil Rights, 1992).

The Asian American community actually differs substantially from the myth of uniform success. The rapid expansion of the Asian population in the United States means that this population is changing more rapidly than others and that perceptions need to keep changing to keep up with the reality. The Japanese in this country have typically lived here for generations, speak English as their first language, are highly educated, and earn high salaries. The comparatively new Asian communities are composed primarily of recent immigrants who have learned or are learning English as a second language, have less education, and earn much less. If even the Japanese earn less than comparably educated and experienced whites, then never Asian immigrants face much greater obstacles to success.

In the federal service, Asian Americans resemble white non-Hispanics in education, salary, grade, and supervisory authority more than they resemble other minority groups. Nonetheless, they continue to earn lower salaries, attain lower grades, and wield less supervisory authority than comparably educated and experienced whites. Among men, grade gaps between comparable Asians and whites have shrunk over the past decade and have essentially disappeared among the college educated. Sizable gaps remain, however, between Asian and white men who have not completed college. Among women, being Asian rather than white appeared to be no particular disadvantage in 1978, but the disadvantage has become apparent over the past 12 years, especially among the least- and best-educated women. These Asian women are still closing the gap relative to white men, but not as rapidly as white women. Being Asian has become a disadvantage for women more so than in the recent past.

The grade and salary gaps between Asians and comparable whites are smaller than for any other minority group, but even this model minority faces discrimination. Policy makers should not ignore this evidence and assume that the battle against discrimination has been won for Asian Americans. A problem remains, especially for those without a college education and probably for recent immigrants, although data currently available do not allow a clear test of the latter hypothesis. Diversity training needs to obtain the truth about Asian Americans to battle false stereotypes and lessen discrimination. Recent immigrants from rural areas, where values and customs differ greatly from the predominant U.S. culture, may need special help to familiarize them with modern technology and American common culture. For a diverse group of Asian Americans, long-term recruitment and placement strategies, commitment to higher education funding, and trancultural programs that include job-related social services should be developed or expanded to attract them to the public service. Increasing the representation of Asian Americans in higher grade positions is a slow process. The Asian American national contingents still lack the numbers to mount a strong political influence by themselves, so pan-Asian efforts and pan-Asian organizations could promote opportunities for the establishment and expansion of Asian political and economic interests.

NOTE

The authors are grateful to the U.S. Equal Employment Opportunity Commission, Public Programs Division, for sponsoring this research and for providing some of the data analyzed; to the U.S. Office of Personnel Management, Division of Workforce Information, for providing the statistical sample of the Central Personnel Data File analyzed in this article; and to The American University for funding purchase of these data.

REFERENCES

Chun, Ki Taek, 1980. "The Myth of Asian American Success and Its Educational Ramifications." *IRCD Bulletin* 15 (Winter/Spring), pp. 1-12.

Daniels, Roger, 1988. *Asian America: Chinese and Japanese in the United States Since 1850.* Seattle: University of Washington Press.

Hurh, Won M. and Kwang C. Kim, 1989. "The Success Image of Asian Americans: Its Validity, and Its Practical and Theoretical Implications." *Ethnic and Racial Studies* 12 (October): 512-538.

International City Management Association, 1991. *The Municipal Year Book.* Washington, DC: International City Management Association.

Kellough J. Edward, 1990. "Integration in the Public Workplace: Determinants of Minority and Female Employment in Federal Agencies." *Public Administration Review* 50 (September/October), pp. 557–564.

Kim, Pan Suk, 1993. "Racial Integration in the American Federal Government: With Special Reference to Asian Americans." *Review of Public Personnel Administration* 13 (Winter), pp. 52–66.

Kranz, Harry, 1976. *The Participatory Bureaucracy* Lexington MA: Lexington.

Krislov, Samuel, 1967. *The Negro in Federal Employment.* Minneapolis: University of Minnesota Press.

———, 1974. *Representative Bureaucracy*, Englewood Cliffs, NJ: Prentice-Hall.

Lewis, Gregory B., 1988. "Progress Toward Racial and Sexual Equality in the Federal Civil Service." *Public Administration Review* 50 (March/April), pp. 220–227.

Meier, Kenneth J., 1975. "Representative Bureaucracy: An Empirical Analysis." *American Political Science Review* 69 (June), pp. 526–542.

———, 1984. "Teachers, Students and Discrimination: The Policy Impact of Black Representation." *Journal of Politics* 46 (February), pp. 252–263.

O'Hare, William P. and Judy C. Felt, 1991. *Asian Americans: America's Fastest Growing Minority Group.* Washington, DC: Population Reference Bureau.

Petersen, William, 1970. "Success Story, Japanese American Style." In *Minority Responses*, edited by Minako Kurokawa, pp. 169–178. New York: Random House.

Rosenbloom, David H., 1977. *Federal Equal Employment Opportunity.* New York: Praeger.

Takaki, Ronald, 1989. *Strangers from a Different Shore: A History of Asian Americans.* Boston: Little, Brown.

Taylor, Patricia A. and Sung-Soon Kim, 1980. "Asian Americans in the Federal Civil Service in 1977." *California Sociologist* 3 (Winter), pp. 1–16.

U.S. Bureau of the Census, 1983. *General Social Economic Characteristics of U.S. Summary, 1980 Census.* Washington, DC: U.S. Government Printing Office.

———, 1988. *We, the Asian and Pacific Islander Americans.* Washington, DC: U.S. Government Printing Office.

———, 1991. *Statistical Abstract of the United States 1990.* Washington, DC: U.S. Government Printing Office.

———, 1992a. *Current Population Reports: Population Projections of the United States by Age, Sex, Race, and Hispanic Origin, 1992 to 2050.* Washington, DC: U.S. Government Printing Office.

———, 1992b. *Current Population Reports: The Asian and Pacific Islander Population in the United States, March 1991 and 1990.* Washington, DC: U.S. Government Printing Office.

U.S. Commission on Civil Rights, 1980. *Success of Asian Americans: Fact or Fiction?* Washington, DC: U.S. Government Printing Office.

———, 1992. *Civil Rights Issues Facing Asian Americans in the 1990s.* Washington, DC: U.S. Government Printing Office.

U.S. Equal Employment Opportunity Commission, 1990. *Annual Report on the Employment of Minorities, Women and Handicapped Individuals in the Federal Government.* Washington, DC: U.S. Government Printing Office.

———, 1991. *Indicator of Equal Employment Opportunity: Status and Trends.* Washington, DC: U.S. Government Printing Office.

U.S. General Accounting Office, 1990. *Asian Americans: A Status Report.* Washington, DC: U.S. General Accounting Office.

U.S. Office of Personnel Management, 1990. *Affirmative Employment Statistics.* Washington, DC: U.S. Office of Personnel Management.

Usdansky, Margaret L. 1992. "Report Spotlights Asian Diversity." *USA Today* (September 18), p. A10.

Reading 17

San Francisco Guards Punished for Their Accents: Discrimination Spoken Here

Richard J.P. Cavosora

"My colleagues and I were devastated by our removal," laments Perfecto Estrada. "I was unemployed for six months; I almost got divorced because of the problems caused by my unemployment." Estrada and four other Filipino security guards of the American Mutual Protective Bureau (AMPB) were banished from their posts last year because they allegedly do not speak English well. Now the five guards are suing their employer and a United States government office for discrimination.

At first there were only rumors. Filipino security officers assigned at the U.S. Department of Treasury offices at 390 Main Street in downtown San Francisco were to be removed from their assignment because of their alleged inability to speak English. So the gossip went among the guards of AMPB, an Oakland-based security firm contracted by the U.S. General Services Administration (GSA) to provide security services in various federal facilities in San Francisco and the East Bay.

"I wasn't concerned at first," recalls Estrada in well-articulated English with a distinct Visayan inflection. "I knew that I did not have any problem communicating in English. I had worked with AMPB for over five years without any complaints about it." Indeed, Estrada had no reason to believe the rumors. First hired by AMPB in 1983, he rose through the ranks first to sergeant and first lieutenant, then to captain and deputy chief. He also served as field supervisor at one point. The

Source: *Filipinas* July 1993, pp. 16–18, 46. Reprinted by permission.

titles did not mean much to him. His promotions, he thought, were a reflection of his leadership and command experience, having served for twenty-eight years in the Armed Forces of the Philippines as an intelligence officer and later on as a district commander of a Philippine Constabulary highway patrol unit with the rank of major.

But the rumors came true. Estrada remembers how their tribulations began. In December of 1991, AMPB, having received a new contract from GSA to provide security at the Treasury offices, permanently assigned Perfecto Estrada, Cabrito Rose, Florentino Ramirez, Teodolfo Loyola, Cayetano Decena and another Filipino guard to work swing, graveyard and weekend shifts at the Department of Treasury offices.

"We were selected for that assignment because of our qualifications," asserts Estrada. "At that time, we were the most qualified to meet strict GSA requirements for the new posts. We had passed all the necessary firearms and written tests, and we were experienced in securing federal facilities."

At the Treasury post, the guards' standing duties were to secure the hallways and emergency exits and to operate the video camera controls. It entailed walking the halls, checking peoples' identification when necessary, and monitoring video security screens. Since the guards were assigned during hours when the building was closed to the public, there were very few occasions that required communicating with other people in the building.

In either January or February of 1992, GSA allegedly received a complaint from a Treasury building official about an incident in which the official had trouble communicating with an unnamed AMPB guard at Treasury. Not much is known about this purported incident. None of the guards recall it, or being involved in it. The Treasury official, however, reportedly claimed to have telephoned a guard station and allegedly had difficulty communicating with the person who answered the call, and who then abruptly hung up. The guard in question was assumed to be a Filipino.

Following the alleged incident, a GSA official of the Federal Protective Services division asked AMPB to remove all five Filipino guards from their Treasury assignments. The official complained of a "language barrier," citing the purported telephone incident as an example. At a meeting, the AMPB management told Estrada, Ramirez and Rose that GSA had requested their removal because of "communication problems."

Their removal hit the security guards hard. Reassignment to various posts was a routine part of a security guard's work, but reassignment due to their allegedly faulty English was, the guards felt, particularly discriminatory and demeaning. "We felt humiliated especially after the long number of years we had worked for AMPB." Estrada says. "We felt embarrassed among friends, co-workers and relatives because we were removed for not being able to speak English." Estrada was not assigned to any posts for some six months after being yanked from the Treasury assignment.

"All of us had emotional, mental and physical distress" he says. "We have also suffered from financial hardships and family problems caused by the loss of income. We felt shame and pain for not being able to support our family here and in the Philippines. Some of our relatives who depend on us for educational support have been forced to quit school."

In March 1992, the five guards sought the help of the Asian Law Caucus. Attorneys from the American Civil Liberties Union of Northern California and the Employment Law Center later joined as co-counsel. In April 1992, the attorneys filed a complaint with the Equal Employment Opportunity Commission charging that AMPB and GSA had discriminated on the basis of national origin, a violation of Title VII of the Civil Rights Act of 1964. A similar complaint was filed with the GSA's Equal Employment Office.

"What these guards experienced has been outrageous!" declares ALC attorney Lora Jo Foo. She describes it as a case of an employer who failed to stand up for the rights of its employees. It's also a case of the GSA—a federal agency mandated by law not to contract various services with businesses that discriminate—discriminating against and "causing profound suffering to people who basically guard facilities and records for the public's benefit."

Ed Chen of the American Civil Liberties Union of Northern California says "the men were highly qualified for the jobs—most had extensive security experience and two had long records of military training and service." All but one had college education in the Philippines where the language of instruction is English. "No one had ever complained about their performance as security guards nor had anyone made unfavorable comments about their English proficiency," explains Chen.

"In other posts, we dealt with the public many times, helping them in directions, telling them where to go. No one complained about our English," Cabrito Rose states ironically. "Yet, at Treasury, there was no one to talk to. *Kami Lang mga guardia* (Just ourselves, the guards). And that's where we were accused of having a 'language barrier.'"

"Their removal was unwarranted," adds Christopher Ho of the Employment Law Center. "Each of them is sufficiently fluent and comprehensible in English to satisfactorily perform his job. Their removal was unlawfully based on their accent, race and national origin—not on their ability to perform their jobs." After they had filed the complaint with the EEOC, AMPB and GSA officials, the guards, particularly Estrada and Rose, had to endure a series of retaliatory harassment. On May 12, 1992, about one month after the guards filed their charges, GSA sent a letter to AMPB ordering their removal from all federal buildings under GSA contract. (However, AMPB did not comply because of the pending EEOC charges. Instead, AMPB appealed the May 12 order to another GSA officer who rescinded it.) In August 1992, AMPB restored some of the guards to the same number of work hours per week they had. They were, however, reassigned to other AMPB-guarded federal facilities. Moreover, once reinstated, other retaliatory actions followed.

"Additional obstacles were placed to make it difficult for us to pass qualifying examinations in the firing range and in written examinations," claims Estrada. "We were scolded and shouted at in public situations for minor infractions, which in the past would have been ignored." After a series of incidents, the guards' lawyers filed additional retaliatory harassment charges against GSA and AMPB. Estrada went on disability leave after being involved in a car accident. Rose, under intense pressure and not being given enough preparation time, failed a qualifying written exam and was terminated by AMPB in April 1992. The rest were not given any other assignments.

A year after their removal, the guards filed a separate civil rights lawsuit accusing the AMPB, GSA and certain federal officials of discriminating against them on the basis of their national origin and violating state anti-discrimination laws and the federal Constitution. The suit seeks an injunction ordering AMPB and GSA to reinstate the five men as security guards at the Department of Treasury with retroactive seniority, back pay, removal of adverse references from their personnel records and compensatory and punitive damages. The suit also seeks an injunction against future discrimination.

In a major triumph for the guards, the EEOC upheld the national origin discrimination complaint they filed against AMPB in April of 1992. Only three percent of such complaints filed with the EEOC are upheld. With the findings, the guards will add "violation of Title VII" charges to their federal lawsuit. The breakthrough, however, is only the beginning of what may be a bigger battle. With its issuance of a "reasonable cause determination," the EEOC also issued an invitation to both parties to engage in settlement negotiations. . . . On the side of the guards, attorneys Alan Sparer and Linda Foy from the private law firm Howard, Rice, Nemerovski, Canady, Robertson & Falk have joined ALC, ACLU, and ELC attorneys as pro bono co-counsel in possible litigation efforts if negotiations do not come about, or if these fail.

Challenging a private security company and a huge federal bureaucracy to a legal battle is a complex and nerve-wracking affair. The experience has taken its toll on the men, most of whom are middle-aged. It took a lot of courage and energy to even start the fight. Yet, despite the humiliation they've suffered, Perfecto Estrada, Cabrito Rose, Teodulfo Loyola, Florentino Ramirez and Cayetano Decena are open to negotiations. But if that does not happen, they have also decided to fight the battle to its very end because, in their own words, "it's a matter of *principio.*"

Reading 18

Immigrant Asian Women in Bay Area Garment Sweatshops: "After Sewing, Laundry, Cleaning and Cooking, I Have No Breath Left to Sing"

Miriam Ching Louie

Helen Wong recalls that when she first arrived in Oakland from Hong Kong in 1988 with her husband and five kids in tow, "I just followed everyone else into the garment shops." Helen's first U.S. job was in a tiny, ten-machine storefront shop on Clay Street tucked behind City Hall. Although Helen spoke no English at the time, she recalls, "Getting a job was easy. But the pay was really low." Working for piece rates, her average wage fluctuated between one and two dollars an hour. Helen and her immigrant co-workers churned out women's dresses and pantsuits. The women usually worked Monday through Saturday, but came in Sundays when there was a special rush order to complete. Helen says, "The pay rate is just the same on Sunday. There is no such thing as overtime. You can take a break if you want to. But sewing by the piece means you don't get paid for it."[1]

Like Helen, thousands of Asian immigrant women bend over machines in sweatshops tucked in Chinatowns, Little Saigons, and Koreatowns across the country. At the beginning of the century, America's seamstresses were likely to be immigrant, young and single. Now at the cusp of the twenty-first century, seamstresses are still likely to be immigrant, but they are married with children and they come, not from southern or eastern Europe, but from South America, East Asia, and the Caribbean. The change in color and languages followed the industry's thrust beyond U.S. borders.

Source: *Amerasia Journal* 18:1 (1992): 1–26. Reprinted by permission.

American consumers sport clothes assembled anywhere from Hong Kong to Mexico, Haiti, South Korea, the Philippines, Guatemala, Sri Lanka, or Costa Rica. With the globalization of labor came international competition between workers.[2]

This article analyzes the impact of this globalization of the garment industry on wages and working conditions of Asian immigrant seamstresses in the San Francisco–Oakland Bay Area. The garment industry is the largest manufacturing sector in San Francisco and employs over 25,000 workers. Ninety percent of these workers are women, and in San Francisco over 80 percent are Chinese-speaking, according to the International Ladies Garment Workers Union (ILGWU). Less than 8 percent of these workers are unionized.[3]

This article draws heavily from the experiences of Asian Immigrant Women Advocates (AIWA), an organizing project concentrated in garment, hotel, restaurant, electronics assembly, and nursing home industries. While this article focuses on the garment industry, AIWA has also found large concentrations of Asian immigrant women working in several other Bay Area industries:

- San Francisco's tourist industry employs 12,900 hotel and 16,900 restaurant and bar workers. Hotel and Restaurant Employees and Bartenders Union Local 2 has 12,000 members—30 percent are Asian and 27 percent Latinos. Fifty percent of the members are women.[4]
- In Santa Clara county, the "Silicon Valley" electronics assembly industry employed at least 195,000 workers in 1980. By 1988 Asians made up

a fifth of the work force, compared to one-tenth in 1980. Asians now account for 43.1 percent of semi-skilled operatives, with Asian women comprising 24 percent, and Asian men 19.1 percent.[5]

- Service Employees International Union (SEIU) organizer Luisa Blue predicts that "in the 1990s, Filipinos alone will be 30 percent of the Bay Area's hospital and healthcare workers."[6]

This article focuses on the status of Asian immigrant women workers in the garment industry, especially the resurgence of ethnic-based community labor organizations. While trade unionists regard these organizations as "pre-union," given the decline in union membership to only 17 percent of all U.S. workers, such formations may well prove to be "post-union." Thus, this study contributes to the current debate among workers, organizers, and researchers over new strategies for organizing America's increasingly female, minority and immigrant work force.

GLOBALIZATION OF THE GARMENT INDUSTRY

Until the 1950s almost all of the nation's clothing was "Made in the U.S.A." Only expensive specialty items, like British woolens, Irish knits, or Italian silks were imported. Now, foreign imports have grown to over 50 percent of all the clothing sold in this country.[7]

Waldinger summarizes the factors that render the production process dependent on cheap labor all over the globe:

Made of soft material, a garment cannot be mechanically fed into a machine: a worker needs to hold a garment or garment part and guide it through the sewing machine. Material-handling problems are compounded by the effects of style. Fashions change regularly; and since these changes alter the tasks of workers who sew the new fashions, the tasks cannot be fully broken down and standardized. For these reasons, labor counts for a very high percentage of total costs. . . .[8]

The simple technology enabled developing countries to enter the international market. During the industrial revolutions of Europe and the U.S., female labor was used in textile and garment production under the rationale that women could easily adapt to such work as a logical extension of their domestic role. Today developing nations still use the cheap labor of women garment workers to accumulate capital and attract foreign exchange to finance industrial growth. During 1988, the U.S. imported $16,426,598,000 worth of garments from developing countries, almost 11 percent of its total imports from developing nations.[9]

Textile and garment workers' labor helped fuel the "economic miracles" of Asia's "Four Little Dragons"—Hong Kong, South Korea, Taiwan, and Singapore. When these women attempt to unionize, they are condemned as a threat to economic development and national security.[10]

As garment production fled overseas, manufacturers and garment workers' unions pressured the U.S. government to place quotas on foreign imports. The government now negotiates quotas with nations exporting large numbers of garments. Rick Shattuc, a U.S. customs agent in San Francisco, explains that Hong Kong, Singapore, South Korea, and Taiwan all have quota restrictions. The quota may change every year. Some nations, like Hong Kong, will apportion parts of their quota to other countries. Garment imports from other Asian countries like India, Bangladesh, Sri Lanka, and the Philippines are also increasing.[11] During 1989 the volume of textile and apparel imports increased 13 percent. During the same period domestic employment fell 3 percent, resulting in a loss of two thousand jobs.[12]

While one group of manufacturers railed against foreign imports, another group moved to take advantage of Third World women's cheap labor through a handy little loophole called "Item 807." Item 807 of the U.S. Tariff Code permits U.S. firms to send cut pieces of fabric to be assembled "offshore," i.e., overseas, and then pay tariffs only on the "value added," which basically amounts to the cheap wages paid to foreign female workers. Because of the cost of shipping, U.S. manufacturers mainly use Item 807 to send cut fabric to nearby Mexico and the Caribbean for assembly. Export manufacturing plants called *maquiladoras* in garment and electronics assembly are mainstays of Mexico's Border Industrialization Program (BIP) and the Caribbean Basin Initiative (CBI). Both the BIP and CBI were encouraged by the U.S. government to stimulate economic development so the countries could pay back their debts to U.S. banks, as well as bind their economies to U.S markets.[13] As a result, in 1990 the Dominican Republic sent $581 million worth of apparel into the United States under Item 807, followed by Mexico with $449 million.[14]

While manufacturers profit from globalization of the industry, immigrant seamstresses in the U.S. are losing jobs unless they work at the "Third World wages" paid to women overseas. In June 1990, Koret of California, one of the last unionized shops in the Bay Area, closed down its three remaining plants and moved production to Guatemala. Koret's San Francisco plants employed over three hundred workers. Another five hundred at subcontracting shops were also affected. Guatemalan seamstresses make an average of $1.50 for an eight-hour day compared to the six dollars an hour Koret workers used to get. Wendy Tjon, a Chinese ILGWU organizer, labeled Koret's move a "blatant effort to bust the union."[15]

According to ILGWU organizers, workers made concessions in 1986 to keep Koret from going abroad, agreeing to cuts of up to 25 percent in piece rates, and allowing Koret to import more items sewn abroad. [In 1987] two-thirds of Koret's production was in the U.S., and one-third abroad. By 1989 the ratio was reversed. The company says it shut down its San Francisco sewing plant in order to reduce overhead and consolidate production. But increasing offshore production appears to coincide with rising profits. In 1987 Koret reported gross profits of approximately $48 million. By 1989, gross profits had risen to $65 million.[16]

In Guatemala where Koret has sent its work, the assembly for export, or *maquiladora* industry, has grown from virtually nothing five years [earlier] to some 225 plants employing 50,000 seamstresses who sew for such brand names as Levi-Strauss, Van Heusen, Calvin Klein, Liz Claiborne, Arrow, and Koret. Charles Ford, a U.S. embassy diplomat stationed in Guatemala, says, "It's not an issue of whether these kinds of jobs are in the States any more, but whether they will be in Korea or in Central America. . . . At least *maquila* will keep jobs alive for those in America who make the fabric and the threads, and keep the other jobs in the hemisphere. Also, to the extent you keep jobs here, you keep people from emigrating."[17]

But Asian immigrant women who lost jobs because of the Koret closure do not share this official's sanguine view. Jenny Chung worked for Koret at the Seal 1 plant for seventeen years, Huan Quing Huang for seven, Anna Lee for nineteen, and Un Un Kwan for twelve years. They complained, "We feel like we give, give, give, but they don't give back. First comes the earthquake. Then at Thanksgiving we find out we are going to lose our jobs with Christmas and Chinese New Year's on the way. Koret is still making money. They just would not make as much money if they [did not] send our jobs overseas to nonunion sweatshops. But they owe us something for the work we have done for them all these years."[18]

THIRD WORLD COMES TO THE U.S.

While more women overseas began sewing for the U.S. market, others were immigrating to the U.S. Ironically, many ended up working in garment sweatshops in the U.S. The globalization of the garment industry coincided with two U.S. demographic revolutions: 1) the jump in immigration from Asia, Latin America, Africa, and the Middle East following the relaxation of racially discriminatory quotas in 1965;[19] and 2) the entry of massive numbers of U.S. women into the paid work force during World War II which has continued unabated. These changes opened up a vast new reserve of workers ready and willing to work in secondary labor market jobs.[20]

Historically, the labor force participation rate of Black, Latina, Asian, and/or immigrant women has run higher than that of white women. To a large extent, this reflected the phenomenon that minority and immigrant men are not paid a "family wage," i.e., enough to support a family on a single salary. Low wages and persistent patterns of occupational segregation make these families more dependent than ever on the work of female family members. In the Asian community, despite low wages and onerous working conditions, necessity drives many immigrant women to become bread or "rice winners."

The influx of immigrants also reinvigorated the garment industry by generating a new wave of contractors. Just as sewing is the first job for many immigrant women, a sewing shop is the first business of many immigrant entrepreneurs. The initial investment for opening a shop is low compared to other businesses. For example, in its San Francisco edition, the Hong Kong–based Chinese language daily *Sing Tao* usually runs a dozen ads for garment shops. Telephone inquiries to owners who ran ads revealed that in Oakland $25,000 is sufficient to start a ten to fifteen person shop, which includes different kinds of sewing and pressing machines as well as access to the previous owner's clients. Rents for storefront space are slightly cheaper farther away from Oakland Chinatown and near East 12th and 14th Streets, called the "China Hill" area where many Vietnamese, Cambodian, and Chinese immigrants have settled in the last few years. Owners surveyed indicated that if the buyer pays cash, the price will be lowered.[21]

The San Francisco Bay Area garment industry is now the third largest in the country after New York and Los Angeles. The industry is estimated to do an annual business of six billion dollars, and accounts for one out of every five manufacturing jobs. The number of jobs in the industry has increased over 20 percent in the last decade,

according to the ILGWU. Most of the workers come from China, Hong Kong, and Taiwan, with smaller numbers from Vietnam, Cambodia, the Philippines, Korea, Mexico, and Central America.[22]

An estimated half to three-quarters of the clothes are produced in small sweatshops. In 1960 there was only one sewing subcontractor listed in the "Yellow Pages" of the Oakland telephone book. By March 1, 1990, 150 East Bay shops were registered with the Department of Industrial Relations' Division of Labor Standards Enforcement, with 478 more shops in San Francisco. The actual number of shops is higher because some owners simply do not register.[23]

Business analysts confirm that on-shore production of textiles and apparel is increasing. The growth in clothing imports slowed for the first time during 1988, according to a U.S. Department of Commerce report.[24] A *Business Week* article entitled, "Why Made in America Is Back in Style" (November 7, 1988), observes that the quicker turnaround time for locally produced goods provides a critical competitive edge in the ever-changing fashion industry. Clothing produced more cheaply overseas must often be ordered in bulk quantities, far in advance. By the time the goods reach U.S. shores, American consumers may have latched on to newer fashion trends, forcing manufacturers to mark down prices to get rid of the now out-of-fashion merchandise. Economists also cite quota restrictions and shipping costs as reasons why manufacturers are returning to on-shore production. *Business Week*, however, neglected to mention the availability of low-paid immigrants as a major attraction for garment manufacturers.

The labor of Chinese seamstresses produces a multiplier effect that ripples far beyond the garment industry itself. In *The New Chinatown*, Peter Kwong examines the class and political contradictions within New York's Chinese community. Entrepreneurs who begin as sewing contractors frequently reinvest profits into bigger ventures in their communities. Women working ten to twelve hours a day, six to seven hours a week, buy prepared food on their way home, thus boosting local businesses. Kwong tracks the growth of sweatshops in Chinatown and cites a 1983 ILGWU study which says that the Chinatown garment industry raises at least $125 million annually for New York's economy with about $32 million spent in Chinatown. The number of Chinatown shops multiplied from eight in 1960 to 500 in 1984. Between 1969 and 1982 Chinese female employment in Chinatown garment factories jumped from 8,000 to 20,000.[25]

Asian women have revitalized the garment industry and ethnic economies in the Bay Area, New York and elsewhere.[26] Yet the women themselves receive little reward for the many hours they spend hunched over machines. Conditions in many of today's sweatshops read like a page lifted from a nineteenth century description of the first sweatshops. Based on interviews of federal labor law enforcement officials, a report entitled "Sweatshops in the U.S.," in 1988 found that

> Hispanics and Asians are thought to be the groups most heavily represented in restaurants and apparel manufacturing establishments that are multiple labor law violators. . . . Hispanics were said to represent from 25 to 98 percent of the workers in restaurants that are sweatshops (an average of 53 percent) and 30 to 95 percent (an average of 60 percent) of the workers in apparel manufacturing shops that violate multiple labor laws. Comparable figures for Asians were 5 to 60 percent (an average of 25 percent) in restaurants and 5 to 70 percent (an average of 35 percent) in apparel.[27]

THE PYRAMID STRUCTURE OF THE GARMENT INDUSTRY

These violations of immigrant workers' rights grow out of the very structure of the industry. Dennis Hayashi, an attorney with the Asian Law Caucus, has taken on numerous cases representing garment workers. According to Hayashi:

> The garment industry is hard to organize because of the way it is structured. You have a mid-level group

of primary capitalists—manufacturers—then contractors, and sewers. The real problem is that contractors basically act as insulation. You have to work at two levels. First, it is legally tough to get contractors to comply with wage and hour regulations. They might just end up going out of business before they can pay wages and still make profits. But then the manufacturers say, "It's not our responsibility." So legally you're already starting in a hole. Politically, the garment workers see the contractors as their immediate employers.[28]

The industry is like a pyramid. At the base, *contractors* employ seamstresses, cutters, trimmers, and pressers. Contractors compete with each other to win contracts from larger manufacturers, and are generally not paid by the manufacturer until the order is completed and accepted. Contractors are legally responsible for any labor law violations. There are about 6,000 contractors in California. Shop size runs from fifty to 5,000 square feet.

Jobbers purchase materials, give cut and uncut pieces to contractors, and tell contractors where to ship finished products.

Manufacturers design garments, determine the cost of the material, labor and products, as well as retail prices and the profit margin. Manufacturers also search out buyers and retailers. By California law, manufacturers are not legally responsible for wage and labor law violations in the shops of their contractors. Furthermore, use of the subcontracting system allows manufacturers to cut the cost of labor and facilities, and leave contractors holding the bag. There are about 5,000 manufacturers in California.

Retailers, like Macy's, Bloomingdale's, and J. C. Penney, buy garments, adding a markup price averaging 31 percent (according to *Business Week*), which is passed along to the customer.[29]

The pyramid structure of the industry also presents problems for government officials investigating labor law violations. "From our surveillance we know that women are working overtime and taking home work," says Frank Conte, District Director of the U.S. Department of Labor, Employment Standards Administration,

Wage and Hour Division. "But their time cards say they work from eight to twelve, two to four. Employers say that workers come in early to drink tea, then take an early lunch, then pick up their kids from school, that they come for 'social club activities' on Saturdays. Unfortunately employees often agree with the employers, sometimes out of a sense of fear, sometimes out of loyalty."[30]

Seamstresses who perform what is known as "homework" also shoulder the cost of electricity and utilities used to produce the clothes. Conte's investigators have seen women leave work with cut pieces and return the next day with finished garments. He notes that an estimated 30 percent of the garments produced are suspected to be "homework," but says that the exact number is impossible to know since many are paid in cash and do not show up on any company payroll records. Children and other family members often help seamstresses finish the work. Undocumented refugees and immigrants who are not legally registered to work are particularly vulnerable to this type of exploitation.

The owner of a garment shop on Third Street in San Francisco complains that the "real culprits" for industry abuses are the large manufacturers who almost always award contracts to low bidders. He laments, "These manufacturers don't care whether we can afford to pay our workers the minimum wage."

PROFILE OF SEAMSTRESSES

A survey of 166 seamstresses conducted by Asian Immigrant Women Advocates offers several insights into the working conditions of local seamstresses.[31] The major findings indicate the following:

- Seamstresses span the age spectrum. Sweatshops, however, are willing to employ older immigrant women who often are unable to find a job elsewhere. Twenty-six percent of the seamstresses are

fifty years and older. All the women have children, and 20 percent have four or more kids.

- The English language proficiency of the women is generally very low. Very few have taken English language classes, and find they do not have the time to take them.

- The vast majority of women (93 percent) list their husbands' jobs as unskilled or semi-skilled, including waiter, bus boy, gardener, day-laborer, and the like.

- The women's previous occupations in their home countries vary: 26 percent had been seamstresses; 15 percent cooks, cashiers, and clerks; 10 percent peasants; and 5 percent housewives.

- In terms of working conditions, 57 percent work six days or more a week, one-third are paid less than minimum wage, and one-half at minimum wage. Twenty-seven percent get paid by the piece, 66 percent by the hour, and 7 percent by the month. Fifty-eight percent work for Asian contractors, and 42 percent for Whites.[32]

- Besides the long work week and sub-minimum pay, the seamstresses lack fringe benefits: 86 percent do not know their rights in hiring and firing procedures; 85 percent get no paid sick leave; 77 percent get no paid vacation leave; 75 percent get no salary increases; 73 percent get no overtime pay; 69 percent get no paid holidays; 69 percent get no health insurance coverage from employers; 57 percent get no break time. In addition, 80 percent report that they get no workers' compensation—in many instances, employers may not inform workers when they are covered.

- Asked to rank the three issues (out of fourteen) they would like to change most in the near future, 68 percent list health insurance, 48 percent minimum wage, and 37 percent annual wage increases.

A study by Chalsa Loo and Paul Ong published in 1982 entitled "Slaying Demons with a Sewing Needle: Feminist Issues for Chinatown's Women" discovered that 47 percent of all women who lived in Chinatown and worked outside the home were employed as sewing machine operators. They found that 84 percent of the 108 working women interviewed did not want their children to be doing the same kind of work, and 72 percent did not feel proud of the kind of work they did.

WORKING FROM "CAN'T SEE" IN THE MORNING TILL "CAN'T SEE" AT NIGHT

Besides examining statistics, we can gain an understanding of the dramatic inequities of the industry's structure by contrasting the lives of manufacturers and their Asian immigrant workers. A *San Francisco Business Times* profile of manufacturer Jessica McClintock begins with her speeding toward "the lacy, elegant office where she runs her multimillion-dollar business." Her company produces 150 fashion lines a season (with five seasons a year) under five different labels, plus bridal dresses. A former teacher, she began her business with an initial investment of $5,000 in the late 1960s and now lives in the wealthy Pacific Heights area of San Francisco. Retail sales run from $75 million to $100 million a year. According to the article, company employees are given pension plans and profit-sharing programs and bonuses far beyond industry standards to make the company more successful.[33]

In contrast, Chan Wai Fun (not her real name) has sewn for the McClintock labels for the last three years in a twenty-person shop in Oakland Chinatown. She receives no pension plan, no profit-sharing, no bonuses. Wai Fun worked as an office manager at the port of Guangzhou in southern China before immigrating to the U.S. in 1985. She used to sing Chinese opera at holiday and workers' union events and on tours to the countryside, but sighs, "I don't practice singing anymore. After sewing, laundry, cleaning and cooking, I have no breath left to sing."

Wai Fun got paid by the piece at her first job which averaged two dollars an hour. She says, "At first it was hard learning to sew on an industrial machine. I touched the pedal and the machine gobbled up the fabric." Now she earns five dollars an hour and works a minimum of nine-and-a-half hours a day, six days a week without benefits or overtime pay. She says, "We keep two sets of timecards, one to punch in the time clock and one where we write down our real hours."

Wai Fun admits that she doesn't like her sewing job, but says that because she doesn't know English or have time to study, she has no choice but to continue working there. Her husband installs carpets and is trying to start his own business. "My husband says I shouldn't work so much because I'm always tired. But the money isn't all for me anyway. My father is retired but gets no Social Security. I have to support an older brother in China and my younger sister and brother are still in school."[34]

Tam Le (not her real name) also sews for the Gunne Sax label owned by Jessica McClintock. She works under a Chinese immigrant contractor from Vietnam in a shop with fifty workers near East 12th and 14th Streets in the China Hill area. "You love your native country better because that is where you grew up. But I wanted my kids to have a better life, so I gave up everything," she explains. That is what compelled her to send her daughters to America by themselves on a dangerous boat ride from Vietnam. They lived in refugee camps in Malaysia, Indonesia, and the Philippines before arriving in the U.S. Loan, now sixteen, and Anh, now fifteen, were only nine and eight years old when they left Vietnam. Tam Le did a two-year stint in an Indonesian refugee camp where she earned money sewing before she was allowed to come to the U.S. to join her daughters in 1985.

After spending a year on welfare and attending some English classes, Tam Le sewed in shops around China Hill for the past four years. At the beginning, she worked at piece rate and brought work home, but now gets paid a straight $4.75 an hour. She says raises are minuscule. Workers receive no paid vacation, sick leave, or overtime or, as Tam Le puts it, "no work, no pay." She desperately wants to learn English to get a better job.

Tam Le's day starts by dropping off her daughters at the bus stop so they can travel to better public schools across town from the Fruitvale district where they live. Then she goes to work at her sewing job all day. On the way home she picks up some food to prepare dinner for her girls. After dinner Tam Le returns to her sewing job and gets home after the girls have finished their homework and are fast asleep. On Sunday, her only day off, she does laundry, buys groceries and cooks a fancy meal in quantity so that the girls can eat leftovers during the week. She tries to spend some time with Loan and Anh watching television and doing their fingernails together.

Tam Le's eyes fill with tears when she talks about how much she misses her husband who is still in Vietnam. "It is so hard to take care of the girls alone." Her husband who was a teacher was drafted into the army in South Vietnam. He was imprisoned after the war and worked in the mines. Now fifty years old, his health is failing, she weeps. Tam Le does not have enough money to sponsor her husband to come to the U.S. Talking about her work and life stirs up feelings of pain and frustration. She wipes her eyes as she says, "I'm working so much I don't have many friends. It's hard for me to take care of the girls by myself. But I do everything for them. They really love me so much."[35]

ORGANIZING ASIAN IMMIGRANT WOMEN: AIWA'S COMMUNITY-BASED STRATEGY AND POPULAR LITERACY

Asian Immigrant Women Advocates (AIWA) is one of many organizations to sprout from conditions within the garment industry. Since its beginning in 1983, AIWA has patiently cultivated a base. Through its projects, it has reached approximately seven hundred Chinese garment workers, twenty-five Vietnamese garment and electronics workers, and twenty-five Korean hotel maids. AIWA initiated outreach to Korean electronics assemblers in the Silicon Valley in 1990. It has worked with these women through use of popular literacy and community-based organizing techniques.

AIWA's base is simultaneously worker, female, Asian, and immigrant, and the organization has developed by blending together several different organizing techniques. As compared to the traditional union organizing strategy, AIWA's approach focuses on the needs of its constituency. *Popular literacy/conscientization/ transformation* is a learning and teaching method which taps into people's life experiences as part of a broader reality, source of knowledge, and guide to action. *Community-based organizing* takes a holistic view of racial/ethnic people and organizes for social change, not only so that the people can win immediate improvements in their lives, but so that they can also develop their own power in the course of waging the fight.

AIWA's use of these methods has evolved out of its specific constituency, namely Asian immigrant women workers. Although AIWA actually uses various methods of organizing in combination, for purposes of clarity each method is separately summarized below. To help readers visualize the culturally specific character of the organization and its base, each section begins with "snapshots" from AIWA's "scrapbook" of organizing, then elaborates on the organizing techniques behind the "snapshot."

POPULAR LITERACY/ LEADERSHIP DEVELOPMENT/ TRANSFORMATION

Sunday School—AIWA Style. Immigrant women will tell you that their biggest stumbling block is that they cannot speak English. But how can they learn when they have to go work to support their families? In response to workers' requests, AIWA set up "Sunday School" for seamstresses who sew late into the night and work Saturdays, and "Night School" for hotel maids and electronics assemblers. Worker-students drill in grammar, pronunciation, and new vocabulary at the same time that they learn to express their ideas and practice standing up for their rights. English phrases memorized in advance often come in handy in a pinch. Hotel maids complain that they're tired of having their supervisors yell at them in English that they can't understand. Mrs. Kim says proudly, "At least now I can tell her, 'take it easy, take it easy, you don't have to yell.' "

"Reverse Journey" to Angel Island. Asian American Studies students know that Angel Island in the middle of the San Francisco Bay acted as Ellis Island/purgatory for the first generations of Asian immigrants. There, U.S. immigration officials inspected and grilled our ancestors, deciding how long they would be imprisoned on the island, and whether they would be allowed to stay in America or sent back to Asia. In May 1990, AIWA organized a "Reverse Journey" to Angel island for immigrant women workers and their families. Workers left their homes and jobs in Oakland and San Francisco, caught a ferry to the island, and trekked up the hill to visit the barracks where their country women were imprisoned and scratched poetry/graffiti on the walls. Historian Judy Yung "talks story," so that today's immigrants can understand more about racism and the hopes of those who came before them. At the same time, many have their first opportunity to get away from the sweatshop/ghetto to hike, soak up some sun, and enjoy the fresh sea breeze.

Texas-bound with the Workers Board. AIWA's bilingual organizers are about to tear out their hair, and they have not even gotten on the plane to El Paso, Texas. They pick up Workers Board members, head for the First Congress of Working Women, co-sponsored by La Mujer Obrera of Chicana/Mexicana seamstresses in El Paso, Common Ground Economic Development Corporation of African American women in Dallas, Ramah Weavers Association of Navajo women in New Mexico, and AIWA. But Workers Board members have never traveled within the U.S. before. Talk about "overpacking"—they want to bring blankets, pillows, sheets, chopsticks, food, and enough clothes for both hot and cold weather.

After being coaxed into leaving some of their belongings home, workers make it to El Paso, where they hear the histories of Mexican, Black,

and Navajo women for the first time. Mexican seamstresses open up their homes to the visitors and organize a trip across the border to see the *maquiladoras.* Upon return, AIWA board members send thank you letters to their new friends in Texas and write an article for AIWA's newsletter which says,

> The women workers in El Paso, Dallas and New Mexico have the same problems we do. We did not know the history of people could be so full of suffering. You can hear the facts, but it is difficult to understand the emotions, to translate the suffering. We all need human rights as minority people.[36]

AIWA's popular literacy, leadership development, and transformation techniques are based on the assumption that if provided with the right tools, workers have the capacity to step beyond the role of "victims" and "objects" to become "subjects" able to work collectively to change the structures oppressing them and exert greater autonomy and self-determination within their lives.

In the example of the English classes, the organizing "tactic" is supplied by workers who are frustrated by not being able to speak enough English to get better jobs, or to understand what is going on at work or with their kids, etc. But there are many ways to teach/learn English. The challenge to AIWA organizers is to use the classes so that workers can reflect on their own lives, determine what is fair, visualize alternatives to oppressive conditions, and practice demanding their rights in a supportive setting. Organizers must also transform themselves through the process. Organizers are still learning how to alter the traditional teacher-student, active-passive, all knowing–blank slate restrictions to draw out workers and listen actively. The classes act as an "intelligence gathering" vehicle and "grapevine" about workplace and community happenings, as well as a way to make new friends and build trust.

The Angel Island trip is an example of how the process of popular education extends outside the classroom and back into history. For Asian immigrant women workers, history punctures illusions about the "American Dream." And like other AIWA events, the outing allows women to have fun as they broaden their horizons beyond the sewing machine, kitchen, and immediate family.

The Congress of Working Women shows how leadership development does not come from just dealing with one's own ethnic group in isolation. Asian women had to figure out how to communicate their story to other women of color. In turn, they learned from these women's stories. AIWA members returned from the Congress with a sharper understanding of racism, exploitation of workers, and women's roles.

The six-session Leadership Development Project (LDP), led by Workers Board members each summer, is another example of AIWA's approach. The sessions include discussions based on a slide show on the history of Asian immigrant women in America; the videotape "Dust & Threads" which contains interviews of seamstresses and hotel maids; role-playing based on "know your rights" information presented by union and community labor advocates; and an economic literacy session. The economic literacy session was designed for AIWA by the Center for Ethics and Social Policy and helps women visualize and discuss the structure of the garment industry. At the end of LDP 1990, Workers Board and graduates organized an "accountability session" with government officials where workers presented personal experiences in the sweatshops and pressured officials to hire Chinese-speaking staff and translate complaint forms into Asian languages.

Additional examples of popular literacy, leadership development, and transformation are testimonies by workers at hearings on raising the minimum wage, protests by workers concerning lack of county services for women and children, as well as the current organizing underway to hold health screenings for electronics assemblers to increase awareness about occupational health hazards.[37]

COMMUNITY-BASED ORGANIZING

Seamstress Survey. In order to find out seamstresses' priority issues, AIWA sends a Chinese language survey to over five hundred seamstresses. To get these "tired out" women to make their way through the lengthy questionnaire, AIWA's Workers Board recruited thirty seamstress' friends to set up a phone bank and explain the questionnaire. Raffle prizes solicited from local Asian businesses are offered as enticements for workers to return questionnaires quickly. The raffle strikes a responsive chord in a community that plays the lotto and *mah jong,* and has buses headed for Reno double-parked on its main street. Results of the 166 questionnaires returned are tabulated and announced in a community meeting, which also features the raffle drawing for women who returned the questionnaire. From that meeting, forty workers are recruited into discussion groups to design a health care campaign, which was the main preoccupation among seamstresses surveyed.

"Losing Face" Campaign. Chinese seamstresses are steamed over how Mei Fun Wong was forced out of her job. The boss told her not to bother coming back after an injury because she was "too old to work anyway." Mrs. Wong labored for ten years as a janitor for slumlord real estate owners. Owners wrote a "blackmail" letter to her saying that she had resigned and asked for cash payment under the table. In fact, Mrs. Wong had done none of these things. While the owners are prominent among Asian community social service organizations for philanthropy, workers say that they "treat their own workers like shit."

In a gripe session about the incident, workers come up with the idea of shaming the owners and making them "lose face" in the community to force them to rehire Mrs. Wong and improve working conditions. Workers decide that it is "fair" to demand that the employers also give Mrs. Wong unpaid vacation leave for eight years and unpaid health benefits for seven years. The women chuckle as they draw up a list of organizations to contact because the owners had bragged about belonging to these groups. If employers can blacklist workers in Chinatown, why can't workers turn the tables?

AIWA's identification as a community-based organization requires taking a holistic view of Asian immigrant women and tuning into the particular culture, language, history, and socioeconomic structure shaping their lives. This includes both the culture women bring with them from their countries of origin as well as their attempt to "resocialize" into the U.S. While women generally have a subordinate position within Asian societies, there are often culturally specific ways through which women do express their autonomy. Organizing must take into account the women's multi-layered heritage.

For example, in Korea, organizing outside of the pro-government union federation is seen as a very radical act for which workers have been arrested, tortured and killed. In the People's Republic of China, although unions exist, they tend to support the party, government and management structure, and serve more of a social function, e.g., as a way for workers to get discount tickets to events. In Vietnam, unions are often seen as communist, and therefore bad.

In community-based organizing, workers and organizers devise "winnable campaigns" and "organizing handles." Through these campaigns, improvements can be won; the "bad guys/gals" targeted, pressured, and exposed; and the "good guys/gals" educated and trained to exercise their power.

AIWA surveyed garment workers to get a sharper profile of seamstresses for a campaign to address these concerns. But even before the survey could be collected, workers' leadership was needed to get the word out and the surveys in. Being tuned into the popularity of raffles and other games of chance in the community allowed AIWA to increase women's participation.

The "Losing Face" campaign is an example of how an "organizing handle" presents itself spontaneously out of an incident that "pisses people off." In the tight-knit ethnic community, "losing face" and blacklisting have been used by those with power to stifle workers, and these tactics can be turned around and creatively used by women workers to gain more autonomy.[38]

As a community-based workers' organization, AIWA must take into account women's roles in the family and the "double day" of work inside and outside the home. Many immigrant women work a "triple day," i.e., they do an extra shift at their job, take work home, or "moonlight" at other places to compensate for low wages. Activities must be organized at night or Sundays, close to job and/or home, and often arrangements must be made for food and children. Meetings cannot go too late, and women must have a compelling reason to participate in activities instead of using the time for their families or working additional hours for pay.

By getting women to attend activities that essentially "steal time" away from waiting on their families, AIWA gets women to focus on their own individual opinions, needs, and self-expression. Getting women to take time out for themselves could be considered a revolutionary act, given women's subordinate role in many Asian cultures. Events like the annual Christmas party and Angel Island tour let the rest of the family in on the fun every now and then, so that they won't feel threatened or left out.

CHALLENGES TO AIWA'S ORGANIZATIONAL DEVELOPMENT

The answer to the question, "does AIWA have any shortcomings?" is easy—yes, plenty! Since its inception in 1983, AIWA has patiently cultivated a base, built a leadership core, and developed a repertoire of organizing techniques. But its progress has only confronted the organization with another set of challenges: dealing with its lack of resources; making the transition from "soft-core" to "hard-core" organizing; and intensifying the process of worker leadership and membership development.

According to AIWA Board member Luisa Blue, "AIWA's biggest stumbling blocks are a lack of funding and no ready-made pool of trained bilingual organizers from which to draw." As a long-time Service Employees International Union organizer who recently worked as a trainer for an AFL-CIO leadership development pilot project, Blue is in a position to know the importance of resources—human and material.[39] With few exceptions, AIWA's bilingual organizers must be trained either from the ranks of the workers or "off the street," and both processes necessitate big investments of time and resources.

In terms of financial resources, AIWA lives a year-to-year, hand-to-mouth existence. The organization has (miraculously) managed to survive and even grow since 1983. Income sources include annual worker membership dues of $5, community fundraisers such as ethnic lunch plate sales at street fairs, direct mail drives and assistance from foundations and churches sympathetic to the issues of minorities, immigrants, women and workers.

"SOFT-CORE" VS. "HARD-CORE" ORGANIZING

When AIWA first opens up work in a new industry or geographical location or with a new ethnic group, it has used what organizers call "soft-core" techniques. Soft-core techniques—characterized by "getting a feel for the land"—are non-threatening ways to establish contacts, build trust with workers, and draw them closer to the organization without immediately asking them to take risks that might get them fired and blacklisted.

This stage in organizational development allows AIWA and other groups like it to make inroads where unions have not tread. New union organizing often necessitates an immediate polarization in the workplace where management uses slick union-busting campaigns to "win the hearts

and minds" of the workers. Workers who side with the union get fired, and if the union loses the election (authorizing it to represent the shop), fired workers will never get their jobs back.

Perhaps this is why some unions like the International Ladies Garment Workers Union (ILGWU) have begun to experiment with the concept of "associate membership," where workers can join a union-affiliated organization and gain access to certain services but not have to be members of union shops. Today 83 percent of U.S. workers are not in unions. In the Bay Area, at least 92 percent of seamstresses were not unionized *before* the closure of Koret, the largest union shop. The Silicon Valley electronics industry remains unorganized despite previous attempts by three different unions. Even with associate membership, however, unions still face the challenge of transforming associate members' consciousness to stand up for their rights as workers, immigrants, women, and minorities.[40]

After AIWA built a base within the garment industry through soft-core tactics, it began to redirect its energies into "hard-core" organizing campaigns geared toward improving a focused aspect of women's working conditions. Hard-core organizing—"taking risks for change"—focuses on institutional change. This transition requires higher consciousness among women workers, as well as organizational flexibility to redistribute resources tied up in soft-core projects. Workers have often grown quite comfortable with seeing soft-core projects, like AIWA's "Sunday School" ESL classes or the job training and placement program.

One major warning, however, is that the distinction between soft- and hard-core organizing cannot be rigidly applied. For example, hard-core organizing opportunities sometimes present themselves right away when workers get fired or otherwise abused by employers and therefore feel they have "nothing to lose" by fighting the boss. Given limited resources, AIWA must decide whether its support of the worker will only help one individual or will lead to a broader advance in the collective consciousness for the workplace as a whole. Hard-core organizing also is not necessarily equivalent to confrontational tactics. But hard-core tactics are premised on a higher level of consciousness among a group of workers to devise and lead the campaign.

Aspects of soft- and hard-core organizing can occur simultaneously in different areas of AIWA's work, or even within a single campaign. AIWA has built a sufficient base and core leadership to undertake this organizing simultaneously.

AIWA'S NEXT STAGE OF DEVELOPMENT: BUILDING A MEMBERSHIP-DRIVEN ORGANIZATION AND A NEW POOL OF LEADERS

Recently, with help from community organizing consultant Omowale Satterwhite, the AIWA staff, Workers Board, and Board of Directors held a series of meetings to reformulate goals and objectives. In contrast to the soft-core vs. hard-core approach described above, in the next stage AIWA will attempt to simultaneously build a workers' membership-driven organization and develop a broader pool of leaders. AIWA sees these leaders as emerging from a series of campaigns designed to improve various aspects of women's working lives.

The objectives during the next two years include having members take ownership of the organization's mission statement; building a core of thirty to forty members in various committees; getting members together to develop an election process based on worker activism on issues campaigns; and working for broader ethnic representation on the Workers Board.

Campaigns will be the main vehicles for building the membership base and developing leadership. The campaigns will involve members in legislative and workplace change; create publicity around issues from the workers' standpoint; enable workers to organize demonstrations, rallies, and protest actions; and provide opportunities for members to participate in networks and coalitions.

Leadership development includes political education for members in all aspects of AIWA's work, and is based on the principle of drawing from the knowledge and expertise of the workers themselves. AIWA will provide specific training on internal and external organizational development, social justice issues, and campaign strategy and tactics.

THE BIGGER PICTURE: LINKING UP WITH NATIONAL AND INTERNATIONAL NETWORKS

Despite its specific history, AIWA is by no means unique, and is only one of many grassroots groups of workers, immigrants, and women to spring up during the past decade. The transformation of AIWA members depends on their ability to see themselves as part of a larger reality, to recognize and identify with others dominated by class, race, sex and other forms of oppression. Though its resources are limited, AIWA builds networks with other grassroots organizations in order to benefit from the mutual sharing of experiences.

AIWA Director Young Shin explains, "We were all feeling isolated. So we got together with La Mujer Obrera and the Chinese Staff and Workers Association and talked about the development of a new workers' movement made up of workers who had not been unionized, immigrants, people of color who work in the most marginal sectors of the economy, and workers who are not part of the elite, of any aristocracy of labor."[41]

Interchange between sister organizations helps organizers see their work with a fresh eye. For example, sister organization La Mujer Obrera in El Paso, Texas, shares what it calls the "Transformation Model," based on its experiences in consciousness-raising and organizing among Chicana/Mexicana seamstresses. Using these techniques, a group of seamstresses affiliated with La Mujer Obrera in 1990 chained themselves to their machines in 1990 when an employer laid them off and refused to pay them for time worked.[42]

Another sister organization, the Women's Committee of the Chinese Staff and Workers Association (CSWA), organizes seamstresses in New York Chinatown. CSWA emerged when the Italian-run Restaurant Workers Union Local 100 refused to accept Chinatown waiters into its membership, forcing Chinese to form their own independent union. In 1988 the CSWA Women's Committee was formed to draw in seamstresses. CSWA organizers Wendy Lau and Christine Yue explain that Women's Committee members do not just "talk shop," but that "we talk about work, family and social issues, and how women do not have equal rights with men in Chinese culture." One of the first discussions of the Women's Committee was on domestic violence within the community after a man killed his wife.

CSWA has a broad range of organizing experience that other groups can learn, such as in building an independent union of immigrants, a workers center, an immigrant labor rights project, the Women's Committee, and a low-cost housing reclamation project made up of Chinese and Puerto Rican families.[43]

According to Center for Third World Organizing founder Gary Delgado, some thirty-five such groups exist nationwide.[44] AIWA belongs to several networks, including a new coalition with Micro Electronics Safety Alliance (MESA) in Portland, Oregon, the Santa Clara County Occupational Health and Safety in Silicon Valley, and the Southwest Organizing Project based in Albuquerque, New Mexico.

Given the global character of exploitation of Third World women workers, AIWA also seeks to learn more about the struggles of women internationally, and has established contacts with groups in Hong Kong, Japan, Mexico, the Philippines, South Korea, and Thailand. AIWA plans to build relations overseas in order to raise women workers' consciousness here, and develop joint actions against the transnational corporations that exploit Third World women seamstresses, hotel maids, and electronics assemblers at home and abroad.

Thus, AIWA is an example of how "grounded theory" based on a methodology from women of color can break through the dominant paradigms of organizing and provide a new approach by "listening real loud" to the voices of immigrant women workers.[45] These women, like Chan Wai Fun who "after sewing, laundry, cleaning and cooking have no breath left to sing," still manage to join AIWA and fight for basic rights. Young Shin asserts, "The indigenous leadership is there. You just have to figure out how to tap into it. Some day things will change. We are just building the momentum, building the base for change."[46]

NOTES

Thanks to AIWA Worker's Board and organizers, especially Young Shin, for articulating the outlines of the solution. Thanks also to Linda Burnham of Women of Color Resource Center, Professors Julia Curry and Alex Saragoza of Chicano Studies at UC Berkeley and Gary Delgado of Center for Third World Organizing for their helpful critiques.

1. Helen Wong interview, August 7, 1990.
2. The garment industry has been studied extensively. Especially during the United Nations "Decade of Women" (1975–1985), feminist studies proliferated on what has come to be known as "global assemblyline" of garment and electronics workers, and on the use of women's labor in development strategies. See, for example, June Nash and Maria Patricia Fernandez-Kelly, eds., *Women in the International Division of Labor* (Albany, New York: SUNY Press, 1983); Maria Patricia Fernandez-Kelly, *For We Are Sold, I and My People: Women and Industry on Mexico's Frontier* (Albany, New York: SUNY Press, 1983); Annette Fuentes and Barbara Ehrenreich, *Women in the Global Factory* (Boston, Massachusetts: South End Press, 1985); and Rachel Kamel, *The Global Factory: Analysis and Action for a New Economic Era* (Philadelphia, Pennsylvania: American Friends Service Committee, 1990).

   Domestically, women researchers also contributed scholarship on labor market segmentation based on the combined impacts of racial, gender, and nationality oppression. See, for example, Denise Segura, "Labor Market Stratification: The Chicano Experience," *Berkeley Journal of Sociology* 29 (1984):57–80; Vicki L. Ruiz, *Cannery Women, Cannery Lives: Mexican Women, Unionization and the California Food Processing Industry, 1930–1950* (Albuquerque, New Mexico: University of New Mexico Press, 1987); Patricia Zavella, *Women's Work and Chicano Families: Cannery Workers in the Santa Clara Valley* (Ithaca, New York: Cornell University Press,

1987); Palmira N. Rios, "Puerto Rican Women In the United States Labor Market," paper delivered at the Seminar on the Situation of the Black, Chicano, Cuban, Native American, Puerto Rican, Caribbean and Asian Communities in the U.S., sponsored by Casa de las Américas and Center for the Study of the Américas in Havana, Cuba, 1984; Women's Task Force/National Congress for Puerto Rican Rights, "*Moliendo Café:* Puerto Rican Women Against All Odds," position paper, New York, May 1985; and Linda Burnham, "Struggling to Make the Turn: Black Women in the Post-industrial Economy," paper delivered at Shomberg Center for Research and Black Culture, New York, June 1989.

Roger Waldinger in *Through the Eye of the Needle: Immigrants and Enterprise in New York's Garment Trades* (New York: New York University Press, 1986) summarized changes in the garment industry and the phenomena of ethnic sewing contractors in New York. Peter Kwong in *The New Chinatown* (New York: Noonday Press, 1987) analyzed how the work of Asian immigrant women seamstresses revitalized New York's garment trade and Chinatown's ethnic economy.

Asian American academics wrote several articles on the emerging Chinatown garment industry. See Diane Yen-Mei Wong and Dennis Hayashi's update on working conditions and labor organizing among Chinatown seamstresses in "Behind Unmarked Doors: Developments in the Garment Industry" in *Making Waves: An Anthology of Writings By and About Asian American Women* , edited by Asian Women United (Boston, Massachusetts: Beacon Press, 1989), 159–171; Morrison C. Wong, "Chinese Sweatshops in the U.S.: A Look at the Garment Industry," in *Research in the Sociology of Work,* edited by Ida Harper Simpson and Richard L. Simpson (Greenwich, Connecticut: JAI Press, 1983); Dean Lam, "Chinatown Sweatshops," in *Counterpoint: Perspectives on Asian America,* edited by Emma Gee (Los Angeles, California: UCLA Asian American Studies Center, 1976); and Paul M. Ong, "Immigrant Wives' Labor Force Participation," *Industrial Relations* 26 (Fall 1987): 296–303.

3. This percentage was determined based on the ILGWU's figures of 2,000 members before 300 members were laid off during the closure of Koret's San Francisco facility in June 1990.

4. Economics Research Associates, "The Economic and Employment Impacts of Visitors to San Francisco," August 1987, 9. Also, Kim Jackson of Hotel and Restaurant Employees and Bartenders Union Local 2 provided information on the ethnic composition of the union during an Interview on December 6, 1990.

5. Compilation of EEOC statistics was summarized in the newsletter, *Global Electronics* 101 (February 1990). The newsletter was edited by Lenny Siegel and published by the Pacific Studies Center, Mountain View, California.

6. Luisa Blue Interview, June 19,1989. Blue's estimate was also confirmed by Greg Lim, Research Director for SEIU Local 250 during an interview on December 6, 1990.

7. Waldinger, *Through the Eye of the Needle,* 72.

8. *Ibid.,* 54–55.

9. U.S. Department of Commerce International Trade Administration, *U.S. Foreign Trade Highlights,* 1988, 61.

10. See Committee for Asian Women (CAW) newsletters, and its booklet, *Moving On: Education in Organizing* (Kowloon, Hong Kong: CAW, 1990). CAW is a pan-Asian organization based in Hong Kong which "assists in consciousness raising of women workers in Asia towards the realization of the commonalities of their situations, problems and analysis; seeks to consolidate organizing efforts of women workers to effect favorable changes in their lives; and facilitates networking and linkages amongst women workers and related groups within Asia and outside for solidarity and support." CAW has assisted and publicized the work of various Asian garment workers organizations. See also, Miriam Ching Louie, "First International Exchange of Women Unionists, *off our backs* (March 1990), 18–19.

11. Rick Shattuc interview, April 24, 1990.

12. David Hackett, "Both Good and Bad Trends in '89: ATMI (American Textile Manufacturers Institute)," *DNR* (Daily News Record) (December 18, 1989), 2.

13. Waldinger, *Through the Eye of the Needle,* 76–79.

14. American Apparel Manufacturers Association, *Focus 1991* (Arlington, Virginia: AAMA, 1991), 35.

15. Miriam Chin Louie, "S.F. Chinese Seamstresses Fight Closure of Plant," *Asian Week* January 19, 1990): 4.

16. Datatek on-line computer service, November 12, 1990. For information on Koret Foundation, sale and purchase of Koret, Inc., see James Leung, "S.F. Formally Asks Clothing Maker Not to Close Factories," *San Francisco Chronicle* (May 8, 1990): A-12; and Tim Turner, "Koret Gets Land for Warehouse; Chico Gets Jobs," *San Francisco Business Times* (October 19, 1987): 3.

17. Mary Jo McConahay, "U.S. Garment Jobs Fleeing to Guatemala,"' Pacific News Service, San Francisco (May 31, 1990).

18. Louie, *Asian Week* (January 19, 1990). For information on a similar plant closure affecting Mexican and Chicana seamstresses, see Jeannie Kevet, "What Price Layoffs?," *San Francisco Examiner* (November 18, 1990): D-1. The article describes how Levi Strauss & Co. closed its plant in San Antonio, Texas, in January 1990, laying off 1,115 workers, of whom 92.4 percent were Latina. Levi Strauss already has eleven production facilities overseas and will send work from the San Antonio plant to contractors in Costa Rica and the Dominican Republic. San Antonio plant workers were not unionized. However, workers managed to slap Levi Strauss with a $11.6 billion lawsuit jointly filed on their behalf by a local legal firm and the Mexican American Legal Defense and Education Fund.

19. With the change in immigration laws, the ratio of immigrants from Europe relative to the Third World reversed. Thus, in the two decades following passage of the 1965 Immigration Act, European immigration declined from 42 percent to 12 percent of the total, while Asian immigration grew from 8 to 43 percent of legal immigration. See Morrison G. Wong, "Post-1965 Immigrants: Demo-

graphic and Socioeconomic Profile," in *Urban Ethnicity in the United States, Urban Affairs Annual Reviews*, vol. 29 (Beverly Hills, California: Sage Publications, 1985), 54. The Bay Area's Asian American population is estimated to be between 1.3 and 1.5 million people, a figure more than six times the size it was in 1970. That is about a quarter of the population projected for the nine Bay Area counties in 1990.

20. The labor of women of all races has become vital to the U.S. economy, especially in the expanding sectors of the job market, such as the service and retail trades. Women now constitute 45 percent of the work force, compared to 37 percent twenty years ago. By the year 2000, the Department of Labor predicts a 25 percent increase in the numbers of women in the job market; more than 80 percent of women between the ages of 25–54 will be working outside the home. Between now and the year 2000, eight of the ten occupations that will produce the most jobs are in traditionally female labor markets—mainly service, unskilled and low-paying. See Ruth Needleman, "Women Workers: A Force for Rebuilding Unionism," in a special issue on "Feminizing Unions," *Labor Research Review* 11 (Spring 1988), Midwest Labor Research, Chicago, Illinois.

21. Phone interviews with shop owners conducted in May 1990 by Elaine Lam, a Chinese bilingual staff member of Asian Immigrant Women Advocates, San Francisco, California.

22. Editorial, "Koret: What Would Keep You?," *San Francisco Chronicle* (May 10, 1990).

23. See Mark Thompson, "Threadbare Justice," *California Lawyer* (May 1990): 30, for conditions in Los Angeles garment industry, and organizing strategies and legal tactics for reforming the industry. In Southern California, Department of Industrial Relations Bureau of Field Enforcement regional manager Roger Miller estimates that one-quarter of all the sewing shops inspectors spot from the street, and many shops are not even registered. The Los Angeles garment industry, which mainly employs immigrant women from Mexico, had 3,510 registered shops as of June 22, 1990, according to the Division of Labor Standards Enforcement. San Francisco County had 444 registered shops; Orange County, 191 shops; Alameda County, 137; and San Diego County, 110.

24. U.S. Department of Commerce International Trade Administration, *Foreign Trade Highlights* , 61.

25. Kwong, *The New Chinatown*, 29–33.

26. Through its work, AIWA learned there are Asian immigrant seamstresses in New York, Boston, Philadelphia, Chicago, Los Angeles, Orange County, Dallas, and Hawaii. See for example, Constance L. Hays, "Immigrants Strain Resources in Chinatown," *New York Times* (May 30, 1990); Sonni Efron's series in the *Los Angeles Times*, "Sweatshops in Suburbia: Old Problem, New Twist" (November 26, 1989): A1, "Mother's Plight Turns a Home into Sweatshop" (November 27, 1989): A1; and "Hot Goods' Law Revived as Anti-Sweatshop Tool" (November 29, 1989): A3; Peter J. Howe, "Laid-off

Garment Workers Celebrate Retraining Benefits Won after Fight," *Boston Globe* (November 2, 1986); "Dallas' Hidden Apparel Workers," *Women's Wear Daily* (March 4, 1988); and Beverly Fujita, "Styles of the Isles," *Spirit of Aloha* (August 1989).

27. U.S. Government Accounting Office, "Sweatshops in the U.S.," August 1988.

28. Interview with Dennis Hayashi, July 23, 1989.

29. Asian Law Caucus, "'Facts about the Garment Industry." See also ILGWU, "Sweatshops Reference" leaflet.

30. Interview with Frank Conte, April 27, 1990.

31. The unusually high rate of hourly wages in this largely piece-rate industry may be accounted for by those working in white-owned shops.

32. Questionnaires were sent to over five hundred women. Thirty seamstresses volunteered their time to make evening phone calls encouraging workers to complete the surveys. A total of 166 women filled out questionnaires.

33. Jan Shaw, "Jessica McClintock Fashions Business World with Romance," *San Francisco Business Times* (August 15, 1988), 10.

34. Interview with Chan Wai Fun, June 25, 1990; translated by Yin Ling Leung of AIWA.

35. Interview with Tam Le, May 29,1990; translated by Mrs. Le's daughter, Loan, and by Thoa Nguyen.

36. "AIWA Attends Congress of Working Women in El Paso, Texas," *AIWA Newsletter* (November 1989).

37. See also Paulo Freire, *Pedagogy of the Oppressed* (New York: Continuum, 1970); Myles Horton and Paulo Freire, *We Make the Road by Walking: Conversations on Education and Social Change* (New York: Bergen & Garvey, 1990). Freire is the *maestro* of popular literacy, and Horton is founder of the Highlander School in Tennessee which trained labor organizers in the 1930s and '40s, civil rights workers in the '50s and '60s, and Appalachian workers today. See also the popular literacy material produced by Center for Ethics and Social Policy, 1442A Walnut St., Berkeley, CA 94709, (415) 846-1674; and by the Debt Crisis Network, c/o Institute for Policy Studies, 1901 Q St., NW, Washington, D.C. 20009.

38. For more information on community organizing methods, contact Center for Third World Organizing, 3861 Martin Luther King Way, Oakland, CA 94609, (510) 654-9601.

39. Interview with Luisa Blue, April 1, 1991.

40. Interview with Peter Olney, June 6, 1989. Olney was ILGWU organizer in Los Angeles for three years, then in the Bay Area for one year. See Olney's article, "The Rising of the Million: Some Strategies for Change," *LA Weekly* (February 24–March 2,1989), 47, for more ideas on the need for union experimentation and initiative to organize immigrant workers. Olney currently works for Service Employees International Union Local 399 in Los Angeles. See also Miriam Ching Louie, "Quan Heads Garment Workers Union in S.F., *Asian Week* (January 5, 1990), based on Quan interviews on September 14, 1989, and December 22, 1989. See also ILGWU Pacific Northwest

District Council, "Proposal: Garment Workers' Service Center," May 28, 1990; and Mark Thompson, ILGWU Southwest District Council newsletter, for more information on the Los Angeles center and associate membership organization. See also Beatriz Nava interview, May 21, 1990. Nava heads the Los Angeles garment workers center.

41. Interview with Young Shin, April 22, 1991.

42. See also Lisa Belkin, "Abuses Rise among Hispanic Garment Workers," *New York Times* (November 28, 1990), for a description of industry conditions in El Paso and the organizing work of La Mujer Obrera.

43. See Wing Lam, "Can Unions Transform Their Members?" Chinese Staff and Workers Association paper, 1990. For a profile of CSWA's work, see Miriam Ching Louie, "New York Chinese Union Thrives on Controversy: Organizing Chinese Kitchen Men, Sewing Women," *Asian Week* (July 6, 1990), based on interviews with Jackson Chin, Wendy Lam, Wing Lam, and Christine Yue on June 4, 1990. For more information about the independent Chinatown, Restaurant Workers Union, Local 318, and the work and perspectives of the Women's Committee, see *CSWA News: The Voice of Chinese American Workers* , and Constance L. Hays, "Waiters Win $760,000 in Union Case," *New York Times* (February 2, 1989).

44. Interview with Gary Delgado, April 11 and May 3, 1991.

45. *Listen Real Loud* is the name of the American Friends Service Committee newsletter reporting on grassroots organizing among women internationally. The phrase also concisely captures the essence of grassroots organizing.

46. Interview with Young Shin, May 3, 1991.

CHAPTER 6

Popular Culture, Imagery, and Stereotypes

Asian American images in the popular media have always been a complex matter. For the most part, the media has depicted Asians in Asia, virtually ignoring Asian Americans. Historically, Asians in films have been seen in mostly negative terms through the eyes of white filmmakers, who reflected the popular "yellow peril" and "white supremacy" sentiments. Recently, audiences have welcomed a variety of high-quality films from Asia and have become accustomed to seeing Asian faces on the big screen. This transition has had only minimal effect at bringing attention to Asian American sensibilities into the popular culture. The Disney animated movie *Mulan* does feature Asian Americans providing the voices, yet the story takes place in medieval China. Is there a motion picture in the theaters where the story revolves around Asians living in the U.S.? Do the television characters Ling Woo (Lucy Liu) on *Ally McBeal* and Sammo Law (Sammo Hung) on *Martial Law* reinforce or counter media stereotypes of Asians and Asian Americans? This chapter examines how Asian Americans have been seen in film, theater, and television. These depictions of Asian Americans in the popular media are significant because how others see Asian Americans has an important impact on how Asian Americans see themselves.

Chapter 6 begins with an edited selection from Gina Marchetti's book, *Romance and the "Yellow Peril."* Marchetti focuses on two films, *The Cheat* (1915) and *Broken Blossoms* (1919), to analyze early depictions of Asians in the United States. In both films, it is evident that the "yellow peril" is the sexual danger posed by contact between Asian males and white women. Marchetti shows how the rape of the white woman serves as a powerful and conscious metaphor for Western national-cultural and personal fears about Asia. The reader is challenged to examine film narratives as more than simple entertainment. Indeed, her thoughtful critique of *The Cheat* and *Broken Blossoms* provides powerful insights into how broader social concerns and ideologies find their way into and throughout popular culture. This theme resonates throughout the chapter.

James S. Moy takes a historical look at the image of Asians in the theater, and his analysis is similar to that of Marchetti. Early representations of Asians were tied to Western colonialism of the East, and the exoticization of the "other." Stereotypes about Asians continued unchallenged until the late 1960s and early 1970s, when Asian American playwrights aggressively attacked Asian stereotypes and their negative consequences on Asian American self-identity. One of the first and most prolific writers of this period was Frank Chin. His plays, *The Chickencoop Chinaman* (1972) and *The Year of the Dragon* (1974) were powerful statements against cultural imperialism, but the plays failed to generate much interest from the popular audience. Similarly, feature films by Asian Americans produced throughout the late 1980s lacked any significant appeal to a mainstream audience. Moy concludes that general audiences can understand Asians and Asian Americans only through stereotypical images.

Essays by writer Jessica Hagedorn, actor Steve Park, and journalist William Wong offer interesting personal perspectives on popular images and stereotypes and their influence. Hagedorn describes her response to watching images of Asian women in contemporary U.S. and foreign-made films. Until recently, Asian women were commonly seen as objects of desire for white men or as suffering victims of war, or both. Depictions of Asian women have changed somewhat in recent years but not significantly, according to Hagedorn. Similarly, Wong critically reviews the 1994 debut of comedian Margaret Cho's television comedy, *All-American Girl*. He acknowledges his hope for the show to be a hit as well as a positive Asian American image on television screens across the nation. Unfortunately, *All-American Girl* was a major disappointment for Wong because the show offered little distinction from any of the bland situation comedies so often seen on television. Park shares his own painful experiences as an actor and the difficulties he's faced while trying to make a living in a career that is particularly unfriendly to Asian American men. Hagedorn, Wong, and Park do not believe that Asian and Asian American characters should be seen *only* as heroes and heroines, but they all recognize that the images of Asians seen in the media are overwhelmingly stereotypical and unbalanced.

The Rape Fantasy: *The Cheat* and *Broken Blossoms*

Gina Marchetti

The narrative pattern most often associated with Hollywood dramas involving the "yellow peril" features the rape or threat of rape of a Caucasian woman by a villainous Asian man.[1] With roots deep within the Euroamerican melodramatic tradition, these fantasies present the white woman as the innocent object of lust and token of the fragility of the West's own sense of moral purity. However, these tales often point to a contradictory suspicion that the masochistic virgin may secretly desire her defilement. Much of the raw violence of these narratives, then, involves not only the eradication of the threat of racial otherness by lynching the Asian rapist but also the brutal punishment of the white woman through both the spectacle of her assault and the humiliation of her rescue.

Two of the most notable silent feature films dealing with interracial rape are Cecil B. DeMille's *The Cheat* (1915) and D. W. Griffith's *Broken Blossoms* (1919). Although *The Cheat* xenophobically calls for the exclusion of people of color from the American bourgeois mainstream, while *Broken Blossoms* seems to ask for a more liberal toleration of some interracial relationships, both narratives use the fantasy of rape and the possibility of lynching to reaffirm the boundaries of a white-defined, patriarchal, Anglo-American culture. By looking at these two early film narratives, the nature of popular fantasies surrounding changes in both the racial composition of America and the place of women

Source: Gina Marchetti, *Romance and the "Yellow Peril": Race, Sex, and Discursive Strategies in Hollywood Fiction* (Berkeley and Los Angeles: University of California Press, 1993). Reprinted by permission.

within the bourgeois patriarchy comes more clearly to the surface. However, before examining this narrative pattern in detail, it may be helpful to look broadly at the melodrama to better understand how these films operate within this specific genre. . . .

THE CHEAT AND THE PORNOGRAPHY OF LYNCHING

In *Anatomy of Criticism*, Northrop Frye observes that a type of modern crime melodrama he labels "the brutal thriller" comes "as close as it is normally possible for art to come to the pure self-righteousness of the lynching mob."[2] Although Cecil B. DeMille's *The Cheat* (1915) is technically not a thriller, it does seem to capture the moral indignation, the melodramatic flourishes, and the invitation for arousal and catharsis necessary to bring it close to the type of fiction Frye describes. A lurid story of a bargain struck by an extravagant socialite with a Japanese merchant for cash in exchange for sex, *The Cheat* climaxes in a scene in which the white woman is branded by the Asian when she refuses to go through with the transaction. After she shoots her attacker, a trial ensues in which the socialite's husband takes the blame for her assailant's wound. Critics have noted that audiences for *The Cheat* would cry out during the famous courtroom scene in support of the mob that nearly lynches the Asian villain. A reviewer for *Moving Picture World*, for example, wrote, "One of the men that sat behind me in the Strand Theatre said, 'I would like to be in that mob.' "[3]

Indeed, the editing, cinematography, and mise-en-scène of the courtroom scene all seem to invite the audience in the theatre to adopt the perspective of the mob at the trial. Unable to control herself after her husband has been falsely convicted of shooting her attacker, Edith Hardy (Fannie Ward) becomes hysterical and rushes up to the judge's bench. She pulls down her dress to reveal the brand on her bare shoulder. A long shot of the packed courtroom stands in for the film audience. In medium close up, Edith pulls back her blonde curls to frame the brand on her pale shoulder. The film, then, cuts between shots of the violent gesticulations of Edith and medium shots of the faces of the jury, her assailant, and the anonymous, sneering faces of white men in attendance. Their looks are directed at both Edith and Tori (Sessue Hayakawa), the man she accuses of her violation, and the camera positions both as objects of scrutiny (and, by implication, moral judgment) for the film viewers.

Ironically, the "lynch mob" in *The Cheat* forms within the "halls of justice," further legitimizing the viewer's shared perspective with the angry mob. When the judge sets aside the guilty verdict, the rioting mob turns into a cheering, appreciative crowd that flanks each side of the courtroom's main aisle as Edith and her husband, Richard (Jack Dean), walk toward the camera as an iris closes in on the couple to conclude the film.

In her essay, "Ethnicity, Class, and Gender in Film: DeMille's *The Cheat*," Sumiko Higashi notes that the courtroom crowd "recalls lynch mobs that murdered blacks."[4] In light of the commercial and critical success (as well as controversy) surrounding Griffith's *The Birth of a Nation*, which was released earlier that same year, public lynchings and moral indignation over interracial sexual relations seem to have been very much a part of the narrative lexicon of the American film in 1915. . . .

Even though the film pulls back from depicting an actual lynching, just as it declines to show Edith as a victim of rape, *The Cheat* still contains all the other elements associated with the public discourse surrounding rapes and lynchings at the time. The film serves, then, as a cinematic retelling of the public display and humiliation of the white victim coupled with the nearly uncontrollable rage of the white mob. Edith's husband serves as stoic patriarch and Tori functions as the rapist, finally exposed publicly, threatened with lynching, and implicitly punished suitably (i.e., legally) by the court. The mob action follows on the sexual arousal accompanying Edith's self-exposure and is, then, expressed through violence toward Tori. Rage against the woman who uses her sexuality for her own gain, outside the boundaries of the patriarchal family, turns against the man of color, who becomes the embodiment of both a sexuality and a social order out of control. . . .

Given that the period from the turn of the century through World War I saw a post-Reconstruction advancement of and subsequent backlash against African Americans as well as the rise of the woman's movement demanding reproductive as well as voting rights, it comes as little surprise that stories about rapes and lynchings would become so popular. Indeed, both acts of violence are linked in the popular imagination as agents for white male control over Caucasian women and men of color. In *Against Our Will: Men, Women, and Rape,* Susan Brownmiller draws a striking parallel between rapes and lynchings:

> Rape is to women as lynching was to blacks: the ultimate physical threat by which all men keep all women in a state of psychological intimidation.
>
> Women have been raped by men, most often by gangs of men, for many of the same reasons that blacks were lynched by gangs of whites: as group punishment for being uppity, for getting out of line, for failing to recognize "one's place," for assuming sexual freedoms, or for behaviour no more provocative than walking down the wrong road at night in the wrong part of town and presenting a convenient, isolated target for group hatred and rage. Castration, the traditional *coup de grace* of a lynching, has its counterpart in the gratuitous acts of defilement that

often accompany a rape, the stick rammed up the vagina, the attempt to annihilate the sexual core.[5]

Just as there seems to be an imaginative coupling of rape and lynching within public discourse, films and other fictions like *The Cheat* appear to serve the same double function as warnings to women that their independence leads to their humiliation and to blacks and other people of color that their desire to assimilate into the American mainstream will never be tolerated. Beyond these warnings, however. the discourse on rapes and lynchings in the American popular media also brings white women and men of color together as transgressors against the domination of white men. Potentially, then, these fantasies hide a resistant core underneath their brutal surfaces. If Tori and Edith somehow recognized their similar victimizations at the trial, then the moral universe of *The Cheat* would collapse. The tease of this possibility as well as its violent suppression fuel the passions explored within the film.

However, focusing exclusively on *The Cheat's* conclusion does little to explain other aspects of the film fantasy. The specifics of its depiction of Japanese Americans, the Long Island social set, the world of Wall Street speculators, and the early-twentieth-century bourgeois home also exist as somehow related to the raw image of sexual humiliation and racist rage that ends the film. Thus, it becomes necessary to unravel how the threat of rape and the possibility of a lynching relate ideologically to these other aspects of the fantasy in order to understand the roots of any ambivalence felt during the film's denouement.

THE JAPANESE VILLAIN

As Sumiko Higashi has aptly pointed out in her analysis of ethnicity in *The Cheat,* the depiction of the assailant as Japanese was part of the yellow peril and anti-immigration rhetoric prevalent on the eve of World War I.[6] However, discourses on the issues of immigration, American imperialism, race,

and ethnicity promulgated by the mass media, government, and other purveyors of ideology were highly contradictory. Such rhetoric as the "white man's burden," "manifest destiny," and the "yellow peril" coexisted with the ideals of the "melting pot," "liberty and justice for all," and the concept of the American Dream. Because of America's peculiar relationship with Japan and the military strength of Japan during the latter part of the nineteenth century and the early twentieth century, fantasies involving that nation and its people proved to be particularly complicated. For example, although *The Cheat's* villain was originally calculated to represent the height of evil as a *Japanese* threat to American identity, the villain's ethnicity was easily switched because of pressure from the Japanese government. Thus, when America entered World War I as an ally of Japan, the film's anti-Japanese intertitles were changed for the 1918 release print to make the villain Burmese.

This ambivalence predates World War I, however. America has had a particularly strong and peculiarly contradictory relationship with Japan and the Japanese since Commodore Perry forcibly opened up the country to trade with the United States in 1853. Japan has been seen as both a country of tremendous power, culture, and wealth with coveted merchandise ready to be commercially exploited and as a weak nation peopled by nonwhite, pagan, uncivilized inferiors also ripe for exploitation by expanding American capitalism. As the Meiji government of the late nineteenth and early twentieth century rapidly modernized the country, Japan's traditional policy of isolation and ban on emigration were lifted. Particularly after the institution of the anti-Chinese Exclusion Act of 1882, Japanese laborers immigrated to Hawaii and the West Coast of the United States in record numbers to take up the slack. Unlike the comparatively weak Chinese government, a strong Japanese position internationally enabled the country to protect its citizens abroad to a certain degree. Moreover, in order to set its citizens apart from the maligned Chinese, Japan scrutinized all potential émigrés carefully and encouraged the emigration of women to prevent the social problems associated with Chinatown's "bachelor society," for example, prostitution, gambling, opium smoking, and general vice.

Few of these measures, however, eased anti-Japanese sentiments. Particularly after Japan's stunning defeat of Russia in 1905, American observers began to worry about the expansionist tendencies of an Asian country that had not been colonized by the West yet had still managed to defeat a major European power in battle. Seeing Japan as a threat to its interests in the Philippines and Hawaii, the American government had to respond cautiously both to domestic calls for the exclusion of the Japanese from the United States and Japan's insistence on equity made from an uniquely powerful position among the nations of Asia. In 1908, President Theodore Roosevelt worked out the "Gentlemen's Agreement" with Japan that restricted the immigration of laborers to the United States. However, "picture brides," other relatives of Japanese workers already in the United States, merchants, scholars, and students were still allowed to enter, and the Japanese were not excluded altogether until 1924.[7]

This ambivalence toward Japan and the Japanese finds its way into the depiction of Hishuru Tori. Both brutal and cultivated, wealthy and base, cultured and barbaric, Tori embodies the contradictory qualities Americans associated with Japan. Like Japan itself, Tori is powerful, threatening, wealthy, and enviable; however, his racial difference also codes him as pagan, morally suspect, and inferior. Moreover, just as Japanese attempts to assimilate Western technology and material culture to strengthen itself economically and militarily during the Meiji era posed a threat to American domination of Asia, Tori's attempts to adapt to and adopt elements of Western society also pose a threat to America's conception of itself. Like any new Asian immigrant seeking to assimilate into the mainstream, Tori threatens America's definition of itself as white, Anglo-Saxon, and Protestant.

Beyond this, Tori poses a further danger to America's national identity by being able to transcend racial boundaries and move fairly easily between Japanese and American cultures, obtaining possessions and gaining status from both worlds. In the title sequence. Tori is introduced in Japanese dress with Asian-style brass brazier, poker, and ivory statuette. Key lights set off his facial features as well as these tokens of his ethnicity against the black background.[8] The chiaroscuro lighting adds to Tori's exoticism, mystery, and the implicit danger conjured up by the peculiar satisfaction he seems to get from branding his possessions.[9]

However, if Tori is associated with darkness, shadows, and the threatening exoticism of Japan in the title sequence, his introduction within the narrative itself shows him in quite a different light (literally). In the flat, high key lighting of daytime, Tori drives up to the Hardy residence in a sporty roadster. Shown in a medium long shot from a high angle, Tori looks like any other wealthy, insouciant young man in a Hollywood film of the time. Because of the distance of the camera, his racial otherness is barely noticeable. Jauntily, he gets out of the car and walks up to the house. Wearing a long duster, cap, casual tweed suit, and bow tie, his relaxed appearance belies any threat he might pose to the American bourgeois domestic sphere he enters. His body language (the self-assured way he perches on the drawing-room desk, the implied intimacy of his picking up Edith's purse and parasol) points to his ability to insinuate himself into this world with apparent ease.

An earlier title indicated that Tori was one of the darlings of the Long Island society set, and the implication is that he gained entry into this world not only from his wealth but also from this ability to "blend in" and create a certain intimacy between himself and Edith, who serves as his liaison with this otherwise racially "exclusive" society. This Americanized Tori innocently attends Edith by holding her coat and accessories, patting her hand, agreeing to help further her status in her set by hosting a charity ball, and unthinkingly grabbing her when she stumbles. Implicitly unable to find a place within the more rigidly racist society of the men on Long Island, Tori finds his niche among the women. However, although his feminization seems to confirm his symbolic castration, it also holds within it the potential threat of an ability to transgress gender along with racial barriers. Tori promises a different type of masculinity (soft, effeminate yielding, "Asian") that may displace the banal paternalism represented by Edith's husband.

When contained within his exclusively Japanese domain, Tori poses no threat, however. In the title sequence, he exists as a self-contained image of otherness outside the narrative, Similarly, when Tori appears as Edith's completely assimilated companion, he functions as what Eugene Franklin Wong has termed the Asian eunuch, an asexual, subservient foil for the white protagonists.[10] Accepted as escort, confidant, and pet in white society, Tori poses no threat to its racial exclusivity because he appears to be totally asexual. Edith's ability to take his apparently innocent loyalty to her for granted is validated by a tradition in American popular culture of emasculated, faithful Asian servants and companions.

Separation of the two spheres, Japan and the West, seems to be the ideological key. When Tori begins to embody both, to merge both into a figure that can no longer be excluded as completely alien or assimilated as impotent and harmless, he becomes a provocative villain. At the charity event held at his mansion, Tori, elegantly dressed in tuxedo, white tie, and patterned vest, moves between two worlds—the American social set of society matrons and stuffy stockbrokers all in Western attire enjoying themselves in the large ballroom and his own private study filled with a large statue of Buddha, incense, rich silks, ivory figurines, and a potted tree with falling petals resembling Japanese cherry blossoms.

When Edith steps into his parlor, she enters a world that offers the forbidden possibility of a meeting of Japan and America within the sexual realm. For a moment, the fantasy seems to be more enticing than dangerous. When Edith caresses a piece of Japanese cloth and Tori gives it to her as a gift, her willingness to be seduced by Tori's wealth and sensuality seems evident. Although Edith backs away as Tori describes the branding of his possessions, she does not leave. Perhaps this can be read as an interest in Tori's brooding, implicitly sadistic sexuality outweighing her fears.

The moment is interrupted when a stockbroker, who had talked her into gambling away Red Cross charity funds on the stock market, comes in to tell her that she has lost the stolen money. The broker leaves, Edith faints, and Tori takes advantage of the opportunity to kiss the unconscious Edith. Much has been made of rape fantasies, their appeal to women, and the sadistic sexuality of silent screen stars like Rudolph Valentino, Erich von Stroheim, and Sessue Hayakawa.[11] The fantasy has been discussed as the internalization of a patriarchal ideology that insists on female passivity and submission to male domination, as an expression of some deep-rooted masochistic desire, and as a way in which society toys with forbidden sexuality to make it acceptable as "punishment" rather than as "pleasure." Whatever the psychological roots of the rape fantasy's appeal to male and female viewers may be, it clearly both disturbs and fascinates, and it plays a key role in Hollywood's depiction of sexuality.

In this case, *The Cheat* links the crossing of racial boundaries with the rape fantasy. It plays on all the ambivalence associated with that fantasy. On the one hand, Edith seems drawn to all those things repressed in her white, American, bourgeois home, for example, open sexuality, the sensual pleasures of clothing, and other objects of consumption. In light of the rapidly changing sexual mores and life-styles of the World War I era, a certain amount of guilt and desire would likely be a part of any erotic fantasy involving a character like Tori. Tori represents indulgence of the senses, of the body, free from the Protestant denial of sexual desire. However, a willing affair with Tori would all at once completely subvert those strictures, ripping apart marriage, the bourgeois family, the Protestant ethic, as well as the racial status quo.

Although a fantasy that toys with this extreme would likely be inviting to many in the audience (women, the working classes, people of color) for a number of reasons, the pull to contain it wins out ideologically. Thus, a desired indulgence may come with the kiss, but it is still a *stolen* kiss, taken not given. As in many Hollywood narratives, forbidden desires find their fulfillment against the will of the protagonist. In this case, Edith can remain a part of the white, bourgeois family because this kiss can be read as a rape rather than the culmination of a love affair.

Moreover, while the kiss for women can be looked at as a fulfillment of secret, forbidden desires for the pleasures and freedoms promised by a love affair with a man of another race, it also marks the beginning of Edith's punishment and the turning point that moves away from any ambivalence about Tori's villainous character that may have been felt earlier. Here, Tori emerges as the archetypal "yellow peril" ravisher of white women. The object of desire, he too becomes the instrument of punishment for that forbidden desire. For male viewers, he can freely indulge sadistic desires "guiltlessly," "naturally," since he is Japanese and beyond Christian notions of morality. He can punish the wayward Edith without violating any code of chivalry, leaving her husband (and, by implication, the white men in the audience) pure. Thus, Tori's ethnicity becomes a necessary part of his ability to fulfill a number of erotic desires for both male and female spectators. His racial otherness allows him to function as a symbol of erotic indulgence and as an instrument of punishment for women's sexual self-assertion. Thus, white men can be free of the dark, brutal side of their own sexuality while maintaining the gender status quo through the threat of rape linked to the supposedly perverse sexuality of the Asian male.

However, the fantasies surrounding the Japanese villain Tori may be even more complicated than this. If Tori's sadistic, punitive masculinity functions to maintain patriarchal strictures legitimately tied to the white male authority of Edith's husband, then the subservient, eunuch-like, impotent aspect of Asian masculinity also associated with the character brings him closer to Edith's position on the social hierarchy. As in many rape fantasies, this offers a peculiar invitation to women to identify with the attacker, to see themselves as pitted against the same authority that he opposes in trying to possess her.

Frightened by the apparition of her husband silhouetted on the sliding paper panel (shoji) doorway as she regains consciousness in Tori's arms and hears the confirmation of her monetary loss, Edith allows herself to be persuaded to agree to Tori's bargain. Although it is never explicitly spelled out, the assumption is that Edith will give herself to Tori sexually in exchange for ten thousand dollars. Visually on the same side of the shoji, Edith and Tori, duplicitous, self-serving, and self-indulgent, are also on the same side morally. Neither can fulfill his or her desires within the bounds of the white bourgeois patriarchy represented by the husband on the other side of the screen.

The visual and moral equivalence between Tori and Edith becomes absolutely clear during the branding and its aftermath. Not unlike the trial scene, this part of the narrative plays with the mercurial nature of the positions of victim and vanquisher in the rape scenario. Again, Tori's costume, which combines Asia and the West with a white tie and tuxedo shirt covered by a Japanese kimono, indicates the possible transgression he represents, that is, the sensual meeting of Japan and America, the erasure of racial borders through eroticism. Edith is dressed in a black gown covered by a white wrap. The contrast not only indicates her divided, duplicitous nature but also points to the racial contrasts at issue—the dark and the light.

When Edith arrives at Tori's home, she brings the $10,000 she has finally gotten from her newly wealthy husband. Although her offer to pay Tori with money instead of herself is refused, the existence of the check places her on an even footing with him. If Tori was below Edith socially before their bargain was struck and above her financially afterward, they, at this point, have attained a certain financial, moral, and social equality.

The balance struck, the film teeters between masochistic and sadistic positions for both Tori and Edith. When Edith masochistically responds to Tori's advances with a threat to kill herself, Tori offers her a pistol from his desk. However, whether the offer is a sadistic jaunt or a masochistic invitation for her to shoot him remains unclear. They struggle. Tori grabs Edith, and Edith strikes at his face and beats him with an iron poker. Tori pulls back Edith's hair, revealing her white shoulder, takes the hot poker from the brazier, and, with the camera fixed on his face, drives the poker down into her flesh (offscreen) and withdraws it. In a wider shot, Tori flings Edith to the tatami floor; the camera pulls back to a high angle shot of her clutching her burned shoulder. She picks up the gun and shoots Tori (offscreen). In a shot paralleling Edith's violation and fall to the tatami, Tori clutches his shoulder and falls to the floor. With this play of anger, violation, and revenge, both parties, technically at least within the narrative economy, seem vindicated. Both have been "cheated" and both have "cheated." Each has exacted revenge on the other. In fact, both find themselves in this position because of the overpowering control of the white, bourgeois, patriarchal status quo, which forbids any resolution of either Tori's desire for Edith or Edith's desire for independence, wealth, and sensualism through any means other than violence. Indeed, Sumiko Higashi views the parallel shots as a "visual example of how both characters share inferior status under white male hegemony.[12] . . .

By the time Edith makes her escape and her husband appears on the scene to save his wife (who has already avenged and "saved" herself), Tori has become a completely emasculated figure. Ironically, no potent Asian rapist exists for Edith's husband to vanquish. Instead, Tori appears as a fallen shadow on the shoji screen; a trickle of blood seeping through the paper signals his wound. When Edith's enraged husband bursts through the screen door, this classic gesture of the chivalrous white patriarch coming to "save" the threatened white woman from the "fate worse than death" seems empty.

Thus, although Edith is brought back into the white bourgeois patriarchy on the arm of her husband during her final march down the courtroom aisle, the foundations of male domination have already been shaken by her actions and the sadomasochistic play of the fantasy. Her husband's stoicism has been totally ineffectual. Even though Tori and her husband have both tried to punish and contain her, Edith has managed to defy both, so that the success of her reabsorption into the bourgeois family must remain at least somewhat problematic.

Wounded, exposed, and nearly lynched at *The Cheat's* conclusion, Tori returns to his place as the emasculated Asian male. The threat he has posed to the white status quo has been obviated. However, interestingly, despite the male figures of judge, jury, enraged mob, and husband, it is the white woman, Edith, who finally acts as the instrument of his castration. Complications, then, arise. Edith may be punished for her independent decision to become involved with Tori, but she is vindicated for her equally independent actions of shooting Tori and publicly assuming responsibility for her revenge. The racist aspect of *The Cheat*, coupled with a call for female self-sufficiency, seems linked to certain elements in the suffrage movement, which pointed to the potential threat of the political power of African Americans and new immigrants from southern and eastern Europe as a reason to grant white, Protestant, Anglo-Saxon women the vote. Similarly, women viewers may look at this triumph over the Japanese villain as an apology for emancipation, since Edith's husband has been so completely ineffectual in protecting his wife, or as an acceptable expression of a desire to dominate men, to indulge in a sadistic fantasy usually denied them. From a totally different perspective, men in the audience might look at both contact between the races and female emancipation as an explosive combination that the text rightly condemns. Whether Edith's final outburst in court, then, can be looked at as an ambivalent nod toward the necessity of female independence or as a racist call for increased vigilance because of threats to the purity of the white woman seems moot.

Looked at either way, however, Edith functions as the gateway into American society that excludes those who cannot fit in because of their race or ethnicity. *The Cheat* gives the white woman this charge, then, to include and exclude the foreign, the alien, and the unacceptable through her sexuality. Thus, the text can simultaneously acknowledge, exploit, and condemn women's increased visibility in the public sphere, as well as their growing demands for sexual self-expression, by placing Edith in the shadow of the Asian villain, who both threatens and embodies all those secret desires that put the white patriarchy on unsteady ground. . . .

BROKEN BLOSSOMS: SEXUAL PERVERSITY AND SPIRITUAL SALVATION

D. W. Griffith's *Broken Blossoms* (1919) has sparked more critical interest than any other film in this study. Based on Thomas Burke's story, "The Chink and the Child," from his collection *Limehouse Nights* on the slum areas of London, *Broken Blossoms* tells a lurid tale of the love of a Chinese, opium-smoking merchant for the abused illegitimate daughter of a brutal boxer.

Given the links between American and British relations with China, the fact that an English story about the Limehouse slums should strike a responsive cord with Griffith and the 1919 film audience should come as no surprise. Since the time of Marco Polo, European trade with China has had an impact on the cultures of both the West and Asia. Tea, silk, and porcelain, in fact, put Britain so in debt to China that England encouraged illegal commerce in its opium from India to redress the trade imbalance. When the trade began to reach epidemic proportions, the Chinese imperial government launched a campaign to suppress it militarily, leading to the Opium War of 1840–1842 and the Treaty of Nanjing that forced China to concede lucrative ports and special privileges to the West. Also involved in the opium trade, American merchants benefited greatly from this blow to Chinese sovereignty. The commercial opening of China further led to increased contact more generally, and missionaries from the United States as well as Great Britain poured into China along with merchants, sailors, and a legion of bureaucrats. Ironically, the missionaries went to China to save it from the "decadence" of its pagan ways, including, of course, the opium use that the West had helped to promote.

In light of the pressure of these colonialist incursions and the internal strife occasioned by the decay of the Manchu-ruled Qing Dynasty, the impoverishment of China seemed certain, and many Chinese, particularly from the southern coastal areas, went to Britain, Australia, and America to seek their fortunes. Many went to California in search of gold and stayed on as laborers to work on the American railroads. However, owing in part to the political weakness of China internationally and racist elements within the labor movement of the latter part of the nineteenth century, the U.S. government instituted a series of exclusionary laws to keep out the Chinese. Those who did manage to stay or enter illegally tended to live isolated lives in the Chinatowns of major metropolitan areas. In Great Britain, an inhospitable climate led to similar conditions, so that the Limehouse of Burke's story would certainly strike a responsive cord with anyone familiar with Chinatown in San Francisco, New York, or in the pulp fiction of the time.[13]

Unlike the short story, however, which simply tries to sketch slum life for the prurient imaginations of outsiders, *Broken Blossoms* attempts to make a moral lesson and elevate the characters and situations of the original story into the realm of what critics have called "poetry" or "art."[14] In addition to the early praise it received as an "art film," *Broken Blossoms* has been studied seriously by film scholars interested in Griffith as an auteur,[15] Lillian Gish as a performer,[16] the production and commercial exploitation of the film as "high art,"[17] its contribution to the history of cinematography with the use of the soft focus Sartov lens,[18] the relationship of the film to melodrama,[19] the importance of the film to the history of Asian representations in the cinema,[20] as well as the film's depiction of gender relations.[21]

Perhaps the most telling studies of the film, however, have dealt with it as a tale of sexual perversity or as an example of Griffith's own well-documented penchant for young girls as objects of erotic desire.[22] Indeed, in many ways, the film can be looked at as a catalog of what society considers as sexual crimes, excesses, or perversions, including rape, incest, sadism, masochism, pedophilia, necrophilia, fetishism, voyeurism, and prostitution as well as miscegenation. In fact, given this list of sexual deviations, interracial sexuality. which remains on the level of controlled lust and innocent affection, may be the most innocuous part of the fantasy.

Given the very thinly disguised sexual deviations depicted in the film, approaching *Broken Blossoms* as a pornographic text seems appropriate. Like pornography, *Broken Blossoms* uses spectacle to arouse the sexual interest of the spectator, while narrative structure permits, controls, and legitimizes this arousal by symbolically punishing the principals (and through them the viewer who identifies with them) for their erotic excesses. However, spectacle wins out, and the evocation of an atmosphere, an image, a feeling that stimulates the erotic involvement of the male viewer takes precedence over the moral imperatives of the plot.

By looking at the erotic fantasies depicted in *Broken Blossoms* in their rawest form, the text's ambivalent treatment of the relationship between sexuality and race may also be exposed. The film is a contradictory mix of high-minded moralizing and lasciviousness, of racial stereotypes and pleas for tolerance, of aestheticism and exploitative violence.

RAPE AND LYNCHING: *THE CHEAT* AND *BROKEN BLOSSOMS*

In many ways, *Broken Blossoms* is the obverse of *The Cheat* and a part of Griffith's post–*The Birth of a Nation* response to charges of racism. While DeMille's *The Cheat*, like *The Birth of a Nation*, argues for a racist exclusionism upheld by violence, *Broken Blossoms*, like Griffith's epic *Intolerance* (1916), attempts to make a case for racial tolerance and respect for foreign cultures. While *The Cheat* sees the intrusion of Asia into American culture as a threat to the white, bourgeois, patriarchal family, *Broken Blossoms* sees the Western patriarchy as a site of violence, decay, and exploitation. Rather than lionizing capitalism and consumerism as the source of new vitality for the bourgeois home, *Broken Blossoms* depicts the poverty and squalor of the proletariat and subproletariat as a hopeless mire that the traditional, bourgeois, domestic virtues can do little to remedy. Ostensibly, the film seems to present the West as brutal, violent, racist, and corrupt and criticizes it for its base treatment of women and outsiders. It praises Asia for its elevated sense of morality and white women for their virtue and purity.

However, underneath this plea for racial harmony and compassion for women can be found a rape-lynching fantasy remarkably similar to . . . the narratives of both *The Cheat* and *The Birth of a Nation*. Like *The Cheat*, *Broken Blossoms* deals with a relationship triangle. Like Tori, Cheng Huan (Richard Barthelmess) referred to in the credits as the "Yellow Man" and called "Chinkie" in the titles is a merchant, associated with the forbidden sensuality and decadence of Asia. Battling Burrows (Donald Crisp), like Richard Hardy, represents the Western patriarch who is losing control of the woman in his charge. Lucy (Lillian Gish), like Edith Hardy, acts as a token of property, power, and moral legitimacy that circulates between them. Like Edith, she seeks solace from the Asian merchant because of inadequacies in her own household. Edith, however, escapes from boredom and a relatively minor shortage of petty cash, whereas Lucy tries to escape from poverty, regular beatings, and implicit sexual abuse. Just as Tori and Richard Hardy struggle to possess Edith sexually, Cheng Huan and Battling Burrows vie for Lucy.

Broken Blossoms begins with the idealistic Cheng Huan departing China to bring the message of Buddhist tolerance and passivity to the West. Yet after unsuccessfully trying to stop a fight between some American sailors while still in China, Cheng Huan seems doomed to failure from the outset. The film then cuts years later to the Limehouse district of London, where Cheng Huan has become a merchant and opium smoker. He becomes enamored of Lucy there, as she pitifully tries to stretch her meager allowance while shopping in Chinatown. When her father nearly beats her to death, she escapes to Chinatown and collapses in front of Cheng Huan's shop. He takes her in and treats her like a goddess. At one point, overtaken by lust, Cheng Huan advances on the innocent Lucy but pulls back before violating her purity. When Burrows learns of his daughter's whereabouts, he becomes enraged, takes her away from Cheng Huan's shop, and beats her to death back at his own hovel. Cheng Huan exacts revenge by shooting Burrows. He carries Lucy's body back to Chinatown and commits suicide next to her corpse.

As the basic elements of *Broken Blossom's* plot indicate, hidden complications of *The Cheat's* rape fantasy, buried behind a facade that denies the power of the association between the white Edith and the Asian Tori as victims of white, patriarchal power, surface in the Griffith film. Kindred spirits, Lucy and Cheng Huan, like Tori and Edith, share a bond of aestheticism and sensual delight in objects of beauty. Like Tori, Cheng Huan embodies the "feminine" qualities linked in the Western imagination with a passive, carnal, occult, and duplicitous Asia. Cheng Huan is feminized in the film not only by his close association with the world of women but also by his elaborate, exotic dress, his languid posture and gestures, and the use of soft focus and diffuse lighting to render his features less angular, more "womanly." However, while this bond is severed by the eruption of Tori's very masculine libido in *The Cheat,* the relationship between Lucy and Cheng Huan remains (as an intertitle states) a "pure and holy thing" as Cheng Huan draws back before consummating his love for Lucy.

Nevertheless, just as Tori's branding of Edith functions as a rape, Cheng Huan's ominous

advance on Lucy and last minute sublimation of his desire, indicated by his kissing the hem of her sleeve rather than her lips, also symbolically marks his possession of the white woman. Battling Burrows reacts to the theft of Lucy as a rape. A title reads: "Battling discovers parental rights— A Chink after his kid! He'll learn him!" The enraged father, then, summons the aid of two of his cronies to form a "lynch mob" to avenge this wrong and retrieve Lucy. An ironic title encourages the viewer to distance himself or herself from Burrows's racist rage: "Above all, Battling hates those not born in the same great country as himself." Thus, the authorial voice of the intertitles promotes a reading that sees Burrows as a racist brute rather than as a brutal but still rightly possessive father. However, in light of Hollywood's consistent support of the rights and virtues of the patriarchy, this vilification of the parental role, no matter how excessively violent its manifestation, must conjure up a certain ambivalence for many in the audience. . . .

If Cheng Huan's advances on Lucy approach rape, then Burrows's abuse of his daughter also approximates rape. Just as Burrows calls together his cronies to form a lynch mob to attack Cheng Huan and retrieve Lucy, Cheng Huan also is cast in the role of avenger of the white woman when he tries to rescue Lucy from her father. As Burrows tears down the closet door to get at Lucy, Cheng Huan collects himself, gets a pistol, and goes to Lucy's aid. Crosscutting between Cheng Huan in the streets of Limehouse, Lucy pitifully running in circles in the closet and Burrows with his ax, the montage pattern established at this point brings *Broken Blossoms* close to the parallel editing associated with Griffith's "last minute rescues" in other films. However, in this case, given that Lucy has been doubly violated and that neither Cheng Huan nor Burrows can function as the avenging patriarch who can save the purity of white womanhood for the perpetuation of the Anglo-Saxon, Protestant, ruling elect, the "rescue" seems pointless. Indeed, Lucy dies before Cheng Huan can arrive.

Although Cheng Huan does manage to avenge Lucy's death by shooting Burrows, this inverted "lynching" of the white father by the Asian male loses much of its force as Cheng Huan returns to his emasculated, passive, masochistic position when he commits suicide on the floor next to Lucy's corpse. This scene, in fact, is crosscut with Burrows's buddies at the police station enlisting the help of the authorities to avenge Burrows's death. Ironically, the official authorities finally appear in the film after all the violent action has taken place. As in many rape-lynching fantasies, the legitimate agents of the government are shown to be ineffectual in keeping the racial and sexual order intact. In this case, Cheng Huan punishes himself symbolically for his transgression through suicide, usurping the role of the state and essentially "lynching" himself.

Like *The Cheat,* then, *Broken Blossoms* maintains a fundamental separation between Asia and the West played out dramatically and violently through a doomed romance in which the effeminate Asian man finds a "perverse" potency in his desire for an unobtainable Caucasian woman. Just as Tori's entrance into American high society marks a transgression of the barriers separating the races, Cheng Huan's emigration from an idyllic China of temple bells, Buddhist statues, and innocent maidens dooms him to the "hell" of Limehouse. As in *The Cheat,* it is the mixture of cultures that indicates a disturbance in the social order. Just as the American sailors wreak havoc in China in the film's opening scenes, Cheng Huan reemerges in England as a grotesque, as alien to British society as the sailors were out of place in the quaint and idealized China of the film. The intrusion of one culture into the other's domain marks the narrative disequilibrium.

In *Broken Blossoms,* the "perversity" of Limehouse is indicated by the opium den that Cheng Huan frequents "where the Orient squats at the portals of the West," as a title indicates. Interracial couples smoke opium together; drugged Caucasian women are shown in languid, sexually suggestive poses. Opium indicates the intrusion of Asia into the West as an unwelcome passivity, sensuality, mystery, and languor.

Although there does seem to be a clear line drawn between the sympathetic Cheng Huan and the villainous Burrows, it cannot be denied that both are creatures of Limehouse. As Burrows flirts and drinks with the "loose" women who also frequent the opium den and as his daughter Lucy is mesmerized by the material pleasures of Chinatown, it becomes quite clear that part of what makes Limehouse and its inhabitants disturbing and peculiar to the middle-class outsider is the erasure of social boundaries between the races. The film's ostensible call for racial tolerance becomes clouded by its insistence that any meeting of Asia and the West must somehow be either violent or "perverse." Thus, it can be argued that *Broken Blossoms*'s bleak view of Limehouse goes beyond a bourgeois suspicion of the working classes whose poverty must somehow be linked ideologically to moral inadequacy rather than to economic exploitation by the ruling order. Limehouse is not only a threat because it is a slum but also because it creates an environment in which the unprotected white virgin can be possessed by the Asian other. Burrows's dissipation and Lucy's inability to escape her father spring from this Limehouse ambience in which troubled families, prostitution, brutality, shiftlessness, and opium all become part of a "perverted," culturally and racially mixed slum.

Thus, while *Broken Blossoms* seems to praise Asian sensitivity and passivity and condemn Western callousness and violence, a closer look at the rape-lynching fantasy reveals a deeper, less liberal perspective. Stripped to its barest elements, *Broken Blossoms* still features the white virgin exposed and humiliated by contact with a man of another race, who loses his life for daring to presume he could possess her. While seeming to condemn the hypocritical white patriarch Burrows for his misplaced desire to avenge the "wrong" done his daughter through her contact with Cheng Huan, the text also allows that "wrong" to be symbolically avenged by Cheng Huan's suicide and tacit acceptance of his own culpability in loving a woman forbidden to him. . . .

Made during the final days of World War I (with references to war casualties and munitions workers), *Broken Blossoms* seems to be part of the rhetoric of universalism, pacificism, and tolerance that formed part of the Versailles Treaty and League of Nations political discourses then current.[23] Given the deep-rooted hatred of the Chinese prevalent in the American popular media since the mid-nineteenth century, the fact that Cheng Huan could emerge as a sympathetic character in *Broken Blossoms* likely would be linked to this broader public interest in burying the hatchet and accepting former enemies as brothers. Thus, Cheng Huan could really be marked as an "outsider" in any respect and function in the same way in the text as the romantic, troubled aesthete saved by the sanctity of the pure, white virgin. The specifics of Cheng Huan's Chinese ethnicity and racial difference simply add a veneer of exoticism to *Broken Blossoms,* encouraging a familiar fantasy of Asia as feminine, passive, carnal, and perverse.

As in many subsequent texts featuring an interracial romance between Asians and Anglo-Americans, the "whiteness" and pure innocence of the Caucasian woman elevates and enables the "base" qualities of the Asian other. Lucy, in *Broken Blossoms,* becomes the token of Cheng Huan's moral salvation through the beauty of romance. Thus, despite its critique of Western brutality and masculine cruelty, the film remains rooted in the very Western ideology of romance where spiritual salvation rests on the possession of the white woman even if that inevitably means total destruction for the man of color who loves her. The West, then, again "saves" the inferior, dependent, lost Asian male by annihilating him.

NOTES

1. For further discussion of race and the rape fantasy in Hollywood, see Ella Shohat, "Gender and Culture of Empire: Toward a Feminist Ethnography of the Cinema," *Quarterly Review of Film Studies* 13, nos. 1–3 (May 1991): 45–84.

2. Northrop Frye, *Anatomy of Criticism: Four Essays* (Princeton: Princeton University Press, 1957): 47.

3. Quoted in Marshall Deutelbaum, "The Cheat," in *The Rivals of D. W. Griffith: Alternate Auteurs 1913–1918,* ed. Richard Koszarski (Minneapolis: Walker Art Center, 1976): 44. From *Moving Picture World,* 25 Dec. 1915, 2384.

4. Sumiko Higashi, "Ethnicity, Class, and Gender in Film: DeMille's *The Cheat,*" in *Unspeakable Images: Ethnicity and the American Cinema,* ed. Lester D. Friedman (Urbana: University of Illinois Press, 1991): 130.

5. Susan Brownmiller, *Against Our Will: Men, Women, and Rape* (New York: Bantam Books, 1975): 281. Although Brownmiller attempts to be evenhanded as in the passage quoted here, she has also been criticized by black feminists for her insensitivity to racial issues. For example, see Angela Y. Davis, *Women, Race, and Class* (New York: Vintage, 1981).

6. Higashi, "Ethnicity, Class, and Gender in Film," 130.

7. For more information, see Kevin Brownlow, *Behind the Mask of Innocence* (New York: Alfred A. Knopf, 1990); Ronald Takaki, *Strangers from a Different Shore: A History of Asian Americans* (New York: Penguin, 1989); Eugene Franklin Wong, *On Visual Media Racism: Asians in the American Motion Pictures* (New York: Arno Press, 1978).

8. The so-called Rembrandt or Lasky lighting in the film creates a chiaroscuro effect and has been discussed in detail by film historians. For example, see David Bordwell, Janet Staiger, and Kristin Thompson, *The Classical Hollywood Cinema: Film Style and Mode of Production to 1960* (New York: Columbia University Press, 1985): 225.

9. As Higashi points out in her essay, the temple gate of Tori's brand has the same sound, "torii," as the character's name.

10. See Wong, *On Visual Media Racism.*

11. A great deal has been written on the appeal of rape fantasies for women. For an overview, see Brownmiller, *Against Our Will.*

12. Higashi, "Ethnicity, Class, and Gender in Film," 131.

13. For information on United States, British, and Chinese relations see James C. Thomson, Jr., Peter W. Stanley, and John Curtis Perry, *Sentimental Imperialists: The American Experience in East Asia* (New York: Harper Colophon Books, 1981).

14. See contemporary reviews of the film anthologized in George C. Pratt, *Spellbound in Darkness: A History of the Silent Film* (Greenwich, Conn: New York Graphic Arts Society, 1973): 250–251; and the critics cited in Lewis Jacobs, *The Rise of the American Film: A Critical History* (New York: Teachers College Press, Columbia University, 1968): 389–390.

15. See Harry M. Geduld, *Focus on D. W. Griffith* (Englewood Cliffs, N.J.: Prentice-Hall, Inc., 1971).

16. Charles Affron, *Star Acting: Gish, Garbo, Davis* (New York: E. P. Dutton, 1977): 12–36.

17. See Vance Kepley, Jr., "Griffith's *Broken Blossoms* and the Problem of Historical Specificity," *Quarterly Review*

of Film Studies 3, no. 1 (Winter 1978): 37–47; Dudley Andrew, "*Broken Blossoms*: The Art and Eros of a Perverse Text," *Quarterly Review of Film Studies* 6, no. 1 (Winter 1981): 81–90.

18. For example, see Bordwell, Staiger, and Thompson, *The Classical Hollywood Cinema*, 287.

19. Robert Lang, *American Film Melodrama: Griffith, Vidor, Minnelli* (Princeton: Princeton University Press, 1989); Nick Browne, "Griffith's Family Discourse: Griffith and Freud," in *Home Is Where the Heart Is: Studies in Melodrama and the Woman's Film*, ed. Christine Gledhill (London: British Film Institute, 1987): 223–234.

20. Brownlow, *Behind the Mask of Innocence*; Dorothy B. Jones, *The Portrayal of China and India on the American Screen, 1896–1955*; Wong, *On Visual Media Racism*. In "Chinky: The Uneasy Other of *Broken Blossoms*" (unpublished paper presented at the 1991 Society for Cinema Studies Conference at the University of Southern California), Phoebe Chao discusses the film's depiction of race in relation to the original Burke short story. For a discussion of the film's depiction of race in relation to the work of photographer Arnold Genthe, see John Kuo Wei Tchen, "Modernizing White Patriarchy: Re-viewing D. W. Griffith's *Broken Blossoms*," in *Moving the Image: Independent Asian Pacific American Media Arts*, ed. Russell Leong (Los Angeles: UCLA Asian American Studies Center and Visual Communications, Southern California Asian American Studies Central, Inc. 1991): 133–143.

21. Sumiko Higashi, *Virgins, Vamps, and Flappers: The American Silent Movie Heroine* (Montreal: Eden Press, 1978); Julia Lesage, "Artful Racism, Artful Rape: Griffith's *Broken Blossoms*," in *Home Is Where the Heart Is*, ed. Christine Gledhill (London: British Film Institute, 1987): 235–254; Marjorie Rosen, *Popcorn Venus* (New York: Avon, 1973).

22. See Lesage, "Artful Racism, Artful Rape"; Andrew, "*Broken Blossoms*"; and Browne, "American Film Theory in the Silent Period." Also, Angela Carter, *The Sadeian Woman and the Ideology of Pornography* (New York: Harper and Row, 1978): 60.

23. Point made by Brownlow as well as Wong.

The Death of Asia on the American Field of Representation

James S. Moy

The Spectacle presents itself as something enormously positive, indisputable and inaccessible. It says nothing more than "that which appears is good, that which is good appears." The attitude which it demands in principle is passive acceptance which in fact it already obtained by its manner of appearing without reply, by its monopoly of appearance.

—Guy Debord

In her recent treatment of the "undoing of women," Catherine Clement asserts that only through her death does the character Cho-Cho san in *Madama Butterfly* emerge as a true Asian character: "Butterfly, whose Japanese name is masked in Italian by the English signifier for an insect, regains her country at the same time she dies a Japanese death" (Clement 58). While this is merely a passing comment in Clement's impressionistic feminist reading of opera, it provides the outline for a larger trajectory which I intend to trace in this essay, as I look at the rather troubling tendency for Asians (both female and male) to find death on the American field of representation.

Generally speaking, despite the realities of Asian life on America's western frontier, theatrical events displaying Asianness prior to the end of the nineteenth century were part of a benign colonialist institution of representation. While the images were relatively unflattering, they at least did not constitute a real threat to Asian American life.

The earliest advertised representations of Asians on the American stage seemed to be limited to the popular entertainment mode. For example, in 1808,

Source: Shirley Geor-Lim and Amy Ling, eds., *Reading the Literatures of Asian America* (Philadelphia: Temple University Press, 1992), pp. 349-357. Reprinted by permission.

a circus troupe in New York featured "THE YOUNG CHINESE" who would "display a variety of comic attitudes and Vaulting, over his Horse in full speed." In 1834, the *Commercial Advertiser* announced the presence of a "Chinese Lady" at the American Museum in New York City. Later that same year, Afong Moy, presumably the aforementioned "Chinese Lady" was again displayed at 8 Park Place, "in native costume." A contemporary print dated 1835 seems to suggest that the display included an appropriate chinoiserie setting (Fessler 6). From the illustration it seems the simple foreigness of Afong Moy was deemed sufficient novelty to warrant her display. Likewise, beginning in the 1830s, P.T. Barnum's displays of the "Siamese Twins," Chang and Eng, the most famous stage display of Asianness in the nineteenth century, further contributed to the institutionalization of this pattern (Bogdan 202–04). Clearly, the context for this type of display is the anthropological gaze associated with modern museums in which the power and authority of an audience member's privileged look is affirmed, usually at the expense of the novel "primitive" objectified dead Other. Thus, the audience members could become "masters of all they survey."

Beyond the pure anthropological display of Anglo-American constituted Otherness, Asian stage representations are found inserted into literary theatrical texts beginning in the second half of the nineteenth century. These generally offered a neutralized Asian—usually Chinese male—character in some comic form. The methods employed in the disfigurement of this type of Asian character are significant, and were doubtless wildly entertaining to Anglo-American audiences of the late nineteenth century. A moment in

James J. McCloskey's *Across the Continent; Or, Scenes From New York Life and the Pacific Railroad* (1870) provides some insight into how such a "Chinese" character might have amused:

CHI: [*Runs up to her*] You like some riceе—[*Aunt Susannah turns back on him. . . . Sits down and takes drink out of bottle*]
CHI: Ah ha—Melican woman like jig water. Me likee, too. [*Takes bottle of water out of her hand and drinks. Offers it back several times, but fools her and drinks himself, talking Chinese all the time, and keeps this up till the bottle is empty*] Me makee mashee. [*Sits beside her*] Ah, there my sizee—me stealee you. [*Tries to put his arm around her. She jumps quickly—he falls, then chases her*]
JOE: Here—what is the matter, Tart?
CHI: [*Joe comes forward with Tom*] Melican woman fightee.
JOE: Come here, Tart. [*To others*] Watch me telephone to China. [*Takes Tart's cue*] Hello, Tart!
CHI: Hello!
JOE: You're crazy.
CHI: Me, too. [*Joe turns away laughing*] Now me talkee. [*Takes end of cue*] Hello—hello—hello—[*Jerks his cue disgusted—jumps on box*]. (McCloskey 107)

While the McCloskey piece can be dismissed as mere popular entertainment or touristic travelogue, attempts by writers who were revered as serious in their desire for greater literary realism did little better.[1]

In *Ah Sin* (1877), Mark Twain and Bret Harte attempt to provide a realistic treatment of a growing and increasingly problematic California Chinese population, "sympathetically" referring to the title character as a "slant eyed son of the yellow jaunders, . . . you jabbering idiot, . . . you moral cancer, you unsolvable political problem."[2] The audience is instructed, "Don't mind him—don't be afraid. . . . Poor Ah Sin is harmless—only a little ignorant and awkward." Another character complains that "when he shakes his head it makes me nervous to hear his dried faculties rattle" (*Ah Sin* 52–53).

Visually, Mark Twain and Bret Harte constituted the Chinese as a "poor dumb animal, with

his tail on top of his head instead of where it ought to be" (*Ah Sin* 52–53). In this regard some of Bret Harte's earlier "John Chinaman" writings are revealing. "The expression of the Chinese face in the aggregate is neither cheerful nor happy. . . . There is an abiding consciousness of degradation, a secret pain or self-humiliation, visible in the lines of the mouth and eye. . . . They seldom smile, and their laughter is of such an extraordinary and sardonic nature—so purely a mechanical spasm, quite independent of any mirthful attribute—that to this day I am doubtful whether I ever saw a Chinaman laugh" (Harte, "John Chinaman" 14:220). Harte described the typical Chinese face: "His complexion, which extended all over his head except where his long pig tail grew, was like a very nice piece of glazed brown paper-muslin. His eyes were black and bright, and his eyelids set at an angle of 15 [degrees]; his nose straight and delicately formed, his mouth small, and his teeth white and clean" (Harte, "Wan Lee, the Pagan" 2:264). Later, Harte claims that despite the surface cleanliness, the Chinese "always exhaled that singular medicated odor—half opium, half ginger—which we recognized as the common 'Chinese smell'" (Harte, "See Yup" 16:144). A figure composed of the most obvious aspects of difference, Ah Sin exists on the margins and is intended to disrupt the orderly progress of narrative. Here, then, Ah Sin serves as little more than comic relief despite his title character status.

This tendency to show the Asian as witless, sexless, and therefore harmless beings emerged as the Western colonialist powers were consolidating their economic subjugation of East Asia. This forced "opening" of Asia required that the victors return with trophies of their greatness. As the ancient Romans articulated their imperial power through the display of foreign slaves and curious animals, so the nineteenth-century apparatus of representation produced harmless human entities for display and amusement. Asians, of course, were just one of many stereotypical immigrant ethnic creations of the nineteenth century. Unlike the Irish, the Germans, or the Italians, whose initial stereotypical representations would ultimately be replaced by dominant title role characters in realistic dramas, Asians in America were never allowed to emerge into the realm of the real.

Beyond this, however, a new troubling tendency emerges by the end of the nineteenth century. For it seems that at this point in American representational history, what had previously been simply nonthreatening stereotypical-comic portrayals of Asianness developed into displays which increasingly included dead Asian representations. It may be significant to note that at about this time one of these newly "opened" and supposedly subjugated East Asian powers was beginning to behave in a fashion not unlike its European mentors. Japan early on understood the need to confront the West on its own terms. In colonizing pieces of Korea, China, and other parts of East Asia, its agenda began to resemble that of the European powers. To the extent that it defeated Russia in the Russo-Japan War of 1904–05, it clearly constituted a threat to the Eurocentric perception of the world order. As is all too often the case, the Western response was to simply have the threat eliminated, killed. In representational terms this meant the previously nonthreatening laughable portrayals of Asianness had to be transformed into figures of death, or preferably mystified figures worthy of death.

Inspired by the success of John Luther Long's short story, "Madame Butterfly" (1898), New York director David Belasco in 1900 collaborated with Long to produce the mythic stage representation of *Madame Butterfly*. While these early projects enjoyed some success, it was not until Puccini's operatic rendering of *Madama Butterfly* (1904) that the killing of Asia on stage achieved truly international dimensions.

The story of *Madama Butterfly* is well known. Pinkerton, a bored U.S. Naval captain stationed in Nagasaki, fakes a wedding to develop a liaison with a local Japanese woman. After he departs, she gives birth to his child and then anxiously awaits his return. Pinkerton returns, of course, with his elegant American wife, but only to claim his child. As "death with honor is better than life with dishonor," the only action left open to Cho-Cho san is suicide.

In the story of Madame Butterfly, then, the Asian ceased to be a novelty from which the West could learn. Asia ceased to exist as a place whose ancient wisdom might provide secrets to help America. Rather, Asianness was reconstituted as an object to be looked at as before, but now pinned to a board with a precisely placed needle through its heart; now, framed like a butterfly arranged for survey in a museum diorama display. Despite the potential for real understanding and exchange resulting from the increased contact between Asia and America, there developed a tendency to kill off Asians. As if to articulate an unwillingness, an impatience, or simply a lack of desire to understand, to learn from. This tendency finally articulates a Eurocentric colonialist way of looking at the world, a kind of tunnel vision, a provincialism. As these collocated aspects of difference hardened into stereotypes on the stage of America's east coast, the representational apparatus of the newly emerging cinema fixed it permanently, enshrined it, inscribed, and inserted it into the popular text of American consciousness.

One of the first feature-length films to exploit the neutralized suicidal Asian male was D. W. Griffith's *Broken Blossoms* (originally titled *The Chink and the Girl*, 1919). The piece features Lillian Gish as Lucy, the daughter of a murderously brutal prize fighter. After a vicious beating administered by her father, Lucy collapses before the "Chink" storekeeper whose subsequent developing love for the girl can only end in tragedy. Characterized as dreamy, frail, and sensitive, the "Yellow Man" here can offer only a love devoid of sexuality. A love so pure, so exquisitely sacred, and ultimately so tediously maudlin, that only suicide seems to provide a proper closure for the piece. Indeed, the elements of the film fit so well together that any other ending would be unacceptable. Death, it would seem, is this "yellow man's" destiny. Still, intended as a sympathetic treatment of the Asian character, the piece displays the latent anti-Asian racism inherent even in such "liberal" representational projects of the time.

The subsequent popular cinematic text is full of such representational figures. The list of suicidal Asians as Emperors, princesses, soldiers, now turned evil seems endless, while whole careers (like Anna May Wong's) in the industry centered on death by one's own hand.

The pervasiveness of this strategy of representation and the hopelessness of transcending this deadly stereotype can be seen in ("Father of American Drama") Eugene O'Neill's feeble attempt to contrast the decadent Babbit-like commercialism of the West with the "Oriental" wisdom of the East in *Marco Millions* (1927). Here, again, while O'Neill clearly hoped to offer a "liberal's" positive view of Asia, he finally could provide little more than a reinscription of the suicidal "Oriental" in an exotic setting. As Kucuchin dies for the love of Marco Polo who in turn loves only money and commerce, the viewer comes away with little more than a touristic view of an imaginary China while apprehending only the failure of the supposed wisdom of the Orient.

Not until the cultural awareness of the 1960s do plays by Asian Americans emerge to counter the institutionalized dead or dying Asian representational figure. David Henry Hwang in his Tony Award–winning *M. Butterfly* (1988) summarizes the attack:

> It's one of your favorite fantasies, isn't it? The submissive Oriental woman and the cruel white man. . . . Consider it this way: what would you say if a blond homecomming queen fell in love with a short Japanese businessman? He treats her cruelly then goes home for three years, during which time she prays to his picture and turns down marriage from a young Kennedy. Then, when she learns he has remarried, she kills herself. Now, I believe you would consider this girl to be a deranged idiot, correct? But because it's an Oriental who kills herself for a Westerner—ah!—you find it beautiful. (Hwang 17)

In addition, an angry Philip Kan Gotanda assails the results of such displacements as one of his characters in *Yankee Dawg You Die* (1988) complains that the only roles open to Asians are "waiters, viet cong killers, chimpanzees, drug dealers, hookers, sexless houseboys. . . . They fucking cut off our balls and made us all houseboys on the evening soaps. 'Get your very own neutered, oriental houseboy!'" (Gotanda 36). Unfortunately such overt, powerful attacks have been for nought as many recent Asian American playwrights have chosen to attack the stereotype while reinscribing it in newly disfigured characters to gain popular Anglo-American audience acceptance.[3] The failure of this self-subverting attack on the dead stereotype can be seen in the fact that even before *M. Butterfly* had completed its run, *Miss Saigon* (1989), a new variant on the *Madama Butterfly* theme, opened in London with a much anticipated New York production scheduled for 1991.

This failure suggests the need for a reassessment of the very possibility of identifying a representation of Asianness which can succeed with Anglo-American audiences. For it seems that only representations which reinscribe the stereotype in some form can find success on the popular stage.

Few playwrights have tried to circumvent this imperative to reinscribe the stereotype while attacking the representational apparatus of Anglo-America. In the 1970s, Frank Chin provided some of Asian America's earliest overt attacks on Anglo-American representational practice. Both his *The Chickencoop Chinaman* (1972) and *The Year of the Dragon* (1974) largely avoided the reinscription of the stereotype by providing Asian characters with significant, if eccentric, substance while often relegating Anglo characters to stereotype. Particularly amusing is the Anglo in-law character, Ross, in *The Year of the Dragon* who as a "sincerely interested student of all things Chinese" fancies himself "more Chinese" than his Chinese American wife (Chin 78–79). Further, Chin's portrayal of domestic tensions in Chinatown in *The Year of the Dragon* disfigures the colorful touristic perception of a community that in reality is often a deadend economic ghetto for many of its inhabitants. Such uncompromising portrayals did not meet with success on the popular American stage. Chin's lack of success in the face of *M. Butterfly's* subsequent popularity clearly confirms the need for the reinscription of stereotype if a playwright is to be accepted by Anglo-American audiences.

Indeed as the film/TV media has taken over the lead in the creation of mediated representational desire it becomes clear that realistic portrayals of domestic Asian American life will continue to have difficulty finding an audience while projects featuring Asians involved in violence and death will command the popular consciousness. Accordingly, films like *An Unremarkable Life* (1989), a quiet piece relating problems in interracial love relations in retirement years; *The Wash* (1988), a film that examines the disintegration of an Asian American family; *Eat a Bowl of Tea* (1989), which offers a glimpse of Chinese American domestic life in the years following World War II; *Dim Sum* (1985), which places filial piety in tension with a Chinese daughter's self-actualization; and *Chan Is Missing* (1982), a breakthrough independent production that spoofs traditional Hollywood film noir practice while providing a look at Chinese attitudes as they impact on a search for a missing person, continue to be relegate to positions of very limited release due to low audience interest. Pieces centering on violence and death, like *Year of the Dragon* (1985), *China Girl* (1987), and *Casualties of War* (1989) maintain relatively high visibility. Thus, the extent to which the popular stereotypes shape audience expectations becomes visible through the box office.

Less clear is the extent to which this same popular consciousness finally shapes Asian American racial desire as well. Arthur Dong's recent film *Forbidden City* (1989) treats this subject. And, it is awkward to admit that after watching the many interviews with Asian American dancers who wished for all the world to be Las Vegas show girls, one can come away with the uneasy conclusion that Asian American desire often coincides with Anglo-American expectations. This desire for

complicity is troubling and is perhaps most clearly seen in the current controversy surrounding the proposed Broadway production of *Miss Saigon*. Even the producers admit that the piece is merely an updating of *Madama Butterfly*. Though David Henry Hwang has attacked the opera as a racist myth, he was one of the strongest voices advocating the casting of an Asian American in the lead role of the Engineer (played in London by Jonathan Pryce, an Anglo made up to look Eurasian). The desire for greater Asian American complicity in racist projects is at best confusing. In any case, it is clear that in the popular consciousness Asianness has fled from the real into the realm of representational desire. Unfortunately, in a piece like *Miss Saigon* the representational Asia carries with it a requirement of self destruction. Indeed, as Catherine Clement says, only through its death, or representational self-effacement, does Asia become real for Western audiences.

NOTES

1. Indeed, this touristic agenda was still being played out as late as 1927 in O'Neill's *Marco Millions*. See my "Eugene O'Neill's *Marco Millions*: Desiring Marginality and the Dematerialization of the Orient," in *Eugene O'Neill in China*, ed. Haiping Lui and Lowell Swortzell (New York: Greenwood Press, 1992).

2. Mark Twain and Bret Harte, *Ah Sin*, ed. Frederick Anderson (San Francisco: Book Club of California, 1961), 10–11, 87.

3. See my "David Henry Hwang's *M. Butterfly* and Philip Kan Gotanda's *Yankee Dawg You Die*: repositioning Chinese American Marginality on the American Stage," *Theatre Journal* 42 (March 1990), 48–56.

WORKS CITED

Bogdan, Robert. *Freak Show: Presenting Human Oddities for Amusement and Profit*. Chicago: University of Chicago Press, 1988.

Chin, Frank. *Chickencoop Chinaman/The Year of the Dragon: Two Plays by Frank Chin*. Seattle: University of Washington Press, 1988.

Clement, Catherine. *Opera, Or the Undoing of Women*. Minneapolis: University of Minnesota Press, 1988.

Fessler, Loren W., ed. *Chinese in America*. New York: Vantage Press, 1983.

Gotanda, Philip Kan. *Yankee Dawg You Die*. Chicago: Wisdom Bridge Theatre Company, 1988.

Harte, Bret. "John Chinaman." In *Writings of Bret Harte*, vol. 14. Boston: Houghton Mifflin, 1896.

————. "See Yup." In *Writings of Bret Harte*, vol. 16. Boston: Houghton Mifflin, 1896.

————. "Wan Lee, The Pagan" In *Writings of Bret Harte*, vol. 2. Boston: Houghton Mifflin, 1896.

Hwang, David Henry. *M. Butterfly*. New York: New American Library, 1988.

McCloskey, James J. *Across the Continent; Or Scenes from New York Life, and the Pacific Railroad*. In *America's Lost Players*, vol. 16, ed. Barret H. Clark. Bloomington: Indiana University Press, 1963.

Moy, James S. "David Henry Hwang's *M. Butterfly* and Philip Kan Gotanda's *Yankee Dawg You Die*: Repositioning Chinese American Marginality on the American Stage." *Theatre Journal* 42 (March 1990).

————. "Eugene O'Neill's *Marco Millions*: Desiring Marginality and the Dematerialization of the Orient." In *Eugene O'Neill in China*, ed. Lui Haiping and Lowell Swortzell. New York: Greenwood Press, 1992.

O'Neill, Eugene. *Marco Millions*. London: Jonathan Cape, 1927.

Twain, Mark, and Bret Harte. *Ah Sin*, ed. Frederick Anderson. San Francisco: Book Club of California, 1961.

Asian Women in Film: No Joy, No Luck

Jessica Hagedorn

Pearl of the Orient. Whore. Geisha. Concubine. Whore. Hostess. Bar Girl. Mama-san. Whore. China Doll. Tokyo Rose. Whore. Butterfly. Whore. Miss Saigon. Whore. Dragon Lady. Lotus Blossom. Gook. Whore. Yellow Peril. Whore. Bangkok Bombshell. Whore. Hospitality Girl. Whore. Comfort Woman. Whore. Savage. Whore. Sultry. Whore. Faceless. Whore. Porcelain. Whore. Demure. Whore. Virgin. Whore. Mute. Whore. Model Minority. Whore. Victim. Whore. Woman Warrior. Whore. Mail-Order Bride. Whore. Mother. Wife. Lover. Daughter. Sister.

As I was growing up in the Philippines in the 1950s, my fertile imagination was colonized by thoroughly American fantasies. Yellowface variations on the exotic erotic loomed larger than life on the silver screen. I was mystified and enthralled by Hollywood's skewed representations of Asian women: sleek, evil goddesses with slanted eyes and cunning ways, or smiling, sarong-clad South Seas "maidens" with undulating hips, kinky black hair, and white skin darkened by makeup. Hardly any of the "Asian" characters were played by Asians. White actors like Sidney Toler and Warner Oland played "inscrutable Oriental detective" Charlie Chan with taped eyelids and a singsong, chop suey accent. Jennifer Jones was a Eurasian doctor swept up in a doomed "interracial romance" in *Love Is a Many Splendored Thing*. In my mother's youth, white actor Luise Rainer played the central role of the Patient Chinese Wife in the 1937 film adaptation of Pearl Buck's novel *The Good Earth*. Back then, not many thought to ask

why; they were all too busy being grateful to see anyone in the movies remotely like themselves.

Cut to 1960: *The World of Suzie Wong*, another tragic East/West affair. I am now old enough to be impressed. Sexy, sassy Suzie (played by Nancy Kwan) works out of a bar patronized by white sailors, but doesn't seem bothered by any of it. For a hardworking girl turning nightly tricks to support her baby, she manages to parade an astonishing wardrobe in damn near every scene, down to matching handbags and shoes. The sailors are also strictly Hollywood, sanitized and not too menacing. Suzie and all the other prostitutes in this movie are cute, giggling, dancing sex machines with hearts of gold. William Holden plays an earnest, rather prim, Nice Guy painter seeking inspiration in The Other. Of course, Suzie falls madly in love with him. Typically, she tells him, "I not important," and "I'll be with you until you say—Suzie, go away." She also thinks being beaten by a man is a sign of true passion, and is terribly disappointed when Mr. Nice Guy refuses to show his true feelings.

Next in Kwan's short-lived but memorable career was the kitschy 1961 musical *Flower Drum Song*, which, like *Suzie Wong*, is a thoroughly American commercial product. The female roles are typical of Hollywood musicals of the times: women are basically airheads, subservient to men. Kwan's counterpart is the Good Chinese Girl, played by Miyoshi Umeki, who was better playing the Loyal Japanese Girl in that other classic Hollywood tale of forbidden love, *Sayonara*. Remember? Umeki was so loyal, she committed double suicide with actor Red Buttons. I instinctively hated *Sayonara* when I first saw it as a child; now I understand why. Contrived tragic resolutions were the only way Hollywood got past

Source: Ms. January/February 1994, pp. 74–79. Copyright © 1994 by Jessica Hagedorn. Reprinted by permission of the author and her agents, Harold Schmidt Literary Agency.

the censors in those days. With one or two exceptions, somebody in these movies always had to die to pay for breaking racial and sexual taboos.

Until the recent onslaught of films by both Asian and Asian American filmmakers, Asian Pacific women have generally been perceived by Hollywood with a mixture of fascination, fear, and contempt. Most Hollywood movies either trivialize or exoticize us as people of color and as women. Our intelligence is underestimated, our humanity overlooked, and our diverse cultures treated as interchangeable. If we are "good," we are childlike, submissive, silent, and eager for sex (see France Nuyen's glowing performance as Liat in the film version of *South Pacific*) or else we are tragic victim types (see *Casualties of War*, Brian De Palma's graphic 1989 drama set in Vietnam). And if we are not silent, suffering doormats, we are demonized dragon ladies—cunning, deceitful, sexual provocateurs. Give me the demonic any day—Anna May Wong as a villain slithering around in a slinky gown is at least gratifying to watch, neither servile nor passive. And she steals the show from Marlene Dietrich in Josef von Sternberg's *Shanghai Express*. From the 1920s through the '30s, Wong was our only female "star." But even she was trapped in limited roles, in what filmmaker Renee Tajima has called the dragon lady/lotus blossom dichotomy.

Cut to 1985: There is a scene toward the end of the terribly dishonest but weirdly compelling Michael Cimino movie *Year of the Dragon* (cowritten by Oliver Stone) that is one of my favorite twisted movie moments of all time. If you ask a lot of my friends who've seen that movie (especially if they're Asian), it's one of their favorites too. The setting is a crowded Chinatown nightclub. There are two very young and very tough Jade Cobra gang girls in a shoot-out with Mickey Rourke, in the role of a demented Polish American cop who, in spite of being Mr. Ugly in the flesh—an arrogant, misogynistic bully devoid of any charm—wins the "good" Asian American anchorwoman in the film's absurd and implausible ending. This is a movie with an actual disclaimer as its lead-in, covering its ass in advance in response to anticipated complaints about "stereotypes."

My pleasure in the hard-edged power of the Chinatown gang girls in *Year of the Dragon* is my small revenge, the answer to all those Suzie Wong "I want to be your slave" female characters. The Jade Cobra girls are mere background to the white male foreground/focus of Cimino's movie. But long after the movie has faded into video-rental heaven, the Jade Cobra girls remain defiant, fabulous images in my memory, flaunting tight metallic dresses and spiky cock's-comb hairdos streaked electric red and blue.

Mickey Rourke looks down with world-weary pity at the unnamed Jade Cobra girl (Doreen Chan) he's just shot who lies sprawled and bleeding on the street: "You look like you're gonna die, beautiful."

Jade Cobra girl: "Oh yeah? [blood gushing from her mouth] I'm proud of it."

Rourke: "You are? You got anything you wanna tell me before you go, sweetheart?"

Jade Cobra girl: "Yeah. [pause] Fuck you."

Cut to 1993: I've been told that like many New Yorkers, I watch movies with the right side of my brain on perpetual overdrive. I admit to being grouchy and overcritical, suspicious of sentiment, and cynical. When a critic like Richard Corliss of *Time* magazine gushes about *The Joy Luck Club* being "a fourfold *Terms of Endearment*," my gut instinct is to run the other way. I resent being told how to feel. I went to see the 1993 eight-handkerchief movie version of Amy Tan's best-seller with a group that included my ten-year-old daughter. I was caught between the sincere desire to be swept up by the turbulent mother-daughter sagas and my own stubborn resistance to being so obviously manipulated by the filmmakers. With every flashback came tragedy. The music soared; the voice-overs were solemn or wistful; tears, tears, and more tears flowed onscreen. Daughters were reverent; mothers carried dark secrets.

I was elated by the grandness and strength of the four mothers and the luminous actors who portrayed them, but I was uneasy with the passivity of the Asian American daughters. They seemed to exist solely as receptors for their mothers' amazing life stories. It's almost as if by assimilating so easily into American society, they had lost all sense of self.

In spite of my resistance, my eyes watered as the desperate mother played by Kieu Chinh was forced to abandon her twin baby girls on a country road in war-torn China. (Kieu Chinh resembles my own mother and her twin sister, who suffered through the brutal Japanese occupation of the Philippines.) So far in this movie, an infant son had been deliberately drowned, a mother played by the gravely beautiful France Nuyen had gone catatonic with grief, a concubine had cut her flesh open to save her dying mother, an insecure daughter had been oppressed by her boorish Asian American husband, another insecure daughter had been left by her white husband, and so on. . . . The overall effect was numbing as far as I'm concerned, but a man sitting two rows in front of us broke down sobbing. A Chinese Pilipino writer even more grouchy than me later complained, "Must ethnicity only be equated with suffering?"

Because change has been slow, *The Joy Luck Club* carries a lot of cultural baggage. It is a big-budget story about Chinese American women, directed by a Chinese American man, cowritten and coproduced by Chinese American women. That's a lot to be thankful for. And its box office success proves that an immigrant narrative told from female perspectives can have mass appeal. But my cynical side tells me that its success might mean only one thing in Hollywood: more weepy epics about Asian American mother-daughter relationships will be planned.

That the film finally got made was significant. By Hollywood standards (think white male; think money, money, money), a movie about Asian Americans even when adapted from a best-seller was a risky proposition. When I asked a producer I know about the film's rumored delays, he simply said, "It's still an *Asian* movie," surprised I had even asked. Equally interesting was director Wayne Wang's initial reluctance to be involved in the project; he told the New York *Times*, "I didn't want to do another Chinese movie."

Maybe he shouldn't have worried so much. After all, according to the media, the nineties are the decade of "Pacific Overtures" and East Asian chic. Madonna, the pop queen of shameless appropriation, cultivated Japanese high-tech style with her music video "Rain," while Janet Jackson faked kitschy orientalia in hers, titled "If." Critical attention was paid to movies from China, Japan, and Vietnam. But that didn't mean an honest appraisal of women's lives. Even on the art house circuit, filmmakers who should know better took the easy way out. Takehiro Nakajima's 1992 film *Okoge* presents one of the more original film roles for women in recent years. In Japanese, "okoge" means the crust of rice that sticks to the bottom of the rice pot; in pejorative slang, it means fag hag. The way "okoge" is used in the film seems a reappropriation of the term; the portrait Nakajima creates of Sayoko, the so-called fag hag, is clearly an affectionate one. Sayoko is a quirky, self-assured woman in contemporary Tokyo who does voice-overs for cartoons, has a thing for Frida Kahlo paintings, and is drawn to a gentle young gay man named Goh. But the other women's roles are disappointing, stereotypical "hysterical females" and the movie itself turns conventional halfway through. Sayoko sacrifices herself to a macho brute Goh desires, who rapes her as images of Frida Kahlo paintings and her beloved Goh rising from the ocean flash before her. She gives birth to a baby boy and endures a terrible life of poverty with the abusive rapist. This sudden change from spunky survivor to helpless, victimized woman is baffling. Whatever happened to her job? Or that arty little apartment of hers? Didn't her Frida Kahlo obsession teach her anything?

Then there was Tiana Thi Thanh Nga's *From Hollywood to Hanoi*, a self-serving but fascinating documentary. Born in Vietnam to a privileged family that included an uncle who was defense minister in the Thieu government and an idolized father who served as press minister, Nga (a.k.a. Tiana) spent her adolescence in California. A former actor in martial arts movies and fitness teacher ("Karaticize with Tiana"), the vivacious Tiana decided to make a record of her journey back to Vietnam.

From Hollywood to Hanoi is at times unintentionally very funny. Tiana includes a quick scene of herself dancing with a white man at the Metropole hotel in Hanoi, and breathlessly announces: "That's me doing the tango with Oliver Stone!" Then she listens sympathetically to a horrifying account of the My Lai massacre by one of its few female survivors. In another scene, Tiana cheerfully addresses a food vendor on the streets of Hanoi: "Your hairdo is so pretty." The unimpressed, poker-faced woman gives a brusque, deadpan reply: "You want to eat, or what?" Sometimes it is hard to tell the difference between Tiana Thi Thanh Nga and her Hollywood persona: the real Tiana still seems to be playing one of her B-movie roles, which are mainly fun because they're fantasy. The time was certainly right to explore postwar Vietnam from a Vietnamese woman's perspective; it's too bad this film was done by a Valley Girl.

1993 also brought Tran Anh Hung's *The Scent of Green Papaya*, a different kind of Vietnamese memento—this is a look back at the peaceful, lush country of the director's childhood memories. The film opens in Saigon, in 1951. A willowy ten-year-old girl named Mui comes to work for a troubled family headed by a melancholy musician and his kind, stoic wife. The men of this bourgeois household are idle, pampered types who take naps while the women do all the work. Mui is a male fantasy: she is a devoted servant, enduring acts of cruel mischief with patience and dignity; as an adult, she barely speaks. She scrubs floors, shines shoes, and cooks with loving care and never a complaint. When she is sent off to work for another wealthy musician, she ends up being impregnated by him. The movie ends as the camera closes in on Mui's contented face. Languid and precious, *The Scent of Green Papaya* is visually haunting, but it suffers

from the director's colonial fantasy of women as docile, domestic creatures. Steeped in highbrow nostalgia, it's the arty Vietnamese version of *My Fair Lady* with the wealthy musician as Professor Higgins, teaching Mui to read and write.

And then there is Ang Lee's tepid 1993 hit, *The Wedding Banquet*—a clever culture-clash farce in which traditional Chinese values collide with contemporary American sexual mores. The somewhat formulaic plot goes like this: Wai-Tung, a yuppie landlord, lives with his white lover, Simon, in a chic Manhattan brownstone. Wai-Tung is an only child and his aging parents in Taiwan long for a grandchild to continue the family legacy. Enter Wei-Wei, an artist who lives in a grungy loft owned by Wai-Tung. She slugs tequila straight from the bottle as she paints and flirts boldly with her young, uptight landlord, who brushes her off. "It's my fate. I am always attracted to handsome gay men," she mutters. After this setup, the movie goes downhill, all edges blurred in a cozy nest of happy endings. In a refrain of Sayoko's plight in *Okoge*, a pregnant, suddenly complacent Wei-Wei gives in to family pressures—and never gets her life back.

"It takes a man to know what it is to be a real woman."

—Song Liling in *M. Butterfly*

Ironically, two gender-bending films in which men play men playing women reveal more about the mythology of the prized Asian woman and the superficial trappings of gender than most movies that star real women. The slow-moving *M. Butterfly* presents the ultimate object of Western male desire as the spy/opera diva Song Liling, a Suzie Wong/Lotus Blossom played by actor John Lone with a five o'clock shadow and bobbing Adam's apple. The best and most profound of these forays into cross-dressing is the spectacular melodrama *Farewell My Concubine*, directed by Chen Kaige. Banned in China, *Farewell My Concubine* shared the prize for Best Film at the 1993 Cannes Film Festival with Jane Campion's *The Piano*. Sweeping through 50 years of tumultuous history in China, the story revolves around the lives of two male Beijing Opera stars and the woman who marries one of them. The three characters make an unforgettable triangle, struggling over love, art, friendship, and politics against the bloody backdrop of cultural upheaval. They are as capable of casually betraying each other as they are of selfless, heroic acts. The androgynous Dieyi, doomed to play the same female role of concubine over and over again, is portrayed with great vulnerability, wit, and grace by male Hong Kong pop star Leslie Cheung. Dieyi competes with the prostitute Juxian (Gong Li) for the love of his childhood protector and fellow opera star, Duan Xiaolou (Zhang Fengyi).

Cheung's highly stylized performance as the classic concubine-ready-to-die-for-love in the opera within the movie is all about female artifice. His sidelong glances, restrained passion, languid stance, small steps, and delicate, refined gestures say everything about what is considered desirable in Asian women—and are the antithesis of the feisty, outspoken woman played by Gong Li. The characters of Dieyi and Juxian both see suffering as part and parcel of love and life. Juxian matter-of-factly says to Duan Xiaolou before he agrees to marry her: "I'm used to hardship. If you take me in, I'll wait on you hand and foot. If you tire of me, I'll . . . kill myself. No big deal." It's an echo of Suzie Wong's servility, but the context is new. Even with her back to the wall, Juxian is not helpless or whiny. She attempts to manipulate a man while admitting to the harsh reality that is her life.

Dieyi and Juxian are the two sides of the truth of women's lives in most Asian countries. Juxian in particular—wife and ex-prostitute—could be seen as a thankless and stereotypical role. But like the characters Gong Li has played in Chinese director Zhang Yimou's films, *Red Sorghum*, *Raise the Red Lantern*, and especially *The Story of Qiu Ju*, Juxian is tough, obstinate, sensual, clever, oafish, beautiful, infuriating, cowardly, heroic, and banal. Above all, she is resilient. Gong Li is one of the few Asian Pacific actors whose roles have been drawn with intelligence, honesty, and depth. Nevertheless, the characters

she plays are limited by the possibilities that exist for real women in China.

"Let's face it. Women still don't mean shit in China," my friend Meeling reminds me. What she says so bluntly about her culture rings painfully true, but in less obvious fashion for me. In the Philippines, infant girls aren't drowned, nor were their feet bound to make them more desirable. But sons were and are cherished. To this day, men of the bourgeois class are coddled and prized, much like the spoiled men of the elite household in *The Scent of Green Papaya*. We do not have a geisha tradition like Japan, but physical beauty is overtreasured. Our daughters are protected virgins or primed as potential beauty queens. And many of us have bought into the image of the white man as our handsome savior: G.I. Joe.

BUZZ magazine recently featured an article entitled "Asian Women/L.A. Men," a report on a popular hangout that caters to white men's fantasies of nubile Thai women. The lines between movies and real life are blurred. Male screenwriters and cinematographers flock to this bar-restaurant, where the waitresses are eager to "audition" for roles. Many of these men have been to Bangkok while working on film crews for Vietnam War movies. They've come back to L.A., but for them, the movie never ends. In this particular fantasy the boys play G.I. Joe on a rescue mission in the urban jungle, saving the whore from herself. "A scene has developed here, a kind of R-rated *Cheers*," author Alan Rifkin writes. "The waitresses audition for sitcoms. The customers date the waitresses or just keep score."

Colonization of the imagination is a two-way street. And being enshrined on a pedestal as someone's Pearl of the Orient fantasy doesn't seem so demeaning, at first; who wouldn't want to be worshiped? Perhaps that's why Asian women are the ultimate wet dream in most Hollywood movies; it's no secret how well we've been taught to play the role, to take care of our men. In Hollywood vehicles, we are objects of desire or derision; we exist to provide sex, color, and texture in what is essentially a white man's world. It is akin to what Toni Morrison calls "the Africanist presence" in literature. She write[...] [...]cters who look like us represented tainers, through or by associati[...] [...] have also learned to view between could render permissible top[...] [...]o add what is missing. For many of would have been taboo, so Am[...] [...] of watching has always been a neces-able to employ an imagined A[...] [...] in the gaps. If a female character is articulate and imaginatively act out the [...]is a mute, willowy beauty, we convince in American culture." The same analogy could be ourselves she is an ancestral ghost—so smart she made for the often titillating presence of Asian doesn't have to speak at all. If she is a whore with woman in movies made by white men. a heart of gold, we claim her as a tough feminist

Movies are still the most seductive and pow-icon. If she is a sexless, sanitized, boring nerd, we erful of artistic mediums, manipulating us with embrace her as a role model for our daughters, ease by a powerful combination of sound and rather than the tragic whore. And if she is pre-image. In many ways, as females and Asians, as sented as an utterly devoted saint suffering nobly audiences or performers, we have learned to settle in silence, we lie and say she is just like our for less—to accept the fact that we are either dec-mothers. Larger than life. Magical and insidious. orative, invisible, or one-dimensional. When A movie is never just a movie, after all.

Reading 22

What Hollywood Should Know: A Call to Action from an Asian American Actor

Steve Park

In the spirit of *Jerry Maguire*, I submit this mission statement to the Hollywood community: I am a Korean American actor. You can see my work in one of the most highly acclaimed movies of 1996 and in one of the most talked about scenes of that year. I play the distraught Japanese American ex-schoolmate of Marge Gunderson, Mike Yanagita, in the Academy Award winning movie *Fargo*. Working with the Coen brothers and Frances McDormand was one of the high points of my career. Not so much because they are brilliant artists, but because they are decent, down to earth people who treated me and the rest of the cast and crew with respect and admiration.

Being an Asian American actor, I continue to struggle to find roles for myself that are not insulting and stereotypical. My career started with *Do The Right Thing*, I was a series regular on *In Living Color*, and I just finished working as a guest star on one of the highest rated shows on television, which brings me to my next point.

Working with the people involved with this show was an extremely painful experience for me. A disturbing lack in generosity of spirit and basic human courtesy in addition to a racial incident on the set has forced me to speak out. These people, by virtue of their status, money, and power are among the most privileged people walking the face of the earth, yet they behaved as if they were bankrupt in spirit and incapable of expressing simple human kindness.

Not only did various key people on the set not have the courtesy to introduce themselves as we began to work together, they created an environment of fear and insecurity. One production assistant spoke of having worked on the show for almost a full year without one cast member having said hello to him in that entire time. And on top of this, the 1st assistant director, in a short tirade, called an Asian American actor to the set over a walkie-talkie with the words, "I don't have time for this! Where's Hoshi, Toshi or whatever the f—k his name is—get the Oriental guy!" He did not even have the respect to learn the name of the actor, a veteran of 40 years. I was the only one who took notice while all others proceeded as if it was business as usual. Given the atmosphere on the set, I did not feel safe to say anything. After all, on the average Hollywood set, finding a person of color is much like trying to find Waldo. It is a white, exclusionary culture.

If this was an isolated incident, I would not have felt compelled to write this mission statement. Unfortunately, I find this attitude and behavior commonplace in the Hollywood culture. I know many people who have experienced this kind of indignity on a movie or television show set, and you can be sure this kind of thing is going on in corporate culture as well. There are many who would argue that the status and power people achieve here is part of the attraction and glamour of Hollywood, and others who climb this ladder of success and are dealt these indignities are just "paying their dues." I believe those who hold this opinion are part of the problem.

Asian Americans are under attack in this country right now. Americans of Asian descent who contributed to the Democratic National Committee are being investigated and harassed, having to prove beyond what is reasonable and just that they are actually citizens of this country.

Source: *AsianWeek*, April 18, 1997, p. 7. Reprinted by permission.

It is no accident that political contributors from places like Europe, Australia or Canada have never suffered from such scrutiny. A recent issue of the *National Review* displays on its cover the Clintons and Al Gore in yellowface with buck teeth and slanted eyes. You can be sure the *National Review* would never have dared to paint the Clintons in blackface on their cover. The fact that they had the grotesque audacity to do this in America in 1997 is nothing less than a call to action, not only for Asian Americans but for all Americans. When the rights of one group of Americans are threatened, America itself is threatened, and we shame the ideal of America.

In movies and television, Asian characters, mostly men, are subjected to indignity and/or violence or are tokenized, while Asian women are exploited as objects of sexual desire. You rarely see Asian characters in leading roles that contain any significant power or influence.

The award-winning documentary *Who Killed Vincent Chin* tells the story of a young Chinese American man in Detroit who was brutally murdered by two white men who mistook him for Japanese, and thereby held him responsible for their unemployment in the automobile industry. These two men were acquitted and never spent a day in jail. Hate crimes against Asian Americans are on the rise in this country, and negative portrayals of Asians in the media only encourage this trend.

There are many who believe Asian Americans have nothing to complain about and that we are the "model minority." But the model minority myth is just that—a myth. As immigrants, we are often not welcomed. We are treated as outsiders regardless of how many generations we have been in this country. We are viewed as "people of color," and face the oppression of racism. We make up more than one half the world's population, yet in spite of our numbers and contributions to the world, our images and perspectives are seldom seen. Our histories and our cultures are obscured, overlooked, buried, or tokenized in a world dominated by Western classism. Our voices are seldom heard, our stories are left untold, and our realties are seldom represented by those who control the means and resources to name and shape a picture of reality. In spite of our diversity, in spite of our unique histories and cultures, we are often represented as a single homogenous group. Asians are the nearly silent, nearly invisible, majority of the world.

In Los Angeles, we live in one of the most racially divided cities in the world, still recovering from the aftershocks of a racial uprising and the O.J. Simpson trial, which made it clear to all in America that white people and black people live in entirely different worlds. This does not even speak to the many issues involving all the other people of color in this country who struggle with racism but are left out of the dialogue by people who see the issues only in black and white.

Other cities may choose to ignore these problems. Los Angeles cannot afford to. The state of affairs in this city, as well as the attitudes and ignorance of many in Hollywood are what will lead us to our next crisis unless we talk openly and honestly about what we can do together to solve these issues. It is my passionate, heartfelt belief that the level of despair being felt in Los Angeles, as well as around the world, makes this state of affairs in Hollywood completely and unequivocally unacceptable.

"Four score and seven years ago, our forefathers brought forth, upon this continent a new nation, conceived in liberty, and dedicated to the proposition that all men are created equal." Do you remember these words? Do you know who said them? Abraham Lincoln in his Gettysburg Address. I first heard these words in the fourth grade in upstate New York, and I memorized the entire speech so that I could deliver it to my classmates, all of whom were white, as part of a public speaking exercise. This memory has just now come upon me, and I am astounded by this memory. As a young Korean American boy, I barely knew what I was saying. I was only concerned that I spoke clearly, memorized all the words, and that I continued to move my head left and right so everyone could see my face. As I remember these words now, as a Korean American man, that all men (and women) are created equal, I realize these words are coming back to me now so that I may save my own life.

Movies are America's greatest export. It is the one industry that America has always been the best at in the world. Communication is our greatest resource. Wake up Hollywood! Wake up America! The world is in a horrible crisis—the time has come for us to muster up our courage and open our hearts against the cruelty of our time and live out and communicate the most important message of all: Love. In the process, we will save ourselves from ourselves.

A Disappointing *All-American Girl*

William Wong

It may not seem so, but the name of San Francisco comedian Margaret Cho's new situation comedy on ABC-TV, *All-American Girl*, is nothing if not political. Many Asian Americans resent how other Americans regard them. They are "Orientals" or a slew of slurs. More benignly, they are "Asians," "Chinese," "Japanese," "Koreans," "Filipinos," or whatever.

But, to many people, they are not "Americans," when in fact a good number were born in the United States and others have become naturalized U.S. citizens. It is true some people of Asian descent who live legally in the United States aren't yet citizens but their U.S.-born children are.

The term "American" remains stubbornly in the public imagination as a description of white people of different European ethnicities. Curiously, African Americans aren't excluded as "Americans" but they are frequently excluded because of their racial heritage.

Cho, an American-born woman of immigrant ethnic Korean parents, has used her dual cultural identities in her stand-up comedy routine. Now she's hit the big time, a TV star.

Her show is one of many trying to crack TV's magic kingdom of high ratings and enduring stardom, or as enduring as our disposable popular culture will allow. (Which usually means 15 minutes, in Andy Warhol time.)

For many Asian Americans, however, *All-American Girl* has inordinate meaning, being the first prime-time television show featuring an acting ensemble that is mostly of Asian descent.

Source: *The Oakland Tribune*, October 9, 1994. Reprinted by permission.

ASIAN AMERICANS VALIDATED

So, at one level, the show validates the existence of Americans of Asian ancestry. How does it do so, you ask? One theory is that if you don't see yourself reflected, in some way, on the ubiquitous tube or other forms of mass media, you don't exist. You are nothing. You have no value.

People of Asian descent, of course, have appeared in the American mass media. But almost never are they the stars, the heroes. When they haven't been invisible (and that's a lot of the time), they are mostly sidekicks, assistants, servants, background noise, or a mute distant presence, anonymous.

On *All-American Girl*, Asian Americans are the stars. In addition to Cho, there's Clyde Kusatu, a veteran character actor; Jodi Long; Amy Hill, who cut her acting teeth in San Francisco; and B.D. Wong, a San Francisco actor of accomplishment who won a Tony award for his complex and demanding role in David Henry Hwang's "M. Butterfly" on Broadway.

This symbolic success, of having Asian-American actors starring in a mainstream TV comedy, isn't enough, however.

At other levels, *All-American Girl* is a disappointment and commits the biggest show-business sin: It isn't funny. That it is very much in the mold of other TV comedies starring white and black actors means it is banal entertainment, a specialty of commercial television.

If Asian Americans were hoping for a TV show that genuinely reflects Asian cultural sensibilities, they'll have to wait for some future show.

In the first four episodes, there have been superficial Asian cultural references. Some have been laughably inept, like rice that's brown and loosely packed, à la an Uncle Ben's recipe. People of Asian descent who eat rice generally eat white rice and, when cooked, it is of a stickier consistency.

AUTHENTICITY IN QUESTION

Drop-in lines about kimchee and "foong sur," a Chinese system of harmonizing a home or office with natural forces (wind, water), simply don't provide enough authentic Asian cultural sustenance. Then again, that's not the goal of *All-American Girl*. If it were, that would probably mean instant extinction of the show.

The Hollywood mentality is to dumb everything down so few people in the vast wasteland of America will be offended. Offending Asian Americans, who make up only three percent of the U.S. population, is no big deal to the show's producers, who are aiming for the other 97 percent of the American population. At the same time, they can say to Asian American nags, "See, we have a show with a lot of Asian Americans as stars. So stop complaining."

The lesson of *Quiz Show*, the provocative film directed by Robert Redford about the TV quiz show scandals of the late 1950s, reminded me of TV's soul. It has none, other than money. TV's all about selling, products first, values that reinforce capitalism second.

The "villains" of *Quiz Show*, the TV producers, network executives and corporate sponsors, sacrificed truth and morality for the sake of high ratings and money. They survived and prospered, while the individual contestants, including a member of the ruling class, were resigned to the anonymous slag heap of American life.

If you want to be TV star, you have to accept the premise that TV is show business, with the emphasis on the latter word. Otherwise, you will reside in Couch Potatoland, where the pay is bad and fame nonexistent. That leaves little choice for ambitious entertainers like Margaret Cho.

CHAPTER 7

Families, Identities, and Culture

There is relatively little research written on Asian American families due to their historically small population and their contemporary image of not being a "problem group." Early social science research on Asian American families tended to focus on the rich cultural resources of Asia to explain the more important features of Asian American family life. This attention to culture is problematic for two major reasons. First, the diversity of Asian Americans makes it extremely difficult to make any reliable generalizations about the Asian American family or culture. Second, culturally based explanations are ahistorical and do not give attention to important sociohistorical factors, such as changing immigration policies or institutional discrimination that affect family formation. Awareness of distinctly different family patterns corresponding to historical periods and generational change reveals the inadequacy of culture-based explanations of Asian American families. Recently, Asian American scholars have taken these concerns into their analysis to fully recognize the adaptive ability of Asian American families and identities, as well as the fluidity of culture.

The work of Evelyn Nakano Glenn and Stacey G. H. Yap directly addresses the deficiencies of culture-based explanations by using an institutional framework and explains how Chinese American families have adapted in response to changing institutional restraints. They point out three distinct Chinese American family types: (1) split household, (2) small producer, and (3) diverse Chinese American families. The existence of three separate Chinese American family types underscores the significance of larger social, political, and economic factors, as well as the resourcefulness of Chinese American families to survive even under harsh conditions.

The impact of dramatic change on family patterns is also important to Nazli Kibria. Her work examines the effects of refugee settlement in the United States, with an emphasis on intergenerational and gender relations. Within this, any understanding of the Vietnamese family experience must take into account distinctive factors of the Vietnamese experience prior to the arrival in the United States. Among these factors are the unusual conditions of migration from Vietnam, the large proportion of young men in the population, the high percentage of migration of disrupted families, and the significant differences of social class among Vietnamese Americans. Taken together, Kibria describes a rise in conflicts between older and younger Vietnamese Americans, complex restructuring of extended family units, and serious challenges to the traditional male and female roles within the family.

Snehendu B. Kar et al. also concentrate on migration and gender but include generational change in their analysis. The authors conducted survey and focus group research to study the psychosocial factors that affect the quality of life of Indo-Americans (from India, Bangladesh, and Pakistan). The researchers found considerable cultural and generational conflict between first-generation Indo-American parents and their second-generation, college-aged children. The greatest sources of intergenerational tension within the Indo-Asian families were the issues of dating and marital preferences of the younger generation. Traditional Indo-American parents believe that dating and marriage are family matters and are family decisions, while the more Americanized younger generation, especially women, want the freedom of individual choice.

Cultural conflicts between generations in Asian American families cannot be denied; however, traditional cultural practices and belief systems do have a significant place in the lives of Asian Americans. Journalist Katherine Kam reports on the traditional cultural rituals that were needed in the aftermath of the 1989 schoolyard shootings in Stockton, California. In that incident, a gunman opened fire on a playground filled with children during their recess break. Five children, ranging in age from six to nine, were shot and killed, while another thirty-one were wounded. Four of the slain children were Cambodian American and one was Vietnamese American. It quickly became apparent that the mainstream mental health professionals who had rushed to the scene after the shooting could offer little help to this predominantly Southeast Asian community. As a result, the school allowed a Buddhist monk to perform a purification ceremony and called on other religious leaders to pray for the dead children. Kam describes how culturally sensitive and culturally appropriate responses were necessary parts of the grieving process that these families had to undergo. Over the years the families and friends of the victims in the Stockton schoolyard tragedy have tried to cope as best they could. Sadly, the April 1999 shooting at Columbine High School in Littleton, Colorado, and the media attention given to it, brought back painful memories of a decade ago. (See Joan Ryan, "Colorado Horror Evokes Painful Memories of '89," in the *San Francisco Chronicle*, April 24, 1999.)

Reading 24

Chinese American Families

Evelyn Nakano Glenn with Stacey G. H. Yap

Today, when the academic achievements of Asian American "whiz kids" are widely touted in the popular media, it is easy to forget that for much of their history, Chinese Americans were among the most vilified minorities in the United States. In the late nineteenth and early twentieth centuries Chinese immigrants were depicted as backward, immoral, filthy, rat-eating, opium-crazed heathens (Dower 1986; Miller 1969; Saxton 1971). They constituted a "yellow peril," an unassimilable horde whose willingness to work long hours for low pay threatened the livelihood of white working men.

Public attitudes took a 180-degree turn in the post–civil rights era, as Chinese Americans, along with the Japanese and other Asian Americans, came to be proclaimed a "model minority." It was asserted that through sheer hard work, they had overcome racism and poverty to reach educational and income levels exceeding even those of European Americans. Seeking an explanation for the extraordinary "success" story, observers turned to the family and cultural values. Strong family ties, discipline and close control over children, and emphasis on collective solidarity over individual interest, made for children who were motivated, well behaved, and obedient in school (Sollenberger 1968; Tsai 1986:162). Many of these characteristics could be traced to traditional Chinese culture, in particular to Confucianism, with its emphasis on filial piety, respect for elders, and reverence for tradition.

The praise heaped on the Chinese American family, although seemingly beneficent, has less

Source: Ronald L. Taylor (ed.) *Minority Families in the United States*, 2d ed. (Upper Saddle River, NJ: Prentice Hall, 1998), pp. 128–158. Reprinted by permission.

benign implications. It tends to gloss over the long history of legal and political assaults on Chinese American family life: laws and policies that restricted immigration, economic activity, residence, political participation, and legal rights. It also shifts attention away from the economic and social difficulties that many immigrant families experience today, some of which are a legacy of past policies. The elevation of the Chinese American family also serves to deny the needs of other minority groups who are deemed less worthy. Thus, the supposed fortitude of Chinese American families is contrasted to the alleged "family disorganization" of blacks and Hispanics. The case of the Chinese, along with other Asian American groups, seems to support the argument that some groups have cultural resources that enable them to resist the demoralizing effects of poverty and discrimination. By implication, the lack of success of other groups can be attributed in some measure to weaknesses in their cultures. The Chinese family is held out as an object lesson to other minority groups that if they only emulated the Chinese, they too could pull themselves up by their bootstraps.

Social science treatments of the Chinese American family have shared the tendency to focus on supposedly unique aspects of Chinese American family structure and to rely on cultural explanations. In contrast to the weight given to economic and political constraints shaping black and Hispanic family life, social science research on Chinese families has interpreted characteristics of Chinese American families as expressions of traditional Chinese values and practices. This approach has grown out of the dominant assimilationist school of race relations. The assimilation model focuses on the initial cultural and social differences of the immigrant groups and attempts to trace the process of assimilation over time. In the case of family, studies have typically begun by examining traditional Chinese family patterns, then discussing how these patterns are expressed in a new setting and undergo gradual change through acculturation (for example, Haynor and Reynolds 1937; Hsu 1971; Kung 1962; Weiss 1974). The features identified as typical of Chinese American families and as evidence of cultural continuity are (1) stability, indicated by low rates of divorce and illegitimacy; (2) close ties between generations, shown in low rates of adolescent rebellion and delinquency; (3) economic self-sufficiency, demonstrated by avoidance of welfare and a propensity toward involvement in family businesses; (4) conservatism, expressed by retention of Chinese language and customs in the home (Glenn 1983); and (5) female subordination, shown in close controls over women and wives' responsibility for domestic work.

Each of these characteristics can be interpreted in terms of specific aspects of Chinese culture. For example, familism—the valuing of family over the individual—is credited for the rarity of divorce. Similarly, the principles of Confucianism, filial piety, respect for elders, and reverence for tradition are cited as the philosophical bases for absence of adolescent rebellion and retention of Chinese language and customs in the home. The family-based agricultural system is seen as the precedent for immigrants' involvement in family enterprise. Patrilineal inheritance, patrilocal residence, and ancestor worship are seen as elevating the status of men and devaluing that of women. Changes in the patterns over time are seen as evidence of acculturation. Thus, for example, changes in husband-wife relations are expected to become more egalitarian as Chinese Americans adopt dominant culture (that is, "American") norms.

A close examination of the history of Chinese American family life and of the dynamics within contemporary families, however, reveals the inadequacy of the cultural assimilationist model. The cultural approach emphasizes the uniqueness and homogeneity of Chinese American families. In actuality we find considerable diversity among classes and subgroups and variation in family structures in different historical periods. Further, we find evidence of similarities between Chinese American families and those of other oppressed minorities, groups subjected to similar constraints. Although the assimilation model emphasizes continuity and gradual, linear change, we find dramatic shifts in family organization correlated with alteration in external constraints.

The perspective that we adopt in this chapter starts at a different point, not with Chinese culture but with conditions Chinese Americans have confronted in the United States; of special note are legal and administrative practices governing immigration, labor market structures restricting economic mobility, and laws limiting political rights. Our focus is on the dialectic between institutional structures that constrain family formation and the efforts of individuals and households to carry out the production and reproduction needed to maintain themselves both on a daily basis and intergenerationally. Within this schema, culture is not an autonomous determinant, but a resource that individuals and households actively shape and mobilize for survival. In short, we recognize the interaction of social structure, culture, and human agency.

In line with recent Third World, feminist, and Marxist critiques of family sociology (see Glenn 1987), we challenge the view of the family as a bounded private sphere separate from "nonfamily." Indeed, it is precisely the interaction between larger political economic forces and family dynamics that needs to be understood. Also in line with these critiques, we reject the view of family as a monolithic entity with unitary interests. Although the family is bound together by economic interdependence and survival needs, it is also divided along gender and generational lines. The interests of husbands and wives, children and parents, are not the same; family members do not make equal contributions or gain equal benefits. Therefore, conflicts arise over division of labor and distribution of resources. Different family forms have different patterns of gender and generational relations. Looking at the Chinese American family in this way leads us to recognize areas of continuities and discontinuities with experiences of other oppressed racial groups. . . .

1850 TO 1920:
THE SPLIT-HOUSEHOLD FAMILY

During the first 70 years of Chinese presence in the United States, from 1850 to 1920, one can hardly talk about family life among the immigrants . . . the population was overwhelmingly composed of adult men with very few women and children. Between 1860 and 1910, the gender ratio fluctuated between 13 and 27 men for every woman. In 1900, the Chinese population consisted of less than 4 percent children 14 and under, compared with 37.4 percent of the U.S. population of whites of native parentage.

The first 30 years, from 1850 to 1882, was a period of relatively open immigration. An estimated 300,000 Chinese left Guangdong Province to work in California and the West. The vast majority were male laborers, about half of whom left wives behind (Coolidge 1909). Many were too poor to pay for their own passage and came on the credit ticket system, which obligated them to work for a term of 7 years to pay off the transport. These "birds of passage" intended to return after accumulating enough to acquire land and retire; in the meantime, they sent remittances to support relatives. At least two-thirds succeeded in returning, so that the population of Chinese never exceeded 110,000.

A small segment of the immigrants were merchants who were allowed to bring wives or concubines and children. Thus the few Chinese families in the United States were of the wealthier merchant class. We know little about what went on in the households, because outsiders rarely penetrated their walls. Women had bound feet and seldom ventured abroad (Haynor and Reynolds 1937). An observer of New York's Chinese quarters noted, " . . . especially is the wife thus carefully excluded from view, except to those of her own sex; and if she has occasion to visit another woman every precaution must be taken to avoid observation. Usually a closed carriage is employed to convey her, even though the distance be less than a block away." Another writer described the living quarters of merchants in San Francisco as modest: "Married people indulge in a little more room than the bachelor of the same class, but the furniture even of the merchant's family home is of the simplest, and more limited than at the store establishment save an extra plant or so. Indeed the wife is kept so secluded that all show may be dispensed with." (quoted in Lyman 1968:325)

At the other end of the scale of "respectability" was the only other sizable group of Chinese women, prostitutes (Goldman 1981; Hirata 1979). Most of these were "indentured" or "enslaved" women who had been lured, bought from impoverished parents, or kidnapped by Chinese procurers working for the tongs that controlled the trade. Once transported to the United States, the women were sold, forced to sign long-term contracts, and held in bondage in brothels in the Chinese quarters of San Francisco and other Western cities and in Western mining camps. According to Pascoe (1990), the severe shortage of women subjected them to severe exploitation but also presented them with some opportunities. Escaping from prostitution was difficult, because the tongs and individual pimps who reaped enormous profits from their exploitation relentlessly tracked down runaway women. Women who were unable to escape rarely lived out the 4- or 5-year terms of their contracts. Fortunate women were rescued by a lover or a missionary group or were redeemed by a wealthy client. Because of the shortage of women, they had a good chance of becoming respectable wives. Pascoe (1990) found records showing that the Presbyterian

Mission House in San Francisco arranged for several hundred marriages for rescued prostitutes in the peak years of operation between 1874 and 1928. The largest group of husbands came from the stratum of small merchants, just below the Chinatown elite, who came to form the "middle class" in Chinatown.

It seems likely that many Chinese laborers in America eventually would have sent for wives, as overseas Chinese did in Singapore and Hawaii (Glick 1980; Purcell 1965). Or they might have married native women, as their compatriots in the Philippines and Peru did (Hunt and Walker 1974; Wong 1978). Both these possibilities were precluded for Chinese men in the United States. An antimiscegenation statute in California forbade marriages between Chinese and other races, and in 1870 the Page Law, designed to curb the Chinese prostitution trade, was passed. The application process for Chinese women was made difficult and arduous, and female applicants were subjected to repeated questioning and badgering. Its effect, according to Pfeffer (1986), was to discourage and bar laborers' wives, resulting in a decline in the proportion of women among the immigrant population. Whereas the male population increased by 42,000, the female population grew by a mere 213 between 1870 and 1880. Passage of the Chinese Exclusion Act of 1882 cut off any possibility of wives of laborers entering.[1] Renewals of the act in 1892 and 1902 further restricted entry and return. Finally, all immigration from Asia was cut off by the 1924 Immigration Act. By that time the various restrictions had had their desired effect. The population of Chinese had dwindled from a high of 107,000 in 1890 to 61,000 by 1920. Chinese men left in this country confronted a stark choice. They could return to China to face the same economic hardships that drove them to migrate in the first place, or they could remain, condemned to eternal bachelorhood or to permanent separation from wives and children.

A small loophole remained: Relatives of U.S. citizens—Chinese born in the United States—were allowed entry. This group was small, but the 1906 earthquake and fire that destroyed most municipal records in San Francisco expanded the number of those who could make the claim without its being disprovable. After that event, Chinese residents could claim American birth, visit China, report the birth of a son, and thereby create an entry slot. Years later the slot could be used by a relative, or the papers could be sold to a young man wanting to immigrate. In such cases the "paper son" assumed the name and identity of the alleged son. These slots enabled many families to adopt sojourning as a long-term economic strategy. Successive generations of men were sent abroad as paper sons to work and remit money to support the kin group. In some Guangdong villages, remittances from overseas workers constituted the main source of income. It has been estimated that between 1937 and 1940 alone, overseas Chinese in the United States, Southeast Asia, and other overseas locations remitted $2 billion.

This sojourning strategy gave rise to a distinct family formation, the *split-household family* (Glenn 1983). In this arrangement, production or income earning was separated from the main household and carried out by a member living abroad, while reproduction—that is, maintaining the family home, socializing children, caring for the elderly, and infirm, maintaining family graves, and the like—was the responsibility of wives and other relatives in the home village. The family as an interdependent economic unit thus spanned two continents. This arrangement allowed maximum exploitation of the male worker. His labor could be bought cheaply because the cost of reproduction was borne by the labor of wives and other relatives in the home village.

Gender and Generational Relations.   The split household is perhaps the ultimate form of gender segregation, with husbands and wives leading completely separate lives. Men abroad lived in "bachelor" societies (Nee and Nee 1973). Employed as laborers or engaged in small business, they resided in rented rooms or shared quarters with other men. Lacking actual kin ties, they constructed fictive "families," district, dialect, and clan associations, the latter based on descent from a mythical ancestor (Lyman 1986). These associations provided security, sociability, and mutual aid. As is common in predominantly male communities, many sojourners found outlets in opium, gambling, and prostitutes. The irregular legal status of "paper sons" made them especially vulnerable to exploitation; fearful of exposure, they were forced to work long hours in shops, restaurants, and factories for low pay and to remain obedient to the associations that provided aid. Those frugal or lucky enough to save passage money returned periodically to China to visit and father more children. Others, either through ill fortune or personal problems such as gambling, never accumulated passage money and had to stay on year after year.

For women left behind, it was a period of massive social change and political upheavals, and they struggled to keep the family together against daunting odds. The ideal was for wives to reside with the husbands' kin group; the in-laws were responsible for safeguarding their chastity and keeping them under the ultimate control of their husbands. Yet a Chinese American sociologist who lived in villages inhabited chiefly by women, children, and older folks left behind by sojourners in the 1930s and 1970s reported that wives had a great deal of power and independence: "They had to make the daily decisions affecting the life of the family, and they learned how to handle money and deal with people outside the home. Naturally these women became extremely self-reliant." (Sung 1987:175)

Maxine Hong Kingston's stories of three women in her family illustrate the diverse fates of women left behind by husbands. The first, about a young unnamed aunt who became pregnant by another man, suggests that the community imposed heavy penalties on women who "strayed," even if she were the victim of rape. Another aunt was abandoned by her husband, who married another woman in America and never visited or sent for her, despite repeated pleas. Unlike some husbands who "disappeared,"

he at least continued to send remittances. Her own mother exercised considerable initiative during her father's absence. She attended a traditional Chinese medical college and became a village doctor to support herself and three children. Her father, a small laundry owner, sent for her after nearly 20 years abroad; the couple established a new family with several more children. Kingston's mother's story and Sung's observations remind us that assumptions about Chinese women's complete lack of self-determination need to be questioned. Many women displayed considerable resourcefulness to ensure their own and their children's survival.

Generational relations were inevitably affected by parental separation. The life story of Lao T-ai-t'ai, a Han woman who lived from 1867 to 1938, suggests that for Chinese women the uterine family—based on ties between mother, children, and grandchildren—rather than the patriarchal family was the emotional center of life (Pruitt 1967; see also Wolf 1972). With fathers gone, these ties became even more central; Sung (1987:175) reported, "Female influence in child-rearing was dominant. The children were surrounded by their mothers, aunts, grandmothers, and perhaps grandfathers returned from abroad." The mother-child tie, especially with the eldest son, normally an important source of leverage in the extended kin household, was further strengthened. In contrast, the father-child tie was weakened by prolonged absence. Because many years passed between visits, children were spaced far apart, and the father was often middle-aged or elderly when the youngest child was born. The age difference increased the formality and distance of the relationship.

1920 TO 1965: THE SMALL PRODUCER FAMILY

Despite obstacles to family formation, we start to see the growth of families in urban Chinatowns in the 1910s. The increase of women and children in the population reflects this growth. Between 1910 and 1930 the ratio of men to women fell from about 14:1 to 4:1, and the percent of children (14 and under) rose from 3.4 percent in 1900 to 20.4 percent by 1930. . . . Most of these early families were formed by small entrepreneurs, former laborers who had managed to accumulate sufficient capital to start a small laundry or shop, often in partnership with other men. They could then register as merchants and send for wives. Aside from sentimental reasons—a desire for companionship and affection—small entrepreneurs had sound economic motives for wanting families in America because women and children were a source of free labor. The intensive exploitation of family labor gave hand laundries and grocery stores the margin needed to make a profit.

The number of families took an even more dramatic leap in the 1930s, 1940s, and 1950s because of changes in immigration regulations. The 1924 immigration law was modified in 1930 to permit wives of merchants and women married to American citizens before 1924 to immigrate (Chinn and others 1969), and in recognition of its alliance with China in World War II, the U.S. government repealed the Chinese Exclusion Act in 1943 and created a token quota of 105 entrants a year. More openings were created by two other changes: "Bride's Act" of 1946, which permitted entry to wives and children of permanent residents (as well as citizens), and the Immigration Act of 1953, which gave preferential entry to relatives of citizens. The vast majority of those who entered under these two acts were women. They fell into two general categories: wives who had been separated from sojourning husbands, sometimes for decades, and brides of servicemen, citizens, and residents who had visited China and had a "hasty" marriage arranged (Lee 1956; for a novelistic treatment, see Chu 1979).

During this period, roughly 1920 to 1960, the typical immigrant and first-generation family operated as a unit of production, with husband, wife, and children engaged in work in the family business—a laundry, restaurant, or small store.

Members worked long hours for no wages. For convenience or lack of means, living quarters were often located above or behind the shop. Thus family and work life were fused. Production and reproduction were integrated and carried on simultaneously. Responsibilities for both were allocated along gender and generational lines. A woman who grew up in a family laundry in the 1930s and 1940s noted that the family's work day started at 7 A.M. and ended at midnight 6 days a week. Although the laundry was sent out for washing it was dried, sprinkled, starched, and ironed in the back room. Tasks were assigned by age and gender. Father did the difficult hand ironing of shirts, while mother operated the collar and cuff press, younger children folded laundry and made up parcels, and older children ironed handkerchiefs and underwear. At the same time, mother supervised their children's homework, related folk stories and legends, and prepared meals. Fathers admonished children and chatted with relatives. Older children entertained and supervised younger children (for popular accounts see Kingston 1976; Lowe 1943; Wong 1950).

Gender and Generational Relations. The small producer family was in many ways a continuation of the peasant family in China and similar to agrarian families engaged in family production around the world (see Young and Wilmott 1973). In sharp contrast to the complete separation of men and women in the split household, husband and wife were constantly together as partners. Husband and wife were mutually interdependent in that he needed her as much as she needed him. Another circumstance contributing to relative egalitarianism was the absence of in-laws. This freed wives from subordination to their husbands' parents. Many of the informants who grew up in a small producer family recalled their mothers as the disciplinarians and dominant figures in the household (Glenn 1983).

The interdependence did not mean that husband-wife relations were necessarily harmonious. Women who had rejoined their husbands or who were "hasty brides" suffered many adjustment problems. Many were appalled by the squalor of their living quarters and dismayed by having to work as hard as or harder than they had in China (Yung 1986:43). They often suffered from isolation because they spoke little English and had no friends or relatives for support and sympathy. This isolation often put them at a disadvantage in relation to husbands, who had resided in the United States for years. Long separation made even long-time mates strangers to each other. Brides who came over after arranged marriages scarcely knew their husbands. Relations were sometimes strained by age disparity. In many cases, men in their forties, who had worked in the United States for years before returning, married women in their teens or twenties.

Working long hours in cramped, damp, or overheated conditions took its toll on the health of family members, a burden felt especially by women, who were primarily responsible for the welfare of children. Tuberculosis and other diseases were rampant in Chinatown (Lee and others 1969). Although men typically worked hard, wives worked longer hours, first up to fix the morning meal and last to bed after cleaning up and preparing for the next day.

Despite the stresses, most marriages remained intact. The low divorce rate may reflect lack of choice. Spouses could not survive on their own, and there was no place for divorced women in the community. Some women believed that their only recourse was suicide. Sung (1967) found that the suicide rate among Chinese in San Francisco was four times that of the city as a whole and that victims were predominantly women.

Close parental control of children was fostered by living and working conditions. There was constant interaction, with parents speaking to children in Chinese and supervising them.[2] Language and cultural tradition were transmitted through this daily interaction. With so many individuals working in close quarters for extended periods of time, conflict had to be kept to a minimum. Discipline and cooperation were stressed, and self-expression was curbed. Children were expected to obey parents; older brothers and sisters helped discipline younger siblings, who were expected to defer to older siblings.

A circumstance limiting parental authority was the family's location in an "alien" culture. Arriving as adults, they rarely acquired more than a rudimentary knowledge of English. Children, once they reached school age, rapidly learned to speak and write English. They became cultural mediators and agents for the family. Children of 8 or 9 years accompanied their parents to the bank, read documents, translated notices in stores, and negotiated with customers. They could exercise considerable discretion in deciding what information to relay to their parents (see Tan 1989). Thus the normal pattern of dependence was reversed.

Among families in which the father was abroad for many years before sending for wife and children, the dominance of the mother-child tie often continued after reunification. Initially the father seemed a virtual stranger to the children, so mother continued to play the central role in child-rearing, education, and discipline. Although Sung calls this pattern matriarchal, it is probably more accurate to call it matrifocal (cf. Stack 1974). Women did not have economic power or authority, but they were the emotional centers of the household. Women were the keepers of family tradition, keeping track of ancestors' anniversaries, passing on family stories, and organizing activities for New Year's and other festival days. If we recall the importance of the uterine family to Chinese women, we see matrifocality not as a departure from the past but as an adaptation of established relationships.[3]

1965 TO THE PRESENT: DIVERSE CHINESE AMERICAN FAMILIES

The 1950s and 1960s were a period of growing heterogeneity among Chinese Americans along class and generational lines. Although there have

always been class divisions, particularly between
the merchants who controlled the large businesses
in Chinatown and workers employed in those
businesses, a number of factors contributed to
ethnic solidarity. Almost all immigrants prior the
1940s came from a few villages in Guangdong
Province and thus shared a common language and
culture. Despite many internal conflicts, forced
ghettoization and the hostility of the outside
world made for a degree of defensive cohesiveness. Most Chinatown residents depended in one
way or another on the tourist trade and had a
common interest in keeping down open conflict
(Light and Wong 1975). The tightly organized
community, made up of clan and other voluntary
organizations and headed by the Chinese Consolidated Benevolent Association, integrated men of
different social classes (Kuo 1982). Vertical ties
were strengthened at the expense of horizontal
ties between men in a similar class position. In
addition, color barriers prevented Chinese from
entering white-collar occupations and the skilled
crafts. Even those with educational and technical
credentials were often forced into small businesses or other forms of self-employment, like
their less educated compatriots. Ethnicity often
took precedence over class in determining one's
economic niche.

This situation changed during and after World
War II, as color barriers began to fall in the professions. Opportunities expanded further as a result of
the civil rights movement in the 1960s, and sizable
numbers of Chinese Americans were able to enter
occupations consistent with their education and
training. Increased social mobility of this educated
segment created a class division between better-
educated professionals and business owners
(middle class) and less educated manual workers
and petty entrepreneurs (working class).

A second factor contributing to diversity was
the entry of several different cohorts of immigrants after 1943. These new immigrants were
much more varied in background than earlier
immigrants. True, those who entered under the
1943 and 1946 Bride's Act and under the family

reunification provisions of the 1953 act came
from the same regions and class backgrounds as
the earlier immigrants. However, a significant
cohort of young professionals and students also
came in the 1940s and 1950s to study at American
universities. Thousands were stranded by the revolution and were allowed to stay on as refugees.[4]
Other migrated for economic reasons, entering as
students and applying for a change to permanent
resident status once they arrived.

The biggest change in immigration took place
with passage of the Immigration Act of 1965,
which scrapped the national-origin quotas and
made family reunification and the filling of
needed occupations the chief criteria for entry.
Each country was given a 20,000-person annual
limit, but spouses, parents, and children were
exempt from the quota. Under these provisions,
between 20,000 and 30,000 Chinese have entered
every year, primarily from Hong Kong (see Wong
1986). These post-1965 immigrants range from
working-class families who arrived with little
except what they carried to those with substantial
assets who were seeking a secure place to invest
their capital.

Linked to both occupational mobility and new
immigration is increased residential dispersion.
Some observers differentiate between suburban
and Chinatown-based Chinese families. This distinction correlates with generation, class, and
recency of immigration. Working-class immigrants often settle initially in or near urban Chinatowns to get acclimated; they can get by speaking
only Chinese and can find ready-made contacts to
get jobs. After establishing themselves, they may
move out into other areas of the city or to the
suburbs, often to areas already settled by Chinese,
forming satellite Chinatowns. More affluent
immigrants often go immediately to locations
outside of Chinatown and can afford to purchase a
home. Professionals, whether immigrants or
American-born, are more likely to live in predominantly white suburbs. These choices have implications for whether Chinese culture and identity
are maintained in the next generation.

These divisions have given rise to numerous subtypes of families, of which four are fairly sizable.

Old Immigrant Families. These are an aging segment of the small producer families, formerly split households who are now united and residing together in the United States. The fathers immigrated before 1965, starting out as sojourners, but were able to send for family members under the war bride, refugee, or family reunification laws mentioned earlier. They often started as laborers but now own a business. These families are Chinatown connected, coming from the same areas around Canton as the late-nineteenth-century founders of Chinatown and speaking the same Toysan dialect. Wong (1985) describes the old immigrant family as traditional in outlook, retaining Chinese notions of a gender and age hierarchy of authority, filial piety, and collectivity. Although only recently formed as a family group, their roots in the United States often go back a century or more. In families in which sojourning was a long-term family strategy, several generations of men in the same family immigrated and passed on a family business from generation to generation. In one family history recounted to Glenn by a 21-year-old college student the great-grandfather arrived as a paper son in the 1890s, worked for 20 years, and sent for his son, the student's grandfather. Grandfather helped great-grandfather run a small business. Great-grandfather later returned to China, leaving grandfather to carry on the business and forward remittances. In the 1940s, grandfather sent for father. Up to that point none of the wives had left China; then, in the late 1950s, father returned to China and brought back his wife. Finally, after nearly 70 years, the first birth of a child on American soil took place. The student was only a first-generation American even though four generations of her family had been in the United States.

Professional Immigrant Families. These consist of an older segment, who arrived as students in the 1940s and 1950s, and a younger segment, who entered after the Immigration Act of 1965. The lowering of discriminatory barriers mentioned earlier speeded the integration of professional immigrants. These immigrants differed not only in education, but also in linguistic and regional background from earlier immigrants. They came from urban backgrounds, were educated in Hong Kong, mainland China, or Taiwan, and are Mandarin-speaking, in contrast to the Cantonese-origin, Toysanese-speaking resident Chinese population. These differences increased the social gulf between scholar-professionals and Chinatown-based Chinese.

The scholar-professional immigrants live in white middle-class neighborhoods in the city or in white suburbs and are employed in mainstream institutions. Although their work and neighborhood contacts are primarily with European Americans, they may socialize with other Chinese of similar backgrounds. A survey of Chinese professionals in California found that 70 percent of the respondents spent either an equal amount of time with Chinese and non-Chinese or more time with non-Chinese.

Wong (1985) describes this group as considerably westernized even before immigrating; having come from major cities, they had adopted Western clothing, recreation, eating, and living habits. Clausen and Bermingham (1982) found that a high percentage of professional immigrants in California had grown up in homes where members spoke Western languages, principally English, and that they themselves had been guests in Western homes and had part of their education in Western-style schools. Some are Christian converts, who are especially likely to subscribe to Western cultural practices, such as free marriage and the primacy of the husband-wife tie.

Households are generally nuclear in form. However, some professional immigrants have taken advantage of the opening up of relations between the United States and China to sponsor parents' immigration. Thus some extended families have been reconstituted. Wives usually also have college or postgraduate degrees, and many are employed in professional, managerial, and administrative support occupations and may also manage their own investments. Our impression from interviewing Chinese professional women for a study of high-tech industries is that when both husband and wife are professionals, they have a sense of economic partnership between them and therefore relative equality. Parents are concerned about their children's education, and they have the resources to provide them the experiences they need to succeed, from music lessons to summer jobs in business. A professional immigrant woman employed as a high-level manager in a high-tech firm told Glenn that she and her husband bought a small resort in the mountains and put their teen-aged sons in charge to give them the opportunity to run a business.

Because of the sojourning strategy adopted by Chinese in response to racist immigration policies, the growth of *American-born Chinese families* was retarded. Despite their continuous presence in the United States, the Chinese American population remained largely "foreign-born" for almost 100 years. Most immigrant groups shift over time to English as a first language and lose traditional cultural practices. The Chinese were often viewed as unassimilable because they retained their language and customs decade after decade. What was not apparent to many people is that the resident population was constantly being replaced by new immigrants. Thus it was not until 1940 that the majority of Chinese were American born; by 1960, more than 60 percent of the Chinese in this country were born here. It seemed that the Chinese were at long last becoming assimilated. The huge influx of immigrants after 1965 dramatically changed the balance once again, and by 1980, 63.3 percent of the Chinese population were foreign born. Thus American-born families, although a sizable segment, have once again become the minority Because of the many different cohorts of immigration, American-born Chinese are quite heterogeneous, ranging from fourth- or fifth-generation descendants of nine-

teenth-century pioneers to fifth-generation children of postwar immigrants. This segment tends to be college educated, and with the fall of discriminatory barriers, they can find white collar jobs outside the ethnic enclave. In 1980, fully 38.8 percent of all American-born men 15 and over were employed as professionals and managers and another 29.7 percent as technical, sales, and administrative support employees (U.S. Bureau of the Census 1988).

Many were born in Chinatown, but they aspire to better living conditions outside of Chinatown. This move represents a shift in economic orientation from immigrant parents. Immigrants were concerned with minimizing current spending in order to save money to invest in business or real estate, to send children to China for education, or to save for the future. They were willing to put up with cramped and substandard housing to save on rent. American-born Chinese are less willing to sacrifice present comfort for the future; perhaps they also feel more secure about the future. In any case, Wong (1985) notes that this group seems to spend more on household goods and other consumer items, even buying on credit. They seek housing that is consistent with their occupational status and income. They often end up in predominantly white neighborhoods and suburbs where, they perceive, schools will be better for their children. Pioneer families who moved into predominantly white areas in the 1960s sometimes encountered prejudice. One mother recalls that her family was the first Asian family to move into a suburban town near Boston. Her children were harassed and called names at school, so she made a special effort to be a good citizen. She got involved in the PTA, scouting, and other community activities to ease her children's acceptance. Her account accords with Wong's observation in New York that American-born Chinese parents tend to participate in organizations such as the PTA. Their participation is eased by their facility in English. The lack of participation by other immigrant parents does not mean that they are less concerned about their children's schooling, but they feel that school policy is the teachers' and administrators' responsibility.

Gender and Generational Relations. Wives have high rates of labor force participation, either as professionals or white collar workers. Almost one third (31.7 percent) of American-born Chinese women are professionals or managers, and 53.1 percent are technical, sales, or administrative support workers (U.S. Bureau of the Census 1988). Husband and wife are thus coequal breadwinners. One observer claims that gender and generational relations are "American," that is, egalitarian, with husband and wife sharing housework and child care and children being allowed to make their own decisions. However, no systematic study has been done of the actual division of labor.

Although children socialize with non-Chinese peers and thus grow up with attenuated ties to other Chinese, parents still make frequent visits to Chinatown to shop and eat. Parents vary in the degree of concern with maintaining cultural tradition, although American-born Chinese usually do not speak Chinese at home. Parents may try to get their children interested in Chinese culture, even sending them to language school. Children rarely learn the language and are more interested in fitting in with their peers. However, when they reach college, some American-born Chinese experience an "identity crisis." They may go through a search for their ethnic roots by taking courses in Asian American history, getting involved in Asian American social life, or joining political organizations aimed at helping the poor and elderly in Chinatown.

Countering the trend toward "assimilation" among immigrant and American-born professionals has been the huge influx of *new working-class immigrant families* since 1965. About half of the post-1965 immigrants can be classified as working class, having been employed as service workers, operatives, craftsmen, or laborers in Hong Kong. Of those classified as professional or managerial at entry, a significant portion experienced downward mobility into blue collar and service occupations because of language difficulties or nonacceptance of foreign credentials.

This group consists primarily of families, either immigrating as a nuclear family group or in a relay fashion, with one member immigrating first and sending for the others. A common motive for immigration is the parents' desire to ensure greater educational and economic opportunities for their children. Because of the preference given to relatives under the 1965 act, most immigrants use kinship ties with previous immigrants to gain entry. They in turn sponsor other kin, so that over time an extended kin network is reassembled. Equal weight is given to husband's and wife's ties under this law, thereby negating the traditional emphasis on male lineage. Thus, for example, a couple might be sponsored by the wife's sister. The couple in turn might sponsor the husband's mother, who later sponsors another of her children, and so on in a chain of relations on both sides. Over time an extended family group is reconstituted. Typically, they do not all reside in one household, although several related households may be involved in a family business, such as a restaurant or garment factory (Wong 1985).

For new arrivals, Chinatown is often the first stopping place. Having given up property, businesses, or jobs and having exhausted their resources or even gone into debt to pay for transportation and settlement, working-class immigrants must quickly find a way to make a living. Those who arrive with capital have some choices—they can take time to learn English and perhaps get some job training or buy a small business. For those without resources, language problems and discrimination in construction and craft trades limit options. The most common strategy is for husband and wife to find employment in the secondary labor market, the labor-intensive, low-capital service and small manufacturing sectors. A typical constellation is a husband employed as a waiter, cook, janitor. or store helper, and a wife employed as a stitcher in a garment shop. Although each individual's wages are low, the pooled income is enough to support the family at a modest level. Full-time employment is a new experience for women. Although many were employed in Hong Kong, they usually did so part-time or engaged in piecework at home, sewing garments or assembling plastic flowers. In the United States, they must learn to juggle a full-time job outside the home with housework and child care.

In the dual-earner working-class household, production and reproduction are completely segregated. In contrast to the round-the-clock togetherness of the small producer household, family members spend most of the day apart. Parents' lives are regulated by the demands of the job, whereas children's lives outside of school hours are relatively unstructured, usually in the company of peers whose parents also work. Children see mothers more than fathers, mostly because many mothers take children to the factory with them, have their school-age children come to their work place after school, or go home to cook the evening meal before returning for an evening shift (Chao 1977; Ikels and Shang 1979; Sung 1987). Still, a study by Betty Sung showed that 17 percent of Chinese high school students in New York did not see their mother once during the week. Even less contact occurs between father and children. If they are employed in a restaurant, fathers' hours often prevent them from seeing children at all. The most common shift for restaurant workers is 2:00 in the afternoon until 11:00 or 12:00 at night. Thirty-two percent of the students in Sung's survey did not see their fathers at all during a typical day. This finding accords with student informants in Boston, who reported that they saw their father only on his days off.

Husbands' and wives' responsibilities for production and reproduction tend to be symmetrical: Both are responsible for breadwinning. Because it is in the form of wages, women's contribution is highly visible. This contribution constitutes a larger portion of family income than in Hong Kong because of the downward shift of the husband's occupational status. A college student

who immigrated with her parents as a young teenager reported that after immigration, relations between her parents were much more equal. The father started helping with housework, and the mother had more say in decision-making.

With two working parents, ties between generations break down. Children complain about the parents' long hours away from home and fatigue when at home. Lack of common experiences leaves little for them to talk about. One young student noted, "We can discuss things, but we don't talk that much. We don't have that much to say." In addition many parents underwent traumatic experiences from World War II, the Chinese Revolution, or uprooting to Hong Kong that they refuse to discuss. Taboos against certain topics become a barrier to intimacy. Parents in turn complain that they have lost control over their children. They attribute their loss of authority to their children's becoming too Americanized. Because parents are not around much to speak to them in Chinese, the children often lose their ability or willingness to speak Chinese. An immigrant mother lamented,

> Because the family budget is too great, the parents usually have to work and leave the children at home with no one to care for them. That's why our children pick up bad social habits and become Westernized to the point that their own culture gets washed away. Their faces are Chinese but their action and language are all western. How could our children not learn to be bad? (Chinese American Workers: Past and Present 1980:55)

When they reach adolescence, children can find a part-time job, which gives them independence. The absence of close-knit family life among these new immigrants has been blamed for the eruption of youth rebellion, delinquency, and gang violence in Chinatowns during the 1960s and 1970s (Fong 1968; Lyman 1970; Sheu 1986). In addition, adolescents made up a larger proportion of the new immigrants than in previous cohorts; they encounter difficulties in school because of language, and when they leave school, they face unemployment or a low-wage job. Similar difficulties were experienced by earlier immigrants, but they may seem less tolerable in an era when expectations are higher and there is more resentment of institutional racism. . . .

CONCLUSIONS: REVISIONING THE CHINESE AMERICAN FAMILY

As changes go on in Chinese American families, we need to begin reformulating our approaches to studying the Chinese American family. Just as family sociology itself has been subject to critical revision, so must the sociology of the Chinese American family be rethought.

First, we need to give a more central place to women's experiences in the family. Until recently Chinese and Chinese American women have been largely invisible; where they appeared, they did so in stereotyped, one-dimensional guises. Recent feminist scholarship on the situation of Chinese peasant women suggests that women were not simply passive victims of a patriarchal family system. Although showing that indeed women were oppressed, these studies also reveal that women actively struggled and sometimes resisted victimization. They fought to preserve ties with children and grandchildren and to keep this uterine group together. Women also cooperated across households and sometimes gained considerable power and influence. In the United States, Chinese American women have played active roles in maintaining culture by transmitting folk legends and family histories to children. Ties between women, especially mothers and daughters, are the bonds that hold the family together. And they continue to maintain contact with far-flung family members, to observe traditional celebrations, and to keep track of family news. They were and are the "kin-keepers." As they moved out into the community, they became vital links between the family and schools and ethnic organizations.

Women are active in the community, in part because they see this as an extension of their responsibilities as mothers (Yap 1989). They were active in political movements to support China during World War II and in support of the revolution in the 1930s (Yung 1990); today their daughters are active in organizing garment workers and fighting violence against Asian Americans.[5]

Second, just as study of black families has led to questioning the nuclear household as the "normal" mode of family, the study of Chinese American families leads us to question the universality of the nuclear family. In the earlier period, we saw in the split-household forms that income pooling and reproduction may occur between individuals separated by an ocean. In the current period, among new immigrants, domestic sharing and production may involve several related households. Even though extended kin do not reside together, they may cooperate in running a common family business. They may also live nearby, pool income, and share certain domestic functions, such as meals.

Third, we need to overcome the tendency to see the family either as a passive product of outside forces or as an autonomous, self-contained unit operating according to different principles from the "outside" world. To understand the Chinese American family, we must recognize the impacts of racism and economic structure on family formation and intrafamily relations. We must simultaneously recognize the assaults that have been perpetrated on Chinese families by racist immigration policy, a race segregated labor system, and legal and political restrictions on mobility and the active struggle on the part of the Chinese to build family life despite the assaults. The Chinese American family has been a "culture of resistance." (Caulfield 1974)

Fourth, we need to recognize the family not as a monolithic entity with singular interests, but as a differentiated institution. Careful reading of descriptions and personal accounts reveals considerable conflict between generations and between men and women. Power is not equally distributed and shapes relationships among members. Each member has a different position in the division of labor. Therefore, each has a unique point of view. Multiple points of view have been better addressed by fictional sources than by social scientists; for example, Amy Tan's novel, *[The] Joy Luck Club*, has alternate chapters written from the point of view of daughters and mothers. Much more systematic study is needed of the gender and generational "politics" within the household. Systematic studies of gender politics and generational relations in Chinese American families need to replace impressionistic generalizations.

Finally, we need to develop a concept of Chinese and Chinese American culture as dynamic. Like culture in general, Chinese American culture is not static but is constantly being created. The Chinese culture that recent immigrants bring is not the same as the Chinese culture that nineteenth-century immigrants brought. The interaction and mixing of these influences and varying political, legal, and social conditions of life in the United States have created a rich and diverse Chinese American culture. The family is the crucible within which culture is created, maintained, and passed on.

NOTES

1. This act specifically excluded laborers and their relatives, although it exempted officials, students, tourists, merchants, relatives of merchants, and citizens.

2. A social worker in Boston's Chinatown claimed that children of laundry owners tended to do better in school than children of wage workers because of the constant parental supervision.

3. It is interesting that the literature for the most part focuses on the father-son tie and secondarily on the husband-wife and mother-son ties. The mother-daughter tie has been ignored. Yet, judging from two important literary treatments and a film, the mother-daughter dynamic is emotionally charged. Identification with and differentiation from the other are central to the Chinese American daughter's identity formation, and getting daughter married and perhaps established in

a career is seen as crucial to mother's identity (cf. Kingston 1976; Tan 1989). Kingston has said in a talk that she began writing at an early age as a way of making private space for herself in a household where her mother constantly intruded upon and took up most of the psychic space.

4. Many of them, along with visitors and seamen, were stranded by the Chinese Revolution and given permanent resident status by the Displaced Persons Act of 1948. Others were allowed to stay under the Refugee Relief Act of 1953 and a presidential directive in 1962 that permitted refugees from mainland China to enter via Hong Kong (Wong 1988).

5. The neglect of women is being redressed in literary accounts. Whereas memoirs and novels before 1950 (for example, Chu 1979, orig. 1961; Lowe 1943; Wong 1950) focus on the father as the central authority figure and influence, memoirs and novels of the 1970s and 1980s focus on mothers as emotional centers and on the ambivalence of mother-daughter relations (for example, Kingston 1976; Tan 1989).

REFERENCES

Caulfield, Minna D. 1974. "Imperialism, the Family and Cultures of Resistance." *Socialist Revolution* 20:67–85.

Chao, Rose, 1977. *Chinese Immigrant Children*. New York: Department of Asian Studies, The City College, City University of New York.

Chinese American Workers. 1980. *Chinese American Workers: Past and Present—An Anthology of Getting Together*. New York.

Chinn, Thomas, H. Mark Lai, and Philip Choy. 1969. *A History of the Chinese in California: A Syllabus*. San Francisco: Chinese Historical Society of America.

Chu, Louis. 1979. *Eat a Bowl of Tea*. Seattle: University of Washington Press (orig. 1961).

Clausen, Edwin G., and Jack Bermingham. 1982. *Chinese and African Professionals in California: A Case Study of Equality and Opportunity in the United States*. Washington, DC: University Press of America.

Coolidge, Mary. 1909. *Chinese Immigration*. New York: Henry Holt.

Dower, John W. 1986. *War Without Mercy: Race and Power in the Pacific War*. New York: Pantheon.

Fong, Stanley L. M. 1968. "Identity Conflict of Chinese Adolescents in San Francisco." In *Minority*

Group Adolescents in the United States, edited by Eugene B. Brody, 111–132. Baltimore: Williams and Wilkins.

Glenn, Evelyn Nakano. 1983. "Split Household, Small Producer and Dual Wage Earner: An Analysis of Chinese-American Family Strategies." *Journal of Marriage and the Family* 45:35–46.

———. 1987. "Gender and the Family." In *Analyzing Gender*, edited by Beth Hess and Myra Marx, 348–380. Newbury Park, CA: Sage.

Glick, Charles E. 1980. *Sojourners and Settlers: Chinese Migrants in Hawaii*. Honolulu: University Press of Hawaii.

Goldman, Miriam. 1981. *Golddiggers and Silverminers*. Ann Arbor: University of Michigan Press.

Haynor, Norman S., and Charles N. Reynolds. 1937. "Chinese Family Life in America." *American Sociological Review* 2:630–637.

Hirata, Lucie Cheng. 1979. "Free, Indentured and Enslaved: Chinese Prostitutes in Nineteenth Century America." *Signs* 5:3–29.

Hsu, Francis L. K. 1971. *The Challenge of the American Dream: The Chinese in the United States*. Belmont, CA: Wadsworth.

Hunt, C. I., and L. Walker. 1974. "Marginal Trading Peoples: Chinese in the Philippines and Indians in Kenya." In *Ethnic Dynamics: Patterns of Intergroup Relations in Various Societies*, ch. 4. Homewood, IL: Dorsey Press.

Ikels, Charlotte, and Julia Shang. 1979. *The Chinese of Greater Boston*. Interim Report to the National Institute of Aging.

Kingston, Maxine Hong. *1976. The Woman Warrior: Memoirs of a Girlhood among Ghosts*. New York: Knopf.

Kung, Shien-woo. 1962. *Chinese in American Life: Some Aspects of Their History, Status, Problems, and Contributions*. Seattle: University of Washington Press.

Kuo, Chia-ling. 1982. *Social and Political Change in New York's Chinatown: The Role of Voluntary Associations*. New York: Praeger.

Lee, L. P., A. Lim, and H. K. Wong. 1969. *Report of the San Francisco Chinese Community Citizen's Survey and Fact Finding Committee* (abridged ed.). San Francisco: Chinese Community Citizen's Survey and Fact Finding Committee.

Lee, Rose Hum. 1956. "The Recent Immigrant Chinese Families of the San Francisco–Oakland Area." *Marriage and Family Living* 18 (February): 14–24.

Light, Ivan, and Charles Choy Wong. 1975. "Protest or Work: Dilemmas of the Tourist Industry in American Chinatowns." *American Journal of Sociology* 80:1342–1368.

Lowe, Pardee. 1943. *Father and Glorious Descendent*. Boston: Little, Brown.

Lyman, Stanford. 1968. "Marriage and the Family among Chinese Immigrants to America, 1850–1960." *Phylon* 29(4):321–330.

———. 1970. "Red Guard on Grant Avenue: The Rise of Youthful Rebellion in Chinatown." In *The Asian in the West*, 99–118. Santa Barbara, CA: ABC Clio Press.

———. 1986. *Chinatown and Little Tokyo: Power, Conflict and Community among Chinese and Japanese Immigrants in America*. Millwood, NY: Associated Faculty Press.

Miller, Stuart Creighton. 1969. *The Unwelcome Immigrant: The American Image of the Chinese, 1785–1882*. Berkeley: University of California Press.

Nee, Victor G., and Brett Nee. 1973. *Longtime Californ'*. Boston: Houghton Mifflin.

Pascoe, Peggy. 1990. "Gender Systems in Conflict: The Marriages of Mission-educated Chinese American Women, 1874–1939." In *Unequal Sisters*, edited by Ellen Carol DuBois and Vicki L. Ruiz, 123–140. New York: Routledge.

Pfeffer, George A. 1986. "Forbidden Families: Emigration Experiences of Chinese Women under the Page Law, 1875–1882." *Journal of American Ethnic History* 6(2):28–46.

Pruitt, Ida. 1967. *Daughter of Han: The Autobiography of a Chinese Working Woman*. Stanford, CA: Stanford University Press.

Purcell, Victor. 1965. *The Chinese in Southeast Asia*. London: Oxford University Press.

Saxton, Alexander. 1971. *The Indispensable Enemy: Labor and the Anti-Chinese Movement*. Berkeley: University of California Press.

Sheu, Chuen-Jim. 1986. *Delinquency and Identity: Juvenile Delinquency in an American Chinatown*. New York: Harrow and Heston.

Sollenberger, Richard T. 1968. "Chinese American Child-rearing Practices and Juvenile Delinquency. *Journal of Social Psychology* 74(February):13–23.

Stack, Carol. 1974. *All Our Kin: Strategies for Survival in a Black Community.* New York: Harper and Row.

Sung, Betty Lee. 1967. *Mountain of Gold.* New York: MacMillan

———. 1987. *The Adjustment Experience of Chinese Immigrant Children in New York City.* New York: Center for Migration Studies.

———. 1990. *Chinese American Intermarriage.* New York: Center for Migration Studies.

Tan, Amy. 1989. *The Joy Luck Club.* New York: Putnam.

Tsai, Shih-Shan Henry. 1986. *The Chinese Experience in America.* Bloomington: Indiana University Press.

U.S. Bureau of the Census. 1988. *Census of the Population: 1980.* Vol. 2. *Subject Reports. Asian and Pacific Islander Population of the United States: 1980.* PC80-2-1E.

Weiss, Melford. 1974. *Valley City: A Chinese Community in America.* Cambridge, MA: Schenkman.

Wolf, Margery. 1972. *Women and the Family in Rural Taiwan.* Stanford: Stanford University Press.

Wong, Bernard. 1978. A Comparative Study of the Assimilation of the Chinese in New York City and Lima, Peru. *Comparative Studies in Society and History* 20:335–358.

———. 1985. "Family, Kinship and Ethnic Identity of the Chinese in New York City, with Comparative Remarks on the Chinese in Lima, Peru and Manila, Philippines." *Journal of Comparative Family Studies* 16:231–254.

Wong, Jade Snow. 1950. *Fifth Chinese Daughter.* New York: Harper and Brothers.

Wong, Morrison G. 1986. "Post-1965 Asian Immigrants: Where Do They Come From, Where Are They Now, and Where Are They Going?" *Annals of the American Academy of Political and Social Sciences* 487 (September):150–168.

———. 1988. "The Chinese American Family." In *Ethnic Families in America,* edited by Charles H. Mindel, Robert W. Habenstein, and Roosevelt Wright. Jr., 230–258. New York: Elsevier.

Yap, Stacey G. H. 1989. *Gather Your Strength, Sisters: The Emerging Role of Chinese Women Community Workers.* New York: AMS Press.

Young, Michael, and Peter Wilmott. 1973. *The Symmetrical Family.* London: Routledge and Kegan.

Yung, Judy. 1986. *Chinese Women of America: A Pictorial History.* Seattle: University of Washington Press.

Vietnamese Families

Nazli Kibria

With the settlement of about 0.5 million refugees from 1975 to 1985, Vietnamese Americans became one of the largest Asian-origin populations in the United States.[1] In 1985, they were estimated to be the fourth largest Asian American group, following those tracing their origins to China (1,079,400), the Philippines (1,051,600), and Japan (766,300) (Gardner and others 1985). Given current growth rates, in the future the Vietnamese are expected to be a significant presence, particularly in California and Texas.[2] This chapter provides a descriptive overview of the family life of Vietnamese immigrants in the United States, paying particular attention to the effects of the migration process on Vietnamese American family patterns. Data from historical and demographic studies of Vietnamese refugee families are supplemented with materials from an ethnographic study, based on in-depth interviews and participant-observation of Vietnamese refugees in Philadelphia during the mid-1980s (Kibria 1993).

The chapter begins with a brief description of the historical context of Vietnamese settlement in the United States. This is followed by a discussion of the key demographic characteristics of the Vietnamese American population, such as its age and gender composition and rates of marriage, divorce, and childbearing. The next sections of the chapter deal with family and household structures and the dynamics of family roles and authority.

THE VIETNAMESE EXODUS

The exodus of refugees out of Vietnam, which began in 1975 and continues to the present day, is a process that has deep and complex roots in the contemporary history of Vietnam, including the military, political, and economic involvement of the United States with South Vietnam. Vietnam was colonized by France in 1883. The French presence in Vietnam continued until 1954, when the country was partitioned across the middle into the "North" and "South." South Vietnam became closely allied with the West, particularly with the United States, which was interested in supporting the South Vietnamese government's efforts to defeat the Communist regime that had been established in the North. The U.S. military, political, and economic involvement in South Vietnam escalated during the 1960s as the conflict between the two Vietnamese regimes grew in scope. The long war ended in 1975, soon after the military withdrawal of the United States from Vietnam, when Northern forces gained control of the South and the country was reunited under Communist rule. Shortly before the fall of Saigon to Communist rule, about 130,000 Vietnamese were flown into the United States as part of an evacuation effort designed to aid South Vietnamese employees and associates of the U.S. government. Often referred to as the "first-wave" refugees, the 1975 arrivals tended to be from the elite strata of South Vietnamese society, with high levels of education and occupational attainment (Baker and North 1984).

Largely unanticipated by the U.S. government was the continuing flow of refugees out of Vietnam after the 1975 evacuation. These later waves of Vietnamese refugees were driven to leave the homeland by the political and eco-

Source: Ronald L. Taylor (ed.) *Minority Families in the United States*, 2d ed. (Upper Saddle River, NJ: Prentice Hall, 1998), pp. 176–188. Reprinted by permission.

nomic policies of the Communist government. Many had been persecuted by the new government because of association with the former South Vietnamese government. For example, some were sent to the "'reeducation camps" set up by the new government to indoctrinate and punish those associated with the former regime. Those South Vietnamese who had drawn on the urban business and service sectors for their livelihood were also affected by the new government's economic policies, particularly the efforts to nationalize businesses. These policies particularly impacted the Chinese minority in Vietnam a group that had been prominent in commerce and trading activities. In the late 1970s, the Chinese were also subject to discriminatory policies such as reduced food rations and the forced closure of Chinese-language newspapers and schools. As a result, during the 1978 to 1979 period, the Chinese Vietnamese accounted for about 70 percent of the "'boat people" leaving Vietnam (Wain 1981). Another factor that spurred the outflow of people from Vietnam was the compulsory military draft imposed by the Vietnamese government in the late 1970s in order to cope with ongoing military conflicts in the region. Motivated by a desire to escape compulsory military service. young men have constituted a large portion of Vietnamese arrivals to the United States.

As a group, post-1975 Vietnamese refugees differ from the 1975 evacuees in a number of ways. Unlike the 1975 evacuees, these later arrivals (often referred to as "boat people") have left Vietnam via covert boat journeys, taking them to nearby asylum countries such as Thailand, Malaysia, and Hong Kong. In the refugee camps that have been set up by those countries they have waited for resettlement decisions, for periods of time ranging from six months to more than two years. The major countries of Vietnamese resettlement have included Australia, Canada, China, and the United States. In order to cope with the growing number of refugees from Vietnam (as well as Cambodia and Laos), in 1980 the U.S.

government instituted the Refugee Act, which specified a set of formal guidelines for the entry, resettlement, and assistance of refugees.

This brief discussion of the history of Vietnamese migration to the United States provides some background for understanding the characteristics of Vietnamese family life in the United States. As suggested by the discussion, Vietnamese refugees are a diverse group. There are, for example, significant differences in the socioeconomic background of the 1975 "wave" and the later arrivals. Whereas many of the "first-wave" Vietnamese held white-collar or high-level military jobs in Vietnam, a large proportion of those who have arrived since 1977 occupied blue-collar or sales/service positions. Levels of educational attainment and English language proficiency have also been lower for the later arrivals (Rumbaut 1989; Strand and Jones 1985). Furthermore, the Vietnamese refugees include the Chinese Vietnamese, a group that has in many ways a cultural identity and experience distinct from those of the ethnic Vietnamese. In Vietnam, many Chinese had maintained a distinct identity from Vietnamese by living in enclaves and maintaining their own schools and newspapers. We can expect these differences in social class and ethnic background to enter into the family patterns of Vietnamese Americans in important ways.

Besides the diversity of the Vietnamese American population, what is also relevant to understanding the group's family patterns is the fact that migration from Vietnam has by necessity been a selective process. The costly, secretive, and hazardous nature of the boat journeys out of Vietnam has meant that it has not usually been possible for entire family units to migrate. The process of resettlement from refugee camps has also contributed to family disruption, given the greater favor with which resettlement officials view smaller family units (Haines 1988). In short, the disruption of family structure and relations due to the migration process is an important dimension of the Vietnamese American family experience.

DEMOGRAPHIC TRENDS

Age and Gender Composition

Both the age and gender compositions of the Vietnamese American population have some unusual qualities. The Vietnamese American population is extremely young, reflecting both the greater proclivity of young persons to undertake the difficult journey out of Vietnam and the high rates of fertility among the group. Data from a longitudinal study of Southeast Asian refugees in San Diego County show that for the 93 Vietnamese households surveyed in 1983, children under 18 years of age comprised 44 percent of the total household members. In 1984, for the same group of households, the percentage of children (42.4 percent) had changed little (Rumbaut 1989). The Office of Refugee Resettlement (1985:10) reports that in 1984, the median age of all Vietnamese arrivals was 20 years.

Some evidence suggests that the age composition of the 1975 Vietnamese arrivals is somewhat less skewed toward the younger ages, reflecting perhaps the lower rates of fertility within this group.[3] Nonetheless, the 1980 census, which surveyed mainly 1975 arrivals, found a median age of 21.5 years for the Vietnamese compared with 30 years for the general U.S. population (Gardner and others 1985). This suggests that despite some internal variations, children and young adults comprise a large proportion of the Vietnamese American population.

A predominance in the number of men over women is another important characteristic of the Vietnamese American population. In 1975, males composed 49 percent of the general U.S. population. In comparison, 55 percent of the "first-wave" Vietnamese settlers to the U.S. were men. The proportion of Vietnamese men to women climbed to 58.4 percent among 1982 arrivals, reflecting in part the efforts of young Vietnamese men to escape the compulsory military draft (Baker and North 1984:25). From the study in San Diego, Rumbaut (1989) reported a

gender ratio of 120 males to 100 females for the Vietnamese. Evidence also suggests that the gender ratio is particularly skewed for Vietnamese Americans aged 12 to 24 years. For example, the Office of Refugee Resettlement (1985) reported that among the Vietnamese who entered the United States in 1984, men outnumbered women by more than two to one in the 12 to 24 year age group.

The male-dominated gender ratio of the Vietnamese American population raises some interesting questions. The "shortage" of Vietnamese women suggests that significant numbers of men in the group may either remain single, postpone marriage, or marry across ethnic boundaries. Each of these possibilities has important implications for the shape of Vietnamese American family life and ethnicity in the future. The male-dominated gender ratio may also affect the organization and ideology of gender roles and relations in the group (for a discussion of the effects of gender ratios on gender relations, see Guttentag and Secord 1983). An ethnographic study of Vietnamese refugees showed that although married Vietnamese refugee women did not derive benefit from the high gender ratio, young unmarried women did experience greater power in their sexual relationships with men owing to the "shortage" of women in the group (Kibria 1993).

Marriage, Divorce, and Childbearing

The marriage and divorce patterns of Vietnamese Americans have not been widely explored, and thus information on this topic is preliminary in nature. There may be some special problems in gathering accurate information on marital dissolution because of the stigma attached to divorce in Vietnamese culture, particularly for women.

In an analysis of data on the 1975 Vietnamese arrivals, Baker and North report 49 percent of those 15 years or older to be married at the time of arrival. A small number of the group, all women, indicated that they were divorced (0.3 percent) or widowed (0.1 percent). The 1970 census showed about 58 percent of the eligible U.S. Vietnamese population to be married and 1.3 percent divorced or widowed. Thus, compared with the U.S. population, a smaller proportion of the "first-wave" Vietnamese refugees were either married or divorced/widowed at the time of arrival.

From his survey study in San Diego, Rumbaut (1988) reported the average age of marriage for Vietnamese Americans as 21.4 years for women and 25.8 years for men. The study also shows extremely low rates of marital dissolution through either death or separation/ divorce. For example, of the 157 Vietnamese adults who were surveyed in 1983, none were divorced or separated, and less than 1 percent indicated that they were widowed. The same respondents were questioned about what their marital status had been in 1975. Sixty-four percent indicated that they were married in 1975, compared with 87.3 percent in 1983. There was little difference in the proportion of widowed and divorced persons in 1975 and 1983. A Bureau of Social Science Research study (Dunning and Greenbaum 1982; Dunning 1986) of 555 Vietnamese refugees (including Chinese Vietnamese) in the New Orleans, Houston, and Los Angeles areas also reveals fairly low rates of marital dissolution. The study found that of those who had ever been married, 83 percent were with their initial spouse at the time of the study.

Far more information is needed to clarify the marriage and divorce rates of Vietnamese Americans and the variations of these patterns within the group due to differences of social class and ethnicity. Contrary to the picture of stability and continuity suggested by the preceding information, a number of qualitative, in-depth studies suggest that there has been a rise in separation and divorce due to the strains on marriages generated by settlement in the United States (Gold 1989; Kibria 1993; Kinzie 1981; Masuda and others 1980). The male-dominated gender ratio, because of its impact on the "pool" of eligible female partners, also raises questions about both the current rate and age of marriage for Vietnamese American men.

Fertility rates in Vietnam are significantly higher than in the United States (Rumbaut and Weeks 1986). For Vietnamese Americans, rates of childbearing continue to be high, owing to both the large proportion of persons of childbearing age and traditional values concerning fertility. The 1980 census shows the number of children ever born per 1,000 Vietnamese American women (aged 15 to 44) as 1,785. This figure is close to that recorded for Hispanic (1,817) and African American women (1,806) and higher than that of the general U.S. population (1,429) or other Asian American groups (Gardner and others 1985:17).

Rumbaut and Weeks (1986) suggest that the 1980 census figures (which provide information mainly on the 1975 arrivals) may underestimate the current fertility rates of the Vietnamese because of the higher socioeconomic background of the 1975 arrivals, a condition that tends to depress rates of childbearing. Using data from a study in San Diego, they report a child-woman ratio[4] of 574 children (aged 0 to 4) per 1,000 Vietnamese American women of childbearing age. This figure is somewhat higher than that found for the Chinese Vietnamese (511) and substantially higher than that of the general U.S. population (309). They found the subgroup of 1975 arrivals within their sample of Vietnamese respondents to have lower fertility rates than later arrivals. The authors also found that increased length of residence as well as a higher level of economic and cultural adaptation to the United States significantly lowered childbearing rates. On the basis of these findings, they predict a decline in childbearing over time for Vietnamese Americans. However, given current rates of childbearing, we can expect a large proportion of children and young persons to be an important characteristic of the Vietnamese American population in the near future.

HOUSEHOLD AND EXTENDED FAMILY

In traditional Vietnamese culture, the family was seen as an extended structure, a group that stretched beyond immediate or nuclear family ties to include a wide range of kin (Haines 1984; Luong 1984; Whitmore 1984). Households, which could include nuclear or extended family members, were enmeshed in a large and active web of kinship relations in the neighborhood and general vicinity. These relations with kin often functioned as important sources of economic and social support (Hickey 1964).

A number of studies have emphasized the continued significance of extended family ties for Vietnamese in the United States. Data on the size and composition of Vietnamese American households provide some evidence for this idea. The 1980 census reports an average household size of 4.4 for Vietnamese Americans. Other relatives beyond the householder's immediate family (that is, householder, spouse, children) were found to account for 55 percent of total household members. Seven percent of those living in the household were found to be unrelated to the head of household. In comparison, among whites, the immediate family accounted for 94 percent of total household members (Gardner and others 1985:23). A Bureau of Social Science Research study (Dunning and Greenbaum 1982) reports an average household size of 4.5 for Vietnamese refugees. For purposes of comparison, respondents were also asked about the size and composition of their households in Vietnam. Average household size in Vietnam was larger (6.5 persons), and there were also a greater number of three-generational households in Vietnam than in the United States.

From his study in San Diego, Rumbaut (1988; 1989) reports a mean household size of 5.5 for the Vietnamese American sample in 1983. Nuclear family members accounted for about four and extended family members for one of all household members. Unrelated persons composed a relatively small proportion (0.43) of total household members. There was little change in these figures in 1984, when the same respondents were questioned again (Rumbaut 1988). Data from this study also show few differences in household size and composition between the first "wave" and later arrivals. However, the average household size of the Chinese Vietnamese sample was somewhat larger than that of the Vietnamese. Further investigation is needed into both the diversity and the processes of change that are most likely occurring in the composition of Vietnamese American households.

The resurfacing of extended family household structures in the United States is in some ways unexpected, given the considerable disruptions to family relations that have been part of the migration process for the group. Studies suggest that the presence of extended family ties in the United States has been made possible by the vigorous efforts of Vietnamese Americans to rebuild their families in the face of the disruption to family ties caused by the migration process (Gold 1989: Kibria 1993). One expression of this family reconstruction process is the heavy secondary migration of Vietnamese Americans within the United States to areas of the country where kin and friends reside. Crucial to this process of reuniting and rebuilding has been the popular Vietnamese conception of family as a large and inclusive circle of significant kin. In effect, this fluid and inclusive conception has allowed for the incorporation of people into the extended kin network who would perhaps not have been part of it in the past. More specifically, Kibria's (1993) study shows three means by which family networks are reconstructed. First, relationships with distant kin are elevated in importance. In other words, relatives who were previously marginal members of the family circle in Vietnam are incorporated into the network of active kin relations. Second, compared with the past, distinctions based on paternal versus maternal descent or the ties of blood versus marriage were considered less important in determining the closeness of family ties. Third, close friends were incorporated into the family circle and treated as kin members.

The efforts to reconstruct kin networks clearly reflect the cultural importance placed on familial relations by Vietnamese Americans. But in addition, studies have suggested that extended family ties have material significance for Vietnamese Americans, playing an important part in the processes by which the group copes with the economic conditions and institutions of U.S. society. Kin are often involved in relations of mutual aid with each other, exchanging goods, services (for example, child care, cooking), and information on how to deal with such U.S. institutions as hospitals and welfare agencies. Family members are often a source of job referrals as well as investment capital for opening small businesses or purchasing homes (Finnan and Cooperstein 1983; Gold 1989; Haines and others 1981; Kibria 1993).

FAMILY ROLES AND AUTHORITY

The rebuilding of kinship ties highlights the continuities of Vietnamese American family life and the ways in which families may be a source of support in the process of adaptation to U.S. society. At the same time, many aspects of the traditional Vietnamese family, particularly patterns of family roles and authority, are being challenged by the conditions of life in the United States. In the following sections, I explore the effects of migration to the United States on intergenerational and gender relations in the family.

Intergenerational Relations

The traditional Vietnamese ideal of the family, derived from Confucian principles, was of a hierarchical entity in which the young were subordinate to the old, as were women to men. For the young, ideal behavior entailed obedience to the elderly and the submission of individual needs and desires to those of the family collective.

These principles were given meaning and legitimacy through the practice of ancestor worship, in which rites were performed to remember and honor the spirits of ancestors. For Vietnamese, the practice of ancestor worship helped to socialize children into ideal family values through its symbolic expression of the unified, sacred, and hierarchical quality of the kin group. Slote (1972) further suggests that traditional modes of child-rearing in Vietnamese families helped to generate qualities of dependence rather than independence in children, thus supporting the prescribed behaviors of obedience and submission to the family collective.

In the United States, these core traditional familial values—the authority of the old over the young and the primacy of the family collective over the individual—continue to be emphasized by the older Vietnamese immigrant generation in their interactions with the young. However, a number of conditions have eroded the ability of parents and other family elders to influence the younger generation. First, there is the youthful age structure of the Vietnamese American population and the small number of Vietnamese elderly in the United States (Eckles and others 1982). And particularly in recent years, many Vietnamese youth have arrived in the United States without older family members. Migration to the United States has thus often created situations in which the elderly are simply not present to enforce their authority over the Vietnamese American young. The growth of Vietnamese American youth gangs is at least partly a reflection of the significant number of young Vietnamese refugees who are in the United States without their parents or other family guardians (Vigil and Yun 1990).

Besides an absence of guardianship, settlement in the United States has also enhanced the economic and social resources of the young compared with those of the old. In a number of Vietnamese American families observed (Kibria 1993), the better language skills, opportunities for education and job training, and familiarity with

U.S. cultural norms have placed children in a position of greater advantage than their parents in dealing with the institutions of U.S. society, a condition that has eroded parental authority. Along with their diminished power and authority over the young, Vietnamese American parents and other family elders also complain about the cultural assimilation of the young, fostered by such powerful cultural agents as U.S. television, popular music, and schools. Of particular concern to the Vietnamese immigrant generation is the growing individualism of the young. Studies document intergenerational clashes within Vietnamese American families, involving attempts by parents or older guardians to ensure that the young behave in ways that meet traditional Vietnamese cultural expectations (Indochina Refugee Action Center 1980; Kibria 1993; Pennsylvania Department of Public Welfare 1979).

However, to suggest that the intergenerational relations of Vietnamese Americans are characterized solely or even primarily by change and conflict would be misleading. A study of Simon (1983) pointed to the considerable consensus of values and expectations between Vietnamese American parents and their adolescent children. Kibria's study (1993) found considerable attachment among younger Vietnamese Americans to traditional Vietnamese family values, including the collectivist and hierarchical qualities of traditional Vietnamese family life.

Gender Relations

The ideal traditional Vietnamese family, modeled on Confucian principles, was one in which women were subordinate to men in all phases and aspects of their lives. The realities of traditional Vietnamese family life of course deviated from this normative model in many ways. For example, older women often exercised considerable power in their household. As part of their domestic caretaking role, women often controlled the family budget and exerted influence over the family economy. And although men controlled key economic institutions, Vietnamese women did have access to economic resources through their extensive involvement in small business and trading. Although such activities may have enhanced the resources and power of women in the family, there is little evidence that they weakened the fundamental subordination and dependence of women on men (Kibria 1990).

Scholars have observed that migration to the United States has challenged the traditional Vietnamese bases of male authority and thus generated a rise in conflicts between men and women. They note how there has been a reversal of traditional male/female roles, a situation that has given rise to conflict. More specifically, Vietnamese American women often assume the "breadwinner" role because service sector jobs are more easily available than the kinds of unskilled blue-collar or professional jobs that men seek. In some cases, the woman economically supports the family while the man undergoes educational or technical training for a skilled job (Gold 1989; Kinzie 1981; Masuda and others 1980).

Although the employment rates of Vietnamese women in the United States are relatively high (see Haines 1986), it is not clear that the economic activities of women have taken on primary significance compared with those of men. The unemployment rate of Vietnamese American women is higher than that of men in the group (Dunning and Greenbaum 1982; Haines 1987). Perhaps the crucial difference in Vietnamese refugee men's and women's employment is revealed in a comparison of their wages and income. For example, the Bureau of Social Science Research study (Dunning and Greenbaum 1982) showed the wages and income of women to be far less than those of men. Whereas, on average, the income of women constituted 36 percent of total household income, the comparable figure for men was 64 percent. Kibria's (1989) study also showed Vietnamese refugee women to be working in unstable, low-paying jobs, often in the underground or informal economy. In short, the evidence suggests that the elevation of Vietnamese American women's economic activities to primary significance compared with men's activities may be a reality for only a small number of families.

Although migration may not have generated a sharp reversal in the economic roles of Vietnamese refugee men and women, it has certainly resulted in a decline in men's ability to obtain jobs that ensure a middle-class standard of living for their families. By the mid-1980s, those Vietnamese immigrants who had arrived as part of the 1975 evacuation had achieved parity in their household income levels with the general U.S. population (Office of Refugee Resettlement 1988:147). But the later cohorts of Vietnamese refugees have had less economic success (Haines 1987). A 1984 survey of Vietnamese refugees in San Diego found 22.4 percent of respondents to be unemployed and 61.3 percent to have incomes below the poverty level. Of those who were employed, 29.2 percent indicated that they received no fringe benefits at work, and 48.7 percent said that there was no possibility for promotion at their jobs (Rumbaut 1989). Caplan and others (1985) note that although the economic self-sufficiency of Vietnamese American families tends to rise over time, this condition is usually achieved not through a rise in individual wages but through the use of multiple wage-earner household strategies. Tensions concerning traditional conceptions of male authority may become apparent when men who were the sole or primary family breadwinners in Vietnam find themselves dependent on the income of other wage-earners in the household. More generally, we can expect the conditions of economic scarcity and insecurity faced by many Vietnamese American families to be a source of strain on marriages and other family relationships.

Besides economic conditions, other factors have affected gender relations in Vietnamese American families. Kibria's (1993) study shows how the cultural and legal conceptions of male authority that are prevalent in the majority U.S. society may work to challenge and shift Vietnamese American normative attitudes regarding men's and women's behavior. Also important was the expansion of Vietnamese refugee women's homemaking activities beyond such traditional work as child care and housework to include negotiation with social institutions located outside the household, such as schools, hospitals, and welfare agencies. The expanded "intermediary" role played by women is a potentially important source of power for women in their relations with men.

CONCLUSIONS

This chapter provides an overview of research on Vietnamese families in the United States. Many studies of Vietnamese American family life have focused on patterns of continuity as evidenced, for example, by the presence of extended family household structures. In these studies, the continued significance of the traditional values and organization of Vietnamese family life in the U.S. context is emphasized. In contrast, other studies have stressed the theme of conflict, or the clashes between traditional expectations of family life and the conditions and orientations of U.S. society. Incorporation of these two themes into a unified perspective may provide a better understanding of ongoing processes of change or the ways in which Vietnamese American families are being shaped and constructed by both the past and the present.

Future research on Vietnamese American families must take into account some distinctive aspects of the Vietnamese experience prior to arrival in the United States. This observation includes not only the group's complex cultural and historical heritage but also the somewhat unusual conditions that have surrounded the migration from Vietnam. For example, the predominance in number of young persons and of men will most likely have important effects on Vietnamese American family life for some time into the future. Also relevant is the considerable disruption of family ties experienced by most Vietnamese refugees. Because of the difficulties of leaving Vietnam, chain migration processes or the gradual migration of entire family units has been less prevalent among the Vietnamese than among many other immigrant groups.

Finally, the diversity of the Vietnamese American population is another important key to understanding the group's family life. As I have discussed, there are significant differences of social class among Vietnamese Americans in terms of both past and current socioeconomic status. Differences between the Chinese Vietnamese and ethnic Vietnamese are also important to consider. In short, rather than viewing Vietnamese Americans as a monolithic population. future research must take into account the differences in social class and ethnic background within the group and the ways in which they are affecting family experiences.

NOTES

1. The 1990 census reported 614,547 Vietnamese in the United States.
2. The 1990 census showed California to be home to 45.6 percent of the Vietnamese population in the United States, with Texas following at 11.3 percent.
3. Baker and North (1984) present information on the socioeconomic background of the 1975 arrivals. They found that 19 percent of the adults had had postsecondary (13 to 16 years) education, whereas 51 percent had received secondary (12 years) level education. Twenty-five percent held professional jobs in Vietnam. Others held mainly clerical and service sector jobs.
4. Child-woman ratio = (Total number of children aged 0–4)/Women of childbearing age × 100.

REFERENCES

Baker. Reginald P., and David S. North. 1984. *The 1975 Refugees: Their First Five Years in America.* Washington, DC: New Transcentury Press.

Caplan, Nathan, John K. Whitmore, and Quang L. Bui. 1985. *Southeast Asian Refugee Self-Sufficiency Study: Final Report.* Ann Arbor, MI: The Institute for Social Research.

Dunning, Bruce B. 1986. "Vietnamese in America: Domain and Scope of Adjustment among 1975–79 Arrivals." Paper presented at the Annual Meeting of the American Association for the Advancement of Science. Philadelphia, Pennsylvania.

———, and J. Greenbaum. 1982. *A Systematic Survey of the Social, Psychological and Economic Adaptation of Vietnamese Refugees Representing Five Entry Cohorts, 1975–1979.* Washington, DC: Bureau of Social Science Research.

Eckles, Timothy J., L. S. Lewin, D. S. North, and D. J. Spakevicius. 1982. *Portrait in Diversity: Voluntary Agencies and the ORR Matching Grant Program.* Lewin and Associates: Office of Refugee Resettlement Report.

Finnan, Christine R., and Rhonda Cooperstein. 1983. *Southeast Asian Refugee Resettlement at the Local Level.* Office of Refugee Resettlement Report.

Gardner, Robert Bryant Robey, and Peter C. Smith. 1985. "Asian Americans: Growth, Change and Diversity." *Population Bulletin* 40.

Gold, Steven J. 1989. "Differential Adjustment among New Immigrant Family Members." *Journal of Contemporary Ethnography* 17:408–434.

Guttentag, Marcia, and Paul F. Secord. 1983. *Too Many Women? The Sex Ratio Question.* Beverly Hills, CA: Sage.

Haines, David. 1984. "Reflections of Kinship and Society under Vietnam's Le Dynasty." *Journal of Southeast Asian Studies* 15:307–314.

———. 1986. "Vietnamese Women in the Labor Force: Continuity or Change?" *International Migration: The Female Experience*, edited by R. J. Simon and C. B. Brettell. Totowa. NJ: Rowman & Allenheld.

———. 1987. "Patterns in Southeast Asian Refugee Employment: A Reappraisal of the Existing Research." *Ethnic Groups* 7:39–63.

———. 1988. "Kinship in Vietnamese Refugee Resettlement: A Review of the U.S. Experience." *Journal of Comparative Family Studies* 19:1–16.

———, Dorothy Rutherford, and Patrick Thomas. 1981. "Family and Community among Vietnamese

Refugees." *International Migration Review* 15:310–319.

Hickey, Gerald C. 1964. *Village in Vietnam.* New Haven, CT: Yale University Press.

Indochina Refugee Action Center. 1980. *An Assessment of the Needs of Indochinese Youth.* Washington, DC: IRAC.

Kibria, Nazli. 1989. "Patterns of Vietnamese Refugee Women's Wagework in the U.S." *Ethnic Groups* 7:297–323.

———. 1990. "Power, Patriarchy and Gender Conflict in the Vietnamese Immigrant Community. *Gender and Society* 4:9–24.

———. 1993. *Family Tightrope: The Changing Lives of Vietnamese Americans.* Princeton, NJ: Princeton University Press.

Kinzie, J. D. 1981. "Evaluation and Psychotherapy of Indochinese Refugee Patients." *American Journal of Psychotherapy* 35:251–261.

Luong, Hy Van. 1984. "Brother and Uncle: An Analysis of Rules, Structural Contradictions and Meaning in Vietnamese Kinship." *American Anthropologist* 86:290–315.

Masuda, Minoru, Keh-Ming Lin, and Laurie Tazum. 1980. "Adaptation Problems of Vietnamese Refugees: Life Changes and Perception of Life Events." *Archives of General Psychiatry* 37:447–450.

Office of Refugee Resettlement. 1985. *Refugee Resettlement Program—Report to Congress.* U.S. Department of Health and Human Services.

———. 1988. *Refugee Resettlement Program—Report to Congress.* U.S. Department of Health and Human Services.

Pennsylvania Department of Public Welfare. 1979. *National Mental Health Needs Assessment of Indochinese Refugee Populations.* Philadelphia: Office of Mental Health, Bureau of Research and Training.

Rumbaut, Ruben G. 1988. *Southeast Asian Refugees in San Diego County: A Statistical Profile.* San Diego: Indochinese Health and Adaptation Research Project, San Diego State University.

———. 1989. "Portraits, Patterns and Predictors of the Refugee Adaptation Process: Results and Reflections from the IHARP Panel Study." In *Refugees as Immigrants: Cambodians, Laotians and Vietnamese in America,* edited by David W. Haines. Totowa, NJ: Rowman & Littlefield Publishers.

———, and John R. Weeks. 1986. "Fertility and Adaptation: Indochinese Refugees in the United States." *International Migration Review* 20:428–466.

Simon, Rita J. 1983. "Refugee Families' Adjustment and Aspirations: A Comparison of Soviet Jews and Vietnamese Immigrants." *Ethnic and Racial Studies* 6:492–504.

Slote, Walter H. 1972. "Psychodynamic Structures in Vietnamese Personality." In *Transcultural Research in Mental Health,* edited by William Lebra. Honolulu: University of Hawaii Press.

Strand, Paul J., and W. Jones, Jr. 1985. *Indochinese Refugees in America: Problems of Adaptation and Assimilation.* Durham, NC: Duke University Press.

Vigil, James Diego, and Steve Chong Yun. 1990. "Vietnamese Youth Gangs in Southern California." In *Gangs in California,* edited by R. Huff. Beverly Hills, CA: Sage.

Wain, Barry. 1981. *The Refused: The Agony of the Indochinese Refugees.* New York: Simon and Schuster.

Whitmore, John K. 1984. "Social Organization and Confucian Thought in Vietnam." *Journal of Southeast Asian Studies* 15:296–306.

Invisible Americans: An Exploration of Indo-American Quality of Life

Snehendu B. Kar, Kevin Campbell, Armando Jimenez, and Sangeeta R. Gupta

This article, based upon our ongoing multinational study: "Effects of Acculturation on Quality of Life among Selected Asian Immigrant Groups,"[1] explores important psychosocial factors which affect quality of life of Indo-Americans. Three sets of primary data were used, including quantitative data from surveys of two Indo-American samples in California: (1) parents/first generation and (2) college students/second generation. The third set of qualitative information is derived from intensive focus groups, seminar presentations and student project reports in a course on "Indo-American Immigration Experience and Quality of Life" taught by Professor Snehendu Kar, the senior author of this article.[2]

While the published literature relevant to Asian Indians and Indo-Americans is extensive, it consists almost exclusively of historical, literary, anecdotal and isolated case studies.[3] Several on-line searches by the writers failed to identify a single published empirical study on psychosocial factors affecting Indo-American quality of life, including health status and needs, using an acceptable sample design and social science methodology. While pioneering studies by Kitano,[4] Sue[5] and few others provide us with insights into issues and health problems affecting Japanese and Chinese Americans, we need comparative studies including samples from other major ethnic groups to understand the common issues which affect all Asian Americans including Indo-Americans. The effects of acculturation and diversity on quality of life of Indo-Amer-

icans remains a major uncharted area of research and policy deliberations.

Recently, several writers have begun to address specific aspects of the Indo-American experience; but these tend to be limited to a specific issue or very small sample of case studies. Notable examples include an examination of mental health of Asian Indians,[6] the use of traditional "Ayurvedic" medicine,[7] and case studies of Indo-American experience using very small sample numbering less than thirty cases.[8] Other scholarly studies of Indo-Americans are limited to early Punjabi farmers in northern California and their ordeal with social integration and family formation.[9] While we commend these authors for raising issues affecting the Indo-American experience, their reports do not study Indo-Americans as a whole social group. To the best of our knowledge, our ongoing multinational study, "Effects of Acculturation on Quality of Life among Selected Asian Immigrant Groups," is the first empirical study which includes intergenerational study of Indo-American quality of life as one of its major components. It is important to note that our survey of a sample of college students and comparison of our survey results with findings from studies of other ethnic groups are still in process, therefore we are unable to compare the Indo-Americans with other Asian groups on many measures.

SOCIAL REALITIES OF THE INDO-AMERICAN EXPERIENCE

We begin with a recognition of social realities which define the Indo-American experience. Within some subgroups of South and East Asian

Source: *Amerasia Journal* 21:3 (Winter 1995/1996): 25–52. Reprinted by permission.

Americans, more than 80 percent are foreign born. Consequently, their level of acculturation and familiarity with the social, medical and health care systems of the United States is limited. Available epidemiological and community-based needs assessments show that recent immigrants, as compared to established immigrants (second generation or earlier), immigrants suffer from different health risks which are uncommon in the United States (tuberculosis, malaria, intestinal worms, etc). Immigration history (including push-pull motivation for migration, socio-political background), acculturation and identity have significant effects on their assimilation into the dominant culture of the host nation. This, in turn, affects the quality of social, personal and physical well-being within the immigrant community.

According to the 1990 Census data and a recent study,[10] among all ethnic groups in the United States, Indo-Americans rank highest in educational achievements and rank among the top in income. A recent analysis by Ong and Azores[11] shows that Indo-Americans, compared to their proportion in the general population, occupy significantly greater numbers of positions in several professional categories. For instance, among all recent immigrant physicians of Asian origin, over 50 percent are Indo-Americans. Indo-Americans are also employed in larger proportions than their share in the general population as academics, and in engineering and mathematical sciences. Yet, relative to several other Asian American groups, Indo-Americans are less visible socially, geographically and politically (with the exception of the popular stereotypes of Indo-Americans in hotel/motel establishments and in 7–11 stores). The extent of diversity within the Indo-American community, dependency on one's own ethnic group for social and economic survival, and a high level of achievement among the English-speaking professionals are some of the factors which make Indo-Americans different from other Asian and Hispanic immigrants from less privileged social stratas. It is important to understand

how these realities affect Indo-Americans, their social relations with other segments of American society, and their overall quality of physical, mental and social well-being.

Demographics

Depending upon how one counts, Indo-Americans are the third or fourth largest group of Asian Americans. Indo-Americans who number 815,447 are the fourth largest Asian American group (after Chinese Americans, 1,645,472; Filipino Americans, 1,406,770; and Japanese Americans, 847,562); they are also among the fastest growing population segment. Between 1980 and 1990, the Indo-American population grew by 126 percent as compared to the 108 percent growth of all Asian Americans combined. The growth rate of the total American population was 9.8 percent. Indo-Americans would be considered the third largest Asian American group and the fastest growing among all major ethnic groups if all immigrants from India, Bangladesh and Pakistan are combined into a single ethnic group as customarily done for Chinese Americans, Korean Americans and others. For instance, Chinese Americans are not divided into different ethnic groups based upon whether their ancestors originated from areas now under the governments of the People's Republic of China or Taiwan or Hong Kong; neither are Korean Americans divided into separate groups based upon whether they originated from places now under the North or South Korean governments. Using this logic, if we were to combine the immigrants who originated from areas under the prepartitioned India but now under three separate governments (India, Bangladesh and Pakistan), their combined number would be 908,656; this would make the Indo-Americans considerably larger than the Japanese Americans. The growth rate of this combined group from the Indian subcontinent, between 1980–1990 would be an astounding 239 percent (estimated from the 1990 U.S. Census).

Diversity

Indo-Americans are the most diverse among all other ethnic groups originating from any one nation for the following reasons. a) Language: India is linguistically more diverse than any other single nation. The government prints its currency bills in fifteen distinct and official languages—not dialects. An Indian originating from one state often cannot speak with a fellow Indian from another state in his/her own primary language. b) Religion: No single nation can match India in terms of its religious diversity. Indians, in large numbers, practice all major religions in the world. While all variations of Hinduism combined form the dominant religion among the Indians, India also has the second largest Muslim population in the world (an estimated 11 percent of Indians constitute over 100 million Muslims thus comprising a group which is second only to Indonesia). Other major religious groups are the Sikhs, Jains, Buddhists and Christians (even if as estimated, only 2 percent of Indians are Christians there would be nearly twenty million of them). c) Provincialism: Most Indians in India identify with their province first and nation second. For example, the linguistic and cultural diversity including lifestyle, religious festivities, food habits and regional attire make Indians from one state very distinct from another. Thus the extent of cultural and linguistic differences between the Bengalis, Punjabis, Gujratis, Madrasis, etc., can hardly be overcome through an appeal to a unified cultural or national identity. Indeed, the residual effects of provincialism are very strong among the first generation Indo-Americans (parents) of our sample resulting in significant differences in self-identities between the parent and student samples of our study. d) Caste System: Caste hierarchy is a closed system—providing only horizontal mobility—and is a powerful determinant of social interactions, family formation and economic achievements. Although the rigid caste system is slowly giving way to modernism in India, most

first generation Indo-Americans who arrived after the immigration liberalization law in 1965 were raised in India by their parents during the thirties, forties and fifties and before the recent modernization weakened the stronghold of practices such as arranged marriages within a specific caste. On the other hand, their children, who are now college students in the United States, grew up in a highly industrialized nation in which individual freedom of choice and responsibility are valued above loyalty to caste, kinships and traditional customs. e) Invisibility: Indo-Americans are the most invisible of all ethnic minorities. Other Asian American groups, including those which are much smaller in number, are more visible socially, politically and geographically. Major American cities have a Chinatown and a Japantown; more recently Koreatowns and other ethnic localities are becoming common in metropolitan areas. This is not true in the case of Indo-Americans. They are also politically rather inactive which make them more invisible.

It is important to understand the socioeconomic and motivational factors which make them socially invisible and the implications of their passive social and political existence for their well-being. An overwhelming majority of Indo-Americans are foreign born first-generation immigrants; according to the 1990 U.S. Census over 80 percent of them are foreign born (98 percent of our parent sample are first-generation immigrants). An overwhelming majority of this cohort arrived after the Immigration Reform Act of 1965; they were highly educated professionals educated in the English medium and they spoke English fluently. Unlike many recent Asian and South American immigrants who do not speak English well or were not economically self-reliant, these Indo-Americans did not have to depend upon localized ethnic networks for financial and/or occupational support. Consequently, following available employment opportunities, they dispersed geographically. This geographic dispersion combined with the extreme internal diversities due to their primary languages, provin-

cialism, religious affiliations, and other preferences do not encourage the Indo-Americans to
form ethnic clusters in defined geographic areas.
They became lost within the vast expanse of the
American mass society; they became functionally
invisible as a separate ethnic group.

STUDY METHODOLOGY

A self-administered questionnaire in English was
used to survey the two Indo-American samples:
parents (n=264), and college students (n=225);
hereafter named as parents and students respectively. The two versions of the questionnaires
contained over 115 items measuring these
domains: (1) socio-demographic background
including immigration history, (2) acculturation,
identity, and assimilation, (3) quality of life, life
satisfaction, and aspirations and concerns, (4)
health status, risks and behavior, (5) intergenerational dynamics and areas of conflicts and congruence, (6) health care utilization, and (7)
communication and social participation. The
items included were selected from several survey
instruments and sales designed for measuring the
variables included in our study. These include: a
scale for measuring "Quality of Life and subjective satisfaction,"[12] Cantril's "Self-Anchoring
Striving Scale" for measuring aspirations, hopes
and fears,"[13] items on acculturation and assimilation frequently used in ethnic studies,"[14] and
health risks, status and behavior items from the
CDC's Behavioral Risk Factor Surveillance
System.[15] In addition, original items specific to
Indo-American culture and family dynamics were
designed for this study (e.g., caste, religion, place
of origin, dating and mating behavior, sources of
intergenerational conflicts).

Selection of a representative sample of Indo-
Americans was the biggest problem for us. It
became clear that it is impossible to find comprehensive lists of Indo-Americans from which we
could select a systematic sample for our study.
Due to the diversity and invisibility of Indo-

Americans, it was not possible for us to use sur-
names from telephone directories or geographic
clusters to select respondents for our study (e.g.,
Chinatown, Koreatown, Japantown). Since
according to the 1990 Census data and another
national study, the Indo-Americans have among
the highest level of educational and occupational
achievements, we chose to publish the parents'
questionnaire in the *India West*, the largest circu-
lating weekly serving Indo-Americans in California. The respondents were asked to complete
and return their anonymous responses to the
senior author. In order to improve the response
rate, twenty-five cash awards were offered as an
incentive. The questionnaire was printed in the
centerfold of the newspaper with a bold headline
announcing that twenty-five winners would be
randomly selected from all respondents who
returned their completed questionnaires within
the announced deadline (five awards of $200 each
and twenty awards of $100 each). The winners,
identified only by the last four digits of their
phone numbers, were to be published in the next
issue of the paper after the deadline. In addition,
a separate news item was released by the editor of
India West and a special article by a reporter
encouraged the readers to support this first ever
survey of Indo-Americans jointly sponsored by
UCLA's Asian American Studies Center, the Federation of Indo-American Associations and the
India West newspaper. We received over 280
responses; several incomplete and ineligible
responses were excluded from our analyses.

Several respondents offered to collaborate
with us for future studies. The questionnaires for
the student sample were administered by the
Indian Student Associations on several campuses
in Southern California which have large enrollments of Indo-American students. The questionnaires were administered in conjunction with
several campus events and at the end of class sessions in which Indo-American students gathered.

Our exploratory study has several limitations;
these include: use of convenient samples due to
the difficulties in obtaining representative

samples described earlier, the differences in data gathering techniques from the parent and student samples and lack of comparable data from other ethnic minorities for comparing the relative quality of life of various ethnic groups using a common set of measures. Despite these limitations, to the best of our knowledge we obtained data from the largest number of Indo-Americans in a single study in the United States to date. The results are presented in two segments. In the first section we present the highlights of our overall survey results with special emphasis on intergenerational and gender role conflicts. In the second segment we integrate the important qualitative and quantitative results under policy and social imperatives. Due to the complex realities described earlier and several unavoidable limitations of this exploratory study, our article does not offer broad generalizations on the status and determinants of quality of life of all Indo-Americans; we rather present our findings as exploratory observations and raise critical issues in policy and research which require our collective attention.

OVERALL RESULTS

On several conventional indicators of social standing (education, income, occupation), Indo-Americans appear to be successful. The high level of subjective quality of life measured through a widely used Cantril's scale of personal aspirations also reflects their socioeconomic achievements. Table 1 presents a summary of comparison of Indo-Americans (parents) with Hispanics, Blacks and Whites on selected variables using secondary data from comparison groups (see Tables 1–5. . .). On measures of education, occupation and income, the Indo-Americans outrank the comparison groups. The median educational level of our respondents is eighteen years; over 50 percent of women have four years of college education (Table 1). Over seven out of ten (71 percent) respondents report families income

above $50,000 per year; compared to 40.5 percent Whites, 21.5 percent Blacks, and 19.7 percent Hispanics with family income above $50,000 (UW/LA 1994). Over 84 percent of respondents hold professional or managerial positions compared to 39 percent Whites, 24.5 percent Blacks and 9.9 percent Hispanics holding similar occupations.[16] These findings are consistent with a recent national survey which reported that Indo-Americans have the highest level of education (median 15.6 years) and have the fourth highest family income among all thirty-three population groups in the United States.[17] The findings on both objective and subjective measures of quality of life for Indo-Americans are favorable. The level of subjective quality of life among the parents and students are high and roughly comparable although the students rated themselves slightly better than the parents.

Using Cantril's Self-Anchoring Life-Satisfaction scale, subjects were asked to judge where on a 10-point ladder of quality-of-life (10 = best and 1 = worst) they felt they belong at the present time, where they would rank themselves five years ago and where they hope to be in five years. On a subjective rating of expected quality of life for the future the averages for the students and parents were 8.6 and 8.2 respectively (P < .001). Researchers who have used this scale before consider a score above 7 as a "high" level of life satisfaction." The parents and students also rate their educational and occupational opportunities rather favorably (a little over 4.0 on a maximum possible score of 5 (see Table 2.v).

Correlation matrix analyses show statistically significant relationships between quality of life and acculturation measures for both parent and student samples. For the parent sample quality of life is related to three acculturation measures in this order: friendship network not exclusively limited to Indians (.22), comfort level with a westernized lifestyle (.18), and preference to speak in English at home (.17); these are all statistically significant at the .001 level. For the student sample, two of these correlation coeffi-

TABLE 1
A Multi-Cultural Health Indicator Comparison[1]

Variable/Indicator	Indo-American			Hispanic*	Black*	White*
	Total Sample	Male	Female	Total Sample	Total Sample	Total Sample
Demographics						
Age (median age)	45	45	39	26	40.3 (mean)	42.2 (mean)
Years of education	18	18	16	9.3 (mean)	10.95 (mean)	12.6 (mean)
No children	25.2	20.8	36.8	19.6		
1 or 2 children	60.3	63	55.6	39.6		
2 or more children	14.5	16.2	7.6	38.2		
Occupation						
Professional	67.3	72.1	54.4	4	12.5	19.3
Managerial	16.8	13.6	6.3	5.9	12	20
Self-employed	6.1	6.5	3.5	4	3.9	10.36
Sales	3.7	5.2	0	41	50	40
Semi-skilled	1.9	.6	5.3	44.8	21.2	11
Income						
50+K	71	77.9	52.6	19.7	21.5	40.5
30–50 K	15	9.1	29.8	17.7	15.2	17.5
16–29 K	11.2	11.1	12.2	38.4	25.1	26.1
0–15 K	2.8	1.9	5.3	24.2	31.2	16.4
Health Care Behavior						
Have no health insurance	9.8	9.7	8.8	39	20	15
# of visits to MD in last year (median)	2	2	2	2	2	2
Always use western medicine	48.6	47.4	49.1			
Never use western medicine	20.6	19.5	24.6			
Never use traditional healer	64.5	63.6	66.7			
Sometimes or always use traditional healer	12.6	13.6	8.8	4.2 curandero		
Health Problems						
Have high blood pressure	8	9.6	0	18	48.8	31
Have diabetes	4.2	5.8	0	7	3.3	3.3
Health Behavior						
Currently smoke	5.6	7.8	0	19.6	27.3	23.2
Had 1 drink in last year	54.7	61.7	36.8	53		

[1]Numbers are percentages unless otherwise indicated.
*Comparison data source: United Way: *Los Angeles 1994: State of the County Databook*

cients are higher and are in this order: friendship network not exclusively limited to Indians (.31), comfort level with a western lifestyle (.23), and preference to speak English at home (.10). There is a slight gender difference in degree of acculturation within the parent and student samples; but the difference is not statistically significant. There are other notable positive attributes. Indo-Amer-

TABLE 2
Indo-American Quality of Life[1]

Variable/Indicator	Parents			Students		
	Total Sample	Male	Female	Total Sample	Male	Female
I. Demographics						
Age (median)	45	45	39	21	22	21
Born In U.S.	1.9	.06	3.5	48.4	44.4	52.3
Gender	100	73	27	100	49.6	50.4
Education (median years of school)	18	18	16	15	15	14
Years in the U.S. (if not U.S. born)	14	15	12	14	14	15
II. Acculturation						
English spoken at home	44.8	43.5	49.1	69	68.3	69.7
All or most of friends are Indians	52.3	53.5	49.2	44.5	38.7	50
Indian festivals are important or extremely important	43.5	42.2	45.6	52.8	46	59.7
Diwali is the most important festival or holiday	34.6	31.8	43.9	44.6	38.9	50
Christmas is the most important festival or holiday	15.9	14.3	21.2	12.5	18.5	6.9
Women wear Indian dress most or all of the time	27.5	29.9	21	28.1	30.2	24.2
III. Intergenerational Conflict[2]						
Source of conflict:						
Dating	—	—	—	46.3	40.9	52.6
Education	—	—	—	7.3	6.8	13.2
Marriage (choice)	19.2	20.8	14	21.9	15.9	29
Career	20.1	16.2	31.6	14.6	15.9	7.9
Parental control	25.7	27.2	33.3	—	—	—
Children's behavior	38.8	37	42.1	—	—	—
IV. Marital Preference[3]						
Marry someone of the same ethnicity	57	57.8	52.6	56.9	50	63.9
Marry someone of the same religion	51.4	54.5	42.1	49.6	43.56	55.4
Marry someone in the same caste	25.7	27.2	22.8	18.1	16.4	20.9
Marry someone who speaks same language	31.8	31.2	35.1	31.9	24.6	39.3
Marry someone from same state/province	22.5	24	19.3	27.1	19.7	34.4
V. Quality of Life						
QOL in present	6.83	6.91	6.64	6.8	6.9	6.72
(standard deviation)	1.79	1.65	2.16	1.76	1.69	1.82
QOL in past 5 years	5.86	5.9	5.85	6.68	6.75	6.6
(standard deviation)	2.14	2.07	2.83	2.14	2.13	2.17
QOL 5 years in the future	8.19	8.27	8.07	8.59	8.57	8.6
(standard deviation	1.85	1.69	2.12	1.43	1.39	1.4
VI. Health Care Behavior						
Satisfied or extremely satisfied with quality of health care	66.9	68.8	59.6	65.1	69.3	63.9
2 or less doctor visits in last year	72.7	72	75	67	71.7	63
Sometimes or always use traditional medicines	12.6	13.6	8.8	15.8	14.3	17.2
Have no health insurance	9.8	9.7	8.8	—	—	—

(*continued*)

TABLE 2 *(continued)*
Indo-American Quality of Life[1]

Variable/Indicator	Parents			Students		
	Total Sample	Male	Female	Total Sample	Male	Female
VII. *Health Behavior*						
Current smokers	5.6	7.8	0	16.8	21.5	12.1
1 or more drinks in the last year	54.7	61.7	36.8	60.3	63.1	57.6
Marijuana in the past month	—	—	—	11.5	18.5	4.5
Cocaine in the past month	—	—	—	2.3	3.1	1.5
Chew tobacco now	—	—	—	3.1	6.2	0
VIII. *Subjective Health Status*						
Health is good or excellent	77.6	78	78.6	84.7	90	79.7

[1]Numbers are percentages unless otherwise indicated.

[2]For respondents to the Adult survey the number represents the percent who indicated the specified area is a source of conflict. For respondents to the Student survey the number represents the percent who "disagree" or "completely disagree" with their parents in the specified area.

[3]Indicated that the characteristic is "important" or "extremely important."

ican women less frequently smoke tobacco and consume alcoholic beverages, the two leading health risk factors for all Americans as a whole.

However, these and other positive findings may reinforce the "model minority myth" which often diverts attention of the social planners and service providers away from the special needs of Asian Americans in general and of Indo-Americans in particular. For instance, while on overall measures of socioeconomic status Indo-Americans appear to be relatively affluent, our data show that they also suffer from psychosocial stressors primarily due to issues around identity and assimilation, intergenerational conflicts, gender-role conflicts and concerns about interracial conflicts.

Identity and Assimilation. To what extent Indo-American assimilation into American culture (or lack of it) and highly diversified self-identities affect the Indo-American quality-of-life is unclear. However, as expected, the student respondents are more comfortable with the American lifestyle than the parents. The students speak English at home more often than their parents (70 and 45 percent, respectively), feel more comfortable with the American lifestyle and, for obvious reasons, less frequently have friends exclusively of Indian ancestry (see Tables 2.II and 6). When asked: "How do you describe your own ethnicity?" the parents and students show some significant differences. Compared to the parents, the students are more often self-identified as bi-cultural (Indo-American); only 27 percent of the students identify themselves as "Indian" compared to 58 percent of the parents. Nearly six-out-of-ten male parents identified themselves as "Indian," only 8 percent as "Indo-American," and less than one percent as "American" (among the mothers these percentages are very similar at 54, 11 and 1, respectively). In contrast, the largest proportion of the students (36 percent) identified themselves as "Indo-Americans," although this is still not a majority, the students four times more frequently identified themselves as bi-cultural (Indo-American) than the parents; and only a little over one-fourth of the students (27 percent) identified themselves as "Indian." It is significant to note that about one-third of the fathers and mothers still retained their Indian provincial identity (34 and 35

TABLE 3.
Acculturation Indicators

Indicators	Students	Parents
How often speak English at home[1]	3.9	3.4***
How often speak English outside home[1]	4.7	4.4*
How often eat Indian foods outside home[1]	3.5	3.8*
Lifestyle and culture most comfortable with[2]	3.4	3.7*

[1]Response range from 1 ("Never") to 5 ("Always")
[2]Response range from 1 ("Indian only") to 5 ("U.S. only")
*p<.05   **p<.01   ***p<.005

Quality of Life Indicators[1]

Indicator	Students	Parents
Quality of life 5 years ago	6.7	5.9***
Quality of life 5 years in future	8.7	8.2*

[1]Response range from 1 ("worst possible life") to 5 ("best possible life")
*p<.05   **p<.01   ***p<.005

Most Frequently Identified Health Concerns[1]

Indicator	Health Concerns for Self		Health Concerns for Family	
	Students	Parents	Students	Parents
Cardiovascular[2]	24.4	28	53.7	28***

[1]Percent identifying concern, up to three concerns could be specified
[2]Includes concerns about "cardiovascular illness," "cholesterol," "heart attack," and "blood pressure"
*p<.05   **p<.01   ***p<.005

Types of Health Care Used[1]

	Students	Parents
Self Care	54.1	80.9***
Western Medicine	92.1	77.6***

[1]Percent reporting using specified type of care "sometimes" or "always/almost always" when they fell ill
*p<.05   **p<.01   ***p<.005

percent respectively); that is they still identified themselves as Punjabi, Gujrati, Bengali, etc. Only about 2 percent of the students and 1 percent of the parents identified themselves as "Americans." Due to space consideration, much of the data cited are not presented in tables, however, all data are available in master files with the authors; the differences cited are statistically significant at least at .01 level).

Intergenerational Conflicts. The most important source of intergenerational conflicts and psychological distress is due to the clash of values between parents and students regarding the dating

TABLE 4

Responses to Open-Ended Question on Issues Not Directly Asked: Interest in Issues Not Covered in the Questionnaire[1]

	Students	*Parents*
Culture Clashes	21.1	30.8
Family Issues[2]	5.3	18.9
Politics	15.8	15.4
Health	2.6	9.1

[1]Of those answering the question percent reporting that the specified topic was an area of concern not fully covered in the questionnaire. 76.8% of the adult population answered the question and 46.3% of the student population responded.

[2]Includes husband/wife relations, conflict with children, and treatment of the elderly.

and mating/marriage preferences of the younger generation (Table 2.III). Any expression of individualism and assimilation of western customs by the younger generation (e.g., smoking or drinking in presence of elderly, disagreement and open expression of it, personal choices not consistent with parental wishes) is perceived by the parents as a threat to their parental status and their right to control their children's behavior. By extension, such behavior is a threat to their time-honored cultural traditions and values which many parents believe must govern individual behavior within their family and social systems. It appears that the parents' wish to hold on to the highly structured roles of parents and children in traditional Indian

families, impose an added burden on second-generation Indo-Americans. The students, on the other hand, are raised and socialized in the American social milieu which places a special emphasis on individualism and search for a personal identity of their own in the absence of clear role models. Female students significantly more often than the men (52 and 41 percent respectively) reported dating preferences as the major source of conflict and stress with their parents (Table 2.III). Over one-fifth of the total student sample reported their marriage preferences as the major cause of conflict with their parents; women nearly twice as frequently (29 and 16 percent, respectively). About four out of ten parents (39 percent) report that the behavior of their children is the most important cause of conflicts within the family; the mothers more frequently see this as a problem than the fathers (42 and 37 percent, respectively). Unlike the prevalent values and norms held by most parents in Euro-American cultures, a significant proportion of Indo-American parents do not perceive dating and mating are matters of individual responsibility or personal freedom of choice.

For the parents, the second most important source of intergenerational conflict is their lack of parental control over their children's behavior in general. One-out-of-four parents stated that challenges to, or disrespect for, parental authority is a

TABLE 5

Source and Quantity of Health Information

Source	*Indian Parents Survey[1]*	*Mexican-American Survey[2]*
Magazines	61.7	43.1
Doctors	58.7	59.5
Family	51.5	33.8
Television	52.4	45.9
Newspapers	58.2	41.9
Friends	47.8	20.3
Radio	31.2	21.6
Pharmacist	13.3	9.5
Nurse	20.8	17.6

[1]Percent reporting receiving "a lot" or "a moderate amount" of health information from the sources listed.

[2]Percent reported receiving "a great deal" or "pretty much" health information from the sources listed.

major problem; interestingly more often the mothers than the fathers believed this (33 and 27 percent, respectively). Roughly equal proportions of parents and students (19 and 22 percent, respectively) reported that decisions regarding marriage by the younger generation are the most important source of intergenerational conflicts. According to the parents, career choices by the younger generation are yet another major source of intra-family conflict; about 32 percent of the mothers and 16 percent of the fathers reported this as a major problem (Table 2.III). Our results also show that self-reported prevalence of psychological distress and depression among the students (how often one thinks about death and suicide) is two times more frequent than that among the parents (12 and 6.5 percent, respectively). Our questions on parent-child communication also revealed an interesting reflection of the effects of traditional roles of parents and children within a family. When we asked our student sample to name the topics which they consider taboo or most inhibited to discuss with their parents, the ranking was as follows: dating, sex, and drinking. It is interesting that Indo-American college students find discussions about dating are more inhibiting than talking about sex with their parents. Perhaps the parents believe that sex is an integral part of dating and therefore see dating as a serious threat to the traditional Indian systems of selection of marital partners through arranged marriage or elaborate matchmaking by the elderly members of the family and/or relatives.

Criteria of marital preferences. Our data show considerable similarities and differences between the parent and student samples in their preference of characteristics in a marital partner (Table 2:IV). We asked our respondents to rate on a 5-point scale (most important = 5; least important = 1) the criteria they consider important in choice of a marital partner. The three criteria considered most important in a marital partner by the parents and the students are to have a partner with same ethnicity, religion and language, in that order. A person from "same ethnicity" is the leading criterion for all subgroups by generation and gender; at least one-half or more respondents in each subgroup state that a person from "same ethnicity" is the most important criteria in a marital partner. The women students prefer "same ethnicity" in a marital partner (63 percent) more often than any

FIGURE 1

Health Behavior Matrix: Modern and Traditional Societies

Cultural	*Modern Societies*	*Traditional Societies*
*BVKAP Disease Etiology	(e.g., USA, UK, Canada) Modern Scientific, specialized (e.g., genetic, germs, toxins, & trauma)	(e.g., China, India) Unitary Cosmic & Magico-Religious (e.g., Chi, Yin/Yang, Karma, Tridosha) & Modern Scientific
Preferred Treatment Modality	Modern Clinical & Surgical Specialist Driven	Traditional Medical, Spiritual and Self-Care Augmented by Modern Medicine
Locus of Decision	Individual & Personal	Collective, Familial & Hierarchic & Compliant
Communication/ Social Relation	Mass: Printed & Electronic Formal & Impersonal	Informal Personal Network Augmented by Modern Media
Accessibility of Services	Highly Variable, Low/No Access for Disadvantaged	Traditional Services More Accessible & Affordable

*Beliefs, values, knowledge, attitude and practice.

Source: S. B. Kar, in "Health Promotion in Asian-Pacific Region," WHO/WPRO, 1993.

other subgroup; followed by the fathers (58 percent). Given the diversity in ethnic identity among the Indo-Americans, specially between the parents and students, one wonders what it means when a majority of both groups prefer a marital partner from "same ethnicity." A person from the same religion is considered important by about one-half of all respondents; it is more frequently mentioned by male parents (55 percent) followed by women students (50 percent). A person speaking the same language is listed as the third most important criteria (32 percent parents and 31 percent students, respectively).

Our findings challenge the popular belief about the significance of caste in marital decisions among Indo-Americans. The importance of caste in marital decisions is reinforced in matrimonial advertisements in newspapers serving Indo-American communities across the United States. One is expected to marry within his/her caste and if an individual marries above or below their caste, the husband's caste remains unchanged. Content analysis of matrimonial announcements in a recent issue of *India Abroad* showed the following specifications: over 90 percent specified caste, over 80 percent emphasized social standing of the family (inherited and father's or brother's earned status), and over 75 percent specified the province of origin. As expected, personal characteristics such as physical appearance with emphasis on complexion, age, education, and occupation are always stated. As a residual influence of traditional arranged marriage, rarely, if ever, the candidate places the announcement. While caste appears to be a major criterion in marital choices in these announcements, caste is considered to be among the least important factors in marital decisions by our respondents. Only 19 percent of the students believed caste is an important consideration; nearly three-fourths of the parents did not consider caste as an important factor (Table 2:IV). These findings suggest that the traditional Indian caste system quickly dissipates into a minor factor affecting only a minority of first genera-

tion Indo-American immigrants. Our results suggest that caste is not a closed system after all, and that the acculturation process in a modern industrialized society can overcome what was historically considered to be immutable.

The parents and students also share several concerns which they believe adversely affect their quality of life. First is their feeling of inadequate social networks and professional support necessary to cope with the sources of their intergenerational conflicts and psychological distress. Communication between parents and children on those topics which cause the most distress (e.g., dating, marriage) are the ones they feel most inhibited to discuss. Many are also reluctant to seek help for personal problems from professional care providers; when ill many (specially the elderly and women) tend to use self-care and traditional medicine with unknown benefits. In response to our request for write-in responses and suggestions about factors affecting their quality of life which they felt were not covered by our questionnaire, a surprisingly high 77 percent of the parents and 46 percent of the students wrote in their responses. Concerns about interracial conflicts were most frequently mentioned by both parents and students (31 and 22 percent, respectively). (See Table 4). The second most frequently mentioned concern among the parents was intergenerational and family conflicts (19 percent). The third important concern among the parents and students is the adverse effects of politics on their quality of life (15 and 16 percent, respectively). In spite of these concerns about factors adversely affecting their quality of life, there seems to be a void in the instrumental support systems they need to cope with these sources of concerns. While intergenerational conflicts due to value clashes identified earlier is a major concern for both parents and students, they do not use professional help nor do they have access to networks or support systems to deal with these problems. While they are concerned about the adverse effects of interracial tensions, negative political environment, "glass ceiling effects," and "model minority myth," the Indo-Americans are also least active in community organizations or political structures that address these concerns. These findings underscore the importance of organized response from within the Indo-American communities and of appropriate public policy analyses by social planners and academic institutions responsible for studying and addressing community needs in our increasingly multicultural societies.

Gender-Role Conflicts. One cannot look at the status of Indo-American immigrant women without considering the cultural heritage they bring from India. Equally important are the concepts of Indo-American immigrant men. In large part, Indo-American immigrant women still define their identity in terms of the patriarchal nature of Asian Indian society. Indo-American women, if single, are defined by their fathers' position and status; if married, by their husbands and later, their sons'. Very rarely are they considered to be or consider themselves to be individuals in their own right. Their status comes from their adherence to socially constructed gender roles.[18] These gender roles attempt to limit their identities to those of a daughter, wife and mother. These narrow confines can result in a great deal of pressure to suppress the natural growth process towards developing a concept of oneself as an autonomous individual. Indian identity is the "network of social roles, traditional values, caste customs and kinship regulations with which the treads of individual psychological developments are interwoven."[19] Upon immigration to the U.S., Indo-American women find an independence of thought that they had not previously believed possible. As they attempt to expand beyond the narrow boundaries of their culturally defined existence, they often clash with the expectations of the older generation and also of the males of their own generation. In attempting to build a new sense of self, they often find themselves torn between the expectations of their natal culture and the possibilities available in their new homes. Even when Indo-American women work outside the home,

they are still expected to come home and maintain the appropriate submissive attitude of their traditional gender role. It is emotionally difficult for these women to assert their newly developing sense of self within these restrictive roles. This can lead to great emotional stress as they attempt to juggle two diametrically opposed ways of being: one culture stresses individuality and the other, conformity. This is not the "double-duty" syndrome which working mainstream American women face in attempting to juggle both a career and their responsibilities at home. It goes beyond that to include emotional and psychological stress as women are literally forced to develop two "different personalities"—one as the assertive career woman appropriate to the dominant Euro-American working culture and the other as the subordinate woman in the home. The development of two "different personalities," can have devastating long-term effects. This phenomena was illustrated in the recent film *Knowing Her Place* (1992) by Indu Krishnan. This film depicts an Indo-American woman who is trapped in these two roles; as a result, she attempts suicide.

Marriage and Divorce. The phenomenon of divorce among Indo-Americans is a complicated issue. In the larger Euro-American population divorce is understood as a life-altering experience that requires an examination of self at a very basic level. Indo-American women also undergo this restructuring of their lives and a redefinition of identity but with further complications due to the nuances of their patriarchal heritage. This situation is further complicated by the fact that divorce among Indo-Americans is a fairly recent phenomenon but one that is increasing. According to the 1990 Census, 13.4 percent of Asian Indian women were classified as residing in "maritally disrupted" homes (this includes separated, divorced and widowed). Indo-American society as a whole and the individual families concerned are not socially or emotionally prepared to handle the upheaval that divorce can create. There is no infrastructure established to ease these women and men into new societal roles. A divorced woman who is independent is an anomaly within an Indo-American society; the community is not adequately equipped to incorporate her into a family setting and to ascribe her appropriate social roles to ease her painful transition. Therefore, many times, these women are at the periphery of society. This situation creates a great deal of psychological stress. With the knowledge that divorce may have such consequences, many women continue in marriages that may not be healthy and therefore, suffer stress and depression.

Policy and Societal Implications. Nearly seventy-five years ago, the philosopher-poet Rabindranath Tagore cautioned Indian political and educational leaders: "When races come together, as in the present age, it should not be merely the gathering of a crowd; there must be a bond of relation, or they will collide with each other."[20] The Los Angeles Uprising of 1992 proved this prophecy. An effective social policy and program must promote "a bond of relation" at first and then channel this force to build bridges between peoples' needs, aspirations and resources. Multiethnic communities consist of culturally diverse groups which vary from one another in terms of objective needs and subjective priorities, interethnic stereotypes and relations affecting social participation, culturally rooted beliefs and values affecting health related practices, language and communication behavior, social network and leadership structures. Cultures may also vary significantly from one another in terms of the values and beliefs they hold about birth, death, illness and major life events; meanings, causes and consequences of these events; and appropriate preventive and healing practices. Finally, multicultural and disadvantaged urban communities consist of high-risk groups with special needs. Effective public policy strategy in such communities must be based upon a sound understanding of the way a culture affects quality of life and social relations of various ethnic groups and their special needs. In recognition of the needs of special populations; the

landmark report which defined our national strategy for disease prevention and health promotion states: "Special population groups often need targeted preventive efforts, and such efforts require understanding the needs and the disparities experienced by these groups. General solutions cannot always be used to solve specific problems."[21]

We highlight now three levels of policy and social action relevant to Indo-Americans in the following areas: (a) civic participation and community, (b) education and schooling, (c) health and human services, and (d) media and private organizations.

Civic Participation and Community

Due to their apparent achievements, the "model minority myth" may be specially applied to Indo-Americans resulting in a denial of their special problems and needs by the policy planners and professionals alike. In addition, a study by Nakanishi and colleagues indicated that Indo-Americans are least likely to register to vote.[22] The relative lack of political participation and social passivity by the Indo-Americans deprives them of the opportunity to publicize their special needs and to participate in public policy debates affecting their lives. To a large extent this model minority myth is based upon the relative successful educational and economic achievements of a few groups of established early immigrants (mainly Japanese and Chinese) who have had over a century of acculturation and adaptation experience in this country.

Extreme diversity among Indo-Americans makes it difficult, if not impossible, for Indo-Americans to organize around common issues. However, our study revealed at least three issues common to the Indo-American community. They include: the educational, occupational and psychological well-being of children; intergeneration conflicts and lack of support systems; and, concerns about adverse effects of racial discrimination. These concerns may serve as common issues to unite Indo-Americans.

Education and Schooling

Typically, social science theories and methods which guide public policy and service strategies in the United States are based upon research conducted primarily among the dominant segment of the American population; we cannot assume that what is true for a dominant majority is valid for ethnic minorities. The social reality is more complex in communities where there is no single dominant majority (e.g., South Central Los Angeles and UCLA School of Public Health with five academic departments each with its own ideology and priorities). In such a diverse community, an effective public policy deliberation will require a "bottom-up" situation analysis, participatory needs assessments and social planning process in partnership with the diverse segments of the public and organizations serving them. A new perspective of multiculturalism for conducting social research, public policy debate and community interventions is long overdue. Academic centers and research universities should reexamine their commitment to the multicultural community they purportedly study and serve. The quality of our understanding of the realities and dynamics of multiculturalism will, in the final analysis, determine the quality of public policy and quality-of-life of all peoples. Practically no generalizable research is available on Indo-Americans; nor does there appear to be an active interest in studying them. Most mainstream researchers, sponsors of research and professionals, without support of any empirical evidence, tend to hold that Indo-Americans as a group are too small, or that they have no problems which warrant professional attention. Indeed, when we initiated the study, many academic colleagues advised us to abandon this line of inquiry. The situation outside the university is no different. Recently the Los Angeles County Department of Health Services had widely solicited and received numerous requests for information and financial support for developing innovative health promotion and disease prevention projects targeted at ethnic minorities; not a single request or proposal dealt with the Indo-American community.[23] Since Indo-Americans are among the largest and fastest growing Asian American minorities, and at the same time almost no empirical study exists on their health risks and factors affecting their quality of life of this important ethnic group, researchers, professional service providers and the community alike will gain from any pioneering work in this area.

Academic institutions have a special obligation to develop a better understanding of the Indo-American experience through original research, formal courses on campus and through an on-going dialogue between policy analysts, scholars, professionals and the Indo-American community. The second-generation Indo-Americans will also benefit from discovering their heritage through culture, literature and language studies and through study abroad programs in the Indian sub-continent. Most Indo-American students tend to follow their parents' footsteps and focus on the hard sciences or professional specialties (physics, engineering, medicine, law, etc). There is a need for recruiting Indo-American youths for the social studies and in professions serving communities directly (e.g., education, public health, social welfare). For those within academic fields, it is imperative to emphasize . . . not only theoretical research but also . . . multidisciplinary research on multicultural communities in general and of the Indo-Americans in particular.

Our findings suggest that the Indo-American college students suffer from a high level of psychological distress, intergenerational conflicts and interracial tensions. At the same time the providers of standard professional and health service are not familiar with the unique problems of this population. Academic institutions with large and increasing numbers of Asian Americans and Indo-American students (e.g., UCLA, UC Berkeley) have a special responsibility to develop culturally sensitive counseling and service programs addressing this population. Given the increasing financial constraints faced by most academic institutions, innovative solutions must be explored. For example, peer-counseling is now a standard feature in most student health service programs; efforts should be made to recruit, train and place Indo-American students as peer counselors to serve this group. Existing campus counselors and providers of psychological services would benefit from cultural sensitivity programs addressing the needs of Asian Americans in general and Indo-Americans in particular.

Continuing education is a requirement for several professions including health care providers serving our communities. Professional education and university extension programs have a responsibility for developing appropriate programs to educate and reeducate social service professionals to become more effective with multicultural populations. Cultural sensitivity training and a working understanding of the subtleties of Asian-American cultures should be incorporated into all professional education programs for social services and health care specialists (e.g., medicine, nursing, law, public health, social welfare).

Universities with large numbers of Asian-American and other ethnic minority students should initiate classes and seminar series on issues of multiculturalism and cultural diversity in their regular curriculum. However, this idea has yet to find its place in academic programs which are driven by established disciplines and professional specialties. For example, while over 42 percent of UCLA's 1994–95 incoming freshman class are Asian Americans and only 28.7 percent are white,[24] yet there are no regular course/s dealing with multiculturalism for the student population as a whole, nor on cultures and languages of several major Asian American groups. Studies on recent immigrants who have distinctly different needs than the established/early immigrants are practically absent. Formal courses and special seminar classes would serve as an important medium to provide essential background towards understanding the culture specific stressors and risk factors which affect various ethnic groups including Indo-Americans. Classes in Indo-American experience and general immigrant experience will help the second generation to understand the subtleties of the impact of their cultural identity on the formation of their individual identity. The classes will also provide a forum for them to explore these issues with other students of non-European and Indian origin. . . .

Dissemination of information regarding the issues which affect the quality of life of Indo-Americans is the first step towards increasing awareness and social support among the general public. It is this public, who, in the final analysis, must support any policy initiative for improving the quality of life of Indo-Americans, and other minority groups.

NOTES

Acknowledgments: The authors are grateful to the Asian American Studies Center at UCLA and particularly to Professor Don Nakanishi for providing us with valuable institutional and financial support without which this study would not have been possible. We thank the UC Pacific Rim Research Program for providing the funds needed to expand the study. We wish to thank Dr. Gauri Bhattacharya, Principal Investigator, National Development Research Institutes Inc., New York for her critical and constructive feedback. We thank the Federation of Indo-American Association (FIAA) and its National President, Mr. Inder Singh, and Mr. Ravi Murarka, the Publisher of the *India West* for co-sponsoring the survey.

1. The study of Indo-American quality of life was sponsored by the UCLA Asian American Studies Center and was directed by Professor Snehendu Kar. This intergenerational study served as the parent project for our subsequent multinational study of Asian immigrants. The ongoing multinational study is sponsored by the University of California systemwide Pacific Rim Research Program and is directed by Snehendu B. Kar. This multiuniversity collaborative research project is codirected by Professors Nelly Candeias and Ruy Laurenti of the University of Sao Paulo, Brazil; Professor Kyoichi Sonoda of the University of Tokyo, Japan; and Professor Eung Im Kim of the Seoul National University in Korea. The study involved surveys of samples of Japanese and Korean immigrants in the United States (California), Sao Paulo (Brazil), and Tokyo and Osaka (Japan).

2. This course was jointly offered by the Asian American Studies Center and the School of Public Health at UCLA.

3. Sripati Chandrasekhar, ed., *From India to America* (La Jolla: Population Review, 1984), Ronald Takaki, *India in the West* (New York: Chelsea House, 1995), Susan Gordon, *Asian Indian* (New York: Franklin Watts, 1990), *California's Punjabi Mexican Americans* (Philadelphia: Temple University Press, 1983*)*, Maxine Fisher, *The Indians in New York City* (New York, Columbia University Press, 1980), Sucheta Mazumder, "Racist Response to Racism: The Aryan Myth and South Asians in the United States," *South Asian Bulletin* 9:1 (1989), 47–55, The Women of South Asian Descent Collective, eds., *Our Feet Walk the Sky: Women of the South Asian Diaspora* (San Francisco, Aunt Lute Books, 1993), and literary works by Bharati Mukherjee.

4. Harry Kitano, *The Japanese Americans* (New York: Chelsea Press, 1993) and Harry Kitano and Roger Daniels, *Asian Americans: The Emerging Minority* (Englewood Cliffs, New Jersey: Prentice Hall, 1988).

5. Stanley Sue, "The Changing Asian American Population: Mental Health Policy," see #2.

6. Priya Aagarwal, A Passage from *India: Post 1965 Immigrants and their Children* (Palos Verdes, California: Yuvati Press, 1991); Pranab K. Nandi, *The Quality of Life of Asian Americans: An Exploratory Study in a Middle Size Community* (Chicago: Pacific-Asian American Mental Health Research Center, 1980).

7. Jayasree Ramakrishna and Mitchell G. Weiss, "'Health, Illness, and Immigration: East Indians in the United States," *The Western Journal of Medicine* 157 (1992):265–270.

8. Ramini S. Durvasula and Gaithri A. Mylvaganam, "Mental Health of Asian Indians: Relevant Issues and Community Implications," *Journal of Community Psychology* 27 (April 1994):97–108.

9. L. A. Wenzel, "The Rural Punjabis of California: A Religio-Ethnic Group," *Phylon* 29, *Atlanta University Review of Race and Culture* (1969):245–256; A. K. Flaueret, "Incorporation into Networks among Sikhs in Los Angeles" *Urban Anthropology* 78 (1974), 773–782; Karen Leonard, *Making Ethnic Choices: California's Punjabi-Mexican Americans* (Philadelphia: Temple University Press, 1994).

10. T. W. Smith, A Report on the Socio-Economic Status of Ethnic Groups in the U.S. (Chicago: University of Chicago, National Research Center 1992).

11. Paul Ong, ed., *The State of Asian Pacific America: Economic Diversity, Issues & Policies, A Public Policy Report* (Los Angeles: LEAP Asian Pacific American Public Policy Institute and UCLA Asian American Studies Center, 1994), Table 2, 152.

12. Ian McDowell and Claire Newell, eds., *Measuring Health: A Guide to Rating Scales and Questionnaires* (New York: Oxford University Press, 1987), John P. Robinson and Philip R. Shaver, *Measures of Personality and Social Psychological Attitudes* (San Diego: Academic Press, 1991).

13. Hadley Cantril, *Pattern of Human Concerns* (New Brunswick: Rutgers University Press, 1965).

14. Anthony Padilla, *Acculturation: Theory, Models and Some New Findings* (Boulder: Westview Press, 1980); G. Marin, F. Sabogal, B. Marin et al., "'Development of a Short Acculturation Scale for Hispanics," *Hispanic Journal of the Behavioral Sciences* 9 (1987):183–205.

15. Centers for Disease Control (CDC), *Behavioral Risk Factor Surveillance System (BRFSS).*

16. United Way, *The Los Angeles Fact Book, 1994 also a Report on Asian American Needs Assessment (1988).*

17. T. W. Smith, ibid.

18. The Women of South Asian Descent Collective, *Our Feet Walk the Sky*; and Sangeeta Gupta, "Shattered Dreams: Shattered Lives?: Indo-American Women and Divorce," unpublished thesis (UCLA), 1994.

19. S. Kakar, *The Inner World: A Psychoanalytical Study of Childhood and Society in India* (New York: Oxford University Press, 1981).

20. Rabindranath Tagore, "On Education,'" *A Tagore Reader*, Amiya Chakravarty, ed. (Boston: Beacon Press, 1961), 216.

21. M. Heckler, *Report of the Secretary's Task Force on Black and Minority Health* (Washington D.C., USDHS, 1985), 39.

22. Armando Jimenez, LADHS, personal communication (1995); Don T. Nakanishi, *The UCLA Asian Pacific American Voter Registration Study* (Asian Pacific American Legal Center, 1987); Aminder Dhillon, *India Journal* 5, (Nov. 25, 1994):2.

23. Jimenez, 1995.

24. *UCLA Today* (December 9, 1994).

A False and Shattered Peace

Katherine Kam

In a corner of a sparsely furnished living room, Keut Chun, a frail man bundled into a heavy jacket, sits on a floor mat and watches a videotape of the funeral for his daughter, Ram. On an altar above him, incense and flowers adorn a photograph of a little girl with bangs shading her eyes. The eight-year-old and four other youngsters died at the hands of a gunman who sprayed bullets across their school playground in Stockton during morning recess. Speaking through a Cambodian interpreter, Chun's wife, Im Chan, says her husband has watched the videotape every day since their daughter was buried two months earlier.

The shattering loss dredged up layers of old pain for Chun. Flashbacks of the four years the family endured beatings and hard labor in the Khmer Rouge camps in Cambodia. Nightmares of communist leader Pol Pot trying to kill him. The 42-year-old farmer lost more than 50 relatives before escaping in 1979 with his wife and son to a Thai refugee camp, where Ram was born. To this day, Chun refuses to tell even close friends how he became blind in one eye. He weeps when they ask him about it. And he weeps when his daughter is mentioned.

No one can say for sure what motivated Patrick Purdy, a young white drifter with a history of mental problems, to vent his rage upon 400 elementary schoolchildren before shooting himself through the head. Some believe racism drove him; others think he was too crazed to care what color his victims were. Purdy's bullets struck children of various races. But because four of the slain were Cambodian, one Vietnamese, and the majority of the 29 injured students also

Southeast Asians, Purdy's 106 rounds of fire ripped into the psyches of a refugee people who had already suffered some of the worst mass atrocities in recent history.

The shooting served as a grim reminder that perhaps there is no safe place in the world, not even for the children. "For a long time, I've never heard the guns," one refugee told reporters after his grand-daughter was injured. "This brought it all back."

Ironically, refugees came to this valley seeking sanctuary from their hardships. San Joaquin County's agricultural economy, low living costs and familiar climate have attracted 31,000 Southeast Asians since the mid-1970s. The majority are Cambodian or Vietnamese, although Laotians, Hmong, and Mien also reside in the valley. Most live in Stockton. Southeast Asians are more heavily concentrated in Stockton (pop. 189,000) than any other California city. Stockton houses the University of the Pacific but has a blue-collar feel, with industry centered around agricultural production and food processing. Many less educated refugees depend on public assistance. But some perform farm labor, and those with educational backgrounds have found jobs as bilingual aides, nurses, and accountants, or have opened small businesses.

Although Stockton offers relative peace compared to war-torn homelands, refugees face new problems such as racism, vandalism and discrimination in a job-scarce county that often resents and misunderstands them. Southeast Asians have been spat upon and called racial epithets. But no one was prepared for the events of January 17, 1989. Nor could anyone foresee the cultural collisions that would arise from starkly opposed Asian and western approaches to handling mental disorders and emotional crises.

Source: *California Tomorrow* (Summer 1989) pp. 8–21. Reprinted by permission.

UTTER TERROR

When news of the shooting broke out, hundreds of distraught parents converged on Cleveland Elementary, a cluster of brown buildings surrounded by homes and churches on a tree-lined street near the heart of town. Keut Chun and his wife heard about the shooting from a neighbor. Chun's wife, Im Chan, 36, a pretty woman with long, thick hair, ran to the school several blocks away. As emergency crews tended to the wounded, parents swarmed around the school, screaming and pleading for their children. Unable to speak much English, Im Chan panicked as she ran about trying to find Ram, the third oldest among her five children, and her son, Rann, who also attended Cleveland. Like other Southeast Asian parents, she clung to one of the few interpreters rushed to the scene. School staff worked frantically to reunite parents with youngsters, a task hindered by the fact that Cambodian women take neither the first nor last names of their husbands, while their children do. Im Chan found Rann unharmed, but Ram died alongside her best friend, Sokhim An. Their bodies had already been removed. The mother found her daughter's name on a list of injured. As Im Chan began screaming and shouting, school staff told her Ram was dead. "At first, nobody even told me," she says months later, still suspecting that the school was trying to hide the death from her. She ran home to tell her husband about Ram. Keut Chun was struck with violent chest pains that hospitalized him for four days.

The shooting terrified Stockton's entire Southeast Asian community, but the majority of the slain and injured were Cambodian. Many Cambodians congregate in certain apartment complexes around town, such as the Park Village Apartments within blocks of Cleveland School. The low-income, 230-unit stucco complex is considered a "first stop" for new arrivals. Families spread woven floor mats in living rooms with no furniture. Doors are often left open during the day, and residents, most unemployed, visit each other's homes casually. Women often cook outdoors. Many families of slain and injured children, including the Chuns, live in Park Village.

After years of persecution, many Southeast Asians worried that the shooting was not an isolated incident. Rumors ran rampant within Park Village. "There was a lot of fear that there was perhaps more than one gunman," recalls Dr. Steve Shon, a cross-cultural psychiatric specialist who journeyed to Stockton after the shooting. "There were fears that people were trying to kill them, exterminate them, kill their kids."

The refugees' initial instinct was to protect their children from another attack. At Cleveland, seven out of 10 students are Southeast Asian—mostly Cambodian and Vietnamese. Many are still trying to learn English. The school also has many Latinos and a large deaf population among its 1,000 students. The Southeast Asian aggregation had not been left to chance; the school district had grouped the children into three of the district's 21 elementary schools to make efficient use of limited numbers of bilingual aides. "But it doesn't look that way to people who have lived for decades in a traumatized situation," says San Joaquin County Mental Health Director Nita Rienhart. "It looks like we're out to do their children in." Anguished parents begged the school district to disperse the children so that no school would be, in their minds, as obvious a target as Cleveland. In the days after the shooting, most Southeast Asian parents kept their children out of Cleveland. Refugees throughout Stockton also kept their children home.

At Park Village, a throng of refugees listened as Cleveland principal Patricia Busher, speaking through a loudspeaker from a balcony, reassured them about the school's safety. Mental health authorities held meetings in community leaders' homes to soothe fears. But refugees still wondered whether the attack was racist or random. By week's end, Cleveland's enrollment returned to almost normal, but some parents had sent their children back only after warning them not to eat cafeteria food because it might be poisoned.

Fear and depression dominated the first days and weeks. Many Southeast Asian parents were numb with grief and shock. At the county's special Transcultural Mental Health Clinic, Cambodian women, dressed in attire ranging from colorful traditional cotton skirts to western pantsuits, sat in a circle during one somber session. Clinic social worker Lonny Mayeda, who is white, knew that Cambodian patients—considered among the most traumatized of Southeast Asians—had lost an average of six to nine close relatives in their lifetimes, compared to one or two for Laotians. A 1987 state-sponsored study found that Southeast Asians are more than four times more likely than the general population to have severe mental health needs because of the horrors they have endured. But Mayeda was unprepared for the chilling revelations she heard. Most of the women in the group had already lost spouses and entire sets of children in Cambodia. Some remained childless widows, but others had remarried and given birth to new offspring. Some of these children attended Cleveland School—and some had been injured.

Since the shooting, the women reported mental flashbacks of past horrors, sleeplessness, lack of appetite, hallucinations, withdrawal, anxiety and depression. Unfamiliar with western medicine, one Cambodian woman feared that upon release from the hospital, her injured son would die under her care at home. Said Mayeda: "They're ten times more afraid than their kids."

But the children were frightened, too. At the hospital, one wounded Cambodian girl became so terrified that she didn't utter a word for more than 24 hours. Not until a psychologist and Cambodian paraprofessional talked to her in her own language and asked her to draw pictures did she feel secure enough to talk again.

At Cleveland, children wanted the drapes closed. They talked of nightmares. Some feared going out on the playground again. They asked for reassurance that the "bad man who hurt little kids" was really dead, according to school psychologist Mike Armstrong.

Ram Chun's nine-year-old brother Rann had been on the playground with his sister when the gunfire erupted. He spotted Purdy quickly and fled to safety. Though he claims he is not afraid, his parents say he and his two younger siblings, James and Mary, stopped playing along the footpaths that wind through Park Village. The slim youngster with sad, questioning eyes feared going down the apartment's short hallway to the bathroom alone. At school, he refused to play on the playground.

Fear was mixed with anger and withdrawal. One eight-year-old girl came to Cleveland frustrated and fell asleep at her desk frequently. The school learned her mother was so retraumatized by the shooting, even though none of her own children had been wounded or killed, that she stayed in bed all day. It was up to the girl to care for four younger siblings after school.

In a flat located one block from the funeral home that held the bodies of the Cambodian children, Touch Lim and his wife, Mak Inn, mourned the loss of daughter Oeun, who was eight. Her picture hung prominently in the living room amid those of the other Lim children. An autographed photo of Michael Jackson hung in the corner, a souvenir from the singer's visit to Cleveland School three weeks after the shooting.

The Lims' small home was decorated for the Asian new year with festive streamers, but Mak Inn's face was crumpled with grief. The couple had already lost three children during Pol Pot's murderous reign from 1975 to 1979. "We come here and another child dies. Why?" her husband asked. The family put fresh food at an altar for Oeun at every meal because her spirit still might be hungry, they said. But Touch Lim felt no peace. "I am angry," he told one of the multitude of newspaper reporters who came to his home. "I need to get this anger off my chest, but I don't know what to do about it. There is nothing I can do about it."

Funeral arrangements only increased the sense of helplessness. Southeast Asians wanted their customary large, elaborate ceremony—a symbol of healing and transition—rather than a small, somber western funeral. But the Buddhist families feared that a Buddhist ceremony with cremation, instead of a Christian one with burial, would offend Americans. The legally required autopsies upset parents greatly, especially the Buddhists, who believed cutting the bodies would interfere with proper reincarnation. The parents also were distressed by laws that prevented them from taking the bodies of their children home to prepare them for burial, as they would have done in their native countries.

Nonetheless, on January 23, six days after the shooting, the Chuns, the Lims and other families felt honored and comforted when dignitaries such as state Superintendent of Schools Bill Honig, Governor George Deukmejian and state Attorney General John Van de Kamp joined more than 3,000 mourners of all colors in a Buddhist-Christian service at the city's civic auditorium. Each slain child was remembered with a minute of silence. Sokhim An. Ram Chun. Oeun Lim. Rathanar Or. Thuy Tran. Later, Sokhim and Ram, best friends in life, were buried side by side.

THE MENTAL HEALTH RESPONSE

The larger community responded dramatically to the shooting. Southeast Asian organizations from all over the state sent relief workers. International donations poured into memorial funds set up to help the families and school. Outpourings of sympathy filled Cleveland with cards, flowers, and drawings made by schoolchildren throughout the country. Legislation to ban assault weapons was proposed in several states.

Likewise, the normally fragmented mental health system came together immediately to treat the victims. Just after the shooting, counselors arrived at the school and the county Mental Health Department dispatched one-quarter of its 120 clinicians to do around-the-clock duty at local hospitals. With instructions no more elaborate than to "saddle up," counselors consoled the gathering families and prepared parents for the

injuries they were about to see. From the beginning, it was clear that the catastrophe was compounded by vast cultural differences. Says social worker Lonny Mayeda, who was with the families at the hospital: "We didn't know what we were doing culturally. We were trying to do what was sensitive, but there were no rules."

Two days after the massacre, the Stockton Unified School District brought in Dr. Steve Shon, a psychiatrist who heads the state Mental Health Department's three-year Refugee Mental Health Project, to coordinate a system plunged into crisis. Shon, a soft-spoken, neatly groomed man in his forties, is the grandson of Korean immigrants. He went to college and medical school in the late 1960s and early 70s, when mental health came to the forefront of U.S. public consciousness. His parents were perplexed when he decided to become a psychiatrist, but the specialty catered to Shon's fascination with the "different ways people think and view the world," he says. As a medical student in San Francisco, he created an Asian health caucus to make physicians aware of cross-cultural issues. In the 1970s, the appearance of traumatized Southeast Asians in mental health clinics prompted Shon to broaden his scope.

Shon's strategy in Stockton was community-wide. During the weeks after the tragedy, almost everyone connected with the shooting—teachers, school staff, ambulance drivers, paramedics, emergency room workers, firefighters—received "psychological debriefings" or group counseling. Shon was particularly concerned that Southeast Asians would experience flare-ups of the little-understood Post-Traumatic Stress Disorder (PTSD), thought to be a lifelong condition that waxes and wanes. Reminders, such as the anniversary of a traumatic event or a new trauma like the shooting, could trigger flashbacks after a period of calm. To avoid reawakening distressing memories, counselors should avoid pushing Southeast Asian parents to talk before they were ready, Shon warned. At Cleveland, school psychologists monitored children during the critical period up to eight weeks after the event, during which PTSD symptoms could first be expected.

Shon knew that Southeast Asian communities such as Park Village were insular and did not know where mental health services were available. "They don't use the media the way most people do," he says. "They don't watch the news at 6 o'clock and at 10 o'clock and read the newspaper. A lot of them have trouble with English." A different tactic would be required to reach them. "We knew we couldn't just open a clinic and say, 'Come on in. We have to talk to you and debrief you all,'" Shon says. The morning after the shooting, families of all five slain children were summoned to the county mental health center and assigned case workers to help with funeral arrangements and other practicalities. School psychologists, public health nurses and social workers monitored families of all the wounded children. Refugees whose children escaped physical harm were sought out too. Mental health workers scattered throughout Park Village and other Southeast Asian enclaves, distributing fliers printed in Vietnamese, Cambodian, Lao and Hmong. The fliers listed a multilingual hotline and also referred refugees to the Transcultural Mental Health Clinic.

Unlike their parents, Cleveland School youngsters would benefit from immediate counseling, Shon and others believed. The children were more expressive and generally have experienced fewer traumas, although older ones might have witnessed violence in refugee camps. In small groups, the children talked. Those with limited English drew pictures about their feelings. While some youngsters believed a dead classmate would never come back, others, mainly Buddhists, believed the child would be reincarnated to live another life. One Southeast Asian girl described intrusive thoughts about the shooting:. "The Spirit God in my head is showing me the pictures again." Cambodian Buddhist children said they were afraid of evil spirits in the bathrooms on the playground. Many wanted spiritual answers to their fears.

The school used cultural rituals to allay these fears. Upon Buddhist parents' request, the school allowed Buddhist monks to perform a purification ceremony that involved sprinkling holy water on the playground. The Chuns refused to attend—Keut Chun is still angry that his daughter's body was removed from the playground before he had a chance to see her—but other families were visibly relieved. Vietnamese leaders also came to Cleveland to hold a joyous new year's ceremony. Men in robes and hats prayed for the slain and beseeched ancestors and local spirits to watch over the San Joaquin Valley.

Despite these successes, Cleveland soon faced stark realities. One month after the shooting, the initial crush of counselors left and a school clinic—staffed by one psychologist—was set up in a donated ship's cargo container. By the time the clinic opened, there were already 19 referrals, some for post-traumatic stress. Children complained of headaches or strange flu-like symptoms. One child stopped eating because of delusions that all the food was infested with vermin. Another child hallucinated that tap water turned to blood when he washed his face. Others needed escorts to go from classroom to classroom, or regressed into bed-wetting. The clanging of tetherball chains terrified youngsters into believing the shooting was happening all over again.

Soon teachers—themselves traumatized—complained publicly that the school district was not providing enough psychologists and bilingual aides. California has few licensed Southeast Asian mental health professionals. Stockton has only one, a Vietnamese psychologist. A Buddhist priest who works as a licensed behavioral specialist in Long Beach might be the state's only Cambodian mental health professional. After the shooting, Stockton brought up one Vietnamese psychiatrist from Los Angeles, but otherwise had to rely on Southeast Asian paraprofessionals who came from other cities. When these workers left, the language and cultural differences grew sorely obvious, and the teachers' charges of inadequate psychological resources grew more compelling. The children, who seemed to benefit from mental health treatment, were not getting enough help.

THE FAMILIES TURN ELSEWHERE

To the contrary, the initial onslaught of help and media attention overwhelmed parents such as the Chuns. In the weeks after the shooting, a parade of news reporters, camera operators, victims witness advocates, social workers, psychologists, and public health nurses visited the families. So many faces passed through the Chuns' door that when asked to recall who came and for what purposes, Keut Chun draws a blank, then produces a packet of dozens of business cards he has collected. "If they came maybe two or three times a week, that would be all right," he says. "But they came four or five times a day, sometimes as late as midnight. I wanted to be left alone. I felt sick when they came."

Particularly confusing were offers of mental health assistance. Typically, Southeast Asians believe someone is either normal or "crazy," with no shades in between. A person only seeks help from outsiders if he is insane. Nor do Southeast Asian cultures have a history of psychotherapy. Instead, "crazy" ones are locked away in institutions, with great stigma visited upon the patients and their families.

Unlike westerners, who may speak of emotional distress in terms of feelings, many Southeast Asians manifest generalized physical complaints—back pains, stomach aches, headaches and dizziness. Often, they seek medical treatment and dismiss as incompetent psychiatrists and counselors who prescribe no medication but talk only. One month after the shooting, Im Chan suffers dizziness and headaches. She pulls back her shirt collar to reveal medicinal patches below her throat. Deep purple creases line her eyes. "I'm very sick," she whispers.

The whole concept of mental health escapes Im Chan and her husband. An interpreter's attempt to translate the term in ways the couple might understand proves futile. Im Chan says "two ladies"—she does not know what department they come from—tell her "not to worry, stay

quiet, have peace of heart, don't think so much about my daughter," but she finds it more helpful when people at her Christian church pray and lay hands on her. Keut Chun says he welcomes help from the "system," but that he doesn't know what to ask for because he doesn't understand its rules. In the refugees' old countries, the government would not have dispatched mental health workers after a tragedy. The victims would have looked to their own, as they had always done. Stockton's Southeast Asian community set up transportation and interpretation services for the stricken families and held home gatherings for them. A dozen extended family members flocked to the Chun home the night of the shooting. News of Ram's death reached relatives in Dallas, where the Chuns lived after coming to the U.S. in 1984. The relatives telephoned Sophal Ung, a Cambodian Christian pastor in Stockton, and implored him to help the family.

Like the Chuns, Southeast Asian families affected by the tragedy turned to religious leaders after the shooting. Two of the dead children were Buddhist, three Christian. In Stockton, free flow and friendship exist between the two bodies of believers, despite theological differences. Ung's church had sponsored the Chuns in the U.S. Like them, Ung knows tragedy first-hand. He labored for four years in the Khmer Rouge camps, suffering beatings and coming near death many times. He lost several friends and family members, including an infant daughter, before making his escape to Thailand. When he reached the U.S. with his family, his wife succumbed to cancer at age 34, leaving him a widower with six children. The Chuns attend church with Ung, who also visits them regularly. A month after the shooting, a vivid dream pierced Im Chan's nightmares. She told Ung she saw her slain daughter "living with God in heaven. She was wearing a white dress, clapping her hands and smiling down at me."

The Chuns trust Ung. Together, they come from a culture influenced by strong Confucian ethics that emphasize coping, family stability, maintaining personal dignity and the dignity of one's family—in short, not losing face by exposing problems to outsiders other than village elders or religious leaders. "If I know someone, I will tell him everything in my heart," Im Chan says. "If I don't know him, I will say nothing."

Other families of injured and slain Southeast Asian children journeyed to a yellow house on a country road hear the edge of town. There, they sought comfort from Dharmawara Mahathera, a high-ranking, 100-year-old monk considered the spiritual head of Stockton's Cambodian Buddhists. Dharmawara's saffron robes cloak a serene old man who speaks and moves deliberately. The house he shares with other Buddhist monks and nuns is filled with religious icons and a large altar with a multitude of Buddha statues surrounded by lights.

The families don't say much when they come. They ask "Bhante," as the monk is respectfully addressed by his followers, to chant mantras over them and to meditate with them. About one month after the shooting, a little boy whose sister died at Cleveland began crying uncontrollably because he thought he had seen a vision of the girl dancing before his eyes. His parents brought him to Dharmawara, whose prayers calmed the child down.

In Dharmawara's world, the concept of mental health is suspect. The monk is baffled by what he sees as a contradiction: psychiatrists treat mental illness with drugs, while psychologists treat clients with counseling. Dharmawara sees the mental health establishment's flurry of activity as an overreaction that underestimates the families' ability to overcome their grief eventually. He reflects a quiet Buddhist acceptance of his people's difficulties. Asked about the holocaust Cambodians have faced, he only says, "It is true that we are suffering more than others."

Naren Lor, a well-educated, elderly Cambodian visitor at Dharmawara's home, ridicules mental health notions. "In my country, they put all the crazy people in one hospital," she says. "When you are crazy, they don't help you. All my family, the good people, they don't go there." She suspects that Southeast Asians who voluntarily use mental health services are merely trying to find a way to receive disability payments. Another visitor, the boyfriend of a slain child's mother, disparages the way the family was "assigned" to go for county mental health appointments.

Dharmawara believes the answer to the families' distress is prayer and meditation. Compared to his ancient religion, he says, western mental health is a very young field that doesn't recognize the spiritual side of human beings. Because the field lacks spirituality, many Cambodians distrust it. "Priests go deeper into the hearts and minds of the hearer," Dharmawara says. "This matter concerns the mind. It concerns spirituality. I don't think any crude remedy will solve the problem. Prayer is enough."

THE LONG ROAD AHEAD

But offering victims no mental health assistance goes deeply against the instincts of U.S. practitioners. It is also politically unacceptable. The mental health response to the tragedy reflects a well-intentioned but perhaps subconsciously paternalistic American need to intervene.

Shon, a sympathetic physician who has devoted his entire career to Asian mental health, has no objections to Southeast Asians' tendency to turn to religion for help. Too often, he says, western practitioners are trained to view religious beliefs as sources of conflicts that can lead to psychological disorders. Shon believes that practitioners who understand the cultures of Southeast Asian patients should incorporate religious practices in therapy. "This is what you encourage them to do—things that are part of their experience to help them reduce anxiety, feel better about what's going on—whether it's going to see the monk, taking herbal medicines, giving offerings—the kinds of rituals and routines they've been used to all their lives."

But he views the refugees' flashbacks, severe depressions and other stress symptoms as requiring professional mental health treatment.

Leaving the conditions unattended is no option. "There are problems with that because there are long-lasting effects that limit people's lives. The native culture is not necessarily doing anything better, not that mental health is going to take [all the problems] away."

He disagrees that prayer is the only way. "I think that when you think there's only one way, that's always dangerous. There are a lot of roads to roam." Reliance on spirituality alone, no matter how effective it may be in its original context, ignores the fact that the refugees now live in a bicultural society and must deal with prejudice, poverty, family upheaval and cultural shock, some mental health specialists argue. In this view, treatment should combine Asian and western notions. . . . Ideally, proponents say, there would be many U.S. trained Southeast Asian mental health professionals who can bridge the language, cultural and religious gap.

Some refugees are amenable to culturally sensitive western mental health treatment and may benefit from it. For other refugees, however, mental health treatment may be of no help. Clearly, the concept is not understood or welcomed: refugees prefer their own way of coping. Still others, who have experienced such incredible trauma, may simply be lost. Says Dharmawara: "They are lost in all these waves of violence and they can't recover themselves now."

As it stands, the dispute remains largely theoretical. County case workers, without a common tongue for counseling and without spiritual beliefs to share with parents, truly cannot do much more than offer comfort and an extra pair of arms. "I don't think of mental health therapy and counseling even as a first choice [of treatment]," says social worker Janet Gedigian, an Armenian whose own grandparents fled the Turkish massacres. She admits she had doubts about how she could best aid the families. "Most people have their own skills and ways of coping preferable to what we have to offer if they work. These families are survivors or they wouldn't be here. Somebody from the welcome wagon didn't pick them up to bring them here. They went through hell to get here."

But the struggles are enormous and the future often uncertain. Keut Chun and Im Chan grow more afraid. In the U.S., their family life has turned upside down. Increasingly, the couple's 16-year-old son challenges their authority. He has been caught fighting at school and has skipped class for weeks at a time to hang out with streetwise friends. In Cambodia, such rebellion is almost unheard of, and the Chuns are at a loss. They have asked trusted Cambodian church leaders to reason with the boy.

Keut Chun's partial blindness, stress, severe headaches and depression, combined with his lack of job and language skills, keep him from working. In Cambodia, he was the strong head of his household. Here, he sits dejectedly and defers to his wife when outsiders come. When the family lived in Dallas, Im Chan was able to find several temporary work assignments. She answers simple questions in English, but her husband cannot.

Chun seems resigned to his fate. He had escaped to Thailand with hopes of returning to Cambodia once the country's turmoil eased. He never intended to be resettled in a country where people move so fast and ways are so strange. He has given up his life. "I am already old," he says. "When I came here, I wanted my children to grow up to be good, to have good educations, to be doctors or teachers, to have a better life in this country."

There is hope for the children. Already, Rann Chun has grown a little less fearful of going into the bathroom alone.

But in the living room, his father continues to watch the videotape of Ram's funeral day after day. Pallbearers march across the screen carrying coffins mounted with huge photographs of the youngsters. Mourners chant prayers in Cambodian. Keut Chun lowers his head as his eyes mist. "I will never believe my daughter is dead."

CHAPTER 8

New Asian American Families, Identities, and Culture

The previous chapter highlighted the diverse and changing Asian American families and identities. This chapter takes the theme of diversity and change even further. One of the most exciting areas of research in Asian American studies today centers on new and emerging families, identities, and cultural formations. The selections featured in this chapter concern Asian American intermarriage, multiraciality, and the gay and lesbian experience. Much of the research done in these areas is being conducted by a younger generation of Asian American scholars, writers, and activists who recognize that there must be expansion of Asian American perspectives.

Larry H. Shinagawa and Gin Y. Pang present the latest analysis of Asian American intermarriage. Much of the scholarly literature in the 1980s and early '90s focused on Asian American interracial marriage, or the marriage of two people from different races. On the other hand, Shinagawa and Pang show a marked increase in intraethnic marriage between Asian American groups. This research is significant because it provides an overview of Asian American intermarriage patterns and identifies a number of factors that may explain the most recent shift toward intraethnic marriage. Among these factors are the growth in population and concentration, similarities in socioeconomic and educational achievements, and increased racial consciousness.

The interest in Asian American interracial marriage has been greater than on intraethnic marriage because of the emergence of a growing number of biracial and multiracial Asian American offspring. The most well known is golf superstar Tiger Woods, who is one-eighth Native American, one-eighth African American, one-quarter white, one-quarter Thai, and one-quarter Chinese. Angelo Ragaza describes how mixed-race Asian Americans are redefining the Asian American experience. When mixed-race individuals refuse to make the forced choice of being one race or another, they challenge society's racial stereotypes and limited categories. Asian American images of mixed-race people are often quite negative and biased, and this is especially true with those who have mixed African American and Asian American heritage. Mixed-race people often have to rely on one another for support to create a sense of identity. As a result, they have begun to organize together around specific issues of special significance to them. One example is the proposed change in the U.S. Census that allows individuals to select a mixed-race category, rather than being forced to designate only one race.

Another emerging change in the Asian American family, identity, and cultural structure is the acceptance of the Asian American gay and lesbian experience. Journalist Carlos Mendez offers a provocative profile of Asian American gay activist and attorney. J. Craig

Fong. In the article, Fong expresses his candid views on a number of issues important to the Asian American, as well as to gay and lesbian communities. In 1993 Fong was named the West Coast Director of the Lambda Legal Defense and Education Fund, the nation's premier gay and lesbian civil rights organization. Prior to his appointment with Lambda, Fong was the Immigration Project Director for the Asian Pacific American Legal Center. The transition from an Asian American civil rights organization to a gay and lesbian civil rights organization was not difficult for Fong because he believes civil rights for gays and lesbians are no different from civil rights issues for everyone else. Despite Fong's ability to serve as a bridge to both communities, he acknowledges the sensitive topic of homophobia among Asian Americans, and raises several other controversial issues.

The complexity of Asian American homophobia is at the center of the article by Alice Y. Hom. Hom interviewed thirteen Asian American parents of gay and lesbian children, and several themes emerged from her research. Her article focuses on the attitudes and reactions of parents before and after they found out about their children's sexuality, the parents' abilities to discuss their children with friends and others, and what advice the Asian American parents would offer to other Asian American parents of gay and lesbian children. Asian American gays and lesbians have published their own "coming out" stories, but there is nothing written from or about their parents' perspectives. Hom's article begins an honest and healthy dialogue between parents and children about sexuality.

Reading 28

Asian American Panethnicity and Intermarriage

Larry Hajime Shinagawa and Gin Yong Pang

Yen Le Espiritu describes Asian American panethnicity as "the development of bridging organizations and solidarities among several ethnic and immigrant groups of Asian ancestry."[1] Espiritu depicts panethnicity as a political and social construction, heavily influenced by the continuing discrimination and oppression of racial minorities. Although there are centrifugal forces that threaten ethnic conflict, Espiritu is confident in the continual development of Asian panethnicity. As long as outside forces treat and perceive Asians as a "race," and as long as Asian Americans can benefit from fusion and shared identification, Espiritu believes that panethnicity will continue to evolve as a dynamic and powerful center of identity.

Since Asian Americans are treated as racial minorities and because they proactively forge new identities, panethnicity should become evident in the most consciousness-related and intimate of relationships—marriages. As Espiritu states:[2]

This book [*Asian American Panethnicity*] focuses primarily on the institutionalization of pan-Asian consciousness. An important next step would be to quantify this consciousness by studying interpersonal pan-Asian ethnicity—most important, its marriage patterns. Most often used to study rates of overall assimilation, intermarriage between ethnic subgroups is an equally good measure of panethnicity at the individual level. Just as intermarriage between major ethnic groups can obliterate boundaries, so intermarriage within these categories can fuse subgroups into one panethnic group.

Source: Amerasia Journal 22:2 (1996): 127–152. Reprinted by permission.

This article examines Asian American marriage patterns. We start with a description of terms to clarify our understanding of the processes of racial and ethnic identification and the development of panethnicity. We next discuss our methodology, where we employ 1980 and 1990 Census data for California to study marriage patterns. We end with a discussion of the possible reasons for the increase in Asian panethnic marriages and explore the implications of this increase for race relations and Asian Americans in particular. Our implicit thesis is that Asian panethnicity, and consequently, Asian interethnic marriage, is growing because Asian Americans are acculturating and learning the main text of American race and ethnic relations: that race, coupled with a growing sense of shared socioeconomic and cultural considerations, defines the primary experiences and affiliations of American society more so than does ethnicity.

THEORETICAL UNDERPINNINGS OF TERMINOLOGY: RACE, ETHNICITY, ETHNIC IDENTITY, AND IDENTI-FACTUAL IDENTITY

Before we investigate the marriage patterns of Asian Americans, we need to define several concepts. Although there are a variety of perspectives in the literature of race and ethnic relations, we use terms with specific definitions which we feel are relevant to panethnicity. More important, these terms are theoretically viewed by researchers as having seminal importance to this topic.

By *race,* we agree with Omi and Winant[3] that it is a social and political construction, but we underscore the relationship between conception, perception, and phenotype rather than emphasizing race as a situs of social conflict and significance. Whereas Omi and Winant define race as "a concept which signifies and symbolizes social conflicts and interests by referring to different types of human bodies," we define race as a group of individuals who are given a set of values, beliefs, and stereotypical behaviors based upon their perceived visible averaged phenotype, most especially by their perceived skin color. Using our concept, a person can belong to a race without necessarily identifying with such a race. They belong because others *perceive* and *evaluate* them to be part of a race and because they are given imputed characteristics and behaviors based on what people choose to perceive.

By *ethnicity,* we refer to a group of individuals who share, communicate and act from the basis of a common history and culture, sometimes a language or slang, and who at one time or another in their collective experiences came from some part of the earth, either actually or mythically.[4] Most ethnic groups are formed by the process of migration; that is, they left some part of the world and forged a new sense of shared community that links this past with the present. Most ethnic groups in the United States tend to be associated with the broad races that have been created through the process of racial formation[5]— Chinese American with Asian, Polish American with White, and Nigerian American with Black.

By *ethnic identity,* we refer to how an individual chooses to identify with ethnic and/or racial group(s).[6] Ethnic group and ethnic identity are not one and the same. Persons can, to different degrees, choose how they wish to express their ethnic attachments. Some may act to distance their membership so as not to be mistaken and suffer the blame for the presumed misdeeds of that group.[7] Others, as Herbert Gans suggests, may strongly identify with their ethnic group and derive meaning and rootedness from such membership.[8]

While there are many forms of ethnic identity, we wish to take note of what we call *identi-factual* ethnic identity. Under identi-factual identity, the community, the family, and the larger society mutually reinforce and mold the ethnic identity of the individual. Identi-factual identity is, therefore, in part, a *given* ethnic identity. In this sense, it shares with race an aspect of objectification (that is, part of their identity exists whether the person chooses to identify with their own ethnic background or not, because others continue to perceive differences or commonalties). In turn, since it is reinforced so substantially by others, the individual tends to be continually aware of one's own identi-factual identity. For example, many, perhaps most, racial minority individuals tend to exhibit identi-factual identity because the larger white society continues to discriminate against them and sets them apart on the basis of perceived "racial" phenotype. On the other hand, most white Americans do not unless they were raised in white-ethnic communities (e.g., Jewish "ghettoes" or Italian neighborhoods). Perceiving themselves as the American mainstream, Whites are not constantly forced to identify with their ethnicity and race because it is not *prescribed* to them.[9] For them, ethnic identity is largely voluntary choice in contrast to racial minorities.[10]

RACE AS REPRESENTATION

Part of the reason for identi-factual identity among racial minorities is the congruence or lack of congruence between *race* and *race as representation.* While race is an objectification and blanket-statement of a group of individuals on the basis of perceived phenotype, *race as representation* is the intersubjective meaning an individual has with the given identification of his or her race as shown to others. A strong relationship between race and race as representation tends to verify social preconceptions of racial categorizations, providing social support for individuals from their own racial group and sometimes recognition from those outside of their group, while a lack of congruence can lead to accusations of "betrayal" and being inattentive to the needs of one's "own" race.[11]

PANETHNICITY

We now return, fortified by this theoretical discussion, to the original focus on panethnicity. In the United States, where race and ethnicity meet and where identi-factual identity is most present among individuals is where panethnicity develops. Panethnicity typically originates from racist stereotyping and race-lumping of distinct ethnic groups. At first, race-lumping is more a reflection of racist perceptions by the majority than a reflection of shared identity among the minorities Yet, eventually, members of disparate groups begin to recognize that they have a shared identity that is shaped by common experience. In time, they not only recognize a utilitarian use of racial identification, but they begin to proactively perceive that their identities, which were once outside of themselves and objectified by the Other, are now simultaneously objectified and intersubjective, enfused with new meaning. They form webs of social and political organizations and institutions and, in turn, develop a new panethnic consciousness. As they acculturate and realize the importance of race in social relations in the United States, members of separate Asian ethnic groups begin to also identi-factually perceive themselves as Asian Americans.

With new interlocking institutions and a shared consciousness, the possibilities for social, intimate interaction for individuals of different ethnic groups increase. An example is the growth of interethnic Asian marriages.

METHODOLOGY

ifornia and the United States as a whole,[12] using weights provided by the U.S. Bureau of the Census.[13] Cross-classification tables were constructed to describe marriage patterns by various social factors. In all cases, the cross-classification tables were statistically significant at the .01 level according to chi-square tests.

Marriage patterns are defined by the researchers as the four most likely variations by race/ethnicity: intraethnic marriages, interethnic marriages, minority-minority marriages, and minority-majority marriages. Intraethnic marriages are those involving spouses of the same ethnicity (e.g., Chinese American to Chinese American). Interethnic marriages are those in which a person marries a spouse of another ethnicity but of the same race (e.g., Chinese American to Korean American). Minority-minority marriages are those involving spouses of two different minority races (e.g., Chinese American to African American). Minority-majority marriages, which have historically been the most prevalent among racial minorities,[14] are those where one spouse is minority and the other is non-Hispanic White (e.g., Chinese American to White).

Asian Pacific interethnic marriages involve both spouses being from the following groups: Chinese, Filipinos, Japanese, South Asians, Koreans, Vietnamese, Cambodians, Hmongs, Laotians, Thais, and other Asian Americans, Hawaiians, Samoans, Tongans, Chamorros, and other Pacific Islanders. This article focuses on the marriage patterns of the largest groups in California: Chinese, Filipinos, Japanese, Koreans, and Vietnamese Americans.[15]

Marriage tables were constructed for the San Francisco Bay area, Los Angeles County, Orange County, San Diego County, Sacramento County, Central Valley urban areas, other high Asian Pacific American concentration counties, and low concentration counties. The following analysis will focus primarily upon the general results

FINDINGS

National Asian Pacific Marriage Patterns, 1980 and 1990

There has been a dramatic shift in the intermarriage patterns of Asian Pacific Americans from the 1980s to the 1990s. On a national level, in 1980, the majority of Asian Pacific intermarriages were inter-racial—mostly with Whites.[16] However, ten years later, the number of interethnic marriages involving spouses from other ethnic backgrounds has now approached or has exceeded interracial marriages.

According to Lee and Yamanaka in 1980, 25.4 percent of all Asian American marriages were intermarriages: 22.7 percent were interracial, and 2.7 percent were interethnic.[17] By 1990, on a national level, our research found that 31.2 percent of all Asian Pacific husbands and 40.4 percent of wives were intermarried. Specifically, 18.9 percent of husbands were interethnically married, and 12.3 percent were interracially married. Asian Pacific men married to Whites dramatically decreased as a proportion of all marriages; only 9.9 percent had married Whites. Similarly, for Asian Pacific women, 16.2 percent were interethnically married, and 24.2 percent were interracially married. Among the interracially married, 20.8 percent had married Whites.

We can draw from these national figures a clear pattern: the proportion of interethnic marriages had risen significantly, 400 to 500 percent in the ten-year span. In contrast, interracial marriages with the white population decreased substantially as a proportion of all Asian Pacific marriages, while interracial marriages with other racial minority groups rose slightly.

State of California Asian Pacific Marriage Patterns, 1980 and 1990

But what happens in a state where 39.2 percent of all Asian Pacific Americans reside? Would large and thriving Asian ethnic communities inhibit or encourage interracial and interethnic marriages?

Would marriages to Whites decrease as a result of the larger population concentrations of Asians? In order to explore these questions, we examined the marriage patterns in California by nativity, region, generation, and sociological age cohort.

Table 1 depicts the marriage patterns of Asian Pacific men and women for California in 1990, where 71.1 percent were married within their ethnic group. Several observations can be made in a comparison of the aggregate marriage patterns. There are 72,375 more women than men among wives and husbands living together in the same domicile. How can this be? Part of the answer lies in the influx of Asian wives of U.S.-servicemen, who had married overseas and came here through international marriages.[18] Another reason is the immigration of foreign-born, Asian female students and nurses who married in the United States.[19] A third reason, relating to U.S.-born (and those born elsewhere but raised in the United States, i.e., the 1.5 generation), may be the greater tendency among biracial women than men to identify with being Asian Pacific American on the census categorizations.[20]

Another observation is that, across the board, women were more likely to intermarry than men in 1990. This pattern has been evident since 1950, when marriages shifted from mainly hypogamous involving Asian men with white women to hypergamous involving Asian women and white men.[21]

Interestingly, though, the proportion of those intermarrying with Whites decreased from 1980 for both Asian Pacific men and women. In 1980, 54.2 percent of all men who intermarried had non-Hispanic white partners, while 72.7 percent of all intermarried women were married to non-Hispanic Whites. By 1990, the proportion of intermarriages to Whites decreased substantially: for men, only 26.6 percent, and for women, 45 percent.

Meanwhile, there was a dramatic rise in the number of interethnic marriages. From 1980 to 1990, interethnic marriages for Asian Pacific men increased from 21.1 percent to 64 percent. From

TABLE 1
Marriage Patterns of Asian Pacific Americans by Nativity, California, 1990

Husband's Ethnicity	General Marriages	% of APA* Marriages				FB Marriages	% of FB APA Marriages				US-Born Marriages	% of U.S.-Born APA Marriages			
		IT	IE	MM	MJ		IT	IE	MM	MJ		IT	IE	MM	MJ
Chinese American	183,567	75.8	16.7	1.5	6.0	150,686	79.8	15.1	1.0	4.0	32,881	57.1	23.9	3.6	15.4
Filipino American	149,256	73.8	13.9	4.3	8.0	127,943	78.9	12.9	3.2	5.0	21,313	43.3	19.4	10.9	26.4
Japanese American	89,187	62.1	21.2	3.6	13.1	27,487	65.7	22.5	2.1	9.7	61,700	60.5	20.6	4.2	14.6
South Asian American	46,456	65.3	23.7	3.3	7.8	45,482	66.3	23.5	2.8	7.4	974	18.9	31.5	22.5	27.1
Korean American	65,360	78.1	18.3	0.5	3.1	63,550	79.6	17.8	0.4	2.2	1,810	25.9	35.9	3.3	34.9
Vietnamese American	48,786	75.5	19.9	1.3	3.3	48,436	75.6	19.9	1.3	3.3	350	71.1	18.6	2.3	8.0
Cambodian American	11,224	80.4	17.2	0.7	1.7	11,159	80.6	17.0	0.7	1.7	65	40.0	60.0	0.0	0.0
Hmong American	7,587	79.8	16.7	0.9	2.7	7,550	79.7	16.8	0.9	2.7	37	100.0	0.0	0.0	0.0
Laotian American	11,051	76.9	18.8	2.3	2.0	10,987	76.9	18.8	2.3	2.0	64	75.0	25.0	0.0	0.0
Thai American	6,481	54.0	35.2	3.2	7.6	6,391	54.3	34.7	3.3	7.7	93	31.2	68.8	0.0	0.0
Other Asian American	9,614	44.3	30.8	6.7	18.2	7,704	47.2	30.7	6.5	15.6	1,910	32.6	31.2	7.4	28.8
Hawaiian American	7,809	15.6	31.6	13.5	39.3	145	69.7	30.3	0.0	0.0	7,664	14.5	31.6	13.8	40.1
Samoan American	5,019	54.5	28.8	5.2	11.6	2,035	62.5	27.0	4.4	6.1	2,984	49.1	30.0	5.7	15.3
Tongan American	963	68.3	20.6	3.0	8.1	906	69.2	19.0	3.2	8.6	57	54.4	45.6	0.0	0.0
Chamorran American	5,035	39.7	28.1	9.9	22.3	745	41.7	39.9	13.8	4.6	4,290	39.3	26.1	9.2	25.4
Other Pacific American	2,470	56.8	29.5	3.4	10.3	2,257	60.3	27.8	3.3	8.5	213	19.7	47.4	3.8	29.1
Total	649,968	71.1	18.4	2.8	7.7	513,463	76.1	17.3	1.9	4.7	136,405	52.3	22.7	6.0	18.9

(Continued)

Wife's Ethnicity	General Marriages	% of APA* Marriages				FB Marriages	% of FB APA Marriages				US-Born Marriages	% of U.S.-Born APA Marriages			
		IT	IE	MM	MJ		IT	IE	MM	MJ		IT	IE	MM	MJ
Chinese American	186,967	74.3	13.9	1.4	10.4	153,542	79.2	11.6	1.1	8.2	33,425	51.7	24.4	3.0	20.9
Filipino American	184,114	59.9	15.0	5.5	19.7	159,624	63.7	13.7	4.5	18.2	24,490	35.2	23.2	12.0	29.6
Japanese American	115,099	48.1	20.0	4.4	27.5	48,220	44.9	16.7	4.8	33.7	66,879	50.4	22.4	4.2	23.1
South Asian American	37,852	80.1	12.0	1.4	6.4	36,608	80.8	11.5	1.4	6.3	1,244	58.4	29.1	2.9	9.6
Korean American	74,622	68.5	16.1	2.5	12.9	71,802	70.3	14.9	2.4	12.4	2,820	22.2	46.6	6.5	24.6
Vietnamese American	52,383	70.7	19.4	1.6	8.3	51,735	71.1	19.4	1.4	8.2	648	45.4	21.3	18.7	14.7
Cambodian American	12,115	74.8	19.8	1.3	4.2	12,115	74.8	19.8	1.3	4.2	—	—	—	—	—
Hmong American	6,900	89.2	8.6	0.9	1.4	6,850	89.5	8.2	0.9	1.4	50	42.0	58.0	0.0	0.0
Laotian American	10,686	80.6	14.9	1.7	2.9	10,612	80.4	15.0	1.7	2.9	74	100.0	0.0	0.0	0.0
Thai American	9,016	38.7	26.7	5.3	29.3	8,912	39.1	26.4	5.1	29.4	104	0.0	56.7	20.2	23.1
Other Asian American	11,460	35.6	28.4	4.0	31.9	8,513	41.6	26.2	2.6	29.6	2,947	18.2	35.0	8.1	38.7
Hawaiian American	7,474	15.7	29.9	12.0	42.5	242	44.6	41.7	8.3	5.4	7,232	14.7	29.5	12.1	43.7
Samoan American	4,709	54.7	21.4	10.8	13.0	2,258	58.9	18.6	9.0	13.6	2,451	50.8	24.1	12.5	12.6
Tongan American	1,340	55.5	25.0	6.0	13.4	1,265	58.8	22.4	6.4	12.4	75	0.0	69.3	0.0	30.7
Chamorran American	5,153	38.8	25.2	12.2	23.8	572	46.7	25.3	12.4	15.6	4,581	37.8	25.2	12.2	24.9
Other Pacific American	2,453	57.3	14.7	4.5	23.5	2,185	63.1	12.3	2.7	21.8	268	9.7	34.3	19.0	36.9
Total	722,343	64.0	16.4	3.4	16.2	575,055	68.9	14.4	2.7	14.0	147,288	44.8	24.3	6.2	24.8

Source: Calculations by Larry Hajime Shinagawa, Ph.D., based upon the 5 percent Public Use Microdata Sample (PUMS), U.S. Bureau of the Census, 1990.

Copyright © 1996, Larry Hajime Shinagawa, Ph.D., Assistant Professor, Department of American Multi-Cultural Studies, Sonoma State University.

*APA = "Asian Pacific American"; IT = "Intraethnic Marriage"; IE = "Interethnic Marriage"; MM = "Minority-Minority Marriage"; MJ = "Minority-Majority Marriage"; FB = Foreign-Born.

1980 to 1990, interethnic marriages for women increased from 10.8 percent to 45.5 percent of all intermarriages.

Marriage Patterns of Specific Asian Pacific Ethnic Groups, 1980 and 1990

Evidently, much of the rise of interethnic marriages can be accounted for by the increasing number of foreign-born who tend to intraethnically and interethnically marry, more so than the U.S.-born. A closer examination of specific ethnic groups also demonstrates a rise in the proportion interethnically married. In addition, when we control for nativity, we find that U.S.-born groups show a similar increase.

We examined the marriage patterns of Chinese, Filipino, and Japanese Americans for 1980 and 1990. These populations were chosen because they were the only major Asian ethnic groups with substantial U.S.-born populations. According to our research, interethnic marriages have increased for each of these groups as a proportion of all marriages.

1990 Asian American Marriage Patterns by Area

We also examined marriage patterns for specific regions in California: the San Francisco Bay area, Los Angeles County, San Diego County, Sacramento County, Central Valley metropolitan areas, other counties with high concentrations of Asian Pacific Americans, and counties with low concentrations.[22] We examined whether residential patterns had an effect on marriage patterns. We found that areas with high Asian Pacific concentration tended to have lower proportions of intermarriage and more inmarriages. The exception was in San Diego and Orange County, where there were large populations of foreign-born Asian wives of U.S. servicemen and biracial children from these marriages. Meanwhile, areas with low Asian Pacific concentrations tended to have higher proportions of intermarriage and less inmarriages. Even in

areas of high Asian Pacific concentrations, where there tended to be fewer minority-majority marriages, there remained a gender difference. More Asian women married Whites than for Asian men.

1990 Asian American Marriage Patterns by Area, Sociological Cohort, and Generation

Traditionally, marriage patterns of Asian Americans have been examined by generation.[23] This approach often overemphasizes the differences between U.S.-born and foreign-born. Implicitly, the underlying theoretical argument in this dichotomous approach is to show the assimilation of Asians into the dominant white population over time. However, we feel that this approach alone is not adequate to show the kinds of marriage patterns of Asian Americans. It is critical to recognize the important political, social, cultural, and historical developments that shape people's lives and their marriage choices.

Utilizing a socio-historical framework, we created a different methodological approach. We divided the generations into first, 1.5,[24] and second generations, rather than the traditional foreign-born and U.S.-born. We also felt that historically and sociologically, Asian Americans' experience growing up in specific milieus would affect their marriage choices. We called these experiences a *sociological cohort*.[25] What follows is an examination of the effect of sociological cohort, modified generation, and area on the marriage patterns of Asian Americans. We start by describing the specific sociological cohorts.

We have devised sociological cohorts that represent both age groups and the major social and historical influences that shaped these age groups. These are: the Pre-WWII and WWII (prior to 1946), Post-WWII (1946 to 1962), the Civil Rights Era (1963 to 1974), the Post-60s (1975 to 1981), and the Vincent Chin cohorts (1982 to 1990). These cohorts represent groups of individuals who came of age (16 years) during a specific period. We describe the cohort characteristics and their general marriage patterns below:

THE PRE-WWII
AND WWII COHORT

This cohort grew up during an era of intense racial animosity, where Asian Americans had few opportunities.[26] Citizenship and immigration were restricted.[27] In addition, anti-miscegenation laws were in place. For all Asian groups, there were more men than women. Despite the anti-miscegenation laws, more Asian men intermarried than women because of the sex imbalance and immigration restrictions (they did so by marrying in states where anti-miscegenation laws were not in effect).[28]

THE POST-WORLD WAR II
COHORT

This cohort grew up during a period of overt discrimination although significant legal strides were beginning to occur in the area of civil rights for racial minorities. Integration of the military had been achieved, desegregation of education was mandated, Asian immigrants could become citizens, and anti-miscegenation laws in the major states where Asian Americans resided were lifted. The majority of racial minorities believed in integration and assimilation into the dominant white society, although very few actually made inroads during that period. Overseas, American military troops served as Occupation forces in Europe and in Asia. Some of these servicemen married Asian women and brought them to the United States (the Warbrides Act of 1946, 1948, and 1958 allowed servicemen to marry overseas, regardless of the racial background of the wife).[29]

THE CIVIL RIGHTS ERA
COHORT

This cohort came of age when major struggles were occurring in American society on a variety of social, political, economic, and cultural fronts. The Vietnam War heightened tensions in American society, racial minorities struggled for equal rights, and sexual and cultural mores were loosening and in flux. For the first time, members of racial groups were interacting in large numbers and in many social settings (especially in colleges and universities). The Civil Rights Act of 1964 passed, barring discrimination on the basis of race.[30] The Immigration Act of 1965 led to a resumption and surge of immigration from Asia.[31]

Asian Americans began to make educational, occupational, and residential inroads into mainstream society because of civil rights protections. By 1966, *The New York Times* and *U.S. News and World Report* characterized Asian Americans (in particular, Japanese Americans), as the "model-minority" who, despite racism, had achieved middle-class status.[32] By 1967, the U.S. Supreme Court declared all anti-miscegenation laws null and void in the *Loving v. Commonwealth of Virginia* decision.[33] For the first time Asian Americans (excluding the Asian wives of U.S. servicemen) could intermarry with the white population. Since there were still few Asian Americans in universities at the time, some college-educated men and women interracially married with the white population. During this period, considerably more Asian women also intermarried with the white population as compared to Asian men.[34]

POST-60s COHORT

This cohort came of age during a time of racial resentment and backlash by Whites against the gains made by racial minorities. The Vietnam War ended ignominiously; other nations seemed to challenge America's economic and military dominance. Most Americans worried about America's declining world influence. The malaise was not confined to international arenas. On the domestic front, Whites increasingly worried about their own status and privilege. The 1978 Bakke decision of the U.S. Supreme Court signaled a retreat from affirmative action and indicated growing antagonism against racial minorities. Some Whites started to claim "reverse discrimination," began to move away from urban centers, and settled increasingly within racially homogeneous suburbs.[35] Urban decline, deindustrialization, and poverty characterized major metropolitan areas where large racial minority populations were centered.[36]

During this period, Asian communities experienced a "rebirth." The 1965 Immigration Act created a phenomenal growth in immigration. Intact families immigrated for the first time in large numbers, college-educated professionals represented a significant proportion of the immigrant population, long-separated families reunited, and traditions were reaffirmed and celebrated.[37] Economic networks and social and political organizations began to sprout within specific ethnic communities and, to a lesser extent, on a broader Pan-Asian basis. Asian American Studies programs, which had begun during the 60s, began to spread throughout the West Coast and in some sections of the Midwest and East Coast. Pan-Asian student organizations evolved on campuses from their 60s base, with many focusing on community service and political activism.[38] Partly as a result of student activism, social service agencies were formed to service the growing immigrant communities.[39] Asian Americans were also rediscovering their roots. Chinese Americans learned about the Chinese Exclusion Act and Angel Island; Japanese Americans about the forced internment during World War II; and Filipino Americans about the contributions of the *Pinoys*, *Pensionados*, and *Manongs* of the first wave of immigrants.[40]

On the political level, the redress and reparations movement began in earnest among Japanese Americans. The movement educated many about the significance of race and racism in shaping the Asian American experience. In addition, the fall of the I-Hotel in San Francisco in 1976, which had historically been the home of many immigrant "bachelors" (most of whom were elderly Filipino and Chinese men from the first wave of immigration), galvanized Asian American support, especially among students.[41] For Korean Americans, the plight of Chol Soo Lee awakened the immigrant community. For the first time, organizations, especially the churches, college and high school students, and even the elderly became actively involved in his struggle for justice.[42] Because Chol Soo Lee was victimized by his race, not his Korean ethnicity, other Asian Americans also participated and sympathized with his plight.

During this period, intermarriages increased as the social distance between Asian Americans and Whites decreased. The majority of intermarriages, among both Asian men and women, were with Whites. Interethnic Asian marriages increased slowly, while intermarriages with other racial minorities remained a very small number. Asian women continued to intermarry more than men, mostly with the white population.[43] Most scholars during this period saw intermarriage as the key index signaling the eventual assimilation of Asians into the white population.[44]

THE VINCENT CHIN COHORT

We name this cohort in remembrance of Vincent Chin and the phenomenal impact that his murder in 1982 has had upon the Asian American communities. The Vincent Chin case, in the words of journalist William Wong, took on "mythic proportions," symbolizing anti-Asian violence and the continuing discrimination against Asian Americans.[45] Fundraising and consciousness-raising campaigns were mounted throughout the United States, the U.S. Commission on Civil Rights began investigating anti-Asian violence[46] and numerous organizations (Japanese American Citizens League, Organization of Chinese Americans, Filipinos for Affirmative Action, and National Asian Pacific American Legal Consortium)[47] began collecting information on anti-Asian violence, hate crimes, and hate groups. For the first time at the nationwide-level, Asian Americans rallied together to fight discrimination directed against them.[48]

During this era, within Asian American communities, there was a tremendous development of economic, social, political, and cultural networks. Ethnic-specific and pan-Asian community-based organizations and professional associations emerged, providing opportunities for networking for both career advancement and personal benefits.[49] Religious institutions such as churches and temples provided spiritual sustenance and affirmation of ethnic traditions.[50] Politically, Asian Americans began to organize campaigns for office at many levels of government.[51] Asian Americans also developed or renewed political and economic ties to their homelands. Proactively, they forced the U.S. government to retain and expand ethnic categories for Asians and Pacific Islanders in the major federal database programs such as the census and health information systems.[52]

Ethnic Studies programs throughout the 1980s continued to expand and to influence Asian American college students. Because many courses emphasized comparative experiences among Asian groups, students developed a strong sense of pan-Asian heritage and racial awareness. For many students, going to colleges where there were many other Asian Americans and taking classes about the Asian American experience led to consciousness-raising and the development of a pan-Asian identity. Socially, there were many opportunities for friendship, dating, and long-term relationships with other Asian Americans.

Pan-Asian consciousness and racial identity was also spurred by tremendous population growth. Between 1970 and 1990, the Asian Pacific population increased by 262 percent, to 7.3 million individuals. By 1990, 39.2 percent (3.4 million) of all Asian Pacific Americans lived in California,[53] constituting 9.6 percent of the state's total population.[54]

In the context of these developments, we predicted a substantial increase in interethnic marriages among Asian Pacific Americans. Coupled with the heightened racial awareness brought on by the trends described above, conditions became ripe for large-scale social interaction among Asian ethnic groups and individuals within these groups. Asian Americans had developed a critical mass[55] where it was possible to maintain, develop, and augment ethnic and community interests, especially when people interacted on a pan-Asian basis. We felt that pan-Asian consciousness would be most present in the Vincent Chin cohort as evidenced by the increased numbers of interethnic Asian marriages.

THE APPLICATION OF SOCIOLOGICAL COHORTS AND GENERATION BY AREA IN STUDYING THE MARRIAGE PATTERNS OF ASIAN AMERICANS

We conducted analyses for the five most numerous Asian American groups by area, sociological cohort, and modified generation.[56] The specific groups were Chinese, Filipino, Japanese, Korean, and Vietnamese Americans. Regionally, we studied marriage patterns for the San Francisco Bay area, Los Angeles, other areas with high concentrations of Asians, and overall for California.

According to our research, the Pre-WWII and WWII cohort had the highest proportion of interethnic marriages and the lowest proportion of interracial marriages. These patterns reflect the significant impact of anti-miscegenation laws and racism directed against Asian Americans. Because intermarriages with Whites were not allowed, many Asian Americans opted, with their limited choices, to marry intraethnically or with other Asian Americans.

After World War II, race relations began to liberalize. In 1948, the State Supreme Court in the *Perez v. Sharp* decision overturned all antimiscegenation laws in California.[57] Beginning with the Post-WWII cohort, we begin to see an increasing proportion of interracial marriages. For the Post-WWII and Civil Rights cohort, there was also a slight decrease in interethnic marriages.

Beginning with the Post-60s cohort, we see interethnic marriages increasing. By the Vincent Chin cohort, interethnic marriages surpassed interracial marriages. In particular, interethnic marriages became more prevalent than minority-majority marriages.

The rise in pan-Asian interethnic marriages is evident in every generation, although most apparent among the 1.5 generation for Chinese Americans, the second generation and beyond for Filipino Americans, the second generation and beyond for Japanese Americans, the second generation and beyond for Korean Americans, and the 1.5 generation for Vietnamese Americans.

Interestingly, given the gender and racial dynamics of American society where, historically, there have been more interracial marriages between Asian women and white men (than Asian men with white women), we find that by 1990, Asian women have shifted dramatically toward interethnic marriages. Thus, the gap between the genders in their proportion married to Whites has decreased substantially. Asian men, meanwhile, show a growing tendency toward both interethnic and minority-majority marriages, although interethnic marriages are much more common overall.

Using California data, we summarize in Table 2 the percentages of interethnic and minority-majority marriages for Asian Americans for the Civil Rights, Post-60s, and Vincent Chin cohorts.

Table 3 depicts the marriage patterns for second generation and beyond Chinese, Filipinos, and Japanese and for 1.5 generation Korean and Vietnamese Americans. Second generation Korean and Vietnamese Americans are not shown due to small sample size.

We found that region had a significant effect upon marriage patterns. Areas with large concentrations of Asian Americans, such as the San Francisco Bay area and Los Angeles, are likely to have (1) much higher proportions of both intraethnic and interethnic marriages, and (2) greater tendencies toward pan-Asian marriages.

Finally, when we define inmarriage as intraethnic marriages, the tendency for intermarriage among younger cohorts and among 1.5 and second generation individuals increases and becomes a substantial proportion of those married. On the other hand, when we define inmarriage as the combination of both intraethnic and interethnic marriages, then there has been only a slight increase in intermarriage overall, and for some ethnic groups, no increase whatsoever. For example, for U.S.-born Chinese American females for 1980, 71.7 percent intraethnically married and 6.4 percent interethnically married (for a combined 78.1 percent inmarriage rate). In 1990, 51.7 percent intraethnically married and 24.4 percent interethnically married (for a combined 76 percent inmarriage rate). Comparing these two "inmarriage" figures (78.1 percent and 76 percent) shows there has not been a major shift toward "intermarriage" for U.S.-born Chinese American females.

SUMMARY OF MAJOR FINDINGS FROM 1980 AND 1990 CENSUS DATA

Analysis of census data reveals the following key points regarding Asian intermarriage and panethnicity:

For a span of ten years (1980 to 1990), nationally and for California, the number of Asian interethnic marriages approaches or now exceeds interracial marriages. Meanwhile, interethnic marriages for Asian Pacific men increased from 21.1 percent in 1980 to 64 percent in 1990, and for women from 10.8 percent to 45.5.

Population size and residential concentrations affect the likelihoods of intramarriage and intermarriage. In areas of high Asian Pacific concentrations in California, as compared to areas of low

TABLE 2
Marriage Patterns of Select Asian American Groups by Recent Sociological Cohorts

	Civil Rights	*Post-60s*	*Vincent Chin*
Chinese American Marriages			
Husbands			
Interethnic	15.3	20.5	35.5
Minority-Majority	6.0	8.8	16.0
Wives			
Interethnic	11.2	14.3	26.2
Minority-Majority	12.1	12.2	16.6
Filipino American Marriages			
Husbands			
Interethnic	12.1	15.9	22.4
Minority-Majority	8.7	10.4	15.7
Wives			
Interethnic	12.8	13.6	23.5
Minority-Majority	19.0	25.7	28.7
Japanese American Marriages			
Husbands			
Interethnic	20.6	30.2	43.7
Minority-Majority	19.1	20.1	26.8
Wives			
Interethnic	17.5	21.5	40.2
Minority-Majority	29.8	33.7	29.9
Korean American Marriages			
Husbands			
Interethnic	15.3	22.1	44.0
Minority-Majority	3.0	5.1	6.0
Wives			
Interethnic	12.6	13.2	27.0
Minority-Majority	14.6	13.2	16.1
Vietnamese American Marriages			
Husbands			
Interethnic	18.0	20.5	42.8
Minority-Majority	2.6	3.9	9.3
Wives			
Interethnic	15.7	16.8	32.9
Minority-Majority	9.2	5.3	10.7

Source: Special tabulations by Larry Hajime Shinagawa, Ph.D., of the 1990 5 percent Public Use Microdata Sample.

concentrations, immigrants had higher proportions of intraethnic marriages; and, among the 1.5 and second generations, there were higher proportions of intraethnic and interethnic marriages.

In specific regions with high numbers of Asians, interethnic marriages were the dominant form of intermarriage, regardless of nativity. The only exceptions were in the areas where there was a large concentration of U.S. servicemen with Asian wives and their biracial children.

Among the younger age cohorts, men and women showed an increasing tendency toward

TABLE 3
Marriage Patterns of Select Asian American Groups by Recent Sociological Cohorts 1.5 and 2nd Generation

	Civil Rights	Post-60s	Vincent Chin
Chinese American Marriages (2nd +)			
Husbands			
Interethnic	28.1	26.3	22.1
Minority-Majority	21.4	12.4	19.9
Wives			
Interethnic	20.6	27.8	40.9
Minority-Majority	25.4	26.2	28.5
Filipino American Marriages (2nd +)			
Husbands			
Interethnic	17.6	22.5	21.0
Minority-Majority	35.8	28.0	27.4
Wives			
Interethnic	21.2	20.3	35.5
Minority-Majority	36.6	35.5	20.5
Japanese American Marriages (2nd +)			
Husbands			
Interethnic	19.9	34.5	41.9
Minority-Majority	26.2	27.0	28.2
Wives			
Interethnic	21.3	28.4	38.2
Minority-Majority	32.4	37.0	35.1
Korean American Marriages (1.5)			
Husbands			
Interethnic	32.3	28.9	45.8
Minority-Majority	18.5	14.3	6.0
Wives			
Interethnic	43.6	26.3	35.1
Minority-Majority	39.3	20.3	25.1
Vietnamese American Marriages (1.5)			
Husbands			
Interethnic	—	41.3	38.8
Minority-Majority	100.0	9.9	15.3
Wives			
Interethnic	—	17.1	31.5
Minority-Majority	—	19.4	15.6

Source: Special tabulations by Larry Hajime Shinagawa, Ph.D., of the 1990 5 percent Public Use Microdata Sample.

interethnic marriages as compared to minority-majority marriages. For the older age cohorts, men and women tended to interracially marry with the white population. The exception was the Pre-WWII and WWII age cohort, who were legally proscribed from marrying Whites.

The wide gap between the genders in intermarriage decreased substantially by 1990. Previously the gender gap was largely due to the greater number of women married to white men, as compared to men who were married to white women. By 1990, this gap had narrowed not because of large increases in the number of men marrying Whites, but because of the increases of both men and women who married interethnically with other Asian Americans.

DISCUSSION

Factors in the Rise of Interethnic Marriages

This research has shown the increasing tendency toward pan-Asian interethnic marriages, regardless of gender, nativity, region, and generation. What factors contributed to this dramatic change? In this discussion, we hypothesize several key reasons linked to the rise of panethnicity among Asian Americans.

The first factor is the growing size and increasing concentration of Asian Americans in the United States in general and California, in particular. Between 1970 and 1990, the Asian Pacific population grew 362 percent nationally. In select California cities, Asian Pacific Americans constituted a significant proportion of the overall population: 57.5 percent of Monterey Park, 45.2 percent of Cerritos, 43.8 percent of Daly City, 34.7 percent of Milpitas, 32.4 percent of San Gabriel, and 29.1 percent of San Francisco.[58] In several universities and colleges in California, such as UC Berkeley, San Francisco State, UCLA, Cal State Long Beach, and UC Irvine, Asian Americans by 1990 constituted at least 25 percent of the total student body.[59] The large concentrations led to the development of a substantial marriage availability pool within the Asian American population.

The second factor is the growth of social and personal networks that have developed from these population changes. These include economic and social institutions and professional associations, which have facilitated interaction between Asian ethnic groups, and, in turn, have led to intimate social relationships.

The third factor is the growing similarity in socioeconomic attainment among Asian Americans. As many achieve middle-class status, individuals move out of ethnic enclaves and into mixed-Asian and white suburbs. Growing numbers of Asian Americans are attending colleges and universities, where they are likely to meet other Asian Americans. Class, by itself, however, does not determine the high rates of intermarriage. U.S.-born Japanese American males, for example, are still not as likely to marry white females, despite their similar class status. We believe that racial stereotyping by gender still affects marital choices, despite similar socioeconomic attainment.

The fourth factor is the acculturation of Asian Americans. The use of a common English language and shared American cultural experiences (e.g., media and education) bridged ethnic differences and forged interaction. Rather than focusing upon the homelands of their parents and grandparents from Asia, younger Asian Americans established cultural roots in the American context.

The fifth factor is a feeling of shared identity among Asian Americans, especially in the context of a racially diverse society. Symbols, foods, behavioral traits, and beliefs about family, community and common histories are shared by many Asian Americans. There is a growing sense of comfort and familiarity with one another.

The final and most important factor is a growing racial consciousness in American society, which is perceived by many Asian Americans as increasingly racially polarized and stratified. This racial awareness is especially acute in California. Deindustrialization, white flight, increased economic competition, anti-immigrant sentiments, hate violence against Asians, the growing sense of despair and hopelessness in the inner cities, and interracial conflicts not only between Whites and Asian Americans but also between racial minority groups all signify the importance of race in American society and have heightened the racial consciousness of Asian Americans. Race, increasingly more so than ethnicity, shapes the experiences and the development of identity among Asian Americans.

The importance of race and racial consciousness was repeatedly expressed in interviews we conducted, especially among Asian Americans who attended colleges and universities.[60] Many had taken Asian American Studies courses, where they learned that *race,* not necessarily *ethnicity,* had shaped Asian American experience. Additionally, Asian American Studies programs may have affected their pan-Asian consciousness by minimizing ethnic differences and emphasizing common concerns. While they acknowledge that ethnic differences exist, many recognize the need to work together on the basis of *race* if Asian Americans are to protect the needs of their particular ethnic group.

"Sophie," a 1.5 generation Korean American, echoed many of the sentiments of a growing number of young, college-educated Asian Americans. She said:

> Ethnically I am Korean. But I would identify myself as "Korean American." I'm very much Korean, but politically, after taking Asian American Studies courses, I would identify myself as "Asian American." Asian American—it's a very political term for me. I think that because of the fact that in the United States we are treated as a homogeneous, monolithic group, they [Whites] kind of see us as one group. And because of that, a lot of the ethnic groups like Chinese Americans, Japanese Americans, Korean Americans, and all the other Asian groups rally around a common cause. It's this huge thing called racism. Because they treat us as one huge monolithic group. That's when I think about the term, "Asian Pacific American." It's a very political term. It's there to unify the 3 percent Asian American population that we have in this country to try to do something for ourselves to empower our communities.

CONCLUSION AND IMPLICATIONS

Our findings show an increasing tendency toward pan-Asian interethnic marriages. One can argue that the increase in pan-Asian marriages signals a movement toward the consolidation of racial lines and social boundaries in contrast to minority-majority interracial marriages which signal assimilation into the white population.[61] We have argued in this article, supported by our census analysis, that the rise in pan-Asian consciousness is based on the lessening of social and physical distance among ethnic groups due to growing population size and concentration, the establishment of economic and social networks, similarities in socioeconomic status among ethnic groups, increasing acculturation, recognition of cultural similarities among ethnic groups, and a heightening racial awareness. This consciousness, while not necessarily a prerequisite, has been instrumental in the development of Asian panethnicity. One important index of this trend has been the growth of interethnic Asian marriages.

If current trends are indicative of the future, Asian Americans may not necessarily distinguish between intraethnic and interethnic marriages. As with the white population, where interethnic white marriages are the norm,[62] a similar pattern of interethnic Asian marriages will probably become commonplace. Especially as society becomes more racially polarized, Asian Americans may place greater emphasis on a close correspondence between race and race as representation in their social and interpersonal relationships. As they approach that point, aspects of culture and the social construction of race and identity will become infused Asian panethnic consciousness, influencing their behavior and the choices they make.

NOTES

1. Yen Le Espiritu, *Asian American Panethnicity: Bridging Institutions and Identities* (Philadelphia: Temple University Press, 1992), 15.
2. Ibid., 167–168.
3. Michael Omi and Howard Winant, *Racial Formation in the United States: From the 1960s to the 1990s,* 2nd ed. (New York: Routledge, 1994), 54–55.

4. Not all members of ethnic groups can genealogically trace their ethnic origin from a specific part of the earth. For example, many Jewish Americans cannot demonstrably trace their lineage to Israel or Judea directly, yet the concept of Israel as a "homeland" can have symbolic meaning to unify their shared community. Similarly, many Chicanos embrace the mythical Aztlan as part of their Chicano ethnic identity. The historical "reality" of such homelands does not have to be proven in order for their symbolic importance to have meaning to such ethnically identified individuals and act as a basis for common and shared community.

5. Omi and Winant, 53–76.

6. Here, more than a matter of semantics, we choose not to use the term racial identity, and opt for ethnic identity instead, even when referring to identities forged by perceptions of race. Those identified by others as members of a particular race may not necessarily identify with that race, and race does not imply specific cultures or histories of a group intrinsically. People who identify with a race have taken an objectified perception and have incorporated it into their own perception of self. In so doing, they have many times added a culture, history (many times of subjugation, oppression, and discrimination), and common fate to race. Race has become ethnicized, and ethnicity has become racialized. For further discussion, see Tamotsu Shibutani and Kian M. Kwan, *Ethnic Stratification: A Comparative Approach* (New York: The Macmillan Company, 1965), 154–158.

7. David M. Hayano, "Ethnic Identification and Disidentification: Japanese-American Views of Chinese-Americans," *Ethnic Groups* 3:2 (1981): 157–171.

8. Herbert Gans, The *Urban Villagers: Group and Class in the Life of Italian–Americans*, 2nd ed. (New York: Free Press, 1982).

9. Ruth Frankenberg, *White Women, Race Matters: The Social Construction of Whiteness* (Minneapolis: University of Minnesota Press, 1993); and Gin Yong Pang and Larry Hajime Shinagawa, "Intermarriage and the Language of Denial," paper presented at the 1994 meeting of Association of Asian American Studies, Ann Arbor, Michigan.

10. See Mary C. Waters, *Ethnic Options: Choosing Identities in America* (Berkeley: University of California Press, 1990); Stanley Lieberson and Mary C. Waters, *From Many Strands: Ethnic and Racial Groups in Contemporary America* (New York: Russell Sage Foundation, 1988); Richard Alba, *Italian Americans: Into the Twilight of Ethnicity* (Englewood Cliffs, New Jersey: Prentice Hall, 1985); and Richard Alba, *Ethnic Identity: The Transformation of White America* (New Haven, Connecticut: Yale University Press, 1990).

11. A classic example of the conflict between race and race as representation is shown in the example of Walter White and his second wife, Poppy Cannon, as described by Paul Spickard in his book *Mixed Blood: Intermarriage and Ethnicity in the 20th Century* (Madison, Wisconsin: University of Wisconsin Press, 1989). During the 1930s and 1940s Mr. White served as the executive secretary of the NAACP. A socially committed civil rights activist coming from a very respected light-skinned African American family, White served as the executive secretary of the NAACP for twenty years. One of his great achievements was the racial integration of the military during World War II brought about by executive order of Harry S. Truman due to White's advocacy. During most of those years, he was married to an African American woman, but he divorced in 1949 to marry a white woman, Poppy Cannon, a prominent journalist. White was blond-haired and blue-eyed. His first wife was appreciably darker than himself. His second wife, too, was darker by several shades than himself, but was recognized by the larger white society as white. Upon marrying Poppy Cannon, despite his many years of meritorious service on behalf of the African American community, he became the brunt of many accusations of "selling out" by other African Americans, and was described by some white segregationists as an example of the "true" intent of black integration: the desire of black men to have sexual access to white women. Here, White was caught in a double bind. In terms of visible phenotype, he was categorized as white. Yet, he grew up and participated in a community where he was recognized as African American. Since his race was questionable, race as representation became very important. In his actions, both of civil activism and his marriage choice of a darker-skinned woman, he reinforced his identification with African Americans. But when he divorced his first wife and married a white woman, he marginalized and "de-centered" himself from the mainstream of African Americans. He had become "illegitimate."

The example highlights how race is both a visual perception and a social formation. Race involves boundaries and categorizations that are shaped and maintained in part by *how individuals and interest groups interpret and choose to represent criteria for membership within the race.* Skin color, body shape, mannerisms, language, political orientations, personal relationships, interests, and shared antagonisms all shape intersubjective identification with a race. When many of the cues to race categorization and identification do not conform to the normative understanding of what characterizes affiliation and allegiance with that group, the individual who "transgresses" has an ambiguous identity and status, according to other members of the group.

12. Within each dataset, we converted the original hierarchical format into a flat file which matched husbands and wives with their characteristics. Each paired husband and wife had indicators regarding their race and ethnicity, in addition to nativity, age, education, income, years since arriving to the United States, and their sex. These datasets represent the largest and most statistically accurate source of information regarding the marriage patterns of Asian Americans. The 1980 dataset is composed of 25,666 individuals, of whom 12,010 were Asian husbands and 13,656 were wives. In 1990, the dataset was

substantially larger, as a result of continuing immigration, in-migration from other states, and natural increase. The 1990 dataset consisted of 67,362 individuals, of whom 31,897 were Asian men and 35,465 were women. The dataset descriptions are found in two technical documents from the U.S. Bureau of the Census: *Census of Population and Housing: 1980, Public Use Microdata Samples, Technical Documentation* (Washington, D.C.: Government Printing Office, 1983); and *1990 Census of Population and Housing, Public Use Microdata Samples, United States* (Washington, D.C.: Government Printing Office, 1993).

13. Since the dataset is a sample, and because the 1990 dataset is not self-weighted (as compared to the 1980 Census), the use of appropriate weights to designate the relative representativeness of each case was very important. Without proper weighting, major statistical sampling errors and faults in interpretation could result from analyzing unweighted data. Since there is variability to the weight assigned each case by the 1990 Census team, most cases tend to represent about eighteen to twenty-two individuals. With this in mind, where rows or columns of statistical information represent less than 400 individuals in the 1990 tables (approximately twenty cases), statistically generalizable statements about marriage patterns are questionable.

14. Larry D. Barnett, "Interracial Marriage in California," *Marriage and Family Living* 25 (1963): 424–427; and Larry Hajime Shinagawa and Gin Yong Pang, "Intraethnic, Interethnic, and Interracial Marriages among Asian Americans in California, 1980," *Berkeley Journal of Sociology* 13 (1988):95–114.

15. We did not have comparable information in 1980 for Asian Indian Americans or South Asian Americans. Figures for South Asian Americans in the 1990s are available from the authors. Please send all correspondence to Professor Larry Hajime Shinagawa, Department of American Multi-Cultural Studies, Sonoma State University, 1801 East Cotati Avenue, Rohnert Park, California 94928. His e-mail address is shinagaw@sonoma.edu.

16. Sharon M. Lee and Keiko Yamanaka, "Patterns of Asian American Intermarriage and Marital Assimilation," *Journal of Comparative Family Studies* 21 (1990):287–305.

17. Ibid., 292.

18. See Bok-Lim Kim, "An Appraisal of Korean Immigrant Service Needs," *Social Casework* 57 (1980):139–148; Elfrieda Berthiaume Shukert and Barbara Smith Scibetta, *War Brides of World War II* (Novato, California: Presideo Press, 1988); and Michael C. Thornton, "The Quiet Immigration: Foreign Spouses of U.S. Citizens, 1945–1985," in *Racially Mixed People in America*, edited by Maria P. P. Root (Newbury Park, California: Sage Publications, 1992):64–76.

19. Marianthi Zikopoulos, ed., *Open Doors: 1987/88: Report on International Educational Exchange* (New York: Institute of International Education, 1988).

20. Larry Hajime Shinagawa, "Racial Classification of Asian Americans," paper presented at the OMB Hearing, San Francisco, July 15, 1994.

21. Harry H. L. Kitano, Dianne C. Fujino, and Jane S. Takahashi, "Interracial Marriages: Where Are the Asian Americans and Where Are They Going?"

22. These tables are available from the authors.

23. In the study of intermarriage, most social scientists have used nativity and generation interchangeably, even though they are not one and the same. Nativity is usually differentiated between the foreign-born and U.S.-born. Immigrants who come here to the United States are considered as first-generation, the children of immigrants as second-generation, and the children of U.S.-born parents of immigrant stock as third-generation. See Akemi Kikumura and Harry H. L. Kitano, "Interracial Marriage: A Picture of the Japanese Americans," *Journal of Social Issues* 29:2(1973), 67–81; and Harry H. L. Kitano et al. "Asian American Interracial Marriage," *Journal of Marriage and the Family* 46:1 (February 1984), 179–190.

   The interchange of nativity with generation poses several problems. First, because the census dataset does not contain information specifically about second, third, or fourth generation, researchers are forced to simplify generation into just first (equivalent to foreign-born nativity) and second (equivalent to U.S.-born nativity, knowing full well that second means second and beyond). Second, the foreign-born are termed as first generation, without much regard to the differences between foreign-born who are born and raised elsewhere and those who are born elsewhere but raised in the United States.

   While there is little that can be done to the first problem (other than to control for sociological age cohorts), the second problem can be addressed by separating the foreign-born into first generation (those who are born and raised elsewhere) and 1.5 generation (those who are born elsewhere but raised in the United States). For the purposes of this study, we defined a person as 1.5 generation if they had come to the United States prior to age of thirteen. We justify this cutoff by recognizing that this is approximately during the onset of puberty, of entering into junior high school, and before the determinative years of educational tracking and selection. Our fundamental assumption is that the 1.5 generation acculturates and adapts to American society more than the first-generation. Thus, we separate the first generation into first and 1.5 generation.

24. 1.5 generation refers to those who are born elsewhere but raised in the United States. For the purposes of this study, our cutoff was to define a person as 1.5 generation if they had come to the United States prior to age of thirteen. Among specific Asian American ethnic groups, the 1.5 generation was a sizable population. For example, among Chinese Americans, there were 23,128 1.5 generation husbands and wives; among Filipino Americans, 24,629; among Japanese Americans, 2,788; among Korean Americans, 7,994; and among Vietnamese Americans, there were 1,118. Among Korean Americans and Vietnamese Americans, there were more 1.5 generation than second generation and beyond husbands and wives.

25. Generations by themselves do not depict historically and socially-formed groupings because members of these generations can come from a diverse range of ages. For example, a Japanese American Sansei, third generation, who came of age during the Civil Rights Era would probably have a very different set of experiences and attitudes compared to a third-generation Sansei who was raised during the 1980s. Without accounting for age and social and historical influences during their formative years, it would be difficult to assess trends in intermarriage among these husbands and wives.

26. Harry H. L. Kitano, *Asian Americans: Emerging Minorities* (Englewood Cliffs, New Jersey: Prentice-Hall, 1988); Ronald T. Takaki, *Strangers from a Different Shore: A History of Asian Americans* (New York: Little, Brown, and Company, 1989); and Sucheng Chan, *Asian Americans: An Interpretive History* (Boston: Twayne, 1991).

27. For a detailed account of Asian Americans as they were affected by American immigration policy, see Bill Ong Hing, *Making and Remaking Asian America Through Immigration Policy, 1850–1990* (Stanford, California: Stanford University Press, 1993).

28. See Emory S. Bogardus, "Filipino Americans," in *Our Racial and National Minorities*, edited by F. S. Brown and J. S. Roucek (New York: Prentice Hall, 1937), 510–525; Constantine Panunzio, "Intermarriage in Los Angeles, 1924–33," *American Journal of Sociology* 47 (March, 1942), 690–701; Robert Risdon, "A Study of Interracial Marriages Based on Data for Los Angeles County," *Sociology and Social Research* 39 (1954), 92–95; John H. Burma, "Interracial Marriage in Los Angeles, 1948–1959," *Social Forces* 42 (December, 1963), 156–165; and Barnett's 1963 article.

29. Shukert and Scibetta, 185–220.

30. For a discussion of changing attitudes after the passage of the Civil Rights Act, see Howard Schuman, Charlotte Steeh, and Lawrence Bobo, *Racial Attitudes in America: Trends and Interpretations* (Cambridge, Massachusetts: Harvard University Press, 1985), 18–40.

31. Hing, 79–120.

32. See *U.S. News and World Report*, "Success Story of One Minority Group," (December 26, 1966), 73–76; and William Petersen, "Success Story: Japanese-American Style," *The New York Times* (January 9, 1966).

33. *Mixed Blood*, 279–280.

34. Kikumura and Kitano.

35. Omi and Winant, 1–8.

36. For a discussion of inner-city decline and its reasons, see Charles Murray, *Losing Ground: American Social Policy, 1950–1980* (New York: Basic Books, 1984); and William Julius Wilson, *The Truly Disadvantaged: The Inner City, the Underclass, and Public Policy* (Chicago: University of Chicago Press, 1987).

37. Pyong Gap Min, *Asian Americans: Contemporary Trends and Issues* (Thousand Oaks, California: Sage Publications, 1994), 10–28.

38. Takaki, *Strangers*, 474.

39. Espiritu, 91–97, 166.

40. Ibid., 19–52.

41. Takaki, *Strangers*, 4.

42. Recollections of Gin Yong Pang, who was an active participant of the Committee to Free Chol Soo Lee.

43. Shinagawa and Pang, 1988.

44. John N. Tinker, "Intermarriage and Assimilation in a Plural Society: Japanese Americans in the United States," in *Intermarriage in the United States*, edited by Gary A. Cretser and Joseph J. Leon (New York: Hayworth Press, 1982); Robert W. Gardner, Bryant Robey, and Peter C. Smith, "Asian Americans: Growth, Change and Diversity," *Population Bulletin* 40:4 (October, 1985), 32–44; and Lee and Yamanaka, 1990.

45. Espiritu, 153.

46. U.S. Commission on Civil Rights, *Civil Rights Issues Facing Asian Americans in the 1990s* (Washington, D.C.: Government Printing Office, 1992), 22–48.

47. Communications with all of these organizations, 1984 to present.

48. Vincent Chin had come to symbolize the plight of every Asian American, regardless of ethnicity, nativity, and gender. The murder of Vincent Chin reminded Asian Americans that the larger white society did not distinguish amongst them as individuals or by their separate ethnic backgrounds. Instead, white society continued to treat them on the basis of their common racial background. In many ways, the racialization of Vincent Chin's death reflected the increasing awareness of race among all segments of American society and signaled the onset of self-conscious racial awareness among Asian Americans.

49. Espiritu, 53–81.

50. A. J. Pais and E. Sanders, "Transplanting God: Asian Immigrants Are Building Buddhist and Hindu Temples across the U.S.," *Far Eastern Economic Review* 23 (June, 1994), 34–35; and Barbara A. Weightman, "Changing Religious Landscapes in Los Angeles," *Journal of Cultural Geography* 14:1 (Fall/Winter 1993), 1–20.

51. Asian American Institute, *Asian American Political Empowerment* (Chicago: Asian American Institute, 1994); Larry Hajime Shinagawa, *Asian Pacific American Electoral Participation in the San Francisco Bay Area* (San Francisco: Asian Law Caucus, 1995); and Larry Hajime Shinagawa, *Asian Pacific American Electoral Participation: A Study of the Exit Poll and Survey Results of the November 8, 1994 Elections for the San Francisco Bay Area, New York City, and Los Angeles* (Washington, D.C.: National Asian Pacific American Legal Consortium, 1995).

52. Espiritu, 112–133; Henry Der, "Statement of Henry Der, Executive Director, Chinese for Affirmative Action, on Behalf of National Coalition for an Accurate Count of Asian/Pacific Americans," in US. House, Committee on Post Office and Civil Service, *Review of 1990 Decennial Census Questionnaire Hearing*, 100th Congress, 2nd session, 14 April; E. Aoki, "Which Party Will Harvest the

New Asian Votes?" *California Journal* (November 1986), 545–546; and "Asian Victory: Census Bureau Drops 1990 Plan," *Asian Week*, March 18, 1988, 1.

53. Asian and Pacific Islander Center for Census Information and Services (ACCIS), *Asian Pacific Americans: State of California, 1990* (San Francisco: Asian and Pacific Islander American Health Forum, 1993).

54. Paul Ong, *Asian Pacific Islanders in California, 1990* (Los Angeles: Public Policy Project, Asian American Studies Center, UCLA, 1991).

55. By critical mass, we mean that Asian American communities had achieved a large enough population size and concentration (approximately 10 to 15 percent of the total population of an urban area), attained a sufficiently adequate socioeconomic standing, and had taken advantage of transnational links to more effectively assert control and independence over their economic, social, political, and cultural interests. With its own developing center of gravity, Asian American communities and individuals no longer had to rely solely upon the mainstream white society for their livelihood, opportunities, status, and identity. But in order to develop critical mass, it became necessary for Asian Americans to interact beyond their specific ethnic group and in a greater pan-Asian identity. A normative base, different than that of white society, now provided an alternative and competing framework for economic, social, political, cultural, and moral development among Asian Americans.

56. Tables are available upon request.

57. *Perez v. Sharp*, 32 c2d 711, 198 P2d 17, 1948. For further details about laws prior to *Perez* and the impact of *Perez*, see L. Tragen, "Statutory Prohibitions Against Interracial Marriage," *California Law Review* (September 1944), 270–280; and Mi-Anne Sumcad, "Filipinos Constitute the Most Intermarriages of Any Asian Group," *Philippine News* (October 3, 1984), 13–14.

58. Ong, 2.

59. According to university research staff at the CSU Chancellor's Office (March 5, 1995) and University of California Office of the President (August 24, 1995).

60. Due to space considerations, we did not include in-depth interviews of Asian Americans that substantiate and support many of these factors. In our interviews conducted between 1988 and 1992 with over fifty Asian Americans from diverse ethnic backgrounds, we found a strong perception of race and gender consciousness, which influenced the marital choices and preferences of Asian Americans.

61. It may still be too early to discount the eventual assimilation of Asian Americans into the dominant White population. There is the possibility that growing Asian panethnicity can be heavily affected by transnational tensions between Asian nations and between Asian nations and the United States. If such tensions were to increase, then they may mitigate the degree of panethnicity and, consequently, interethnic marriages. Moreover, if Asian Americans began to disperse in their regional, residential, and occupational patterns, we may see greater degrees of structural assimilation and eventually some movement toward social and cultural assimilation. Another possibility may be "wedge" race relations which would ally Asian Americans with Whites against African Americans and Latinos. This, too, may lessen the social distance between Asian Americans and Whites and lead toward greater integration with the white population. For further information, see Milton Gordon, *Assimilation in American Life: The Role of Race, Religion, and National Origins* (New York: Oxford University Press, 1964).

62. See Lieberson and Waters, *From Different Strands*, conclusion.

Reading 29

All of the Above

Angelo Ragaza

At ever increasing rates, mixed-race Asian Americans enter a community which has seen sweeping changes in numbers, visibility, power, and consciousness. Will biracial Asian Americans identify as Asian American? Will the Asian American community embrace biracial Asians? Or, as some would have it, does the growing number of biracial Asian Americans threaten to undermine Asian American solidarity just as it is beginning to grow?

Population specialists have quietly noted that America is in the midst of a biracial baby boom. Between 1968 and 1989, children born to parents of different races more than tripled, from one per cent of total births to 3.4 per cent. According to the 1980 U.S. Census, there were approximately 2 million children living in multiracial households. The largest proportion lived in Asian-white households, usually with Asian mothers and white fathers. This is because rates of outmarriage in the Asian American community are high: in Los Angeles County in 1977, 60 per cent of Japanese Americans married non-Japanese, while 49.7 per cent of Chinese Americans and 34.1 per cent of Korean Americans married outside their community: on a national level, the rates have likely since grown. In the Japanese American community, mixed-race births currently outnumber monoracial births: for every 100 births to two Japanese parents in the U.S., there were 139 births to a Japanese and a non-Japanese parent.

PLEASE CHOOSE ONE

How biracial people identify themselves has a lot to do with who is asking and how the question is

Source: A. *Magazine* 3:1 (1994): 21–22, 76–77. Reprinted by permission.

framed. In 1979, Dr. Christine Hall, a University of Arizona sociologist who is herself Japanese/African American, completed one of the nation's first dissertations on biracial individuals. In it she asked 30 subjects, all Japanese/African American, to define their racial and cultural identity. When asked to choose among standardized racial categories—black, Hispanic, Asian, Native American, other—19 chose "black" and 11 choose "other." "When you give people a forced choice," Dr. Hall says, "they choose the way that society wants them to."

But when asked to rate their "blackness" and their "Japanese-ness" on a scale from 1 to 6, 28 out of 30 rated themselves high on both. "For me, that proved that people were very multicultural," Hall says. "But society never gives you a question like that. . . . They force you to choose one or the other."

When my Dad died, there were of course feelings of loss. But underneath, this strange question popped into my head: Now that he's gone, does that mean I'm not Korean anymore? I thought that I had figured it all out for myself. To have the "Korean community" that I'd grown up with taken away from me rattled me for a while. I think I certainly identify much more as Korean. But finding out how to be Korean on my own terms rather than my father's is proving to be quite a process.

—Andrew Ko, 30, Dutch, English, French/Korean American

Parents exert critical influence on how their children grow to perceive their cultural identity. While biracial Asian Americans often say that their Asian parent did not consciously educate them about Asian culture—aside from how to prepare Asian food and certain customs and expressions: rarely do biracial Asian Americans

349

say they learned about both parents' cultures equally. In some cases, one parent acted to ensure that the children get a thorough feel for his or her own culture, without emphasizing similar education in the other parent's culture. "These days I'm exploring my Asian side more," says Lisa, 25, who is half African half Korean American. "Because my father was raising Black children, and that was unequivocal. He resented any inquiries about our Korean heritage. He kept us ignorant about it, and my mother did, too."

Michael Thornton, a Japanese/African American sociologist, and a professor of Asian American Studies and Afro-American Studies at the University of Wisconsin, says that until recently many interracial parents didn't fully understand the impact mixed heritage might have on their children. Often parents educate their children about race only after they'd had negative experiences. "For example, when I was about five or six, I was assaulted by a number of white kids in the street," he says," "because they identified me as black *and* Japanese, and they didn't quite know what that was. I talked to my mother and my father, and they sat me down and explained what was happening. It wasn't as if they had long term plans and [were] cognizant of the effect being mixed-race would have on me."

Of course, identity isn't so cut and dried: a biracial individual's sense of cultural identity can go through different stages as he or she grows up. In the groundbreaking anthology *Racially Mixed People in America*, psychologist George Kitahara Kich found that biracial adults of white and Japanese heritage progressed through three major stages in identity development. From age three through 10, they noticed a difference between how they perceived themselves and how others perceived them. This was followed by a struggle, from age eight until young adulthood, to gain acceptance from others. He notes that as biracial individuals mature, they feel less compelled to choose between one race or the other and are able to conceive of their racial and cultural identity as multidimensional.

But what does being "multicultural" really mean? Since biracial individuals cannot rely on standard monoracial vocabulary to define their identity, often they must define it on their own. For Chinese/African American Randall Wilson, now 40 years old, identity is still a work in progress. "I had no role models," he says. "Most of my life there has been a lot of conflict, because I didn't ever fit into one camp. Now I am creating my *own* camp."

THE ANTI-MINORITY AND THE DOUBLE MINORITY

Biracial Asian Americans who are half-white may deny experiencing prejudice while growing up. Nevertheless, many remember comments from Asians, both in Asia and America, that were accusations of cultural inauthenticity. "When I was in Korea, I'd walk down the street and all I ever heard behind me was '*mi gook-saram,*' which means 'white person,' " says Ko. "Most Koreans don't treat me like I'm Korean, because I don't look Korean enough, I don't speak Korean well enough, even though I was raised in some respects as Korean as they were."

One Asian American community which has seen its mixed-race population increase dramatically is Vietnamese Americans. As Kieu-Linh Caroline Valverde writes in *Racially Mixed People in America*, Amerasians, whether half white or half black, are seen by the Vietnamese community as "illegitimate, resulting from passing relationships that brought Vietnamese bar girls and American GIs together." The stereotype persists, despite the fact that the vast majority of relationships between GIs and Vietnamese women during the Vietnam War lasted at least two years, and often resulted in common-law marriage. But because it is assumed that Amerasians' mothers were bar girls or prostitutes, Amerasian females are often confronted with the same stereotype.

Biracial Vietnamese also say that there is a perception that Amerasians are uneducated. In

Vietnam, many Amerasians receive little education; some do not attend school at all. By the time many are permitted to immigrate to the United States, they have passed the age of 17 and are therefore too old to benefit from the Preparation for American Secondary Schools (PASS) program. As a result, many Amerasians are deprived of language skills and a fair chance to further their education.

On the other hand, biracial Asian Americans who are half-white are often thought to have better access and more acceptance in white communities, because they represent the combination of a social majority and, in America, a "model minority." Some biracial Asian Americans who are half-white say they never felt isolated or experienced overt prejudice, even though they grew up in all-white neighborhoods. "There was a time when, if someone asked if I'd ever encountered racism, I'd say, no, race has had no bearing on me," says Paul Pfeiffer, who is Filipino/German American. Still, Pfeiffer feels that people may have felt comfortable making racially insensitive comments about Asians and other people of color in front of him because he is half white and half Asian, and therefore "safe."

But to many biracials, who strongly identify themselves as Asian American, that "one of us" safety is an offense.

"My Asian heritage is very important. It's something that I'm constantly enforcing," says Paul Berges, who is Japanese/French/German American. "It shatters that whole myth that all Asians want to do is assimilate." Because of the ambiguity of his features, Berges has been told that he could pass for white. "It would be really easy for me," he says, "but I have no interest in doing it."

I can see them look at me and some don't think that I can understand Korean. I hear them making derogatory remarks about the fact that I'm mixed. And then they start making derogatory remarks about my mother, because how could an Asian woman marry someone who is black? She must have been a prostitute! I'll walk into a market and see someone behind the counter who looks like my Mom, and I'll feel a certain affection. But then she'll treat me with complete lack of respect and cordiality. Differently than she would treat a white person who comes into the market. . . . When a white person comes in, they'll be very friendly. Then I'll come in, and they'll sort of look me up and down and try to figure out what I am. Unless I come in a suit: then it's a different story. But it's hurtful.

—Song Richardson, 26
Korean/African American

Biracial Asian Americans who are half African American, on the other hand, represent two minority communities. Because the hierarchy of race in America posits Asians, as the "model minority," slightly "below" whites but "above" other people of color, many monoracial Asians are even less prepared to accept half black Asian Americans than they are to accept half white Asian Americans.

Part of the extent to which this hierarchy has been internalized by the Asian American community stems from negative stereotypes held about people of African descent in Asia. "There's been research on mixture groups in Japan," says Hall. "The kids who are half-white got along much better than kids who are half black." In Vietnam and the Philippines, as in many Asian countries, dark skin is associated with lower socioeconomic class and with ethnic minorities. Such attitudes are carried over into Asian communities in America.

Kimiko Roberts, 17, whose mother is Japanese American and whose father is African American, says when her parents married, her mother was "disowned, for the most part." Roberts still has disturbing childhood memories of the tension from her mother's family.

"There were a lot of really awful things, really mean thoughts, like telling people that I was going to be the 'bad seed,' really ignorant things that didn't make any sense and were based on fear," she says. "I can remember Christmases where people wouldn't speak to me directly; they would tell so-and-so to go and tell me something.

At family functions, I felt neglected. I know it hurt my mother, because she really didn't like taking me to those kinds of situations, but she wanted me to know my family."

African/Asian Americans say they are not perceived as unusual among other African-Americans, and that acceptance comes more readily from that community. Crystal Wong, 19, who is African/Vietnamese American, attributes this to the diversity of black physical types—a result of extensive interbreeding with whites and Native Americans. "In the black race, there's such a wide variety," she says. "From very, very light to very dark. You blend in a lot easier, regardless of what you look like." By contrast, many Americans, non-Asian as well as Asian, perceive the range of Asian physical types to be much more limited, even though in actuality Asians are as physically diverse as any other race. "Insofar as skin color and hair texture," Wong explains, "I couldn't cross over as an Asian woman." Roberts has had similar experiences. "People who are Japanese always rule me out as being not Japanese," she says. "But if I'm just meeting somebody who is black for the first time, they'll say, 'Are you half black?'"

But in spite of apparent acceptance, African/Asian Americans experience a tacit pressure to prove their blackness. Richardson recalls an incident at Harvard in which black students had a meeting about her and a friend who is half black, half white. "It was a meeting about why we were not acknowledging the fact that we were black and pretending to be someone else," she explains. "It was very bizarre for me; it made me not want to hang out with them either. Even now, I feel like I have to make an extra effort to be with African Americans just to prove that I'm black."

THE BODY BIRACIAL

I didn't do anything with my hair. It was really unruly. I didn't think it was attractive, and I didn't really make any effort. Other black kids in my school, the few that were there, ridiculed me,

because I needed no-lye. I needed Dark and Lovely or something, and I wouldn't use it—part of me thought that I should be as black as I can be. It wasn't until sophomore, junior year, which is relatively late to get your hair straightened as a black woman, that I did it. But I didn't really keep it up. My relatives don't understand what my problem is. I have an aunt who's like, "You've got long, beautiful hair. You could have everything you want! You've got a good job. Just fix your hair and you'll be fine." Hair is a big political statement in the African American community. By not making a statement, I'm making a statement. Although I'm trying as hard as I can to figure out what it is.
—Lisa, 25, Korean/African American

People who are biracial experience an exaggerated emphasis on their physical appearance; after all, their features can mean acceptance from one community and rejection from another. Wong, who has found acceptance in the black community, says, her brother, who looks more Asian, has had a very difficult time fitting in with African Americans. "He's just a little darker than me, but his hair is a lot straighter," she says. "I noticed that when he went to high school, he met a lot of Asian friends and tended to stick with that group more—wanted to be part of them."

Biracial people are often told they are "exotic," "beautiful," and "fascinating." The subjects in Hall's study and many people interviewed for this article said they felt content—in some cases, very pleased—with their physical appearance. "I do think I'm an attractive person. I've been led to believe that by response," Filipino/German Sue Delara says. "I have some of my mother's height, but I have a little Filipino 'roundness,' so I look more voluptuous. I think I got the best of both worlds."

But not all biracial people appreciate the attention. Richardson views compliments about how "exotic" she appears as a cheap way for men to start conversations with her. "It really pisses me off, actually," she says. "Especially because of the stereotypes some men have about Asian women." At the same time, Richardson, who is half black, has to contend with sexual stereotypes about *black* women. "It's a nightmare," she says.

Wong resents what "biracial beauty" implies about monoracial people of color. She remembers one friend who told her that he thought biracial children were "the prettiest kids that there were."

"I thought that was a terrible thing to say, because he was a black guy. I would hope that he would think that his own race was beautiful," she says. "To say that some other race has to come in and beautify the black race means that all-black kids are not as beautiful as racially mixed ones."

FREE LOVE AND THE FUTURE?

Hall says that racial identity processes seem to begin around adolescence: dating age. The ethnicities of the people biracial individuals choose to date reflects the level of diversity in their community. People who grow up in predominantly white neighborhoods date white people. But in diverse neighborhoods, the dating choices of biracial individuals reflect their own considerations of identity. Not surprisingly, many biracial people express a striking openness toward the ethnicity of their partners. "My first boyfriend was Filipino. I've dated black guys, I've dated Puerto Rican guys, white guys—I've done them all," Delara jokes, with a giggle. "I'm into the rainbow coalition."

For Pfeiffer, who is gay, his exploration of his Filipino identity and his deepening involvement in the gay Asian American community were intertwined processes. He is currently in a long-term relationship with another Filipino American. "I basically just dated white men before I came to New York," he says. With a couple of exceptions, everyone he has dated since moving to New York

two years ago has been a man of color. "I would be lying if I said I now find white men less attractive," he says. "But I recognize the value of not having to put up with certain kinds of bullshit."

"I was dating a Latino guy for two years," says Roberts. "I just recently started to date a guy who's African American. I pretty much feel like I can date whoever I want to date. My parents were an interracial couple, and I feel if they can do it, then of course I can too."

In choosing not to let the boundaries of race keep them from "doing it," the parents of biracial people have unwittingly lifted the rhetoric of race which obscures America's multiracial reality. As Maria Root notes in *Racially Mixed People in America*, 30 to 70 per cent of African Americans are estimated to be of multiracial ancestry. Filipinos and Latinos are virtually all multiracial, as well as the majority of Native Americans, and native Hawaiians. Moreover, a significant proportion of the white-identified population is multiracial. The U.S. Census continues to deny this reality, in refusing to create special categories for people of mixed race—partially because of a justified wariness in communities of color toward the creation of new categories, since any subtraction from the African, Asian, Latino and Native American populations could be politically expensive.

The growing biracial population constitutes a challenge to the definitions of identity from which people of color in America now draw strength and pride after generations of shame. But multiracial and monoracial Asian Americans have much to share: Both live in America with an ambiguous status. Both are confronted by the dilemma of defining their identity between two cultures—between commonality and difference. But both also enjoy the benefit of drawing on two cultures, two perspectives, every single day of their lives.

A Fighter for Gay Rights

Carlos Mendez

The Lambda Legal Defense and Education Fund—the nation's premier law firm and chief litigator for the gay and lesbian community—celebrated its 20th anniversary last year, as J. Craig Fong marked his first year as Lamba's West Coast regional director.

Lambda's new west coast office is miles and a seeming galaxy away from its previous downtown Los Angeles location of towering corporate complex and corporate law firms. It is now situated in the heart of L.A.'s mid-Wilshire district along a strip of asphalt once known as the Miracle Mile.

Though only a block away from the new and improved L.A. County Museum of Art, the new location abuts the boarded and abandoned art deco and '50s L.A.—modern structures of two retail giants which opted for the suburban shopping malls. In Lambda's new office this summer afternoon, the air hums with the sound of air-conditioning and the relaxed but determined activity of staff, interns and volunteers.

In Fong's very functional second floor office overlooking Wilshire Boulevard a Mozartian opera plays quietly in the background. Stacks of assorted papers and documents sit neatly atop his desk. On one corner, in a plexiglass frame is a photo of Fong and his partner in romance—one wears a tank top, the other a crimson red T-shirt. In a smaller, metal enclosed frame, Fong proudly points out his godson, Jason. Before his Lambda appointment, Fong was Immigration Project Director for the Asian Pacific American Legal Center from 1987 to 1991.

Source: AsianWeek, July 29, 1994, pp. 1, 14–15. Reprinted by permission.

As a Chinese American, explains a very forthright Fong, "I feel very close to the Asian Pacific Islander community. I'm also a gay man. And this community means a lot to me. It is a community I have wanted to work for. I had done some tangential work before coming on board with Lambda, but not nearly as much as I'm doing now. I also realize as an Asian man, as a gay man and as someone who has done a lot of work in the Latino community, I have sitting at this table a number of bridges I can help build. That I can link communities that normally don't talk to one another. Or that are not familiar with one another. That's an enormous opportunity."

The fall of '91 and winter of '92 was a difficult time for the New York-based organization and its Los Angeles branch just two years in existence, Fong explains. While Asian American professional guilds rallied in protest at the casting of an English actor for the Eurasian lead in Miss Saigon, Lambda blithely went ahead and accepted the producer's offer of a fund-raiser. At headquarters, dismay turned to dissension, and later some staff resignations. Terming the fallout "a tempest in a teacup," Fong admits there is no one in the organization today who would not say using the Broadway production as a fund-raiser was a mistake. "It was distinctly a lack of cultural sensitivity," Fong readily replies. "Everyone affiliated with the organization now knows it and acknowledges it. And the truth is, like anything else when you're working across communities and across cultures, it's about learning."

Fong is fairly certain the fact that he is an Asian American was not lost on the Lambda board members when hiring for his position. "It makes good sense," Fong continues, "if you think about it. Los Angeles, and California, generally, has a large people of color population. And regardless of that diversity, we are quite different from New York. I think they realized it was to their benefit to have an Asian American at the helm of their West Coast office. So I think that probably had something to do with it. But hopefully, I think they realized I am well qualified in other ways."

Modesty may prevent Fong from singing his own praises. He is a 1981 University of Pennsylvania Law School grad, and in between stops at University of Madrid, UC-Berkeley's Boalt Hall, and an assistant professorship in English at Gregg International College in Yokohama, Japan, Fong graduated in 1978 with a B.A. in clinical and social psychology from Yale University. Before Fong's four-year tenure with the Asian Pacific American Legal Center, he worked as a staff attorney for the Security Pacific Corporation in Los Angeles, and an associate in the mergers and acquisition department of Chapman & Cutler in Chicago.

According to the organization's quarterly newsletter, The Lambda Update, "lambda" is the eleventh letter in the Greek alphabet. As a pictograph it was originally used as a symbol to represent the scales of justice, and later came to represent the concept of balance. Painted on the battle shields of soldiers in Spartan Greece, it signified the balance of the demands of the state against the freedom of the individual. Lambda was adopted in 1974 by the International Gay Rights Congress as the international symbol for gay and lesbian civil rights.

Two years ago, explains Fong, before his appointment, Lambda's focus was almost completely on litigation. Like the NAACP Legal Defense and Education Fund, from which all subsequent civil rights organizations have taken their suffix and lessons, the objective is setting legal precedent and slowly chipping away at exclusionary and prejudicial legal and social barriers. "That is of course still Lambda's primary mission," continues Fong. "To change the law and do something that will change the way gay

men and lesbians are treated and perceived by the legal system."

In the annals of Lambda's history, no court case better illustrates the nature of the opposition to come than its first. In 1972 a New York court denied Lambda nonprofit status. The court ruled that Lambda's "stated purposes are on their face neither benevolent nor charitable, nor, in any event, is there a demonstrated need for this corporation. . . . It does not appear that discrimination against homosexuals, which undoubtedly exists, operates to deny them of legal representation." That decision was overturned the next year on appeal.

"I think Lambda's vision now, here," two years later, Fong explains, "is the same but expanded. We're still doing the impact cases. For example, the Hawaii marriage case, HIV discrimination cases, a company denying health benefits to an employee and his partner. But in addition to these test cases, we're also doing more education. That is to say, we're taking the victories that we've won, and we're going into the community and trying to teach how you can now use the law to your own benefit. I'm really proud of that. Although our organization has always done its best work in the field of test cases, when we go into the community we suddenly no longer are just these lawyers who argue cases before the Supreme Court. We become a resource for the community."

Putting his immigration law background back into high gear, Fong is also actively involved in two high stakes political asylum cases. In one, he is representing (with Lambda staff attorney Suzanne Goldberg) a Russian lesbian, Alla Pitcherskala, who was denied asylum based on her well-founded fear of sexual persecution. In the second, Fong is representing Jacob Rivas, a gay Nicaragua man with AIDS, in his fight against deportation. In the high stakes and high profile gays in the military court battle, Lambda represents three of the most nationally prominent defendants.

The thing that's important to know about gays in the military, Fong begins, warming to the subject, "is that Lambda has been fighting these cases for 18 years. People in the media and other gay and lesbian organizations have been talking about it for two. Lambda has been fighting and losing these cases all the way up the line. We have always believed that gay men and lesbians have an equal right to serve in the U.S. armed forces. Over the last couple of years we have had some victories." Fong readily admits to his own incompatibility with military service, but addresses the constitutional and sociological points.

Though unmentioned, over the aerial survey of his own personal history, at 40, Fong, like Bill Clinton and the baby boomers in bloom in the nation's capital, can recall the tragedy that was Vietnam. "There are many gay men and lesbians who want to serve their country," says Fong. "And I will say this, now, in a time when the economy is very tight, the military is often the employer of last resort. Two, especially for women, the military is a place that offers a remarkable opportunity for advancement—more so than in the civilian world. Yes, there are problems. Yes, there is sexism. But I think many women find the possibility of quickly being able to take leadership and responsible roles very attractive."

Gay civil rights, explains Fong, are nothing more than the same civil rights everybody else has. "The radical right and those people who are campaigning against us," explains Fong, "who think that we're somehow this community that wants special rights—that's just wrong. They don't understand that all we are asking for as a community is to be treated like everybody else. No special treatment, just the same treatment."

As examples, Fong gives the military, marriage, and work place discrimination. "If I'm not doing my job, yeah, fire me," Fong continues, his voice rising with indignation. "But don't fire me simply because of my sexual orientation. Don't forbid me from marrying simply because of my sexual orientation. Don't give me different benefits on the job simply because of my sexual orientation. All I want is simply to be treated like everybody else."

Lambda, explains Fong, has been in existence for 21 years. For most of those 21 years it took its cases to court, fought, and more often than not lost. "What we are seeing now . . . especially over the last three to five years, and especially over the last two to three years, is an acceleration in the number of courts that are willing to open-mindedly listen to the arguments we have been making for 21 years." Fong sees the changes in the judicial temper as a direct result of a change in the cultural climate.

"What has happened," continues Fong, "is there are now courts, judges and the culture willing to listen to the national argument. Before they just made their irrational decisions: We can discriminate against gay men and lesbians. Why, because we always have. Why, because we always will. And that was enough. Forget the law. Forget the [U.S.] Constitution."

Fong speaks of the Washington state case of *Commemeyer v. U.S. Army*, brought on behalf of a 27-year veteran discharged in 1992 for publicly acknowledging that she was a lesbian, and the Steffan case in Washington, D.C., over a cadet discharged from the Naval Academy. "Both cases are saying, unless you have a good reason for treating gay men and lesbian differently, you can't do that. And the military doesn't have a good reason for treating them differently."

Prior to the gay liberation landmark protest over police brutality at the Stonewall Tavern in New York City 20 years ago, gay and lesbian life was hidden. After Stonewall, the gathering anger led to a movement that united gay men and then lesbians for the first time. Fong says, "Not that we all look alike, or think alike, or act alike, because we don't. But there is a presence that is visible. And there is a courage that comes from being aligned with more and more people."

THE SEXUAL QUESTION

Fong, when asked how much of the fight for gay rights is also a fight for the right to party, takes a deep breath, sighs, and with lawyerly precision, replies: "I think it is very important for us to draw a distinction between simple sexual, biological activity, and the rights we enjoy as individuals and as a community. To the extent that there are members in our community that express their sexuality in ways that may be different from the straight mainstream community, it is important to Lambda that these people be allowed to do that. But that is not all of who we are."

Fong emphatically notes that gays and lesbians have done much more than simply create a community based on its sleeping arrangements. Gays and lesbians, says Fong, have come together to create a community to meet a variety of needs for people whose needs are different from mainstream Americans. "It goes beyond simply the right to sleep with whom we please, or to party when we please. I'm really much more concerned with the quality of our interaction with the straight community. In terms of our need to fight for the right to sleep with whom we please, that is only in my view important insofar as straight people try to judge us based on whom we sleep with. I'm really not concerned with what the boys in the bathhouses are off doing whatever it is they are doing. They have the right to do that. That's inside the gay community. That's in and amongst ourselves.

"I'm much more concerned when that gay man leaves the bathhouse and puts on a suit to go to work the next morning. I am much more concerned with how he is treated by his employers. Because they may make decisions about him, they may hire him, fire him, pay him and give him benefits differently, simply because of what he did last night. To me that's the big difference. That's something they should not be doing."

While Fong sees similarities with the other civil rights movements, particularly the African American and women's movements, he says each has its own identity because of their separate histories and the manner of groups that have lined up in opposition to them. "The gay and lesbian community and movement," Fong explains, "crosses

all races, all classes, all income groups, all religions and all nationalities. So we are somewhat broader. The other movements have laid good groundwork for us. We are the beneficiaries of those experiences. But I would say we are very different from them."

Being Asian American and gay "is a mess!" says Fong, breaking out in a rueful and exasperated grin. "If you're talking about who in the gay community marginalizes Asian Pacific Islanders, I would say gay and lesbian mainstream white people do." Asian Pacific Islanders, Fong notes, are a small percentage of the American population in general, and of the gay and lesbian community, in particular. "It is difficult," Fong continues, "because the mainstream white community, especially in the gay and lesbian community, have certain stereotypes about what Asian Pacific Islanders are. And those stereotypes work distinctly against us."

"We are seeing more and more groups like the Gay Asian Pacific Support Network [GAPSN] in Los Angeles and the Gay Asian Pacific Alliance [GAPA] in San Francisco. These organizations, which function as support groups are trying to encourage a sense of pride and identity among and within Asian Pacific Islander gay men and lesbians. So that we can rise above the stereotypes the mainstream gay and lesbian community would put on us."

"Being Asian and being queer," Fong observes, "are a different set of interests and balances. I'm not saying that it's easier or harder. But it's different. How you deal with those differences is something you look to other Asians to help you with because white folks don't understand."

It is the Confucian and Buddhist roots of many of the Asian cultures that is at the heart of the great cultural divide, explains Fong. "That is, you are nothing until you become an ancestor. If I don't make my father an ancestor—what that means is giving him a grandson. So that when my father dies, my son will grow up remembering and revering his grandfather." What Confucian and Buddhist cultures teach, explains Fong, is what makes the individual's importance comes after his lifetime when he is an ancestor. "And you don't become an ancestor until you have people alive today worshipping you when you are dead. So the idea, even for me, a fourth generation Chinese American, that I will never be an ancestor. Why? Because I don't have kids. Who will burn incense on my grave?"

Fong describes a Holcaust poster hanging on the office wall of a friend he calls his rabbi. In the center around signs commemorating persons who died of AIDS is a candle surrounded by barbed wire. The inscription reads: "Who Will Say Kaddish For Me?"

"That's exactly it," explains Fong. "Who is going to say Kaddish for me? Who is going to burn incense at my grave?"

"It's not about the future. It's about the past. It's about maintaining a link to the people who came before you. When we try to explain that to the mainstream gay and lesbian community, they don't get it. And that is the Asian equivalent of 'Who Will Say Kaddish For Me?' "

"You become brave," Fong continues. "You remind yourself that it is not so much whether or not your family burns incense at your grave. You condition yourself to remember that the honor and memory to who you are lives on in those who continue after you.

"And those people who remember your contribution are those who will symbolically burn incense at your grave. And those are the people you need to cultivate now. Because most of us, as Asian gay men and lesbians, will not have children."

These are the kinds of things I've had to think about, says Fong, of his middle years. But the gay and lesbian community itself, he continues, has had to create new communities, new self-identi-ties, and its own set of morals and values. Asians within the gay and lesbian community have to do so also. "But the thing that is hardest," Fong confides, "is not dealing with the mainstream, gay or straight, it's dealing with other Asians. The amount of prejudice that exists, the amount of misunderstanding that exists among straight Asian Pacific Islanders (against Asian gays and lesbians) in the United States is unbelievable."

Fong reasons Asian homophobia is a combination of the Confucian Buddhist beliefs carried firmly down the line of generations. And in the process of Asian American assimilation, the wholesale adoption of certain American cultural values, particularly those that have long held gay and lesbian life in contempt, or fear.

But there is also something else at work, says Fong. "American society already emasculates Asian men."

In the end, Fong allows his struggle for identity, "and finding a place for myself in this world is not atypical. I would say what is probably the best lesson to be taken away from this, whether you're straight or gay, Asian or not, is that finding your identity is an exercise in great courage. It is particularly so for marginalized people, for minorities, for people doubly marginalized." Fong continues, his voice rising with anger, "And I am not going to let the straight people tell me what I can and can't do. I am not going to let the white people tell me what I can and cannot do. And I'm not going to let the mainstream queers tell me as an Asian queer what it is I can and cannot do."

Fong, once again the clinical and social psychology major at Yale, concludes, "However you want to slice that, it's an exercise in courage of all of us to find, nurture, cultivate and ultimately adopt the identities and beliefs that make us up as human beings."

Reading 31

Stories from the Homefront:
Perspectives of Asian American Parents
with Lesbian Daughters and Gay Sons[1]

Alice Y. Hom

Having been a classroom teacher since 1963, I have new knowledge that ten percent of all the students who came through my classroom have grown up and are gay and lesbian. . . . Because I cannot undo the past, I want to teach people the truth about homosexuality so people will not abandon these children.[2]

These are stories from the homefront; the emotions, responses, and attitudes of Asian American parents about their lesbian daughters or gay sons. The stories attempt to shed some light on parents' attitudes, and inform lesbians and gay men various ways parents may react and respond to their coming out.

I focus on four themes that illustrate important concepts around understanding Asian American parents and their views on homosexuality. These themes emerged from the interviews: 1) the attitudes of parents before disclosure/discovery; 2) the attitudes and reactions of parents after disclosure/discovery; 3) disclosure to friends and their communities; and 4) advice for other parents.

Sexuality is an issue rarely or never discussed amongst Asian families, yet it remains a vital aspect of one's life. What are the implications of alternative sexualities in family situations? Coming out stories and experiences of Asian American lesbians and gay men have had some exposure and publication,[3] however the voices of the parents are rarely presented or known.

I found the majority of interviewees through personal contacts with individuals in organizations such as Asian Pacifica Sisters in San Francisco, Mahu Sisters and Brothers Alliance at UCLA and Gay Asian Pacific Alliance Community HIV

Source: Amerasia Journal 20:1 (1994): 19–32. Reprinted by permission.

Project in San Francisco. I met one set of parents through the Parents and Friends of Lesbians and Gays group in Los Angeles. Obviously this select group of people, who were willing to talk about their child, might represent only certain perspectives. Nonetheless, I managed to pool a diverse set of parents despite the small size in terms of disclosing time and time lapse—some parents have known for years and a few have recently found out. I did receive some "no" answers to my request. I also offered complete anonymity in the interviews; most preferred pseudonyms. Names with an asterisk sign denote pseudonyms.

I interviewed thirteen parents altogether, all mothers except for two fathers.[4] The interviewee pool consisted of four single mothers by divorce, a widower, two couples, and four married mothers. The ethnicities included four Chinese, four Japanese, three Pilipinas, one Vietnamese, and one Korean. Most live in California with one in Portland and another in Hawaii. All of the interviews occurred in English with the exception of one interview conducted in Japanese with the lesbian daughter as translator. Ten out of the thirteen interviewees are first generation immigrants. The other three are third generation Japanese American. I interviewed four mothers of gay sons including one mother with two gay sons. The rest had lesbian daughters including one mother with two lesbian daughters. Six were told and seven inadvertently discovered about their children's sexual orientation.[5]

Most books on the topic of parents of lesbian and gay children report mainly on white middle-class families.[6] *Beyond Acceptance: Parents of Lesbians and Gays Talk about Their Experiences* by Carolyn W. Griffin, Marian J. Wirth and Arthur

G. Wirth, discusses the experiences of twenty-three white middle-class parents from a Midwestern metropolitan city involved with Parents and Friends of Lesbians and Gays (PFLAG).[7] Another book titled, *Parents Matter: Parents' Relationships with Lesbian Daughters and Gay Sons*, by Ann Muller, relates the perspectives of lesbian and gay children with a few stories by the parents. Seventeen percent of the seventy-one people interviewed were black.[8] These examples present mainly an Anglo picture and fail to account for the diversity of lesbian and gay communities as well as different experiences of parents of color.

ATTITUDES OF PARENTS TOWARDS GAYS AND LESBIANS PRE-DISCLOSURE

The knowledge of lesbians and gay men in their native countries and in their communities in the United States serves as an important factor in dismantling the oft-used phrase that a son or daughter is gay or lesbian because of assimilation and acculturation in a western context. The parents interviewed did not utter "it's a white disease," a phrase often heard and used when discussing coming out in an Asian American community and context. Connie S. Chan in her essay, "Issues of Identity Development among Asian American Lesbians and Gay Men," found in her study that nine out of ninety-five respondents were out to their parents. Chan suggested that this low number might be related to, ". . . specific cultural values defining the traditional roles, which help to explain the reluctance of Asian-American lesbians and gay men to 'come out' to their parents and families."[9]

Nonetheless, the parents interviewed recounted incidents of being aware of lesbians and or gays while they were growing up and did not blame assimilation and Anglo American culture for their children's sexual orientation. One quote by Lucy Nguyen, a fifty-three-year-old Vietnamese immigrant who has two gay sons, does however, imply that the environment and

attitudes of the United States allowed for her sons to express their gay identity. She stated

> I think all the gay activities and if I live at this time, environment like this, I think I'm lesbian. You know, be honest. When I was young, the society in— Vietnam is so strict—I have a really close friend, I love her, but just a friendship nothing else. In my mind, I say, well in this country it's free. They have no restraint, so that's why I accept it, whatever they are.[10]

This revealing remark assumes that an open environment allows for freedom of sexual expression. Nevertheless, it does not necessarily suggest lesbians and gay men exist solely because of a nurturing environment. Rather lesbians and gay men must live and survive in different ways and/or make choices depending on the climate of the society at the time.

Midori Asakura*, a sixty-three-year-old Japanese immigrant with a lesbian daughter, related an example of lesbianism in Japan. She remembered, while studying to be a nurse, talk in the dorm rooms about "S" which denotes women who had really close friendships with one another.[11] She recalled,

> One day you'd see one woman with a certain blouse and the next day, you'd see the other woman with the same blouse. They would always sit together, they went everywhere together. There was talk that they were having sex, but I didn't think they were. . . . People used to say they felt each other out. I thought, "Nah, they're not having sex, why would they?" Everyone thought it was strange but no one really got into it.[12]

When asked what she thought of the "S" women, Midori replied, "I didn't think much of it, although I thought one was manlike, Kato-san, and the other, Fukuchi-san, who was very beautiful and sharp-minded was the woman."[13]

Another parent, George Tanaka,* a fifty-three-year-old Japanese American who grew up in Hawaii and has a lesbian daughter, remembers a particular person known as *mahu*.[14] Toni Barraquiel, a fifty-four-year-old Pilipina single mother with a gay son, commented on gay men in Manila because of their effeminacy and admission of being gay. Toni asserted these men would be in certain careers such as manicurists and hairdressers. When asked of the people's attitudes towards them she replied,

> that they look down on those gays and lesbians, they make fun of them. . . . It seems as if it is an abnormal thing. The lesbian is not as prominent as the gays. They call her a tomboy because she's very athletic and well built.[15]

Maria Santos*, a fifty-four-year-old Pilipina immigrant with two lesbian daughters, spoke of gays and lesbians in Luzon. She said, "There were negative attitudes about them. 'Bakla' and 'Tomboy'— it was gay-bashing in words not in physical terms. There was name-calling that I did not participate in."[16]

Lucy Nguyen* had lesbian classmates in her all-girls high school. She said, "They were looked down upon, because this isn't normal. They were called 'homo'."[17] A common thread throughout the observations of the parents about gays and lesbians lies in stereotypical gender role associations. For example, Margaret Tsang*, a sixty-year-old Chinese single parent who has a gay son, recalled a family member who might possibly be gay, although there was not a name for it. She observed, "He was slanted towards nail polish and make-ups and all kinds of things. And he liked Chinese opera. He behaved in a very feminine fashion."[18]

Similarly, Liz Lee, a forty-two-year-old Korean single parent with a lesbian daughter, clearly remembered lesbians in Seoul. "My mother's friend was always dressed like man in suit. She always had mousse or grease on her hair and she dressed like a man. She had five or six girlfriends always come over."[19] Liz related that she did not think anything about it and said they were respected.[20] When asked of people's attitudes toward these women, Liz responded, "They

say nature made a mistake. They didn't think it was anybody's choice or anybody's preference."[21]

For the most part the interviewees, aware of gays and lesbians during their growing up years, associated gender role reversals with gays and lesbians. The men were feminine and the women looked male or tomboy with the women couples in a butch-femme type relationship. The belief and experiences with lesbians and gay men who dress and act in opposite gender roles serve as the backdrop of what to compare their children with when faced with their coming out. Most of what these parents see is a part of homosexuality, the dress or behavior. They have not seen the whole range of affectional, emotional, intellectual and sexual components of a person. Although I asked the interviewees if they had any thoughts or attitudes about lesbians or gay men, most said they did not think about them and did not participate in the name calling or bashing. This might not be necessarily true because they were able to relate quite a few incidents of homophobic opinions which might have been internalized. Moreover, once they know they have a lesbian or gay child, that distance or non-judgmental attitude radically changes. As one mother remarked, "the fire is on the other side of the river bank. The matter is taking place somewhere else, it's not your problem."[22]

DISCLOSURE OR DISCOVERY

For the most part, parents experience a wide range of emotions, feelings and attitudes when they find out they have a lesbian daughter or gay son. Parents find out through a variety of ways, ranging from a direct disclosure by the child themselves, discovering the fact from a journal, confronting the child because of suspicions or by walking in on them.

For example, Liz Lee, who walked in on her daughter Sandy, said, "[it was] the end of the world. Still today I can't relate to anything that's going on with my daughter, but I'm accepting."[23] She found out in 1990 and said,

I was hoping it was a stage she's going through and that she could change. I didn't accept for a long time. I didn't think she would come out in the open like this. I thought she would just keep it and later on get married. That's what I thought but she's really out and open. . . . I said to myself I accept it because she is going to live that way.[24]

Because Sandy serves as the co-chair of the Gay, Lesbian and Bisexual Association at school, her mother sees Sandy as happy and politically fulfilled from this position which assists her process in accepting Sandy's sexual orientation. However, like many of the parents interviewed, she initially thought she had done something wrong. "I didn't lead a normal life at the time either. But Sandy always accept me as I was and she was always happy when I was happy and I think that's love. As long as Sandy's happy."[25]

Toni Barraquiel responded differently when Joel told her at an early age of thirteen or fourteen that he was gay back in the mid 1980s. She plainly asked him if he felt happy which he replied affirmatively. Thus her response, "well, if you're happy I'll support you, I'll be happy for you."[26] Their relationship as a single mother and only child has always been one of closeness and open communication so problems did not arise in terms of disclosing his sexual orientation. Toni Barraquiel experienced confusion because at the time he had girlfriends and she did not think of him as a typical feminine gay man, since he looked macho. She also wondered if her single mother role had anything to do with Joel's gay orientation:

Maybe because I raised him by myself, it was a matriarchal thing. I have read now that these gays, there is something in the anatomy of their bodies that affect the way they are. So it is not because I raised him alone, maybe it's in the anatomy of the body. Even if I think that because I raised him alone as a mother, even if he came out to be gay, he was raised as a good person. No matter what I would say I'm still lucky he came out to be like that.[27]

In the end she accepted Joel no matter what caused his sexual orientation.

Katherine Tanaka*, a fifty-three-year-old Japanese American from Hawaii, found out about Melissa's lesbianism through an indirect family conversation. George Tanaka* brought up the issue of sexuality and asked Melissa* if she was a lesbian. He suspected after reading her work on the computer. Katherine* remembered her response:

I was in a state of shock. I didn't expect it, so I didn't know how to react. It was the thing of disbelief, horror and shame and the whole thing. I guess I felt the Asian values I was taught surface in the sense that something was wrong. That she didn't turn out the way we had raised her to be.[28]

George Tanaka* recalled, "After we hugged, she went off to her bedroom. As she was walking away from us, all of a sudden I felt like she was a stranger. I thought I knew [her]. Here was a very important part of her and I didn't know anything about it."[29] The idea of not knowing one's children anymore after discovering their sexual orientation remains a common initial response from the interviewees. Because of this one aspect, parents believe their child has changed and is no longer the person they thought they knew. For example one parent said:

The grieving process took a long time. Especially the thing about not being a bride. Not having her be a bride was a very devastating change of plans for her life. I thought I was in her life and it made me feel when she said she was a lesbian that there was no place for me in her life. I didn't know how I could fit into her life because I didn't know how to be the mother of a lesbian.[30]

Upon finding out the parents interviewed spoke of common responses and questions they had. What did I do wrong? Was I responsible for my child's lesbian or gay identity? What will others think? How do I relate to my child? What role do I have now that I know my child is a lesbian or gay man? The emotions a parent has ranged from the loss of a dream they had for their child to a fear of what is in store for them as a gay or lesbian person in this society.

Nancy Shigekawa*, a third-generation Japanese American born and residing in Hawaii, she recalled her reaction:

> I had come home one night and they were in the bedroom. Then I knew it wasn't just being in the room. My reaction was outrage, to say the least. I was so angry. I told them to come out . . . and I said [to her girlfriend] "I'm going to kill you if you ever come back." That's how I was feeling. I look back now and think I must have been like a crazy lady.[31]

Maria Santos* remembered her discovery.

> I found out through a phone call from the parents of [her] best friend. They [Cecilia* and her friend] were trying to sneak out and they had a relationship. I thought it would go away. Let her see a psychiatrist. But she fooled me. In her second year at college she told me she was a lesbian. It broke my heart. That was the first time I heard the word lesbian, but I knew what it meant. Like the tomboy.[32]

She also had a feeling about her youngest daughter, Paulette*:

> At Cecilia's graduation I saw them talking secretly and I saw the pink triangle on her backpack. I can't explain it. It's a mother's instinct. I prayed that it would not be so [starts to cry]. Paulette told me in a letter that she was a lesbian and that Cecilia had nothing to do with it. I wanted it to change. I had the dream, that kids go to college, get married and have kids.[33]

Maria Santos* did not talk to anyone about her daughters. She grew up having to face the world on her own without talking to others. However, she said, "But I read books, articles all about gays and lesbians as members of the community. They are normal people. I did not read negative things about them."[34]

In this sense parents also have a coming out process that they go through. They must deal with internalized homophobia and reevaluate their beliefs and feelings about lesbians and gay men. One method in this process includes reading about and listening to gay men and lesbians talk about their lives. Having personal contact or at least information on lesbian and gay life takes the mystery out of the stereotypes and misconceptions that parents might have of lesbian and gay people. What helped some women was the personal interaction and reading about lesbian and gay men's lives. They had more information with which to contrast, contradict, and support their previous notions of lesbians and gay men.

Yet sometimes some parents interviewed have not yet read or do not seek outside help or information. Some of the parents did not talk to others and have remained alone in their thinking. This does not necessarily have negative effects. Liz Lee said, "Still today I don't think I can discuss with her in this matter because I can't relate. . . . I can't handle it. I wouldn't know how to talk to her about this subject. I just let her be happy."[35]

MG Espiritu*, a sixty-year-old Pilipina immigrant, believes her daughter's lesbianism stems from environmental causes such as being with other lesbians. Nonetheless, less than a couple of years after finding out about her daughter Michelle, she went with her daughter to an Asian Pacific lesbian Lunar New Year banquet. MG* did so because her daughter wanted it and she wanted to please her. When asked how she felt at the event, MG* replied, "Oh, it's normal. It's just like my little girls' parties that they go to."[36] She speaks of little by little trying to accept Michelle's lesbianism.

PARENTS, FRIENDS AND THEIR ETHNIC COMMUNITIES

For some parents having a lesbian or gay child brings up the issue of their status and reputation in the community and family network. Questions such as: What is society going to think of me? Will the neighbors know and what will it reflect upon us? Did they raise a bad child?

> I told her we would have to move away from this house. I felt strongly neighbors and friends in the community would not want to associate with us if they knew we had a child who had chosen to be homosexual.[37]

The above quote reflected one parent's original reaction. Now she feels differently but is still not quite out to her family in Hawaii. Some parents have told their siblings or friends. Others do not talk to relatives or friends at all because of fear they will not understand.

The following quote highlighted a typical anxiety of parents:

> I was ashamed. I felt I had a lot to do with it too. In my mind I'm not stupid, I'm telling myself, I know I didn't do it to her. I don't know if it's only because I'm Japanese . . . that's the way I saw it. I felt a sense of shame, that something was wrong with my family. I would look at Debbie* and just feel so guilty that I have these thoughts that something's wrong with her. But mostly I was selfish. I felt more for myself, what I am going to say? How am I going to react to people when they find out?[38]

Despite her apprehension in the beginning, she did disclose Debbie's lesbianism to a close friend:

> I have a dear friend who I finally told because she was telling me about these different friends who had gay children. I couldn't stand it, I said, "You know, Bea, I have to tell you my daughter is gay." She was dumbfounded. I'm starting to cheer her up and all that. That was a big step for me to come out.

Nancy Shigekawa's* quote emphasizes the complexity of feelings that parents have when adjusting to their children's sexual orientation.

If parents are not close to their immediate family, they might not have told them. Others have not spoken because they do not care whether or not their family knows. Some parents do not disclose the fact of their gay son or lesbian daughter to protect them from facing unnecessary problems.

When asked how their respective ethnic communities feel about lesbians and gay men, some parents responded with firm conviction. Liz Lee, who spoke about the Korean community, said, "As long as they're not in their house, not in their life, they accept it perfectly."[39] She mentioned her daughter's lesbianism to a nephew but not to others in her family. "I'm sure in the future I have to tell them, but right now nobody has asked me and I don't particularly like to volunteer."[40] Jack Chan*, a sixty-one-year-old Chinese immigrant claimed, "Shame, that's a big factor. Shame brought upon the family. You have to remember the Chinese, the name, the face of the family is everything. I don't know how to overcome that."[41]

Lucy Nguyen* gave this answer about the Vietnamese community, "They won't accept it. Because for a long, long time they say they [gays and lesbians] are not good people, that's why."[42] Lucy felt that by talking about it would help and teach the community to open their minds. The frankness and openness of speaking out about gay and lesbians will inform people of our existence and force the issue in the open. In this way having parents come out will make others understand their experiences and allow for their validation and affirmation as well.

Although most of these parents have negative views about the acceptance level of friends and particularly with ethnic communities, some have taken steps to confide in people. One must also realize their opinion reflects their current situation and opinion which might change over time. Three of the parents have participated in panels and discussions on Asian American parents with lesbian and gay kids.

ADVICE TO OTHER PARENTS

In many ways the mere fact these parents agreed to the interview has much to say about their feelings or attitudes towards lesbian and gay sexuality and their kids. Although some parents might feel some unease and reservations, they had enough courage to speak to me and voice their opinions. Many of the parents did so out of love and concern for their children. A few thought that they did not have anything to say but agreed to talk to me. In the process of these interviews, some parents expressed appreciation and comfort in talking to someone about their experiences. Their struggle of coming to terms with their lesbian daughters and gay sons merits notice.

One of my last questions related to helping other parents. While some did not have an answer to the question, "What advice do you have for other parents with lesbian and gay kids?" a few responded with the following suggestions. For example,

> Love them like a normal individual. Give all the compassion and understanding. Don't treat your child differently because the person is gay, because this is an individual. . . . I cannot understand why it is so hard for these parents to accept their child is gay. What makes them so different, because they are gay? The more you should support your kid, because as it is in society, it has not been accepted one hundred percent.[43]

> I cannot throw them out. I love them so much. Even more now because they are more of a minority. They are American Asian, women and lesbian. Triple minority. I have to help fight for them. . . . Accept them as they are. Love them more. They will encounter problems. It will take years and years to overcome homophobia. Make them ambitious, well-educated, better than others so they can succeed.[44]

Tina Chan*, a fifty-eight-year-old Chinese immigrant, offers similar advice. Other parents concurred:

> My advice is to accept them. They haven't changed at all. They're still the same person. The only thing different is their sexual orientation. They should really have the support from the family, so they would not have this battle like they're not even being accepted in the family. They should look at them like they have not changed. Parents can't do it.

> They think the whole person has changed and I think that's terrible because they haven't. I mean it's so stupid.[45]

Jack Chan* also leaves us with advice to take to heart:

> Don't feel depressed that their parent [is] coming around so slow or not coming around at all. Remember when you come out to them the parent generally go[es] into the closet themselves. However long it take you to come out, it'll probably take them longer to accept. It's a slow process. Don't give up.[46]

CONCLUDING REMARKS

George Tanaka* relates an incident where he and his wife told their coming out process in front of ten Asian American gay men and in the end found some of the men crying. "The tears surprised me. . . . We were representing the sadness that there could not be loving parents. Representing some hope their parents would likewise be able to become loving about it."[47] The belief that parents can change and go through a process where eventual acceptance and supportiveness appear to have a basis in reality, although a happy ending might not always be the case.

From these interviews one can sense some of the thoughts, actions, and experiences of Asian American parents. These stories are not the last word but signal the beginning of a more informed dialogue.

What would the stories of their daughters and sons look like against their parents' perceptions? It would be helpful to have the stories side by side to evaluate the differences. Moreover, gay and lesbian children might have perspectives that inform parents. Other issues such as socialization processes, religious, language and cultural issues, and spouses' opinions need further exploration. I did not include a discussion on the origins of lesbian and gay sexual identity. I hope these stories from the homefront can serve as an initial mapping of a complex sexual territory that is part of Asian American family dynamics.

NOTES

1. The desire to work on this project came after listening to two Japanese American parents, George and Katherine Tanaka, talk about their lesbian daughter. They revealed a painful process of going through their own coming out while grappling with their daughter's sexual identity and their own values and beliefs. As members of Parents and Friends of Lesbians and Gays (PFLAG) they mentioned they were the only Asian Americans, the only parents of color, for that matter, in this organization. Despite being the Asian American contact Katherine has received less than ten calls during a two year time span and not one Asian American parent has ever come to PFLAG. She recounted her feelings and belief of being the only Asian parent with a gay child. That feeling of loneliness and alienation struck me deeply because as an Asian American lesbian I could identify with her feelings.

2. Interview with Katherine Tanaka. Los Angeles, California, February 21, 1993.

3. See Kitty Tsui, *the words of a woman who breathes fire* (San Francisco: Spinsters Ink, 1983). C. Chung, Alison Kim, and A.K. Lemshewsky eds., *Between the Lines: An Anthology by Pacific/Asian Lesbians* (Santa Cruz: Dancing Bird Press, 1987). Rakesh Ratti, ed., *A Lotus of Another Color: The Unfolding of the South Asian Gay and Lesbian Experience* (Boston: Alyson Press, 1993). Silvera Makeda, ed., *A Piece of My Heart: A Lesbian of Colour Anthology* (Toronto: Sister Vision Press, 1993).

4. Mothers comprise the majority of the parents interviewed. Perhaps mothers are more apt to talk about their feelings and emotions about having a gay son or lesbian daughter than the father. Mothers might be more understanding and willing to discuss their emotions and experiences than the fathers who also know.

5. I did not interview parents who had a bisexual child. I believe a son or daughter who comes out as bisexual might encounter a different set of questions and reactions, especially since the parent might hope and persuade the daughter or son to "choose" heterosexuality instead of homosexuality.

6. See Carolyn W. Griffin, Marian J. Wirth and Arthur G. Wirth, *Beyond Acceptance: Parents of Lesbians and Gays Talk About Their Experiences* (New York: St. Martin's Press, 1986).

7. Parents and Friends of Lesbians and Gays (PFLAG) has chapters all around the United States. One couple and a father interviewed are involved with PFLAG in their respective locales.

8. Ann Muller, *Parents Matter: Parents' Relationships with Lesbian Daughters and Gay Sons* (Tallahassee: The Naiad Press, Inc., 1987), 197.

9. Connie S. Chan "Issues of Identity Development among Asian-American Lesbians and Gay Men." *Journal of Counseling and Development*, 68 (Sept/ Oct, 1989), 19.

10. Interview with Lucy Nguyen. Los Angeles, California, February 20, 1993.

11. Interview with Midori Asakura. Los Angeles, California, April 18, 1993.

12. Midori Asakura.

13. Ibid.

14. Mahu does not necessarily mean gay but defines a man who dresses and acts feminine. However, its common usage does denote a gay man.

15. Interview with Toni Barraquiel. Los Angeles, California, April 18, 1993.

16. Telephone interview [with] Maria Santos. Portland, Oregon, May 9, 1993.

17. Lucy Nguyen.

18. Interview with Margaret Tsang. San Francisco, California, February 5, 1993.

19. Interview with Liz Lee. Los Angeles, California, May 11, 1993.

20. Liz based this respect on this particular woman's election to something similar to a city council and her standing in the community.

21. Liz Lee.

22. Midori Asakura.

23. Liz Lee.

24. Ibid.

25. Ibid.

26. Toni Barraquiel.

27. Ibid.

28. Katherine Tanaka.

29. Interview with George Tanaka. Los Angeles, California, February 21, 1993.

30. Katherine Tanaka.

31. Telephone interview with Nancy Shigekawa. Kaneohe, Hawaii, March 20, 1993.

32. Maria Santos.

33. Ibid.

34. Ibid.

35. Liz Lee.

36. Interview with MG Espiritu. Northern California, July 20, 1993.

37. Katherine Tanaka.

38. Nancy Shigekawa.

39. Liz Lee.

40. Ibid.

41. Interview with Jack Chan. Northern California, July 18, 1993.

42. Lucy Nguyen.

43. Toni Barraquiel.

44. Maria Santos.

45. Interview with Tina Chan. Northern California, July 18, 1993.

46. Jack Chan.

47. George Tanaka.

CHAPTER 9

Asian American Political Empowerment

For years Asian Americans have been considered the missing link in U.S. electoral politics. Numerous studies on Asian American participation in electoral politics have shown low voter registration rates relative to the general population. All of these studies conclude that the high percentage of foreign-born Asian Americans is the primary factor for low voter registration rates and, therefore, low voter participation. This chapter features articles regarding various Asian American political empowerment issues, including voting, redistricting efforts, the recent political campaign controversy, and local level organizing.

Paul Ong and Don Nakanishi provide an interesting analysis of the potential of Asian American political participation. The authors acknowledge that Asian American voter participation has historically been quite low relative to other groups. One major reason for this is the high percentage of immigrants within the Asian American population who are not citizens and are ineligible to vote. However, Ong and Nakanishi use an empirical approach to underscore the fact that the naturalization rate for Asian immigrants is higher than for any other immigrant group, and that Asian immigrants who have lived in the United States for the longest time have the highest rate of voter registration and voter participation. The authors believe that the Asian American electorate is in the process of a transition and that future Asian American voter participation and political activism will be determined by newly naturalized Asian immigrants.

Despite the prospects for increased Asian American political participation, Leland Saito recognizes the need for Asian Americans to join with other groups to achieve political goals. In his article, Saito reviews an effort in Southern California in which Asian Americans and Latinos worked together to redraw the boundaries of a state assembly district. The process of political redistricting occurs after each decennial census and is intended to reflect demographic changes in the area. Historically, politicians have purposely divided concentrations of ethnic groups into separate voting districts in order to dilute their political influence. Saito's work is significant because it illustrates the political emergence and sophistication of Asian Americans as their population grows. Asian Americans and Latinos demonstrated that it is possible to put aside their differences and combine their resources for the political benefit of both groups.

Another strategy for increasing Asian American political participation and representation is found in the article by Tito Sinha, who looks at the single-transferable vote (STV) process. In the New York City School Board elections, several candidates vie for a limited number of available seats in a wide open at-large election. STV allows voters to list favored candidates in order of preference. When a candidate reaches a certain "threshold" of first-choice votes to win the election, "surplus" votes are then transferred to the remaining candidates. In addition, votes are also transferred from the candidate with the fewest first-choice votes to the other remaining candidates. A study was conducted by the Asian American Legal Defense and Education Fund (AALDEF) concerning the effects of STV on Asian American candidates running for the school board. In a conventional "winner-takes-all" style of election, the top vote-getters in districtwide elections would be the winners. In many cases, if there are more than one Asian American candidate, the Asian American vote is split and all Asian American candidates suffer. In an STV election, Asian American votes would not be "wasted," but transferred to the second-preference candidate, who is often another Asian American. According to the study, STV has a positive effect on the election process because it encourages various Asian American ethnic groups to work together in order to solidify the Asian American voter base. STV also encourages different groups to work together, rather than against each other, because everyone depends on transfer votes to win an election.

Attention to Asian Americans in politics is not always positive. This is witnessed by the recent controversies over illegal fundraising activities by foreign Asian influence peddlers to both the Clinton reelection campaign and to the Democratic National Committee (DNC). One article by Ling-chi Wang and another by Phil Tajisu Nash and Frank Wu focus on this issue and its impact on Asian Americans. Wang angrily denounces the attention given to a small handful of individuals whose activities have nothing to do with advancing the political and civil rights interests of Asian Americans. According to Wang, the fundraising scandal has single-handedly undone decades of work by Asian American activists to overcome the perpetual foreigner stereotype commonly found in the hearts and minds of most non-Asians. Nash and Wu agree with Wang and write about the way Congress has chosen to investigate the charges. They argue that the expansive attention on allegedly illegal campaign contributions has a distinctive racial undertone, which only serves to divert attention away from legitimate concerns for genuine campaign finance reform and unfairly targets Asian Americans. Nash and Wu agree that campaign finance reform is long overdue, but that it should not be accomplished by playing the "race card."

It is important that the campaign reform scandal not draw attention away from other important political and civil rights issues for Asian Americans. One of the major issues is anti-Asian violence. On April 29, 1997, police officers shot and killed Kuanchung Kao, 33, in front of his home in Rohnert Park, California, a community one hour north of San Francisco. Asian Americans in the community believe the use of deadly force was racially motivated. The local district attorney further enraged Asian Americans when he ruled the case to be justifiable homicide, clearing the officers involved of all criminal charges. A coalition of Asian American civil rights organizations united to seek justice for the Kao family. They organized protests to draw attention to the killing, demanded a federal investigation into the police shooting, supported a civil lawsuit against the police department, and established a fund for Kao's wife and three young children. This incident underscores that Asian Americans must still use direct forms of protest in order to fight for basic rights.

Becoming Citizens, Becoming Voters:
The Naturalization and Political Participation
of Asian Pacific Immigrants

Paul Ong and Don Nakanishi*

In his address to the national conference of the Southwest Voter Registration Project in 1995, Vice President Albert Gore heralded naturalization as the final stage of incorporating an immigrant into American society.[1] Naturalization is not merely a technical change in immigration status. The passage to citizenship also is more than the required level of acculturation defined by a basic command of the English language and knowledge of U.S. history and its political institutions. With this act, immigrants abandon allegiance to their country of origin and pledge loyalty to the United States.

The acquisition of citizenship marks the beginning of full political and social membership in this country. The individual acquires new civil and legal rights, with the opportunity to vote and to participate in the electoral process perhaps the most important. The stakes are also economic. In today's growing anti-immigrant climate, citizenship has become a litmus test for inclusion in America's social contract. Consider, for instance, current proposals to require citizenship for programs such as SSl (Supplementary Security Income) for the elderly and AFDC (Aid to Families with Dependent Children) for families with children.[2]

Naturalization and political participation have profound implications for groups, as well as individuals. The political strength of an immigrant-dominated population within our electoral system

Source: Bill Ong Hing and Ronald Lee, eds., *Reframing the Immigration Debate* (Los Angeles: LEAP Asian Pacific American Public Policy Institute and UCLA Asian American Studies Center, 1996), pp. 275–305. Reprinted by permission.

hinges on two interrelated but distinct processes: (1) the groups naturalization rate, that is, the relative proportion of immigrants with citizenship; and (2) the rates by which naturalized and native-born citizens both register to vote and actually vote during elections. Low rates in either situation dilute an immigrant-dominated group's potential electoral power, and thus diminish its influence on legislation and public policy. Citizenship and civic participation also are regarded by the general public as indicators of the ability and willingness of a group to assimilate and become "Americanized" rather than to separate from the mainstream. While high rates of naturalization and civic participation do not guarantee that members of a group will be accepted as equals, low rates foster a sense of political isolation and provide fodder for nativist movements.

Although becoming a citizen and a voter are often viewed as simultaneous processes, they are distinct and temporally distant forms of membership and participation. Most adult immigrants and refugees acquired their fundamental political values, attitudes, and behavioral orientations in counties that have sociopolitical systems, traditions, and expectations that are different from those in the United States. Indeed, many came from countries where voting was not permitted, limited to a privileged few, or was widely viewed as being inconsequential because of the dominance of a single political party. As a result, these immigrants must undergo a process of political acculturation beyond the rudimentary exposure to the basic structure of the U.S. government presented in adult citizenship classes. The general notion of participating in electoral politics is a prolonged and complicated process of social learning for immigrants—as it may be for many native-born citizens as well.

Using an empirical approach, this essay examines rates of naturalization, voter registration, and voting behavior for Asian Pacific immigrants and refugees. The first section explores the overall trends in naturalization between Asian and other groups of immigrants during the past three decades. Factors that have the greatest influence on whether Asian immigrants become naturalized are also measured. The second section analyzes the political participation of immigrant and native-born Asian Pacific Americans, with special attention to voter registration and electoral involvement. Comparisons are made between Asian Pacific Americans and other groups in American society, and the analysis explores factors that account for differences in participation rates. A concluding section summarizes major findings and offers several policy recommendations.

BECOMING CITIZENS: NATURALIZATION AND ASIAN IMMIGRANTS

The status of Asian Pacific Americans, as an immigrant-dominated population, is greatly affected by the rate of naturalization. While the number of U.S.-born citizens doubled between 1970 and 1990, the foreign-born population grew over eight-fold because of the Immigration Act of 1965. As a consequence, the proportion of U.S.-born citizens in Asian Pacific America declined from 52 percent to 21 percent. Although U.S.-born citizens continued to comprise a large majority of the Japanese American community from 1970 to 1990, newer and rapidly growing groups such as Southeast Asians, Koreans, and Asian Indians were predominantly foreign-born. Since the early 1970s, immigrants have constituted a growing majority of the Asian Pacific American adult population; each decade the number of foreign-born

adults has more than doubled (See Table 1). Given these demographic trends, naturalization rates very directly determine the size of the Asian Pacific American population eligible to vote and also its political future.

This section of the report examines naturalization rates and influences for Asian Pacific immigrants over the minimum eligibility age of 18.[3] The analysis is based on samples from the three census periods that looked at individuals. The advantage of this data source is the large sampling which allows for detailed tabulations and reasonable estimates of the characteristics of the entire population.[4] While the 1970 sample includes only 1 percent of the total U.S. population, the 1980 and 1990 samples include 5 percent of the population. The samples also contain information on nativity, racial and ethnic identity, demographic characteristics, educational attainment, and a host of other variables.

TABLE 1

Nativity of Asian Pacific Americans 18 Years and Older

	1970	1980	1990
Population (in thousands)			
Total Asian Pacific Americans	969	2,498	4,938
U.S.-Born Citizens	502	741	1,022
Immigrants	468	1,758	3,916
Percent U.S.-Born Citizens	52%	30%	21%
Distribution by Ethnicity			
Japanese	411	567	706
Chinese	288	598	1,261
Filipino	214	538	1,033
Koreans	57	227	548
SE Asians	—	143	592
Asian Indians	—	274	555
Percent U.S.-Born Citizens			
Japanese	73%	68%	65%
Chinese	39%	26%	19%
Filipino	30%	19%	20%
Koreans	43%	7%	8%
SE Asians	—	2%	2%
Asian Indians	—	17%	6%

Estimates from Public Use Micro Samples

U.S.-born category includes those born to U.S. citizens

There are limitations, however. The census does not distinguish between legal immigrants, undocumented aliens, and some foreign visitors. Foreign tourists (without an established residence) are excluded, but those on employment or student visas are included. Thus the immigrant population in the census can be best described as the foreign-born population with an established U.S. residence. The census data also do not follow individuals over a period of time; the data refer to the characteristics of the sample at one point in time. But profiles, rates, and other demographic features of the 1970, 1980 and 1990 populations can be compared.

The census uses five categories to define U.S. citizenship: (1) those born in the United States (citizens by *jus solis*), (2) those who are citizens through birth in a U.S. territory, (3) those born abroad to U.S. citizens (citizens by *jus sanguini*), (4) alien immigrants, and (5) naturalized immigrants.[5] For the purpose of this report, the foreign-born population is comprised of those in the last two categories, and the naturalized population is comprised of those in the last category. The terms "foreign-born" and "immigrant" are used interchangeably.

The data reveal the following: (1) Asian Pacific immigrants are naturalizing at a rate comparable to that of non-Hispanic white immigrants. (2) Length of residence in the United States is the single most important factor in determining naturalization rates. (3) This time-dependent process, along with the underlying acculturation process, appears remarkably stable over the decades. (4) While time is the most important factor, ethnicity, age, and level of education are among other influential factors.

OVERALL PATTERN OF NATURALIZATION

Between 1970 and 1990, the naturalization rate for all immigrants fell 24 percentage points from 67 percent to 43 percent (See Table 2). Two

TABLE 2

Naturalization Rates by Years in U.S. and by Race All Immigrants 18 Years and Older

	1970	1980	1990
All Immigrants (in thousands)	8,468	12,423	17,612
Distribution by Years in U.S.			
0 to 10 years	25%	34%	39%
11 to 20 years	19%	23%	26%
21 or more years	55%	43%	35%
Distribution by Race			
Non-Hispanic Whites	76%	53%	37%
Blacks	2%	5%	7%
Latinos	16%	27%	37%
Asians	6%	14%	22%
Overall Naturalization Rates	67%	54%	43%
Naturalization Rates by Years in U.S.			
0 to 10 years	20%	20%	15%
11 to 20 years	64%	49%	45%
21 or more years	90%	85%	74%
Naturalization Rates by Race			
Non-Hispanic Whites	77%	71%	63%
Blacks	45%	43%	36%
Latinos	35%	31%	28%
Asians	41%	36%	43%

Estimates from Public Use Micro Samples

Excluding those born abroad to U.S. Citizens

factors are behind this decline. The first relates to a resumption of large-scale immigration in 1960s, and the second simply reflects actual changes in naturalization rates within certain groups.

After the 1965 immigration changes, the adult immigrant population more than doubled from less than 8.5 million in 1970 to over 17.5 million in 1990. Renewed large-scale immigration altered the proportion of immigrants who resided in the United States for a lengthy period of time.[6] A majority (55 percent) of the 1970 adult immigrants had lived in the United States for 21 or more years, but two decades later only about a third (35 percent) had lived in the United States for that length of time. This decline in the number of long-term immigrants occurred despite an increase in the absolute number of long-term residents from 4.9 million to 6.2 million. On the other hand, newer immigrants (those in the country for no more that 10 years) increased from

25 percent to 39 percent of all adult immigrants. In absolute numbers, their ranks grew from 2.2 million to 6.9 million.

Given the large number of recent immigrants, the decline in the relative number of citizens among adult immigrants from 1970 to 1990 is no surprise. In fact, this recomposition accounts for nearly half of the overall decline.[7]

The rest of the decline is attributable to the second factor, changes in the naturalization rate. Comparing groups who have resided in the United States for different periods of time presents a clear picture. In 1970, 20 percent of those who had been in the country for ten years or less were naturalized. In 1990, only 15 percent of that group was naturalized. For those who had resided in the country for more than two decades, the naturalization figure dropped from 90 percent in 1970 to 74 percent in 1990.[8] Some social, cultural, and economic explanations for this decline are considered below.

RACIAL VARIATIONS

A racial recomposition of the foreign-born population has accompanied the renewal of large-scale immigration.[9] Sources of modern immigration differ dramatically from that of earlier immigration. For the first two-thirds of the century, Europeans dominated immigration flows into the United States. After the elimination of racially biased quotas in 1965, people from the Asia Pacific and Latin America have dominated. Non-Hispanic whites comprised 75 percent of all adult immigrants in 1970 but less than 20 percent in 1990. Latinos and Asian Pacific Islanders were less than a quarter of all immigrants in 1970, but today they constitute the vast majority.

The racial recomposition has favored some populations that have low naturalization rates. Mexicans, for example, are not only the single largest group of recent immigrants but also a group with a substantially lower than average rate of naturalization (Skerry, 1993; Tomas Rivera Center,

1994). They generally are not proficient in English; they maintain ties to Mexico through occasional visits; and, relative to other immigrants, they are less educated. These factors may contribute to their low naturalization rate. The shift to non-European immigrants, however, cannot solely explain the drop in naturalization rates, because recent non-Hispanic white immigrants *also* maintain a lower than average naturalization rate.

Naturalization rates for Asian immigrants over three decennial censuses did not decrease. Overall rates have fluctuated around 40 percent (See Table 2). Although all non-Hispanic white immigrants exhibited higher overall rates, rates are directly related to the fact that most long-term residents for the three census years were non-Hispanic whites (See Table 3). On the other hand, newer immigrants were predominantly Asian and Pacific Islanders.

Over time, naturalization rates for Asian Pacifics have changed for both new and long-term

TABLE 3
Naturalization Rates
Asian and Non-Hispanic White Immigrants
18 Years and Older

	1970	1980	1990
Years in U.S.			
Non-Hispanic Whites			
0–10 years	17%	16%	20%
11–20 years	19%	18%	16%
over 20 years	64%	66%	64%
Asians			
0–10 years	56%	66%	54%
11–20 years	19%	20%	32%
over 20 years	25%	13%	14%
Naturalization Rate by Years in U.S.			
Non-Hispanic Whites			
0–10 years	20%	16%	15%
11–20 years	69%	53%	48%
over 20 years	92%	89%	81%
Asians			
0–10 years	17%	19%	19%
11–20 years	67%	67%	66%
over 20 years	68%	79%	81%

Estimates from Public Use Micro Samples

residents. In 1970, Asian rates were consistently low for all cohorts, especially for long-term residents. The substantially lower rate for long-term Asian residents versus non-Hispanic whites (68 percent versus 92 percent, Table 3) is a historical legacy. Prior to 1952, most Asian immigrants were ineligible for citizenship (Hing, 1993). Historical restrictions not only delayed naturalization for those who wanted to become citizens, but years of discrimination alienated many other Asian immigrants and dampened their desire to naturalize. By 1980, however, the naturalization rates for non-Hispanic whites declined while those for Asians improved. Asians had a higher rate among those in the country for ten years or less. By 1990, an Asian rates were at least equal to, or considerably higher than, those of non-Hispanic whites.

The fact that many immigrants return to their native lands permanently should be taken into account for a more accurate naturalization rate calculation. Return migration is more extensive for non-Hispanic whites than for Asians (Liang, 1994; Jasso and Rosenzweig, 1990). Calculations by the Immigration and Naturalization Service that include return-migrants show that immigrants from Asian Pacific countries have the highest naturalization rates (INS, 1990). The top three Asian Pacific communities are Vietnamese (78 percent), Chinese (63 percent), and Filipino Americans (63 percent).[10] Among the bottom five nationality groups are Canadians (12 percent), the British (20 percent), and Italians (23 percent).[11]

TIME-DEPENDENT ACCULTURATION

As noted, length of residence in the United States is the most powerful determinant of whether a person will naturalize. This is partly a product of the residency requirement for naturalization, which is usually five years, although the period for spouses of citizens is reduced to three. Other constraints on naturalization may be more impor-

tant. Acculturation, the broad process of learning and adopting the language, values, and norms of the host society, is a central factor.

A strong correlation between time in the United States and the level of assimilation has been demonstrated. The level of economic assimilation, as measured by immigrant earnings compared to that of U.S.-born ethnic counterparts with similar education and years of work experience, starts from a low point at the time of entry and gradually improves over a fifteen-year period; at that point, immigrants reach parity (See Borjas, 1990). Understanding English and societal institutions also improves over time.

Naturalization rates of Asian immigrants show a remarkably similar pattern for all three censuses. Graph 1 compares the rates in five-year increments.[12] Prior to five years, few naturalizations occur, due largely to the five-year residency requirement for most immigrants.[13] The greatest increase occurs among those in the country between 5 and 15 years. The data suggest that two-thirds of all naturalizations take place within this range.[14] The naturalization rate continues to increase after residency of more than 15 years, but in smaller increments. The one exception to the overall pattern is for those who have been in the country for over a quarter century. In 1970, only a third of this cohort were citizens, due to the legacy of discrimination encountered by earlier immigrants. Over time, this effect faded as the number of pre-World War II immigrants declined. By 1990, 84 percent of the Asian Pacific immigrants in the country for more than 25 years were citizens.

The influence of length of residence on the naturalization rate can also be seen in data for comparable groups in different census years. Although the census does not identify and follow the same groups each census, a dynamic process can be inferred from observed differences among groups at the same point in time. For example, because the naturalization rate in 1990 for those in the country for 11 to 15 years was higher than the rate for those in the country for 6 to 10 years, the inference is that the increase was due to being in the country an additional five years.[15] This is a reasonable assumption given the relative stability of the pattern of naturalization rates observed in Graph 1.

This type of analysis allows a further step in determining how naturalization rates change with time. While the census data are not longitudinal, samples can be used to estimate changes for a given cohort over time. For example, the group whose members were from 18 to 40 years old in 1970 would be roughly the same group with members from 28 to 50 in 1980, and 38 to 60 in 1990.[16] While the census sample does not include the same individuals in all three decades, statistical principles permit the use of the data to develop representative profiles as this cohort aged over time. This method can be further refined by dividing the cohort by period of entry into the United States and tracking each group over time. Using this approach, longitudinal changes in naturalization for each cohort can be estimated. Table 4 compares the results of this exercise with the rates observed in cross-sectional analysis. In spite of minor differences, patterns are remarkably similar.

While time in the United States is perhaps the single most important factor in determining the naturalization rate, the entire process is not simple. Changes in the rate are based on a more fundamental phenomenon: acculturation that unfolds over time, such as learning [the] English language, acquiring a knowledge of U.S. institu-tions, and strengthening one's sense of identity as an American. These changes are no doubt influenced by demands of everyday life. Like most residents, immigrants work to earn a living, while coping with family responsibilities.

Larger societal forces also influence the process. Historically, the dampening effect of discrimination was clear. More recently, the growth of anti-immigrant sentiments, particularly in California, has also affected the behavior of immigrants. The fear created by efforts such as Proposition 187 has led to a noticeable increase in naturalization applicants.

INTRA-COHORT VARIATIONS

In addition to length of residence and the acculturation process, naturalization rates are also affected by ethnicity, age, English language ability, and education. Table 5 presents an analysis on those falling between the ages of 6 and 20, the range when changes in rates are most dramatic.

Among major ethnic groups, the difference between the highest and lowest naturalization rates is about 50 percentage points. Japanese immigrants exhibited the lowest rates: for those in the country from 6 to 10 years, only 1 in 14 was a citizen. Although the rate increased as residency increased, only 1 in 3 Japanese immigrants in the country 16 to 20 years was a citizen. This strikingly low level of naturalization may be tied to Japanese transnational corporations. With increased trade with the United States, many of these companies establish operations in the country and bring a significant number of nationals to work. Sizable and visible communities of these employees and their families have been established in places like New York City and parts of Southern California. This transpacific movement in turn fostered the migration of other Japanese who work in restaurants, clubs, and other businesses serving corporate-based Japanese communities. Many of these Japanese do not regard

TABLE 4
Estimated Naturalization Rates of Asian Immigrants

Years in U.S.	Cross-section Average (70–90)	Pseudo Panel Estimates
0–5	7%	8%
6–10	36%	33%
11–15	63%	64%
16–20	74%	77%
21–25	81%	81%

Estimates from Public Use Micro Samples

GRAPH 1
Naturalization Rates Among Asian Pacific Immigrants by Years in the United States

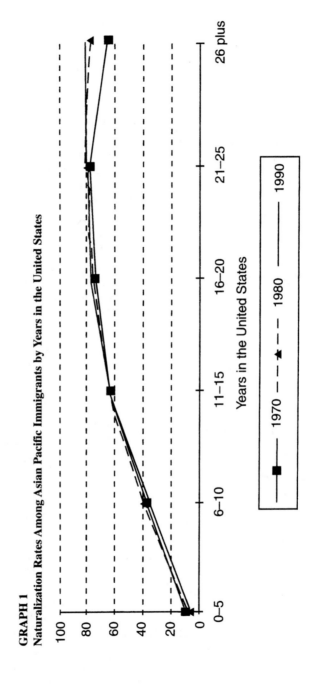

TABLE 5
Detailed Naturalization Rates of Asian Immigrants

	Years in the United States		
	6–10	*11–15*	*16–20*
By ethnicity			
Japanese	7%	18%	35%
Chinese	34%	67%	80%
Filipinos	45%	73%	83%
Koreans	27%	62%	82%
SE Asians	32%	62%	N.A.
Asian Indians	26%	53%	68%
By age			
18–29	34%	67%	80%
30–39	35%	65%	76%
40–49	33%	64%	77%
50–59	29%	59%	75%
60 plus	23%	44%	60%
By education level			
0–8 years	17%	36%	56%
9–11 years	29%	54%	69%
High School	34%	61%	71%
Some College	43%	70%	77%
Bachelor's	39%	73%	83%
Master's	25%	67%	79%
Doctorate	15%	49%	75%
By English language ability			
None	6%	12%	26%
Poor	22%	47%	66%
Good	39%	69%	76%
Very good	38%	68%	79%
Only English	33%	62%	77%

Estimates from Public Use Micro Samples

themselves as immigrants, even after residing in the country for a number of years.

Filipinos represent the other end of the spectrum with the highest naturalization rates. In many respects, they are the most "Americanized" of Asian Pacific immigrants. The history of U.S. colonization from 1898 to 1946 has left a legacy in the Philippines where English, once the official language, remains the language of choice for many Filipinos. Many aspects of U.S. culture also have become deeply embedded in Filipino society and identity. This pre-migration acculturation has facilitated the naturalization process for Filipino immigrants in the United States. This "headstart" is reflected in the 1990 census, in which nearly

half of those who had been here for 6 to 10 years were citizens.

Naturalization rates of other Asian Pacific immigrant groups fall between those of the Japanese and Filipinos (See Table 5). As length of residence increased, however, the naturalization level for the other groups approached that for Filipinos. In other words, the early advantage enjoyed by Filipinos in terms of "Americanization" disappeared as the other groups acculturated. The rate for Southeast Asians was similar to that of Chinese and Koreans. This may be surprising because Southeast Asians are less likely to have formed a pre-migration sense of attachment to the United States because they are predominantly refugees. On the other hand, refugees may be more likely to sever ties with the home country because of a revolutionary change in government, thus prompting the formation of allegiance to the United States.

Younger immigrants are also more likely to be citizens (See Table 5). Having spent most of their lives in another society and culture, older immigrants may find that breaking their attachment is not easy. Middle-age immigrants are also burdened by the daily demands of working and raising a family. Younger immigrants, on the other hand, are being raised and educated in the United States, so *American* behaviors and values become *their* behaviors and values.

Differences in English-language ability also generate variations in the naturalization rates (See Table 5). Among those who do not speak English, only 1 in 10 was a citizen in 1990. Even among those who had lived in the country for 16 to 20 years, only 1 in 4 was naturalized. Rates generally increased with improved English language ability. Those whose English proficiency was "very good," for example, were 3 to 6 times more likely to be naturalized than those who did not speak English.

Educational attainment also influences the likelihood of being a citizen but not in a linear fashion. The naturalization rate increased with years of schooling up to an undergraduate education. For example, among immigrants in the country for 6 to 10 years, those with some college education were more than twice as likely to be naturalized than those with no more than an elementary school education. This pattern suggests that more formal education enabled an immigrant to acquire more quickly the knowledge required to pass the naturalization exam. This educational effect, however, was smaller among those in the country for 16 to 20 years.

Graduate school experience played a different role. Those with a doctorate degree had lower naturalization rates than those with a masters degree,[17] who in turn had lower rates than those with a bachelors degree. This outcome was particularly noticeable among those in the country for 6 to 10 years. Although this pattern may be puzzling at first glance, the result in fact is not surprising since many of those with more than an undergraduate education are in the country on temporary visas to pursue additional graduate and post-doctorate training, and thus are not eligible for citizenship (Ong, et al., 1992). Naturalization rates of doctorate degree holders—even those with over 11 years U.S. residency—were lower than those with bachelor's degrees.

The data support the thesis that age, English language ability, and education influence the naturalization rate in an interrelated way. Elderly immigrants, for example, may be more likely to have a poor command of English or to have less education. Those with advanced degrees may be more likely to have a better command of English. An analysis to determine if these factors have an independent effect on odds of an immigrant becoming a citizen sheds some light.[18] Results are consistent with patterns discussed above: (1) the likelihood of naturalization decreases with age but increases with English language ability, and (2) the effect of education is nonlinear, with the odds increasing up to an undergraduate education and then decreasing with additional graduate training. Moreover, ethnic variations discussed earlier also hold, with Filipinos having the highest probability of being citizens and the Japanese the lowest.

BECOMING VOTERS: THE ELECTORAL PARTICIPATION OF ASIAN IMMIGRANTS

In recent years, a number of political commentators and scholars have speculated about whether Asian Pacific Americans will become a major new force in American electoral politics, because of their dramatic demographic growth and concentration in certain key electoral states like California, New York, and Texas (Tachibana, 1986; Cain, 1988; Stokes, 1988; Nakanishi, 1991; Karnow, 1992; Miller, 1995). Many believe that if Asian Pacific American—like American Jewish—voters come to represent a proportion of the electorate that is comparable to, if not greater than, their share of the total population, then they could become a highly influential "swing vote" in critical local, state, and presidential elections. In California, for example, the state with the most congressional seats and electoral college votes, if Asian Pacific Americans, who are 1-in-10 residents of the state also became 1-in-10 voters, then they could play a strategically important role in national and local elections. Indeed, their voting potential coupled with their proven record of campaign funding could elevate Asian Pacific Americans to the status of leading players in the grand theater of American politics (*Asianweek*, 1994).

During the past decade, the increase in the political participation and presence of Asian Pacific Americans in electoral politics is unmistakable. The 1995 edition of the "Asian Pacific American Political Roster and Resource Guide" (Nakanishi and Lai, 1995) listed over 1,200 Asian Pacific American elected and major appointed officials for the federal government and 31 different states. In contrast, the first edition of this directory, published in 1978, listed several hundred politicians, primarily holding offices in Hawaii and California (Nakanishi, 1978). The vast majority of 1978 officials were second and third generation Asian Pacific Americans, primarily Japanese Americans. Today, a growing number of recently elected officeholders are immigrants, such as Jay Kim of Walnut, California, the first Korean American elected to Congress; David Valderrama, the first Filipino American elected as a delegate to the Maryland Assembly; and City Councilmember Tony Lam of Westminster, California, the first Vietnamese American elected to public office. In the past few years, Asian Pacific American candidates also have run well-financed, professional—though ultimately unsuccessful—mayoral campaigns for some of the nations largest cities, including Los Angeles, San Francisco, and Oakland.

There is more, however, to this seemingly optimistic and glowing assessment of Asian Pacific American electoral achievements. In reality, this immigrant-dominant population has yet to reach its full political potential, especially in transforming its extraordinary population growth into comparable proportions of registered voters who actually vote. In California, for example, Asian Pacific Americans may represent 1-in-10 residents but are no more than 1-in-20 of the states registered voters and only 3 out of 100 of those who actually vote (The Field Institute, 1992).

The size, characteristics, and impact of the Asian Pacific American electorate are constantly evolving in relation to historical and contemporary conditions. Institutional structures as well as individual personalities are relevant at both the grassroots and leadership levels. Early Chinese and Japanese immigrants were disenfranchised and excluded from fully participating in American life because of discriminatory laws and policies, such as the 1870 naturalization law, *Ozawa v. United States* (1922), and *Thind v. United States* (1923), which forbade Asian immigrants from becoming naturalized citizens. These legal barriers prevented early Asian Pacific immigrants from being involved in electoral politics of any form—be it the type of ward politics practiced by European immigrants in East Coast and Midwest cities or simply to vote for their candidate in a presidential election.

Barriers significantly delayed the development of electoral participation and representation by Asian Pacific Americans until the second and subsequent generations, decades after their initial period of immigration. Early Asian immigrants and their descendants were scapegoated for political gain by opportunistic politicians and anti-Asian social movements and political parties. The most disastrous example was the wholesale incarceration of 120,000 Japanese Americans during World War II.

This legacy of political exclusion and isolation has many contemporary manifestations. Asian Pacific American civil rights groups remain vigilant in seeking the elimination of a number of "political structural barriers (Kwoh and Hui, 1993), such as the unfair redistricting of Asian Pacific American communities and the lack of bilingual ballots and voting materials, which prevents less English-proficient Asian Pacific Americans from exercising their full voting rights (Bai, 1991). Likewise, grassroots voter registration campaigns in Asian Pacific American communities have had to confront and overcome deep-seated views of political inefficacy, political alienation, and mistrust of government held by large segments of the immigrant Asian Pacific American population. And elected officials and major political parties pay little attention to the unique public policy and quality-of-life needs and issues of Asian Pacific Americans.

This section of the report analyzes levels and determinants of voter registration and voting by naturalized Asian Pacific immigrants over the age of 18, compared to native-born Asian Pacific Americans and other racial and ethnic populations. The analysis is based on the Census Bureau's 1990, 1992, and 1994 Current Population Surveys (CPS). The 1994 CPS data, which will be the primary focus of analysis, was particularly useful because it provided detailed information on the citizenship status of individuals similar to the decennial census, as mentioned in the previous section on naturalization. This made it possible to differentiate between

Asian Pacific Americans who were foreign-born and native-born, as well as immigrants and refugees who were naturalized and those who were not.

Unfortunately, this data source does not enable an analysis of differences in electoral participation among the array of Asian Pacific ethnic communities. Previous studies have found that rates of voter registration vary markedly, with Japanese Americans having the highest proportion of registered voters and Southeast Asians having the lowest percentage (Nakanishi, 1991). Despite their limitations, advantages of the CPS data are that they allow an examination of both national and regional trends with a sufficiently large sample of Asian Pacific Americans,[19] and an analysis of potential differences in registration and voting rates in relation to native-born and naturalized citizens, which has rarely been examined rigorously (Din, 1984; Nakanishi, 1991; Horton, 1995; Shinagawa, 1995; Tam, 1995).

Major findings are that naturalized Asian Pacific immigrants and refugees have lower rates of voter registration than native-born citizens. Asian Pacific naturalized citizens who have been in the country for over 20 years, however, have registration rates that are comparable to, or exceed those of, the native-born, while those who arrived over 30 years ago have higher rates for both registration and voting. As in the case of naturalization rates, statistical analysis revealed that year of entry was the single most important factor in determining voter registration rates. In terms of actual voting, best predictors included not only year of entry but also educational attainment and age. And finally, characteristics of Asian Pacific American voters as a whole, as well as between native-born and foreign-born, reflect an ethnic electorate that is far from being monolithic with respect to political party affiliations, ideological preferences, and voting preferences. Rather, these groups have many dimensions of diversity, which are influencing their continued development.

RATES OF VOTER REGISTRATION

The Asian Pacific population in the United States is characterized by the largest proportion of individuals over the age of 18 who cannot take the first step towards participating in American electoral politics, that is, registering to vote, because they are not citizens. In 1994, 55 percent of adult Asians were not citizens in contrast to 44 percent of the Latinos, 5 percent African Americans, and 2 percent Non-Hispanic whites. The proportion of non-citizens varied by geographic region, with Honolulu having the lowest percentage of non-citizens among its adult Asian population (21 percent), and New York (73 percent) having the highest. Sixty-three percent of adult Asians in Los Angeles County and 52 percent in the Oakland-San Francisco region also were not citizens.

Nationwide, in 1994, approximately 1,166,450 Asian Pacific American were registered to vote, of whom 58 percent (680,750) were U.S.-born and 42 percent (485,700) were foreign-born (Table 6). California's Asian Pacific American electorate, which accounted for 40 percent of the country's Asian Pacific American registered voters, mirrored the nation's composition of U.S.-born (58 percent) to foreign-born (42 percent) voters. Hawaii, on the other hand, which has witnessed far less recent immigration than many mainland states, had an overwhelmingly U.S.-born Asian Pacific American electorate (88 percent).

Native and naturalized Asian Pacific American citizens exhibited very low overall rates of voter registration. Nationally, 1994 CPS census data estimated that only 53 percent of all Asian Pacific American citizens—as well as 53 percent of Latino citizens—were registered in contrast to 61 percent of African Americans and 69 percent of Non-Hispanic whites. Similar patterns were observed in 1992 for these population groups in Los Angeles, Oakland-San Francisco, New York, and Honolulu. Indeed, in some regions, differences in voter registration rates between Asian Pacific Americans and Non-Hispanic whites, who

TABLE 6
Distribution of Naturalized and U.S-Born Asian Pacific American Registered Voters, 1994

	California	*Hawaii*	*Rest of Nation*	*National Total*
U.S.-born	271,820 (58%)	218,580 (88%)	189,790 (42%)	680,190 (58%)
Naturalized	194,840 (42%)	29,170 (12%)	261,680 (58%)	485,710 (42%)
Total	466,660	247,770	451,470	1,165,990
% of national total	40%	21%	39%	100%

Current Population Survey, 1994

usually have the highest rates of registration, were quite substantial. In 1992, for example, in the Oakland-San Francisco region, 56 percent of all adult Asian Pacific American citizens were registered to vote compared to 86 percent of Non-Hispanic whites, 73 percent African Americans, and 63 percent Latino American citizens. At the same time, regional differences in voter registration rates for Asian Pacific American communities were apparent, with Los Angeles having the highest (64 percent) and New York having the lowest (54 percent).

Many previous studies have found that Asian Pacific Americans have lower rates of voter registration than African Americans and non-Hispanic whites, and usually the same or somewhat lower rates than that of Latinos. The findings here are consistent, and remain extremely puzzling, because of the relatively high, group-level attainment levels of Asian Pacific Americans in education and other socioeconomic variables. These factors have been long associated with active electoral participation in political science research (Nakanishi, 1986a, 1991; Cain, 1988; Field Institute, 1992; Erie and Brackman, 1993; Lien, 1994).

Among Asian Pacific American citizens, those who were born in the United States have a higher *overall* rate of voter registration than those who were born abroad and have become naturalized. In 1994, as Table 7 illustrates, 56 percent of all U.S.-born Asian Americans were registered compared to 49 percent of those who were naturalized.

Indeed, foreign-born Asian Pacific American citizens had among the lowest rates of any group, including Latino naturalized citizens (53 percent). In terms of electoral participation beyond registration, however, both Asian Pacific American naturalized and native-born voters had among the highest rates of voting during the 1994 elections. Therefore, Asian Pacific immigrants appear to reflect a provocative series of discrete, non-linear trends from becoming citizens to becoming registered voters and then to becoming actual voters: they have one of the highest rates of naturalization

TABLE 7
Voter Registration and Turnout Rates, 1994

	% Registered to Vote	*% Voted in 1994 Elections*
Asian Pacific Americans		
U.S.-born	56%	78%
Foreign born	49%	74%
Overall	53%	76%
Latinos		
U.S.-born	53%	62%
Foreign born	53%	74%
Overall	53%	64%
African Americans		
U.S.-born	61%	63%
Foreign born	58%	78%
Overall	61%	63%
Non-Hispanic Whites		
U.S.-born	69%	73%
Foreign born	68%	78%
Overall	69%	73%

Current Population Survey, 1994

after immigrating, but one of the lowest rates of voter registration after becoming citizens. Once registered, however, Asian Pacific American naturalized citizens have among the highest rates of voting of any group.

A closer and more detailed examination of Asian naturalized citizens indicates that those who immigrated over 20 years ago, prior to 1975, have rates of voter registration comparable to, if not greater than, those who were born in the United States (See Tables 8 and 9). Indeed, this was the case for practically all age groups, educational attainment levels, and for women. On the other hand, Asian Pacific naturalized citizens who immigrated within the past twenty years have rates of registration that are substantially lower than native-born citizens and naturalized citizens who arrived before 1975. This was consistent for practically all age and educational attainment levels, as well as for men and women. Like naturalization, statistical analysis revealed that year of entry was the best predictor of voter registration for Asian naturalized citizens. For voting, year of entry, educational attainment, and age were the strongest explanatory variables for Asian naturalized registered voters.

Like the process of naturalization, the importance of time-dependent variables for electoral participation is consistent with the view that immigrants and refugees must often undergo a

TABLE 9

Detailed Rates of Voter Registration of Asian Pacific-American Naturalized and Native-Born Citizens, 18 Years and Older

	Number of Years in the U.S. (Naturalized Citizens)				
	6–10	11–14	15–19	20+	U.S.-Born
By age					
18–24	0%	20%	15%	10%	26%
25–29	13%	16%	0%	31%	25%
30–39	3%	15%	4%	40%	31%
40–49	8%	37%	42%	20%	24%
50–59	0%	19%	20%	51%	22%
60 plus	0%	0%	12%	41%	40%
By education level					
0–8 years	0%	11%	26%	33%	24%
9–12 years	0%	0%	13%	45%	16%
High school	16%	20%	335	28%	16%
Some college	1%	18%	23%	28%	32%
BA	5%	12%	27%	45%	43%
Graduate Degree	0%	66%	18%	41%	45%
By gender					
Males	6%	20%	23%	29%	32%
Females	6%	21%	27%	39%	29%

Current Population Survey, 1994

prolonged and multifaceted process of social adaptation and learning before fully participating in their newly-adopted country. Becoming actively involved in American electoral politics and politically acculturated may be one of the most complex, lengthy, and least understood learning experiences. Adult Asian Pacific immigrants and refugees, like other groups of migrants (Gittleman, 1982), largely acquired their core political values, attitudes, and behavioral orientations in sociopolitical systems that differed from that of the United States. Some of their countries of origin did not have universal suffrage, others were dominated by a single political party (which made voting nearly inconsequential), and still others were in extreme political upheaval as a result of civil war or international conflict. Indeed, one of the major reasons why many Asian refugees left their homelands was to escape some

TABLE 8

Registration and Voting by Year of Immigration for Naturalized and U.S.-Born Citizens, 1994

	% Registered to Vote Year of Immigration for Naturalized Citizens	% Actually Voted
Pre-1965	77%	92%
1965–1974	57%	66%
1975–1985	43%	71%
1986–1994	26%	81%
Overall	49%	74%
U.S.-born	56%	78%

Current Population Survey, 1984

of the most horrendous political situations like the killing fields in Cambodia.

As a result, previously learned lessons and orientations toward government and political activities may not be easily supplanted nor supplemented. For example, adult education classes in American civics and government which immigrants usually take to prepare for naturalization examinations expose them to the most rudimentary facts about American government. At the same time, though, they probably have little or no impact on preexisting political belief systems, the general sense of political efficacy and distrust toward government, or knowledge of American political traditions, current policy debates, and political party agendas. Learning about and becoming actively involved in politics "American style" through registering to vote and voting in elections take place through a range of personal and group experiences that go beyond citizenship classes. Over time, this evolution occurs in conjunction with other aspects of acculturating to American life and society.

The Asian Pacific American electorate is clearly in the process of transformation and change. Its future characteristics and impact will be largely determined by the extent to which newly naturalized Asian immigrants and refugees are incorporated into the political system and encouraged to register to vote and to cast their ballots. An electorate that "looks like Asian Pacific America," in all of its dimensions of diversity, especially in becoming predominantly foreign-born rather than reflecting its current native-born majority profile, may have far different partisan preferences and public policy priorities.

The Asian Pacific American voters in the city of Monterey Park in Los Angeles County may be illustrative (See Table 10). In 1984, the city had a plurality of Democrats (43 percent) over Republicans (31 percent) among Chinese American voters, and also a high proportion of individuals (25 percent) who specified no party affiliations and considered themselves to be independents.[20]

By 1989, Chinese American voters, who accounted for the vast majority of new registered voters in Monterey Park since 1984, were nearly evenly divided among Democrats (35 percent), Republicans (37 percent), and independents (26 percent) (Nakanishi, 1986a, 1991). The Asian Pacific American electorate in the city changed its overall partisan orientation through the addition of these new, largely Chinese American registered voters. In 1984, the city's Asian Pacific American voters as a whole showed a slight majority for the Democrats. By 1989, with an increase of over 2,500 new registered voters, the Asian Pacific American electorate in the city could no longer be characterized in this manner. In an analogous fashion, the Asian Pacific American electorate at both the grassroots and leadership levels nationally have undergone, and will continue to undergo, significant changes with the increased future political participation of Asian Pacific immigrants and refugees.

CONCLUSION AND RECOMMENDATIONS

Large-scale immigration from Asia since the enactment of the Immigration Act of 1965 has had a dramatic impact on many states and regions across the nation, as well as on the Asian Pacific American population.[21] From a largely native-born group of 1.5 million in 1970, Asian Pacific Americans became a predominantly immigrant population of 3.5 million in 1980. By 1990, the population had doubled again to 7.2 million nationwide, of which 66 percent were foreign-born. Recent projections estimate that Asian Pacific Americans will continue to increase to nearly 12 million by 2000, and nearly 20 million by 2020. The foreign-born sector is expected to remain the majority beyond 2020 (Ong and Hee, 1993).

The issues of naturalization and electoral participation will remain compelling and critical for both the Asian Pacific American population and

TABLE 10
Asian Pacific American Registered Voters, Monterey Park, California, 1984 and 1989

	# Registered	Democrats	Republicans	Other No.	Parties
'84 Citywide	22,021	13,657	5,564	368	2,290
	(100%)	(62%)	(25%)	(2%)	(10%)
'89 Citywide	23,184	13,243	6,684	369	2,888
	(100%)	(57%)	(29%)	(2%)	(13%)
'84–89 Net Gain/Loss	+1,163	−414	+1,120	+1	+598
'84 Asian Pacific Total	6,441	3,265	1,944	54	1,178
	(100%)	(51%)	(30%)	(1%)	(18%)
'89 Asian Pacific Total	8,988	3,754	3,198	168	1,868
	(100%)	(42%)	(36%)	(2%)	(21%)
'84–89 Net Loss/Gain	+2,547	+489	+1254	+114	+690
'84 Non-Asian Pacific Total	15,438	10,392	3,620	314	1,112
	(100%)	(67%)	(23%)	(2%)	(7%)
'89 Non-Asian Pacific Total	14,196	9,489	3,486	201	1,020
	(100%)	(67%)	(25%)	(1%)	(7%)
'84–89 Net Loss/Gain	−1,242	−903	−134	−113	−92
'84 Chinese Americans	3,152	1,360	972	23	797
	(100%)	(43%)	(31%)	(1%)	(25%)
'89 Chinese Americans	5,356	1,868	1,989	100	1,399
	(100%)	(35%)	(37%)	(2%)	(26%)
'84–89 Net Gain/Loss	+2,204	+508	+1,017	+77	+602
'84 Japanese Americans	2,586	1,429	838	21	298
	(100%)	(55%)	(32%)	(1%)	(12%)
'89 Japanese Americans	2,919	1,516	99142	370	
	(100%)	(52%)	(34%)	(1%)	(13%)
'84–89 NET Gain/Loss	+343	+87	+153	+21	+72

Source: UCLA Asian Pacific American Voter Registration Project, 1995.

for American society generally for many years to come. Asian immigrants have the highest rates of naturalization of any group, including those who came from Europe, and do not remain permanent aliens in this country. They "Americanize," become full citizens, participate actively in all sectors of American life, and should be entitled to all their citizenship rights and privileges. At the same time, Asian Pacific immigrants like their native-born counterparts have extremely low overall rates of voter registration when compared with other groups. Asian Pacific immigrants appear, however, to attain levels of political involvement that are the same, if not better, than those of native-born Asian citizens with the passage of a substantial period of time—over two decades—and with increased acculturation.

The political incorporation of naturalized *(and native-born)* Asian Pacific Americans into the American electoral system needs to be accelerated. Challenging contemporary remnants of the political exclusion and isolation that Asian Pacific Americans experienced in the past is a responsibility to be shared with the two major political parties and others who believe that citizens should be able to exercise fully their right to vote. Unfair redistricting of Asian Pacific American communities, lack of bilingual voter registration application forms and ballots, and opposition to the implementation of legislation like the National Voter Registration Act of 1993 (a.k.a. the Motor Voter Act) perpetuate "political structural barriers," which must be challenged and replaced by fair and inclusive political practices and policies. Asian immigrants have much to contribute to all aspects of American political life—as voters, campaign workers, financial donors, policy experts, and elected officials—and must be allowed and encouraged to participate fully. To do so is to continue a political tradition as old as the nation itself of benefiting from the special leadership talents and contributions of individuals who came to the United States from all corners of the world and shaped its domestic and international programs and policies.

In recent years, the incentive and necessity for Asian Pacific immigrants and their native-born counterparts to naturalize and become more involved in electoral politics have been greatly enhanced in both obvious and unexpected ways. Politicians and the major political parties, who had long neglected to address the unique interests and concerns of Asian Pacific Americans, have become increasingly responsive and attentive, especially to the growing sector of the Asian Pacific American population that contributes sizable donations to campaign coffers. Less interest, however, has been shown toward augmenting the long-term voting potential of Asian Pacific Americans, and few attempts have been made by either the Democratic or Republican party to finance voter registration and education campaigns in Asian Pacific American communities.

The increasing number of Asian Pacific Americans, especially those of immigrant background, who are seeking public office appears, however, to be stimulating greater electoral participation among Asian Pacific Americans at the grassroots level. For example, Asian Pacific American candidates are now regularly making special efforts to seek monetary donations and register new voters among Asian Pacific Americans in juris-

dictions in which they are running for office. These activities provide Asian immigrants with important and direct vantage points from which to understand the workings of the American political system, thereby facilitating their political acculturation. At the same time, a wide array of advocacy and social services groups have formed in Asian Pacific American communities across the nation, and a number of different community-based outreach campaigns have been launched to promote citizenship and to register individuals, particularly those who have just been naturalized. Finally, disastrous events like the 1992 civil unrest in Los Angeles, in which over 2,000 Korean American and Asian-owned businesses were destroyed, have underscored the need for immigrant-dominant communities to place greater organizational and leadership activities toward augmenting their access to, and influence in, local government and other policy arenas, as well as to increasing their representation in voter registration rolls.

The decade of the 1990s and the start of the new century are often viewed in glowing and optimistic terms because of seemingly positive demographic trends. The period will be important to witness and analyze because of the extraordinary challenges and opportunities that it will undoubtedly present for Asian Pacific Americans in seeking realization of their full potential as citizens and electoral participants. The level of success that they will achieve in the future, however, will not be solely determined by the Asian Pacific American population, or its leaders and organizations. Success will require the partnership, assistance, and intervention of a wide array of groups and leaders in both private and public sectors. Whether Asian Pacific Americans become a major new political force in the American electoral system is nearly impossible to predict with any precision. Our ability to raise and seriously entertain such a question in the context of the disenfranchisement and exclusion that Asian Pacific Americans faced in the past is quite revealing in itself.

NOTES

1. Albert Gore, "Keynote Address." (Pasadena, Calif., 14 July 1995).

2. The 1995 Personal Responsibility Act.

3. To become citizens, immigrants: (1) must be at least 18 years of age; (2) have been lawfully admitted to the United States for permanent residence; (3) have lived in the United States continuously for five consecutive years; (4) are able to speak, read and write English; (5) pass an exam on U.S. government and history; (6) be of good moral character; and (7) are able to show loyalty to the United States by taking an oath of allegiance. There are exceptions to these rules: (1) the spouse or child of a United States citizen becomes eligible in three years; (2) a child who immigrates with his or her parent may become a citizen when the parent naturalizes; (3) an adopted child is eligible for administrative naturalization; (4) an alien who served in World War I, World War II, Korean War, Vietnam, or Grenada may naturalize without permanent residence requirements in some situations; (5) an alien who has served in the Armed Forces for three years may be able to naturalize without meeting certain requirements: (6) former U.S. citizens may waive some requirements; and (7) employees of organizations that promote the U.S. interests in foreign countries may naturalize without meeting these requirements.

4. The number of adult Asian immigrants in the samples are over 10,000 for 1970, 87,000 for 1980, and 182,000 for 1990.

5. The 1970 Census used only four categories: naturalized U.S. citizen, alien, born abroad of American parents, and native-born.

6. The number of years in this country is estimated based on time of entry into the United States. The census does not report whether a respondent has been in the country continuously.

7. The observed change can be decomposed into three components: (1) the difference due to a change in the composition of the population holding naturalization rates for each subgroup constant, (2) the difference due to a change in naturalization rates holding the composition constant, and (3) the difference due to the interaction of the changes in rates and composition. Calculations indicate the compositional shift accounts for just slightly less than half of the decline—that is, 11.2 of the 23.5 percentage points difference in the 1970 and 1990 naturalization rates.

8. The contribution of lower rates with each cohort can be estimated through decomposition with one component being the change in within-group rates between 1970 and 1990, holding the composition by years in the United States to that observed for 1970. Calculations indicate that the within-group drop in naturalization rates accounts for 53 percent of the overall decline for all immigrants— that is, 12.5 of the 23.5 percentage points difference in the naturalization rates for 1970 and 1990.

9. For the purpose of this paper, the four major racial groups are defined as Asians, African Americans, non-Hispanic whites, and Hispanics. The Hispanic classification is nominally an ethnic classification, but being Hispanic in U.S. society is often ascriptive in a manner similar to membership in a racial group.

10. Rates are based on administrative records on the total number of legal immigrants admitted and the total number of persons who naturalized. Rates reported in the text are for the cohort of immigrants who entered between 1970 and 1979. The number of persons from this cohort who naturalized is based on INS records from 1970 to 1990.

11. The two other nations are Mexico (14 percent) and the Dominican Republic (22 percent).

12. Categories beyond 20 years for the 1980 Census differ from those for the other two censuses. For the 1980 Census, the categories are 21–29 and 30-plus years.

13. The low rate is also due to the inclusion of foreign-born persons on temporary visas in the United States. As stated earlier, the census does not differentiate between permanent immigrants and those on temporary visas. The latter are likely to be here for a short time and thus are concentrated among newly-arrived aliens.

14. The estimate depends on assumptions regarding the naturalization rate in the fifth year and the fifteenth year and the relative number who would never naturalize. One difficulty making an estimate is the nonlinear nature of the naturalization rates, with a noticeable decrease in the change with more years in the United States. If we assume that the rates are 10 percent in the fifth year and 70 percent in the fifteenth year, and that 10 percent would never naturalize, then two-thirds of all naturalization would have occurred in the 5-15 year range.

15. Repeated for the 6-to-10 year group over the next five years; consequently, the difference in the naturalization rates between the two groups observed in the cross-sectional data would not be an accurate predictor of the increase in rate experienced by the 6-to-10 year group over the subsequent five years.

16. There are changes in the cohort from one census to another due to death, emigration, and changes in how respondents report their time of entry into the United States. It is, however, beyond the scope of this study to examine how these factors may affect our estimates.

17. This includes those with a non-doctorate professional degree.

18. The results of this multivariate analysis based on logit regressions are available from the authors.

19. The 1994 CPS included 3,317 Asians out of a total sample of 102,197. The 1990 survey included 2,914 Asians among 105,875; and the 1992 had 3,443 Asians among 102,901. Both weighted and unweighted data were analyzed for this report.

20. Other studies have also found that some groups of Asian American voters register in higher than expected propor-

tions as "no party" or independents. See Din, 1984, and Chen, *et al.*, 1989.

21. These population figures include both Asian Americans and Pacific Islanders (*e.g.*, Hawaiians, Samoans, Guamanians, Tongans, Fijians, Palauans, Northern Mariana Islands, and Tahitians). From 1980 to 1990, Pacific Islanders increased by 41 percent from 259, 566 to 365, 024.

REFERENCES

"Asians Called a 'Major National Force' in Political Fund-raising." *Asianweek.* 1 June 1994.

Bai, Su Sun. "Affirmative Pursuit of Political Equality for Asian Pacific Americans: Reclaiming the Voting Rights Act." *University of Pennsylvania Law Review* 139, no. 3 (1991): 731–767.

Borjas, G. *Friends or Strangers: The Impact of Immigrants on the U.S. Economy.* New York: Basic Books, 1990.

Cain, Bruce E. "Asian-American Electoral Power: Imminent or Illusory?" *Election Politics* 5 (1988): 27–30.

Chen, Marion, Woei-Ming New, and John Tsutakawa. "Empowerment in New York Chinatown: Our Work as Student Interns." *Amerasia Journal* 15 (1989): 299–306.

Din, Grant. "An Analysis of Asian/Pacific American Registration and Voting Patterns in San Francisco." Master's Thesis, Claremont Graduate School, 1984.

Erie, Steven P., and Harold Brackman. *Paths to Political Incorporation For Latinos and Asian Pacifics in California.* Berkeley: The California Policy Seminar, 1993.

The Field Institute. "A Digest on California's Political Demography," 1992.

Gittleman, Zvi. *Becoming Israelis: Political Resocialization of Soviet and American Immigrants.* New York: Praeger, 1982.

Hing, Bill Ong. *Making and Remaking Asian Pacific America through Immigration Policy, 1850–1990.* Stanford: Stanford University Press, 1993.

Horton, John. *The Politics of Diversity: Immigration, Resistance, and Change in Montery Park, California.* Philadelphia: Temple University Press, 1995.

Jasso, Guillermina, and Mark R. Rosenzweig. *The New Chosen People: Immigrants in the United States*

(The Population of the U.S. in the 1980's Census Monograph Series). For the National Committee for Research on the 1980 Census. New York: Russel Sage Foundation, 1990.

Karnow, Stanley. "Apathetic Asian Pacific Americans? Why Their Success Hasn't Spilled Over into Politics," *Washington Post* 29 November 1992, sec. C.

Kwoh, Stewart, and Mindy Hui. "Empowering Our Communities: Political Policy." *The State of Asian Pacific America: Policy Issues to the Year 2020.* Los Angeles: LEAP Asian Pacific American Public Policy Institute and the UCLA Asian Pacific American Studies Center, 1993: 189–197.

Liang, Zai. "On the Measurement of Naturalization." *Demography* 32, no. 3 (1994): 525–548.

Lien, Pei-te. "Ethnicity and Political Participation: A Comparison between Asian and Mexican Americans." *Political Behavior* 16, no. 2 (1994): 237–264.

Miller, John. "Asian Pacific Americans Head for Politics." *The American Enterprise,* 6 (1995): 56–58.

Nakanishi, Don T. *The National Asian American Roster, 1978.* Los Angeles: UCLA Asian American Studies Center, 1978.

———. "Asian Pacific American Politics: An Agenda for Research." *Amerasia Journal* 12 (1986a): 1–27.

———. "The Next Swing Vote? Asian Pacific Americans and California Politics." In *Racial and Ethnic Politics in California,* edited by Byran Jackson and Michael Preston. Berkeley: Institute for Governmental Studies, 1991, 25–54.

Nakanishi, Don T. and James S. Lai. *Asian Pacific American Political Roster and Resource Guide.* Los Angeles: UCLA Asian American Studies Center, 1995.

Ong, Paul, Lucie Cheng, and Leslie Evans. "Migration of Highly-Educated Asians and Global Dynamics." *Asian and Pacific Migration Journal* 1, nos. 3–4 (1992): 543–584.

Ong, Paul, and Suzanne Hee. "The Growth of the Asian Pacific American Population: 20 Million in 2020." In *The State of Asian Pacific America: Policy Issues to the Year 2020.* Los Angeles: LEAP Asian Pacific American Public Policy Institute and the UCLA Asian Pacific American Studies Center, 1993, 11–24.

Shinagana, Larry H. "Asian Pacific American Electoral Participation in the San Francisco Bay Area: A Study of the Exit Poll Results of the November 8,

1994 Elections for the Cities of Daly City, San Francisco, and Oakland," an unpublished report commissioned by the Asian Law Caucus, Inc. and funded by the Ford Foundation, 1995.

Skerry, Peter. *Mexican Americans: The Ambivalent Minority.* New York: Free Press, 1993.

Stokes, Bruce. "Learning the Game." *National Journal,* no. 43 (22 October 1988): 2649–2654.

Tachibana, Judy. "California's Asians: Power from a Growing Population." *California Journal* 17 (1986): 534–543.

Tam, Wendy. "Asians—A Monolithic Voting Bloc?" *Political Behavior* 17, no. 2 (1995): 223–249.

Tomas Rivera Center. *Mexican Americans: Are They an Ambivalent Minority?* Claremont, CA: The Tomas Rivera Center, 1994.

U.S. Immigration and Naturalization Service. *Statistical Yearbook of the Immigration and Naturalization Service, 1990.* Washington D.C.: U.S. Government Printing Office, 1991.

Asian Americans and Latinos in San Gabriel Valley, California: Ethnic Political Cooperation and Redistricting 1990–92

Leland T. Saito

After the racial turmoil of the 1960s and 1970s, the relative calm of the 1980s seemed to indicate that the United States was entering a period of improved race relations. However, the racial rhetoric of politicians such as Jesse Helms, the popularity of ex–Ku Klux Klan member David Duke in the Louisiana elections, and the rise in racial hate crimes once again brought race and ethnic relations to the forefront of public attention. In addition to the conflicts of Anglos versus African Americans that have long dominated the discourse on race and ethnic relations, conflict between ethnic groups, such as Korean small business owners and their African American clientele, have now emerged.

Interethnic struggle reached a high point following the acquittal of the four Los Angeles police officers accused of using violent force against Rodney King, an African American. Following the verdict, hundreds of businesses owned by Koreans and other ethnic groups were looted and burned down by African Americans and Latinos.

Against this backdrop of racial tension, I examine political relationships between Asian Americans and Latinos in the San Gabriel Valley, located in Los Angeles County. I examine an Asian American organization that was established around the issue of redistricting and reapportionment and how the group formed an alliance with its Latino counterpart in the region. In this case, the Asian American and Latino organizations were able to reach agreement on plans that accom-

Source: Amerasia Journal 19:2 (1993): 55–68. Reprinted by permission.

plished the complex task of protecting the political interests of Latinos and Asian Americans.

What were the circumstances in the San Gabriel Valley that led to cooperation in the redistricting process between Asian Americans and Latinos? The Asian American and Latino communities overlap in the region so that district plans would affect both groups.

The San Gabriel Valley is an ideal place to study ethnic relations because of its demographics. Beginning in the 1970s, the formerly Anglo population experienced rapid change when large numbers of Asian Americans and Latinos entered the region. For example, Monterey Park has become the first city outside of Hawaii with a majority (57.5 percent) Asian American population.[1] At the regional level, Latinos have become the majority population in the valley and they hold all elected state and federal offices that cover Monterey Park. Yet, vestiges of Anglo political dominance remain on the local level in the form of Anglo control of some city councils.

This study primarily uses data from ethnographic fieldwork and interviews collected from 1990 to 1992. Census and voter registration data were also utilized. Ethnographic fieldwork was critical for documenting and analyzing events emerging from the historical and contemporary factors that formed the context for ethnic relations in the San Gabriel Valley.

This paper differs in three ways from other studies in race and ethnic relations. First, community studies traditionally examine one ethnic group, or compare an ethnic group with Anglos;

this study examines two groups, Asian Americans and Latinos.[2] Second, most studies examining ethnic relations examine conflict,[3] whereas my research examines the circumstances around the volatile process that led to ethnic cooperation rather than conflict. Third, while one school of thought suggests that ethnicity is decreasing in importance politically, my study supports the persistence of ethnicity in politics.

Theoretically, one school of thought suggests that economic class is increasing in importance with a relative decline in ethnicity. Milton Gordon, in his formulation of assimilation theory, believed that ethnicity, "defined or set off by race, religion, or national origin," was a temporary condition which would disappear as groups "assimilated" into the mainstream.[4] In politics, Robert Dahl focused on the overlap of generation and economic class, concluding that ethnic politics would lose its meaning when an ethnic group made the transition from an immigrant group which is economically homogeneous to the third generation which becomes economically heterogeneous.[5] As a result, economic interests among members of the ethnic group would vary tremendously and would take precedence over ethnic group interests. Nathan Glazer's and Daniel Moynihan's work showed that ethnic groups in New York city continue to have importance as "interest groups" and refocused attention on the political consequences of ethnicity.[6] This paper examines the conditions supporting the persistence of ethnicity in politics, using redistricting as an example.

REDISTRICTING: ASIAN AMERICANS

After each decennial census, the state political districts (assembly, senate, and congressional) are reconfigured to reflect changes in population. Redistricting is critical for ethnic politics because it creates state and federal districts from which officials are elected. Historically, politicians have divided geographic concentrations of ethnic groups into many districts diluting their political influence.

Organizing along ethnic lines is made possible through legal precedent and federal laws. The Voting Rights Act of 1965 and 1982 amendment prohibit minority vote dilution by fragmenting communities.[7] Recent court cases have established the legal basis for creating electoral districts that preserve the political integrity of ethnic groups by keeping communities intact within districts. One of the most important for the Los Angeles region was the 1990 case of *Garza* v. *County of Los Angeles*, which ruled that Latinos had been consistently divided into separate districts. As a result, the Los Angeles County supervisorial districts were redrawn and a Latina, Gloria Molina, was elected to office in the newly created district where Latinos became the majority population group. Oral and written testimony submitted by Asian Americans to the state senate and assembly committees on redistricting focused on these laws and court rulings, stressing the need to keep Asian American communities whole within a district, rather than fragmented in a number of districts.

In their oral and written testimonies submitted to the state assembly and senate committees on redistricting, the Coalition of Asian Pacific Americans for Fair Reapportionment outlined the issues that followed ethnic lines and established the fact that there was such an entity as an "Asian American" community. Anti-Asian American activities, such as hate crimes and English-Only movements, employment discrimination, lack of social service funding, immigration policy, discriminatory admission policies of California state universities, and racist rhetoric by politicians linking immigration to social problems were some of the issues mentioned in the testimony.

Judy Chu, former mayor of Monterey Park and a current member of the city council, addressed some of these issues in her testimony before the Senate committee on elections and reapportionment:

Without concentrated districts, the ability for Asian Americans to express their concerns about issues will be diluted. For instance, Monterey Park faced an anti-immigrant movement in the mid to late 1980s. There were attempts to restrict languages other than English from being spoken in public, from being written on city materials that went to the public, and from being on commercial signs. There were attempts to prevent foreign-language books from being in our library. While these efforts have been defeated in Monterey Park, some of the issues are still being pushed in other parts of the San Gabriel Valley where there is no organized opposition. . . . Asians need advocates for programs that will help Asian immigrant children and adults learn the English language and make the transition to American society successfully. Unfortunately, those programs are sparse or have long waiting lists.[8]

Leland Saito, in testimony submitted to the assembly committee, cited employment discrimination in Alhambra, the city that borders Monterey Park to the north:

In 1990, the United States Justice Department sued the city of Athambra and its Fire and Police Departments with charges of employment discrimination against minorities. The U.S. Justice Department does not sue a city unless there is strong evidence of discrimination in hiring and employment procedures and an egregious disparity between the ethnic makeup of the department and surrounding region.[9]

Redistricting was a key issue for Asian Americans, given that no Asian American had been elected to the state legislature in over a decade. The basis for any claim starts with the raw numbers of population and the 127 percent increase of California's Asian American population over the last decade due primarily to immigration. The increase during the past ten years of the Asian American population in cities in the San Gabriel Valley was dramatic. Monterey Park's Asian American population increased by 90.6 percent, bringing the Asian American population to 57.5 percent of the city's population. Similarly, in the nearby cities of Alhambra, Rosemead, and

San Gabriel, the Asian American population increased between 289 to 372 percent, forming between 32 to 38 percent of the population in those cities.[10]

The statewide Coalition of Asian Pacific Americans for Fair Reapportionment was formed in 1990 to advocate the interests of Asian Americans and Pacific Islanders to the state legislature which is in charge of the redistricting and reapportionment process.

The Southern California part of the coalition targeted three areas in Los Angeles County with large and rapidly growing Asian American and Pacific Islander populations. They were the Central Los Angeles, South Bay, and San Gabriel Valley areas. Regional coalitions were organized and the San Gabriel Valley Asian Pacific Americans for Fair Reapportionment was established.

The goals included reversing the fragmentation of Asian American and Pacific Islander communities into separate political districts, educating the community about the politics of redistricting and reapportionment, and establishing working ties between ethnic groups in the Asian American and pacific Islander community as well as with Latinos and African Americans.

Judy Chu, speaking on behalf of the San Gabriel Valley coalition about the fragmentation of the community in testimony to the Senate Committee on Reapportionment, stated:

Our votes are fractionalized. The cities (in the west San Gabriel Valley). . . . are divided into two supervisorial districts, three assembly districts, three senatorial districts, and three congressional districts. It is no wonder that Asians in California are virtually unrepresented anywhere beyond the local level.[11]

Reflecting the demographic mix of the area, most of the members of the San Gabriel Valley group were Chinese American, along with some Japanese American. Republicans and Democrats were active in the non-partisan organization.[12]

The statewide and regional coalitions established themselves before the state legislature as the voices of the Asian American and Pacific Islander community in the redistricting process. However, over time the agenda appeared to be controlled primarily by the native-born and established immigrants, while the more recent immigrants supplied their numbers to give the coalitions legitimacy as representatives of the different communities. Experience with politics, networks with political activists in the different ethnic communities, technical skills needed for the analysis of data, and the knowledge required to testify at government hearings were resources that existed largely among certain members of the community. Employees of social service agencies, college students and professors, staff workers of elected officials, and attorneys were the primary participants in the coalitions.

As a result, negotiations between Asian Americans and Latinos were carried out by a small group of highly-educated professionals who were acutely aware of the need for coalitions because of the tremendous amount of work and resources required to counter the history of gerrymandering that fragmented ethnic communities.

ASIAN AMERICANS AND LATINOS

There were major problems to overcome in the development of an alliance between the two ethnic groups. Asian Americans were well aware of the large numbers of Latinos in the San Gabriel Valley and of the fact that Latinos held all county, state, and federal elected offices that included Monterey Park. The needs of Asian Americans could easily be lost in an alliance.

Latinos were concerned about the rapidly growing number of Asian Americans and the threat this posed to growing Latino political power. In fact, when the Southwest Voter Registration and Education Project, a Latino organization, held one of the first voter registration drives in the area for Asian Americans, some Latinos in the region complained about it, saying that resources should be used only for Latinos.[13]

However, despite their differences, several factors encouraged the development of an alliance. Each group recognized the strengths of the other. As newcomers to the process, Asian Americans involved in redistricting were well aware of the need to work with the more experienced Latinos. Asian Americans had much to learn from Latino organizations that had gained political and legal knowledge through their successful court cases, such as *Garza* v. *County of Los Angeles*. Latinos also had the support of organizations with much larger budgets, such as the Mexican American Legal Defence and Education Fund and the Southwest Voter Registration and Education Project. Even though the Asian American population is growing rapidly in the San Gabriel Valley, Latinos are still the largest population group in the area. Also, there were Latino members in the state legislature who would be open to listening to the Latino coalition.

During the first meeting between the two statewide groups in May 1991, an Asian American stated that we were new to the game and looked to Latinos for guidance:

> Asians and Pacific Islanders are at an early stage. We look to the Latino community for help. We want to nurture the relationship, I am encouraged by the sensitivity expressed at this table. We would appreciate your guidance, steps we should take, direction to go in; it's a new process for many of us. Someone later added that we (Asian Americans) are where the Latinos were in the 1960s or 70s.[14]

Latinos were well aware of the tremendous growth of the Asian American population in the valley documented by the 1990 census. Latinos were also aware that this growth was translating into a political force represented by recent successful campaigns to elect Asian Americans to local city councils and school boards. Also, as the late Jesse Unruh reportedly said, "money is the mother's milk of politics," and Asian Americans had a strong record of donating money. Don Nakanishi writes that Asian Americans have become "a major new source of campaign funds, a veritable mountain of gold."[15] In fact, Nakanishi notes that Asian Americans "In the 1988 presidential election. . . . were second only to the American Jewish population in the amount of campaign money raised by an ethnic or minority group."[16] The fact that this money could also flow to Latino candidates had already been proven in past campaigns when Asian Americans held fund raisers for state Senator Art Torres in his bid for Los Angeles County Supervisor in the newly created San Gabriel Valley district and for Xavier Becerra and his campaign for the Assembly in 1990.

Although they are the majority of the population, Latinos and Asian Americans still lack representatives in elected offices. For example, in 1991, the city council of Rosemead was all Anglo, despite the fact that Asian Americans and Latinos combined were over 80 percent of the population. In August 1991, during one of the Latino and Asian American meetings to discuss plans, one Latino began to talk about the necessity of building links between Latinos and Asian Americans at all levels.

> We have to work together. In local neighborhoods, cities, the region. Working together, Asians and Latinos can offset the disproportionate amount of political power held by Anglos. We can work together on a project, or elections. The perception among Latinos is that Asians have a lot of money, are organized. The newspapers have given this a lot of coverage. I have all the articles since this began. We can pool our resources, Asians have money and we have numbers.[17]

Asian Americans responded by saying that they were committed to working together because of common issues. Realistically, political realities dictated that Asian Americans must work with Latinos. In fact, Asian Americans already had a long history of working with Latinos and they listed a number of examples.

> I can say that Asians are committed to working with Latinos because the political reality is that Asians

need Latinos more than Latinos need Asians because our population is smaller and we have a low number of registered voters. We know we need Latino support to win. In fact, we have already started making links. Tomorrow, the local Asian Pacific Democratic Club, many of the members of the coalition are part of that, are meeting with the San Gabriel Valley LULAC to discuss redistricting. The Asian Democratic club walked for Xavier Becerra's campaign. Asians volunteered for Art Torres during his last campaign. One of the Latinos replied that this was true, he had worked on Becerra's campaign and was impressed by the Asian turnout.[18]

Asian Americans and Latinos understood that the political clout of both groups supporting one set of redistricting plans for the region would increase the possibility of the legislature adopting the plan. Most important, they also knew that if Asian Americans and Latinos were pitted against one another, both groups could end up losing.

In conclusion, Latinos and Asian Americans recognized that each group could benefit through combined efforts. The enemy was the political establishment and its history of political gerrymandering which fragmented each community, diluting political power and leaving them with leaders who did not have to respond to issues of the Asian American and Latino communities.

BUILDING A STATE ASSEMBLY DISTRICT

The main concern of the Asian American group was keeping their population together and getting as many Asian Americans as possible into an assembly district. The group checked the 1990 census data and picked out the cities with the largest numbers of Asian Americans. Using this rough guide, the group drew a line around Monterey Park, Alhambra, Rosemead, San Gabriel, South Pasadena, San Marino, and Temple City. To achieve the required amount of about 370,000 people for an assembly district, the group experimented with portions of cities to the north, such as Arcadia, and cities to the east and south, such as El Monte, and Montebello. The group ended up with districts where the Asian American population ranged around 35 percent.

Checking political parties, the districts varied from slightly more Democratic to slightly more Republican. The major difference was going north and east into cities like Arcadia which included more Anglo Republicans while going south brought in more Latino Democrats.

What really interested the group was the voting record in the 1990 California secretary of state election. Flores, an Anglo Republican, was a Los Angeles City Council person for the southern area and little known in the San Gabriel Valley. It is possible that Latinos may have thought that she was Latina because of her last name, acquired through marriage. Checking the data, in the Republican northern cities such as San Marino, Flores won by a wide margin whereas in the Democratic Latino cities, Eu won by a wide margin. The group thought that this was interesting because even though Flores had a Latino last name, incumbency and political party seemed to be more important to the Latino vote. The group was concerned about the northern cities. What did it mean when a very popular moderate Asian American Democrat could not win? After all, Eu had won some past elections with the highest vote totals of anyone running for a statewide office.

Examining the areas of population concentration and growth collided with several political realities. First, creating a district that would maximize Asian American political influence does not necessarily result from just grouping the largest number of Asian Americans possible in one district. The northern cities were areas of heavy Asian American growth but also contained large numbers of politically conservative Anglos who may not support issues important to Asian Americans, such as more open immigration policies and bilingual voting materials. Discussion during a meeting of the Asian American coalition

brought out these points as members expressed their concern:

Some residents in the northern cities were very conservative and the John Birch Society was active there. Another person added, it goes beyond political partisanship because the anti-Asian activity in the north was scary. A recent newspaper article in the *Los Angeles Times* listed a number of incidents, including cross-burnings on lawns of Asian homes. What will inclusion of these areas mean for Asian political interests? Will our interest be served best by someone responding to the interests of conservative Anglos or moderate to liberal Latinos? If a moderate Democrat like March can't win (in the northern cities), what chance does another Asian have? Maybe even an Asia Republican with a strong record with the party may not have a chance.[19]

As one Latino mentioned:

If the cities with high Asian concentrations were put in one district, would we be creating a district which will not be an Asian influence district? It could possibly be a district where the Asian population would be high, but Anglo registered voters may be the dominant group. If that is so, then an Asian or Latino influence district would be lost in the area.[20]

Second, there was difficulty in reconciling the political rights of the Asian American population, which was under the protection of the Voting Rights Act, and the Latino assemblyman, who as a minority elected official, also came under the Voting Rights Act. He lived in Monterey Park and had expressed his desire to stay there. How would you create a single district which protected his rights as an ethnic incumbent, and also protected the rights of Asian Americans? Adding cities like South Pasadena and San Marino would be out of the question because along with Asian Americans were high numbers of Anglo Republicans who were not likely to vote for a Latino Democrat. Also, the Asian American group did not want to ignore the concerns of the Latino group and damage efforts to build a coalition.

Also, the possibility of a lower voter turnout in the southern cities as compared to the northern cities may favor an Asian American candidate.

If we go north, we get Republican, high propensity voters, people who may not vote for an Asian. Going south or east, we get Latinos, Democrats. They may not vote for an Asian either, but even in areas like Montebello which are considered middle-class Latino strongholds, their voting frequency may be less than in northern areas. Because their voter turnout is less, it may be better to go south than north.[21]

The group studied the current 59th district and discussed ways to modify it. Adding Rosemead and San Gabriel would keep the core Asian American population together. The four cities (along with Monterey Park and Alhambra) with the largest and fastest growing Asian American populations would be together. At the same time, by going south, a Latino majority population would be maintained. Solidly Democratic, the area did support March Fong Eu.

With these proposals in mind, the Asian American and Latino groups got together to work out a final plan. One Latino said that they were working hard to develop a plan that considered the concerns of the Asian American community. Therefore they moved Rosemead from the 60th to the plans for the 59th Assembly district. The Latinos agreed that because of its large (34.3 percent) and rapidly growing (371 percent over the past decade) Asian American population, it should go along with Monterey Park. This would also benefit Latinos because it would weaken the Anglo incumbent (assembly district) by taking away a city where she received many of her votes.[22] The strength of the Anglo vote in the city was clear since all the city council members at that time were Anglo.

Adding San Gabriel was tougher for the Latino group. Not currently in the 59th Assembly district, it would add yet another city to Xavier Becerra's Latino district, an additional burden for his reelection campaign. Although there was a solid middle-class community of Latino voters, there was also a large number of high propensity Republican Anglo voters.

Ultimately, adding the four cities of Asian American concentration and growth to the 59th district could be done while still maintaining a district where Latinos and Democrats were well over 50 percent of the population, giving the Latino incumbent a strong base to run on if he decided to seek reelection.

On August 30, 1991, the San Gabriel Valley Latino and Asian American groups, along with representatives from both statewide organizations, held a press conference in Monterey Park's city hall to announce that they had reached agreement on plans for districts in their region. In September, a group of Latinos and Asian Americans went together to Sacramento and met with a number of elected officials to lobby for their joint plan.

The Governor of California, Pete Wilson, vetoed the plans submitted by the state legislature. The state Supreme Court took over the redistricting task and appointed a "special masters" committee to create a new plan. The San Gabriel Valley Asian American and Latino groups coordinated their testimonies to support one another when they spoke before the masters committee.

The state Supreme Court adopted the new plan on January 27, 1992. The plan created a new assembly district, 49, which followed the recommendations of the valley coalition by grouping the four cities of Asian American concentration. The San Gabriel Valley was the only region in the state where such close working ties existed between Asian Americans and Latinos.

CONCLUSION

Perhaps one of the reasons why Asian Americans and Latinos were able to reach agreement over plans was the demographic balance of the San Gabriel Valley. Clearly, although the Asian American population was rapidly growing, their numbers in terms of registered voters were too small to be a threat to a strong Latino candidate. Therefore, Latinos could agree to the Asian American plan of grouping four cities together without endangering the reelection chances of the incumbent Latino assemblyman. As the Asian American population continued to grow and gain political power, changing the balance of power in the region, forging an alliance could prove to be a much more difficult task.

Asian Americans understood that they were newcomers to the redistricting process and that they would benefit from an alliance with Latinos who had the experience of winning major battles in court which established political rights, had powerful organizations backing their efforts, held all major political offices in the region, and had the largest ethnic population in the state to give them a strong foundation for their claims. In the year 2000, when the next census is taken and the redistricting process occurs again, Asian Americans will no longer be newcomers to the process. The question is, will Asian Americans find it necessary to form a coalition with Latinos? Uniting two groups proved to be much easier when a common enemy existed, the state legislature, which was interested in pitting the two groups against one another. Judging from the experience of the 1990s and the fragmentation of many Asian American and Latino communities throughout the state in the final redistricting plans, the common goal of protecting the political rights of their respective communities could again prove to be a powerful inducement for forming a coalition.

Latinos and Asian Americans also have similar concerns which should continue to provide a basis for a coalition. With large numbers of immigrants in both groups, some of the issues they share include bilingual voting materials, English language classes, and immigration policy. As ethnic groups, they both face employment discrimination as shown in cases filed against the city of Alhambra. Although Latinos had made some headway in terms of electing officials, both groups were faced with politicians who were unresponsive to their concerns.

Unlike the conditions in Los Angeles that sparked the events following the Rodney King decision, such as class divisions following ethnic lines, an educational system in crisis, high unemployment, few services, and deteriorating housing stock, the San Gabriel Valley had a significant middle class population. Also, there were a number of Latino and Asian American individuals and organizations in existence that had a history of working together.[23] The difficult task of building working relations was made easier because of such existing ties. Politically experienced and economically stable, the residents were able to get involved with what is for the average person, an abstract political concept that seemed to have little to do with the reality of their day-to-day lives.

In contrast to the San Gabriel Valley coalitions around a set of plans, the Los Angeles downtown Asian American and Latino groups basically agreed to disagree and not attack one another. Major differences between Los Angeles and the San Gabriel Valley might explain why agreement was reached in one place but not the other. First, the Asian American population mix in downtown was much more complex, with well developed Japanese, Chinese, Korean, and Filipino communities as compared to the San Gabriel Valley which was dominated by Chinese and Japanese Americans.[24] Organizing the individual Asian American communities and then meeting together as a unified group was a more complicated and lengthy process.[25] In addition, the San Gabriel Valley Asian American population was more experienced politically because of its longer history of working on the campaigns of local Asian American candidates. Networks and organizations were already in place which could begin work on redistricting.

Second, the downtown Asian American and Latino populations were spread out over a much larger area, with miles separating some of the communities as compared to the four contiguous cities in the San Gabriel Valley Asian American plan. Third, the overall demographic mix of the downtown area was more complicated with a large population of African Americans who were nearly absent (about 1 percent) in the San Gabriel Valley. This required taking into consideration the political rights of another group, making the process much more complex. Fourth, downtown Los Angeles contained some of the most expensive real estate in the state, making it the site of much larger political battles than in the San Gabriel Valley. As a result of these four factors, Los Angeles presented a more complex set of circumstances that had to be worked out among more participants.

In summary, organizing along ethnic lines was made possible by federal law and legal precedent which established the political rights of communities as defined by ethnicity. Understanding the political nature of redistricting, Asian Americans and Latinos put aside their differences and combined their resources to fight the common enemy, the political establishment and its history of political gerrymandering, which had fragmented Asian American and Latino communities for so long.

NOTES

This research was supported in part by a Rockefeller Foundation Fellowship in the Humanities administered by the UCLA Asian American Studies Center and an American Sociological Association Minority Fellowship funded by the National Institute on Mental Health.

1. Paul M. Ong, *Asian Pacific Islanders in California, 1990* (Los Angeles: Asian American Studies Center, University of California, Los Angeles, 1991).

2. Illsoo Kim, *New Urban Immigrants: The Korean Community in New York* (Princeton, New Jersey: Princeton University Press, 1981); Peter Kwong, *The New Chinatown* (New York: Hill and Wang, 1987); S. Frank Miyamoto, *Social Solidarity among the Japanese in Seattle* (Seattle, Washington: University of Washington Press, 1984); Victor G. Nee, and Brett de Bary Nee, *Longtime Californ': A Documentary Study of an American Chinatown* (Stanford: Stanford University Press, 1986).

3. Edward Chang, "New Urban Crisis: Korean-Black Conflict in Los Angeles" (Ph.D. Dissertation, University of California at Berkeley, 1990); Melvin L. Oliver and James H. Johnson, "Inter-Ethnic Conflict in an Urban Ghetto: The Case of Blacks and Latinos in Los Angeles,"

Research in Social Movements, Conflict and Change 6 (1984):57–94.

4. Milton M. Gordon, *Assimilation in American Life* (New York: Oxford University Press, 1964):27.

5. Robert A. Dahl, *Who Governs? Democracy and Power in an American City* (New Haven, Connecticut: Yale University Press, 1973).

6. Nathan Glazer and Daniel P. Moynihan, *Beyond the Melting Pot* (Cambridge, Massachusetts: MIT Press, 1986):17.

7. Chandler Davidson, editor, *Minority Vote Dilution* (Washington D.C.: Howard University Press, 1984).

8. Judy Chu, March 9, 1991. Testimony delivered in Los Angeles to the California Senate Committee on Elections and Reapportionment.

9. Leland Saito, June 28, 1991. Testimony delivered in Los Angeles to the California Assembly Committee on Elections, Reapportionment and Constitutional Amendments.

10. Ong.

11. Chu, March 9, 1991.

12. Don Nakanishi, "The Next Swing Vote? Asian Pacific Americans and California Politics" in Byran O. Jackson and Michael B. Preston, eds. *Racial and Ethnic Politics in California* (Berkeley: IGS Press, 1991).

13. Jose Z. Calderon, "Mexican American Politics in a Multi-Ethnic Community: The Case of Monterey Park: 1985–1990." Ph.D. dissertation, UCLA, 1991.

14. Statement of a member of the Los Angeles Asian American Coalition during a meeting in Los Angeles on May 24, 1991.

15. Nakanishi, 47.

16. Nakanishi, 47.

17. Statement of a member of the San Gabriel Valley Latino Coalition during a meeting between the Valley groups on August 8, 1991.

18. Statement of a member of the San Gabriel Valley Asian American Coalition during a meeting between Valley groups on August 8, 1991.

19. Discussion during a San Gabriel Valley Asian American Coalition meeting on July 30, 1991.

20. A member of the Latino California state coalition during a meeting with the California state Asian American coalition on June 26, 1991, in Los Angeles.

21. A member of the San Gabriel Valley Asian American coalition during a meeting on June 27, 1992.

22. Discussion during meeting between the Asian American and Latino San Gabriel Valley coalitions on August 8, 1991.

23. Leland T. Saito, "Politics in a New Demographic Era: Asian Americans in Monterey Park, California." Ph.D. dissertation, UCLA, 1992.

24. ———, "Japanese Americans and the New Chinese Immigrants: The Politics of Adaptation," *California Sociologist* 12 (1989):195–211. Leland T. Saito and John Horton, "The Chinese Immigration and the Rise of Asian American Politics in Monterey Park, California" in Edna

Bonacich, Paul Ong, and Lucie Cheng, eds. *Struggles for a Place: The New Asian Immigration in the Restructuring Political Economy* (Philadelphia: Temple University Press, 1993).

25. Yen Le Espiritu, *Asian American Panethnicity: Bridging Institutions and Identities* (Philadelphia: Temple University Press, 1992).

P.R. Elections in N.Y.C.: Effects of Preference Voting on Asian American Participation

Tito Sinha

On May 4, 1993, New York City voters cast their ballots in Community School Board elections, which use the single-transferable vote (STV) to elect 32 school boards of nine members each in at-large races.

STV is a form of proportional representation whereby voters list candidates on their ballots in order of preference, with their ballots going to the highest-ranked candidate who can be helped by their votes. Candidates win by obtaining a certain "threshold," which is roughly equal to one-ninth of the electorate in each of the 32 at-large races. Winning candidates thus represent a "constituency" about the size of what a single-member district would be if that system were used.

In the vote count, "surplus" ballots are transferred to remaining candidates both from winning candidates who obtain this threshold (surplus ballots being those beyond the threshold) and from losing candidates who have the least number of first-choice votes. These ballots are transferred according to how voters rank their preferences, with the process continuing until nine candidates have reached the threshold or only nine candidates remain.

The 1993 school board elections were significantly different from past elections for two reasons: A larger number of candidates ran and voter turnout increased dramatically. This increased interest was prompted in large part by debate over the "Children of the Rainbow" curriculum, which prescribes multi-cultural instruction at the elementary school level. Competing coalitions formed to endorse slates of candidates who would support their positions.

With Asian Americans under-represented on New York City's school boards—as they are on all of the city's elected bodies—the Asian American Legal Defense and Education Fund (AALDEF), a New York City-based civil rights organization, undertook to study how the use of P.R. affected Asian American candidates and voters in the 1993 elections.

Overall, seven of the 11 candidates identified as Asian American won seats. AALDEF was most interested in those candidates who ran in districts with a concentration of Asian American residents. This report focuses on two such districts in the Borough of Queens, Districts 24 and 25.

STV AND ASIAN AMERICANS

Thirteen percent of the voting-age population of District 24 is Asian American. The Asian American candidates in District 24 were Louisa Chan and Margaret Pan-Loo, both Chinese Americans, and Daok Lee Pak, a Korean American. Chan ran on a slate with three non-Asians and eventually won with the transfer of ballots from other Asian candidates and from other candidates on her slate. The two other Asian candidates running in the district—Margaret Pan-Loo and Daok Lee Pak—were not elected.

According to the tallies of first choices from the Board of Elections, Chan, Pak and Pan-Loo each received comparable amounts of first-choice votes after the first count: Chan received 634, Pak 613 and Pan-Loo 628. Yet, only Chan was able to accumulate enough votes—the winning threshold

Source: National Civic Review (Winter-Spring 1994): 80–83. Reprinted by permission. Copyright © 1994 National Civic League Press. All rights reserved.

was 1,662—through subsequent transfer of ballots from other non-Asian candidates on her slate after those candidates had either been elected or defeated.

Even though Chan ran on another slate, she was the next-choice candidate on many of Pak's and Pan-Loo's ballots when they were defeated. Pak and Pan-Loo ran together on the same slate—on Pak's slate, they were the only candidates. Consequently, when Pak was defeated in the 13th round of ballot transfers, Pan-Loo received 127 of Pak's 646 ballots. But Chan also benefited by receiving 128 of Pak's ballots. The fact that Chan ran on a separate slate from Pak and Pan-Loo, yet received as many second-choice votes as Pan-Loo among Pak's 646 votes, demonstrates that Pak's supporters did not vote exclusively according to the slates promoted by the candidates.

Similarly, when Pan-Loo was defeated in the 17th round and her ballots were distributed, Chan received more of her transfer ballots than any other candidate. Thus, despite differences of ethnic identity and slate affiliation among the Asian American candidates, a considerable segment of voters who selected one Asian candidate as their first choice chose the other Asian candidates as their second and third choices.

Asian candidates also received ballots from non-Asian candidates who were not on their slate, but shared similar ideological positions. For example, Chan received a significant number of votes from Patricia Hayes, who was not on her slate but who also supported the "Children of the Rainbow" curriculum. When Hayes was defeated in the 14th round, Chan received more of her 664 ballots than any other candidate.

In District 25, where 12 percent of the voting-age population is Asian American, the Asian candidates were Pauline Chu, a Chinese American and Han Young Lee, a Korean American. Entering the election, both Chu and Lee had served two terms, but Chu was re-elected

and Lee defeated in the last round of ballot transfers.

The results from District 25 indicate a pattern of voting for Asian American candidates similar to the results from District 24. In District 25, Chu was able to accumulate enough first-choice ballots to meet the threshold necessary to win before there were any transfers from defeated candidates. Han Young Lee received 74 of her 323 surplus ballots—more than any other candidate—even though she was not the second-choice candidate on Chu's slate.

The District 25 results demonstrate that, as in District 24, Asian American candidates were the primary recipients of ballots transferred from other Asian American candidates, which indicates that there is a solid voter base that prefers to elect Asian Americans over other candidates. It is highly likely that voters with these preferences are Asian Americans.

One explanation for Lee's inability to make the winning threshold in 1993 was the greater number of candidates running and the increased voter turnout attracted by the "Children of the Rainbow" controversy. The greater number of candidates resulted in a higher winning threshold; whereas Lee was able to win in previous years with 500 or 600 votes, in 1993 she needed 1,373. As a result, the role of transfer ballots became more critical, since they could have elevated Lee's vote total to the threshold.

According to Lee, there were more Korean voters in the 1993 election, which should have helped her. But the combination of a larger threshold and the support of conservative candidates by Korean Christians and Korean conservatives may have diluted Lee's support from this traditional voter base.

The impact of P.R. in electing Asian Americans in District 25 was critically different from that in District 24. Preferential voting clearly facilitated the election of Louisa Chan in District 24. She won because a good portion of ballots from the other Asian candidates transferred to her. In the more conventional winner-takes-all system of voting, the vote of those preferring Asian candidates would have been split among the three Asian candidates and likely been "wasted."

While working more closely with other Asian American candidates can help increase the number of transfer ballots Asian American candidates receive from each other as well as solidify a critical base of Asian American voters, the results from Districts 24 and 25 show that the transferred ballots received by Asian Americans from Asian Americans are by themselves not always enough to make the winning threshold. In District 25, even if Lee had received all of Chu's 323 transfer ballots, she still would have fallen 153 votes short of the threshold. In District 24, working with non-Asian candidates enabled Chan to receive the transfer ballots she needed to win.

CONCLUSION

Asian Americans in New York City must better anticipate how critical election issues such as the multi-cultural school curriculum debate will affect voter turnout and, in particular, the pattern of Asian American voting. If the current system is preserved, Asian American candidates who do not have voter bases large enough to be elected on the first count need to build coalitions with each other *and* non-Asian candidates so that they will increase their opportunities for receiving the transfer ballots needed to win.

Perhaps more importantly, we may assume that the coalitions formed for purposes of campaigning will persist long after election day. This raises some hope that policy making will become a less factious, polarized and alienating process.

Reading 35

Foreign Money Is No Friend of Ours

Ling-chi Wang

Not since the anti-Chinese movement of the second half of the 19th century have the Chinese been the focus of more national political controversy and attention in the U.S. than in the past two weeks. At the center of the controversy are millions of dollars in alleged illegal political contributions made by foreign Asians to both the Clinton re-election campaign and the Democratic National Committee (DNC). Among the major contributors are those made by people affiliated with the Chinese Indonesian billionaire Mochtar Riady ($450,000), a South Korean company ($250,000), and the Hacienda Heights Buddhist Temple ($140,000). But the most sensational of all is a reported promise of $15 million by Taiwan's ruling party, Kuomintang, in an attempt to influence U.S. policy toward Taiwan. According to the *Yazhou Zhoukan*, a weekly news magazine published in Hong Kong, powerful Kuomintang official Liu Tai-ying made the offer in a secret meeting with Clinton's former White House assistant, businessman, and DNC fundraiser Mark Middleton in August last year in Taiwan. According to one story, as an assurance to Liu, Middleton bragged about his influence in the Clinton administration, "I am a window to the White House."

In the eye of the election-year political storm is Chinese American John Huang, former vice chair of the Finance Committee of the DNC. According to reports in the *Wall Street Journal, New York Times, Washington Post, Los Angeles Times* and *Newsweek*, Huang has been active in raising millions from foreign sources even though his declared intention was to raise money to help empower Asian Americans.

Source: AsianWeek, November 8, 1996, p. 7. Reprinted by permission.

Since the disclosure, Republican presidential candidate Bob Dole and the national press have been making repeated allegations of political corruption against President Clinton and the DNC. To contain the political damage, John Huang resigned and made himself inaccessible for more than a week before returning to Washington last week.

At the same time, several liberal Asian American leaders and organizations have sounded off on the subject of John Huang. They charged that Huang has been unfairly singled out for influence peddling by a racist media and the Republican Party. Four press conferences were held on Oct. 21 and 22 in four different cities by Asian Pacific American leaders "to object to the unfair portrayal of political contributions from *our* community." By making such an accusation, they seem to suggest that John Huang is a victim of racism and that he should be defended as a symbol of the growing financial clout of Asian Americans and their efforts to empower themselves.

As an Asian American active in advancing Asian American civil and political rights in the past 30 years, I am not so sure.

Without doubt, Mr. Huang has raised big bucks; but most of what he raised appears to have come from questionable foreign sources with intentions quite contrary to his stated objective of empowering Asian Americans. For example, Indonesian politicians have publicly praised the Riadys for advancing the interests of Indonesia with their huge contributions. And Taiwan's sole interest since 1949 is to cause conflict between the U.S. and China and to drag the U.S. into the dispute between China and Taiwan.

From my vantage, not only has Huang's work in no way benefitted Asian Americans, it has contributed to a new moneyed politics that corrupts American democracy and rips off Asian American communities—i.e., using Asian Americans as a shelter for advancing foreign interests. In fact, he has single-handedly undone Asian American efforts since the late 1960s to rid themselves of the stereotype of Asian Americans as "foreigners."

I am not oblivious to the anti-Asian racist sentiments fueling the feeding frenzy over the John Huang affair. Huang's activities are emblematic of what big fundraisers in both Republican and Democratic parties have long been doing. Yet the contributions he's raised are peanuts compared with the funds amassed by his counterparts working for foreign firms—let alone from our Western allies such as Canada, Australia, Mexico, Israel, Britain, Japan, Taiwan, and Korea. (Some of us may remember the machinations of the old pro-Taiwan "China Lobby" in the 1950s and '60s when funds, before the Watergate scandal, were used openly to prevent the U.S. from normalizing relations with China and to prevent China from being admitted into the United Nations. We certainly have not forgotten the Tongsun Park and Sun Myung Moon scandal, the so-called "gifts of deceit" in the 1970s.)

What is different this year is that for the first time Chinese and Asian Americans are getting significantly involved in major-league politics. At the same time, the public class wouldn't be scapegoating John Huang and the Indonesian Chinese connection if it thought Asian Americans had the political juice to defend themselves. Imagine what Jewish Americans would do if similar questions were leveled at one of the major Jewish fundraisers lobbying for U.S. aid to Israel!

This evident anti-Asian racism should not, however, excuse us Asian Americans from taking a careful look at what kind of money is being raised and for what purposes. There is no indication that the big foreign contributors have any interest whatsoever in the concerns and welfare of Asian Americans. For this reason alone, we need to draw a sharp line between those who have a

genuine concern for empowering Asian America in contrast with those who just want to buy influence in high places.

Unfortunately, it is the latter Johnny-come-latelys whose influences seem to be growing by leaps and bounds. Yet they have neither knowledge nor interest in Asian American community concerns. Indonesian businessman Bambang Trihatmokjo and President Suharto's second son said it all in connection with the Riady contributions in the *Strait Times* (Singapore) last week: "I feel that if we look at it from the perspective of its benefit to us, we have a lobbyist who is close to the No. 1 man in the United States."

These opportunists look to milk the genuine Asian American empowerment movement for their own political and business mileage, often seducing well-intentioned but naive activists into jumping onto their lucrative bandwagons. Some Asian Americans anxious to gain access to power most likely think there is nothing wrong with hitching a free ride. Yes, the political corruption in the mainstream has also reached the budding Asian American movement.

This is why I have not been actively involved in political activities, as apposed to community activities, in the last eight years. It occurs to me that the original vision of the Asian American movement—activating ordinary Asian Americans to identify and promote their immediate community interests and well beings—has been pushed aside in favor of transnational moneyed politics in which opportunists buy instant recognition and influence with cold, hard cash. Worse yet, they did it in the name of Asian Americans, but for quite different purposes. This is nothing short of adding insult to injury.

Since money has become the lifeline of American democracy and politicians are always hungry for cash, some Asian Americans go along with these opportunists, pretending they are responding to grassroots concerns. But the opportunists could care less about the community. John Huang himself has never, to my knowledge, identified himself actively and in a sustained manner with any community causes, from immigration to welfare, anti-Asian violence to affirmative action. He is more interested in buying influence for his clients, both domestic and foreign. The only thing that distinguishes him in this regard from other influence peddlers in Washington is his race, his indiscretion or arrogance, and his perceived political vulnerability.

I know John Huang is a victim of racism. But given his involvement in the corrupt system of moneyed politics, I have no sympathy for him. Nor do I feel obligated as an Asian American to defend him in the name of our community. Instead of feeling sorry for John Huang and depicting him as a victim of Republican and media racism, Asian Americans should be angry with him and denounce him for using Asian Americans as a cover to channel foreign money for purposes other than advancing the rights and welfare of Asian Americans, and for contributing to the restoration of Asian Americans as "foreigners" again.

Asian Americans Under Glass: Where the Furor Over the President's Fundraising Has Gone Awry—and Racist

Phil Tajitsu Nash and Frank Wu

As revelations of suspect campaign contributions emerge almost daily—lately, F.B.I. warnings of possible Chinese influence, and a $50,000 donation taken at the White House by Hillary Rodham Clinton's chief of staff—the Democratic National Committee has gone on the offensive, taking an inexcusable guilt-by-association approach. With the announcement that after auditing its contributions from the last election cycle it would refund approximately another $1.5 million in donations, the D.N.C. also confirmed that it had been making telephone calls to its Asian-American supporters to ask whether they were citizens; how much money they earned; who employed them; and whether they would authorize the party to obtain a credit report on them.

Responding to the controversy surrounding former D.N.C. official John Huang, the party hired accountants and lawyers to conduct a review of seven categories of funding sources, but focused five of them racially on Asian Americans—for example, "contributions made in connection with any DNC fund-raising event targeting the Asian Pacific American community."

D.N.C. general chairman Roy Romer, governor of Colorado, faced a barrage of questions about the campaign finance fiasco. But he answered only a few inquiries about the racialization of the controversy. He tried to make amends by saying, "Callers were not properly trained. . . . To every member of the Asian-American community, we . . . very much want to heal any of the

pain and wounds that have been caused by that." He added, however, "We had to do it."

Unfortunately, Romer's explanation is hardly persuasive. The party's callers did exactly what they were told to do: The D.N.C. released its script, which showed the exact wording of questions about citizenship, along with tips such as employing female interviewers on the premise that they would be less threatening, and avoiding leaving messages that would reveal the purpose of the call. In any event, the questions aimed at Asian Americans reflect the same stereotyping that has portrayed all Asian-derived people as foreigners, even if they are fifth-generation Californians.

The interrogation of Asian Americans focused mainly on innocent people, of course. According to the D.N.C.'s own figures, Huang solicited 424 contributions, and eighty-eight are in the process of being returned. So 336, or approximately 80 percent, were legitimate and appropriate. Singling out which funds to return should have been determined by using a nonracial category, such as one targeting donors who gave more than $10,000.

The initial D.N.C. review covered only donors who gave more than $2,500; another review will include those who gave less. As Bob Sakaniwa, Washington representative of the Japanese American Citizens League, observed, "That's even more troubling, because those are probably rank-and-file people in the party who wanted to help out." The major media outlets didn't bother to ask about the racial angle to the audit, perhaps because they have helped generate the frenzy over foreign influence—thus neglecting the real issue

Source: The Nation 264:12 (March 31, 1997): 15–16. Reprinted by permission.

of campaign finance reform. Phrases like The American Spectator's "Bamboo Network" or William Safire's favorite, "The Asian Connection," perpetuate the stereotyping that formerly brought us the "Yellow Peril" and the "Asiatic Hordes."

As Congress irons out committee funding and structure to carry out its own investigations of the money connections in the presidential election, it is imperative that the focus remain on influence-buying as an issue, without assuming that this is a problem to which people of Asian descent are almost genetically predisposed. Huang's case has overtones of the Koreagate scandal, in which four Democratic Representatives were reprimanded in 1978 for accepting bribes from Tongsun Park, a foreign businessman. Then, as now, some people believed that the influence of big money over our representative democracy could be ameliorated by blaming foreigners while merely tinkering with campaign finance reform. To further compound the insult, on January 21 the D.N.C. announced it would no longer accept legal contributions from noncitizen permanent residents, who pay taxes and are by law entitled to take part in the political process. Senator Dianne Feinstein has done the same and, after F.B.I. warnings, said she became "very cautious" about Asian American contributions.

Donations connected to foreign sources have accounted for only a tiny percent of the hundreds of millions of dollars in "soft money" delivered to the parties, the sluiceway that is the real scandal. Yes, former Clinton aide Webster Hubbell has been linked to payments originating from Indonesia's Riady family (for whom Huang worked before joining the U.S. government), and the funds accepted on White House premises by the First Lady's aide came from a California businessman of Asian descent. Yet liberals and conservatives alike have taken to framing the campaign finance scandal as a cover-up by using Asian-Americans as a "race card." The problem with this is that it conflates two issues. The first is a justifiable concern about campaign finance

fraud; the second is an unjustifiable tarring of Asian-Americans. Defending Huang and the very American system of which he is a part is different from objecting to racial assumptions bound up in the investigation.

Given its own activities, the D.N.C. may well be using the race card to deflect attention from itself. But it is equally true that Asian-Americans are facing real racial stereotyping as they attempt to participate in the electoral process. On the campaign trail last fall, would-be-populist billionaire Ross Perot recited the names of Asian American campaign contributors in a November 3 speech at the University of Pennsylvania and then declared, "So far, we haven't found an American name." He asked rhetorically whether the audience wouldn't rather have someone named "O'Reilly" instead of "Huang" working for them. Later, citing Mark Middleton and James Wood, two other Americans linked to allegations of illegal campaign fundraising by the D.N.C. in Taiwan, Perot said, "Now that's two names you can relate to." Many major media outlets reported Perot climbing in the polls as he began condemning campaign finance problems in this way, but none saw fit to print his actual remarks. The racialization of the controversy thus continued without acknowledgment.

For the vast majority of Asian Americans who had never heard of John Huang before the scandal broke in the press—or Little Rock restaurateur Charles Yah Lin Trie, or California engineer Johnny Chung, apparently connected to each other only in that they gave large sums of money now being returned by the Democratic Party—it's been a harsh lesson in U.S. politics. "This is the classic example of throwing the baby out with the bath water," says consumer advocate Professor Carol Izumi of George Washington University Law School. "It doesn't address the problem of Asian corporate influence, and further isolates Asian-Americans, who were just coming into their own politically."

Indeed, for most Asian Americans, before the Huang scandal broke, the real story of Campaign

'96 was decidedly upbeat. For the first time, national Asian-American organizations worked together to mobilize voter registration campaigns in New York, Los Angeles and other cities. Washington State voters elected a second-generation Chinese-American governor, Gary Locke. Most important for the future, many thousands of Asian-Americans ran for office, made small campaign contributions or worked as campaign staff for Republican, Democratic and independent candidates. All this from a community that is two-thirds immigrant and that has been criticized for its apathy toward public life.

Asian-Americans constitute about 3 percent of the U.S. population, but the percentages are far higher in key electoral states like California and major cities like New York, Los Angeles and San Francisco. With Clinton winning more than 60 percent of the Asian-American vote, according to some exit polls, and Republicans now backing away from the harshest measures aimed at legal immigrants, their political muscle was beginning to be felt.

Luckily, a group of Asian-Americans with an understanding of history has started to guide public outrage about electoral infractions back to the main issue and away from John Huang's name. Led by Professor Ling-chi Wang at the University of California, Berkeley, Asian-Americans for Campaign Finance Reform calls for a full airing of the complaints against Huang in an impartial hearing; appointment of a special prosecutor; real and substantial campaign finance reform; and a climate that does not play up racial tensions. Campaign finance reform can come in many guises, but at the least it must protect the right of every individual to participate in politics and government.

Ultimately, Huang, the Riadys, the D.N.C. and others under suspicion deserve to be presumed innocent and given a fair hearing. The American people deserve a campaign financing system that does not favor large, multinational corporate donors over small, community-based sources. And all of us deserve political and media leaders who will denounce race-based guilt by association whenever it appears.

S.F. Rally Spotlights Kao Killing

Bert Eljera

Ayling Wu's face contorts in anguish each time she recalls the April 29 shooting-death of her husband at the hands of a Rohnert Park public-safety officer—a tragedy Wu feels she could have prevented had she been more assertive. In her first interview following the death of her husband, Kuanchung Kao, Wu said that sometimes she blames herself for not doing enough and allowing her respect for authority to get the better of her.

"I could have taken the stick away," Wu said, referring to the stick her husband was holding that prompted Public Safety Officer Jack Shields to shoot him, when he refused to drop it. "There was no danger to anybody. I don't know why they had to shoot him." Wu said she moved away from her husband when Shields shouted at her to back off. Then, after Kao was shot in the chest, she attempted to give him first aid, being a nurse herself. Again, instead of insisting, she followed police orders not to get near the body, she said. For several hours, Kao's body lay by their driveway while a female police officer watched her inside their house, Wu said. Her 6-year-old daughter, Karolyn, saw the body. "The police are serial killers," the girl said to her, according to Wu.

"It's so hard," she said. "I'm taking it one day at a time. I have to be strong for my kids." There are two other children of Kao and Wu—twin boys Kyle and Kallen, nearly 2 years old. The family has lived in Rohner Park for the past seven years.

The tragedy ended the Kaos' pursuit of a better life in the United States, having emigrated from Taiwan in 1989 with hopes of earning a college degree, getting good jobs, and raising a family in America.

Kao graduated with a degree in genetic engineering from South Dakota University in 1989, and then moved to Rohnert Park to be close to his studies at Sonoma State University, where he earned his degree in microbiology in 1993. Six months after Kao moved to Rohnert Park, Wu arrived from Taiwan, and the couple found a home at Maria Place, a middle-class neighborhood of single-family homes.

At the time of his death, Kao, 33, was a quality-control manager at Genesis Technology in Hayward. Wu is the director of nursing at the Alzheimer's Center in Petaluma. She is now back at work. But Wu said the death of her husband has left her with few options. "I can't afford to move right now," she said. "Even if I love to, I can't," because of financial reasons. Her sister is staying with her and her children right now, but she is expected to go back to Taiwan next month, she said. The support from the Asian Pacific American community helps her to get going, Wu said. "My children also keep me going. They deserve a future, but I'm not sure I can give them that future," she said.

According to the Sheriff's Department investigation, and an independent inquiry by the Asian Law Caucus, a co-counsel for the Kao family, Kao's misfortunes on that fateful night did not begin at his residence. He went to a Cotati bar just outside Rohnert Park, to meet a friend with whom he was discussing the possibility of starting a business. A familiar face at the bar, Kao stayed there for about seven hours and got drunk. Police later said his alcohol level was 0.23, three times the legal limit.

Source: AsianWeek, August 22, 1997, pp. 12–13. Reprinted by permission.

While at the bar, a group of individuals, who police did not identify, started taunting Kao, who became enraged. Several scuffles ensued, and at one point, he was stabbed above an eye with a dart.

When police offers responded, Kao demanded that they arrest those who had provoked him. Seeing that he was very drunk, police instead put him in a taxicab, which took him home at about 2 a.m. After he was dropped off at his house; Kao began screaming in the middle of the street, yelling, "Neighbors, please help me." He removed his shirt, and knelt in the middle of the street, crying for help.

Several neighbors called the police and reported that a man was screaming and acting crazy. Wu tried to get her husband to come inside the house, but he refused. It was at this point that Shields and another public-safety officer, Mike Lynch, responded to the calls. What transpired after that—and Kao's shooting—will become the subject of a lawsuit the Kao family is planning to file against the Rohner Park police.

The key issue: Did Officer Shields use excessive force against Kao?

An investigation by both the Sonoma County Sheriff's Department and the Rohnert Park Office of Public Safety found Shields not guilty of any wrongdoing. In a 600-page report, the Sheriff's Department concluded that Shields shot Kao out of fear that his life was in danger. The Rohnert Park police said the officer also followed proper police procedure in handling the situation. Sonoma County District Attorney Michael Mullins decided in June not to press charges against Shields.

But John Burris, who was a co-counsel in Rodney King's civil suit against the Los Angeles Police Department and now represents the Kao family, said the police "forced a confrontation."

"They forced the action when they could have easily backed off, bide their time, and call for backup," Burris said. "He [Shields] created the environment that forced him to shoot." Burris said he has six months from the April incident to file the case. "We have to make sure we're on solid ground," he said.

The case has outraged the Asian Pacific American community, and a rally held Saturday was the latest in a series of events intended to focus public attention on the need for a more thorough investigation, possibly by the Justice Department and the U.S. Commission on Civil Rights. "If they [authorities] think we're invisible, if we do not speak out, they will do nothing," said Supervisor Mabel Teng, one of the dozens of speakers at the rally at Union Square in San Francisco, which was attended by about 300 people, mostly Chinese Americans from the Bay Area. "We have to mobilize our community."

Teng drew parallels between the Kao shooting and the slaying of Vincent Chin, who was killed 15 years ago by two Detroit autoworkers who mistook him for being Japanese. Although they admitted to the killing, neither spent time in jail. Both incidents involved Chinese Americans, and both may have been killed because of their ethnicity. In the case of Kao, his being Chinese may have been the reason Rohnert Park police assumed he was a martial-arts expert, and therefore dangerous with a stick, Teng said.

"The Vincent Chin case changed my life forever," said Teng, who abandoned plans to become a doctor, and instead became a community activist and politician. "In Vincent Chin, we were looking for justice," said Les Hata, dentist from Oakland and member of the San Francisco chapter of the Japanese American Citizens League. "There needs to be justice for the Kao family. The case needs further exploration."

Felicia Sze, a graduate student at UCLA, said every Asian American should be involved in the case. "You cannot say this is an isolated case, and that it happened once," she said. "It's wrong that it happened in the first place, but we have to make sure that it does not happen again."

Wu sobbed uncontrollably when asked how her children are taking the death of their father. She said her daughter told her about a dream last week. "She said she saw her father standing by her bedside and praying for her," Wu said.

CHAPTER 10

Future Directions in Asian American Studies

No one can predict the future. However, it is clear that the future of Asian America is centered on the issue of its diversity. At the onset of Asian American movement in the late 1960s, Asian American activists downplayed differences between Asian American ethnic groups in favor of political unity. As we enter the beginning of a new millennium, the Asian American experience has expanded to include new voices and new perspectives. Unity without diversity results in an inability to adapt to changing historical conditions. At the same time, acknowledging Asian American diversity without recognizing the need for social and political unity is a native and ahistorical stance. It is clear that unity cannot be forged by ignoring differences; the presumption of "sameness" is dangerous, whether imposed externally by society or perpetuated internally. Unity comes only with embracing differences in the particulars, affirming the broader issues that diverse people have in common. This chapter features articles that offer a theoretical challenge to the dominant ideology that concentrates on uncritically categorizing groups and experiences into arbitrary and distinct parts.

Lisa Lowe was one of the first to analyze the importance of recognizing diversity within the Asian American experience. Drawing examples from poetry, novels, and film to highlight what she calls heterogeneity, hybridity, and multiplicity of the Asian American experience, Lowe directly challenges the "dominant" versus "minority" discourse over who and what is Asian American. The dominant society's insistence on Asian American homogeneity has historically led to violence and the exclusion of "yellow peril" Asian immigrants, as well as quotas against "model minority" Asian American students. However, while Lowe recognizes the need for various Asian American groups to unify to resist discrimination, this should not be done at the expense of denying important intragroup differences such as class, gender, and national differences. Her article focuses on the need to look at identity and culture as fluid and dynamic, rather than as fixed and stagnant, phenomena. This seemingly obvious concept has frequently been lost during periods of intense social conflict and political hegemony.

Keith Osajima takes Lowe's arguments to another level, forwarding the notion of "oppositional" postmodernism, which utilizes the postmodernist insights from the Lowe article but maintains the progressive "emancipatory" vision central to the beginnings of the Asian American studies movement of the 1960s. Osajima cites Lowe's use of "strategic essentialism" to acknowledge that there are times when political unity among various Asian Americans is absolutely imperative, but he also recognizes the need for Asian Americans to work beyond the narrow self-interests of the group to develop a broader and stronger sense of social justice. Osajima's insights harken back to Ronald Takaki's position regarding the strength that comes with recognizing both "particularism" and "pluralism" to understand the significance of cultural change within groups and society (Chapter 4).

Sau-Ling Wong's work is similar to Osajima's in that it critiques a popular theoretical position and attempts to reposition it in a more progressive emancipatory stance consistent with the founding ideas of the Asian American movement. Wong describes the theoretical trend in Asian American studies toward what she calls "denationalization," that has brought forth an easing of cultural nationalist concerns and increasing permeability between "Asian" and "Asian American," as well as a shift from the domestic perspective to one that is diasporic. While these global perspectives are appealing and analytically useful, Wong is concerned that theoretical ideas may lose sight of the social, economic, and political challenges confronted by Asian Americans today. She, like Osajima, does not want to forget the founding principles of ethnic studies and Asian American studies, amid the rush to embrace "denationalism."

Lastly, Dana Takagi addresses the important and timely issue of Asian American sexuality. She argues that anyone interested and involved in Asian American studies needs to be thinking about sexuality for two main reasons. First it offers another element to the broader discussion of diversity among Asian Americans. Second, recognizing Asian American sexuality helps to better understand the distinctions and intersections between sexual and racial identity. Takagi recognizes that sexual identity among Asian Americans has been kept silent, for the most part, under the more dominant concept of racial identity. "Breaking the silence" is a term often used by Asian American activists to speak up against racial injustice. Takagi believes the term should confront homophobia and self-censorship within Asian American communities as well.

Heterogeneity, Hybridity, Multiplicity: Marking Asian American Differences

Lisa Lowe

In a recent poem by Janice Mirikitani, a Japanese-American *nisei* woman describes her *sansei* daughter's rebellion.[1] The daughter's denial of Japanese-American culture and its particular notions of femininity reminds the *nisei* speaker that she, too, has denied her antecedents, rebelling against her own more traditional *issei* mother:

> I want to break tradition—unlock this room
> where women dress in the dark.
> Discover the lies my mother told me.
> The lies that we are small and powerless
> that our possibilities must be compressed
> to the size of pearls, displayed only as
> passive chokers, charms around our neck.
> Break Tradition.
> I want to tell my daughter of this room
> of myself
> filled with tears of shakuhatchi,
>
> .   .   .   .
>
> poems about madness,
> sounds shaken from barbed wire and
> goodbyes and miracles of survival.
> This room of open window where daring ones
>   escape.
> My daughter denies she is like me . . .
> her pouting ruby lips, her skirts
> swaying to salsa, teena marie and the stones,
> her thighs displayed in carnivals of color.
> I do not know the contents of her room.
> She mirrors my aging.
> She is breaking tradition. (9)

The *nisei* speaker repudiates the repressive confinements of her *issei* mother: the disciplining of

Source: *Diaspora* 1:1 (1991): 24–44. Reprinted by permission of University of Toronto Press Incorporated.

the female body, the tedious practice of diminution, the silences of obedience. In turn, the crises that have shaped the *nisei* speaker—internment camps, sounds of threatening madness—are unknown to, and unheard by, her *sansei* teenage daughter. The three generations of Japanese immigrant women in this poem are separated by their different histories and by different conceptions of what it means to be female and Japanese. The poet who writes "I do not know the contents of her room" registers these separations as "breaking tradition."

In another poem, by Lydia Lowe, Chinese women workers are divided also by generation, but even more powerfully by class and language. The speaker is a young Chinese-American who supervises an older Chinese woman in a textile factory.

> The long bell blared,
> and then the *lo-ban*
> made me search all your bags
> before you could leave.
>
> Inside he sighed
> about slow work, fast hands,
> missing spools of thread—
> and I said nothing.
>
> I remember that day
> you came in to show me
> I added your tickets six zippers short.
> It was just a mistake.
>
> You squinted down
> at the check in your hands
> like an old village woman peers
> at some magician's trick.

That afternoon
when you thrust me your bags
I couldn't look or raise my face.
Doi m-jyu.

Eyes on the ground,
I could only see
one shoe kicking against the other. (29)

This poem, too, invokes the breaking of tradition, although it thematizes another sort of stratification among Asian women: the structure of the factory places the English-speaking younger woman above the Cantonese-speaking older one. Economic relations in capitalist society force the young supervisor to discipline her elders, and she is acutely ashamed that her required behavior does not demonstrate the respect traditionally owed to parents and elders. Thus, both poems foreground commonly thematized *topoi* of diasporan cultures: the disruption and distortion of traditional cultural practices—like the practice of parental sacrifice and filial duty, or the practice of respecting hierarchies of age—not only as a consequence of immigration to the United States, but as a part of entering a society with different class stratifications and different constructions of gender roles. Some Asian American discussions cast the disruption of tradition as loss and represent the loss in terms of regret and shame, as in the latter poem. Alternatively, the traditional practices of family continuity and hierarchy may be figured as oppressively confining, as in Mirikitani's poem, in which the two generations of daughters contest the more restrictive female roles of the former generations. In either case, many Asian American discussions portray immigration and relocation to the United States in terms of a loss of the "original" culture in exchange for the new "American" culture.

In many Asian American novels, the question of the loss or transmission of the "original" culture is frequently represented in a family narrative, figured as generational conflict between the Chinese-born first generation and the American-born second generation.[2] Louis Chu's 1961 novel *Eat a Bowl of Tea*, for example, allegorizes in the conflicted relationship between father and son the differences between "native" Chinese values and the new "westernized" culture of Chinese-Americans. Other novels have taken up this generational theme; one way to read Maxine Hong Kingston's *The Woman Warrior* (1975) or Amy Tan's . . . *The Joy Luck Club* (1989) is to understand them as versions of this generational model of culture, refigured in feminine terms, between mothers and daughters. However, I will argue that interpreting Asian American culture exclusively in terms of the master narratives of generational conflict and filial relation essentializes Asian American culture, obscuring the particularities and incommensurabilities of class, gender, and national diversities among Asians; the reduction of ethnic cultural politics to struggles between first and second generations displaces (and privatizes) inter-community differences into a familial opposition. To avoid this homogenizing of Asian Americans as exclusively hierarchical and familial, I would contextualize the "vertical" generational model of culture with the more "horizontal" relationship represented in Diana Chang's "The Oriental Contingent." In Chang's short story, two young women avoid the discussion of their Chinese backgrounds because each desperately fears that the other is "more Chinese," more "authentically" tied to the original culture. The narrator, Connie, is certain that her friend Lisa "never referred to her own background because it was more Chinese than Connie's, and therefore of a higher order. She was tact incarnate. All along, she had been going out of her way not to embarrass Connie. Yes, yes. Her assurance was definitely uppercrust (perhaps her father had been in the diplomatic service), and her offhand didacticness, her lack of self-doubt, was indeed characteristically Chinese-Chinese" (173). Connie feels ashamed because she assumes herself to be "a failed Chinese"; she fantasizes that Lisa was born in China, visits there frequently, and privately disdains Chinese-Americans. Her assumptions about Lisa prove to be quite wrong, however; Lisa is even more critical of herself for "not being genuine." For Lisa, as Connie eventually discovers, was born in Buffalo and was adopted by non-Chinese-American parents; lacking an immediate connection to Chinese culture, Lisa projects upon all Chinese the authority of being "more Chinese." Lisa confesses to Connie at the end of the story: "The only time I feel Chinese is when I'm embarrassed I'm not more Chinese—which is a totally Chinese reflex I'd give anything to be rid of!" (176). Chang's story portrays two women polarized by the degree to which they have each internalized a cultural definition of "Chineseness" as pure and fixed, in which any deviation is constructed as less, lower, and shameful. Rather than confirming the cultural model in which "ethnicity" is passed from generation to generation, Chang's story explores the "ethnic" relationship between women of the same generation. Lisa and Connie are ultimately able to reduce one another's guilt at not being "Chinese enough"; in one another they are able to find a common frame of reference. The story suggests that the making of Chinese-American culture—how ethnicity is imagined, practiced, continued—is worked out as much between ourselves and our communities as it is transmitted from one generation to another.

In this sense, Asian American discussions of ethnicity are far from uniform or consistent; rather, these discussions contain a wide spectrum of articulations that includes, at one end, the desire for an identity represented by a fixed profile of ethnic traits, and at another, challenges to the very notions of identity and singularity which celebrate ethnicity as a fluctuating composition of differences, intersections, and incommensurabilities. These latter efforts attempt to define ethnicity in a manner that accounts not only for cultural inheritance, but for active cultural construction, as well. In other words, they suggest that the making of Asian American culture may be a much "messier" process than unmediated vertical transmission from one generation to another, including practices that are partly inherited and partly modified, as well as partly invented.[3] As the narrator of *The Woman Warrior* suggests, perhaps one of the more important stories of Asian American experience is about the process of receiving, refiguring, and rewriting cultural traditions. She asks: "Chinese-Americans, when you try to understand what things in you are Chinese. how do you separate what is peculiar to childhood, to poverty, insanities, one family, your mother who marked your growing with stories, from what is Chinese? What is Chinese tradition and what is the movies?" (6). Or the dilemma of cultural syncretism might be posed in an interrogative version of the uncle's impromptu proverb in Wayne Wang's film *Dim Sum*: "You can take the girl out of Chinatown, but can you take the Chinatown out of the girl?" For rather than representing a fixed, discrete culture, "Chinatown" is itself the very emblem of fluctuating demographics, languages, and populations.[4]

I begin my article with these particular examples drawn from Asian American cultural texts in order to observe that what is referred to as "Asian America" is clearly a heterogeneous entity. From the perspective of the majority culture, Asian Americans may very well be constructed as different from, and other than, Euro-Americans. But from the perspectives of Asian Americans, we are perhaps even more different, more diverse, among ourselves: being men and women at different distances and generations from our "original" Asian cultures—cultures as different as Chinese, Japanese, Korean, Filipino, Indian, and Vietnamese—Asian Americans are born in the United States and born in Asia; of exclusively Asian parents and of mixed race; urban and rural; refugee and nonrefugee; communist-identified and anticommunist; fluent in English and non-English speaking: educated and working class. As with other diasporas in the United States, the Asian immigrant collectivity is unstable and changeable, with its cohesion complicated by intergenerationality, by various degrees of identification and relation to a "homeland," and by different extents of assimilation to and distinction from "majority culture" in the United States. Further, the historical contexts of particular waves of immigration within single groups contrast with one another; the Japanese-Americans who were interned during World War II encountered quite different social and economic barriers than those from Japan who arrive in southern California today. And the composition of different waves of immigrants differs in gender, class, and region. For example, the first groups of Chinese immigrants to the United States in 1850 were from four villages in Canton province, male by a ratio of 10 to 1, and largely of peasant backgrounds; the more recent Chinese immigrants are from Hong Kong, Taiwan, or the People's Republic (themselves quite heterogeneous and of discontinuous "origins"), or from the Chinese diaspora in other parts of Asia, such as Macao, Malaysia, or Singapore, and they are more often educated and middle-class men and women.[5] Further, once arriving in the United States, very few Asian immigrant cultures remain discrete, impenetrable communities. The more recent groups mix, in varying degrees, with segments of the existing groups; Asian Americans may intermarry with other ethnic groups, live in neighborhoods adjacent to them, or work in the same businesses and on the same factory assembly lines. The boundaries and definitions of Asian American culture are continually shifting and being contested from pressures both "inside" and "outside" the Asian origin community.

I stress heterogeneity, hybridity, and multiplicity in the characterization of Asian American culture as part of a twofold argument about cultural politics, the ultimate aim of that argument being to disrupt the current hegemonic relationship between "dominant" and "minority" positions. On the one hand, my observation that Asian Americans are heterogeneous is part of a strategy to destabilize the dominant discursive construction and determination of Asian Americans as a homogeneous group. Throughout the late nineteenth and early twentieth centuries, Asian immigration to the United States was managed by

exclusion acts and quotas that relied upon racialist constructions of Asians as homogeneous;[6] the "model minority" myth and the informal quotas discriminating against Asians in university admissions policies are contemporary versions of this homogenization of Asians.[7] On the other hand, I underscore Asian American heterogeneities (particularly class, gender, and national differences among Asians) to contribute to a dialogue within Asian American discourse, to negotiate with those modes of argumentation that continue to uphold a politics based on ethnic "identity." In this sense, I argue for the Asian American necessity—politically, intellectually, and personally—to organize, resist, and theorize *as* Asian Americans, but at the same time I inscribe this necessity within a discussion of the risks of a cultural politics that relies upon the construction of sameness and the exclusion of differences.

1

The first reason to emphasize the dynamic fluctuation and heterogeneity of Asian American culture is to release our understandings of either the "dominant" or the emergent "minority" cultures as discrete, fixed, or homogeneous, and to arrive at a different conception of the general political terrain of culture in California, a useful focus for this examination since it has become commonplace to consider it an "ethnic state," embodying a new phenomenon or cultural adjacency and admixture.[8] For if minority immigrant cultures are perpetually changing—in their composition, configuration, and signifying practices, as well as in their relations to one another—it follows that the "majority"' or dominant culture, with which minority cultures are in continual relation, is also unstable and unclosed. The suggestion that the general social terrain of culture is open, plural, and dynamic reorients our understanding of what "cultural hegemony" is and how it works in contemporary California. It permits us to theorize about the roles that ethnic immigrant groups play in the making and unmaking of culture—and how these minority discourses challenge the existing structure of power, the existing hegemony.[9] We should remember that Antonio Gramsci writes about *hegemony* as not simply political or economic forms of rule but as the entire process of dissent and compromise through which a particular group is able to determine the political, cultural, and ideological character of a state (*Selections*). Hegemony does not refer exclusively to the process by which a dominant formation exercises its influence but refers equally to the process through which minority groups organize and contest any specific hegemony.[10] The reality of any specific hegemony is that, while it may be for the moment dominant, it is never absolute or conclusive. Hegemony, in Gramsci's thought, is a concept that describes both the social processes through which a particular dominance is maintained and those through which that dominance is challenged and new forces are articulated. When a hegemony representing the interests of a dominant group exists, it is always within the context of resistances from emerging "subaltern" groups.[11] We might say that hegemony is not only the political process by which a particular group constitutes itself as "the one" or "the majority" in relation to which "minorities" are defined and know themselves to be "other," but it is equally the process by which positions of otherness may ally and constitute a new majority, a "counterhegemony."[12] . . .

2

In regard to the practice of "identity politics" within Asian American discourse, the articulation of an "Asian American identity" as an organizing tool has provided a concept of political unity that enables diverse Asian groups to understand our unequal circumstances and histories as being related; likewise, the building of "Asian American culture" is crucial, for it articulates and empowers our multicultural, multilingual Asian origin community vis-à-vis the institutions and apparatuses that exclude and marginalize us. But I want to suggest that essentializing Asian American identity and suppressing our differences—of national origin, generation, gender, party, class—risks particular dangers: not only does it underestimate the differences and hybridities among Asians, but it also inadvertently supports the racist discourse that constructs Asians as a homogeneous group, that implies we are "all alike" and conform to "types": in this respect, a politics based exclusively on ethnic identity willingly accepts the terms of the dominant logic that organizes the heterogeneous picture of racial and ethnic diversity into a binary schema of "the one" and "the other." The essentializing of Asian American identity also reproduces oppositions that subsume other nondominant terms in the same way that Asians and other groups are disenfranchised by the dominant culture: to the degree that the discourse generalizes Asian American identity as male, women are rendered invisible; or to the extent that Chinese are presumed to be exemplary of all Asians, the importance of other Asian groups is ignored. In this sense, a politics based on ethnic identity facilitates the displacement of intercommunity differences—between men and women, or between workers and managers—into a false opposition of "nationalism" and "assimilation." We have an example of this in recent debates where Asian American feminists who challenge Asian American sexism are cast as "assimilationist," as betraying Asian American "nationalism."

To the extent that Asian American discourse articulates an identity in reaction to the dominant culture's stereotype, even to refute it, I believe the discourse may remain bound to, and overdetermined by, the logic of the dominant culture. In accepting the binary terms ("white" and "non-white," or "majority" and "minority") that structure institutional policies about ethnicity, we forget that these binary schemas are not neutral descriptions. Binary constructions of difference use a logic that prioritizes the first term and subordinates the second; whether the pair "difference" and "sameness" is figured as a binary synthesis that considers "difference" as always contained within the "same," or that conceives of the pair as an opposition in which "difference" structurally implies "sameness" as its complement, it is important to see each of these figurations as versions of the same binary logic. My argument for heterogeneity seeks to challenge the conception of difference as exclusively structured by a binary opposition between two terms by proposing instead another notion of difference that takes seriously the conditions of heterogeneity, multiplicity, and nonequivalence. I submit that the most exclusive construction of Asian American identity—which presumes masculinity, American birth, and speaking English—is at odds with the formation of important political alliances and affiliations with other groups across racial and ethnic, gender, sexuality, and class lines. An essentialized identity is an obstacle to Asian American women allying with other women of color, for example, and it can discourage laboring Asian Americans from joining unions with workers of other colors. It can short-circuit potential alliances against the dominant structures of power in the name of subordinating "divisive" issues to *the* national question. . . .

3

As I have already suggested, within Asian American discourse there is a varied spectrum of discussion about the concepts of ethnic identity and culture. At one end, there are discussions in which ethnic identity is essentialized as the cornerstone of a nationalist liberation politics. In these discussions, the cultural positions of nationalism (or ethnicism, or nativism) and of assimilation are represented in polar opposition: nationalism affirming the separate purity of its ethnic culture is opposed to assimilation of the standards of dominant society. Stories about the

loss of the "native" Asian culture tend to express some form of this opposition. At the same time, there are criticisms of this essentializing position, most often articulated by feminists who charge that Asian American nationalism prioritizes masculinity and does not account for women. At the other end, there are interventions that refuse static or binary conceptions of ethnicity, replacing notions of identity with multiplicity and shifting the emphasis for ethnic "essence" to cultural hybridity. Settling for neither nativism nor assimilation, these cultural texts expose the apparent opposition between the two as a constructed figure (as Fanon does when he observes that bourgeois assimilation and bourgeois nationalism often conform to the same colonialist logic). In tracing these different discussions about identity and ethnicity through Asian American cultural debates, literature, and film, I choose particular texts because they are accessible and commonly held. But I do not intend to limit *discourse* to only these particular textual forms; by *discourse*, I intend a rather extended meaning—a network that includes not only texts and cultural documents, but social practices, formal and informal laws, policies or inclusion and exclusion, and institutional forms of organization, for example, all of which constitute and regulate knowledge about the object of that discourse, Asian America. . . .

Before concluding, I want to turn to a final cultural text which not only restates the Asian American narrative that opposes nativism and assimilation but articulates a critique of that narrative, calling the nativist/assimilationist dyad into question. If *Joy Luck* poses an alternative to the dichotomy of nativism and assimilation by multiplying the generational conflict and demystifying the centrality of the mother-daughter relationship, then Peter Wang's film *A Great Wall* (1985)—both in its emplotment and in its very medium of representation—offers yet another version of this alternative. Wang's film unsettles both poles in the antinomy of nativist essentialism and assimilation by performing a continual geographical juxtaposition and exchange between a variety of cultural spaces. *A Great Wall* portrays the visit of Leo Fang's Chinese-American family to the People's Republic of China and their month-long stay with Leo's sister's family, the Chao family, in Beijing. The film concentrates on the primary contrast between the habits, customs, and assumptions of the Chinese in China and the Chinese-Americans in California by going back and forth between shots of Beijing and Northern California, in a type of continual filmic "migration" between the two, as if to thematize in its very form the travel between cultural spaces. From the first scene, however, the film foregrounds the idea that in the opposition between native and assimilated spaces, neither begins as a pure, uncontaminated site or origin; and as the camera eye shuttles back and forth between, both poles of the constructed opposition shift and change. (Indeed, the Great Wall of China, from which the film takes its title, is a monument to the historical condition that not even ancient China was "pure," but co-existed with "foreign barbarians" against which the Middle Kingdom erected such barriers.) In this regard, the film contains a number of emblematic images that call attention to the syncretic, composite quality of all cultural spaces: when the young Chinese Liu finishes the university entrance exam his scholar-father gives him a Coca-cola; children crowd around the single village television to watch a Chinese opera singer imitate Pavarotti singing Italian opera; the Chinese student learning English recites the Gettysburg Address. Although the film concentrates on both illustrating and dissolving the apparent opposition between Chinese Chinese and American Chinese, a number of other contrasts are likewise explored: the differences between generations both within the Chao and the Fang families (daughter Lili noisily drops her bike while her father practices tai chi; Paul kisses his Caucasian girlfriend and later tells his father that he believes all Chinese are racists when Leo suggests that he might date some nice Chinese girls); differences between men and women (accentuated by two scenes, one in which Grace Fang and Mrs. Chao

talk about their husbands and children, the other in which Chao and Leo get drunk together); and, finally, the differences between capitalist and communist societies (highlighted in a scene in which the Chaos and Fangs talk about their different attitudes toward "work"). The representations of these other contrasts complicate and diversify the ostensible focus on cultural differences between Chinese and Chinese-Americans, as if to testify to the condition that there is never only one exclusive valence of difference, but rather cultural difference is always simultaneously bound up with gender, economics, age, and other distinctions. In other words, when Leo says to his wife that the Great Wall makes the city "just as difficult to leave as to get in," the wall at once signifies the construction of a variety of barriers—not only between Chinese and Americans, but between generations, men and women, capitalism and communism—as well as the impossibility of ever remaining bounded and impenetrable, of resisting change, recomposition, and reinvention. We are reminded of this impossibility throughout the film, but it is perhaps best illustrated in the scene in which the Fang and Chao families play a rousing game of touch football on the ancient immovable Great Wall.

The film continues with a series of wonderful contrasts: the differences in the bodily comportments of the Chinese-American Paul and the Chinese Liu playing ping pong, between Leo's jogging and Mr. Chao's tai chi, between Grace Fang's and Mrs. Chao's ideas of what is fitting and fashionable for the female body. The two families have different senses of space and of the relation between family members. In one subplot, the Chinese-American cousin Paul is outraged to learn that Mrs. Chao reads her daughter Lili's mail; he asks Lili if she has ever heard of "privacy." This later results in a fight between Mrs. Chao and Lili in which Lili says she has learned from their American cousins that "it's not right to read other people's mail." Mrs. Chao retorts: "You're not 'other people,' you're my daughter. What is this thing, 'privacy'?" Lili explains to her that "privacy" can't be translated into Chinese. "Oh, so you're trying to hide things from your mother and use western words to trick her!" exclaims Mrs. Chao. Ultimately, just as the members of the Chao family are marked by the visit from their American relatives, the Fangs are altered by the time they return to California, each bringing back a memento or practice from their Chinese trip. In other words, rather than privileging either a nativist or assimilationist view, or even espousing a "Chinese-American" resolution of differences, *A Great Wall* performs a filmic "migration" by shuttling between the various cultural spaces; we are left, by the end of the film, with a sense of culture as dynamic and open, the result of a continual process of visiting and revisiting a plurality of cultural sites.

In keeping with the example of *A Great Wall*, we might consider as a possible model for the ongoing construction of ethnic identity the migratory process suggested by Wang's filming technique and emplotment: we might conceive of the making and practice of Asian American culture as nomadic, unsettled, taking place in the travel between cultural sites and in the multivocality of heterogeneous and conflicting positions. Taking seriously the heterogeneities among Asian Americans in California, we must conclude that the grouping "Asian American" is not a natural or static category; it is a socially constructed unity, a situationally specific position that we assume for political reasons. It is "strategic" in Gayatri Spivak's sense of a "strategic use of a positive essentialism in a scrupulously visible political interest" (205). The concept of "strategic essentialism" suggests that it is possible to utilize specific signifiers of ethnic identity, such as Asian American, for the purpose of contesting and disrupting the discourses that exclude Asian Americans, while simultaneously revealing the internal contradictions and slippages of Asian American so as to insure that such essentialisms will not be reproduced and proliferated by the very apparatuses we seek to disempower. I am not suggesting that we can or should do away with the notion of

Asian American identity, for to stress only our differences would jeopardize the hard-earned unity that has been achieved in the last two decades of Asian American politics, the unity that is necessary if Asian Americans are to play a role in the new historical bloc of ethnic Californians. In fact, I would submit that the very freedom, in the 1990s, to explore the hybridities concealed beneath the desire of identity is permitted by the context of a strongly articulated essentialist politics. Just as the articulation of the desire for identity depends upon the existence of a fundamental horizon of differences, the articulation of differences dialectically depends upon a socially constructed and practiced notion of identity. I want simply to remark that in the 1990s, we can afford to rethink the notion of ethnic identity in terms of cultural, class, and gender differences, rather than presuming similarities and making the erasure of particularity the basis of unity. In the 1990s, we can diversify our political practices to include a more heterogeneous group and to enable crucial alliances with other groups—ethnicity-based, class-based, gender-based, and sexuality-based—in the ongoing work of transforming hegemony.

NOTES

Many thanks to Elaine Kim for her thought-provoking questions, and for asking me to deliver portions of this essay an papers at the 1990 meetings of the Association of Asian American Studies and of the American Literature Association; to James Clifford, who also gave me the opportunity to deliver a version of this essay at a conference sponsored by the Center for Cultural Studies at UC Santa Cruz; to the audience participants at all three conferences who asked stimulating questions which have helped me to rethink my original notions; and to Page duBois, Barbara Harlow, Susan Kirkpatrick, George Mariscal, Ellen Rooney, and Kathryn Shevelow, who read drafts and offered important comments and criticism.

1. *Nisei* refers to a second-generation Japanese-American, born to immigrant parents in the US; *Sansei*, a third-generation Japanese-American. *Issei* refers to a first-generation immigrant.

2. See Kim, *Asian*, for the most important book-length study of the literary representations of multi-generational Asian America.

3. Recent anthropological discussions of ethnic cultures as fluid and syncretic systems echo these concerns of Asian

American writers. See, for example, Fischer; Clifford. For an anthropological study of Japanese-American culture that troubles the paradigmatic construction of kinship and filial relations as the central figure in culture, see Yanagisako.

4. We might think, for example, of the shifting of the Los Angeles "Chinatown" from its downtown location to the suburban community of Monterey Park. Since the 1970s, the former "Chinatown" has been superseded demographically and economically by Monterey Park, the home of many Chinese-Americans as well as newly arrived Chinese from Hong Kong and Taiwan. The Monterey Park community of 63,000 residents is currently over 50% Asian. On the social and political consequences of these changing demographics, see Fong.

5. Chan's history of the Chinese immigrant populations in California, *Bittersweet*, and her history of Asian Americans are extremely important in this regard. Numerous lectures by Ling-chi Wang at UC San Diego in 1987 and at UC Berkeley in 1988 have been very important to my understanding of the heterogeneity of waves of immigration across different Asian-origin groups.

6. The Chinese Exclusion Act of 1882 barred Chinese from entering the U.S. the National Origins Act prohibited the entry of Japanese in 1924, and the Tydings-McDuffie Act of 1934 limited Filipino immigrants to 50 people per year. Finally, the most tragic consequence of anti-Asian racism occurred during World War II when 120,000 Japanese-Americans (two-thirds of whom American citizens by birth) were interned in camps. For a study of the anti-Japanese movement culminating in the immigration act of 1924, see Daniels. Takaki offers a general history of Asian origin immigrant groups in the United States.

7. The model minority myth constructs Asians as aggressively driven overachievers; it is a homogenizing fiction which relies upon two strategies common in the subordinating construction of racial or ethnic otherness—the racial other as knowable, familiar ("like us"), and as incomprehensible, threatening ("unlike us"); the model minority myth suggests both that Asians are overachievers and "unlike us," and that they assimilate well, and are thus "like us." Asian Americans are continually pointing out that the model minority myth distorts the real gains, as well as the impediments, of Asian immigrants; by leveling and homogenizing all Asian groups, it erases the different rates of assimilation and the variety of class identities among various Asian immigrant groups. Claiming that Asians are "overrepresented" on college campuses, the model minority myth is one of the justifications for the establishment of informal quotas in university admissions policies, similar to the university admission policies which discriminated against Jewish students from the 1930s to the 1950s.

8. In the last two decades, greatly diverse new groups have settled in California; demographers project that by the end of the century, the "majority" of the state will be comprised of ethnic "minority" groups. Due to recent immigrants, this influx of minorities is characterized also by greater diversity within individual groups: the group we call Asian American no longer denotes only Japanese, Chinese, Koreans, and Filipinos, but now includes Indian, Thai, Vietnamese, Cambodian, and Laotian groups; Latino communities in California are made up not only of Chicanos, but include Guatemalans, Salvadorans, and Colombians. It is not difficult to find Pakistani, Armenian, Lebanese, and Iranian enclaves in San Francisco, Los Angeles, or even San Diego. While California's "multiculturalism" is often employed to support a notion of the "melting pot," to further an ideological assertion of equal opportunity for California's different immigrant groups, I am, in contrast, pursuing the ignored implications of this characterization of California as an ethnic state: that is, despite the increasing numbers of ethnic immigrants apparently racing to enjoy California's opportunities, for racial and ethnic immigrants there is no equality, but uneven development, nonequivalence, and cultural heterogeneities, not only between, but within, groups.

9. For an important elaboration of the concept of "minority discourse," see JanMohamed and Lloyd.

10. This notion of "the dominant"—defined by Williams in a chapter discussing the "Dominant, Residual, and Emergent" as "a cultural process . . . seized as a cultural system, with determinate dominant features: feudal culture or bourgeois culture or a transition from one to the other"—is often conflated in recent cultural theory with Gramsci's concept of hegemony. Indeed, Williams writes: "We have certainly still to speak of the 'dominant' and the 'effective,' and in these senses of the hegemonic" (121), as if the dominant and the hegemonic are synonymous.

11. See Gramsci, "History." Gramsci describes "subaltern" groups as by definition not unified, emergent, and always in relation to the dominant groups:

> The history of subaltern social groups is necessarily fragmented and episodic. There undoubtedly does exist a tendency to (at least provisional stages of) unification in the historical activity of these groups, but this tendency is continually interrupted by the activity of the ruling groups; it therefore can only be demonstrated when an historical cycle is completed and this cycle culminates in a success. Subaltern groups are always subject to the activity of ruling groups, even when they rebel and rise up: only 'permanent' victory breaks their subordination, and that not immediately. In reality, even when they appear triumphant, the subaltern groups are merely anxious to defend themselves (a truth which can be demonstrated by the history of the French Revolution at least up to 1830). Every trace of independent initiative on the part of subaltern groups should therefore be of incalculable value for the integral historian. (54–55)

12. "Hegemony" remains a suggestive construct in Gramsci, however, rather than an explicitly interpreted set of relations. Contemporary readers are left with the more specific task of distinguishing which particular forms of challenge to an existing hegemony are significantly transformative, and which forms may be neutralized or appropriated by the hegemony. Some cultural critics contend that counterhegemonic forms and practices are tied by definition to the dominant culture and that the dominant

culture simultaneously produces and limits its own forms of counter-culture. I am thinking here of some of the "new historicist" studies that use a particular notion of Foucault's discourse to confer authority to the "dominant," interpreting all forms of "subversion" as being ultimately "contained" by dominant ideology and institutions. Other cultural historians, such as Williams, suggest that because there is both identifiable variation in the social order over time, as well as variations in the forms of the counter-culture in different historical periods, we must conclude that some aspects of the oppositional forms are not reducible to the terms of the original hegemony. Still other theorists, such as Ernesto Laclau and Chantal Mouffe, have expanded Gramsci's notion of hegemony to argue that in advanced capitalist society, the social field is not a totality consisting exclusively of the dominant and the counterdominant, but rather that "the social" is an open and uneven terrain of contesting articulations and signifying practices. Some of these articulations and practices are neutralized, while others can be linked to build important pressures against an existing hegemony. See Laclau and Mouffe, especially pp. 134–45. They argue persuasively that no hegemonic logic can account for the totality of "the social" and that the open and incomplete character of the social field is the precondition of every hegemonic practice. For if the field of hegemony were conceived according to a "zero-sum" vision of possible positions and practices, then the very concept of hegemony, as plural and mutable formations and relations, would be rendered impossible. Elsewhere, in "Hegemony and New Political Subjects," Mouffe goes even further to elaborate the practical dimensions of the hegemonic principle in terms of contemporary social movements.

WORKS CITED

Adamson, Walter. *Hegemony and Revolution: A Study of Antonio Gramsci's Political and Cultural Theory.* Berkeley: U of California P, 1980.

Cabral, Amilcar. *Unity and Struggle: Speeches and Writings of Amilcar Cabral.* Trans. Michael Wolfers. New York: Monthly Review, 1979.

Chan, Sucheng. *Asian Americans: An Interpretive History.* Boston: Twayne, 1991.

———. *This Bittersweet Soil: The Chinese in California Agriculture, 1860–1910.* Berkeley: U of California P, 1986.

Chang, Diana. "The Oriental Contingent." *The Forbidden Stitch.* Ed. Shirley Geok-Lin Lim, Mayumi Tsutakawa, and Margarita Donnelly. Corvallis: Calyx, 1989. 171–77.

Chu, Louis. *Eat a Bowl of Tea.* Seattle: U of Washington P, 1961.

Clifford, James. *The Predicament of Culture: Twentieth Century Ethnography, Literature, and Art.* Cambridge: Harvard UP, 1988.

Daniels, Roger. *The Politics of Prejudice.* Berkeley: U of California P, 1962.

Fanon, Frantz. *The Wretched of the Earth.* Trans. Constance Farrington. New York: Grove, 1961.

Fischer, Michael M. J. "Ethnicity and the Postmodern Arts of Memory." *Writing Culture.* Ed. James Clifford and George Marcus. Berkeley: U of California P, 1986.

Fong, Timothy. "A Community Study of Monterey Park, California." Diss. U of California. Berkeley.

Gong, Ted. "Approaching Cultural Change Through Literature: From Chinese to Chinese-American." *Amerasia* 7 (1980): 73–86.

Gramsci, Antonio. "History of the Subaltern Classes: Methodological Criteria." *Selections,* 52–60.

———. *Selections from the Prison Notebooks.* Ed. and trans. Quinton Hoare and Geoffrey Nowell Smith. New York: International, 1971.

A Great Wall. Dir. Peter Wang. New Yorker Films, 1985.

JanMohamed, Abdul, and David Lloyd, eds. *The Nature and Context of Minority Discourse.* New York: Oxford UP, 1990.

Kim, Elaine. *Asian American Literature: An Introduction to the Writings and Their Social Context.* Philadelphia: Temple UP, 1982.

———. "'Such Opposite Creatures': Men and Women in Asian American Literature." *Michigan Quarterly Review* (1990): 68–93.

Kingston, Maxine Hong. *The Woman Warrior.* New York: Random, 1975.

Laclau, Ernesto, and Chantal Mouffe. *Hegemony and Socialist Strategy.* London: Verso, 1985.

Laurentis, Teresa de. *Technologies of Gender.* Bloomington: Indiana UP, 1987.

Lowe, Lydia. "Quitting Time." *Ikon 9, Without Ceremony: a special issue by Asian Women United.* Spec. issue of *Ikon* 9 (1988): 29.

Minh-ha, Trinh T. *Woman, Native, Other: Writing Postcoloniality and Feminism.* Bloomington: Indiana UP, 1989.

Mirikitani, Janice. "Breaking Tradition." *Without Ceremony,* 9.

Mouffe, Chantal. "Hegemony and New Political Subjects: Toward a New Concept of Democracy." *Marxism and the Interpretation of Culture.* Ed. Cary Nelson and Lawrence Grossberg. Urbana: U of Illinois, 1988. 89–104.

Sassoon, Anne Showstack. "Hegemony, War of Position and Political Intervention." *Approaches to Gramsci.* Ed. Anne Showstack Sassoon. London: Writers and Readers, 1982.

Spivak, Gayatri. *In Other Worlds.* London: Routledge, 1987.

Takaki, Ronald. *Strangers From a Different Shore: A History of Asian Americans.* Boston: Little, 1989.

Tan, Amy. *The Joy Luck Club.* New York: Putnam's, 1989.

Williams, Raymond. *Marxism and Literature.* Oxford: Oxford UP, 1977.

Yanagisako, Sylvia. *Transforming the Past: Kinship and Tradition among Japanese Americans.* Stanford: Stanford UP, 1985.

Postmodern Possibilities: Theoretical and Political Directions for Asian American Studies

Keith Osajima

Over the past two decades, the upsurge of interest in postmodern theories has led to a critical rethinking of longstanding theoretical paradigms and practices. The interest in postmodern theories has contributed to the reshaping of intellectual life—inspiring a critique of traditional disciplinary boundaries, a reconfiguring of fields like literary studies, and the formation of new interdisciplinary units, such as Cultural Studies. In this essay, I present some thoughts on how postmodern theories might contribute to the development of Asian American studies as an intellectual field of inquiry and a vehicle for political and social change. My goal is to raise issues about theoretical possibilities and limits to serve as a basis for further discussion.

I have argued elsewhere that to make sense of postmodern theories, it is useful to think of them as a relational phenomena, as perspectives situated in opposition to the power and practices associated with modernism.[1] Postmodern theorists argue that modernist claims, such as the unequivocal value of science and reason, the ideal of the autonomous subject, and the notion of linear, progressive development, are not universal, but constructed "metanarratives" which represent only a narrow worldview emanating from a western European experience. Metanarratives constitute closed systems of knowledge which subsume difference and diversity by imposing singular, homogenizing models of explanation or development.[2] They are exclu-

sionary for they narrowly define what is acceptable and legitimate, while simultaneously excluding, silencing, and rendering invisible other views.

By revealing the normalizing and exclusionary tendencies of modern metanarratives, postmodern critics seek to unveil the constructed nature of "truth" claims, and to open new areas of inquiry and understanding. As Rosenau notes, postmodern theorists focus onl "all that the modern age has never cared to understand in any particular detail, with any sort of specificity."[3] David Harvey adds: "The idea that all groups have a right to speak for themselves, in their own voice, and have that voice accepted as authentic and legitimate is essential to the pluralistic stance of postmodernism."[4] Breaking from disciplinary boundaries and seamless reductionist explanatory models, postmodern theorists develop interdisciplinary analyses that reveal the heterogeneity, complexity, and plurality of local social conditions. Critical of modernist views that privilege autonomy, coherence, and rationality as the essential qualities of the self, postmodernists bring into view the multiple, complex, and often contradictory ways people craft themselves as raced, gendered, and classed subjects.[5]

The postmodern direction toward inclusion, multiplicity, and heterogeneity is particularly well-suited to an analysis of the contemporary Asian American experience. The tremendous influx of immigrants and refugees over the past thirty years has dramatically altered the composition of the Asian American population. "Asian America" now signifies an extremely diverse entity, composed of

Source: Amerasia Journal 21:1 & 2 (1995): 79–87. Reprinted by permission.

people from widely different cultural, ethnic, gender, educational, class, generational, and political backgrounds. Postmodern theories, which focus on the complexly constructed nature of social conditions and identities, can provide a framework for understanding the dynamic changes in the Asian American experience.

We need not go far to realize the analytic benefits of postmodern perspectives. Lisa Lowe's article "Heterogeneity, Hybridity, Multiplicity: Marking Asian American Differences"[6] is an excellent example of how postmodern perspectives can contribute to insightful analyses of Asian Americans. Taking a critical stance against modernist metanarratives, Lowe argues that the representations of Asian American culture and identity in novels and films are often dominated by conceptualizations which essentialize and homogenize the Asian American experience, producing images that oversimplify a complex phenomena. She notes, for example, that many Asian American novels cast cultural issues exclusively in terms of "generational conflict and filial relation(s)."[7] Similarly, discussions of Asian American identity often simplistically characterize identity issues in binary terms—as conflicts between those who identify closely with the immigrant or nationalist positions versus those who are more Americanized and assimilated.[8]

Avoiding the homogenizing effects of the master narratives, Lowe advocates an analysis that examines the multiplicity and complexity of the Asian American experience. She maintains that "what is referred to as 'Asian America' is clearly a heterogeneous entity" and Asian American identity is better understood as a matter of "cultural hybridity" than of simple binary categories. "The boundaries and definitions of Asian American culture are continually shifting and being contested from pressures both 'inside' and 'outside' the Asian origin community."[9]

Lowe offers Peter Wang's film, *A Great Wall*,[10] as an example of a cultural text which captures the heterogeneity, multiplicity, and hybridity of the Asian American experience. The film, which

is complexly constructed to reveal differences between Chinese America and China, "unsettles" the dominant nativist-assimilationist opposition found in more traditional Asian American representations. She writes:

> *A Great Wall* performs a filmic "migration" by shuttling between the various cultural spaces; we are left, by the end of the film, with a sense of culture as dynamic and open, the result of a continual process of visiting and revisiting a plurality of cultural sites.[11]

Lisa Lowe's article reveals the analytic gains to be made when one questions the limiting effect of modern discourses and turns toward postmodern perspectives to describe and analyze the diversity and heterogeneity of Asian America. Perhaps more important, the article illustrates how postmodern theories can help us to develop a critical self-assessment of Asian American studies itself.

The postmodern critique of metanarratives implores us to "think about how we think."[12] The strength of postmodern perspectives is their insistence on analyzing the construction of powerful discourses and the ways they limit and define social life. This critical stance can promote a rethinking of the foundations of Asian American studies. By turning the analytic gaze inward—making Asian American studies the subject of a postmodern inquiry—we can think critically about "how we think" about the field and consider alternative conceptualizations.

One product of this inquiry is a critical assessment of our theoretical development. Gary Okihiro notes that one of the failures of Asian American studies has been its inability to critically challenge and break free of the theoretical paradigms inherited from traditional disciplines. He writes: "Despite the radical origins of the field, very few Asian American scholars have truly challenged the 'tyranny of received paradigms.'"[13] Instead, many Asian Americanists have been relatively conservative in their theoretical thinking, relying on European ethnic studies.

From a postmodern perspective, the tyranny of received paradigms can be understood as a power effect of modern academic discourses and accompanying institutional practices. Most Asian American scholars in the social sciences adhere closely to the normative standards set forth in traditional academic disciplines. These privilege certain modernist discourses, such as the value of objective positivist science in the search for universal laws and reductionist explanatory models. In part this adherence is simply a matter of survival (as any graduate student or assistant professor will testify to), but it also appears to be a matter of choice—an uncritical acceptance and privileging of traditional academic practices. In either instance, the tyranny of received paradigms reflects the power of modern discourses to define and oftentimes limit the range of theoretical tools we use to study Asian Americans. As Foucault notes, modern discourses create "regimes of truth" in which a circumscribed set of ideas and practices are deemed legitimate and truthful.[14] By revealing the Eurocentric, constructed nature of dominant regimes of truth in academe, Asian Americanists may find it easier to rethink theoretical positions and to consider alternative approaches.

Turning the postmodern gaze inward on Asian American studies also raises critical questions about the fundamental assumptions of identity politics that have organized the field. The field emerged at a time when representing the Asian American experience was a simpler task. In the late 1960s, the majority of young students, scholars and activists pioneering the development of Asian American studies shared many common characteristics. Most were educated, American-born, English-speaking and middle class, and were either Japanese, Chinese or Filipino. Racism and economic exploitation were privileged, in our analyses and practices, as the main forms of oppression. The cohesiveness of the panethnic "Asian America" hinged on forging a common identity and politics grounded in the shared experience with racism and economic exploitation.[15]

The social realities of a changing Asian American population, along with postmodern impulses toward inclusivity and heterogeneity call these developments into question. Lowe challenges us to think about the viability of an Asian American studies and politics organized principally around an ethnic identity. She worries that while such identity politics have been beneficial, there are potential risks as well. An "essentializing" Asian American identity may suppress our differences and suggest an oversimplified Asian American experience which "inadvertently supports the racist discourse that constructs Asians as a homogeneous group" and excludes the experiences of the more recently arrived Asian groups.[16] An Asian American studies that "generalizes Asian American identity as male" is also problematic for it renders women, gays and lesbians invisible.[17] Extending this analysis further, an Asian American studies that is grounded in elite, middle-class academic institutions may be unable to address the needs of working class Asian communities. Perhaps most important, as postmodern theories call attention to the impact of multiple oppressions and to the multiplicitous nature of our constructed identities, an Asian American studies that has organized primarily around issues of race may be too narrowly focused.

What do these challenges imply for the direction of Asian American studies? Can we turn to postmodern theories for some guidance? Here, I find that postmodern perspectives do a better job raising critical issues than resolving them. Indeed, one of the major problems of postmodern theories is that their celebration and privileging of uncertainty, ephemerality, fragmentation, and multiplicity acts as a centrifugal analytic force which makes it difficult to find effective political strategies for change. Best and Kellner write: "For extreme postmodernists, social reality is therefore indeterminate and unmappable, and the best we can do is live within the fragments of a disintegrating social order."[18] Postmodern analyses can affirm a sense of pessimism and meaninglessness that fuels hopelessness, malaise and political paralysis.[19] They help to formulate compelling depictions of the complexities of life in postmodern societies, but offer little vision for an alternative future. If we were to follow these postmodern tendencies to their extreme, we would have to seriously consider abandoning the project of building an Asian American studies and an accompanying anti-racist politics.

I am not quite ready to abandon the project (though critics on both the left and right might seem ready to jettison identity politics). But I'm also not willing to dismiss the postmodern critique and adopt a closed stance in rigid defense of Asian American studies. We need to think hard about the real and important questions raised by postmodern theories, without slipping into a nihilist chasm. How can our research and teaching move toward multiplicity, complexity and diversity, while avoiding fragmentation, disconnection, and political paralysis? How can the postmodern impulse toward local and specific analyses be brought together with the incisive structural analyses of oppression developed in Asian American studies? How can we maintain our historically effective role of combatting racism against Asians (a task that is likely to go unaddressed if an Asian American identity politics is abandoned), without privileging race to the point where it masks or excludes the effects of other oppressions operating within Asian American communities? Here, I think a major contribution of postmodern and feminist analyses of multiple oppressions is that it forces us to think about how our simultaneous positions in oppressed and oppressor roles impact on social relations and political practice. For straight, middle-class, Asian American males, like myself, it means confronting the reality that it is often easier to champion anti-racist causes than to deal with our sexism, classism and homophobia.

If the centrifugal tendencies of extreme postmodern positions cannot answer these questions, perhaps a synthetic approach to theory which avoids dogmatism and the reified labels that define rigid borders between schools of thought

can move us closer to viable answers.[20] I am persuaded by Barry Smart's notion of an "oppositional" postmodernism,[21] which utilizes postmodern insights and critiques, yet holds on to a progressive, emancipatory vision of possibility born out of modernism. This means, for example, paying analytic attention to the specificities of local conditions, but situating those within analyses of broader structural, global relations. It means utilizing insights gained from an analysis of discourse and power, but not privileging the text at the expense of human agency. It means recognizing the exclusionary and hierarchical effects of modernity's emphasis on reason and rationality,[22] but not abandoning reason as tool for change. An oppositional postmodernism leaves open the possibility that a critical use of reason to interrogate oppressive facets of modernism can lead to a politics of change.[23]

For Asian American studies, an oppositional postmodernism requires us to pay serious attention to the multiplicity, complexity, and hybridity of the Asian American experience—what Michael Omi has called an "elegant chaos,"[24] while guarding against a fragmentation that renders a broader, panethnic Asian American studies impossible. It requires that our analyses not end at the moment of critique, but, attendant to the history of Asian American studies, also includes ways for turning postmodern analyses into concrete strategies for change.

How might this difficult melding of apparently contradictory tendencies be realized in an Asian American politics? One common strategy has been to argue for a politics of pan-Asian coalition building, where divergent groups come together to work toward a goal of some common relevance. Yen Espiritu's important book, *Asian American Panethnicity*,[25] offers a number of examples of how panethnic, coalition building has resulted in significant political victories. Lisa Lowe's discussion of "'strategic essentialism" follows somewhat similar lines where people from different groups adopt an Asian American identity for the specific, strategic purpose of "contesting and disrupting the discourses that exclude Asian Americans."[26]

While coalition building is a valuable approach, I would not hitch the future of Asian American studies to this strategy alone. As Papusa Molina notes, coalitions can be problematic for they are short-lived; tend to disappear when the battle is won or lost; are often motivated more by pragmatic instrumental goals than deep commitment; and often require individuals to sacrifice their needs for the benefit of the cause.[27]

As a complement, she proposes that coalitions and other political organizing be built upon deep alliances in which people commit to work with others, not simply for political expediency, but because people feel strong connections, commitment, and responsibilities toward each other. These alliances develop when people come to fully understand and appreciate the unique struggles and experiences that make up an individual's life as well as the points of shared experience. The alliances also hinge on people's commitment to working for a just society, supporting and participating in efforts to fight against the inequality and forms of oppression that impact on their allies' lives. In these ways, alliances are consistent with a synthetic oppositional postmodernism. That is, they seek to develop a shared vision of liberation from oppression which is part of the modernist project. But they account for the contextual complexities of postmodern life, and do not require that people gloss over all differences in order to find a common ground to work together.

As Asian America moves toward the next century, it is certain that the complexities and heterogeneity of today will continue to increase. Understanding those complexities, and forging an effective politics for change is the task faced by Asian American studies. As I have tried to show on a general level, an oppositional postmodern Asian American perspective can assist in that effort. What remains is to think more specifically about how tools like postmodern theories and alliances can concretely inform our research, pedagogy and political practice.

NOTES

1. Keith Osajima, "Postmodernism and Asian American Studies: A Critical Appropriation," in *Privileging Positions: The Sites of Asian American Studies* (Pullman: Washington State University Press, 1995).
2. Pauline M. Rosenau, *Post-modernism and the Social Sciences* (Princeton, New Jersey: Princeton University Press, 1992).
3. Ibid., 8.
4. David Harvey, *The Condition of Postmodernity* (Cambridge: Basil Blackwell, 1989), 48.
5. Dorrine Kondo, *Crafting Selves* (Chicago: University of Chicago Press, 1990).
6. Lisa Lowe, "Heterogeneity, Hybridity, Multiplicity: Marking Asian American Differences," *Diaspora* 1:1 (1991): 24–44.
7. Ibid., 26.
8. Ibid., 32.
9. Ibid., 27.
10. Ibid., 27–28.
11. Ibid., 39.
12. Dana Takagi, "Postmodernism from the Edge: Asian American Identities," presentation at the Association for Asian American Studies Conference, Ithaca, New York, June 1993.
13. Gary Y. Okihiro, "African and Asian American Studies: A Comparative Analysis and Commentary," in *Asian Americans—Comparative and Global Perspectives*, edited by Shirley Hune, Hyung-chan Kim, Stephen S. Fugita and Amy Ling (Pullman: Washington State University Press, 1991), 17–28.
14. Michel Foucault, *Power/Knowledge,* edited by Colin Gordon (New York: Pantheon, 1980).
15. Yen Le Espiritu, *Asian American Panethnicity* (Philadelphia: Temple University Press, 1992).
16. Lowe, 30.
17. Ibid., 30.
18. Steven Best and Douglas Kellner, *Postmodern Theory—Critical Interrogations* (New York: Guilford Press, 1991), 258.
19. Rosenau, 15.
20. George Ritzer, "The Current Status of Sociological Theory: The New Syntheses," in *Frontiers of Social Theory—The New Syntheses,* edited by George Ritzer (New York: Columbia University Press, 1990), 1–30.
21. Barry Smart, *Modern Conditions, Postmodern Controversies* (London, England: Routledge, Inc., 1992), 178.

22. Nancy Fraser and Linda J. Nicholson, "Social Criticism without Philosophy: An Encounter between Feminism and Postmodernism," in *Feminism/Postmodernism*, edited by Linda J. Nicholson (New York: Routledge, Inc., 1990) 19–38.

23. Smart, 181.

24. Michael Omi, "Elegant Chaos: Postmodern Asian American Identity," in *Asian Americans: Collages of Identities*, edited by Lee C. Lee (Ithaca, New York: Asian American Studies Program, Cornell University, 1992), 143–154.

25. Espiritu.

26. Lowe, 39.

27. Papusa Molina, "Recognizing, Accepting and Celebrating Our Differences," in *Making Face, Making Soul*, edited by Gloria Anzaldua (San Francisco: Aunt Lute Foundation Books, 1990), 325–331.

Denationalization Reconsidered: Asian American Cultural Criticism at a Theoretical Crossroads

Sau-Ling C. Wong

In this essay, I would like to address what I consider to be a theoretical crossroads at which Asian American cultural criticism has found itself. For some time now, Asian American cultural criticism—by which I simply refer to implicit or explicit analysis of Asian American subject formation and cultural production—has been undergoing dramatic changes from whose influences no one in the field of Asian American studies can be exempt. Not only have these changes been shaping the practice of individual scholars, but they have been exerting mounting pressure on the field to reflect on its own operating assumptions and, if necessary, modify them. I will use the term *denationalization* to try to capture the complexity of these cultural phenomena, of which I will single out three for scrutiny.

The first is the easing of cultural nationalist concerns as a result of changing demographics in the Asian American population as well as theoretical critiques from various quarters ranging from the poststructuralist to the queer. This has made possible a complication of identity politics as articulated in the 1960s and 1970s, as well as opened up other axes of organization and mobilization including class, gender and sexuality. Concomitantly, permeability has been increasing in the boundaries between Asian Americans and "Asian Asians," once a rallying point for the Asian American movement; as well

Source: *Amerasia Journal* 21:1 & 2 (1995): 1–27. Reprinted by permission.

as between Asian American studies and Asian studies, two disciplines with very distinct histories and institutional locations, and vexed, at times openly antagonistic, relations. The expanding intercourse between the two fields is, among other things, a response to new patterns of economic and political power affecting the relative positioning of Asia and America. In turn, this repositioning arises from a larger global movement of transnational capital, whose cultural consequences include a normalization of multiple subjectivities, migrations, border-crossings.[1] The sweep of the postmodern condition has made it more and more acceptable to situate Asian Americans in a diasporic context—the third component of the denationalizing trend I wish to investigate. A *diasporic perspective* emphasizes Asian Americans as one element in the global scattering of peoples of Asian origin, in contrast to what I call a *domestic perspective* that stresses the status of Asian Americans as an ethnic/racial minority within the national boundaries of the United States. Together, these three changes have taken on the force of something of a paradigm shift in Asian American studies.

. . . I believe a political question of constituency and mission underlies questions of application encountered daily by academic practitioners of cultural criticism. This question must be addressed collectively in the face of a trend that, to some, appears to promise novelty, intellectual excitement, delivery from the institutional ghetto of ethnic studies, or even, perhaps, better funding.

THE EASING OF CULTURAL NATIONALIST CONCERNS

I will begin with a clarification. The switching between "Asian American cultural criticism" and "Asian American studies" in the preceding paragraphs is not done randomly. My remarks will concentrate on the former domain, although I believe their implications concern the field as a whole.

On the issue of denationalization, within the Asian Americanist community there has actually been a kind of disjuncture between the history/social science contingent and the literature/cultural studies contingent. The national boundaries of the United States have never been as intense a point of contention for the former as for the latter. From the start, Asian American historians and social scientists have been interested in immigration; of course, in immigration studies border-crossing is more a given than a cultural proposition to be debated.

Furthermore—and I will elaborate on this later—in a sense it is misleading to cast the current debates on "theory" in Asian American studies (of which denationalization is one manifestation) solely in terms of an unprecedented contemporary occurrence due to external influences. The "pre-post" period—the period before concepts from poststructuralism and postmodernist theories found a hearing in Asian American studies—was already witness to much critical interest beyond the domestic American scene. The activists who founded Asian American studies in the late 1960s and early 1970s were influenced as much by the Cultural Revolution in China as by "domestic" American events like the civil rights movement or the black power movement.[2] The anti-Vietnam War movement, which jolted many Asian Americans into recognizing their commonality with the "gooks" as well as among themselves, is inherently transnational in outlook. So too is the internal colonialism model, which, by drawing analogies between colonies in the traditional mode in the Third World and race relations within U.S. boundaries, allowed Asian Americans to talk about their

history beyond terms set by narratives of Americanization dominant in the 1940s and 1950s. As Sucheta Mazumdar puts it, "the very genesis of Asian American Studies was international."[3] (In this sense, my term "denationalization" is something of a misnomer, as it suggests deconstruction of an establishment where seeds of that deconstruction have been present from the start. For lack of a comparably complex organizing term, however, I will continue to use "denationalization.") . . . .

GROWING PERMEABILITY BETWEEN "ASIAN" AND "ASIAN AMERICAN"

Denationalization in the second sense entails a relaxation of the distinction between what is Asian American and what is "Asian," and between Asian American studies and Asian studies. To quote Elaine Kim's succinct formulation in a key document in the denationalization debate, her foreword to Shirley Lim and Amy Ling's 1992 critical anthology, *Reading the Literatures of Asian America* (framed as a revision of the 1982 Introduction to her *Asian American Literature*), "The lines between Asian and Asian American, so important to identity formation in earlier times, are increasingly being blurred."[4] As a corollary of this blurring, something of a rapprochement between Asian studies and Asian American studies has been taking place.

There are obvious material bases for this second component of denationalization, chief among them the ascendancy of Asia as an economic power of global impact, the coalescence of the Pacific Rim as a geoeconomic entity, and the circulation of Asian transnational capital.[5] Thus instead of being mere suppliants at the "golden door," desperate to trade their sense of ethnic identity for a share of America's plenty, many of today's Asian immigrants regard the U.S. as simply one of many possible places to exercise their portable capital and portable skills. In other words, whereas political instability and economic depression used to occur hand in hand, the Asia of "little dragons" has disentangled the two, creating a situation in which phenomenal economic growth coexists with political uncertainty or repression.[6] While the U.S. is still wildly romanticized in many parts of Asia, the concept of the Pacific Rim as an interconnected economic unit underscores the unevenness of this vast region in which migration is but a rationale means of trade-off between security and profit. (In fact, the direction of movement can no longer be assumed to be from Asia to America; many Asian Americans in science and technology are relocating to Asia.)[7] Segments of the Asian professional class have developed their own patterns of trans-Pacific commuting, which obviously affect identity formation in unprecedented ways.

Christopher L. Connery has deftly traced the gradual rise of what he terms Pacific Rim Discourse in the mid-1970s, which has diffused into American culture as an Asia-facing orientation (as opposed to an earlier preoccupation with Europe) and a general awareness of the interconnectedness of Asian and U.S. fortunes.[8] Among the contributing factors he lists are the thaw in U.S.-China relations, the end of the Vietnam War, the recognition of Japan's economic power, and the worldwide economic downturn that forced the U.S. to acknowledge its loss of hegemony. Although Connery notes a decline in Pacific Rim Discourse and an American retreat from internationalism in the late 1980s, the discourse's hold on the American population imagination is still to be reckoned with.

When cultural projects involve trans-Pacific collaboration in material terms, delimiting and designating them as either Asian American or "Asian" become much more difficult, maybe ultimately irrelevant. One good example is the work of film director Ang Lee (*Pushing Hands, The Wedding Banquet,* and *Eat, Drink, Man, Woman*), who grew up in Taiwan, received an American education, draws from both sides of the Pacific for funding, actors and film crew, and deals with characters of varying degrees of biculturality. How exactly should one classify him and his

oeuvre, not just at credit-claiming time but in a conscientious attempt at valid conceptualization?

Apart from the issue of classification, cultural dissemination, maintenance, and transformation for Asian Americans—a group with a sizable aggregate disposable income—are very different matters today than they were before the advent of cheap jet travel, fax and e-mail, pocket translators, long-distance phone services competing for clients with multilingual support, satellite-typeset Asian-language newspapers, and video and laserdisc rental outlets featuring Asian films. While "trans-Pacific families"[9] have been a long-standing reality among Asian Americans, today's voluntary immigrants and their descendants, especially middle-class ones, lead a kind of life that tends to blunt the acute binarism between Asian and American with which earlier generations have had to contend strenuously. They need no longer conform to a paradigm of identity formation developed in the steamboat era, when entry into the U.S. more often than not meant a one-way experiment in adaptation. Instead, the voice of family across the ocean could be just a push-button phone call away, and Asian-language media could be brought into one's living room.[10] To paraphrase the title of a book on Southeast Asian Americans, the Far East has come near.[11] . . .

Not to be overlooked as part of post-1965 demographic changes in the Asian American community is the influx of Asian-born academics (among whom I count myself), whose outlook and research activities further make for closer interactions between Asian and Asian American studies. On the one hand already Westernized before immigration to the U.S.—as Rey Chow points out, this complicates, for good reason, the stereotypical belief in a pristine "native" origin[12]—these academics, unlike many of their American-born counterparts, are bilingual and biliterate, often retaining a keen interest in the transformations in the Asian cultures in a postcolonial context. To them, the continuities between Asian and Asian American are more abundant, the disjunctures less absolute, than to the early cultural nationalists. Especially apparent to the immigrant scholars is the need to denaturalize the U.S. borders as a sort of invisible fence around Asian American cultural criticism. . . .

SHIFTING FROM A DOMESTIC TO A DIASPORIC PERSPECTIVE

The third aspect of denationalization—the shift from a domestic American to a diasporic perspective—follows from the first two but has its own additional set of contributing causes. The increased porosity between Asian and Asian American is but one constituent in a global trend; to paraphrase a character in Salman Rushdie's *Satanic Verses*, the universe is shrinking.[13] In light of the aforementioned combination of multinational capital, cultural homogenization through commodification, and advanced communications technology, not only the Pacific Rim regions, but all regions of the world can be said to be interpenetrating.[14] Furthermore, as Edward Said remarks, in our century forced uprootings of entire populations have attained proportions that are humanistically and aesthetically incomprehensible. "Our age—with its modern warfare, imperialism and the quasi-theological ambitions of totalitarian rulers—is indeed the age of the refugee, the displaced persons, mass immigration."[15] Though Said's observation is not made in reference to denationalization, the mass movements he describes do point to a world in which identity and culture are increasingly decoupled from geopolitics. . . .

Not only scholars but creative writers as well are participating in denationalization in the third sense. Russell Leong's volume of poetry, *The Country of Dreams and Dust*, maps the full sweep of the Chinese diaspora with glances at the Vietnamese diaspora.[16] Jessica Hagedorn describes her own works as being filled with "edgy characters who superficially seem to belong nowhere, but actually belong everywhere"[17]—a phrase that she endows with paradigmatic force and exemplifies in the character Joey Sands in the novel

Dogeaters, a mixed race homosexual prostitute with the adaptability of a chameleon.[18] Hagedorn stresses the inspiration she gets from the "elegant chaos" of the Philippines' hybrid culture, as well as from the worldwide pop culture perceived as "American." She asserts that "as Asian Americans, as writers and people of color in a world still dominated by Western thinking," we should affirm "a literature that attempts to encompass the world."[19] For her, Asian American identity formation is not correlated with a sense of belonging to any geographical or political entity. Hagedorn's recent anthology, *Charlie Chan Is Dead*, applies principle of selection consonant with this belief.[20]

A similar valorization of fluid subjectivity and cultural world citizenship has been voiced by David Mura. In his 1991 memoir *Turning Japanese*, Mura links his "sense of homelessness and defiance of limits" to a ludic aesthetic, citing Yeats, "One day, the poet will wear all masks."[21] Mura's view suggests that denationalizing moves are not peculiar to the foreign-born or those from a heritage as hybrid as the Philippines'. Mura is a Sansei from Minnesota who grew up in a Jewish neighborhood; in his personal life, he has had to grapple with some of the issues with which the Asian American movement contended in the 1960s and 1970s, as one of his earlier essays shows.[22] Yet Mura, too, appears to have come to regard an Asian American identity as limiting. Poststructuralism is obviously a mediating influence in the case of Barthes-quoting Mura, a product of graduate studies in literature, but one hardly needs it to respond to the alluring possibility of an ever-evolving, never-resolved subjectivity, characterized by instability, endless movement, boundary transgressions, and multiple reference points.

RESERVATIONS

The above, then, are some material circumstances and discursive practices that have contributed to the emergence of a larger, more diverse, more cosmopolitan, one might say more intractable (from a theoretical standpoint) Asian American population. This population calls for vocabularies and concepts about subject formation and cultural production adequate to its perceived realities.

While I have been an early proponent of broadening Asian American literary studies to include immigrant works, which presupposes noteworthy continuities between Asian and Asian American historical experiences and cultural expressions, I have found myself raising questions about the consequences of an uncritical participation in denationalization, as if it represented a more advanced and theoretically more sophisticated (in short, superior, though proponents rarely say so directly) stage in Asian American studies. A developmental or maturational narrative about reconfigurations in Asian American cultural criticism, whether implicitly or explicitly presented, to me poses some serious risks. For convenience in discussion, these risks can be grouped into two categories that are, in fact, inseparable: unwitting subsumption into master narratives (despite a mandate to subvert master narratives built into the ethnic studies approach), and depoliticization occluded by theoretical self-critique.[23] While conceding the intellectual and emotional excitement generated by the sense of identity expansion, the benefits of interdisciplinary commerce, indeed the irreversibility of the material forces fueling Asian diasporas, I contend that at this juncture in the evolution of our field, we need to historicize the push to globalize Asian American cultural criticism. Without such historicizing, one of the most important aspirations of denationalization—to dialogize and trouble American myths of nation—may end up being more subverted than realized. . . .

It is in this context that I wish to examine a much cited model of identity formation proposed in Lisa Lowe's influential theoretical essay, "Heterogeneity, Hybridity, Multiplicity: Marking Asian American Differences."[24] Among other things, Lowe calls for a redefinition of Asian American subjectivity by holding up, as a "pos-

sible model for the ongoing construction of ethnic identity," the transnationally mobile Chinese American family in Peter Wang's film *A Great Wall*. She valorizes "the migratory process suggested by [Peter] Wang's filmic technique and emplotment": namely, a "shuttling between . . . various cultural spaces," so that "we are left, by the end of the film, with a sense of culture as dynamic and open, the result of a continual process of visiting and revisiting a plurality of cultural sites."

> We might conceive of the making and practice of Asian American culture as nomadic, unsettled, taking place in the travel between cultural sites and in the multivocality of heterogeneous and conflicting positions.[25]

I do not quote this passage here as a summation of the complex arguments in the essay, which, in deconstructing Asian American identity and revealing its internal contradictions, scrupulously affirms the continued need for a Spivakian "strategic essentialism." Lowe's main point is to interrogate the definition of "Asian American" . . . and open up the possibility of "crucial alliances with other groups—ethnicity-based, class-based, gender-based, and sexuality-based—in the ongoing work of transforming hegemony."[26] In that sense, the *Great Wall* example supports but one argument in that essay.

Nevertheless, in view of how central a theoretical document Lowe's essay is in contemporary Asian American studies, and how frequently the passage on *A Great Wall* has been cited by students, Asian Americanists, and other scholars,[27] I would like to raise several issues suggested by it. One is the danger of decontextualization. When the Chinese American father in *A Great Wall* is extracted from his environment to serve as a model of cultural dynamism, what get left out of the picture are the character's socioeconomic positioning as well as the historical juncture at which the film was made. In the film, the computer scientist's trip to China is precipitated precisely by the kind of career frustration in a racist corporate structure that I touched on above. (He is passed over for a deserved promotion.) In the pre-Tiananmen honeymoon in U.S.-China relations, this frustration could be made into a comic mechanism to trigger a journey of cultural reconsideration and discovery for the entire family; conflicts, where they surface, could be an occasion for light-hearted cross-cultural comparisons. But the hopeful cast to the journeying is less a function of cultural mobility per se than a function of less somber times.

What is more, I wonder to what extent a class bias is coded into the privileging of travel and transnational mobility in Lowe's model—and this is a questioning I extend to some other articulations of denationalization. I understand fully that Lowe's "cultural sites" need not be geographic; however, it is also not entirely accidental, I believe, that *A Great Wall* is about an affluent Chinese American family of the professional class that can take vacationing for granted and have a comfortable home to return to, even when the father has quit his job. After all, as Elaine Kim observes, it is middle-class Asian American youth who can "spend the summer in Seoul or Taipei almost the way middle-class American youth of yore went to summer camp."[28] In other words, Lowe's model of identity and cultural formation celebrating is, at least in part, extrapolated from the wide range of options available to a particular socioeconomic class, yet the class element is typically rendered invisible. It is from a similar premise, if in much harsher terms, that E. San Juan has faulted Jessica Hagedorn's celebration of her global family and her freedom to put together a fluid, transnational, and cosmopolitan identity. The celebration betrays traces of her own upper-class background: consuming of imported goods is now extended to consuming of cultural products and practices.[29]

Class can also be erased when an exilic sensibility is promoted as less narrow than an immigrant one.[30] A preference for exile status is sometimes expressed by middle or upper-middle class immigrant intellectuals who do not want to confront their complicity in emigration and settlement. That is, the severity of the circumstances propelling their exit and preventing their return could have been exaggerated in the interest of ennobling one's self-image. I began pondering this issue when, some years ago, I interviewed two well-known Chinese immigrant writers whose works I taught in a course on Chinese immigrant writing. Even though both left Taiwan under less than life-threatening circumstances and had been living as permanent residents in the U.S. for years, both repudiated the category of "immigrant" (to them probably too materialistic in connotation), preferring to be known as exiles, victims of the cataclysms in recent Chinese history who were displaced from their troubled homeland against their will. Without claiming to know how widespread this phenomenon is,[31] I submit that an elastic definition of "forcible removal" encouraged by the favoring of an exilic identity does have a tendency to depoliticize. Of course, a prolonged exilic sensibility could have been accounted for as well by the less than enthusiastic reception that the U.S. has historically offered Asians. This point has been frequently made in defense of Asian American "sojourning"; further, in his recent typology of Chinese American identity, Ling-Chi Wang has demonstrated the complexities of identification even within a single individual's lifetime.[32] Nevertheless, the potential to glamorize a noncommittal political stance in one's land of principal residence is, to me, a real danger, one that Asian American cultural critics need to recognize. . . .

But what of the opportunity to build political coalitions *across* national boundaries? Doesn't diaspora studies provide that?[33] Admittedly formed without as much deep study as I would have liked, my tentative view on this question is that, while I have seen political alliances formed between Asian Americans of different ethnicities to support struggles elsewhere—for example, in aid of pro-democracy dissidents in China or Korean students fighting for reunification—the more typical transnational political alliances seem to be those based on "blood," as a matter of "helping one's own." And given the history of Asian American studies, in which political coalitions formed with other racial/ethnic *domestic* minorities made the very existence of the field possible, I would argue for a continued primacy for this type of association. Elliott Butler-Evans made the point that Rodney King was beaten as a member of an American minority, not as a member of the black diaspora.[34] I think what he meant was that although the violence against African-Americans could be cast in a diasporic context, it is the more immediate context—the status of African-Americans as a domestic American minority—that provides the more compelling explanation and makes for more effective political intervention (at least in the short run.) This understanding should thus take precedence over one framed by the African diaspora; that the latter might provide a more theoretically comprehensive account, or be more intellectually gratifying, is a matter of lesser urgency. In the same spirit, I submit that coalitions of Asian American and other racial/ethnic minorities within the U.S. should take precedence over those formed with Asian peoples in the diaspora.

Furthermore, denationalization seems to me to have different valences in the Asian American and African-American contexts. A shift from an African-American domestic to an African diaspora perspective might be more politicizing for African-Americans, while a corresponding move might be depoliticizing for Asian Americans. For African-Americans, the study of diverse other African-origin groups might help counter the group's sense of beleaguerment and constriction imposed by the United States variant of slavery and racism. Connecting to African origins is a powerful means of undoing the cultural amnesia white society attempted to impose. In contrast, a denationalized Asian American cultural criticism may exacerbate liberal pluralism's already oppressive tendency to "'disembody," leaving America's racialized power structure intact.

In tracing her own evolving reaction to Theresa Hak Kyung Cha's *Dictee* from the 1980s to the 1990s, Elaine Kim states that this radically destabilizing text demonstrates how "we can 'have it all' by claiming an infinity of layers of self and community."[35] While Kim is careful to enumerate the possibilities so claimed, the very fact that a critic like her, known for political commitment and a deep appreciation of historical particularities, should employ a vocabulary of limitlessness testifies to the rhetoric's allure. I believe we can "have it all" only in our consciousness; the infinity of layers of self and community inevitably shrinks when one attempts to translate the claim into material reality. Not only are one's time and energy for action finite, but whatever claiming one does must be enacted from a political location—one referenced to a political structure, a nation. Theoretically I could ascribe a great deal of power to interstitiality and subjectivity-shuttling, which may be wonderful prompters of denaturalizing insights; in practical political terms, however, I can't see how an interstitial, shuttling exercise of power is done.[36] Nations dispense or withhold citizenship, identity cards, passports and visas, voting rights, educational and economic opportunities. For every vision of a borderless world extrapolated from the European Union or NAFTA, there are countless actual instances of political struggles defined in terms of national borders and within national borders. By definition, a world where most travel requires passports and visas is not ready for "world citizenship," a phrase that to me means as much as, or as little as, "just a human being." As ideals both are unimpeachable in their generosity of spirit, their expressed desire to abolish all divisions, all oppositions; as points of purchase for political action both are severely limited in utility, oftentimes disappointingly irrelevant.

In the same sentence where she affirms an "infinity of layers of self and community," Elaine Kim takes care to highlight a word that has an almost old-fashioned ring in today's world—

roots: "our rootedness enables us to take flight."[37] To Asian Americans the term "roots" could evoke contradictory meanings: either "origin," where one or one's family hails from in Asia; or else commitment to the place where one resides.[38] The second meaning, on which Asian American studies was founded, is what today's Asian Americanists must not lose sight of amidst the enthusiastic call for denationalization.

A PERSONAL POSTSCRIPT

On the door of the Asian American Studies Program office at UC Berkeley is a sign: THIS IS NOT ASIAN STUDIES, SOUTH—AND SOUTHEAST ASIAN STUDIES, OR EAST ASIAN LANGUAGES. Though born out of a practical concern—the frustrated secretary's attempt to minimize misdirected inquiries and interruptions—this sign to me epitomizes the institutional reality within which Asian American studies still operates today. It is a reminder of the precariousness of Asian American studies's discursive space: despite the increasing porosity of boundaries, Asian studies and Asian American studies are still distinct, and collapsing the two will work to the detriment more of Asian Americans as a minority within U.S. borders than of "Asian Asians." For the dropping of the "American" in "Asian American studies" is not only a widespread error—I have yet to hear of someone mistaking Asian American studies for American studies—it is one with potentially serious political consequences. As one of the immigrant academics whose presence has contributed to denationalization, I am mindful of contradictions in my position,[39] and I know that many of the research and teaching interests that come readily to me are not always the ones most needed in the field. Given that, I can no more wish myself out of priority-setting by citing the postmodern condition as my alibi, than I can conjure up an unproblematic multiple subjectivity through an assemblage of poststructuralist terms.

Times are bad, no question about it. Ling-Chi Wang has identified four founding principles of ethnic studies: self-determination, solidarity among American racial minorities, educational relevance, and an interdisciplinary approach (ridiculed as "undisciplined" in the 1960s and 1970s but, like marginality, now fashionable in academia).[40] Though these principles might not yield an exhaustive account of Asian American studies, I don't think any of them has been invalidated by changing times. The political imperatives informing Asian American cultural criticism in the early days have not been so firmly achieved that they can be comfortably retired now. In fact, in the age of Newt Gingrich, Rush Limbaugh, Proposition 187, and increasingly vicious attacks on affirmative action and other policies safeguarding the rights of peoples of color, there seems to me to be an even greater need for Asian Americanists to situate themselves historically, to ask where denationalization comes from and where it is headed. To what extent do we want to denationalize our field? To what extent do we want a diasporic perspective to supersede a domestic one? Without subscribing to a narrow, either/or alarmism, I submit these questions for the consideration of my fellow Asian Americanists.

NOTES

I am indebted to many colleagues for reading earlier drafts of this paper, being exceptionally generous with their critiques and insights, suggesting readings, sharing their work in progress, offering encouragement and support, and providing opportunities for my ideas to be publicized; for lack of space their contributions cannot always be specified: Kum-Kum Bhavnani, Chen Kuan-Hsing, King-Kok Cheung, Inderpal Grewal, Abdul JanMohamed, Caren Kaplan, Elaine Kim, Russell Leong, Lisa Lowe, Colleen Lye, Michael Omi, David Palumbo-Liu, David Parker, Steve Rumpel, Dana Takagi, Dick Walker, Ling-Chi Wang. King-Kok Cheung and I exchanged work in progress; on some issues we independently arrived at shared views, while on others we differ; see her Introduction to *An Interethnic Companion to Asian American Literature* (Cambridge University Press, 1997). I am also grateful for feedback from the students in my graduate seminar on Asian American literature, Spring 1993, as well as from the audiences at the following gatherings when earlier versions of the paper were presented: the "Decentering Identity, Recentering Politics" conference at UC Santa Barbara, April 1993, organized by Kum-Kum Bhavnani; the Asian American Literature Discussion Group session at the MLA Convention, Toronto, December 1993; the Townsend Center Humanities Fellowship meetings, 1993–4; the Ethnic Studies Colloquium Series, UC Berkeley, Spring 1994; the American Cultures Summer Seminar for Community College Teachers, June 1994. I thank Dorothy Wang and John Zou for their skillful and prompt research assistance, often at short notice.

1. Paradoxically, another cultural consequence may be just the opposite: the rise of various forms of fundamentalism worldwide, with their insistence on purity, absoluteness, and inviolable borders. I am indebted to Abdul JanMohamed for pointing out this phenomenon, which, however, lies beyond the scope of this paper.

2. Sucheng Chan, *Asian Americans: An Interpretive History* (Boston: Twayne Publishers, 1991), 174–175.

3. Sucheta Mazumdar, "Asian American Studies and Asian Studies: Rethinking Roots," in *Asian Americans: Comparative and Global Perspectives*, eds. Shirley Hune et al. (Pullman: Washington State University Press, 1991), 40.

4. Shirley Geok-lin Lim and Amy Ling, eds., *Reading the Literatures of Asian America* (Philadelphia: Temple University Press, 1992), xiii.

5. This phenomenon has generated a great deal of scholarship; see, for example, Frederic C. Deyo, ed., *The Political Economy of the New Asian Industrialism* (Ithaca, New York: Cornell University Press, 1987); Nigel Harris, "The Pacific Rim" (review article), *Journal of Development Studies* 25:3 (April 1989), 408–416; Miyohei Shinohara and Fu-chen Lo, eds., *Global Adjustment and the Future of Asian-Pacific Economy: Papers and Proceedings of the Conference on Global Adjustment and the Future of Asian-Pacific Economy Held on 11–13 May, 1988 in Tokyo* (Tokyo: Institute of Developing Economies and Kuala Lumpur: Asian and Pacific Development Centre, 1989); Ziya Onis, "The Logic of the Developmental State" (review article), *Comparative Politics* 24:1 (October 1991), 109–126.

    Parenthetically, the prospect of sharing in Asian prosperity is so attractive that the former British colonies of Australia and New Zealand, previously Europe-oriented and white-identified, are now attempting to redefine themselves as Asian. See, for example, Shi Zhongxin, "Australia 'Merging into Asia,' " *Beijing Review* 36:3–4 (Jan. 18, 1993), 13; Colin James, "Bye-bye Britannia: Asia Looms into the National Consciousness," *Far Eastern Economic Review* 157:17 (Oct. 20, 1994), 26–27; Bruce Grant, "Australia Confronts an Identity Crisis," *New York Times* vol. 143, sec. 4 (March 20, 1994), E5, col. 1. See Rob Wilson and Arif Dirlik, "Introduction: Asia/Pacific as Space of Cultural Production," in Wilson and Dirlik, eds., *Asia/Pacific as Space of Cultural Production*, special issue of *boundary* 2 21:1 (Spring 1994), 1–14, for a broader contextualization of this redefinition.

6. A recent *Wall Street Journal* article notes that Taiwan, Hong Kong, Singapore, and South Korea are now considered part of the First World. See Dan Biers, "Now in First World, Asian Tigers Act Like It," *Wall Street Journal* February 28, 1995, A-15.

7. Ashley Dunn, "Skilled Asians Leaving U.S. for High Tech Jobs at Home," *New York Times* 144:1, February 28, 1995, 1, col. 1.

8. Christopher L. Connery, "Pacific Rim Discourse: The U.S. Global Imaginary in the Late Cold War Years," in Wilson and Dirlik, 30–56.

9. The term is Liu Haiming's, in "The Trans-Pacific Family: A Case Study of Sam Chang's Family History," *Amerasia Journal* 18:2 (1991), 1–34.

10. A few images from my own experience illustrate the magnitude of this cultural phenomenon: an encyclopedic Chinese video store in Lion City, a giant suburban Asian shopping mall in San Jose, California; AT&T and MCI vying for Asian customers through language- and culture-specific ads designed to tug at the heartstrings of trans-Pacific families; second-generation college students at UC Berkeley telling me that they have managed to keep up with their Cantonese through watching Hong Kong movies at home.

11. Lucy Nguyen-Hong-Nhiem and Joel Martin Halpern, eds., *The Far East Comes Near: Autobiographical Accounts of Southeast Asian Students in America* (Amherst: University of Massachusetts Press, 1989).

12. Rey Chow, *Woman and Chinese Modernity: The Politics of Reading between West and East* (Minneapolis: University of Minnesota Press, 1991), xi–xii.

13. As cited in Jessica Hagedorn, "The Exile Within/The Question of Identity," in Lee C. Lee, ed., *Asian Americans: Collages of Identities Proceedings of Cornell Symposium on Asian America: Issues of Identity* (Ithaca, New York: Asian American Studies Program, Cornell University, 1992), 25.

14. Frederick Buell, *National Culture and the New Global System* (Baltimore: The Johns Hopkins University Press, 1994), provides one account of this interpenetration that minimizes the effects of cultural imperialism.

15. Edward Said, "Reflections on Exile," in Russell Ferguson et al., eds., *Out There: Marginalization and Contemporary Cultures* (New York: The New Museum of Contemporary Art and Cambridge, Massachusetts: The MIT Press, 1990), 357.

16. Russell Leong, *The Country of Dreams and Dust* (Albuquerque, New Mexico: West End Press, 1993). This . . . publication is particularly intriguing given the fact that Leong, the editor of *Amerasia Journal*, has been a significant presence in Asian American studies since the cultural nationalist period.

17. Hagedorn, "Exile," 28.

18. Jessica Hagedorn, *Dogeaters* (New York: Pantheon, 1990).

19. Hagedorn, "Exile," 28.

20. Jessica Hagedorn, ed., *Charlie Chan Is Dead: An Anthology of Contemporary Asian American Fiction* (New York: Penguin, 1994).

21. David Mura, "Preparations" [excerpts from Chapter 1 of *Turning Japanese: A Sansei Memoir*, Boston: Atlantic Monthly, 1991], in Lee C. Lee, *ibid.*, 23.

22. David Mura, "Strangers in the Village," in Rick Simonson and Scott Walker, eds., *The Graywolf Annual Five: Multi-Cultural Literacy* (Saint Paul, Minnesota: Graywolf Press, 1988), 135–153.

23. For a particularly incisive critique of the tendency among some Asian American cultural critics to align Asian American literature with a postmodernist aesthetic while bypassing contemporary political history, see David Palumbo-Liu, "The Ethnic as 'Post-': Reading the Literatures of Asian America," *American Literary History* 7:1 (1995), 161–168. Palumbo-Liu's essay in this volume, "Theory and the Subject of Asian American Studies," raises this pointed question: "does the postmodern present the moment for the ethnic to be conjoined with the universal, as everything is now in a correlate condition of fragmentation and revision, or does this condition erase at that moment the very specificity of ethnicity?"

24. Which, interestingly, appeared in the inaugural issue of a journal named *Diaspora*. "Heterogeneity, Hybridity, Multiplicity: Marking Asian American Differences," *Diaspora* 1:1 (1991), 24–44.

25. Lowe, "Heterogeneity," 39.

26. Ibid., 39, 40.

27. Buell, 194–196, represents a recent example of a non-Asian Americanist using Lowe's essay.

28. "Foreword," in Lim and Ling, xiv.

29. E. San Juan, Jr., "From Identity Politics to Strategies of Disruption: USA Self and/or Asian Alter?" in Lee C. Lee, 129–131.

30. I consider "exilic'" and "diasporic" to be overlapping, both being referenced to a point of origin and both entailing dispersal. In this essay I use "exilic" when the forcibleness of the removal and the sense of involuntary expulsion are foregrounded by the subject.

31. Nerissa Balce-Cortes observes that some Filipino Americans have been criticized for adopting an "exile" label while enjoying a relatively privileged and terror-free life abroad during the Marcos era. Remark made at a 1993 meeting of the Filipino Studies Working Group, University of California, Berkeley.

32. L. Ling-Chi Wang, "Roots and the Changing Identity of the Chinese in the United States," in Tu Wei-ming, ed., *The Living Tree: The Changing Meaning of Being Chinese Today* (Stanford: Stanford University Press, 1994),185–212.

33. I am indebted to Angela Davis for raising the question of political alliances at the "Decentering Identity, Recentering Politics" conference, and to Barbara Christian for comparing notes with me on the political meaning of the diasporic perspective in African-American and Asian American studies at the 1994 American Cultures seminar at UC Berkeley.

34. Comment made at the "Decentering Identity, Recentering Politics" conference.

35. Elaine Kim, "Forward" in Shirley Goek-Lim and Amy Ling, eds., *Reading the Literatures of Asian America* (Philadelphia: Temple University Press, 1992), xvi.

36. Except maybe in a state of revolutionary anarchy?

37. Kim, "Foreword," xvi.

38. Wang, "Roots," 187.

39. For a relevant analysis of the intellectual's location, see Aijaz Ahmad, *In Theory: Classes, Nations, Literatures* (London: Verso, 1992), 73–94 and 159. I am indebted to Colleen Lye for this source.

40. "Asian American Studies/Ethnic Studies: Politics of Reception and Acceptance," unpublished paper presented to Columbia University's Graduate School of Education, November 5, 1993.

Maiden Voyage: Excursion into Sexuality and Identity Politics in Asian America

Dana Y. Takagi

Like black men and women who refused to be the exceptional "pet" Negro for whites, and who instead said they were "niggers" too (the original "crime" of "niggers" and lesbians is that they prefer themselves), perhaps black women writers and non-writers should say, simply, whenever black lesbians are being put down, held up, messed over, and generally told their lives should not be encouraged, *We are all lesbians.* For surely it is better to be thought a lesbian, and to say and write your life exactly as you experience it, than to be a token "pet" black woman for those whose contempt for our autonomous existence makes them a menace to human life.[1]

Alice Walker

The topic of sexualities—in particular, lesbian, gay, and bisexual identities—is an important and timely issue in that place we imagine as Asian America. *All of us* in Asian American Studies ought to be thinking about sexuality and Asian American history for at least two compelling reasons.

One, while there has been a good deal of talk about the "diversity" of Asian American communities, we are relatively uninformed about Asian American subcultures organized specifically around sexuality. There are Asian American gay and lesbian social organizations, gay bars that are known for Asian clientele, conferences that have focused on Asian American lesbian and gay experiences, and as Tsang notes in this issue, electronic bulletin boards catering primarily to gay Asians, their friends, and their lovers. I use the term "subcultures" here rather loosely and not in

the classic sociological sense, mindful that the term is somewhat inaccurate since gay Asian organizations are not likely to view themselves as a gay subculture within Asian America any more than they are likely to think of themselves as an Asian American subculture within gay America. If anything, I expect that many of us view ourselves as on the margins of both communities. That state of marginalization in both communities is what prompts this essay and makes the issues raised in it all the more urgent for all of us—gay, straight, somewhere-in-between. For as Haraway has suggested, the view is often clearest from the margins where, "The split and contradictory self is the one who can interrogate positionings and be accountable, the one who can construct and join rational conversations and fantastic imaginings that change history."[2]

To be honest, it is not clear to me exactly *how* we ought to be thinking about these organizations, places, and activities. On the one hand, I would argue that an organization like the Association of Lesbians and Gay Asians (ALGA) ought to be catalogued in the annals of Asian American history. But on the other hand, having noted that ALGA is as Asian American as Sansei Live! or the National Coalition for Redress and Reparation, the very act of including lesbian and gay experiences in Asian American history, which seems important in a symbolic sense, produces in me a moment of hesitation. Not because I do not think that lesbian and gay sexualities are not deserving of a place in Asian American history, but rather, because the inscription of non-straight sexualities in Asian American history immediately casts theoretical doubt about how to do it. As I will suggest, the recognition of different

Source: *Amerasia Journal* 21:1 (1994): 1–17. Reprinted by permission.

sexual practices and identities that also claim the label *Asian American* presents a useful opportunity for re-thinking and re-evaluating notions of identity that have been used, for the most part, unproblematically and uncritically in Asian American Studies.

The second reason, then, that we ought to be thinking about gay and lesbian sexuality and Asian American Studies is for the theoretical trouble we encounter in our attempts to situate and think about sexual identity *and* racial identity. Our attempts to locate gay Asian experiences in Asian American history render us "uninformed" in an ironic double sense. On the one hand, the field of Asian American Studies is mostly ignorant about the multiple ways that gay identities are often hidden or invisible within Asian American communities. But the irony is that the more we know, the less we know about the ways of knowing. On the other hand, just at the moment that we attempt to rectify our ignorance by adding say, the lesbian, to Asian American history, we arrive at a stumbling block, an ignorance of how to add her. Surely the quickest and simplest way to add her is to think of lesbianism as a kind of ad hoc subject-position, a minority within a minority. But efforts to think of sexuality in the same terms that we think of race, yet simultaneously different from race in certain ways, and therefore, the inevitable "revelation" that gays/lesbians /bisexuals are like minorities but also different too, is often inconclusive, frequently ending in "counting" practice. While many minority women speak of "triple jeopardy" oppression—as if class, race, and gender could be disentangled into discrete additive parts—some Asian American could rightfully claim quadruple jeopardy oppression—class, race, gender, and sexuality. Enough counting. Marginalization is not as much about the *quantities* of experiences as it is about *qualities* of experience. And, as many writers, most notably feminists, have argued, identities whether sourced from sexual desire, racial origins, languages of gender, or class roots, are simply not additive.[3]

NOT COUNTING

A discussion of sexualities is fraught with all sorts of definition conundrums. What exactly does it mean, sexuali*ties*? The plurality of the term may be unsettling to some who recognize three (or two, or one) forms of sexual identity: gay, straight, bisexual. But there are those who identify as straight, but regularly indulge in homoeroticism, and, of course, there are those who claim the identity gay/lesbian, but engage in heterosexual sex. In addition, some people identify themselves sexually but do not actually have sex, and, there are those who claim celibacy as a sexual practice. For those who profess a form of sexual identity that is, at some point, at odds with their sexual practice or sexual desire, the idea of a single, permanent, or even stable sexual identity is confining and inaccurate. Therefore, in an effort to capture the widest possible range of human sexual practices, I use the term sexualities to refer to the variety of practices and identities that range from homoerotic to heterosexual desire. In this essay, I am concerned mainly with homosexual desire and the question of what happens when we try to locate homosexual identities in Asian American history. . . .

It is vogue these days to celebrate difference. But underlying much contemporary talk about difference is the assumption that differences are comparable things. For example, many new social movements activists, including those in the gay and lesbian movement, think of themselves as patterned on the "ethnic model."[4] And for many ethnic minorities, the belief that "gays are oppressed too" is a reminder of a sameness, a common political project in moving margin to center, that unites race-based movements with gays, feminists, and greens. The notion that our differences are "separate but equal" can be used to call attention to the specificity of experiences or to rally the troops under a collective banner. Thus, the concept of difference espoused in identity politics may be articulated in moments of what Spivak refers to as "strategic essentialism" or in what Hall coins "positionalities." But in the heat of local political struggles and coalition building, it turns out that not all differences are created equally. For example, Ellsworth recounts how differences of race, nationality, and gender, unfolded in the context of a relatively safe environment, the university classroom:

> Women found it difficult to prioritize expressions of racial privilege and oppression when such prioritizing threatened to perpetuate their gender oppression. Among international students, both those who were of color and those who were White found it difficult to join their voices with those of U.S. students of color when it meant a subordination of their oppressions as people living under U.S. imperialist policies and as students for whom English was a second language. Asian American women found it difficult to join their voices with other students of color when it meant subordinating their specific oppressions as Asian Americans. I found it difficult to speak as a White woman about gender oppression when I occupied positions of institutional power relative to all students in the class, men and women, but positions of gender oppression relative to students who were White men, and in different terms, relative to students who were men of color.[5]

The above example demonstrates the tensions between sameness and difference that haunt identity politics. Referring to race and sexuality, Cohen suggests that the "sameness" that underlies difference may be more fiction than fact:

> . . . the implied isomorphism between the "arbitrariness of racial categorizations" and the "sexual order" elides the complex processes of social differentiation that assign, legitimate, and enforce qualitative distinctions between different types of individuals. Here the explicit parallel drawn between "race" and "sexuality," familiar to so many polemical affirmations of (non-racial) identity politics, is meant to evoke an underlying and apparently indisputable common sense that naturalizes this particular choice of political strategy almost as if the "naturalness" of racial "identity" could confer a corollary stability on the less "visible" dynamics of sexuality.[7]

There are numerous ways that being "gay" is not like being "Asian." Two broad distinctions are worth noting. The first, mentioned by Cohen above, is the relative invisibility of sexual identity compared with racial identity. While both can be said to be socially constructed, the former are performed, acted out, and produced, often in individual routines, whereas the latter tends to be more obviously "written" on the body and negotiated by political groups.[7] Put another way, there is a quality of voluntarism in being gay/lesbian that is usually not possible as an Asian American. One has the option to present oneself as "gay" or "lesbian," or alternatively, to attempt to "pass," or, to stay in "the closet," that is, to hide one's sexual preference.[8] However, these same options are not available to most racial minorities in face-to-face interactions with others.

As Asian Americans, we do not think in advance about whether or not to present ourselves as "Asian American," rather, that is an identification that is worn by us, whether we like it or not, and which is easily read off of us by others.

A second major reason that the category "gay" ought to be distinguished from the category "Asian American" is for the very different histories of each group. Studying the politics of being "gay" entails on the one hand, an analysis of discursive fields, ideologies, and rhetoric about sexual identity, and on the other hand, knowledge of the history of gays/lesbians as subordinated minorities relative to heterosexuals. . . . Similarly, studying "Asian America" requires analysis of semantic and rhetorical discourse in its variegated forms, racist, apologist, and paternalist, and requires in addition, an understanding of the specific histories of the peoples who recognize themselves as Asian or Asian American. But the specific discourses and histories in each case are quite different. Even though we make the same intellectual moves to approach each form of identity, that is, a two-tracked study of ideology on the one hand, and history on the other, the particular ideologies and histories of each are very different.[9]

In other words, many of us experience the worlds of Asian America and gay America as separate places—emotionally, physically, intellectually. We sustain the separation of these worlds with our folk knowledge about the family-centeredness and supra-homophobic beliefs of ethnic communities. Moreover, it is not just that these communities know so little of one another, but, we frequently take great care to keep those worlds distant from each other. What could be more different than the scene at gay bars like "The End Up" in San Francisco, or "Faces" in Hollywood, and, on the other hand, the annual Buddhist church bazaars in the Japanese American community or Filipino revivalist meetings?[10] These disparate worlds occasionally collide through individuals who manage to move, for the most part, stealthily, between these spaces. But it is the act of deliberately bringing these worlds closer together that seems unthinkable. Imagining your parents, clutching bento box lunches, thrust into the smoky haze of a South of Market leather bar in San Francisco is no less strange a vision than the idea of Lowie taking Ishi, the last of his tribe, for a cruise on Lucas' Star Tours at Disneyland. "Cultural strain," the anthropologists would say. Or, as Wynn Young, laughing at the prospect of mixing his family with his boyfriend, said, "Somehow I just can't picture this conversation at the dinner table, over my mother's homemade barbecued pork: 'Hey, Ma. I'm sleeping with a sixty-year-old white guy who's got three kids, and would you please pass the soy sauce?' "[11]

Thus, "not counting" is a warning about the ways to think about the relationship of lesbian/gay identities to Asian American history. While it may seem politically efficacious to toss the lesbian onto the diversity pile, adding one more form of subordination to the heap of inequalities, such a strategy glosses over the particular or distinctive ways sexuality is troped in Asian America. Before examining the possibilities for theorizing "gay" and "Asian American" as non-mutually exclusive identities, I turn first to a fuller description of the chasm of silence that separates them.

SILENCES

The concept of silence is a doggedly familiar one in Asian American history. For example, Hosokawa characterized the Nisei as "Quiet Americans" and popular media discussions of the "model minority" typically describe Asian American students as "quiet" along with "hard working" and "successful." In the popular dressing of Asian American identity, silence has functioned as a metaphor for the assimilative and positive imagery of the "good" minorities. More recently, analysis of popular imagery of the "model minority" suggest that silence ought to be understood as an adaptive mechanism to a racially discriminatory society rather than as an intrinsic part of Asian American culture.[12]

If silence has been a powerful metaphor in Asian American history, it is also a crucial element of discussions of gay/lesbian identity, albeit in a somewhat different way. In both cases, silence may be viewed as the oppressive cost of a racially biased or heterosexist society. For gays and lesbians, the act of coming out takes on symbolic importance, not just as a personal affirmation of "this is who I am," but additionally as a critique of expected norms in society, "we are everywhere." While "breaking the silence" about Asian Americans refers to crashing popular stereotypes about them, and shares with the gay act of "coming out" the desire to define oneself rather than be defined by others, there remains an important difference between the two.

The relative invisibility of homosexuality compared with Asian American identity means that silence and its corollary space, the closet, are more ephemeral, appear less fixed as boundaries of social identities, less likely to be taken-for-granted than markers of race, and consequently, more likely to be problematized and theorized in discussions that have as yet barely begun on racial identity. Put another way, homosexuality is more clearly seen as *constructed* than racial identity.[13] Theoretically speaking, homosexual identity does not enjoy the same privileged stability as racial identity. The borders that separate gay from straight, and, "in" from "out," are so fluid that in the final moment we can only be sure that sexual identities are as Dianna Fuss notes, "in Foucaldian terms, less a matter of final discovery than a matter of perpetual invention."[14]

Thus, while silence is a central piece of theoretical discussions of homosexuality, it is viewed primarily as a negative stereotype in the case of Asian Americans. What seems at first a simple question in gay identity of being "in" or "out" is actually laced in epistemological knots.

For example, a common question asked of gays and lesbians by one another, or by straights, is, "Are you out?" The answer to that question (yes and no) is typically followed by a list of who knows and who does not (e.g., my coworkers know, but my family doesn't . . .). But the question of who knows or how many people know about one's gayness raises yet another question, "how many, or which, people need to know one is gay before one qualifies as "out?" Or as Fuss says, "To be out, in common gay parlance, is precisely to be no longer out; to be out is to be finally outside of exteriority and all the exclusions and deprivations such outsider-hood imposes. Or, put another way, to be out is really to be in—inside the realm of the visible, the speakable, the culturally intelligible."[15] . . .

The Coming Out Incident

Once, when I was a teaching assistant in Asian American Studies at Berkeley during the early 1980s, a lesbian, one of only two white students in my section, decided to come out during the first section meeting. I had asked each student to explain their interest, personal and intellectual, in Asian American Studies. Many students mentioned wanting to know "more about their heritage," and "knowing the past in order, to understand the present." The lesbian was nearly last to speak. After explaining that she wanted to understand the heritage of a friend who was Asian American, her final words came out tentatively, as if she had been deliberating about whether or not

to say them, "And, I guess I also want you all to know that I am a lesbian." In the silence that followed I quickly surveyed the room. A dozen or so Asian American students whom I had forced into a semi-circular seating arrangement stared glumly at their shoes. The two white students, both of whom were lesbians, as I recall, sat together, at one end of the semi-circle. They glanced expectantly around the circle, and then, they too, looked at the ground. I felt as though my own world had split apart, and the two pieces were in front of me, drifting, surrounding, and at that moment, both silent. . . .

In the silence that followed the act of coming out, and indeed, in the ten weeks of class in which no one spoke of it again, I felt an awkwardness settle over our discussions in section. I was never sure exactly how the Asian American students perceived the lesbian—as a wannabe "minority," as a comrade in marginality, as any White Other, or perhaps, they did not think of it at all. Nor did I ever know if the lesbian found what she was looking for, a better understanding of the Asian American experience, in the silence that greeted her coming out. . . .

More important, the coming out incident suggests that marginalization is no guarantee for dialogue. If there is to be an interconnectedness between different vantage points, we will need to establish an art of political conversation that allows for affirmation of difference without choking secularization. The construction of such a politics is based implicitly on our vision of what happens, or, what ought to happen, when difference meets itself—queer meets Asian, black meets Korean, feminist meets Greens, etc., at times, all in one person.[16] What exactly must we know about these other identities in order to engage in dialogue?

The Question of Authenticity

What we do know about Asian American gays and lesbians must be gleaned from personal narratives, literature, poetry, short stories, and essays. But first, what falls under the mantle, *Asian American gay and lesbian* writings? Clearly, lesbians and gays whose writings are self-conscious reflections on Asian American identity and sexual identity ought to be categorized as Asian American gay/lesbian writers. For example, Kitty Tsui, Barbara Noda, and Merle Woo are individuals who have identified themselves, and are identified by others, as *Asian American lesbian voices*. Similarly, in a recent collection of essays from a special issue of *Amerasia, Burning Cane*, Alice Hom ruminates on how an assortment of Others—white dykes, Asian dykes, family, and communities—react to her as butchy/androgynous, as Asian American, as a lesbian. These writers are lesbians and they write about themselves as lesbians which grants them authorial voice *as a lesbian*. But they also identify as *Asian American*, and are concerned with the ways in which these sources of community—lesbian and Asian American—function in their everyday lives.

But what then about those who do not write explicitly or self-consciously about their sexuality or racial identity? For example, an essay on AIDS and mourning by Jeff Nunokawa, while written by a Japanese-American English professor, does not focus on issues of racial and sexual *identity*, and as such, is neither self-consciously gay nor Asian American.[17] What are we to make of such work? On the one hand, we might wish to categorize the author as a gay Asian American writer, whether he wishes to take this sign or not, presuming of course, that he is gay since his essay appears in an anthology subtitled, "gay theories," and, in addition presuming that he is Asian American, or at least identifies as such given his last name. On the other hand, we might instead argue that it is the author's work, his subject matter, and not the status of the author, that marks the work as gay, Asian American, or both. . . . In this case, we might infer that since the topic of the essay is AIDS and men, the work is best categorized as "gay," but not Asian American.

This may seem a mundane example, but ı illustrates well how authorial voice and subject matter enter into our deliberations of what counts and what does not as Asian American gay/lesbian writings. . . . The university is filled with those of us, who while we live under signs like gay, Asian, feminist, ecologist, middle-class, etc., do not make such signs the central subject of our research. And what about those individuals who write about gays/lesbians, but who identify themselves as heterosexual? In the same way that colonizers write about the colonized, and more recently, the colonized write back, blacks write about whites and vice versa, "we" write about "them" and so on.

I want to be clear, here. I am not suggesting that we try to locate Asian American gay/ lesbian sensibilities as if they exist in some pure form and are waiting to be discovered. Rather, I think we ought to take seriously Trinh T. Minh-ha's warning that, "Trying to find the other by defining otherness or by explaining the other through laws and generalities is, as Zen says, like beating the moon with a pole or scratching an itching foot from the outside of a shoe."[18] My concern here is to turn the question from one about a particular identity to the more general question of the way in which the concept of identity is deployed in Asian American history.

Thus, not only is marginalization no guarantee for dialogue, but the state of being marginalized itself may not be capturable as a fixed, coherent, and holistic identity. Our attempts to define categories like "Asian American" or "gay" are necessarily incomplete. . . .

RETHINKING IDENTITY POLITICS

Lisa Lowe in her discussion of identity politics affirms the articulation of "Asian American" identity while simultaneously warning us of its overarching, consuming, and essentializing dangers. She (Lowe) closes her discussion saying:

.y to remark that in the 1990s, we can rethink the notion of ethnic identity in of cultural, class, and gender differences, .er than presuming similarities and making the erasure of particularity the basis of unity. In the 1990s, we can diversify our political practices to include a more heterogeneous group and to enable crucial alliances with other groups—ethnicity-based class-based, and sexuality-based—in the ongoing work of transforming hegemony.[19]

I have intended this essay, in part, as an answer to Lowe's call to broaden the scope of Asian American discourse about identity. But there is a caveat. The gist of this essay has been to insist that our valuation of heterogeneity not be ad-hoc and that we seize the opportunity to recognize non-ethnic based differences—like homosexuality—as an occasion to critique the tendency toward essentialist currents in ethnic-based narratives and disciplines. In short, the practice of including gayness in Asian America rebounds into a reconsideration of the theoretical status of the concept of "Asian American" identity. The interior of the category "Asian American" ought not be viewed as a hierarchy of identities led by ethnic-based narratives, but rather, the complicated interplay and collision of different identities.

At the heart of Lowe's argument for recognizing diversity within Asian American, generational, national, gender, and class, as well as my insistence in this essay on a qualitative, not quantitative view of difference, is a particular notion of subjectivity. That notion of the subject as non-unitary stands in sharp contrast to the wholistic and coherent identities that find expression in much contemporary talk and writing about Asian Americans. At times, our need to "reclaim history" has been bluntly translated into a possessiveness about *the* Asian American experience (politics, history, literature) or perspectives as if such experiences or perspectives were not diffuse, shifting, and often contradictory. Feminists and gay writers, animated by post-structuralism's decentering practices offer an alternative, to theorize the subject rather than assume its truth, or worse yet, assign to it a truth.

Concretely, to theorize the subject means to uncover in magnificent detail the "situatedness"[20] of perspectives or identities as knowledge which even as it pleas for an elusive common language or claims to establish truth, cannot guarantee a genuine politics of diversity, that is, political conversation *and* argument, between the margins.[21] Such a politics will be marked by moments of frustration and tension because the participants will be pulling and pushing one another with statements such as, "I am like you," and "I am not like you." But the rewards for an identity politics that is not primarily ethnic-based or essentialist along some other axis will be that conversations like the one which never took place in my Asian American studies section many years ago, will finally begin. Moreover, our search for authenticity of voice—whether in gay/lesbian Asian American writing or in some other identity string—will be tempered by the realization that in spite of our impulse to clearly (de)limit them, there is perpetual uncertainty and flux governing the construction and expression of identities.

NOTES

My special thanks to Russell Leong for his encouragement and commentary on this essay.

1. Alice Walker, *Conditions: Five, the Black Women's Issue* (1984):288–89.
2. See Donna Haraway, "Situated Knowledges: The Science Question in Feminism and the Privilege of Partial Perspective," FEMINIST STUDIES 14:3 (1988), 575–99.
3. See Teresa de Lauretis, "Feminist Studies/Critical Studies: Issues, Terms, and Contexts," in *Feminist Studies/Critical Studies*, edited by Teresa de Lauretis (Bloomington: Indiana University Press, 1986), 1–19; bell hooks, *Yearning: Race, Gender and Cultural Politics* (Boston: South End Press, 1990); Trinh T. Minh-ha, *Woman, Native, Other* (Bloomington: Indiana University Press, 1989); Chandra Talpade Mohanty, "Under Western Eyes: Feminist Scholarship and Colonialist Discourses," in *Third World Women and the Politics of Feminism* edited by Chandra Talpade Mohanty, Ann Russo and Lourdes

Torres (Bloomington: Indiana University Press, 1991), 52–80; Linda Alcoff, "Cultural Feminism versus Post-Structuralism: The Identity Crisis in Feminist Theory," *Signs*, 13:3 (1988), 405–437.

4. Jeffrey Escoffier, editor of *Outlook* magazine made this point in a speech at the American Educational Research Association meetings in San Francisco, April 24, 1992.

5. See Elizabeth Ellsworth, "Why Doesn't This Feel Empowering? Working through the Repressive Myths of Critical Pedagogy," 59:3 (1989):297–324.

6. Ed Cohen, "'Who Are We'? Gay 'Identity' as Political (E)motion," *inside/out*, Diana Fuss, ed. (New York and London: Routledge, 1991), 71–92.

7. Of course there are exceptions, for example, blacks that "pass" and perhaps this is where homosexuality and racial identity come closest to one another, amongst those minorities who "pass" and gays who can also "pass."

8. I do not mean to suggest that there is only one presentation of self as lesbian. For example, one development recently featured in the *Los Angeles Times* is the evolution of "lipstick lesbians" (Van Gelder, 1991). The fashion issue has also been discussed in gay/lesbian publications. For example, Stein (1988) writing for *Outlook* has commented on the lack of correspondence between fashion and sexual identity, "For many, you can dress as femme one day and a butch the next. . . ."

9. Compare for example the histories: Takaki's *Strangers from a Different Shore*, Sucheng Chan's *Asian Americans*, and Roger Daniels' *Chinese and Japanese in America* with Jonathan Katz' *Gay American History*, Jeffrey Week's *The History of Sexuality*, Michel Foucault's *The History of Sexuality*, and David Greenberg, *The Construction of Homosexuality*.

10. See Steffi San Buenaventura, "The Master and the Federation: A Filipino-American Social Movement in California and Hawaii," *Social Process in Hawaii* 33 (1991), 169–193.

11. Wynn Young, "Poor Butterfly" *Amerasia Journal* (1991), 118.

12. See Keith Osajima, "Asian Americans as the Mod Minority: An Analysis of the Popular Press Image in th 1960s and 1980s," *Reflections on Shattered Windows Promises and Prospects for Asian American Studies*, Gary Y. Okihiro, Shirley Hune, Arthur A. Hansen and John M. Liu, eds. (Pullman: Washington State University Press, 1988), 165–174.

13. See Judith Butler, *Gender Trouble* (New York: Routledge 1990); Michel Foucault, *The History of Sexuality, Volume 1: An Introduction*, trans. Robert Hurley (New York: Vintage, 1980); Monique Wittig, *The Straight Mind and Other Essays* (Boston: Beacon 1992); Greenberg, *The Construction of Homosexuality*.

14. Diana Fuss, "Inside/Out," *inside/out*, Diana Fuss, ed., (New York: Routledge, 1991), 1–10.

15. Ibid.

16. All too often we conceptualize different identities as separate, discrete, and given (as opposed to continually constructed and shifting). For an example of how "identity" might be conceptualized as contradictory and shifting moments rather than discrete and warring "homes" see Minnie Bruce Pratt, "Identity: Skin Blood Heart" and commentary by Biddy Martin and Chandra Talpade Mohanty, "Feminist Politics: What's Home Got to Do with It?"

17. See Jeff Nunokawa, "'All the Sad Young Men' AIDS and the Work of Mourning," *inside/out*, Diana Fuss, ed., 311–123.

18. Trinh T. Minh-ha, 76.

19. Lisa Lowe, "Heterogeneity, Hybridity and Multiplicity: Marking Asian American Differences," *Diaspora* (Spring 1991), 24–44.

20. Haraway.

21. I am indebted to Wendy Brown for this point. See Wendy Brown, "Feminist Hesitations, Postmodern Exposures," *Differences* 2:1 (1991).

ontributors

Kevin Campbell completed his Ph.D. in public health from the University of California, Los Angeles, where he is a senior research associate.

Richard J. P. Cavosora is a frequent contributor to *Filipinas*.

Kenyon S. Chan is Dean of the College of Liberal Arts and Professor of Psychology at Loyola Marymount University.

Sucheng Chan is Professor and former Chair of Asian American Studies at the University of California, Santa Barbara. She is the author and editor of numerous books, including *This Bittersweet Soil: The Chinese in California Agriculture, 1860–1910* (1986), *Asian Americans: An Interpretive History* (1991), *Quiet Odyssey* (1990), and *Hmong Means Free* (1994).

Tom L. Chung is the Director of Research at the Massachusetts Executive Office of Elder Affairs.

G. Reginald Daniel is a lecturer in sociology at the University of California, Santa Barbara, and in Latin American Studies and Afro-American Studies at the University of California, Los Angeles.

Bert Eljera is a staff writer for *Asian Week*.

Timothy P. Fong is Director of the Asian American Studies program at California State University, Sacramento. He is the author of *The First Suburban Chinatown: The Remaking of Monterey Park, California* (1994) and *The Contemporary Asian American Experience: Beyond the Model Minority* (1998).

Evelyn Nakano Glenn is Professor of Women's Studies and Ethnic Studies at the University of California, Berkeley. She is the author of *Issei, Nisei, War Bride: Three Generations of Japanese Women in Domestic Service* (1986).

Sangeeta R. Gupta is a graduate student in the Department of History at the University of California, Los Angeles.

Jessica Hagedorn is the author of *Dogeaters* (1990), a novel nominated for a National Book Award, and the editor of *Charlie Chan is Dead: An Anthology of Contemporary Asian American Fiction* (1993).

Alice Y. Hom is coeditor (with David L. Eng) of *Q & A: Queer in Asian America* (forthcoming).

Shirley Hune serves as Associate Dean for Graduate Programs in the Graduate Division at the University of California, Los Angeles. She is also a professor of urban planning in the School of Public Policy and Social Research at UCLA.

Armando Jimenez is a doctoral candidate in public health at the University of California, Los Angeles.

Katherine Kam is a freelance journalist in Northern California and the former coeditor of *California Tomorrow*.

Snehendu B. Kar is Professor of Public Health and Chair of the Asian American Studies Program at the University of California, Los Angeles.

the control and measurement of operations have the same consequences.

The hypothesis that a more sophisticated managerial technology can be fully utilized only when the organization has been designed as a total system, will be examined in accordance with the following model.

In this presentation, my approach will be analytical, or a successive breakdown of the whole into increasingly smaller parts.

ORGANIZATION AS A TOTAL SYSTEM

In Figure 7-1, the business organization is presented in its most simplified form. The basic input is economic resources, the organization is the process, and the output is economic welfare. Other organizations can be represented by changing inputs-outputs. For example, a hospital has a human input (sick patient) and a human output (healthy patient).

In Figure 7-2, the control or feedback mechanism is added to the organization which is represented by management. Or, in terms of control theory, the management segment constitutes the basic control element of the organization. Thus, given a certain welfare objective or expected welfare output (a profit increment),

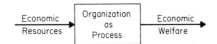

Figure 7-1   *Organization as a system.*

actual welfare is measured against expected welfare. If a difference exists, then a problem is indicated. This information is sent to the management segment which formulates a solution that becomes an input in the organization process. This feedback device will operate until the actual and expected welfares are approximately equal.

In Figure 7-3, the control unit is further broken down into a series of parts in order to provide an adaptive capability for the organization.[4] Given a change in certain environmental inputs, one initially has an input analyzer which indicates the nature of such changes. This is an information gathering or sensory device; and somewhat analogously, market research might be so categorized in terms of sensitizing the organization to some of the external variables as accounting functions for the internal changes. One also has a display device or identifier which indicates the state of the organization or any of its subprocesses at any given time. Hence, if the subprocess was a

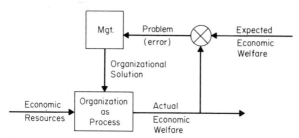

Figure 7-2   Organization with control unit.

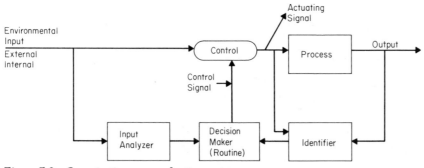

Figure 7-3   Organization as an adaptive system.

production plant, the identifier at a given time might indicate the productive capacity, current running capacity, order backlog, inventory conditions, orders in process, production lines in operation, and machine breakdown. Such information is fed to a decision-making unit along with the information from the environment. We assume that a set of rules has been programmed. One of these rules will be selected, given a particular environmental input, and given the state of the process at some given point of time in order to achieve a certain output.

For example, if the initial input is a large order with a required completion date, the rule may be to go to overtime. This information is called a control signal and is sent to the control unit. The control unit is that element which actually changes the input before it enters the system or the process itself. The order could have been put into a queue. Such information is simultaneously sent to the identifier. Therefore, at any given time, the identifier tells us what inputs have entered the process, the state of the process, and its outputs.

Because the control signal and the control unit are frequently confused, the difference between the two should be noted. The example that is usually given is that of driving an automobile. If one wants to stop an automobile by pressing on the brake pedal, information is relayed to the brakes of the car. It is not the brake pedal that stops the car, but the brakes which constitute the control unit. Similarly, in a man-to-man system, the control signal, and the control unit might appear as in Figure 7-4.

Let us suppose that the total employee population is the basic system and we want a higher work output. Further assume that we know exactly what the relationship is between need satisfaction input and expected work output. Given the figure for expected work output, the decision-maker will increase or decrease the amount of need satisfaction (for example, money) by a control signal to the financial department where need satisfaction is stored in the form of money. This department would release funds until the expected work output was achieved. The control element constitutes the reservoir and release of funds, not the decision to increase work output, its relay to the employee, or even the decision to pay more. In other words, money may be to the employee what brakes are to an automobile.

For our particular purposes, those subparts of the organizational control mechanism, input analyzer, and so on, give the process an adaptive capability: the ability to adapt the changing inputs in order to maintain a desired or expected output.

In Figure 7-5, the organization is further broken down into a series of major subproc-

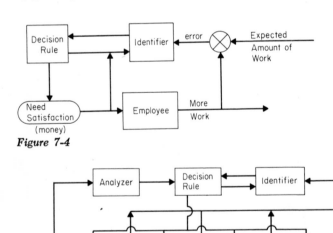

Figure 7-4

Figure 7-5

esses: marketing, production, and so on, each with its own adaptor. The adaptor consists of an input analyzer, decision rules, identifier, and control for each subprocess. Moreover, it is assumed that each of these subprocesses can be identified and separated from other subprocesses. A super adaptor applies a series of decision rules for subdecision makers to assure appropriate adjustment between processes. It is further assumed that each subsystem's adaptor has this same capability concerning sub-subprocesses. Consequently, the production system may have such subsystems as purchasing, inventory control, and maintenance. The inputs and outputs of these subsystems would have to be controlled appropriately with the proper decision rules.

In Figure 7-6, a learning capability in the form of a designer is added to the adaptive system. A learning capability can be thought of as the ability of the system to redesign itself or learn from past mistakes in order to improve system performance. However, although the environmental state of the system and the application of what is thought to be the correct rule is given, the expected output may still not be produced. This indicates design problems.

The designer would receive information as to system performance. Then, in order to increase welfare output, he would attempt to improve the adaptive mechanism by formulating more effective decision rules for the decision-making routine; by improving the identifier in terms of more and better information; by achieving a more rapid response in information from the input analyzer; by improving the sensory devices; and by improving the control mechanism.

In Figure 7-7, we now see the total system in some detail. We have our environmental inputs on the left, both external and internal: psychological, sociological, etc. Two basic subsystems are shown, marketing and production, in which the marketing output becomes a production input. Each of these subsystems has its own adaptor and, although not shown, a coordinating adaptor to integrate the two. Further, each subsystem has its own design capability. The only new feature of the schematic is the box at the top, "Design of System Design." This particular function would integrate the work of subdesigners. For example, if the organization is viewed as an aircraft, design coordination is required for such areas as weight, and structures, air frame, power, and information systems. Moreover, this function would advise as to design technique and strategy, and ideally, one might be able to reach a stage in which the actual design of subsystems could be programmed and routinized.

Thus, in looking at Figure 7-7, we see, in some detail, the organization as a total system that is self-regulating and self-learning and at least partially closed; a system in which the environment can be detailed and in which subsystems are integrated. Further, the adaptor provides for appropriate internal adjustments between subsystems. In other words, the organization, without too much difficulty, can be considered as a total system. All of its essential elements can be incorporated into a design. Also, with an appropriate index, one could detail the subsystems; each subsystem could be broken down into its sub-subsystems, etc. The indexing of the system's subparts schematic to assure appropriate usage is not an insurmountable problem. For example, it is estimated that the blue prints for a new aircraft

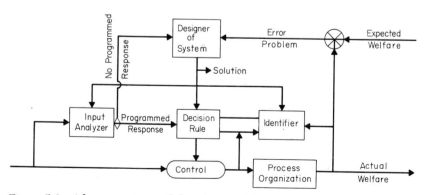

Figure 7-6 Adaptive system with learning capability.

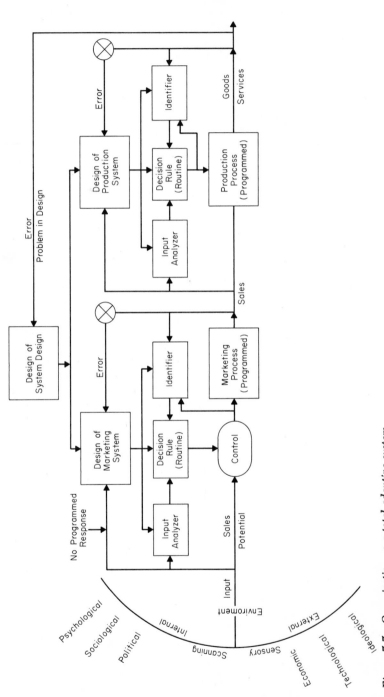

Figure 7-7 *Organization as a total adaptive system.*

may finally weigh two or three tons—more than the aircraft itself!

SYSTEM DESIGN

In Figure 7-8, we can briefly go through the design process which further analyzes the function of the designer. Given a statement of the problem or the type of system with which one is concerned, the next and key step is the construction of a model of the system. Such a model (which I believe should be essentially stochastic in nature) would stipulate the output, or mission, of the system and the inputs, of which there are three: (1) the input upon which the process is to operate or that input which enters the system, (2) environmental inputs which affect the process, and (3) instrumental or control inputs which modify the operation of the process or the process itself. (This last set of inputs concerns the technology of processing the load inputs.)

For example, in a marketing subsystem, if the initial input is a potential customer, he has to be processed through the subsystem so that a sale is secured. The system's logic relates to the set of decision rules or, given certain inputs, the state of the system and a certain control capability, such as the extent of advertising, what particular decision rule should be utilized to achieve some expected output? Information requirements relate to the classification, amount, and timing of information for the system to operate as expected. Concerning the environmental variables, it is necessary to know what information about which variables should be gathered and how often, how much, and how soon this information has to reach the decision rule.

At the outset, it would be a highly worthwhile investment to construct a fairly complete stochastic model of the proposed system in which output is the dependent variable and environmental and instrumental inputs are the independent variables. For example, one might be concerned with a personnel selection subsystem in which the output is a certain number of qualified employees. The environmental inputs might include labor demand for certain occupations, amount of unemployment, and the number of graduates. The instrumental variables might include the recruiting budget, the number of recruiters, and the training program.

What is being suggested is that it is more efficient to construct one model to which various decision rules can be applied than to construct a new model every time a new decision rule is formulated. With the latter approach, one would always be reconstructing the model when there is a change in tools.

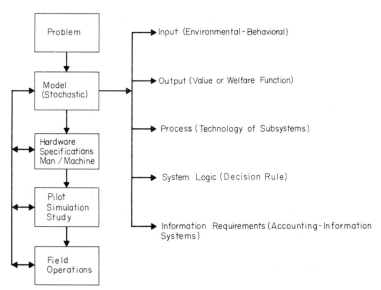

Figure 7-8 System design. For a full explanation of this design process see Harry Goode and Robert Machol. System Engineering. *New York: McGraw-Hill, 1957.*

Assuming the model can be constructed, the research and development begins. One can experiment and try different decision rules and different hardware specifications, which lead to the next two steps in the design process. Given a new rule on a pilot basis, one can apply it to actual hardware. Naturally, one has to be sure that the data from pilot studies are meaningful in terms of the total system with which one is concerned. Experimentation is costly and uncertain, but there is little doubt that the payoff is greater than using an intuitive approach.

If it is successful, the new rule can be applied and data can be fed back regularly to the designer so that he can continually improve and refine his initial model. Although one may begin with a relatively unrefined model, with successive experimentation and field experience, hard data will constantly flow back to the designer. This will enable him to improve his model in terms of the nature of variables, the preciseness of the parameters, and predictability.

As for hardware specifications, apart from the consideration of costs, one is concerned with providing components that will execute the operations as specified. In Figure 7-8, Schematic, the hardware problem how to convert what is essentially a paper model into something that approaches operating reality is of particular concern. (It seems to me that this is the area of greatest deficiency as far as the state of the arts is concerned.) We can construct reasonably good stochastic or econometric models, which can be used to simulate different decision rules, but the conversion of those models into operating reality with appropriate hardware is a different matter.

In operating context, the stochastic model or identifier becomes an information panel for a decision or rule-maker. In terms of hardware, what is needed are information collection or sensory devices which survey the environment and send such data to a central location so that the values of the variables of the model can be displayed. An example of this is the control room in a public utility in which the operator continually watches the changing values of significant variables. Only with such a display can appropriate action be taken. However, wiring such a system is a particularly difficult task.

For example, I am a member of a team that has been given the responsibility of designing a metropolitan poverty program as a total sys-tem. The primary inputs are poverty families and the output is supposed to be self-sufficient economic units. Although there exists some technical assurance that a stochastic model can be constructed, we have not been able to reach this design step because we are at the very primitive stage of inventing sensory mechanism that will give us some running idea of the nature of our changing inputs. In this instance the changing inputs are the changing mix of the characteristics of our poverty family inputs. This program appears in Figure 7-9.

Another area that requires additional work is the control element, which actually modifies the operation of the system. In a man-to-man system, we do not have sufficient information about which variables to vary and the degree of variation necessary to achieve the desired human behavior. The crude reward and punishment system that we have all too often gives us dysfunctional results. Presumably, in the design process, when serious deficiencies arise, research and development should be directed to those areas.

MANAGERIAL TECHNOLOGY AS UTILIZED IN SYSTEM DESIGN

Although this view of an organization as a total adaptive system and the design process has been brief, perhaps it has been sufficient to indicate how one can take advantage of the newer managerial techniques in the use of system analysis.[5] It is necessary to know where and how these techniques fit in terms of the system presented. As for the behavioral sciences, our environmental inputs or variables are behavioral in nature. To build a model, and eventually a display panel, such knowledge is essential. In the decision box we would utilize our various decision rules such as Linear Programming, Game Theory, Dynamic Programming, and Pert.

Because system design requires eventual concern with a total subsystem such as marketing, we will probably become increasingly concerned with the problem of combining various decision rules. For example, Gerald Thompson has indicated that we must combine appropriate decision rules to achieve the most satisfactory system output. We must know under what conditions it is advisable to move from Linear Programming to rule of thumb and then back to Linear Programming. There is an over-concern with single decision rule,

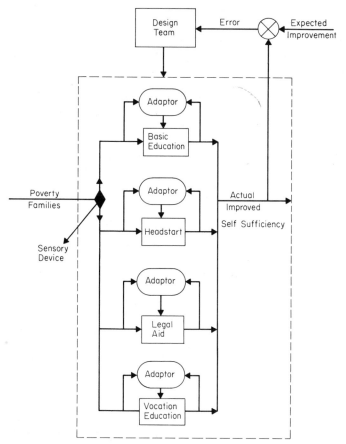

Figure 7-9   Poverty programs system.

and we must learn how to use different combinations of rules under a variety of operating conditions. As Professor Thompson has noted, "We need to develop heuristics about using heuristics. That is, an executive program that would accept a problem and then decide which of a list of heuristics (decision rules) should be employed to give its solution."[6]

The information sciences relate to the input analyzer, collection, manipulation, and relay of information. Here we have all of our data, collection, and processing problems. The control element relates to the relatively new area of control theory; specifically, the direction of human effort. Finally, in designing a specific subsystem, such as personnel or marketing, we should have some knowledge with regard to the technology of these systems. For example, we should be able to use employment tests correctly in the selection process.

In designing an organization as a total system, it would appear that we would have to be familiar with and capable of using, a wide array of reasonably sophisticated managerial techniques and knowledge. The understanding and use of managerial techniques is an integral part of the design process. This is a counterdistinction to the bureaucratic structure, which merely attaches such techniques to the system with little purpose or place.

DESIGN CRITERIA

Design criteria are rules which are utilized to evaluate the acceptability of designs. Given a number of designs, we must determine which one is the best. Although there are numerous rules, the most widely used are measurability, feasibility, optimality, reliability, and stability. We will consider only the first three. Measurability is the system's ability to evaluate its performance. If its performance cannot be measured, a system's desirability or undesirability cannot be established and its particular excellences or deficiencies cannot be known. When models are measurable, the superior system can be inferred from the specific measuring devices used in each. In the model which I have suggested, the identifier as a display panel is the primary measuring mechanism since we would know the actual inputs, process, outputs, and decision rules. If the model is not working as expected, the errors would be fed to the designer on a more or less continual basis so that the system could be redesigned for more effective results.

One of the most serious weaknesses of the bureaucratic design as a management system is that it lacks measurability. When the bureaucratic system is redesigned from a product to a functional arrangement or when the line of command is lengthened by the introduction of additional levels of managers, no measuring devices exist, either in the previous or subsequent design, that will indicate what improvements, if any, have occurred.

Feasibility relates to the question of whether or not the model will operate as planned. A model must be realistic; it must be capable of being installed, of achieving expected payoff, and of performing its task requirements within the environment of the system. If a particular quantitative decision-making tool is suggested, we must be reasonably certain that it can be employed in an operational context.

The use of pilot studies or experimental models relates to the question of feasibility. Given any managerial device, we want to know whether it will increase organizational payoff when it is utilized; whether stockholders, employees, and consumers will be better off than before. Organizations are normative systems. All too often, the student and practitioner are exposed to quantitative manipulations and behavioral research that is interesting, but either no directions are provided as to how these findings are to be incorporated into the operations of the firm, or no measuring devices are suggested that will actually establish the quantity of welfare that the research results will actually produce. Frequently, we are highly impressed with the elegance and sophistication of the research and the virtuosity of the analyst, and then discover that the extent of research usefulness is limited.

The end purpose of the manager, as it is viewed in this analysis, is to design subsystems which will actually increase human well-being. The manager is not, per se, a mathematician, statistician, sociologist, or psychologist. However, he must rely on these disciplines in much the same way as the engineer has to rely on physics.

This does not mean that continuous research is unnecessary in these disciplines, but it does mean that such research will not automatically lead to improvements. It is only when the designer is able to incorporate findings into an operating reality that he can achieve the full value of the research.

A corollary to the feasibility criterion relates to balance between parts of the system. All parts of the system must not only be integrated, but also mutually consistent. We would not put a primitive input analyzer into practice and follow this with a complex regression analysis in the identifier. The final system output would be no more productive than the least productive part of the system. Each part acts as a constraint on all other parts. Consequently, the identifier can never be any better than the input analyzer, and so on.

The absence of integration and/or balance is self-defeating. For example, we frequently find information systems personnel providing voluminous data; that is, the input analyzer is well developed. However, the rest of the system may be missing—there is no identifier, set of decision rules, etc. In other instances, we may have an analysis of the use of a single decision rule, as linear programming, but nothing else.

As long as we find this "bits and pieces" type of analysis, managers will always revert, out of necessity, to the most primitive part of the total system because this part represents the primary constraint. In such a context, increasing sophistication will not meet the criterion of feasibility. Even if it is used, no increment in organizational payoff will result.

For example, in the design of the poverty program system previously mentioned, the staff's initial impulse was to design an econometric model of the program, including exogenous variables. We immediately ran into the constraints of the rest of the system and realized that until we had a relatively effective input analyzer, a set of decision rules, and a control element, we could not move to the sophisticated model we wanted. In other words, when we design a total system, we are generally forced to start with a fairly elementary model. Then, when all the parts are developed, we can progress to a more complex system.

It seems to me that we are overly concerned with the optimality criterion in the "management sciences," while we tend to ignore such other criteria as measurability and feasibility on the assumption that, if one has an optimal solution, there is little else that has to be done. But unless all criteria are considered, we will not get the hoped-for results. To have a solution that is optimum but not feasible is meaningless. Obviously, a solution has to be measurable, feasible, and reliable before we can consider its optimality. For the most part, operating managers stress the feasibility criterion. At the outset, they want something that will work and actually function at this stage. They are not overly concerned with optimality. In dealing with a complex system, I am not sure of what constitutes an optimal solution. Engineers, for example, have told me that they really don't know what an optimal aircraft would be like.

Russell Ackoff has said, "One of the things Operations Research has learned about putting results to work is having considerable effect on its methods. This means the team must either translate elegant solutions into approximations that are easy to use, or side-step the elegance and move directly to a quick and dirty decision rule. Operations Research is learning that an approximation that is used may be a great deal better than an exact solution that is not."[7] Because design methodology imposes a specific discipline on the designer, we can be assured that new techniques will be effectively utilized.

SOME IMPLICATIONS

While this has been a rather broad treatment of the organization as a total system, nevertheless, certain implications can be inferred. First, on a normative basis, organizations should be viewed as a total system if we are to increase organizational output. Different organizations, corporations, universities, poverty programs, and so on, can be so categorized. Further, although this is by and large an article of faith, some empirical evidence does exist; certainly in the area of complex weapons systems. If organizations are viewed as a total system, better results will be obtained. We are in the initial stages of this development and, at this time, we can only block out the basic characteristics of total systems. I am quite convinced, for example, that the poverty program on the local metropolitan operating level can only be designed as a total system.

Second, I have attempted to demonstrate that the systems approach is a highly conducive vehicle for the incorporation of current managerial technologies, unlike the bureaucratic structure. Irrespective of the developing managerial concepts, the bureaucratic structure itself represents such a serious constraint that only minimal advantages would occur.

Third, when viewed in this context, the essential role of the manager is that of designer of organizational or behavioral systems, just as the engineer is the designer of machine systems. The design of a large complex system will, however, necessitate a team effort of mathematicians, psychologists, and information specialists. But, as in the case of large machine systems, system specialists will be required to integrate the team effort. There is little reason why efforts cannot be organized to design a marketing system in the same fashion as the F-111 aircraft was designed.

If we were to speculate about the future, eventually the organization might be divided into two basic divisions, planning and operations. The computer, behavioral scientists, information specialists, and quantitative personnel would comprise the planning unit. This planning division would be comparable to the engineering division currently found in organizations. The organization of the poverty program, for instance, is divided between planning and control on the one hand, and operations on the other. Planning has the primary responsibility of total system design. This unit is an interdisciplinary team under the direction of a systems specialist. This is in contrast to the typical operations research arrangement in which a line manager may use operations research for assistance if he has a problem. In the poverty program, the manager is viewed as the operator of the system developed by the team.

Similarly, if the organization is to fully utilize the systems approach, the first step would be to establish a design team with planning responsibility. Also there is no reason why a particular team has to be concerned entirely with one subsystem, such as marketing or personnel. Once the development work has been done regarding one subsystem, the team should have the capability of designing any other subsystem. In the poverty program, the same team is dealing with headstart, legal aid, health, and manpower training subsystems.

There are educational implications suggested by this analysis; namely, a division of business education into two relatively distinct areas. One would represent the traditional bureaucratic approach and contain the basic principles, material and functional areas. The other would stress the organization as a total system (the alternative to principles), and would be the basic course upon which the newer management technologies (as exemplified by such courses as statistics) would be systematically built and integrated. At the University of Massachusetts, we have moved in this direction on the graduate level.

Thus, rather than offer behavioral and quantitative courses in a curriculum with little rhyme or reason, the new technologies can be integrated in the systems fabric. This is a rational program for the student because he now knows why and where the parts fit, why he has to be able to construct a stochastic model, and so forth.

In all probability, the two basic approaches —bureaucratic and systems—will exist side by side in the curriculum over a number of years. Gradually, however, one would expect the bureaucratic material to be phased out in order to reflect changes in the real world. In form, organizations may continue as bureaucratic structures; in substance, they will take on systems orientation with a continual integration of operations and elimination of authority boundaries.

My final observation concerns the ultimate development in systems. It is hoped that, in the long run, the systems approach will result in a more "human use of human beings" in an organizational setting which the Father of Cybernetics, Norbert Wiener, suggested.[8] The ultimate goal of the designer of man systems is to increase the human welfare of the organization's membership. This will occur because the nature of the design process is to continually create a system that most closely fits the basic material of the system—man himself. I certainly concur with Chris Argris' comments upon the non-human characteristics of bureaucracy.[9]

The ideal organization or system would be a cybernetic one—a self-regulating mechanism in which individuals adjusted and adapted to their environment because they were self-motivated to do so. Such an organization would have the characteristics of the purely competitive economic mode. Yet, if we are to reach such an ideal state, such systems will have to be invented. To observe that the traditional bureaucratic structure has serious drawbacks, or that principles of management are not very rigorous, is not enough. If the present hierarchical scheme is deficient, then only a better one will rectify the situation. There is little question that we are at last in a position to invent better social systems. I have attempted to demonstrate, when we view the organization as a total system, we have taken the first step in this forward direction.

References

1. For example see: Joseph Litterer. *Analysis of Organizations.* New York: John Wiley, 1965. Claude McMillan and Richard Gonzalez. *Systems Analysis.* Homewood, Illinois: Richard Irwin, 1965, chs. 11–14. Ross Ashby. *An Introduction to Cybernetics.* New York: John Wiley, 1958, chs. 10–14. Adrian McDonough, and L. J. Garrett. *Management Systems.* Homewood, Illinois: Richard Irwin, 1964. Richard Johnson, Fremont Kast, and James Rosenzweig. *The Theory and Management of Systems.* New York: McGraw-Hill, 1963 and Stafford Beer. *Cybernetics and Management.* London: English Universities Press, 1959.

2. For example see: G. Donald Malcolm, Alen Rowe, and Larimer McConnell. *Management Control Systems.* New York: John Wiley, 1960.

3. See: Cornelius Leondes. *Computer Control Systems Technology.* New York: McGraw-Hill, 1961, chs. 15–20.

4. For a review of adaptive systems see: Eli Mishkin and Ludwig Braun, Jr. *Adaptive Control Systems.* New York: McGraw-Hill, 1961. John H. Westcott, *An Exposition of Adaptive Control.* New York: Macmillan Company, 1962.

5. For a more complete review, see: Harry H. Goode and Robert Machol. *System Engineering.* New York: McGraw-Hill, 1957.

6. Gerald L. Thompson. "Some Approaches to the Solution of Large Scale Combinatorial Problems." Working Paper. Carnegie Institute of Technology, Pittsburgh, p. 25.

7. Rusel L. Ackoff. "The Development of Operations Research as a Science," in *Scientific Decision Making in Business,* ed. by Abe Shuchman. New York: Holt, Rinehart and Winston, 1963, pp. 59–60.

8. See: Norbert Wiener. *The Human Use of Human Beings.* Garden City, New York: Doubleday and Company, 1954.

9. Chris Argris. *Personality and Organization.* New York: Harper and Brothers, 1957.

READING 8

A SYSTEMS APPROACH TO RESEARCH MANAGEMENT:
Part 1. Scientific Research *

R. E. Gibson

INTRODUCTION

"Research and development" has now become big business with many complex ramifications within itself and even more complex and far-reaching interactions with the rest of society. According to the estimates made by the National Science Foundation the annual expenditures for R&D in the United States exceeded 11 billion dollars in 1959, were close to 12.5 billion in 1960 and they are still growing. Research and development is now one of the principal components of modern industry[1] and has become a powerful instrument in economic development and in national prestige. International competition in this field is extending and intensifying. The supremacy of the United States is being seriously challenged. The Soviet

* Reprinted with permission from Research Management, vol. V, 1962.
[1] *In 1960 the expenditures for R&D were made as follows: Government organizations $1.8 billion, Universities $1.0 billion, other non-profit organizations $0.25 billion, Industry $9.4 billion.*

Union is a prominent challenger in the minds of most of us but the United Kingdom, Sweden, Germany, France, Japan, and Italy are by no means negligible contenders in certain areas and the growing threat of Red China looms in the offing. From a national as well as a private or company viewpoint, it is expedient that we make the fullest use of the potential inherent in our public and private research and development organizations.

This potential is realized through two channels: (1) the intellectual growth of our society, and (2) the growth of modern technology. Although from many points of view the first is the more important, I shall treat it only incidentally in this paper and will concentrate attention on the second, dealing mainly with the role of research and development as components of technology. Because the subject is complicated, we can miss very important points if we attempt to deal with it piecemeal. I shall, therefore, use what may be called a "systems approach" to develop an overall general picture of technology, including research and development and the problems that arise in managing organizations to advance it.

The "systems approach" to a complex subject is a "synthetic" one, as opposed to an "analytic" one. Indeed, we might have called this paper "A synthetic approach to research management" except that the word synthetic emphasizes other meanings, and, therefore, I use the term "systems." Although the words, "system" and "systems," are becoming hackneyed, they do convey an important idea which has proven very fruitful in technical thought and expression. Indeed, the exploitation of this idea is forming the main bridge between the classical sciences of physics and chemistry and the newer sciences associated with biology and medicine. In order to bring out the connotation of the systems approach, I shall discuss what I consider to be some important concepts associated with the term system.

SYSTEMS CONCEPTS

A system may be defined as an integrated assembly of interacting elements designed to carry out cooperatively a predetermined function. Those elements may vary from mechanical components to biological ones, from units in an organization to segments of intellectual activity, but the idea of cooperation with a purpose is always present. Examples include a radio set, an automobile, a guided missile system, an automatic factory, biological organisms ranging from amoeba to homo sapiens, an industrial corporation, a symphony orchestra, a church, a society, a civilization.

The term system conjures up the picture of a group of individual entities, each of which has a peculiar and essential part to play but each of which is entirely dependent for its effectiveness on the communications established between it and its fellows.

Inherent in the idea of a system are the following concepts:

1 The key concept conveyed is a network of elements, each of which develops information peculiar to itself from the inputs it receives, and passes on this information, its outputs, with appropriate *precision* and *timeliness* to the other elements so that they can perform the parts effectively.
2 To be considered a system, an assembly must contain all the sources of significant inputs to its elements. For example, an animal cannot be divorced from its food supply, a plant from solar radiation, or a factory from its markets.

3 The definition of a system that we have just given emphasizes the importance of objectives or the predetermined functions that the elements of the system are to achieve cooperatively—the stability and breadth of the objective reflects itself in the character of the system designed to carry it out. An objective of ephemeral value tends to produce a flimsy system. However, the objective of the human organism, namely, survival in a competitive and changing world, is one towards which it has worked for millions of years and if we use the term survival to mean that of the race as well as the individual, it seems we have an objective that will challenge our biological system for many years to come.

4 Consideration of a system places the communication lines which link the various elements upon an equal footing with the elements themselves. The ability of these links to transmit timely and precise information, in other words the phasing and band width of the communications, can play a determining role in the growth and functioning of the system.

5 A very important family of communication links are called *feedback links*. When part of the output of a machine or system is applied to affect or control its input, a feedback is established. Familiar examples are the oscillator in a radio transmitter, a governor on a steam engine, automatic control on a radio, the mechanism of balancing, homeostasis, etc., in human beings. It is convenient to distinguish two special cases of feedback, namely, negative feedback and positive feedback. Negative feedback is established when the increase in the output of the system tends to cut down the input, as in the action of a governor on a steam engine. Such feedbacks lead to a condition of equilibrium and are the basis of automatic control. Positive feedback exists when an increase in output acts to increase the input—as in an oscillator. The result is unstable operation. No equilibrium is established, but rather the output of the system increases at an exponential rate. Explosives, epidemics, and the initial growth of populations in an environment of plenty are examples of the working of positive feedbacks.

The phasing or timeliness with which information is transmitted along feedback links is of great importance. Indeed the difference between negative and positive feedback is 180° in phase. Time delays causing phase changes can convert signals intended to produce negative feedback into ones giving positive feedback and vice versa. It can be shown quite simply that positive feedback in a system causes its output to grow exponentially whereas negative feedback leads to stability of control and keeps the system in equilibrium, that is to say prevents its output from growing. In the following discussion I shall refer frequently to the feedbacks in many types of systems; practically all will be positive.

The block diagram so familiar to engineers these days serves to summarize important aspects of the systems approach to complicated subjects. In such a diagram we can divide the subject into definable entities whose internal contents can be treated separately and whose reactions on the operation of the system can be specified through the inputs they require and the outputs they generate. As long as these are kept within tolerances, the exact contents of the blocks are immaterial. With this in mind, we can look at many very different assemblages from the systems point of view. Our system may consist of all those human activities that go to make up a civilization. We may apply it to the individuals that make up society—we may apply it to the brains and skills whose products are research and development. We shall apply it to scientific research—the components or blocks of the system being the ideas

and ratiocinations that go on in one man's mind or in the minds of a number of people. Sometimes the system we are talking about will be composed of tangibles like the people and machines, sometimes of intangibles like ideas, intellectual or manual activities.

DEFINITION OF SCOPE OF RESEARCH MANAGEMENT

Discussion of research management frequently flounders in a morass of arguments between those who claim that management has no place in research and those who claim that unless research is well managed it is ineffective. In order to avoid this type of argument, I should like to comment on the place and scope of management in research operations using the block diagram of technology shown in Figure 8-1 as a frame of reference. Figure 8-1 shows in block diagram form the various activities which make up modern technology.

Scientific Research

Near the bottom of Figure 8-1, we see a block labelled, "scientific research," which is still a very individual activity. It is motivated by curiosity or an uneasy feeling that a discrepancy exists between preconceived ideas and our observations of natural phenomena. Its ob-

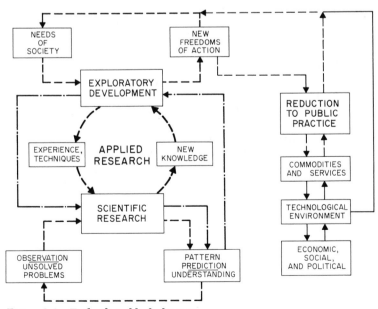

Figure 8-1 Technology block diagram.

jective is understanding or the fitting of new and strange observations into patterns of established fact. In this type of research the role of management is one of complete restraint and noninterference. A decision is made to invest some money in an individual and his assistants in the hope that their talents, intuition, and skill will lead them to the discovery of new and significant knowledge and the broadening of the basis of our understanding of nature. Thereafter they are best left alone.

Exploratory Development

A second activity shown in Figure 8-1 is called "exploratory development" and is the field that used to be the territory of the inventor. Its incentives are the realization that limitations to human activity can be broken down by the application of knowledge and ingenuity to produce new devices, commodities, or services that give us new freedoms of action. The invention of the steam engine, Daimler's invention of a *high speed* internal combustion engine, the Wright Brothers' demonstration at Kittyhawk, Goddard's liquid fuel rockets in 1926—were all events that made available to man new freedoms of action which he has exploited with far-reaching social consequences. In this area, the role of management is a tenuous one and depends primarily on the number of people that are involved in a given exploratory enterprise. Indeed, in both of the activities that I have mentioned, scientific research and exploratory development, it seems that management in the classical sense of the word can play a role only in getting the expeditions started. When, like a band of explorers, they penetrate into the unknown, they are on their own and decisions for action must be taken in the light of the new and strange situations that arise. As the size of the band increases, the need for management goes up, but it is emphasized that the important decisions must be made by those closest to the front line.

Applied Research and Development

In the middle of the diagram is an area entitled "applied research" which bridges the gap between scientific research and exploratory development. Its functions are to provide the exploratory developer with accurate and systematized knowledge and understanding from scientific research, and to carry the unsolved problems uncovered in the course of a development back to the laboratories for solution and understanding. This is the area in which the large research and development laboratories of government, industry, and nonprofit corporations now operate. It is an area where time scales are important, where the product interacts closely with the environment described in the next paragraph. It is the area to which I shall refer when I speak of management of research and development in this paper.

Reduction to Public Practice

New freedoms of action become effective in society only after they are reduced to public practice and this entails the investment of large sums of money and manpower, an investment which must be amortized by the returns brought in by products. Here, of course, is a place where management, business acumen, and an intimate knowledge of the technological, economic, social, and political environment are of paramount importance. Since the operation of an applied research organization involves expenditures of considerable sums of money and the investment of intellectual and practical talents of a number of scientists and engineers, it becomes important that those responsible for the management of this work also know intimately the interactions of its products or potential products with the technological, political, economic, and social world, and the processes whereby new freedoms of action are reduced to public practice. This knowledge is fundamental to the initiation of research and development programs likely to obtain "profitable" results at the right time. I think, therefore, that we can safely assume that the subject before us is not irrelevant and that management of the right kind has a very important part to play in the realization of the maximum potential inherent in an applied research organization.

The function of research management is to operate effectively the system referred to as applied research in Figure 8-1 and in order that we may see how this may be accomplished, we must understand something about its objectives—the elements it contains, and the interactions among these elements. I propose, therefore, to proceed now with a detailed systematic discussion of the activities which make up modern technology, namely, scientific research, exploratory development, and reduction

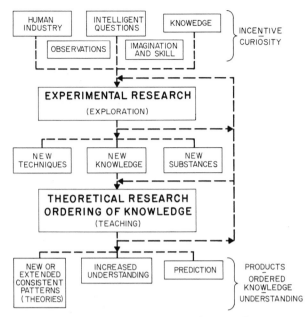

Figure 8-2   Some feedbacks in scientific research.

to public practice with the conviction that a knowledge of the nature of these activities is fundamental to any discussion of their management.

Before doing so, however, it might be wise to say a word or two about "management." The word itself has an unfortunate history. It originally meant training horses to do the exercise of the manége. It still conjures up in the minds of many people a set of manipulations or manipulators promoting the exploitation of human resources for more or less worthy ends. Over the past twenty-five years there has grown up an influential school of thought that regards "management" in the sense of organizing, controlling, and exploiting the brains and skills of people as a profession in itself. The rise of this school parallels that of the rise of the schools of education at the beginning of this century, a movement which placed emphasis on *how* to teach rather than on *what* to teach.

There is no doubt at all that the modern "management" school is making extremely important contributions by attacking objectively the complicated problems that arise when human beings cooperate in a system. It is questioning the dogmas, studying and systematizing the methods of successful practitioners, and evolving new techniques and broadening our basis of understanding. However, along with very sound results there has grown up and

been widely sold a mythology that gives the impression that "professional management" can be substituted for leadership, glib expertise for hard earned experience, and academic formulae for common sense. Discrimination is of the essence in management.

This paper may be regarded as a delineation of my own definition of "management" as applied to an R&D organization or program. What I have in mind is really "leadership" or "generalship" where the prime object of the exercise is to advance technology by means of an organization and the secondary objective is to operate the organization smoothly.

SYSTEMATIC DISCUSSION OF THE COMPONENTS OF MODERN TECHNOLOGY—THEIR INTERACTIONS AND FEEDBACKS

Scientific Research[2]

Figure 8-2 gives a simplified picture of scientific research in block diagram form. The first block in this system is labelled "experimental research." Its inputs are human industry, intelligent questions, existing knowledge, accurate observation of phenomena, imagination and

[2] *This subject is discussed more fully in an article "Cultural Implications of Scientific Research," R. E. Gibson, J. Wash. Acad. Sci. 47, 249 (1957).*

skill—all motivated by curiosity to understand exactly what is going on, through the establishment of valid facts determined by controlled experiments. I cannot dwell here on the immense amount of hard work and ingenuity that must be expended to establish one fact, to be sure that it can be reproduced exactly by any competent observer and that it can be expressed unambiguously in quantitative terms. The outputs of this box are new knowledge, new techniques, new substances.

The second block, of equal or even greater importance than the first, is labelled "theoretical research or the ordering of knowledge." The input to this block is new and old knowledge and the function of this block is to arrange the new facts and the old knowledge in consistent and satisfying patterns which we call theories. Its outputs are new or extended consistent patterns of knowledge—increased understanding that comes when the new and strange are logically related to the old and familiar and the power of predicting new facts by extrapolation from well established theories. In other words, the primary function of this block is to reduce the myriad facts emerging from experimental research to systematic and manageable form.

Figure 8-2 brings out several important feedbacks: the first is the "interplay of experimental theory and experimental practice" to quote Claude Bernard; the second is the feedback from the output to the input of the experimental research box; and the third the feedback from the output of theoretical research not only to its own input but also to the input of the experimental box. These are discussed in more detail in the following paragraphs.

1 From observation and careful study of phenomena or events, facts are obtained which may then be fitted together in an experimental pattern, i.e., a working hypothesis. If the facts fit well into the hypothesis, the latter immediately suggests new subjects for observation or new experiments from which come new facts and so the activity in the circuit builds up, and with it, *confidence in the validity of the facts and the consistency of the theory.* On the other hand, if the facts do not fit into a recognized pattern, one must first make a further study of their validity to ensure that they have not been vitiated by some error (and errors may arise in very subtle ways). At the same time, it may be necessary to reexamine the pattern or theory and, if necessary, modify it to ac-

commodate the new facts. The process is a cyclic one and only when the *facts and the experimental theory fit together* can we be content with either. The product of this circuit is a satisfying pattern or general theory which enables us to understand the phenomena or events in the field of study, which comprehends all the facts, links them with facts from other fields, and enables us to predict verifiable new phenomena or events. The outputs of this circuit are the major theories or patterns which accommodate large bodies of facts such as the Laws of Thermodynamics, the Laws of Motion, the Theory of Relativity, the Quantum Theory, Maxwell's Electromagnetic Equations, the Mendelian Laws.

2 In order to extend and integrate the patterns and to assay their consistency over wide ranges of facts, it has been found necessary to seek facts in every region susceptible to precise observation. The new substances, instruments, and techniques—we may even include concepts—discovered and developed in the course of one series of researches may be used to explore other new regions for more facts. The build-up in the circuit due to this positive feedback has been most spectacular; indeed the history of natural philosophy is marked by milestones, each indicating the discovery of a new device or technique which opened up to human experience regions that were hitherto inaccessible. These devices were means to an end, but the end would never have been achieved without the means. Telescopes, microscopes, x-rays, radioactivity, alpha-particles, neutrons, cyclotrons, chemical analysis, electronics, highspeed computing machines, have all been means of opening up new continents for valid experiences. The positive feedback from its output to its input gives experimental research an ever expanding potential to break down existing barriers to its own advances.

3 The arrow from the output of theoretical research to the input of the whole system also indicates a positive feedback, the autocatalytic effect of *understanding.* A satisfactory theory or pattern of facts broadens and deepens understanding, pointing the way to new fruitful fields where facts of significance, interest, and potential for application are likely to be discovered. In short, it permits the asking of more *intelligent* questions. It helps research men to make more intelligently the most important decision of all, namely, the choice of problems in which to invest years of their lives. With the aid of new instruments, techniques and methods,

both experimental and theoretical, these decisions may be implemented and the investigators may pursue their researches into new and more complex fields with increasing facility and confidence.

The effects of these feedbacks on the growth of scientific knowledge and understanding have been really extraordinary. It is very difficult to get a quantitative expression of the size and extent of scientific knowledge at any one time but all indices that have been examined indicate that scientific knowledge doubles each 10–15 years and has done so steadily since 1700 [D. J. Price, *Discovery*, 17, 240 (1956)].

There are regions of interest in science where it is not possible to make precise observations or accumulate facts under completely controlled conditions. In such cases the system works in a deductive mode through the feedback from "satisfying patterns" to observation. In cosmogony or petrogenesis for example, it is not practical to build up a theory of the origin of the universe or of rocks from reproducible facts obtained from direct observation of the processes concerned. However, starting from a comprehensive pattern of facts from physics and chemistry and certain assumptions, it is possible to draw a theoretical picture of the origin of the universe or rocks in *sufficient* detail that certain critical consequences which are susceptible to observation may be deduced. Facts extracted from observations may then be compared with those deduced from theory. The history of the sciences I have mentioned shows clearly that as our satisfying patterns grow in depth and breadth, the deductions drawn lead to more and more pertinent and refined observations and our confidence in them grows accordingly. This circuit has found wide application in attacks on complicated problems or those dealing with past or future events. Its power depends on the existence of broadly based, established patterns of facts, a condition which is sometimes not fully appreciated in attempts to apply "scientific methods" in new or complicated fields such as social sciences.

There is one interesting philosophical implication of the role of positive feedbacks in scientific research. When positive feedback exists, we may say that the output is coherent with the input and the subject *grows*. When, however, the outputs of either block are erroneous (facts being contaminated with error or theories with fallacy) they will be out of phase with the input when fed back; in other words, the outputs and inputs are incoherent in this case. Positive feedback may become negative. We might suggest, therefore, that the criterion of truth can be related to the coherence of the outputs and inputs of these blocks.

Truth leads to rapid growth of knowledge—error leads to stagnation. Examples of incoherence of output and input are not hard to find in the history of science. For example, Lord Kelvin's theory of the cooling of the earth caused a temporary but significant stagnation in the science of geophysics which started again on a rapid growth only after the growing knowledge of radioactivity corrected the error in Kelvin's theory. The struggles of the kinetic theory to explain quantitatively the properties of gases in pre-quantum theory days is another striking example.

It is also interesting to notice two rather important differences between science and art. Positive feedbacks are strong in science and their effects are of greatest significance. In art the feedbacks are quite weak—one masterpiece seldom paves the way for a greater one. The absence of strong positive feedbacks has resulted in the arts growing much less steadily than the sciences. A second difference is to be found in the communications which must be exact and quantitative in science—they need not be so in art.

I cannot leave the subject of scientific research without emphasizing the extreme importance of ordering our knowledge into patterns that make it interesting and manageable. "Order is remembered—chaos is forgotten." Since knowledge grows only in the minds of people, we must recognize the key role of the teacher in ordering new knowledge and experience into interesting and stimulating patterns that excite the interest of the student to assimilate this knowledge in his mind. The teachers who inspire students and write text books systematizing the knowledge in a given field play just as important a role in the advancement of science as do those who discover new knowledge by experimental research. However, it is present day fashion to underrate the former, and the road to academic promotion is paved with reprints without too much regard to their quality. The quality of our scientific education reflects this distressing imbalance.

READING 9

A SYSTEMS APPROACH TO RESEARCH MANAGEMENT:
Part 2. Technology and Its Environment*

R. E. Gibson

INTRODUCTION

In Part 1 of this series [Reading 8] we sketched an outline of technology and its components, pointing out those areas where management has a specific contribution to make. We also discussed in some detail the workings of scientific research as a subsystem in the larger system. An understanding of this subsystem is essential for the intelligent management of any technological enterprise, although the purely management functions associated with this subsystem are more concerned with restraint than action. In this part, we will deal with exploratory development and reduction to practice, and the influence of environment on these activities, noting that this is an area in which management functions play a more fundamental part.

* Reprinted with permission from Research Management, vol. V, 1962.

EXPLORATORY DEVELOPMENT

In the words of Howard Wilcox, "By exploratory development we mean the practice of investigating, creating, and designing new techniques and devices which promise to break through limitations hitherto set by nature on man's freedom of choice and action." Although the techniques and methods employed in exploratory development are often similar to those employed in scientific research, and there has always been a close connection and interchange of results between the two, their objectives are quite different. Scientific research seeks new and uncontaminated knowledge from which to make patterns of facts and ideas that lead to a deeper understanding of man and his environment. The exploratory developer, sensing the need for a new freedom of choice and action, uses all the knowledge he can glean from any source whatever, and exerts his ingenuity to put it together to give a new device, commodity, technique, or service that supplies this need. In the field of photography the close relation between scientific research and exploratory development is well seen. Actually photography has always been an exploratory development. It has used scientific knowledge wherever available but the exploratory development of new processes and techniques has so outrun the scientific understanding that C. E. K. Mees once remarked, "photography has done more for science than science has for photography."

The general nature of exploratory development is illustrated by the block diagram in Figure 9-1. Its inputs are human industry, existing knowledge, and understanding, existing arts, imagination, and skill; its outputs are new devices and techniques that are capable of giving us new possibilities for action.

It is through this system that human knowledge, imagination, ingenuity, and skill contribute to the material progress of mankind. Exploratory developments such as the domestication of animals, the invention of the sail, the steam engine, the high speed internal combustion engine have literally changed the

ecological patterns of the world and determined the course of civilization. The correlation between the availability of wind driven ships as by far the best means of hauling heavy loads over long distances and the rise of centers of populations adjacent to rivers and sea coasts is ample evidence of this. Exploratory development is a much older activity than scientific research; it goes back to and perhaps even marks the dawn of civilization. For thousands of years it remained the field of the lone inventor or the master artist and his apprentices. The old inventors used whatever knowledge they could find—some of it sound but most of it unsound. Hence, invention was a haphazard game with chances of success rather slim, so that when successful and profitable results were obtained, the techniques and processes were held in tight secrecy. Positive feedbacks were severely limited or nonexistent. The Edisonian method of invention emerged during last century. It was based on empirical knowledge systematically obtained by the combined trial and error of a team of workers. It was successful in its day, but the growth of scientific knowledge

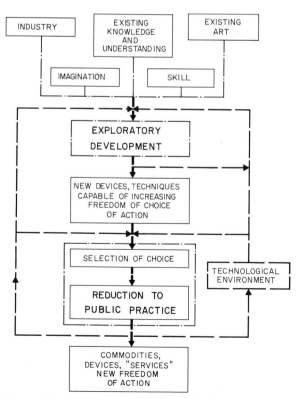

Figure 9-1   Feedbacks in exploratory development.

has brought about its obsolescence. Modern exploratory development now relies heavily on systematic knowledge and understanding, the product of scientific research, and the applied research organization I have described in connection with Figure 9-2 provides its inputs. The arrows on the dashed lines in Figure 9-1 indicate important feedbacks that now exist in exploratory development—all are positive, and our new devices, techniques, and freedoms of choice and action are increasing exponentially.

REDUCTION TO PUBLIC PRACTICE

In the overall realm of technology, the function of the research scientist is to seek and understand new human experiences; that of the exploratory developer is to apply established experience to create new devices and techniques which widen our freedom of choice and action in all fields of human endeavor. However, the selection of courses of action to be taken from the variety of choices available are not made by the scientist or the inventor but by the entrepreneurs of the business, financial, military, and political world. The introduction of a new commodity or service into use by the public at large (reduction to public practice) is an undertaking that requires capital and facili-

ties and in the past has been motivated either by a known demand or by the probability that a demand for a product or a service may be created when it is attractively presented to the public.

Thus, when the potentialities of a new development are demonstrated, a decision to choose it as the basis for a course of action must be taken in the light of the investment in money, manpower, and skill that must be made to prepare it for public use. Its promised performance must be realized with safety, reliability, and ease of operation when it is placed in the hands of the using public. In the absence of other compelling circumstances, its cost must be within the means of potential users and must of course be favorable when compared with competing items designed to do the same job. All these attributes must be engineered into the commodity before it can be said to be *reduced to public practice*. Even then, the economic atmosphere must be such that the demand for the commodity will be large enough to justify the investment in it. The same applies to the introduction of a new service or technique—for example, a new drug or surgical operation must be tested under all conceivable conditions, the results evaluated carefully, and necessary precautions defined. The techniques and methods must be reduced to a routine that

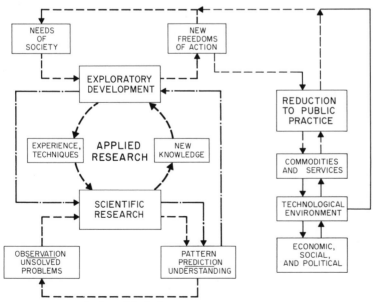

Figure 9-2 Technology block diagram.

can be safely followed by any qualified practitioner. What I have said applies to automobiles, hairdryers, washing machines, television sets, as well as to the practice of medicine, surgery, agriculture, or even the operation of machine tools.

An important factor in determining the reduction to public practice of new knowledge or developments is the "technological environment" prevailing at the time. By "technological environment" I mean the products of former developments that have been reduced to public practice. This comprises the sum total of all the know-how, skills, techniques, tools, materials, and appurtenances that are items of commerce, readily available for producing a new device or perfecting a service so that it can be presented to the using public in simple, reliable, and economical form. For example, if we wish to make a modern loudspeaker cabinet, the technological environment that affects us is the kind of wood we have available, the hand or power tools we have, the screws, the glue, the paint that we can obtain. If we had to cut down a tree, dress it with an adze, drill it with red hot irons and chisels, and hold the pieces together with wooden pegs, the job would be much slower and more difficult than it is when we have plenty of plywood, a well-stocked modern basement fortified by a good neighborhood hardware store. Indeed, it might be so difficult that we would find it impossible.

The interactions between the new development and the "technological environment" give rise to a system of feedback loops as shown in

Figures 9-1, 9-2, and 9-3. A new development not only enriches the technological environment by itself but also by the demands it makes for auxiliary materials, tools, techniques, and so forth. On the other hand, the resources of the prevailing technological environment have a great effect on the speed at which a development is reduced to public practice—a lack of such resources may even prevent the exploitation of a development. It was many years after Newcomen first demonstrated the feasibility of a steam engine that artisans were able to bore a cylinder more than 8 in. in diameter, round enough to accommodate a tight-fitting piston. The introduction of the steam engine into public practice was delayed for a long time. Indeed, one can say without exaggeration that the interactions with the technological environment have played a dominant role in determining the direction of technological progress. The technological environment is only one of the external elements that influence the course of technology. Figure 9-3 shows diagrammatically other environments that influence the direction of technological growth.

The economic environment plays an important role in determining the reduction to public practice of a potential commodity or service. Indeed, in countries encouraging and practicing free enterprise, the operation of the economic feedback loops has played the most important part in determining the direction of technological progress except in time of emergency. The "reduction to public practice" of a new development has depended strongly on its ability

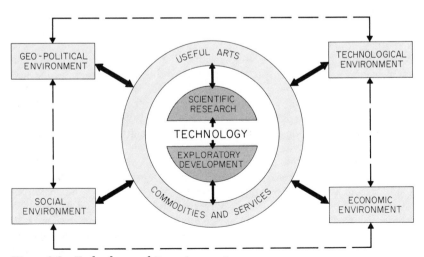

Figure 9-3   Technology and its environment.

to fulfill a need for which people not only *wanted* to pay but for which they *could* pay. The result has been intense efforts to reduce prices without apparent loss of performance, to stimulate wants by advertising, and ability to pay by extension of credit. These factors have had a strong influence on the course technology has taken. On the other hand, a healthy technology has raised its economic environment to a point where standards of living are high and the ability to assimilate more technological developments is correspondingly great.

Recently another feedback has become apparent, or rather, has spread its sphere of influence. I refer to the geopolitical or national prestige feedback. This has existed for centuries in the military sphere where nations whose technology could support development and production of advanced weapons rose to positions of eminence. However, in nonmilitary fields, the economic loop was the determining factor. The competition in space rendered acute by the successful launching of Sputnik I in October 1957 has extended the national prestige value of technological developments beyond the purely military sphere and the geopolitical feedback loop is becoming important in stimulating technological advances. The question of how long the political feedback will be a dominating factor in a free enterprise society is a very interesting one, but somewhat beyond the scope of this paper. It is my opinion, however, that its effects are more likely to grow than to diminish during the next decade.

It will be seen that the successful conduct of modern research and development activities requires that those responsible for planning and execution broaden their thinking to include the whole system shown diagrammatically in Figure 9-3. We cannot think of technology without considering its interactions with the environment of which the four main elements are shown in this diagram. The size and cost of R&D programs and the short time scale between new ideas and new commodities and services demands that the interactions with environment be taken into account even before the initiation of a substantial program.

Probably the most difficult set of problems in the management of research and development is not immediately apparent in an idealized diagram such as Figure 9-3. I refer to those arising from all the noise in the com-munication links. The signals in the lines to technology from its environments and back again are always buried deep in a background of noise coming from the caprices and conflicts that envelop human beings. The detection of the true meaning of these signals is an art that the research director must learn.

Through scientific research, experience is being accumulated and understood at a rapidly accelerating rate, thereby furnishing an ever growing wealth of organized knowledge for new exploratory developments. Through these exploratory developments, natural limitations to freedom of action are being broken down at an even more rapid rate. The problem is shifting from one of removing limitations to freedom of action, to one of choosing wisely from the plethora of choices presented to us. The technological environment is becoming increasingly richer and consequently the technological problems associated with the reduction of a development to public practice are becoming easier. The time between the completion of a radically new development and its reduction to public practice is shortening to a few years. Over a hundred years elapsed between the first demonstration of Newcomen's engine and the first commercial railroad train. It was 50 years after Faraday first demonstrated a generator of electrical energy that the first electrical generating station supplying power to the public was opened by Edison. It was only 20–25 years after Daimler's invention of a lightweight gasoline engine that the automobile became a reasonably reliable and widely used means of transportation. Within 18 years after Goddard's 200-lb. thrust liquid fuel rocket performed successfully for the first time, the German V-2, with a thrust of 50,000 lb., was being produced in large quantities. Less than three years after the Chicago atomic pile first went critical, large scale atomic piles were operating to produce plutonium and the first bomb had exploded. Within 10 years practical atomic fuel power plants were operating and within 15 years atomic powered submarines were in commission and large-scale atomic plants were providing the public with electric power. Science, technology, and their environments now form an integrated system in which causes in any one part of the system lead rapidly to effects in another. The manager of research must now regard this whole system as his province. Even this is not enough, for technology must now be regarded as a game played in a world arena.

Migration of Technology

Although a technology may be developed and flourish in one particular country, it actually knows no national boundaries. There is a world-wide recognition that technology offers high standards of living and is actually necessary to support the tide of urbanization which is sweeping inexorably over all the world. It is an established fact that any nation which has the will to develop itself technologically can do so, and an increasing number of nations throughout the world are becoming convinced that their only hope for escaping poverty lies in modern technology.

We must, therefore, expect that the rate of growth of world-wide technology will by no means diminish in the future, and that we shall be faced with increasing competition in fields of technology and industry where we have held the leading position.

Indeed, two very old and fundamental limitations to the migration of technology are being removed, namely the limitations imposed by supplies of energy and trained manpower. The effects of the removal of these limitations will be felt more and more strongly in the next decade. With the development of atomic energy and of solar energy, the ready availability of fossil fuels need no longer be the dominant factor in the location of industries. The rapid advances in the field of automatic control, the automatic operation and control of industrial processes are removing the requirements for large numbers of highly skilled workers as a critical factor controlling the technological expansion of a society. Very shortly a handful of highly trained technicians will be able to supply a large population with industrial products. Recognition of the ease with which technology migrates throughout the world and that many of our own developments may be more easily used advantageously by others than by ourselves, with no disruption of vested interests, raises matters of grave concern to those charged with the planning of technological efforts at all levels.

Our vulnerability to the threats of international competition demands more than merely holding a Maginot line of our present industrial might. It requires a dynamic and far-sighted policy to explore new capabilities and objectives in which we can excel for a reasonable length of time. Such policy calls for an increased national investment in scientific research and education, in exploratory development to find new freedoms of action and potential capabilities, and for wise policy planning on the part of the entrepreneurs in the industrial, political, and military world to see new objectives in new capabilities and reduce them to practice at the proper time.

Objectives and Functions of Management of Research and Development

On the basis of the above discussion of scientific research and exploratory development as components of technology and of the relation of technology to society as a whole, it is possible to deduce some of the fundamental functions associated with the management of R&D organizations, for these organizations themselves are systems with communications, feedbacks, coherence and incoherence of inputs and outputs, and with constraints imposed upon them from external organizations in the economic, political, and social world. We have seen that the internal feedbacks in technology are responsible for its exponential growth—the same is true of R&D organizations. We have seen that the external feedbacks existing between technology and its environments are responsible for the *direction* of its growth—the same is true of an R&D organization. Thus, an intimate knowledge of these feedbacks and their implications is an essential part of the equipment of the management of an R&D organization.

Expanding growth is a characteristic of technology and all its components. It seems highly probable that the capacity for expanding growth and change must also be an important characteristic of an R&D organization if it is to remain dynamic and successful. This growth, however, need not be reflected in terms of commonly accepted criteria such as number of staff, floor space, volume of sales, profits, etc., indeed, these may not measure growth but merely inflation. Real growth is measured by the slope of the output curve and significant outputs of lasting value are: (*1*) hardware, exploratory developments that find a permanent place in the useful arts and in public practice, (*2*) patents, (*3*) publications in scientific literature, (4) men of experience and judgment. These outputs are not arranged in order of importance. Their quality and quantity may or may not depend on the size of the organization but they do depend on its vitality and on the functioning of important positive feedbacks associated with internal and external links.

In the first place, a network of communication channels to carry clear, certain, and timely information must be established. This requires a common basis of understanding throughout an organization, not only among groups trained in the same discipline but also among groups and individuals trained in diverse disciplines. An important function of management is to promote this common basis of understanding and a common set of values throughout the organization. Without it, the channels shown in Figure 9-2 are not effective. Vertical channels are essential for spreading a sound knowledge of the objectives throughout the organization and for ensuring that new ideas generated at any level receive prompt attention at the top. Effective horizontal communications are the best assurance of avoiding the negative effects of duplication and enhancing the positive effects of exchanging knowledge and critical discussion. A positive feedback arises from the fact that a basis of mutual understanding promotes better internal communications and better communications broaden the common basis of understanding.

A second feedback that repays attention is that existing between the outputs and the inputs of a group in an organization. This will be positive if the output of the group is of such a quality that it is coherent with the inputs. If, however, the quality and timeliness of the output of a group drops through causes such as sloppy thinking, shoddy workmanship, poor planning, or tardy communications, this feedback ceases and even becomes negative. In most research and development activities, timeliness and clarity of communications are extremely important—the delays in communicating results may well destroy the positive nature of the feedbacks.

It is generally agreed that one of the most baffling problems in the management of research and development is the establishment of criteria for evaluating the productivity of a group or organization. It is suggested that the feedbacks from output to input of the group constitute a focal spot for such an evaluation.

If these are highly positive, the group cannot fail to be productive; if they are low or negative, remedial measures are imperative.

The *external* links involving interactions with the technological, economic, social, and political environments are the channels through which the raw material for policy making flows into an organization. They provide the basis for estimating the compatibility of the products of R&D with the potential and demands of the environment; and of assessing the probability that a development will not only be excellent technically but that it can be reduced to public practice with "profitable" results, using the term in its broadest sense. Because of lead times and "noise," these environmental interactions present particularly difficult problems to the management of R&D organizations who must know not only the present state of environments but must be able to forecast future economic, social, and geopolitical demands years before they become acutely obvious.

These problems are difficult and important enough to warrant the full time attention of a staff group, specializing in a study of environmental interactions and operations analysis or other methods of assessing the relative potential values of different developments. Such staff groups are absolutely essential if the implications of the complex environmental interactions are to be reduced to understandable form.

Probably the chief function of the research manager is to ensure that the organization over which he presides and all its members make the most effective use of time, as measured in years rather than hours. Time is the commodity in shortest supply and is a basis on which all compete on equal terms. The effective use of time not only requires skillful planning, it also requires a scrutiny of all activities in an organization to ensure that they contribute positive feedbacks. If they do not, their usefulness is in question. For example, a reporting system should be such that each stage contributes a real feedback to the previous one as well as a significant communication forward. This feedback should always clarify or add to the ideas of the person writing the report as well as those of the reader.

Summarizing this part we emphasize the following points:

1 A systems approach to the management of research and development focusses the at-

tention of the manager on the formulation of the larger system *in which* he has to operate as well as on the subsystem (laboratory or group) which is his particular responsibility. The larger system must not only contain the subsystem but also *all* the sources of significant information (significant inputs) to the subsystem that influence the outputs of the subsystem. This is essential for recognition of the phase and amplitude of the external feedbacks that determine direction of healthy growth.

2 Systems approach to the management of research and development draws attention to the control of internal feedbacks both in amplitude and phase as a prime function of the management of a program or organization. These are the mechanisms determin-

ing growth or stagnation. They provide an index of progress and a point of entry for effective action. They are particularly significant as an index of the health of the overall communications of the organization.

3 The systems approach to research management places utmost emphasis on choice of objectives and the boundary conditions that influence this choice. These conditions arise from internal sources, external sources, and time considerations. The objectives chosen must be within the competence of the organization to deliver at the proper time products that meet the requirements imposed by the environment at that time.

4 Making the most effective use of time is the chief responsibility of research management.

READING 10

A SYSTEMS APPROACH TO MANPOWER MANAGEMENT*

Edgar G. Williams

Automation, data processing, and other technological developments are forcing personnel executives to reappraise their traditional roles and functions. The conventional specialization that has been their stock in trade is proving to be overly microscopic and myopic.

Manpower management must be viewed as a total system, interrelated and interacting with the other systems of work—the creative, the financial, and the distribution systems—with which a business or social institution operates. The ideas that follow attempt to expedite understanding such an approach.

People and their problems absorb much of every manager's time. The responsibility for manpower management in a leadership position cannot be extracted without managerial abdication, although personnel specialists may be assigned some of the work.

Manpower management permeates all organizational levels and units. Competent managers, well-versed in the behavioral and social

* *Reprinted with permission from* Business Horizons, *Summer, 1964.*

sciences, can establish and maintain desirable human relationships that contribute to organizational effectiveness, personal satisfactions, personal growth and development, and productivity and profits.

In any business enterprise, modern manpower management involves four separate but interrelated factors: a manpower philosophy or point of view, the existing personnel climate or environment, the manpower program, and the manpower system.

Concerned with people, their work behavior, and desirable organizational relationships, a *manpower philosophy* consists of fundamental concepts, ideals, principles, and methods relative to manpower resources. Any such system of thought must be suited to the framework of social, economic, technological, and political elements which exist at a particular time and place. This variable combination of internal and external elements that impinge on and influence manpower decisions and actions is the *personnel climate.*

A manpower philosophy adaptable to a particular climate makes it possible to create a *manpower program* directed toward establishing and maintaining an adequate and satisfactory work force. The program represents a set of potential values which must be converted through action into actual values in the form of desired human relationships that are conducive to cooperation and coordination of effort.

Transforming the potential of the manpower program is accomplished through a *manpower system*. This is the total flow of work required to make the program operate. It consists, in the main, of a number of inputs and outputs, and a number of sequentially related subsystems, processes, and activities. It provides for information retention and feedback from which the evaluation of results, corrective actions, and innovations may be undertaken and even new plans created. Successful operation of the system depends upon the various interrelated work flow systems that are activated through the release of information and authority.

A total manpower system is comprised of at least five separate subsystems: *employment, development, utilization, compensation,* and *maintenance* (see Figure 10-1). The shaded areas show possible divisions of work between personnel staff specialists and operating managers.

In brief, the climate and the nature of the work to be performed supply us with job-related information about the human requirements—skills, knowledge, attitudes, and performance standards—as well as required nonanimate factors. These inputs provide the means through which manpower is employed and capacities are developed, and through which both are put to best use.

Monetary and other values must be provided for satisfying individual wants and needs. Through safety and medical plans and proper consideration of employee relations, the work force is maintained. Feedback from each of the subsystems or from the total system takes a variety of forms and provides a built-in corrective feature.

The utilization system is perhaps the most vital of the subsystems because the effective use of manpower as a resource actually takes place within it. Herein is the greatest opportunity for professional personnel executives to increase their real value to both employees and managers. They are or should be uniquely qualified to communicate to operating managers by translating the findings of the behavioral science researchers into meaningful everyday language. As a result, leadership styles and expected work group behavior may become more compatible, satisfying, and productive.

A systems-oriented approach to manpower management integrates the role and function of the professional personnel executive with those of operating managers who will benefit most from his support.

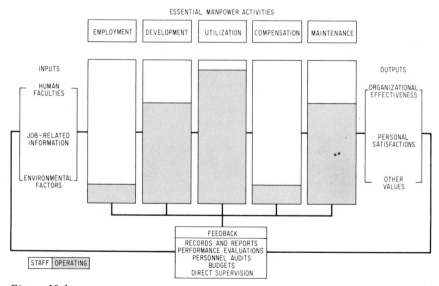

ESSENTIAL MANPOWER ACTIVITIES

| EMPLOYMENT | DEVELOPMENT | UTILIZATION | COMPENSATION | MAINTENANCE |

INPUTS

HUMAN FACULTIES

JOB-RELATED INFORMATION

ENVIRONMENTAL FACTORS

OUTPUTS

ORGANIZATIONAL EFFECTIVENESS

PERSONAL SATISFACTIONS

OTHER VALUES

FEEDBACK
RECORDS AND REPORTS
PERFORMANCE EVALUATIONS
PERSONNEL AUDITS
BUDGETS
DIRECT SUPERVISION

STAFF OPERATING

Figure 10-1

READING 11

DEFENSE SYSTEMS MANAGEMENT: THE 375 SERIES*

Edward J. Morrison

Significant changes have recently been instituted in contracting arrangements between the Department of Defense and the aerospace industry. Through spelling out specific rules and approaches to sharpen systems management, the Department of Defense and the Air Force have taken an important step toward a revision of management practices in that important area. However, the total implications of these changes for aerospace management today, and for government-industry relationships in the future, while still unclear, are likely to be considerable.

Although the exposition of this article is limited to relationships between the Air Force and the aerospace industry, such relationships may prove to be a pattern acceptable to, and adopted by, other governmental agencies in their contracting with private industry. Widespread adoption of these relationships would signal a basic departure from current business

* *Reprinted from* California Management Review, *vol. IX, no. 4, Summer, 1967. Copyright 1967 by The Regents of The University of California.*

practice. Under the new systems management concept:

A new structural relationship has been created in which the Air Force, as a buyer, makes specific management decisions about policy and detailed procedures within aerospace companies that sell defense systems to the Air Force.

The manuals prescribing new systems management concepts and procedures are very large, full of detail, and subject to varying interpretation by officials in government and private contractor organizations. As a result, private contractors may find it difficult to know if they are "in conformance" with new systems management requirements.

Questions may be raised about centralization of power, as government makes industry decisions that were previously made by private contractors.

Managers in private contracting firms may begin to worry more about satisfying government requirements than about producing the most effective weapons systems.

I do not intend to be negatively critical of

the parties involved, but rather seek to examine efforts to date in this field and to point out some of the potential gains and potential problems inherent in such a management accommodation.

A HUGE PLANNING TASK

National defense is a costly business. Maximum efficiency in Department of Defense operations requires a clear statement of national objectives, defense objectives, and a careful consideration of potential weapons systems that will satisfy those objectives. The Department of Defense is concerned with balancing the cost and advantages of any single weapons system against the costs and performance of every other system. This huge planning task must consider short-range requirements as well as those five, ten, or twenty years in the future.

When management decisions involve hundreds of millions, or even billions of dollars, even a small percentage error in estimating by the Department of Defense may result in sizable mistakes. Large sums of money may be wasted if the government finds out, months or years after letting a contract, that the weapons system is not technically adequate or feasible. Also, if there is not a thorough evaluation of the objectives upon which acquisition of a weapons system is made, later examination of these objectives may result in scrapping an entire system into which millions of dollars have been invested. Sophisticated planning tools are required for such a large, important task. For years the government has looked hopefully to private companies in the aerospace industry to develop and standardize management planning and controlling tools throughout the industry; for the most part, standardization did not occur.

During the years since World War II, the Air Force let contracts for weapons systems and utilized a system of Air Force plant representative officers to supervise contractors' performance and to assure conformance to contract specifications and system requirements. Often assistance in this task was hired from technically competent independent firms. However, for a number of reasons, occurring in part from government actions and in part from private contractor practices, serious management and technical problems often beset the achievement of aerospace contract objectives.

In 1964 the Air Force announced a series of manuals that set up a management program designed to enforce consistent management logic and control over acquisition of all future weapons systems to be procured by the Air Force. In its scope and specificity it sounded a significant, and to some an ominous, change in the relationship between government and private business. Public announcements[1] left little doubt that the Air Force was going to try to instill and require the same management discipline in its own Systems Command and in all companies that wish to do business with the Air Force. The tool selected to effect management discipline was a series of Air Force Systems Command Manuals, referred to as the 375 Series.

To those in industry who have expressed fear that government would stifle creativity, government spokesmen replied that they preferred the word "limit" to stifle and then said further that limits should be established to make an innovator conform to the total integrated impact of a program.[2]

The 375 Series was not conceived in a vacuum. Several years of intense management effort in the Department of Defense (DOD) resulted in a more coherent way of doing defense business as well as in the isolation of many problems and problem symptoms. DOD management is concerned with many problems, some of genuine interest to private industry, including:

Excessive growth of program costs.
Serious schedule slippages.
Too frequent redirection and cancellation.
Inadequately defined mission, performance, and operating requirements.
Unrealistic cost and schedule estimates.
Frequent engineering and program management changes.
Inadequate consideration of production unit costs or reliability and the ease of maintenance of hardware.

PROGRAM PACKAGE CONCEPT

In order to combat these problems, the Department of Defense developed a program package concept that relates planning and budgeting to mission-oriented defense requirements. Where previous budgets requested so much for hardware, personnel, operations, etc., the program package concept identifies nine basic defense programs and further segregates each of these into program elements. Each program element is dollar-costed and time-phased functionally. Collectively, these program elements, when costed in a five-year time frame, represent a five-year force structure.[3] This force structure demonstrates the DOD's ability to meet national defense objectives during the next five years. If a new weapons system is to be included and budgeted in the force structure, a program change proposal must first be approved by the Secretary of Defense.

Other concepts were promulgated to facilitate handling the urgencies and complexities of an effective defense posture. The "concurrency concept" stated that several portions of a system can be developed at the same time in order to shorten the time between initiation of a project and its completion. Contract definition has been refined: to speed engineering development by early approval by the Secretary of Defense; to define fully structured fixed price or incentive price contracts; to facilitate system project management; and to extend management planning and control techniques applied to DOD contracts. These changes sound complex (and in operation they are) but later portions of this article should provide some clarification of their nature and effect on the DOD agencies and private contractors doing business with the government.

THE SYSTEM LIFE CYCLE

Phases of a defense system life cycle. Before discussing the impact of the 375 Series manuals upon government agencies and private contractors, it will be helpful to examine the Defense System Life Cycle in which they are applied. Very briefly a system goes through the following stages:[4]

1 *Concept formulation.* Develop the concept of a system and establish its feasibility.
2 *Contract definition.* Sufficiently define the system and the engineering and development effort necessary.

3 *Acquisition phase.* Physically acquire the system (detail design, development, procurement, and testing).
4 *Operational phase.* Deliver and place the system in use.

As Figure 11-1 indicates, the acquisition and operational phases overlap. As the first end items of hardware and software are developed, produced, tested, and accepted by the Air Force, they are transferred to a using command and made operational with active logistic support. These phases will be covered in more detail.

On July 1, 1965, DOD Directive 3200.9 redefined the relationships and interfaces[5] between government and contractors during the first two phases of a system life cycle. This redefinition is important because it shows the intent of DOD and identifies a complex and somewhat unique relationship between the Air Force as a buyer and the aerospace industry as a seller. As one reads the following paragraphs, it might be interesting to imagine these relationships as if they applied to one's own business' buyer-seller relationships.

Concept formulation. Completed during this phase are the experimental tests—engineering and analytical studies that provide the technical, economic, and military basis for a decision to develop the equipment or system. Certain steps must be accomplished and demonstrated by a contractor to the Air Force, then by the Air Force to the DOD:[6]

Establish that primarily engineering, rather than experimental, effort is required and that the technology needed is sufficiently in hand.
Define mission and performance envelopes.
Select best technical approaches.
Make thorough trade-off analyses.
Assure that cost effectiveness of the proposed item is determined favorably in relationship to cost effectiveness of competing items (on a DOD-wide basis).

CONCEPT FORMULATION	CONTRACT DEFINITION			ACQUISITION (Operational)	
	A	B	C	DEVELOPMENT	PRODUCTION

Conditional Approval for Development   Ratification of Approval for Development   PRODUCTION DECISION   KEY DECISIONS

Figure 11-1 Defense system life cycle.

Assure that cost and schedule estimates are credible and acceptable.

One or more contractors may be involved in this concept formulation phase, and one or more contractors may be paid for its work. Obviously, the Air Force Systems Command must be interested in the project if it is to be submitted and recommended to the Office of the Secretary of Defense for consideration. If all of the steps above are accomplished, the Office of the Secretary of Defense may give conditional approval for engineering development and appoint a source selection authority that will eventually make the choice of contractor(s) to define, develop, and produce the equipment or system.

Contract definition.   Having established the desirability and feasibility of a certain weapons concept, the DOD will finance contract definition efforts, usually by two or more contractors, each working in close collaboration with the DOD component having development responsibility. DOD Directive 3200.9 states that after contractors have been selected,

> . . . A fully competitive environment shall be established with the competition in terms of concept, design approach, trade-off solutions, management plans, schedule, and similar factors as well as over-all cost.[7]

The screening and negotiating processes occur in phase A of contract definition (see Figure 11-1). During phase B, the work in the competitive environment described immediately above is done. As a result of phase B, competing contractors each submit a contract definition report and a complete technical, management, and cost proposal for development of the proposed system.

These outputs accomplish the following:[8]

Provide a basis for a fixed price or a fully structured incentive contract for engineering development.
Establish firm and realistic performance specifications.
Precisely define interfaces and responsibilities.
Identify high-risk areas.
Validate technical approaches.
Establish firm and realistic schedule and cost estimates for engineering development (in-cluding production engineering, facilities, construction, and production hardware that will be funded during engineering development because of concurrency considerations). Establish schedule and cost estimates for planning purposes for the total project (including production, operation, and maintenance).

During phase C of contract definition the proposals submitted by each competing contractor are evaluated by the source selection evaluation board with assistance from the source selection advisory council (cf. DOD Directive 4105.2, April 6, 1965). After the development contractor has been selected, the evaluation board may also recommend what is known as "technical transfusion,"[9] i.e., concepts, management plans, etc., may be taken from one DOD-financed contract definition proposal or another previously contracted technical study and incorporated in another proposal in order to make it stronger. The government may do this since it contracted for unlimited rights to technical data produced in a DOD-financed contract study.

As a result of technical transfusion, the desired changes are incorporated in a contract proposal which is then submitted with a DOD-component recommendation. (Not all proposals are recommended for additional action.) The Secretary of Defense then rules on the recommendation, and, if it is approved, a definite engineering development contract is negotiated and executed, usually with only one private contractor.

Contractor organization.   As a side note, it might be mentioned that three types of contractor organization structures have been considered closely by the Air Force. One type of contractor organization currently in effect is called "functionally oriented" in which the mode of organization is by technical disciplines, such as electrical engineering, mechanical engineering, mathematical department, etc. This type of organization lacks central project control and is not looked on very favorably by the customer (e.g., the Air Force). A second mode of organization is called "fully project oriented," and under this arrangement each project within the contractor's company has its own engineering, manufacturing, and other departments. A third mode of organization is sometimes called a "bi-lateral line" organization (Figure 11-2). It has the strength of a

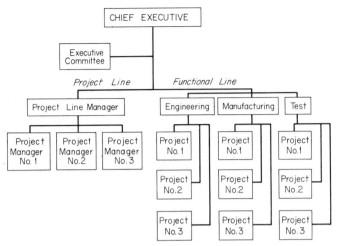

Figure 11-2   Contractor organization: bilateral line.

single project manager within the contractor's firm who is responsible for budget, schedule, and technical performance of each project. Under this type of arrangement the customer (AF) has a single responsible source for contact, and the company may retain the advantages of a concentrated technical discipline within a functional department.[10] In many respects, this type of organization closely parallels the relationship between the systems program office and other participating governmental organizations and civilian contractors. (See AFSCM 375–3, Chapter 3, June 15, 1964.)

Because of the detail specified in the 375 Series manuals, the acquisition and operational phases will be discussed in the following section.

One of the major problems of defense systems management is the immensity of the task. Time spans between system conception and phase-out are often long; many government and private organizations are usually involved. The size of some systems, such as the TFX airplane, is huge, and the technology is often complex. In fact, the same factors that make systems management difficult also make it mandatory.

The Department of Defense has insisted that its systems command be organized to impose more vigorous systems management on their operations. The vehicle for communicating **how** systems management should be performed is the so-called "375 Series." A number of DOD directives and Air Force regulations prescribe and refer to the 375 Series of Air Force Systems Command Manuals, the most important of which are the following:

AFSCM 375–1   Configuration Management
AFSCM 375–3   System Program Office Manual
AFSCM 375–4   System Program Management
AFSCM 375–5   System Engineering Management Procedures
AFSCM 375–6   Development Engineering
AFSCM 310–1   Management of Contractor Data and Reports.

In addition, many other related manuals, program management instructions, AF Headquarters operating instructions, pamphlets, and regulations are relevant to, or prescribe the performance of, systems management. Some of these documents speak solely to government agencies, while others specify required private contractor management practices. In many instances, the systems command requires extensive standard information outputs for all contractors so that it may make valid comparisons. These requirements will affect contractors' internal management information gathering and reporting procedures as well as their management decision-making practices.

The scope and interrelationship of the 375 Series may be seen within the framework of the systems program office which has systems management responsibility for every authorized project (Figure 11-3).

One of the most difficult problems of working with the 375 Series is their sheer size. Moreover, much of the material is covered in

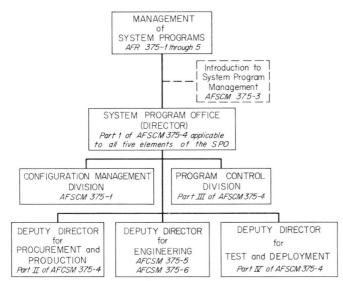

Figure 11-3   Relationship of systems management manuals.

great detail. It is, therefore, difficult for a private contractor to know the extent to which his normal management practices will be affected when he "gets into conformance" with the requirements of the 375 Series.

There is a logic inherent in the manuals, but unfortunately it is not reflected in their numbering system. Perhaps the uninitiated should begin with 375–3, then read 375–4 and DOD Directive 3200.9. The 375–4 manual indicates when other references are necessary to follow the complete sequence of systems management events, and it directs one to 375–1, 375–5, and 310–1 for more detailed explanations of the functions they describe.[11] In this article the manuals are treated in that order, omitting DOD Directive 3200.9 which was covered earlier.

System program office manual, AFSCM 375–3.   This manual contains introductory information and is written in a casual style to familiarize those who may be interested in defense systems management. It discusses basic systems management concepts, systems program office organization, control techniques, functional areas of systems management, and organizational relationships among the various members of the "government/industry team."

System program management procedures, AFSCM 375–4.   Appropriately, AFSCM 375–4 may be considered to be the "parent" manual of this series. This manual establishes the scope, objectives, and procedures for the conceptual, definition, acquisition, and operational phases of a system program. By using the systems program office as a focal point, it prescribes the significant management activities for integrating and fulfilling responsibilities of organizational elements involved in managing a system program. AFSCM 375–4 is a mandatory standard for all future systems command programs and projects.[12]

Part I defines the basic requirements for program control, configuration management, procurement and production, engineering and test, and deployment. These basic requirements are to be implemented by AFSCM 375–1, AFSCM 375–5, AFSCM 310–1, and Parts II, III, and IV of AFSCM 375–4.[13]

A series of "road maps" portrays the sequence of management activities and organizational interaction during the four phases of a system life cycle. These "road maps" are described and explained in considerable detail in the body of AFSCM 375–4, and they provide the reader with the sequential flow of activities involved in systems management. When the details of these activities become too complex, or when higher authority is needed to authorize action, the reader is invited to refer to other documents as appropriate, such as regulations, directives, or further portions of the 375 Series.

By following sequenced events and guidelines described in AFSCM 375–4, as augmented by 375–1, 375–5, and 310–1, program managers should achieve an integrated management information system that will:

Measure progress in meeting program objectives of schedule, cost, and technical performance.

Rank problems in terms of their criticality in meeting program objectives.

Provide each level of management with information in necessary detail for decision-making purposes.

Managing the system life cycle of a defense system of the magnitude of the TFX or the C-5A airplane programs is a Herculean task, and one would expect management guidelines to expand into considerable proportions. The problems of configuration management, systems engineering, and data management are immense.

Configuration management during the definition and acquisition phases, AFSCM 375–1. This function is concerned with identifying, controlling, and accounting for all hardware and facility requirements. During each phase of the life cycle of a system, it is essential to describe fully the picture or profile of each element of the system at that time. These specifications may then be used as a bench mark or baseline against which activities of the next phase may be controlled.

Three major requirements baselines are employed in defense systems management. The contract definition phase is controlled against a **program requirements baseline** which is established by a system specification. During the contract definition phase, hardware and facilities design requirements are further defined and finally established as a **design requirements baseline** against which detailed design and production may be controlled.[14] When the customer formally accepts the first article produced and agrees that it satisfies contractual requirements of technical performance, a third bench mark, the **product configuration baseline,** is established. This baseline is used to control future builds and tests of the article.

During engineering development and production, there are inevitably going to be changes in established baselines. Before such changes may be authorized, each one must be examined to insure that it is compatible with all other system elements, as well as with in-service equipment. The change must also be timely, feasible, and necessary. Further, any changes that are finally agreed upon must be reflected in the baseline against which they are made.

Another function of configuration management is to report the current status of baselines: of contracts, of specifications, of designs, and of facilities, hardware, and associated software. When the technology of a product is complex, these baselines must be thoroughly defined in detail and the critical interfaces identified to permit control. It is easy to see why electronic data-processing equipment is used to handle the extensive data necessary for effective configuration management. In programs of great complexity or magnitude, it is vital to provide maximum visibility of high-risk technical interfaces and to maintain high standards of technical control.

System engineering management procedures, AFSCM 375–5. The intent of this manual is to introduce the concept of **total systems design** into Air Force systems command management thinking and into private contractors' engineering organizations. As explained by the manual, total systems design will be accomplished through systems engineering, using a uniform design process. These three terms are further defined and elaborated.

As a result of usage, states the manual, the term "systems" includes:

> . . . prime mission equipment; computer programs; equipment for training, checkout, test, and maintenance; facilities required to operate and maintain the system; selection and training of personnel; operational and maintenance procedures; instrumentation and data reduction for test and evaluation; special activation and acceptance programs; and logistics support for test, activation, and operational aspects of the program.[15]

Obviously, this is a broad definition of the term that necessitates a broad consideration of engineering management problems.

Systems engineering is concerned with deriving a total system design to achieve stated objectives—a single set of optimum outputs based on given inputs. Total systems design includes engineering all system elements and components and their interrelationships for the duration of the total program. Program objectives require that schedule, cost, and technical performance should all be weighed in the evaluation of engineering results.

The manual directs that a uniform design process be followed in systems engineering. It is recognized, in the manual, that:

> No two systems are ever alike in their developmental requirements. However, there is a uniform and identifiable process for logically arriving at systems decisions regardless of systems purpose, size, or complexity. This manual describes and specifies such a process, i.e., a systems engineering management process.[16]

Under this systems engineering management process, there would be an integration of all relevant design disciplines and single control over evaluation of requirements and design. A planned flow of technical information permits dynamic updating of engineering results. Further, basic data would be readily accessible for determining detailed requirements for personnel subsystems, logistics, and procedural publications. The manual prescribes detailed procedures that are designed to facilitate each of the above processes.

By enforcing adherence to this systems engineering management process, the Air Force hopes to achieve several innovations to its past practices, for example:

Develop and identify performance and design specifications before the fact (of detailed design).

Require management to make earlier identification of control, accounting, and system requirements.

Provide a mandatory flow of documentation to the systems command earlier in the program, identifying problem areas and recommending courses of action.

Provide necessary data for making systems management and command decisions.

Generally, systems engineering encourages:

1 Greater visibility of engineering performance.
2 Earlier systems engineering management action.
3 Earlier program management decisions.

Management of contractor data and reports, AFSCM 310–1/AFLCM 310–1. Although this manual does not bear the "375 Series" designation, adherence to its specifications is required by AFSCM 375–4 (cf. pp. 57 and 91), as well as AFSCM 375–5 (cf. p. 3). Further, AFSCM 375–3 states that the systems program office is responsible for acquisition of all data, including engineering management, and logistics information and must assure that it is available at the proper time and location. To accomplish this mission, a data management officer is appointed by the system program office.[17]

Data management is a significant and complicated requirement for both the governmental and private contractors. This manual alone is over 1,200 pages long, and is very detailed in its requirements. It specifies types of reports, their form, layout, and contents, and sometimes the size and requirements of each data element included.

Effective performance of data management results in adequate, timely documentation of activities and decisions that have occurred in previous phases of a system life cycle. In fact, contractor data are often a large part of the "product" that is bought under contracts for defense systems. Much work has been done and is being done in this area of data management. However, anyone associated with this function, either in government or out, will agree that much more effort is required before completely meaningful, useful, and manageable systems will be obtained.

CHANGE IN THINKING

From the foregoing exposition, one may discern a major change in the Department of Defense's thinking about systems management. Previous defense contract relationships were characterized by government's stating broader objectives and policies, while leaving the specifics of implementation to private contractors. Determination of satisfactory contractor performance usually came after completion of a project and was accomplished by comparing contract specifications with documentation and hardware performance. In too many instances, the comparisons were inconclusive or less than satisfactory.

Expanded government authority. Under systems management concepts embodied in the 375 Series, the government's role is considerably enlarged and made much more specific. A systems program director is responsible for program objectives of cost, schedule, and technical performance. He is also responsible for management decisions about specific engineering management disciplines employed by private contractors. He is responsible for detailed management control and reporting procedures and for many other decisions about how well a private contractor's management is doing a job. Under the 375 Series procedures, the government's management authority does not wait until after a product is produced; it works actively while the project is in progress.

Basic structural change.   A realignment of roles played by government agencies and private industry has been described in this article, and this realignment will undoubtedly have significant, lasting effects on the parties involved. Whenever a basic structural change occurs between two large, powerful parties in our economy, one may expect to find significant changes of several kinds. This last statement is predicated on the notion that other government agencies will follow the lead of the 375 Series (such as the National Aeronautics and Space Agency [NASA] is doing with its "500" Series") and that eventually many nonaerospace companies will have to deal with similar requirements imposed by nondefense-oriented governmental agencies that procure private industry goods and services. From observation of the present situation, several problems may result.

THE POSSIBLE CONSEQUENCES

Emerging problems.   It should be obvious that the government enjoys a somewhat privileged relationship as a customer dealing with private business. Typically, a customer buys a product that meets his desired specifications and leaves the process of achieving that product to those who manage the producing organization. By virtue of prescribing extensive management systems and practices that must be followed by companies wishing to do business with it; by reserving (and exercising) the right of review and possible rejection of internal management procedures and operating practices; and by passing technical judgment on the validity, accuracy, and adequacy of technical data, the Air Force places itself in an interesting position. Several possibilities are apparent.

Who is responsible?   Aerospace companies' executives may begin to manage their operations more with an eye to satisfying customer-designed management system requirements than to producing a product they think will perform best in a manner that they feel is most expeditious and most technically fruitful. This reorientation of management attention is more than just a matter of "stifling creativity." It places the right and responsibility for critical management decisions with the Air Force rather than with the contractor. If a wrong decision is made, a forceful argument can be presented that the Air Force had the right of technical review and disapproval and that, in not disapproving, it did, in fact, give tacit approval to the decision in question. This raises a disturbing question of legal liability for payment by the Air Force, even when performance of an end item is not according to prescribed specifications.

Management interpretation.   It is inevitable that a document such as the 375 Series will contain words or paragraphs that are somewhat ambiguous, leaving room for varying interpretation by private contractors or government officials. Examination of current practice shows that variation in interpreting managerial specifications has, in fact, occurred. This variance has the effect of establishing a confusion in personal relationships between a program office and private contractors and may result in some firms being much more controlled than others.

Too much centralization?   A further problem inherent in this customer-contractor relationship may be found in the question of where and by whom technical and management decisions can best be made—the level of decision making inherent in decentralization. Much has been reported in the literature to indicate that decisions should be made as close as possible to the level of occurrence of problems and by people most fully informed about the problems and technically capable of making those decisions.[18] According to this literature, it would seem inadvisable to give the right of review and responsibility for disapproval of problem solutions to an "outside agency" not "in the business" of producing the items in question. Delay of decisions is inevitable. Also, even with technical assistance, it is still difficult to understand fully the intricacies of operating situations and to make better decisions from a remote location and organization that can be made by persons more closely involved in such a situation.

Tons of data—how useful? In reporting data to the customer, many useless or even dysfunctional reports may be generated and forwarded for review and storage. The massive data requirements for aerospace development, acquisition, and operation would stagger the casual observer and impress even the trained practitioner. The impact of this problem is evidenced by subcontractors who refuse to accept business with aerospace companies because of unrealistic documentation requirements imposed on them. Although discipline in handling data requirements is admittedly necessary, the complexity of this subject area reveals a need for careful analysis and much better systems. One primary danger lies in developing reports that provide prescribed data but that result in little management analysis and decision. Those people involved in electronic data processing, management systems, and contractual data requirements understand the critical nature of this problem far beyond the scope of this article's elaboration of it.

Stifling innovation? A fundamental question is raised about what is the most fruitful business environment for technical innovation. There seems to be no great customer complaints with technology created under existing management systems; however, greater management control is desired in acquiring systems embodying that technology. The 375 Series inaugurates extensive engineering management controls and a uniform design process, and it remains to be seen whether technical innovation will occur at a satisfactory rate under this system.

In conclusion, one is faced with a certainty and an uncertainty. It is certain that the Department of Defense has expressed its conclusions that previous government/industry relationships were not a satisfactory method of acquiring defense systems. Since the Department of Defense is certainly by far the largest customer for aerospace products, the government has the power to change those relationships. But responsibility must accompany power, and, as government assumes its new management role, it should assume a greater responsibility of some sort toward private in-dustry. It may be concluded that in entering these uncharted relationships the long-run management consequences of changes attempted through application of the 375 Series are still very uncertain.

References

1. Philip Geddes, "Customer Closes Loopholes in Program Management," *Aerospace Management*, April 1964.

2. *Ibid.*

3. *Air Force Systems Command Manual* (AFSCM) 375–4, p. 4, Final Coordination Draft, June 1965.

4. *Ibid.*, p. 1.

5. The word "interface" is a useful part of aerospace industry jargon. The word indicates a meeting or tangency of two or more elements—technical elements or organizational elements—but it does not indicate the nature of the relationship that exists. However, if one is aware of a meeting point, further consideration may be given to defining the nature and criticality of that relationship.

6. DOD Directive 3200.9, July 1, 1965, p. 4.

7. *Ibid.*, p. 6.

8. *Ibid.*, p. 3.

9. *Ibid.*, p. 9 and AFSCM 375–4, p. 85.

10. Some work has been done in describing the nature of matrix organizations; cf. John Mee, "Matrix Organization," *Business Horizons*, VII:2 (Spring 1964), 70–72, and Fremont A. Shull, "Matrix Structure and Project Authority for Optimizing Organizational Capacity" (Business Science Monograph, No. 1, Business Research Bureau; Carbondale, Illinois: Southern Illinois University, n.d.). More work should be done on the effects of such arrangements.

11. AFSCM 375–2 covers management surveys, is not mentioned in AFSCM 375–4, and is not currently in use. AFSCM 375–6 deals specifically with development engineering and will not be covered in this article.

12. Cf. AFSCM 375–4, p.*i.*

13. *Ibid.*, p. 4.

14. AFSCM 375–3, p. 39.

15. AFSCM 375–5, p.*i*, Dec. 14, 1964.

16. *Ibid.*

17. AFSCM 375–3, p. 42.

18. For a discussion of this subject as regards individual firms, see R. C. Davis, *Fundamentals of Top Management* (New York: Harper and Brothers, 1951), pp. 306–316, and Koontz and O'Donnell, *Principles of Management* (New York: McGraw-Hill Book Company, Inc., 1964), chap. 17.

SECTION 3

Planning

Planning involves preparing to meet the future. However, since we shall all meet our future, whatever it may be, and since we are not all planners, a more precise description is necessary. The key word is "preparing." To be prepared to meet the future means that one is able both to adapt effectively and efficiently to the changes which the future will surely bring, but also, that one is able to take advantage of the opportunities which the future presents.

Planning, especially that of the "long-range" variety, is receiving a great deal of attention in the literature of management and associated fields of specialization. Many different views of the planning function are popular, ranging from the simple relationship of planning to forecasting to a view of planning which encompasses a systems view of the management process. The view taken in this section is somewhat temperate but it is more nearly the latter than the former.

Planning is one of the central functions of management. Without planning, it is not possible for the manager to perform his other functions, e.g., organizing, controlling, etc. If the organization has any goal other than self-perpetuation, it is necessary for the manager to direct it toward the future accomplishment of these goals. Indeed, even if self-preservation is the only goal, the organization is more likely to achieve it in a changing environment through planning than it is without planning.

Crucial to the planning function are the organization's objectives. Many large organizations have little idea what their objectives are. Indeed, the idea of an organization perceiving its objectives really means that the humans who control the organization's destiny do so, and it is vividly clear that many do not. Although an objective of most industrial firms is growth, *many have failed to delineate those areas in which growth is both practical and profitable. In failing to do so, they have precluded themselves from taking advantage of the future. As a result, they will be forced to* react *to a changing environment, and unless they are very fortunate, will be in a position of "catching up" with trends rather than leading them.*

A variety of forces have influenced the planning activities carried on in modern organizations. The Department of Defense embarked on organized planning activities in advance of most industries. Yet, the interplay between government and industry planning is made apparent when one reviews the literature to find papers which emphasize what industry has learned about planning from government (witness the excellent paper by Smalter) and those which treat the impact of industry's planning activities on government. Indeed, both are valid, for the interaction has been great, and the transfer has operated in both directions.

Another major force which has led to increased formal planning emanates from the success achieved by quantitative decision analysis. The fields of concern, e.g., operations research, systems analysis, management science, etc., have demonstrated that analysis can be applied to strategic planning. In doing so, they have provided both techniques to aid planners and a framework on which planning can be performed and evaluated.

During the past few years many companies have established full-time positions with a function variously referred to as "top management planning" or "long-range planning." The continued establishment of these positions indicates that the development of corporate strategy and a system of plans to support that strategy is evolving as a major function in many U.S. Corporations. Although executive personnel have always performed a degree of long-range planning, it is still a rather recent innovation, particularly in the degree of formality being established in organizational arrangements and modus operandi. *The recent furor over long-range planning has produced only a few books; the periodical literature has been enriched with some very perceptive articles on the subject. In this section some of the better articles are reflected; the articles deal with the conceptual framework of long-range planning as well as describing some of the tools that can be used in performing long-range planning.*

READING 12

WHERE LONG-RANGE PLANNING GOES WRONG*

E. Kirby Warren

In comparatively recent years, the emphasis in business planning has moved from adapting to change to actively anticipating and planning for change. With the growth of large corporations and the increased amount, speed, and magnitude of change—economic, social, technological, and competitive—adaptation alone has often proved inadequate to insure corporate survival and profitability.

This is not to say that long-range planning is a new activity; farsighted businessmen have devoted their time and energy to it for at least the last half century. But the increased size and complexity of business have made long-range planning of vital importance in recent years, and companies today ignore it at their peril.

Moreover, the increasing size of corporations —and, indeed, of the economy itself—have taken such planning out of the realm of activities that can be handled informally by a top execu-

* Reprinted from Management Review, by permission of the American Management Association, Inc., May, 1962.

tive. The magnitude of the task and the growing number of other responsibilities that must be handled by top management have made it necessary to delegate major portions of the job to other levels of the organization. With this delegation has come the need for more formalized procedures; with it, also, has come the increased danger of error in the performance of any one of its parts or, more important, in the assembly of these parts into a meaningful and integrated whole.

Thus it happens that, at the very time companies are depending most heavily on long-range planning and devoting the greatest efforts to it, they often find that the resulting long-range plans are inadequate, inappropriate, and sometimes extremely harmful to the company.

To see why this should be so, we can take a look at the four major functional parts of long-range planning and see the ways in which the planners involved most often go wrong. Long-range planning can be separated into four basic types of activities that must be performed:

1 Forecasting activities.
2 Budget and financial accounting activities.
3 Setting goals and designing action programs.
4 Direction, supervision, and coordination of planning activities.

FORECASTING

There is a great deal of circularity in the sequencing of these functions, but given a basic sense of the broad goals sought, the first basic phase of long-range planning is forecasting. Despite the difficulties brought on by a rapidly changing business environment, the potential ability to carry out this function has greatly increased in recent years. Not only do improved forecasting techniques enable the planner to make more valid estimates about the future, but there is also considerable increase in the availability of information on virtually every facet of business and economic life. The many surveys and special studies sponsored by governmental agencies provide a wealth of data that not too long ago would have been costly if not impossible for business to obtain. Less directly, government regulations requiring corporations to disclose information that had previously been carefully concealed made still more valuable information available. And the growing sense of professionalism in business management has paved the way for voluntary exchange of business data. Trade associations play an active role in this area by fostering the exchange of information and encouraging the pooling of corporate resources and experience.

Despite these advances, the quality of current long-range forecasting falls considerably short of both what is desirable and what is possible. Time and again, instead of representing estimates of expected or desired future states, given projected internal and external changes, the forecasts or planning assumptions are only mechanical extrapolations of trend.

Rose-colored Glasses

There are two basic causes for this, both stemming from apparent misconceptions about the purpose and nature of forecasting. The fundamental reason for making forecasts is the desire to estimate as accurately as possible the expected outcome of a number of controllable and uncontrollable actions. Despite this, the first major cause of poor forecasting is the feeling of many forecasters that their projections often have to represent what management wants to see, rather than what they are likely to see.

A corporate-level "plans analyst" in one decentralized heavy-industry firm showed unusual candor in confirming this conclusion:

"In many cases, [division planners] show corporate management what they feel corporate management wants to see. They paint a picture that may be unrealistic, but it usually takes two or three years for this to become apparent. Often, they attain their goals for totally different reasons than were planned. Even more often, as might be expected, they fail to realize their objectives.

"Division management seems to take the view that if things don't work out as well as expected, they have the uncertainty of the future to fall back on. At worst, once every three or four years they may get a real going-over, but this is accepted as the price paid for freedom to work on the myriad operational problems faced today, rather than tackle problems that may be several years away."

The Best Guesses

The line of reasoning behind the second form of poor forecasting is more common. One executive explained it this way: "We can estimate what kinds of changes are likely to occur, but for the most part we are just guessing. Rather than base our plans on guesses, we assume that the future will be largely a continuation of current trends. We know that many of our assumptions will prove incorrect, but so would our guesses. This way we have something to start with that can be modified as we approach the time period involved and greater certainty."

This tendency is not limited to estimates of external, uncontrollable variables. One divisional director of research and development pointed out that the work of this group in looking for new products and improving existing product lines, along with work done by product- and market-development groups, was seldom reflected in the division's five-year plan. It was mentioned in the "prose plan" as one of the factors that would produce growth and greater profits, but the tie between this work and action steps to produce such increases was seldom made.

Thus, even the type of change that is quite certain—change the company is actively working on—is often ignored in preparing forecasts and planning assumptions. The usual explanation is that, although change will result, "it is hard to predict the specific impact of this change."

Again, the basic misconception of the purpose of a forecast is evident. Prediction is seldom possible. The purpose of the forecast is to provide the best guesses with regard to the future so alternative plans can be developed. The appropriate alternative can be chosen and modified when the proper time arrives, but current decisions can reflect the best estimates of the future. It is seldom easy to arrive at meaningful estimates, but it is far better to work with even imperfect guesses than with static and unimaginative extrapolations of trend. And the greater the uncertainty of the future, the more does the company need to anticipate possible future changes.

Estimates and Ulcers

The view that to be useful forecasts must be close to certainty has a secondary effect. The men who are actually developing the forecasts often complain that the executives for whom they prepare projections "simply do not understand the nature of forecasting. They don't understand the value of working with alternative estimates of the future. They want *answers.*"

With their responsibility for making decisions involving thousands if not millions of dollars, it is not surprising that executives want answers, not estimates. To be sure, they recognize that a long-range forecast is at best a carefully formulated guess, but it is not really surprising that they should rebel at the idea of receiving these guesses in a form that emphasizes their uncertainty.

In an effort to come to grips with this limiting outlook and to improve the quality of long-range forecasting, some companies require that all major forecasts or assumptions be stated in terms of "best," "worst," and "most likely" estimates, and that the ensuing plans be designed to cope with each eventuality.

Basically, forecasting is a technical function performed by specialists. The specialists have developed techniques for producing better forecasts: Great advances have been made in data-processing, storage, and retrieval, and procedures for making decisions under uncertainty are emerging. But for this progress to have meaning, those who direct the technicians must seek and use true forecasts rather than extrapolations. The importance of this vital element of planning cannot be overemphasized. If preliminary forecasts are inadequate, programs designed to move the company from expected to desired future states will in all likelihood be misdirected.

BUDGETING AND ACCOUNTING

If forecasting receives too little attention in long-range planning, the budgeting and financial accounting function often receives too much. The confusion between budgeting and planning is unfortunately quite common, and the result is most undesirable. If planning and budgeting are viewed as being virtually synonymous, then major portions of the planning responsibility, including much implied objective-setting and program design, may be turned over to the "budgeteers"—men whose financial accounting background often has not prepared them to carry out complete planning jobs.

Budgeting is, after all, largely the translation of objectives and programs into financial form. To turn over major portions of the responsibility for planning to budget specialists is like turning over major portions of the responsibility for international policy-making and speech-writing to the technicians at the United Nations who translate such statements into other languages.

The Budgeteer's Limits

In annual planning, this abandonment of responsibility for objective-setting and program design is somewhat less critical, since much short-term planning is really little more than the allocation of available resources within the framework of existent policy. But for the elements of current decision-making that must reflect change in policy because of environmental changes, and for the aspects of longer-range planning that are designed to alter the company's course, planning must go beyond the limits of the budgeteer.

The Budgeting Job

Budgeting and financial accounting activities constitute only one aspect of long-range planning, but it is an important aspect. The primary function of the budget group is the translation of plans into financial terms. Although many of the financial implications of various objectives and programs are self-evident, a second function of the budget and accounting group is analyzing financial plans and reporting to management on the less obvious indications. A third and related group of responsibilities involves working with division officers to help them achieve their desired goals along desired lines, but in such as way as to produce better-balanced and more desirable financial results.

Members of the units performing these budgetary and financial accounting activities are, as would be expected, men with financial accounting backgrounds. Their leaders are men who have moved up in the financial accounting end of the business, and many have received their basic training in public accounting.

Considerable effort is being expended in many companies to broaden the background of this group, from the individuals working on the detailed elements of the budget up to the controller himself. This effort is certainly commendable, but it does little good if the men involved do not have time to bring this broader viewpoint to bear on their work. There is a tendency in some companies to overload the capacities of those responsible for this work, so that despite their "broadening," they simply do not have time to do more than unimaginative clerical work. Failure to pick out more than the financial errors before departmental plans are summarized places an even greater burden on corporate management with regard to appraisal: By the time plans reach corporate review, only perceptive digging by top management will unearth faulty premises, inadequate program design, or other errors that may be buried in the summary nature of departmental plans.

As is true of forecasting, the greatest single need for improving the quality of budgeting and financial accounting functions is the need for clarifying the true nature of these activities and understanding what should not be done as well as what should be done.

SETTING GOALS AND DESIGNING ACTION PROGRAMS

Commenting on the fairly common problems created by confusing budgeting with planning, particularly when combined with poor forecasting, David Hertz wrote: "Some managements develop 'budgets' based on subjective forecasts and stick to them through thick and thin. Each decision is made in accordance with an arbitrary plan that was established without any forecasting of probable changes in the uncontrollable variables.... Does this sound unlikely? It is possible to point out [cases where] the budget called for adding twenty men to several specific companies that had year-to-year budgets for expansion in their product line and [they] proceeded with those plans on schedule, despite clear portents of future difficulties for these products."

Vital Ingredients

This kind of thing occurs when several vital ingredients of planning are left out. When arbitrary objectives are set and budgets are designed to "meet" these objectives, what has not been done is (1) to analyze projections of expected goals in order to realistically set desired goals, (2) to analyze the specific problems standing in the way of filling the gap between expected and desired, and (3) to design a program of *action steps,* not mechanical allocations of wishful thinking, designed to overcome these problems. These three activities comprise the third group of planning functions.

In many cases, programs laid out for years two to five of a five-year plan fail to reflect more than a degree of qualified effort in this area. Because of inadequate forecasting, the best possible picture of the expected future state had not been drawn. Therefore, to begin with, objectives are necessarily arbitrary, since they reflect neither an accurate projection of the external environment nor an accurate projection of internal change. Starting with unsound forecasts and arbitrary goals, it is not difficult to see why less-than-adequate efforts have been made to identify and analyze the problems faced in "filling the gap." What is the gap, after all, other than the distance between desired and expected? If the gap cannot be identified, how can problems and needs be clarified—and, going one step further, how can programs be meaningfully designed?

Obviously, they cannot be, and what results is a vague approximation of long-range plans or merely a stimulus to longer-range thinking. Such a plan is sometimes defended as "a blueprint for what we will do, given a rather conservative allowance for change." But why do you need a blueprint if change is conservative? It may be defended as "a starting point, a point of departure from which we can make changes as the future becomes more certain." But is this doubtful gain really worth the time and expense incurred, when this activity falls so far short of its potential contribution to business management?

Boon or Boondock?

Such poor planning may be defended as a stimulus to reflection, but this also is quite doubtful. If a best effort is made and falls short of perfection, those involved, knowing that their best efforts are expected, will reflect and perhaps be stimulated; but where the best is not demanded and less meaningful efforts are accepted, the first people to realize that "not much is expected of our plans" are those working on them. This is one of the major reasons for poor planning.

A senior staff officer of a large electrical company, commenting on some of the examples of bad five-year planning he had seen, raised the question of whether such planning might not be worse than none: "I am not altogether certain that, when we work with such imperfect devices and accept such poor plans, we may not only be failing to get improved long-range planning, but we may be interfering with those few people whose natural foresight and inclination for future thinking would have been looked to in the past to provide informally what we need in this area."

Who Does What?

Much of the blame for poor objective-setting, inadequate analysis of future problems, and mechanistic program designs has been laid to uncertainty about the future, but it seems likely that the training and ability of the men who are called on to carry out these responsibilities are equally responsible.

The bulk of the long-range planning work should and often does rest with line management. Staff groups do leg work, run down ideas, and occasionally put together program recommendations that are finally decided on by line management, but a major portion of this work usually rests with line officers. There are many cases, however, in which a great deal of the program-design responsibility has been taken over by staff or budget men. Vaguely sketched goals and general strategies are determined by the line manager, and the detail work of indicating how much will be spent in which areas and in what specified ways is left to others. David Ewing has pointed out an important reason: "Long-range planning puts possibly a greater premium on conceptual skills of the manager (as opposed to technical and human-relations skills) than does any other phase of top management. Looked at diagrammatically, a company's long-range plan at any moment would appear as a vast cobweb of short-term and long-term interrelationships between marketing, production, finance, industrial relations, executive development, and all the rest. All of these plans are built on certain assumptions, and the individual plans in turn become premises and assumptions for each other."

How many line managers possess these "conceptual skills"? How many have the experience, breadth of knowledge, attitudes, and time to make use of them? Or, getting closer to the source of the difficulty, how many are hired and promoted with these skills in mind? There is ample evidence that many men charged with long-range planning responsibilities do not possess these attributes to the necessary degree or, if they do, they lack the time or incentive to use them.

Needed Skills

As was the case with the forecasting and financial accounting functions, a necessary first step in improving this third part of long-range planning is the development of a clear sense of what good performance demands. The people performing these activities should possess the skills necessary to analyze the problems involved in moving from the expected to the desired future state in order to identify the specific objectives that need to be realized. They must have the capacity to develop a series of action steps designed to meet these objectives. And they must have the ability to develop alternative programs to meet the contingencies that may arise.

This does not mean that line officers should be chosen solely on the basis of their long-range planning potential. Operational, technical, and administrative skills cannot be overlooked; the line officer must be able to get things done as well as conceptualize and plan. If, in selecting men to fill these posts, a review of their strengths and weaknesses reveals deficiencies in one area or the other, efforts can be made to overcome those weaknesses—either directly or by providing staff assistants in a manner that will assure their use in compensating for these limitations.

DIRECTION, SUPERVISION, AND COORDINATION

Clarifying the nature of these first three groups of long-range planning activities, selecting people qualified to perform them, directing and supervising their efforts, and coordinaitng the separate parts of the plan are among the major responsibilities of those chosen to carry out the fourth aspect of planning.

Although the company president or, in decentralized companies, the division general manager is ordinarily the titular head of division long-range planning, as a matter of fact he usually confines his direct efforts to rather broad and summary analysis and review. He gives direction by decision, supervises by reaction, and coordinates by arbitration, but he is a reactor rather than an active participant in the administrative element of planning. Perhaps all that can be expected of a chief executive or division manager is that he use his influence to stimulate others and support the individual or individuals who play a more direct role in the direction, supervision, and coordination of planning. If this is the case, however, the choice of men to supplement him should be made with a full realization of the responsibilities involved.

Although carrying out these functions necessitates some degree of planning skill, the "director" of long-range planning is not so much a planner as he is a supervisor and coordinator of planning. He will be called upon to advise on planning, but his principal responsibilities are to direct and coordinate its conduct.

The Controller as Director

The job of the planning director in evaluating and coordinating the elements of the long-range plan can be made much easier by effective budget and analysis work. Because of this partial dependency on the budget function, a great many companies and divisions formally or informally turn the direction function over to the head of this group, the controller. There is strong evidence to suggest that although the controller, through his budget and analysis group, can make a significant contribution to planning, he is usually not a good choice to serve as director of long-range planning. Richard G. Martens, an executive with much experience in this field, has presented one of the strongest statements in support of this viewpoint:

> The controller's main job is to see that the resources of the business are conserved and being used efficiently. In accomplishing this task he uses the tools of accounting, auditing, and more recently, budgeting and forecasting. Because of his interest in conservation and efficiency, the controller normally has a functional bias in the direction of saving rather than spending money. His work is primarily with figures and, of necessity, is oriented toward recording and examining the results of past operations. His task is to measure the results of risks taken by other functions of the business rather than to take risks himself.... Within such a setting, it is only to be expected that forecasting, as developed by the controller, has tended to be a projection of past trends into the future.
>
> Long-range planning, on the other hand, must contend with the risks of innovation and deal with the exceptional and improbable future. It must be concerned with risk-taking—spending money to make money. The measure of the effectiveness of long-range planning is not efficiency but how well the course of business has been charted on the sea of future risk. Above all, those entrusted with the responsibility for long-range planning must be oriented toward the future—not the past. They must be able to take risk in their stride—not pass the risk to others or act as a passive observer or measurer. The long-range planner must lead—not follow....
>
> Placing the long-range planning function under the average controller will assure its sterility.

Although this may overstate the case, the general conclusion seems justified. Even when an effort has been made to broaden the background and perspective of the controller and his budget and analysis group, they may of necessity continue to be primarily "number" men. If this is not the case, their major work, budget and financial accounting, will suffer.

When the controller assumes responsibility for the direction, supervision, and control of long-range planning, he is charged with what amounts to two somewhat conflicting responsibilities, and the duality of his functions cannot help but reduce his efficiency in one or both areas. On the one hand, he is to direct and assist in planning, and on the other hand he must continue to discharge the control responsibilities that have often led to his being characterized as an "all-seeing eye."

A number of corporate divisions have sought to develop a new post at the division level to relieve the division general manager of a portion of these direction functions. The man chosen, usually called director of long-range planning, is given a very small staff and presumably is expected to act as an extension of the general manager. In some cases, this group also provides assistance in the other elements of long-range planning.

Ideally, the people selected for such posts should possess considerable experience in line operations so they will be regarded as men who know the score. They must also possess the skills and leadership qualities necessary to this vital function. Quite surprisingly, there are many instances in which these factors have been disregarded.

In some cases, the man chosen to serve as planning director and his assistants are younger men who were put in these posts because of the broad experience it would offer them. These key jobs are regarded primarily as good training positions. Perhaps such appointments do provide broad training, but it is virtually certain that they will not provide effective direction and coordination of long-range planning activities.

A somewhat more common type of unfortunate appointment is the assignment of these posts to men regarded as planning theorists. To the men they are supposed to assist in developing plans, they are usually regarded as staff eggheads who are filled with ivory-tower ideas about planning but who lack a working knowledge of practical operating problems.

At the extreme, there are cases where men assigned to this work are generally considered corporate misfits. Although they are talented people in many respects, top management has been unable to find a place for them in either line or other staff positions, and they are put in long-range planning work because "they can stay out of trouble there."

Lack of Concern

The appointment of younger men out to learn the business, planning theorists, or corporate misfits to such vital positions indicates either considerable confusion as to the requirements for such jobs, or, more likely, lack of real concern for long-range planning. There are instances where the division manager or corporate officer who makes the appointment is actually far from convinced that long-range planning is worth the trouble. Where this is the case, formal long-range planning is almost certainly doomed to ineffectuality.

Much vital progress will begin to take place when long-range planning has passed through the early stages of fashionability and is subjected to more objective scrutiny. At that point, planning will no longer be a stylized "must" but will be accepted on its own strengths, and companies that now merely go through the motions will exert more meaningful and effective efforts. Toward this end, an essential first step is a clearer understanding of these four key elements of long-range planning.

READING 13

WHAT ARE YOUR ORGANIZATION'S OBJECTIVES? *
A General-Systems Approach to Planning

Bertram M. Gross

There is nothing that managers and management theorists are more solidly agreed on than the vital role of objectives in the managing of organizations. The daily life of executives is full of such exhortations as:

"Let's plan where we want to go . . ."
"You'd better clarify your goals . . ."
"Get those fellows down (or up) there to understand what our (or their) purposes really are . . ."

Formal definitions of management invariably give central emphasis to the formulation or attainment of objectives. Peter Drucker's (1954) idea of "managing by objectives" gave expression to a rising current in administrative theory. Any serious discussion of planning, whether by business enterprises or government agencies, deals with the objectives of an organization.

* *Reprinted from* Human Relations, *vol. 18, no. 3, 1965 by permission of The Tavistock Institute of Human Relations, London, England.*

Yet there is nothing better calculated to embarrass the average executive than the direct query: "Just what are your organization's objectives?" The typical reply is incomplete or tortured, given with a feeling of obvious discomfort. The more skilful response is apt to be a glib evasion or a glittering generality.

To some extent, of course, objectives cannot be openly stated. Confidential objectives cannot be revealed to outsiders. Tacit objectives may not bear discussion among insiders. The art of bluff and deception with respect to goals is part of the art of administration.

But the biggest reason for embarrassment is the lack of a well-developed language of organizational purposefulness. Such a language may best be supplied by a general-systems model that provides the framework for "general-systems accounting," or "managerial accounting" in the sense of a truly generalist approach to all major dimensions of an organization. It is now possible to set forth—even if only in suggestive form—a general-systems model that provides the basis for clearly formulating the performance and structural objectives of any organization.

Let us now deal with these points separately —and conclude with some realistic observations on the strategy of planning.

THE NEED FOR A
LANGUAGE OF PURPOSEFULNESS

Many managers are still too much the prisoners of outworn, single-purpose models erected by defunct economists, engineers, and public administration experts. Although they know better, they are apt to pay verbal obeisance to some single purpose: profitability in the case of the business executive, efficiency in the case of the public executive.

If profitability is not the sole objective of a business—and even the more tradition-ridden economists will usually accept other objectives in the form of constraints or instrumental purposes—just what are these other types? If efficiency is not the only objective of a government agency—and most political scientists will maintain that it cannot be—what are the other categories? No adequate answers to these questions are provided by the traditional approaches to economics, business administration, or public administration. Most treatises on planning—for which purpose formulation is indispensable—catalogue purposes by such abstract and nonsubstantive categories as short-range and long-range, instrumental and strategic (or ultimate), general and specific. One book on planning sets forth thirteen dimensions without mentioning anything so mundane as profitability or efficiency (LeBreton & Henning, 1961). Indeed, in his initial writings on management by objectives, Drucker never came to grips with the great multiplicity of business objectives. In his more recent work Drucker (1964) deals with objectives in terms of three "result areas": product, distribution channels, and markets. But this hardly goes far enough to illuminate the complexities of purpose multiplicity.

Thus far, the most systematic approach to organizational purposes is provided by budget experts and accountants. A budget projection is a model that helps to specify the financial aspects of future performance. A balance sheet is a model that helps to specify objectives for future structure of assets and liabilities. Yet financial analysis—even when dignified by the misleading label "managerial accounting"—deals only with a narrow slice of real-life activi-

ties. Although it provides a way of reflecting many objectives, it cannot by itself deal with the substantive activities underlying monetary data. Indeed, concentration upon budgets has led many organizations to neglect technological and other problems that cannot be expressed in budgetary terms. Overconcentration on the enlargement of balance-sheet assets has led many companies to a dangerous neglect of human and organizational assets.

The great value of financial analysis is to provide a doorway through which one can enter the whole complex domain of organizational objectives. To explore this domain, however, one needs a model capable of dealing more fully with the multiple dimensions of an organization's performance and structure. To facilitate the development of purposefulness in each of an organization's subordinate units, the model should also be applicable to internal units. To help executives to deal with the complexities of their environment, it should also be applicable to external competitors or controllers.

THE GENERAL-SYSTEMS APPROACH

As a result of the emerging work in systems analysis, it is now possible to meet these needs by developing a "general-systems model" of an organization. A general-systems model is one that brings together in an ordered fashion information on all dimensions of an organization. It integrates concepts from all relevant disciplines. It can help to expand financial planning to full-bodied planning in as many dimensions as may be relevant. With it, executives may move from financial accounting to "systems accounting." It can provide the basis for "managerial accounting" in the sense of the managerial use not only of financial data (which is the way the term has been recently used) but of all ideas and data needed to appraise the state of a system and guide it towards the attainment of desirable future system states.[1]

Before outlining a general-systems model,

[1] *"General-systems theory" often refers to theories dealing broadly with similarities among all kinds of systems—from atoms and cells to personalities, formal organizations, and populations. In this context the term refers to a special application of general-systems theory to formal organizations— an application that deals not merely with a few aspects but generally with all aspects of formal organizations.*

it is important to set aside the idea that a system is necessarily something that is fully predictable or tightly controlled. This impression is created whenever anyone tries to apply to a human organization the closed or non-human models used by physicists and engineers. A human organization is much more complicated.

Specifically, when viewed in general-systems terms, a formal organization (whether a business enterprise or a government agency) is

1 a man-resource system in space and time,
2 open, with various transactions between it and its environment,
3 characterized by internal and external relations of conflict as well as cooperation,
4 a system for developing and using power, with varying degrees of authority and responsibility, both within the organization and in the external environment,
5 a "feedback" system, with information on the results of past performance activities feeding back through multiple channels to influence future performance,
6 changing, with static concepts derived from dynamic concepts rather than serving as a preliminary to them,
7 complex, that is, containing many subsystems, being contained in larger systems, and being criss-crossed by overlapping systems,
8 loose, with many components that may be imperfectly coordinated, partially autonomous, and only partially controllable,
9 only partially knowable, with many areas of uncertainty, with "black regions" as well as "black boxes" and with many variables that cannot be clearly defined and must be described in qualitative terms, and
10 subject to considerable uncertainty with respect to current information, future environmental conditions, and the consequences of its own actions.

THE PERFORMANCE-STRUCTURE MODEL

The starting-point of modern systems analysis is the input-output concept. The flow of inputs and outputs portrays the system's performance. To apply the output concept to a formal organization, it is helpful to distinguish between two kinds of performance: producing outputs of services or goods and satisfying (or dissatisfying) various interests. To apply the input concept, a three-way breakdown is helpful: ac-

quiring resources to be used as inputs, using inputs for investment in the system, and making efficient use of resources. In addition, we may note that organizational performance includes efforts to conform with certain behaviour codes and concepts of technical and administrative rationality.

These seven kinds of performance objective may be put together in the following proposition:

> The performance of any organization or unit thereof consists of activities to (1) satisfy the varying interests of people and groups by (2) producing outputs of services or goods, (3) making efficient use of inputs relative to outputs, (4) investing in the system, (5) acquiring resources, and (6) doing all these things in a manner that conforms with various codes of behaviour and (7) varying conceptions of technical and administrative rationality.

In simplified form, the relations between these categories of performance may be visualized as follows:

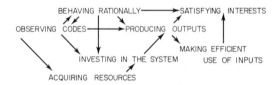

Let us now turn to system structure. The minimum elements in a machine system are certain physical components, including a "governor" (or "selector"), an "effector," a "detector," and lines of communication between them and the environment. For a formal organization these may be spelled out more specifically as subsystems in general, a central guidance subsystem, internal relations among the subsystems, and relations with the external environment. It is helpful at times to consider separately the people and the physical assets grouped together in the subsystems. It may also be helpful to give separate attention to the values held by individuals and the various subsystems.

These seven sets of structural objectives may be put together in the following proposition:

The structure of any organization or unit thereof consists of (1) people and (2) non-human resources, (3) grouped together in differentiated subsystems that (4) interrelate among themselves and (5) with the external environment, (6) and are subject to various values and (7) to such central guidance as may help to provide the capacity for future performance.

In the language of matrix algebra, one can bring the two elements of system performance and system structure together into a 2×1 "nested" vector which may be called the "system state vector." Let P symbolize system performance and S system structure. Then the following sequence of vectors may symbolize changing system states over a period of time:

$$\begin{bmatrix} P \\ S \end{bmatrix}^1 \qquad \begin{bmatrix} P \\ S \end{bmatrix}^2 \quad \dots \begin{bmatrix} P \\ S \end{bmatrix}^n$$

The vector is "nested" because both the performance element and the structure element consist of seven subelements and are themselves 7×1 vectors. Each subelement, in turn, is a multidimensional matrix.

The performance vector, it should be noted, includes among its many components the basic elements in income statements and revenue-expenditure budgets. The structure vector includes all the assets (and claims against them) measured in a balance sheet. Indeed, the former may be regarded as a greatly enlarged performance budget, the latter a balance sheet that includes human and institutional assets as well as financial assets. The relations between the two are even closer than those between an income statement and a balance sheet. Almost any aspect of system performance will have some effect on system structure. Any important plans for future performance inevitably require significant changes in system structure. Changes in system structure, in turn, are invariably dependent upon some types of system performance. In everyday affairs, of course, executives often make the mistake of

—planning for major improvements in performance without giving attention to the structural prerequisites, and
—planning for major changes in structure (sometimes because of outworn or unduly abstract doctrines of formal organization) without considering their presumed connection with performance.

The skilful use of a performance-structure model may help to avoid these errors.[2]

The first elements in both structure and performance, let it be noted, are human: people and the satisfaction of people's interests. All the other elements and their many decisions —both financial and technological—are ways of thinking about people and their behaviour. An organization's plans for the future are always plans made by people for people—for their future behaviour and for their future relations with resources and other people. Financial and technological planners may easily lose sight of these human elements. Another virtue of general-systems analysis, therefore, is that it helps to bring together the "soft" information of human relations people with the "hard" data of accountants and engineers.

PERFORMANCE OBJECTIVES

Any one of the seven elements of system performance, as baldly stated above, may be used in a statement of "where we want to go" or as a criterion of "doing an effective job." But none of them is meaningful unless broken down into its subelements. When this is done, indeed, the basic subelements may be rearranged in many ways. There is no magic in any one ordering.

Within the present space limits I shall merely touch upon some of the major dimensions of each element and subelement. Additional details are available in *The Managing of Organizations* (Gross, 1964, Pt. V, Chs. 20–29).

Some random illustrations for both an organization (an aircraft company) and a unit thereof (its personnel office) are provided in Table 13-1. Tables 13-2 and 13-3 provide more detailed illustrations in two areas of special complexity: output objectives and input-output objectives. In these tables "goal" refers to a specific type of subelement and "norm" to a more specific formulation of a goal. To save space, reference to the tables will not be made in the text.

[2] *This performance-structure model represents a major adaptation of what has long been known as "structural-functional" analysis. It is more dynamic than traditional structural-functional analysis, however, since it starts with action (performance) and works back to structure as the more regularized aspect of action. Also, instead of assuming a single function such as "system maintenance," it broadens the idea of function to cover the major dimensions of performance.*

TABLE 13-1   PERFORMANCE OBJECTIVES: SOME GENERAL ILLUSTRATIONS

Performance Objectives	Aircraft Company Goals	Aircraft Company Norms	Personnel Unit Goals	Personnel Unit Norms
1. Satisfying Interests				
(a) *Members*	Higher morale	Reducing labour turnover to 6%	Professional prestige	Leadership in professional organizations
(b) *Clientele network*	Meeting airlines' needs	5% rise in total sales	Meeting needs of line	Fewer complaints
(c) *Others*	Investors	Maintaining 3% yield on common stock	Serving all employees	Reducing labour turnover to 10%
2. Producing Output				
(a) *Output mix*	Adding short-range jets	End-product production schedule	New management training programme	End-product services
(b) *Quantity*	Increased market penetration	15% of industry sales	Greater coverage	150 "trainees" per year
(c) *Quality*	Safer planes	Wing improvements	Better designed courses	Better consultants
(d) *Output flow*	Work-flow	Detailed schedules	Work-flow	Detailed schedules
3. Making Efficient Use of Inputs				
(a) *Profitability*	Higher profits on net worth (or total assets)	20% on net worth	—	—
(b) *Costs per unit*	Lower engine costs	8% reduction	Total costs per trainee	$200 per week
(c) *Partial input ratios*	More output per man-hour	10% increase	Teacher costs	$150 per training-hour
(d) *Portion of potential used*	Reducing idle equipment-time	5% reduction	Full participation in training programme	No vacancies
4. Investing in the Organization				
(a) *Hard goods*	Re-equipment programme	Detailed specifications	New files	No vacancies
(b) *People*	Management training programme	50 trainees per year	"Retooling" of old-timers	Participation in "refresher" courses
(c) *Internal units*	Reorganization of personnel unit	Higher status for training section	Maintenance of existing organization	Maintaining present status for training section
(d) *External relations*	More support in Congress	Support by specific senators	More support from "line" executives	Support by specific executives
5. Acquiring Resources				
(a) *Money*	More equity	Selling securities	Larger budget	5% increase
(b) *People*	Better managers	Recruitment programme	More professional staff	Recruitment programme
(c) *Goods*	New machines	Procurement programme	New files	Procurement programme

6. *Observing Codes*				
(a) External codes	Obeying anti-trust laws	Competition within limits	Living within budgets	Controls on commitments
(b) Internal codes	Obeying company regs.	Control of deviations	Loyalty to unit	Social exclusiveness
7. *Behaving Rationally*				
(a) Technical rationality	Aeronautical research	Specific studies	Personnel research	Specific studies
(b) Administrative rationality	Formal reorganization	More decentralization	More "democracy"	Monthly staff meetings

TABLE 13-2 OUTPUT PERFORMANCE OBJECTIVES: SOME DETAILED ILLUSTRATIONS

Output Production Objectives	Aircraft Company Goals	Aircraft Company Norms	Personnel Unit Goals	Personnel Unit Norms
A. Output Mix	Continued output of long-range jets / New short-range jet / Parts production / Research for government / Advisory services for users	Detailed production schedule	Maintaining personnel records / Recruitment services / Classification system / Job analysis and evaluation / Training programme	Operating programme
B. Output Quality				
1. Client satisfactions			Training programme:	
(a) *Presumed results*	Faster, safer flights	Specific speed and safety standards	Better managers	Subsequent performance of trainees
(b) *Choices made*	Popularity among passengers	Prosperity of airline customers	Popularity of programme	Backlog of applications
(c) *Payments given*	Rising volume of airline sales	15% of industry sales	Budgets allocated	Specific budget figures
(d) *Opinions expressed*	Low complaint level	Decline in pilots' complaints	Trainees' opinions	Specific statements
2. *Product characteristics*	Conformance with specifications	Detailed specifications	Improved curriculum	Emphasis on decision-making skills
3. *Production processes*	Careful testing	Specific tests	Improved teaching methods	Use of field studies
4. *Input quality*	Outstanding productive personnel	Acquiring best designers	Outstanding teachers	Acquiring teachers of high repute
C. Output Quantity				
1. Monetary value	Planes:			
(a) *Total sales value*	15% of industry sales	X million dollars	—	—
(b) *Value added*	Lower proportion of value added with more sub-contracting	$\dfrac{X}{3}$	—	—
(c) *Value added adjusted for price changes*	20% beyond 1960	$\dfrac{X \cdot 9}{3}$ (price deflator)	—	—
(d) *Imputed value of non-marketed output*	Advisory services: Input value	Specific cost figures	Input value	Specific cost figures

	Planes:		Training programme:
2. Physical volume			
(a) Tangible units	Number to be produced		—
(b) Surrogates for intangible services	Advisory services:		
(i) clients	More clients ⎱		More trainees ⎱
(ii) duration	Longer periods ⎰ Specific figures		Longer courses ⎰ Specific figures
(iii) intermediate or subsequent products	Memoranda produced		Field studies undertaken
		Detailed production schedule	
		Specific figures	
(iv) input value			
Total costs	Total costs		Total costs

TABLE 13-3   INPUT-OUTPUT PERFORMANCE OBJECTIVES: SOME DETAILED ILLUSTRATIONS

Efficiency (Input-Output) Objectives	Aircraft Company		Personnel Unit	
	Goals	Norms	Goals	Norms
A. Profitability				
1. Unit profits	Short-range jet: higher profits with rising volume	Specific figures	—	—
2. Total profits				
Before taxes	Higher profits	10% increase	—	—
After taxes	Higher profits	12% increase	—	—
Total profits	Lower (with replacement of debt by equity)	10% decrease	—	—
3. Net worth	Higher	10% increase	—	—
4. Total assets			—	—
5. Sales	Lower (with higher volume of sales)	10% decrease	—	—
B. Costs per Unit	New short-range jets: Declining total costs with rising volume	10% decline per unit over first year	Training programme: Rising costs with longer duration and higher quality	20% more per trainee
C. Partial Input-Output Relations				
1. Labour-output ratios	For a specific output unit:			
(a) Labour time	More output per direct man-hour	10% increase	More teacher-time per trainee	10% more per trainee
(b) Labour cost	No increase in direct costs	Same	Higher teacher fees	20% more per trainee
	Small increase in direct plus indirect labour costs	5% increase	Higher overhead costs	5% increase
(c) Output per $1 of labour cost	Lower total value	−6%	—	—
	Lower added value	−29%	—	—
2. Capital-output ratio	For specific machines: fuller use of rated capacity	Specific figures	Low-cost residential facilities	Specific figures
D. Portion of Output Potential Used				
1. Waste	Less scrap material	Specific figures	Less waste	Elimination of unnecessary paperwork
	Better utilization of scrap			
2. Gap between actual and potential	Fuller use of capacity	Reaching 80% in 2 shifts	Fuller use of computers (on personnel records)	Reaching 35% of capacity
	Higher fulfilment of profit potential	8% on total assets	Higher fulfilment of service potential	Specific data on quality and quantity of end-products

1. Satisfying Interests

Although the satisfaction of human interests is the highest purpose of any organization, interest-satisfaction objectives (often referred to as *benefits, welfare, utility, value,* or *payoff*) are the most difficult to formulate.

First of all, such objectives always involve a multiplicity of parties at interest—or "interesteds." These include the members of the organization, the organization's "clientele network," and other external groups and individuals. They vary considerably in visibility and in the extent to which their interests are affected by an organization's performance.

Second, their interests are usually multiple, often hard to identify, always divergent, and sometimes sharply conflicting. In psychological terms these interests may be described in terms of the human needs for security, belonging, status, prestige, power, and self-development. Many of these needs are expressed in terms of services and goods designed to meet them and the monetary income which, in a market economy, is necessary to provide such services and goods. They may also be expressed in terms of the needs for both employment and leisure. The terms "public interest" or "national interest" are ways of referring to the great multiplicity of interests that many people and groups throughout a society have in common. There are always conflicting views concerning the nature of "public interests."

Third, it is immensely difficult to specify the extent of satisfactions desired or attained. Satisfactions themselves are locked in the hearts and minds of the people whose interests are presumed to be satisfied. They are inextricably associated with dissatisfactions and frustration. The most we can do is use certain indirect indicators expressed in terms of the observable behaviour of the behaviour of "interesteds." Two of the most immediate forms of behaviour are the choices they make (in participating in the organization or using its product) and money they are willing to pay (in the form of consumer purchases, taxes, or dues). Other indicators are their expressed opinions (complaints or praise) and their subsequent behaviour as a presumed result of the satisfactions obtained. Such indicators with respect to clientele satisfactions provide the most important measures of output quality.

2. Producing Output

Output production objectives are much easier to formulate. They may best be expressed in terms of an "output mix" listing the types of services or goods supplied to the organization's (or unit's) clientele. For each type quality and quantity objectives may then be set.

Yet there are at least five major problems in this area. First of all, output quality has many dimensions. As already indicated, clientele satisfaction, the most important dimension of output quality, is exceedingly difficult to measure. Less direct indicators—such as product specifications, production processes, and the quality of input factors—may also be needed. The objective of higher quality often conflicts with the objective of higher quantity.

Second, although monetary aggregates are the only way of measuring total output, they must be used with considerable care. Important distinctions may be needed between the total value of output and value added, between marginal value and total or average value, between different ways of allocating value to time periods. For comparisons over time, adjustments for price changes may be needed; for international comparisons, adjustments in the value of international currencies.

Third, in the case of services and goods that are not sold (and this includes most of the intermediate output within business organizations) the only direct measure of output quantity is physical units. In most instances this means that there is no common denominator for the total quantity of different kinds of unit. All that can be done to aggregate quantity objectives is to use input costs or some administratively determined "price" (as in internal pricing systems) as an indirect quantity indicator.

Fourth, in the case of intangible services there are no physical units that can readily be identified. Here one can set objectives only in terms of such indirect indicators as the number of clients, the duration of services, certain intermediate products that are more tangible, and the volume or value of input factors.

Fifth, considerable confusion may develop between intermediate products and the end-products supplied to an organization's clientele. This readily happens with intangible end-product services that are provided on a

TABLE 13-4   STRUCTURAL OBJECTIVES: SOME GENERAL ILLUSTRATIONS

Structural Objectives	Aircraft Company		Personnel Unit	
	Goals	Norms	Goals	Norms
1. People				
(a) Types	Fewer "blue-collars"	Specific manning tables	More professionals	Specific manning tables
(b) Quantity	No overall increase	Specific manning tables	Larger staff	4 new positions
(c) Quality	Better-educated staff	90% college graduates above supervisory level	Better educational background	All college graduates with a few PhDs
2. Non-human resources				
(a) Physical assets	More modern plant	Specific re-equipment programme	More adequate space	5 more rooms
(b) Monetary assets	More liquid position	2:1 current liability ratio	Larger reserves	More transferable budget items
(c) Claims against assets	Higher ratio of equity to long-term debt	$10 million equity increase	—	—
3. Subsystems				
(a) Units	Improved divisional structure	Stronger jet-plane divisions	Improved internal structure	Stronger training group
(b) Committees ·	Improved committee structure	Inter-divisional task force on new jets	Better representation on committees	Participation in jet-plane task force
4. Subsystem relations				
(a) Cooperation-conflict	Settlement of inter-divisional disputes	Compromise on jet-plane design	Settlement of inter-unit disputes	Compromise on location of training division
(b) Hierarchy	Stronger central control	Fewer levels	Stronger unit position	Direct line to top manager
(c) Polyarchy	Dispersed responsibility	New clearance procedures	Dispersed responsibility	New clearance procedures
(d) Communication	Better communication among divisions	Weekly paper	Better communication with line executives	Liaison units in line divisions
5. External relations				
(a) Clients and suppliers	Better distribution channels for parts	Relations with specific distributors	More support from line executives	Support by specific executives
(b) Controllers and controllees	More support in Congress	Support by specific Senators	More support by budget unit	Support for 4 new positions
(c) Associates and adversaries	Limits on competition	"Understandings" on division of markets	Rivalry with budget unit	Less budget opposition to training programme funds
6. Values				
(a) Internal-external orientation	Public service	Safer planes	Professionalism in personnel management	Advancement of unit's interests

(b) *Conformity and individualism*	Initiative	Proposing of company policy by divisions	Loyalty to unit	Subordination of external interests
(c) *Activism-passivity*	Progress	Faster planes	Progress	All-round improvement
7. *System management*				
(a) *Higher level*	More "professional" approach	Specific planning and control methods	More "human" approach	More emphasis on personnel management
(b) *Lower level*	More effective supervision	Participatory activation methods	More effective supervision	Better check of supervisors

non-sale basis to an intangible, unorganized, or reluctant clientele. More tangible intermediate products—particularly when supplied by hard-driving, ambitious units—may then receive disproportionate attention. One remedy is to formulate objectives in terms of work-flow—that is, a series of intermediate outputs leading to the production of the organization's end-products.

3. Making Efficient Use of Inputs

When resources available for use as inputs are perceived as scarce, an organization or unit becomes interested in making efficient use of inputs relative to outputs. Since there are many ways of calculating input and output and of relating the two, there are many varieties of input-output performance.

Profitability is the most useful input-output relation, since it provides a common measure of value for both input and output. Profitability measures may be used in many ways, however, depending upon whether one (1) relates profits to net worth, total assets, or sales, (2) focuses on unit profits or total profits, or (3) thinks in short- or long-range terms. Depending upon a variety of techniques for handling difficult accounting problems, they are subject to considerable statistical manipulation. They may also reflect an organization's monopoly power and its ability to obtain subsidies, as well as its efficiency. Nevertheless, in many circumstances—particularly over a long time period—profitability is the best single measure of efficiency, output quantity and quality, and interest satisfaction.

The most generally applicable efficiency objective is attaining the lowest possible total costs for a given unit of output. This cost-accounting measure is an essential instrument in attaining—even in formulating—profitability objectives. It is relevant to non-marketed products as well. In developing cost-accounting goals, however, it is essential not to neglect the quality dimensions of output. In the case of intangible services, as already indicated, the identification of the unit is extremely difficult. Where capital and material inputs are involved, it is necessary to make difficult—and sometimes arbitrary—decisions with respect to depreciation, the distinction between current and capital expenditures, and the value of withdrawals from inventories.

Partial input-output ratios are those relating some measure of input—usually either labour or capital—to some measure of total output. Such a ratio is particularly meaningful when the volume of other input factors may be presumed to remain unchanged. It will be very misleading, however, whenever there is any significant change in any other input factor—as when increased output per employee is counterbalanced, and in fact caused, by increased capital per unit of output.

Another efficiency measure is the proportion of potential actually used. This may be expressed in terms of a reduction in waste, a higher utilization of capacity (potential output), or profits in relation to potential profitability.

4. Investing in the System

In addition to producing current output, an organization must invest in its capacity for future production. Investment objectives involve the expansion, replacement, conservation, or development of assets. They are essential not only for survival, but to prevent decline or promote growth.

The most obvious investment objectives relate to hard goods and monetary reserves. The hard goods may include land, buildings, equipment and machinery, and stocks of materials. The monetary reserves may include cash, deposits, securities, receivables, and any other funds that can be drawn upon.

Less obvious, although equally important, is investment in people, subsystems, subsystem relations, external relations, and the development of values. Investment in the guidance subsystem itself—that is, in the management structure—is particularly important.

In other words, investment performance may deal directly with any element of system structure. Accordingly, the specifics of investment objectives may be presented in the subsequent discussion of system structure.

In general, however, it should be pointed out that investment objectives often mean a diversion of resources from use in current output. Thus there are often important conflicts not only among different forms of investment but between investment and output production.

5. Acquiring Resources

Neither output production nor investment is possible without resources that can be used as inputs. These must be obtained from the external environment or from within the organization. Under conditions of scarcity and competition this requires considerable effort. Thus resource-acquisition objectives usually receive high priority. Indeed, long-range planning is often oriented much more to acquiring resources than to utilizing them.

Organizations that sell their output may acquire external resources from the consumer market (through sales revenue), the capital market (through investment), and banks (through loans). Their sales, investment, and borrowing objectives are closely related to the extent of clientele satisfactions. Organizations and units that do not sell their output must depend mainly upon budgetary allocations.

In both cases monetary terms provide the most general expression of resource-mobilization objectives. But the monetary objectives are meaningful only when they reflect the specific resources to be acquired with money —people, information, facilities, goods, or organizations. In many circumstances it is also necessary to include (1) specifications for the resources desired, (2) specific terms and conditions, (3) selection methods, (4) the maintenance of supply lines, and (5) inspection of resources received.

The logical justification of an organization's "requirements" for additional resources is best provided by a set of objectives that moves back from (1) interest satisfactions and (2) output mix to (3) efficiency and (4) investment. In the budget-allocation process "acquisition logic" also requires efforts to appeal to the interests of those with most influence in the allocation decisions.

6. Observing Codes

Every organization aims at doing things in the "right" way. To some extent the "right" way is set forth in external codes—laws, regulations, moral and ethical prohibitions and prescriptions, and professional principles. It is also determined by the codes of the organization—its written and unwritten rules and rituals.

Some may prefer to think of code observance as a restraint upon efforts to attain other objectives. None the less, a considerable amount of purposeful activity in organizations is involved in containing inevitable tendencies towards code deviation.

The greatest attention is usually given to internal codes. In the case of external codes that are not "internalized," the organization will often tolerate deviation. Indeed, the deception of external inspectors may itself become part of the internal code. Similarly, the deception of the organization's code-enforcement efforts may become part of the internal code of various units. These tendencies towards deviation are facilitated by the difficulty of understanding—or even keeping up with—complex regulations. They are promoted by recurring code conflicts.

These difficulties may be handled only in part by formal enforcement measures. Successful code observance also requires widespread internalization of codes and the continuing adjustment of conflicting and confusing codes.

7. Behaving Rationally

An organization or unit also aims at doing things "rationally." This means the selection of the most satisfactory means of attaining a given set of objectives—from interest satisfaction and output production down to rational behaviour itself. Thus rationality is an all-pervasive instrumental objective.

Perfect rationality is an impossible objective. The instruments of rational calculation—information, knowledge, and skill—are always imperfect. The dimensions of rational behaviour —desirability, feasibility, and consistency—are themselves frequently conflicting. The more desirable objective will frequently be less feasible, the more feasible objective less consistent with other goals, the more consistent objective less desirable.

Technical rationality involves the use of the best methods devised by science and technology. With rapid scientific and technological progress, it is constantly changing. On the one hand, the rational methods of a few years ago may be irrational today. On the other hand, new techniques are often adapted on the basis of "technological faddism" rather than truly rational choice. In either case, there are usually serious disputes among technicians, disputes that cannot be entirely settled within the confines of technical rationality.

Administrative rationality is a much broader type of rationality. It involves the use of the best methods of guiding or managing organizations. This involves the interrelated processes of planning, activating, and evaluating with respect to all significant dimensions of both performance and structure. It provides the framework for resolving technical disputes. Yet administrative rationality, although highly developed on an intuitive basis, still awaits systematic scientific formulation. Many so-called "principles" of administration neglect the major dimensions of performance, deal formalistically with structure, and ignore the relation between the two. Management theory has not yet gone far enough in encouraging managers to think and communicate explicitly in connexion with such delicate subjects as the development and use of power and the management of internal and external conflict.

STRUCTURE OBJECTIVES

In thinking of system structure we should beware of images derived from the "non-human" structure of a building. The structure of an organization is based upon the expectations and behaviour of people and human groups. It has informal as well as formal aspects. It can never be understood (not even in its formal aspects) from an inspection of written decisions alone. It is never free from internal conflicts and inconsistencies. Unlike the frame of a building, it is always changing in many ways. Indeed, structure is merely the more stabilized aspect of activity. It consists of interrelations that provide the capacity for future performance and that can be understood only in terms of performance objectives. Some random illustrations of objectives for structural change are provided in Table 13-4.

1. People

The people in an organization are the first element in an organization's structure. Thus structural objectives may be formulated in terms of the types of personnel, their quality, and their quantity.

Personnel may be classified in terms of specific positions with such-and-such titles, salaries, and perquisites; abilities, knowledge, and interests; experience; educational background; health; and various personality characteristics. Other characteristics relate to age, sex, race, religion, geographical origins. Some combination of these dimensions is usually employed in objectives for recruitment, replacement, and promotion.

The formulation of quality objectives involves consideration of the place of various people within a specific subsystem. Without reference to any subsystem, however, it also involves attention to people's capacity for learning and self-development. It involves objectives for promoting the utilization of such capacity.

The number of people in an organization is one of the simplest measures of its size. Larger numbers are often sought as a prelude to obtaining other assets, as a substitute for them, or as compensation for the lack of quality. Even with high-quality personnel and an adequate complement of non-human resources, larger numbers are often needed to supply essential reserves or the basis of major output expansion.

2. Non-human Resources

With advancing science and technology, non-human resources become increasingly essential as instruments of human activity.

Certain natural resources—if only a piece of land—are an essential foundation of human activity. Physical facilities provide the necessary housing for human activity. Equipment and machinery, particularly when driven by electrical energy, make it possible for people to move or process things with little expenditure of human energy. Data-processing machinery replaces human labour in the processing of information. Thus investment objectives must deal with the structure of these physical assets.

As indicated in the discussion of investment performance, they may also include objectives with respect to monetary assets and—where balance-sheet accounting is used—to the structure of claims against them (liabilities).

3. Subsystems

Within any organization people and non-human resources are grouped together in various subsystems. Each subsystem, in turn, is often subdivided still further. The smallest subdivision is the individual person.

Each subsystem is identifiable mainly by its role or function. The major element in role definition is the output expected from the subsystem. In larger organizations, particularly those based upon advancing technology, role differentiation tends to become increasingly specific and detailed. It also tends to undergo change—but at uneven and varying rates in response to recurring new environmental conditions, new technology, and adjustments in the quantity and quality of the organization's output mix. This means an internal restructuring of the subsystems. With growth of the organization as a whole, the subsystems change in a disproportional manner. Some expand, some decline, and some must be liquidated.

Important distinctions must be made between individuals and roles. People may come and go, while a role remains. Moreover, one person may play a number of roles—that is, "wear many hats." Some roles are substantially developed by the people who play them. Most people are substantially affected by the roles they play.

There are many kinds of subsystem. Some are hierarchically organized units; others are committees. Some are organized to perform functions peculiar to a specific organization; others provide certain kinds of services (personnel, budgeting, accounting, procurement, methods analysis, public relations) that are widely used by many organizations. Some are called "line," others "staff." Some are informal only. The most important subsystem is the management or guidance subsystem (discussed separately under 7 below).

4. Internal Relations

By itself subsystem differentiation is divisive. The system as a whole exists only to the extent that the parts are brought together in a network of internal relations.

The first element in internal relations is co-operation among and within the subsystems. This cooperation must be based upon certain commonly accepted objectives for future performance. Otherwise work-flows will not mesh. A large part of this cooperation may consist of routinized, habitual expectations and activity. At the same time cooperation is always associated with conflict relations within and among subsystems. If carried too far, conflict and tension may impair—even destroy—the internal structure. Within limits they may help to invigorate it.

Hierarchic relations are an indispensable element in the cooperation-conflict nexus. These consist of superior-subordinate relations,

usually confined to certain spheres of behaviour. The lines of hierarchic authority provide formal channels of internal communication and ladders for career advancement. The upper positions in a hierarchy provide valuable points for conflict settlement and important symbols of organizational unity. At the same time, the growing role differentiation in modern organizations leads inevitably towards the subdivision of hierarchic authority and the growth of "multiple hierarchy" (see Gross, 1964, pp. 377–9).

Hierarchy is always accompanied by polyarchy—sometimes referred to as "lateral relations." One form of polyarchy is "joint authority." Thus committee members (often representing different units) may operate together as equals rather than as superiors and subordinates. Another is "dispersed authority." In budget procedures various units negotiate and bargain with each other—at least up to the point where hierarchic authority may be brought into play.

The communication network is an all-pervasive part of internal relations. A critical role in this network is always played by the various lines of hierarchic authority. But many other multi-directional channels and media—some of them informal—are also needed.

5. External Relations

The immediate environment of any organization includes not only individuals but also various groups that may be classified as enterprises, government agencies, and various types of association. The relations between an organization and this immediate environment may be expressed in terms of the roles played by such individuals and groups:

(a) Clients and suppliers
The clients are those who receive, or are supposed to benefit from, an organization's output. The suppliers are those who supply the goods, services, information, or money acquired by the organization.

(b) Controllers and controllees
The controllers are the external regulators or "superiors." The controllees are the organization's regulatees or "subordinates."

(c) Associates and adversaries
The associates are partners or allies engaged

in joint or cooperative undertakings. The adversaries include rivals for the same resources, competitors in producing similar outputs, and outright enemies interested in limiting or destroying the organization's performance or structure.

The same external organization often plays many—at times even all—of these roles. In so doing it will use many forms of external persuasion, pressure, or penetration.

Resistance to external influence usually involves an organization in preventive or counter measures of persuasion, pressure, or penetration. A more positive approach to external relations involves efforts to isolate, neutralize, or win over opponents and build up a farflung structure of external support through coalitions, alliances, and "deals." Such efforts may be facilitated by persuasive efforts aimed at unorganized publics.

6. Values

The individuals and subsystems in any organization are always guided by some pattern of values—that is, general attitudes towards what is desirable or undesirable and general ways of looking at the world. Some of the most important elements in this value structure may be defined in terms of the continua between

(a) *Internal and external orientation*
Internal orientation emphasizes the interests of members—in terms of their income, status, power, or self-development. External orientation emphasizes the interests of nonmembers; these may range from investors (owners) to clients to the society as a whole. Some organizations aim at integrating the two sets of values.

(b) *Conformity and individualism*
In many organizations conformity is a high value—sometimes to the point of the complete subordination of individual initiative. Nevertheless, highly individualistic values may be hidden behind a façade of superficial conformism.

(c) *Passivity and activism*
Among many members or organizations passivity is a highly cherished value. It leads to "playing it safe," "taking it easy," "following the book," and waiting for orders.

Activist values, in contrast, lead to risk-taking, initiative, and innovation. Although apparently conflicting, the two are often intertwined.

Other values relate to freedom and control, authoritarianism and democracy, material and non-material interests, equity and equality, impersonality and particularism, and ascription and achievement.

7. Guidance Subsystem

Some amount of coordinated action is always provided by the autonomous action—both routinized and spontaneous—of an organization's subsystems. But sufficient capacity for effective performance is not possible without the coordinating and promotional functions of a special subsystem with the responsibilty for system guidance, or management. This guidance subsystem is composed of a network extending from a general directorate and top executives down through the middle and lower levels of managerial or supervisory personnel. At any level the members of this subsystem play various roles in decision-making and communication with respect to the making of plans, the activating of people and groups, and the evaluating of plans made and action taken. The interrelation among these roles helps to determine the structure of the guidance subsystem.

An important aspect of management structure is the balance between centralization and decentralization. Both centralization and decentralization may be thought of in terms of the distribution of responsibility and authority by (a) vertical levels, (b) horizontal levels, and (c) geographical location. The extent of centralization or decentralization in any of these dimensions can best be specified with reference to specific roles or functions. The prerequisite for effective decentralization of some functions is the centralization of other functions. With increasing size and complexity, it usually becomes necessary to delegate greater responsibility and authority to lower levels and to field offices. This, in turn, requires the strengthening of certain planning, activating, and evaluating functions *of* the "centre," as well as various horizontal shifts in the centralization-decentralization balance *in* the centre.

Another vital aspect of management structure is its power base. This includes the resources at its disposal. It includes the support it obtains from the membership and major points of internal influence. It includes the support obtained externally—from associates, from clients and suppliers, and from controllers and controllees. Top business executives need support from their boards of directors and banks; government executives from President or Governor, legislators, and external interest groups.

Other important dimensions of management structure relate to managerial personnel and tenure. Admission to the upper ranks of management may be dependent upon a combination of such factors as sponsorship, ability, education, personality characteristics, and social origins. Some top managers seek a self-perpetuating oligarchy, with little or no provision made for inevitable replacement. Others set as major objectives the development of career and recruitment systems that make for high mobility within managerial ranks.

THE STRATEGY OF PLANNING

Planning is the process of developing commitments to some pattern of objectives.

The preceding section set forth the major categories of objectives.

Let us now turn to some of the strategic considerations involved in deriving a pattern from these categories.

1. The Selectivity Paradox

As specialists develop comprehensive ways of looking at systems, they often tend to overemphasize the role of comprehensive objectives in planning. Thus economists often give the false impression that national aggregates of income, product, investment, and consumption are the major goals in national policy-making. In the process of "selling their wares," budgeteers and accountants often give the impression that comprehensive projections of budgets, income statements, or balance sheets can define an organization's major goals. If this approach should be automatically transferred to general-systems accounting, we should then find ourselves recommending that an organization's planners should formulate comprehensive objectives for all the elements of system performance and system structure.

Yet this would be a misleading position. The essence of planning is the *selection of strategic objectives in the form of specific sequences of action to be taken by the organization.* These critical variables must be selected in terms of:

(a) The major interest satisfactions that must be "promised" to obtain external and internal support.

(b) Present, imminent, or foreseeable crises or emergencies. These may require "contingency plans."

(c) Their decisive impact upon preceding, coordinate, or subsequent events.

(d) The long-range implications of action in the present or the immediate future. These are the critical considerations with respect to the "sunk costs" of investment programmes and the immediate steps in extended production processes (such as the building of houses, ships, or aircraft).

With these strategic elements selected, many elements of performance and structure may be detailed in subsystem plans or handled on the basis of current improvisation. A passion for comprehensive detail by either the organization or its subsystems may undermine selectivity. It may easily result in a loss of perspective, in document-orientation instead of action-orientation, and in an information supply that overloads communication channels and processing capacity. It may thus lead to serious waste of resources.

But—and here is the paradox of selectivity—strategic objectives can be selected rationally *only if the planners are aware of the broad spectrum of possible objectives.* Otherwise, objectives may be set in a routinized, arbitrary, or superficial fashion. The very concept of selection implies the scanning of a broad range of possibilities.

The solution to this paradox may be found in the use of general-systems accounting to provide *a comprehensive background for the selection of strategic objectives.*

2. The Clarity-Vagueness Balance

There is no need to labour the need for clarity in the formulation of an organization's objectives. Precise formulations are necessary for delicate operations. They provide the indispensable framework for coordinating complex activity. They often have great symbolic significance.

Yet in the wide enthusiasm for "crystal-clear goals," one may easily lose sight of the need for a fruitful balance between clarity and vagueness. The following quotation is an effort to contribute to this balance through a "crystal-clear" statement on the virtues of vagueness:

> If all the points on a set of interrelated purpose chains were to be set forth with precise clarity, the result would be to destroy the subordination of one element to another which is essential to an operating purpose pattern. The proper focusing of attention on some goals for any particular moment or period in time means that other goals must be left vague. This is even more true for different periods of time. We must be very clear about many things we aim to do today and tomorrow. It might be dangerously misleading to seek similar clarity for our long-range goals.
>
> Apart from its role in helping provide focus, vagueness in goal formation has many positive virtues. It leaves room for others to fill in the details and even modify the general pattern; over-precise goals stifle initiative. Vagueness may make it easier to adapt to changing conditions; ultra-precision can destroy flexibility. Vagueness may make it possible to work towards many goals that can only be attained by indirection. Some of the deepest personal satisfactions from work and cooperation come as by-products of other things. If pursued too directly, they may slip through one's fingers; the happiest people in the world are never those who set out to do the things that will make them happy. There is something inhuman and terrifying about ultrapurposeful action proceeding according to blueprint and schedule. Only vagueness can restore the precious element of humanity.
>
> Above all, vagueness is an essential part of all agreements resulting from compromise. When a dispute is resolved, some degree of ambiguity enters into the terms of settlement. Hence the wide-open language often used in the final language of statutory law. Similar ambiguities are found in most constitutions, charters, declarations of purpose, policy manifestos, and collective bargaining agreements. Certain anticipated situations are always referred to in terms that mean different things to different people, and are valuable because of, not despite, this characteristic. (Gross, 1964, p. 497.)

3. Whose Objectives?

Whose objectives are an organization's objectives?

The crystal-clear answers to this question point to (1) the people who wrote the charter (law or articles of incorporation) under which the organization operates, (2) the holders of formal authority over the organization (legislators or stockholders), (3) the members of the organization as a whole, (4) the organization's specialized planning people, or (5) the organization's top managers.

Yet each of these answers is incomplete. The charter-writers and the holders of formal authority can deal with only a small portion of an organization's objectives. The members, the subsystems, and the specialized planners have or propose many objectives that the organization never accepts. The managers' objectives may be accepted only in part by the rest of the organization. All of these groups have many conflicting objectives.

A better, although vaguer, answer is one that defines an organization's objectives as those widely accepted by its members. These objectives may (to some extent, they *must*) reflect the objectives of charter-writers, the holders of formal authority, and other external groups. They must represent a common area of acceptance on the part of the organization's subsystems and members, albeit within a matrix of divergent and conflicting purposes. The technical planners play a major role in helping to formulate planning decisions. The top managers make (or legitimate) the decisions and play a major role in winning their acceptance throughout the organization. Whether recognized in formal planning procedures or not, the entire management structure is involved *de facto* in the daily operation of formulating and winning commitment to objectives for future performance and structure.

4. Conflict Resolving and Creating

As already indicated, the process of organizational planning involves dealing with many conflicting objectives and with divergent or conflicting parties at interest both inside and outside an organization.

Hence planning—rather than involving nothing but the sober application of technical rationality—is an exercise in conflict management. In this exercise systematic technical calculations are exceedingly valuable as a means both of narrowing areas of conflict and of revealing possibilities for conflict resolution. Yet technical calculations are never enough. Over-reliance upon them can lead to administrative irrationality.

Rational planning, in contrast, requires realistic attention to the power for and against alternative plans. It requires the resolution of conflicts through the use of power in various combinations of persuasion and pressure. It also requires the building of a power base through various methods of conflict resolution.

The most widespread mode of conflict resolution is compromise, through which some interests are sacrificed. A more creative—but more difficult—method is integration. This involves a creative readjustment of interests so that all parties may gain and none lose. In some cases, total victory may be obtained for one point of view, with consequent defeat for its opposition. To prevent defeat on some objectives, it is often necessary to tolerate deadlock or avoid an issue entirely. Any real-life planning process may be characterized as *a stream of successive compromises punctuated by frequent occasions of deadlock or avoidance and occasional victories, defeats, and integrations.* All these outcomes lead to new conflicts to be handled by the planners and managers.

Successful planning is often possible only when the key members of an organization see themselves threatened by an imminent crisis. In non-crisis conditions the subsystems tend to move in their own directions. They will most readily accept common objectives when the alternative is perceived as an onslaught of acute dissatisfactions, that is, a crisis. With crisis as the alternative, conflicts may be more quickly and effectively resolved. This is particularly relevant to subsystem resistance against plans for significant structural change.

In developing an organization's purposes, therefore, managers are frequently involved in crisis management. They try to anticipate crises around the corner. They try to respond promptly to crises that emerge. They may even try to create crises by setting high aspirations and accentuating fears of failure. These are delicate activities. For managers without a broad perspective on an organization's performance, structure, and environmental relations, they are dangerous undertakings —with much to be lost on one front as the price of victory on another. Even with such a broad perspective, they involve considerations that may not always be publicly discussed with complete frankness.

Hence a better-developed language of organizational purposefulness will not provide an outsider with a satisfactory answer when he asks a manager, "Just what are your organization's purposes?" The most it can do is help the managers themselves in the difficult and unending process of asking the question and finding workable answers.

References

Drucker, Peter F. (1954). *The practice of management.* New York: Harper.

Drucker, Peter F. (1964). *Managing for results.* New York: Harper & Row.

Gross, Bertram M. (1964). *The managing of organizations* (2 vols). New York: Free Press.

LeBreton, Preston P. & Henning, Dale A. (1961). *Planning theory.* Englewood Cliffs, N.J.: Prentice-Hall.

READING 14

SHAPING THE MASTER STRATEGY OF YOUR FIRM*

William H. Newman

Every enterprise needs a central purpose expressed in terms of the services it will render to society. And it needs a basic concept of how it will create these services. Since it will be competing with other enterprises for resources, it must have some distinctive advantages—in its services or in its methods of creating them. Moreover, since it will inevitably cooperate with other firms, it must have the means for maintaining viable coalitions with them. In addition, there are the elements of change, growth, and adaptation. Master strategy is a company's basic plan for dealing with these factors.

One familiar way of delving into company strategy is to ask, "What business are we in or do we want to be in? Why should society tolerate our existence?" Answers are often difficult. A company producing only grass seed had very modest growth until it shifted its

* *Reprinted from* California Management Review, *vol. IX, no. 3, Spring, 1967. Copyright 1967 by The Regents of The University of California.*

focus to "lawn care" and provided the suburban homeowner with a full line of fertilizers, pesticides, and related products. Less fortunate was a cooperage firm that defined its business in terms of wooden boxes and barrels and went bankrupt when paperboard containers took over the field.

Product line is only part of the picture, however. An ability to supply services economically is also crucial. For example, most local bakeries have shut down, not for lack of demand for bread, but because they became technologically inefficient. Many a paper mill has exhausted its sources of pulpwood. The independent motel operator is having difficulty meeting competition from franchised chains. Yet in all these industries some firms have prospered—the ones that have had the foresight and adaptability (and probably some luck, too) to take advantage of their changing environment. These firms pursued a master strategy which enabled them to increase the services rendered and attract greater resources.

Most central managers recognize that master strategy is of cardinal importance. But they are less certain about how to formulate a strategy for their particular firm. This article seeks to help in the shaping of master strategies. It outlines key elements and an approach to defining these. Most of our illustrations will be business enterprises; nevertheless, the central concept is just as crucial for hospitals, universities, and other nonprofit ventures.

A practical way to develop a master strategy is to:

Pick particular roles or niches that are appropriate in view of competition and the company's resources.

Combine various facets of the company's efforts to obtain synergistic effects.

Set up sequences and timing of changes that reflect company capabilities and external conditions.

Provide for frequent reappraisal and adaptation to evolving opportunities.

NEW MARKETS OR SERVICES

Picking propitious niches. Most companies fill more than one niche. Often they sell several lines of products; even when a single line is produced an enterprise may sell it to several distinct types of customers. Especially as a firm grows, it seeks expansion by tapping new markets or selling different services to its existing customers. In designing a company strategy we can avoid pitfalls by first examining each of these markets separately.

Basically, we are searching for customer needs—preferably growing ones—where adroit use of our unique resources will make our services distinctive and in that sense give us a competitive advantage. In these particular spots, we hope to give the customer an irresistible value and to do so at relatively low expense. A bank, for example, may devise a way of financing the purchase of an automobile that is particularly well-suited to farmers; it must then consider whether it is in a good position to serve such a market.

Identifying such propitious niches is not easy. Here is one approach that works well in various situations: Focus first on the industry —growth prospects, competition, key factors required for success—then on the strengths and weaknesses of the specific company as matched against these key success factors. As we de-

scribe this approach more fully, keep in mind that we are interested in segments of markets as well as entire markets.

The sales volume and profits of an industry or one of its segments depend on the demand for its services, the supply of these services, and the competitive conditions. (We use "service" here to include both physical products and intangible values provided by an enterprise.) Predicting future demand, supply, and competition is an exciting endeavor. In the following paragraphs, we suggest a few of the important considerations that may vitally affect the strategy of a company.

ELEMENTS OF DEMAND

Demand for industry services. The strength of the **desire** for a service affects its demand. For instance, we keenly want a small amount of salt, but care little for additional quantities. Our desire for more and better automobiles does not have this same sort of cut-off level, and our desires for pay-television (no commercials, select programs) or supersonic air travel are highly uncertain, falling in quite a different category from that of salt.

Possible **substitutes** to satisfy a given desire must be weighed—beef for lamb, motorboats for baseball, gas for coal, aureomycin for sulfa, weldments for castings, and so forth. The frequency of such substitution is affected, of course, by the relative prices.

Desire has to be backed up by **ability to pay,** and here business cycles enter in. Also, in some industries large amounts of capital are necessarily tied up in equipment. The relative efficiency, quality of work, and nature of machinery already in place influence the money that will be available for new equipment. Another consideration: If we hope to sell in foreign markets, foreign-exchange issues arise.

The **structure of markets** also requires analysis. Where, on what terms, and in response to what appeals do people buy jet planes, sulphuric acid, or dental floss? Does a manufacturer deal directly with consumers or are intermediaries such as retailers or brokers a more effective means of distribution?

Although an entire industry is often affected by such factors—desire, substitutes, ability to pay, structure of markets—a local variation in demand sometimes provides a unique opportunity for a particular firm. Thus, most drug-stores carry cosmetics, candy, and a wide variety of items besides drugs, but a store located in a medical center might develop a highly profitable business by dealing exclusively with prescriptions and other medical supplies.

All these elements of demand are subject to change—some quite rapidly. Since the kind of strategic plans we are considering here usually extends over several years, we need both an identification of the key factors that will affect industry demand and an estimate of how they will change over a span of time.

SUPPLY SITUATION

Supply related to demand. The attractiveness of any industry depends on more than potential growth arising from strong demand. In designing a company strategy we also must consider the probable supply of services and the conditions under which they will be offered.

The **capacity** of an industry to fill demand for its services clearly affects profit margins. The importance of over- or undercapacity, however, depends on the ease of entry and withdrawal from the industry. When capital costs are high, as in the hotel or cement business, adjustments to demand tend to lag. Thus, overcapacity may depress profits for a long period; even bankruptcies do not remove the capacity if plants are bought up—at bargain prices—and operated by new owners. On the other hand, low capital requirements—as in electronic assembly work—permit new firms to enter quickly, and shortages of supply tend to be short-lived. Of course, more than the physical plant is involved; an effective organization of competent people is also necessary. Here again, the case of expansion or contraction should be appraised.

Costs also need to be predicted—labor costs, material costs, and for some industries, transportation costs or excise taxes. If increases in operating costs affect all members of an industry alike and can be passed on to the consumer in the form of higher prices, this factor becomes less significant in company strategy. However, rarely do both conditions prevail. Sharp rises in labor costs in Hawaii, for example, place its sugar industry at a disadvantage on the world market.

A highly dynamic aspect of supply is **technology.** New methods for producing established products—for example, basic oxygen conversion of steel displacing open-hearth furnaces and mechanical cotton pickers displacing century-old hand-picking techniques—are part of the picture. Technology may change the availability and price of raw materials; witness the growth of synthetic rubber and industrial diamonds. Similarly, air cargo planes and other new forms of transportation are expanding the sources of supply that may serve a given market.

For an individual producer, anticipating these shifts in the industry supply situation may be a matter of prosperity or death.

CLIMATE OF INDUSTRY

Competitive conditions in the industry. The way the interplay between demand and supply works out depends partly on the nature of competition in the industry. **Size, strength, and attitude of companies** in one industry—the dress industry where entrance is easy and style is critical—may lead to very sharp competition. On the other hand, oligopolistic competition among the giants of the aluminum industry produces a more stable situation, at least in the short run. The resources and managerial talent needed to enter one industry differ greatly from what it takes to get ahead in the other.

A strong **trade association** often helps to create a favorable climate in its industry. The Independent Oil Producers' Association, to cite one case, has been unusually effective in restricting imports of crude oil into the United States. Other associations compile valuable industry statistics, help reduce unnecessary variations in size of products, run training conferences, hold trade shows, and aid members in a variety of other ways.

Government regulation also modifies competition. A few industries like banking and insurance are supervised by national or state bodies that place limits on prices, sales promotion, and the variety of services rendered. Airlines are both regulated as a utility and subsidized as an infant industry. Farm subsidies affect large segments of agriculture, and tariffs have long protected selected manufacturers. Our patent laws also bear directly on the nature of competition, as is evident in the heated discussion of how pharmaceutical patents may be used. Clearly, future government action is a significant factor in the outlook of many industries.

CRUCIAL FACTORS

Key factors for success in the industry. This brief review suggests the dynamic nature of business and uncertainties in the outlook for virtually all industries. A crucial task of every top management is to assess the forces at play in its industry and to identify those factors that will be crucial for future success. These we call "key success factors." Leadership in research and development may be very important in one industry, low costs in another, and adaptability to local need in a third; large financial resources may be a *sine qua non* for mining whereas creative imagination is the touchstone in advertising.

We stressed earlier the desirability of making such analyses for narrow segments as well as broad industry categories. The success factors for each segment are likely to differ in at least one or two respects from those for other segments. For example, General Foods Corporation discovered to its sorrow that the key success factors in gourmet foods differ significantly from those for coffee and Jello.

Moreover, the analysis of industry outlook should provide a forecast of the **growth potentials** and the **profit prospects** for the various industry segments. These conclusions, along with key success factors, are vital guideposts in setting up a company's master strategy.

The range of opportunities for distinctive service is wide. Naturally, in picking its particular niche out of this array a company favors those opportunities which will utilize its strength and bypass its limitations. This calls for a candid appraisal of the company itself.

POSITION IN MARKET

Market strengths of company.   A direct measure of **market position** is the percentage that company sales are of industry sales and of major competitors' sales. Such figures quickly indicate whether our company is so big that its activities are likely to bring prompt responses from other leading companies. Or

our company may be small enough to enjoy independent maneuverability. Of course, to be most meaningful, these percentages should be computed separately for geographical areas, product lines, and types of customer—if suitable industry data are available.

More intangible but no less significant are the relative standing of **company products** and their **reputation** in major markets. Kodak products, for instance, are widely and favorably known; they enjoy a reputation for both high quality and dependability. Clearly, this reputation will be a factor in Eastman Kodak Company strategy. And any new, unknown firm must overcome this prestige if it seeks even a small share in one segment of the film market. Market reputation is tenacious. Especially when we try to "trade up," our previous low quality, service, and sharp dealing will be an obstacle. Any strategy we adopt must have enough persistence and consistency so that our firm is assigned a "role" in the minds of the customers we wish to reach.

The relationship between a company and the **distribution system** is another vital aspect of market position. The big United States automobile companies, for example, are strong partly because each has a set of dealers throughout the country. In contrast, foreign car manufacturers have difficulty selling here until they can arrange with dealers to provide dependable service. A similar problem confronted Whirlpool Corporation when it wanted to sell its trademarked appliances publicly. (For years its only customer had been Sears, Roebuck and Company.) Whirlpool made an unusual arrangement with Radio Corporation of America which led to the establishment of RCA-Whirlpool distributors and dealers. Considering the strong competition, Whirlpool could not have entered this new market without using marketing channels such as RCA's.

All these aspects of market position—a relative share of the market, comparative quality of product, reputation with consumers, and ties with a distributive system—help define the strengths and limitations of a company.

SERVICE ABILITIES

Supply strengths of a company.   To pick propitious niches we also should appraise our company's relative strength in creating goods and services. Such ability to supply services fitted to consumer needs will be built largely on the firm's resources of labor and material, effective productive facilities, and perhaps pioneering research and development.

Labor in the United States is fairly mobile. Men tend to gravitate to good jobs. But the process takes time—a southern shoe plant needed ten years to build up an adequate number of skilled workers—and it may be expensive. Consequently, immediate availability of competent men at normal industry wages is a source of strength. In addition, the relationships between the company and its work force are important. All too often both custom and formal agreements freeze inefficient practices. The classic example is New England textiles; here, union-supported work habits give even mills high labor costs. Only recently have a few companies been able to match their more flourishing competitors in the South.

Access to **low-cost materials** is often a significant factor in a company's supply position. The development of the southern paper industry, for example, is keyed to the use of fast-growing forests which can be cut on a rotational basis to provide a continuing supply of pulpwood. Of course, if raw materials can be easily transported, such as iron ore and crude oil by enormous ships, plants need not be located at the original source.

Availability of materials involves more than physical handling. Ownership, or long-term contracts with those who do own, may assure a continuing source at low cost. Much of the strategy of companies producing basic metals —iron, copper, aluminum, or nickel—includes huge investments in ore properties. But all sorts of companies are concerned with the availability of materials. So whenever supplies are scarce a potential opportunity exists. Even in retailing, Sears, Roebuck and Company discovered in its Latin American expansion that a continuing flow of merchandise of standard quality was difficult to assure, but once established, such sources became a great advantage.

Physical facilities—office buildings, plants, mines—often tie up a large portion of a company's assets. In the short run, at least, these facilities may be an advantage or a disadvantage. The character of many colleges, for instance, has been shaped by their location, whether in a plush suburb or in a degenerating urban area, and the cost of moving facilities is so great that adaptation to the existing neighborhood becomes necessary. A steel company, to cite another case, delayed modernizing its plant so long that it had to abandon its share of the basic steel market and seek volume in specialty products.

Established organizations of highly talented people to perform particular tasks also give a company a distinctive capability. Thus, a good research and development department may enable a company to expand in pharmaceuticals, whereas a processing firm without such a technical staff is barred from this profitable field.

Perhaps the company we are analyzing will enjoy other distinctive abilities to produce services. Our central concern at this point is to identify strengths and see how these compare with strengths of other firms.

FINANCES AND MANAGEMENT

Other company resources.   The propitious niche for a company also depends on its financial strength and the character of its management.

Some strategies will require large quantities of capital. Any oil company that seeks foreign sources of crude oil, for instance, must be prepared to invest millions of dollars. Five firms maintain cash reserves of this size, so **financial capacity** to enter this kind of business depends on: an ability to attract new capital —through borrowing or sale of stock—or a flow of profits (and depreciation allowances) from existing operations that can be allocated to the new venture. On the other hand, perhaps a strategy can be devised that calls for relatively small cash advances, and in these fields a company that has low financial strength will still be able to compete with the affluent firms.

A more subtle factor in company capacity is its **management.** The age and vitality of key executives, their willingness to risk profit and capital, their urge to gain personal prestige through company growth, their desire to insure stable employment for present workers— all affect the suitability of any proposed strategy. For example, the expansion of Hilton Hotels Corporation into a world-wide chain certainly reflects the personality of Conrad Hilton; with a different management at the helm, a modification in strategy is most appropriate because Conrad Hilton's successors do not have his particular set of drives and values.

Related to the capabilities of key executives is the organization structure of the company. A decentralized structure, for instance, facilitates movement into new fields of business, whereas a functional structure with fine specialization is better suited to expansion in closely related lines.

PICKING A NICHE

Matching company strengths with key success factors.   Armed with a careful analysis of the strengths and limitations of our company, we are prepared to pick desirable niches for company concentration. Naturally, we will look for fields where company strengths correspond with the key factors for success that have been developed in our industry analyses described in the preceding section. And in the process we will set aside possibilities in which company limitations create serious handicaps.

Potential growth and profits in each niche must, of course, be added to the synthesis. Clearly, a low potential will make a niche unattractive even though the company strengths and success factors fit neatly. And we may become keenly interested in a niche where the fit is only fair if the potential is great.

Typically, several intriguing possibilities emerge. These are all the niches—in terms of market lines, market segments, or combinations of production functions—that the company might pursue. Also typically, a series of positive actions is necessary in order for the company to move into each area. So we need to list not only each niche and its potential, but the limitations that will have to be overcome and other steps necessary for the company to succeed in each area. These are our propitious niches—nestled in anticipated business conditions and tailored to the strengths and limitations of our particular company.

An enterprise always pursues a variety of efforts to serve even a single niche, and, typically, it tries to fill several related niches. Considerable choice is possible, at least in the degree to which these many efforts are pushed. In other words, management decides how many markets to cover, to what degree to automate production, what stress to place on consumer engineering, and a host of other actions. One vital aspect of master strategy is fitting these numerous efforts together. In fact, our choice of niches will depend in part, on

how well we can combine the total effort they require.

Synergy is a powerful ally for this purpose. Basically, synergy means that the combined effect of two or more cooperative acts is greater than the sum which would result if the actions were taken independently. A simple example in marketing is that widespread dealer stocks combined with advertising will produce much greater sales volume than widespread dealer stocks in, say, Virginia and advertising in Minnesota. Often the possibility of obtaining synergistic effects will shape the master strategy of the company—as the following examples will suggest.

COMBINATION OF SERVICES

Total service to customer.   A customer rarely buys merely a physical product. Other attributes of the transaction often include delivery, credit terms, return privileges, repair service, operating instructions, conspicuous consumption, psychological experience of purchasing, and the like. Many services involve no physical product at all. The crucial question is what combination of attributes will have high synergistic value for the customers we serve.

International Business Machines, for instance, has found a winning combination. Its products are well designed and of high quality. But so are the products of several of its competitors. In addition, IBM provides salesmen who understand the customer's problems and how IBM equipment can help solve them, and fast, dependable repair service. The synergistic effect of these three services is of high value to many customers.

Each niche calls for its own combination of services. For example, Chock Full o' Nuts expanded its restaurant chain on the basis of three attributes: good quality food, cleanliness, and fast service. This combination appealed to a particular group of customers. A very limited selection, crowded space, and lack of frills did not matter. However, if any one of the three characteristics slips at an outlet, the synergistic effect is lost.

ADDING TO CAPABILITIES

Fuller use of existing resources.   Synergistic effects are possible in any phase of company operations. One possibility is that present activities include a "capability" that can be applied to additional uses. Thus, American watch companies have undertaken the manufacture of tiny gyroscopes and electronic components for spacecraft because they already possessed technical skill in the production of miniature precision products. They adopted this strategy on the premise that they could make both watches and components for spacecraft with less effort than could separate firms devoted to only one line of products.

The original concept of General Foods Corporation sought a similar synergistic effect in marketing. Here, the basic capability was marketing prepared foods. By having the same sales organization handle several product lines, a larger and more effective sales effort could be provided and/or the selling cost per product line could be reduced. Clearly, the combined sales activity was more powerful than separate sales efforts for each product line would have been.

VERTICAL INTEGRATION

Expansion to obtain a resource.   Vertical integration may have synergistic effects. This occurred when the Apollo Printing Machine Company bought a foundry. Apollo was unsatisfied with the quality and tardy delivery of its castings and was looking for a new supplier. In its search, it learned that a nearby foundry could be purchased. The foundry was just breaking even, primarily because the volume of its work fluctuated widely. Following the purchase, Apollo gave the foundry a more steady backlog of work, and through close technical cooperation the quality of castings received by them was improved. The consolidated set-up was better for both enterprises than the previous independent operations.

The results of vertical integration are not always so good, however; problems of balance, flexibility, and managerial capacity must be carefully weighed. Nevertheless, control of a critical resource is often a significant part of company strategy.

UNIQUE SERVICES

Expansion to enhance market position. Efforts to improve market position provide

many examples of "the whole being better than the sum of its parts." The leading can companies, for example, moved from exclusive concentration on metal containers into glass, plastic, and paper containers. They expected their new divisions to be profitable by themselves, but an additional reason for the expansion lay in anticipated synergistic effects of being able to supply a customer's total container requirements. With the entire packaging field changing so rapidly, a company that can quickly shift from one type of container to another offers a distinctive service to its customers.

International Harvester, to cite another case, added a very large tractor to its line a few years ago. The prospects for profit on this line alone were far from certain. However, the new tractor was important to give dealers "a full line"; its availability removed the temptation for dealers to carry some products of competing manufacturers. So, when viewed in combination with other International Harvester products, the new tractor looked much more significant than it did as an isolated project.

NEGATIVE SYNERGY

Compatibility of efforts.   In considering additional niches for a company, we may be confronted with negative synergy—that is, the combined effort is worse than the sum of independent efforts. This occurred when a producer of high quality television and hi-fi sets introduced a small color television receiver. When first offered, the small unit was as good as most competing sets and probably had an attractive potential market. However, it was definitely inferior in performance to other products of the company and, consequently, undermined public confidence in the quality of the entire line. Moreover, customers had high expectations for the small set because of the general reputation of the company, and they became very critical when the new product did not live up to their expectations. Both the former products and the new product suffered.

Compatibility of operations within the company should also be considered. A large department store, for instance, ran into serious trouble when it tried to add a high-quality dress shop to its mass merchandising activities. The ordering and physical handling of merchandise, the approach to sales promotion, the sales compensation plan, and many other procedures which worked well for the established type of business were unsuited to the new shop. And friction arose each time the shop received special treatment. Clearly, the new shop created an excessive number of problems because it was incompatible with existing customs and attitudes.

BROAD COMPANY GOALS

Summarizing briefly: We have seen that some combinations of efforts are strongly reinforcing. The combination accelerates the total effect or reduces the cost for the same effect or solidifies our supply or market position. On the other hand, we must watch for incompatible efforts which may have a disruptive effect in the same cumulative manner. So, when we select niches—as a part of our master strategy—one vital aspect is the possibility of such synergistic effects.

Master strategy sets broad company goals. One firm may decide to seek pre-eminence in a narrow specialty while another undertakes to be a leader in several niches or perhaps in all phases of its industry. We have recommended that this definition of "scope" be clear in terms of:

Services offered to customers.
Operations performed by the company.
Relationships with suppliers of necessary resources.
The desirability of defining this mission so as to obtain synergistic effects.

But master strategy involves more than defining our desired role in society. Many activities will be necessary to achieve this desired spot, and senior executives must decide what to do first, how many activities can be done concurrently, how fast to move, what risks to run, and what to postpone. These questions of sequence and timing must be resolved to make the strategy operational.

STRATEGY OF SEQUENCE

Choice of sequence. Especially in technical areas, sequence of actions may be dictated by technology. Thus, process research must precede equipment designs, product specifications must precede cost estimation, and so forth. Other actions, such as the steps necessary to form a new corporation, likewise give management little choice in sequence. When this occurs, normal programming or possibly PERT analysis may be employed. Little room—or need—exists for strategy.

Preordained sequences, however, are exceptional in the master strategy area. A perennial issue when entering a new niche, for instance, is whether to develop markets before working on production economies, or vice versa. The production executive will probably say, "Let's be sure we can produce the product at a low cost before committing ourselves to customers," whereas the typical marketing man will advise, "Better be sure it will sell before tooling up for a big output."

A striking example of strategy involving sequence confronted the Boeing company when it first conceived of a large four-engine jet plane suitable for handling cargo or large passenger loads. Hindsight makes the issue appear simple, but at the time, Air Force officers saw little need for such a plane. The belief was that propeller-driven planes provided the most desirable means for carrying cargo. In other words, the company got no support for its prediction of future market requirements. Most companies would have stopped at this point. However, Boeing executives decided to invest several million dollars to develop the new plane. A significant portion of the company's liquid assets went into the project. Over two years later, Boeing was able to present evidence that caused the Air Force officials to change their minds—and the KC 135 was born. Only Boeing was prepared to produce the new type of craft which proved to be both faster and more economical than propeller-driven planes. Moreover, the company was able to convert the design into the Boeing 707 passenger plane which, within a few years, dominated the airline passenger business. Competing firms were left far behind, and Convair almost went bankrupt in its attempt to catch up. In this instance, a decision to let engineering and production run far ahead of marketing paid off handsomely.

No simple guide exists for selecting a strategic sequence. Nevertheless, the following comments do sharpen the issue:

Resist the temptation to do first what is easiest simply because it requires the least initiative. Each of us typically has a bias for what he does well. A good sequence of activities, however, is more likely to emerge from an objective analysis.

If a head start is especially valuable on one front, start early there. Sometimes, being the first in the market is particularly desirable (there may be room for only one company). In other cases, the strategic place to begin is the acquiring of key resources; at a later date limited raw materials may already be bought up or the best sites occupied by competitors. The importance of a head start is usually hard to estimate, but probably more money is lost in trying to be first than in catching up with someone else.

Move into uncertain areas promptly, preferably before making any major commitments. For instance, companies have been so entranced with a desired expansion that they committed substantial funds to new plants before uncertainties regarding the production processes were removed.

If a particular uncertainty can be investigated quickly and inexpensively, get it out of the way promptly.

Start early with processes involving long lead-times. For example, if a new synthetic food product must have government approval, the tedious process of testing and reviewing evidence may take a year or two longer than preparation for manufacturing and marketing.

Delay revealing plans publicly if other companies can easily copy a novel idea. If substantial social readjustment is necessary, however, an early public announcement is often helpful.

In a particular case, these guides may actually conflict with each other, or other considerations may be dominant. And, as the Boeing 707 example suggests, the possible gains may be large enough to justify following a very risky sequence. Probably the greatest value of the above list is to stimulate careful thought about the sequence that is incorporated into a company's master strategy.

RESOURCE LIMITATIONS

Straining scarce resources. A hard-driving executive does not like to admit that an objective cannot be achieved. He prefers to believe, "Where there's a will there's a way."

Yet, an essential aspect of master strategy is deciding what can be done and how fast.

Every enterprise has limits—perhaps severe limits—on its resources. The amount of capital, the number and quality of key personnel, the physical production capacity, or the adaptability of its social structure—none of these is boundless. The tricky issue is how to use these limited resources to the best advantage. We must devise a strategy which is feasible within the inherent restraints.

A household-appliance manufacturer went bankrupt because he failed to adapt his rate of growth to his financial resources. This man had a first-rate product and a wise plan for moving with an "economy model" into an expanding market (following rural electrification). But, to achieve low production costs, he built an oversized plant and launched sales efforts in ten states. His contention was that the kind of company he conceived could not start out on a small scale. Possibly all of these judgments were correct, but they resulted in cash requirements that drained all of his resources before any momentum was achieved. Cost of the partially used plant and of widely scattered sales efforts was so high that no one was willing to bail out the financially strapped venture. His master strategy simply did not fit his resources.

The scarce resource affecting master strategy may be managerial personnel. A management consulting firm, for instance, reluctantly postponed entry into the international arena because only two of its partners had the combination of interest, capacity, and vitality to spend a large amount of time abroad, and these men were also needed to assure continuity of the United States practice. The firm felt that a later start would be better than weak action immediately—even though this probably meant the loss of several desirable clients.

The weight we should attach to scarce resources in the timing of master strategy often requires delicate judgment. Some strain may be endured. But, how much, how long? For example, in its switch from purchased to company-produced tires, a European rubber company fell behind on deliveries for six months, but, through heroic efforts and pleading with customers, the company weathered the squeeze. Now, company executives believe the timing was wise! If the delay had lasted a full year—and this was a real possibility—the consequence would have approached a catastrophe.

Forming coalitions. A cooperative agreement with firms in related fields occasionally provides a way to overcome scarce resources. We have already referred to the RCA-Whirlpool arrangement for distributing Whirlpool products. Clearly, in this instance, the timing of Whirlpool's entrance into the market with its own brand depended on forming a coalition with RCA.

EXAMPLES OF COALITIONS

The early development of frozen foods provides us with two other examples of fruitful coalitions. A key element in Birdseye master strategy was to obtain the help of cold-storage warehouses; grocery wholesalers were not equipped to handle frozen foods, and before the demand was clearly established they were slow to move into the new activity. And the Birdseye division of General Foods lacked both managerial and financial resources to venture into national wholesaling.

Similarly, Birdseye had to get freezer cabinets into retail stores, but it lacked the capability to produce them. So, it entered into a coalition with a refrigerator manufacturer to make and sell (or lease) the cabinets to retail stores. This mutual agreement enabled Birdseye to move ahead with its marketing program much faster. With the tremendous growth of frozen foods, neither the cold storage warehouse nor the cabinet manufacturer continued to be necessary, but without them in the early days widespread use of frozen foods would have been delayed three to five years.

Coalitions may be formed for reasons other than "buying time." Nevertheless, when we are trying to round out a workable master strategy, coalitions—or even mergers—may provide the quickest way to overcome a serious deficiency in vital resources.

THE RIGHT TIME TO ACT

Receptive environment. Conditions in a firm's environment affect the "right time" to make a change. Mr. Ralph Cordiner, for example, testifies that he launched his basic reorganization of General Electric Company only when he felt confident of three years of high business activity because, in his opinion, the company could not have absorbed all the internal readjustments during a period of declining volume and profits.

Judging the right time to act is difficult. Thus, one of the contributing factors to the multimillion-dollar Edsel car fiasco was poor timing. The same automobile launched a year or two earlier might have been favorably received. But buyer tastes changed between the time elaborate market research studies were made and the time when the new car finally appeared in dealer showrooms. By then, preference was swinging away from a big car that "had everything" toward compacts. This mistake in timing and associated errors in strategy cost the Ford Motor Company over a hundred million dollars.

A major move can be too early, as well as too late. We know, for instance, that a forerunner of the modern, self-service supermarket—the Piggly Wiggly—was born too soon. In its day, only a few housewives drove automobiles to shopping centers; and those that could afford cars usually shunned the do-it-yourself mode so prevalent today. In other words, the environment at that time simply was not receptive to what now performs so effectively. Other "pioneers" have also received cool receptions—prefabricated housing and local medical clinics are two.

NO SIMPLE RULES

The preceding discussions of sequence and timing provide no simple rules for these critical aspects of basic strategy. The factors we have mentioned for deciding which front(s) to push first (where is a head start valuable, early attention to major uncertainties, leadtimes, significance of secrecy) and for deciding how fast to move (strain on scarce resources, possible coalition to provide resources, and receptivity of the environment) bear directly on many strategy decisions. They also highlight the fundamental nature of sequence and timing in the master strategy for a firm.

Master strategy involves deliberately relating a company's efforts to its particular future environment. We recognize, of course, that both the company's capabilities and its environment continually evolve; consequently, strategy should always be based, not on existing conditions, but on forecasts. Such forecasts, however, are never 100 per cent correct; instead, strategy often seeks to take advantage of uncertainty about future conditions.

This dynamic aspect of strategy should be underscored. The industry outlook will shift for any of numerous reasons. These forces may accelerate growth in some sectors and spell decline in others, may squeeze material supply, may make old sources obsolete, may open new possibilities and snuff out others. Meanwhile, the company itself is also changing—due to the success or failure of its own efforts and to actions of competitors and cooperating firms. And with all of these internal and external changes the combination of thrusts that will provide optimum synergistic effects undoubtedly will be altered. Timing of actions is the most volatile element of all. It should be adjusted to both the new external situation and the degrees of internal progress on various fronts.

Consequently, frequent reappraisal of master strategy is essential. We must build into the planning mechanisms sources of fresh data that will tell us how well we are doing and what new opportunities and obstacles are appearing on the horizon. The feedback features of control will provide some of these data. In addition, senior managers and others who have contact with various parts of the environment must be ever-sensitive to new developments that established screening devices might not detect.

Hopefully, such reappraisal will not call for sharp reversals in strategy. Typically, a master strategy requires several years to execute and some features may endure much longer. The kind of plan I am discussing here sets the direction for a whole host of company actions, and external reputations and relations often persist for many years. Quick reversals break momentum, require repeated relearning, and dissipate favorable cumulative effects. To be sure, occasionally a sharp break may be necessary. But, if my forecasts are reasonably sound, the adaptations to new opportunities will be more evolution than revolution. Once embarked on a course, we make our reappraisal from our new position—and this introduces an advantage in continuing in at least the same general direction. So, normally, the adaptation is more an unfolding than a completely new start.

Even though drastic modification of our master strategy may be unnecessary, frequent incremental changes will certainly be required to keep abreast of the times. Especially desirable are shifts that anticipate change before the pressures build up. And such farsighted adjustments are possible only if we periodically reappraise and adapt present strategy to new opportunities.

Master strategy is the pivotal planning instrument for large and small enterprises alike. The giant corporations provide us with examples on a grand scale, but the same kind of thinking is just as vital for small firms.

AN EXAMPLE

A terse sketch of the central strategy of one small firm will illustrate this point. The partners of an accounting firm in a city with a quarter-million population predicted faster growth in data processing than in their normal auditing and tax work, yet they knew that most of their clients were too small to use an electronic computer individually. So they foresaw the need for a single, cooperative computer center serving several companies. And they believed that their intimate knowledge of the procedures and the needs of several of these companies, plus the specialized ability of one partner in data processing, put them in a unique position to operate such a center. Competition was anticipated from two directions: New models of computers much smaller in size would eventually come on the market—but even if the clients could rent such equipment they would still need programmers and other specialized skills. Also, telephonic hook-ups with International Business Machines service centers appeared likely—but the accounting firm felt its local and more intimate knowledge of each company would give it an advantage over such competition. So, the cooperative computer center looked like a propitious niche.

The chief obstacle was developing a relatively stable volume of work that would carry the monthly rental on the proposed computer. A local insurance company was by far the best prospect for this purpose; it might use half the computer capacity, and then the work for other, smaller companies could be fitted into the remaining time. Consequently, the first major move was to make a deal—a coalition—with the insurance company. One partner was to devote almost his entire time working on details for such an arrangement; meanwhile, the other two partners supported him through their established accounting practice.

We see in this brief example:

The picking of a propitious niche for expansion.

The anticipated synergistic effect of combining auditing services with computing service.

The sequence and timing of efforts to overcome the major limiting factor.

The project had not advanced far enough for much reappraisal, but the fact that two partners were supporting the third provided a built-in check on the question of "how are we doing."

References

This article is adapted from a chapter in *The Process of Management*, second edition, Prentice-Hall, Inc., 1967. Executives who wish to explore the meaning and method of shaping master strategies still further can consult the following materials: E. W. Reilley, "Planning the Strategy of the Business," *Advanced Management*, XX (Dec. 1955), 8–12; T. Levitt, "Marketing Myopia," *Harvard Business Review*, XXXVIII:4 (July-Aug. 1960), 45–66; F. F. Gilmore and R. G. Brandenburg, "Anatomy of Corporate Planning," *Harvard Business Review*, XLI:6 (Nov.-Dec. 1962), 61–69; and H. W. Newman and T. L. Berg, "Managing External Relations," *California Management Review*, V:3 (Spring 1963), 81–86.

READING 15

THE CRITICAL ROLE OF TOP MANAGEMENT IN LONG-RANGE PLANNING*

George A. Steiner

There is no substitute for long-range planning in the development of profitable and healthy organizations. It is not, of course, the only requirement, but it is a major one. Too few companies, particularly the smaller and medium-sized ones, and too few government organizations try or do effective long-range planning.

In examining many long-range planning programs, I have come to two major conclusions. First, the fundamental concept of an effective long-range planning program is deceptively simple. Second, creating and maintaining a first-rate long-range planning program is deceptively difficult and demands, for its success, devoted attention by chief executives. I should like to discuss these two points, but first I should like to say a few words about the importance of effective long-range planning.

* Reprinted with permission from Arizona Review, April, 1966.

IMPORTANCE OF LONG-RANGE PLANNING

There exists in some business and government quarters surprising resistance to developing systematic and comprehensive planning. Naturally there are a great many reasons for such resistance, but failure to grasp the significance of effective planning is more important than it should be.

Several years ago, Mr. S. C. Beise, then President of the Bank of America, observed that for many years before World War II commercial banks did not aggressively seek savings deposits. As a result, the industry did not involve itself importantly in the related field of real estate financing. After World War II building boomed and little financial firms grew dramatically to fill the home financing need.

Today these once-small savings and loan companies constitute a big industry in the United States and have given banks stiff competition for savings funds.

The commercial banking industry today has made a strong comeback in the fields of savings and real estate lending, but due to its lack of foresight some twenty years ago, the banking industry gave birth to one of its own biggest competitors. I believe the industry has learned its lesson well, and it is one every industry and company should note.[1]

A recent study of the thirteen fastest growing companies in the United States revealed that all give high priority to long-range planning and manage to inspire most levels of managers to think about the future.[2]

Not only are more companies discovering the advantages of comprehensive and effective planning programs, but governments are developing organized long-range planning programs. This movement is particularly rapid among Western European governments and some developing nations. Last August President Johnson dramatically announced that the planning-programming-budgeting system introduced into the Pentagon by Secretary McNamara must be applied throughout the government.

There are many reasons why systematic and structured long-range planning is considered so important by progressive businesses and non-business organizations. Effective planning prevents ad hoc decisions, random decisions, decisions that unnecessarily and expensively narrow choices for tomorrow. Effective planning gives an organization a structural framework of objectives and strategies, a basis for all decision making. Lower-level managers know what top management wants and can make decisions accordingly. But there are also ancillary benefits. An effective planning organization, for example, provides a powerful channel of communications for the people in an organization to deal with problems of importance to themselves as well as to their organization.

It is difficult to exaggerate the importance of effective comprehensive planning to an organization. It has, for many companies, provided that margin needed for outstanding growth and profitability.

A CONCEPTUAL MODEL OF LONG-RANGE PLANNING

A conceptual model of planning at a sufficiently low level of abstraction is a guide in establishing a complete system. The words *long-range planning* are useful in emphasizing a time dimension to planning. In describing an effective planning program, however, I prefer to speak of comprehensive, corporate or total planning.

Planning in this sense may be described from four points of view. First, a basic generic view of planning as dealing with the futurity of present decisions. This means that current decisions are made in light of their long-range consequences. It means also that future alternatives open to an organization are examined and decisions made about preferred alternatives. On this basis, guidance is provided for making current operating decisions. There are also many other conceptual views of planning; one concept, for example, recognizes planning as reasoning about how you get from here to there.

Planning is also a process. It is a process which establishes objectives; defines strategies, policies and sequences of events to achieve objectives; defines the organization for implementing the planning process; and assures a review and evaluation of performance as feedback in recycling the process.

Planning may be considered from a third point of view—namely, as a philosophy. Planning has been described as projective thought, or "looking ahead." Planning in this sense is an attitude, a state of mind, a way of thinking.

Finally, planning may be viewed in terms of structure. Long-range planning, as the term is typically used in the business world, refers to the development of a comprehensive and reasonably uniform program of plans for the entire company or agency, reaching out over a long period of time. It is an integrating framework within which each of the functional plans may be tied together and an overall plan developed for the entire organization.

Broadly, this structure includes four major elements (Figure 15-1). The first consists of strategic plans. These are a loose, written and unwritten set of major objectives, strategies and policies. The second is a detailed, uniform

---

[1] S. C. Beise, *"Planning for Industrial Growth: An Executive View,"* remarks before the Milan Conference on Planning for Industrial Growth, sponsored by Stanford Research Institute, 1963, mimeographed.

[2] Jack B. Weiner, *"What Makes a Growth Company?,"* Dun's Review and Modern Industry, November 1964.

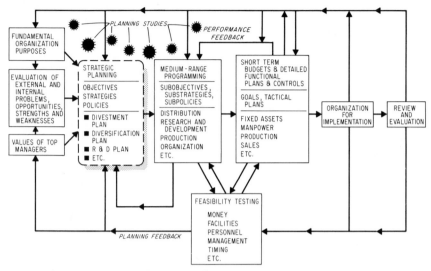

Figure 15-1   A structure and process of business planning.

and a rather complete medium-range set of plans (two to seven, but generally five, years) covering major areas of organizational activity. The third part is short-term plans and budgets. The fourth structural part consists of planning studies which frequently are projections of things to come. A government agency, for example, may make a study of future revenues and demands for funds. A public utility may make population projections for its area. An automobile company may study changing consumer tastes, likely competitor moves and developing automotive technology. Such forecasts are not plans. The results of such studies, however, are important in actually making plans.

Long-range planning as the term is typically used in the business world does not refer so much to the future span of time covered as to the idea of management grappling systematically with future opportunities, problems and alternative courses of action. Many companies typically have the pattern of plans and the concepts of planning already defined. This can be and often is called long-range planning. But I prefer other words to describe this structure.

LONG-RANGE PLANNING
IN LARGE AND SMALL BUSINESSES

All companies plan ahead in some degree. But not all have the sort of concept and structure noted here. While statistics on this subject are

rather poor, I think it is probably true that close to a majority of the largest companies throughout the world have some sort of overall business planning program and a staff assigned to help executives do the work. Two years ago I held a research seminar at the Palais de Fontainebleau, France to discuss strategic business planning. About one hundred directors of corporate planning or top line managers of the largest multi-national corporations of the world were present. One of the surprising conclusions reached at the seminar was that, despite the great surface diversities of planning among these companies, there was a large degree of comparability among basic planning definitions, principles, procedures and structures.[3]

There are relatively fewer numbers of medium and small-sized companies with comprehensive planning programs, but their numbers are growing. They are beginning to realize that, despite their limited resources, they have about the same fundamental planning requirements as the larger companies. Their salvation is not to ignore the problem but to develop short-cuts and rough-cut techniques for dealing with it.[4] There are many

[3] *See George A. Steiner and Warren M. Cannon, eds.,* Multinational Corporate Planning *(New York: The Free Press, Spring 1966).*
[4] *For suggestions about how to do this, see Roger A. Golde, "Practical Planning for Small Business,"* Harvard Business Review, *September-October 1964; Myles L. Mace, "The President and*

ways for a small company to get outside help at a reasonable price. Local banks can give advice. Many consulting agencies are available. Even professors are sometimes handy as consultants. Placing on his board of directors some persons who can contribute to long-range planning may also be attractive to a small businessman.

Systematic and reasonably well-structured planning programs are required by all organizations to survive and progress in the most healthy and effective manner. This is not something that only large companies need and are able to do. The requirement for effective planning exists for small companies, trade associations, industrial development agencies and for governments.

Professor Frank Gilmore of Cornell University presents the necessity for better planning in small businesses with this warning:

> The swing to strategic planning in large organizations constitutes a serious threat to small business management. It challenges one of the important competitive advantages which the small company has enjoyed—being faster on its feet than the larger company in adapting to changing conditions. It is perfectly clear that mere adaptation in the short run will no longer suffice. Trends must henceforth be made, not simply coped with.[5]

His point, of course, is that strategic planning among small businesses and smaller nonprofit organizations must accompany the better planning of the larger organizations. Smaller organizations can plan ahead systematically and continuously. First, however, there must be a recognition by the chief executive that this is possible. Then the smaller organization must devise ways and means to perform planning at a cost under benefit.

Naturally, different organizations go about meeting their planning responsibilities in different ways. Many big corporations have a large central planning staff reporting to the chief executive through a senior vice president. Each of the divisions of such a company may also have a planning staff. At the other extreme are the very small firms where the chief executive does almost all the planning. As firms increase in size, the chief executive may get help by hiring a special assistant, by using his vice presidents in ad hoc advisory planning committees or by using his vice presidents and functional officers as a permanent planning staff to help him develop plans.

In a similar fashion, basic principles essential for effective planning apply to all organizations—large and small, profit and nonprofit. Precisely how the principles are applied, however, does differ among organizations and among problems and over time.

Of cardinal importance in creating and maintaining useful comprehensive planning programs is the role played by chief executives.

TOP MANAGEMENT'S KEY ROLE IN PLANNING

There can and will be no effective long-range planning in any organization where the chief executive does not give it firm support and make sure that others in the organization understand his depth of commitment. Yet one competent observer finds:

> Probably the single most important problem in corporate planning derives from the belief of some chief operating executives that corporate planning is not a function with which they should be directly concerned. They regard planning as something to be delegated, which subordinates can do without responsible participation by chief executives. They think the end result of effective planning is the compilation of a "Plans" book. Such volumes get distributed to key executives, who scan the contents briefly, file them away, breathe a sigh of relief, and observe, "Thank goodness that is done—now let's get back to work."[6]

This, of course, shows a lack of understanding of the planning task and the responsibility of the top executive. Another competent ob-

Corporate Planning," Harvard Business Review, *January-February 1965; and Raymond M. Haas, Richard I. Hartman, John H. James and Robert R. Milroy,* Long-Range Planning for Small Business, *Bureau of Business Research, Graduate School of Business, Indiana University, 1964.*
[5] *Frank F. Gilmore, "Strategic Planning's Threat to Small Business," mimeographed, 1966.*

[6] *Mace, op. cit., p. 50.*

server says the matter is not so much a lack of understanding but abdication of responsibility. Professor O'Donnell has said:

> I think one of the outstanding facts about corporate planning at the present is that the presidents of corporations have been ducking their jobs.... They seem to be following the practice of setting in a fuzzy way some objectives to be accomplished in the future and establishing a committee, with the staff help of a planning group, to come up with a plan for achieving the objectives. From this point until the plan is presented to him, the president almost abdicates his responsibilities. When the plan is placed on his desk it is often too late for him to exert much influence on it.[7]

It is essential that the chief executive assume primary responsibility for his organization's long-range planning. When he hires an assistant to help him, or establishes a planning staff, he is merely extending his reach. These people are helping him do *his* job. This is a recognition that the world is too large for one man to grasp completely, and that to the extent he can get others to help him he will be more able to examine a wider range of threats to and opportunities for his organization.

Issues concerning the role of the chief executive in the development of plans are subtle and complex. I participated in one conference with chief executives where the major focus was on the relationship of the president with his staff in the development of corporate plans. These executives were dedicated to the idea of comprehensive planning but were uncertain about many matters relating to their participation. The range of alternatives is very wide. Effective planning, for example, requires that the top executive "buy it." He must believe in planning as being important to the success of his enterprise. He must give more than "lip service" to the effort. He must feel committed, and his support must be visible to others in the corporation. By his actions the chief executive will set the psychological climate in which planning is done.

How an executive does these things will depend upon his style of management, the way his company is organized, the personalities involved and his own sense of commitment. For example, if the chief executive devotes most of his attention to short-range problems, this emphasis will not be lost on his subordinates. Even if he is interested in long-range planning, can he find the time to do it properly? I agree partly with Senator Jackson for example, when, speaking about the federal government, he observed:

> ... I am convinced that we never will get the kind of policy planning we need if we expect the top-level officers to participate actively in the planning process. They simply do not have the time, and in any event they rarely have the outlook or the talents of the good planner. They cannot explore issues deeply and systematically. They cannot argue the advantages and disadvantages at length in the kind of give-and-take essential if one is to reach a solid understanding with others on points of agreement and disagreement.[8]

While this observation does have an important element of truth in it for a large government department or a large multinational business, it has much less for a small enterprise where the chief executive must plan if any planning is to be done. But even in the largest companies and government agencies the chief executives must get involved in the substance of planning. If they do not they will clearly be abdicating one of their major responsibilities. At the very least they will be captives of their planning staffs and thereby lose some element of control of their enterprises.

But the question still exists: how shall the chief executive participate in the substance of planning? There is no simple answer. For the first planning effort, the chief executive of any organization—large or small, profit or non-profit—ought to be deeply involved. Once the planning program has gotten on a solid footing, with periodic cycling, general understanding and acceptance, the chief executive will know more clearly at what points and how much his participation is required. If a company, for example, has just begun the planning process and is pounding out long-

---

[7] *George A. Steiner, ed.,* Managerial Long-Range Planning *(New York: McGraw-Hill Book Co., Inc., 1963), p. 17.*

[8] *Henry M. Jackson, "To Forge a Strategy for Survival,"* Public Administration Review, *Vol. XIX (Summer 1959), p. 159.*

range objectives, the chief executive should be intimately involved. Once those objectives are established, he must help make and approve strategies to reach them. When this work is done, he may get involved in subsequent cycles of planning only with selected changes in specific objectives and strategies. Both he and his staff will know better with experience what these points are. There is no ready answer for any chief executive, however, to the question of when and how much he can delegate to and rely upon his staff—both line and functional—what are, in the end, his planning responsibilities.

It is not enough that the chief executive participate in the planning exercise. His relationship to it must be visible to others in the organization. By various methods open to him, the chief executive must have others know about and understand his interest in the process.

DEVELOPING THE PLAN

It is a major responsibility of the chief executive to see that the proper planning system is developed and maintained. In this effort, of course, he will have help from subordinates—both line managers and their staffs. But it is his responsibility to make sure that the system is appropriate to his enterprise, and that it is done at a cost (using this word broadly) under benefit which produces optimum values.

Many years ago I had the job of helping an organization develop its first comprehensive planning program. In preparing procedures and suggesting roles of people in the organization I ran into grave difficulties. People were not sure of their responsibilities, or did not want to assume the responsibility I suggested. Different people wanted to do different things which did not necessarily mesh. There were also other points of dispute. To solve the entire problem I prepared a letter for the signature of the chief executive which set forth the essential elements of the planning program, how it should be developed and who was responsible for what. This worked like a charm. From that day to this the top executives of that company have watched over the planning process. It is an outstanding system.

I am not saying, of course, that chief executives must get enmeshed in all the grubby details of a total planning program. What I do say is they must see that the job of planning

the plan is done, that it is appropriate and put into operation.

Clarification of roles of participants in the planning process is important and raises complex issues. For example, since corporate planning staffs are direct aids to the chief executive he must see that their roles are clear and generally understood.

A staff, for example, which fails to distinguish between strategic planning and tactical planning may lose top management if it gets too deeply involved in the details of tactical planning. Top management is interested in both strategic and tactical planning, but principally strategic planning. I once knew a staff that simply could not get itself out of the morass of details involved in short-range tactical planning. It was not long before the top management and its planning staff stopped talking to one another. There have been managers who simply could not differentiate between their responsibilities for strategic as distinguished from short-range tactical planning. Their concentration on the latter got them involved in a sort of Gresham's law of planning: short-range planning tends to drive out long-range planning.

Subtle problems of staff role arise in the development of strategic plans by central planning staffs and plans and operations of divisions. Long-range plans made in one area of a company often make sense only when considered in light of other areas and of the company as a whole. In this light, corporate planning staffs inevitably get involved in this interrelationship. Their role in modification of plans to relate better to the company as a whole may result in bitter conflict with line officers if large issues are involved. No matter how clear staff roles may be this sort of conflict will arise. It is less likely to arise and less likely to be serious if roles are clearly specified and understood.

There is no question about the fact that planning should not be separated from doing. Upon examination, however, this is not as simple as it sounds. In the strategic planning area, for example, plans may be developed for divisional execution, and the divisions may not have much if any participation in their preparation. Even with close line and staff interrelations at central office headquarters, staff inevitably will make decisions. The mere choice of alternatives to present to line managers, for example, may implicitly be decision-making by staff. Problems of drawing a line of demarcation between staff and line decision-making, and planning and operations, vary from case to case in the development of plans, and from time to time. There can be no simple formula. But efforts to clarify staff role can prevent unnecessary conflict.

Even when the staff role is clear, however, difficult problems of relationships may arise. In larger companies with comprehensive planning programs, corporate functional staffs, including long-range planning staffs, review divisional plans at the request of top management. Plans are submitted up the line, but staffs help line managers review them. In one instance a president asked his director of long-range planning to review the plans of a powerful division manager. The president insisted upon a rigorous examination of the plans because of the substantial capital outlays sought by the divisional manager. The planner did so and provided the rationale for rejecting the plans. He was not very happy about his role. He had been cultivating this divisional manager for a long time in order to develop a better planning program in his division and to arrange better communications to help them both do a better planning job. Now the divisional manager felt he had been double-crossed. The corporate planner will have problems in rebuilding his lines of communication with this division.

The planning process is complex. There must be understanding of authority, responsibility, procedures and timing. The chief executive is responsible for seeing that this need is met.

BASE DECISIONS ON PLANS

Comprehensive planning done with and on behalf of top management should result in operating decisions. Without decisions the planning process is incomplete. Failure to take action on prepared plans, or continuous vacillation, will weaken staff efforts. People simply will not be motivated to exert the energy, develop the creativity and use the imagination needed to make quality plans if top management ignores them or cannot seem to act upon them.

In one company I know, one month after a five-year long-range plan had been developed for the first time and approved by top management, the president announced a flat seven percent budget cut for all division budgets. This was his method to reduce costs. The announced reason was the need to bring costs within the year's anticipated revenues. With this announcement, the longer-range projects naturally were abandoned and the benefits of long-range planning cast in grave doubt.

The extent to which divisional line managers make decisions in light of strategic corporate plans raises a different type of problem. In some companies the connection between the corporate strategic plan and the divisional intermediate-range plans is very close. The two may, in effect, be prepared together. In one small company of about five hundred people making a variety of electronics equipment, there was a planning program where strategic plans were developed for the company as a whole and the divisions tied their sub-strategies and detailed long-range plans clearly and closely into the corporate plan. These were intermeshed because the two were done by about the same people and at about the same time. In other instances, the corporate strategic plan constitutes an umbrella under which the divisional plans are made but the interrelationship between the two is rather loose.

A somewhat different type of problem arises very subtly if divisional managers think that corporate planning staffs are making plans for them to execute. It can arise if chief executives do not get involved in the planning and accept staff recommendations without much or any reservation. In such cases divisional managers are likely to take this position to the corporate staff: "You made the plans, now execute them. Don't ask me to."

One of the major attributes of comprehensive corporate planning is that the structure, especially when written, permits managers down the organizational chain to make decisions with a reasonable degree of certainty they are in line with the objectives sought by higher level management. Naturally, if decisions made throughout an organization do not relate to the planning program, it will not be long before the planning program disappears.

This, of course, does not mean blind devotion to plan. Depending upon circumstances, it may be wise for a manager to make decisions which are very different than those planned. Flexibility must be injected into planning. There are a number of techniques to do this. One major method is for the chief executive to inject a philosophy and understanding of flexibility into the planning and operational decision-making process.

In sum, chief executives have an important role in assuring that decisions throughout the organization are made in light of plans and evolving cumstances—not blindly, not without reference to plans, but related meaningfully within a planning framework.

PLANNING TAKES TIME

While conceptually simple, a comprehensive long-range planning program for a large organization cannot be introduced overnight and expected to produce miraculous results immediately. Several years ago I calculated that about five years were required for a medium-sized or large company to develop an effective comprehensive planning system.[9] This was confirmed by another study.[10] Since there is so much more known today about how to develop effective comprehensive planning programs, it is possible to reduce this time span. Much depends upon the organization and what is going on inside it.

Among most initial efforts to develop comprehensive long-range planning programs with which I have been familiar, the first effort

[9] *Steiner, op. cit., p. 19–21.*
[10] *R. Hal Mason, "Organizing for Corporate Planning," Proceedings of the Long Range Planning Service Client Conference, February 7–9, 1962, Menlo Park, Calif., Stanford Research Institute.*

did not produce much of immediate substantive value. Yet, all those involved felt the effort worthwhile. This was so, I found, because the effort introduced a new point of view into the company which appeared to have important possibilities in future planning. It also was seen as a focal point for communicating in a common language about major problems. There are many other reasons why managements have been pleased with the first attempt at long-range planning even though it did not provide immediate substantive values. But first efforts do not always provide important bases for immediate decision.

An effective planning program of one company cannot be lifted intact and applied to another. While the fundamental process and structure may be removed from one company to another, the details of operation will vary. Furthermore, since an organization is a living, dynamic institution in a rapidly changing environment, the procedures for planning change.

RESUMÉ

Two major underlying considerations in the development of effective long-range planning are, first, understanding of an operational conceptual model of plans, and second, understanding and acceptance by the chief executive of his role in creating and maintaining quality planning.

George Humphrey used to say that the best fertilizer ever invented was the footsteps of the farmer. Similarly, the best assurance of effective planning in an organization is the active participation of the chief executive in doing it.

READING 16

THE INFLUENCE OF DEPARTMENT OF DEFENSE PRACTICES ON CORPORATE PLANNING*

Donald J. Smalter

Over the past several years I've conducted a personal study of Department of Defense practices and activities.

My company has no business whatsoever with the Department of Defense, so my interest related strictly to the observation of D-O-D methodologies, their analytical techniques and the usefulness of these to the management of large corporations. In particular, this question puzzled me: Why were many observers labeling Robert McNamara a "great" manager?

I found this: There are *many* significant "values" in observing the D-O-D, as their managerial problems are bigger and more complex. They must, of necessity, formalize and systematize many more of their practices and procedures than managers in smaller organizations.

Some of the concepts and techniques that are useful to industrial corporate planners and managers are:

* *Reprinted with permission from* Management Technology, *vol. 4, no. 2, December 1964.*

1 Strategic planning by missions with special attention to resource allocation, using an annual scheduled planning cycle, linked to the budgeting process.
2 The use of systems analysis and planning, embodying quantitative techniques, incorporating the application of game theory and subjectively judged probabilities.
3 NEEDS research, i.e., formalized study to perceive needs.
4 An approach which might be termed "Management by Priority-of-Challenge."
5 The unique planning/analysis organizational alignment, and its potential applications.
6 The use of logic-sequence network diagrams for project planning and implementation; and finally
7 The utilization of a strategic planning "decision center" in the Pentagon.

Table 16-1 lists inadequacies reportedly found by McNamara and his Assistant Secretary, Charles Hitch, when they assumed their D-O-D responsibilities in January 1961. I compiled this list after reading numerous articles in the public literature. Further, I corresponded briefly with several people in the D-O-D, received literature on their planning process and procedures. Charles Hitch, incidentally, is the Assistant Secretary for Budgeting and Control.

First, McNamara and Hitch claim to have found poor coordination with State Department policies. The D-O-D people apparently had limited liaison with the State Department staff concerning military responses that might be anticipated to be necessary in the various segments of the world—if some specific enemy action occurred. For instance, one of the first things that happened unexpectedly in the Kennedy administration was the Russian erection of the Berlin wall. The late President was reportedly disturbed to find that the military had drawn inadequate contingency plans for the Berlin Wall Crisis.

Next, they concluded that the Pentagon allotted inadequate time for strategy studies of what they should be striving to accomplish. Come budget time each year, there was a tendency for the service heads to allot a billion here, a billion there for continuation of present commitments, without proper analysis of their changing needs. Strategic plans then were assembled in a relatively short period of time, in order to meet budget deadlines.

There was rather poor coordination between strategic planning and functional budgeting, or, in other words, between the long-term mission requirements and the annual budgeting by service branch. The fifth point: There were unilateral service plans and not unified DOD plans, with imbalances in the allocated resources for a given mission. To illustrate: While the Army had a number of divisions on standby at airfields for emergency airlift, the Air Force leadership was dubious about spending their limited funds for airlift capability. They much preferred to use most of their appropriations for nuclear retaliation bombers. Thus, the Air Force possessed far too few planes to airlift these divisions overseas. Another example: The number of bombers, Polaris missiles, and ICBM missiles, all strategic nuclear retaliation devices, were not determined through detailed study, but rather tended to be determined subjectively by the service leadership.

Sixth, the total financial implications of program decisions were poorly determined. For instance: The chiefs-of-staff authorized development of numerous major weapons systems and yet hadn't projected the total cost of *developing* each beyond a year. Further, they had not pre-determined how much it would cost to *operate* these weapons over an extended period of time. Too frequently a poorly conceived project consumed gigantic expenditures. DYNASOAR and SKYBOLT, as examples, are now cancelled.

Seventh, strategic alternatives were selected intuitively, not through dispassionate analysis. The best example to illustrate perhaps would be the B-70 supersonic bomber, a project which made numerous headlines. General Curtis LeMay insisted on vast future reliance on the B-70. But, the chiefs-of-staff had *not* conducted strategy research of the B-70 versus the Polaris missile versus land-based intercontinental missiles. When McNamara assumed responsibility, he initiated the "dispassionate" studies which resulted in a sharply accelerated Polaris program, an expedited, enlarged Minute-Man program, with a drastic cut-back on the B-70 program. This was accomplished through a detailed analysis of alternatives by a section called the Systems Analysis group, primarily an Operations Research type staff.

The eighth point logically follows the previous comment: There was inadequate use of cost/effectiveness as a basis for measurement of weapon system alternatives. Service leadership did *not* possess a sound grasp of the *total* cost for supporting a B-70. The Polaris submarine proved far cheaper to maintain for the same unit of retaliation effectiveness. Prior to this, the Pentagon conducted few, if any, studies for cost comparisons of strategic alternatives.

Ninth, there was inadequate DOD analysis on weapon *NEEDS*. Note the emphasis on the word "needs." McNamara found that the initiative for weapons systems ideas was coming mainly from the outside and that the military inside the DOD were not systematically studying their needs to identify new weapon system concepts.

Finally, the span of time to precipitate major program decisions was far too long to satisfy the new Secretary of Defense. In the huge DOD organizational pyramid, specific responsibility tended to be elusive. The Secretary wanted to see decisions faced with much less delay. I'll speak later about this in relation to the Pentagon's decision room, or "BIG BOARD."

Many of these points in Table 16-1 are

TABLE 16-1   DOD SHORTCOMINGS PER McNAMARA & HITCH. . . .

1. Poor coordination with State Department policies.
2. Poor contingency planning for political "upheavals."
3. Inadequate time allotted for strategy studies.
4. Poor coordination between strategic planning & functional budgeting.
5. Unilateral service plans, NOT unified DOD plans.
   —Imbalance in resources for missions
   —Poorly defined missions
6. Financial implications of program decisions poorly determined
   —Poor regard for resource constraints
   —Frequent cancellations of poorly conceived projects
7. Strategic alternatives selected intuitively, NOT thru dispassionate analysis
8. Inadequate cost/effective measurement of weapon system alternatives.
9. Negligible DOD analysis of weapon NEEDS.
10. Long span-of-time to precipitate major program decisions.

criticisms that in an analogous way apply to industrial corporations.

Due to numerous complaints from the military, Secretary McNamara was called before a Congressional Committee to explain his reforms. This is how he stated his philosophy: "We must first determine what our foreign policy is to be, formulate a military strategy to carry out that policy, then build the military forces to successfully conduct this strategy."

He initiated several key organization changes. He enlisted the aid of a scholarly thinker named Charles J. Hitch from Rand Corporation who had studied the Defense Department problems for many years and published several perceptive articles analyzing managerial needs. That move was probably among the more significant he made, for Hitch is Operations Research oriented. Hitch assumed responsibility for the budgeting and operations research functions.

McNamara also created or strengthened several key jobs related to planning. First, the position of Assistant Secretary for Policy Planning and International Security Affairs was provided to better coordinate strategy with State Department policies, to formulate the strategic planning and to determine the broad requirements for conflict contingencies.

Next, he created the high level office of Deputy Assistant Secretary for Systems Analysis. This office and supporting staff were created to make cost-effectiveness studies of major strategic and weapons systems alternatives, using quantitative techniques. Naturally, these mathematical experts, trained in the operations research approach, were sympathetic to the use of computers for solving complex problems.

Further, McNamara and Hitch created the position of Deputy Assistant Secretary for Programming, whose task required maintenance of a "running" five-year program-budget, which would completely reflect all the strategic decisions and all the projected expenditures. This program-budget is updated monthly, based on a managerial system that Hitch created (Reference 1) in which the military may propose "program-changes." These are processed for approval to be inserted into the "running" 5-year plan. This system is a tremendous managerial asset. It did not exist three years ago.

LESSON 1 FOR THE CORPORATE PLANNER

Prior to the McNamara regime, the Army, Navy, Air Force budgeted rather independently and almost ignored coordination of each other's programs. What McNamara instituted was planning by missions, illustrated in Figure 16-1. Key missions were identified, e.g., a nuclear retaliation mission, a "hot-spot response" mission requiring high-capacity airlift of police type forces, etc. In a complete 5-year plan, strategic elements and their supporting expenditures were assembled in what has been popularly termed "mission program-packages." Any mission package-plan then often had elements from the Army, the Navy, and the Air Force. Nuclear retaliation capability serves as a prime example: The Navy possessed the Polaris; the Air Force had the B-70 or other long-range planes, plus Minute-Man and Atlas ICBM's; the Army possessed Pershing missiles with a 400 mile range. The quantity and use of these was planned rather disjointedly. McNamara's staff then determined the *needs* for

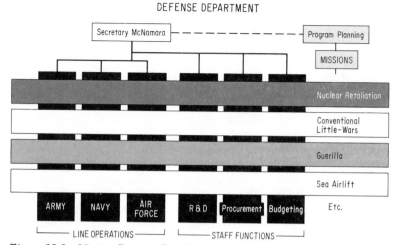

Figure 16-1   Mission "crosscut" on functions.

TABLE 16-2   DEPT. OF DEFENSE FINANCIAL SUMMARY (IN BILLIONS OF DOLLARS)

	FY 1961 Actual	FY 1962 Original	FY 1962 Final	FY 1963 Current Estimates	FY 1964 Budget Estimates
1. *Strategic Retaliatory Forces*		$7.6	$9.1	$8.5	$7.3
2. *Continental Air & Missile Defense Forces*		2.2	2.1	1.9	2.0
3. *General Purpose Forces*		14.5	17.5	18.1	19.1
4. *Airlift/Sealift Forces*		.9	1.2	1.4	1.4
5. *Reserve & Guard Forces*		1.7	1.8	2.0	2.0
6. *Research & Development*		3.9	4.3	5.5	5.9
7. *General Support*		12.3	12.7	13.7	14.6
8. *Civil Defense*			.3	.2	.3
9. *Military Assistance*		1.8	1.8	1.6	1.6
Proposed Legislation for Military Compensation, etc.					.9
Total Obligational Authority	$46.1	$44.9	$51.0	$52.8	$55.2
Less Financing Adj.	−3.0	−1.2	−1.6	−1.5	−1.5
New Obligational Authority	$43.1	$43.7	$49.4	$51.3	$53.7
Adj. to Expenditures	+1.6	+1.0	−1.2	−1.3	−1.3
Total Expenditures	$44.7	$44.7	$48.2	$50.0	$52.4
TOA by Dept. & Agency					
Army	$10.5	$10.6	$12.8	$12.2	$13.1
Navy	12.8	12.5	14.9	15.2	15.5
Air Force	20.1	18.7	20.0	20.9	20.7
Civil Defense			.3	.2	.3
Defense Agencies	.3	.4	.3	1.8	1.9
Retired Pay	.8	.9	.9	1.0	1.2
Military Assistance	1.5	1.8	1.8	1.6	1.6
Proposed Legislation					.9
*Total**	$46.1	$44.9	$51.0	$52.8	$55.2

* Excludes cost of nuclear warheads.

any one mission. Such study resulted in significant moves, e.g., a drastic cut-back in B-70 planned expenditures. Table 16-2 illustrates the plan by mission for 1962 as originally budgeted, (Reference 2) and then after hurried study, the whole requirement as rebudgeted. Studies revealed inadequate air and sea-lift forces which needed to be supplemented as well as a certain number of other requirements. Nuclear retaliation capabilities were modified with greater dependence on stationary missiles, cutting out B-70's and Minute-men on railroad cars.

In the middle of Table 16-2 is a comparison of the original budget versus the revised budget. Observe that the Army received more money for limited warfare, and the Air Force was appropriated additional funds for airlift capacity. There were the short-term 1st year changes, and these McNamara initiated promptly after assumption of responsibility. Note that these expenditures are expressed in *billions* of dollars.

What lessons can be gained from this? Permit me to try to clarify the fundamental concept of mission planning. The top management job might best be described as allocating limited resources, for selected mission purposes in the dimension of *time*. This task may be visualized as a 3-dimensional cube shown in Figure 16-2. (Note my extensive use of colorful visuals. One of the major problems corporate planners must recognize is the necessity to better communicate *concepts* to other executives. We in IMC have used diagrams and charts liberally, as such visuals tend to concisely clarify concepts. Consequently, I highly recommend their use to you. Planners must better communicate the concepts of formal planning and what it can accomplish.) The first time "slice" (vertical) is the annual profit-plan or budget, and the next 5 "slices" are the 5-year corporate program plan.

This conceptualization is useful in clarifying responsibilities to various high-level managers. As illustrated in Figure 16-3, complete program balance is difficult to attain! (This is not meant to be indicative of IMC's true position, but merely serves to illustrate the point).

In examining product-lines or missions, it is often readily apparent that a more adequate job might be done in planning goals and programming expenditures for each different mission.

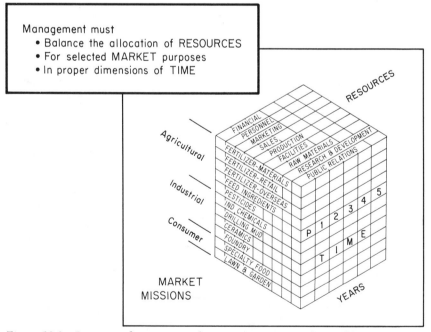

Management must
  • Balance the allocation of RESOURCES
  • For selected MARKET purposes
  • In proper dimensions of TIME

Figure 16-2 Program cube concept with mission, resource, *and* time *dimensions.*

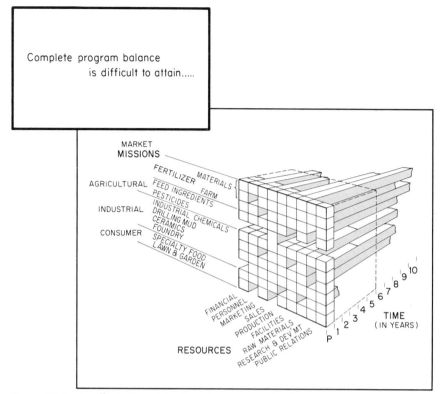

Figure 16-3   An illustration of inadequate program planning.

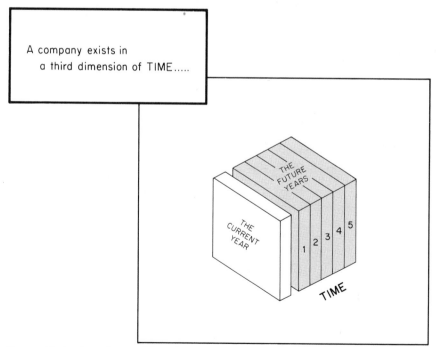

Figure 16-4   Annual time *"slices."*

Let's segregate the time factor as shown in Figure 16-4, isolating the current year's "slice." How can the annual profit-plan which tends to be a functional budget, be integrated with strategic plans for the 5 years? McNamara organized DOD planning in an annual sequenced relationship, leading up to the deadline date when he had to submit an annual budget to Congress.

In strategic planning then, it is essential to conduct studies on key issues, and this should continue preferably on a year round basis. In the case of the DOD, the program change concept permits monthly changes. As illustrated in Figure 16-5—Annual Planning Calendar, the first phase covers study of the problems, needs, and opportunities as researched and identified. Next, the organization should investigate these issues in detail, and attempt to resolve their strategy, i.e., what they are striving to do. Next, specific targets or goals should be set for a five year plan, followed by preparation of a one year budget. The Defense Department calls this their *planning, programming, budgeting* sequence.

We at IMC essentially adopted the same process: Strategic planning, Step 1; Programming, Step 2; and Budgeting, Step 3. This process has been very useful! As our fiscal year runs from July through June, we present our 5-year plan to the Board of Directors every March. As a result, sales and profit projections in a skeletal plan are already prepared for a detailed 1-year budget. This facilitates the preparation of the 1-year budget or profit-plan on a soundly conceived basis. All the strategic aspects are essentially resolved as ample time has been allotted to the strategic thinking.

With minor imperfections, IMC has operated on this basis for two consecutive years. We pioneered this approach without the benefit of observing the DOD. After studying DOD practice, it sharpened our comprehension, enabling us to do a better job.

Our company identified 9 missions of interest (as shown in Figure 16-6), several where our present involvement was relatively minimal, but our goals ambitious. The DOD coincidentally also has 9. Although IMC has been essentially a mining company, even before we instituted market-mission planning we had significantly progressed toward a greater emphasis on market orientation. Examination of our motives and purpose from a mission viewpoint leads to the obvious conclusion that we're in business to serve customers. Consequently, our thinking must be oriented to the market environment, rather than an emphasis on our internal structure and skills. Our thoughts must give dominant attention to the *market* challenges. Corporations possess certain "internal" opportunities (e.g., process cost reduction), but the majority of our opportunities will exist "externally."

With improved insight, we realized our product-markets fell into three distinct market groupings: agricultural, industrial, and consumer. Segmenting this further, we easily identified a prime mission for plant nutrition —or fertilizer, the latter being our largest business, and one with a tremendous demand growth rate. Other missions were also identified, e.g., animal health and nutrition, and foundry supply (as shown in Figure 16-7). Additionally, we were involved in specialty foods and flavors. Ac'cent, a flavor enhancer, is one of our products. This change in perspective influenced our thinking. We found ourselves analyzing possibilities for future growth with a new discernment.

Secretary McNamara initiated planning in "program-packages" around his DOD missions. His method is to maintain a book in which all pertinent master plans are contained. Plans for any given mission are in this book on his desk. Though it is under security restrictions, we can speculate on its contents. What might be in such a book and what should an analogous industrial program-package contain? First, a program-package ought to possess a *charter* which states the scope of the mission as well as the objectives to be fulfilled. What is the vital difference between objectives and goals? Objectives are timeless, immeasurable, without quantification. Goals are measurable and possess a time parameter as well. In addition, the charter should contain a "product-line concept" as cited in Table 16-3. Many commercial development authors profess that a product-line should establish its own "ecological niche" in the market place, i.e., that management should strive to offer unique customer values. What proprietary directions for growth are desirable? What pioneering aims are sought?

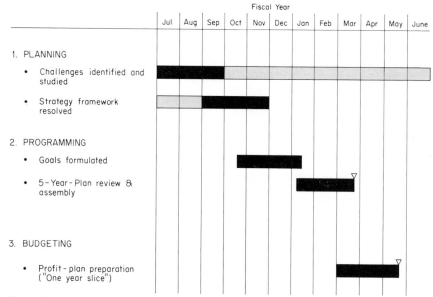

Figure 16-5   Annual planning calendar (3 steps).

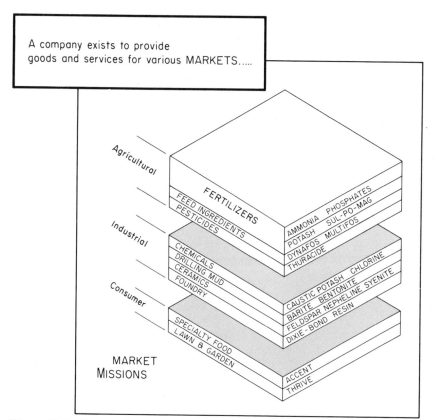

Figure 16-6   Horizontal mission "slices."

INTERNATIONAL MINERALS & CHEMICAL CORPORATION

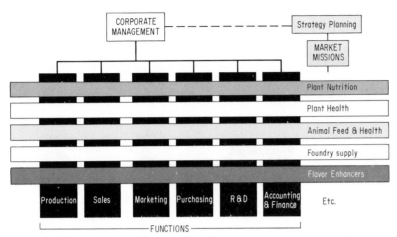

Figure 16-7 IMC mission "crosscut" on functions.

TABLE 16-3   MISSION "PROGRAM-PACKAGE" PLANNING CHECKLIST

CHARTER
Scope/Purpose/Objectives
Product-Line Concept
  Unique "values" offered
  Proprietary Directions
  New-Frontier Aims

POSITION (Present & Future)
Industry Structure & Character
Profit Sources
Product Life-Cycle Status
Market Share & Area
Capacity Utilization etc.

ATTRIBUTES (or Capabilities)
Strengths
Weaknesses

ENVIRONMENT (Present & Future)
Market Demand Outlook
Competition and Price
Distribution Channels
Changing Technology
Economy Trends
Regulatory Constraints
Community Constraints

IMPACT ON IMC
Problems & Needs ⎫
Threats   ⎬ Priorities in Response?
Opportunities   ⎭

MOMENTUM—PRESENT OPERATIONS
Prospects/Goals
Premises
P&L Summary

BUSINESS DEVELOPMENT ACTION—
PROGRAMS
Response to Attributes ⎫
                         ⎬ How?
Response to Challenges ⎭
Alternatives Considered/Selected
Resource "Handling"
  Capital Projects
  Geographical Expansion
  Raw Material Needs
  Services & Merchandising
  Acquisition Goals
  Financial Demands

TECHNICAL PROGRAM
Support
  Cost reduction
  Product improvement
  Sales service
  Market application development
Innovative

ORGANIZATION—NEEDS & PLANS

GOALS
Sales   ⎫
        ⎬ Performance (& Comparison w/others)
Profits ⎭

QUESTIONS: Completeness? Soundness? How
  Execute?

Next, it's desirable to understand your basic *position* through conduct of an audit. What's your participation in the industry structure? Where are the greatest profit margins? What's the product life-cycle status of each product? What market share do the products possess? How well are existing capacities being utilized? Next, the relevant *environment* must be examined. It's vital that management look outward to be aware of the rapidly changing environment in which the company exists. What is the market demand outlook for the product-line?

What are the present distribution channels, and the possibilities of advantageously altering those channels? What impact is changing technology going to have? In the Annual Planning Calendar, the first step involves the creation of a technological forecast as well as a market audit/forecast. These analyses lead to the identification of corporate *attributes,* i.e., strengths and weaknesses in resources and capabilities.

We must then ascertain our relative position in this ever-changing environment. What are the problems, needs, threats, and opportunities? What are the most important challenges?

Next, we must establish what our *momentum* is going to achieve. What are the prospects anticipated? Are we going to have continued growth? Or do we have some major product that will become obsolete? What are the premises or assumptions behind this projection? A profit and loss summary based on our momentum must then be assembled on a year-by-year basis. In business and sales development, what will we be striving to accomplish above and beyond our momentum? How will we respond to our attributes? How will we respond to the challenges that we have identified? But, most importantly, how will we manipulate our limited resources for maximum profit? What capital investments should we make and where? Which should have priority? What degree of raw material insurance is desirable? This question is particularly vital to a mining company because of limited mineral reserves. What are the financing demands from this total program?

What level of technical expenditures is justified, both for product-line support, and for innovative possibilities? What program

balance is desirable? Are there any "gaps" in the total program? Next, what are the organizational needs, training plans, and recruiting requirements? And finally, what are the goals for sales and profits? Most important, what's the performance level of return on investment, return on sales, so that we may compare one mission versus the other? What's the return on the incremental investments that we're planning to install, so that we can determine in which mission our capital will be most productive? In review, the manager should ask himself: Is it complete? Is it soundly conceived? How satisfactorily is the organization prepared to execute the plans?

Our planning organization at the corporate-level issues to the various divisions a "call" for plans and goals with guideline formats. It is preferable *not* to *do* the planning, but to assist, guide, and stimulate those who must execute mission strategy. Our staff does work closely with division planners in attempting to resolve appropriate courses of action. An indispensable component of our corporate planning and development division is a sizeable operations research department. In particular, the use of operations research tools and techniques must be initiated at the corporate level first in order to demonstrate to others their usefulness.

The "program-package" contents then as finally condensed and assembled contains about 9–10 pages for each mission:

1 The charter and mission attributes.
2 The company's relative position summarized.
3 The future environment described.
4 A summary of strategy statements, i.e., what we're striving to accomplish.
5 Specific sales goals, the capital allocations, and the anticipated performance.
6 Acquisition criteria, and prospects ranked in order of priority.
7 A sequenced action-plan; and finally,
8 What we term our "green-arrow" diagram.

(It is simply a means to illustrate the items this program supports plus an identification of other corporate activities which are synergistically linked, e.g., logistical investment opportunities.)

Studies of the *process* of planning in the DOD also have been of great assistance. Two professors from Cornell, F. E. Gilmore and R. G. Brandenberg analyzed the thought process used by the Army War College, (Reference 3), and constructed a network diagram for analogous corporate mission planning.

Though not utilized precisely as designed, it has been of significant help in understanding the total corporate planning process. The fundamental step-by-step procedure is as follows: First, what are the challenges facing the corporation? Next, how do these affect our missions, e.g., what justification is there to add new missions? What are the desired missions? What are the attainable goals to be sought? What are the competitive strategies to follow? And finally, what action-plans are necessary to implement these strategies?

The term strategy has been used repeatedly here. What do we mean? It may be defined simply as: "How best to deploy limited resources in order to maximize profits in the changing environment, against competition, in pursuit of goals." Note the resemblance to the military definition of strategy.

This definition is useful to our understanding of the planning task in a number of ways. The planner must determine how to allocate (and even control) the way resources are used. Figure 16-8 illustrates resources as the vertical slices of the cube.

Management has these four fundamental strategies at its fingertips: diversification; product development; market development; market penetration, per Figure 16-9. Around these fundamentals, we at IMC have created a system of plans, which illustrates the interrelationships and hierarchy of these plans. This system helps to clarify the jurisdictional authority and responsibility within the total plan. Fundamental function however, of the corporate planning organization is a "call" for sales and profit goals to be sought by the divisions for present products. This is accomplished in the programming (2nd) phase of the annual corporate planning calendar.

In the task of resource allocation, we, as managers, must maneuver these resources, allocating them rationally to the different market or product missions. With which ones must the corporate planner be most concerned? The

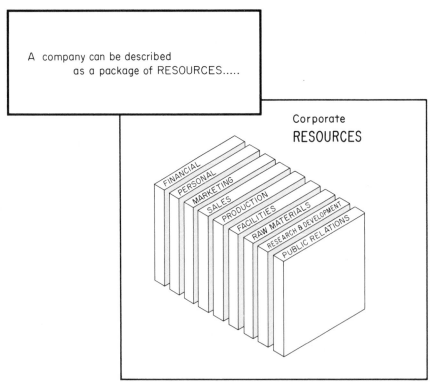

A company can be described as a package of RESOURCES.....

Corporate **RESOURCES**

FINANCIAL
PERSONAL
MARKETING
SALES
PRODUCTION
FACILITIES
RAW MATERIALS
RESEARCH & DEVELOPMENT
PUBLIC RELATIONS

Figure 16-8   Vertical resource slices.

TABLE 16-4   RESOURCE ALLOCATIONS

MUST BE ESTABLISHED FOR—

ACQUISITION CAPABILITIES

NEW CAPITAL INVESTMENTS AND
JOINT VENTURES

R&D PROGRAM EMPHASIS
POSTURE   OFFENSIVE
DEFENSIVE

MARKETING EMPHASIS
MOST PROFITABLE PRODUCTS
UTILIZE INCREMENTAL CAPACITY

MANPOWER FOR NEW BUSINESS
DEVELOPMENT

most critical are listed in Table 16-4. First, where will we strive to make acquisitions? (Obviously, we can't consummate acquisitions in *all* fields.) Second, which missions deserve the lion's share of our capital investment monies? Next, where are we going to place our emphasis in R&D, and in marketing? Where will we allocate expensive business development people with their creative, entrepreneurial talent?

Certainly, one of the more important allocation tasks is capital budgeting. All capital plans are processed through our department before they're scheduled for review and final approval by executive management. Our budgeter-planner reviews all major proposals with appropriate experts. If necessary, projects are postponed, revised or perhaps cancelled.

The Capital budgeting problem may be best illustrated per Figure 16-10. A corporation has a limited source of funds and MUST try to obtain the best possible rate-of-return. The corporate planner must determine where the funds cut-off line should fall. He must pose this question: Does the corporation possess ample opportunities to warrant moving this cut-off out to the right. If not, why not?

IMC then has been utilizing the mission concept, finding it quite useful in turning our thinking "outward" to the ever-changing environment.

LESSON 2 FOR THE CORPORATE PLANNER

Another of the DOD approaches useful to industry planners is their application of operations research principles to complex strategy research questions. Within 3 weeks after Robert McNamara assumed his Secretary of Defense duties, he produced what are popularly called his "76 trombones." These were seventy-odd questions, each beginning with "why." Why are you doing this? Why couldn't it be done in a cheaper, more effective way? He assigned responsibility for each question, asked for the answers within 3 weeks. These were important fundamental questions. From these answers he concluded that changes were urgently needed.

Much publicity was produced recently when McNamara questioned the need for air-

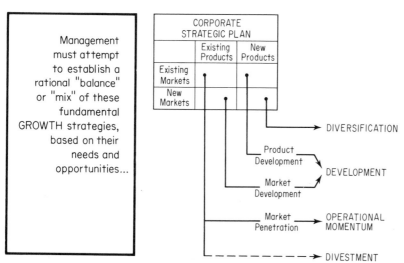

Figure 16-9   Four fundamental growth strategies.

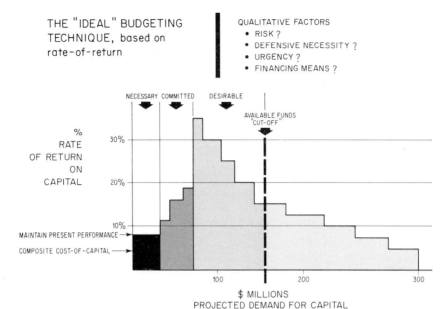

THE "IDEAL" BUDGETING TECHNIQUE, based on rate-of-return

QUALITATIVE FACTORS
- RISK ?
- DEFENSIVE NECESSITY ?
- URGENCY ?
- FINANCING MEANS ?

NECESSARY   COMMITTED   DESIRABLE

AVAILABLE FUNDS "CUT-OFF"

%
RATE
OF RETURN
ON
CAPITAL

30%

20%

10%

MAINTAIN PRESENT PERFORMANCE →

COMPOSITE COST-OF-CAPITAL →

100   200   300

$ MILLIONS
PROJECTED DEMAND FOR CAPITAL

Figure 16-10

craft carriers suggesting their vulnerability perhaps outdated their usefulness. He turned the operations research group to studying this query. Naturally, Navy top leaders were terribly upset. I do not know what the answer proposed or concluded. Obviously, the Defense establishment is not going to abandon aircraft carriers tomorrow, although, they may have some longer-term plans. But, McNamara did ask that and similar questions on military strategy, weapons systems cost/effectiveness, and administrative cost reduction.

The following quotation is taken from one of the research articles (Reference 4) on McNamara:

> McNamara is called the virtual master of the Defense Department, the greatest managerial genius of our times.

What is his secret? Answer: The question *Why,* sent to his staff and the military with a deadline for the answers. The study of these questions, mainly strategic in nature, and the asking of more questions, keeps these people thinking and responding with adequate programs. Part of the McNamara technique is to write his questions and insist on written answers. The Secretary maintains on his desk a black, looseleafed notebook containing his annual list of 120 of the most basic questions.

Each February they go out to his advisers. The answers are due the end of the summer, when they will be the basis of his changes in the five year program-budget.

This question posing is a very useful managerial tool. Some of the problems are so complex that McNamara assigns them to a study group, the operations research group. This small group is headed by Dr. Alain Enthoven, who recently has attained much prominence. His title is Deputy Assistant Secretary of Defense for Systems Analysis.

Recently, Dr. Enthoven (Reference 5) cited his fundamental task as:

> Systems Analysis can best be described as a continuing dialogue between the policy maker and the systems analyst, in which the policy-maker (McNamara), asks for alternative solutions to his problems; while the analyst attempts to clarify the conceptual framework in which the decisions must be made, to define alternative possible objectives and criteria, and to explore in as clear terms as possible (and quantitatively), the cost and effectiveness of these courses of action.

That quotation seems particularly descriptive and clear. Fortunately, IMC's chairman and chief executive officer, a graduate Industrial Engineer, sympathizes and understands the values of applying mathematics to complex business problems. IMC has used these techniques in mine planning for more than a decade. We next turned the application of quantitative analysis to marketing strategy questions. As shown in Figure 16-11, an econometric model was created for world phosphate rock supply-demand about three years ago. To gather the required inputs, skilled people were actually sent over to North Africa, to Jordan, to Morocco and other sources where phosphate is mined. A geologist was even assigned to view operations in the South Sea Islands of the Pacific. With input facts gathered from many sources, we estimated our competitors' costs and volumes from numerous mining sources distributed to markets in 45 countries. From this analysis, we ascertained our delivered cost advantages in certain markets. It would have been nearly impossible to have assimilated or manipulated this information without our computer.

The Defense Department civilian staff has been severely criticized on their extensive use of computers for problem solving. To place the use of computers in proper perspective, this quotation by Assistant Secretary of Defense Charles Hitch (Reference 6) in response to that criticism seems particularly apropos:

It cannot be stated too frequently or emphasized enough that economic choice is a way of looking at problems and does not necessarily depend on the use of any analytical aids. Computational devices are quite likely to be useful in analysis of complex problems, but there are many problems in which they have not proved particularly useful, where, nevertheless, it is rewarding to array alternatives and think through their implications in terms of objectives and cost. Where mathematical models and computations are useful, they are in no sense alternatives to, or rivals of good intuitive judgment. They supplement and complement it. Judgment is always of critical importance in designing the analysis, choosing the alternatives to be compared, and selecting the criterion.

LESSON 3 FOR THE CORPORATE PLANNER

Fundamental to the planning task is an understanding of the stepwise thought process to be applied in problem solving. Table 16-5 "Commander's Estimate of Situation" (Reference 7) stems from an Army field manual. It addresses itself to mission planning as a commander analyzes a given situation; identifies

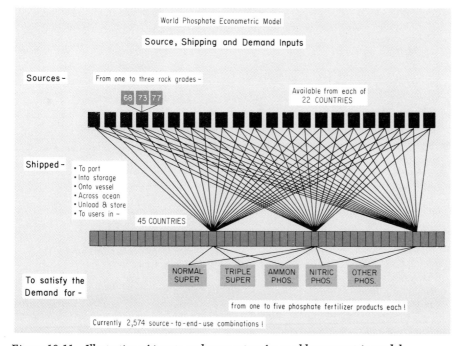

Figure 16-11   Illustration of inputs *and parameters for world econometric model.*

the possible alternatives; compares these courses-of-action; determines the best, and translates this into an action-plan. An unqualified comprehension of these steps is quite essential.

Table 16-6 illustrates the "attack" procedure of operations researchers in solving a problem.

There are other analogous problem solving techniques: as shown in Table 16-7, the weapons systems analyst solves his problems by starting with an identification of military needs.

Systems engineers have developed the most sophisticated methodology. After looking at all the thought processes that various disci-

TABLE 16-5   COMMANDER'S ESTIMATE OF SITUATION

1. MISSION
   task statement & purpose

2. THE SITUATION & COURSES-OF-ACTION
   gather relevant facts
   list difficulties
   list feasible courses-of-action

3. ANALYSIS OF OPPOSING COURSES-OF-ACTION
   deduce consequences
   determine strengths & weaknesses inherent in each course-of-action

4. COMPARISON OF COURSES-OF-ACTION
   deduce relative merits

5. DECISION
   select best alternative
   translate into complete statement
   who
   what
   when
   where
   how
   why

TABLE 16-6   EXAMPLES OF STEPS IN PROBLEM SOLVING BY VARIOUS DISCIPLINES

Major Steps	Military Strategy	Operations Research
1	—	—
2	Situation observed	—
3	—	Problem identification
4	Mission description	Problem formulation
5	Situation objectives	Construct model
6	Identify all feasible courses of action	Derive model solution
7	Analysis of each course	Test model & solution
8	Compare	—
9	Decision on best	Establish controls
10	—	Report results
11	—	—
12	Action-plan assembled	—

TABLE 16-7   ADDED EXAMPLES OF STEPS IN PROBLEM-SOLVING

Major Steps	DOD Weapons Systems	Systems Engineering
1	(Strategy & Tactics Analysis)	—
2	—	Environmental/Needs Research
3	Military need identified	Unsatisfied need identified
4	Need specified	Problem definition
5	Objectives defined	Select objective criteria
6	Concept proposals solicited	System synthesis alternatives
7	Conceptual & feasibility studies	Systems analysis
8	Cost/effectiveness comparison	Comparison
9	Selection of best	Selection
10	System Package-Plan defined	Communicating results in prospectus
11	—	—
12	Action-Planning	Action-Planning

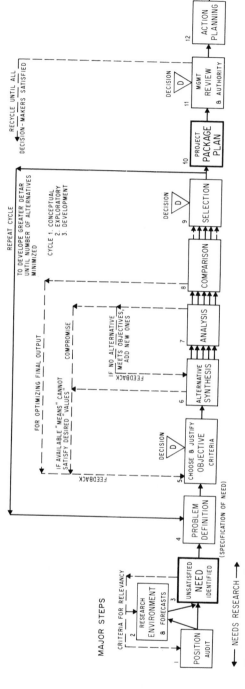

Figure 16-12 A derived problem-solving procedure.

plines apply to the solution of problems, the systems engineering technique was most valuable, as was the military strategy approach. But, the facet with particular merit is comprehension of the "needs research" concept (Reference 8).

Where does the definition of a problem, need, or opportunity begin? At what starting point? Usually it begins by perceptual awareness of the company's position or capability; this awareness plus an imperfect knowledge of the environment precipitates the identification of a problem or opportunity as illustrated in Figure 16-12, "Methodology for Project Exploratory Planning (P-E-P)."

Preferably, relevant facts pertaining to the company's position in the forecasted environment must be examined to identify a problem, need, or opportunity. This might be termed *needs* research. The word "challenge" is more suitable as it covers all the terms: problems, needs, threats, and opportunities.

In Step 5, objectives must be precisely chosen and justified. Step 6 is the process of creating and/or inventing alternatives; Step 7 and 8, their analysis and comparison; Step 9, the selection of the best course-of-action; Step 10 requires the assembly into a "package-plan;" Step 11 is the final decision point before proceeding. The final step is action-planning/scheduling, a useful point to apply network planning techniques.

IMC's Corporate Planning & Development Division organization was designed on the basis of a sound understanding of this process. Emphasis should be on the establishment

of priorities, more clearly demonstrated in Figure 16-13, "Management by Priority-of-Challenge" where the managerial problem is linked with the determination of budget levels. Figure 16-14 shows the organization and broad responsibilities of our planning and development division, a sizeable corporate-level staff division, employing 25 professionals. Notice that the first department consists of an environment analysis group, with primarily market-research type skills.

The second department, strategic planning primarily provides leadership to the assembly of IMC's 5-year plan. Next, a venture development group which endeavors to precipitate appropriate projects, particularly those that the operating divisions are not organized to execute. Finally, a management planning department, which predominantly performs operations research type studies. This division, with its complement of high caliber people is having a sizeable impact on the corporation's activity. Note the striking similarities between this organization and those in McNamara's DOD.

LESSON 4 FOR THE CORPORATE PLANNER

The use of logic sequence network diagrams provides yet an additional lesson from the study of DOD planning techniques. We are in the midst of building a $58 million plant, as a joint venture with Standard Oil of California and E. I. D. Parry of India on the east coast of India. In order to more efficiently execute

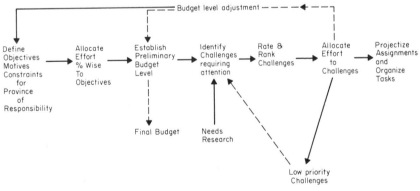

Need: Optimum allocation of effort to assure systematic concentration on the most important problems and opportunities.

Figure 16-13   Management by "priority-of-challenge."

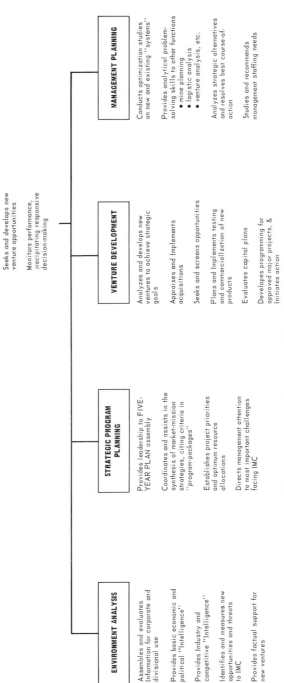

Figure 16-14 Functions and responsibilities—corporate planning and development.

CORPORATE PLANNING & DEVELOPMENT DIVISION

Provides environment "Intelligence" and measures Impact on IMC

Develops strategic plans responsive to challenges

Determines optimum resource allocations

Seeks and develops new venture opportunities

Monitors performance, precipitating responsive decision-making

ENVIRONMENT ANALYSIS

Assembles and evaluates Information for corporate and divisional use

Provides basic economic and political "Intelligence"

Provides Industry and competitive "Intelligence"

Identifies and measures new opportunities and threats to IMC

Provides factual support for new ventures

STRATEGIC PROGRAM PLANNING

Provides leadership to FIVE-YEAR PLAN assembly

Coordinates and assists in the synthesis of market-mission strategies, citing criteria in "program-packages"

Establishes project priorities and optimum resource allocations

Directs management attention to most important challenges facing IMC

VENTURE DEVELOPMENT

Analyzes and develops new ventures to achieve strategic goals

Appraises and Implements acquisitions

Seeks and screens opportunities

Plans and Implements testing and commercialization of new products

Evaluates capital plans

Developes programming for approved major projects, & Initiates action

MANAGEMENT PLANNING

Conducts optimization studies on new and existing "systems"

Provides analytical problem-solving skills to other functions
● mine planning
● logistic analysis
● venture analysis, etc.

Analyzes strategic alternatives and resolves best course-of-action

Studies and recommends management staffing needs

this project in its early phases, we created a network task sequence for the general manager. Say for example, the first task is approval by the Indian government for a license; the next task may be hiring a sales manager; the next, to conduct a market seeding program, and so on. These steps are predetermined for him in the necessary sequence and inter-relationship. It gives the manager a discipline of stepwise tasks as he progresses in the construction of the plant and effectively marketing its output. This technique is an adaptation of a similar method devised by Boeing Aircraft and the Air Force (Reference 9) for more effective contract liaison, re: Figure 16-15.

Network sequence diagrams have an added advantage when used to minimize time through the use of the well publicized Navy PERT or critical-path planning techniques. For example, we have utilized this in the case of an ammonia plant we recently built on the Mississippi River, Nitrin, Inc., a $22.5 million joint venture with Northern Natural Gas of Omaha. This is the technique first created and used in development of the Polaris Missile.

Note that we *not* only sequence planned the construction of the plant, but, also scheduled

all merchandising programs, and a build-up of the market distribution system.

LESSON 5 FOR THE CORPORATE PLANNER

Now for the last lesson from the DOD management. In the huge, complex organization of the DOD, McNamara perceived the necessity to expedite decision making. There were excessive committee meetings, too many reports being passed around, tending to delay decisions on program changes. Consequently, a specially designed room was created under the management of the Office of Programming, who are also in charge of maintaining the "running" 5-year plan. In this room are four Vu-graph type projectors that display against 4 adjacent screens, as shown in Figure 16-16. On one side of the room is a tramrail which brings forward on floor-to-ceiling charts, the approved program package data. On the opposite side, the tramrail displays added posters that relate to the specific elements under examination. The decision-making party sits in the center area, and can refer to the side panels for perspective data. The visualization is flexible and provides needed support for the proposal or problem under examination.

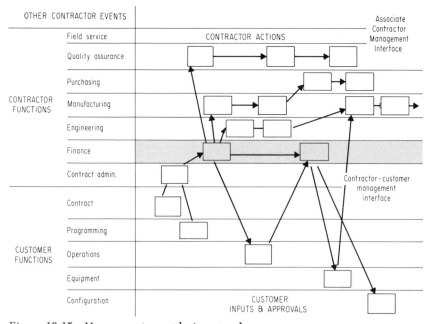

Figure 16-15 Management event-logic network.

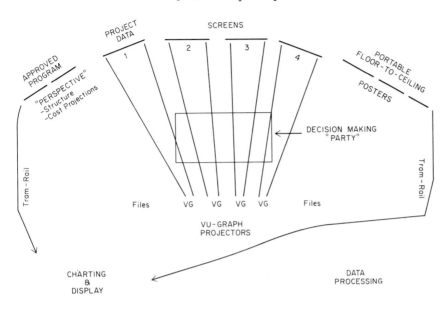

Figure 16-16

There is a computer located behind the projectors in the preparation area which also contains the charting and display requirements. The DOD planners assert that they have the capability, if somebody asks a resource allocation trade-off question, to run it through the computer, type the answer, prepare a visual, and project it back on the screen in seven minutes time.

It can be safely claimed that there are many values in observing DOD management practices. Lesson 1, mission planning, its application, and the organization related to it are useful concepts. Lesson 2, there are significant values in observing the use of quantitative analyses techniques in response to posed questions. Lesson 3, there are values in Needs Research as an unrecognized starting point for problem solving. Lesson 4, logic sequence networks are valuable tools for project execution and coordination. Lesson 5, decision making "centers" are worthwhile devices for expediting review/approval decisions in complex organizations.

Yes, our Defense Department is still providing useful "spin-offs" for industrial application.

References

1. "Programming System for Office of Secretary of Defense"; OASD (c) Programming, Directorate for Systems Planning, 25 June 1962.

2. *Missiles and Rockets Magazine,* Vol. 12, No. 12, March 1963, page 30.

3. Gilmore, F. F. and Brandenburg, R. G., "Anatomy of Corporate Planning"; *Harvard Business Review,* Vol. 40, No. 6, Nov./Dec. 1962, page 61–69.

4. "Secretary McNamara's One Magic Word"; *This Week Magazine,* 4 August 1963.

5. "The Whizziest Kid"; *Time Magazine,* 28 June 1963.

6. Hitch, Charles J., "The New Approach to Management in the U. S. Defense Department"; *Management Science,* Volume 9, No. 1, October 1962, page 1–8.

7. *Defense Department Staff Officers' Field Manual,* FM 101–5, (1960 edition), page 142.

8. Smalter, D. J., "Management by Priority-of-Challenge"; *Chemical Engineering Progress,* Vol. 60, No. 6, June 1964, page 25–27.

9. Kast, F. E., et al., "Boeing's Minuteman Missile Program," *Science Technology, and Management,* McGraw-Hill Book Company, 1963, page 233.

SECTION 4

PLANNING, PROGRAMMING, AND BUDGETING

Elements of several basic concepts—the systems view, long-range planning, and formal decision analysis—have been combined into a framework for decision-making at the highest levels of the Federal government. The institution of a planning, programming, and budgeting system (PPBS) in the Federal government resulted from its successful application in the Department of Defense. Subsequently, these ideas have been adopted at the state, city, and other governmental levels. In business similar ideas have been applied using terms dictated by the firm's product orientation.

The concept of planning-programming-budgeting puts organizational strategy into the proper context. Long-range planning should encompass all the functional areas of the enterprise; the concept of a program and a budget facilitates the relating of objectives and the means of attaining these objectives. Also, planning-programming-budgeting forces recognition of what the organization is trying to achieve both in near-term and long-term, and the alternative ways of achieving ends.

The PPBS was instituted in the Federal government to obviate management difficulties which are succinctly spelled out by the original government directive:*

* *Bureau of the Budget Bulletin 66–3, "Planning-Programming-Budgeting," October 12, 1965.*

> *... program review for decision-making has frequently been concentrated within too short a period; objectives of agency programs and activities have too often not been specified with enough clarity and concreteness; accomplishments have not always been specified concretely; alternatives have been insufficiently presented for consideration by top management; in a number of cases the future year costs of present decisions have not been laid out systematically enough; and formalized planning and systems analysis have had too little effect on budget decisions.*

Essential to the Federal government's PPBS is an output-oriented program structure *which provides data on all of the activities of each agency and which spells out the relationship of each to overall objectives. Complementing this program structure are* analyses and comparisons of alternative objectives and of alternative ways of achieving objectives. *The third essential element of PPBS is a* time cycle *which provides analytic results, information, and recommendations at a time which facilitates decision-making.*

The other aspect of timing which is critical to PPBS is the compilation of the costs and benefits derived from various activities over a meaningful time span. This means that projections of future costs and benefits must be made. More importantly however, it means that these factors need be considered at the time at which programs are to be embarked upon. *PPBS provides the framework through which such timely consideration can be given to program decisions.*

READING 17

A CONCEPTUAL FRAMEWORK FOR THE PROGRAM BUDGET*

Arthur Smithies

I. BUDGETING, PROGRAMMING AND POLICY

The need for program budgeting arises from the indissoluble connection between budgeting and the formation and conduct of national policy, or the policy of a state, a city, or a town, as the case may be. Governments, like private individuals or organizations, are constrained by the scarcity of economic resources at their disposal. Not only the extent to which they pursue particular objectives, but the character of the objectives themselves, will be influenced by the resources available. On the other hand, the extent to which the government desires to pursue its objectives will influence the resources it makes available to itself by taxation or other means. Budgeting is the process by which objectives, resources, and the interrelations among them are taken into account to achieve a coherent and com-

* Reprinted with permission from The RAND Corporation, RM-4271-RC, September, 1964, The RAND Corporation, Santa Monica, California.

prehensive program of action for the government as a whole. Program budgeting involves the use of budgetary techniques that facilitate explicit consideration of the pursuit of policy objectives in terms of their economic costs, both at the present time and in the future.

To be more specific, a modern government is concerned with the broad objectives of Defense; Law and Order; Health, Education and Welfare; and with Economic Development, together with the conduct of current business operations, notably the Post Office. No government, whatever its resources, can avoid the need for compromises among these objectives. No country can defend itself fully against all possible external threats. It takes certain risks with respect to defense for the sake of increasing the domestic welfare of its citizens. It must also compromise between the present and the future. The more actively it promotes defense and welfare at the present time, the more it may retard the long-run economic development of the country, by curtailing both private and public investment in the future. The country will be frustrated in the pursuit of all its objectives if it neglects the effective maintenance of law and order. Yet, compromises are made in this area also. No country supports a police force that will detect every crime, and no country enforces every law up to the limit.

Moreover, the character of each major program will depend on the total resources the government can appropriate to its purposes. A small country (at the present time) cannot afford nuclear weapons. Few countries can, or at any rate do, attempt to educate as wide a segment of their population as does the United States. However, countries may vary in their willingness to pursue their national objectives. With much smaller natural resources, the Soviet Union is prepared to make efforts comparable to the United States in both the fields of defense and education.

The task of making the necessary compromises among various objectives is the function of budgeting. To make those compromises it is necessary that the various government activities be expressed in terms of a common denominator, and the only common denominator available is money. It is difficult to compare the relative merits of an additional military division and an additional university. It is often more feasible to compare the relative merits of spending an additional billion dollars in one direction or the other. But to make that comparison it is necessary to know how much an additional billion dollars will add to military strength and how much to university education. While defense and education cannot be measured in simple quantitative terms, quantitative information can throw light on the consequences of spending money in various directions.

There are, however, a multitude of ways in which money can be spent on defense or education. To make intelligent comparisons, each of these major functions must be broken down into meaningful subfunctions. Modern defense at least requires considerations in terms of strategic forces and limited war forces. Education must be broken down at least into primary, secondary, and tertiary education. Major programs should thus be considered in terms of sub-programs, and at the end of the scale one reaches the manpower, material, and supplies used by the government in support of these activities. Such considerations and calculations should lead to the concept of resources (money) used in optimal ways to achieve policy objectives.

Some government decisions relate only to the immediate future in the sense that if they turn out to be wrong, they can be readily reversed. Others, however, relate to a distant future that can be only dimly foreseen. Pure research, particularly, is in this category, since its consequences are in the nature of the case unknown. But governments nevertheless must make critical decisions with respect to the resources they devote to particular kinds of research as well as to research in the aggregate. At a lower order of difficulty, critical decisions with respect to transportation, resource development and the development of weapons systems relate to the next decade rather than the next year. Budgeting is essentially a matter of preparing for the future, but modern budgeting involves long-range projections into a highly uncertain future.

The basic point of view of this Memorandum is that a government can determine its policies most effectively if it chooses rationally among alternative courses of action, with as full knowledge as possible of the implications of those alternatives. The requirement of choice is imposed on it by the fact that any government is limited by the scarcity of resources. It is fundamental to our culture that rational choice is better than irrational choice. The government must choose not only among various courses of government action, but also between the government's total program and the private sector of the economy. The task of choice is not rendered easier by the fact that a substantial part of the government's program is designed to affect the future performance of the private economy.

Programming and budgeting are the focus of the process of comparison and coordination. In line with the foregoing paragraphs it involves:

1 Appraisals and comparisons of various government activities in terms of their contributions to national objectives.
2 Determination of how given objectives can be attained with minimum expenditure of resources.
3 Projection of government activities over an adequate time horizon.
4 Comparison of the relative contribution of private and public activities to national objectives.

5 Revisions of objectives, programs, and budgets in the light of experience and changing circumstances.

These operations are inherent in any budgetary process. Program budgeting involves more explicit recognition of the need to perform them than has been traditional. It also involves the application of new analytical techniques as an aid to the exercise of the human judgment on which choices must ultimately rest.

It should be clear from this statement of the budgetary problem that the traditional distinction between policy-making and budgeting, or between setting of goals and deciding on how to attain them, is inadequate and misleading. While the government can have a general desire and intention to defend the country, it cannot have a defense objective that is operationally meaningful until it is aware of the specific military implications of devoting resources to defense; and as part of that awareness, it should know the consequences of using defense resources in alternative ways. The question of allocative efficiency is thus intimately bound up with the question of the determination of goals. An adequate programming system must serve both purposes.

Governments can differ by temperament and institutional arrangements in the relative weights they give to the formulation and pursuit of goals, and the attainment of efficiency in the sense of minimizing costs of particular activities. A "crash program" devised with scant attention to efficiency may reach the moon in 1970. Preoccupation with efficiency may delay the successful event until 1980. However, crash programs can fail utterly, through lack of consideration of factors that would emerge in deliberate analysis.

Even in World War II, however, the overriding condition of scarcity placed limits on the pursuit of military abundance. As mobilization proceeded, competition between military output and civilian supply became acute. While many public and private investment projects could be deferred, supplies of canned foods, clothing, and transportation had to be maintained for the sake of the war effort itself. Basic materials—notably steel, copper, and aluminum—and manpower were closely allocated. Special programs were set up for rubber and petroleum. Even though allocation through financial controls receded into the background, the need for efficient allocation asserted itself strongly in other ways.

On the other hand, the successful strategy of World War II consisted of producing more of everything that was needed, so that military commanders could concentrate on military victory unhampered by the limitations of scarcity.

The United States, nevertheless, had options denied to most other countries. The political radical can deride preoccupation with efficiency as a delaying tactic. Conservatives can emphasize it for the same reason. Other countries have less freedom of choice. The plans of many of the underdeveloped countries have been frustrated through failure to pay attention to the elementary economics of choice. Considerations of comparative advantage have been ignored as encouraging indiscriminate *import* substitution. Public enterprises have been inefficiently planned and operated. As a result of such experiences, realization is dawning that, from the point of view of development, the basic principles of efficient allocation cannot be ignored.

Since all governments are confronted with the problem of scarcity, the logic of the decision-making process is independent of the form of government, even though outcomes may differ widely. All governments are concerned with defense, welfare, development, and law and order. In an authoritarian government initial preferences among these objectives depend on the ambitions and values of a central authority. But authority is constrained to those among them by resource limitations, and by the fact that any authority is less than absolute in its ability to enforce its will on the people.

In a democratic government the process is more indirect. Democracies also depend on leadership, but they depend on democratic consent. Leaders must educate and respond to public opinion. They must propose programs that will serve the national interest and also maintain them in power. Whichever of these objectives is uppermost in their minds, the basic task of allocation remains; and its performance reflects the combined judgment of the leadership and the public, concerning the contribution of government expenditures to national objectives. The thesis of this Memorandum rests on the assumption that society benefits to the extent that such choices are made in the light of the fullest possible information concerning their implications.

II. PROGRAM BUDGETING IN THE FEDERAL GOVERNMENT

For half a century there has been dissatisfaction in the United States with traditional budgetary methods, and some notable improvements have been made. A brief survey of that history will help to indicate the possibilities, as well as the difficulties, of further improvement.

Traditionally, budgeting has been conducted in terms of executive departments and their subdivisions. The traditional method of reviewing a department budget is to scrutinize proposed increases or decreases in objects of expenditure, with particular emphasis on personnel of various grades, and with emphasis on supplies and equipment as the activities of the department dictate. Such a system has advantages from the point of view of administrative control and, in highly simplified situations, could meet the requirements set out above. To the extent that every department or subdivision performed an identifiable function, the total expenditures, and particularly changes in them, might serve as rough indicators of the government's program. In the pre-World War II Army, numbers of officers and men were better indicators than they are today. In the Department of Justice, changes in the number and grades of lawyers in the various divisions are some indication of changes in the orientation of the policy of the department. If such indicators are relied on, the task of the budget reviewer is simply to see to it that the Army does not house itself too comfortably or that the lawyers do not have too many secretaries.

The traditional method is not and never has been adequate. The name of a department or a bureau is not sufficient to describe what it does. Nor are numbers or types of personnel employed an adequate measure of the functions they perform. Furthermore, the traditional budget period of a single year throws little light on the significance of expenditures whose effects may be spread over the next decade.

The inadequacies of the traditional system, however, have long been apparent. As early as 1912, President Taft's Commission on Economy and Efficiency recommended drastic changes in existing procedures. The Commission stated:

> The best that a budget can do for the legislator is to enable him to have expert advice in thinking about policies to be determined. His review of the economy and efficiency with which work has been done should be based on facts set forth in the annual reports of expenditures which would supplement the budget.
>
> To the administrator (i.e., the head of an executive department) the advantage to be gained through a budget is the ability to present to the legislature and to the people, through the Chief Executive or someone representing the administration, a well-defined, carefully considered, lucidly expressed welfare program to be financed, and in presenting this, to support requests for appropriation with such concrete data as are necessary to the intelligent consideration of such a program.
>
> To the Executive (i.e., the President) the advantage to be gained lies in his ability to bring together the facts and opinions necessary to the clear formulation of proposals for which he is willing actively to work as the responsible officer. To the people the advantage is the fact that they are taken into the confidence of their official agents. Therein lie the practical use and purpose of the budget.

Consequently, the Commission proposed first, a comprehensive executive budget (which had not previously existed); secondly, a classification of the budget in terms of programs or functions, and also a classification based on the distinction between capital and current items; and, thirdly, thorough and systematic review of the budget *after the fact*. These innovations were to be added to the traditional budget, and resulted in a proposal of extraordinary complexity.

While the Commission laid the foundation for all subsequent reforms, the political climate of the time did not permit action. In fact, nothing was done until 1921, when the drive for economy after World War I produced the

Budget and Accounting Act of that year, which required the President to submit a comprehensive executive budget, and set up the Budget Bureau as the staff agency to assist him. The comprehensive budget was an essential step in achieving the comparison of alternatives in the executive branch, but the Act left departmental budgets and procedures for preparing them unchanged.

Further progress toward a program budget was delayed until after World War II, when the movement again gained impetus—a generation after the Taft Commission. In 1949 the Hoover Commission recommended that "the whole budgetary concept of the federal government should be refashioned by the adoption of a budget based upon functions, activities, and projects: this we designate a 'performance budget'." The recommendation was made a legislative requirement by the National Security Act Amendments of 1949 and the Budgeting and Accounting Act Procedures Act of 1950. The Second Hoover Commission in 1955 recommended a "program budget" and proposed improvements in the government accounting system that would facilitate budgeting on a cost basis.

The result has been significant change and improvement in the presentation and the format of the federal budget, and the change in format has produced a significant change in the methods by which the budget is prepared and considered both in the Executive Branch and with Congress. The old "greensheets" of detailed personnel requirements, which once formed the central pivot of budget examination, have now receded into the background, and are now included merely as an appendix to the President's Budget.

In the immediate postwar period, and of course before, personal services were the heart of the matter. Budget examination in both the Executive Branch and the Congress consisted mainly of "marking up" the greensheets. Even in a construction agency like the Bureau of Ships of the Navy, procurement of material appeared on a one-line item in the President's Budget, while details of personal services occupied 300 lines. Classification by activities was rudimentary; and in many bureaus at the present time the budget for each bureau is classified by objects and by significant activities.

The recent changes in classifications are by no means formalities. They reflect changes in the approach of budget officers and congressional committees to their tasks of review and appraisal. Able and conscientious efforts are being made throughout the government to appraise activities in terms of their effectiveness in promoting national objectives. In this respect the idea of program budgeting has been accepted in principle. The main problem at the moment is not to inject a new idea, but to improve on what has already been done, and there is still abundant room for improvement.

In two major respects there is still need for reconsideration or revision of previous practice. In the first place, programs or activities are still propounded and considered mainly within the limits of the existing bureaus or departments in which they occur. Even if two or more bureaus or departments conduct activities that are essentially complementary or competitive with each other, those activities are not considered together. To take some obvious examples: In agriculture, the price support program has to contend with a wheat surplus. At the same time, its research program is devising methods for increasing wheat production! At the departmental level, the failure to achieve coordination among the water-resource programs of Interior, the Corps of Engineers, and Agriculture has been a long standing embarrassment to the government. The President's Budget Message, however, is arranged in terms of major programs that cut across department lines. For instance, all expenditures in natural resources are grouped as a single major program, irrespective of what department conducts them. But this does not mean that decisions are made in a similar way.

A second major defect of the present budget is its short time span of one year. It is still mainly concerned with appropriations and expenditures for the succeeding year, and contains figures only for the year just completed, estimates for the current year, and for the year to which it relates. This may be adequate for many administrative activities, but, as pointed out above, it is thoroughly inadequate for procurement of long-lead items and for construction projects. Whether projections over a number of years should be published in the formal budget is an open question. But there can be little doubt that they should be available to the executive and congressional authorities who review the budget.

The Defense Budget is a special case that will be discussed in detail later. At this stage, it will suffice to indicate with great brevity what has been done since World War II. Despite the creation of the Department of Defense in 1947, the defense budget consisted essentially of budgets for the three separate Services. The total arrived at by the President and the Secretary of Defense was shared among the Services according to some fairly arbitrary formula, rather than by consideration of the contribution of the Services to the defense program as a whole or by consideration of programs that cut across Service lines.

In 1949, Congress ordered so-called "performance budgets" to be submitted for each Service. Prior to that time, budgets had been prepared for the Army and the Navy, based on estimates made by their technical services. In the Army, for instance, separate budgets were prepared for the Quartermaster Service, the Transportation Service, the Ordnance Service, and so forth. Such an arrangement had little merit from the point of view of determining requirements with reference to the mission of the Army.

The new "performance" budget adopted a new classification, which is now in use. The major headings are Military Personnel; Operation and Maintenance; Procurement; Military Construction; and Research, Development, Test and Evaluation.

From the point of view of relating the budget to national strategy, this arrangement has little apparent advantage over the old one. A budget constructed on these lines does not permit the Secretary of Defense or the President to tell what provision is being made to increase capacity to defend the United States, to engage in operations in Asia, and so forth. However, this budget is an improvement in some respects. It corresponds to major areas of general staff responsibility.

Moreover, it also makes some distinction between the present and the future. Military personnel and operation and maintenance are mainly concerned with current operation. Procurement and construction mainly relate to the investment in equipment for the future, while research and development relates to the more remote future. Thus, if each of the Services had a clear cut mission, a projection of the present budget over, say, a five-year period could give a coherent picture of military costs for each mission. There would still remain the vital problem of assessing the military effectiveness of the costs incurred.

In 1961, a major change was made by adding a programming system to the existing budget system. Since then decisions have been made on the basis of five-year programs relating to the defense program as a whole, regardless of Service distinctions. These decisions are subsequently translated into the existing annual budget categories for each Service. During the process of translation and compilation of the budget, minor but not major revisions are made. The President's Budget is presented on both a program basis and on a conventional basis for the budget period. The five-year projections are not published for general use.

The major programs are Strategic Retaliatory Forces, Continental Air and Missile Defense Forces, General Purpose Forces (including most of the Army and the Navy), Airlift and Sealift Forces, Reserve and National Guard Forces, Research and Development, and General Support. In addition, Retired Pay, Civil Defense, and Military Assistance are included as separate programs.

Budget and Program procedures in the Defense Department will be the subject of a separate paper. For the present, we shall be concerned with the logic of the program structure that has been adopted, as a complicated and revealing case study of the nature, the possibilities, and the limitations of program budgeting.

III. WHAT IS A PROGRAM?

In the federal government, the terms "program," "performance," "activity" and "function" are all used more or less interchangeably. While there may be shades of difference among them, there is no consistent pattern. Research, for instance, may be designated by some organizations as an activity and by others as a program. Program and performance are often used synonomously. But the federal budget often uses the term "program and performance." The performance budget of the Defense Department does not correspond to the present program structure. These ambiguities and inconsistencies of language reveal the ambiguities of the underlying situation. As we shall see, there are a number of criteria for the designation of an operation as a program. The defense program structure itself reveals a variety of criteria which will be discussed in a moment. Meanwhile light may be shed on the problem by beginning with a hypothetical example outside government.

Consider the question of the organization of a highly integrated automobile manufacturer, which not only produces automobiles, but also produces rubber, iron and steel. The objective of the corporation is to maximize its profits. But it is hard to imagine its conducting its operations simply by reference to that objective. If it produces several brand names, it is likely to have a separate program and separate organizations for each of them. Each brand name presumably is intended to appeal mainly to a separate section of the market. Or the company may, as General Motors does, put brands in active competition with each other.

Programming of final products is hardly likely to be sufficient. Increased demands for rubber and steel from the top do not immediately evoke increases in supply; this may not be forthcoming unless capacity to produce steel and rubber has been built in anticipation of increased demand for automobiles. Consequently the corporation would probably have both a steel and a rubber program that would attempt to anticipate final demands. Moreover, there would be no point in having separate steel and rubber programs for each of the final products. Errors could be avoided and economies achieved by having single organizations supply steel and rubber to the several final product divisions. Furthermore, those concerned with the manufacture of final products are unlikely to be expert in steel and rubber technology. The effective division of labor commends a vertical division of functions.

The long run future of the organization will depend on the research and development it conducts. Some research and development may be connected with specific brands, the production of which can be anticipated; in that event it can be included in the final product programs. But some research is of common benefit to all final products, and some will relate to the models of the future that will come into production beyond the horizon of any feasible production plans. Consequently, a separate research program is likely to be called for.

It should be noted from this example that the question of programming and that of organization are closely connected. A central management might control the entire operation, in which case the separate programs would aid it in its thinking about its problems. What is more likely is that the need to program will also pattern the administrative shape of the organization and will dictate some decentralization of authority.

Another example from outside government, very different from the corporation, is a liberal arts college. Its objectives are not to make money, and not directly to equip its students to make money. It does not measure its success by the incomes subsequently earned by its alumni—although it is not entirely uninterested in that subject. For objectives, it must rely on general statements, such as the advancement of knowledge and equipping its students for citizenship in a free society. Such general statements do not tell it what to teach or what to investigate. And it would not accept the view that its function is simply to teach students what they want to learn. Yet the college resources are limited. It must allocate its resources.

It solves its problems by setting up programs that it believes will throw light on its objectives. It thinks of its faculty as concerned broadly with science and the humanities, and with teaching and research within these categories. While it cannot define its objectives *precisely*, it believes that their attainment will be furthered by its performance in these areas.

The college begins with some allocation and then from year to year considers reallocations that it believes will further its (undefined) objectives. It may be able to make sensible choices among alternative courses of action, even though its objectives are not clearly defined.

In pursuing its policies, the administration of the university is subject to a number of constraints. It has to persuade its students to accept the relative emphasis it gives to science and the humanities, and its faculty the allocation between teaching and research. Otherwise, it may lose both students and faculty in competition with other institutions.

The programming problems of the college are not unlike those of government in fields such as defense or welfare. When government undertakes to produce the marketable goods, its problem is closer to that of the private business.

Let us now examine the new program structure of the Department of Defense. While we do not know precisely why that particular structure was adopted, it is instructive to guess at the possible reasons.

The structure clearly derives from the strategic doctrine that distinguishes between general war and limited war; and the view that the use of large strategic weapons for limited purposes is "unthinkable." It implies that one of the main programming tasks is to achieve the most effective balance between strategic and limited war forces.

Strategic Retaliatory Forces qualifies as a program for a number of reasons. First, it is directly related to a major objective of defense policy, and, in principle, requirements for these forces can be calculated from knowledge of the enemy threat and of the capability of our own weapons. Secondly, the program can be neatly broken down into a number of program elements—Polaris, Minuteman and manned bombers. These elements are to a large degree substitutes for each other, so that there is a problem of determining an optimum mix of the elements. Thirdly, the program cuts across service lines. The program concept thus serves as an instrument of coordination of the services.

Continental Defense could be regarded as an element of strategic deterrence. The main purpose of it at the present time is to protect and to warn the strategic forces; and when force requirements are reduced, the better the forces are defended. However, if extensive and effective defense of cities ever becomes a reality, continental defense would have more meaning as a separate program, although still linked to strategic concepts.

General Purpose Forces occupy about 35 per cent of the budget and include the forces designed to meet non-strategic attacks in the Western Hemisphere, in the Far East, in Southeast Asia—in fact, all over the world. The threat is not clearly defined, and neither are the requirements for meeting it. Clearly this program is of a very different character from the other two, and does not lend itself readily to analysis either in terms of its components or of its contribution to defense objectives. One possibility of improvement that suggests itself is that the program should be broken down on a regional basis; but this meets with the serious objection that forces can be transferred from one region to another, and one cannot predict whether threats will appear in isolation, in sequence, or simultaneously.

Airlift and Sealift is logically a component of general purpose forces. It is designed to increase mobility and hence permit economies with respect to the size of forces. It is presumably considered as a separate program because its components, airlift and sealift, should be considered as substitutes for each other, and the best mix should be achieved.

Research and Development is allocated to particular programs when it can be directly related to them. It is properly considered separately when it is conducted for purposes beyond the horizons of other programs.

The large item General Support, which includes nearly 30 per cent of the budget, includes not only items such as general overhead which in its nature cannot and should not be allocated to specific programs, but also an amount which it has not yet proved feasible to allocate.

Other programs such as Reserves and Military Assistance have presumably been considered separately for administrative or political reasons.

These comments on defense programming are not intended to disparage the important advances that have been made. They are intended, rather, to indicate the difficulties and the variety of criteria involved in breaking up a highly complicated operation into neat program categories.

Almost all the difficulties of devising a satisfactory program system arise in the field of international relations (apart from defense); and because of the complexity of the problem, budgeting and programming in this area is still in an unsatisfactory condition.

In the first place, the objectives of foreign policy are diverse, complicated, and amorphous. Only a few years ago the situation seemed simpler. Foreign policy appeared to consist of containing Russian expansion in Europe, ostracizing China, and promoting economic development elsewhere. With that degree of simplification three major programs suggest themselves. Political and military means would implement the first two, and economic aid the third. At the present time, Russia must be distinguished from the Eastern European Communist countries, which also must be distinguished from each other; our allies trade with China; Russia and China are active in the underdeveloped countries, and for our part, sharp distinctions must be drawn among Asia, Africa, and Latin America. Foreign programs must be devised with the realization that a simple foreign policy doctrine is not available.

A second major difficulty is that foreign policy cuts across department lines; not only the Department of State and the Department of Defense, but the AID agency, the Department of Agriculture, the Treasury, the Department of Commerce, the Tariff Commission, and a growing number of international agencies are concerned with it. Moreover, especially in the economic area, there is an intimate relation between foreign and domestic policy. A serious depression in the United States would be more harmful to underdeveloped countries than calling off the entire aid program.

A third difficulty, which is closer to the province of this Memorandum, is the age-old conflict between the regional and the functional point of view. Or more accurately, should a regional or country breakdown be the primary classification, with the functional breakdown secondary, or should it be the other way around? Emphasis on the functional approach tends to center authority in Washington, and creates confusion in the field. Emphasis on the country approach may produce coherence in the field and confusion in Washington. Advocates of either emphasis are encountered with strong counter arguments. Administration must be based on one approach or the other. But in the purpose of planning for the future, perhaps both should run in awkward double harness.

Quite different problems and approaches occur in connection with the programming of resource development, such as power, navigation, and flood control. Such activities are designed mainly to improve the economic performance of the country in the future. Unlike defense or foreign policy, they are intended to produce economic benefits. The difficulties arise because they must be formulated in the context of a mixed economy; and in most cases there are direct or indirect private alternatives which are not subject to government planning. (Even though navigation is the exclusive province of the government, there are private transportation alternatives to inland waterways.)

The programming method used by the Government is to attempt to assess the costs and benefits of individual projects, in comparison with private and other public alternatives. The program, then, consists of the most meritorious projects the budget will accommodate. Meritorious projects excluded from the budget provide arguments for increasing its size, in the same way that excluded defense or foreign aid activities provide a case for increasing those segments of the budget.

There are difficulties inherent in the specific project approach. The attempt is to apply profit criteria to public projects, analogous to those used in valuing private projects. This involves comparison of monetary values of present and future costs and benefits. But, in many important cases, such as urban highways, recreation parkways, free bridges, and flood control dams, the product of the government's investment does not directly enter the market economy. Consequently evaluation requires imputation of market values. For example, the returns on a bridge have been estimated by attempting to value the time saved by users. Such measurements necessarily contain a strong element of artificiality.

In other cases, the purposes of government investment are to alter the character of the market economy, either for the nation as a whole or for particular regions within it. In such cases, returns should be measured in terms of the market values that will exist as a result of the investment, rather than those that prevail before it is undertaken. This difficulty has led economists and planners to attempt to construct "shadow" prices as a basis for their measurements.

In still other cases, government undertakes investments that require a longer view of the future than private enterprise is willing to undertake. It is therefore prepared to accept a lower rate of return than that which is yielded by private investment in other directions. But how much lower the return should be is not revealed by market prices.

These remarks indicate that project evaluation cannot be achieved entirely by objective economic analysis. In most cases, there is a strong political element in the choice of projects. To serve the national interest, such choices should be made in the light of overall policies with respect to economic development. Attempts to build up such policies from the consideration of particular projects seem to give undue scope for the influence of particularistic political interests, and do not appear to add to the formulation of inherent national objectives. The question is therefore raised whether, in fields such as transportation and natural resources, overall programs should not be formulated into which particular projects can be fitted.

If so, what should such programs contain? Description of an area as an activity or a program implies that its components are more closely in competition with each other than they are with elements outside the program. Should urban transport be placed more closely in competition with international transport than with other aspects of urban development? Should international transport be regarded as a component of transportation or foreign trade, or both? In much current discussion, it seems to be taken for granted that transportation is a natural program category. But that conclusion is by no means obvious.

Similar problems and difficulties arise in connection with other fields such as education, health, and welfare. Some aspects of education and health are designed to increase the economic effectiveness of the labor force. Others are designed to enrich the social and intellectual lives of individuals. Education in particular is held essential for the political health of the country. Possibly the economic aspects of education and health should be considered not only as components of education and health generally, but also as parts of a national manpower program.

In the United States, in particular, there is a further major difficulty connected with activities in the resource and welfare fields. The activities of the federal government are designed to supplement those of the private economy, or to supplement and stimulate state and local governments. Should plans in these areas relate to the nation as a whole, covering the activities of the private economy and all levels of government? To what extent should the federal government attempt to implement such overall plans by controls over the private economy or conditional grants-in-aid to other levels of government? Presumably our belief in the competitive market economy and our commitment to the federal system preclude thorough-going resort to central planning and control in any important area. The federal government is thus faced with a dilemma with which it must live as best it can.

This discussion shows that designation of activities as programs is no easy or trivial matter. The way in which a program structure is set up for the government as a whole or for any major segment can have a profound effect on the decisions that are reached, so that the design of programs should be regarded as an important part of the decision-making process. The following paragraphs indicate some of the criteria that should be taken into account.

1 An important criterion for a program structure is that it should permit comparison of alternative methods of pursuing an imperfectly determined policy objective. Thus the need for public assistance can be clarified and analyzed by breaking the problem down into the needs arising from old age, economic dependence, physical disability, and unemployment. Limited resources prevent provisions for all cases under these categories. Despite the absence of a clear cut concept of social welfare, a satisfactory comparison among these various categories must be formed.

2 Even though objectives may be clearly defined, there are usually alternative ways of accomplishing them. Thus Airlift and Sealift is designated as a separate program, largely because a requirement can be accomplished by various combinations of air and sea transports.

3 Programs may also consist of a number of complementary components, none of which can be effective without the others. A health program requires doctors, nurses, and hospitals in the right proportions.

4 A separate program may be needed where one part of an organization supplies services to several others. Economies are likely if a department has a single computer operation rather than separate ones in each bureau. Since the acquisition of computer facilities is likely to have an appreciable lead time, departmental planning is likely to require that computers be budgeted as a separate program, even though they are far removed from the end objectives of the department.

5 An organization's objectives may require it to adopt overlapping structures. This need is evident in foreign affairs where both geographical and functional programs are required. It is also evident within the country, where regional as well as national requirements must be considered.

6 A further criterion relates to the time span over which expenditures take effect. The uncertainties of the future usually preclude firm estimates of requirements for government services beyond a limited period, say five years. Yet, research and development and investment must be undertaken to provide for a longer-run future. Even where such activities can be identified with some major program, they should be dealt with as separate sub-programs, since the uncertainties of the longer-run future should affect the character of the activities undertaken. In other cases, such long range activities may not be identifiable with any current end product program. In that event, it is obvious that they should be dealt with separately. In fact, differences in time spans of various activities may be the leading characteristic of an organization's program structure. A growing undertaking may think primarily in terms of the division of its functions among production, investment, and research and development.

The need for programming arises from the limitations of human beings and the obstinacy of the physical environment. In the first place, it is not sufficient to invoke the Constitution and seek to promote the general welfare. The general welfare can only be understood in terms of components and by choosing among them. Secondly, the process of relating ends to means is immensely complicated in a modern society. The process must be broken down into a hierarchy of optimizations and suboptimizations. Thirdly, results cannot be achieved instantaneously, and frequently long lead times are involved. Moreover, resources once committed to a purpose are not readily transferable elsewhere. Consequently, programming is required.

A general distinction that may be useful is that between the final and intermediate programs of an organization. Final programs can be regarded as those that contribute directly to its general objective. Intermediate programs are operations singled out for treatment as programs that contribute to final programs in the immediate or remote future. Thus in the Department of Defense, strategic forces, general purpose forces and possibly air defense can be considered final, while all others are intermediate. From the point of view of the government as a whole, however, defense becomes the final program and its components intermediate.

IV. PROGRAM PREPARATION, APPRAISAL, AND ANALYSIS

Preparation

Up to this point in the discussion, programming and budgeting have not been distinguished from each other, and program budgeting has been regarded as a budgetary process that pays due regard to policy objectives, costs, and time dimensions. We must now modify these simplifications and regard programming and budgeting as different but complementary components of the same operation. Every organization, in or out of government, finds it necessary to have an annual budget which represents a detailed and feasible plan of action for the ensuing year. Every organization, however, must look beyond the next year, even to make coherent plans for that year. An explicit projection beyond the end of the following year will be called a program. Programs and budgets should clearly be consistent with each other. Departures of the budget from the program call for revisions of the program, and program revisions call for changes in the budget.

In some instances, budgeting and programming may be identical processes. In the Anti-Trust Division of the Department of Justice, for instance, the basic cost factor is the number and types of lawyers employed. The requirement derives from the vigor of the government's enforcement policy, and the nature of the cases that fall within its net. Anti-trust cases cannot be disposed of in one year; consequently, budgeting must look beyond a single year. Apart from the fact that typewriters and secretaries can be adequately dealt with on an annual basis, there is unlikely to be any difference between the requirements of effective programming and effective budgeting.

In other cases, programming and budgeting methods should differ markedly. Consider, for instance, the Federal Prison System. The system should program for a number of years, because it must have a cell for every prisoner. The number of prisoners will depend on future crime rates and enforcement policies. If techniques of detention, punishment and correction remain the same, the program and its cost can be derived from the expected number of prisoners, changes in price levels, wage rates, conviction costs, and so forth. Further refinements should take into account change in prison methods that could lead to economies or increased costs: changes in length of sentences, the effects of civil rights legislation, of abolition of capital punishment, and so forth. Program estimates of this character require human abilities, research methods and procedures far different from those required to produce a detailed estimate of cost for the ensuing year. While next year's budget should be derived from the program and consistent with it, it should also be separate.

In contrast to the prison system, programming for defense is vastly more complicated. Defense consists of a number of major programs that are in competition with each other for the resources available for defense, and whose program elements are in competition with each other. The President and the Secretary of Defense should be able to decide whether an increase in one area should result in contraction in another or an increase in the total size of the budget. Changes in external threats, technology, management techniques, and strategic doctrine all demand that programs be subject to continual revision. Consequently, it is clear that programming in defense and other agencies responsible for interrelated programs should be a highly centralized operation, carried out by flexible methods and capable of rapid revision. But the centralized operation should not be permitted to occur in a vacuum. Its success will depend heavily on the extent to which ideas and experience at all levels of the Department can be fed into it.

Ideally, the process of revision should be continuous and comprehensive. Every year should, in principle, be the first year of a new program. The need for comprehensive revision derives from the fact that the elements of a program are frequently highly interdependent. Revision of any one element should call for reconsideration of all others. In practice comprehensiveness may be too costly in time, effort, uncertainty, and confusion. However, the built-in tendencies towards rigidity in any system must be guarded against. In this respect a centralized programming system is likely to be more flexible than a conventional budget system, which is particularly responsive to the forces of inertia throughout the organization.

The need for flexibility has an important bearing on the time span that programs should cover. The very existence of a program implies some loss of flexibility. By reason of having adopted it, the organization reduces its freedom to do something different in future years, since a conscious act of revision is required. On the other hand, investment projects, to say nothing of research and development, undertaken now must be based on some view of a highly uncertain future. Time spans should be long enough but not unnecessarily long.

The dilemma could be partially resolved if programs could be expressed in terms of ranges rather than single figures. If the ranges included genuine upper and lower limits, it would become clear that projection beyond a limited period was not operationally meaningful. Ranges and more elaborate methods for taking uncertainty into account have been frequently advocated, but rarely adopted. One approach is to program for limited time horizons, but to recognize that important items in the program will yield their benefits beyond the horizon. The imposition of a horizon and the knowledge that there is something beyond it should stimulate the design of projects that can be adapted to conditions that at the present time can be only dimly foreseen.

Appraisal

Both the usefulness and feasibility of programming depend on one's ability to appraise and analyze past experience. The directions and techniques of future policy depend critically on the quantitative and the qualitative data derived from the past. Rational planning can be applied to new departures, such as ballistic missiles, only to the extent that they are comparable with something that was done in the past. The cost-effectiveness of missiles could be appraised initially only by comparison of their expected performance with that of the manned bomber. Once missiles exist, new generations could be compared with their predecessors.

Fortunately for the ordinary conduct of life, dramatic breaks with the past are rare. The decision to construct the atomic bomb was such an example. It may have been thought at the time that comparison with the destructive power of high explosives afforded a basis for comparison. But subsequent experience has shown how naive were simple and vulgar criteria such as "a bigger bang for a buck." However, once the world became imprisoned in the atomic age, the feasibility of rational calculation began to assert itself within that world. We are now at the dawn of the space age. Rational processes do not tell whether we should go to Mars at all or how soon we should get to Mars. Once we are there, we may be able to think more clearly about Venus.

Even though the adoption of space exploration as a goal may not be a matter of rational calculation, problems of efficiency arise as soon as the goal is adopted. The resources that the government is prepared to devote to its pursuit are limited by competing claims on the budget. The efficiency with which the operation is carried out may mean the difference between success and failure, given the constraint on available resources. Even though the objective differs from anything that has been undertaken in the past, experience with the design of research, development, and investment in other areas that were once new can be highly useful and relevant.

Consequently, a successful decision-making process depends heavily on systematic and thorough accumulation of evidence about the past as a guide to the future. A knowledge of the past is necessary not only to provide experiences analogous to those of the present but to point to methods of improving on past performance.

While this point may seem obvious, it nevertheless needs emphasis. Governments seem prone to two kinds of error in this connection. On the one hand past experience is simply reproduced through failure to analyze its relevance for the present. One striking example is provided by the Korean war mobili-

zation—both the pattern of government organization and the long range strategy, such as building up an industrial base. Preparations for the long-run future (as distinct from merely fighting the Korean engagement) showed remarkably little awareness of the nature of nuclear war—although we were already in the atomic age. The reason was that those who were called upon to organize the Korean undertaking had little to go on except their World War II experience. No systematic attempts had been made to appraise that experience and adapt it to future requirements. But governments also tend to make the opposite kind of mistake, by failing to recognize that history does afford instances of problems closely analogous to those of the present. The United States is not exempt from these tendencies. The government does not preoccupy itself extensively with historical analyses.

In the budgetary area, narrowly defined, recording one aspect of the past has been an important preoccupation. Budgeting has been traditionally associated with accounting. But government accounting systems have been largely designed to check on the honesty of officials and to limit their exercise of discretion. This type of accounting has in turn been reflected in traditional methods of budgeting for the future. As in business, the government in recent years has recognized the need for cost accounting. Improvements have been most marked in the corporation area. They are far less evident among the regular departments and agencies. But it is doubtful whether any accounting system will provide all the cost information needed for adequate program analysis.

Reporting on costs, however, is only one side of the problem. Equally important, and far more difficult, are the questions on the benefit side. How well is a long range research program succeeding? Is public health being improved, or is it deteriorating? Does the fact that we have no war mean that potential enemies are being deterred by our forces? How do we compare a world with foreign aid with a world without it? Can such questions as these be answered systematically? Or must detailed information on costs be associated with crude intuition on benefits? This may be true. The assessment of benefits depends largely on judgment and intuition, rather than on precise measurement.

Analysis

When attention moves from the past to the future, two major questions arise separately or in combination. First, how effective is a program in attaining its intended objective; and second, can existing program results be accomplished at lower cost? These questions attempt to draw a distinction between the *effectiveness* of a program in achieving its objective and the *efficiency* with which it is carried out. For instance it may be possible to consider the effectiveness of the antitrust program under the present organization of the division. It should also be possible to decide whether the same results could be more efficiently achieved by reorganizing the division. For instance, efficiency may be increased by having fewer senior lawyers and more assistants, or vice versa.

The distinction between effectiveness and efficiency, when it can be made, is useful for analytic purposes. But in important instances, the distinction is arbitrary, and possibly misleading. Consider an analogy from the market economy. If an automobile is perfectly standardized, it is possible to consider separately the demand for it and the cost of production. But suppose a new technology produces a different kind of car that has greater consumer appeal. The distinction between efficiency and effectiveness becomes much more difficult. If the technology produced helicopters that displaced automobiles it might be meaningless. In these circumstances, total value produced must be compared with total costs. The number of cars loses significance as a precise measurement. It becomes instead an index of automobile transportation. As such, of course, it may have significant uses.

Likewise in government, the feasibility of distinguishing between effectiveness and efficiency depends on the possibility of quantitative measurement of programs. Such measurement is possible in a limited number of cases. Electric power can be measured in kilowatts. Volume of mail handled may be a useful measure of the activities of the Post Office, although the citizen may disagree as he waits impatiently for his mail. Miles of highway constructed again is a measure, but one wants to know where the highways lead to. Numbers of children educated is a significant figure, but is not a measure of the quality of education.

In other areas, notably defense, and law and order, this type of cardinal measurement is clearly impossible. Nevertheless, it may still be possible to apply the criterion "more or less" to a program. Even though strategic deterrence cannot be measured in any units, it still seems meaningful to say that deterrence has increased, decreased or remained the same. If this is possible, the efficiency of the program at any level can be examined separately.

The possibility of ordinal measurement can be increased if trade-off factors can be established among various program components. The effectiveness of airlift and sealift will depend on the numbers of troops transported and the speed of the operation. Experience and analysis may show that to transport 100,000 men in one month is preferable to transporting 200,000 in two months. One may, therefore, be able to say that "airlift and sealift" has increased or decreased, even though the composition of the program has changed materially.

The concepts of efficiency and effectiveness have been emphasized because they serve to indicate the areas where objective analysis may be possible and those where it is not.

The efficiency concept implies that measures taken to achieve economies will not affect the attainment of the objectives of the program, when it is carried out at a given level. Consequently, efficiency can be dealt with by analytical methods. The relatively new techniques of operations research and cost-effectiveness analysis (as usually conceived) are all concerned with efficiency questions.

The distinction between effectiveness and efficiency must, however, be used with extreme care. Measures that purport to increase efficiency may have pronounced effects, good or bad, on effectiveness. Government economy campaigns, for instance, often reduce effectiveness, sometimes intentionally, in the guise of eliminating waste. On the other hand, the elimination of undeniable waste may improve the effectiveness of government operations generally. With respect to particular programs, increasing the number of students per teacher will affect the quality of education. On the other hand, removal of cumbersome equipment from aircraft on grounds of efficiency may have unforeseen beneficial effects in terms of range and maneuverability. Where such possibilities exist, questions of cost and effectiveness become thoroughly intermingled.

Economic factors probably dominate the cost side of the government's activities, but there are non-economic costs as well. Probably the most decisive objection to a civil defense program has been not its economic costs, but the destruction of social values it might involve. The destruction of the beauty of the countryside by superhighways, and of cities by freeways, represents non-economic costs that are too infrequently recognized. In some cases, the final purpose of a program, insofar as the government is concerned, is to produce outputs with economic value. Government production of marketable electric power is a clearcut example. But as was pointed out above, the purported economic valuation of many government activities necessarily involves political judgments concerning critical elements in the valuation.

Many government activities are designed to yield both economic and non-economic returns. Education is a good example. One of its objectives undoubtedly is to produce an enterprising and skilled labor force that will contribute to economic prosperity. Another is to preserve and enlarge the cultural heritage of the country, and, hopefully to sustain its capacity to govern itself, despite technological advance. Another example is public health. Reduction of working time lost by sickness is one of its benefits. But measures to reduce suffering in old age are not undertaken for economic reasons. The idea of economic measurement has great attractiveness because of the analytic possibilities, especially to economists, that it offers. But it is a perversion of human values to push it into areas where it does not belong.

Even where the effectiveness of programs can be measured in terms of money, that is not the end of the story; they must be undertaken or not undertaken in competition with other programs that are not so measurable. The President, for instance, may have to decide whether to spend his marginal billion dollars on a new (measurable) dam or on (non-measurable) hospitals for the aged. Such decisions are necessarily political. Also within

major programs, choices are frequently political rather than technical. There is no purely technical basis for deciding the relative emphasis that should be given to strategic deterrence compared with limited war capabilities. In agriculture, the decision to support agricultural incomes at some desired level is a political rather than a technical matter.

Some authorities argue that political choices can best be made if politicians listen merely to voices in the air, observe straws in the political wind, or regard their occupation as an amusing bargaining game. Our position is that political choices can be improved if politicians are aided by information and technical analysis concerning the probable consequences of their acts. The technician may be able to point out that some courses of political action will not yield the results desired. For instance, in a poor country overemphasis on welfare, compared with development, may destroy the country's chances of both welfare and development.

Ultimately decisions are made by individuals, groups, or legislative bodies exercising their informed judgment. One can hope that such decisions will be improved if they are made in the light of all available evidence and the evidence is marshalled in an orderly way. Furthermore, such procedure may help to avoid the political bargaining and logrolling that mars rather than makes the political process.

There is a useful parallel to be drawn between political and legal processes. The decisions of judges or juries cannot be appraised by objective standards. They depend on adversary procedures that follow well-established rules. If those rules are violated, decisions are upset on appeal. Otherwise, they stand.

A programming approach to government decision-making can be thought of as an adversary process. Decision-making is arranged so as to permit the competition of ideas, in the light of which decision-makers make choices among relevant alternatives.

V. PROGRAMMING AND ORGANIZATION

Our discussion has indicated that there is a close connection between programming and organization. Programs cannot be formulated or carried out unless they are under the direction of a responsible authority. Also, programs cannot be compared and related to each other except by a superior authority responsible for all of them. The question then arises whether the considerations that determine the best program structure for the government are an equally good guide to its organizational structure. Or are there additional or alternative criteria that should govern its pattern of organization? Since differing programming and organizational structures are found to give rise to conflict, there should clearly be no unnecessary incompatibility between them.

At the highest executive level, there is no incompatibility. The President is the head of the administrative executive branch, and since the Budget and Accounting Act of 1921, it has been definitely established that he is responsible for recommending a comprehensive program to the Congress.

There should be a strong presumption that the responsibilities of executive departments should be determined by program criteria. Each department should be assigned responsibility for closely related programs that serve the same general objective. The department head in his recommendations to the President should be personally responsible for achieving the best comprehensive program within the scope of his jurisdiction.

Within departments, the organization of bureaus, divisions and sections should be organized on a programmatic basis unless there are good reasons for departing from that rule.

Unfortunately, the problem is not as simple as this. There are good reasons why the requirements of effective administration may diverge from those of effective programming. There are also reasons, not necessarily good, why, in fact, programming cuts across administrative lines rather than coincides with them.

1 The existing organization of the government has deep historical roots which the strongest President (to say nothing of the Congress) is reluctant to disturb violently. Although Presidents have been repeatedly granted reorganization powers, they have been disinclined to use those powers to make major changes.

2 There may be strong arguments for not disturbing the historical situation, even though contemporary programming requirements seem to demand it. There are many propo-

nents of the virtues of competition among the military services, provided the competition is given coherence by a programming system. Moreover, today's programming structure may not be suitable for tomorrow. Stability in the organization may be worth the price of some inconsistency with the structure that contemporary logic seems to require.

3 When overlapping program structures are required, the organization cannot do full justice to both of them. This difficulty is particularly evident when the regional-functional issue arises.

4 A particular activity may be concerned with more than one program, in which case it cannot be assigned without question to one department. The Corps of Engineers is an essential part of military defense, even though its main peacetime concern is civil works. It should not necessarily be transferred to the Department of the Interior, even though that transfer might improve resource programming. The Department of Agriculture has important international as well as domestic activities. Those activities should not necessarily be transferred to the Department of State. International agricultural programs may be evolved more effectively in an agricultural rather than a foreign service environment.

5 The organization required for effective administration of programs may differ from that required for effective formulation. Good administration may require the setting up of a separate research department, even though all the research done in it can be identified with other programs. Efficiency may be increased by having scientists working together, under the supervision of scientists rather than by having them scattered through a departmental bureaucracy. In the case of the Post Office, questions relating to construction, mail deliveries and technical improvement can be formulated on a functional and nationwide basis. Yet the administration of the Post Office must necessarily be decentralized on a regional and local basis. Furthermore, a single general counsel's office, a single supply organization, and a single carpool is likely to be enough for one department—simply on grounds of administrative efficiency.

These examples suffice to indicate that apart from the forces of tradition and inertia, the criteria for programming and those for effective organization do not coincide, and may diverge materially. Conditions will differ from department to department. In some instances programming may be a highly centralized operation only indirectly concerned with administration. In simpler situations there need be no incompatibility. In still others, programs are intended to overcome the organizational incongruities that cannot feasibly be altered.

The distinction between programming and administration is not as clear-cut as it may appear at first sight. Administration does not consist simply of carrying out directives. In fact, successful administration implies the exercise of discretion by administrators, hopefully in the direction of measuring the efficiency of their operations. Their operating experience should be brought to bear on future program and policy decisions. Moreover, a powerful administrator has his own ideas concerning future policy, and may not willingly accept the views of planners and programmers. He may even have useful ideas to contribute. It is hard to conceive of the three military services carrying out their missions successfully if they had no ideas on national strategy. A central planning organization is unlikely to be successful if it is insulated from operating experience.

Where programming and administration diverge, the way in which the organization as a whole works thus depends largely on the means employed to ensure that administrators in fact carry out programs. The mere announcement of a program, however well conceived, is not enough. The world is full of national planning organizations that have remarkably little influence on powerful departments. The critical factor is the head of the organization. Without his authority and support, departments or bureaus are likely to go their own way. Moreover, programming, as Defense Department experience has shown, can be a potent instrument for increasing the authority of the department head. In fact, some uneasy critics of Defense Department programming allege that that is its main purpose.

Our main concern in the present discussion is the role that the annual budget can play in synchronizing administration with program decisions. The structure of the budget and the financial controls embodied in it can make for harmony and discord. If, for instance, appropriations are made to separate bureaus, as

they used to be, the bureaus acquire a large degree of autonomy and freedom from central control. On the other hand, if they are made to the secretary of a department, and he is free to allocate them at his discretion, he is provided with a powerful instrument of coordination. These matters will be discussed in the next section.

VI. PROGRAMMING AND THE ANNUAL BUDGET

Most governments, as well as other organizations, find it necessary to have an annual, or at most a biennial, budget, even though a coherent program may require projections over a much longer period. Governments are concerned with the immediate impact of their budgets. They may attach importance to a budgetary rule, such as a requirement of budget balance, or they may be concerned with the short-run economic impact of the budget. Furthermore, governments require budgets to be prepared with a degree of detail that would be meaningless if extended over a number of years. Although much has been done since 1950 to eliminate irrelevant detail from the budget, effective administration still requires an impressive amount of it. Thus the budget is to be distinguished from a program with respect both to its detail and its time horizon. The need for greater detail also means that it should be prepared by methods that differ from, but are consistent with, those used in programming.

Budget Preparation and Consideration

If programs are reviewed annually in the manner we have proposed, the annual budget process would result in a more detailed and precise estimate of the costs of the first year of the continually updated program.

The traditional method of preparing the annual budget has been to begin with initial requests from organization units in terms of their objects of expenditure. In some cases this operation has broken down under its own weight. In defense, for instance, budget preparation is in fact largely centralized, even though all installations go through the motions of the traditional method. In other and simpler situations, where there is no conflict between programs and organization, budget and program preparation can be part of the same operation.

In general, budgeting should be associated both with the programming process and with the traditional organization unit method. For the program itself to be realized it must be supported by the financial controls of the budgetary process. On the other hand, the methods of cost estimation by factors that are necessary for a central operation are not precise enough for the preparation of administrative budgets. Factors cannot be satisfactorily used to provide precise estimates of requirements for personnel, office supplies, foreign travel and the like. Moreover, commitment to factors such as those implied by military tables of organization tend to prevent improvements in organization. On the other hand, they may prevent Parkinsonian expansion.

One possibility would be to use centralized methods to arrive at a first approximation to the budget on a program basis. Tentative allocations among organization units could then be made. They would then submit their detailed budgets in the form of revisions to the initial allocations. These revisions would then form the basis of a second approximation to the budget submitted by the department to the President and by him to the Congress.

A more radical departure from traditional budget practice would be to rely entirely on centralized methods for the preparation of the President's budget. This would mean that both the President and the Congress would have to consider the budget in programmatic terms, through lack of any other kind of information.

After the budget was enacted by Congress, the various bureaus would then submit their budgets as part of a separate administrative budget process. This would be an internal affair whereby the Secretary of the department arrived at a final allocation of funds.

This suggestion is not as radical as it sounds. Already, in the Department of Defense, money is allocated after enactment of appropriations through an internal funding program. This is necessary because the detailed estimates that go into the budget have already become out of date one year later, when the budget goes into operation.

Objection would be raised, however, that elimination of detail from the budget would deprive the Congress and the Budget Bureau of an opportunity to review matters such as personnel which have always been one of its main preoccupations. The answer to this objection is that the Congress could still require full reporting by organization units. They could review performance after the fact, and the impressions made by this review would naturally influence attitudes towards appropriation ratios for the future. In fact, appropriation hearings now are as much concerned with review after the fact as with consideration of next year's estimates. Progress in the direction we suggest is not out of the question.

Appropriations should, in general, be made for major programs and perhaps some of their major subdivisions, and within programs separate appropriations would probably be desirable for research and development, construction, major procurement, and for current operations. Those for current operations could be made for obligation within the financial year. For long-lead items, however, longer-term funding would be necessary in order to facilitate effective programming. However, in fluid situations, where the program structure is and should be subject to change, a more stable appropriation structure may be desirable. The Department of Defense retains its old appropriations side by side with its new program system. Whether this should be a transitional or a permanent arrangement remains to be seen.

Fund Allocation: Consumer Budgeting

Designation of appropriations for such purposes, however, does not settle the question of how the funds are allocated within a department. There can be no question but that appropriations should be made to the Secretary of the department and that he should have considerable freedom to transfer funds among closely related activities. Where programs cut across departmental lines they can be made either to the head of the major department concerned, or to the President.

The need for freedom to transfer has already been recognized. Before World War II there were more than 2000 separate appropriation items in the Federal Budget. By the Act of 1950, the President was given authority to simplify the budget, and consequently by 1955 the number of items for the whole government had been reduced to 375, implying a great increase of freedom to transfer among activities. Agreement to this change represents recognition by Congress that it cannot achieve economy by highly specific appropriations. Rather it must rely on considerable discretion of administrators to achieving economy in a time sense, by attempting to allocate funds in order to achieve efficiency.

The question that is still unsettled is how funds should be allocated within departments. Here there are two broad alternatives: consumer allocation and supplier allocation. With consumer allocation the final user of the goods gets the money initially and he "purchases" from the supplier. The supplier gets money only for working capital and long-run capital purposes. With supplier allocation, the supplier gets all the money, but is required to supply on requisition to the user—without a financial transaction taking place. With the first system the commander of a fleet would get the money and he would purchase from the Naval supplying bureaus. Under the present system the money is allocated to the bureaus and they supply ships, men, guns, and ammunition to the fleets.

Commanders of fleets and armies, in time of war, have more important concerns than finance. But in other areas, including many defense activities, the principle of consumer allocation has important advantages. It gives the ultimate user some freedom to choose among alternatives, and, hence, to economize. He also has a financial opportunity to influence the type of product supplied to him. While he is not allowed to make a personal profit, he has some of the incentives of a private business man.

Supplier allocation, on the other hand, tends to neglect questions of cost-effectiveness and, hence, encourages inefficiency. In the absence of compelling reasons to the contrary, such as those already noted, the consumer principle is generally preferable.

Applying that principle means that funds should be allocated initially to the directors of final programs. They should purchase from organization units or from the directors of intermediate programs. Funds provided directly to the latter would be for capital purposes.

With such a system, financial controls could help in implementing program decisions, and in achieving coordination in the face of the inevitable divergences between the organizational structure and the programming structure.

Obligations and Expenditures

Annual budgeting has always involved a dilemma. The principal concern of those concerned with fiscal policy has been the total level of expenditures, which in conjunction with the yield of taxation leads to surpluses, deficits, or budget balance. Yet the primary instrument of control available to the government has been the granting of obligational authority, or appropriations. An appropriation gives an administrator authority to incur obligations either by the letting of formal contracts, or by making more informal commitments to spend money.

Especially where procurement is concerned, expenditures made in any year result largely from earlier obligations and from still earlier grants of obligational authority. Similarly, obligational authority granted this year may only result in expenditures in future years. Consequently, efforts by the President or the Congress to regulate annual expenditures are frequently frustrated because control actions are not taken long enough in advance. Or else those efforts must be concentrated on those obligations that do result in expenditures in the very near future.

Program budgeting could assist annual budgeting by giving a time profile of the government's activities. Ideally, programs should be prepared for a number of years in advance in terms of the obligational authority to be requested, the obligations to be incurred and the expenditures to be made in each of the future years. In these circumstances, future expenditures could be foreseen and a more firm basis for control would exist.

Some critics of the present budgetary process have urged that attention should be focused on still another concept: costs incurred during the year rather than on cash expenditures. Such costs would emphasize resources consumed during the year—e.g., equipment spares and spare parts used in a maintenance activity, regardless of the year in which they were procured. Thus, account would be taken of beginning and year-end inventories. Costs incurred may give a clearer picture of program progress than do expenditures. On the other hand, cash expenditures may be more relevant for fiscal policy. Choice between these concepts is of secondary importance, however, compared with the need to relate them to prior obligations and appropriations.

Concluding Comments

The effectiveness of the programming-budget system will depend strongly on the staff arrangements made to carry it out. The first point to emphasize is that the entire operation must be the personal responsibility of the executive head of the organization. No one at a lower level has the authority or the right or the ability to acquire the knowledge required to perform the necessary tasks of coordination. This point was explicitly and emphatically recognized with respect to the President in the Budget and Accounting Act of 1921. The Budget Bureau has no authority except as a presidential staff agency. To underline the point, the Budget Director is not subject to Senate confirmation, and as a further indication of his staff position he was provided with a lower salary than befitted his importance.

Similarly at the departmental level, the Secretary must be responsible for both programs and budgets, for the same reasons.

The second point to stress is that programming, budgeting, and review after the fact are separate but highly interrelated operations. Programming is concerned with policy objectives, long-range projections and analytic methods that go far beyond the scope of traditional budgetary procedures. Programming, however, may remain merely a useful academic exercise unless it is implemented through the budget, which should provide an essential link between policy and administration. Finally, both programming and budgeting depend in essential ways on the information that can only be obtained through perceptive reviews of past performance, which require the exercise of analytic skills that go far beyond usual concepts of government accounting.

A conceptual framework for program budgeting will not in itself achieve the desired results. The objectives can only be achieved through the exercise of a wide variety of human skills of the highest caliber.

PROGRAM BUDGETING AND THE SPACE PROGRAM *

Murray L. Weidenbaum

The implementation of the Planning-Programming-Budgeting System (PPBS) by all major Federal Government agencies presents both important opportunities and major problems to the Nation's space program. The first part of this paper describes the main features of the PPBS effort. The second part analyzes possible applications to and impacts on space activities.

THE PLANNING-PROGRAMMING-BUDGETING SYSTEM[1]

Economists have long been interested in identifying policies that would promote economic welfare by improving the efficiency with which a society uses its resources, particularly in the public sector. For many years, the Corps of Engineers and the Bureau of

* Reprinted from Walter R. Johnson (ed.), The Management of Aerospace Programs, vol. 12 of the American Astronautical Society Science and Technology Series, 1967. With permission of the author and the American Astronautical Society.

Reclamation have applied benefit/cost analysis to evaluate prospective projects. Despite important difficulties, such as choosing an appropriate discount rate which would correspond to a realistic estimate of the social cost of capital, the use of benefit/cost analysis has improved the allocation of government resources. It has served as a partial screening device to eliminate obviously uneconomical projects—those whose prospective gains are less than estimated costs. Perhaps the overriding value has been to demonstrate the possibility of making objective analyses of essentially political actions, thus narrowing the area in which political forces operate.

A related development has been the application of cost/effectiveness analysis to military budget decision-making. For military programs, ordinarily the benefits or results cannot be expressed in dollars terms. However, the end objective, such as the capability to destroy X number of enemy targets under stipulated conditions, can be expressed in quantitative terms. Hence, the alternative ways of achieving the objective—Y bombers versus Z missiles or some combination—can be priced out and a least-cost solution arrived at.

This latter approach has been at the heart of the Planning-Programming-Budgeting System introduced in the Pentagon. It clearly has been the success of the Pentagon approach which has led to adoption of a government-wide PPBS effort. A fundamental shift has occurred in military resource allocation methods. Previously, each service competed for a larger share of the defense budget and, within the service totals, strategic weapons such as ICBM's competed for funds with tactical programs. Under the new system, close substitutes for performing the same or similar missions are compared with each other, although different services may be involved.

In August 1965, President Lyndon Johnson required each large Federal agency to set up a PPBS activity. Through this combination of planning and budgeting, it was hoped that broad national goals would be identified, specific government programs related to them, and the most economical method of carrying them out arrived at. Four major steps are being taken to accomplish this rather tall order.

Identifying national goals. The specific goals which are deemed appropriate for the Federal Government to be seeking will be selected, in the light of a comprehensive evaluation of national needs and objectives.

Relating broad goals to specific programs. Specific alternative programs which may help to achieve the broad national goals and objectives will then be examined. The ones that appear to be most promising, given the various constraints under which the government operates, will have to be selected. Many government agencies have little discretion in selecting the optimum combination of programs which can assist in achieving broad national goals in their area of operations. They often find vague or conflicting congressional guidance on goals but clear and precise legislative directive as to which specific programs—and in what amounts—are to be conducted. The task here may be to infer the goals from the specific programs and then develop new or improved means of achieving these goals.

Relating programs to resource requirements. Specific costs of alternative programs will then

need to be estimated, in order to compare their efficiency in achieving the goals. To those acquainted with benefit/cost or cost/effectiveness analysis, this will be no minor achievement in many elusive program areas.

Relating the resource inputs to budget dollars. Finally, the manpower facilities, and other resource requirements will need to be translated into budget dollars, so that decisions can be made to implement the PPBS plan through the budget process.

The main product of PPBS is designed to be a comprehensive multi-year Program and Financial Plan for each government agency, which will be updated periodically and systematically. This Plan will show projected outlays for each major program area of an agency or department. Hence, determining the output-oriented categories is an important step.

Many difficulties are involved in measuring the output of a government program. Conceptually, only the end-product should be measured rather than intermediate outputs. For example, in the post office, the end product might be the number of letters delivered, and not the number of times these letters were handled at the various post offices.

Similarly, in the case of hospital programs it might be possible to look at output in terms of patient-days. However, the mission of a hospital might be described better as proper treatment of patients. Within a broad framework, the mission of a health program might be viewed as maintenance of good health and the output measure might reflect days of good health rather than incidents of illness.

The Federal agencies are encouraged to consider comparisons and possible trade-offs among program elements which are close substitutes, even though the activities may be conducted in different agencies. This is an attempt to introduce some competition among programs and hopefully to achieve greater effectiveness from budgetary outlays.

Table 18-1 is a hypothetical sketch of this new approach. Transportation is a good example of a major program category which consists of a variety of activities in different departments, with little attention to gaps or overlapping functions or conflicting objectives.

The major agencies involved are the Department of Commerce (Bureau of Public Roads and the Maritime Administration), the Federal Aviation Agency, the Department of

TABLE 18-1   ILLUSTRATIVE OUTLINE OF A NATIONAL TRANSPORATION PROGRAM

Elements	Fiscal Years
General Inter-City Transport	1967, 1968, 1969, 1970, 1971, 1972

General Inter-City Transport

    Interstate Highways
        Interstate Highway Program
        Primary System Highways

    Domestic Water Transport
        Inland Waterways Facilities
        Maritime Programs

    Aviation
        CAB Subsidies to Airlines
        FAA and NASA Aircraft Technology

Urban Commuter Transportation
    Urban Highway Systems
    Urban Transit Systems

Rural Access
    Secondary System-Roads
    Forest, Public Lands, National Parks Roads
    Aid to Local Service Aviation

Military Standby Transportation

the Army (Corps of Engineers, civil functions), the Department of Agriculture (Forest Service), The Department of the Interior (National Park Service), the Treasury Department (the Coast Guard), the Department of Housing and Urban Development (mass transit assistance program), and regulatory agencies, such as the ICC, CAB, and Federal Maritime Board. Significantly, only a few of these agencies are scheduled to be absorbed by the proposed Federal Department of Transportation.

Table 18-2 illustrates the possible specific elements which might comprise one of the

TABLE 18-2   ELEMENTS OF A TRANSPORTATION PROGRAM CATEGORY: URBAN COMMUTER TRANSPORTATION

Urban highways

Passenger-miles carried
Ton-miles of freight carried
Number of miles of way completed
Number of miles of way placed under construction

Urban transit systems

Passenger-miles carried
Number of passenger miles carried
Number of miles of way completed
Number of miles of way placed under construction

From the above information, some comparisons might be made between urban highways and urban transit systems in terms of:
   1. Capital cost per mile of way.
   2. Operating cost per mile of way.
   3. Average commuter travel time per mile of way.

transportation subcategories, urban commuter transportation. These elements may vary from the number of miles of way placed under construction (a measure of capital investment) to the number of passenger-miles carried (a measure of output). Tables 18-1 and 18-2 are indicative of the broader horizons of the new breed of governmental budgeteers and represent an initial step along a relatively new path in governmental resource allocation.

IMPACTS OF PPBS ON THE SPACE PROGRAM

The formal transition to PPBS should be relatively straightforward for the major space agencies. Both the Department of Defense and NASA already develop their budget proposals around programs and specific systems. Certainly the task would seem to be less formidable than for agencies in such elusive areas as justice, social welfare, and beautification. For example, a basic program breakdown of NASA outlays already is contained in the Budget document and can be developed into a rudimentary program budget (see Table 18-3).

Identifying national space goals. Nevertheless, the complete adaptation of the PPBS mechanism and concepts might create or highlight important policy problems for the space program. It might be helpful to return to each of the four major steps of PPBS described earlier. The first step is "identifying national goals." Two basic and quite different approaches have been suggested for identifying the goals relevant to the space program.

The first approach is that of the recent report of the Senate Committee on Aeronautical and Space Sciences[2] which, although dealing with aeronautics, may be almost equally relevant. The Committee states that "national aeronautical goals (for our purposes, we may substitute 'astronautical goals') support, and interact with, a group of more general goals." Four so-called more general goals are identified: national transportation goals, national defense goals, social and economic development goals, and international relations and prestige goals. From this point of view, space exploration would be considered essentially as an intermediate good, a step toward achieving other, more fundamental goals.

The second approach to identifying national space goals is that of the National Planning Association contained in a recent study by Leonard Lecht.[3] In identifying the major American goals and objectives, Lecht lists space research along with national defense, consumer living standards, and other fundamental needs of our society. He states that, "There is general agreement in the United States that a sustained space research program is an important and continuing national objective" (p. 277).

That these are two different approaches to space goal-setting may be seen by reference to some of the fundamental questions involved in budgeting for space programs. For example, are Project Apollo and the develop-

TABLE 18-3   RUDIMENTARY PROGRAM BUDGET FOR NASA IN FISCAL YEAR 1967 (IN MILLIONS)

Activity (Budget Plan)	Appropriation Categories			
	Research and Development	Construction of Facilities	Administrative Operations	Total
Manned space flight	$3,024	$54	$310	$3,387
Scientific investigations in space	530	6	69	605
Space applications	88	—	13	101
Space technology	248	11	192	451
Aircraft technology	33	21	50	104
Supporting activities	325	9	30	364
Total	$4,248	$101	$664	$5,012

Source: Derived from materials in *Budget of the United States Government for the Fiscal Year Ending June 30, 1967*, Washington, U.S. Government Printing Office, 1966, pp. 867, 870, and 872.

ment of a supersonic transport alternative means of achieving a similar goal—successful scientific competition with the communist nations? According to the Senate approach, it would appear that this would be a sensible tradeoff, and that the two programs are to some degree substitutes. Under the NPA approach, this would not be the case. A manned lunar landing would be considered basic to space research while the SST would be treated together with other transportation programs.

However somewhat different results may be obtained in attempting to answer the question: on what basis should space funds be allocated to DoD or NASA? Under our variant of the Senate approach these would not be viewed as substitutable items. Military space programs would be considered to be part of a national defense goal while NASA programs would be related to one or more civilian national goals. Conversely, under the NPA approach both DoD and NASA could be viewed as, at least in some cases, alternative instruments for performing space research and development.

Clearly, the proper identification of the national goals which each Federal agency's programs are designed to serve is fundamental to the effective application of PPBS. Without doing so, the process can readily degenerate into routine filling out of tedious forms. Although the matter of goal-setting is essentially subjective, the present writer opts for the NPA approach to the space program, that it has become an important national objective. On that basis, it may be useful to proceed to the next PPBS steps.

Relating broad space goals to specific space programs. As Margolis and Barro have pointed out, a set of mission categories that is useful in practice must be based on well-defined characteristics of projects at a lower level of abstraction than "ultimate objectives" or "national goals." They call for an "end-product" rather than "end-objective" set of categories, having the following characteristics:

1 They should group projects that are functionally related in an operationally well-defined sense. This might be according to type of payload or region of space in which they operate.
2 They should separate projects that serve distinct concrete objectives. For example,

projects that provide economic benefits or military capabilities should be separated from purely scientific efforts.
3 They should reflect the space program as currently constituted and projected but should be flexible enough to allow for growth in program scope and variety of subjects.[4]

It should be recognized that there may be fundamental limitations to as well as advantages of the Margolis-Barro approach. Their "end-product" categories do provide a method of budget allocations on a program basis which is rather operationally simple and clear cut. However, it hardly is a format for making the key decisions about the scope and structure of the space program. Rather, it requires that these broad "political" decisions already have been made, so that the PPBS technicians can go about their job of precisely costing out launching schedules and tracking facilities requirements.

Indeed, they state that "the whole question of 'space program goals' has been discussed at too vague and abstract a level to be relevant to the program bugeting process, and it has been obscured by public controversies over the wisdom of undertaking particular space missions" (p. 133). In view of the pioneering nature of the Margolis-Barro effort to develop a space program budget, we should be charitable in belaboring their shortcomings. However, it is somewhat disappointing to see the technician lamenting that his chore of choosing between 80% and 85% learning curves is obscured because the nation has not clearly determined that the overall mission is worth undertaking at all.

On a technical basis, the space program may appear to be readily adaptable to PPBS. Witness the ease with which the standard budget materials were able to be converted into at least a rudimentary space program budget (Table 18-3). However, on a substantive basis, it appears that such program budget materials do not throw up the basic policy alternatives for the space program which is at the heart of the PPBS approach—the choice among alternative programs for achieving a given mission. It is only on the basis of alternative choices that benefit/cost or cost/effectiveness analyses can be made to assist the policy makers in their decision-making.

It may be recalled that for the transportation area, the hypothetical program analysis presented choices among modes—air, water, and land—and between systems—highways and mass transit for the urban commuter function (see Tables 18-1 and 18-2). Despite greater sophistication in the important area of cost methodology, available program analyses for space activities do not present such basic choices, but assume that they already have been made. It is the contention of the present writer that following this less ambitious route will result in PPBS degenerating into a low-level accounting operation. Indeed, the desire to fill out the formats neatly should not take priority over the fundamental need to improve the allocation of government resources among alternative uses. Although any first attempts inevitably will be crude, it is suggested that program budgeting for space activities throw up alternatives such as the following:

1 Continuation of the current effort at a manned lunar landing by 1970.
2 A slow-down in the manned lunar program and an expansion in unmanned planetary exploration, both within the same budget total as (1).
3 A slow-down in the manned lunar landing and an expansion in efforts to utilize the fruits of space technology on earth, both within the same budget total as (1).
4 Continuation of the current effort at a manned lunar landing by 1970 and beginning a major effort at exploring Mars, thus raising the space budget substantially above (1), particularly in later years.
5 Continuation of the current manned lunar landing program and a substantial expansion of NASA's aeronautical R&D with the aim of expanding the use of commercial aircraft in short-haul markets and by personal rather than primarily business travelers. This alternative might require levels of budgetary support at various ranges between (1) and (4).

Undoubtedly the above questions require more precise formulation and in some cases detailed development of missions which have been stated too broadly. However, they are designed to indicate the types of basic choices which should not be ignored in the Planning-Programming-Budgeting System but which are the fundamental reason for establishing the detailed budgetary procedures and forms.

Relating space programs to resource requirements. Given the identification of the specific programs which could help to achieve broad national space goals, the problem of estimating resource requirements would seem to be a less formidable one. Here, the path-breaking work of the Rand Cost Analysis Department[5] reduces this formidable task to relatively manageable proportions. However, important technical problems do arise.

As Margolis and Barro point out, the interdependence among space activities makes it difficult to compute the true incremental cost of carrying out an individual project. It follows from the principle of the learning curve that the cost of hardware items procured for a particular project depends not only on the number of units required by that project but also on the number required by all projects using those particular items. If a project is eliminated and, hence, the demand for a particular hardware item reduced, then the unit cost of the item increases to all other projects that require it concurrently or at a later date.[6]

To further complicate estimating the requirements of space programs, it should be noted that major space vehicle systems and ground installations are often used in many different flight projects. Items that are most likely to have multiple uses—boosters, propulsion systems, launch facilities, tracking networks—have tended to be expensive relative to items that are peculiar to individual projects.[7] No single method among the many suggested for dealing with this problem is really satisfactory. The present procedure whereby such items are segregated into separate categories appears to be as reasonable as any.

The fundamental problem to be encountered at this step of the process perhaps is the fact that, as in the case of defense activities, so much of the results of the space program cannot be expressed in dollar terms. Hence, benefit/cost analyses cannot be made. To some degree, we must be content with relying on Leonard Lecht's conclusion that "The space effort involves the incurring of large expenditures in the present or near future for benefits at a more remote future date which, at best, can be very imperfectly foreseen . . . the unanticipated consequences are likely to exceed in importance those which can be anticipated in advance."[8]

Again relying on the experience of military analysts, cost/effectiveness studies can be utilized at this step of the space PPBS process to identify the least cost alternatives to achieving already-identified space goals.

Relating the space resource inputs to budget dollars. In a sense, this last step may seem to be a backward taking one. After identifying the total system resource inputs, PPBS now requires that they be reduced to the common and crude denominator of budget dollars. Upon reflection, it can be seen that this is an essential step of the entire process. Supposedly or hopefully the basic program decisions have been made in the context of a complete analysis of the entire system being considered, including its costs and benefits to the nation as a whole as well as to the Federal Treasury.[9] However, for the *results* of the PPBS analysis to become operationally useful in terms of government budget-making and expenditure allocation, they must be incorporated into the formal budget submissions in the customary manner.

Indeed, this may be the fundamental double contribution of PPBS: to make possible the implementation of long-range planning through the budget process, thus giving practical application to the planning and analysis effort and improving the intellectual content of budget-making.

CONCLUSION

By raising fundamental questions concerning the alternative uses of the Federal Government's funds and resources and by providing some concepts and methodology for answering them, the Planning-Programming-Budgeting System is an important attempt both to sharpen the government's budgetary preparation and review process. Perhaps more fundamental, it ultimately—if carried out in spirit as well as in letter—will increase the benefits achieved by the Nation from its public investments and outlays.

References

1. For a more detailed treatment, see M. L. Weidenbaum, "Program Budgeting: Applying Economic Analysis to Government Expenditure Decisions," *University of Missouri Business and Government Review*, Vol. VII, No. 4, July-August 1966, pp. 22–31.

2. U.S. Senate, Committee on Aeronautical and Space Sciences, *Policy Planning for Aeronautical Research and Development*, Washington, U.S. Government Printing Office, 1966.

3. Leonard A. Lecht, *Goals, Priorities, and Dollars*, New York, Free Press, 1966.

4. Milton A. Margolis and Stephen M. Barro, "The Space Program" in David Novick, editor, *Program Budgeting, Program Analysis and the Federal Budget*, Cambridge, Harvard University Press, 1965, pp. 133–135.

5. Cf. Harold Asher, *Cost-Quantity Relationships in the Airframe Industry*, Santa Monica, Rand Corporation, July 1956; David Novick, *Weapon-System Cost Methodology*, Santa Monica, Rand Corporation, February 1956; David Novick, *System and Total Force Cost Analysis*, Santa Monica, Rand Corporation, April 1961.

6. Margolis and Barro, *op. cit.*, pp. 128–129. The procedure described by Margolis-Barro raises the question of marginal versus average cost pricing. If the canceled project were the marginal recipient and marginal cost pricing were used, there would be no effect on the projects that were higher up on the curve (to the left on a negative sloping improvement curve). However, under an average cost pricing system, the effects would be as they indicate.

7. *Ibid.*, p. 129.

8. Lecht, *op. cit.*, p. 285.

9. Such externalities are dealt with at length in the pertinent economic literature. See the sources cited in (1).

SECTION 5

SYSTEMS ANALYSIS

Systems analysis is the name which has been popularized by Department of Defense analysts for the application of scientific methodology and economic models to the analysis of strategic decision problems. The areas of study called operations research *and* management science *are so closely allied with systems analysis that, although formal distinctions are made between the fields in particular organizations, the exercise involved in making the distinctions is unlikely to be worth the effort.*

Systems analysis involves the evaluation and comparison of alternative ways of achieving objectives on the basis of the resource costs and the benefits associated with each alternative. Critical to this process is the use of models, abstractions of the real world, which can be analyzed in lieu of experimentation in the real world. Through the use of models, the best alternative can be determined, and if the model is a good one, the best alternative as determined from the model will indicate an action in the real world which is a "good" one (if it is not "the" best of all those which are available).

The similarities among the fields variously called systems analysis *and* operations research *are more important than are the differences. However similar are the concepts, the practical differences which have evolved serve to place the role of each in proper focus. First, systems analysis usually is more concerned with the* invention of new alternatives *than is operations research. Many operations researchers have confined themselves to problems involving the comparison of a prescribed set of alternatives whereas systems analysts have set out to develop new ones. Of course, the level of rigor involved in the determination of the "best" alternative is therefore usually lower in the latter case than in the former, but the possibility of finding alternatives which are radically different from and superior to those obvious ones is also greatly enhanced.*

Another practical difference between the fields lies in the nature of the problems which have been attacked. Systems analysts have tended to concentrate on higher-level "ill-structured" problems in which objectives are less precisely defined and less sophisticated analysis is possible. Although all decision-problem analysis relies heavily on the use of human judgment, systems analysts have perhaps made greater use of judgment than have operations researchers.

Systems analysis is an intrinsic part of the Federal government's planning, programming, and budgeting system. Moreover, some variety of formal analysis is a necessary part of the fulfillment of any manager's planning function.

READING 19

SYSTEMS ANALYSIS TECHNIQUES FOR PLANNING-PROGRAMMING-BUDGETING *

E. S. Quade

INTRODUCTION

Broadly speaking, any orderly analytic study designed to help a decisionmaker identify a preferred course of action from among possible alternatives might be termed a systems analysis. As commonly used in the defense community, the phrase "systems analysis" refers to formal inquiries intended to advise a decisionmaker on the policy choices involved in such matters as weapon development, force posture design, or the determination of strategic objectives. A typical analysis might tackle the question of what might be the possible characteristics of a new strategic bomber and whether one should be developed; whether tactical air wings, carrier task forces, or neither could be substituted for U.S. ground divisions in Europe; or whether we should modify the test ban treaty now that the Chi-

* Reprinted with permission from The RAND Corporation, P-3322, March, 1966, The RAND Corporation, Santa Monica, California.

nese Communists have nuclear weapons and, if so, how. Systems analysis represents an approach to, or way of looking at, complex problems of choice under uncertainty that should have utility in the planning-programming-budgeting (PPB) process. Our purpose is to discuss the question of extending military systems analysis to the civilian activities of the government, to point out some of the limitations of analysis in this role, and to call attention to techniques that seem likely to be particularly useful. I will interpret the term "technique" broadly enough to range from proven mathematical algorithms to certain broad principles that seem to be often associated with successful analysis.

Some fifteen years ago a similar extension raised quite some doubt. When weapons system analysts (particularly those at The RAND Corporation) began to include the formulation of national security policy and strategy as part of their field of interest, experienced "military analysts" in the Pentagon and elsewhere were not encouraging. They held that the tools, techniques, and concepts of operations analysis, as practiced in World War II, or of weapons system optimization and selection—in which analysts had been reasonably successful—would not carry over, that strategy and policy planning were arts and would remain so.

Fortunately, these skeptics were only partially right. It is true that additional concepts and methodologies significantly different from those of earlier analysis had to be developed. But there has been substantial progress, and the years since 1961 have seen a marked increase in the extent to which analyses of policy and strategy have influenced decision-makers on the broadest issues of national defense.

Today's contemplated extension to PPB is long overdue and possibly even more radical. Systems analysis has barely entered the domain of the social sciences. Here, in urban planning, in education, in welfare, and in other nonmilitary activities, as Olaf Helmer remarks in his perceptive essay:

> . . . we are faced with an abundance of challenges: how to keep the peace, how to alleviate the hardships of social change, how to provide food and comfort for the inaffluent, how to improve the social institutions and the values of the affluent, how to cope with revolutionary innovations, and so on.[1]

Since systems analysis represents an approach to, or way of looking at, any problem of choice under uncertainty, it should be able to help with these problems.

Actually, systematic analysis of *routine* operations is widespread throughout the civil government as well as in commerce, industry, and the military. Here analysis takes its most mathematical form—and, in a certain sense, its most fruitful role. For example, it may help to determine how Post Office pick-up trucks should be routed to collect mail from deposit boxes, or whether computers should be rented or purchased to handle warehouse inventories, or what type of all-weather landing system should be installed in new commercial aircraft. Such problems are typically an attempt to increase the efficiency of a man-machine system in a situation where it is clear what "more efficient" means. The analysis can often be reduced to the application of a well-

understood mathematical discipline such as linear programming or queuing theory to a generic "model," which, by a specification of its parameters, can be made to fit a wide variety of operations. An "optimum" solution is then obtained by means of a systematic computational routine. The queuing model, for example, is relevant to many aspects of the operations of the Post Office, airports, service facilities, maintenance shops, and so on. In many instances such models may actually tell the client what his decision or plan ought to be. Analysis of this type is usually called operations research or management science rather than systems analysis, however.

There are, however, other decisions or problems, civilian as well as military, where computational techniques can help only with subproblems. Typical decisions of this latter type might be the determination of how much of the Federal budget should be allocated to economic development and what fraction of that should be spent on South America, or whether the needs of interstate transportation are better served by improved high speed rail transport or by higher performance highway turnpikes, or if there is some legislative action that might end the growth of juvenile delinquency. Such problems will normally involve more than the efficient allocation of resources among alternative uses; they are not "solvable" in the same sense as efficiency problems in which one can maximize some "pay-off" function that clearly expresses what one is trying to accomplish. Here rather, the objectives or goals of the action to be taken must be determined first. Decision problems associated with program budgeting are mainly of this type—where the difficulty lies in deciding what ought to be done as well as in how to do it, where it is not clear what "more efficient" means, and where many of the factors in the problem elude quantification. The final program recommendation will thus remain in part a matter of faith and judgment. Studies to help with these problems are systems analyses rather than operations research.°

Every systems analysis involves, at one stage, a comparison of alternative courses of action in terms of their costs and their effectiveness in attaining a specified objective. Usu-

---

° *For a further discussion of this distinction, see Reference 2.*

ally this comparison takes the form of an attempt to designate the alternative that will minimize the costs, subject to some fixed performance requirement (something like reduce unemployment to less than 2% in two years or add a certain number of miles to the interstate highway system), or conversely, it is an attempt to maximize some physical measure of performance subject to a budget constraint. Such evaluations are called cost-effectiveness analyses.† Since they often receive the lion's share of attention, the entire study also is frequently called a cost-effectiveness analysis. But this label puts too much emphasis on just one aspect of the decision process. In analyses designed to furnish broad policy advice other facets of the problem are of greater significance than the comparison of alternatives: the specification of sensible objectives, the determination of a satisfactory way to measure performance, the influence of considerations that cannot be quantified, or the design of better alternatives.

THE ESSENCE OF THE METHOD

What is there about the analytic approach that makes it better or more useful than other ways to furnish advice—than, say, an expert or a committee? In areas such as urban redevelopment or welfare planning, where there is no accepted theoretical foundation, advice obtained from experts working individually or as a committee must depend largely on judgment and intuition. *So must the advice from systems analysis.* But the virtue of such analysis is that it permits the judgment and intuition of the experts in relevant fields to be combined systematically and efficiently. The essence of the method is to construct and operate within a "model," a simplified abstraction of the real situation appropriate to the question. Such a model, which may take such varied forms as a computer simulation, an operational game, or even a purely verbal "scenario," introduces a precise structure and terminology that serve primarily as an effective means of communication, enabling the participants in the study to exercise their judgment and intuition in a concrete context and in proper relation to others. Moreover,

† Or, alternatively, cost-utility and cost-benefit analyses.

through feedback from the model (the results of computation, the countermoves in the game, or the critique of the scenario), the experts have a chance to revise early judgments and thus arrive at a clearer understanding of the problem and its context, and perhaps of their subject matter.‡

THE PROCESS OF ANALYSIS

The fundamental importance of the model is seen in its relation to the other elements of analysis.§ There are five all told, and each is present in every analysis of choice and should always be explicitly identified.

1 *The objective (or objectives).* Systems analysis is undertaken primarily to help choose a policy or course of action. The first and most important task of the analyst is to discover what the decisionmaker's objectives are (or should be) and then how to measure the extent to which these objectives are, in fact, attained by various choices. This done, strategies, policies, or possible actions can be examined, compared, and recommended on the basis of how well and how cheaply they can accomplish these objectives.

2 *The alternatives.* The alternatives are the means by which it is hoped the objectives can be attained. They may be policies or strategies or specific actions or instrumentalities and they need not be obvious substitutes for each other or perform the same specific function. Thus, education, antipoverty measures, police protection, and slum clearance may all be alternatives in combating juvenile delinquency.

‡ C. J. Hitch in Reference 3, p. 23, states "Systems analyses should be looked upon not as the antithesis of judgment but as a framework which permits the judgment of experts in numerous subfields to be utilized—to yield results which transcend any individual judgment. This is its aim and opportunity."

§ Olaf Helmer in Reference 1, p. 7, puts it this way: "The advantage of employing a model lies in forcing the analyst to make explicit what elements of a situation he is taking into consideration and in imposing upon him the discipline of clarifying the concepts he is using. The model thus serves the important purpose of establishing unambiguous intersubjective communication about the subject matter at hand. Whatever intrinsic uncertainties may becloud the area of investigation, they are thus less likely to be further compounded by uncertainties due to disparate subjective interpretations."

3 *The costs*. The choice of a particular alternative for accomplishing the objectives implies that certain specific resources can no longer be used for other purposes. These are the costs. For a future time period, most costs can be measured in money, but their true measure is in terms of the opportunities they preclude. Thus, if the goal is to lower traffic fatalities, the irritation and delay caused to motorists by schemes that lower automobile speed in a particular location must be considered as costs, for such irritation and delay may cause more speeding elsewhere.

4 *A model (or models)*. A model is a simplified, stylized representation of the real world that abstracts the cause-and-effect relationships essential to the question studied. The means of representation may range from a set of mathematical equations or a computer program to a purely verbal description of the situation, in which intuition alone is used to predict the consequences of various choices. In systems analysis (or any analysis of choice), the role of the model (or models, for it may be inappropriate or absurd to attempt to incorporate all the aspects of a problem in a single formulation) is to estimate for each alternative the costs that would be incurred and the extent to which the objectives would be attained.

5 *A criterion*. A criterion is a rule or standard by which to rank the alternatives in order of desirability. It provides a means for weighing cost against effectiveness.

The process of analysis takes place in three over-lapping stages. In the first, the formulation stage, the issues are clarified, the extent of the inquiry limited, and the elements identified. In the second, the search stage, information is gathered and alternatives generated. The third stage is evaluation.

To start the process of evaluation or comparison (see Figure 19-1), the various *alternatives* (which may have to be discovered or invented as part of the analysis) are examined by means of the *models*. The models tell us what consequences or outcomes can be expected to follow from each alternative; that is, what the *costs* are and the extent to which each *objective* is attained. A *criterion* can then be used to weigh the costs against performance, and thus the alternatives can be arranged in the order of preference.

Unfortunately, things are seldom tidy: Too often the objectives are multiple, conflicting, and obscure; alternatives are not adequate to attain the objectives; the measures of effectiveness do not really measure the extent to which the objectives are attained; the predictions from the model are full of uncertainties; and other criteria that look almost as plausible as the one chosen may lead to a different order of preference. When this happens, we must take another approach. A single attempt or pass at a problem is seldom enough. (See Figure 19-2.) The key to successful analysis is a continuous cycle of formulating the problem, selecting objectives, designing alternatives, collecting data, building models, weighing cost against performance, testing for sensitivity, questioning assumptions and data, re-examining the objectives, opening new alternatives, building better models, and so on, until satisfaction is obtained or time or money force a cutoff.

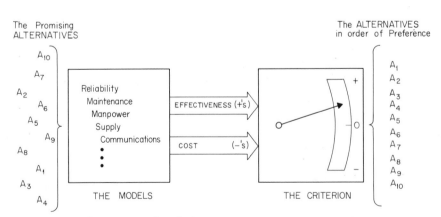

Figure 19-1   The structure of analysis.

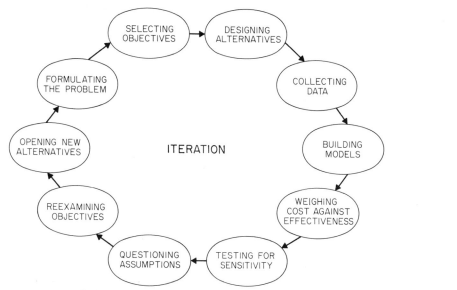

Figure 19-2   The key to analysis.

In brief, a systems analysis attempts to look at the entire problem and look at it in its proper context. Characteristically, it will involve a systematic investigation of the decisionmaker's objectives and of the relevant criteria; a comparison—quantitative insofar as possible—of the cost, effectiveness, risk, and timing associated with each alternative policy or strategy for achieving the objectives; and an attempt to design better alternatives and select other goals if those examined are found wanting.

Note that there is nothing really new about the procedures I have just sketched. They have been used, more or less successfully, by managers throughout government and industry since ancient times. The need for considering cost relative to performance must have occurred to the earliest planner. Systems analysis is thus not a catchword to suggest we are doing something new; at most, we are doing something better. What may be novel though, is that this sort of analysis is an attempt to look at the entire problem systematically with emphasis on explicitness, on quantification, and on the recognition of uncertainty. Also novel are the schemes or models used to explore the consequences of various choices and to eliminate inferior action in situations where the relationships cannot be represented adequately by a mathematical model.

Note that there is nothing in these procedures that guarantees the advice from the analysis to be good. They do not preclude the possibility that we are addressing the wrong problem or have allowed our personal biases to bar a better solution from consideration. When a study is a poor one it is rarely because the computer wasn't powerful enough or because the methods of optimization were not sufficiently sophisticated, but because it had the wrong objective or poor criteria. There are some characteristics of a study, however, that seem to be associated with good analysis. Let me identify some of these.

PRINCIPLES OF GOOD ANALYSIS

1 It is all-important to tackle the "right" problem. A large part of the investigators' effort must be invested in thinking about the problem, exploring its proper breadth, and trying to discover the appropriate objectives and to search out good criteria for choice. If we have not chosen the best set of alternatives to compare we will not discover the best solution. But if we have chosen the wrong objective then we might find a solution to the wrong problem. Getting an accurate answer to the wrong question is likely to be far less helpful than an incomplete answer to the right question.

2 The analysis must be systems oriented. Rather than isolating a part of the problem by neglecting its interactions with other

parts, an effort should be made to extend the boundaries of the inquiry as far as required for the problem at hand, to find what interdependencies are important, and to study the entire complex system. This should be done even if it requires the use of purely intuitive judgment.

An interdisciplinary team of persons having a variety of knowledge and skills is helpful here. This is not so merely because a complex problem is likely to involve many diverse factors that cannot be handled by a single discipline. More importantly, a problem looks different to, say, an economist, an engineer, a political scientist, or a professional bureaucrat, and their different approaches may contribute to finding a solution.

3 The presence of uncertainty should be recognized, and an attempt made to take it into account. Most important decisions are fraught with uncertainty. In planning urban redevelopment we are uncertain about city growth patterns, about the extent to which freeways or rapid transit systems will be used, about costs, about tax revenues, about the demand for services. For many of these things, there is no way to say with confidence that a given estimate is correct. The analyst attempts to identify these uncertainties and evaluate their impact. Often he can say the value of a parameter will be more than A but less than B. Sometimes it is possible to indicate how the uncertainty can be reduced by further testing and how long that will take. Most important, the analysis should determine the effect of uncertainty on the answers. This is done by a sensitivity analysis that shows how the answers change in response to changes in assumptions and estimates.*

The study report should include the presentation of a contingency table showing the effectiveness and cost associated with each significant alternative for various future environments and for each set of assumptions about the uncertainties.

4 The analysis attempts to discover new alternatives as well as to improve the obvious ones. The invention of new alternatives can be much more valuable than an exhaustive comparison of given alternatives, none of which may be very satisfactory.

5 While in problems of public policy or national security, the scientific method of controlled repeated experiment cannot be used,

See, for example, Reference 4, pp. 12–41.

the analysis should strive to attain the standards traditional to science. These are (1) intersubjectivity: results obtained by processes that can be duplicated by others to attain the same results; (2) explicitness: use of calculations, assumptions, data, and judgments that are subject to checking, criticism, and disagreement; and (3) objectivity: conclusions do not depend on personalities, reputations, or vested interests; where possible these conclusions should be in quantitative and experimental terms.

THE MODELS

As mentioned earlier, systems analysis is flexible in the models it uses. Indeed, it has to be. Mathematics and computing machines, while extremely useful, are limited in the aid they can give in broad policy questions. If the important aspects of the problem can be completely formulated mathematically or represented numerically, techniques such as dynamic programming, game theory, queuing theory, or computer simulation may be the means of providing the best solution. But in most policy analyses, computations and computers are often more valuable for the aid they provide to intuition and understanding, rather than for the results they supply.

While a computer can solve only the problems that the analyst knows conceptually how to solve himself, it can help with many others. The objection that one cannot use results which depend on many uncertain parameters represents a lack of understanding of how systems analysis can help a decisionmaker. For a study to be useful it must indicate the *relative* merit of the various alternatives and identify the critical parameters. The great advantage of a computerized model is that it gives the analyst the capability to do numerous excursions, parametric investigations, and sensitivity analyses and thus to investigate the ranking of alternatives under a host of assumptions. This may be of more practical value to the decisionmaker than the ability to say that a given alternative will have such and such a rank with high confidence in a very narrowly defined situation.

The type of model appropriate to a problem depends on the problem and what we know or think we know about it.

For example, suppose we are concerned with long-range economic forecasting or decisions about the development of a national economy. The type of model to use will depend on the particular economy and on the kind of questions that must be answered. If the questions were about the United States, the model might be mathematical and possibly programmed for a computer because of its size and complexity. (By a mathematical model I mean one in which the relationships between the variables and parameters are represented by mathematical equations.) In the case of the United States, because of the vast amount of data available in the form of economic and demographic time series regarding just about every conceivable aspect of economic life, numerous mathematical and computer models have been formulated and used with more or less success.

If we are not able to abstract the situation to a series of equations or a mathematical model, some other way to represent the consequences that follow from particular choices must be found. Simulation may work. Here, instead of describing the situation directly, each element making up the real situation may be simulated by a physical object or, most often, by a digital computer using sets of random numbers, and its behavior analyzed by operating with the representation. For example, we might use computer simulation to study the economy of some Latin American country. The distinction between a computer simulation and the use of a computer to analyze a mathematical model is often a fuzzy one, but the fundamental difference is that in simulation the overall behavior of the model is studied through a case-by-case approach.

For studying the economy of a newly emerging nation such as is found in Africa, where the situation is even more poorly structured and where we have little firm knowledge of existing facts and relationships, a possible approach would be through the direct involvement of experts who have knowledge of the problem.

Ordinarily, we would like to have the judgment of more than one expert, even though their advice usually differs. There are several ways to try for a consensus; the traditional way has been to assemble the experts in one place, to let them discuss the problem freely,

and to require that they arrive at a joint answer. They could also be put to work individually, letting others seek methods for the best combined use of their findings. Or they could be asked to work in a group exercise—ranging from a simple structured discussion to a sophisticated simulation or an "operational game"—to obtain judgments from the group as a whole.

This latter approach is a laboratory simulation involving roleplaying by human subjects who simulate real-world decisionmakers. To study the economy of an underdeveloped country the various sectors of the economy might be simulated by specialized experts (see Reference 5). They would be expected, in acting out their roles, not so much to play a competitive game against one another, but to use their intuition as experts to simulate as best they could the attitudes and consequent decisions of their real-life counterparts. For instance, a player simulating a goods producing sector of the economy might, within constraints, shut down or expand manufacturing facilities, modernize, change raw material and labor inputs, vary prices and so on. There would also need to be government players who could introduce new fiscal or monetary policies and regulations (taxes, subsidies, tariffs, price ceilings, etc.) as well as social and political innovations with only indirect economic implications (social security, education, appeals to patriotism, universal military service, etc.) In laying down the rules governing the players' options and constraints and the actions taken within these rules, expert judgment is essential. It is also clear that for this problem political and sociological experts will be needed, as well as economists.

There is, of course, no guarantee that the projections obtained from such a model would be reliable. But the participating experts might gain a great deal of insight. Here the game structure—again a model—furnishes the participants with an artificial, simulated environment within which they can jointly and simultaneously experiment, acquiring through feedback the insights necessary to make successful predictions within the gaming context and thus indirectly about the real world.

Another useful technique is one that military systems analysts call "scenario writing." This is an effort to show how, starting with the present, a future state might evolve out of the present one. The idea is to show how this might happen plausibly by exhibiting a reasonable chain of events. A scenario is thus a primitive model. A collection of scenarios provides an insight on how future trends can depend on factors under our control and suggests policy options to us.

Another type of group action, somewhat less structured than the operational game, attempts to improve the panel or committee approach by subjecting the views of individual experts to each other's criticism without actual confrontation and its possible psychological shortcomings. In this approach, called the Delphi method, direct debate is replaced by the interchange of information and opinion through a carefully designed sequence of questionnaires. At each successive interrogation, the participants are given new refined information, and opinion feedback is derived by computing consensus from the earlier part of the program. The process continues until either a consensus is reached, or the conflicting views are documented fully (see References 6 and 7).

It should be emphasized that in many important problems it is not possible to build really quantitative models. The primary function of a model is "explanatory," to organize our thinking. As I have already stated, the essence of systems analysis is not mathematical techniques or procedures, and its recommendations need not follow from computation. What counts is the effort to compare alternatives systematically, in quantitative terms when possible, using a logical sequence of steps that can be retraced and verified by others.

THE VIRTUES

In spite of many limitations, the decisionmakers who have made use of systems analysis find it extremely useful. In fact, for some questions of national defense, analysis is essential. Without calculation there is no way to discover how many missiles may be needed to destroy a target system, or how arms control may affect security. It may be essential in areas also; one cannot experiment radically with the national economy or even change the traffic patterns in a large city without running

the risk of chaos. Analysis offers an alternative to "muddling through" or to settling national problems by yielding to the strongest pressure group. It forces the devotees of a program to make explicit their lines of argument and talk about the resources their programs will require as well as the advantages they might produce.

It is easy, unfortunately, to exaggerate the degree of assistance that systems analysis can offer the policymaker. At most, it can help him understand the relevant alternatives and the key interactions by providing an estimate of the costs, risks, payoffs and the timespan associated with each course of action. It may lead him to consider new and better alternatives. It may sharpen the decisionmaker's intuition and will certainly broaden his basis for judgment, thus helping him make a better decision. But value judgments, imprecise knowledge, intuitive estimates, and uncertainties about nature and the actions of others mean that a study can do little more than assess some of the implications of choosing one alternative over another. In practically no case, therefore, should the decisionmaker expect the analysis to demonstrate that, beyond all reasonable doubt, a particular course of action is best.

THE LIMITATIONS

Every systems analysis has defects. Some of these are limitations inherent in all analysis of choice. Others are a consequence of the difficulties and complexities of the question. Still others are blunders or errors in thinking, which hopefully will disappear as we learn to do better and more complete analyses.

The alternatives to analysis also have their defects. One alternative is pure intuition. This is in no sense analytic, since no effort is made to structure the problem or to establish cause-and-effect relationships and operate on them to arrive at a solution. The intuitive process is to learn everything possible about the problem, to "live with it," and to let the subconscious provide the solution.

Between pure intuition, on one hand, and systems analysis, on the other, other sources of advice can, in a sense, be considered to employ analysis, although ordinarily a less systematic, explicit, and quantitative kind. One can turn to an expert. His opinion may, in fact, be very helpful if it results from a reasonable and impartial examination of the facts, with due allowance for uncertainty, and if his assumptions and chain of logic are made *explicit*. Only then can others use his information to form their own considered opinions. But an expert, particularly an unbiased expert, may be hard to find.

Another way to handle a problem is to turn it over to a committee. Committees, however, are much less likely than experts to make their reasoning explicit, since their findings are usually obtained by bargaining. This is not to imply that a look by a "blue ribbon" committee into such problems as poverty or the allocation of funds for foreign aid might not be useful, but a committee's greatest utility is likely to be in the critique of analysis done by others.

However, no matter whether the advice is supplied by an expert, a committee, or a formal study group, the analysis of a problem of choice involves the same five elements and basic structure we discussed earlier.

It is important to remember that all policy analysis falls short of being scientific research. No matter how we strive to maintain standards of scientific inquiry or how closely we attempt to follow scientific methods, we cannot turn systems analysis into science. Such analysis is designed primarily to recommend—or at least to suggest—a course of action, rather than merely to understand and predict. Like engineering, the aim is to use the results of science to do things well and cheaply. Yet, when applied to national problems, the difference from ordinary engineering is apparent in the enormous responsibility involved in the unusual difficulty of appraising—or even discovering—a value system applicable to the problems, and in the absence of ways to test the validity of the analysis.

Except for this inability to verify, systems analysis may still look like a purely rational approach to decisionmaking, a coldly objective, scientific method free from preconceived ideas and partisan bias and judgment and intuition.

It isn't, really. Judgment and intuition are used in designing the models; in deciding what alternatives to consider, what factors are relevant, what the interrelations between these factors are, and what criteria to choose; and in interpreting the results of the analysis. This fact—that judgment and intuition permeate all analysis—should be remembered when we examine the apparently precise results that seem to come with such high precision analysis.

Many flaws are the results of pitfalls faced by the analyst. It is all too easy for him to begin to believe his own assumptions and to attach undue significance to his calculations, especially if they involve bitter arguments and extended computations. The most dangerous pitfall or source of defects is an unconscious adherence to a "party line." This is frequently caused by a cherished belief or an *attention bias*. All organizations foster one to some extent; RAND, the military services, and the civilian agencies of the government are no exception. The party line is "the most important single reason for the tremendous miscalculations that are made in foreseeing and preparing for technical advances or changes in the strategic situation" (Reference 7). Examples are plentiful: the political advisor whose aim is so fixed on maintaining peace that he completely disregards what might happen should deterrence fail; the weaponeer who is so fascinated by the startling new weapons that he has invented that he assumes the politician will allow them to be used; the union leader whose attention is so fixed on current employment that he rejects an automatic device that can spread his craft into scores of new areas. In fact, this failure to realize the vital interdependence among political purpose, diplomacy, military posture, economics, and technical feasibility is the typical flaw in most practitioners' approach to national security analysis.

There are also pitfalls for the bureaucrat who commissions a study or gives inputs to it. For instance, he may specify assumptions and limit the problem arbitrarily. When a problem is first observed in one part of an organization, there is a tendency to seek a solution completely contained in that part. An administrator is thus likely to pose his problems in such a way as to bar from consideration alternatives or criteria that do not fit into his idea of the way things should be done; for example, he may not think of using ships for some tasks now being done by aircraft. Also, to act wisely on the basis of someone else's analysis one should, at the very least, understand the important and fundamental principles involved. One danger associated with analysis is that it may be employed by an administrator who is unaware of or unwilling to accept its limitations.

Pitfalls are one thing, but the inherent limitations of analysis itself are another. These limitations confine analysis to an advisory role. Three are commented on here: analysis is necessarily incomplete; measures of effectiveness are inevitably approximate; and ways to predict the future are lacking.

Analysis Is Necessarily Incomplete

Time and money costs obviously place sharp limits on how far any inquiry can be carried. The very fact that time moves on means that a correct choice at a given time may soon be outdated by events and that goals set down at the start may not be final. The need for reporting almost always forces a cutoff. Time considerations are particularly important in military analysis, for the decisionmaker can wait only so long for an answer. Other costs are important here, too. For instance, we would like to find out what the Chinese Communists would do if we put an end to all military aid to Southeast Asia. One way to get this information would be to stop such aid. But while this would clearly be cheap in immediate dollar costs, the likelihood of other later costs precludes this type of investigation.

Still more important, however, is the general fact that, even with no limitations of time and money, analysis can never treat all the considerations that may be relevant. Some are too intangible—for example, how some unilateral U.S. action will affect NATO solidarity, or whether Congress will accept economies that disrupt cherished institutions such as the National Guard or radically change the pattern of domestic military spending. Considerations of this type should play as important a role in the recommendation of alternative policies as any idealized cost-effectiveness calculations. But ways to measure these considerations even approximately do not exist today, and they must be handled intuitively. Other immeasurable considerations involve moral judgments—for example, whether national security is better served by an increase in the budget for defense or for welfare, or under what circumstances the preservation of an immediate advantage is worth the compromise of fundamental principles. The analyst can apply his and others' judgment and intuition to these considerations, thus making them part of the study; but *bringing them to the attention of the decisionmaker*, the man with the responsibility, is extremely important.

Measures of Effectiveness Are Approximate

In military comparisons measures of effectiveness are at best reasonably satisfactory approximations for indicating the attainment of such vaguely defined objectives as deterrence or victory. Sometimes the best that can be done is to find measures that point in the right direction. Consider deterrence, for instance. It exists only in the mind—and in the enemy's mind at that. We cannot, therefore, measure the effectiveness of alternatives we hope will lead to deterrence by some scale of deterrence, but must use instead such approximations as the potential mortalities that we might inflict or the roof cover we might destroy. Consequently, even if a comparison of two systems indicated that one could inflict 50 per cent more casualties on the enemy than the other, we could not conclude that this means the system supplies 50 per cent more deterrence. In fact, since in some circumstances it may be important *not* to look too dangerous, we encounter arguments that the system threatening the greatest number of casualties may provide the *least* deterrence!

Similarly, consider the objective of U.S. government expenditures for health. A usual measure of effectiveness is the dollar value of increased labor force participation. But, this is clearly inadequate; medical services are more often in demand because of a desire to reduce the every day aches and pains of life. Moreover, we cannot be very confident about the accuracy of our estimates. For example, one recent and authoritative source estimates the yearly cost of cancer to the United States at $11 billion, while another, equally authoritative, estimates $2.6 billion (Reference 8).

No Satisfactory Way to Predict the Future Exists

While it is possible to forecast events in the sense of mapping out possible futures, there is no satisfactory way to predict a single future for which we can work out the best system or determine an optimum policy. Consequently, we must consider a range of possible futures or contingencies. In any one of these we may be able to designate a preferred course of action, but we have no way to determine such action for the entire range of possibilities. We can design a force structure for a particular war in a particular place, but we have no way to work out a structure that is good for the entire spectrum of future wars in all the places they may occur.

Consequently, defense planning is rich in the kind of analysis that tells what damage could be done to the United States given a particular enemy force structure; but it is poor in the kinds of analyses that evaluate how we will actually stand in relation to the Soviets in years to come.

In spite of these limitations, it is not sensible to formulate policy or action without careful consideration of whatever relevant numbers can be discovered. In current Department of Defense practice quantitative estimates of various kinds are used extensively. Many people, however, are vaguely uneasy about the particular way these estimates are made and their increasingly important role not only in military planning but elsewhere throughout the government.

Some skepticism may be justified, for the analytical work may not always be done competently or used with its limitations in mind. There may indeed be some dangers in relying on systems analysis, or on any similar approach to broad decisions. For one thing, since many factors fundamental to problems of Federal policy are not readily amenable to quantitative treatment, they may possibly be neglected, or deliberately set aside for later consideration and then forgotten, or improperly weighed in the analysis itself or in the decision based on such analysis. For another, a study may, on the surface, appear so scientific and quantitative that it may be assigned a validity not justified by the many subjective judgments involved. In other words, we may be so mesmerized by the beauty and precision of the numbers that we overlook the simplifications made to achieve this precision, neglect analysis of the qualitative factors, and overemphasize the importance of idealized calculations in the decision process. But without analysis we face even greater dangers in neglect of considera-

tions and in the assignment of improper weights!

THE FUTURE

And finally, what of the future? Resistance by the military to the use of systems analysis in broad problems of strategy has gradually broken down. Both government and military planning and strategy have always involved more art than science; what is happening is that the art form is changing from an ad hoc, seat-of-the-pants approach based on intuition to one based on analysis *supported by* intuition and experience. This change may come more slowly in the nonmilitary aspects of government. For one thing, the civilian employees of the government are not so closely controlled "from the top" as those in the military; also the goals in these areas are just as vague and even more likely to be conflicting.* The re-

---

* *James R. Schlesinger in Reference 2 has a slightly different view: "Thus the mere uncovering of ways to increase efficiency is not sufficient. Even where a decision is clear to the disinterested observer, it is difficult to persuade committed men that their programs or activities should be reduced or abandoned. The price of enthusiasm is that those who have a commitment will be "sold" on their specialty and are incapable of viewing it in cold analytical terms. This may be especially true of the military establishment, where the concepts of duty, honor, and country when particularized lead to a certain inflexibility in adjusting to technological change and the new claims of efficiency. But it is also true in the civilian world: for conservationists, foresters, water resource specialists, businessmen, union leaders, or agrarians, some aspects of their value-systems run directly counter to the claims of efficiency. The economic view strikes them all as immoral as well as misleading. (After all, is it not a value judgment on the part of economists that efficiency calculations are important?)*

"Even in the case of fairly low-level decisions, if they are political, systematic quantitative analysis does not necessarily solve problems. It will not convince ardent supporters that their program is submarginal. Nevertheless, quantitative analysis remains most useful. For certain operational decisions, it either provides the decisionmaker with the justification he may desire for cutting off a project or forces him to come up with a nonnumerical rationalization. It eliminates the purely subjective approach on the part of devotees of a program and forces them to change their lines of argument. They must talk about reality rather than morality. Operational research creates a bridge to budgetary problems over which planners, who previously could assume resources were free, are forced, willingly or unwillingly, to walk."

quirements of the integrated Planning-Programming-Budgeting system will do much to speed the acceptance of analysis for other tasks, however.

With the acceptance of analysis, the computer is becoming increasingly significant—as an automaton, a process controller, an information processor, and a decision aid. Its usefulness in serving these ends can be expected to grow. But at the same time, it is important to note that even the best computer is no more than a tool to expedite analysis. Even in the narrowest decisions, considerations not subject to any sort of quantitative analysis can always be present. Big decisions, therefore, cannot be the *automatic* consequence of a computer program or of any application of mathematical models.

For broad studies, intuitive, subjective, even ad hoc study schemes must continue to be used—but supplemented to an increasing extent by systems analysis. The ingredients of this analysis must include not only an increasing use of computer-based models for those problems where they are appropriate, but for treatment of the nonquantifiable aspects, a greater use of techniques for better employment of judgment, intuition, and experience. These techniques—operational gaming, "scenario" writing, and the systematic interrogation of experts—are on the way to becoming an integral part of systems analysis.

CONCLUDING REMARKS

And now to review. A systems analysis is an analytic study designed to help a decisionmaker identify a preferred choice among possible alternatives. It is characterized by a systematic and rational approach, with assumptions made explicit, objectives and criteria clearly defined, and alternative courses of action compared in the light of their possible consequences. An effort is made to use quantitative methods, but computers are not essential. What is essential is a model that enables expert intuition and judgment to be applied efficiently. The method provides its answer by processes that are accessible to critical examination, capable of duplication by others, and, more or less, readily modified as new information becomes available. And, in contrast to other aids to decisionmaking, which share the same limitations, it extracts everything possible from scientific methods, and therefore its virtues are the virtues of those methods. At its narrowest, systems analysis has offered a way to choose the numerical quantities related to a weapon system so that they are logically consistent with each other, with an assumed objective, and with the calculator's expectation of the future. At its broadest, through providing the analytic backup for the plans, programs, and budgets of the various executive departments and establishments of the Federal Government, it can help guide national policy. But, even within the Department of Defense, its capabilities have yet to be fully exploited.

References

1. Helmer, O., *Social Technology*, The RAND Corporation, P-3063, February 1965; presented at the Futuribles Conference in Paris, April 1965.

2. Schlesinger, J. R., "Quantitative Analysis and National Security," *World Politics*, Vol. XV, No. 2, January 1963, pp. 295–315.

3. Quade, E. S., (ed.), *Analysis for Military Decisions*, Rand McNally, Chicago, 1964.

4. Fort, Donald M., *Systems Analysis as an Aid in Air Transportation Planning*, The RAND Corporation, P-3293, January 1966.

5. Helmer, O., and E. S. Quade, "An Approach to the Study of a Developing Economy by Operational Gaming," in *Researche Operationale et Problems du Tiers-Monde*, Dunod, Paris, 1964, pp. 43–54.

6. Helmer, O., and Norman C. Dalkey, "An Experimental Application of the Delphi Method to the Use of Experts," *Management Sciences*, Vol. 9, No. 3, April 1963, pp. 458–467.

7. Helmer, O., and Nicholas Rescher, "On the Epistemology of the Inexact Sciences," *Management Sciences*, Vol. 6, No. 1, October 1959, pp. 25–52.

8. Kahn, H., and I. Mann, *Ten Common Pitfalls*, The RAND Corporation, RM-1937, July 17, 1957.

9. Marshall, A. W., *Cost/Benefit Analysis in Health*, The RAND Corporation, P-3274, December 1965.

10. McKean, R. N., *Efficiency in Government Through Systems Analysis*, John Wiley & Sons, Inc., New York, 1958.

11. Hitch, C. J., and R. N. McKean, *The Economics of Defense in the Nuclear Age*, Harvard University Press, Cambridge, Massachusetts, 1960.

12. Peck, M. J., and F. M. Scherer, *The Weapons Acquisition Process: An Economic Analysis,* Harvard University Press, Cambridge, Massachusetts, 1962.

13. Ellis, J. W., Jr., and T. E. Greene, "The Contextual Study: A Structured Approach to the Study of Limited War," *Operations Research,* Vol. 8, No. 5, September-October 1960, pp. 639–651.

14. Novick, D., (ed.), *Program Budgeting: Program Analysis and the Federal Budget,* Government Printing Office, Washington, D.C., 1965; and Harvard University Press, Cambridge, Massachusetts, 1965.

15. Mood, Alex M., "Diversification of Operations Research," *Operations Research,* Vol. 13, No. 2, March-April 1965, pp. 169–178.

16. Dorfman, Robert, (ed.), *Measuring Benefits of Government Investments,* The Brookings Institute, 1965.

17. Fisher, G. H., *The World of Program Budgeting,* The RAND Corporation, P-3361, May 1966.

READING 20

THE ANALYTICAL BASES OF SYSTEMS ANALYSIS *

G. H. Fisher

INTRODUCTION

My assigned topic is "The Analytical Bases of
Systems Analysis." This subject may be approached from several points of view. The
usual one, I suppose, is to translate "analytical
bases" into "tools and techniques," and then
to proceed to talk about linear programming,
Monte Carlo techniques, computer simulation
models, and the like. Since a lot has already
been written and said on these subjects, I prefer to take a different tack.

I want to focus on a discussion of the role
of analysis in the decisionmaking process. This
is important because different people in the
analytical community have differing views on
the matter and depending on which view is
held, one can arrive at various alternative conclusions regarding the conceptual and procedural bases for analysis in support of the deci-

* *Reprinted with permission of The RAND Corporation, P-3363, May, 1966, The RAND Corporation, Santa Monica, California.*

sion process. Let me say at the onset that my
views are probably somewhat controversial,
and that no doubt many attendees at this symposium will tend to take issue with some of my
arguments. This, however, should help stimulate lively discussion!

Let me also emphasize at this point that my
remarks are focused primarily on a *long-range-
planning military decision context;* but hopefully many of the points made will have more
general applicability.

WHAT IS SYSTEMS ANALYSIS?

Before launching into a discussion of the role
of systems analysis in the long-range-planning
process, I think I had best take a few moments
to tell you what the term "systems analysis"
means to me. This seems necessary because the
term itself apparently has various meanings
today; and also there are *other* terms which
are sometimes used as being synonomous with
systems analysis: e.g., cost-effectiveness analysis, cost-benefit analysis, operations analysis,

and the like. Now I do not want to get tangled up in a semantics jungle here. So let me just say that in the context of my talk, systems analysis is an analytical process having the following major characteristics:

1 A most fundamental characteristic is the systematic examination and comparison of alternative courses of action which might be taken to achieve specified objectives for some future time period. Not only is it important to systematically examine all of the relevant alternatives that can be identified initially, but also to *design additional ones* if those examined are found wanting.[1] Finally, the analysis, particularly if thoroughly and imaginatively done, may frequently result in modifications of the initially specified objectives.

2 Critical examination of alternatives typically involves numerous considerations; but the two main ones are assessment of the cost (in the sense of economic resource cost) and the utility (the benefits or gains) pertaining to each of the alternatives being compared to attain the stipulated objectives.

3 The time context is the future—often the distant future (five, ten, or more years).

4 Because of the extended time horizon, the environment is one of uncertainty—very often great uncertainty. Since uncertainty is an important facet of the problem, it should be faced up to and treated explicitly in the analysis. This means, among other things, that wherever possible the analyst should avoid the exclusive use of simple expected value models.

5 Usually the context in which the analysis takes place is fairly broad (often very broad) and the environment very complex with numerous interactions among the key variables in the problem. This means that simple, straightforward solutions are the exception rather than the rule.

6 While quantitative methods of analysis should be utilized as much as possible, because of items (4) and (5),[2] purely quantitative work must often be heavily supplemented by qualitative analysis. In fact, I stress the importance of *good* qualitative work and of using an appropriate combination of quantitative and qualitative methods.

7 Usually the focus is on research and development and/or investment type decision problems, although operational decisions are sometimes encountered. This does not mean, of course, that operational considerations are ignored in dealing with R&D and investment type problems.

THE ROLE OF SYSTEMS ANALYSIS IN THE LONG-RANGE-PLANNING DECISION PROCESS

Given this general conception of systems analysis, let me now turn to a discussion of the role of analysis in the long-range planning-decision process.

I suppose, as analysts, we would always like to try to come up with "preferred solutions" when studying alternative future courses of action. Ideally this means determining *"the optimum"*—that is, the point on some well-defined surface where all the partial derivatives are equal to zero and the appropriate second order conditions prevail. I submit, however, that in most of today's long-range-planning decision problems of any consequence, it is rarely possible to even approach anything like a hard core optimization. Most likely we will be lucky if we can get some notion as to the *signs* of the partial derivatives—i.e., whether we are moving "up the hill," so to speak, toward the saddle point in a maximization problem, or away from the saddle point ("down hill"). In fact, I would even argue that in most studies that I have worked on in recent years, it is often difficult to determine what "hill" we are on, or should be on! This rather crude analogy begins to convey the flavor of my thoughts on the role of analysis in the long-range decision process. Let me now be more specific.

Here I shall take as a text for my remarks the following statements by the Assistant Secretary of Defense, Systems Analysis:

> Ultimately all policies are made . . . on the basis of judgments. There is no other way, and there never will be. The question is whether those judgments have to be made in the fog of inadequate and inaccurate data, unclear and undefined issues, and a welter of conflicting personal opinions, or whether they can be made on the basis of adequate, reliable

[1] *E. S. Quade*, Military Systems Analysis, *The RAND Corporation, RM-3452-PR, January 1963, p. 1.*
[2] *And also because of inadequate data and information sources.*

information, relevant experience, and clearly drawn issues. In the end, analysis is but an aid to judgment .... Judgment is supreme.[3]

The analyst at this level is not computing optimum solutions or making decisions. In fact, computation is not his most important contribution. And he is helping someone else to make decisions. His job is to ask and find answers to the questions: "What are we trying to do?" "What are the alternative ways of achieving it?" "What would they cost, and how effective would they be?" "What does the decisionmaker need to know in order to make a choice?" And to collect and organize this information for those who are responsible for deciding what the Defense program ought to be.[4]

The Assistant Secretary's remarks pretty much reflect my own views on the subject. I would put the argument in the following manner:

Contrary to what some of the more enthusiastic advocates of quantitative analysis may think, I tend to visualize systems analysis as playing a somewhat modest, though very significant, role in the overall decisionmaking process. In reality most major long-range-planning decision problems must ultimately be resolved primarily on the basis of intuition and judgment. I suggest that the main role of analysis should be to try to *sharpen* this intuition and judgment. In practically no case should it be assumed that the results of the analysis will "make" the decision. The really critical problems are just too difficult, and there are too many intangible (e.g., political, psychological, and sociological) considerations that cannot be taken into account in the analytical process, especially in a quantitative sense. In sum, the analytical process should be directed toward assisting the decisionmaker in such a way that his intuition and judgment are better than they would be without the results of the analysis.

We might say that there are two extreme positions regarding the role of analysis in the decisionmaking process. On the one hand, one might argue that the types of long-range-planning decision problems under consideration here are just too complex for the current state of analytical art to handle. Decisions must be made purely on the basis of intuition, judgment, and experience: i.e., the zero analysis position. At the other extreme are those who tend to think that all problems should be tackled in a purely quantitative fashion, with a view to essentially "making" the decision. Such a view implies explicit (usually meaning quantitative) calculations of cost and utility for all the alternatives under consideration. This may be possible, at times, for very narrowly defined, low level sub-optimization problems; but even this is questionable.

More generally, in dealing with major decision problems of choice, if the analyst approaches the analytical task in an inflexible "hard core" frame of mind, he is likely to be in for trouble. For example, he may soon give up in complete frustration, he may wind up with such a simplified model that the resulting calculations are essentially meaningless, or the result might be that his conclusions are presented two years after the critical time of decision and therefore useless to the decisionmaker.

My viewpoint is that in most cases the relevant range is between the extremes mentioned above, and that in such a context there is a wide scope of analytical effort that can be useful. Furthermore, even when only a relatively incomplete set of quantitative calculations of cost and utility can be made (probably the general situation), much can be done to assist the decisionmaker in the sense that I am using the term assistance. To repeat: The objective is to *sharpen* intuition and judgment. It is conceivable that only a small amount of sharpening may on occasion have a high payoff.

One other point seems relevant here. In that rare circumstance when a fairly complete set of calculations of cost and utility is possible and a resulting conclusion about a preferred alternative reached, it just may be that the conclusion itself may not be the most useful thing to the decisionmaker. In the first place, as pointed out earlier, the analysis usually cannot take everything into account—particularly some of the nebulous non-quantitative considerations. The decisionmaker has to allow for

---

[3] *A. C. Enthoven, quotation contained in an article in* Business Week, *November 13, 1965, p. 189.*
[4] *A. C. Enthoven, article in* The Armed Forces Comptroller, *Vol. IX, No. 1, March 1964, p. 39.*

these himself. But more important, most high-level decisionmakers are very busy men, with the result that they do not have time to structure a particular problem, think up the relevant alternatives (especially the *subtle* ones), trace out the key interaction among variables in the problem, and the like. This the analyst, if he is competent, can do, and should do. And it is precisely this sort of contribution that may be most useful to the decisionmaker. The fact that the analysis reaches a firm conclusion about a preferred alternative may in many instances be of secondary importance.

WHY IS OPTIMIZATION SO DIFFICULT?

At this point you may well ask the question: "Why is hard core optimization so difficult for the class of decision problems under consideration here?" Part of the answer, of course, is that in dealing with long-range-planning problems major uncertainties are always present; and the theory of choice under conditions of uncertainty does not always give us a definite set of rules to follow. Should we use expected values and ignore variances? Should we take variances into account; and if so, how? Should we use a minimax rule? And so on.

Another part of the answer concerns the basic nature of the decision questions themselves—their complexity and the scenario dependency of assumptions that must be made to formulate and to deal with the questions. Let me illustrate this point by referring to an area where in the past some of us thought that something approaching optimization might be attained. (We could have been wrong, of course; and I suspect we were!) I have in mind the general war problem area.

In the past—and still to a large extent today—general war decision problems have been formulated in terms of a "spasm response" scenario; and analyses of these problems have for the most part been conducted in that context. Spasm response involves a fairly mechanistic set of considerations. One side lets go with all (or a major part) of his strategic forces, and the other side retaliates in kind. Many of the major facets of this problem can be modeled, and numerous sets of quantitative results can be calculated—and have been calculated. Now I do not suppose any of us would argue that

we have ever attained "hard core" optimization in dealing with the spasm response case. There are still major uncertainties involved. But I do think some of us thought we were moving in that direction.

Now let us see what happens when we move away from the spasm response case (today usually called the pure *assured destruction* case) and begin to consider other strategies and scenarios. While not at all underplaying the importance of having an assured-destruction deterrent capability, many people today feel that in addition, other concepts of general war involving *controlled response* capability should be seriously considered. The main idea here is that in future time periods it might be desirable, even mandatory, that the national leaders have a wider range of options available to use in dealing with crisis situations—that is, a wider range than that available from a force mix tailored primarily to the notion of spasm response. Examples of these other options may be summarized under headings like:

1 Damage limiting capability.
2 Coercion and bargaining capabilities to be used in an escalation process stemming from a crisis situation.
3 Intrawar deterrence of countervalue exchanges.
4 War termination.

In addition, we have the problem of the proliferation of nuclear weapons in the future—the "N-country" problem—and the question of what this means for the future force posture of the United States.

Now I obviously cannot get into a detailed discussion of these topics here. Each is a complex subject in itself. But the main point I am trying to make is, I think, clear. Once controlled response strategies and scenarios are taken into consideration, the analytical problems increase astronomically when compared with the spasm response case. The uncertainties compound, scenario dependencies abound, a force mix that might seem preferred in one case might not look so good in another, non-quantifiable variables (e.g., political and psychological factors) are just very important, and the like. In sum, any notion of anything approaching hard core optimization goes out the window; and we begin to wonder whether classical systems analysis can contribute very much in dealing with problems of this kind.

Perhaps something can be done in the way of very low level suboptimizations for small pieces of the total problem. And some of this may be useful to a limited extent. But the long-range force planners have to grapple with the general war *force mix* problem (including force size) for future time periods; and the real question is whether analysis of *some kind* can sharpen the intuition and judgment of the decisionmakers in this complicated area.

I think the answer is probably "yes," but I confess that at this time I cannot be specific as to how analysis might help. At RAND we have just recently launched a major study of the whole question of controlled response in general war. Initially we shall probably experiment with various combinations of the more conventional methods, including war gaming (manual), war game simulations, classical systems analysis, and the like. Here we recognize that any one method alone will not do the job, and we also realize that the political scientists will have to provide a substantial input, particularly in the form of a menu of rich scenarios of various controlled response environments. Our main goal, of course, is to try to come up with some *new* concepts, methods and techniques of analysis, as well as to say something substantive about the complicated issues involved. We may fail, of course; but we think it is very important to give the problem a good try.

Let us turn now to a different problem area: the question of the mobility of the general purpose forces. Here again is a case where one might, at first glance, think that something approaching a reasonably good optimization might be possible. I haven't time to even outline all of the issues involved in this problem. So I shall discuss a few of them (staying within the bounds of an unclassified discussion) to illustrate my point.

Until recently most studies tended to focus on the "big lift" part of the total problem—that is, the intercontinental transportation question. The central issue here, of course, is the preferred mix of airlift, sealift, and prepositioned supplies and equipment. Some very good work has been done in this area, and I think something fairly close to good *sub*optimizations has been attained. However, when one

begins to think more deeply about the *total* problem—the problem the force planners have to grapple with—then questions begin to arise.

Two key factors in the big lift problem are: (1) the high cost of airlift vs. sealift and prepositioning; and (2) the payoff in terms of *very* rapid response time available from force mixes containing a relatively high proportion of expensive airlift capability. So the question of the value of very rapid response is a dominant consideration. However, if one wants to get serious about delving into the matter of quick response, it is immediately obvious that the boundaries of the original problem have to be broadened. Total response time is made up of intra-Z.I. mobility and intra-theater (or objectives area) mobility in addition to the big lift. And there are *interactions among all three*. So we have to look at the total before we know what kind of a response we really have for various alternatives. Here the problem begins to get very complicated. For example, when the intra-objectives area is added to the analysis, things get particularly messy. The ground battle cannot be ignored, nor can the questions of re-deployment and resupply. Furthermore, the final outcomes are just *very scenario dependent*.

Although I have barely scratched the surface, I think I have said enough to illustrate my point: that hard core analysis of the mobility problem facing the long-term planners is very difficult—particularly in an optimization sense. Does this mean that all the study effort expended in this area to date is worthless to the decisionmakers? I think nothing could be further from the truth. Recently, some very interesting work has been done on the intra-theater (or objectives area) mobility problem, to supplement the studies already done in the big lift area. While no over-all "preferred solutions" have been forthcoming, these studies have provided major insights into the key variables involved, some of the more important interrelationships among the variables, the sensitivity of results to variations in key parameters and assumptions, and the like. As a result, I feel that the decisionmakers have a much better basis for their judgments regarding future mobility force mixes than they would have had without the studies. But in my view, this is the real value of analysis. That is my main point.

WHAT CAN BE DONE?

If you agree with even half of what I have said up to this point, you may wonder about whether systems analysis can contribute very much to the long-range planning process in the area of national security—or any other realm, for that matter. Perhaps systems analysts had best apply for job re-training and transfer to other occupations!

I do not think such a conclusion is warranted. Given the appropriate view regarding the role of analysis in the planning decision process, I think that the analyst can pull his own weight many times over in assisting the decisionmakers to sharpen their intuition and judgment. Let me try to illustrate my point by offering some simple examples.

For these examples, I have deliberately chosen "sticky" (but not atypical) problem areas. I have also deliberately chosen what some people might call fairly "low level" examples of analytical work in these problem areas. Actually, I think that in many cases, much more in the way of analysis can in fact be done than is indicated in any illustrations. However, I want to try to make an *a fortiori*

argument, so to speak. If I can show that relatively simple type analyses can be useful, then I shall be well on the way toward demonstrating my point without having to resort to arguments based on more sophisticated forms of analytical effort. Another point is relevant here. In most fast-moving decision environments, the analyst is quite often called on to try to do something useful in a relatively short period of time. Usually this means that he does not have time to structure and carry out a complicated, complete analysis of the problem. He will have to settle for much less if he is to have any impact at all on the decision process.

For a change of pace, let us start out with an example outside the national security area. Suppose that we are concerned with deciding among alternative proposed water resources projects, and that we have a given budget to spend on such projects in the future. The budget is such that all of the proposed projects cannot be undertaken. We therefore want to choose the "preferred mix." Suppose further that we have an analytical staff and that it comes up with a summary of results of systems analyses of the problem in the following format:

TABLE 20-1

Analytical Factor	Proposed Projects			
	1	2	3	4 ... n
(1) Present worth[a] ($):				
(a) Discounted @ $2\frac{1}{2}\%$ (50 yr)				
(b) Discounted @ 5% (50 yr)				
(c) Discounted @ 8% (50 yr)				
(2) Possible variability of outcome:				
(a) "Most likely" range of present worth (low-high $)				
(b) Range of present worth outside of which outcome is "very unlikely" to fall				
(3) Effect on personal wealth distribution:				
(a) Number of farms affected				
(b) Average value of land and buildings per farm in the watershed ($)				
(c) Average net benefit per farm owner ($)				
(4) Effect on regional wealth distribution:				
(a) Average increase in per family income in the Basin ($)				
(b) Percentage increase in average income in the Basin due to project				
(5) Internal rate of return of project (%)[b]				

[a] Present value of estimated benefits minus present value of estimated costs.
[b] The rate of discount which reduces present worth to zero.

Assume that in addition to the quantitative data presented in the table, the analytical staff has supplemented the numerical calculations with *qualitative* discussion of some of the more relevant nonquantifiable issues involved in the decision: e.g., political factors, non-quantifiable "spillover" effects, and the like.

Now decision problems regarding alternative water resources projects are usually very complex. The analyst can rarely come up with a preferred solution—particularly in the sense that one mix of alternatives completely dominates all others. I submit, however, that even in such a context, analytical results of the type portrayed above can go a long way toward sharpening the intuition and judgment of the decisionmakers. I think you will all agree that in the above illustrative case, the decisionmakers would be better off if they had the results of the analytical effort than if they did not have such information. Their decision is likely to be a more informed one.

Let me now turn briefly to another example to illustrate a somewhat different point. Actually, I want to show two things with this example: (1) how wrong conclusions can be drawn from a systems analysis—particularly in the face of uncertainty; and (2) how the results of the same study can be interpreted differently, and how the second interpretation can be of assistance to the decisionmakers.

I have in mind here the results and conclusions of a study that was actually performed by one of the military departments in the Department of Defense and submitted to the Secretary of Defense and his staff. We need not get into the substantive national security issues involved in the study to illustrate the methodological points that I want to emphasize.

The structure of the analysis was an equal cost comparison of several alternative future courses of action; that is, for a specified budget level to be devoted to a particular military mission area, the alternatives were compared on the basis of their estimated effectiveness in accomplishing the stipulated task. The final quantitative results took the following form.

The stated conclusion of the study, based almost exclusively on these quantitative results, was that alternative C is preferred over A and B for a wide range of circumstances and contingencies. (The context of the study, I should point out, involved a time period some

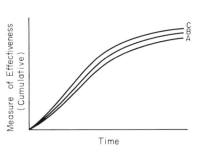

Figure 20-1 Comparison of equal cost alternatives.

10 to 15 years into the future.) Yet the difference in estimated effectiveness of the alternatives (for a constant budget level) was *at most 15 percent!* Now my point is simply that the context of the problem was clouded by so many uncertainties and the model used in the analysis was so aggregative, that calculated differences among the alternatives averaging less than 15 percent *just cannot be regarded as significant.* Thus, the stated conclusions of the study, if taken literally, could in a real sense be misleading to the decisionmakers.[5] In decision problems of this type where uncertainties are very great, the analyst is generally looking for much larger differences among the alternatives being examined. How great? There is no general rule. However, I can say that in the past when experienced analysts have been dealing with problems of this type, differences in the neighborhood of a *factor or 2 or 3* have been sought. I personally feel that in most long-range planning problems where major uncertainties are present, quantitative differences among alternatives must be *at least* a *factor of two* before we can even begin to have any confidence that the differences are significant. In any event, when they are smaller than that, the analyst must exercise extra caution in interpreting the results, and he must not make statements that are likely to mislead the decisionmakers.

There is another side to the coin, however. When quantitative differences among alternatives fall within a relatively narrow range, does this mean that the study is of no use to the decisionmaker? Not necessarily. If the

---

[5] *Needless to say, the Secretary of Defense and his analytical staff were not misled in this case. They are too experienced in interpreting the results of analytical studies to be overly impressed by small differences.*

quantitative work has been carried out in a reasonably competent manner and the differences among alternatives do tend to be relatively small, this fact in itself can be of considerable interest to the decisionmaker. This is especially true if sensitivity analyses have been made showing that as key parameters in the problem are varied over their relevant ranges, the final results are still within relatively narrow ranges. Given results of this kind, the decisionmaker can be less concerned about making a mistake regarding the quantitative aspects of the problems, and he may then feel somewhat more comfortable about focusing more of his attention on the *qualitative* factors —political, psychological, sociological considerations. In fact, if the analyst has done a reasonably thorough job, he might include a discussion of these factors in a qualitative supplementation to the purely quantitative part of the study.

The main point here is that while one of the main goals of analysis is to search for "pre-ferred alternatives" characterized by quantitative results *significantly* different (better) from other alternatives, the fact that a strong case cannot be made for a preferred alternative does not mean that the study is worthless. The results, and the sensitivity analysts supporting the results, can still be very enlightening to the decisionmaker. And again I emphasize that this is the main purpose of analysis.

As a final example, let us consider a military decision environment where the analyst is called upon to come up with something in a relatively short period of time in a rather complex problem area. The question is what can be done, if anything? If we take the position that the objective is to provide something that will help sharpen the decisionmakers' intuition and judgment, I think a great deal can be done. Something far short of a type of analysis involving a relatively complete set of calculations of utility and cost may be very useful. For one thing, a mere enumeration of all the relevant alternatives may be very helpful. If

TABLE 20-2 SELECTED DATA BEARING ON UTILITY CONSIDERATIONS FOR ALTERNATIVE SYSTEMS A, B, C, D AND E

Description	Alternative System				
	A	B	C	D	E
Quantitative Information					
Effective range (n mi)					
Cruise speed (kn)					
Penetration speed (kn)					
Warhead yield (MT)					
Circular error probability (CEP)					
Single-shot-kill probability					
Against soft targets					
Against hard targets					
Extended strike option time (days)					
.					
.					
.					
etc.					
Qualitative Information[1]					
"Show of force" capability					
Multi-directional attack capability					
Ground vulnerability					
In-flight vulnerability					
Controlled response capability					
.					
.					
.					
etc.					

[a] Some of these items have quantitative aspects to them; but they are very difficult to assess in a study with a short time deadline.

the analyst can go beyond this and furnish data and information bearing on utility and cost of these alternatives, so much the better.

One thing that can be done is to develop summary analyses of cost and utility and present them along with a qualitative statement of some of the key implications. Examples are contained in Figure 20-2 and Table 20-2.

Figure 20-2 shows total system cost (research and development, investment, and operating cost[6]) vs. force size for several alternative systems. Here some of the alternatives are ground-based missile systems, others are airborne-alert, long-endurance-aircraft systems, with the aircraft serving as missile-launching platforms. In the case of the missile systems, force size means number of missiles in position ready to go. For the aircraft platform systems, force size means number of missiles continuously airborne on station ready to go.

Used in conjunction with data pertaining to utility (as in Table 20-2), system cost vs. force size curves can be useful. For example, suppose that alternatives A and C are in the same ball park with respect to certain key utility variables—say, penetration capability and single-shot kill probability—but that C is clearly more vulnerable to an initial enemy strike than is A. The difference in the system cost curves for A and C in Figure 20-2, then, essentially represents what we pay for getting reduced vulnerability. But there are other ways

to play this game. Suppose the decisionmaker has a given budget (B_0 in Figure 20-2) to spend for supplementation of the already planned strategic forces. For B_0 he can get a force size of F_1 for alternative A, or a much larger force (F_2) of system C. He may judge that the larger force of C may more than compensate for its higher vulnerability. Or he may decide that F_2 of C is roughly equivalent to F_1 of A and decide to go for C for other (qualitative) reasons: e.g., C may have more of a show-of-force capability than A, or be preferable from a controlled response point of view.

In any event, *the decisionmaker is clearly in a better position to sharpen his intuition and judgment if he has the benefit of Figure 20-2 and Table 20-2 than if he did not have them.*[7] This is an illustration example of what was meant earlier when I indicated that there are numerous things that can be done between the extremes of no analysis whatever and "hard core" cost-utility analysis. The above example is certainly far short of the latter; but it nevertheless may be useful.

CONCLUDING REMARK

I see that my allotted time has expired. I hope that my remarks have served to sharpen your intuition and judgment regarding the analytical bases of systems analysis. Thank you.

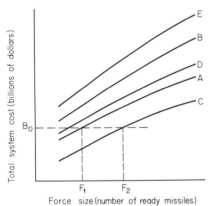

Figure 20-2 Total system cost versus force size for alternative systems A, B, C, D, and E.

[6] *Operating cost is usually computed for a fixed period of years—say, 5 or 7.*

References

Enthoven, A. C., "Decision Theory and Systems Analysis," *The Armed Forces Comptroller*, March 1964.

Fisher, G. H., *The Role of Cost-Utility Analysis in Program Budgeting*, The RAND Corporation, RM-4279-RC, September 1964.

———, *Analytical Support for Defense Planning*, The RAND Corporation, P-2650, October 1962.

Fort, Donald M., Systems Analysis as an Aid in Air Transportation Planning, The RAND Corporation, P-3293-1, March 1966.

Hitch, C. J., *An Appreciation of Systems Analysis*, The RAND Corporation, P-699, August 1955.

[7] *It is assumed, of course, that a textual discussion goes along with the figure and the table, so that the decisionmaker has the benefit of any interpretive comments that the analyst may have.*

————, and R. N. McKean, *The Economics of Defense in the Nuclear Age,* Harvard University Press, Cambridge, 1960.

Hoag, M. W., *Increasing Returns in Military Functions,* The RAND Corporation, P-3309, February 1966.

McKean, R. N., *Efficiency in Government Through Systems Analysis,* John Wiley & Sons, Inc., New York, 1958.

Novick, David, *Program Budgeting: Program Analysis and the Federal Government,* Harvard University Press, Cambridge, 1965.

Prest, A. R., and R. Turvey, *"Cost-Benefit Analysis: A Survey," The Economic Journal,* December 1965, pp. 683–735.

Quade, E. S. (ed.), *Analysis for Military Decisions,* Rand McNally & Co., Chicago, 1964.

————, *Systems Analysis Techniques for Planning-Programming-Budgeting,* The RAND Corporation, P-3322, March 1966.

————, *Cost-Effectiveness: An Introduction and Overview,* The RAND Corporation, P-3134, May 1965.

————, *Pitfalls in Military Systems Analysis,* The RAND Corporation, P-2676, November 1962.

————, *Military Analysis,* The RAND Corporation, RM-4808, November 1965.

————, *The Limitations of a Cost-Effectiveness Approach to Military Decision-Making,* The RAND Corporation, P-2798, September 1963.

READING 21

SYSTEMS ANALYSIS—CHALLENGE TO MILITARY MANAGEMENT*

Laurence E. Lynn, Jr.

The question is whether . . . judgments have to be made in the fog of inadequate and inaccurate data, unclear and undefined issues, and a welter of conflicting personal opinions, or whether they can be made on the basis of adequate, reliable information, relevant experience, and clearly drawn issues.

Dr. Alain C. Enthoven

Essentially we regard all military problems as, in one of their aspects, economic problems in the efficient allocation and use of resources . . . The job of economizing, which some would delegate to budgeteers and comptrollers, cannot be distinguished from the whole task of making military decisions.

Hon. Charles J. Hitch

* Reprinted with permission of Commandant, U.S. Army Management School, Fort Belvoir, Virginia.

. . . how decisions are reached greatly influences what the decisions are.

Capt. Stanley M. Barnes, USN

SECTION 1 INTRODUCTION

Defense and the nation's resources. To fail to provide an adequate military defense capability for the United States would expose not only this country—its inhabitants, its institutions, and its material wealth—but also the entire non-Communist world to the threat of conquest or destruction.

Annual defense budgets are now in the neighborhood of fifty billion dollars. Yet both despite and because of the enormity of this sum, public debate as to the adequacy of our defenses continues among those who could fairly be said to subscribe to the initial statement of this section. Some regard the current budget as insufficient; criticisms range from "we could do more" to the dramatic claim that the size and composition of the budget represent "unilateral disarmament." On the other hand, it is claimed by some who believe in the need for active defenses that the budget compounds a defense posture which already represents a diabolical overkill capacity far exceeding the requirements of deterrence.

Apparently, then, commitment to the goal of "an adequate defense capability" does not imply a clear-cut policy recommendation. Should we utilize more or less resources than the current budget allows? If so, how much more or less should we utilize, and on what? If not, are the resources obtained with currently budgeted funds utilized in the most effective manner, or should we be allocating more to some activities and less to others? A mere recognition of the need for defense does not automatically provide answers to questions as to what kind of defense and how much of it we need.

This paper focuses primarily on an economic and quantitative approach to defense planning at the national policy level which is known as *systems analysis*, or, what amounts to the same thing, *cost-effectiveness*. As employed by Secretary of Defense McNamara, systems analysis "assists in selecting weapon systems and choosing among alternative courses of action for purposes of designing and procuring a force structure adequate to our needs."[1] A mission-oriented planning, programing and budgeting process has been implemented which facilitates the use of such analyses in defense planning and procurement.

The need for quantitative defense analysis at the national policy level arises from several economic considerations: (a) The resources available for defense are limited. Hence, duplication of effort is a luxury which we can ill afford. Nor can we afford to allow imbalances in our defense capabilities to develop through a lack of effective planning. (b) The point has been reached in weapon system acquisition at which, in general, relatively large increases in expenditure may yield relatively small increments in defense effectiveness. Wasteful commitments of resources to projects with only marginal value must be avoided. (c) Because implementing the rapid developments in mili-

tary technology is both enormously costly and time consuming, great care must be taken to insure sound decisions in the planning stages. It is unnecessarily wasteful to abandon poorly-conceived projects only after large amounts of resources have been expended on them. On the other hand, care must be taken not to abandon promising developments prematurely.

Considerations such as these suggest that defense planning must be vitally concerned with quantitative issues. Decision makers and managers must be concerned not only with whether or not a particular proposal will add to our capabilities, but also, to the greatest extent possible, how much our capabilities will be augmented. It is important as well to know how much a particular proposal will cost and how the cost of augmenting capabilities in this way compares with the costs of achieving similar results in other ways. The availability of such quantitative information, when used properly in light of the many nonquantitative factors that must be considered, can help insure that the total volume of resources available for defense is most effectively employed to achieve military objectives. Systems analysis, which assists in providing and evaluating quantitative information, is properly viewed as effectiveness-maximizing, not cost-minimizing.

The relevance of quantitative analysis is by no means limited to the allocation of resources at the national policy level. Operations research techniques have long been applied to problems concerning the efficient utilization of defense resources at many levels in the defense establishment. The importance of using resources efficiently is growing as rapid changes in weapons technology and the increasing sophistication of strategic and tactical doctrine place ever greater demands upon our defense capabilities. Throughout this paper the logical similarities of systems analysis as used at the national policy level and other quantitative problem-solving approaches used throughout the defense establishment will be stressed.

The objectives of achieving optimum allocation and efficient utilization of defense resources can be justified from another viewpoint: resources devoted to defense represent resources which are not devoted to other desirable uses such as private consumption and investment, expenditures for education, highways, water pollution control, the alleviation of poverty and disease, and the like. Systems

[1] *Robert S. McNamara, "Managing the Department of Defense,"* Civil Service Journal, *April-June 1964.*

analysis can help insure that what we get in terms of defense for what we give up in terms of other, non-military, objectives is maximized. To put it another way, systems analysis can help insure that given defense capabilities are attained with a minimum sacrifice of other objectives. This is an important economic and social objective. As Kermit Gordon, Director of the Bureau of the Budget, stated, a billion dollars ". . . is a lot bigger in civilian terms than it is in military terms. With it we can underwrite the anti-poverty program for a year."[2] When resources have such a high potential yield in social benefits if devoted to civilian uses, it is incumbent upon defense decision-makers to employ these resources to maximum effect in military uses.

Quantitative analysis and defense planning. This discussion is addressed to all military decision-maker/managers, though its subject matter should be of interest to anyone concerned with defense planning. It is recognized that relatively few military managers are connected with the decision making process at the national policy level at any given time. The probability is increasing, however, that the typical military manager, no matter at what level in the defense establishment he is working, will be in positions to initiate, supervise, evaluate or participate in some phase of quantitative analysis. It is of considerable importance, therefore, that managers obtain sufficient understanding of what is involved in quantitative analysis so that they can effectively confront the needs and issues as they arise. The systems analysis approach is chosen as a fulcrum for the discussion because (1) it is a useful introduction to the application of quantitative reasoning to problems concerning the allocation and efficient utilization of resources at all levels, and (2) it is an essential element in the education of those who want to know more about how and why the tools of the military profession are chosen.

The thesis which emerges in the subsequent discussion can be stated in two parts, as follows:

a. Economic concepts and quantitative reasoning are tools of management. The careful and intelligent application of such concepts

[2] *Quoted by Daniel Lang in "An Inquiry into Enoughness,"* The New Yorker, *10 October 1964.*

and methods in the allocation of limited defense resources among a variety of alternative uses and the efficient utilization of resources in given uses can materially assist the military manager in solving many of the complex problems involved in mission accomplishment and in achieving the most with the resources available to him.

b. The meaningful application of quantitative economic analysis can enhance the role of military judgment and experience in the decision-making process by permitting the decision maker to focus his attention on the essential relationships and critical values of the problem. All military managers need not possess the technical and academic skills of the analysts, though there is a growing need for trained analysts in the military. If the manager will familiarize himself with the analytical approach and know the characteristics of good quantitative analysis, he will be able to communicate effectively with the specialists both to insure the proper consideration of his judgment and ideas in the analyst's work and to incorporate analytical results meaningfully into his decisions.

Section outline. In Section 2 we will describe more specifically what is meant by systems analysis—also pointing out what is not meant—and why it makes sense to employ it in solving military problems. The logical relationship of systems analysis both to traditional military problem-solving frameworks such as the staff study and the estimate of the situation and to other scientific problem-solving techniques is discussed in Section 3.

SECTION 2
WHAT IS SYSTEMS ANALYSIS?

Some basic ideas. *Systems analysis/cost-effectiveness is the process by which the costs and effectiveness of alternative courses of action are determined and compared for the purpose of assisting the decision maker in choosing the best course, or combination of courses, of action to accomplish his mission.*

A course of action is the commitment of a volume of resources to some specific configuration or use, where the term resources refers to an aggregation of men, materiel and facilities. A course of action may be a decision to utilize productive facilities to fabricate materials into some particular kind of product or class of products such as weapons or vehicles and to organize these into effective elements of our defense posture. In other problems, a course of action may be a decision to use existing resources in some specified way, perhaps by reorganizing or relocating them, modifying them or augmenting them with additional equipment or personnel. These organized aggregations of resources, designed to perform certain definite missions, can be termed "systems."

The important thing to realize is that a decision to commit resources to some specific use, or to utilize more rather than less resources for a particular use, is simultaneously a decision not to commit these resources to some alternative use or configuration. What these resources would accomplish if committed to other uses represents the opportunities foregone, or *opportunity cost*, of choosing the given course of action.

"Opportunity cost" is not a familiar term in military activities. It is common to think of the costs of a course of action as the resources used up in its undertaking, i.e., the amounts of inputs required. Costs in this sense are generally measured in terms of the dollar value of the resources or in terms of actual manhours, supplies and services of equipment and facilities. But the value of the outputs which these resources could produce if used in some other way is an equally valid way of expressing cost. The user "trades in" or gives up these outputs, or opportunities, in order to undertake the given course of action and gain its output. We generally cannot place a monetary value on the outputs of military activities as can be done in many business problems. But we can approximate the value of military activities by attempting to quantify their effectiveness in achieving designated missions. Thinking in terms of opportunity costs is a way of focusing attention on the fact that there are many effective ways of using resources in accomplishing defense missions. The decision maker must concern himself with these alternatives in order to insure that what is given up by taking a particular course of action is not more important than what is gained.

The cost effectiveness dilemma.

The military decision maker obviously cannot consider the infinitely large number of useful ways that resources can be employed. He must confine himself to the ways resources can be used to accomplish a given objective or mission in which he is interested. Systems analysis can help the decision maker approach this task systematically by revealing to him the differences in effectiveness associated with differences in resource costs for those courses of action which contribute to the attainment of a given objective or set of objectives. Then it is up to the decision maker to establish a choice criterion which will answer the question: Is the difference in effectiveness which I get by choosing action A instead of action B worth the difference in cost?

The answer to this question is simple if, when comparing two courses of action, for example, greater effectiveness is associated with lower costs. In most problems, however, the decision maker is confronted with the need to make a judgment in cases in which greater effectiveness is associated with higher costs. The decision maker must then attempt to decide whether the more costly alternative adds sufficiently to defense capabilities to make the added expenditure worthwhile.

Systems analysts have a way of making these difficult problems at least manageable. We can illustrate this point with an example. Let two courses of action under consideration be the development and procurement of two alternative surface-to-air missiles for defending against attacking enemy bombers. Missile A might have a higher kill probability than Missile B, but it may also be more expensive to deploy. Missile A might, for example, have a more complex and costly guidance and control system which makes it more accurate when operational. On the other hand, this complex guidance and control system may reduce the probability that Missile A is launched successfully, i.e., reduce its reliability. However, the probability that an air defense missile will kill an attacking enemy bomber is assumed to depend both on accuracy and on reliability, and the greater accuracy of Missile A in our example may be supposed to outweigh its lower reliability.

But consider this hypothetical experiment. Suppose that instead of spending X dollars on Missile A, we spend the same amount on Missile B. That is, suppose that we buy more cheap missiles instead of fewer expensive ones. It might be discovered that the level of effectiveness which can be obtained with these B missiles exceeds the effectiveness obtainable with fewer expensive A missiles. Effectiveness, then, depends not only on reliability and accuracy, but also on the number of missiles that can be launched at an attacker. For a given budget outlay, Missile B is more effective than Missile A.

Exactly the same conclusion would result if, instead of using the conceptual device of a given budget outlay, a given level of effectiveness were specified and the question asked: Which missile system will achieve this effectiveness more economically?

The use of this last conceptual device sounds a little suspicious. It seems to imply that the best system is the cheapest system. Or, alternatively, it may imply that all that must be done is to compute the ratio of effectiveness to cost and the highest ratio wins. No one with any understanding of weapons and technology, or with any concern for the absolute degree of effectiveness of a system, is going to accept such rules of choice.

But something else in the statement must be noted. A given level of effectiveness is specified. This point is of crucial importance. Failure to recognize its implications is the source of a great deal of misunderstanding. A comparison of ratios is meaningless unless the value in the numerator or the value in the denominator of the ratio is held constant.[3] The analyst, when considering ratios, is careful to specify that either effectiveness—the numerator —or cost—the denominator—is the same in all comparisons. This is, as was noted, a conceptual device which clarifies the "more-expensive-but-more-effective" dilemma.

Clearly, if a given level of effectiveness is desired, *all things considered,* the most economical means of achieving it is the best choice. And if the allowable budget outlay is fixed, the decision maker will prefer the system which provides the greater effectiveness, *all things considered,* for that fixed outlay. This is a far different thing than simply comparing cost-effectiveness ratios and picking out the highest one. No competent systems analyst

advocates the latter procedure. These comparisons could look quite different for different budget outlays, or at different levels of effectiveness. It is up to the decision maker to decide which level of effectiveness he wants, or which budget outlay will be allocated to the problem.

Systems analysts typically use graphs to describe the relationships that have been discussed. In Figure 21-1, effectiveness is measured along the vertical axis and cost is measured along the horizontal axis. Notice the following characteristics of this graph: (1) For any given level of costs, or alternatively, for any given level of effectiveness, development and procurement of Missile B is the preferred course of action, because of the greater number of B missiles that can be successfully launched. (2) Beyond level of cost outlay X, effectiveness is increased only negligibly. This reflects a phenomenon termed *diminishing marginal returns:* in using resources to accomplish given objectives, it is usually the case that ever greater amounts of additional resources must be utilized to obtain given increments of effectiveness. At point X in Figure 21-1, diminishing marginal returns have reached the extent that it simply isn't worthwhile to allocate any more resources to either system.

The word "marginal" is one of the most frequently encountered in a systems analyst's vocabulary. Analysis "at the margin" means considering the impact on effectiveness of adding or subtracting "a little bit more" resources with respect to a given allocation. Consider again point X in Figure 21-1. Adding a little more to budgeted outlay for the two air defense missiles hardly affects the effectiveness of either missile system. Returns "at the margin" are nearly zero. The average returns of the two systems—*total* effectiveness divided by

[3] *If the ratio of effectiveness to cost for one system is greater than that for another system at every level of effectiveness or cost, ratio comparisons will indicate the preferred system but will not indicate how much of it is desirable. The analyst's device must still be employed to answer the latter question.*

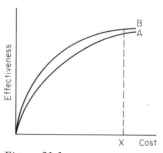

Figure 21-1

total resource outlay—may be impressive. But what the decision maker/manager should really want to know is what happens when he spends a little *more* or a little *less* on the systems. This information will tell him the real impact that extra spending or budget cutting will have on system effectiveness.

By using graphs, the decision maker can visually examine the implications of any budget outlay for optimum force structure, or he can determine approximately how much it costs to attain any specified level of effectiveness. In some cases he may discover that a large increase in outlays on a particular system will produce only a negligible increase in effectiveness. It is likely that these funds would be far better used for some force component which would add materially to defense capabilities. In other cases, it may become apparent that what is being spent yields very little effectiveness and that increased expenditure would increase effectiveness a great deal.

In the particular example under discussion, the systems analyst has provided a particularly useful piece of information to the decision maker. His analysis so far has revealed that Missile B is a better weapon than Missile A in accomplishing the specified objectives. Provided that the objective has been correctly stated, the decision maker now has a basis for making a decision that he probably could never obtain by being able to consider only the statement, "Missile A is both more effective and more expensive than Missile B."

The parametric study.   Even the hypothetical example. we have been discussing is too simple to be illustrative of many of the problems with which analysis must contend. It may be supposed, for example, that the kind of attack initially envisioned by the analyst was enemy bombers approaching from a high altitude. If, instead, we consider bombers approaching in low altitude attack patterns, the missile with the better guidance and control system might become more effective. Missile A might have a complex over-the-horizon radar which is able to identify and engage targets when Missile B's simpler line-of-sight radar is ineffective. The graphs might appear as in Figure 21-2. The situation is now reversed. If the enemy attacks at low altitudes, Missile A is the preferred weapon at every level of expenditure.

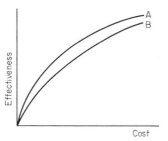

Figure 21-2

Figures 21-1 and 21-2 together represent a highly simplified version of a "parametric study." In each cost-effectiveness graph, a different assumption is made concerning the altitude of the enemy's attack. In technical terms, each assumption concerning the altitude of attack is a parameter with respect to graphs relating the variables cost and effectiveness. For each different assumption concerning altitude, a new graph must be drawn. By comparing these graphs the analyst can get a feel for the sensitivity of his missile comparisons to changing values of the parameter.

The altitude of the enemy's attack is one thing, the timing of his attack quite another. How sensitive are the two weapon systems under analysis to this factor?

Let us suppose that expensive Missile A has a reprograming capability. That is, if the missile fails to fire after the first attempt to launch, steps can be taken to make additional launch attempts possible. The greater the number of times that attempts to launch the missile can be made, the greater the reliability of the system. However, this reprograming capability assumes that time is available to accomplish the necessary actions. The more time that is available after an initial failure to launch, the more attempts to launch that can be made. We may describe the relationship between missile reliability and time as in Figure 21-3.

This consideration enters into the analysis in the following way. Attacking enemy bombers need not arrive over a target area simultaneously. This was assumed to be the case in the preceding analysis. It can be argued, however, that since a large wave of incoming bombers is highly vulnerable to U. S. manned interceptors, the enemy may prefer to time phase his attack. If a non-simultaneous attack is considered to be a possibility, our preference for air defense missiles may be affected

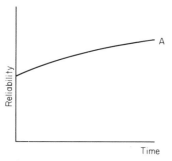

Figure 21-3

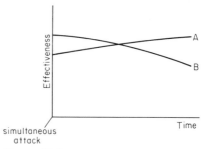

Figure 21-5

just as it was when low altitude attacks were considered. As we have seen, the reliability of Missile A increases with the length of time over which an attack takes place. If we assume that bombers attack over a lengthy time span, the cost-effectiveness graph may appear as in Figure 21-4.

Missile A now is preferred at every level of expenditure over Missile B. The increased reliability of Missile A, resulting from its reprograming capability, and its greater accuracy combine to offset the cost advantage of Missile B. Presumably, there exists some assumption concerning the time phasing of an enemy attack for which we would be indifferent between Missile A and Missile B. In fact, we can construct the following graph: for a given budget expenditure on missiles, and also assuming a high altitude attack, we can describe the relationship between effectiveness and the timing of an attack for both Missile A and Missile B. This graph is presented in Figure 21-5.

For a simultaneous attack, Missile B is more effective. Missile B's margin of superiority gradually is overcome, however, as the amount of time utilized by the enemy in his attack is increased.

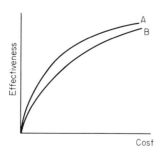

Figure 21-4

"Parameterizing," that is, drawing new cost-effectiveness graphs which incorporate different assumptions concerning factors which may have an important bearing on systems comparisons, is a convenient way of analyzing the sensitivity of the comparisons to these factors. We have discovered in our example that comparisons between Missile A and Missile B are highly sensitive to both the altitude and the time-phasing of the enemy's attack. If we pursued the analysis further, we might find that the comparisons were insensitive to certain other factors.

Such information is of the utmost importance to the decision maker. If analysis reveals that system comparisons are insensitive to certain factors, he need not worry about these factors in making his decision. He will want to focus his attention on those factors which do affect system comparisons. Uncertainty concerning any of these latter factors must weigh heavily on his decision.

Analysis and decisions. The decision maker now knows that the optimum choice of weapons is strongly influenced by the altitude of attack adopted by the enemy and by the timing of the attack. Since these factors are beyond his control, the decision maker will not want to commit himself to a choice of weapons which is appropriate for only one or two contingencies. He may want to "take out insurance" against the possibility of a variety of contingencies by procuring a mix of weapons. He may now feel he is in a position to go ahead with development and initial investment in both Missile A and Missile B. On the other hand, he may feel that only Missile A should be developed and procured, even though it is an inferior missile under certain contingencies. He may feel, for example, that the existence of a manned interceptor force is sufficient insurance against simultaneous attack. The more sophisticated capabilities of Missile A might make the most valuable additions to air defense.

Note that the decision to procure Missile A, which the hypothetical analysis revealed as a reasonable course of action, is a decision to buy the weapon with the greater unit cost. Systems analysis relates costs to effectiveness for a range of threats. The aim is to find the system which, for a given outlay, best counters these threats. This may be the least expensive weapon, but it may well be the most elaborate and expensive weapon if its effectiveness in countering the threats is sufficiently great.

The decision maker has some ideas, too, as to how his decisions may in fact affect enemy decisions. The deployment of a missile capable of defending against low altitude attacks may mean that the enemy will have to increase his force considerably, at great cost, if he is to penetrate these defenses. Or he may have to employ additional weapons, say ICBMs, to suppress the U. S. defenses and permit penetration by bombers. The enemy may be forced to abandon low altitude attack plans in favor of alternatives which are less costly but also less effective from his point of view.

The graphs and analysis that have been discussed by no means constitute a complete study. No attempts were made to evaluate such innovations as a shoot-look-shoot capability resulting from the use of a radar which is "farsighted" enough to permit us to look and see if an incoming bomber has been destroyed and, if not, to shoot at it again. The effects of varying the number of bombers in an attacking force and their dispersal within an attack pattern were not considered. Nor were varying assumptions concerning the target system which the enemy is attacking treated explicitly. Such factors should be "parameterized" as were altitude and timing. The decision maker may want to see further studies which consider more sophisticated versions of enemy strategy and tactics, perhaps incorporating detailed intelligence information, in order to get a better idea of exactly how much of each type of weapon he will want in the force.

Moreover, effectiveness has been defined in only one of several possible ways: increase the probability of killing attacking enemy bombers. Perhaps the real objective is to limit the damage inflicted on the U. S. population or on its economic strength, and effectively meeting this objective may call for expenditures on passive defense, i.e., blast and fallout shelters, as well as on active bomber defense, or perhaps even increased capability of destroying enemy bombers before they reach the CONUS defenses. Further analysis might clarify these issues in terms of the tradeoffs among costs and effectiveness.

But is all this analysis worthwhile? The decision might have been made without knowing the results of analysis. The decision maker might have announced that Missile A would be developed because it was more accurate and had more sophisticated radar. On the other hand, the decision maker might have decided to go ahead with both missiles because they were both good weapons, and it is always wise to have a diversified arsenal since you never know what the enemy will come up with. It is by no means obvious that either of these decisions, based purely on judgment and experience, is inferior to decisions backed by analysis. Moreover, not so much time and talent has been wasted on studies.

Intuitive judgment does not necessarily produce inferior decisions. Yet two points must be made:

a. The decision maker who has no analysis to assist him may actually have less opportunity to bring his experience to bear on a problem and to exercise effective judgment. Good analysis will have succeeded in identifying the real objectives and key variables of a problem. It will indicate how sensitive the analytical findings are to changes in the values of the key variables or in the assumptions on which the analytical model is constructed. Of vital importance, it will point out remaining areas of uncertainty, which may call for additional information or further study. Uncertainty can never be eliminated when the actions of a devious enemy must be taken into account. Analysis can, however, explicitly identify areas of uncertainty and indicate how the likelihood of mission accomplishment is affected by them. And by bringing these uncertainties into the open, analysis can frequently succeed in squeezing them into the smallest area.

Dealing explicitly with uncertainty—and indicating the relative significance of what we do know compared to what we do not know—is one of the most important contributions of analysis to the decision-making process. Uncertainty as to how an ICBM force would perform in a nuclear exchange, could (and has!) lead to the conclusion that "we can't rely on missiles" or even "missiles have no deterrent value." This type of reaction implies that if we are not completely sure about a future event, we are obliged to be completely unsure. Analysis which reveals that a particular weapon is, on the basis of the best information available, 80% reliable—thus expressing our uncertainty explicitly in the form of a probability—can lead to more fruitful reactions. For example, launching two weapons instead of one can increase reliability to 96%. Design improvements or better maintenance policies might increase the reliability of a given missile. Moreover, the fallibilities of human judgment being what they are, the weapon or alternative we "feel" sure about may be no more reliable in fact than the missile. Explicit treatment of uncertainty will serve the planning process much better than unaided intuitive judgment.

With the aid of analysis, then, the decision maker can focus his attention on clearly-defined issues, utilizing his judgment to evaluate assumptions, criticize the numbers and probabilities the analyst has employed, weigh the uncertainties with which facts and assumptions must be accepted, temper and modify analytical conclusions with experience factors, predict the future consequences of actions taken now, evaluate how and to what extent factors not considered by the analyst should affect the decision. The opportunities which the decision maker has to exercise critical and meaningful judgment, and the likely consequences of his judgments, are much more clearly delineated when major aspects of the problem have been quantified and analyzed.

b. When only intuitive, unsupported judgment is used, the danger exists that the premises and assumptions which the decision maker consciously or unconsciously has in mind, and which may be wholly appropriate in some problems, may lead to conclusions which are far wide of the mark in other problems, and lead to serious imbalances or vulnerabilities in our capabilities. Willingness consistently to draw upon the results of analysis can add an important element of objectivity to the decision-making process (provided, of course, that the military and civilian analysts are encouraged to be objective in their analyses). This is important in view of the consequences that can follow on a biased or uninformed decision.

Does the possibility exist, however, that quantitative analysis can lead to worse decisions than those that would be made without it? The answer is yes. One reason is that the analysis may be faulty. A second reason, related to the first, may seem paradoxical. The more the military decision maker/manager fails to exercise his judgment and draw upon his experience in participating in and evaluating analyses, the greater the possibility that analytical results will be misinterpreted, misused, or used indiscriminately to the detriment of national defense.

Analysis cannot, and must not, substitute for military judgment; it can however, serve as an exceedingly valuable input to inform military judgment. However, successful analysis depends on two-way communication between the analyst and the user. The challenge to military decision maker/managers is to become sufficiently conversant with the purpose, scope and methods of systems analysis and the other quantitative problem-solving approaches so that they can communicate effectively with the technically trained analysts.

Challenge to military managers. If what has been said so far is true, the military decision maker/manager, far from being replaced by the analysts, will be confronted with the need both to understand what the analyst is doing and to integrate the results of analysis into the management process. Yet considerable skill and judgment are involved in designing and conducting studies. Establishing quantifiable objectives for a given problem, identifying the courses of action which will accomplish the objectives, and measuring the costs and effectiveness of each course of action are complex and difficult tasks. It may seem to many that a specialist's skills are required if one is to begin to make sense of quantitative analysis and analytical findings.

While there is a rapidly growing need for specially trained military personnel to participate in quantitative analysis, there is perhaps a greater need for managers who are able to supervise or evaluate quantitative analysis, or to envision how quantitative analysis could be useful to them and to initiate the necessary studies. To perform these roles successfully, military managers should be familiar with elementary economic and quantitative concepts, comprehend both the value and the limitations of the scientific approach and know the characteristics of good quantitative analysis. Military managers should be able to evaluate the quality of studies in terms of the measures of effectiveness which are defined, the analytical assumptions, procedures and techniques, the elements included in the cost calculations and choice criteria.

This general ability to evaluate quantitative analysis does not necessarily depend upon formal training in the technical and academic skills of the specialist. The essential requirement is a willingness to learn new concepts and to acquire some new attitudes and to utilize these concepts and attitudes objectively whenever the need or the opportunity arises. As we previously noted, the needs and opportunities may arise not only at the national policy level but at any level in the defense establishment.

Some practitioners have found it conceptually useful to describe the many possible levels of analysis in terms of a hierarchy, as follows (from highest to lowest): system, sub-system, assembly, sub-assembly, component, and part.[4] It is apparent that as we ascend in the hierarchy, we are considering progressively more complex aggregations of resources. Problems can be classified by considering where in the hierarchy of resource aggregation the elements of analysis are to be found.

At lower levels in the hierarchy, problems tend to be relatively narrow in scope and more readily quantifiable. These problems are frequently of a repetitive or routine nature, involving the efficient organization or utilization of the resource elements under study under conditions in which there is general agreement as to what efficiency means. For these reasons, they are frequently amenable to the sophisticated mathematical techniques of operations research or the detailed technical considerations of value engineering. Examples of these types of problems are those concerning optimum maintenance scheduling and procedures, transporting items from a variety of origins to a variety of terminals, managing inventories, loading and unloading cargo vehicles, servicing customers.

This is not the case at the systems analysis level. Earlier we described a system as an integrated organization of men, material and facilities designed to perform some specific service or set of services in support of major defense establishment missions. In systems analysis, as the term implies, systems, taken *in toto*, are the elements of analysis. It is instructive to consider how a system analyst views his task. "We . . . tend to compare a small number of different systems under varying circumstances and objectives. No simple criteria of performance are used. The major attention is focused on uncertainties. A system is preferred when it performs reasonably well under probable circumstances in terms of the high-priority objectives, and yet hedges against less probable or even improbable situations and does more than just pay lip service to medium and low priority objectives."[5]

Far from dealing with routine tasks and/or relatively narrow objectives, systems analysis is concerned with mission accomplishment and broad strategic objectives at the national policy level. At this level there is rarely an accepted view as to the meaning of mission accomplishment or the precise nature of strategic objectives. Thus systems analysis must be centrally concerned with problem definition and the selection of appropriate objectives. It must concern itself with all of the risks, uncertainties and unknowns of contingency planning for national defense.

The challenge to the analyst and the manager at the national policy level is to develop better ways of thinking about problems and assigning better alternatives for handling them, not to acquire technical virtuosity in solving them. The problem orientation of systems analysis and the need to consider a great range of uncertainties and strategies are readily apparent in the hypothetical air defense analysis presented in the previous section.

Many military problems, for example, those involving tactics or the costs and effectiveness of sub-systems such as particular battlefield weapons or support items, occupy an intermediate position in the hierarchy. Such problems frequently involve contingency analysis and hence are influenced by uncertainties and parameters which are difficult to quantify. On the other hand, their scopes are limited relative

---

[4] *I am indebted to Wayne Allen, Member of the Technical Staff at IDA, for helpful discussions on this point.*

[5] *Herman Kahn,* On Thermonuclear War, *Princeton: Princeton University Press, 1961, pp. 119–120.*

to those encountered at the national policy level and the analyst may be able to confine himself to a narrower range of issues and uncertainties and benefit from somewhat better opportunities for agreement on objectives, quantification and even experimental verification of assumptions.

It may be noted finally that problem packages may involve analysis at all levels. Information may be generated by operations analysis and war gaming, with the results serving as inputs to a higher level systems analysis. Extensive interactions among analytical conclusions and techniques at the various levels may take place, and the methodologies may range from intuition to sophisticated mathematical programing.

The importance of making this somewhat artificial distinction among problems is this. The senior military decision maker/manager may become involved in problems at any or all of these levels. Each type of problem may, however, involve different tests of his competence and require different responses and different degrees of personal involvement. In some cases, a few hours of discussion to define the problem may be all that is necessary before it is handed to the experts to arrive at a solution. In others, military assistance may be required in problem formulation, in data gathering and analysis, in constructing new alternatives, problem reformulation and so on. In still others, objective evaluation and critique by military management of completed analysis may be necessary. Some may require experience with equipment performance, logistics, operations; others may involve strategic or doctrinal judgments and insights. All involve the integration of this knowledge and experience with scientific principles of problem solving. It is to prepare him for this varied role that it is necessary for the military manager "to be familiar with the analytical approach, comprehend both its value and its limitations, and know the characteristics and good quantitative analysis." We advocate, in other words, an intuitive understanding on the part of the military of scientific quantitative problem solving.

We will describe more fully the logic of systems analysis in the following section. At this point we want to introduce some general guidelines for the manager to assist him in initiating, supervising, and evaluating quantitative analysis.

Does the Study Ask the Right Questions?

Analytical studies are built around some measure or measures of performance or effectiveness. Measures of effectiveness should accurately describe some desirable military objective. To be truly quantifiable, they must be defined at less than the ethereal level of "winning the war" or "destroying the enemy's will to resist." Beyond this general comment, the narrowness or breadth of the specified objectives depends upon the kind of problem which is subjected to analysis. The higher the level of the problem, the more the analysis should be cognizant of the trade-offs that exist among narrowly-defined objectives. Mobility versus firepower, missile accuracy vs. missile reliability, vehicle land speed vs. the capability of negotiating rugged terrain—desirable capabilities may be competitive rather than complementary, and this must be recognized in good analysis.

Frequently objectives are framed in terms of requirements which are generated by the need or the desire to handle particular contingencies. Studies based on such objectives may lead to recommendations which represent uneconomical uses of defense resources when considering more broadly conceived tactical or strategic missions. Hence measures of effectiveness should be conceptually sound in that they are consonant with strategic and/or tactical doctrine or with general policy directives. Depending, of course, upon the level of the problem, proposed courses of action should be evaluated in terms of their contribution to relatively broadly-defined defense missions. Their capability of handling narrower problems can be evaluated within the more general framework.

It is important to emphasize that careful definition of the questions which a study is to answer is an analytical step in itself. Ideally, optimum solutions are obtained by relating a set of known, defined preferences to a set of available alternatives for satisfying such preferences. The mix of alternatives chosen is that which most fully satisfies preferences. Military analysis cannot be so conceptually neat. It is frequently an iterative procedure, and initial formulations of the problem and the initial list of alternatives to be considered may be revised considerably as analysis proceeds. Yet the tendency to define objectives so that they are in line with *hoped for* outcomes or to define and analyze alternative courses of action in a manner which is slanted toward yielding particular answers, is not likely to produce optimal solutions. These tendencies can be minimized by concentrating on achieving a careful, comprehensive and sound definition of objectives and missions and attempting to evaluate all relevant alternatives impartially in terms of these objectives and missions. If it proves necessary or desirable to revise objectives or design new alternatives, this should be justified by the analysis itself, and successive rounds of analysis should proceed in the same impartial manner.

Are the Answers to the Questions Reasonable in Light of the Evidence?

Closely connected with the definition of objectives is the selection of a criterion or criteria for choosing among courses of action in terms of objectives attainment. Sometimes, through analytical devices such as those described on pp. 219–222 above, the choices can be described in relatively unambiguous terms. For example, the system which provides a satisfactory level of effectiveness at least cost will be chosen. In others, such as our air-defense problem, a variety of characteristics and capabilities must be balanced against a variety of uncertainties and risks. Subjective judgments inevitably enter to resolve complex choice problems. The military manager should determine what the choice criteria are and if they appear to be reasonable and consistent in light of available evidence and the assumptions and procedures of the analysis itself.

Has the Evidence Been Evaluated Objectively, Consistently, and Comprehensively?

The manager must be able and willing to discount or reject study assumptions, analytical techniques and concepts, and interpretations which appear to reflect undue attention to irrelevant considerations, personal prejudices or preconceived opinions. A careful and objective study will make its assumptions explicit and will provide adequate justification for them. The manager should be able to verify from the study report precisely how conclusions were arrived at.

The manager should also examine the content of the study and ask some probing questions. Are the concepts, assumptions and procedures sound? Are they consistent with the specified objectives? Are they sufficiently comprehensive of the key elements of the problem?

If the manager is himself consistent and objective in asking these questions of his analysts and analysis, as well as asking these questions of himself when he is engaged in problem solving, he is beginning to acquire facility in handling quantitative analysis.

Some misconceptions. Though good systems analysis and cost effectiveness studies, properly used, can be a useful input to the decision-making process, some misleading impressions tend to be created when the value to military decision makers of making quantitative estimates of costs and effectiveness is asserted. We label these impressions "misconceptions" and list them as follows:

Misconception 1: Systems analysis requires that all factors within its purview be strictly measurable—factors which are not measurable are ignored.

Systems analysis, indeed all quantitative analysis, presupposes that important elements of military problems can be quantified and that it is desirable to do so. Verbal generalizations are difficult to analyze, compare and apply. Moreover, as we have tried to show, generalizations may lead to erroneous conclusions. Even if intuitive reasoning could tell us which of many courses of action are "better" or "best," the crucial questions are likely to be (a) how much better and under what conditions? and (b) what are the trade-offs in terms of effectiveness and cost among desirable courses of action? What intuitive reasoning and clever insight can do most effectively is handle the non-measurable and non-comparable factors and integrate them with analytical results to produce wise decisions. ". . . the significance of the numbers in an analysis depends upon the importance of effects not encompassed by these numbers, and the recognition of this dependence should not be left to chance. . . . As a minimum (such factors) can be displayed and talked about."[6] They can never be ignored.

Misconception 2: The output of a systems

6 *Charles J. Hitch and Roland N. McKean,* The Economics of Defense in the Nuclear Age, *Cambridge: Harvard University Press, 1961, p. 184.*

analysis is a decision as to which of the alternatives considered is "best"—the best alternative is always the one with the lowest cost.

The quality of analysis and its usefulness to the decision maker are not judged on the basis of how many definitive conclusions are contained in it. Definitive answers are much less desirable than a plausible formulation of the problem accompanied by analysis which explores the sensitivity of results to alternative assumptions for a broad range of budget outlays and levels of effectiveness. Good analysis points out those areas which are characterized by a high degree of uncertainty or are in need of further study. Definitive conclusions are the decision-maker's job. He must evaluate the information contained in analysis and arrive at his decision.

A premise of systems analysis is that it is only common sense to consider costs when evaluating alternative ways of achieving given objectives. If a particular objective is agreed upon, and if a given level of effectiveness can be achieved in several ways, it is common sense to prefer the most economical way of achieving this level of effectiveness. The decision maker could use an uneconomical way of achieving his objective, but this would mean that he was using up resources which could be used to better advantage in some other way. But, as we have emphasized, this does not mean that analysis is biased toward cheap weapons. Analysis is biased in favor of effectiveness, and if the procurement of expensive weapons will produce the greatest effectiveness for a given budget outlay, analysis will reveal these weapons to be the preferred choice.

Misconception 3: The techniques of systems analysis, because they are quantitative, are inherently complex and must be performed on computers.

Computers are frequently useful to the analyst. Cost computations, for example, may require the summarization of a large volume of raw data which computers can accomplish quickly and efficiently. Yet the essence of analysis is not the placement of giant computers in a harness of sophisticated mathematical models. Decision makers are more likely to be bounced out of the saddle by failure to assure adequate problem design and definition, or by selection of inappropriate rules of choice and erroneous interpretation of results, than by galloping computers.

Misconception 4: Systems analysis is used when problems are too complicated for ordinary human judgment.

Quantitative reasoning does not require incomprehensible mathematical expressions. A grasp of relatively simple quantitative concepts coupled with an aggressive application of objectivity and common sense can yield good analyses and good interpretations of analyses even when complicated problems are involved. Systems analysis is used whenever a means of making a systematic evaluation of alternatives is desired and whenever the problem lends itself to quantification. The results of analysis are inputs to the decision-making process. But the decision maker is still in control. Systems analysis helps to focus judgment—it does not replace it.

It is reiterated, however, that systems analysis, as any other endeavor undertaken by human beings, can be good or bad, sound or faulty. These are numerous pitfalls in systems analysis which must be carefully and studiously avoided. In fact, good systems analysts are the first to enumerate these pitfalls and point out the consequences of ignoring them. It is entirely disingenuous, therefore, to chronicle these pitfalls and allege them to be "weaknesses" or shortcomings of the systems analysis approach. All systems analysts are not superficial and narrow any more than all doctors are quacks. The basic procedures and characteristics of systems analysis/cost-effectiveness have been shaped by the need to account for complex situations full of pitfalls and problems.

SECTION 3 SYSTEMS ANALYSIS: THE COLD, HARD LOOK

Scientific problem solving and military tradition. Does the use of quantitative concepts such as those employed in cost-effectiveness analyses represent a revolutionary break with military problem solving traditions embodied in the estimate of the situation and staff research? Have military judgment and experience, which form the backbone of military problem-solving approaches, thus been downgraded?

It must be noted immediately that some types of quantitative analysis, indeed some of the most sophisticated and complex analyses, have been done continuously in the military for over 20 years. Operations research techniques have been applied to military problems since World War II. But these applications were mainly in areas in which there was little serious dispute as to how the problem ought to be defined and no serious doubts that sophisticated techniques were required. Military users of such studies readily conceded the need for highly-trained experts to arrive at the answers.

The controversies have arisen as scientific problem solving approaches have been applied to problems which the military have solved before without experts and without explicit reference to the scientific method. It is in connection with such problems that questions as to the relationships of systems analysis/cost-effectiveness to traditional problem solving approaches, and suspicions as to the confidence being placed in military judgment, arise. Many of these questions are profound and are related to military professionalism in its broadest sense. Still others arise out of misunderstandings or a lack of familiarity with scientific problem solving. We want to begin to shed some light on these issues in this section.

Staff research and systems analysis both begin when problems arise that are too big to be solved by one man using his unaided brain power and paper and pencil. These problems are generally empirical, i.e., arising from observation or experience with some difficulty in planning, operations, procurement or the like. The question becomes one of approach: how are possible solutions to these problems to be determined?

The logic of problem solving.   No matter which problem-solving approach is chosen, four phases can generally be identified. In empirical inquiries:

a. The problem must be formulated in a precise manner: Exactly what are the questions which are to be answered? This may involve a statement of objectives to be attained, performance to be evaluated, or perhaps hypotheses to be verified. Whatever form the problem statement takes, it must be consistent with the overall goals or missions of the organization in which the problem has arisen.

b. Data, facts and information which bear upon the questions to be answered must be assembled. The nature of these information "raw materials" is determined both by the

problem and by the prospective methods of evaluation or analysis to be employed. They may consist of numerical information such as design or performance characteristics and descriptive statistics and sets of alternative possibilities for objectives attainments, evaluation of probabilities.

c. Procedures for processing the data and facts so that they relate directly to the problem statement must be decided upon and employed. These procedures may be formal or informal, sophisticated or casual.

d. Conclusions may be arrived at, decisions recommended, or courses of action suggested on the basis of results obtained from the problem solving procedures employed in Step 3 and then communicated to the decision maker.

We may summarize the four phases of empirical inquiry as:

a. Problem Formulation
b. Assembly of Facts
c. Analysis
d. Conclusions and Recommendations

How do traditional staff research procedures, outlined, for example, in Army FM 101-5, relate to this schema? The steps of staff research are study and understanding of the problem (problem formulation); preparation of basic work plan, collection, evaluation and organization of data (assembly of facts); analysis of data (analysis); and the drawing of sound conclusions and the formulation of recommendations (conclusions and/or recommendations). Similarly, the steps in an estimate of the situation can be similarly organized: the mission (problem formulation); the situation and courses of action (assembly of facts); analysis, opposing courses of action, and comparison, own courses of action (analysis); decision (conclusion and/or recommendations).

We can similarly analyze the procedures of systems analysis. According to one description[7] the problem is formulated by describing the context in which it arises, the objectives in tentative form, the criteria needed to determine success or failure, and the hypotheses of action to achieve objectives (problem formulation); the relevant data are sought out as facts,

[7] *Captain Stanley M. Barnes, USN, "Defense Planning Processes," U. S. Naval Institute Proceedings, June 1964, p. 34.*

possibilities, alternatives, and costs (assembly of facts); the application of these data to the problem as formulated, is worked out with models ("a set of relationships, mathematical or logical"), approximations, computation and results (analysis); the results obtained are translated into conclusions after interpretation of the effect of nonquantifiables, incommensurables, and uncertainties (further analysis and conclusions and/or recommendations).

The breakdown of staff research estimate of the situation and systems analysis into the four problem-solving phases is summarized in Table 21-1.

To emphasize the generality of this scheme, it is useful to apply it to more sophisticated and technical problem solving approaches. The basic concepts of operations research have been described as the measure of effectiveness, the model, the role of experimentation, and the necessity for decision.[8] In operations research, the measure of effectiveness describes

[8] *Cyril C. Herrmann and John F. Magee, "Operations Research for Management," in Edward C. Bursk and John F. Chapman, editors,* New Decision-Making Tools for Managers, *Cambridge: Harvard Univ. Press, 1963, p. 6.*

the extent to which the objectives of the operation are met. Hence a problem formulation phase must clearly establish these objectives or goals. The model "is generally built up from observed data or experience . . ." A careful study of the operation and assembly of relevant facts, perhaps involving experimentation, must precede analysis. A model is constructed which represents those aspects of the operation which relate to effectiveness as defined. The model is then manipulated in the analytical phase to produce information which will be of importance to the decision maker in deciding how best to manage his operation. The operations researcher should finally clearly indicate, on the basis of his analytical findings, how alternative courses of action available to the decision maker are related to the decision maker's goals.

In a similar manner, the procedures for conducting a linear programing analysis can be described as: determination of a measure of effectiveness (problem formulation): determination of alternative means, or processes, of accomplishing the objective and their rates of efficiency, together with the linear constraints binding upon the operation (assembly of facts),

TABLE 21-1

	Staff Research	Estimate of Situation	Systems Analysis
1. *Problem Formulation*	Study and understanding of the problem	Mission	Formulation: describe problem context, objectives, criteria, hypotheses.
2. *Assembly of facts*	Preparation of work plan Collection, evaluation of data Organization of data	The situation and courses of action.	Seeking out facts, possibilities, alternatives and costs.
3. *Analysis*	Analysis of data	Analysis, opposing courses of action. Comparison, own course of action.	Application of data to problem using models, approximations, computations, results. Interpret effects of nonquantifiables, incommensurables, uncertainties.
4. *Conclusions and/or recommendations*	Drawing of sound conclusions Formulation of recommendations	Decision	Results translated into conclusions.

construction of an objective function and a linear equation system relating the various processes to objectives obtainment subject to the linear constraints (analysis); description of the solution(s) and their implications (conclusions and/or recommendations).

There are no fundamental differences among the various problem-solving approaches, either traditional or scientific, in the logic of what has to be accomplished. The differences are rather in methods—how the problem gets solved—and to some extent, in emphasis. The military manager should desire to find and apply the most effective method or approach for resolving his problems. Systems analysis, or any kind of quantitative approach, is one way—one set of tools and procedures—available to the manager to assist him in making effective plans and good decisions. As we suggested in the preceding section, there is nothing inherent in quantitative analysis which downgrades military judgment or experience. What quantitative analysis brings to the decision-making process are objectivity, a concern for explicit, quantitative treatment of the key factors and relationships in the problem, a belief that costs and effectiveness have to be consid-

ered simultaneously in the decision-making process, and an emphasis on *how* answers are arrived at as opposed to arriving at answers.

Analysis is, as General Decker has put it, *"the cold, hard look which individuals or organizations directly involved in the problem find difficult to take."*[9]

The interrelationships among the many problem-solving methods is depicted in Figure 21-6. Systems analysis and cost effectiveness studies are viewed as integrating, either explicitly or implicitly, four different kinds of inputs: (1) a problem in defense planning which needs to be solved; (2) the judgment and experience of military men, together with their acknowledged background in solving problems; (3) the objective and comprehensive thinking characteristic of scientific quantitative methods; and (4) the results of many other studies dealing with related problems of narrower scope and perhaps using highly sophisticated techniques.

[9] *General George H. Decker, "Costing Strategy,"* Armed Forces Management, *September 1963, p. 40.*

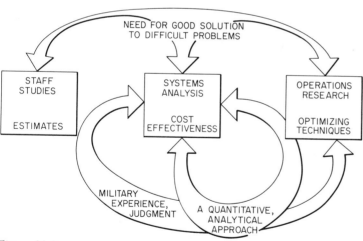

Figure 21-6

SECTION 6

APPLICATIONS OF SYSTEMS ANALYSIS

In this section, system analyses in a number of major decision areas are discussed by the people who were involved in the analyses. Of necessity, the level of formality is higher in a few of these papers than in the rest of the book. However, in no case is any high-level mathematics used, and in all of the papers, the essence of both the problem and the salient analytic aspects can be gained from the informal portions of the discussions.

John Haldi's paper on issues of analysis serves to place in perspective the current and future role of systems analysis in government.

READING 22

SYSTEMS ANALYSIS IN THE WAR ON POVERTY *

Robert A. Levine

Last summer [1965] the Office of Research, Plans, Programs and Evaluation of the Office of Economic Opportunity put together an anti-poverty plan and a four-year program based on that plan, for OEO and for the total War on Poverty of which OEO-funded programs are a part. OEO was probably the first civilian agency to do this. It was done hurriedly with the due date of Labor Day and with a planning staff that did not come on board until the first of July.

I want to share some experiences of this planning process. Although planning of this type was first done by the U.S. Government in 1961, in the Department of Defense, our problems as a civilian agency are quite different from those of Defense.

1 Welfare is easier to define than national security. That is, we know what we mean and can measure what we mean in terms of improvement of people as defined by income and other variables. Deterrence is much more difficult to measure.

2 We had a lot of data to begin with—more than Defense. Good economic data have been gathered and tabulated in this country for 30 years or more, and for the 20 years since the Employment Act of 1946 created the President's Council of Economic Advisers, the data have been quite good. Unfortunately, as most users will testify, these data are almost always out of phase with operational needs. There are problems such as the need for series on time and geographical bases different from the bases on which the data are gathered.

3 Unlike the Defense Department, we play a game against nature which makes our task considerably easier. We do not have to contend with a malevolent enemy.

These first three make our job easier than Defense; the next makes it more difficult, however.

4 Unlike many of the Defense programs, our results are testable. They have not really

* Reprinted with permission of the author. Paper presented at the 29th National Meeting of the Operation Research Society of America, Santa Monica, California, May 18–20, 1966.

been tested yet, although, when the 1965 Current Population Survey reported a drop of one million in the number of poor people from 1963 to 1964, a copy of the release was sent to OEO by a White House staffer who had written across it "nice going Sarge." Unfortunately, the change had taken place before OEO had really gotten into the business. In any case, the results of our activities are testable and are being tested and that means that our concepts will come into direct contact with what one of my colleagues calls the "real world out there." Thus far, deterrence theory has made no such contact.

5 Perhaps our greatest difficulty compared to the Department of Defense is that we started with no long history of accumulated systematic analysis in the field of poverty and social welfare. There had been, of course, much writing by economists and sociologists on related topics, but remarkably little of it systematically related costs and benefits of suggested policies or made systematic ,comparison of alternatives. The Department of Defense in 1961 had a huge backlog of accumulated analyses and policy recommendations from organizations like RAND, and much of what was done in 1961 and 1962 resulted directly from the intellectual investments started in 1951 and 1952.

I think we in OEO did a good quick planning job in this first year, but it was narrow and shallow because of the time constraints. It was narrow in that we did not consider as many alternatives as we should have; it was shallow because analysis did not go as deep as it should have. But, at least we know where the bodies are buried—we know what shortcuts we took and what simplifications we made.

What I would like to do today is to describe what we did and to draw some conclusions, but first, I want to expose a prejudice. We have done a set of system analyses of which we are pretty proud and I think that systems analysis properly done is bound to improve government planning and operations. Nonetheless, I am a bit skeptical of some of the uses made of systems analysis. For one thing the numbers used in systems analysis are always imperfect and to make decisions on the basis of small quantitative differences derived from very fuzzy inputs is wrong and is dangerous.

If differences are small, then an entirely different basis for decision should be arrived at. Indeed, if quantitative results do not accord with one's intuition, one had better check his numbers very carefully, because by and large intuition is the better guide.

A similar danger is that too much concentration on quantity, as is sometimes the case with systems analysis and systems analysts, can lead to asking the wrong questions. It is all too easy to substitute the concrete for the important, and it is frequently done.

I know some pretty horrible examples of misuse of analysis from my time at RAND and in the Defense establishment, but these are classified Secret, so I will give two other examples of systems analysis badly used.

The first comes from the cost-benefit analysis of water resource projects. (Incidentally, cost-benefit analysis and systems analysis are not identical. Cost-benefit analysis can be an important part of systems analysis but it is not the whole. The imposition of non-quantitative systems on decision making—the construction of qualitative alternatives, for example, can be just as important.) In any case, some work on water resource projects goes into an immense amount of intricate detail to try to establish the interest rate which should be used to discount future benefits from the water in order to match them against current costs of the project. Should it be the interest rate the government must pay for its borrowed funds, should it be the opportunity cost of using the same funds for private capital projects, or what should it be? To me, this whole debate is meaningless when estimates of proper interest rates are very imprecise and the final choice of an interest is arbitrary. If a Go-no-Go decision were made on the basis of such an arbitrary choice of interest rate it would be the wrong decision half the time.

Fortunately, the study I have in mind came out with the answer that at *any* interest rate the particular project under consideration was uneconomical. The costs, no matter how defined, were substantially greater than the benefits. The water system proposed would have provided a major subsidy to agricultural programs which would otherwise have been uneconomic. Now, this is the best use of highly legitimate cost-benefit analysis; the analytical discovery of *large* quantitative differences on the basis of simple generally acceptable *ceteris paribus* assumptions. The project was clearly unjustified.

And to end the story, the uneconomical project was adopted with great popular and political fanfare which shows another sort of limit on the application of cost-benefit analysis.

The second example of the dangers of systems analysis comes from some of our own work in the War on Poverty. Again it is a question of the use of cost-benefit analysis. It illustrates the possible use of quantity to narrow the focus down to the wrong questions. We of course avoided the error, but we could have made it.

In our OEO programs we do much training. For the evaluation of training programs, a frequently used method is that of matching the cost of the program against estimated increases in lifetime earnings derived from the training. If lifetime earnings, discounted properly, are greater than the cost then the training is justified. But for the purposes of War on Poverty training, in order to bring policy logic to this sort of computation, it must be assumed that if a training project is uneconomical—that is, if discounted earnings are less than cost—a preferable alternative would be to provide transfer payments for the less expensive direct support of those who would otherwise have been trained more expensively.

But our objective, as stated by our legislation, is not just removal of people from poverty by simple devices such as transfer payments. We operate under the Economic Opportunity Act and our primary mandate is to provide the opportunity for people to get themselves and their families out of poverty. In this case, therefore, the rationale of transfer payments as an equal-value alternative to training, is incorrect. Even if discounted earnings were less than cost we might want to do the training anyhow because of the social value placed on ending poverty through personal opportunity.

All this, I think, demonstrates some skepticism about classical (10–15 years old) systems analysis as a solution to all problems. Nonetheless, a standard *caveat* of systems analysis is that one should not look for perfect optimum but rather for any available improvement. Let me look now—under this *caveat* about systems analysis being imperfect and sometimes dangerous—to all we did to try to *improve* policy-

making through the use of such an analysis. My last point about the training programs provides a start. To my mind the most important contribution of systems analysis is to demand a definition of objectives, and to make that definition operational. I have already pointed out that in the hierarchy of our objectives, opportunity comes above the direct cure of income-defined poverty as such. But that initial definition of objectives does not end our problem; it begins them.

How do we define the objectives of providing opportunity and reducing poverty? We decided that our major measure would be the number of people moved past a family-income benchmark we call the poverty line. To move people past an arbitrary line is *not* our objective but it is a measure which can be applied to our real objectives. It is a necessary compromise in the name of systematic decision making. So we try to move people by a line. What line? We decided to use an *annual* income measure. This is not completely satisfactory—it ignores assets for example, and thus it includes as poor some people that may be really rich. Similarly by selecting annual income, it ignores those who may have an income in one year that may be atypically low and who may not be really poor at all. We have been struggling with refinements of the definition, but in the meantime, in order to get something done we have made compromises in the name of system and have used annual income. Having decided on income as a measure, we made one immediate advance; we changed from the simple poverty line adopted some years ago by the Council of Economic Advisers of $3,000 for a family and $1,500 for an individual to a more detailed, more variable line. Our current line, adapted from the work of Mollie Orshansky of the Social Security Administration, varies according to family size and according to farm versus non-farm residence. For a non-farm unrelated individual, the poverty line is $1,540, for a four-person family, it is $3,130, and it varies between these numbers and above them up to much larger families (which are too typical among the poor). Farm families are set at 70% of the nonfarm level.

Still more advance is necessary. We are working on regional variations, and in addition there is a question as to whether the poverty line should change over time as it has done in the past. But again in order to get going with our planning, we made the necessary compromise in the name of system.

Another definitional question still bothers us, and this one is also connected with our objectives. An individual and family line is certainly proper for the measurement of those dimensions of the poverty problem which can properly be called individual and family problems. But is such a line relevant to the community problems which Community Action programs (half the OEO total budget in fiscal 1966) are designed to attack? Even in the worst urban slums more than half the residents are above the individual-family poverty lines. Should we not extend our programs to them because of this fact? I doubt it; I feel we may need a different sort of standard to operate on and measure the progress against the problem of the community. For the moment, however, we are still using a single standard, another compromise among detail, system, and the need to get on with the job.

Getting on with the job, the necessary step was to divide this defined poor population into subgroups. Here, one's first intuition about the groups to use is wrong. It's very tempting to use age groups—that is apparently the first impulse of anyone starting into the question. But age groups are not completely workable in terms of the above kinds of problems, and the kinds of programs with which we are trying to attack these problems. Youth—say ages 16–21—is a usable age group, because youth have separately definable problems and we have separately definable programs for these youth. The aged provide another quite distinct and separable group whose needs—primarily for money alone—are distinct from those of the rest of the poor population. Children provide a less tractable group. In part there are separable children's programs, in the education field and elsewhere, but difficulties arise because programs to approach children *as* children are not the only ones. Operationally, a major way to reach a poor child is through his family. And most families understandably have people in a variety of age groups. So families provide another category we must look at and one which is not neatly parallel to the others. And families ought to be further divided between those whose heads are in or should be in the labor force and those who are

out or should be out; the problems and programs are quite different for the two categories. So we end up with a complex and overlapping set of categories—youth, aged, children, labor-force families, non-labor-force families. One really cannot divide the problems of poverty without looking at the programs designed to attack these problems, and we end up with a cross-classified matrix with objective groups on one axis and programs on the other.

Turning to our treatment of programs, what our summer analysis first did was to look at the whole range of existing government programs which might, without too much stretch of the imagination be called poverty programs. We estimated that the Federal Government was spending about $20 billion in this, with state and local governments spending about $10 billion more. The scope of OEO in the overall War on Poverty is indicated in part by the fact that this fiscal year we are disposing of only a billion and a half dollars. In any case what we should have done last summer was to attempt to re-allocate the entire $20 billion of Federal expenditures for greatest effectiveness against poverty. The charge of our legislation is that the Director of OEO should coordinate all anti-poverty programs. Last summer, however, we did not attempt this overall re-allocation because we did not have time. Rather we tried to allocate our own OEO programs and suggested major *additions* to other anti-poverty programs, but made no recommendations for internal re-allocation. Certainly, in our second planning cycle we are attempting the larger job.

To get a handle on programs then, we divided these programs into three functional groups according to the particular portion of the poverty problem that they were designed to attack. This division, a qualitative one, is the guts of our systems analysis. The three functional groups were *jobs, social programs* and *transfer payment* programs. These are three reinforcing categories—three legs on a stool—rather than being alternatives.

The importance of jobs is demonstrated definitionally. If opportunity is our primary objective then, in the American economy and American society as they exist, jobs are the name of the game. Opportunity means opportunity for self support which in turn means the opportunity to work in a useful and gainful job at non-poverty wages. If there are not enough jobs (and there were not at the time this analysis was made, last summer, although this has drastically changed since) we need programs to correct this deficiency. Job programs are important both because they provide immediate concrete and symbolic results from the War on poverty, but they are also vital to the long-run effectiveness of our remedies.

Second in order, although not particularly second in importance, come social programs. These are programs for basic individual and environmental change. We must realize that many of the poor do not have decent jobs because they are not capable of taking and holding decent jobs. Their individual education and training may be too low; their health may be too bad; family situations such as a large family headed by a female may make work difficult; families may be too large even for acceptable work to bring them above the poverty line; people cannot get jobs because of racial discrimination. Therefore in order to make job programs successful we must change the personal, family and environmental factors which make people and families unable to take jobs. These social programs thus reinforce the job programs but the job programs also reinforce the social programs. The worst thing that could happen would be for us to educate and to train people, to change their environments to raise their hopes and then not to fulfill their hopes because there are not enough jobs in the economy.

The third leg is transfer payments—pure money payments for no services rendered. Transfer payment programs are not primarily opportunity. They are recognition that some people cannot use work or training opportunities. The aged can make little fruitful use of such opportunities and the same can be said for many female family heads. Transfer payments also provide interim money for those who are waiting for opportunity programs to pick them up. But in one major way transfer payment programs also do provide opportunity. Money means ability to choose. A man with a family to support may, if given money, have the choice of taking training for a decent job instead of having to grab the first available job of any type in order to feed his family.

This is the structure of our analytical system and note that I have described it without mentioning cost-effectiveness or cost-benefit once. Nonetheless it is systems analysis made systematic by organizing problems and programs into a structure where it becomes possible to examine alternatives and magnitudes in relationship to one another. Of course that is not all of it. Let me give some further examples of the kinds of analysis we did internally within this structure.

1 I have already mentioned the crucial nature of the definition of objectives with Opportunity in the top position, and the quantitative measurement of these objectives, even though this measurement must be oversimplified.

2 We used quantitative analysis to confirm intuitions. Our intuitions told us, for example, that family planning would be a highly cost-effective program. We looked at family planning and discovered that this was indeed the case. Program costs were estimated to be low and effectiveness was estimated to be high. Our estimate is that, had family planning programs for the poor been started a generation ago, there would be about 4½ million fewer poor people in the country today. This is highly cost-effective, although not quite as good as suggested by the summer intern who burst in and told us that a particular family planning program had proved effective after only six months of operation. In any case the family planning case also provides a good example of the political constraints on the uses of analysis. We are pushing ahead with family planning programs, but cautiously.

3 We also used quantity to make at least one discovery we did not expect, although please note that it is a large rather than a small quantitative difference. In the Job category of programs, we started out with the aggregate demand hypothesis that tight overall employment would take care of almost all the job problems of the poor. We made estimates however, of the size and projected changes of unemployment in various categories of the poor and discovered that it just ain't so. Our estimates have since been confirmed by the fact that even at the lowest unemployment rate in 13 years, the poor still do not have enough jobs. On the basis of these estimates we recommended substantial job creation programs, although with unemployment at current levels (much lower than the time we made our proposals) job creation is no longer our major emphasis.

4 We made numerical evaluations of alternative programs. Looking again at the job category, we looked in last summer's con-

text of over four percent unemployment, at
job training, aggregate demand programs
and housing construction programs and estimated that none of these would provide
enough jobs for the poor. We therefore became quite interested in community employment programs to take poor people into
useful public service jobs such as teachers'
aides, health aides, other subprofessional
categories and maintenance jobs as well.
This seemed the most cost-effective mode
of creating jobs and at the same time it
would help fill the vast need in this country
for an increase in public services.

5 Our definition of objectives implies that
what we are out to do is cure rather than
ameliorate poverty and thus in looking for
effectiveness, we looked for the causal relationships between various problems and
poverty and we looked for fundamental
rather than ameliorative programs. Because
we had questions about whether things such
as poor housing and bad health care caused
poverty rather than being spectacular symptoms of poverty, we gave programs in these
areas relatively low priority relative to jobs
and education—whose causal connection to
poverty is clear.

6 We looked for the universes within which
our programs could be most effective. The
Job Corps technique of intensive training in
a residential program is hoped to be successful for a wide variety of youths. Relative
to cheaper alternatives, however, we believe
its differential effectiveness is likely to be
highest for hard core, hard-to-reach youth
who simply cannot be reached any other
way. And we recommended Job Corps concentration on these. For easier youths,
cheaper programs are likely to be more
cost-effective. Similarly Community Action
can be a useful technique almost anywhere.
But it is more likely to be more useful
where the poor live among the poor in
urban slums and rural depressed areas. In
these environments where facilities, sur-
roundings, and neighbors are all likely to be
poor, the expenditure of Community Action
dollars is likely to be most effective, because
there is far more to be done—we are not
working at a sparse margin. Because these
dollars are limited, we recommend they be
confined primarily to such areas of "concentrated" poverty even though they would not
be ineffective elsewhere.

7 My last example describes a technique for
getting the total budget down to a prescribed level. We used it not necessarily
because it was the best technique but because in the short time available to us it
seemed the only technique. In retrospect,
it may be the best anyhow. Rather than trying to add up programs to reach a certain
specified budget level, we started out with
what we called an unconstrained budget—
unconstrained by fund availability. That is,
we estimated how large our programs could
be, subjected only to constraints other than
dollars, constraints such as the number of
doctors available for medical programs. This
added up to a sum higher than there was
any likelihood of our obtaining. We then
cut programs back by priority, cutting out
the least cost effective first. We started with
programs universes which included all the
34 million poor, then in order to get our
budgets down we cut back for example to
the hard-core universe of greatest need I
have described for Job Corps and the universe of concentrated poverty which is in
greatest need of Community Action, for
example. We have not considered the general applicability of this sort of method compared to other modes of budget analysis for
other programs but it did work well for us.

Let me conclude with two points. First,
what I have been talking about is planning
analysis and should be carefully distinguished
from operations. For example, in talking about
concentrated poverty, we defined this poverty
to be that which existed in the lowest 25 percent of urban census tracts and the lowest 40
percent of rural counties. This was based on
the greatest-need rationale described above,
but what we were aiming at was a definition
which would enable us statistically to measure
the slums and rural depressed areas. For operational purposes, it is necessary to look
directly for areas describable as slum or depressed areas, rather than arbitrarily decide on
the particular tracts and counties we used for
statistical purposes. Census tracts and counties
are arbitrary definitions, and the only data currently available for these definitions are from
the 1960 Census and are now six years old.
The rationale of concentrated poverty by
which we arrived at these definitions was not
arbitrary, but it is the rationale rather than the
superannuated statistics which must be used
to apply programs to these areas. For statistical and budgeting purposes, the Law of
Large Numbers implies that we are likely to
be okay but the Law of Large Numbers cannot be applied to detailed local operations.

More generally, planning does not control operations and one problem we have not yet solved is how to control operations to meet the plan.

Finally let me mention evaluation. The plan I have described is based on theory. For better or for worse, OEO very rapidly built up spending commitments for over one billion dollars which preceded the conclusion of the planning processes described. The planning, however, preceded the first results of the programs so that we planned and allocated on the basis of how these programs *ought* to have worked. This year it is different. We are beginning to get evaluative results on how our programs are working. What we can do now and are beginning to do is much closer to true cost-effectiveness analysis—matching actual effectiveness against actual costs. My skepticism about the over-use of such analysis still applies. Decisions should still be made only on the basis of big quantitative differences and the right questions should be asked whether or not the answer is quantifiable. Now, however, the quantities we are working with are real numbers and not hypotheses, which is a very substantial change. As I have said at the outset, our results are testable. They are being tested, and next year, I may speak with less confidence.

READING 23

A PROPOSED METHODOLOGY FOR COMPARING FEDERALLY ASSISTED HOUSING PROGRAMS*

William B. Ross

Sheerly by coincidence, the launching of the new Federal Department of Housing and Urban Development followed shortly on the heels of the new presidential directive[1] for increased formal emphasis on more precise identification of national goals and on more systematic analysis of alternative means of reaching them most effectively. From the beginning, there have been no illusions either

that the desired objective of effective public administration was a new one or that all the sought-after improvement in the precision and quality of analysis would be achieved overnight—or in a single year—or in a single administration.

The urgency of the presidential instruction was clearly of the "let us begin" variety. But the full burden falls on individual agencies to translate into their own operational setting an analytic approach long pioneered—but still conceded to be in the development stage[2]— in the analysis of defense goals and alternatives. The launching of so many simultaneous diverse efforts—without benefit of the extensive developmental work which preceded the formal Defense Department system—has inevitably resulted in analysis ranging from the un-

* Reprinted with permission of the American Economic Association from American Economic Review, vol. LVII, no. 2, May, 1967. The opinions expressed in this article are those of the author and do not necessarily represent those of the Department of Housing and Urban Development. Grateful acknowledgment is extended for comments on an earlier draft to several individuals but especially to Robert C. Caldwell, Charles W. Wiecking and George W. Wright.
1 President's Memorandum to Heads of Departments and Agencies, Aug. 25, 1965; U.S. Bureau of the Budget, Bulletin No. 66–3, Oct. 12, 1965, and Supplement to Bulletin No. 66–3, Feb. 21, 1966.

2 Alain C. Enthoven, "Introduction," A Modern Design for Defense Decision: A McNamara-Hitch-Enthoven Anthology (Washington, Industrial College of the Armed Forces, 1966), p. 7.

even to the unsatisfactory and, often, to the unproduced. Each agency making this effort faces its own particular version of generalized national goals supported by broad individual program objectives leading to loosely related program activities on which voluminous records are kept on everything but how the program activities support the program objectives and lead specifically and measurably to the fulfillment of concrete national goals.

When everything depends on everything else, it is not immediately clear whether better analysis can be started most effectively: at better specification of national goals; at clearer development of relationships between overall program objectives and national goals; at testing of the relationships between specific program activities and program objectives; or at development of better data on any or all of the preceding relationships.

The present paper is, at best, a progress report on how one analytic staff in one agency is attempting to approach one specific policy problem cycle. The aim of the paper is to describe what we believe to be useful analytic methodology for the federal decision-maker; we try to be explicit about the stages of analysis in which we choose to defer concentration while presenting for critical review those tentative proposals which now appear to us both to be relevant and to lead in useful directions.

Federal Goals in Housing

Since 1949, the nation has had the expressed goal "of a decent home and a suitable living environment for every American family. . . ."[3] The directness, simplicity, grandeur, and scope of this expression have been the envy of presidential speechwriters and of legislative draftsmen ever since. None has topped it, and most have sensed the futility of even trying.

But the process of refining this broad goal into operational terms—even setting aside for present purposes the phrase "a suitable living environment"—is neither direct nor unambiguous. Certainly, the refinement process must consider the broad variety of action programs enacted under the "decent home" banner. Not

[3] *Declaration of National Housing Policy, Section 2, Housing Act of 1949 (Public Law 171, 81st Cong.; 63 Stat. 413).*

all of the relevant programs are the responsibility of the Department of Housing and Urban Development, but even those that are represent a diversity which we feel incapable of encompassing altogether within a single analytic framework.

For initial clarity, we have chosen somewhat arbitrarily to subdivide HUD's housing programs between those which appear to fit most logically under the phrase "to facilitate effective private housing market mechanisms" as distinguished from programs whose ultimate purposes appear to include overt assistance in the provision of housing at below-market costs. This dichotomy is neither a clean one nor of indefinite value. But, for the present, we find it to be a useful distinction.

The "assisted" housing programs are not themselves by any means a homogeneous group. Interpretation and interpolation of recorded legislative histories, inductive reasoning from obvious relationships, and even interrogation of participants in the legislative process all have a part in trying to identify just what unique combination of contributions a particular program was (and is) expected to make toward the overall decent home goal.

Essentially, each well-established federal activity has been the product of a unique, continued exercise in group dynamics involving interaction between (1) proposers of legislation (executive and legislative); (2) subcommittees, full committees, and leadership groups in the legislative process; (3) executive branch program administrators; (4) executive and legislative participants in the budgetary process; and (5) the "target group" of individuals or institutions. The net programmatic result has both the strengths and the weaknesses of the processes of democracy; above all, however, it means that single-dimensional measurement and single-criteria evaluation and even single-disciplinary study are inadequate—or even misleading.

The unraveling of the mixture of motivations and goals is the most difficult and the most critical part of analytic efforts—and, potentially, the most productive. But, the complexity of these patterns means that analysis cannot start at a logical beginning of clear identification of unambiguous goals and proceed in orderly, martial fashion to conclusions. The program grouping with which this paper deals is merely one special case of this problem.

At this stage, for example, we do not find it useful to insist on a direct separation of the income-redistribution goals of housing assistance programs from the development goals—both economic and social—of providing more housing of socially acceptable quality for various population groups. Yet, we cannot ignore the existence of "low" income groups too "poor" to be aided directly through existing housing assistance mechanisms. The evidence of constraints on the utility of functional programs for income-maintenance objectives requires more careful delineation of objectives/means relationships but cannot be regarded as a prima facie case for abandonment.

The Concept of Output

In the past, it would have been relevant, or even necessary, to debate at length whether the "outputs" of housing assistance programs should be quantified in "goods" terms (e.g., units produced) or "service" terms (e.g., unit months of occupancy). This dilemma appears to us to have been resolved by increased reliance on upgrading of existing substandard housing units and by the initiation of new assistance methods which involve temporary support of units for varying periods of time. Thus, for the present, at least, we find it necessary to use output concepts of the flow-of-service in order to compare those programs which we now administer, let alone the infinite varieties of alternative assistance devices which could be considered.

Again, the choice is a tentative one, and the probabilities are high that we will, for some parts of the analysis, need to return to production or "goods" output measurements. For either choice, considerably more thought will need to be given to the "standard-substandard" concepts and definitions.

"Housing Assistance" Programs

Any listing of federal "programs" is tentative and subject to expansion or contraction as analysis focuses, at one stage, on relevant characteristics which require separate consideration of distinctions within an administratively cohesive program or, at another stage, on characteristics which blur the distinctions between programs administered by totally different organizations or agencies.

With these reservations, we consider that seven administratively separate programs constitute the "assisted housing" category:

1 Low-rent public housing (including new construction; acquisition of new units; acquisition of existing units, with or without rehabilitation; and leasing of existing units).
2 Rent supplements with mortgage insurance (with or without federal acquisition of the insured mortgage).
3 Direct loans at below-market interest rates for rental housing for the elderly and handicapped.
4 Below-market interest rate loans to higher educational institutions for housing and related facilities (including faculty housing and married student apartments).
5 Insured mortgages at below-market interest rates coupled with federal acquisition of the insured mortgage.
6 Below-market interest rate loans for rehabilitation of owner-occupied dwellings in urban renewal areas.
7 Partial grants to low-income homeowners in urban renewal areas for rehabilitation.

Economic Characteristics of "Assisted Housing" Programs

While this group of programs has the common economic characteristic that the housing for some period of time is provided to the occupant at less than the private market costs, the significant differences within the group may be categorized, tentatively, as: (1) differences in degree (level or proportion) of assistance; (2) differences in time pattern of gross and net federal outlay or cost; (3) differences in time pattern of benefits; (4) differences in the physical unit provided; (5) differences in total cost of the unit provided.

For purposes of this paper, it is necessary only to describe the range of these differences rather than the full array of them.

The degree of assistance can be as high as a partial contribution to operating costs plus the full capital costs of building new units as represented by the maximum annual federal contribution under low-rent public housing; it can be as low as a small fraction of the cost of a fix-up job as in the owner-occupant rehabilitation assistance programs. It may be as fixed as the maximum dollar limit for rehabilitation grants; it may be as indeterminate as the rent supplement payment which depends more on the future incomes of the tenants than it does on initial construction costs.

The time pattern of net federal outlays or cost can be as simple and as short as the one-check disbursement of a rehabilitation grant; it can be as long as the fifty-year maximum repayment period on a college dormitory loan; it can be as complex as the forty years of annually calculated net federal contributions to a low-rent public housing project plus the estimated federal loss on tax-exemption of the bonds sold to finance the project.

The time pattern of benefits can last as long as the housing unit stands in many cases; it could change or even terminate at the first annual tenant income reexamination of a rent supplement project; it can be linked to specific time periods as in the case of public housing leased units; or a residual part of it could be capitalized into the net selling price of a unit rehabilitated with great assistance when the property subsequently changes hands.

The physical units provided show large distinctions within each program group as well as between them—even when reduced from "structures" to "dwelling unit" terms. The range can be from the sleeping/study room shared by two or four college students to the multibedroom apartment for a large family in public housing or a rent supplement project.

Over and above the unit cost differences attributable to differences in average unit size, there are other major cost factors of great policy relevance. Quality of construction standards are among the most significant of these. Quality standards of size, equipment, and allowable amenities are administratively established pursuant to general legislative standards or guidance (e.g., "not be of elaborate or extravagant design or materials")[4] and thus differ most between programs which have been administered separately. The scope of "related facilities" included can also be significant as when a public housing project includes community rooms for recreational or social services activities. Equal size and quality units can be provided in large- or small-scale projects or in single units with greatly differing production costs. And, highly significantly, local land values and construction costs for the same product can differ within the nation by nearly 100 percent.

Relevant Policy Issues

Given a going concern which carries on, among its activities, a series of related programs with this range of diversity, the policy questions most frequently raised are likely to be along the lines of: What changes, if any, ought to be made in the multitude of administratively established constraints? What alternative devices could be proposed to better serve all or part of the objectives of this program group? And, most of all, what should be the incremental change in the relative proportions in which these related—and sometimes complementary—programs should be offered in the next annual budget?

The first of these questions is literally always relevant. The others become pressing on at least an annual cycle and become increasingly intense in those years in which a program exhausts its previously authorized time or money limits and must, in effect, have its option renewed. In each such policy question, varying degrees of partial goal reexamination and refinement are necessarily involved, but the complex nature of the composite goal mixture seldom permits abstract, total goals formulation except in the context of a policy issue along one of these lines.

At this stage of development, our approach to the assisted housing program group focuses on the income redistribution (housing cost savings to tenants) aspects which are their most common denominator but not necessarily the dominant goal of any one program nor of equal weights in the goal mix as between programs.

Measuring "Costs"

For present purposes, we believe it appropriate to measure "costs" of the assisted housing programs in terms of net federal payments, although more sophisticated measures may

---

[4] *Section 401(a), Housing Act of 1950 (Public Law 475, 81st Cong.; 64 Stat. 48).*

become more useful at later stages of analysis; e.g., in dealing with macroeconomic aspects of national housing investments. Our federal cost measure cannot, however, be restricted solely to direct outlays and recoveries of the Department. The nature of financing mechanisms used in this program group requires consideration of interest costs (only parts of which may be reflected in the agency's books) and the effects of exemption from federal income taxes. These factors are considered not for the sheer joy of complicating the analysis but solely out of the necessity that they be taken into account in reducing the disparate programs to a meaningful common basis.

The consideration of interest costs is present in another form when we attempt to make comparisons between the disparate time patterns of disbursement and repayment possible within this program grouping. Discounted present values are an obvious device for handling this problem, and the use of federal borrowing rates is an equally obvious first approximation of an appropriate rate of discount when we are comparing alternative federal methods of spending money to achieve the same or related ends. Again, more complex discount rate concepts, e.g., taxpayer's marginal value of consumption foregone, are only appropriate in the analysis of more aggregate aspects of the housing problem.

Measuring "Benefits"

Isolating the income-redistributional results of the housing assistance programs can be regarded as a first approximation of one aspect of the "benefits" of these programs, although we will most certainly want subsequently to look at the pattern of "savings" against the beneficiary income patterns to make a judgment on how well the income-redistributional results correspond to public goals. Initially, we may assume that the assisted tenants are those for whom income benefits are intended to accrue.

While the rents (or monthly housing costs for owner-occupants) of the units aided under the various programs are determinable, we need a base concept against which to compare these rents. Comparison with rents paid by the tenants in their previous housing has immediate but superficial attractiveness. It suffers from the defect that varying quality, size, and location of the previous unit make this comparison unreliable at best.

A better concept—which both avoids the uncertainty-of-previous-condition problem and adapts to the variety of factors influencing unit costs—is that of "private market housing of comparable quality." This standard has considerable flexibility in analysis and appears to be useful for a wide variety of comparisons, provided one keeps in mind the weakness of its implicit assumption that the tenant would have chosen housing of this size, quality, location, etc.

At its simplest stage, this standard can be applied to analysis of the pure cost differences to the federal government involved in its choices of financial devices. This can be accomplished by applying the financial assistance parameters of each program in turn to a standard housing unit to determine the variations in net federal cost and net rent savings yielded by each of them. This assumes that the unit would have cost the same to construct and would have served the same tenants under each of the programs compared.

The next stage would involve the assumption that private construction cost of the comparable unit would have equaled that experienced by the assisted unit. By holding unit costs constant and applying the financial parameters of the going private mortgage market (regular FHA mortgage insurance terms and conditions may be useful for this purpose), we may approximate the net rental savings to tenants for each of the programs in turn.

Since, in either case, these rental savings accrue over an extended period of time, they must also be aggregated in some way to compare the relative "rental savings per dollar of federal cost" efficiencies of the various programs. Because these savings are effectively felt by the recipients as the (reduced) rent becomes due, the temptation is very strong to ignore discount factors and simply add the savings over the period in which they are expected to occur even though the costs would be aggregated on a discounted basis. The natural compulsion toward symmetry and reversibility in analysis argues otherwise. In addition, it may be useful in evaluating income-redistributional effects of programs to consider the stream of benefits as equivalent to a stream of cash payments. Thus, by discounting rental savings also at the federal borrowing rate, we have automatically calculated the present value of a stream of payments which can be compared with the present value of the pattern of federal costs incurred to yield that income benefit through an indirect (or multiple-goal) device.

Subsequent relaxation of the "equality-of-cost" assumption will be feasible through successive stages of architectural-engineering analyses of the products of each assistance program to approximate more accurately the private reproduction costs of assisted units. As sufficient operating and maintenance cost data become available, it will also be possible and desirable to put overall construction and operating costs on comparable bases to evaluate differences in total life ("systems"?) costs resulting from differences in construction standards as between programs.

In any event, the relative values of private "rental savings per dollar of federal cost" among the various federal assisted housing programs provide one benefit-cost ranking—one that measures the income redistribution benefit. We may term the highest benefit-to-cost ratio "the income redistribution optimum."

In addition to the income redistribution effects, there are other aspects of the effects of assisted housing programs requiring equal attention, in their turn, such as the unit output/cost optimum or "most bang for the buck" target.

Over and above direct financial/cost benefit comparisons, there are differential benefits associated with the separate housing assistance programs in terms of how each program contributes or fails to contribute to the strategy of providing rebirth to dying cities or critical improvements to decaying neighborhoods. In short, if we were to give to the poor—through a negative income tax or some alternative device—the dollar equivalent of the income benefits they receive through these housing programs, we would still face the problem of saving our cities and neighborhoods; and this effort, too, would have its very substantial money cost.

Thus, should we identify two alternative housing programs which are comparable in their income redistribution benefits (or comparable in cost to the federal government), but

one makes a notable contribution to urban redevelopment or neighborhood improvement and the other does not, then clearly the one making the dual contribution is to be preferred on efficiency grounds.

Accordingly, we would next want to identify the nonquantifiable environmental impacts of the alternative housing solutions and the long-term versus short-term implications. By and large, this would consist of identifying the favorable and unfavorable consequences worthy of note for each relevant housing alternative, including implications with regard to meeting other urban objectives such as the creation of sound neighborhoods and economically viable cities. We would also assess the relative significance of these factors, considering such things as the relationship to overall area needs in terms of roads, facilities, and commercial establishments; the impact on the neighborhood subculture; the hostility or acceptance of nearby residents; the ease of assembling suitable real estate; the probable timing; and the number of persons affected, etc. This could culminate in the creation of a table of descriptive summary data along the following lines: housing alternative; cost disadvantage (over least total cost solution); unfavorable environmental consequences; favorable environmental consequences; significance of consequences.

The final stages of this approach to an optimum solution would consist of a new ranking from "most preferred" to "least preferred" which considers both housing cost/benefit factors and environmental consequences. The theoretical optimum at this stage may be defined as one of the following: (1) the "least total cost" alternative whose net environmental disadvantages are not sufficient to offset its cost advantage over higher cost alternatives, or (2) the alternative whose net favorable environmental consequences provide the most significant offset (nonquantitative judgmental offset) to its cost disadvantage. We will call this approximation the "environmental optimum."

The suggested handling of nonquantitative data is not a mechanical or arithmetic one, and it does not yield a numeric solution. For that reason, it will be unsatisfactory to some. We are all familiar with the horse and rabbit stew problem implicit in any decision involving both quantitative and nonquantitative data.

However, we believe that this approach provides the opportunity to quantify everything that can be quantified in a practical situation and to compare systematically alternative packages of concomitant net benefits associated with each alternative as offsets to cost factors.

The President has placed strong emphasis on the careful definition of program objectives and on careful analysis of alternative means for achieving these objectives efficiently. At the federal level, the general strategy in housing and urban development programs will almost certainly be (1) to encourage efforts by local governments to identify and pursue the most efficient local solutions, (2) to develop national data and analyses which identify the most effective overall programs and administrative practices, and (3) to seek expansion of these efficient programs and general and broad application of creative new approaches. We invite your attention to these matters and seek constructive suggestions on the analytical methods we have outlined.

READING 24

GOVERNMENT-INDUSTRY DEVELOPMENT OF A COMMERCIAL SUPERSONIC TRANSPORT *

Stephen Enke

The U.S. government is expected to spend $2 billion or more to develop a commercial supersonic transport (SST) that will be safe, profitable, and available for airline use around 1974.

Among the major policy questions now being raised by the U.S. SST program are: (1) Is a U.S. SST economically justifiable? (2) Why is federal assistance necessary? (3) How much of its expenditures on the SST should the federal government recover, and through what means? (4) How can government finance an SST monopoly, and yet protect the public interest without concerning itself with aircraft prices, flight frequencies, and passenger fares? (5) Are the benefits of the SST sufficiently general to justify a federal subsidy of its development and possible manufacture?

The answers to these questions are of very broad interest because the U.S. SST may be

* Reprinted with permission of American Economic Association from American Economic Review, vol. LVII, no. 2, May, 1967.

the first of several federal government programs to develop products of advanced technology for commercial use.

SST's Economic Justification

The President has declared that the U.S. SST must be safe and "profitable," but what is the interpretation of profitable and how can it be estimated far in advance?

Airline managements presumably will not buy an SST unless it can earn as much on its investment cost as can be earned on the advanced subsonics of the 1970's (e.g., the Boeing 747). Practically, this means that SST prices, flight costs, and receipts must permit a return of about 20 percent before taxes and interest. (Publicized "orders" for SST's are revocable until performance and prices are known.)

What airframe and engine manufacturers must ordinarily expect to earn from a new aircraft is more uncertain. Realizations have often been far worse than expectations, and several new commercial aircraft of the past ten years have lost money for their manufacturers (e.g., Convair 880). Expectations of profit must presumably be higher the greater are the sums to be risked and the greater the dispersion of possible financial outcomes.

If the U.S. government is initially to finance 80-90 percent of the U.S. SST's development costs, and if up to $4 or $5 billions of American resources must somehow be invested in development and manufacture before the program generates a net cash inflow from sales to airlines, an obvious economic test of the U.S. SST's justification is its ability to earn the 10-15 percent rate of return earned on an average by domestic resources employed in U.S. industry.

Whether the resource and money costs sunk in the U.S. SST's development and manufacture can earn a 10-15 percent rate of return depends upon: (1) costs of development, for airframe and engine; (2) costs of manufacture, for airframe and engine, as a function of production rate, cumulative output, and calendar date; (3) operating costs per plane mile, as a function of various performance parameters (e.g., specific fuel consumption) and permissible altitude of transonic acceleration; (4) operating receipts per plane mile, as a function of seating capacity, load factor (percentage capacity sold), and fare levels; (5) availability of supersonic passengers, as a function of number of long-haul passengers, subsonic passenger fares, willingness to pay more for less time in the air, and extent to which sonic boom nuisance restricts available routes and schedules. All of these factors remain shrouded in uncertainty.

Development costs of aircraft have often been underestimated by a factor of two—especially where the necessary state of art has yet to be attained.

SST operating profits are extremely sensitive to specific fuel consumption, lift-drag ratio (a measure of aerodynamic efficiency), and aircraft weight empty. Of its maximum gross take-off weight of maybe 650,000 pounds 10 percent or less will be payload and about 45 percent will be fuel. An X percent improvement in fuel economy, if translatable into greater seating capacity, could increase net flight receipts by perhaps $3X$ percent, proportionately increasing the selling price the aircraft can command.

Supersonics will have to compete with subsonics. Advanced subsonics may have costs per seat mile 20-30 percent below those of the U.S. SST. Airlines, unless they acquire SST's at subsidized prices, will hence buy relatively few SST's so that load factors are exceptionally high (e.g., 70 percent of seats are filled instead of the 55 percent typical of today's jets) and have to levy a surcharge (e.g., 10-20 percent) on SST tickets. No one knows how many long-haul passengers would be diverted to subsonics by such fare differentials. Estimates are that one-half may be lost.

The growth rate of passenger demand is also uncertain. Long-haul revenue passenger miles have increased at an average of 14 percent during the past ten years, but this rate is expected by most to decline. Continued growth will presumably vary with quality of service, per capita incomes, and population growth. The lowest estimate of passenger volume growth between 1966 and 1990 is five times.

Public acceptance or nonacceptance of frequent sonic booms by commercial aircraft remains doubtful. If commercial overland supersonic flight is not permitted by the U.S. and most foreign governments, no more than 40 percent of long-haul passengers remains to be shared with subsonics on the available routes over water. Conversely, as the SST's engines are "sized" for high altitude transonic acceleration (above 35,000 feet) and fuel consumption per mile at subsonic speeds is much higher, the economics of the SST are improved if it is permitted to cross the sound barrier at lower altitudes nearer to airport terminals. Unfortunately, as SST designs increase in gross take-off weight to permit more seats and hence lower seat mile costs, the severity of expected sonic boom increases and the possibility of operating restrictions (e.g., curfews on transcontinental flights) is increased. The prudent assumption, until more conclusive predictions can be made of public reaction to boom, is that commercial supersonic flights over populated land areas will be prohibited.

Anyone who has been intimately involved in econometric assessments of SST "profitability" realizes full well that its prospects will remain most uncertain at least until prototype flight tests and possibly until regular commercial operations begin. The total market for SST's to 1990 is probably somewhere between 150 to 600 aircraft. The profitability of the program is sensitive to numbers of SST's sold. Under certain sets of favorable assumptions the over-all rate of return could be 10-15 percent. But under other sets of equally plausible assumptions the return is negative. Perhaps a best guess is an overall program rate of return of 0 to 5 percent.

The simple truth, however, is that such a complex and technically advanced aircraft must be an investment gamble in its first generation.

Necessary Federal Assistance

There is general agreement that, if there is to be a U.S. SST program, the federal government must finance it, past flight test and possibly certification, by means of outright grants, advances to be recouped later, and/or guarantees of borrowings by the airframe and engine contractors from the financial community.

Three of the principal manufacturers and their suppliers lack both the ability and willingness to provide $4 billion or so for the development and production funds required before the date around 1975 at which time net cash inflows commence. Their collective net worths, including that of some of their probable subcontractors, do not approach such a figure. Besides, even if able, why should airframe and engine manufacturers risk such sums on an SST? They have alternative investment opportunities involving fewer technical uncertainties, smaller investments, and shorter "dry" periods before recovery of principal. That one airframe and one engine manufacturer are expected to be selected around January 1, 1967, for continued development with government assistance, almost guaranteeing a limited monopoly of a usable design eventually, is not enough apparently to evoke more than 10-20 percent participation in development costs by the manufacturers.

Potential airline customers are not expected to be a significant source of funds. No way remains of compelling the airlines to depart from their usual policy of "wait and see" before purchasing. Firm orders cannot be expected until after successful prototype flight tests in 1970 perhaps. And even then it seems unlikely that more than half the aircraft's fly-away price can be extracted through progress payments six to twelve months before delivery. (Although the first fifty or so SST's delivered probably have a special premium value of several million dollars each, because of high load factors during their initial two to three years of service, the first hundred-odd U.S. SST's have already been allocated for refundable deposits of $100,000 each.)

The combination of high technical risks and large dollar magnitudes makes it most improbable that the manufacturer, or indirectly the financial community, will provide the needed funds. Thus the federal government must either provide assurance against certain risks (e.g., accidental loss of a prototype) and/or become a sort of silent partner (providing say 80 percent of the net cash outflows and sharing say 80 percent of the net cash inflows). Such a scaling down of the private sums at risk to one-fifth of the total funds involved, with a commensurate scaling down of cash surpluses later, might be sufficient to evoke limited private financing despite the program's many uncertainties.

In addition to the funds required for development and production of an SST, safe and economical operation of SST's will be possible only if government expenditures are made for improved air traffic control, solar and cosmic radiation monitoring systems, and an improved meteorological forecasting capability.

The SST will cruise at 65,000 as compared to 35,000 feet for subsonics. The effects of wind and temperature on SST fuel consumption and the consequent impact on SST operating costs and payload make better data on these parameters vital. At supersonic speeds more advance warning is required to maneuver around unfavorable weather. In the period from 1970 through 1990 meteorological improvements alone could cost governments over a billion dollars.

These negative "externalities" should be considered part of the price of having an SST.

How Should the Government Recover?

The manufacturers will not risk even limited sums unless they and the government can agree on a financial plan that specifies at least the formula by which government will recoup its share of development and other "sunk" costs.

Unless there are significant and "external" national interests served by the program, a controversial issue discussed below, the federal government must be placed in a position to obtain the same rate of return on its investment as do the manufacturers if an impolitic and unwarranted subsidy is to be avoided. Thus if the program is continued because the $4 billions-odd worth of resources invested in it are expected to earn 10 to 15 percent before taxes or interest, and if the government were to accept say 5 percent on an 80 percent share of costs, the manufacturers would be expected to earn 30 percent to 55 percent on their investments. The only way government can avoid paying such a subsidy and still accept say 5 percent for itself, is to continue a program that prospectively wastes some of the nation's resources by promising a return less than that ordinarily obtained from domestic labor and capital used by industry in the U.S.

Thus government must be expected to share in profits if (1) the program appears economically justifiable and (2) unjustified subsidies to manufacturers are to be avoided. There is no logical escape. This requirement for government profit sharing has nothing to do with "socialism."

A major issue is whether government recovery should be either through some sort of tax or through sharing in net cash inflows as a silent partner.

Levies most often mentioned are:

1 A "royalty" or tax "off the top," added to the manufacturer's price of the aircraft: this would probably mean a 10 million tax added to say a $35 million manufacturer's price, and such a tax would lose sales to competing subsonics and possible supersonics.
2 An annual tax on SST aircraft operated by U.S. airlines: this would advantage foreign airlines, and a tax adequate for full government recovery plus an equity risk return would have the same present discounted value and incidence on price and sales as would an adequate royalty on delivery.
3 A tax of 10-20 percent on fares charged all SST passengers originating or terminating in U.S. territory: such a tax would further divert passengers to subsonic aircraft.

A tax on jet fuel purchased in the U.S. by all commercial supersonics may have to be reserved to pay for the special SST flight support services discussed above.

The alternative to a tax is sharing through a financial partnership or "pooling" arrangement. There could be one pool on the airframe and another on the engine. In each case the selected manufacturer and the federal government would be the initial members—able to sell their shares later to financial intermediaries. They would contribute, quarter by quarter, development and production costs in some agreed upon ratio. And, when net cash inflows start around 1975, these would be shared by the contractor and the government in proportion to their credits in the pool. Such credits should include both advances and an equity rate of return, preferably the same for each partner, of from 10 to 15 percent compounded.

One advantage of pooling as against taxing is that there is less likelihood of handicapping U.S. SST manufacturers or U.S. airlines operating SST's.

Another potentially important advantage of pooling is that the self-interests of the airframe and engine manufacturers are made coincident with the interests of the federal government. If the contractor believes some design change will more than pay for itself, i.e., that it will earn a good rate of return on the extra cost of making a change, government will similarly be advantaged if the contractor knows his business. And ordinarily, because airframe and engine manufacturers are experienced in commercial air transport and presumably know the airlines' needs better than FAA officials, pooling could permit the federal government to give the manufacturers the maximum degree of private initiative possible. Such freedom may be needed to make the program an economic success. Certainly, the SST program should not be administered as though the U.S. were developing and procuring a bomber say, for hopefully it is airlines and not the federal government that will buy and use this aircraft.

Another recoupment issue is whether the government should share in manufacturers' receipts or net cash inflows forever or only until such time as the government has realized some previously stipulated rate of return on its outlays.

Making either the royalty or pooling claims to SST sales revenue transferable would enable the government to sell its rights to future revenues to the private sector if and when success of the program seems assured.

Why should government seek to recover all its advances from those who buy or use the SST, for are there not other broad national interests being served?

The most intangible and commonly suggested "external" benefits are (1) technological "fall-out," (2) contingent military use, and (3) national prestige, but each of these proclaimed grounds has been vigorously denied by others.

A more explicit argument is that the sale of U.S. SST's at $35 million or so each will benefit the U.S. balance of payments in the 1970's. Such claims ignore many substitution effects. Traditionally, half U.S. aircraft exports have been financed in the U.S. Each U.S. SST exported may mean at least one less U.S. subsonic exported. If the U.S. sells competitive aircraft to foreign airlines, U.S. airlines may lose passengers to them. Estimates suggest that, over five years from date of sale, the net balance-of-payments credit for the U.S. from the sale of an SST is no more than 5-10 percent of its U.S. export price (and may even be negative if increased U.S. tourist spending abroad is considered).

Nevertheless, some gross external benefits must exist, although not necessarily net of special high altitude meteorology costs, etc. In the end the program's Phase I and II (design competition) costs to the federal treasury might be "forgotten" as an alleged contribution of $300 million-odd to some vague "national interests." But beyond that, and starting with Phase III (prototype development) in 1967, the program should be treated as a commercial risk enterprise of manufacturers and government in partnership.

Mitigating the Monopoly

The federal government in early 1967 may select a single SST airframe and engine contractor to continue prototype development. The selected manufacturers will emerge with considerable monopoly power that could be of considerable value. How can the government use public funds to create a monopoly and yet protect the public interest without destroying the managerial prerogatives and efficiency of private manufacturers and airlines?

First, the monopoly will be limited, for there may be some competition from the supersonic Anglo-French Concorde; but more important should be the rivalry of growth subsonics, competition that compels the selected U.S. SST manufacturers to provide the best possible performance at a price.

Second, the selected prime development contractors will have many subcontractors, especially on the airframe. These subcontractors will acquire a competence that later could be used by a rival prime contractor. Also key employees have been known to transfer at higher salary to a rival manufacturer.

Third, the federal government is expected to have the right to license patents at zero cost, together with shop drawings, to any other airframe and/or engine manufacturers who might later seek to compete.

Hence, if a really large and profitable SST market were to prove itself, it is not evident that rival manufacturers could not materialize. The DC-8 did follow the Boeing 707. A first generation manufacturer is not always sure of developing a profitable aircraft that excludes competition.

A single airframe and single engine manufacturer for the U.S. SST should create other novel problems more easily overlooked.

One is division of the flyaway aircraft's price between airframe and engine. There is a very large range of indeterminacy. The engine for example might be priced almost down to its marginal production cost. But its price could be as high as the aircraft price minus marginal airframe cost. The maximum conceivable engine price could be three times the minimum. Previously an airframe company had some choice among engine firms to narrow the range of possible engine prices.

The airlines will be face to face with a limited monopolist able to charge variable (i.e., discriminatory) prices unless prevented by government. Some of the earlier deliveries, assuming they can maintain schedules, have potentially higher load factors and hence should command premium prices. Should the competition of Concorde and the subsonics prove minor, some airlines may ask for federal ceilings on U.S. SST prices.

This could be a dangerous step. If government regulates SST prices, should it not more energetically regulate SST fares so that airlines do not receive unjustified profits, and perhaps depress load factors through excessive competition in flight frequencies on approved SST routes? The situation of the U.S. merchant marine should be enough to deter any airline management from inviting government intervention.

The remaining alternative would be to develop two airframe-engine combinations—which practically would mean also producing two rival aircraft. This would double development costs. It would also lose some "learning curve" efficiencies in manufacturing. These extra costs would be justified only if, attributable solely to prolonged competition, operating costs were reduced by about a quarter.

Are the Benefits General Enough?

Costly public enterprises of great inherent risk are more easily justified if the spending of taxpayers' funds occasions widespread benefits. It is not enough that they provide employment and profits for a few localities and firms. How diffused are the benefits of the SST program likely to be?

About 85 percent of U.S. residents have never flown, those who do fly do not always take long-haul flights, and perhaps less than 5 percent of all Americans will ever fly SST's at their higher fares. Private, nonexpense account, long-haul passengers will mostly continue to fly subsonically. (It is not even certain that the federal government will reimburse its employees and those of its contractors for a supersonic surcharge.)

Further, American SST passengers will tend to travel to and from a few areas, such as New York, Chicago, Los Angeles, San Francisco, Seattle, Washington, D.C., and Miami. Americans living elsewhere may never use an SST except on international flights. But 100 million Americans may find themselves subjected daily to sonic booms if overland SST flights are permitted.

For all these reasons, and as the U.S. SST program is seen increasingly as a rival to expansion of Great Society programs, it is certain to become more controversial.

Conclusions

There are few modern instances of development with public funds of a technologically advanced product that is to be produced—very likely by a monopoly—and used commercially by private firms. Desirable guidelines in such cases are: (1) continuation only so long as the program is expected to earn a rate of return comparable to that expected by U.S. industry in making investments; (2) equal government sharing in such a rate of return, partly to avoid subsidization, but also to provide incentives for only economical design changes, etc.; (3) full recoupment by government, plus an equity or risk-taker's return, except insofar as there clearly are net "external" or national interests; (4) recoupment by government of its advances, not by taxes that reduce sales and use, but through some partnership (pooling) arrangement; (5) avoidance of special controls that will prevent the usual exercise of experienced management by the airframe and engine manufacturers; (6) use of public funds only to the extent that a private and excessively profitable monopoly will not be created; (7) no unrecovered government subsidies except where adequate benefits are likely to be diffused among a large fraction of citizens.

Finally, it is to be hoped and expected that a U.S. prototype of an SST will be flying well before the end of the 1970's, one that promises to be safe and profitable without being a public nuisance because of sonic boom. This means a state of art that will permit a rate of return of at least 10 percent on all resources invested in development after 1966 without supersonic flight over populated land areas. Until proposed designs can give this promise with more confidence it seems premature to begin construction of a prototype aircraft.

READING 25

AN APPROACH TO STRUCTURING TRANSPORTATION COST AND CRITERIA ANALYSIS*

Andrew V. Wittner

FOREWORD

In the coming decade, transportation investment decisions will begin to press even harder on government officials at the Federal, state, and local levels. As the scope and financial implications of transportation programs become more clear, the need for a systematic framework for guiding investments in research and facilities in those programs will be more pronounced.

The need for such a framework especially reflects the absence of any market mechanism adequate to elicit the resources required to support transportation programs. The massive capital inputs to regional transportation systems

* Reprinted with permission of the author. This paper was written in early 1967 as part of an introductory study of the Northeast corridor transportation problem. Many of the ideas given in the paper were developed with the assistance of Dr. Gerald Higgins, now at the University of Texas. The author is presently on the staff of the Chief of Staff, U.S. Army.

are simply too great for private funds to meet alone. If they are to emerge as realities, such transportation systems will probably have to be provided as a public commodity with resources in large measure provided by the government. And the government must be prepared to make these economic decisions without the guidance of a market mechanism.

This paper is intended for those engaged in seeking ways to come to grips with transportation investment criteria. It was not designed to be of use in the analysis of underdeveloped countries, although some sections may have application, but rather to persons concerned with the economics of transportation in the United States. There are few problems of economics and engineering more compelling, and the Federal Government is of course now engaged in establishing an expanding transportation post in the cabinet.

A reasonably complete overview of problem essentials does not seem to exist. We have apparently chosen to bypass sensible structuring of this problem, as with others, in our concern for the niceties of mathematical modeling and the supposed urgencies of rate making. This is not to argue against the need for sophisticated research technique and its potential application value, nor to imply that solutions to the many analytical problems embedded in relating, say, transportation to regional growth, or subsidy to self-sufficiency, will fall immediately from sensible structuring and orderly procedure. The point, instead, is that if such sophistication is to have value in application, we ought to be better advised as to which problems ought to be attacked, and in what order.

It is important to emphasize at the start that a rigid structure for transportation systems analysis is not proposed here. It is entirely possible that such a structure will never exist, or if suggested will be of little analytical value. What is attempted instead is the identification of key analytical issue, discussion of their economic and other dimensions, and suggestions for getting at these problems as study groups define their efforts. Hopefully, managers will find these ideas useful as they guide transportation research.

THE ELEMENTS OF TRANSPORTATION DECISIONS

Decisions to invest in transportation research and facilities will ultimately be governed by the following considerations:

Subsidy and/or regulation problems
Potential contributions to regional growth
Nonsubsidy Federal Government costs, and matching costs
Profitability, short and longer term
System growth potential and lifetime
Technical feasibility, including right-of-way availability
Manageability, if a large system
Prestige factor, if any
Vested interest

This set is neither exhaustive nor are all its elements mutually exclusive. The elements both interact and, clearly, may be rephrased or added to depending on one's viewpoint. Most important, each element *by itself* is extremely difficult to assess. And of course, the underlying problem is not so much establishing individual value measures relating to each factor, but finding some mechanism for tying all elements together such that a reasonably well-weighted decision may be made. The search for this means of integrating elements bearing upon transportation investment is tantamount, at this still early stage of transportation analysis, to a beginning search for criteria. It is well recognized that the development of these criteria will be difficult, as attested to by the Congressional hearings on the proposed Department of Transportation and the controversy concerning the provision in the initial bill giving criteria responsibility to the Secretary of Transportation. But criteria are critically needed, and they can be developed and communicated only through the logical and common sense evaluation of factors like those cited above.

WHY THOSE ELEMENTS?

The selection of these elements is not completely arbitrary. First, each element is itself composed of a set of subelements. These subelements are most often economic; but they are also political, social, technological, psychological, and perhaps other. In the vernacular, each factor is clearly multidimensional, and unfortunately there is even cross relation between the multidimensionality. Technological aspects of, say, a subsidy question can easily involve both economic and political backdrop.

It is this disciplinary multidimensionality, in some combination, that should, as analysis proceeds, characterize the way each factor is approached, dissected, and evaluated. But it is the economic dimension that will probably provide most of the quantitative decision-aiding information, although this will not come easy at first. This defines one of the two most important characteristics of the set: namely, that these factors, with the exception probably of only the last two given in this wholly arbitrary list, are all susceptible to economic analysis. There is much room, still, for improved economic analytical technique, in regional growth and its relation to transportation especially, but the framework for economic analysis is there. There exist costs, and this paper suggests ways to help measure them, and there will exist benefits, however difficult to define.

Underlying this entire question is the stark fact that there exists no clear market-directed mechanism that can now assist, or possibly will ever assist, in the efficient allocation of resources to large-scale transportation problems. Some elements of an economic market exist, but their interaction and lack of definition, coupled with prevailing nonmarket factors, seem to preclude the devising of an economically useful market analysis. Whereas most investment decisions in the private sector are made with thorough rate-of-return analyses, such analyses are likely to be of little value, presuming they might be accomplished, with regard to transportation systems. Uncertainties in the system are so dominant as to make rate-of-return estimating at this juncture little more than problem definition; useful in that sense probably, but not in a decision context. It is not so much the purpose of this paper to propose a surrogate or substitute for an economic market, but simply to look into matters that exert key influence on the total environment. In time, perhaps a surrogate market situation may develop.

Of more practical importance, probably, than each significant factor having an economic or other important dimension, is the straightforward notion that *those factors are the ones that will be framed into questions and asked* in some form or another by the persons most concerned. Here is where common sense appears to transcend analysis, the latter with its difficulty in communication and remaining underdeveloped ability to define and deal with these kinds of very broad problems. In short, we *know* that the factors cited above, or variations, are the important factors; what remains is to make them analyzable. And after all, there is not really too great a fundamental difference between common sense and application of economic analysis, so long as those persons applying the economics take continuing account of the present limitation of their art and those persons distrustful of economic analysis recognize that common sense cannot provide all the answers.

ASPECTS OF CRITERIA ANALYSIS

While the factors cited will undoubtedly bear on transportation criteria as they take shape, their importance and weighing will depend largely on analytical structuring. To rephrase, the importance of each factor will depend to a very great extent on how logically its economic (or other) composition is set forth. The follow-

ing key economic aspects, at least, will pertain to most factors.

Marginal costing—its potential and practicability
Joint cost or cost allocation—source or benefit
Remaining (or salvage) value measurement
Follow-on cost demand or implicit resource allocation, and spillover cost
Estimated total system cost, allocations among systems, and financing options

The above are cost aspects; the following are key benefit aspects.

Benefit definition—is the benefit as stated a true intended benefit or merely a convenient stopgap?
The benefit-time dimension—dynamics and discounting
Gross benefit measurement—does measurability exist?
Marginal and joint (spillover) benefit measurement—practical concepts or not?
Benefit weighting, given joint allocations
Choosing a desirable end-benefit, often without aid of previous analysis

Criteria aspects, some of which are given next, attempt to define relations between costs and benefits and provide a mechanism for choosing between alternative proposals; between alternative levels of resource (cost) allocation and hoped-for benefit realization. Criteria issues are relatively well-known and apply generally to both transportation and other problems, although, of course, in varying degrees.

Can a high level (more aggregate) cost-benefit criterion be chosen?
Are we unwisely relegating *absolute* accomplishment to secondary importance in an attempt to be efficient?
Can ratios, or perhaps a class of ratios, be useful criteria?
Do noneconomic criteria dominate?

In the process of early analysis, criteria discussions and criticisms per se should be set aside and cost and benefit questions should be tackled. From this, sensible treatment or derivation of criteria may come. Reversing things and backing into cost and benefit analyses by way of theoretical criteria study would be less likely to yield useful results or results that may be communicated to persons with less technical training.

This paper, then, is not so much an attempt to isolate criteria as it is an attempt to structure cost-criteria relationships and thereby shed partial light on how to select criteria. Some time is also devoted, in passing, to benefit-criteria relationships; this, of course, is conceptually at least as difficult as the cost aspect and is co-mingled with it.

The following section is directed at discussion of those cost and benefit aspects of criteria that are noted above. This is followed by a brief discussion of approaches to costing and how criteria may evolve.

CRITERIA-COST RELATIONSHIPS

1. Marginal Cost, Its Potential and Practicality

Clearly one would like to be able to pose in transportation analysis the typically sensible marginal query, "Is the additional expenditure a good idea or can I do better in some other way?" Given a cost-single-measure-of-performance function of the sort given by curve OM in Figure 25-1, certain analytical statements are possible.

At point A, where the slope of P-P′ is zero, no additional benefit is obtained at added cost. So if the additional expenditure C_1-C_2 were contemplated, some additional measure of benefit B_2 would have to result; in short, an additional dimension of effectiveness would have to appear at that point. It might perhaps take the functional form S-S′, but it is clearly not commensurable (or additive) with P-P′ as shown.

Of course, this merely indicates what has been known for some time: namely, that the postulating of a transportation "cost-composite benefit" function is exceedingly difficult. So, even if a family of "cost-single performance"

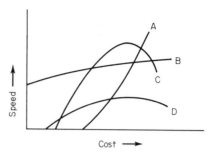

Figure 25-2   Different systems and a single performance measure.

functions for different proposed systems were conceived and drawn, as in Figure 25-2, the question of developing an overall criterion or criterion input is contingent not so much on marginal analysis relating to the *given* performance indicator, but rather to definition of co-mingled performance indicators. (Note: Systems A and B have interesting characteristics; A appears to offer unlimited speed, and B affords some speed at no expenditure. Most cost-speed functions will probably look something like C and D where the downward slope indicates the acquisition of an additional benefit or no added expenditure.)

But this is not to condemn marginal analysis, possibly in association with mathematical programming, as useless. Since the problem of defining all benefits of transportation systems will remain very difficult for some time, if not for always, where there is partial benefit definition (as with speed) there is room for useful marginal analysis. This is of course predicated on careful establishment and error bounding of the cost-single-benefit function. In short, attacking the cost-criterion problem in *stages,* by singling out measurable, individual benefits, should enable *and be encouraged by* useful marginal analysis. This should be a valuable aid to criteria development, at least in providing added insights. But care must be taken to ensure that little more than this is claimed, as yet, for marginal costing.

2. Joint Cost or Cost Allocation; Source and Service

Joint costs, simply defined are expenses incurred in the simultaneous production of two or more commodities or services. However, such costs may be viewed either from the "where generated" position or from the "where payoff"

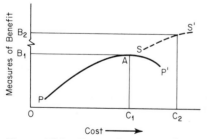

Figure 25-1   Cost-performance relationships.

position; that is, either from the *causing* system or endeavor (like R&D) or from the *caused* benefit or service. In either case, allocation problems must be dealt with early in the search for transportation criteria. Allocation, in the case of transportation systems, is more difficult when viewed from the benefit side. Both source-cost and benefit-cost allocation are discussed below.

As regards the allocation of not-yet incurred costs to alternative causing or planned systems, the problem is in structure like that faced in the military. A crude purpose or mission is hypothesized and a system (or systems) proposed to accomplish the mission. To the extent that costs are measurable, that is, that cost factors are derivable and that good system specification is possible, they may be allocated to that system. Analysis at this stage concentrates on careful specification and cost error analysis, and does not concern itself with subtle distinctions between system objectives, missions, purposes, or benefits. This point is important and often overlooked in a search for sophistication; careful system specification, based on knowledge of operation, is indispensable and must be sought early in the analysis. In fact, solid understanding of how a system functions should result in cost category structuring that will *both permit and facilitate* repeated re-allocation as purposes take on better definition and new systems are suggested.

There has been some question as to the handling of costs already incurred (for existing systems). These of course are sunk costs, yet certain of the more theoretically-minded argue that opportunity costs exist in the sense that previous commitments represent options foreclosed. It must be remembered that opportunity costs are not precisely costs, but rather benefits foregone as the result of taken action. As such, even if measurable, they are not readily combined with costs. Thus, the opportunity cost of an inherited asset is functionally related to both increasingly attractive benefit-cost criteria for present options (because of the cost being sunk), and to foregone benefits which may have resulted from past actions not taken.

These are logical and analytical imponderables, no matter how interesting. Granted that at a present decision point things (options) may be foreclosed because of past actions. But to state that their costs and benefits should be measured is to vastly over-complicate an already complicated problem and to imply that

measuring costs and benefits of still-existing options is easy. It is suggested, in transportation matters, that economists content themselves with trying to measure future streams for still-existing action possibilities. Success here will be reward enough.

In summary, then, from the standpoint of joint cost allocation to causing systems, in addressing the "where generated" allocation problem, there seems to be nothing unique to transportation problems. Note that "spillover" has not as yet been addressed. This is because spillover is defined here as a concept distinct from allocation, and is treated below in the section discussing implicit resource allocation. The following principles, not new by any means, are reemphasized here only because of the complexity of transportation analysis.

System specification, based on functional knowledge, is all-important to criteria development. Yet such specification must be parametric, and indicative of performance regimes in early stages of analysis.

Cost category structuring must relate closely to specification and still be flexible enough to permit re-allocation as designs and purposes are formed.

Sunk costs ought to be treated as they usually are, as sunk. Their opportunity costs are conceptually interesting but remain for economists of the next generation.

As regards allocation to benefits, in addressing the "where payoff" question, the problem cannot be so neatly structured. Benefit *measurement* or *definition* dominates the problem of *allocating* costs to benefits, as does the allocation of costs to benefits dominate the allocation for criteria purposes of costs to causing systems. (The above discussion of causing-system allocation naively assumes away the service or benefit aspect; and assumes away distinctions between services, products, objectives, and other forms of benefits.)

In summary, the whole question of benefit analysis pervades the question of cost analysis, and therefore of cost-criteria relationships. This is not a "finding" of this paper, but it is worth repeating as a warning to those who tempt logic by examining costs in a void. In the early years of military cost-effectiveness work, and still on occasion, the military variant of this was a major problem. Persons responsible for "effectiveness" studies would often seclude themselves, for security or administrative reasons, from persons concerned with resource analysis. A day or so before the due date, it would frequently be found that the two separate groups had produced separate and therefore useless products.

3. Remaining (or Salvage) Value Measurement

The concern here is not so much with how to make such measurements, but whether they are relevant to the decision context. How to make them is a complex question of purposes, estimating system lifetimes, and hypothesizing future buyers. But often they need not even be addressed.[1]

Suppose a transportation system exhibits an annual cost stream, over time, like that shown in Figure 25-3. At Time t the system is withdrawn from service and no further operating costs are incurred. But is the system "worth" anything sitting about idle? Hardly! And in some alternative use it would again begin incurring costs, as indicated by the dotted line. More important, except for modification or something similar, the system would have been "free" or available, an inherited asset, to the follow-on system. From this emerges the often overlooked rule that if a system has a place in a follow-on system, its remaining value at "follow-on time" (Time t above) is zero in any cost-benefit computation involving the new system; that is, remaining value is pertinent only in distinct and not related uses.

Unfortunately, for those who dwell extensively on the theory of remaining value, not too many carefully designed systems have distinct

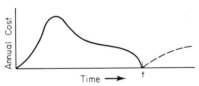

Figure 25-3

[1] *Much has been written on the subject of computation. A good summary was provided by J. W. Noah then of the Center for Naval Analysis in his* Concepts and Techniques for Summarizing Defense System Costs. *He does not, however, seem to be specifically concerned with the question of alternative uses, as in this paper.*

alternative uses (benefits). Even where such uses exist, prices users may be willing to pay are exceedingly difficult, if not impossible, to determine beforehand.

The important thread in this argument is the focus on use, or intended benefit. If, in alternative use, an older system can function, then that system is *inherited or free* except for modification[2] or add-on operating cost. As such, in that use, there is *no* remaining value. If it cannot function in that use, but may in some other, then nothing is inherited or free to the intended system (since it *cannot* "use" the older system). But perhaps there is remaining value if, for a different purpose, a buyer may be found.

However ... if there is remaining value, perhaps in the form of a Latin American entrepreneur or government, since it is by definition *not* related to the new or follow-on system, why should this value be credited to the follow-on system rather than elsewhere in the total economy? This question is interesting but ranges a bit beyond transportation criteria. The salient feature of the argument is to emphasize that residual value often has no meaning; it is not wise to set about such computation without asking why beforehand.

4. Follow-On Cost Demand or Implicit Resource Allocation, and Spillover Cost

These three ideas are often discussed as one, yet represent different sorts of resource allocation dangers. The definitions given below are arbitrary, but are designed to help point up specific problems:

Follow-on cost demand.   The unexpressed requirement for allocation for resources at a *point in time* either explicitly beyond present planning or, although within the span of time being studied, so distant as to be obscured by more pressing problems. Careful scrutiny of the cost-time dimension may lessen the difficulty of estimating or bounding this resource requirement.

Implicit resource allocation.   The unexpressed requirement for resource allocation caused by the *functional nature* of the transportation physical plant or overall complex.

[2] *Modification cost can be high.*

Spillover cost.   Cost or resource allocation sharing; induceable over time or functionally (as in the above two categories), or otherwise, and which, hopefully, is allocable.

Spillover cost has been used too often as a catch-all, to variously mean or suggest follow-on or implied costs, and joint costs. Yet one ought to avoid using "spillover"; it is not a useful analytical term. If a cost element or cost-causing factor does indeed "spill over" onto another, or to another resource source, it should be possible to postulate why this occurs.[3] Thus, spillover cost may be follow-on (time-related), implicit (functionally related), or have its basis in some concept of "jointness" falling outside either a strict time or functional dimension.

One such, for example, might relate to jurisdiction. A particular transportation concept might traditionally have involved participation of Federal, State, and local governments. Hopefully, percents contributed will somehow tie to anticipated jurisdictional benefits, and to call these "spillover costs" is to bypass the very fundamental idea that these costs somehow have roots in benefit/jurisdiction definition.

In summary, the notion of spillover cost as such is not a very helpful one. An effort designed to provide better definition of characteristics that will permit "spillover" to be broken into analytical components would be of considerable potential value in criteria structuring.

5. *Estimated Total System Cost, Allocations Among Systems, and Financing Options*

Possibly the most critical problem for the larger systems, from a practical viewpoint, will be that of raising sufficient capital from alternative sources to provide for whatever systems are chosen. All too often financial problems and methods have so pervaded transportation analysis as to overwhelm consideration of transportation needs and demands, and deter-

mine almost in and of themselves the form of transportation investment.[4]

Not only is the question of adequate total funding important, but the problems of how to relate potential sources to percentage contribution, and how to allocate among systems, are equally important. While the concern here is more with the first two of these questions, it is very important to emphasize that form of allocation will be a major determinant of total demand and distribution, and thereby of return to the various investors; it is in short an economic tool and one to be carefully evaluated.

Of much concern in recent months has been the question of user charges.[5] The three advantages usually cited in favor of such support which, incidentally, not only addresses the question of recovering outlay but also that of raising the money, are:

Users heretofore have often been able to avoid, by living outside the tax base area, a general tax levied by muncipalities to theoretically provide transportation funds.

User charges further enhance the ability of a transportation system to shape and respond to broader economic aims, through the pricing mechanism.

Governments, facing as they do many kinds of competing financial needs and obligations, are to a degree spared the problem of providing transportation funding.

These are compelling arguments. They are countered by those who cite the dangers of imbalanced user charges (equal charges for short versus longer distance), of user charges funding unrelated projects, and of user charges unrelated to demand or in fact causing demand overload (e.g., commuter discounts tending to

---

[3] *Postulating "why," as difficult as this may be on occasion, is only the beginning. This paper in its entirety is directed at suggesting ways to get at "how much."*

[4] *See Wilfred Owen, The Metropolitan Transportation Problem, Chapter V. Brookings, 1966. Owen concludes that present financial policies, as regards urban areas, are badly in need of study and overhaul. He favors a self-supporting system, and goes on to specifically suggest revision of state-aid policies, close ties between costs and charges, better use of the pricing mechanism, more efficient administrative arrangements, and attempts to improve integration and study of the "whole" transport system. His ideas are on the ascendancy.*
[5] *"Charges" and "taxes" are used synonymously here, although they are not precisely the same, to refer to the notion of a transportation beneficiary sharing in cost whether he has agreed to or not.*

encourage peak loadings). But these arguments are primarily management-related, not really bearing on the carefully applied validity of the user charge concept.

So self-support, judging from current discussions, will very possibly mean increased emphasis on user charges in the future; and this, clearly, can encourage investors to participate. Certainly no most-advisable financing or recovery method has stood out from among the many tried,[6] and as more proponents of self-support and newer resource allocation methodology are heard, the increased emphasis on "pay-as-you-go, but reasonably" is probably inevitable. Taxes, in so many cases, have not begun to recover costs associated with transport facility; and these costs over time have often required subsidy.

Since financing will be manifested in allocations to systems, and since these systems will generate use patterns, there exists a strong, if not clear, relationship between financing patterns and investment recovery. Cost structuring of proposed systems must take account of this process; it would not be wise to be wedded to a set of cost accounts (in a model structure) that could neither indicate which costs might be government-borne, or user-charge recoverable, or which cost elements are a direct function of use patterns of demand generated by charges within a certain pricing mechanism.

This is a factor of key importance in the planning of future transportation systems analysis. Much more work in seeking the relations between financing options and cost structuring is needed if decision criteria are to involve, as they should, costs as a function of financing possibilities.

WORKABLE CRITERIA AND APPROACHES TO COSTING

Approaches to costing. By way of summarizing much of what has been said above, the following set of 14 questions is presented. The set, of course, is hardly all-inclusive, and as always the questions do often overlap. Yet

[6] *General and special taxes (e.g., real estate, personal property, gasoline) user charges (fixed and variable, often inequitable), equity and debt (in many forms, as initial capital), and combinations of all, with and without subsidy.*

each question, or a variant, ought to be thought of in considering all proposed sets of transportation system cost elements. There is no clear tie between the questions listed and the several conceptual issues previously discussed. Yet obviously there is strong relation, and a further attempt to integrate these "ways of looking at the problem" ought to be made early in any study effort. Many of the questions are applicable to most kinds of systems analyses, and some especially to transportation, but only explicit consideration can help to ensure that cost structuring gets off on the right foot by including or excluding appropriate cost elements.

1 Is the cost element likely to be significant, relative to total system costs?
2 What is the range of uncertainty about the cost element? How good are related data and experience?
3 Are the costs measurable? Do joint cost and allocation problems dominate?
4 May uncertainty be handled by cost-sensitivity analysis within a specified model structure? (Note: sensitivity analysis, in theory, enables analytical treatment of any cost uncertainty.)
5 Is the cost element common to different transportation systems?
6 Will an aggregate model, possibly with an "operator" function to zero-out inappropriate elements, be more efficient than a series of models?
7 Is the cost element "considered" important, perhaps for a specialized reason as for rate determination, by certain interests?
8 Is the cost element an input to other work and therefore needed in the interest of being responsive?
9 Is system operation or some other system-defining characteristic dependent on a certain, possibly unique, cost element?
10 Is the question of time-phasing, or following year costs, amenable to analysis? Related to this, are lag patterns tying *materiel* availability to *funding* availability desirable? In short, is the particular cost element in question especially time-dependent?
11 Is the cost element one that is marginally measurable? And marginally relatable to joint benefits and benefit measurement?
12 Does the element imply additional or subsequent costs? That is, will "implicit" or "follow-on" resource allocation be overlooked if an element is omitted?

13 Is the question of salvage or remaining value well understood? That is, is the relation between inherited assets, remaining value, and system functioning, with regard to the particular cost element, understandable?

14 Most important, what is the purpose of the costing exercise? The following are but four possible broad purposes of costing transportation systems:

> Understanding total system costs, over time[7]
> Establishing investment or rate-of-return-base
> Establishing basis for Federal government participation
> Providing a quick response answer to specific questions

These are the kinds of questions that should determine the emphasis given a certain cost element as study progresses. Approaches to costing can be roughly based on these questions and answers to them. The actual costing can both begin by building on the less conceptual approaches and the different data that derive, and later address the more subtle questions. The following chart roughly suggests several approaches, as different questions from among the 14 are addressed (Y = addressed; N = not addressed). Approaches 1 to 3 in general address fewer and less difficult questions, and may be somewhat shorter term efforts than approaches 4 to 7. However, both longer and short term efforts may involve difficult ques-

[7] *This could have many sub-purposes in itself. For example, focus might be on right-of-way payments or certain operational aspects.*

tions, as evidenced by questions 11 and 12 being tackled in several approaches.

A simple "yes" or "no" answer, unfortunately, will not provide the final judgment as to whether a given cost element should be included in a specific model format. For the first approach, as an example, although the chart above suggests that only six of the fourteen questions be directed at the proposed set of cost elements, a positive answer to but *one* question could mean including the cost element.

A glance at Question 14 will affirm this. If a cost element is important only because a desired cost estimate has a special purpose, then it must, for that reason alone, be included. These kinds of questions can help those costing large transportation systems to logically arrange their ideas, but the questions must be weighed intelligently.

Workable criteria. The thesis of this paper is that an overall procedure which pointedly addresses those cost-criteria problems very briefly sketched in each section, should help cut the criteria question to a size whereat some solid progress may be made. This is not to say that the suggested approach is as yet well integrated (that is, that the pieces tie together as best they might), that each problem is itself as clearly stated as it might be, or that other aspects of criteria-cost relationships could not profitably be singled out. Rather, the point is that study as suggested of each part of the problem is worthwhile in itself and should help provide basic knowledge as well as further guidance.

Preliminary criteria ought not involve too

Approach	Questions														
	1	2	3	4	5	6	7	8	9	10	11	12	13	14	*
1	Y	Y	N	Y	N	Y	N	N	Y	N	N	N	N	Y	8
2	Y	Y	N	Y	Y	Y	N	Y	Y	N	N	Y	N	Y	5
3	Y	Y	Y	Y	Y	Y	Y	Y	Y	Y	Y	N	N	Y	2
4	Y	Y	?	Y	?	Y	N	Y	N	N	N	N	N	Y	8
5	Y	Y	Y	Y	Y	?	N	Y	Y	N	N	Y	N	Y	4
6	Y	Y	Y	Y	Y	Y	Y	Y	Y	Y	Y	N	Y	Y	1
7	Y	Y	Y	Y	Y	Y	Y	Y	Y	Y	Y	Y	Y	Y	0

Total number of questions not addressed in each approach.

many dimensions of benefit (yet speed often seems to overwhelm commercial transport planning), ought not to be too concerned with benefit *quantification* to the exclusion of benefit *definition*, and should have a firm foundation in sensible costing. In short, the search for transportation investment criteria ought to proceed as a search for resource allocation structure rather than for the criteria themselves. From an orderly structuring will probably derive useful technique application and theoretical insight.

Although benefits and theoretical benefit problems have been mentioned, the list of key benefit aspects given at the beginning of this paper has not been specifically addressed. The emphasis on costing reflects the notion that cost structuring, as difficult as it may be (especially since it is so interwoven with benefits), is easier than benefit structuring. This too might be attempted, but workable criteria are probably best found, in the author's opinion, if the analytical effort is tuned most to the development of cost relationships.

READING 26

THE APPLICATION OF COST-EFFECTIVENESS TO NON-MILITARY GOVERNMENT PROBLEMS *

Olaf Helmer

1. INTRODUCTION

In this paper an attempt will be made to set down general procedural guidelines for the introduction of a systematic cost-effectiveness approach to the budgeting problems of a Department of the federal government. The procedure to be outlined is, in principle, applicable to other cases—for instance to sub-sectors of a Department, to State or city government agencies, or to industry—subject however to obvious adjustments necessitated by considerations of scale and of specific constraints peculiar to each case.

It will almost immediately become apparent that the role of expert judgment cannot be neglected. Indeed, it plays such a dominant part that a portion of this paper will be devoted to a discussion of the efficient use of expertise and to the avoidance of its abuse.

* Reprinted with permission of The RAND Corporation, P-3449, September, 1966, The RAND Corporation, Santa Monica, California.

2. MANDATORY ALLOCATIONS

In allocating a given budget it will invariably be the case that some portions of it are already firmly committed, say for current operations, previously contracted obligations, pension payments, etc. For clarification, let it be understood that from here on we shall concern ourselves only with the remaining portion of the budget, that is, with that part which can be freely disposed within the constraints of feasibility and prudence. In particular, if there is a previous commitment to expend some amount on some particular measure or activity, but if the precise amount is subject to executive discretion, then the minimum amount required to be spent will be considered firmly allocated, while the question of what marginal amount above that minimum is to be allocated to that measure will be considered part of the budgeting process to be treated in this paper.

The conditions prevailing, or expected to prevail, at the beginning of the budgeting period, together with a statement of the mandatory allocations just described as well as of the amount of the freely disposable budget, constitute the initial situation on the basis of which the budgetary decisions have to be made.

3. PROGRAMS

In deciding how to spend a Department's budget (by which, as we noted, we mean the freely disposable part of the total budget), consideration has to be given to numerous competing measures.

Let us assume that

$$M_1, M_2, \ldots, M_z$$

is a complete list of measures worthy of such consideration. A measure M_i is rarely, if ever, of the all-or-nothing kind; that is, one can usually associate with it a degree, q_i, to which such a measure can be executed. As a rule, this is obvious. For example, salary raises, support of scientific research, agricultural subsidies, retraining programs, foreign aid, slum clearance, reforestation all are of this kind. But even in the case of seemingly unitary events, such as building a dam or landing on the Moon, there clearly are aspects under the planner's control —such as expected time of completion or size and quality of effort—which can be reflected in the "degree" of the measure's acceptance.

The construction of a program, then, may be considered to consist of the assignment of numbers

$$q_1, q_2 \ldots, q_z$$

to the above measures (where many of the q_i may be 0, indicating rejection of Measure M_i), such that the total cost of carrying out the given measures to these degrees is not expected to exceed the given budget.

The problem is to devise criteria under which alternative programs can be compared and to describe a procedure by which the preferred program can in fact be selected.

4. NOMINATION AND AGGREGATION

Before a program can be composed it is necessary to arrive at a list of measures deserving of consideration.

There is no hard-and-fast rule for the compilation of such a list. Good government policy depends not only on competent analysis and expert judgment but also on inventiveness and imagination. Therefore, in attempting to compile a list of measures for consideration, it is well to elicit suggestions representing as many different viewpoints as are relevant to the subject matter at hand.

Measures which are strictly complementary, in the sense that neither can be meaningfully adopted in the absence of the other, should be combined and listed as one measure. The measures thus nominated for consideration should be screened by an expert or, better, a panel of experts, in order to eliminate those which, upon closer examination, appear to be technically infeasible or expensive beyond all reason or fraught with highly undesirable incidental consequences. (The procedure for using a panel rather than a single expert, the opportunity for which will recur several times in the program budgeting effort, will be discussed separately in Sec. 10.)

If the total list thus obtained consists of no more than a few dozen items, it can be further processed as a whole. If it is larger, consisting perhaps of the order of a hundred or several hundred items, it is advisable first to aggregate all nominated measures under several subheadings in order to facilitate efficient processing by the planning staff. While a large set of potential measures usually lends itself to a rather natural categorization by subject matter, the precise manner in which this breakdown is achieved is immaterial, as long as items related by (partial) complementarity or by substitutability are relegated to the same subheading and each such category in turn contains no more than at most a few dozen items.

For the case where no such breakdown into categories is required we shall develop a method below of allocating the budget over the measures listed for consideration.

If, on the other hand, the number of measures to be considered is so large as to make a breakdown into, say, s categories,

$$K_1, K_2, \ldots, K_s,$$

advisable, then essentially the same allocation method may have to be used several times, as follows:

First, tentatively allocate portions B_1, B_2, ..., B_s of the budget, B, to K_1, K_2, ..., K_s respectively, where

$$B_1 + B_2 + \ldots + B_s = B.$$

Then solve the allocation problem of each B_i among the measures within K_i. The process of these sub-allocations may reveal that the original allocations of B_i to K_i require revision. Such a revision should be carried out by applying to the apportionment of B among B_1, B_2, ..., B_s precisely the same method that leads to the allocation of B_i among the measures listed in K_i. Let a revised, and thus improved, allocation be

$$B_1' + B_2' + \ldots + B_s' = B.$$

Now, for each B_i' which is actually different from B_i, a revised sub-allocation among the measures contained in K_i has to be carried through. If necessary, this process has to be iterated once again. (This sounds more complex than it is, since most of these revisions will be in the nature of minor marginal adjustments.)

5. REASONABLE ADOPTION BOUNDS

First of all, now, it is necessary to establish for each nominated measure M the unit in which its degree of adoption, q, is to be measured. Sometimes it may be easiest to describe the degree of adoption of a measure in terms of the number of dollars to be devoted to it, so that the dollar will be the unit of measurement. More often, a more natural unit may suggest itself, such as the number of items of a certain kind that are concerned by the measure (e.g., the number of acres to be reforested, the number of housing units or highway miles to be built, the number of workers to be retrained, etc.). The particular choice of unit is immaterial, as long as it is defined without ambiguity, so that "adoption of M to the degree q" has a precise meaning.

Regardless of just how the benefits derived from the adoption of M are to be assessed, its value V, as a function of the degree of adoption q, will typically be represented by an S-shaped curve of the following kind:

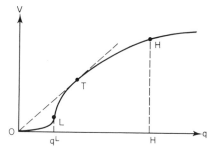

Figure 26-1

That is to say, up to a certain point L, roughly in the vicinity of the point of inflection, the degree of adoption of the measure, q, is too small to produce more than a negligible value, V. While beyond L the marginal value per added adopted unit begins to decrease, still the average value per unit increases up to the point T, where it reaches its maximum. Beyond T it begins to decrease, and from some point H on, the marginal returns decrease so fast as to make further investment in the measure under consideration appear definitely unremunerative.

While these points on the curve are not exactly determinable (nor even exactly defined), it will be possible, for each measure M under consideration, to establish by a panel of experts two approximate bounds, q^L and q^H, representing respectively the lowest and highest reasonable degrees to which the measure might, if at all, be adopted. The inherent conceptual vagueness of these bounds is immaterial; for practical purposes it suffices to obtain a consensus as to a value, q^L, below which the adoption of M would be pointless, and a value, q^H, above which marginal benefits are so small as to make a higher degree of adoption wasteful, or where the cost would exceed the entire available budget. It should be noted that among the causes for diminishing marginal return above q^H may well be nonmonetary resource constraints. That is, while increased adoption of M may eo ipso appear profitable, the entailed depletion of scarce resources may have a deleterious overall effect. This observation should serve to emphasize that, in appraising the value of a measure, a systems viewpoint must be adopted, giving due consideration to the overall effects rather than to the effects of M regarded in isolation.

6. COSTS

Next, the cost of each proposed measure has to be determined. Here we note at once that, since the costs in question are future costs, they are in principle not determinable with absolute accuracy but can only be estimated with a certain, limited, degree of reliability. Hence, while reasonable accuracy is desirable, an exaggerated display of supposed precision is misleading and, moreover, aggravates the planning process unnecessarily.

For most practical purposes it will suffice to estimate the costs, C_i^L and C_i^H, of each measure M_i at the levels of adoption represented by q_i^L and q_i^H respectively, as well as of the marginal costs per unit at each of these two levels of effort, and to assume that intermediate marginal costs can be obtained by interpolation. In extraordinary cases, where a sizeable deviation from such linearity is expected, a suitable annotation to that effect, indicating the need for later correction, will be sufficient at this point.

It is well known that the expected cost of a measure depends to some extent on what other measures are being enacted, and to what degree. This dependence on the systems context can often not be neglected, although it may be assumed to have only a secondary effect. Since at this stage an estimate must be supplied in ignorance of the remaining program, it is necessary to proceed by successive approximation. At this first stage, in fact, the cost of each measure should be estimated on the (fictitious) assumption that it alone be added to what has earlier been referred to as the initial situation. To aid the subsequent process of correcting for systems context, it may be well to annotate each item with appropriate indications as to which other items, if adopted, would noticeably affect the given item's estimated cost-in-isolation.

The recommended procedure for actually arriving at the above cost estimates, C_i^L and C_i^H for each M_i (as well as corresponding marginal costs), is to have a staff of trained cost analysts prepare calculations of costs together with indications of, and reasons for, the degree of their own uncertainty associated with each. These are submitted to a panel of (subject matter and cost) experts, who form a consensus as to the acceptance or modification of the cost figures submitted to them. (For details regarding the operation of such a panel the reader is again referred to the last section of this paper.)

7. BENEFITS

The procedure for ascribing benefits (or effectiveness values) to contemplated measures is conceptually different but in fact not too dissimilar from that of ascribing costs.

The principal conceptual difference lies in the fact that no ready-made unit of measurement, comparable to the dollar in the case of costs, is available. It should be clearly understood that this is not just a temporary deficiency which the passage of time will eliminate. While certain consequences of the adoption of a measure may have objectively measurable effects (e.g., increased earning power resulting from retraining), any measure invariably has a multitude of effects which are in principle incommensurable because the relative evaluation of diverse effects will depend on individual subjective preferences among social utilities. Moreover, superimposed upon the subjectivity of these personal predilections is their inherent vagueness, due to the lack of explicit articulation characteristic of social attitudes.

The best that can be done in view of these circumstances is to resort, again, to the use of a panel of experts (taking care that all relevant aspects are represented). However, in order to make communication among them possible as to the values to be ascribed to various measures, it is necessary—as a minimum—to establish a unit of measurement, however vague. One way to do this (though not the only one) is by the following prescription:

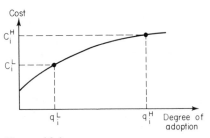

Figure 26-2

Take the initial situation, with no measures adopted (other than precommitted ones), as having zero value. Imagine the (unknown) budget allocation which the appraiser would regard as optimal to have a value of 1000. Assess the contribution of each measure M_i, at degree of adoption q_i, as the number of permills by which it, considered in isolation, would raise the value of the initial situation toward the value of the "ideal" situation (to which the value 1000 had been ascribed). Here again, as in the case of costs, it suffices to fix a few values, among them V_i^L and V_i^H (see Figure 26-1) to be ascribed to M_i if the latter is enacted at levels q_i^L and q_i^H respectively. It may be expedient, though not necessary, to determine the position of T (see Figure 26-1), where the ray from the origin is tangent to the curve. In view of the inherent vagueness of the value concept it is here even more justified to assume for all practical purposes that at intermediate levels the value can be calculated by simple interpolation.

The real value of a measure, even more so than its cost, depends on the systems context, that is, on the remainder of the adopted program. Thus, again, a successive-approximation procedure is indicated, allowing for correction of the values-in-isolation as the planning process zeros in on the finally adopted program. Annotations indicating the adoption of what other measures might particularly affect the value of a given measure would again be a helpful preparation to this effect.

8. COMPOSITION OF THE FIRST-APPROXIMATION PROGRAM

We are now ready to construct a first-approximation program, that is, a program which would be the optimal one, were it not for two considerations: (*a*) the true, systems, costs and benefits are not necessarily identical with the costs and benefits determined for each measure separately in isolation; and (*b*) both costs and benefits are mere estimates, based partly (in the case of costs) or wholly (in the case of benefits) on judgment, and thus subject to some revision as the planning process itself generates among the planners an increasing understanding of the implications of each decision under consideration.

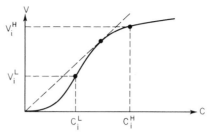

Figure 26-3

Disregarding these caveats for the moment, the matter of constructing an optimal program becomes one of straight-forward calculation, namely by maximization of marginal returns. Geometrically the solution to this problem can be visualized as follows: For each measure, M_i, represent the value, V_i, as a function of the cost, C_i (Figure 26-3), which under our assumptions will be an S-shaped curve similar (if not identical) to the representation of V_i as a function of q_i, but with the point of tangency, T', of the ray from the origin possibly farther to the right than in the latter case (due to the tendency of marginal costs to decrease).

Now represent the revelant parts of all of these curves on one diagram (Figure 26-4), where for simplicity a total of only 5 measures has been assumed, and consider a ray from the origin, with an angle α between it and the V-axis. All points above this ray have a larger benefit-cost ratio, V/C, than those below. Associated with each such ray is a program, obtained by selecting for each measure M_i the point on its curve that lies farthest to the right and on or above the ray. In the example, this program would consist in enacting the measures M_1, M_2, M_3, M_4, M_5 to the degrees q_1, q_2, q_3, 0, q_5 respectively (q_4 being 0 because

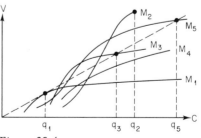

Figure 26-4

the corresponding curve lies entirely below the ray). Associated with this program will be a fixed cost C, where C is a monotonically increasing function of α. Thus, by rotating the ray through increasing values of α, the program cost can be increased until it equals the given budget, B. The resulting values of q_1, q_2, ..., q_z will furnish the desired first approximation to the optimal program.

9. REFINEMENT OF THE PROGRAM

Next, the process just described of obtaining costs and values and an approximate optimal program has to be iterated. However, costs and values are no longer determined on the assumption of measures being isolatedly added to the initial situation, but rather on the hypothesis that the adoption of each item is accompanied by the introduction of the other items at the levels indicated in the first-approximation program.

The result of this effort (which, because only marginal adjustments are called for, will be much simpler than that in the first round) will be a second-approximation program.

It is for the experts to decide whether the quality of this program is sufficient to be accepted as the final one, or whether another iteration is indicated. It may be expected that, while one iteration of the original process is indispensable for the production of a close-to-optimal program, further iterations may often not be required.

10. THE USE OF PANELS OF EXPERTS

As we stated at the beginning of this paper, and as must have become abundantly clear in

Experiments have shown that the best use of a panel of experts is not made by the traditional method of having the issues presented to them and debated in open discussion, until a consensus emerges or a group position has been agreed upon by majority acclamation. In order to avoid the inadvertent psychological drawbacks of such a procedure and to arrange a setting in which the pros and cons of an issue can be examined as systematically and dispassionately as its essentially intuitive character allows, it is preferable to proceed so as to minimize the effects of supposed authority and of specious oratory.

To this end, if time and facilities permit, it is expedient to provide for anonymity of the experts' opinions and of the arguments advanced by them in defense of these opinions. Such a procedure, at least until appropriately sophisticated computing machines come to our aid, is apt to be cumbersome, and compromises may have to be sought that do not violate the basic principle too much.

An anonymous debating procedure, aimed at contriving an eventual group position, might have the following form:

Let us consider the typical situation of having to arrive at a group answer to the question of how large a particular number N should be. (E.g., N might be the estimated cost of a measure, or a value representing its overall benefit, or the portion of the budget to be devoted to it, or an estimate of the smallest reasonable degree of adoption, or the reduction in cost due to the simultaneous adoption of some other measure.) One might proceed in the following steps: (1) Have each expert independently give an estimate of N. (2) Arrange the responses in order of magnitude, and determine its quartiles, Q_1, M, Q_2:

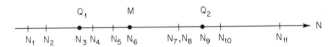

the sequel, the reliance on expert judgment is an indispensible part of budgetary planning. In the particular type of case treated here, of budgeting the expenditures of a Department of the federal government, the range of required expertise is not likely to be provided by a single person; hence almost inevitably a variety of expert advisers needs to be consulted.

so that the four intervals formed on the N-line by these three points each contain one quarter of the estimates. Communicate the values of Q_1, M, Q_2 to each respondent, ask him to reconsider his previous estimate and, if his new estimate lies outside the interquartile range (Q_1, Q_2), to state briefly his reason why, in his opinion, the answer should be lower (or higher) than corresponds to the 75% majority opinion expressed in the first round. (3) The results of this second round, which as a rule will have a less dispersed distribution, are again fed back to the respondents in summary form, that is, by communicating the magnitude of the new quartiles to them. In addition, the reasons for raising or lowering the value, elicited in Round 2 and suitably collated and edited, are fed back to the respondents (always, of course, preserving anonymity as to the proponent). The experts are now asked to consider these reasons, give them what weight they are thought to deserve, and in their light to revise their previous estimates. Moreover, if their answer now falls outside the second round's interquartile range, they are asked to state briefly why they found the argument unconvincing that might have drawn them toward the median or beyond. (4) Finally, in a fourth round, both the quartiles of the third distribution of responses and the counter-arguments elicited in Round 3 are submitted to the respondents, who are now encouraged to make one last revision of their estimates. The median of these Round 4 responses may then be taken as representing the group position as to what N should be.

The above procedure can be refined by requiring each respondent in the first round to state how relatively expert he considers himself to be with regard to the particular estimate required of him. For example, if he is asked—as will normally be the case—to estimate not one but several quantities,

$$N_1, N_2, \ldots, N_z,$$

he may indicate, by assigning respectively A, B, C, or D to approximately one quarter each of the questions, how relatively competent he regards himself with respect to each question. On the basis of this information, it is possible to use as the group consensus, not the median of all fourth-round responses, but the median of only those responses that came from that third, say, of the respondents who had declared themselves relatively most expert with regard to the corresponding question.

The procedure described here would today require the use of questionnaires or of inter-viewers. Eventually it should be possible to have each expert equipped with a console through which he can feed his responses into a computer which would process these inputs, possibly augment them with relevant information automatically drawn from an existing data bank, and feed back the result to each respondent.

Until this day arrives—thus for another five years perhaps—the cybernetic arbitration procedure described above may be too time-consuming to be acceptable without modification. A simplified version, which preserves the anonymity of the estimate but not that of the proffered reasons, has already been tried successfully. This procedure is to have the experts meet in one room and to have each equipped with a device permitting him to select one of a set of numbers (say, from 0 to 10) by pushing an appropriate button. The set of these responses appears in scrambled order on a panel visible to all participants. They engage in a free debate, which produces reasons for raising or lowering the estimates as well as a critique of such reasons. This is then followed up by another (anonymous) vote, and the median is used as the group opinion. (Again, a refinement relying on self-estimates of relative competence, can easily be adjoined to the procedure.)

No matter which version of the technique is used, it may be expected that respondents with well-founded opinions on a subject will be swayed little by counter-arguments or by the opinion of the majority, whereas the opinions of those respondents who feel unsure of their positions will be influenced by valid arguments. The induced process of convergence therefore—one may hope—results from an increased understanding of the issue rather than from specious persuasion.

It is to be hoped that this technique of using expert opinions will be refined through future practice. Efforts at such refinements might aim at increasing either the efficiency, as indicated earlier, or the reliability of the method. But imperfect as it is at present, it appears to be the most promising approach available today toward the meaningful introduction of cost-effectiveness considerations into the operations of government agencies.

READING 27

ISSUES OF ANALYSIS IN COST-EFFECTIVENESS STUDIES FOR CIVILIAN AGENCIES OF THE FEDERAL GOVERNMENT *

John Haldi

The chief purpose of this paper is to discuss a few of the many current Government program issues requiring analysis and, hopefully, to stimulate additional interest in and study of Government programs. As the problems of modern society grow increasingly complex, and as Federal expenditures increase to overcome these problems, the payoff from analysis which helps us use our resources more efficiently will rise commensurately. Admittedly the tools of management science will not give us complete solutions to any of the Government's high-level managerial problems. Nevertheless, people trained to approach management problems objectively and quantitatively have a great deal to offer the Government's decision-making process.

In general, the issues to be discussed here are being raised in connection with the

* *Reprinted by permission of the author. Paper presented at the meeting of The Institute of Management Sciences, Philadelphia, Pa., September 7, 1966.*

Planning-Programming-Budgeting (PPB) System now being installed by all major civilian agencies in the Federal Government. Two important purposes of the PPB system are: (1) to stimulate more and better analysis of Government programs and (2) to see that the results of such analysis are reflected in budget decisions.

The initial instructions implementing PPB required that each agency (1) establish an output-oriented program structure, (2) within the context of this program structure, prepare a multi-year budget (usually for the next five years), and (3) establish new analytical staffs.

Although these instructions were comprehensive, it should not be inferred that Government agencies were completely lacking in all those areas. Rather, the impact varied among agencies. In passing, it ought to be noted that some Government agencies, chiefly on account of the two Hoover Commissions, moved towards program budgeting even before Defense did in 1961. And of course, all Government agencies had at least some in-house analytic capability (some rather well staffed) and all did some multi-year planning before the advent of PPB; in several instances, an agency's forward planning was and still is in excess of that now required by the PPB system. Nevertheless, the new PPB system appears to be having some impact on all agencies, and it is beginning to stimulate increased interest at high levels in the contribution that improved analysis can offer program decisions.

The most important single ingredient in the PPB package is more and better analysis of Government programs. Since Government programs cover such a wide variety of fields—health, highways, education, transportation, urban problems, etc.—the models, skills and types of analysis needed will vary from program to program and from agency to agency. To some extent, this will be illustrated by the examples which follow. First, however, a few general comments about most of the analysis which is being initiated under PPB. I do this because of certain misapprehensions which have been repeatedly brought to my attention.

We have *not* reached that golden millennium of cost-benefit analysis where we can make marginal comparisons, for instance, between hospital, highway and recreation programs. We have discovered no magic formula for quantifying benefits, and therefore, we have no studies underway or contemplated which will attempt marginal benefit-cost comparisons between entirely different programs. The shortcomings of the present state of the art of cost-benefit analyses have been well-summarized in a recent article by Prest and Turvey in *The Economic Journal*.[1]

The type of analysis receiving new emphasis from PPB can best be described as "cost-effectiveness" studies or systems analyses. Cost-effectiveness studies differ from cost-benefit studies in that: (1) certain basic objectives are taken as given and (2) no attempt is made to quantify all benefits in dollar terms. Thus, although cost-effectiveness studies fail to make marginal comparisons between radically different programs, the scope of the analysis is usually broader and somewhat more relevant to top-management problems than it has been in

the past. Two pragmatic reasons for being content with cost-effectiveness studies at this time are: (1) problems are more tractable at this level, and (2) there can be early and great payoff from such studies.

The examples that follow have been chosen to illustrate some of the various management-science problems that need analysis. There are many more like this and, in addition, a great many problems that can be described as "purely economic." A brief description of many of these "purely economic" problems is more or less available in an unpublished but rather widely distributed paper by Kermit Gordon, "Research Opportunities in Applying Rational Calculation to Federal Expenditures," (October 2, 1965), so here I will limit myself to (1) an attempt to present a few new examples in some detail, and (2) a brief mention of other subjects under study.

IN-DEPTH EXAMPLES OF ISSUES FOR ANALYSIS

Harbor deepening by the Corps of Engineers. The general practice of the Corps of Engineers in evaluating harbor improvements currently is to consider each harbor project as an entity. If the project shows a benefit/cost ratio in excess of unity, the project is justified. If the project is of a variable nature; i.e., if there is a range of improvements possible with corresponding ranges of costs and benefits, the project expenditure chosen is that which maximizes the difference between the present value of benefits and costs. In each instance, however, the particular harbor under consideration is analyzed separately from proposed improvements for some other harbor.

This approach is justified when improvements in one area will have no effect on other areas. For example, improving river port facilities along the Mississippi may have no measurable effect on harbor activity along the Northeastern States, and improvements in New York Harbor may have little effect on shipping at St. Louis. Such projects may be considered independent of each other.

But any one change may not be independent with respect to all other areas. Improvements in Boston Harbor may well have an impact on New York Harbor traffic and vice versa. When changes in one river or harbor will affect traffic in another, proposed projects in these competi-

[1] A. R. Prest and R. Turvey, "Cost-Benefit Analysis: A Survey," The Economic Journal, *December* 1965, pp. 683–731.

tive areas may be viewed as interdependent. Analysis of interdependent areas will not yield maximum net benefits (present value of benefits-costs) if the projects for the areas are treated as separate (independent) problems. Current evaluation practice of improvement projects will bias decisions in the direction of over-investment when interdependent areas are considered independently.

Over-investment bias occurs for two reasons:

1 The area over which maximization of net benefits takes place is too localized. Of course, the nature of maximization of benefits will always be localized to some extent because it is not feasible to simultaneously compare and rank all Government investment projects; i.e., investment in moon projects, foreign aid, river and harbor projects, etc. But within an administrative subunit, and particularly with respect to a particular species of expenditure, maximization should be calculated over the broadest possible range, especially where competitive interdependence is large. Instead of maximizing the net benefits for a single harbor improvement, maximization should occur over several interdependent harbors. Such an approach could result in the abandonment of some projects which yield small net benefits even though the benefit/cost ratio for these projects exceeds unity.
2 Benefits are overstated because, when considering the anticipated benefits of a single harbor project, we ignore the impact of projects for different harbors that may currently be under consideration or that may come under consideration in the foreseeable future. Thus, the benefits anticipated as the result of an expenditure on harbor *A* may be eroded in whole or part by expenditures that may be made on harbors *B, C, D*, etc. If this erosion had been considered, a smaller total level of expenditure would have been justified.

Deepening East Coast harbors provides an excellent example of harbor improvement projects which are probably highly interdependent. Demand for deeper harbors, of course, arises from the larger ships now in existence, being built, or planned. A few specifics will give a better feel for the interdependencies. Over the past 10-15 years, there has been a marked trend towards bigger ships, especially tankers. Oil tankers have increased in size from 15,000–25,000 ton up to 200,000 ton giants, and still bigger ships are now on the drawing boards. In addition to oil, other bulk commodities such as bauxite, wheat and coal are beginning to move in so-called "giant" ships (currently up to 70,000–80,000 tons in the case of dry bulk cargo ships). These new ships may draw as much as 80–100 feet of water when fully loaded.

The Corps of Engineers currently maintains the depth of the channels in major harbors such as New York and Philadelphia at about 45–50 feet. This depth is adequate for the average dry cargo ship of 15,000–20,000 tons, but it will obviously be inadequate for these larger ships.

In New York and Philadelphia, existing channels have already been dredged down to bedrock, so that any further deepening will require underwater blasting and drilling—a somewhat expensive operation. In both the New York and Philadelphia harbors, the estimated cost of deepening only 10 additional feet is estimated at $300 million for each harbor; yet 10 additional feet will obviously be insufficient to handle fully loaded giant tankers. Furthermore, any underwater blasting in those areas might do far more extensive damage to the sea life and ecology than dredging has ever done, a disbenefit which any analysis must take into account.

Fortunately, a large number of alternatives and tradeoffs are possible. Since any given harbor usually requires further deepening for only one (or maybe two) specific commodities, it is proper for the analysis to take account of any special physical handling properties of the commodity in question. For discharging oil, for example, offshore loading facilities and lightering are both distinct possibilities at any given harbor. Moreover, consideration of pipelines introduces direct interdependencies and tradeoffs between harbors. Take the case of New York and Philadelphia. While we don't know at this time whether it is worth deepening either harbor, I do know that if we propose to deepen one of these harbors we should certainly investigate the cost of pumping oil 100 miles across New Jersey before committing ourselves to deepening the other harbor. Adequate pumping capacity may cost a lot less than $300 million.

If we broaden the analysis to include an additional stretch of the Eastern Seaboard, interesting possibilities may be available. One intriguing tradeoff possibility reaches from Philadelphia to Portsmouth, Maine. A cross-section profile of the harbor at Portsmouth shows that both the harbor and outside channel are both rather deep, but a substantial rock ledge at the mouth of the entrance restricts deeper ships from entering (See Figure 27-1). It might be possible to remove enough of this ledge, at a reasonable cost, to permit even the deepest tankers to use this harbor fully loaded.

Improving the Portsmouth harbor, plus construction of a large capacity pipeline to Boston, New York, and Philadelphia, might be a much more efficient way, economically, to supply overseas oil to the populous Eastern Seaboard than deepening the latter three ports.

The Corps' PPB unit has just recently begun a study of our East Coast harbor system. This study, far broader in scope than any done heretofore, will attempt to take account of the different commodity flows, usage, interdependencies, etc.

Forest Service timber cutting program.
The U.S. Forest Service (FS) operates 154 National Forests encompassing 186 million acres. Virtually all National Forest (NF) land is managed for a multiplicity of purposes; e.g., timber, recreation, wildlife, grazing and natural beauty. However, current management practice by the Forest Service is to administratively "zone" all NF land according to its *primary* use. For example, land along highways and around lakes, up to the ridge line usually, is set aside for recreation or "natural beauty," and trees in this area are neither managed nor harvested for a commercial return. Any cutting that might occur on this land would be highly selective and would be aimed at enhancing beauty, enlarging campsite areas, or adding to trails for hikers.

Apart from this recreation land, a large amount, perhaps three-fourths of all NF land is

designated primarily as "timber growing," and is managed primarily for commercial timber supply. In these areas timber is harvested regularly on a sustained-yield basis. ("Sustained-yield" is a conservationist measure which says, in essence, "don't cut more timber than you grow.") Last year, the Forest Service allowed approximately 12 billion board feet of timber to be cut from the National Forests on a sustained-yield basis.

For purposes of this discussion, let us completely accept the rather broad sustained-yield philosophy as just stated. A variety of interpretations are still possible. For example, the sustained-yield constraint can apply to the entire country.

On a country-wide basis, sustained-yield means "don't cut more timber than we grow nationally," and within this constraint it might be optimal to cut primarily in high productivity regions like the Pacific Coast and Southeast and use other regions as a sort of "strategic reserve" in the unlikely event that the country should ever be short of timber.

A regional constraint implies "cut no more than grows in each region," and a NF constraint says cut no more than grows annually in a NF. A "working circle," an area big enough to supply one modern mill, generally is somewhat smaller than any of our NF's. Thus the sustained-yield concept applied to the working circle is the most restrictive constraint.

Now if these different constraints could be applied to a programming model which included all timber land in the NF's, and if the objective function were to maximize revenues, then it seems reasonable to expect that revenues maximized under the tightest constraint would be less than revenues maximized under a looser constraint.[2]

Current Forest Service practice is to cut timber within the tightest of the four constraints discussed; i.e., each working circle is on a sustained-yield basis. This policy is followed for a variety of reasons, the most important being maintenance of stable employment in small communities heavily dependent upon timber.

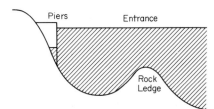

Figure 27-1 Profile of harbor at Portsmouth, Maine.

[2] *This is a simplified presentation, of course. To be useful, such a model would have to take account of many other important restrictions, such as the difference between sawtimber (hardwood and softwood) and pulpwood.*

A major change in the present timber cutting policy of the Forest Service would probably result in changing the occupations of many individuals plus changing the population distribution and the future of many small towns. Resource decisions like this cannot ignore political realities, and these usually dictate that Government organizations take explicit account of the social costs attributable to change. Not only in the timber program, but in most other Government programs, the social costs attributable to change can generally be measured relatively easily in comparison to the difficulty involved in estimating the long-term gains that might flow from changing to other, more efficient practices. But such studies are not being made with sufficient frequency. Alternatives are not automatically more efficient. They must be subjected to in-depth analyses and their merits validated before responsible decision-makers, subject to a myriad of political forces, can seriously consider adopting new and better policies. The lack of good studies showing possible gains from more efficient policies all too often leads to bureaucratic inertia and stifling of desirable program changes. Since the amount of resources now allocated by the Government is so great, we simply cannot afford to assume that the current policy is optimal in any sense. This is where good systems analysis, aided by large computers, can be a significant aid to improved program management.

It should now be possible to comprehensively study the timber program and obtain good estimates of the gains to be derived by shifting harvesting to the most efficient timber-growing lands. With this knowledge in hand we could make a much more realistic reexamination of our present policies.

The post office network.   Currently there are over 32,000 Post Offices in the United States, and mail can originate at any office and receive final delivery from any office. In actual fact, of course, the great bulk of the mail moves between the few hundred largest offices. The volume of mail currently handled is staggering: 70 billion pieces per year. Letters comprise approximately 40 of these 70 billion pieces, with second, third, and fourth class mail making up the balance. Of these 40 billion letters, approximately 2 billion are now deposited as air mail by the senders, with many more moving by air on a space-available, nonpriority basis. Total expenditures by the Post Office are now approaching $6 billion per year, and the amount spent on processing and transportation alone is over $3 billion per year. Hence a 10 percent improvement in the processing-transportation network would yield annual savings of over $300 million.

Distribution of mail requires a great many small steps, each of which is very simple, but which represent a very complex network when considered in their totality. The procedures now used to distribute mail have evolved over a long period of time and are based on a great deal of experience and experimentation. For conditions of the past and the immediate present, these methods may possibly be near-optimal. However, prospective mechanization over the next 10–20 years will question and perhaps make obsolete centuries of time-tested methods, truisms, and tradition. Sophisticated network analysis will likely be required if we are to rapidly assimilate the full potential of improvements just recently available or now in development.

Before describing some mechanization and automation possibilities, let me first describe briefly how mail is currently worked. After collection, letters are simultaneously canceled and faced in the same direction. They then enter the sorting and distribution process. In large processing facilities, outgoing mail receives both a "primary" and "secondary" sort. Virtually all sorting is still done manually, in 49-hole (seven by seven) "cases." The rationale for the size of the case is simple: this is the convenient reach of an average person's arm.

In a major city like Washington or Philadelphia, the second sort customarily results in breaking down outgoing mail to about 2,000 destinations. This means, for example, that if a sufficient volume goes from Washington to Northern California, mail might be made up to San Francisco, Oakland, Sacramento, and "all other Northern California." Mail to each of these four destinations will then be tied in separate bundles up to 4–5 inches thick. If there are sufficient bundles to make up individual pouches or bags, this will be done, otherwise all bundles will go into one bag. Then upon arrival in San Francisco, the mail to Oakland and Sacramento is handled as bundles or bags (depending on how it was shipped), not as individual letters.

The current mail system has several major interdependencies. First, the primary rule of efficient letter-handling is: *always* preserve facing of letters (this undoubtedly is a good rule). Then, because mail is shipped in bags, it is tied into small bundles to preserve facing. And because it is time-consuming and expensive to untie bundled mail and put it back into the sorting process as loose mail, outgoing mail is made up into as many separate destinations as volume justifies, while still loose. (Breaking mail down to about 2,000 destinations tends to utilize secondary sorting clerks to capacity since the theoretical limit from breaking each of 49 initial sorts down another 49 ways would be 2,401 final destinations.)

Our shipping container, the familiar mail bag, is one of the important determinants of the process described. The great antiquity of the mail bag is attested to by the fact that it was reputedly first invented by the Phoenicians. In the Phoenicians' time, when labor was relatively plentiful and space on ships was scarce, the mail bag unquestionably made good sense. Even today no other container minimizes "cube" like the mail bag. However, relative scarcities have changed somewhat in the last 2,000 years, and minimization of space should no longer be presumed a desirable goal. Mail bags are not susceptible to mechanical handling by automatic equipment, and the amount of manual labor required to load and unload mail bags is now reaching enormous proportions. In the coming years, the Post Office will have to move to adopt other containers which can be handled more efficiently.

In addition to containerization, letter-sorting is now mechanizable in various degrees. The Post Office has recently begun experimenting with a "semi-automatic" letter sorting machine, where clerks sort letters by punching keys on a keyboard. This machine enables letters to be sorted about twice as fast as manually and, in addition, the first sort can be to about 225–250 locations, which seems to be the maximum "scheme" that clerks can remember.

By combining the capability of this letter-sorting machine with some kind of tray-like containers which preserve facing but don't require tying into smaller bundles, it might be considerably more efficient to have just a primary outgoing sort, and eliminate the secondary sort. For example, all mail to Northern California would be put into common trays, taken out to the airport and shipped to San Francisco as fast as possible.

A complicating factor which the Post Office lives with and which adds force to this suggestion is the fact that, in large cities, about 70–80 percent of all mail comes into the Post Office between 5:00 p.m.–7:00 p.m., while "late" planes tend to depart between 8:30 p.m.–10:30 p.m. Because of this, the Post Office segregates air mail and gives it first priority to meet the dispatch schedule. Eliminating the secondary sort would unquestionably make it easier to meet the schedule. When "priority mail" becomes a reality, and all long-distance first class mail moves by air, this peaking problem will be accentuated several-fold.

Any major switch in the present scheme is, of course, complicated by the fact that piecemeal experimentation is not possible. If all mail arriving in San Francisco had to be given extra processing, and San Francisco had to process all outgoing mail as it does now, it would be swamped and service would be worse, not better. The inability to experiment is all the more reason why a good systems analysis is virtually a necessary prerequisite to change and improvement.

OTHER EXAMPLES

On the basis of my experience to date, I would say that virtually all programs and all departments in the Federal Government are susceptible to and could profit from more in-depth analysis. In some areas the potential payoff is enormous compared to the investment. Even in programs where the payoff is less, good analysis will still pay for itself by a wide margin.

The poverty program is one of the biggest and most important areas now under study and it undoubtedly will be under study for some time to come. A variety of programs for dealing with poverty now exist (e.g., Job Corps, Neighborhood Youth Corps, Headstart, and VISTA) and many more programs will unquestionably be recommended in years to come. Since the resources available to fight the war on poverty are so small compared to the total need, it is imperative that we study the cost and effectiveness of each program before making major resource commitments.

Another problem area now under active study is motor vehicle accidents, a problem area that was highlighted in recent congressional hearings. It now appears that cost-effectiveness is a good tool for analyzing this problem. Some alternative ways to reduce auto accidents are: (1) improve safety features in cars, (2) improve driver training and driver licensing, (3) improve the driving environment, including better repair of existing roads and better construction of new roads, and (4) better emergency medical services. When these alternatives are reduced to specifics, the cost of each can readily be estimated, and, although subject to wider uncertainty, the effectiveness of each can also be estimated through careful systematic analysis.

Other areas which need the light of systematic analysis can be cited. (1) Water pollution: our current water resources policies seem to favor more expensive methods of reducing pollution over less expensive methods. (2) Other water resources policies encourage people to overbuild in vulnerable flood plains by building or promising flood control projects for such flood plains. (3) Our sugar subsidy program seems to cost three times as much as the total net income of sugar producers. (4) Our maritime policies include an operating subsidy whose structure creates a positive incentive to the overmanned ships. (5) Certain programs are bringing reclaimed land into production while other programs are designed to remove land from production. (6) We invest hundreds of millions of dollars annually to move passengers from airport to airport, but we have paid no attention to the leg of the trip between airport and final destination. The advent of an 1,800 miles per hour SST will make this deficiency in the system even more glaring. (7) We spend over ten times as much on urban roads as on urban mass transit without even examining the balance between these two types of transportation. (8) On different types of crime we spend widely varying amounts of resources on investigation, apprehension, and prosecution without any systematic study to determine whether significant improvements could be made by improving the mix.

This list of examples could be readily extended to include many more which come to mind. However, I believe it is sufficient enough to show that good imaginative analysis is capable of yielding great payoffs in terms of better Government programs. The important tasks immediately ahead are (1) to get our analytic capability organized so as to systematically attack these problems, and (2) to sell decision-makers on the value of good analysis and, in the case of Government programs, to also sell the public on the analytic results. How to accomplish this latter task could itself be the subject of a worthwhile analytic study.

SECTION 7

INTERORGANIZATIONAL MANAGEMENT

An organization consists of an aggregation of resources—human and non-human. Such resources as exist require a meaningful relationship in terms of layout and authority—responsibility relationships. Organizational structure takes many forms, from the simple one-man proprietorship to the complex matrix organization.

As soon as the business firm involves more than one person, it has an organizational structure. Line and staff provides the basic organizational dichotomy of the traditional bureaucratic model. Traditional function specialization and vertical hierarchy have been augmented in terms of the project manager who is given responsibility and authority to manage the development and acquisition of an ad hoc project requiring extensive crossing of the traditional lines of the organization. In the project organization, the authority and responsibility patterns take on vestiges of both the functional and the project organization. The traditional line-staff organizational arrangement is changed, for in such a case, the functional line manager may have to deal with many project managers whose projects are being supported in the line manager's department. Thus, in military and space projects and in the aerospace industry where large ad hoc projects are a way of life, the project organization becomes a dominant influence.

The idea of project management has demonstrated its utility in a wide variety of Defense-Aerospace Industry contexts. So, too, are formal projects important to administration at the highest levels of the Federal government.

Witness, for example, the increasing emphasis being placed on special presidential missions and task forces and the consequent deemphasis of activities which are undertaken solely within a given cabinet-level department.

In the future, these concepts will undoubtedly be extended to such areas as urban renewal programs, transportation systems, and such related endeavors. Increasingly, these projects will have aspects of both business and government organization structure. Indeed, many of them will be performed on joint bases which involve elements of both functional and project techniques.

Again we emphasize that the new evolving theory of interorganizational management, *exemplified in the project environment, complements and refines traditional management theory. It is important to realize that management theory has much to gain from the project-management concepts, especially when one considers that project management is a move towards formalization of the many collateral contacts which are not explicitly considered in the traditional bureaucratic model.*

In this section the illustrations of interorganizational management serve to define the role and scope of applications of project concepts together with the difficulties involved in implementing project management.

READING 28

PROJECT MANAGEMENT*

Major David I. Cleland

Ultimate authority within the Department of Defense rests with the Office of the Secretary of Defense. This authority has its origin from Title II, The Department of Defense, the National Security Act of 1947 (Public Law, 80th Congress). This act reflects the intent of Congress to centralize and strengthen the management of the military, economic, and social aspects of national defense. Subsequent legislation in 1958, under stimulus of President Eisenhower's defense reorganization message, clearly portended subsequent recentralization of authority within the Office of the Secretary of Defense. This increasing centralization has been accomplished in an environment of:

1 Changing roles and missions of the military establishments with respect to the traditional separation of areas of operation; begining erosion and merging of parochial divisions of military operations into land, sea,

* Reprinted with permission from Air University Review, vol. XVI, no. 2, January-February, 1965.

and air employment; continuing unification of certain functions of the armed forces, with indications of a single national system of defense evolving.

2 Increasing and dynamic acceleration in the conception and development of weaponry.[1] Technical breakthroughs, incremental and protracted development cycles, and increasing costs stimulated the need for a distinct type of managerial innovation in the management of large development and production programs.

Within the national military establishment certain weapon acquisitions became so vast and demanding that it was impossible to assign to one single organization total responsi-

[1] Weaponry, *a general term, connotes the varied instruments intended to inflict damage to an enemy through the destruction of physical or mental capabilities. The term* weapon system *means a highly sophisticated weapon composed of a combination of equipment, skills, and managerial know-how, which as an integrated entity is capable of effectively destroying an enemy.*

bility for successful accomplishment of the objective. The increasing demands for more advanced weaponry and the increasing propensity of the Department of Defense to depend on the private industrial complex for research and development efforts intensified the requirement for a management philosophy that went beyond the traditional management theories.

Unfortunately expertise in the science and art of management lagged the state of the art in development and engineering. The military manager, engaged in the development and acquisition of weapons, was confronted with the coordination and integration of large aggregations of human and nonhuman resources, the greater part of which were outside the traditional concept of *line* command. Traditionally, management practitioners and scholars have approached the management function through the medium of the *line* and the *staff*. Line functions are thought of as those activities which have a direct and constitutional role in the accomplishment of organizational objectives. Staff, on the other hand, refers to the specialized assistance and counsel provided the line manager. Traditional management philosophy is pervaded with vertical flow of authority and responsibility relationships. Whatever horizontal relationships did exist were of a collateral and coordinating nature and did not violate the principle of unity of command. Traditional military and business organizations have functioned for the most part on a vertical basis and depend almost exclusively on a strong and inviolate superior/subordinate relationship to ensure unanimity of objective. The existing management theory was found lacking when it was realized that certain management relationships were evolving in the development and acquisition of large single-purpose projects whose development and production cut across interior organizational flows of authority and responsibility and radiated outside to other organizations that were managed as autonomous units. In particular, traditional management theory failed to provide a contemporary philosophy required for the manager to use in defense/industry ventures involved in the inception and development of advanced weapon systems. Singular elements of risk and uncertainty, extensive involvement of resources, and changing concepts in the employment of weaponry forced a management posture calling for a blending and unifying of many defense and industrial organizations directed toward a common objective. An existing multilayered and diffused management structure within the industrial and defense organizations concerned complicated the management function.

The basic objectives involved in the development and acquisition of a weapon system include divergent activities such as research, engineering, test, production, operational support, etc., all of which are time-phased over the life of the project. The result is an interlaced sequential managerial activity encompassing broad spectrums of personnel and resources extending over several years of time. The intimate superior/subordinate relationships found in recurring activities still exist, but the main focus of the task involves the unification and integration of complex input factors into a meaningful pattern of accomplishment. The functional approach, or traditional departmentation based on homogeneity of duties or geographical location, becomes meaningless when the task involves the coordinated single-goal effort of hundreds of organizations and people. Individual managers have a general affinity for identifying boundaries of responsibilities and specializing in these areas. When organizations were relatively small this provided no great problem, since the functional manager could maintain lateral staff contact to ensure mutual support and understanding of interfunctional goals. Traditional management thinking is built on these ideas; the emergence of multiorganizational objectives has shown the provincial management theory of Fayol and Taylor to be lacking.[2]

Since World War II there has been unprecedented acceleration in the advancement of technology in all phases of industrial and military management. Radical changes have occurred in the design and employment of weaponry. These profound changes have forced

[2] *Henri Fayol, a French industrialist, wrote a book titled* General and Industrial Management, *which appeared in 1916. No English translation was published in the United States until 1949 (New York: Pitman Publishing Corporation). Fayol is called by many scholars the father of modern management theory. His writings describe the job of the manager from the viewpoint of a single firm rather than from the unifying requirement demanded of a project manager in today's defense/industry environment. Frederick Taylor's writings appeared around the turn of the present century and described management at the shop level; he was concerned with the efficiency of workers and managers in actual production-line activities.*

innovation in Government- and Defense-oriented industrial organizations. In many cases weapons and strategy have evolved which do not fit the functional organization, and the result has been the emergence of new theories concerning management and organization. Attention is being given to molding the organization around the task. New terms have come into use, such as "systems management" and "systems engineering," which portend the need for a new type of managerial surveillance that has no organizational or functional constraints.

The size and complexity of contemporary and expected future programs discourage the development of a single *autonomous* element of the defense establishment to manage a program successfully. Rather what is required is a blending of the technical know-how of many functionally oriented organizations under one centralized coordinating and managing agency whose prime role is to synchronize and integrate an aggregation of resources. The *project management* philosophy has been developed by the military/industrial complex as a means to satisfy the requirement for the management of defense resources from inception to operational employment. How did this concept develop? Is it a further refinement of traditional management thought and theory, or is it a revolutionary new development which portends radical changes in organizational theory and in the management of activities by the functional approach?

In the aerospace industry/Government relationship there has developed a tendency towards greater and greater use of ad hoc offices concerned exclusively with the managerial integration of a single weapon system or subsystem. The increasing use of this managerial innovation indicates that it is becoming sufficiently ingrained in management thought and theory so that serious questions are being raised about the ability of the pure functionally oriented organization to manage more than one major project successfully. This is particularly so where nonrepetitive production programs are being conducted and in those military and industrial organizations where basic and applied research programs are undertaken. The establishment of a project manager in a functional organization permits managerial concentration of attention on the major considerations in the project or program. This concentration is particularly valuable when the producer is competing in a market

system where the product price is largely determined by reimbursement of costs actually incurred or where the contract involves, on the part of the producer, a total commitment of company resources over an extended period of time and, on the part of the buyer, a monopsonistic situation where an intimate dependence upon the producer to fulfill the contract commitment increases the risk and uncertainty factors. It is a market where the financial and managerial risks of the business center around only one or a few ventures. Consequently there is a much greater propensity on the part of the buyer to enter into the active management of the program in the seller's facility.

Characteristics of Project Management

In a sense project management is compatible with the traditional and functional approach to management, yet it has provided *a way of thinking* with respect to the management of highly technical and costly weapon systems, the development and acquisition of which have spread across several large autonomous organizations. The project manager within Department of Defense organizations has been established to manage across functional lines in order to bring together at one focal point the management activities required to accomplish project objectives. The project manager has certain characteristics which tend to differentiate him from the traditional manager:

1 As project manager, he is concerned with specific projects whose accomplishment requires a great amount of participation by organizations and agencies outside his direct control.

2 Since the project manager's authority cuts through superior/subordinate lines of authority, there is a deliberate conflict involved with the functional managers. The functional manager no longer has the complete authority with respect to the function; he must share the authority relative to a particular project with the project manager.

3 As a focal point for project activities, the project manager enters into, on an exception basis, those project matters which are significant to the successful accomplishment of the project. He determines the *when* and *what* of the project activities, whereas the functional manager, who supports many different projects in the organization, determines *how* the support will be given.

4 The project manager's task is finite in dura-

tion; after the project is completed the personnel directly supporting it can be assigned to other activities.

5 The project manager manages a higher proportion of professional personnel; consequently he must use different management techniques than one would expect to find in the simple superior/subordinate relationship. His attitude regarding the traditional functions of management must of necessity be tempered by increased factors of motivation, persuasion, and control techniques. For many professionals the leadership must include explanations of the rationale of the effort as well as the more obvious functions of planning, organizing, directing, and controlling.

6 The project manager is involved in managing diverse and extraorganizational activities which require unification and integration directed toward the objective of the project. He becomes a unifying agent with respect to the total management function. In effecting this unifying action he has no line authority to act per se but rather depends on other manifestations of authority to bring about the attainment of the objective. Thus the *directing* function is of somewhat less importance from the perspective of the project manager. What direction he does effect is accomplished through the functional managers who support him in the project endeavor.

7 The project manager does not normally possess any traditional line authority over the line organizations involved in creating the goods or services. His motivational tools become different than those available in the more prevalent superior/subordinate vertical relationship.

Evolution of Project Manager

One major difficulty in adjusting to the concept of project management is caused by a failure on the part of management to understand this new and evolving role. The concept of project management is still evolving. Its evolution has gone through stages where different titles and degrees of responsibility have been associated with the position. The construction industry early recognized the need for a management process which permitted the introduction of a unifying agent into the ad hoc activities involved in the construction of single, costly projects such as dams, turnpikes, and large factories and buildings.

During World War II when large aircraft contracts came to the airframe industry, a new method of management arose which integrated the many and diverse activities involved in the development and production of large numbers of aircraft. In the military establishment one sees evidence of the project manager in such endeavors as the Manhattan Project, the ballistic missile program, and the Polaris program.

The need for a unifying agent in these large projects motivated the development of a project-type organization superimposed on the traditional and functional organizational structure. This unifying agent idea reflects contemporary thinking about project management. The forerunners of project managers, designated project expediters, did not perform line functions but instead informally motivated those persons involved in doing the work. The project expediter was mainly concerned with schedules and depended upon his personal diplomacy and persuasive abilities to remove bottlenecks in the management process. The project expediter was perhaps the earliest kind of project manager. Slightly above him in terms of time and responsibility appeared the project coordinator, who had a more formal role in the organization and was concerned with the synchronization of organizational activities directed toward a specific objective in the overall functional activities. This type of coordinator had some independence, reflected by his freedom to make decisions within the framework of the overall project objectives, but he did not actively enter into the performance of the management functions outside his own particular organization. The project coordinator had specific functional authority in certain areas, such as in budgeting, release of funds, and release of authority to act as in the dispatching function in the production control environment.

Today's project manager is in every sense a manager. He actively participates in the organic functions of planning, organizing, and controlling those major organizational activities involved in the specific project. He accomplishes the management process through other managers. Many of the people that feel the force of his leadership are in other departments or organizations separate and apart from the project's manager's parent unit. Since these people are not subject to his operating supervision and owe their fidelity to a superior line manager, unique conflicts of purpose and tenure present themselves. The project manager has real and explicit authority but only over those major considerations involved in the project plan. One of the project manager's biggest problems is how to get full support in the project effort when the functional people are responsible to someone else for pay raises, promotion, and the other expected line superior/subordinate relationships.

Authority and Responsibility of the Project Manager

Since the project manager acts as the focal point within the organization through which major decisions and considerations flow, he must be given a special kind of recognition with respect to the authority and responsibility involved in his relationships with other managers in the organization. Authority is the legal or rightful power to command, to act, or to direct. Ultimate authority derives from the society in which the organized effort exists. Authority is *de jure* in the sense that it exists by rightful title, i.e., specific delineations of the authority of an organizational position are contained in the unit's documents such as policy and procedural instruments job descriptions, and organizational charters.[3] Not to be neglected is the *de facto* authority that can be exercised by the project manager, i.e., the implied authority reflected in the organizational

[3] *Within the Air Force specific and forceful authority has been delegated to the project manager, or in Air Force parlance the system program director. Air Force Regulation 375–3, dated 25 November 1963, states:*

An SPD (System Program Director) is appointed by AFSC (Air Force Systems Command) for each system program not later than receipt of the formal document requiring application of system management techniques.

He manages the collective efforts of participating field organizations in preparing system program documentation, and revisions as requested.

His mission with respect to an approved system program is to:

(1) Manage (plan, organize, coordinate, control and direct) the collective actions of participating organizations in planning and executing the system program.

(2) Propose and/or prepare modifications of, or changes to, the system program within the limits of guidance received from participating organizations or higher authority.

(3) Make changes to the system program consistent with his authority, as required to maintain internal balance of the system program.

position. It is the intrinsic and necessary power to discharge fully the responsibilities inherent in the task or job. Thus an organization receiving public funds has *de facto* authority to create administrative policy stipulating how the funds will be maintained, to appoint a custodian to assume pecuniary responsibility for the safe-guarding and legal obligation of the funds, and to take other necessary measures to adequately control the expenditure of the funds within the specific authority granted when they were accepted. Other aspects of the *de facto* authority include the project manager's persuasive ability, his rapport with extra-organizational units, and his reputation in resolving opposing viewpoints within the parent unit and between the external organizations. Other factors that influence the degree of authority which the project manager can exercise include:

1 Influence inherent in the rank, organizational position, or specialized knowledge of the incumbent.
2 The status or prestige enjoyed by the project manager within the *informal* organizational relationships.
3 The priority and obligation existing within the organization for the timely and efficient accomplishment of the project goals.
4 The existence of a bilateral agreement with a contracting party for the completion of the project within the terms of the contract in such areas as cost, performance (quality, reliability, technology), and schedule.
5 The integrative requirements of the project manager's job in the sense that he has the sole responsibility within the organization to pull together the separate functional activities and direct these diverse functions to a coordinated project goal.

The project manager's authority and responsibility flow horizontally across the vertical superior/subordinate relationships existing within the functional organizational elements. Within this environment the authority of the project manager may often come under serious question, particularly in cases involving the allocation of scarce resources to several projects. Generally the project manager has no explicit authority to resolve interfunctional disputes through the issuance of orders to functional groups outside his office. However, since the project manager is the central point through which program information flows and total project executive control is effected, this individual comes to exercise additional authority over and above that which has been specifically delegated. His superior knowledge of the relative roles and functions of the individual parts of the project places him in a logical position to become intimately involved in the major organizational decisions that might affect the outcome of his project. As the focal point through which major project decisions flow, the project manager's input into the decision process cannot be ignored or relegated to a subordinate role. The unique position of the project manager inherently gives him knowledge superior to that of the personnel responsible for any subsystem or subactivity functioning as part of the integrated whole. (But this superior knowledge does not exist as the single authority within the total organization but only as the single authority with respect to the particular project involved.)

Organizational rank carries both explicit and implied authority. The project manager should have sufficient executive rank within the organization relationship to enable him to exercise a subtle and pervasive authority by virtue of his position or the trappings of his office. He should have sufficient rank (through evidence of seniority, title, status, prestige, etc.) to provide general administrative leverage in dealing with other line officials, with supporting staff personages, and with those in authority but external to the parent unit. This implies that there should be some correlation between the rank of the project manager and the cost and complexity of the project he manages. The more costly the project, the greater the degree of risk involved; and the more complex the internal and external organizational structures involved, the higher the rank of the project manager should be. Within the military services there has been a tendency to increase the authority of a project manager's position by assigning higher ranking officers to it. A brigadier general would be expected to exercise more influence (and thus authority) over his subordinates, his peers, and extraorganizational elements than would a lieutenant colonel or major occupying a similar position.

Management literature has neglected any real definition or discussion of the authority of the project manager. This is to be expected because of the near universality of the functional approach to management education and practice. Until contemporary management thinking has fully conceptualized the unique nature of the project manager's role, extraordinary manifestations of authority will be required. It will be an uphill struggle because of the threat that project management poses to ingrained functional management practices and thinking.

The project manager requires a clear delineation of authority and responsibility in order to balance the considerations involved in the proper development and successful conclusion of the project objective. He is frequently faced with major and minor "trade-offs" involving factors of cost, schedule, and performance of the product. Many times these trade-offs lack clear-cut lines of demarcation and foster internal and extraorganizational conflicts of purpose. Referral of the problem for resolution to the proper functional managers may not resolve it in the best interests of the project, since the functional manager tends to be parochial (and rightly so) in his view and less concerned with individual project objectives than with providing the services of his particular function across all the projects.

The creation of the position of project manager in an organization requires careful planning to prepare existing management groups. Certain criteria are offered for delineating the authority and responsibility of project managers:

1 The charter of the project manager should be sufficiently broad to enable his active participation in the major managerial and technical activities involved in the project. He should be given sufficient policy-making authority to integrate the functional contributions to the project goals.
2 The project manager must have the necessary executive rank to ensure responsiveness to his requirements within the parent organization and to be accepted as the unquestioned agent of the parent organization in dealing with contractors and other external entities.
3 He should be provided with a staff that is sufficiently qualified to provide administrative and technical support. He should have sufficient authority to vary the staffing of his office as necessary throughout the life of the project. This authorization should in-

clude selective augmentation for varying periods of time from the supporting functional agencies.

4 He should participate in making technical, engineering, and functional decisions within the bounds of his project.

5 The project manager must have sufficient authority and capability to exercise control of funds, budgeting, and scheduling involved in the project accomplishment.

6 Where the project management task involves the use of contractors supporting the project effort, the project manager should have the maximum authority possible in the selection of these contractors. After the contractors are selected, the project manager should have direct involvement in the direction and control of the major contractors involved in his particular project. His should be the only authority recognized by the official in the contractor's organization who is charged with contractual actions.

Focal Position of the Project Manager

The typical relationship that would be desirable for a situation involving two organizations having a mutuality of interest in a large project is shown in Figure 28-1. The establishment of a special project office in both the buyer's organization (e.g., the Government) and the seller's organization (e.g., an aerospace company) permits a focal point for concentration of attention on the major problems of the

project or program. This point of concentration forces the channeling of major program considerations through a project manager who has the perspective to integrate relative matters of cost, time, technology, and system compatibility.

This managerial model is not meant to stifle the interfunctional lines of communication or the necessary and frequent lateral staff contacts between the functional organizations of the defense contractor and the military organization. Rather, what is intended is the establishment of a focal point for critical decisions, policy-making, and key managerial prerogatives relating to the project manager when trade-offs between the key elements of the research or production activity are involved. By being in a face-to-face relationship the two project managers can control and resolve both interfunctional and interorganizational problems arising during the course of the project. This organizational relationship precludes any one functional manager from overemphasizing his area of interest in the project to the neglect of other considerations.

Organizational Arrangements for Project Managers

The organizational arrangements for management of industrial projects can vary considerably. One example is the functional organiza-

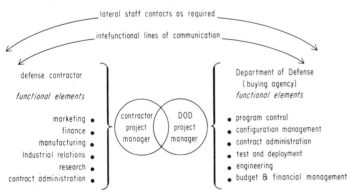

Figure 28-1   Interorganizational project manager relationships. Critical decisions involving policy and managerial prerogatives are directed through the central focal point. Decisions involve cost and cost estimating, schedules, product performance, (quality, reliability, maintainability), resource commitment, project tasking, trade-offs, contract performance, and total system integration.

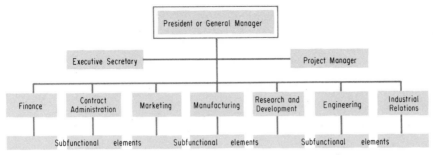

Figure 28-2   Functional organization with project manager in a staff capacity.

tion with the project manager reporting to the company president or general manager in a staff capacity (Figure 28-2). Under this concept the project manager functions as an "assistant to" the chief executive officer in matters involving the project, relieving him of some of the burdensome detail of the project. As a staff official the "assistant to" type of project manager investigates, researches, analyzes, recommends, and coordinates relative to the project. Major decisions are made by the chief executive officer. Although the project manager does not function in a line capacity in this arrangement, he usually has wide use of functional authority and by being in close proximity to the chief executive wields significant influence with respect to the project.

Placing the project manager in a staff capacity degrades his ability to function as a true integrator and as a decision-maker with respect to the major factors involved in the work of the project. With this arrangement there is the risk of having the project manager's responsibilities exceed his authority. If he is relegated to a staff position, his ability to act decisively depends almost solely upon his grant of functional authority, his personal persuasive abilities, or some specialized knowledge he has.

A functional organization exists in which the project manager reports to the chief executive officer in a line capacity (Figure 28-3). In this organizational and authority relationship the project manager's immediate office

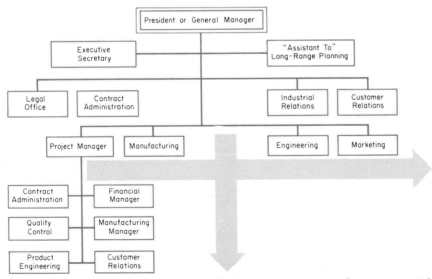

Figure 28-3   Functional organization with project manager in a line capacity. This organizational structure allows for vertical flow of functional authority and responsibility.

staff may vary from a single manager to several hundred people, depending upon the degree of centralization of the project activities. As the project manager's responsibilities increase and more and more of the operating facets of the project are centralized under his control, the organization may seem to have a new company or organizational division formed to manage each major program or project independently. The project manager has authority over the functional managers with respect to the *when* and *what* of the project activities. Functional managers in turn are responsible to both their functional supervisors and the project manager for adequate support of the project.[4] The authority of the project manager in this organizational relationship flows horizontally throughout the organization. It is tempered, however, by direction from the functional managers, who are concerned with the *how accomplished* portion of the project.

The type of functional organization, the size and complexity of the project, and the philosophy of management held by the chief executives of the firm will affect the type of project management to follow. The proponents of total project management would desire to have all project people working directly for the project manager. The choice of organizational arrangement, whether pure functional, completely projectized, or an organizational form in between these extremes, should be made after the effects of the unique environment on the particular project are evaluated as to basic advantages and disadvantages.

---

[4] *This appears to violate the scalar principle described by Henri Fayol in* General and Industrial Administration. *Fayol envisions the scalar chain as the chain of superiors ranging from the ultimate authority to the lowest rank with the line of authority following every link in the chain. He also discusses the unity of command principle, i.e., an employee should receive orders from one superior only. The author of this article believes that these principles can easily be upheld in small organizational arrangements where the management process operates through the vertical superior/subordinate relationship. In today's large organizations where the management of a single project may cut across many internal functional lines of authority and extend into outside organizations, these management principles lack ubiquity. What is required is a discrete differentiation of managerial functions between the functional manager and the project manager as to respective spheres of influence.*

Project Management in DOD

The Department of Defense has something over 100 weapon and support systems managed by project managers. Practically all these project managers are officers with the rank of colonel or lower, though in some of the larger programs (e.g., the F-111 System Program) the project manager has the rank of brigadier general. As military officers, these project managers are subject to permanent change of station in and out of the system program offices. Usually their tenure in any one project manager position is considerably shorter than the four to eight years required for the development and acquisition of a major weapon system. Ostensibly, these project managers plan, organize, and control the activities involved in the development and acquisition of weaponry. They are supported by subsystem managers and other project managers throughout the research, development, and production complexes of both Governmental and industrial organizations. Within the Governmental structure, project managers are identified as the symbol of leadership of the project. Unfortunately, in some cases this leadership is symbolic only, because of the active participation in upper organizational echelons of advisers, delayers, debaters, inspectors, and coordinators. These specialized staff personnel become involved in providing such support as budget, audit, contract surveillance, technical advice, programing, procurement review, facilities control, etc. The proliferation of these special support agencies leads one to fear that the project manager is becoming merely a symbol of leadership for whom there is a lack of authority and responsibility, in both degree and clarification.

The project manager may be located in an organizational position several echelons down the managerial hierarchy of the Department of Defense. In this position he finds it difficult to be selective in the acceptance of the abundant special staff assistance that is made available—and in some cases directed—to him. The increasing trend toward centralization in the Department of Defense and the establishment of certain thresholds in the expenditure of Defense funds have placed constraints on the project manager. The delegations of authority to the project manager vary widely in their charters and perhaps even more widely in practice. One could not reasonably expect the project manager to have complete control of his funds or the final decision on technical problems when his project is part of an overall defense development effort. Logically, a superior organizational unit that has a greater perspective of the total resources to be allocated should retain sufficient control over the project manager to ensure unanimity of national goals. What does become suspect is the use of multilayers of line managers and staff specialists between the project manager and the point of decision in the Department of Defense.

The use of project management techniques had its inception in the military/industrial complex. It has enabled the management of large aggregations of resources across functional and organizational lines directed toward unifying all effort to the common objective. Project management is a relatively recent phenomenon; as business and military organizations continue to become larger and more interdependent, the role of the project manager will come into clearer focus.

READING 29

MAKING PROJECT MANAGEMENT WORK *

John M. Stewart

Late last year [1964], with a good deal of local fanfare, a leading food producer opened a new plant in a small midwestern town. For the community it was a festive day. For top management, however, the celebration was somewhat dampened by the fact that the plant had missed its original target date by six months and had overrun estimated costs by a cool $5 million.

A material-handling equipment maker's latest automatic lift truck was an immediate market success. But a few more successes of the same kind would spell disaster for the company. An actual introduction cost of $2.6 million, compared to planned expenses of $1.2 million, cut the company's profits by fully 10 per cent last year.

A new high-speed, four-color press installed by a leading eastern printing concern has enabled a major consumer magazine to sharply increase its color pages and offer advertisers

unprecedented schedule convenience. The printer will not be making money on the press for years, however. Developing and installing it took twice as long and cost nearly three times as much as management had expected.

Fiascos such as these are as old as business itself—as old, indeed, as organized human effort. The unfortunate Egyptian overseer who was obliged, 5,000 years ago, to report to King Cheops that construction work on the Great Pyramid at Giza had fallen a year behind schedule had much in common with the vice-president who recoils in dismay as he and the chief executive discover that their new plant will be months late in delivering the production on which a major customer's contract depends. The common thread: poor management of a large, complex, one-time "project" undertaking.

But unlike the Egyptian overseer, today's businessman has available to him a set of new and powerful management tools with the demonstrated capacity to avert time and cost overruns on massive, complex projects. These

* Reprinted with permission from Business Horizons, Fall, 1965.

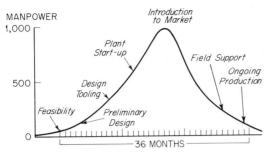

Figure 29-1 Manpower commitment to a new-product introduction project.

Figure 29-2 Manpower commitment to a merger project.

tools, developed only recently, are not yet in common use outside the construction and aerospace industries, where such projects are a way of life. But there is already solid evidence that they can be successfully applied to a host of important, nonroutine business undertakings where conventional planning and control techniques fail—undertakings ranging from a new-product introduction or the launching of a national advertising campaign to the installation of an EDP system or a merger of two major corporations (Figures 29-1 and 29-2).

PROJECT MANAGEMENT ORGANIZATION

Commercial project management is usually a compromise between two basic forms of organization—pure project management and the more standard functional alignment. In the aerospace and construction companies (Figure 29-3), complete responsibility for the task, as well as all the resources needed for its accomplishment, is usually assigned to one project manager. In very large projects, the organization he heads, which will be dissolved at the

conclusion of the project, resembles a regular division, relatively independent of any other division or staff group. Outside the aerospace and construction industries, however, the project manager is usually not assigned complete responsibility for resources (Figure 29-4). Instead, he shares them with the rest of the organization. He may have a project organization consisting of a handful of men on temporary assignment from the regular functional organization. The functional managers, however, retain their direct line authority, monitor their staffs' contributions to the project, and continue to make all major personnel decisions.

Reluctance to adopt new tools is typical in any industry; thus, one should not expect the tools of project management to gain instant acceptance. Outside the aerospace industry, few business executives appreciate their value and versatility. Fewer still are able to recognize the need for project management in specific situations, nor do they know how to use the powerful control techniques it offers. Meanwhile, the few companies that have grasped the significance of the new management concepts and learned to apply them enjoy an extraordinary, if temporary, advantage. They are bringing new products to market faster than their competitors, completing major expansions on schedule, and meeting crucial commitments more reliably than ever before.

Project management, however, is far from being a cure-all for the embarrassments, expenses, and delays that plague even the best-managed companies. First, project management requires temporary shifts of responsibilities and reporting relationships that may disturb the smooth functioning of the regular organization. Second, it requires unusually disciplined executive effort.

Basic to successful project management is the ability to recognize where it is needed and where it is not. When, in short, is a project a project? Where, in the broad spectrum of undertakings between a minor procedural modification and a major organizational upheaval, should the line be drawn? At what point do a multitude of minor departures from routine add up to the "critical mass" that makes project management operationally and economically desirable? Senior executives must have methods to identify those undertakings, corporate or divisional, that cannot be successfully man-

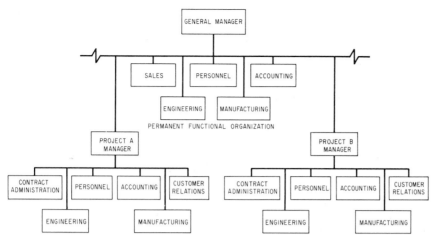

Figure 29-3   *Typical project organization in the aerospace and construction industries.*

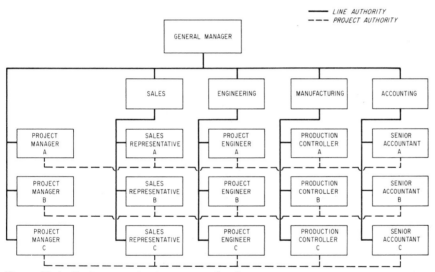

Figure 29-4   *Project organization in general industry.*

aged by the regular functional organization working with routine planning and control methods. Although there are no simple rules of thumb, management can determine whether a given undertaking possesses this critical mass by applying four yardsticks: scope, unfamiliarity, complexity, and stake.

Scope

Project management can be profitably applied, as a rule, to a one-time undertaking that is (1) definable in terms of a single, specific end result, and (2) bigger than the organization has previously undertaken successfully. A project

must, by definition, end at an objective point in time: the date the new plant achieves full production, the date the parent company takes over operating management of the new acquisition, or the date the new product goes on sale in supermarkets across the nation, to name a few.

The question of size is less easily pinned down. But where substantially more people, more dollars, more organizational units, and more time will be involved than on any other infrequent undertaking in the organization's experience, the test result is clearly positive. Such an undertaking, even though its component parts may be familiar, can easily overwhelm a divisional or corporate management. Project management forces a logical approach to the project, speeds decision making, and cuts management's job to a reasonable level. For example, a large service company, with years of experience in renovating district offices, established a project organization to renovate its 400 district offices over a two year period. Even though each task was relatively simple, the total undertaking would have swamped the administrative organization had it been managed routinely.

In terms of the number of people and the organizational effort it involves, a project could typically be charted over time as a wave-like curve, rising gradually to a crest and dropping off abruptly with the accomplishment of the end result. Consider, for example, the introduction of a new consumer product. The project begins with a few people studying the desirability of adding a product to the line. After some early decisions to proceed, perhaps a few dozen engineers are employed to design the product. Their work passes to scores of process planners, tool makers, and other manufacturing engineers, and finally involves entire manufacturing plants or divisions as the first month's production gains momentum. This momentum carries into the field as salesmen increase their effort to introduce the product successfully. Finally, the project effort ebbs as the new product is integrated into routine production and marketing operation.

Again, a merger typically shows a similar "growth and decay" project pattern. Initially, a few senior executives from each company may be involved in discussing the merger possibility. As interest grows, financial and legal advisors are engaged by both sides. Key inside executives are added to the task force to assist in planning. Then, as the deal moves toward completion, widening circles of executives, technical people, and analysts become involved in identifying the changes required after merger. Once the merger has been approved by the directors and stockholders of the two companies, the process of meshing the philosophies, structures, policies, and procedures of the two organizations must begin, possibly requiring the active participation of hundreds or even thousands of people. Eventually, as most of the changes are accomplished, employees return to their normal duties, and the corporation resumes its orderly march toward the end of the fiscal year. The merger project is at an end.

Unfamiliarity

An undertaking is not a project, in our sense of the term, unless it is a unique, or infrequent, effort by the existing management group. Lack of familiarity or lack of precedent usually leads to disagreement or uncertainty as to how the undertaking should be managed. In such a situation, people at the lower management levels need to be told more precisely what they are to do, while senior executives are justifiably troubled by a greater than usual sense of uncertainty about the realism of initial cost estimates, time commitments, or both.

Thus, though a single engineering change to one part of a product would not qualify for project management by this criterion, the complete redesign of a product line that had been basically unchanged for a decade would in most cases call for project management treatment. Individual managers could accomplish the first change easily, drawing on their own past experience, but each would have to feel his way by trial and error through the second.

Complexity

Frequently the decisive criterion of a project is the degree of interdependence among tasks. If a given task depends on the completion of other assignments in other functional areas, and if it will, in turn, affect the cost or timing of subsequent tasks, project management is probably called for. Consider the introduction of a hypothetical new product. Sales promotion plans cannot be completed until introduction dates are known; introduction dates depend upon product availability; and availability depends on tooling, which depends in turn on the outcome of a disagreement between engineering and product planning over performance specifications. There are many comparable interdependencies among marketing, engineering, manufacturing, and finance. If, as seems likely in this situation, no one person can produce a properly detailed plan on which all those concerned can agree; if estimates repeatedly fail to withstand scrutiny; or if plans submitted by different departments prove difficult to reconcile or coordinate, the critical mass of a project has probably been reached.

Stake

A final criterion that may tip the scales in favor of project management is the company's stake in the outcome of the undertaking. Would failure to complete the job on schedule or within the budget entail serious penalties for the company? If so, the case for project management is strong.

The corporate stake in the outcome of a project is commonly financial; that is, the failure of a $50,000 engineering project might jeopardize $12 million in annual sales. But it may also involve costs of a different kind. As more than one World's Fair exhibitor can attest, failure to meet a well-publicized project schedule can sometimes do real harm to a company's reputation. Again, failure to meet time and cost objectives may seriously disrupt corporate plans, as in the case of an equipment manufacturer who was obliged to abandon a promising new product line when a poorly-managed merger soaked up earnings that had been earmarked for R&D on the new line. In all such cases, the powerful controls of project management offer a much firmer prospect of meeting the time, cost, and quality objectives of the major one-time undertaking.

The specific advantages of project management for ventures that meet the criteria just discussed are easily summarized. Project management provides the concentrated management attention that a complex and unfamiliar undertaking is likely to demand. It greatly improves, at very small cost, the chances of on-time, on-budget completion. And it permits the rest of the organization to proceed normally with routine business while the project is underway. But these benefits are available only if top management clearly understands the unique features of project management, the problems it entails, and the steps required to make it work.

THE NATURE OF PROJECT MANAGEMENT

With respect to organization, project management calls for the appointment of one man, the project manager, who has responsibility for the detailed planning, coordination, and ultimate outcome of the project. Usually appointed from the middle management ranks, the project manager is supplied with a team, often numbering no more than half a dozen men for a $10 million project.

Team members, drawn from the various functional departments involved in the project, report directly to the project manager. For the duration of the project, he has the authority to insist on thorough planning, the freedom to challenge functional departments' assumptions and targets, and the responsibility to monitor every effort bearing on the successful completion of the project.

Within the limits of the project, the project manager's responsibility and authority are interfunctional, like that of top management for the company as a whole. Despite this similarity, however, his function cannot safely be superimposed on a top executive's normal workload. Every company I know that has tried giving operating responsibility for the management of a complex project to a division manager has found that he is soon swamped in a tidal wave of detail. Most projects call for more and faster decisions than does routine work, and clear precedents are usually lacking. Thus, a general manager who tries to run one of his own projects seldom has any guidelines for making reliable cost and time estimates, establishing cost control at commitment points, or setting adequately detailed targets for each department. Lacking precedents, he is obliged to invent them. This procedure may drain off far more of his time than the division can afford, without really providing the project with the concentrated attention it needs. He may well find that he is spending better than half his working time trying to manage a project representing less than a tenth of his division's annual budget, while divisional performance as a whole is slipping alarmingly. For these reasons, few projects are ever successfully managed on a part-time basis.

The essence of project management is that it cuts across, and in a sense conflicts with, the normal organization structure. Throughout the project, personnel at various levels in many functions of the business contribute to it. Because a project usually requires decisions and actions from a number of functional areas at once, the main interdependencies and the main flow of information in a project are not vertical but lateral. Up-and-down information flow is relatively light in a well-run project; indeed, any attempt to consistently send needed information from one functional area up to a common authority and down to another area through conventional channels is apt to cripple the project and wreck the time schedule.

Projects are also characterized by exceptionally strong lateral working relationships, requiring closely related activity and decisions by many individuals in different functional departments. During a major product development, for example, a design engineer will work more closely with the process engineering manager and the product manager from marketing than with the senior members of his own department. He will need common sense and tolerance to succeed in the scramble for available resources, such as test-cell time or the help of metallurgical specialists, without hurting relationships of considerable importance to his future career.

Necessarily though, a project possesses a vertical as well as a horizontal dimension, since those who are involved in it at various stages, particularly those who make the technical decisions that determine costs, must often go to their superiors for guidance. Moreover, frequent project changes underline the necessity of keeping senior executives informed of the project's current status.

SPECIAL SOURCES OF TROUBLE

Understandably, project managers face some unusual problems in trying to direct and harmonize the diverse forces at work in the project situation. Their main difficulties, observation suggests, arise from three sources: organizational uncertainties, unusual decision pressures, and vulnerability to top-management mistakes.

Organizational Uncertainties

Many newly appointed project managers find that their working relationships with functional department heads have not been clearly defined by management. Who assigns work to the financial analyst? Who decides when to order critical material before the product design is firm? Who decides to delay design release to reduce unit cost? Who determines the quantity and priority of spares? All these decisions vitally concern the project manager, and he must often forgo his own guidelines for dealing with them. Unless he does so skillfully, the questions are apt to be resolved in the interest of individual departments, at the expense of the project as a whole.

Because of the number of decisions or approvals that may arise in the course of a large project, and the number of departments that have an interest in each, innumerable possibilities always exist for interdepartmental conflicts. Besides coping with these conflicts, the project manager must juggle the internal schedules of each department with the project schedule, avoid political problems that could create bottlenecks, expedite one department to compensate for another's failure to meet its schedule, and hold the project within a predetermined cost. Moreover, he must do all this single-handed, with little or none of the experienced top-management guidance that the line manager enjoys.

Unusual Decision Pressures

The severe penalties of delay often compel the project manager to base his decisions on relatively few data, analyzed in haste. On a large project where a day's delay may cost $10,000 in salaries alone, he can hardly hold everything up for a week to perform an analysis that could save the company $5,000. He must move fast, even if it means an intuitive decision that might expose him to charges of rashness and irresponsibility from functional executives. Decisions to sacrifice time for cost, cost for quality, or quality for time, are common in most projects, and the project manager must be able to make them without panicking. Clearly, therefore, he has a special need for intelligent support from higher management.

Vulnerability to Top-Management Mistakes

Though senior executives can seldom give the project manager as much guidance and support as his line counterpart enjoys, they can easily jeopardize the project's success by lack of awareness, ill-advised intervention, or personal whim. The damage that a senior executive's ignorance of a project situation can create is well illustrated by the following example. A project manager, battling to meet a schedule that had been rendered nearly impossible by the general manager's initial delay in approving the proposal, found functional cooperation more and more difficult to obtain. The functional heads, he discovered, had become convinced—rightly, as it turned out—that he lacked the general manager's full confidence. Unknown to the project manager, two department heads whom he had pressured to expedite their departments had complained to the general manager, who had readily sympathized. The project manager, meanwhile, had been too busy getting the job done to protect himself with top management. As a result, project performance was seriously hampered.

EXECUTIVE ACTION REQUIRED

Because of the great diversity of projects and the lack of common terminology for the relatively new techniques of project management, useful specific rules for project management are virtually impossible to formulate. From the experience of the aerospace and construction industries and of a handful of companies in other industries, however, it is possible to distill some general guidelines.

Guideline 1: Define the Objective

Performing unfamiliar activities at a rapid pace, those involved in the project can easily get off the right track or fall short of meeting their commitments, with the result that many steps of the project may have to be retraced. To minimize this risk, management must clarify the objective of the project well in advance by (1) defining management's intent in undertaking the project, (2) outlining the scope of the project, that is, identifying the departments, companies, functions, and staffs involved, and the approximate degree of their involvement, and (3) describing the end results of the project and its permanent effects, if any, on the company or division.

Defining management's intent. What are the business reasons for the project? What is top management's motive in undertaking it?

A clear common understanding of the answers to these questions is desirable for three reasons. *First,* it enables the project manager to capitalize on opportunities to improve the outcome of the project. By knowing top management's rationale for building the new plant,

for example, he will be able to weigh the one-time cost of plant start-up against the continuing advantage of lower production costs, or the competitive edge that might be gained by an earlier product introduction. *Second,* a clear definition of intent helps avert damaging oversights that would otherwise appear unimportant to lower-level managers and might not be obvious to the senior executive. One company failed to get any repeat orders for a unique product because the project team, unaware of the president's intent, saw their job only in terms of meeting their schedule and cost commitments and neglected to cultivate the market. *Third,* a definition of the intent of the project helps to avoid imbalance of effort at the middle-management level, such as pushing desperately to meet a schedule but missing cost-reduction opportunities on the way.

Outlining the scope of the project. Which organizational units of the company will be involved in the project, and to what degree? Which sensitive customer relationships, private or governmental, should the project manager cautiously skirt? By crystallizing the answers and communicating them to the organization, the responsible senior executive will make it far easier for the project manager to work with the functional departments and to get the information he needs.

Describing the end results. Top managers who have spent hours discussing a proposed project can easily overlook the fact that middle managers charged with its execution lack their perspective on the project. An explicit description of how a new plant will operate when it is in full production, how a sales reorganization will actually change customer relationships, or how major staff activities will be coordinated after a merger, gives middle managers a much clearer view of what the project will involve and what is expected of them.

Guideline 2: Establish a Project Organization

For a functionally organized company, successful project management means establishing, for the duration of the project, a workable compromise between two quite different organizational concepts. The basic ingredients of such a compromise are (1) appointment of one experienced manager to run the project full-time, (2) organization of the project management function in terms of responsibilities, (3) assignment of a limited number of men to the project team, and (4) maintenance of a balance of power between the functional heads and the project manager. In taking these steps, some generally accepted management rules may have to be broken, and some organizational friction will almost inevitably occur. But the results in terms of successful project completion should far outweigh these drawbacks and difficulties.

Assigning an experienced manager. Though the project manager's previous experience is apt to have been confined to a single functional area of the business, he must be able to function on the project as a kind of general manager in miniature. He must not only keep track of what is happening but also play the crucial role of advocate for the project. Even for a seasoned manager, this task is not likely to be easy. Hence, it is important to assign an individual whose administrative abilities and skill in personal relations have been convincingly demonstrated under fire.

Organizing the project manager's responsibilities. While some organizational change is essential, management should try to preserve, wherever possible, the established relationships that facilitate rapid progress under pressure. Experience indicates that it is desirable for senior management to delegate to the project manager some of its responsibilities for planning the project, for resolving arguments among functional departments, for providing problem-solving assistance to functional heads, and for monitoring progress. A full-time project manager can better handle these responsibilities; moreover, the fact that they are normally part of the executive job helps to establish his stature. A general manager, however, should not delegate certain responsibilities, such as monitoring milestone accomplishments, resolving project-related disputes between senior managers, or evaluating the project performance of functional department managers. The last responsibility mentioned strikes too close to the careers of the individuals concerned to be delegated to one of their peers.

For the duration of the project, the project manager should also hold some responsibilities normally borne by functional department heads. These include responsibility for reviewing progress against schedule; organizing for, formulating, and approving a project plan; monitoring project cost performance; and, in place of the department heads normally involved, trading off time and cost. Also, the senior executive must encourage the project manager to direct the day-to-day activities of all functional personnel who are involved full-time in the project. Functional department heads, however, should retain responsibility for the quality of their subordinates' technical performance, as well as for matters affecting their careers.

Limiting the project team. Functional department heads may view the project manager as a potential competitor. By limiting the number of men on the project team, this problem is alleviated and the project manager's involvement in intrafunctional matters is reduced. Moreover, men transferred out of their own functional departments are apt to lose their inside sources of information and find it increasingly difficult to get things done rapidly and informally.

Maintaining the balance of power. Because the project manager is concerned with change, while the department head must efficiently manage routine procedures, the two are often in active conflict. Though they should be encouraged to resolve these disputes without constant appeals to higher authority, their common superior must occasionally act as mediator. Otherwise, resentments and frustrations will impair the project's progress and leave a long-lasting legacy of bitterness. Short-term conflicts can often be resolved in favor of the project manager and long-term conflicts in favor of the functional managers. This compromise helps to reduce friction, to get the job accomplished, and to prepare for the eventual phasing out of the project.

Guideline 3: Install Project Controls

Though they use the same raw data as routine reports, special project controls over time, cost, and quality are very different in their accuracy, timing, and use. They are normally superimposed upon the existing report structure for the duration of the project and then discontinued. The crucial relationship between project time control and cost control is shown graphically in Figure 29-5.

The project in question had to be completed in twenty months instead of the twenty and a half months scheduled by a preliminary network calculation. The project manager, who was under strict initial manpower limitations, calculated the cost of the two weeks' acceleration at various stages of the project. Confronted by the evidence of the costs it could save, top management approved the project manager's request for early acceleration. The project was completed two working days before its twenty-month deadline, at a cost only $6,000 over the original estimate. Without controls that clearly relate time to cost, companies too often crash the project in its final stages, at enormous and entirely unnecessary cost.

Time control.   Almost invariably, some form of network scheduling provides the best time control of a project. A means of graphically planning a complex undertaking so that it can be scheduled for analysis and control, network scheduling begins with the construction of a diagram that reflects the interdependencies and time requirements of the individual tasks that go to make up a project. It calls for work plans prepared in advance of the project

in painstaking detail, scheduling each element of the plan, and using controls to ensure that commitments are met.

At the outset, each department manager involved in the project should draw up a list of all the tasks required of his department to accomplish the project. Then the project manager should discuss each of these lists in detail with the respective departmental supervisors in order to establish the sequence in the project in relation to other departments. Next, each manager and supervisor should list the information he will need from other departments, indicating which data, if any, are habitually late. This listing gives the project manager not only a clue to the thoroughness of planning in the other departments but also a means of uncovering and forestalling most of the inconsistencies, missed activities, or inadequate planning that would otherwise occur.

Next, having planned its own role in the project, each department should be asked to commit itself to an estimate of the time required for each of its project activities, assuming the required information is supplied on time. After this, the complete network is constructed, adjusted where necessary with the agreement of the department heads concerned, and reviewed for logic.

Once the over-all schedule is established, weekly or fortnightly review meetings should be held to check progress against schedule. Control must be rigorous, especially at the

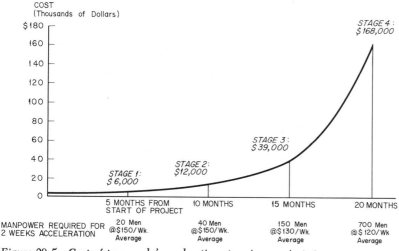

Figure 29-5   Cost of two weeks' acceleration at various project stages.

start, when the tone of the entire project is invariably set. Thus, the very first few missed commitments call for immediate corrective action.

In critical path scheduling, one of the major network techniques, the diagram is similar in principle to that of Figure 29-6 for a very simple hypothetical project.

In the diagram, each arrow represents a defined task, with a clear beginning end, and time requirement, that can be delegated to a single manager or supervisor. Each circle, or node (except the "start" node), represents the completion of a task. Task A, for example, might be "Define the technical objective of the project." The numeral 1 indicates that the allotted time for its completion is one day.

The arrangement of the arrows is significant. As drawn here, B depends upon A; that is, it may not start until A is complete. Similarly, C may not start until B is complete. Also, while B and E may start at different times, neither may start until A is complete. Further along, G may not start until both D and F are complete. This diagram, then, is one of *sequence* and *dependency*.

The time required for the project corresponds to the longest path through the network from Start to Complete in terms of the time requirement associated with each task. In the diagram above, A-E-F-G is the critical path. To meet the over-all schedule, each of these tasks must begin as soon as its predecessor is completed and must end within its allotted time. To shorten the schedule, one or more of the tasks on the critical path must be accelerated.

There are other more complex varieties of network scheduling. Critical path method calculates both normal and crash schedules (and costs) for a project. Program evaluation and review technique (PERT) allows the use of multiple time estimates for each activity. PERT/Cost adds cost estimates, as the name implies. RAMPS (resource allocation and multiproject scheduling) adds the further refine-

ment of a tool for allocating limited resources to competing activities in one or more projects. All, however, rest on the basic network concept outlined above.

Cost control. Project cost control techniques, though not yet formalized to the same degree as time controls, are no harder to install if these steps are followed: (1) break the comprehensive cost summary into work packages, (2) devise commitment reports for "technical" decision makers, (3) act on early, approximate report data, and (4) concentrate talent on major problems and opportunities.

Managing a fast-moving $15 million project can be difficult for even the most experienced top manager. For a first-line supervisor the job of running a $500,000 project can be equally difficult. Neither manager can make sound decisions unless cost dimensions of the job are broken down into pieces of comprehensible size. Figure 29-7, which gives an example of such a breakdown, shows how major costs can be logically reduced to understandable and controllable work packages (usually worth $15,000 to $25,000 apiece on a major project), each of which can reasonably be assigned to a first-line manager.

Cost commitments on a project are made when engineering, manufacturing, marketing, or other functional personnel make technical decisions to take some kind of action. In new-product development, for example, costs are committed or created in many ways—when marketing decides to add a product feature to its product; when engineering decides to insert a new part; when a process engineer adds an extra operation to a routing; when physical distribution managers choose to increase inventory, and so on. Conventional accounting reports, however, do not show the cost effects of these decisions until it is too late to reconsider. To enable the project manager to judge when costs are getting out of control and to decisively take the needed corrective action, he must be able to assess the approximate cost

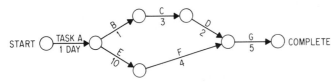

Figure 29-6 A simple critical path network.

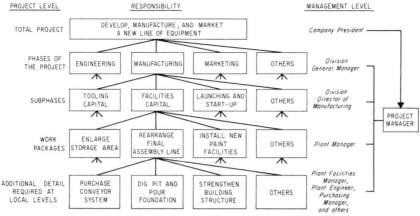

Figure 29-7 Breakdown of project cost responsibility by management level.

effect of each technical decision. In other words, he must have cost commitment reports at each decision stage.

Almost without exception, experience shows, 20 per cent of the project effort accounts for at least 80 per cent of the cost to which the company is committed. With the aid of a detailed cost breakdown and current information on cost commitment, the project manager is able, even after the project is underway, to take people off less important activities in order to concentrate more effort where it will do the most good in reducing costs. One company cut its product introduction costs by over $1 million in this way between the dates when the first print was released and the first machine assembled.

Quality control.   Experience with a wide variety of projects—new-product introductions, mergers, plant constructions, introduction of organizational changes, to name a few—indicates that effective quality control of results is a crucial dimension of project success. Quality control comprises three elements: defining performance criteria, expressing the project objective in terms of quality standards, and monitoring progress toward these standards.

The need to define performance criteria, though universally acknowledged, is generally ignored in practice. Such quality criteria can, however, be defined rather easily, that is, simply in terms of senior executives' expectations with respect to average sales per salesman, market penetration of a product line, ratio of accountants to production workers, processing

time for customer inquiries, and the like. If possible, these expectations should be expressed quantitatively. For example, the senior executive might expect the project to reduce emergency transportation costs from 15 per cent to 5 per cent of total shipping costs. Or he might expect a 30 per cent reduction in inventory costs following installation of a mechanized control system.

Since achievement of these quality goals is a gradual process, the project manager should review progress toward them with the general manager monthly or quarterly, depending upon the length of the project. Sometimes there will be little noticeable change; in other cases major departures from expectation will be apparent. Here, as in the case of time and cost controls, the importance of prompt action to assure that the objectives will be met cannot be overemphasized.

MANAGING THE HUMAN EQUATION

The typical manager in a commercial business who is handed his first project management assignment finds adjustment to his anomalous new role painful, confusing, and even demoralizing. Lacking real line authority, he must constantly lead, persuade, or coerce his peers through a trying period of change.

Too often, in these difficult early weeks, he receives little support from senior management. Instead, he is criticized for not moving faster and producing more visible results. He may be blamed for flaws in a plan that, through the fault of top management, had to be rushed to completion mere days before the project began. Senior managers need to recognize that naming and needling the project manager is not enough. By giving him needed support at the start, by bringing a broad business perspective to bear on the over-all project plan, and by giving the project manager freedom in the details of the doing, the senior executive can greatly enhance his prospects of success.

Another critical point comes at the conclusion of the project, when its results are turned over to the regular organization and the project manager and his team must be returned to their permanent assignments. By virtue of the interfunctional experience gained under pressure, the project manager often matures in the course of a project, becoming a more valuable manager. But he may have trouble slowing down to a normal organizational pace. His routine job is likely to seem less attractive in terms of scope, authority, and opportunity to contribute to the business. Even the best project manager, moreover, can hardly accomplish his project objectives without antagonizing some members of management, quite possibly the very executives who will decide his future. In one instance, a project manager who had brought a major project from the brink of chaos to unqualified success was let go at the end of the project because, in accomplishing the feat, he had been unable to avoid antagonizing one division manager. Such difficulties and dissatisfactions often lead a retired project manager to look for a better job at this time, in or out of the company.

To retain and profit by the superior management material developed on the fertile training ground of the project, senior executives need to be aware of these human problems. By recognizing the growth of the project manager, helping him readjust to the slower pace of the normal organization, and finding ways to put his added experience and his matured judgment to good use, the company can reap a significant side benefit from every successfully managed project.

READING 30

MULTIPLE LADDERS IN AN ENGINEERING DEPARTMENT*

F. J. Holzapfel

Despite the rapid rate of change in technology and products, industry's organization concepts all seem to be variations of the traditional organization of a fighting force such as was used in ancient times. The principle of organization then, as now, was authority.

McGregor[1] sums up the conventional conception of harnessing human energy to organizational needs as "Theory X." This theory states that management directs and controls the efforts of people, modifying their behavior to fit the needs of the organization. Further, this theory implies that without this active intervention, people will be passive or resistant to organization needs and hence must be persuaded, rewarded and punished.

Where this theory is practiced, most people will want to be managers, rather than managed. Oratory about dual ladders or the

equivalence of managerial and technical jobs is hypocritical in such cases. The day-to-day actions belie the words.

In noting that managerial, professional and technical employees have become the largest group in our workforce, Peter Drucker has commented[2] that a different organizational philosophy may be in order. He suggests that we have to organize an information and decision system (that is, a system of judgment, knowledge and expectations) rather than a system of authority, responsibility and command.

As an alternative to Theory X, McGregor suggests "Theory Y." An important element of this theory is that the essential task of management is to arrange organizational conditions and methods of operation so that people can achieve their own goals by directing their own efforts toward organizational objectives. Peter Drucker has called this "management by objectives" in contrast to "management by control." This organization philosophy should not be confused with "permissive management," because attainment of objectives can be the most demanding taskmaster of all.

WHY THE DISSATISFIED ENGINEER?

The literature is full of articles about dual ladders of promotion (manager vs. technical specialists).[4-9] Surveys repeatedly indicate that most engineers are less than satisfied. In my opinion, the engineers are really dissatisfied with the "command and control" organization philosophy that prevails. They recognize that under such circumstances any pronouncements about dual ladders or equivalence of technical and managerial jobs are intended to salve the ego of those who haven't been anointed.

Basically, the various "multiple paths of progression" plans are salary administration devices. Most companies use a salary administration system that divides the entire salary spectrum from office boy to president into a series of overlapping salary ranges. Within broad limits, individuals in the same salary range are considered to be of equal value to the company. It is convenient to assign titles that suggest the type of work done by the individuals.

Very often, administrative or managerial titles are bestowed as status symbols, even though the direct line supervisory aspects of the job occupy only a small part of the man's time. Here too it is necessary to have an intimate knowledge of the particular company, and even of the particular department, since practices vary widely.

Where the "Theory Y," or "Management by Objectives" philosophy, is practiced, the distinction between the two rails of the dual ladder become a matter of degree, rather than of kind. The ability to listen, motivate, and persuade are not only desirable attributes of administrators. The technical specialist will derive greater satisfaction and be more likely to influ-

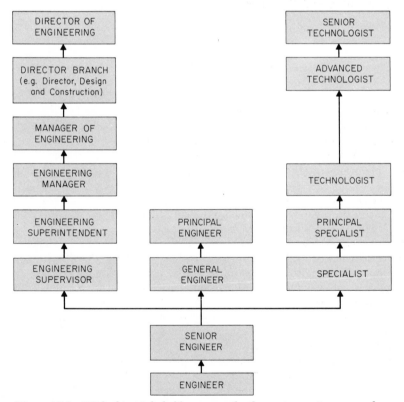

Figure 30-1 With this triple-ladder approach, the senior engineer can choose (or be chosen) for the managerial, generalist, or specialist route to advancement. It is possible to switch from one ladder to the other—e.g., for a qualified principal engineer to move over to the managerial side.

ence events to the extent that he learns and practices these same skills.

A SPECIFIC EXAMPLE

So much for generalities. Let's see how management by objectives applies to the Central Engineering Dept. of Monsanto Co. This department was created in 1965 by the merger of the separate and autonomous engineering departments of the firm's seven operating divisions. Its principal assigned job is the design and construction of all major (more than $100,000 each) capital projects for the entire company. The total capital program has been at the $150 to $200 million per year level.

The long-term objectives of consolidation are to:

Achieve greater organizational flexibility, so that personnel may be shifted to handle large projects faster.

Develop greater technical skill in the many new specialties that are becoming important in engineering.

Have a broad enough base to develop in-house consultants, refresher training programs, etc.

Figure 30-2 shows the basic administrative scheme of Monsanto's Central Engineering

Dept. To achieve organizational stability, to provide for continual technical training in order to combat obsolescence, and to facilitate career counseling and salary administration, the organization is made up of technical sections—such as electrical design, construction, and so on.

Each of these sections is administered by an engineering manager, who must provide adequate numbers of people trained in the particular technical specialty of his section (e.g., electrical design) and who must assign men to provide such specialized design for each project. In the case of his younger men, and those whose technical skills are less than his, the manager must review the work for technical adequacy.

However, the department is really a job shop. Its function is the design and construction of capital projects—some 100 to 150 at any one time, which vary in size from $100,000 to $30 million. Efficient execution of any one project requires that each have a "project manager," and that project management of each of the various simultaneous projects be superimposed upon the basic organization. The real-life organization is thus a "matrix." Figure 30-3 attempts to show this schematically. As far as the usual administrative or managerial role is concerned, the project manager has no

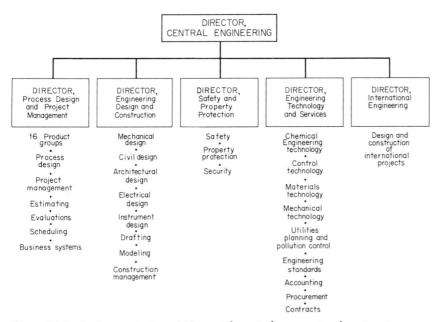

Figure 30-2   Basic organization of Monsanto's central engineering department.

one who reports to him directly, unless it is a large project and he needs one or more assistant project managers. He is not responsible for anyone's salary administration, career counselling, training, or discipline. If his is a small project, he may be a relatively young engineer. On larger projects, his "salary administration" title may be senior engineer, general engineer, principal engineer, specialist, or even engineering supervisor, superintendent, or manager (see below). The project manager title is in effect an assignment, rather than a position, for the duration of the project only. The scope and objectives of the project are established in discussions with the client—the operating division.

Here is the definition of project manager that we have given to our personnel:

> The *Project Manager* is ... charged with primary responsibility for a project so that its engineering objectives are attained within established cost and schedule limitations. He is the chief representative of the Central Engineering Dept. to the client.
>
> Responsibility for the performance of various functions is divided among the different sections of Central Engineering. The Project Manager makes arrangements with each such section for assignment of personnel and execution of its portion of the work, and monitors progress to insure that actions are taken and

decisions made in a fashion that will best satisfy total project objectives. Line authority for the performance of the members of a functional section and for the technical adequacy of their work remains with the manager of the functional section.

There will be occasions where compromises must be made in the interests of achieving total project objectives. The Project Manager is expected to make a reasonable effort to reconcile differences and to minimize the need for compromise, insofar as time and good judgment permit. However, where concurrence cannot be obtained, the project manager shall make such decisions as are required. The various functional sections are expected to implement such decisions. They may appeal the decision through their line organization to the extent that conviction and good judgment dictates, but work is to continue in line with the Project Manager's decision while appeal is pending.

On paper, this system may seem cumbersome. It lacks the comforting hierarchy of decision-making and command. But it does work. In his technical specialty, each man is subject only to his technical superior. The administrative group must set goals for each project. With goals established, each man is able to use judgment to arrive at decisions in his

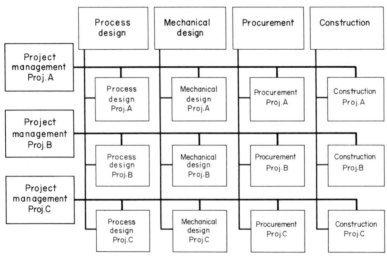

Figure 30-3 Matrix organization shows how project work is handled within the department.

area of expertise. For the most part, conflicts between technical areas can be resolved in the best interest of the project by objective discussion among peers, and few problems need to be arbitrated by the administrative groups.

PERSONAL ADVANCEMENT: THE LADDERS

In the Central Engineering Dept., we are attempting to practice management by objectives, and we do have a "dual ladder" title and salary administration scheme. Figure 30-1 shows the titles used. There are approximately 1,000 people in this department. Of these, about 650 are engineers or members of one of the other professions.

Note that this chart shows the starting engineer at the bottom center. He progresses as a "general practitioner" to senior engineer. From here, he may elect, or be chosen for, an administrative job (shown in the left column), or may decide to concentrate on some technical specialty (shown in the right column). However, he may prefer or be better suited to general practice. The center column indicates that he may make further advances in salary and influence.

The titles that appear on the same horizontal line are in the same salary range. In this connection, it is worth noting that the administrative line of progression is characterized by a series of discrete steps because of the nature of the organization units, whereas the specialist line of progression is really a continuous spectrum of ability.

At periodic intervals, each man should perform an agonizing self-appraisal to establish the type of work from which he derives most satisfaction, the amount of sacrifice he is prepared to make to achieve his goals, and the amount and nature of the competition. If properly done, semiannual or annual discussions between the engineer and his "administrator-coach" can be very helpful in establishing goals, indicating desires, and mapping out plans for achieving such desires. At the earlier stages in a man's career, it is easy to arrange for transfers and temporary assignments, so that the younger engineers may have a taste of each of the types of work.

Maloney, in his articles on ladders for technical status seekers,[3] has some down-to-earth advice that bears rereading. In some cases, an engineer may find it interesting to subject himself to a series of psychological tests that have been validated on engineers and are administered and interpreted by a competent psychologist.

The existence of a multiple-path progression plan, or of an enlightened organization philosophy, will not relieve any engineer of the need for the soul-searching outlined above. Where both exist, however, the conscious choice of one of the nonadministrative roles is less difficult to make. The nature of our modern technology-dependent organizations is such that we must have more people on the technical side. Their work will be more rewarding both to themselves and to the corporation if they have elected this choice, rather than if such choice were by default.

References

1. McGregor, D., "Leadership and Motivation," M.I.T. Press, 1966; also "The Human Side of Enterprise," McGraw-Hill, 1960.

2. Drucker, P. F., "Management and the Professional Employee," *Harvard Bus. Rev.*; also "Managing the Educated," unpublished address.

3. Maloney, P. W., "Ladders for Technical Status Seekers," *Chem. Eng.*, Sep. 13 and Sep. 25, 1965; also "Reward Systems for Technical Men," *Chem. Eng.*, Aug. 2 and Aug. 13, 1965.

4. "Dual Ladder—Theory or Practice," *American Engineer*, Aug. 1966 (staff article).

5. Murdick, R. G., "The Three Jobs of the Technical Specialist in the Engineering Organization," *American Engineer*, Mar. 1966.

6. Campbell, R. O., "Climbing Three Ladders to Success," *Oil & Gas J.*, Nov. 2, 1964.

7. "Three Ways Up at Calresearch," *Chem. Eng. News*, Nov. 13, 1961.

8. Trader, W. D., "Professional Job Levels," *Machine Design*, Sep. 13, 1962.

9. Raudsepp, E., "Engineering or Management," *Machine Design*, Dec. 21, 1961.

READING 31

THE ROLE OF PROJECT MANAGEMENT IN SCIENTIFIC MANUFACTURING *

Keith Davis

Summary—A survey was made of various types of project management organizations used to achieve some measure of managerial unity. Four principal types were identified.

The project expediter achieves unity of communication, the project coordinator gets unity of control, the project confederation achieves unity of direction, and project general management accomplishes the ultimate unity of command. Furthermore, project management may disregard existing levels and functions in superimposing its own structure on the existing organization.

Project organization requires a project manager with considerable role adaptability. He must balance technical solutions with time, cost, resource, and human factors. He is an integrator and a generalist, rather than a technical specialist; and he devotes most of his

* *Reprinted with permission from* IRE Transactions on Engineering Management, *vol. 9, 1962.*

management time to the functions of planning and control. Both the project manager and his superiors may need to give more emphasis to the **management** aspects of his job. To be an effective project manager, the technical man needs to be intellectually sophisticated in the field of management and also to have an attitude which gives some priority to the management aspects of his job.

Project management has become a major device for better management in scientific manufacturing during the last two decades. The project manager generally has complete managerial, budget, and technical responsibility for directing a specialized research or development project. The mix of his group is tailored to fit one specific job, and when that job is finished, he is returned to his "permanent" job or to another project, usually with a different mix of specialists, depending on the requirements of the new project. In this manner, each new project has a separately constituted work group drawn from their permanent or "home-base" assignments within the organization. An arrangement of this type achieves a necessary measure of stability through permanent attachment to the organization, while permitting greater flexibility to adjust each work group to fit the specific manpower requirements of that one job.[1]

PROJECT MANAGER'S ROLE AND FUNCTION

Project management gradually developed in manufacturing as a device for achieving better management of complex development and manufacturing projects. Probably it evolved somewhat from the construction industry, which had practiced something similar to it for years. In the construction of dams, air bases, and factories, separate project organizations were established under a project director. When the job was completed, the project group disbanded to be assigned to other activities of the parent organization. When large manufacturing contracts came to the air frame industry, its members were quick to notice the similarity and to develop a type of project management suited to their own needs for better management. Some of the first companies to make major use of it were Douglas, Lockheed, Martin, and Chance-Vought. Similarities between heavy construction and air frame manufacture may be observed. In each case there is a major job, substantially separate in itself, of finite duration, for one or a very few customers, involving something at least slightly different from what has been done before.

ORGANIZATION FOR PROJECT MANAGEMENT

Fundamental to the project management concept is some form of organization which will help project accomplishment. Emphasis is upon structures and procedures which will integrate the many diverse activities involved in today's complex scientific projects. Each project must be *administratively* tied together in the same

way that its end product must be *physically* put together before it is a workable whole. It follows that *the primary reason for project management organizations is to achieve some measure of managerial unity,* in the same way that physical unity is achieved with the product. Without project organization, the project's activities remain functionally separated in the traditional functional areas of the business, such as production, research, and engineering, and are unified only in the general manager or his equivalent. However, some scientific projects are of such vast complexity or so unique in nature that one general manager is unable to devote the required time to performance of the unifying function; therefore, he establishes a separate unifying agent to perform this function for him. This agent is some form of project organization.

My research with manufacturing firms in the West discloses that there are several types of organization which are sometimes designated "project management." At least four types are readily distinguished. The first type has only a *project expediter.* He does not perform primary management functions, such as directing people, but he does perform two other activities essential to good management. First, he is supposed to expedite the work by dealing with all persons involved to assure that schedules are met; however, he has no power other than persuasion and reporting back to his superior. This reflects his second function, that of serving as a center of communication to be able instantly to report to general management on the *whole* of the project and thus relieve general management of the tedious task of keeping up with all the details. Accordingly, he accomplishes unity of communication, a key necessity in the complex world of advanced technology. Furthermore, he serves as interpreter and translator of complex scientific concepts into the cost, market, and other business interests which general management has.[2] In some cases, he expedites technical aspects only, in which case he is the scientific equivalent of the old production expediter on the factory floor. In other cases, he expedites the whole project, serving more as a staff assistant to a general manager.

---

[1] *See Paul O. Gaddis, "The project manager—his role in advanced technology industry,"* Westing-house Engr., *vol. 19, pp. 102–106, July, 1959.*

[2] *For example, see T. Burns, "Research, development and production: problems of conflict and co-operation,"* IRE Trans. on Engineering Management, *vol. EM-8, pp. 15–23, March, 1961.*

A second type of project organization is directed by a *project coordinator*. He has independent authority to act and is held responsible therefore, but he *does not* direct the work of others. He is more of a staff leader, exercising his leadership through procedural decisions and personal interaction, rather than through line authority. For example, he can independently, or in discussion with others, determine a schedule change and issue procedural changes relating thereto, somewhat like a production control department in a factory, but he cannot direct or discipline others. As another example, his signature may be necessary for release of budget monies, like a controller, but he does not originally set the budget. His control of the budget is perhaps his greatest strength. This forces a unity of control, in addition to the unity of communication which existed in the first type, the production expediter. Like the expediter, the coordinator may cover only the technical aspects of the project, or he may coordinate the entire project.

The third type of project organization is headed by a manager who actually performs the full range of management functions from planning to controlling the work of others; hence, he may properly be called "manager." However, those persons he directs are mostly working in other departments spatially removed from him and are, consequently, not subject to his operating supervision throughout the work day. Though they are assigned to his project, they remain in their permanent departments. In some cases, they may be assigned to the project only part time, but in most cases they are assigned full time. A typical situation is the following one. The project manager determines budgets for his employees, issues instructions to them, sends them on trips, assigns their work, and so on, but much of their housekeeping services and routine supervision are supplied by their permanent departments. Often each person looks to his permanent department for technical leadership also. Since he continues to be a part of his permanent department, he has recourse through his own departmental chain of command to the project manager's superior in case of an irresolvable dispute. Thus, each can administratively go around his project manager without committing the organizational sin of bypassing. The project manager may select his personnel or they may be assigned to him on the basis of

specifications he sets. In either case, he may remove one of them from the project because of poor performance but this act merely returns that person to duty in his permanent department.

This third type of organization is a *project confederation*. In addition to the unity of communication and of control found in types one and two, the confederation achieves a unity of *direction*. All operations, though spatially separated, are focused toward one objective under the *general* direction of one person. In small projects, the project manager manages his departmental people without any intervening level, no matter what level they occupy in their permanent departments. In larger projects the project manager directs *departmental* project managers who then supervise on a face-to-face basis the persons assigned to the project. The project manager may be assisted by several employees and sub-managers working directly with him in his office.

The fourth type of project organization has the ultimate organizational objective of unity of command, which basically means that each person is responsible to one manager only. Persons are temporarily withdrawn from their departments and wholly assigned to the project under the project manager. He is their chain-of-command manager until they are removed or the project plays out. This fourth type is *project general management*. Its manager directs virtually the complete project. He is in many respects a separate branch manager with profit authority and responsibility, subject to general direction by his superior. This type of organization is especially suitable for major projects lasting one year or more.

The four types of project organization which have been discussed represent important differences, but there are many further variations within each type. The concept of project management is a complex one, permitting infinite variations in management design. In all cases the basic objective is some measure of managerial unity. The project expediter achieves unity of communication; the project coordinator gets unity of control, the project confederation accomplishes unity of direction, and project general management accomplishes the ultimate unity of command.

For project unity, there appear to be three avenues open to the chief executive of a firm. One is that he can perform the unifying function himself. Another is that he can have a committee do it, but projects require managerial action rather than deliberative thought, so a committee is rather unfit for managing or coordinating the whole project. This leaves the third choice—a separate project manager or coordinator. My research has disclosed an interesting example of the failure of committee project management. As shown in Figure 31-1, Project Roger was originally designed to be coordinated by AA and BB, who were in separate chains of command. GG was also part of the coordinating "committee," but it was felt that his status was lower since he worked at a lower level in the organization. The project soon bogged down under the weight of coordination problems, lack of authority and responsibility, and red tape. As stated by one of those involved, "I found it simply unworkable. It could not provide the requisite experimental controls, proper procedures, and generally could not keep things going smoothly."

Finally a revised organization was designed for Project Roger as shown in Figure 31-2. The revised organization had the chain of command centering in a project manager. In addition, LL was brought in to provide additional routine task and paperwork coordination, leaving the project manager free to make major decisions. This new organization worked effectively.

It is apparent that *project organization may disregard existing levels and functions in superimposing its own structure on the existing company organization.* It establishes a structure of its own based upon each person's ability to

contribute to that specific project, regardless of his permanent organizational location. Project Roger illustrates this development.

Figure 31-3 shows the permanent organizational assignment of persons in Project Roger. In this chart, AA and BB are at the same level, but in the revised project organization (Figure 31-2), AA is superior to BB. Similarly, GG is ordinarily one level lower than BB, (Figure 31-3), but in Figure 31-2, he is at an equal level with BB in the project. KK and MM are normally at the same level with LL, and in a different chain of command, but in the project (Figure 31-2) they both report to LL. Earlier in the project, (Figure 31-1), KK reported to II, who in the permanent organization was his equal and in a different chain of command.

In one company which used type 3 of project organization (the project confederation), the project managers reported directly to the general manager, even though in their "permanent" organizational assignments they were at least two levels removed from him. They freely admitted that at the end of the project they expected to return to lower levels in their firm. Project management in this firm was looked upon as a testing ground and a broadening experience for promising middle managers.

THE PROJECT MANAGER'S ROLE

Indeed, project management is broadening. It requires a wide range of abilities, judgment, and communication. It may require skills of talking science with a physicist, as well as costs with the general manager and general business relationships with the customer's purchasing agent, engineer, or vice president. It is evident that *project organization requires a project manager with considerable role adaptability.* If he cannot adapt to quick changes in level, function, and interest, in his relations with others, then his multitude of contacts may

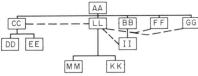

Figure 31-1 Project Group Roger, original design. (Three chains of command loosely coordinated.)

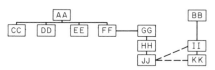

Figure 31-2 Project Group Roger, revised design. (The chain of command with added task coordinator LL.)

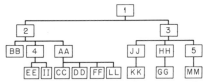

Figure 31-3 Permanent organizational assignment of men in Project Group Roger.

be ineffective. He cannot insist on being an engineer or a physicist all the time, because he is dealing with many other types of people and situations.[3]

The importance of role adaptability is shown in Figure 31-4, which reports 485 minutes of observation of three project managers who directed project confederations (type 3). The data show that project managers during this brief period had a broad range of contacts from the general manager to vendors and from the research to the sales function. During frequent trips which the observer could not record, they were also contacting customers, the home office, and the general public.

Column 2, Number of persons interacting, excluding the manager being observed.

	Minutes	Per Cent
0	103	21
1	199	41
2	53	11
10	38	8
12	92	19

Column 3, Activity.

1. Communication	481	99
2. Contemplation	4	1
3. Personal time, excluding discussion with observer	0	0

Column 4, Interactor level.

0. No interacter	103	21
1. General Manager	1	*
2. Departmental managers	11	2
3. Functional managers (middle management)	156	32
4. Supervisors (operative supervision)	96	20
5. Employees (operative workers)	110	23
6. Vendor	6	1
7. General public	0	0
8. Home office personnel, any level	0	0
9. Field personnel, any level	0	0
10. Not classified	2	*

Column 5, Interacter function.

0. No interacter	103	21
1. Own department (immediate subordinate or superior)	1	*
2. Other in department	0	0
3. Research	16	3
4. Engineering	92	19
5. Production	8	2
6. Sales	91	19
7. Finance	0	0
8. Personnel	0	0
9. Other staff	72	15
10. General management	7	1
11. Miscellaneous, not classified	95	30

Column 6, Communication technique.

	Sending	Receiving
0. No Interacter	3	0
1 or 11. Oral telephone	38	9
2 or 12. Oral face-to-face, two persons (31 per cent)	88	64
3 or 13. Oral face-to-face, over two persons (38 per cent)	73	110
4 or 14. Written letter	0	17
5 or 15. Other written	5	78
10 or 20. Other	0	0
Per cent sending and receiving	43	57

Column 7, Management function.

	Minutes	Per Cent
0. No interacter	3	1
1. Planning	123	25
2. Organizing	1	*
3. Directing	1	*
4. Controlling	341	70
5. Not classified	16	3

* Less than one half of one per cent.

Figure 31-4   Code for dimensions, showing times in minutes and per cent of time for each dimension.

Figure 31-5 provides further evidence of the need for role adaptability. It reports interview responses rather than observations. The respondents are departmental project managers operating under type 4, project general management. Figure 31-5 suggests that the extra-departmental contacts of the project managers are considered time consuming and important. Again contacts ranged widely from customers to operating personnel. (Observe, however, that in all instances the most time was taken in direct supervision of a particular subordinate.)

It follows that *the function of project manager requires a balancing of technical solutions*

[3] See S. Marcson, "Role concept of engineering managers," IRE Trans. on Engineering Management, vol. EM-7, pp. 30–33, March, 1960.

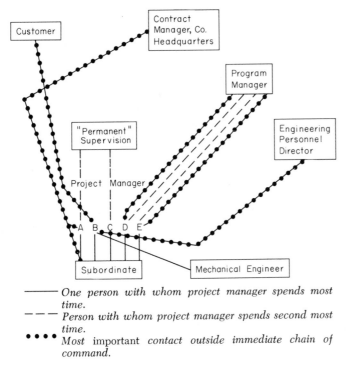

One person with whom project manager spends most time.

Person with whom project manager spends second most time.

Most important contact outside immediate chain of command.

Figure 31-5   Contacts of five departmental project managers.

with time, cost, resource, and human factors. The project manager is an integrator and a generalist, rather than a technical specialist. In the various contacts reported in Figure 31-4 the project manager is largely working with others to achieve a balance of all interests in the project. For example, scientific department X has worked out a bid price for a unit of the project. The project manager points out how the price is out of line with competitors and the unit's heavy weight will cut into the weight allowance for other units of the project. In another case, a technical department insists that a unit cannot be "done right" and still meet the deadline. It demands more time to completely check out all bugs before proceeding. The project manager shows how the reality of deadlines will not permit standard procedures and that "checking bugs" must proceed concurrently with further work on the unit. In the middle of this discussion the customer telephones concerning a proposed conference with the customer about the project.

It is probable that project managers, having mostly a technical background, do not realize the vital significance of broadness and versatil-

ity, rather than specialty, in performing as a project manager. Top managers probably do not realize how difficult it is to get a competent technical man to give genuine first priority to his *management* job when he is a project manager, and accordingly *they* fail to take the time to convince him of the first priority of management.

Reference to Column 7 of Figure 31-4 shows that *project managers devote most of their management time to the functions of planning and control.* Four hundred and eighty-five minutes is a limited period of observation, but the data consistently emphasize planning and control. Referring back to the conclusion that managerial unity is the basic purpose of project management, it is evident that planning and control are organic in achieving this unity. Organizing is primarily a commitment resulting from plans, and it takes very little time. The directing function is mostly achieved in the operating departments, leaving the project manager more involved in controls to assure performance and to report performance. Thus the first and last items in the sequence of management functions—planning, organizing, directing, and controlling—are the functions which require the most project management time and may be of most significance.

CONCLUSION

The primary reason for project management is to achieve some measure of managerial unity. There are four principal types of organization to achieve this objective.

The project expediter achieves unity of communication, the project coordinator gets unity of control, the project confederation achieves unity of direction, and project general management accomplishes the ultimate unity of command. Furthermore, project management may disregard existing levels and functions in superimposing its own structure on the existing organization.

Project organization requires a project manager with considerable role adaptability. He must balance technical solutions with time, cost, resource, and human factors. He is an integrator and a generalist, rather than a technical specialist; and he devotes most of his management time to the functions of planning and control. Both the project manager and his superiors may need to give more emphasis to the *management* aspects of his job. To be an effective project manager, the technical man needs to be intellectually sophisticated in the field of management and also to have an attitude which gives some priority to the management aspects of his job.

SECTION 8

PROJECT PLANNING AND EVALUATION

Managerial controls provide the manager with the tools for determining whether the activity being carried on under his guidance is efficiently proceeding toward the planned objective. Controls provide a means for comparing actual with expected performance. Feedback, the essence of management control, consists of data, arrayed in various forms, which has a predictive value for the manager. In a project, the factors of time, performance, and schedule provide a basis against which control can be exercised. Control is the constant matter of seeking an answer to the question: "How well am I doing in terms of accomplishing that which I set out to do?"

In the development and acquisition of a major project, such as a weapon system or a new product, progress towards the deadlines and cost targets require control techniques that are frequently more advanced than those found in the more traditional commercially oriented firm. As a result, the aerospace industry and the Department of Defense has devoted considerable effort in recent years in advancing methods to track the cost, performance, and schedule of development progress. This section will examine and compare some of these techniques as related to the more conventional methods of control.

READING 32

AN ANALYSIS OF MAJOR SCHEDULING TECHNIQUES IN THE DEFENSE SYSTEMS ENVIRONMENT *

J. N. Holtz

I. INTRODUCTION

The Weapon System Acquisition Environment

The aerospace industry, faced with time deadlines and using sophisticated technology, requires scheduling techniques that are frequently more advanced than those of the more traditional commercially oriented firms. Consequently, the industry has devoted considerable effort in the past decade to advancing the scheduling state of the art. The devices discussed in this Memorandum, however, are not applicable solely to defense-oriented systems. Several are used by industrial firms on various commercial products, and these firms are increasingly adopting the more advanced techniques.

This Memorandum attempts to survey, compare, and evaluate the major scheduling techniques currently available to project management, and to suggest areas for further research that may lead to improving these techniques. To provide a framework for this analysis, the nature of the weapon system acquisition environment must be clearly understood. The following discussion describes several critical dimensions of this environment: the life cycle of a weapon system—its built-in uncertainties and dynamic character—the numerous firms involved in a given project, and the hierarchies of project management existing in corporations and agencies.[1]

The life cycle of a weapon system. Most, if not all, commercial products have a life cycle. Fad items—hula hoops, for example—have a very short life cycle. Other items—such as stoves or refrigerators—have a longer cycle. Each new product must be conceived, re-

* Reprinted with permission of The RAND Corporation, RM-4697-PR, October, 1966, The RAND Corporation, Santa Monica, California.

[1] *Readers already familiar with this environment may prefer to turn directly to the subsequent material.*

searched, designed, tested, produced, sold, and serve its function before it becomes obsolete.

Defense systems likewise have a life cycle, but their period of usefulness is limited by changing operational requirements and advances in technology. This life cycle usually consists of several phases: (a) conceptual, (b) definition, (c) acquisition (including development and production), and (d) operation.

From a scheduling standpoint, perhaps the most significant characteristic of the life cycle is the change in the type of work performed in each phase. In the conceptual and definition phases, emphasis is on specifying the performance characteristics and hardware configurations that will eventually result for the system. Here the effort is primarily analytical, and activities are usually unique and varied.

In the development phase, the design, fabrication, and testing of a limited number of prototypes are usually the primary functions. Frequently, the vehicles used to test individual performance characteristics may be quite dissimilar. The activities in the development phase, although not highly repetitive, have reached the stage where enough information is available to permit the scheduling of resources to specific functions. In a large weapon system development, interactions among the activities are likely to be numerous, complex, and consequently, formidable to manage. A comprehensive scheduling system is therefore required to permit efficient management of the project.

When performance has been demonstrated by the prototypes, production operations usually follow. Contractors are required to produce quantities of the same item on a scale that on occasion approaches mass production. By this time, most of the design uncertainty has been overcome, and reasonably final production drawings exist for the components. It is thus possible to make detailed subdivision of production operations and to control the use of resources on these operations.

Eventually the completed systems, and spares, are turned over to the using commands —Strategic Air Command (SAC), Tactical Air Command (TAC), etc.—which are responsible for their deployment and operation until the systems become obsolete.

Managerial decisions affecting the project must be made throughout all phases of the life cycle. The diverse nature of the activities in each phase requires a variety of scheduling information. This Memorandum will attempt to determine whether any single scheduling technique is sufficiently versatile to be used throughout the entire life cycle of a project.

Numerous industrial suppliers. The development of a new product frequently requires diverse technologies. An example is the recent commercial development of petrochemicals, which was accomplished by forming joint subsidiaries combining technologies adapted to petroleum and chemical firms. Yet the development of defense systems is substantially more complex than the development of most commercial products. The technologies required generally exceed the feasibly attainable capabilities of any one firm. Consequently, defense firms frequently form arrangements similar to a joint venture. The simplest arrangement involves the designation of one firm as a weapon system prime contractor, the other firms being affiliated with it as subcontractors.

Another common arrangement is where several large firms become associate contractors, each being responsible for developing a major segment of the weapon system. For example, one associate contractor is responsible for guidance, another for airframe, another for propulsion, etc. Frequently each associate contractor subcontracts a portion of his project to another firm; the subcontractor may sub-subcontract a smaller portion to yet another firm, etc. Such subcontracting frequently involves thousands of industrial firms in the system development effort.

A third arrangement is one similar to the associate contractor system but with the addition of an integrating contractor whose function is primarily to coordinate systems engineering and checkout for the entire weapon system.

Many governmental agencies often furnish personnel, facilities, or material to develop a system. Each industrial firm and governmental agency, in turn, has more than one level of internal management. The levels vary in number from firm to firm but range in scope from first-line supervision to top management. Consequently, for a significant weapon system there evolve a substantial number of managerial interrelationships. Each managerial group must be informed of plans and progress relating to its sphere of responsibility.

Program monitors. It is obvious that in this environment some group or agency should be responsible for management of the entire project. In the Air Force a System Project Office (SPO) is established in the appropriate division of the Air Force Systems Command (AFSC) to provide this function. The SPO is responsible for the project throughout the weapon acquisition phase. Upon completion and delivery of the hardware, the remaining responsibilities of the SPO are transferred to a weapon system manager in the Air Force Logistics Command (AFLC). Responsibility for operation of the weapon system in the field rests with one of the using commands (i.e., SAC, TAC, ADC, etc.). The SPO, in conjunction with AFLC and the training command (ATC), coordinates the planning for training and for the maintenance and supply which will be required in the operational phase of the system.

If many firms are to make portions of the system, some mechanism should exist to ensure that all components will mate (interface) and function properly in the completed system. The SPO has this responsibility and accomplishes it with technical support either from in-house systems engineering laboratories (those at Wright Field, for example) or from nonprofit engineering concerns.[2]

In defense contracting, the industrial firms deal with only one consumer, the Government, and more specifically with the program manager designated by the Department of Defense. The importance of national defense, coupled with this monopsony (one buyer) situation, naturally leads the Government to take a very active interest in the progress of the system. The SPO is primarily responsible for directing the program, while AFSC, Headquarters USAF, and the Office of the Secretary of Defense (OSD) are also involved in reviewing its progress. In addition, the Bureau of the Budget, Congressional committees, and even the President may become involved in a particular program from time to time.

Again, it is essential that the information systems used for analyzing program status be capable of directing pertinent information to each of the appropriate agencies and individuals concerned.

Dynamic nature of the environment. To be useful in this environment a scheduling sys-

tem also must be responsive to extensive changes in the projects. The project life cycle generally lasts a period of several years; frequently, development effort alone will require four or five years. A mix of various weapon systems is necessary to accomplish the objectives of national defense. From time to time the assessment of the threat to our national security may be modified, which in turn may alter the relative priority of a given project in this mix or affect the amount of funds allocated over time to the project. These factors often result in either an accelerated schedule or a program "stretchout."

Likewise, general technological advances and experience on a specific project frequently lead to design changes that affect the project schedule. The scheduling system must respond to these changes if it is to be useful to management.

Criteria for Comparison of Alternative Scheduling Techniques

It is difficult, if not impossible, to prepare a quantitative assessment of the utility of a particular scheduling technique. It is possible, however, to isolate features that are desirable and then to assess the extent to which these features are satisfied. Although, conceptually, it is possible to assign weights to each feature and thereby construct an index of relative usefulness, this additional step, being inherently subjective, will be left to the reader.

The following criteria are not intended to be comprehensive but are sufficiently basic to be helpful in estimating the strengths and weaknesses of each technique. The discussion in the subsequent sections should indicate the usefulness of these criteria in assessing various systems.

1 *Validity*. The information contained in the system and presented to the appropriate levels of management should reflect genuine progress. For example, suppose a guidance system is required to keep a missile on course, and a gyroscope is an integral component of this guidance system. If the gyroscope is improperly designed, a bias will be introduced into the measurement of spatial relationships. Measurements used in the guidance system will be invalid, that is, they will not reflect the true state of affairs.

2 *Reliability*. The data contained in the system should be consistent regardless of who

[2] *The MITRE Corporation, Aerospace Corporation, etc.*

obtains them or when they are obtained. In the above example, suppose that the gyroscope were properly designed, and thus capable of providing a valid measurement of attitude, but that electrical pulses, external to the gyroscope, frequently altered its motion and generated inconsistent readings. Readings used by the guidance system would then be unreliable. Relating this example to scheduling techniques, the system may be well designed, and consequently valid, yet subject to error because of weaknesses in data collection, and therefore unreliable. Or the reverse, that is, reliable yet invalid results are also possible.

3 *Implementation.* A large number of personnel are likely to be involved in furnishing inputs to and using outputs from a scheduling system. Thus the technique should be easy to explain and understand, and simple to operate.

4 *Universality of Project Coverage.* Ideally, one scheduling system should be sufficient from beginning to end of a project life cycle. All levels of management should be able to use the information in the system, and all relevant factors to be controlled should be encompassed by the one system.

5 *Sensitivity Testing (Simulation).* Since management decisionmaking involves selecting one course of action out of alternative possible courses, it is desirable to assess the scheduling implications of these alternatives. A system that enables management to simulate the impacts of alternative courses of action can facilitate the selection process and lead to better decisions concerning the project.

6 *Forecasting.* One purpose of collecting data is to assess the probability of accomplishing future tasks. Some scheduling systems are oriented more explicitly toward longer term operations than others.

7 *Updating.* Program decisions in a dynamic environment must be based on current data. The scheduling system should be capable of incorporating rapidly, and with ease, information on project progress.

8 *Flexibility.* A desirable feature in a scheduling technique is its ability to adapt easily to changes in the project. This feature is closely related to a simulation capability. The system must be flexible if simulation of alternatives is to be possible, but a system may be flexible without emphasizing simulation potential.

9 *Cost.* The scheduling system should provide the required information at the lowest cost. Cost is a difficult factor to measure for several reasons. First, scheduling costs are not usually uniformly recorded by industry and government, probably because the functions attributable to collection of data in support of the system vary among contractors. Also, total scheduling costs are needed to compare techniques. In a Gantt system, for example, time standards are as much a part of the cost as is chart preparation, yet this factor frequently is not included in estimates of schedule cost.

Second, systems that are the most useful in terms of the above criteria generally involve greater cost. Consequently, the appropriate cost statistic is not total dollar cost, but rather cost per unit of utility, or benefit. This cannot as yet be precisely measured.

Finally, cost is largely a function of the size of the program, and implementation of each system involves both fixed and variable costs. Thus, techniques with high fixed costs tend to be relatively less expensive in large-scale applications and relatively more expensive in small projects.

Missile System Development Example

A hypothetical missile system has been selected to facilitate a comparison of alternative scheduling techniques for the development phase of a project. Although the example is greatly abbreviated, it will suffice to demonstrate the major characteristics of each technique. Various nonstandard illustrations are used in describing applications to production processes.

Table 32-1 contains all the basic data—events, activities, and time estimates—needed to compare the scheduling techniques for the missile system development example. The discussion in the various sections throughout the Memorandum will draw upon this table.

Project status is measured by the accomplishment of *events* representing significant points of partial completion of a project. *Activities,* on the other hand, occur over a time horizon. Each activity is defined by a starting and an ending event. Resources are consumed by activities rather than events. Decisions made by project management may alter the levels and qualities of resources applied to activities. Estimates of the time required to accomplish each activity are given in Table 32-1. These estimates are indicated as "optimistic," "most likely," and "pessimistic,"[3] and serve as the schedule data for the example.

---

[3] *The meaning of* optimistic, most likely, *and* pessimistic *times is explained in Section V.*

Generally, the events and activities required to complete a component or subsystem are *dependent* upon the results of the preceding activities in that subsystem. Frequently, information generated through performance on an activity in one subsystem also is essential to the definition and performance of activities in a different subsystem. For example, information concerning the size, weight, etc., of a missile must be obtained from the missile design before the launching equipment can be designed and fabricated. In general, fabrication of launching equipment is separate from fabrication of the missile except for this information requirement. This relationship makes the activities interdependent. Such interdependencies must be considered in scheduling projects. The relevant interdependencies are identified in footnotes to Table 32-1.

II. GANTT AND MILESTONE CHARTS

Gantt Technique

The Gantt technique was the first formal scheduling system to be used by management.[4] The cornerstone of the technique is the Gantt

[4] *Developed by Henry L. Gantt in the late 1800s, the technique was based on the scientific management approach of Frederick W. Taylor. Prior to the twentieth century, management of productive operations was loosely organized. Few standards existed by which performance could be gauged. In the 1880s, Taylor altered the process of management by attempting to substitute "scientific management" for "opinions" and "hunches" based on little factual data.*

This "scientific method" involved identifying tasks and subtasks to be performed in the productive operations of the plant. The subtasks were refined into elementary work movements, which were "timed" to determine how much time each movement should require under normal working conditions if performed by a "typical" operator. The elementary operations were then assigned to an operator and their accumulated times became a standard by which the operator's performance was measured. The variance, if any, between work planned for the day, week, etc., and work completed for the period was analyzed to determine the factors responsible for underperformance (or overperformance), so that corrective action could be prescribed.

Gantt met Taylor in 1887 and became actively involved in the scientific management movement. Gantt made numerous contributions to management philosophy, but he is remembered primarily for his graphic technique, which he devised to display data required for scheduling purposes.

chart, which is basically a bar chart showing planned and actual performance for those resources that management desires to control. In addition, major factors that create variance (i.e., overproduction or underproduction) are coded and depicted on the chart.

Application to production operations. The Gantt chart was designed for, and is most successfully applied to, highly repetitive production operations. Normally, it assumes that time standards are available for each operation and that the objective of management is to obtain "normal" output from each major resource employed, especially labor and machinery. If, for example, it has been established that an average of 60 seconds (including personal time)[5] is required for a "typical" worker to assemble a cigarette lighter, then each man assigned to that task should be scheduled to assemble 60 per hour and he should meet this quota. Reasons for underperformance should be established.

A similar example can be given for machinery. If a drilling machine is rated as requiring 30 seconds to drill six holes in a two-barrel carburetor, then that machine should be scheduled to perform this function on 120 carburetors per hour. Again, reasons for any variation in performance should be established.

The Gantt charts applicable to these two types of production operation are called "man-loading" and "machine-loading," respectively. An example of a man-loading chart is given in Figure 32-1. The machine-loading chart is similar, except that machine time rather than man time is scheduled. The chart shown in Figure 32-1 provides the following information:

The "✔" indicates that the chart was based on actual production through Friday, July 10.

The space shown for each day represents the output scheduled for that day. The thin line indicates the output actually produced by the worker for the day. In the example, Mr. Braden failed to produce his scheduled output on Monday, Tuesday, and Wednesday. His underproduction on Monday and Tuesday was due to material troubles (M) and Wednesday's underproduction was traced to tool troubles (T). On Thursday, Braden met his scheduled output, and on Friday he ex-

[5] *An allowance for coffee breaks, wash room, etc.*

TABLE 32-1 DATA FOR THE MISSILE SYSTEM DEVELOPMENT EXAMPLE

Event No.	Events	Activity No.	Activities	Estimated Time Required (weeks)		
				Optimistic	Most Likely	Pessimistic
1	Begin project	1-2	Assemble maintenance equipment fabrication facilities	1	3	6
2	Start maintenance equipment fabrication	1-3	Assemble training facilities for operating personnel	3	4	5
3[a]	Start training of operating personnel	1-4	Assemble ground equipment fabrication facilities	0.1	0.2	0.5
4	Start ground equipment fabrication	1-5	Assemble installation and check out equipment fabrication facilities	0.1	0.2	0.5
5	Start installation and check out equipment fabrication	1-6	Assemble missile erection equipment fabrication facilities	1	3	6
6	Start missile erection equipment fabrication	1-7	Assemble missile transportation vehicle fabrication facilities	5	7	8
7	Start missile transportation vehicle fabrication	1-8	Assemble missile fabrication facilities	0.1	0.2	0.5
8	Start missile fabrication	1-9	Assemble emplacement fabrication facilities	4	5	6
9	Start emplacement equipment fabrication	1-10	Assemble training facilities for maintenance personnel	1	2	3
10[b]	Start training of maintenance personnel	1-11	Assemble site construction facilities	3	4	5
11	Start site construction	2-12	Fabricate maintenance equipment	14	19	26
12	Maintenance equipment fabrication	3-13	Train operating personnel	16	19	20
13	Training of operating personnel completed	4-21	Fabricate ground equipment	16	19	21
14	Installation and checkout equipment fabrication completed	5-14	Fabricate installation and checkout equipment	4	6	7
15[c]	Missile erection equipment fabrication completed	6-15	Fabricate missile erection equipment	2	3	5
16[d]	Missile transportation vehicle fabrication completed	7-16	Fabricate missile transportation vehicle	8	9	12
17	Missile functional test completed	8-17	Fabricate missile	27	30	54
		9-19	Fabricate emplacement equipment	26	28	31
		10-29	Train maintenance personnel	8	9	10
		11-30	Construct launch site	18	21	25
		12-25	Transport maintenance equipment to site	0.1	0.2	0.5
		13-23	Transport operating personnel to site	0.1	0.2	0.5
		14-20	Test installation and checkout equipment	5	7	8

Activity	Description			
15-26	Transport missile erection equipment to site	0.1	0.2	0.5
16-27	Deliver missile transportation vehicle to site	0.1	0.2	0.5
17-18	Correct deficiencies in missile	8	10	11
18-27	Transport missile on missile transportation vehicle to site	0.1	0.2	0.5
19-28	Transport emplacement equipment to site	0.2	0.4	1.0
20-22	Transport installation and check out equipment to site	0.1	0.2	0.5
21-24	Transport ground equipment to site	0.1	0.2	0.5
22-32	Install checkout equipment at site	0.1	0.2	0.5
23-32	Operating personnel install ground equipment	0.1	0.3	1.0
24-32	Ground equipment installed at site	0.1	0.2	0.5
25-31	Install maintenance equipment	1	2	3.5
26-33	Install missile erection equipment at site	0.2	0.4	1.0
27-33	Install missile at site	0.1	0.2	0.5
28-33	Utilize emplacement equipment to install missile	0.6	1	2.0
29-33	Perform maintenance operations on missile site	0.1	0.2	0.5
30-34	Check out site construction	0.1	0.2	0.5
31-34	Check out installed maintenance equipment	1	2	3.5
32-34	Check out installation of ground equipment	0.1	0.2	0.5
33-34	Check out missile installation	16	24	34
34-35	Transfer responsibility for operational unit to using command	0.1	0.2	0.5

Event No.	Event
18	Missile fabrication completed
19	Emplacement equipment fabrication completed
20	Preliminary check out of installation and checkout equipment completed
21	Ground equipment fabrication completed
22	Installation and checkout equipment on dock at site
23	Operating personnel at site
24	Ground equipment on dock at site
25	Maintenance equipment on dock at site
26	Missile erection equipment on dock at site
27	Missile on dock at site
28[e]	Emplacement equipment on dock at site
29	Maintenance personnel at site
30	Site construction completed
31	Installation of maintenance equipment completed
32	Installation of ground equipment completed
33	Missile installation completed
34	Launch site completed
35	First operational unit completed

NOTE: Footnotes a through e indicate interdependencies between events. The meaning of interdependency is explained on page 321.

[a] Must be completed before event No. 20.
[b] Must be completed before event No. 20.
[c] Must be completed before event No. 17.
[d] Must be completed before event No. 17.
[e] Must be completed before event No. 34.

ceeded it. The overproduction on Friday is indicated by a second thin line.

Braden's performance for the entire week is shown as a heavy, solid line immediately beneath the thin lines representing his daily performance. It can be readily seen that his cumulative output for the week was less than scheduled. Each worker's performance is analyzed in a similar way.

Because the foreman is responsible for the output of those working under him, the chart records the scheduled output of his combined work force. In the example, the shaded line opposite his name indicates that Mr. Allen did not meet the scheduled output for the week. The reasons for this underperformance can be traced to specific employees on specific days.

The general foreman is responsible for the overall production of the department and thus the row opposite his name represents the scheduled output for the entire department. In the example the solid bar indicates that the output of the department did not meet the week's scheduled production. Consequently, the factors responsible for the poor performance and the areas in which they occurred will need to be determined.

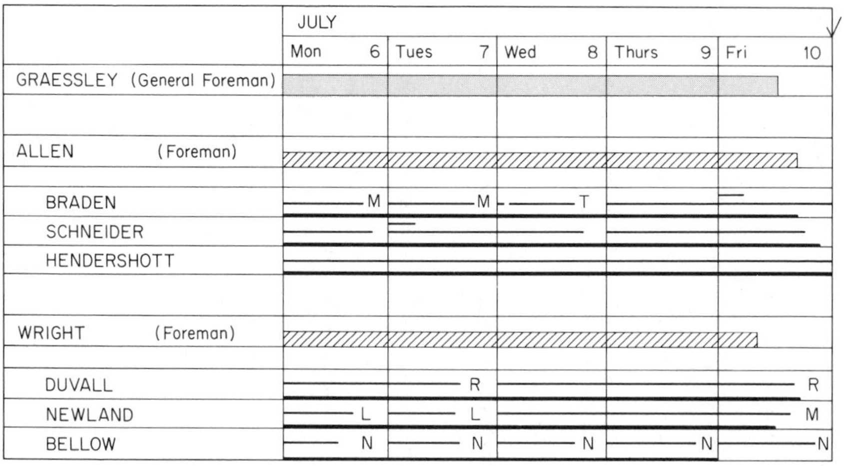

	JULY				
	Mon 6	Tues 7	Wed 8	Thurs 9	Fri 10
GRAESSLEY (General Foreman)					
ALLEN (Foreman)					
BRADEN	— M	— M	— T		—
SCHNEIDER					
HENDERSHOTT					
WRIGHT (Foreman)					
DUVALL		— R			— R
NEWLAND	— L	— L			— M
BELLOW	— N	— N	— N	— N	—N

LEGEND

A. The ordinate (y axis) comprises a discrete listing of the names of employees in a department. The abscissa (x axis) represents a time horizon.

B. Other characteristics

  1. | | Width of daily space represents amount of work that should be done in a day.

  2. ——   Amount of work actually done in a day.

  3. – – –   Time taken on work on which no estimate is available.

  4. ——   Weekly total of operator. Solid line for estimated work; broken line for time spent on work not estimated.

  5. ▨   Weekly total for group of operators.

  6. ▭   Weekly total for department.

  7. Reasons for falling behind:
     A = Absent
     N = New operator
     L = Slow operator
     R = Repairs needed
     T = Tool trouble
     M = Material trouble
     Y = Lot smaller than estimated

Figure 32-1   Gantt man-loading chart.

In a similar manner, the work performance of several departments can be combined on a single chart to show aggregate accomplishment. Charts can also be prepared for various managerial levels so that performance can be depicted and responsibility traced throughout the organization. The graphs are normally maintained on a daily basis to provide up-to-date control.

Frequently, even in production operations, workers perform tasks for which there are no time standards, such as tool repair, housekeeping, etc. The amount of time spent on such tasks is usually represented by a dashed line. This type of effort is not indicated in Figure 32-1, but the line is identified in the legend.

Gantt charts need not be organized along departmental lines only. For example, instead of showing quantity of output for one department, the chart could depict the progress of various departments striving simultaneously toward completion of a *component* or some other appropriate unit. This latter type of chart is more appropriate for prototype development and testing. Its application is discussed below.

Application to Development Operations.

To demonstrate the application of a Gantt chart to nonrepetitive operations we will use the hypothetical missile system development example presented on page 320. A schedule of *planned* activities (taken from Table 32-1) is shown in Figure 32-2.[6]

In constructing such a schedule, it is important to keep in mind that when activities must be performed in series, they cannot be scheduled to begin before their predecessors are completed.[7] Assuming available resources and a desire to complete all activities as soon as possible, the tendency would be to schedule each activity at its *earliest start time*,[8] i.e., as

---

[6] *Activities with a most likely time of less than 1.0 week add little to the illustration at this point and are omitted, reducing the number of activities listed from 43 to 22.*

[7] *Managers do occasionally assign resources to portions of later activities in a series before earlier activities are completed.*

[8] *This term was not formally introduced into the scheduling literature until the critical path technique evolved. However, since it simplifies the description, it is used here in explaining the basis for construction of the Gantt chart.*

soon as the prior activity is scheduled to be completed. Only certain "critical" activities need be scheduled in this fashion; most others can be delayed as long as the scheduled completion of the project is not jeopardized.[9]

Unfortunately, the degree of flexibility which exists in scheduling a project cannot be readily ascertained through the use of the Gantt charts because relationships among activities in a project are not clearly revealed. For example, in Figure 32-2 activities 2-12 (fabricate maintenance equipment), 3-13 (train operating personnel), and 8-17 (fabricate missile) are all scheduled to be completed before activity 17-18 (correct deficiencies in missile) is scheduled to begin. That activities 8-17 and 17-18 are in series, i.e., have a formal predecessor-successor relationship, is not revealed by the chart.

Figure 32-3 is a typical Gantt chart used by management to control activities after the schedule is completely prepared and actual operations are under way. The chart assumes the project has been in operation for 20 weeks and is scheduled for completion in an additional 40 weeks.

The chart indicates that activity 9-19 (fabricate emplacement equipment) and activity 11-30 (construct launch site) are, respectively, four weeks and one week ahead of schedule. However, activities 2-12 (fabricate maintenance equipment) and 4-21 (fabricate ground equipment) are, respectively, two and three weeks behind schedule. On the basis of the information in Figure 32-3, it is not obvious whether the project will be completed on schedule. Actually it is possible to complete the fabrication of maintenance equipment and the fabrication of ground equipment as late as the 60th and 64th week, respectively, and still complete the project on schedule.[10] Since the chart does not provide this information, it is necessary to use other techniques to establish interrelationships and to compute the earliest start and latest completion dates for each activity. A Gantt chart incorporating all of this information would be too cluttered to be easily read and understood.

A Gantt chart based on earliest start times

---

[9] *In subsequent discussion of scheduling techniques, such latter points are called* latest start times, *and the flexibility in scheduling certain activities are termed "float" or "slack."*

[10] *The method for computation of latest completion dates is given in Table 32-7 in Section IV.*

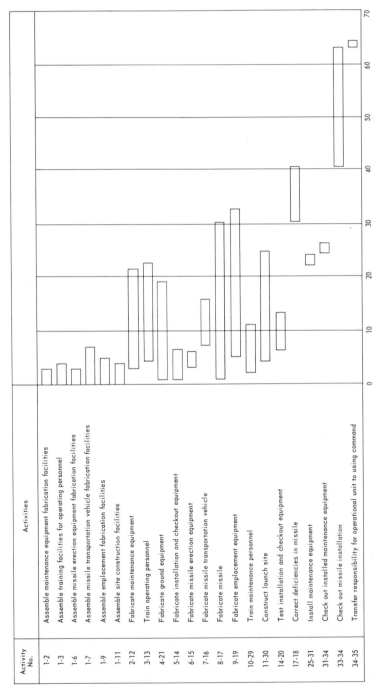

Figure 32-2   Gantt chart showing plan for missile system development.

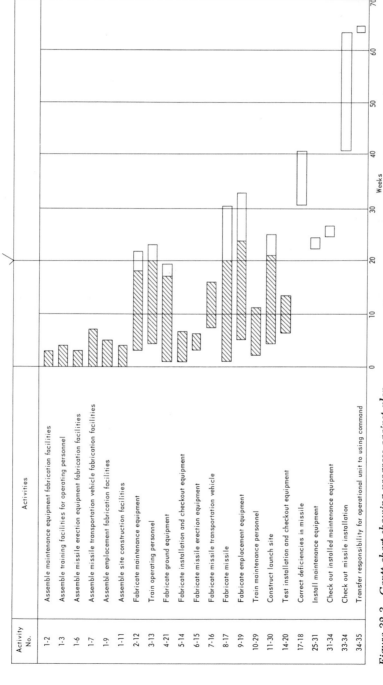

Figure 32–3 Gantt chart showing progress against plan.

combined with a transparent overlay based on latest completion times would provide more of the information useful for scheduling but would still not depict the interrelationships existing among activities.

The Gantt technique was devised originally for use by first-line supervision on repetitive production operations. It is an excellent tool for this type of operation because (1) good estimates of normal production times can be obtained when work is performed repetitively; and (2) production responsibility of first-line supervision is normally limited to a few operations. Thus, significant interrelationships, if any, are obvious at this level. The complex interrelationships evolve when information on many facets of an overall project must be presented to higher levels of management. The large amount of detailed information accumulated at the foreman level must then be compiled and summarized into fewer activities.

The most important strengths and weaknesses of the Gantt technique are summarized in Table 32-2.

TABLE 32-2   GANTT TECHNIQUE—STRENGTHS AND WEAKNESSES

Criteria	Strengths	Weaknesses
1. Validity	Good in production operations. Because of short time duration of each measured operation, only small errors in measurement are likely to occur.	No explicit technique for depicting interrelationships, which are especially important in development.
2. Reliability	Simplicity of system affords some reliability.	Frequently unreliable, especially in development stage, because judgment of estimator may change over time. Numerous estimates in a large project, each with some unreliability, may lead to errors in judging status.
3. Implementation	Easiest of all systems in some respects because it is well understood. (System implies existence of time standards.)	Quite difficult to implement for the control of operations in development phase, where time standards do not ordinarily exist and must be developed.
4. Universality of project coverage	Can comprehensively cover a given phase of a life cycle. Effective at the resource or input level of control.	Less useful in definition and development phases of life cycle.
5. Sensitivity testing (simulation)		No significant capability.
6. Forecasting	In production operations, good technique to assess ability to meet schedule on a given activity if based on good time standards.	Weak in forecasting ability to meet schedule when interrelationships among activities are involved.
7. Updating	Easy to update graphs weekly, etc., if no major program changes.	
8. Flexibility		If significant program changes occur frequently, numerous charts must be completely reconstructed.
9. Cost	Data gathering and processing relatively inexpensive. Display can be inexpensive if existing charts can be updated and if inexpensive materials are used.	The graph tends to be inflexible. Program changes require new graphs, which are time consuming and costly. Frequently expensive display devices are used.

NOTE: Recall that this table is intended only as a summary of certain qualitative information on the relative usefulness of the scheduling technique. As indicated previously, a more formal quantitative evaluation of the extent to which the criteria are met was considered infeasible in this study.

Milestone Technique

The milestone scheduling system is based largely on the same principles as the Gantt system but the technique of displaying project status differs. The milestone system is usually applied to development projects and is frequently used at several of the higher-management levels, for example, corporate, SPO, AFSC, and Hq USAF.

A milestone represents an important *event* along the path to project completion. All milestones are not equally significant. The most significant are termed "major milestones" usually representing the completion of an important group of activities. (Also, events of lesser significance are often called "footstones" and "inch stones" at least in conversation if not in the formal literature.) In reality, of course, there are many gradations of importance.

Events that are designated as milestones vary from system to system. Attempts are currently being made to establish milestones common to all programs, especially within major systems. For example, events such as "Contractor Selected," "Equipment Delivered," and "Final Acceptance Inspection Completed" are common to all systems, while "Aircraft Flyaway" is common to all aircraft systems, but not to missile systems. It is anticipated that milestone standardization, if successful, will be of significant help to program monitors in comprehending the status of the program, as well as in comparing progress on various programs.

Milestone chart. Systems management requirements currently specify that schedule data be furnished in milestone form by the System Project Office (SPO) and various contractors. In the planning phase, milestones are established for the total life cycle of the program. Major milestones are included in a comprehensive development plan, i.e., the System Package Program.[11] Progress in accordance

[11] *Described in* System Program Documentation, *Air Force Regulation 375–4, Department of the Air Force, Washington, D.C., Nov. 25, 1963. Progress information is reported in accordance with a procedure sometimes referred to as the Rainbow Reporting System. When initiated the Rainbow System required status information on cost, manpower, facilities, and technical performance, as well as schedule information. The system was called Rainbow because each type of information required was described on a card of a designated color, the assembled package being not unlike a rainbow.*

with the plan usually is reported for two time periods: (1) milestones scheduled to occur in the current fiscal year and (2) milestones scheduled to be completed during the current month.

A chart showing selected milestones for our hypothetical missile system is presented in Figure 32-4. The milestones are designated by their event number as given in Table 32-1 and are for the current year. The project status is shown as of April 30, 1966. On that date five milestones had been completed on schedule. The milestones for event 16 (missile transportation vehicle fabrication completed) was completed two months behind schedule. Also, it was anticipated that event 19 (emplacement equipment fabrication completed) would not be completed by August as scheduled, but would lag a month; thus it should be rescheduled to be completed in September. The remaining milestones are expected to be completed on schedule.

Collection and reliability of data. The method of collecting and organizing data is similar to that for the Gantt technique. Only the graphic presentation is different. Accordingly, the strengths and weaknesses of the milestone technique are very similar to those summarized in Table 32-2 for the Gantt technique. The milestone reporting system can be automated with relative ease. Data on changes in status can be read into a computer, which prints the required format depicting progress on the appropriate milestones. This innovation tends to reduce the costs of the system and also to improve the timeliness of the data.

III. THE LINE OF BALANCE TECHNIQUE (LOB)

Application to Production Operations

The line of balance technique (LOB) was developed to improve scheduling and status reporting in an ongoing production process. Essentially the technique consists of four elements:

1 The objective,
2 The program or production plan,
3 Measurement of progress, and
4 The line of balance.

The objective. The first step in scheduling production is to obtain the contract delivery

Event No.	Milestones	1965			1966												1967		
		O	N	D	J	F	M	A	M	J	J	A	S	O	N	D	J	F	M
12	Maintenance equipment fabrication completed			↑															
13	Training of operating personnel completed			↑															
14	Installation and checkout equipment fabrication completed				↑														
15	Missile erection equipment fabrication completed				↑														
16	Missile transportation vehicle fabrication completed					⇧		♦											
18	Missile fabrication completed										⇧								
19	Emplacement equipment fabrication completed											⇧	◊						
20	Preliminary checkout of installation and checkout equipment completed						↑												
21	Ground equipment fabrication completed								⇧	◊									
30	Site construction completed										⇧								
33	Missile installation completed																		⇧
35	First operational unit completed																		⇧

LEGEND

↑   Action completed on schedule (completed action)

♦   Action not completed on schedule (actual slippage)

◊   Anticipated delayed accomplishment of future action (anticipated slippage)

⇧   Scheduled (or rescheduled) action

Figure 32-4   Milestone chart applied to missile project.

schedule. The objective of the production operation is to meet a schedule based on cumulative deliveries. Figure 32-5*a* illustrates this *objective* as used in LOB. The chart shows the cumulative number of units scheduled to be delivered and the dates of delivery. The *contract schedule line* represents the cumulative quantity of units scheduled to be delivered over time.

The program.   The second step is to chart the *program*. The program, also called the production plan, comprises the stages in the producer's planned production process and consists, essentially, of key manufacturing and assembly operations sequenced in a logical production scheme over the time period required to complete. A sample program is presented in Figure 32-5*b*. Time is shown in working days remaining until each unit can be completed. Symbols and color schemes can be used to depict different types of activity, such as assembly, machining, purchasing of materials, etc.

Measurement of progress.   To illustrate the control function, let us assume that production has been in progress for a month. We are then able to measure the status of the components (units) in the various stages of completion.

Program progress data are obtained by taking a physical inventory of the quantities of materials, parts, or sub-assemblies that have passed through a series of control points in the production plan. The data are then plotted on a bar chart illustrated by Figure 32-5*c*. For example, if control point 15 in chart *b* were selected, the inventory might reveal that 29 units were completed on that date and hence 29 would be shown on the bar chart, which thus represents actual production progress.[12]

Line of balance.   The last step is to construct the line of balance, which represents the number of units that *should* pass through each control point at a given date if management can reasonably expect the objective, i.e., the delivery schedule, to be met.

The line of balance is constructed in the following manner:

1   Select a particular control point, for example, 15.[13]

[12] *The legend also utilizes shading in parts b and c to indicate the type of material or function involved. This assists in identifying general areas of responsibility.*

[13] *Actually one would probably start with the last control point (42) and work back through the project. For our purposes here control point 15 is of special interest in illustrating the usefulness of the technique.*

2 From the production plan (Figure 32-5*b*) determine the number of days required to complete a unit from the control point to the end of the production plan (i.e., 27 days).

3 Using this number determine the date the units should be completed. (October 29 plus 27 working days is December 8.)

4 Find the point corresponding to this completion date (December 8) on the contract schedule line and ascertain the number of units (35) that should be completed on that date if the delivery schedule is to be met.

5 Draw a line on the production progress chart (Figure 32-5*c*) at that level (35 units) and over the control point (15).

6 Repeat this procedure for each control point and connect the horizontal lines over the control points. The resulting line is the line of balance. It indicates the quantities of units that should have passed through each control point on the date of the study (October 30) if the delivery schedule is to be met.

The production progress chart shows the status of a program at a given point in time. Thus management can determine at a glance how actual progress compares with planned progress. Where actual progress lags planned progress, the variance can be traced to the individual control point(s).

In the example described above, it is evident that without management action the delivery schedule will not be met because several control points, including the last one, are behind schedule. By using both the production plan and the program progress chart, one can begin at the end control point (42) and trace back through the series to find the source of the delay. Working *backward*, we see that control point 37 is a critical point of delay. If 37 were on schedule, then it is quite likely that all the succeeding control points would be on schedule. In trying to determine why 37 is behind schedule, we see that control points 35, 31, and 30 are also behind schedule. Control point 35, however, is in series with 31 and is presumably held up because 31 is not on schedule, which in turn is held up because control point 30 is not on schedule. We note that the control points preceding operation 30 are on schedule and therefore assume that the difficulty probably lies within operation 30 itself. The initial difficulty, however, lies in the sequence of activities preceding operation 31, so that 31 is behind schedule because 15 is behind schedule. Thus control point 15 is the

bottleneck. It is reasonable to assume that with more management surveillance, and perhaps with more resources devoted to operations 15 and 30, operation 31 will be on schedule, and as a result so will 35, 37, 38, 39, 40, 41, and 42.

Application to Development Operations

Although LOB has been widely applied to production operations at the prime and associate contractor level, a variant of this technique can be used in the development stage of a weapon system where only one complete system, or a small number of complete systems, is to be produced. In this case, control of the quantity of items through a given point is not relevant as it is in production operations. Instead, monitoring of progress is directed toward major events, that is, the completion of significant activities in the development process. In our discussion, we assume the development of a single unit using the hypothetical missile system described in Sec. I.

As applied to the development phase, the four elements of the technique are essentially the same as those for production scheduling and control, but their composition is altered.

The objective. Instead of scheduling many units, the delivery schedule is based on the production of a single unit or on a limited number of units. The objectives chart will thus show the required percent completion of individual activities, rather than number of systems through each control point. Figure 32-6 illustrates this possible adaptation of LOB to the hypothetical development project.[14] Supporting data are given in Tables 32-3 and 32-4.

The scheduled starting date of the component begins in the appropriate week at a point on the abscissa representing zero percent completion. The scheduled completion date of each activity is represented in the appropriate week at a point on the abscissa which represents 100 percent completion. A straight line is drawn between these two points. This straight line assumes that the same rate of progress will occur throughout the activity period. If the scheduler has reason to doubt that progress will proceed at a constant rate, the line can

---

[14] *The list of activities has been condensed for purposes of illustration.*

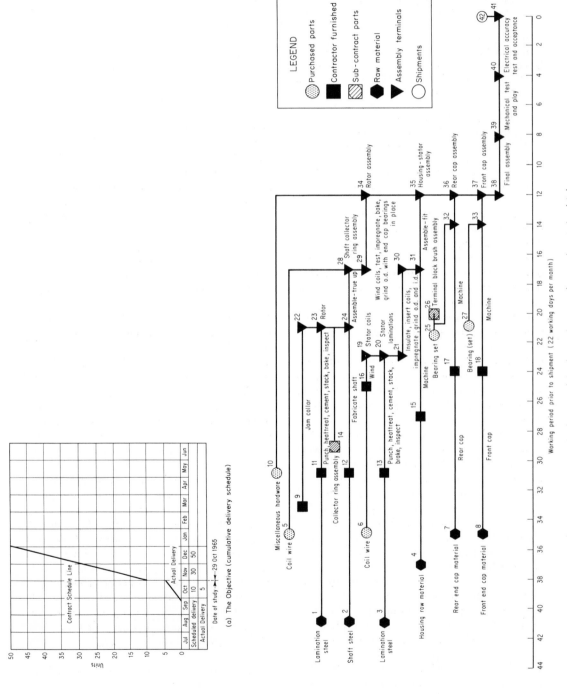

(a) The Objective (cumulative delivery schedule)

(b) The Program or Production Plan (showing major operations and control points)

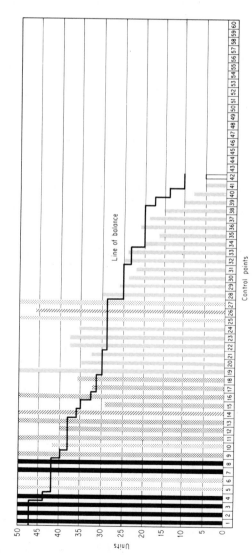

(c) Program Progress Data and Line of Balance (showing progress through major control points)

Figure 32–5   The line of balance technique.

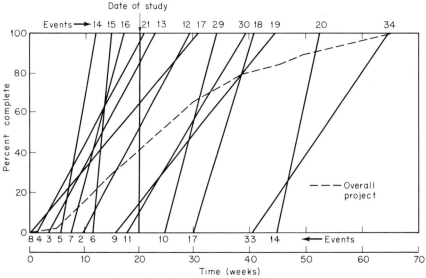

Figure 32-6   LOB prototype development objectives chart.

be drawn in any shape that management feels will correctly depict the expected progress.

Using the data in Table 32-4, an overall project objectives curve can be constructed as follows:

1 Summarize the weeks estimated to complete each activity and thus obtain the total activity-weeks of effort to be involved dur-

ing each incremental time period. (Computations were made for five-week intervals in the example.)

2 Compute the cumulative activity-weeks of planned effort through the end of each time period.

3 Compute the ratio of (1) over (2) for each time period. This ratio is the percent of the project planned to be completed at the respective points. The line connecting these

TABLE 32-3   SUPPORTING DATA FOR FIG. 32-6

Activity No.	Activities	Estimated Activity Time (weeks)	Scheduled Dates	
			Start	Complete
2-12	Fabricate maintenance equipment	19	10	29
3-13	Train operating personnel	19	4	23
4-21	Fabricate ground equipment	19	2	21
5-14	Fabricate installation and checkout equipment	6	6	12
6-15	Fabricate missile erection equipment	3	12	15
7-16	Fabricate missile transportation vehicle	9	8	17
8-17	Fabricate missile	30	0.2	30.2
9-19	Fabricate emplacement equipment	28	16	44
10-29	Train maintenance personnel	9	25	34
11-30	Construct launch site	21	18	35
14-20	Test installation and checkout equipment	7	45	52
17-18	Correct deficiencies in missile	10	30.2	40.2
33-34	Check out missile installation	24	40.6	64.6
Total		204	—	—

TABLE 32-4   DATA FOR OVERALL PROJECT OBJECTIVES CURVE

Time Period (Identified by Final Week)	Estimated Activity-Weeks Required During Period	Cumulative Activity-Weeks to Date	Percent of Planned Completion[a]
0	0	0	0
5	9	9	4.4
10	21	30	14.7
15	30	60	29.4
20	28	88	43.1
25	24	112	54.9
30	24	136	66.6
35	19	155	76.0
40	14	169	82.8
45	9	178	87.2
50	10	188	92.1
55	7	195	95.6
60	5	200	98.0
65	4	204	100.0

[a] Information in this column is basis for dotted line in Figure 32-6.

points is the overall project objectives curve. The completion date of the last activity should coincide with the completion date of the overall project.

The development plan.   A flow chart showing the development plan of the hypothetical missile system is given in Figure 32-7. Procedurally, the development plan chart is taken as a control point for the progress chart (see Figure 32-8). The development plan chart in our example does not show connections between the activities because only 13 activities out of the 34 given in Table 32-1 are included. If all 34 were shown, the activities would follow in sequence to the completed missile system.

Determination of progress.   There is no technique available to determine true overall program status where considerable uncertainty exists concerning completion dates. The origi-

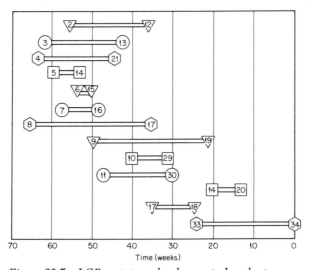

Figure 32-7   LOB prototype development plan chart.

nal estimated time to complete an activity, the length of time devoted to it to date and the current physical state of completion all may be known. However, the actual time required to complete it is not known and must be estimated by the responsible project engineer. The LOB technique for approximating the status of the program is as follows:

$$\text{Percent completion} = 1 - \frac{d}{A}$$

where d = the number of weeks required to complete a particular activity, and A = the gross number of weeks originally estimated for the entire project. As an example, suppose that the time originally required to complete the development phase was 10 weeks, that 8 weeks have already elapsed, and that the current estimate of the time to completion is 4 weeks. According to the LOB formula, the development phase is $100 (1 - (4/10)) = 60$ percent complete.

Two alternative techniques could also be used to estimate percent completion. For example, if it now appears that the total time required for the development phase is 12 weeks, when 4 weeks remain to completion one can consider that the development is actually 8/12 or 67 percent complete, and not 60 percent complete as revealed by the LOB formula.

A second alternative would be to place the 8 actual weeks of effort over the original time estimate (10 weeks); this would indicate that the phase was 80 percent complete.

While the major reference material on LOB discusses the second alternative, it selects the basic LOB technique as the preferable one because "while the prescribed method requires one additional mathematical step, it helps compensate for inaccuracies in the initial estimate of time required for the entire phase."[15] However, in some respects the first alternative appears to be the most realistic because it is based on current information rather than on the original estimate.

On the other hand, it is obvious that no simple algorithm alone can be expected to solve the problem of precisely determining the actual percent completion of a complex project.

The procedure recommended in the LOB technique is applied to our hypothetical missile system in Table 32-5, and the program progress is shown in Figure 32-8. (Control points are the ending events for the activities.)

To determine total project status, sum the estimated weeks required to complete each activity (d), and divide by the total number of weeks originally estimated to be required for the entire project (A). This gives the percentage not completed ($d \div A$). Subtract the percentage not completed from 100 percent, and the result is the percentage of the total project completed $[1 - (d/A)]$.

[15] Line of Balance Technology, *op. cit., p. 19.*

TABLE 32-5 SUPPORTING COMPUTATIONS FOR FIGURE 32-8 (PERCENT COMPLETION: 20TH WEEK)

Activity No.	Activities	d	A	$1 - (d/A)$
2-12	Fabricate maintenance equipment	12	19	37
3-13	Train operating personnel	4	19	79
4-21	Fabricate ground equipment	4	19	79
5-14	Fabricate installation and checkout equipment	0	6	100
6-15	Fabricate missile erection equipment	0	3	100
7-16	Fabricate missile transportation vehicle	0	9	100
8-17	Fabricate missile	11	30	63
9-19	Fabricate emplacement equipment	24	28	14
10-29	Train maintenance personnel	9	9	0
11-30	Construct launch site	17	21	19
14-20	Test installation and checkout equipment	7	7	0
17-18	Correct deficiencies in missile	10	10	0
33-34	Check out missile installation	24	24	0
Total		122	204	40

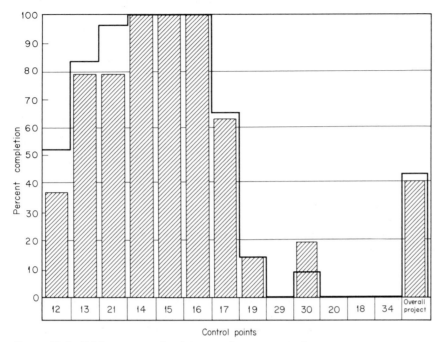

Figure 32-8   LOB prototype development phase progress chart.

In the example (Table 32-5), the total activity-weeks originally estimated were 204. In the 20th week of the project, it is estimated that 122 activity-weeks will be needed to complete the project. Accordingly, the estimated percentage of the overall project completed is $1 - (122/204) = 40$ percent.

Although the LOB technique does not provide any sophisticated way of guiding personnel in the process of estimating time remaining to complete a project, one method frequently used by schedulers is to divide a major phase into a number of individual technical tasks and then relate the number completed to the total. However, such a method has the limitation of assuming that all tasks are of equal difficulty. An alternative, of course, is for the estimator to draw more generally on his own experience in determining estimated time to completion.

The line of balance.   An additional step is necessary to complete the analysis of program progress. That step is "striking the LOB." On the objectives chart (Figure 32-6), construct a vertical line perpendicular to the abscissa at the date of the study. This vertical line will intersect several, if not all, of the percent completion lines for the individual events at a point representing their currently scheduled completion status. Then draw a horizontal line at the percent completion point on the progress chart (Figure 32-8), above the respective events. Thus, both the scheduled status and the actual status of the events and of the overall project are shown for the date of the study. Notice that in the development phase, the line of balance does not necessarily descend continuously in a stepwise fashion as it must in the production plan.

Evaluation of LOB Technique

The LOB technique, like the Gantt technique, was originally designed for production operations. The Gantt technique focused on providing management with information relating to the efficient utilization of resources. Machine and manpower inputs to the production process were emphasized. On the other hand, the LOB technique is *product* oriented. Its information centers on the extent to which the planned production of a quantity of items is actually being realized. It is not directly concerned with the efficient utilization of resources. Its key usefulness is that bottlenecks in the production process are emphasized.

Management must then take appropriate action, generally increasing the level of resources at these bottlenecks. Consequently, Gantt and LOB are complementary techniques.

The LOB technique has some applicability in prototype development when a limited number of components, or operations, are to be controlled. The LOB development plan chart is capable of depicting interrelationships, although seldom is the effort made to include all such relationships.

The LOB technique has several limitations. The inability to precisely state the percent completion of components is one area that can

lead to weakened managerial control of the project.

In addition, if management wishes to examine the impact of alternative approaches to overcoming a bottleneck, the LOB affords no simulation capability for this purpose. The determination of the time to complete a component is left up to the judgment of an engineer, and LOB is silent as to how this estimate should be made. Consequently, inconsistencies occur and reliability is impaired. Finally, the technique is rather inflexible. If there is a change in the development plan, the entire chart system may need to be reconstructed; the

TABLE 32-6   LOB TECHNIQUE—STRENGTHS AND WEAKNESSES

Criteria	Strengths	Weaknesses
1. *Validity*	Uncertainties surrounding completion times in production operations are minimal; consequently LOB affords management a sound technique for judging status of operations.	Uncertainties encountered in the development phase impair judgment on actual project status. The techniques for estimation of percent completion can lead to erroneous decisions concerning project development.
2. *Reliability*	Compares favorably with Gantt technique.	
3. *Implementation*	Only slightly more difficult to comprehend and to implement than Gantt technique.	
4. *Universality of project coverage*	Capable of covering a system life cycle.	Does not emphasize resource allocation directly.
5. *Sensitivity testing (simulation)*		No significant capability for simulating alternative courses of action.
6. *Forecasting*	Depicts status of project well in production stage and can forecast whether or not schedule will be met.	Offers no technique to handle uncertainty in development phase.
7. *Updating*		Considerable clerical effort required to update graphs.
8. *Flexibility*		Inflexible. When major program changes occur, the entire set of graphs must be redrawn.
9. *Cost*	Data gathering and computations can be handled routinely. Expense is moderate and largely for clerical personnel and chart materials.	Charts require frequent reconstruction, which is time-consuming.

NOTE: Recall that this table is intended only as a summary of certain qualitative information on the relative usefulness of the scheduling technique. As indicated previously, a more formal quantitative evaluation of the extent to which the criteria are met was considered infeasible in this study.

up-dating of program progress requires extensive chart changes. Table 32-6 further identifies the strengths and weaknesses of the LOB technique.

IV. THE CRITICAL PATH METHOD (CPM)

Application of CPM[16]

The critical path method (CPM) was the first technique designed specifically for complex, one-of-a-kind operations. Although initially used to plan and control the construction of facilities, it applies equally well to development of new weapon systems and is designed to interrelate diverse activities and explicitly depict important interdependencies. The construction of a chemical plant, for example, requires coordination of numerous functions and activities. A well-coordinated construction schedule can shorten the project by months and thereby significantly reduce project costs. The CPM technique utilizes a network approach and a limited time-cost trade-off capability for organizing data on these types of interactions. Accordingly, the basic elements in CPM are:

1 The flow diagram or network,
2 Critical time paths,
3 Float (scheduling leeway), and
4 The time-cost function.

Network. The development of a network or flow diagram that embraces all events and activities and explicitly recognizes major known interdependencies among activities is an important element in the CPM. It is based on the following simple concepts:

1 An activity (or job) is depicted by an arrow:

2 Each arrow is identified by an activity description:

develop engine

---

16 *The basic development is attributable to M. R. Walker who was with the Engineering Service Division of E. I. DuPont De Nemours & Company Inc., and J. E. Kelley, Jr., Remington Rand Univac (now Sperry Rand Corporation).*

3 A sequence of activities is indicated by linking arrows:

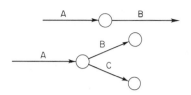

4 Events link activities:

An event occurs at a point in time and signifies either the start or completion of an activity.

5 A grouping of activities and events forms a network. Networks may be either activity- or event-oriented. In activity-oriented networks, the activities (arrows) are labeled; in event-oriented networks, the events (circles, or other symbols) are labeled:

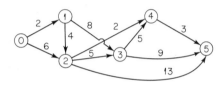

There are certain rules to follow in constructing a network; e.g., no looping is allowed:

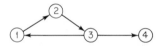

Looping indicates not only that event 1 must be completed before event 2, and event 2 before event 3, but also that event 3 must be completed before event 1. It is logically not possible to require the start of a preceding event that depends on completion of a succeeding event.

6 The length of an arrow has no significance; it merely identifies the direction of work flow. Also, time estimates which are secured for activities represent elapsed or flow time and are not identified—at least initially—with calendar dates.[17]

The critical time paths. In a complex project, involving multiple activities and events,

---

17 *The distinction between flow time and calendar (or scheduled) time will be clarified further under the subsequent section on the PERT system.*

sequences or paths of activities can be identified. These paths vary in length according to the time required to accomplish the component activities. The path or paths requiring the longest time are called the critical paths. When a critical path has been determined, management is advised to devote resources to those activities along this path in an effort to reduce the time requirement and thus shorten the overall program. Of course, as one critical path is shortened, another eventually becomes critical.

Float.   Some leeway exists in scheduling activities not on a critical path. This leeway is called float. The technique for determining float is as follows:

Starting at the beginning of the network, determine the *earliest occurrence time for each event in the program.* Since the first event (which has no preceding activities) must occur before any succeeding activities can begin, assign it an earliest occurrence time (*ES*) of zero. Add to this time the duration of the activity leading to the next event; this yields the *ES* for that succeeding event. If several activities lead to a given event, then its *ES* is the highest value obtained by adding the duration of each predecessor activity to the *ES* of the activity's beginning event. *Thus when an event is a part of two or more paths, the longest path to the event must be completed before any subsequent activities can be started.* Continue the process until the final event has been reached; its *ES* becomes the earliest completion time for the project.

To determine the latest occurrence time (LC) for each event, begin with the time estimate for the completed project, obtained from the *ES* procedure above, and assign this as the *LC* for the final event. Then subtract from this the time duration of the immediate predecessor activity to obtain the *LC* for the activity's beginning event. If an event has several succeeding activities, its *LC* is taken as the smallest value obtained by subtracting the duration of each of these activities from the *LC* of its ending event. In this manner calculate the *LC* for each event, starting at the *end* of the network and working backward along activity paths until the beginning event is reached, which will have *LC* = 0.

If for each event both the earliest and the latest occurrence time are available, the float or leeway in scheduling each event can be readily calculated. Those events and activities with zero float are necessarily on the critical path.

The actual procedure for computing float is as follows: Let i = an event signifying the origin of an activity, let j = an event signifying the termination of the activity, and Y_{ij} = the activity time duration. Note that an activity's earliest start time (ES_{ij}) equals ES_i, the earliest occurrence time of event i; and the activity's latest completion time (LC_{ij}) equals LC_j, the latest occurrence time of event j.

Construct a matrix by entering the Y_{ij} for each activity in the proper cell. For example, using the network shown in item 5 above, a matrix can be constructed as follows:

ES	i \ j	1	2	3	4	5
0	0	2	6	-	-	-
2	1	-	4	8	-	-
6	2	-	-	5	2	13
11	3	-	-	-	5	9
16	4	-	-	-	-	3
20						

0	2	6	11	17	20	LC

Computing Earliest Occurrence Time. The procedure for computing earliest occurrence time (*ES*) is as follows:

1 Enter a zero in the first cell of the *ES* column, which represents the starting time of the project.
2 Add the corresponding values of Y_{ij} to the *ES* values column by column. In our example, $ES_0 = 0$ and $Y_{01} = 2$; hence $0 + 2 = 2$, and we enter 2 in the *ES* column below the zero, indicating that 2 weeks are required before the activities immediately after event 1 can be started.
3 Continue this procedure for each column. For example, the values in column 2 of the matrix are 6 weeks and 4 weeks. The corresponding values in the *ES* column are 0 and 2 weeks. Adding $6 + 0 = 6$ and $4 + 2 = 6$, we see that by either path it will be 6 weeks before event 2 can occur. Consequently, we enter 6 in the *ES* column opposite event 2.
4 Where different times result from this summation process, select the *longest* time

(path) and enter that number in the *ES* column. For example, column 3 of the matrix has Y_{ij} values of 8 and 5; the corresponding *ES* values are 2 and 6. By adding $8 + 2 = 10$ and $5 + 6 = 11$, we see that 11 is the longest time path and place it in the *ES* column.

Computing Latest Occurrence Time. The procedure for computing latest occurrence time (*LC*) is as follows:

1 Enter the longest time path in the project (i.e., 20 weeks, taken from the last cell in the *ES* column) in the last cell of the *LC* row.
2 Subtract the corresponding values of Y_{ij} from the *LC* values row by row. In our example, $LC_5 = 20$, and $Y_{45} = 3$; hence $20 - 3 = 17$, and we enter 17 in the *LC* row to the left of the 20 weeks. This means that event 4 must occur by the seventeenth week if the project is to be completed in 20 weeks. Continue this procedure for each row.
3 Where different times result from the subtraction process, select the *shortest* time (path) and enter that number in the *LS* row. For example, row 3 of the matrix has Y_{ij} values of 5 and 9; the corresponding *LC* values are 17 and 20. By subtracting $17 - 5 = 12$ and $20 - 9 = 11$, we see that the shortest time path is 11 and enter that number in the *LC* row.
4 The last entry in the *LC* row should be a zero, corresponding to the zero in the first cell of the *ES* column.

Identifying Events on the Critical Path. Every event that has an equal *ES* and *LC* time is on the critical path. In our example, event 1 has an *ES* of 2 and an *LC* of 2; hence it is on the critical path. Event 4 has an *ES* of 16 and an *LC* of 17; hence it is not on the critical path. Accordingly, the critical path includes events 0, 1, 2, 3, and 5.

Identifying Total Float. Total float for an activity is the amount of time available for an activity less the amount of estimated time required to complete the activity. In our example, total float for an activity equals $(LC_j - ES_i) - Y_{ij}$. Thus, for event 3, $LC_3 = 11$; $ES_1 = 2$; $Y_{13} = 8$; hence $(11 - 2) - 8 = 1$ week of float.

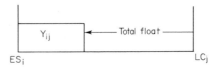

Other Types of Float: Free, Interfering, and Independent. It may be desirable to know how much a preceding activity may be delayed (if at all) without interfering with the earliest start of the succeeding activity. This is called *free* float. At this point, it is necessary to introduce data on an activity's completion time (EC_{ij}). EC_{ij} is derived by adding the estimated time required for an activity (Y_{ij}) to the activity's earliest start time (ES_{ij}). To compute free float: Let ES_{12}, EC_{12}, LC_{12}, and Y_{12} apply to the preceding activity and let ES_{23}, LC_{23}, and Y_{23} apply to the succeeding activity. Then $ES_{23} - (EC_{12} + Y_{12}) =$ free float for activity 1-2.

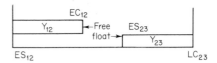

Interfering float is total float minus free float. The concept also can be presented in a diagram. For example, any delay in activity 1-2 beyond the *ES* date of activity 2-3 will delay or interfere with activity 2-3. Hence, part of the total float for activity 1-2 is free float ($ES_{23} - EC_{12}$) and the remainder is interfering float ($LC_{12} - ES_{23}$).

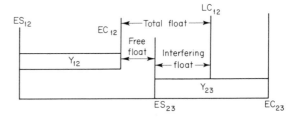

Independent float is computed as $ES_{34} - LC_{12} - Y_{23}$. For example, if all activities prior to activity 2-3 are completed by the LC_{12} date, and all activities succeeding activity 2-3 are started at the ES_{34} date, then $ES_{34} - LC_{12}$ is the amount of time available to perform activity 2-3. Subtracting the actual time required to perform the activity from the available time gives the independent float; i.e., the activity can be displaced forward or backward within this time interval without interfering with any other event.

Time-Cost function.

The contribution to system management embodied in the CPM does not end with the time parameter. It also provides a technique to aid management in making time-cost trade-off decisions.

The technique is quite simple, requiring only four estimates: (1) normal activity time, (2) normal activity costs, (3) activity times on a "crash" basis, and (4) cost on a "crash" basis. These estimates are based on the principle of the time-cost curve, illustrated in Figure 32–9.

In this example, the normal activity time estimate would be six weeks and the cost estimate would be $10,000. On a crash basis, the activity time would be four weeks and the cost $20,000. A simple assumption would be that cost and time are related inversely and linearly (i.e., for each reduction in time there will be a corresponding increment of added cost). For example, according to Figure 32-9, shortening the time by one week (from six to five) would cost $5,000. The decision-maker can compare the costs of shortening the schedule by allocating additional resources to an activity (or activities) on the critical path for which marginal cost is less than for any other activity. Thus the time required on any path can be shortened at least cost. Assumptions other than an inverse linear relationship can also be introduced by properly reflecting them in the shape of the time-cost curve.

The task of calculating these time-cost trade-offs can be quite formidable to accomplish

manually if the project becomes even moderately complex. A computer program assuming linear time-cost relationships has been developed that will automatically schedule the project for the least cost activities. This computer routine requires at least the two time-cost data points—i.e., assuming normal and crash programs for each activity. Non-linear assumptions are more difficult to treat in large projects.

It is not the purpose of this Memorandum to explore time-cost relationships; however, this mechanism is usually considered a component of CPM and should be mentioned when comparing CPM with PERT.[18]

Application to the Model

The CPM can be applied to the hypothetical missile system described in Sec. II. Figure 32-10 represents the planned sequence of activities in network form. The numbered circles correspond to the events in Table 32-1. Note that interdependencies are depicted in the network. For example, event 3 must occur before event 20 can be completed. Such interdependencies can be readily ascertained from the CPM network but would not be clearly evident in a tree diagram or in a Gantt or milestone chart.

It could be argued that engineers responsible for development are usually aware of these interrelationships when the Gantt chart is used, and nothing is gained by the network presentation. This may indeed be the case in simple or small-scale projects. However, when a number of managers are involved in planning and measuring the progress of a complex system, they may not be aware of the effect of interdependencies beyond their immediate sphere of interest. It is possible that a subcontractor

[18] *Several scheduling techniques have since been expanded to incorporate cost considerations, e.g., PERT-Cost, RAMPS, SPAR, etc. See especially PERT-Cost System Description Manual, vol. 3, U.S. Air Force, December 1963; Jack Moshman, Jacob Johnson, and Madalyn Larsen, RAMPS—A Technique for Resource Allocation and Multi-Project Scheduling, Proceedings 1963 Spring Joint Computer Conference; and J. D. Wiest, The Scheduling of Large Projects with Limited Resources, Research Memorandum No. 113, Graduate School of Industrial Administration, Carnegie Institute of Technology, Pittsburgh, 1963.*

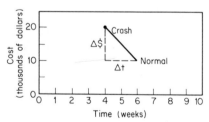

Figure 32-9 CPM time-cost trade-off.

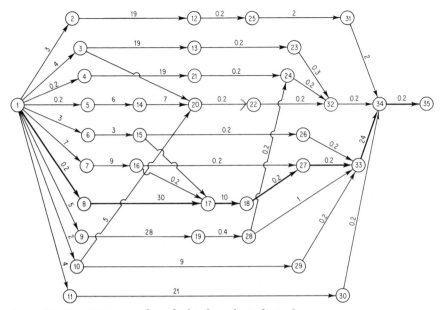

Figure 32–10   CPM network applied to hypothetical missile system.

may be well aware of those relationships within his control, and yet not realize that his schedule is in jeopardy because another department will not be able to deliver its portion of the project on time, or, conversely, that a component he is developing may, if not completed on time, retard another subcontractor and hence the entire project. In making the relationships explicit, the network serves as a communications device to ensure that all parties concerned are aware of the overall plan and their responsibilities in view of the plan.

The problem of keeping the planning and control information system attuned to actual development operations is common to all managerial techniques. A major advantage of the network-type presentation is that it enables the manager to cumulate the activity times along a given path to determine the total estimated time per path. The longest time path is the critical path. In Figure 32-10, for example, the longest time path is 64.8 weeks and is composed of events 1, 8, 17, 18, 27, 33, 34, and 35. All other paths are estimated to be completed in less time. If the tasks are scheduled to take the estimated time, then all paths other than this critical path contain float. Any path on which estimated completion time is greater than, or equal to, the time remaining before a scheduled project completion date is called critical. Hence, there may exist *the* most criti-

cal path, the *second* most critical, etc. In Figure 32-10, events 1, 9, 19, 28, 33, 34, and 35 would comprise the second most critical path (58.6 weeks).

Table 32-7 presents the matrix of task times needed to compute the *ES* and *LC* times for each activity in our hypothetical missile system. For example, activity 14-20 has an earliest start time of 6.2 weeks from the beginning of the project. It must be completed in the 64th week or the activity will "float" the succeeding activity beyond the project completion date. Thus we can compute the various float concepts for activity 14-20:[19]

1 Total float
$$= (LC_{20} - ES_{14}) - Y_{14-20}$$
$$= (64 - 6.2) - 7 = 50.8$$
2 Free float
$$= ES_{20-22} - (ES_{14-20} + Y_{14-20})$$
$$= 13.2 - (6.2 + 7) = 0.$$
3 Independent float
$$= (ES_{20-22} - LC_{5-14}) - Y_{14-20}$$
$$= (13.2 - 57) - 7 = -50.8$$

[19] *For clarity, and to be consistent with the explanation on pages 40–41, LC and ES values are identified by the appropriate activity designator which in turn is composed of both the starting and ending event numbers. Technically, however, ES can be fully defined by the starting event and LC by the ending event number.*

TABLE 32-7

j \ i	1	2	3	4	5	6	7	8	9	10	11	12	13	14	15	16	17	18	19	20	21	22	23	24	25	26	27	28	29	30	31	32	33	34	35
1	0																																		
2		3	4	0.2	0.2	3	7	0.2	5	2	4	19	19								19														
3														6						5															
4															3																				
5																9			28									0.4							
6																	30										0.2								
7																				5						0.2	0.2								
8																		10							0.2				9	21					
9																	0.4			7				0.2											
10																	0.2						0.2									0.2			
11																						0.2										0.3			
12																								0.2							2	0.2			
13																																	0.4		
14																																	0.2	0.2	
15																																	1	2	
16																																	0.2	0.2	
17																																		24	
18																																			0.2
ES	0	3	4	0.2	0.2	3	7	0.2	5	2	4	22	23	6.2	6	16	30.2	40.2	33	13.2	19.2	13.4	23.2	33.6	22.2	6.2	40.4	33.4	11	25	24.2	33.8	40.6	64.6	64.8
LC	0	41.4	44.9	45	51	26.8	21	0.2	11.2	31.4	43.4	60.4	3.9	57	29.8	30	30.2	40.2	39.2	64	64	64.2	64.1	64.2	60.6	40.2	40.4	39.6	40.4	64.4	62.6	64.4	40.6	64.6	64.8

1 *Total float.* Assuming that there are no project changes, and that activity 14-20 is started at the earliest possible date and completed at the earliest possible time, 50.8 weeks will elapse before activity 20-22 will have to be started. Consequently, freedom exists to allocate resources to other more critical tasks up to a maximum of 50.8 weeks before the scheduled completion of activity 14-20 is jeopardized.

2 *Free float.* If activity 20-22 were to start on the earliest possible date, no freedom would exist to allocate resources to other tasks. In other words, there would be no free float in the scheduling of activity 14-20. As mentioned previously, total float can be subdivided into free float and interfering float. Interfering float would delay (interfere with) the start of the subsequent activity (20-22) beyond the earliest start date. In the above example, all of the float for activity 14-20 is interfering.[20]

3 *Independent float.* In the illustration a negative value (--50.8) was obtained and therefore there is no independent float. This negative statistic does indicate that there would be no time available to perform activity 14-20 if the prior activity (5-14) were delayed until its latest completion date and if scheduling the subsequent activity (20-22) on its earliest start date was contemplated. In fact, the latest completion date for activity 5-14 significantly postdates the earliest start date for activity 20-22. This, of course, is of no real concern here because the earliest start date of activity 20-22 (also identified by LC_{20}) can be delayed substantially without jeopardizing project completion. In other words, total float exists, but independent float, being a very restrictive concept, does not in this case.

Evaluation of CPM

The network concept of CPM is an excellent device for explicitly depicting significant interrelationships among events. The flow of all activities is on paper so that those concerned can analyze the work plan and approve or disapprove it. Communication of planned activity is thus facilitated.

Since time estimates lead to the determination of a critical path, the attention of management is focused on the activities along the path so that resources can be applied to them, perhaps by reallocation from other activities where float exists.

One criticism of CPM is that emphasis on critical path activities may obscure the fact that some activities on a second path may be very close to being critical and would become so with slight changes in values. However, this possibility can be alleviated by determining the first most critical path, the second most critical path, etc., and *then* determining the critical activities within this broader context.

The time-cost function, although not fully implemented in actual systems, can provide trade-off information on the relative cost of reducing scheduled time in various activities. This trade-off feature linking cost and schedule is beyond the scope of this study but nevertheless is an important element of the CPM method.

CPM does not provide a capability for handling schedule uncertainty. For example, the development of a component may involve a major engineering improvement, and there may be considerable uncertainty regarding the time required for its accomplishment. In CPM, the responsible individual must provide management with his single best estimate of the time requirement. He may not reflect his uncertainty in terms of a range of estimates. The single value is incorporated into the network and the critical path determined. If the estimate is in error, then the critical path may be incorrectly drawn.

The strengths and weaknesses of CPM are summarized in Table 32-8.

V. PROGRAM EVALUATION AND REVIEW TECHNIQUE (PERT)

PERT Methodology

The program evaluation and review technique (PERT)[21] was formulated at approximately the same time as the critical path method (CPM). Like CPM, PERT is designed for scheduling activities in the development phase and is not directly suitable for application to repetitive

---

[20] *If these resources were allocated, it would be at the cost of delaying the start of task 20–22. This may, nevertheless, be a wise decision since activity 20–22 may be delayed a maximum of 50.8 weeks and the project can still be on schedule.*

[21] *PERT was developed by C. E. Clark, W. Fazar, D. G. Malcolm, and J. H. Roseboom, working with the management consulting firm of Booz, Allen and Hamilton, the Navy Bureau of Ordnance, and Lockheed Corporation.*

TABLE 32-8   CPM TECHNIQUES—STRENGTHS AND WEAKNESSES

Criteria	Strengths	Weaknesses
1. *Validity*		No formula is provided to estimate time to completion; consequently, the technique is as valid as the estimator. The margin of error is generally less in construction than in development.
2. *Reliability*		Numerous estimates in a large project, each with some unreliability may lead to significant errors in judging project status.
3. *Implementation*		Relatively difficult to explain, especially if the various concepts of float are utilized.
4. *Universality of project coverage*	Very good for single-shot activities, such as construction or development projects.	Weak in the production phase of a weapon life cycle. The technique is not well adapted to scheduling production quantities.
5. *Sensitivity testing (simulation)*	Excellent for simulating alternative plans, especially when coupled with the time-cost aspect.	
6. *Forecasting*	Strongly oriented to forecasting ability to accomplish future events on schedule.	
7. *Updating*	Good capability. Activities are clearly identified and time estimates can be obtained as needed.	
8. *Flexibility*	Portions of the network can be easily changed to reflect program changes.	
9. *Cost*		Considerable data are required to use CPM as both a planning and status reporting tool and a computer is almost invariably required. Therefore, the cost outlay can be fairly extensive.

NOTE: Recall that this table is intended only as a summary of certain qualitative information on the relative usefulness of the scheduling technique. As indicated previously, a more formal quantitative evaluation of the extent to which the criteria are met was considered infeasible in this study.

production operations. Both CPM and PERT are based on the network concept; both identify a critical path; both isolate float or slack. CPM, however, pioneered simple time-cost trade-off relationships. PERT, on the other hand, used a more sophisticated approach to the problem of treating schedule uncertainties.

Since the events, activities, and network concepts embodied in PERT are the same as those described for CPM, our discussion of PERT will cover only the major differences between the two techniques.

The PERT planning phase: estimated time. It is essential in the PERT planning process to secure estimates of the amount of time required to complete each activity. PERT recommends that three estimates be obtained rather than a single point estimate:

1 *Optimistic time, a,* (only 1 percent of the time would the activity be completed more quickly),[*]

[*] *This 1 percent requirement is frequently relaxed in practice.*

2 *Most likely time, m* (mode),
3 *Pessimistic time, b,* (only 1 percent of the time would more time be required).[22]

This estimating method has the following advantages. First, estimators usually make more valid estimates if they can express the extent of their uncertainty. Range-of-time estimates are more realistic and informative than a single point estimate. They are particularly worthwhile assuming that the burden of preparation does not become excessive.

Second, a single point estimate is likely to be the mode. In estimating activity time, the mean is generally considered a more representative statistic than the mode. It more nearly represents all possible values in the time distribution because it is based on all the information relative to the distribution, rather than being merely the most frequent single estimate.

The beta (β) distribution is used in the PERT estimation process.[23] A formula approximating the mean of the distribution, called the expected time (t_e), can be derived based on the three time estimates and the beta distribution. For example:

$$t_e = \frac{a + 4m + b}{6}$$

Letting $a = 5$ months, $m = 7$ months, and $b = 15$ months, we obtain

$$\frac{a + 4m + b}{6} = \frac{5 + 4(7) + 15}{6} = \frac{48}{6} = 8 \text{ months}$$

Note that the midpoint of the range is $(15 + 5) \div 2 = 10$ months. The mode is 7 months. The mean (t_e) is 8 months. The mean lies one-third of the distance from the mode to the midpoint of the range.

The critical path.   After the expected time has been determined for each activity in the network, it is possible to compute the critical path, which is simply the longest path of expected times in the network. When more than one time path leads into an event, the longest time path leading into that event establishes the expected time for the event.

Calendar time.   The scheduler is now ready to schedule the start and the completion of each activity, based on the expected time estimates. Several concepts have been developed to aid management in monitoring progress and allocating resources to the activities. The first is that of the earliest expected occurrence date of an event (T_E). Normally, the start of a project is associated with a specific calendar date, and then the elapsed time for an activity is added to that date to determine the calendar date of the next event. This procedure is followed for every event on the PERT network. In working from the start to the end of the project—i.e., the forward pass—the expected earliest occurrence dates for each event can be determined.

After the earliest completion date has been established for the end item in the project, the latest allowable occurrence date (T_L) for each event can be determined by proceeding backward—the backward pass—from the earliest completion date,[24] *or from a promised due date,* and subtracting expected times. The T_L represents the latest date that an event can occur and not jeopardize the project completion date.[25]

It is now possible to determine the amount of *slack* in the project. Slack is the time flexibility available to management in scheduling resources to a given activity and is defined as $T_L - T_E$. If T_L is later than T_E, then positive slack exists and management has some freedom in scheduling the event. If T_L is earlier than T_E, negative slack exists and completion of the project is in jeopardy. The path with the most negative slack, or the least positive slack if there is no negative slack, is necessarily the longest time path—the critical path.

---

[22] *This 1 percent requirement is frequently relaxed in practice.*
[23] *The beta distribution has two interesting characteristics: (1) The range precisely equals six standard deviations (i.e., the "tails" of the distribution do not approach infinity), and (2) using the PERT approximation, the mean of the distribution lies one-third of the distance from the mode to the midpoint of the range. Also, in practice the skewness of activities tends to be toward the right.*

[24] *If the earliest completion date is used as the project completion date (due date) in performing the backward pass, earliest and latest completion dates will be identical for events on the critical path.*
[25] T_E and T_L correspond to the ES and LC measures for events in Sec. IV. A different symbol has been selected to emphasize that the event occurrence times in the PERT model are probabilistic measures—the sum of expected activity duration times.

Negative slack should not exist in the planning phase of a project. If the T_E and T_L were computed as described above, negative slack could not exist, and the critical path would contain, at a minimum, zero slack. Frequently, however, under pressure from the customer or in eagerness to obtain a contract, a contractor will agree to complete a project in less time than is indicated by the preliminary estimates.[26] This directed completion date is then entered on the calendar as the scheduled completion date (T_S) and, in the backward pass, new T_L dates are computed based on the directed date. Thus, negative slack may exist.

Negative slack must be remedied in one of two ways if management expects to complete the project on schedule. First a portion of the resources can be withdrawn from noncritical activities and allotted to critical activities. This, of course, implies that such resources—i.e., skills, equipment, or facilities—are transferable. Second, management can increase the overall level of resources devoted to the project.

From a project management standpoint, an ideal situation would exist if there were zero slack on all activities. Adequate resources would then be optimally allocated, given the completion date of the program.[27]

After analysis of possible trade-offs of resources, acceptable scheduled completion dates (T_S) can be determined and the activities scheduled. As one might suspect, in general T_S should occur between T_E and T_L.

The PERT operating phase.   The acceptance by management of the T_S means the acceptance of a plan of action and the end of the initial PERT planning phase. The authorization of work to be performed as scheduled begins the PERT operating phase. Essentially, this phase involves reporting program status and acting on this information. The following information is reported during the operating phase:

1 Completed activities and their completion dates.

2 Changes in activity time estimates.
3 Changes in schedule.
4 Event and activity additions and deletions.

Input data are prepared and computer printouts of status are distributed periodically (generally every two weeks) to the appropriate levels of management.

The PERT-Time system cycle, with the interrelationships between the planning and the operating phases, is shown in Figure 32-11.

Various types of data are contained in the PERT system. Thus far, the most important use of operating data for control purposes appears to be through the analysis of slack. The amount of slack (often negative) is charted periodically so that management can follow the trend from week to week. Normally, with good control the amount of negative slack on a path should decrease over time. This decrease is generally attributable either to greater management attention to activities on that path or, as described below, to the lessening of uncertainty concerning completion times.

The standard deviation (σ) of an activity. By using three time estimates for each activity, the scheduler can apply probability theory in determining uncertainty in scheduling activities. Assuming that the beta distribution is a valid representation of the distribution of the estimates, the standard deviation for an activity can be approximated by the following equation:

$$\sigma = \frac{b - a}{6}$$

thus the range $(b - a)$ is six times the standard deviation.

To illustrate the standard deviation of an activity, let $a = 10$ months, $m = 13$ months, and $b = 16$ months. Then

$$t_e = \frac{10 + 4(13) + 16}{6} = 13$$

$$\sigma = \frac{(16 - 10)}{6} = 1$$

A common interpretation of this statistic is that a 67 percent chance (67 out of 100 times) exists that the activity will be completed within one standard deviation (12th and 14th months); a 95 percent chance between 2σ of the mean (11th and 15th months); and a 99 percent

---

[26] *It also should be noted that such estimates usually are made with a specified level of funding in mind and are subject to modification if the anticipated funding level is revised.*

[27] *This assumes that the cost-time relationship for individual activities is a continuously decreasing function to the right, as illustrated in part in Figure 32-9.*

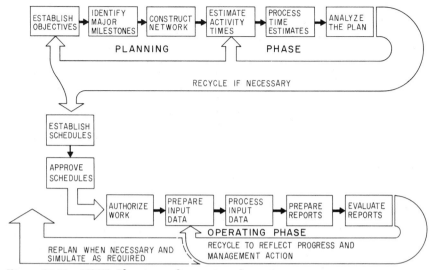

Figure 32-11   PERT: Planning and operating phases.[28]

chance between 3σ of the mean (10th and 16th months). This interpretation is misleading because the above applies to a normal, and not to a beta distribution. Depending on the skewness of the beta distribution one σ from the mean may contain considerably more or less than 67 percent of the observations. The σ has no inherent meaning in quantifying uncertainty for an individual activity; however it is used to compute the σ of an event which is described in the following subsection.

Probability of meeting scheduled date or of having positive slack.   The probability of meeting the scheduled date or, alternatively, of having positive slack can be determined by using the concepts of slack and standard deviation of an activity. While this probability statistic can be computed for any event in the project, the *ending* event is used in the following example.

First, compute the length of the longest path leading into any specific event (T_E), and then compute the standard deviation of that event's earliest occurrence time (σT_E). The σT_E is defined as the square root of the sum of the activity standard deviations squared (σ^2), i.e., the variances of the activities lying on the longest time path leading into that event. Here the

event time (path length) is generally assumed to be normally distributed,[29] not beta distributed. The probability of meeting the scheduled date can then be determined by using tables of the areas under the normal curve.[30] The formula for this normalized statistic is

$$\frac{T_S - T_E}{\sigma T_E}$$

If we assume that an event is scheduled to be completed in 10 months, but the earliest expected date is 12 months from now, and the standard deviation of that event is 1 month, then

$$Z = \frac{T_S - T_E}{\sigma T_E} = \frac{10 - 12}{1} = \frac{-2}{1} = -2$$

From tables of the area under a normal curve we find that a Z of minus two (-2) is associated with 0.0228 of the total area under the curve; in other words, only two times out of

[28] *Taken from* PERT-Time System Description Manual, *vol. 1, U.S. Air Force, September 1963, p. V-3.*

[29] *Through invoking the central limit theorem. Also, the assumption must be made that the activities are independent. This assumption has been challenged on numerous occasions, since many activities are interconnected and also frequently appear on more than one path in a network.*
[30] *Tables of areas under the normal curve can be found in virtually every basic statistics textbook. They are also included in the PERT-Time System Description Manual, Appendix B.*

100 would management expect to complete that event on schedule. Since this represents a small probability, it is clear that the program schedule is in difficulty.

Unfortunately, management usually does not employ this probability measure because of a feeling that too much uncertainty exists in the entire estimation and planning process for this statistical calculation to have meaning. It also appears that management in general is not familiar with probability theory.

Actually, similar information can be presented to management without using formal probability theory. The scheduling section in the Dynasoar (X-20) Program Office derived an interesting surrogate for such probability statistics. A "recovery ratio" was computed that was simply a ratio of the negative slack to the length of the critical path. For example, path A in a project may require 20 weeks to perform and contain 5 weeks of negative slack. Path B may require 3 weeks and have 1 week of negative slack. Slack calculations alone would indicate that Path A was most critical (i.e., $5 > 1$). The recovery ratios for path A would be $(5 \div 20)$, $\frac{1}{4}$, or 0.25; for path B they would be $(1 \div 3)$, $\frac{1}{3}$, or 0.33. This would indicate that in reality path B is more critical than path A, since only 3 weeks would remain to pick up 1 week of negative slack, whereas on A, 20 weeks are available to pick up 5 weeks of negative slack. The recovery ratio is easier to compute and to understand than the probability distribution, and is worth serious consideration by management.

Types of PERT networks. The fact that various levels of management and numerous interrelationships among firms, agencies, and military offices that are involved in weapon system acquisition was brought out in Sec. I of this Memorandum. In such an environment, with its variety of demands, a single network often will not suffice. Accordingly, variations have been evolved to handle various aspects of the planning and control process.

1 *Detailed and Operating Level Networks*

Generally, each prime or associate contractor constructs and uses a network that covers his individual sphere of program responsibility. If a portion of the project is subcontracted to another firm that subcon-

tractor in turn may be required to construct and use a network for his portion of the project. These networks are constructed in considerable detail and frequently comprehend even relatively minor activities and events.[31] Such networks are utilized by operating managements and are termed operating networks, or detailed networks. In addition, since they often cover only a fragment of a project, NASA has referred to them as fragnets (*frag*mentary *net*works).

2 *Integrated Project Networks*

The detailed operating networks prepared by the separate firms and agencies may be combined or integrated, generally at the SPO level, into one comprehensive network encompassing all events in the entire project. Although perhaps not directly involved in detailed operations, the SPO can exercise management surveillance over the progress of the entire project through use of this integrated network.

3 *Condensed or Summary Networks*

Generally, detailed networks contain too much operating data for top project management or other interested parties (i.e., DOD, Headquarters USAF, etc.) monitoring the progress of the program on a more aggregative basis. To accomplish this, a summary, or condensed network is constructed which eliminates much of the detail, yet retains the events of major significance. Such networks frequently are displayed in project control offices.

Accurate translations of activity time estimates must be made when the operating networks are either integrated or condensed. The integration and condensation processes involve identifying, recording, coordinating and storing interface events.[32] Various computer routines are being developed to accomplish this complex and vital task. The relationship among these various forms of networks is indicated in Figure 32-12. This diagram depicts condensation of networks prior to network integration. Either condensation or integration can occur first depending on the requirements of the levels of program management.

Information usually is abstracted from the condensed network and forwarded to agen-

---

[31] *It is evident that the level of detail may vary among contractors.*

[32] *An interface event signals the transfer of responsibility, end items, or information from one part of the project effort to another.*

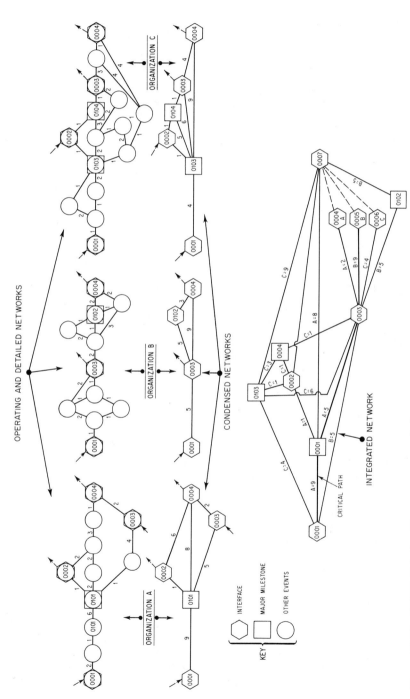

*Figure 32-12   PERT: Relationships among networks.**

* Adapted from Planning and Control Techniques and Procedures (PCT), Headquarters, U.S. Army Material Command, AMC Regulation 11–16, vol. 2, August 1963, Fig. 11-3-5.

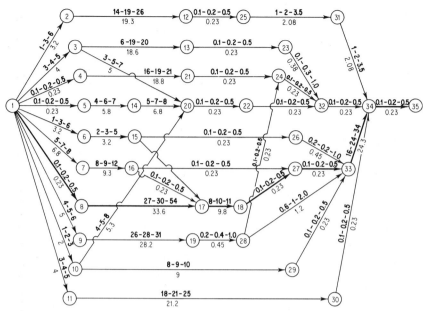

Figure 32-13   PERT network applied to hypothetical missile system.

cies above the SPO in milestone form. The current procedure of selecting information from the networks and listing this information in line item or narrative form appears to have limitations. One relatively simple improvement would utilize the network concept and its relevant information on interrelationships at top project levels. Perhaps this could be accomplished by including a requirement that summary networks be incorporated in the System Package Program[33] and that project progress be reported against these networks.

Application of PERT to Hypothetical Missile System

The PERT network shown in Figure 32-13 for our hypothetical missile system is a summary network. The events and activities are identical to those used in the network illustrating the critical path technique in Sec. IV, and the same "rules" are followed. In each case the work flow envisioned at the time is the same, and thus the networks are the same. However,

---

[33] *As mentioned previously, the System Package Program is the basic management document for major weapon systems programs.*

in the PERT network, three time estimates are used for each activity: optimistic, most likely, and pessimistic. These estimates (taken from Table 32-1) are displayed in bold on Figure 32-13 to emphasize the major difference between CPM and PERT.

The expected times as derived from the three time estimates in PERT frequently will differ somewhat from the single time estimates recorded in CPM. As described above, the mean is conceptually a more comprehensive measure incorporating the extreme (optimistic and pessimistic) values and in this sense reflects the range of uncertainty revealed by the three time estimates. The mean used in PERT will vary from the mode used in CPM in those instances when the time interval between the mode and the optimistic time differs from the interval between the mode and the pessimistic time estimates. The mean and mode will coincide where there is equal uncertainty in positive and negative directions, since the mode will bisect the range between the optimistic and pessimistic times.

Once the expected time for each event has been computed, the techniques are identical in their method of identifying the critical path. In our missile system example, the critical path for PERT is identical with that for CPM (i.e., events 1, 8, 17, 18, 27, 33, 34, and 35). However, the time to complete the project has been lengthened from 64.8 weeks to 68.6 weeks. This difference is the result of the fact that in the estimates for individual activities prepared using the PERT technique, the range between the optimistic and expected times was less than the range between the pessimistic and expected times.

In this simple example, the difference of 3.8 weeks in a project of 69 weeks' duration is only moderately important. It would be difficult to state clearly which estimate (PERT or CPM) was the more accurate. The PERT technique is more sophisticated in that it does attempt to deal with uncertainty. However, various mathematicians have questioned certain of the simplifying assumptions used in the PERT estimation process.[34]

If, in scheduling the activities for our hypothetical missile system, we assume a directed date of 65 weeks from now, that becomes the scheduled date for completion of the project. If the length of the critical path is 68.6 weeks, we have negative slack of 3.6 weeks. Because of the uncertainty inherent in the activities as shown by the estimation intervals, management may require some "feeling" for the likelihood of the project's being completed on schedule. Using the concept of zero slack, this likelihood can be ascertained by computing (1) the standard deviations of the activities on the critical path (σ), (2) the standard deviation of the final event (σ_E), (3) the Z statistic, and, finally, (4) the probability of positive slack. These computations are given in Table 32-9.

Note that the probability is only 0.25. A gambling management might be content to proceed and see what develops, but most managements would probably require at the very least a 50 percent chance of meeting schedule. This would then call either for shifting resources from noncritical events to critical events or for employing a higher level of resources. If positive slack exists, management frequently is content to assume that the project will be completed on schedule.

---

[34] *An analysis of the significance of these arguments is found in K. R. MacCrimmon and C. A. Ryavec, An Analytical Study of the PERT Assumptions, The RAND Corporation, RM-3408, December 1962.*

TABLE 32-9   COMPUTATIONS REQUIRED FOR PROBABILITY OF POSITIVE SLACK

(1) Standard deviation and variance of critical path activities:

Event Number on Critical Path	Standard Deviation of an Activity $[(b-a)/6]$	Variance of an Activity (σ^2)
8	$\dfrac{0.5 - 0.1}{6} = 0.07$	0.0049
17	$\dfrac{54 - 27}{6} = 4.5$	20.2500
18	$\dfrac{11 - 8}{6} = 0.5$	0.2500
27	$\dfrac{0.5 - 0.1}{6} = 0.07$	0.0049
33	$\dfrac{0.5 - 0.1}{6} = 0.07$	0.0049
34	$\dfrac{34 - 16}{6} = 3.0$	9.0000
35	$\dfrac{0.5 - 0.1}{6} = 0.07$	0.0049

Total variance along the critical path... 29.5196 or 29.52

(2) Standard deviation for the final event = $\sqrt{29.52}$ or 5.43.

$$(3) \quad Z = \frac{T_S - T_E}{\sigma T_E} = \frac{65 - 68.6}{5.43} = \frac{-3.6}{5.43} = -0.662.$$

(4) Probability of positive slack. Referring to tables of the area under the normal curve, the Z statistic corresponding to the number −0.662 is approximately 0.25. This means that only 25 times out of 100 could management expect to complete the project on schedule.

Evaluation of PERT

Since its formulation, PERT has been received both favorably and unfavorably. Those who favor it recognize it as a good planning tool. Others feel that it has been offered as a panacea for all scheduling problems. Still others think that the technique is "basically nothing new." PERT, however, does offer several concepts not previously incorporated in scheduling techniques.

Unfortunately, PERT, as conceived by its developers, has never been applied in total to any major system. In particular, the three time estimates and the probability computations have never had a thorough test throughout a full project cycle. Perhaps the most complete attempt was the use of the three time estimates on the Dynasoar program, but that program was cancelled before completion.

Obviously, it is difficult to make a satisfactory comparison between CPM and PERT if the factors unique to PERT—its three time estimates and use of probability theory—are not implemented. Since use of the beta distribution in the PERT technique has been attacked by mathematicians, and engineers have been reluc-

TABLE 32-10   PERT TECHNIQUE—STRENGTHS AND WEAKNESSES

Criteria	Strengths	Weaknesses
1. *Validity*	PERT, like CPM, is capable of depicting work sequence. The use of three time estimates should make it more valid than any other technique.	
2. *Reliability*		On the other hand, securing three time estimates for each activity requires more information which would tend to introduce additional error.
3. *Implementation*		The complete PERT system is quite complex and therefore difficult to implement.
4. *Universality of project coverage*	Very strong in development phase.	Requires adaptation for application to production operations.
5. *Sensitivity testing (simulation)*	Since PERT is usually mechanized, it has good potential for simulating the impact of various resource allocations on the schedule, or the various ways of sequencing work.	
6. *Forecasting*	PERT is strongly oriented to forecasting the ability to accomplish future events on schedule.	
7. *Updating*	Activities are clearly identified and elapsed times can be obtained as needed.	Estimation of activity times is quite time-consuming, and calculation of expected times requires use of a computer.
8. *Flexibility*	As the project changes over time, the network and new time estimates can be readily adjusted to reflect changes, especially if present experimental efforts on automatic plotting of networks are successful.	
9. *Cost*		More data and more computations are required than in any other system; hence the system is more costly.

NOTE: Recall that this table is intended only as a summary of certain qualitative information on the relative usefulness of the scheduling technique. As indicated previously, a more formal quantitative evaluation of the extent to which the criteria are met was considered infeasible in this study.

tant to make the three time estimates because they believe them to be too time-consuming, the probability calculations have usually been abandoned, perhaps justifiably. However, any new system that is to be used by numerous firms requires time to implement. Perhaps PERT should be implemented a portion at a time. Further study might indicate that in most cases expected time estimates do not vary significantly from single point estimates and therefore multiple estimates are not justified in view of the added inconvenience and cost. On the other hand, the problem of dealing with uncertainties in estimates remains. This issue is as yet unresolved.

At first, PERT had no cost-estimating capability. Now the network and critical path features of PERT-Time have proved their worth, and attempts are being made to extend the concept to the cost and reliability aspects of project management. The first full-scale application of the PERT-Cost technique was made on the TFX program. It is important to note that the PERT-type network provides a common framework for incorporating these other factors, and thus PERT provides the basis for a more completely integrated management system.

PERT has earned widespread acceptance in industry and government, and undoubtedly will be the dominant scheduling system for major development programs for some time to come, especially since attempts are being made to integrate it with companion techniques for planning and control of cost. In addition, it appears likely that a related effort will be made to utilize it in the planning and control of technical performance.

Some of the strengths and weaknesses of PERT are summarized in Table 32-10.

READING 33

MANAGING RISKS FOR MORE EFFECTIVE PROGRAM CONTROL*

James R. Polski

Engineers and scientists usually are the world's greatest optimists. In some respects they need to be, in order to ride the waves of opposition while pursuing their intuition into uncharted waters. The Wrights, the Edisons and the Goddards are the classical models of this tenacious breed.

The present day confreres of these titans are urged to temper bubbling optimism with equal doses of realism—regarding the risks of failure —to meet commitments of megabuck magnitude without overruns.

Inherently, the risk of failure to meet objectives shadows all design and development programs. Yet, because it is a negative aspect, the incidence of risk is quite often overlooked in the glare of optimism. Or, even where it is not ignored completely, it may be appraised but not deeply enough, or perhaps not often enough to serve as a significant input for decision-making.

* Reprinted with permission of General Electric Company, Missile and Space Division, from Aerospace Management, vol. 1, no. 1, Spring, 1966.

Risk is a prime variable in a design and development program. It can be defined as the probability that the work being done will miss the triple target of cost, delivery schedule, or technical performance. Reducing this probability is as healthy to a contractor as the reduction of a beltline is to an overweight. Coincidentally, in both cases the achievement of success depends upon discipline.

In the management of a design and development program, the discipline consists of identifying and evaluating the elements of risk on a continuous basis. To use elements of risk as inputs for decision-making, the General Electric Company, Missile and Space Division has developed the Risk Appraisal of Programs System (RAPS). Basically, RAPS provides both a framework for identifying the risks and a comparative measure for expressing the extent of risk associated with each hardware end-item or task.

In general problem-solving, the identification of the problem is the first step to its solution; this holds true also in risk appraisal. A good point to remember, however, is that the RAP

System is not aimed at eliminating risks, but rather at balancing risks across the program. For, better program value is provided if one does not spend money on elaborate attempts to lower risk in one area while excessive risks are going unheeded in another.

An accurate appraisal of risk can serve both the customer and the contractor; first as a planning tool, it can provide bases for trade-offs; secondly, it can function as a communication medium between customer, program manager, and the program team; lastly, when practiced during the course of development, it can be used for assessing the changes in program risks and for verifying conformance to plans.

FACTORS AFFECTING RISK

The many factors which affect risk in a development program can be grouped in two broad categories: (1) factors stemming from resource limitations such as funds and time, as well as from specific mission requirements; (2) factors bearing on the conduct and management of the total task.

For each hardware subsystem "Resource Limitations" risks are appraised using a checklist—from the viewpoint of individuals responsible for the end item. Seven fundamental aspects are considered: inputs, capabilities, knowledge, reliability, margins, schedules and funds.

Based upon the lack of a given resource factor, risk-level estimates may be assigned. These limitations may comprise a lack of capability with respect to critical skilled manpower, or a lack of inputs such as design requirements data on a subsystem.

The risk-level gradation for each of the seven aspects is identified as "High, Moderate, Minor, or Low."

A "High" risk estimate is a judgment that the particular resource limitation could jeopardize the successful fulfillment of the program. This, in effect is a "signal" for management action. "Moderate" risk implies an attenuation of this signal; whereas "minor" signifies a normal amount of risk incident to this type of work; and "low" indicates that additional risk could be assumed in this area—for trade-off purposes.

Where limitations are adjudged to be "High" or "Moderate," substantiation is furnished by providing an explanation and recommendations

for lowering to "Minor"; as well as a rough cost-estimate of direct labor and materials that may be required to lower the risk level.

This substantiation is the guiding philosophy of the RAP System. For it motivates people to focus on potential problem areas and to formulate solutions—without losing sight of cost-time-technical-risk trade-offs. This requirement then, counteracts the natural human tendency to "over-control" in reacting to risks.

INFLUENCE OF MANAGEMENT PRACTICES

Program Risk can also be varied with the use, or lack of use, of certain proven management methods and practices for conducting the work in all the principal functions. Management practices to be followed may differ from program to program. The practices to be used may vary with the nature of the development, the extent of the funding, the criticality of the schedule, as well as the influence of other customer requirements. A point to remember here is that the disciplined approach to risk appraisal is primarily an insurance against the omission of certain practices through oversight. Application of rigorous management practices to the conduct of work can serve to substantially lower the risk.

Risk appraisal for "Management Practices" is conducted on the basis of selected key areas from the various functions. Such key areas include Design Review, Qualification System, Procurement Management, Quality Controls and Schedule Management. Typical examples of proven low-risk practices from these areas are:

Use of outside consultants for Design Reviews.
Incorporation of Qualification requirements in the equipment specification.
Employment of vendor-capability analyses in Procurement Source Selection.
Use of the Quality Audit technique.
Regular reporting of Schedule information for current program status.

SELECTION OF KEY AREAS

A question may be raised at this point, as to how the key areas for management practices, and the practices themselves were selected for risk appraisal, in the first place?

Methods and practices of the greatest practi-

RESOURCE LIMITATIONS
RISK ESTIMATE CHECKLIST

PROGRAM:_____   DATE:_____

ITEM:_____

Based upon your experience and judgement in reference to a program of this nature and based upon the present plan for technical analysis, design, hardware, fabrication, testing and evaluation indicate the Risk due to any lack of the following

Risk Level Estimates
HIGH MOD. MINOR LOW

1. INPUTS – Based upon the clarity and firmness of available customer requirements and/or interface definitions, drawings, or study results, what level of risk is imposed on the program?

2. CAPABILITIES – Considering the need for suitably skilled and experienced manpower and of appropriate facilities for conducting the work, as compared to the availability and allocation of these capabilities, what level of risk is involved?

3. KNOWLEDGE – Based upon the availability of fundamental and accurate information on the environment, technologies, or techniques involved; or upon the test results available or planned, what level of risk is imposed on the programs?

4. RELIABILITY – Considering the degree of proven reliability of parts or components available, as judged by failures and problems that have persistently reoccurred in similar equipments, what level of risk is involved?

5. MARGINS – Based upon the stringency of the reqt. vs. the state-of-the-art supplemented by development plans, what level of risk is involved? (Examples: weight limit in view of past actuals and present research; materials specified in view of fabrication difficulties.)

6. SCHEDULES – Considering the programmed time for significant portions of the work in the current phase or throughout the total development, what level of risk is imposed on the program?

7. FUNDS – Considering the funding available and/or allocated to this work for the immediate period or for the total task, what level of risk is imposed on the program?

The limitations which are adjudged to be of "High" or "Moderate" Risk must be substantiated on the following page by a brief explanation of the action that might be taken and a rough estimate of the cost of such action.

Name/Title Estimator:_____
Form A

Figure 33-1

cal significance were selected in the light of cumulative experience at General Electric and the Air Force. First a study was made, within the General Electric, Missile and Space Division, to earmark practices which consistently contributed to the successful conduct and control of past development programs. Secondly, the chosen practices were compared with the Air Force Systems Command findings reported in AFSCP 375-2, entitled "A Summary of Lessons Learned from Air Force Management Surveys." This report highlights the most repetitive management deficiencies encountered in the aerospace industry, grouped as follows:

Program and Contract Functions
Engineering Functions
Production and Quality
Assurance Functions
Purchasing and Material Functions
Product Support Functions

Correlating these Air Force findings with in-house studies, twenty-one management practice areas were identified as most significant for managing development programs. These are:

Specifications
Design Stage Release System
Design Review
Reliability Plan
Reliability Design Analysis
Qualification System
Make-or-Buy Plan
Material Control
Manufacturing Process Control
Procurement Management
Quality Control & Test Plan
Quality Controls
Failure Analysis
Value Engineering
Configuration Management
Data Management
Logistics/Support Management
Facilities Management
Cost Management
Schedule Management
Audits

Now, as any seasoned manager in a customer or contractor organization knows, when it comes to a management practice, what counts most is not "what's up front" on its label, but what's in it to ferret out program weaknesses and to lower the risks of failure. To this end, the following five fundamental questions are addressed to each management practices area:

What actions are involved?
Who is responsible?
When are these actions to take place?
What format is to be followed?
What follow-up action ensues?

Accordingly, each of the twenty-one management practices are appraised by filling in a checklist of significant requirements. Space has been provided on each checklist for commenting on mitigating circumstances; the overall risk for the function under consideration is then judged, based on the answers to the detailed questions. The same four gradations of risk are used here as in the risk appraisal of "Resource Limitations." The checklist concept used here serves the same purpose as checklists used by pilots in various phases of their flight, or the item-by-item checkout approach used in launch operations.

RAPS IMPLEMENTATION

When should RAP System Implementation begin? As soon as the program team has been organized and operating. The implementation starts with an "Initial Appraisal" that establishes a plan by the Program Manager, and a Risk Appraisal by the program team. Subsequent re-appraisals are made on a periodic basis, generally quarterly. The risk levels and the actions taken to attenuate major risks can then be displayed in reference to the basic plan.

Essentially, here's what the "Initial Appraisal" does:

(1) Establishes a Risk Plan by the Program Manager, as to the risk level acceptable for the "Resource Limitation" factors, and the extent to which the low-risk management practices are to be used. These risk levels together make a "profile" line on the RAPS presentation.

(2) Determines the level of risk for each major hardware end item (generally a subsystem) by "Resource Limitation" factor; also determines the level of risk in each management practices area. Risk levels are assigned depending on the extent the low-risk practices are planned for use.

All appraisals are made by the team members responsible for the hardware item or function involved. "Resource Limitations" checklists are completed for each subsystem by each responsible person in Engineering, Manufacturing, and Quality Control. These are consolidated by subsystem, to review the commonality of the risk estimates and consistency of recommendations made to deal with them.

One of the attributes of the RAP System is that it lends itself to summarization and to tab runs. The data may be recorded on cards so that tab runs can be made by:

Hardware end-item or technology
Resource limitation factor
Gradation of risk
Organization function submitting the data

As a result, the similarity between symptoms, problems and recommendations can easily be recognized and generalized for discussion. The Risk Appraisal for the total program is then formulated by aggregating and summarizing the subsystem appraisals.

Appraisal data is arrayed on a chart with columns set up for each of the four risk levels; the left hand side defines the dual look at risk —the seven Resource Limitations factors followed by the 21 Management Practices areas; the field displays the Program Manager's Plan as a profile line and the percent of appraisals at a given risk level in tabulated form. Percentages exceeding the plan are shaded for emphasis. The scheme for reading the RAPS chart is shown below. This chart is a typical example of a Risk Appraisal. The adjacent RAPS chart is used as a part of the Program Appraisal and Review (PAR) System presentation. As evident in the right half of this data chart, analytical comments are confined to terse statements on risks, as well as the action planned for reducing them.

This chart initially concentrates management attention on planned risks and the basis for the plan; and later it focuses on the extent to which the appraised risks differ from the plan.

BENEFITS, PRESENT AND FUTURE

In essence, then, the benefits of the RAP System can be summarized as follows:

Helps focus management attention on major risk areas.
Provides an opportunity for offering recommendations to lower excessive risks.
Assists management in evaluating how the overall job is being done.

There are also additional side-benefits to performing risk appraisals on a formal, written basis: it improves communications with program management and provides that often-needed memory jog to follow proven practices. Also when problems and suggested solutions are committed to paper, these are less suscepti-

ble to being swept under a carpet of complacency.

The RAPS management system has been used on seven programs in the Division and on the entire activities of the Mississippi Test Support Department. Furthermore it is planned for use on all new major or critical programs in the Division.

This type of look has resulted in program adjustments to accomplish additional analyses, reallocate hardware for qualification, and change funding release dates. In the words of Bob Hammond, Manager of Ballistic System Programs, Re-entry Systems Dept., who has used RAPS on two programs in his Section: "RAPS highlights problem aspects which are not always readily visible. Particularly in view of time limitations this structured approach to looking at a program's problems can be a real help. My program managers are, of course, extremely close to their programs, but even for them this technique may present the problem in a fresh light and in total, provide a useful checklist for the program."

RAPS can provide an effective tool for communicating the risk picture on a program to the customer. It offers the opportunity to jointly review the risks—be they inherent or imposed. RAPS can thus promote full understanding of the approaches and methods to be used to achieve program objectives.

Possibly among the unexplored areas of activity which may in the future furnish fertile grounds for customer applications of this basic idea, are Source Selection and Program Definition. If used in connection with Requests for Proposals, RAPS might improve the definition and presentation of development and management plans. This could contribute to the further refinement of "tools" used in evaluating and comparing proposals.

Systems Program Management procedures are now being required on many of the new contracts awarded by the DOD. The "Self-auditing" feature of the RAPS technique is particularly adaptable to Systems Program Management, for example in identifying compliance with the Air Force 375 requirements, RAPS could be used both by industry and System Program Offices, in addition to independent surveys for identifying compliance with 375.

Presently, the Management Practices check-

DESIGN REVIEW
RISK ESTIMATE CHECKLIST   DATE:_____

PROGRAM:_____

ITEM: _____   _____
          (System, Sub-System, Component or Other Name)   Drawing No.

1. At what point in the program was design review scheduled and conducted?
   a) Before Stage Release I . . . . . . Yes ( )   No ( )   c) Before Stage Release III . . . . . . Yes ( )   No ( )
   b) Before Stage Release II . . . . Yes ( )   No ( )   d) Before Stage Release IV . . . . . . Yes ( )   No ( )

2. Were advanced checklists sent to the engineer and properly completed? . . . . Yes ( )   No ( )

3. Were suitable data supplied to the Design Review Office by responsible parties a reasonable
   time before the review? (Check One)
   a) Yes . . . . . ( )   b) Data not timely . . . . ( )   c) No . . . . . ( )

4) Was item definition provided to design review participants early enough to permit study? (Check One)
   a) Yes . . . . . ( )   b) Marginal . . . . ( )   c) No . . . . . ( )

5. Which of the following technical items were covered adequately during the design review?
   a) Basic approach or features . . . . ( )   m) Maintainability analysis . . . . ( )
   b) Relation to "state-of-the-art" . . . . . ( )   n) Parts Application Review . . . . ( )
   c) Anticipated problems . . . . ( )   o) Design safety factor analysis . . . . ( )
   d) Development required . . . . ( )   p) Tolerance analysis . . . . ( )
   e) Development plans . . . . ( )   q) Utilization of specification design
   f) Aerodynamic analysis . . . . ( )   standards applicable to program . . . . ( )
   g) Stress, vibration & other   r) Development tests . . . . ( )
      mechanical analyses . . . . ( )   s) Qualification tests . . . . ( )
   h) Thermal analysis . . . . ( )   t) Manufacturing plan . . . . ( )
   i) Electrical analysis . . . .( )   u) Schedule information . . . . ( )
   j) Life analysis . . . . ( )   v) Cost information . . . . ( )
   k) Reliability analysis . . . .( )   w) Quantity control plan . . . . ( )
   l) Trade-off analysis, including costs. . .( )   x) Test plan . . . . ( )

6. Was the design review attended by the following technical personnel?
   a) Design Engineer . . . . Yes ( )   No ( )   f) Producibility . . . . Yes ( )   No ( )
   b) Next Product Level Designer . . Yes ( )   No ( )   g) Manufacturing . . . . Yes ( )   No ( )
   c) System Engineer . . . . Yes ( )   No ( )   h) Qualified Consultant (not
   d) Reliability . . . . Yes ( )   No ( )   working on this Program) . . . . Yes ( )   No ( )
   e) Quality Control . . . . Yes ( )   No ( )

7. Were minutes and action item records published? (Check One)
   a) No . . . .( )   c) Yes, usually in 1 to 2 weeks. . . . . ( )
   b) Yes, usually in over 2 weeks . . . . . ( )   d) Yes, usually within 1 week . . . . ( )

8. Did the design review accomplish or provide:
   a) Assurance of design feasibility? Yes ( )   No ( )   e) Assurance that input and output
   b) Adequate producibility? . . . . . Yes ( )   No ( )   requirements and tolerances are
   c) Reliability assurance? . . . . . . Yes ( )   No ( )   compatible with next design
   d) Proper consideration of trade-   level . . . . Yes ( )   No ( )
      off factors . . . . Yes ( )   No ( )

9. What has been the response to action items from prior related design reviews? (Check One)
   a) Performance is always timely and   c) Performance is sometimes
      effective . . . . ( )   inadequate . . . . ( )
   b) Performance is usually adequate   d) Action item response is generally
      technically and timely . . . . ( )   unsatisfactory . . . . ( )
                                                        e) Not applicable . . . . ( )

COMMENTS: (Use Reverse Side or Additional Sheets if required)

DESIGN REVIEW – OVERALL RISK ESTIMATE _ _ _ _ _ _ _ _ _ _ _   HIGH   MOD.   MINOR   LOW

Name/Title Estimator:_____   □ □ □ □

Form E

Figure 33-2

list used in RAPS is being expanded to cover the 375 procedures. This same approach could possibly be used by a System Program Director and his staff to assess the overall risk in the early phases of a program. Both the System Contractor and the System Program Office could thus complete their separate appraisals and compare their risk profiles. The incorporation of key procedural requirements in checklist form could prove a valuable aid to the Contractor's Program Managers and to the System Program Offices alike.

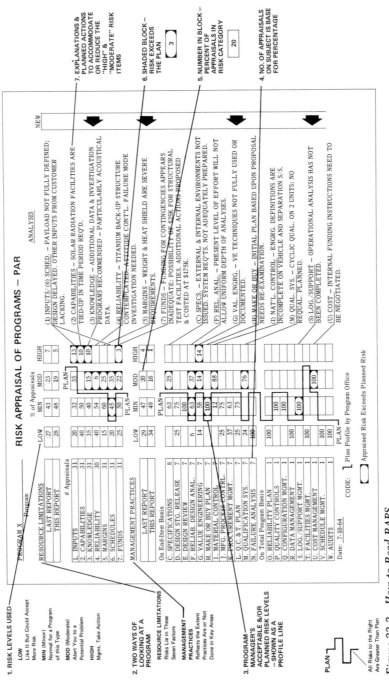

Figure 33-3   How to Read RAPS.

SECTION 9

ORGANIZATION CHARTING

The development of traditional management theory has involved a constant search for a universal organizational concept. Much of the controversy reflected in the literature centers around the attempts to perpetuate the hierarchical model of the organization. Verticality of management practice is apparent in such principles as unity of command, parity of authority and responsibility, the scalar chain, and functional authority. Advocates of the hierarchical model are characterized by their dependence on a nucleus of principles designed to preserve the sanctity of the vertical organization. The concept of the informal organization has been used to explain the unstructured community of people having reciprocal peer relationships in the organization.

There is a growing awareness in management literature of the propriety of peer-colleague relationships in accomplishing organized effort. We have not suddenly discovered these relationships, but we are beginning to see evidence of attempts to develop charting techniques to formalize them.

One might well question the value of the traditional charting methods as a means of analyzing organizational relationships. Perhaps the most frequent complaint about pyramidal organization charts is that they fail to portray the interrelationships of people in their day-to-day activities. But we must remember that the pyramid chart has considerable value in showing how the organization is functionally structured.

The value of linear responsibility charts, systematized linear charts, and the other techniques discussed in this section lie in the fact that such methods go beyond functional, formal lines of authority. These newer methods provide a means of displaying the coordinative interrelationships that unify the basic functional activities.

READING 34

ROLES AND RELATIONSHIPS: CLARIFYING THE MANAGER'S JOB *

Robert D. Melcher

Far too many companies cherish the myth that the publication of organization charts and position descriptions will resolve the majority of problems relating to the role each manager plays in relationship to his work group and to the organization. The organization chart does show basic divisions of work and who reports to whom, but it does not depict detailed functions and how individuals relate to these functions; in other words, it does not show how the organization actually works. The position description delineates the detailed task to be performed, but it cannot show how the organization really functions, either. Position descriptions are far more concerned with defining an individual's tasks than with how, in carrying out his responsibilities, he interacts with his colleagues. The way in which management positions are described often indicates com-

* *Reprinted with permission from* Personnel, *vol. 44, no. 3, May-June, 1967. Copyright 1967 by American Management Association Inc.*

plete independence from other positions—and, more often than not, independent action instead of group participation is encouraged. As a result, there is no opportunity to build a framework that can be used to relate and integrate each manager and the work he does to the organization and its goals.

The human-relations approach to resolving problems relating to interpersonal and intergroup relations concentrates primarily on behavioral approaches and experiences involving sensitivity training sessions, group problem-solving and goal-setting courses, and similar techniques. The primary purpose of the behavioral approach is to develop an awareness within each individual of his own behavioral characteristics, to increase his understanding of the underlying cause of intergroup conflict, and to develop techniques and approaches that can in some way help improve the individual's working relationships.

Unfortunately, many of these human-relations approaches do not involve the work group. Even when the work group is involved, the subject matter seldom relates specifically to the various working roles and relationships of the members of the group. Hence there is little opportunity for the group to focus on their work interface problems and put to productive use the techniques and skills gained through human-relations training experiences —and when experiences cannot be put to use, their value is soon lost.

PLANNING AND PARTICIPATION

A sound and successful organization development process requires a planned, systematic approach that encourages management involvement and participation. In order to meet these criteria and strengthen the organization development process, a number of companies have utilized an approach that enables each manager to actively participate with his superiors, peers, and subordinates in systematically describing the managerial job to be done and then clarifying the role each manager plays in relationship to his work group and to the organization.

The tool that evolved has been called the Management Responsibility Guide. Its development was sparked by a linear charting technique, developed by Ernest Hijams and Serge A. Bern, that is used to relate management positions, functions, and responsibility relationships to each other. Although their Linear Responsibility Chart can be used to describe roles and relationships, its use seems to be somewhat limited, because the functions are not systematically structured and the approach does not actively involve members of the work group in resolving their roles and responsibility relationships. Without a planned and systematic approach, it is very difficult to group and relate managerial functions in the manner best suited to aid an organization to objectively solve its organizational problems. And without the active involvement of the work group, there is little opportunity to actually resolve differences and improve communications. It was out of the recognition that the mating of a behavioral sciences approach to a systems framework was essential, if role and relationship resolution was to take place, that the Management Responsibility Guide approach evolved.

Within every organization there exist specialized managerial tasks or functions that must be acted upon if the organization is to attain its objectives and goals. At the higher management levels, these managerial functions tend to be described in objective-oriented terms; at each subsequent lower level, these functions are broken into more detailed functions and are defined in more task-oriented terms. To be meaningful, these functions must be structured and phrased in a manner that not only describes the managerial functions but highlights the role and relationship problems that need to be clarified and resolved by each work group. Only after the objective delineation and definition of these essential managerial functions have been completed should each manager's responsibility relationships be developed. How each manager's view of his responsibility relationship to each function and each person is resolved determines how effectively the organization works—or does not work.

SEMANTIC SOLUTIONS

One of the primary problems impeding the process of role and relationship resolution is that of developing a set of terms that describe the various responsibility relationships in a way that is meaningful and acceptable to the group. Although there are many responsibility relationship terms that could be developed for a specific organization, the following seven definitions seem to meet the communication requirements of most organizations and, along with the defined functions, serve as a common focal point for the work group:

A. *General Responsibility*—The individual guides and directs the execution of the function through the person delegated operating responsibility.
B. *Operating Responsibility*—The individual is directly responsible for the execution of the function.
C. *Specific Responsibility*—The individual is responsible for executing a specific or limited portion of the function.
D. *Must Be Consulted*—The individual, if the decision affects his area, must be called upon before any decision is made or approval is granted, to render advice or relate information, but not to make the decision or grant approval.

E. *May Be Consulted*—The individual may be called upon to relate information, render advice, or make recommendations.
F. *Must Be Notified*—The individual must be notified of action that has been taken.
G. *Must Approve*—The individual (other than persons holding general and operating responsibility) must approve or disapprove.

It is obvious that a format is required that can be used to relate the organization's managerial functions, positions, and responsibility relationships to each other—and this is where the Management Responsibility Guide format makes its contribution.

DEVELOPING THE GUIDE

How the Management Responsibility Guide is developed by the work group is as important to its successful completion as the elements that it comprises. The first and perhaps most important step pertains to how the work group views and relates to the process that is to take place. Ordinarily, someone outside the work group is needed to work with the group as a consultant in developing the functions and serving as a resource. More often than not, there is a high degree of skepticism within the work group regarding the role of the consultant and his ability to actually help them, as well as considerable concern on each person's part as to how his status will be affected. Because each member of the work group must be afforded the opportunity to understand the process and to express his feelings, a group briefing session should first be held to explain the entire process and ground rules. Questions about the process and its underlying concepts and purposes should be encouraged by the manager of the work group and the consultant.

The functions of the work group can now be developed. Each member of the group is individually interviewed and given the opportunity to describe his job and any problems he wants the consultant to be aware of. In this fact-gathering and problem-definition phase, it is essential that the focus be directed toward objectively describing and grouping managerial functions that logically belong or relate to the same family, regardless of who presently is responsible. If responsibility relationships are also discussed at this time, emotion and subjectivity enter the picture and the probability of objectively delineating what needs to be done is poor. When questions relating to responsibility relationships are raised, the person raising them should be advised that he will have the opportunity to express his views fully at a later stage in the process.

A DOUBLE CHECK

After the key functions have been defined to the satisfaction of each manager, the consultant reviews all the defined functions with the managers' superior and, if necessary, revises the definitions to the satisfaction of the superior and each of the subordinates concerned.

The point has now been reached where the responsibility relationships can be developed. Each individual within the work group is given, in the Management Responsibility Guide format, a list of all functions developed for the group and is requested to enter the relationship code or codes that best express what he thinks his responsibility relationship to each function should be. He is further instructed that if he assigns an operating responsibility (B) to himself for a function, he should enter what he thinks should be the responsibility relationship of all other managers who should have a relationship to that function. In addition, he is requested to review each function and make whatever change in the wording he deems necessary.

After the forms are completed, they are returned to the consultant and the various points of view are entered on a master copy. The chart in Figure 34-1 shows how the master copy might look after the views of all members of the group have been entered on it. (In this case, the group concerned is a large division of the company; other charts would break down each of the functions in more detail and would list managers at lower levels of the organization. This division, in turn, would represent one of the functions on a chart indicating top management's roles and responsibilities.) For each function, the top line of symbols represents the point of view of the person who has indicated that he holds operating responsibility (B) for that function. The symbols in the second line represent the point of view of the person whose position title appears at the top of the column. Since two people considered that they had operating responsibility for the

MANAGEMENT RESPONSIBILITY GUIDE © R. MELCHER 1967

MANAGEMENT POSITION

Number	Function	Vice President Aerospace	Vice President Manufacturing	Director Manufacturing	Director Engineering	Manager Engineering Technology	Manager Quality Assurance	Manager Marketing	Manager Contracts	Manager Master Scheduling	Manager Financial Services
10.1	Coordinate division budgeting & financial planning activities & communicate financial information to division management.	A / AF	EF / DF	EF / E		EF / F	EF / EF	EF / E	E / D		B
10.2	Develop project & program schedule requirements, establish, coordinate & control schedules & report on status.	A / A	EF / (E D)	EF / DF		EF / (C D)	EF / (D)	EF / D	B	B	
10.3	Direct contract activities & evaluate & approve contract provisions of all division sales proposals & contract documents.	A / A		E			EF / (D)	B	EF / DF	EF / DF	C
10.4	Plan & coordinate divisional marketing activities so as to secure the business necessary to maximize division's capabilities.	A / AD	EF / F	EF		E	B	DF / (CG)	EF / (CD)	F / F	F / F
10.5	Develop & design new, & improve existing, electronic & electro-mechanical aerospace products & processes.	A / AF	F / E	B		E	E / DG			F / F	
10.6	Secure materials & tools, coordinate manpower & manufacture products to specified quantity, time & cost requirements.	A / A	B	E		(F / CD)		EF / E	F	EF / E	
10.7	Establish quality assurance policies, procedures & controls to insure that products meet applicable standards & specifications.	A / A	DF / EF	DF / EF		B	EF / E	EF / D	EF	F	
10.8	Develop & design proprietary products & processes utilizing proven technology specifically adapted to industrial automation.	A / AF / A	DF / EF / E	(C / B) / (B / DF)		B	E / EF / DF	E / E / DF	E / E / F	F / F / F	

RELATIONSHIP CODE

- **A** GENERAL RESPONSIBILITY
- **B** OPERATING RESPONSIBILITY
- **C** SPECIFIC RESPONSIBILITY
- **D** MUST BE CONSULTED
- **E** MAY BE CONSULTED
- **F** MUST BE NOTIFIED
- **G** MUST APPROVE

ORGANIZATION IDENTIFICATION	NUMBER 200	MANAGEMENT RESPONSIBILITY GUIDE © R. MELCHER 1967	DATE	PAGE
Aerospace — Aerospace Division		APPROVAL		NO 1 OF 1

Figure 34-1

function on line 10.8, the first two lines represent their points of view, and the third line represents the views of the individuals at the tops of the column. The symbols that are circled indicate major conflicts between the viewpoints of the person with operating responsibility and those at the tops of the columns.

RESOLVING CONFLICTS

After an analysis of the responses has been completed, a determination must be made as to how best to resolve any divergent points of view that have been brought to the surface. At this stage the personalities and backgrounds of the people in the work group influence what is to be done.

One approach is to allow each member of the work group to review the varying points of view, then bring them together at a group meeting to collectively clarify and resolve differences. This approach has the distinct advantage of getting the full participation and involvement of each member of the work group. Ordinarily, interpersonal differences related to the day-to-day job content never get aired; this process permits each member of the group to present his position, and more often than not the individuals themselves resolve differences without their superior's having to intervene or make a decision.

This process is highly educational; it gives each member of the group a better understanding of the interaction that must take place in order for the group to function effectively. Moreover, the superior has an opportunity to sit back and view how his organization operates and how the members of his staff relate to one another.

Of course, there may be sensitive situations that are better handled or resolved on a superior-subordinate basis, but, for the most part, group participation and involvement seem to be more effective. No matter what approach is taken, the objective should be to get differences into the open and encourage the individuals themselves to clarify and resolve their roles and responsibility relationships.

The same general approach is used to resolve differences between work groups. After the group members have reached agreement on their roles and responsibility relationships, other individuals or groups are asked to indicate what they think their responsibility relationships should be to each of the functions. As before, differences between the groups that have been brought to the surface can then be resolved, and copies of the form indicating the agreed-upon roles and responsibility relationships are then issued to each member of the work groups as well as to other members of management within the company. Figure 34-2 shows how the chart might appear after divergent views have been reconciled and the relationships with managers outside the work group have been entered.

The Management Responsibility Guide, as its name indicates, is only a guide; it reflects the work group's view as to how they agreed to work with one another at a specific point in time. Conditions continually change and the Management Responsibility Guide, like any other management tool, should be periodically reviewed and updated.

SOME APPLICATIONS

Because the Management Responsibility Guide serves to clarify and resolve problems relating to working relationships, it can be a means of solving problems relating to duplication of effort and overlapping of responsibility; conversely, it can be used to identify responsibility gaps within the organization. It provides an objective way to bring sensitive relationship problems into the open and helps establish a common understanding of each function and each individual's or group's role in the organization.

The guide can also be used as a means of instituting managerial controls and pinning down responsibilities. Since objective consideration can be given to an individual's strengths and weaknesses, in relation to each function, management is able to tighten or loosen controls as well as clearly determine who is responsible for a given function.

As an organization analysis tool, there are a number of uses. For example, in a management audit, the Management Responsibility Guide can be analyzed to determine workload balance, pattern of delegation, and shifting of responsibility due to cutbacks, additions, or other changes in the workload. Since functions and responsibility relationships are delineated in an orderly and systematic manner, management is able to evaluate the impact of

NUMBER	FUNCTION	President	Vice President Aerospace	Vice President Manufacturing Director	Manager Ind'l Engineering	Manager Technology	Manager Quality Assurance	Manager Marketing	Manager Contracts	Manager Master Scheduling	Manager Financial Services & Treasurer & Controller	Vice President Earth Sciences	Vice President Test Laboratories	Manager Ind'l. Relations
10.1	Coordinate division budgeting & financial planning activities & communicate financial information to division management.	A-F	E-F	E-F	E-F	E-F	E-F	E-F	D	(B)	D-F			
10.2	Develop project & program schedule requirements, establish, coordinate & control schedules & report on status.	A	D-F	D	D-F	D-F	E-F	E-F	(B)	F	E-F			
10.3	Direct contract activities & evaluate & approve contract provisions of all division sales proposals & contract documents.	A-F	E	E	E	E	D-F	(B)	E-F	F	E-F	E		
10.4	Plan & coordinate divisional marketing activities so as to secure the business necessary to maximize division's capabilities.	A-D	E-F	E-F	E-F	E	(B)	D-F	D-F	F	E-F	E		
10.5	Develop & design new, & improve existing, electronic & electro-mechanical aerospace products & processes.	A	E-F	D-F	(B)	E				E			E	
10.6	Secure materials & tools, coordinate manpower & manufacture products to specified quantity, time & cost requirements.	A	D-F	(B)	D-F	E		E	E-F	E	E-F			
10.7	Establish quality assurance policies, procedures & controls to insure that products meet applicable standards & specifications.	A	D-F	E-F	E	E	(B)	D-F	E-F	F	E-F			
10.8	Develop & design proprietary products & processes utilizing proven technology specifically adapted to industrial automation.	A-D	E	E	(B)	E	E-F	E-F	E-F	F	F			

RELATIONSHIP CODE

- A GENERAL RESPONSIBILITY
- B OPERATING RESPONSIBILITY
- C SPECIFIC RESPONSIBILITY
- D MUST BE CONSULTED
- E MAY BE CONSULTED
- F MUST BE NOTIFIED
- G MUST APPROVE

ORGANIZATION IDENTIFICATION	NUMBER	MANAGEMENT RESPONSIBILITY GUIDE © R. MELCHER 1967	DATE	PAGE
Aerospace / Aerospace Division	200	APPROVAL		NO. 1 OF 1

Figure 34-2

major staffing changes and, accordingly, can quickly realign functions and responsibility relationships.

EVALUATING PERFORMANCE

One of the more difficult aspects of evaluating performance is establishing the criteria on which performance is to be judged. Since functions and relationships are systematically delineated, it is possible to use the Management Responsibility Guide as a basis for evaluating performance. The systematic delineation of functions has similar advantages in the field of systems and procedures. At the lower echelons of an organization, functions tend to be described in task-oriented terms; hence, the job of the analyst is simplified, for with the clarification of responsibility relationships, the analyst need only describe the work in greater detail.

Position guides, at best, describe the general responsibilities of a position and generally do not consider organization levels or specific management relationships. Manually, or through the use of data processing techniques, a new type of "guide" can be prepared—one that can be updated instantly and that simultaneously considers organization level, functions, positions, and responsibility relationships. In a similar manner, programs relating to managerial experience inventories and the cross-referencing of similar or identical functions can be instituted.

PARTICIPATION IS THE KEY

Over the past five years, the Management Responsibility Guide has been used in some 30 organizations ranging from large to small, in industry and government, as an aid in solving a variety of management problems relating to managerial roles and relationships. One of the primary reasons for its success is the fact that managers at all levels were drawn into the process and actively participated in resolving problems in which they were personally involved. In each organization, this approach has provided a dynamic means of objectively describing the work to be done and clarifying the role each manager plays in it—and it has proved to be a major factor in improving management communications and interpersonal and intergroup relations.

READING 35

WHAT'S NOT ON THE ORGANIZATION CHART *

Harold Stieglitz

Organization charts come in various sizes, colors and even textures. Most are black and white and printed on paper. Some are affixed to office walls—and made of materials that are easily changed. Some charts are highly detailed; some are very sketchy. Some are stamped *confidential* and secreted in the desks of a chosen few; others are broadly distributed and easily available. Despite these and other variations that might be noted, all organization charts have at least one thing in common: they don't show how the organization works. Or, as some people say, they don't show the *real* organization.

Such a statement, which usually emerges as a criticism of organization charts, goes beyond the fact that the organization chart, like milk, may be dated but not fresh. For it is increasingly understood that no organization chart is 100% current. Rather, the criticism is that

* Reprinted with permission from The Conference Board Record, *September, 1964. Copyright 1964 by National Industrial Conference Board.*

even the most current chart is utterly inadequate as a diagram of the organization.

Few organization planners, even those whose major preoccupation is drawing charts, argue too vehemently against this criticism. They just go on drawing their charts. Most often, the charts they draw are of the conventional type made up of boxes and lines. These usually end up in a pyramidal shape with a box (generally larger) at the top to represent the chief executive.

However, behind the preparation and issuance of the chart, there is, presumably, this basic understanding: An organization chart is not an organization. And there is far more to an organization—even in the limited sense of an organization structure—than can ever be put on a chart.

But while the chartist himself may be aware of it, this knowledge is seldom pervasive. Some companies recognize this and attempt to underscore the fact that a chart is just a two-dimensional representation by placing the following caution at the bottom of the chart:

Level of boxes shows reporting relationships and has no significance with regard to importance of position or status.

Such a caution or demurrer is seldom sufficient to quiet the critics or unruffle ruffled feathers, and is quite often taken with a large grain of salt—sometimes because the chart does show some of the very things that the demurrer may say it doesn't. If nothing else, for example, the head of a unit that doesn't appear on an organization chart can be reasonably sure that his unit is not rated important enough to merit inclusion.

Actually, the conventional organization chart (see the chart) shows very little. It implies a little more than it shows. But the inferences that are drawn from it are limited only by the experience, imagination and biases of the beholder—in or outside of the company. In other words, one of the troubles with charts seems to be the people who read them.

WHAT IT SHOWS

The organization chart of most companies shows—indeed is designed to show—just two things:

1 Division of work into components. These components may be divisions or departments or they may be individuals. Boxes on the conventional chart represent these units of work.

2 Who is (supposed to be) whose boss—the solid lines on the chart show this superior-subordinate relationship with its implied flow of delegated responsibility, authority and attendant accountability.

Implicit in these two are several other things that the chart is designed to show:

3 Nature of the work performed by the component. Depending upon the descriptive title placed in the box, what this shows may be specific (Facilities Engineering), speculative (Planning) or spurious (Special Projects).

4 Grouping of components on a functional, regional or product basis. This is also conveyed to some extent by the labels in the boxes.

5 Levels of management in terms of successive layers of superiors and subordinates. All persons or units that report to the same person are on one level. The fact that they may be charted on different horizontal planes does not, of course, change the level.

It is rather difficult to pinpoint anything else about a structure that is actually shown on an organization chart. Some may argue whether, in fact, even the few items above can be read directly from any or some charts.

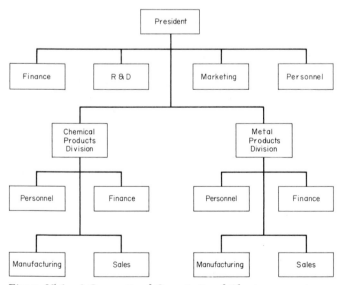

Figure 35-1   A Conventional Organizational Chart.

WHAT THE CHART DOESN'T SHOW

What an organization chart doesn't show is often the most interesting part of the chart—at least to the internal personnel. And it is the inferences that arise from what's missing which companies attempt to deal with in their demurrers or cautions. The demurrers, as already suggested, don't always scotch the inferences. In many cases, the warnings may be erroneous or incomplete.

Degree of Responsibility and Authority

Take, for example, this caution: "Size and position of boxes do not indicate degree of responsibility or authority." Well, it is quite possible that they do. Indeed in the mere process of showing superior-subordinate relationships, the chart does clearly imply varying degrees of responsibility and authority. This is implicit in the process of delegation.

A possibly more accurate demurrer might be "any relationship between size and position of boxes and degree of responsibility and authority may be coincidental, accidental or just plain odd." For what the chart clearly does not show is the degree of responsibility and authority exercised by positions on the same management level. Two persons on the same management level may have vastly different degrees of authority. A man on the third level may have more or less authority than a second-level manager in a different chain of delegation.

Of course, because the chart cannot adequately begin to depict varying degrees of authority, it cannot show the degree of decentralization. Decentralization, organizationally speaking, has relevance only in terms of delegation of decision-making authority. Almost by definition, it refers to the level at which decisions are made.

Inferences about decentralization are often drawn from charts; the company chart that shows activities grouped into product divisions or regional divisions as opposed to a purely functional grouping is often referred to as decentralized. That may or may not be the case. The view from the top may be of a highly decentralized company; the view from the bottom or intermediate layers may be quite the opposite. And a functionally organized company can be as highly decentralized as a divisionally organized company. It all depends on the level at which decisions are being made. The chart cannot depict that, nor can it depict the extent of the restrictions—in the form of policies, budgets, procedures, reports, audits—that make for more or less decentralization.

Staff and Line

Distinguishing between staff and line is an arduous, hazardous, and so far as some organization planners are concerned, an academic chore. Attempting to determine line and staff from an organization chart presents similar hazards. Titles or functional labels alone won't do it. What one company considers line may be staff to another. Again, it depends on the responsibility and authority delegated to the units.

Of course, the nature of the company's business may have clues to what is staff or line. In a manufacturing company, for example, certain functions are traditionally viewed as staff: personnel administration, public relations, legal and secretarial, and finance are examples. In a services company the arrangement may be quite different. But reliance on the nature of the business can be misleading. In manufacturing, for example, divisionalization has brought into being staff units with labels such as manufacturing and marketing—labels that typically would belong to line components in a functionally organized firm.

In some companies, charting methods are used to attempt to distinguish what these firms consider to be line and staff (or service and operating) units. Sometimes the so-called staff units are charted on one horizontal plane, line on another. Other companies use skinny little lines to connect staff, healthier looking lines to connect line or operating units. Still others add labels to underscore this visual aid.

With all these visual distinctions, a chart reader might readily infer what is obviously being implied: there is a difference between the two types of units. To try to interpret these differences in terms of line-staff responsibilities, authorities, and relationships presents the same difficulties as reading the degree of decentralization from the chart.

Status or Importance

To some people, inclusion on the organization chart is, in itself, a status symbol. The physical location on the chart—the linear distance from the chief executive—is viewed as a measure of importance. And there's the rub. Given the limitations of a piece of paper, not everyone can be charted equidistant from the chief executive. Reassurances like "size and position of boxes do not reflect importance or status" are seldom reassuring enough. The incumbent charted in a particular spot may realize the truth of this statement; but he may fear that the "other fellows may not," or vice versa.

There is little question but that position on an organization chart, in some companies, does imply relative importance and status. But it has the same limitations in implying (or covering up lack of) importance as do size of office, titles, parking lot space, etc. Most people still rely on the pay envelope as a more accurate reflection of relative importance. And the organization chart just isn't designed to reflect the pay structure of the company.

In short, the organization chart may imply relative importance or status, but, to rephrase a caution that might appear on a chart, "Any inferences drawn from this chart regarding relative importance or status may or may not be correct."

Lines of Communication

Another caution that shows up is: "This chart does not indicate channels of contact." Actually it does. What it doesn't show is *all* the channels of contact or communication. Possibly a more appropriate warning might be: "This chart indicates a few of the major channels of contact—but if the organization sticks to only these, nothing will get done." For it is a truism of organization that no one unit or individual operates in isolation from all the others. All are linked by an intricate network of communication. (Maze may be a more apt term than network.) Proper organization performance relies on this network and on each unit and individual becoming party to it. To chart the total network is practically impossible. To attempt to chart it—and thus introduce certain rigidities into it—might easily frustrate its workings.

Relationships

In a real sense, lines of communication are really relationships. "You can't have one without the other"—and the picture of either that

shows up on the chart is that of only a few key links in the total network.

Any organization is a hotbed of relationships. Not all of them, of course, necessarily grow out of the nature of the work of the company. Even those that do, however, do not show up on the conventional or even unconventional organization chart.

On occasion a company has noted: "This chart shows relationships only and does not represent levels of management." The caution may have been on the wrong chart, for on the chart in question the opposite seemed true.

More frequently the company notes: "This chart shows reporting relationships only. . . ." Even this seems questionable—it is accurate only if the phrase reporting relationships is understood to mean superior-subordinate reporting relationships.

Organizational relationships—as opposed to social, etc. relationships within a company—grow out of the division of work and delegation of responsibility and authority. A number of functional relationships, authority relationships, staff-line relationships, and just plain work relationships may come into play in reaching any decision or in completing any given piece of work. Most companies long ago gave up any attempt to even begin to show all of these relationships on a chart.

The "Informal" Organization

To some people, that mystical entity known as the "informal" organization is the *real* organization. *It* is how things really get done.

The *it* referred to, however, may be any number of things, depending upon the point of view. To narrow it to just two types—there is the "informal" organization and the *informal* organization.

The "informal" organization, in this makeshift dichotomy, encompasses all relationships and channels of communication that mature, reasonable people are expected to develop and use in order to meet organizational objectives. As mature, reasonable people, they are expected, of course, to also respect their superior's need to be kept informed of matters affecting his area of accountability. This "informal" organization is viewed as a logical and necessary extension of the formal organization. It is informal only in the sense that nobody has found it necessary to inundate the organization with memorabilia that fully spell out its workings.

The *informal* organization, on the other hand, encompasses all the relationships, communication channels, and influences or power centers that mature, reasonable people develop because a lot of other people in the organization are not mature and reasonable—"especially the bosses who needn't be informed because they'll only say 'no.'" Rather than being a logical extension of the formal organization, it comes into being because the formal organization is viewed as being illogical or inflexible or inefficient or just plain inconsistent with the personal and possibly organizational objectives being worked toward. This *informal* organization, according to "informal" organization specialists, gets work done in spite of the formal organization.

Neither shows up on the organization chart: the "informal" because it's too complex to be reduced to a two-dimensional chart; the *informal* because that would make it formal—a heresy that would immediately give rise to another *informal* organization.

For those not fully satisfied with this dichotomy, there may be a third type—the INFORMAL organization. It includes parts of the "informal" and *informal*. By definition, it covers everything not shown on the organization chart; by definition, it can't be charted.

THE INADEQUATE CHART

Attempts to revamp the conventional organization chart in order to overcome these and other limitations have produced many examples of modern, nonobjective art (Alexander Calder's mobiles have been mistaken for organization charts.) There is the circular chart (and its variants) designed to better convey internal relationships and to better camouflage "status." There is the chart with the vertical lines between boxes stretched to reflect similar levels of responsibility or similar levels of pay (scrapped after first attempt—required too long a sheet of paper). There is the chart with the pyramid up-ended to reflect the true flow of authority—from subordinates to superiors (scrapped after first attempt—"That's rubbing it in").

Despite all its limitations, the conventional chart is increasingly used to depict the skeletal structure of the organization. For more complete documentation of what this chart means, companies rely on position guides, linear responsibility charts, statements of general responsibilities and relationships—indeed, the whole organization manual.

The essential value of the chart seems to lie in the fact that it does strip the organization to the skeletal framework. In so doing, it serves a useful purpose both as a tool of organizational analysis and a means of communication.[1] As a complete picture of the organization, it is recognized as being completely inadequate. But it evidently is less inadequate than most substitutes.

[1] *See "Charting the Company Organization Structure," Studies in Personnel Policy, No. 168, for detailed description of charts and their uses.*

READING 36

LINEAR RESPONSIBILITY CHART—NEW TOOL FOR EXECUTIVE CONTROL *

Alfred G. Larke

Every now and then, somebody comes up with an idea so obvious that everybody understands it, and many good men ask themselves, "How could I have overlooked it?" Some, in fact, always wonder if anything so simple could be good, just because it is simple.

The originators of a new and graphic method of analyzing and recording organizational structure, job content, and functional operating responsibilities, seem to have come up with just such a simplification of a number of management control devices.

Called the Linear Responsibility Chart, it compacts within the limits of a single sheet of graph paper much if not most of the information that normally would require dozens of pages of organization manual, organization charts, operating or responsibility flow charts, and job description write-ups to record by usual methods.

The mere packing of a lot of information into a small space does not, of course, necessarily make it more readily available or easier to comprehend, as anyone realizes who may have tried to read the Lord's Prayer engraved on the head of a pin.

The virtue of the new type of chart is that, in presenting much in little space, it presents it in visual rather than verbal form, making good on the fabled Chinese picture, so often said to be worth 1,000 words, but so seldom proven to be.

Whether the Linear Responsibility Chart replaces the many forms of organizational information records whose data it summarizes is open to question.

The Serge A. Birn Company, Louisville, Ky., consulting management engineers who introduced the new chart (a simplification of a European device of similar nature), think it can completely replace at least the usual bulky organization manual.

The Controller's department of Corning

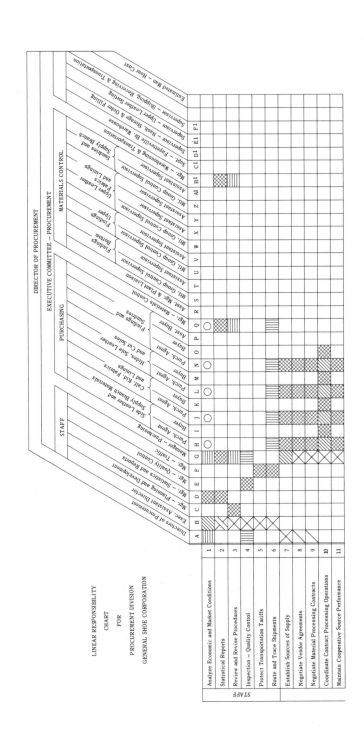

LINEAR RESPONSIBILITY
CHART
FOR
PROCUREMENT DIVISION
GENERAL SHOE CORPORATION

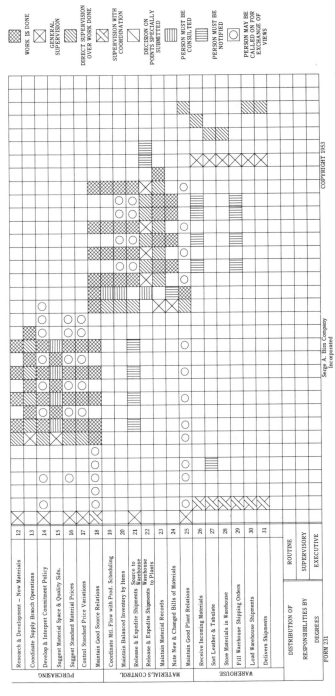

Figure 36-1 Typical Linear Responsibility Chart is this single-sheet description of Purchasing Division of General Shoe Corporation, Nashville, Tenn. A tentative study proposal, rather than a chart of the situation now in effect, it shows how LRC is used. General Shoe study was aimed at (1) More clearly defining authorities and responsibility; (2) Reassigning present personnel to jobs that company experience and testing showed them best fitted for; (3) Providing for an orderly progression of advancement; (4) Pointing up where on-the-job training is needed to fit others for advancement. Note that symbols (see key) in any vertical column describe the job at its head; in any horizontal row, show operating responsibility for function at left. Other charts have been used with quantitative symbols to tally time or to make interplant comparisons of methods. In most applications it has been found to be both clear and concise.

Glass Works, Corning, N.Y., which has worked out variations of its own on the basic chart, sees the LRC rather as a summary of information from many sources, handier to use than the original material because it is compact and visual.

"It does not replace (other) accepted techniques of functional and organizational control," says a Corning Glass internal memo on the subject. "Rather, it is an important supplementary tool which supervisory and other management individuals can use advantageously because it affords the opportunity quickly to scan and assess the actual relationship which exists between an operating group's employees, their functions, and their workloads." (Corning Glass has introduced a quantitative feature into its version of the Linear Responsibility Chart.)

Another consulting engineer, exposed to Birn's LRC idea for the first time, described the chart as "a very handy tool" for executive control but was doubtful it could completely replace older methods of charting organizational relationships.

No company has abandoned the organization manual as a result of adopting the LRC, but that is inconclusive, since the charts have been in use in this country only a little more than a year, and among a very limited number of companies. Some have never had a manual, some are so small it is doubtful they could afford to set up one or, having set it up, afford high-grade talent needed to keep such a manual up to date.

What the Linear Responsibility Chart is, and how it presents its information, are best understood by looking at a typical one, like that made during a study for General Shoe Company (see Figure 36-1).

In its basic form, it uses eight symbols, as shown, to indicate eight relationships that may exist between any position in an industrial organization and any function or piece of work with which he may be associated as policy-maker, supervisor, co-ordinator, or do-er.

On a specially designed sheet of charting paper, the job titles in the department or unit of the company are listed along the horizontal axis, at the top. The functions performed by the organizational unit are listed along the vertical axis, at the left. In the square where job title and function meet, the relationship is indicated by the appropriate symbol. If the job has nothing to do with the function, the square is left blank, of course.

S. H. Durst, works manager of Gamble Brothers, Louisville, Ky., manufacturers of dimension lumber and machined wood parts, gives this description, from his use of the Linear Responsibility Chart:

"On most charts, as you look at the chart, you see the man's name, his department, and to whom he is responsible. The duties that he performs are a separate set of instructions, usually carried in a procedure manual. With the Linear Responsibility Chart, you see the man's duties, what he is responsible for, and to whom he is responsible.

"I think a good example of this chart would be to compare it to a curve sign on the highway. Although the sign says there is a curve, you are in doubt how fast you can take your car around the curve. If you add to that curve sign (the notation) 45 miles per hour, you then have a complete explanation, that there is a curve and that you can proceed around it at a safe speed of 45 miles per hour.

"Thus, a man can look at the Linear Responsibility Chart and also pick off the duties that he is responsible for."

Replacement or supplement, the LRC has a great many uses in which its virtues are to save time and money, or to throw a bright spotlight on an organizational situation that needs study—or both.

Here are some of the uses (in its brief history of use in this country, the LRC has been put to most of them):

1. To simplify and speed up the making of a management audit.

Initially an advantage to the outside consultant making the audit, this is, of course, of advantage to the corporation under study, because a saving in time in making the audit will be reflected in a saving in the cost of making it.

Instead of having to make lengthy notes as he interviews executives, and of then having to study them as he converts them into a verbal description of the organization, the man making the audit can chart his facts on the LRC graph as he gets them—altering them, if need be, as he receives conflicting or additional facts.

Birn and his associates use this method regularly now; it constitutes a kind of organizational shorthand that need not be transcribed.

2. To simplify executive control and speed executive decisions.

The executive wishing to determine responsibility for something that has gone amiss is unlikely to want to ruffle through many pages of an organizational manual every time the need occurs but he will find it simple to check responsibility on a one-page chart that he can keep in his desk, or his pocket.

The president of one sizable company, who has used the LRC for nearly a year now, is jovial about this use. "It used to be," he says, "that when something went wrong, it was almost impossible to pin it on anyone. Now I keep the chart in my desk—these men helped make it; it represents exactly how things are done. So, now when anything goes wrong, I simply open my drawer and take it out. There can be no argument, and there never is."

3. To spot organizational errors, and to make them easy to correct by making their faultiness obvious to everyone concerned.

The "before" charts made in almost any organization the consultants have studied are much more interesting than the "after" charts, but with becoming modesty, no management seems willing to demonstrate how greatly it has improved matters between "before" and "after." The mockup chart (Figure 36-2), a disguised version of a real-life before-and-after set, shows, however, how these faults are detected and remedied.

The "before" chart of this pair shows a situation that had grown up gradually over a long period and worked well so long as the company was operating under large, long-run contracts. Too many production superintendents, however, shared authority to make binding decisions on sequence of operations and other processing details. Time spent in reconciling differences was great—often two hours per man weekly for as many as fifteen men. But, when competition forced the company to go out for new business aggressively, the old methods became suicidally cumbersome.

Bids were late, friction increased among the many men who had authority to decide. Eventually, one week, it took six meetings, totalling twelve hours, for each of those involved, to come to a common decision. At this point, the Linear Responsibility Chart made clear why the company was falling behind.

The conditions had existed before. Management knew something was wrong. But *what*

was wrong, and in what way, did not become clear until a graphic display like this *made* it clear. The "after" chart, concentrating decision in a few hands—the proper ones—and giving only consultative authority to the others, straightened the problem out.

One measure of the method's success was the reduction in "steps required" to settle methods from 41 to 21. Hours saved were almost geometrically proportional.

4. To facilitate changes in assignments of duties and authorities when a change in leading personnel occurs.

Because a new top man usually handles his job differently from his predecessor, delegating some things he did himself and taking on responsibilities he assigned to others, a shift in the work of lower-ranking management is required, too. This is the point at which maintenance of an unwieldy organization manual is first apt to break down. With responsibilities and authorities recorded visibly on a single sheet, as in LRC, the necessary changes are easy to make.

5. Realignment of tasks when activities are expanded or contracted because of varying business.

6. To check on whether a given executive is putting too much time or effort into routine activities—or supervisory—instead of executive.

7. To compare methods and operation of similar departments in a multiplant operation.

Corning Glass Works did this kind of comparative study of accounting departments in fourteen plants with the expenditure of about ten man-weeks of time. Using symbols of its own devising, instead of those proposed by Birn, it was able to get a quantitative measure of time spent on the various functions listed at the left of the chart, as well as of the work done by each individual in the vertical columns.

When the charting survey was finished, data was available for changes: Time per employee spent in payroll preparation varied from plant to plant, as did also total accounting personnel per employee.

These results spotlight areas for further study: Are the wide variations justified in each case, or can a better method be picked up from one plant and made standard procedure in all plants?

The charting, as R. C. Koch of Serge A. Birn Company points out, aids in an effort to make

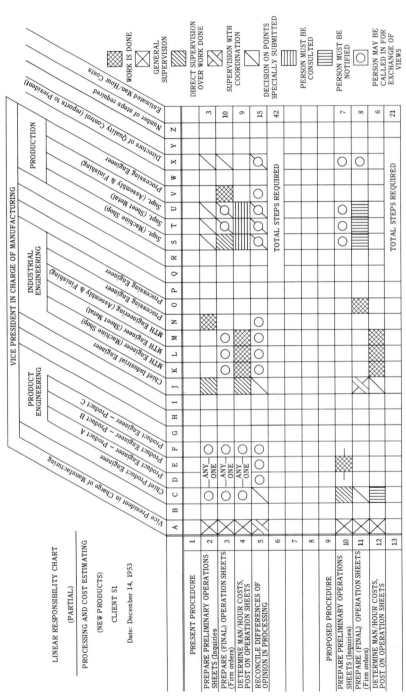

Figure 36-2 Before-and-after charts, disguised, but from a real plant, show how organizational faults are detected, remedied. See text.